The World of Psychology

The World of Psychology

Ellen R. Green Wood

St. Louis Community College—Meramec

Samuel E. Wood

Higher Education Center of St. Louis

Allyn and Bacon

Boston   London   Toronto   Sydney   Tokyo   Singapore

DEDICATION

In honor of our parents, this book is dedicated with love and gratitude to Edna Shores Rosenthal and the late Adam Rosenthal and to Rev. S. E. Wood and Daisy Jernigan Wood.

Editor-in-Chief, Social Sciences: Susan Badger
Developmental Editor: Elizabeth Brooks
Senior Editorial Assistant: Dana Hayes
Cover Administrator: Linda Dickinson
Manufacturing Buyer: Louise Richardson
Signing Representative: Ward Moore
Production Coordinator: Leslie Olney
Editorial-Production Service: Publicom, Inc.
Cover Designer: Studio Nine

Library of Congress Cataloging-in-Publication Data

Wood, Ellen R. Green.
   The world of psychology / Ellen R. Green Wood, Samuel E. Wood ; instructor's section and annotations prepared by Mark Garrison. — Annotated instructor's ed.
      p.   cm.
   Includes bibliographical references and indexes.
   ISBN 0-205-15001-2 (AIE). — ISBN 0-205-13756-3 (SE)
   1. Psychology.   I. Wood, Samuel E.   II. Garrison, Mark (Mark David)   III. Title.
   [DNLM: 1. Psychology.   BF 121 W874w]
   BF121.W665 1993
   150—dc20
   DNLM/DLC
   for Library of Congress   92-48992
                                                                  CIP

Printed in the United States of America

10 9 8 7 6 5 4   97 96 95 94

Credits

Chapter 1
Opener Michael Dwyer/Stock Boston **p. 2 (upper)** Brad Markel/Gamma Liaison **p. 2 (lower)** Brad Markel/Gamma Liaison **p. 3** UPI/Bettman **p. 5** Bob Daemmrich/Stock Boston **p. 18** Courtesy of Cable News Network, Inc. **p. 23** The Granger Collection

The credits continue on the pages following the index. They should be considered an extension of the copyright.

Contents

CHAPTER 1

Introduction to Psychology xxvi

CHAPTER 2

Biology and Behavior   **34**

CHAPTER 5

Learning   150

CHAPTER 6

Memory 188

CHAPTER 7

Intelligence, Thought, and Creativity 226

CHAPTER 8

Child Development 260

CHAPTER 11

Human Sexuality and Gender   366

CHAPTER   12

Personality Theory and Assessment   398

CHAPTER   15

Therapies   510

CHAPTER   16

Social Psychology   546

CHAPTER 17

The World of Psychology: Multicultural Issues and Applications 582

Preface

Our goals in writing this book can be summarized as a desire to introduce the world of psychology accurately, faithfully, and clearly to students in an interesting and memorable format. We have tried to present the principles of psychology by using a clear and engaging writing style in a pedagogically sound learning format that is accessible and appealing to students.

We are sensitive to the many complexities of the teaching/learning process, having taught thousands of students their first course in psychology. Over the years we have witnessed changes in our field of study, in our students, and in ourselves as well. Thus, we sought to create a textbook that is sensitive to the changing needs of modern students and their professors and that would provide a context through which the reader may learn about psychology's past, its present, and its probable future.

To accomplish our goals we set forth the following objectives:

To Maintain a Clear, Understandable Writing Style That Students Will Find Interesting.

First and foremost a textbook is a teaching instrument. It cannot be a novel, nor should it be an esoteric, academic treatise. A good psychology text must communicate to a diverse audience of varying ages and levels of academic ability. Our text will be appealing to the academically accomplished student yet accessible to students whose academic skills are yet to be fully developed.

We seek to achieve this objective by explaining concepts in much the same way we would if the reader were a student in our own psychology classes. Throughout the text we have sought to ensure a flow and continuity by using a dialogic style which avoids abrupt steps in thought. This text is also filled with everyday examples pertinent to the student's life.

To Provide a Series of High-Interest Features That Will Appeal To Today's Students.

In keeping with this goal, every chapter opens with a lively, high-interest vignette to capture student interest and build motivation. Also, we have prepared three types of boxed features: (1) *World of Psychology: Applications* to show practical applications of the principles of psychology, (2) *World of Psychology: Multicultural Perspectives* to explore issues involving race, gender, and ethnic and cultural diversity, and (3) *World of Psychology: Pioneers* to give due prominence to some of our pioneers and to show their human side as well as their contributions to the field.

To Encourage Students To Become Active Participants in the Learning Process.

Reading about psychology is not enough. Students should be able to try, where appropriate, what they have learned. Many of the principles we teach can be demonstrated, often without elaborate equipment and sometimes as the student reads. What better way to teach new material and to make it fresh, interesting, and memorable than to have students demonstrate principles for themselves with *Try It!*, an important and innovative feature of *The World of Psychology*. This feature personalizes psychology and makes it come alive. Student involvement is also promoted through the extensive use of rhetorical questions and by casting the student in the role of the subject in selected studies, such as the role of the "teacher" in the Milgram experiment. Thus, students who use *The World of Psychology* will become active participants in the learning process rather than simply passive recipients of information.

To Promote and Nurture Critical Thinking

Critical thinking does not consist of being critical of all viewpoints other than our own. To live peacefully in an increasingly diverse society, we must learn to develop an understanding and appreciation for conflicting viewpoints in the multitude of issues that divide us—psychological, social, economic, political, moral, and ethical.

Critical thinking is too important to leave to chance. While opportunities for critical thinking are provided throughout the text, we have also developed a systematic method for nurturing critical thinking. A *Thinking Critically* section appears at the end of each chapter and features three categories of critical thinking questions:

1. *Evaluation* questions teach students to think critically as they evaluate psychological theories, techniques, approaches, perspectives, and research studies.
2. *Point/Counterpoint* questions require students to comprehend, to analyze, and to formulate convincing arguments to support *both* sides of important issues in psychology.
3. *Psychology in Your Life* questions allow students to apply psychological principles and concepts in their own lives and in the practical, everyday world.

To Help Students Understand and Appreciate Human Diversity and the Part That Multicultural Issues Play in Modern Psychology

To accomplish this goal, we have dedicated a series of boxed features entitled *World of Psychology: Multicultural Perspectives* to cover a wide range of multicultural issues. Among them are "Cultural Values and Academic Achievement," "Culture, Race, and Care for the Elderly," "Mate Preferences around the World," "The Glass Ceiling: Few Women and Minorities at the Top," and "Gestures: Different Meanings in Different Countries." In addition, human diversity has been considered in relation to dozens of other topics throughout the text.

Finally, issues relating to human diversity are explored in chapter 17, "The World of Psychology: Multicultural Issues and Applications," and in chapter 11, "Human Sexuality and Gender."

To Achieve a Balance between Psychological Principles and Applications.

To present psychological principles alone may leave students wondering what psychology has to do with their own lives. The *World of Psychology: Applications* features help students apply psychology to their personal lives and to contemporary issues or problems in the larger cultural milieu. Some of the topics are "Noise and Hearing Loss: Bad Vibrations," "Date Rape: New Outrage on Campus," "Thinking and Depression: Avoiding Cognitive Traps," "The Effects of Nonmaternal Care on Children," and "The Polygraph: Lie Detector or Emotion Detector?"

In addition, the second half of chapter 17 explores the major areas in applied psychology—I/O, environmental, architectural, forensic, sports, and consumer psychology. Finally, every chapter contains a critical thinking question, "Psychology in Your Life," which requires students to consider the many ways psychological principles can be applied to their own lives and to life in general.

To Be Current in Our Coverage While Preserving the Classic Contributions in Our field.

Advances in knowledge and research are occurring at an ever more maddening pace, and modern authors must keep abreast. Accordingly, our references reflect the most up-to-date state of the science for the many rapidly changing topics we cover. Yet we do not use newness for its own sake. We include, as well, studies that have stood the test of time, and we explore in depth the classic contributions to psychology.

To Give Students an Appreciation of Psychology's History and Its Pioneers, and an Understanding That Psychology Is a Living, Growing, Evolving Science.

A portion of the introductory chapter is devoted to psychology's history. But, in our view, the history of psychology is best understood and appreciated in the context in which the contributions were made. Consequently, topics like learning, memory, intelligence, emotion, and personality, for example, integrate the historical and research contributions to show how psychology has evolved up to the present day. In addition, emphasis is given throughout the text to pioneers in psychology, and selected pioneers—such as B. F. Skinner, Jean Piaget, and Karen Horney—are featured in *World of Psychology: Pioneers*. We focus on the human qualities of the pioneers, their life struggles and successes along with their contributions, to bring the history of psychology alive for students.

To Provide an Accurate and Thoroughly Researched Textbook That Features Original Sources.

To accomplish our goals of introducing the world of psychology accurately, faithfully, and clearly, we have gone back to original sources and have reread the basic works of the major figures in psychology and the classic studies in the field. This has enabled us to write with greater clarity and assurance, rather than having to hedge or write tentatively when discussing what experts in the field have actually said. This book is among the most carefully researched on the market, among the most up to date, and among the most extensively referenced textbooks available.

To Provide a Sound Pedagogical System Woven Throughout the Text and the Learning Package

The pedagogical system consists of the following components:

Learning Objectives/Questions Learning objectives—written in question form—guide student reading, focus attention on key information, provide a framework for a SQ3R approach, and assist students in preparing for exams.

Memory Checks An average of six Memory Checks appear during each chapter to encourage students to pause at the end of sections and test their comprehension of the material just read.

Margin Glossary A margin glossary provides a ready reference for important Key Terms, which appear in boldface print in the text, and for additional terms that appear in italics. All definitions also appear in the end-of-text Glossary. Phonetic pronunciations are provided for hard-to-pronounce terms.

Chapter Summary and Review The Chapter Summary and Review section, arranged according to the major headings in the chapter, provides condensed answers to the learning objectives/questions and also lists the Key Terms for each topic. This feature is useful as a preview to the chapter and as a review in preparing for tests.

All of these features support a modified SQ3R approach, which is explained to the student in chapter 1, in *World of Psychology: Applications—Sharpening Your Study Skills.*

SQ3R The SQ3R technique is a systematic approach to maximize learning, improve retention, and develop more effective study skills. *SQ3R* stands for *Survey, Question, Read, Recite,* and *Review.* Briefly stated, to follow the SQ3R method, students complete these steps:

Survey First students are encouraged to look over the Chapter Outline at the beginning of each chapter, read the opening vignette, read all the topic headings and study questions, glance at the illustrations, and read the Chapter Summary and Review. This will provide an overview of the chapter.

Question Students are encouraged to read the learning objectives and to turn the topic headings into one or more questions before they read each section in the chapter.

Read Next students read a section of the text in an attempt to answer the learning objectives and other questions of their own, and then stop at the Memory Check.

Recite Students are encouraged to write or recite the answers to the learning objectives and their own questions or to write a short summary of the section.

Review Students should complete the Memory Check before beginning the next section of the text. When they have finished the chapter, they should turn to the Chapter Summary and Review section and review each of the study questions and answer them in their own words. The answers provided are given only as condensed, basic answers that they will want to expand on. Finally, students should be sure they understand the Key Terms. Definitions for the Key Terms appear in the margin glossary or tables on the pages indicated in parentheses.

To Provide Instructors and Students with a Complete, Coordinated Teaching and Learning Package of the Highest Quality

The *Annotated Instructor's Edition* has been developed by Mark Garrison of Kentucky State University to encourage student involvement and understanding. It is comprised of two parts: the instructor's section bound into the front of the book, and the detailed annotations that appear in blue type in the margins of the book. The annotations include teaching suggestions, examples, activities, critical thinking topics, multicultural issues, and references to the Test Bank items and the many visual aids that accompany the book.

Along with the *Annotated Instructor's Edition* is a separate *Activities and Demonstrations Manual,* also prepared by Mark Garrison, which provides detailed instructions for all of the activities, plus more than 150 ready-to-duplicate handouts.

The book is also supported by a comprehensive computer-ready test item file and printed Test Bank, prepared by Janet Simons of Central Iowa Psychological Services. The Test Bank includes detailed explanations for answers to each item to help students understand *why* an answer is correct.

An innovative study guide with language enrichment, prepared by Joyce Bishop of Golden West College, is available for students. It was carefully coordinated with the Test Bank and the textbook, and it includes practice multiple-choice tests with explanations for answers, extra help with vocabulary, flashcards, and many other features.

A wide array of additional supplementary materials are also available with this book. These include Allyn and Bacon's exclusive CNN videos of brief, up-to-the-minute reports on current issues in psychology, a Level 3 Video Disk, Allyn and Bacon's extensive video library, a newly revised set of color transparencies, a booklet of current articles from *The Washington Post* relating to multicultural issues, and more. See your Allyn and Bacon representative for information.

Acknowledgments

We first express our appreciation to Russ Boersma, a treasured friend and respected colleague who first encouraged us to write this textbook and whose continued support and encouragement has helped sustain us through the years of effort in making *The World of Psychology* a reality.

Much of *The World of Psychology* was written in New Harmony, a peaceful and picturesque town in Indiana whose charm and serenity was so magnetic that we have made it our home away from home for the last four years. We owe an unbelievable debt of gratitude to Jane Blaffer Owen for her encouragement and support of the project and for allowing us to spend so many productive and enjoyable months in one of the houses that she and we so love and treasure. New Harmony is a magical place, a jewel in the United States, in large measure because Mrs. Owen has provided the vision and unselfishly devoted her resources and limitless energy to making it so. It has been a rare privilege to know Jane Owen, for her life, her work, and her values have touched us and will always be an inspiration to us. We also thank Gary Gerard, Nancy McIntyre, and all the people at Red Geranium Enterprises and the New Harmony Inn for making our stay in New Harmony so memorable.

Our developmental editor, Elizabeth Brooks, epitomizes what a developmental editor should be, and she deserves a string of accolades too long to include here. Through these years of close work with Beth, we have developed not only a profound respect and admiration for her professional skill, but a deep affection as well. She knew where to cut, where to embellish, when to change and how. Her suggestions and her tireless dedication to the project helped make *The World of Psychology* what it is. Her influence is prominent from cover to cover.

The leader of this project is Susan Badger, Editor-in-Chief of Social Sciences at Allyn and Bacon. From beginning to end, Susan was intimately involved in every aspect of the project. All features of design, pedagogy, content, and organization bear the mark of the thought, work, and taste of Susan Badger. She is a most remarkable person—a consummate professional with exceptional intelligence, judgment, and taste, who is relentless in her pursuit of excellence. We stand in awe of her ability to manage, direct, and orchestrate all the components of highly complex projects. Yet Susan somehow manages to merge these dynamic professional qualities with warmth and personal magnetism—a feat accomplished by few.

We owe a large and growing debt of gratitude to Ward Moore, Senior Publisher's Representative, who brought our manuscript to the attention of Allyn and Bacon and is thus responsible for performing the first act that brought us all together. Ward is highly respected in his field and has championed *The World of Psychology* throughout its production.

We express our thanks and appreciation to Judy Fiske, Vice President of Production, who, from our earliest planning meeting, has skillfully supervised the production of the project, and to Linda Dickinson, Cover Administrator, who designed the cover for the book. We also express our thanks and appreciation to Leslie Olney, Production Coordinator, for guiding the book through the final stages of production, and to Patricia White Maka and Meredith Rutter of Publicom, Inc., for their long hours of hard work in copy editing the manuscript and laying out the book. Our sincere thanks to Dana Hayes, Senior Administrative Assistant, for her flawless administration of the review process. Through countless communications by phone and by mail, Dana has always been a pleasure to work with.

Sandi Kirshner, Vice President of Marketing, and Joyce Nilsen, Marketing Manager for Psychology, have worked tirelessly in developing the marketing strategy for the book, and in providing the publisher's representatives with the information and resources they need. Their work will play a giant role in determining the success of the book, and so will the excellent work of Lou Kennedy, Director of Advertising, and Ron Sohn, Assistant Advertising Manager, who are in charge of brochures, catalogs, and all other materials for presenting the book and the ancillary materials.

Everyone at Allyn and Bacon works hard to maintain a standard of excellence in making fine books. Behind the scenes but very much involved in making our book were John Isley, President of Allyn and Bacon, and Bill Barke, Vice President and Editorial Director. We express our sincere appreciation and deep gratitude to them for their confidence in us and for their commitment to and active involvement in the project. We are honored to have the privilege of working in this creative enterprise with all of the publishing professionals at Allyn and Bacon.

We also thank our respected colleagues in the Psychology Department at St. Louis Community College at Meramec—Jim Wheeler, Bob Allbee, Mike Davies, Beth Powell, and Shari Talley for their interest, support, encouragement, and expertise.

Finally, our sincere thanks to the many colleagues around the country whose expertise helped make the book what it is today. It could never have been written without them.

Reviewers

Joyce Bishop
Golden West College

Allen Branum
South Dakota State University

Andre Cedras
Macomb Community College

Samuel Church
Fairmont State College

James Dooley
Mercy College

William Dwyer
Memphis State University

Thomas Fitzpatrick
Rockland Community College

Kathleen Fuhs
J. Sargeant Reynolds Community College

Wayne Hall
San Jacinto College North Campus

Barbara Honhart
Baker College of Flint

Claire Lowder
Illinois Central College

Lynn McCutcheon
Northern Virginia Community College

James Nelson
Parkland College

Diane Owsley
Elizabethtown Community College

Gregory Pezzetti
Rancho Santiago College

Pennie Seibert
Boise State University

Pamela Stewart
Northern Virginia Community College

Thomas Tighe
Moraine Valley Community College

Rene Villa
Hillsborough Community College

Everett Wagner
San Antonio College

Phyllis Walrad
Macomb Community College

Patrick Williams
University of Houston–Downtown

Topics Related to Human Diversity

Following are some of the topics considered from a multicultural perspective

Abnormality, cultural definition (p. 477)
Achievement motivation (pp. 350–351)
Alcohol use and abuse (p. 464)
Antipsychotic treatment for schizophrenia (p. 532)
Attributional biases (pp. 552–553)
Bulimia (p. 302)
Discrimination
   in interview styles (p. 589)
   in the workplace (pp. 590–591)
   overcoming discrimination (pp. 593–594)
   reverse discrimination (p. 592)
Elderly, attitudes toward care of (p. 327)
Emotional display (p. 363)
Emotional expression (p. 361)
Eyewitness identification and race (p. 190)
Health in America (pp. 458–459)
Hearing (p. 88)
Infant mortality (p. 267)
Intelligence (pp. 244–245)
Intelligence testing, cultural bias in (p. 240)
Job stress (p. 598)
Language development (p. 283)
Mate preferences (pp. 558–559)
Maternity leave policy (p. 599)
Minnesota Multiphasic Personality Inventory (MMPI) (pp. 428–429)
Moral development (p. 307)
Multiple personality disorder (p. 490)
Nonverbal behavior, gestures (p. 551)
Perceptual illusions (p. 105)
Personal space, cultural differences in (p. 605)
Pregnancy, teenage (p. 310)
Prejudice (pp. 586–595)
Prosocial behavior (p. 575)
Psychotherapy (p. 539)
Racial tolerance, survey (pp. 594–595)
Scapegoating (p. 577)
School achievement (pp. 290–291)
Sexual behavior, teenage (pp. 310–311)
Shift work (p. 116)
Stereotyping (p. 588)
Surveys (p. 5)
Transition from childhood to adolescence (p. 299)
U.S. population, racial composition (p. 585)

Following are some of the topics discussed in relation to gender differences

Adult development (pp. 313, 315, 316, 317, 318, 320–321)
Aggression (pp. 374, 376)
Alcohol use and abuse (p. 464)
Body fat, gender differences (p. 468)
Body image, gender differences in (p. 301)
Brain differences (pp. 369, 385)
Child care (p. 316)

Cognitive abilities (p. 375)
Discrimination in the workplace (pp. 590–591)
Drug therapy, gender differences in dosage effects (p. 539)
Early and late maturation in boys and girls (pp. 300–301)
Employment (pp. 376, 590–591)
Fear of success (pp. 350–351)
Freud's view of psychosexual development in males and females (pp. 407–408)
Freud's views of women and men (p. 409)
Gender stereotyping (pp. 376–377)
Health care, gender gap (p. 459)
Homosexuality (p. 385)
Horney and feminine psychology (pp. 412–413)
Job stress, women (p. 598)
Jung's concepts of the anima and animus (p. 411)
Marital satisfaction (p. 315)
Medical treatment, seeking of (p. 454)
Menopause (p. 313)
Mental disorder, incidence in males and females (pp. 490, 496)
Moral development (pp. 306–307)
Psychotherapy (p. 539)
Rape (p. 394)
Sexual arousal (pp. 379–382)
Sexual attitudes and behavior (pp. 378, 379)
Sexual behavior, teenage (pp. 310–311)
Sexual dysfunctions (pp. 387–389)
Sex hormones (pp. 369, 381)
Sex-role development, theories of (pp. 371–373)
Sex-role stereotypes (pp. 376–377)
Sex typing and adjustment (pp. 370–371)
Sex typing, parental roles in (p. 371)
Sexually transmitted diseases, differential effects on males and females (pp. 390, 391, 392)
Smoking, gender differences (p. 463)
Suicide (pp. 502–503)
Surveys (p. 6)
Widowhood (p. 326)

Following are some of the topics discussed in relation to aging

Attitude change (p. 327)
Cognitive development (pp. 323–324)
Creative contributions (pp. 313–314)
Exercise, benefits of (pp. 298, 466–467)
Health and coping skills (pp. 312–313, 323)
Hearing loss (p. 88)
Intellectual capacity (pp. 313–314, 323–324)
Life satisfaction (p. 325)
Physical development (pp. 322–323)
Sexuality (p. 323)
Sleep (pp. 120–121)
Stress and lack of control (p. 446)
Suicide (pp. 502–503)
Taste (p. 91)
Vision (p. 77)

1

Introduction to Psychology

CHAPTER OUTLINE

Anita Hill

Clarence Thomas

I n October 1991 the nation witnessed a spectacle unprecedented in American politics. The .confirmation of Judge Clarence Thomas, nominated to the United States Supreme Court, seemed all but certain. Then Professor Anita Hill came forward and accused Judge Thomas of sexual harassment she said occurred in the early 1980s. Even under the hot lights of the TV cameras, Professor Anita Hill sat calmly and coolly, poised and unemotional, as she charged that Clarence Thomas, her former boss, had continually pressured her to date him. She recounted incidents in which he described to her graphically vulgar scenes from pornographic films. She also accused Judge Thomas of making lewd comments to her and bragging about his sexual abilities. Judge Thomas's backers were outraged; the nation was shocked.

Then came Judge Thomas's turn to be questioned by the Judiciary Committee about Professor Hill's allegations. He was not calm and cool. With anger and emotion, he lashed out at the senators, accusing them of presiding over what he called "a high-tech lynching for uppity blacks." "Enough is enough," Thomas said. "I have not said or done the things that Anita Hill has alleged. God has gotten me through, and He is my judge."

As the Judiciary Committee hearings continued, Anita Hill took a lie detector test and passed it. Both Judge Thomas and Professor Hill brought forth supporters and character witnesses who appeared before the committee. As the American people watched, the weight of credibility seemed to swing back and forth between the judge and the professor.

The nation's TV networks carried the spectacle, and it immediately soared to the top of the ratings, surpassing popular soap operas, sports events, and game shows. Why were people so fascinated with the Thomas-Hill hearings? Perhaps this event aroused such interest because it included many intriguing issues in human behavior, subjects that psychologists study and research. This one situation involved issues of race, of gender, of sexual behavior, and of alleged sexual harassment.

The Thomas-Hill hearings also raised many questions about the accuracy of memory. Do we remember events, both recent and remote, exactly as they happened? Or, do we "reconstruct" events and recollect partly truth and partly fiction? How do we perceive events? Do different people perceive the same experiences in vastly different ways—especially if one is male and the other female? Are lie detector tests accurate and reliable? Can we be assured that those who pass lie detector tests are telling the truth, and those who do not are lying?

This case also led many to have questions about motives, the motives of Judge Thomas and of Professor Hill. And what were the motives of the senators, both Democrats and Republicans, on the Judiciary Committee? Were they honestly and objectively seeking the truth, or were they influenced by hidden psychological and political motives?

Never before have so many Americans slipped into the role of amateur psychologist at the same time. But in the world of psychology that you are about to enter, people ask questions, probe issues, and test hypotheses that are far wider and deeper than those involving the judge and the professor.

WHEN MANY PEOPLE CONSIDER THE FIELD OF PSYCHOLOGY, they conjure up images of mental disorders and abnormal behavior. Psychologists do study the strange and unusual, but they are interested in the normal and commonplace as well. In fact, the world of psychology is broad enough to encompass the full range of behavior and mental processes.

Just what is psychology? Psychology has changed over the years, as has its definition. In the late 1800s mental processes were considered to be the appropriate subject matter of psychology. Later there was a movement to restrict psychology to the study of observable behavior alone. Today the importance of both areas is recognized, and **psychology** is now defined as the scientific study of behavior and mental processes.

The goals of psychology are to describe, explain, predict, and control behavior and mental processes. There are two basic types of research that psychologists pursue to accomplish these goals—(1) basic or pure research and (2) applied research. The purpose of **basic research** is to seek new knowledge and to explore and advance our general scientific understanding. Basic research is not intended to solve specific problems. Nor is it meant to investigate ways to apply what is learned to immediate problems of the real world. Yet very often, the findings of basic research are later used in applied settings. **Applied research**, on the other hand, is conducted specifically for the purpose of solving practical problems and improving the quality of life.

Descriptive Research Methods

The goals of psychological research—description, explanation, prediction, and control—are typically accomplished in stages. In the early stages of research, descriptive research methods are usually the most appropriate. *Descriptive research methods* yield descriptions rather than identify causes of behavior. Naturalistic observation, laboratory observation, the case study, and the survey are examples of descriptive research methods.

Naturalistic Observation: Caught in the Act of Being Themselves

Question: What is naturalistic observation, and what are some of its advantages and limitations?

Naturalistic observation is a research method in which the researchers observe and record behavior in its natural setting without attempting to influence or control it. Ethologists are researchers who study the behavior patterns of animals in their natural environment. They might observe their subjects through high-powered telescopes or from blinds that they build to conceal themselves.

Often subjects are not aware that they are being observed. This can be accomplished by using one-way mirrors, a technique researchers often use to observe children in nursery schools or special classrooms. You may have seen episodes of "60 Minutes," "20/20," or "Candid Camera" in which hidden cameras or tape recorders were used to gather information from unsuspecting subjects, "caught in the act of being themselves."

The major advantage of naturalistic observation is the opportunity to study behavior in normal settings, where behavior occurs more naturally and spontaneously than it would under artificial and contrived laboratory conditions. Sometimes naturalistic observation is the only method available to study certain phenomena that would be either impossible or unethical to set up in an experiment, such as how people typically react during disasters like earthquakes or fires.

Naturalistic observation has its limitations, however. Researchers must wait for events to occur; they cannot speed the process up or slow it down. And because they have no control over the situation, the researchers cannot reach conclusions about cause-and-effect relationships. Another potential problem in

psychology: The scientific study of behavior and mental processes.

basic research: Research conducted for the purpose of advancing knowledge rather than for its practical application.

applied research: Research conducted for the purpose of solving practical problems.

descriptive research methods: Research methods that yield descriptions of behavior rather than causal explanations.

naturalistic observation: A research method in which the researcher observes and records behavior in its natural setting, without attempting to influence or control it.

Jane Goodall has observed the behavior of chimpanzees in Tanzania for more than 30 years.

case study: An in-depth study of one or a few subjects consisting of information gathered through observation, interview, and perhaps psychological testing.

survey: A research method in which interviews and/or questionnaires are used to gather information about the attitudes, beliefs, experiences, or behaviors of a group of people.

naturalistic observation is observer bias, which is a distortion in researchers' observations. Observer bias can result when researchers' expectations about a situation cause them to see what they expect to see or to make incorrect inferences about the behavior they observe.

Laboratory Observation: A More Scientific Look at the Subject

Another method of studying behavior involves observation that takes place, not in its natural setting, but in the laboratory. There researchers can exert more control and use more precise equipment to measure responses. Much of our knowledge about sleep, for example, has been gained by laboratory observation of subjects who sleep for several nights in a sleep laboratory or sleep clinic.

The Case Study Method: Studying a Few Subjects in Depth

Question: What is the case study method, and for what purposes is it particularly well suited?

Another descriptive research method used by psychologists is the **case study** or case history. In a case study, a single individual or a small number of persons are studied in great depth, usually over an extended period of time. A case study involves the use of observation, interviews, and sometimes psychological testing. The case study is exploratory in nature, and its purpose is to provide a detailed description of some behavior or disorder. This method is particularly appropriate for studying people who have uncommon psychological or physiological disorders or brain injuries. Often case studies emerge during the course of treatment of these disorders. Much of what we know about unusual psychological disorders such as multiple personality comes from the in-depth analyses provided by case studies.

In some instances the results of detailed case studies have provided the foundation for psychological theories. The theory of the famous Sigmund Freud is based primarily on case studies of his own patients.

Although the case study has proven useful in advancing our knowledge in several areas of psychology, it has certain limitations. Researchers cannot establish the cause of observed behaviors in a case study. Moreover, because so few subjects are studied, researchers do not know how applicable, or generalizable, their findings may be to larger groups or to different cultures.

Survey Research: The Art of Sampling and Questioning

Question: What are the methods and purpose of survey research?

Psychologists are interested in many questions that would not be possible to investigate using naturalistic observation or the case study. The **survey** is a research method in which interviews and/or questionnaires are used to gather information about the attitudes, beliefs, experiences, or behaviors of a group of people the researcher wishes to study. The results of carefully conducted surveys have provided much of the information available about the incidence of drug use, about sexual behaviors of particular segments of the population, and about the incidence of a number of mental disorders.

Question: What is a representative sample, and why is it essential in a survey?

Selecting a Sample: There Are More than Numbers to Consider Researchers in psychology rarely conduct experiments or surveys using all members of the group they would like to study. For example, researchers interested in studying the sexual behavior of American women do not attempt to study every woman in the United States. Instead of studying the whole *population* (the entire group of interest to researchers and to which they wish to apply their findings), the researchers select a sample for study. A *sample* is a part of the population that is selected and studied in order to reach conclusions about the entire larger population of interest.

Perhaps you have seen a carton of Neapolitan ice cream that contains three separate flavors packed side by side—chocolate, strawberry, and vanilla. To properly sample the carton, a person would need a small amount of ice cream containing all three flavors in the same proportions as they are found in the carton—a representative sample. A **representative sample** is a sample that includes important subgroups in the same proportion as they are found in the larger population.

Selecting a representative sample is difficult, but expert organizations like Gallup and Roper can select relatively small samples and get an accurate view of the opinions of large groups of people. In 1968 Gallup polled a mere 2,000 voters in the United States and predicted that Richard Nixon would get only 43 percent of the popular vote. When the final election results were reported, Nixon received 42.9 percent of the votes.

The Use of Questionnaires Researchers using the survey method rely on information gathered through questionnaires, interviews, or some combination of the two. Surveys that use questionnaires can be completed more quickly and less expensively than those involving interviews.

The largest survey ever taken of the sexual behavior of American women was conducted by *Cosmopolitan* magazine (Wolfe, 1981). About 106,000 women— 3.5 percent of *Cosmopolitan* readers—completed and returned a questionnaire that had appeared in the magazine. Two-thirds of the respondents claimed to have had 5 to 25 sexual partners, and a high percentage reported having had intercourse with more than one partner on the same day. Do these results reflect the sexual behavior of the average American woman?

The number of people who respond to a survey is not the critical element. A researcher can generalize findings from a sample only if it is representative of the entire population of interest. The readers of *Cosmopolitan* magazine do not represent a cross section of American women. Its readers tend to be young, single, and relatively affluent women. Furthermore, the response rate was only 3.5 percent of the readers. It is possible that women who chose to respond to the survey were more sexually active than the average reader.

The Interview: A Better Way "The best survey research uses the personal interview as the principal method of gathering information" (Kerlinger, 1986, p. 379). Skilled interviewers asking well-worded questions of a carefully selected sample of subjects can provide accurate information. When respondents feel comfortable with an interviewer, they feel freer to share personal information.

Imagine that you are being interviewed about a sensitive subject such as sexual behavior. Will you be equally comfortable and truthful regardless of whether the interviewer is male or female? young, middle-aged, or old? black or white? Christian or Jewish? middle class or working class? The validity or truthfulness of responses can be affected by personal characteristics such as the "race, age, sex, religion, vocabulary, accent, ethnic background, or social class of the interviewer" (Van Dalen, 1973, p. 329).

population: The entire group of interest to researchers and to which they wish to generalize their findings; the group from which the sample is selected.

sample: The portion of any population that is selected for study and from which generalizations are made about the larger population.

representative sample: A sample of subjects selected from the larger population in such a way that important subgroups within the population are included in the sample in the same proportions as they are found in the larger population.

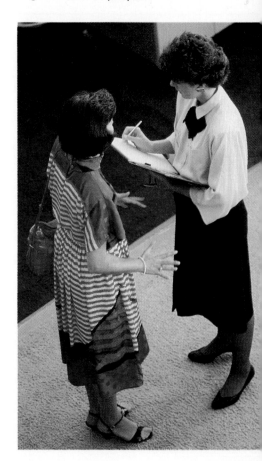

Surveys provide information about large numbers of people.

In general male interviewers obtain less information than female interviewers. People are most inhibited when they give personal information to interviewers who are the same age but of the opposite sex. Skilled survey researchers, therefore, must select interviewers who have personal characteristics that are appropriate for their subjects.

Advantages and Disadvantages of Survey Research   Surveys, if conducted properly, can provide highly accurate information about large numbers of people. Yet large-scale surveys can also be costly and time-consuming. Expertise is required in many areas—selecting a representative sample, interviewing, constructing questionnaires, and analyzing data.

The major limitation of the survey is that the respondents may provide inaccurate information. Subjects may give false information because of a faulty memory or a desire to please the interviewer (saying what they think the interviewer wants to hear). Subjects may desire to present themselves in a good light (called the social desirability response), or they may even deliberately attempt to mislead the researcher.

Memory Check 1.1

1. Researchers using naturalistic observation attempt to control the behavior being observed. (true/false)

2. Much knowledge about sleep and the human sexual response has been gained through:

   a. naturalistic observation   c. the survey
   b. laboratory observation   d. the case study

3. The case study is *not* useful for:

   a. learning about rare physical and psychological disorders
   b. learning the consequences of rare brain injuries
   c. supplying detailed descriptions of behavior that can provide the foundation for psychological theories
   d. studying large numbers of people

4. The survey is most useful when we wish to learn about:

   a. rare psychological and physical disorders
   b. the behavior, beliefs, or attitudes of a large group of people
   c. how people react during natural disasters
   d. all of these

5. The most accurate surveys are those with the largest number of respondents. (true/false)

Answers: 1. false 2. b 3. d 4. b 5. false

The Experimental Method: Searching for Causes

Question: What is the main advantage of the experimental method?

The descriptive research methods (naturalistic observation, the case study, and the survey) are all well suited for satisfying the first goal of psychology—that of description. From their descriptions, researchers may propose possible explanations for the behaviors they study. At some point researchers usually seek to determine the causes of behavior and various other psychological phenomena. What, for example, are the causes of depression, insomnia, stress, forgetting, and aggression? The **experimental method,** or the experiment, is the only research method that can be used to identify cause-effect relationships.

The experiment is designed to test a *hypothesis*—a prediction about a cause-effect relationship between two or more conditions or variables. A variable is any condition or factor that can be manipulated, controlled, or measured. One variable of interest to you is the grade you will receive in this psychology course. Another variable that probably interests you is the amount of time that you will spend studying for this course. Do you suppose there is a cause-effect relationship between the amount of time you will spend studying and the grades you will make?

Consider two other variables—alcohol consumption and aggression. Does the consumption of alcohol cause people to behave more aggressively? Alcohol consumption and aggressive behavior are often observed together. We can assume that there is likely to be more aggression among drinkers in a lively tavern than among a gathering of nondrinkers in a discussion group. But can we assume that the alcohol consumption itself causes the aggressive behavior?

Alan Lang and his colleagues (1975) conducted an experiment to determine if alcohol consumption itself increases aggression, or if the beliefs or expectations about the effects of alcohol cause the aggressive behavior. Subjects in the experiment were 96 male college students who were classified as heavy social drinkers. Half the subjects were given plain tonic to drink; the other half were given a vodka-and-tonic drink in amounts sufficient to raise their blood-alcohol concentration to .10 percent, which is "the legal limit of intoxication in most states" (Marlatt & Rohsenow, 1981, p. 66). Subjects were assigned to four groups:

Group 1: Expected alcohol/ Received tonic (only)
Group 2: Expected alcohol/ Received alcohol (mixed with tonic)
Group 3: Expected tonic/ Received alcohol (mixed with tonic)
Group 4: Expected tonic/ Received tonic (only)

You may think that any heavy social drinker could detect the difference between a drink of vodka-and-tonic and a drink of plain tonic. Yet "pilot testing revealed that drinkers could tell a mixture of one part vodka to five parts tonic water with no more than 50 percent accuracy, or chance odds" (Marlatt & Rohsenow, 1981, p. 62).

After the subjects had consumed the designated amount, the researchers had a confederate—an accomplice who posed as a subject—become involved in the experiment. The confederate purposely provoked half the subjects by belittling their performance on a difficult coordination task. "In a sarcastic and condescending manner, the confederate asked if the subject's attempt had been serious, . . . if he had to cheat to stay in school, and generally questioned the subject's intelligence" (Lang et al., 1975, p. 512). The confederate did *not* provoke the other half of the subjects.

experimental method: The research method in which researchers randomly assign subjects to groups and control all conditions other than one or more independent variables, which are then manipulated to determine their effect on some behavioral measure—the dependent variable in the experiment.

hypothesis: A prediction about the relationship between two or more variables.

All the subjects participated in a learning experiment in which the same confederate posed as the learner. The subjects were told to administer an electric shock to the confederate each time he made a mistake on a decoding task. Each subject was allowed to determine the intensity and duration of the shock. (Although the subjects believed they were shocking the confederate, no shocks were actually delivered.) The researchers measured the aggressiveness of the subjects in terms of the duration and the intensity of the shocks they chose to deliver.

What were the results of the experiment? As you might imagine, the subjects who had been provoked gave the confederate stronger shocks than the subjects who had not been provoked. But the subjects who drank the alcohol were not necessarily the most aggressive. In fact, the unprovoked subjects who expected tonic but received alcohol were less aggressive than any of the groups, provoked or unprovoked, who *expected* alcohol. If not the alcohol, then what caused the aggression? The researchers found that it was the expectation of drinking alcohol, not the alcohol itself, that caused the subjects to be more aggressive. Regardless of the actual content of their drinks, the subjects who thought they were drinking alcohol gave significantly stronger shocks, whether provoked or not, than the subjects who assumed they were drinking only tonic (see Figure 1.1). Evidently it was their thinking, not their drinking, that caused the aggression.

Independent and Dependent Variables

Question: What is the difference between the independent variable and the dependent variable?

Figure 1.1   Mean Intensity of Shock Given by Provoked and Unprovoked Subjects   The Lang experiment convincingly demonstrates that subjects who thought they were drinking alcohol gave significantly stronger shocks, whether provoked or not, than subjects who believed they were drinking only tonic. (Data from Lang, Goeckner, Adesso, & Marlatt, 1975.)

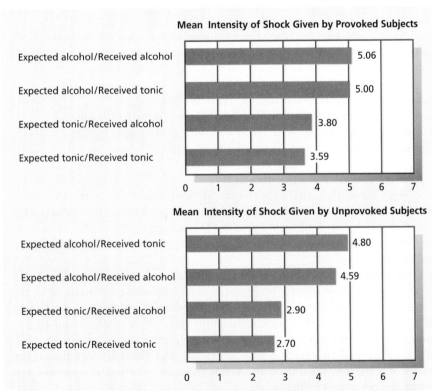

In all experiments there are two types of variables. First there are one or more **independent variables**—variables that are manipulated by the researcher to determine whether they cause a change in another behavior or condition. Sometimes the independent variable is referred to as the treatment. In the Lang experiment, there were two independent variables—the alcoholic content of the drink and the expectation of drinking alcohol.

The second type of variable found in all experiments is the **dependent variable**. It is measured at the end of the experiment and is presumed to vary (increase or decrease) as a result of the manipulations of the independent variable or variables. The dependent variable is presumed to depend on or to be affected by changes in the independent variable. In the Lang study, the dependent variable was the level of aggression. This variable was measured by the intensity and duration of the electric shocks the subjects chose to deliver to the confederate.

Experimental and Control Groups: The Same Except for the Treatment

Question: How do the experimental and control groups differ?

Most experiments are conducted using two or more groups of subjects. There must always be at least one **experimental group**—a group of subjects who are exposed to the independent variable, or the treatment. The Lang experiment used three experimental groups:

Group 1:   Expected alcohol/ Received tonic (only)
Group 2:   Expected alcohol/ Received alcohol (mixed with tonic)
Group 3:   Expected tonic/ Received alcohol (mixed with tonic)

In most experiments it is desirable to have a **control group**—a group that is similar to the experimental group and used for purposes of comparison. The control group is exposed to the same experimental environment as the experimental group but is not given the treatment. The fourth group in the Lang study was not exposed to either of the two independent variables. This group did not expect alcohol and did not receive alcohol. Because this group was similar to the experimental groups and was exposed to the same experimental environment, it should be considered a control group. In an experiment, all groups, including the control group, are measured on the dependent variable at the end of the experiment.

Control in the Experiment: Attempting to Rule Out Chance

By conducting the Lang experiment in a laboratory, the experimenters were able to control the environmental setting in order to rule out other factors that could conceivably have caused the aggressive responses. Frustration, pain, and extreme noise or heat are several conditions that can increase aggressive responses. Consequently the researchers carefully controlled the environment so that none of these conditions were present. They varied only the independent variables: the subjects' expectations and the content of their drinks. Therefore, the researchers could be reasonably sure that the manipulation of the independent

independent variable: In an experiment, the factor or condition manipulated by the researcher to determine its effect on another behavior or condition known as the dependent variable.

dependent variable: The variable that is measured at the end of an experiment and is presumed to vary as a result of manipulations of the independent variable.

experimental group: In an experiment, the group of subjects that is exposed to the independent variable, or the treatment.

control group: In an experiment, a group that is similar to the experimental group and is exposed to the same experimental environment but is not exposed to the independent variable; used for purposes of comparison.

variables (alcohol and expectations) caused the differences in the degree of aggression among the groups.

Generalizing the Experimental Findings: Do the Findings Apply to Other Groups?

What should be concluded from the Lang experiment? Can you conclude that people in general tend to be more aggressive when they believe they are under the influence of alcohol? Before reaching such a conclusion, consider several factors. (1) The only subjects used in this experiment were male college students. You cannot be sure that the same results would have occurred if females or males of other ages had been used. (2) The subjects in this experiment were classified as heavy social drinkers. Would the same results have occurred if nondrinkers, moderate social drinkers, or alcoholics were included? To apply this experiment's findings to other groups, the experiment would have to be replicated, or repeated, using different populations of subjects. (3) The amount of alcohol given to the students was just enough to bring their blood-alcohol level to .10 percent. You cannot be sure that the same results would have occurred if subjects had consumed more or less alcohol.

Potential Problems in Experimental Research

If an experiment is properly designed and conducted, the researcher should be able to attribute changes in the dependent variable to the manipulations of the independent variable. But several factors other than the independent variables can cause changes in the dependent variable and, therefore, destroy the validity of an experiment. Three of these potential problems are selection bias, the placebo effect, and experimenter bias. Researchers must design experiments to control for these and other problems that could invalidate the results.

Question: What is selection bias, and what technique do researchers use to control for it?

Selection Bias: Bias from the Start   One factor that can account for differences between the experimental and control groups' measures on the dependent variable is selection bias. **Selection bias** occurs when subjects are assigned to groups in such a way that systematic differences among the groups are present at the beginning of the experiment. If selection bias occurs, then differences at the end of the experiment may not reflect the manipulation of the independent variable but may be due to pre-existing differences in the groups.

To control for selection bias, researchers must use **random assignment**. This process consists of selecting subjects by using a chance procedure (such as drawing the names of subjects out of a hat) to guarantee that all subjects have an equal probability of being assigned to any of the groups. Random assignment maximizes the likelihood that the groups will be as similar as possible at the beginning of the experiment. If there had been pre-existing differences in the level of aggressiveness of subjects in Lang's alcohol experiment, random assignment should have spread those differences across groups.

Question: What is the placebo effect, and how do researchers control for it?

The Placebo Effect: The Power of Suggestion (the Subject's)   Another factor that can influence the outcome of an experiment is the placebo effect. The

selection bias: The assignment of subjects to experimental or control groups in such a way that systematic differences among the groups are present at the beginning of the experiment.

random assignment: In an experiment, the assignment of subjects to experimental and control groups by using a chance procedure, which guarantees that all subjects have an equal probability of being placed in any of the groups; a control for selection bias.

placebo effect occurs when a subject's response to a treatment is due to the subject's expectations about the treatment rather than to the actual treatment itself. Suppose a drug is prescribed for a patient and the patient reports improvement. The improvement could be a direct result of the drug, or it could be a result of the patient's expectation that the drug would work. Studies have shown that sometimes remarkable improvement in patients can be attributed solely to the power of suggestion—the placebo effect.

The researcher must use a control group to test whether results in an experiment are due to the treatment or the placebo effect. The subjects in the control group are given a fake treatment. In drug experiments, the control group is usually given a **placebo**—an inert, or harmless, substance such as a sugar pill or an injection of saline solution. To control for the placebo effect, researchers do not let subjects know whether they are in the experimental group (receiving the treatment) or in the control group (receiving the placebo). If subjects getting the real drug or treatment show a significantly greater improvement than the subjects who receive the placebo, then the improvement can be attributed to the drug rather than to the power of suggestion. In the Lang experiment, some subjects who expected alcohol mixed with tonic were given only tonic. The tonic without alcohol functioned as a placebo. This enabled the researchers to measure the effect of the power of suggestion alone in producing aggression.

The placebo effect can invalidate the results of experiments when researchers do not take into account the subjects' expectations. But what about the expectations of those who conduct the experiments—the researchers themselves?

Question: What is experimenter bias, and how is it controlled?

Experimenter Bias: The Power of Suggestion (the Experimenter's) The expectations of the experimenter are a third factor that can influence the outcome of an experiment. **Experimenter bias** occurs when researchers' preconceived notions or expectations become a self-fulfilling prophecy and cause them to find what they expect to find. A researcher's expectations can be communicated to the subjects, perhaps unintentionally, through tone of voice, gestures, or facial expression. These communications can influence the subjects' behavior. Expectations can also influence a researcher's interpretation of the experimental results, even if no influence occurred during the experiment.

Robert Rosenthal is one researcher who has had much to say about experimenter bias, or the self-fulfilling prophecy. In one study Rosenthal (1973) tested the effect of teacher expectations on student test scores. A group of 100 cadets at the United States Air Force Academy Preparatory School were randomly assigned to five mathematics classes. The math instructors were told that students had been assigned to their classes according to high or low ability in math. In reality the five classes did not differ in math ability, but the instructors believed they did. Math achievement scores for the five classes should have been about the same. Were they? No. Apparently teacher expectations had influenced achievement because those students who had been labeled as high in math ability outperformed the students who had been labeled low in math ability. It seems amazing that nothing more than a belief held by teachers or experimenters can make a difference in the actual performance of students or subjects.

To control for experimenter bias, researchers must not know which subjects are assigned to the experimental and control groups. The identities of both the experimental and control subjects are coded, and their identities are not revealed to the researcher until after the research data are collected and recorded. When neither the subjects nor the experimenter knows which subjects are getting the treatment and which are in the control group, the experiment is using the **double-blind technique**. The double-blind technique is the most powerful procedure for studying cause-effect relationships.

placebo effect: The phenomenon that occurs when a person's response to a treatment or response on the dependent variable in an experiment is a function of expectations regarding the treatment rather than the treatment itself.

placebo (pluh-SEE-bo): Some inert substance, such as a sugar pill or an injection of saline solution, given to the control group in an experiment as a control for the placebo effect.

experimenter bias: A phenomenon that occurs when the researcher's preconceived notions in some way influence the subjects' behavior and/or the interpretation of experimental results.

double-blind technique: An experimental procedure in which neither the subjects nor the experimenter knows who is in the experimental or control groups until after the results have been gathered; a control for experimenter bias.

Advantages and Disadvantages of the Experimental Method

The overwhelming advantage of the experiment is its ability to reveal cause-effect relationships. This benefit is possible because researchers are able to exercise strict control over the experimental setting. This allows them to rule out factors other than the independent variable as the reason for differences in the dependent variable. But often the more control the experimenter exercises, the more unnatural and contrived the research setting becomes. When subjects know that they are participating in an experiment, their behavior may be different from what it would be in a more natural setting. When a natural setting is considered to be an important factor in a study, researchers may choose to use a field experiment—an experiment conducted in a real-life setting. Although some control over the experimental environment is sacrificed, the advantage is more natural behavior on the part of the subjects.

A major limitation of the experimental method is that in many areas of interest to researchers in psychology, this method is either unethical or not possible. Some treatments cannot be given to human subjects because their physical or psychological health would be endangered, or their constitutional rights violated.

Memory Check 1.2

1. The experimental method is the *only* research method that can be used to identify cause-effect relationships between variables. (true/false)

2. Which of the following statements is *not* true about a control group?

   a. It should be similar to the experimental group.
   b. It is exposed to the independent variable.
   c. At the end of the experiment, it is measured on the dependent variable.
   d. It is used for purposes of comparison.

3. Match the description with the appropriate term.

   ＿＿＿ 1) a prediction about a relationship between two variables   a. independent variable
   ＿＿＿ 2) any condition that can be manipulated, measured, or controlled   b. variable
   ＿＿＿ 3) the variable measured at the end of the experiment   c. hypothesis
   ＿＿＿ 4) the variable manipulated by the researcher   d. dependent variable

4. In experiments that test drugs, the control group is given an inert substance called a ＿＿＿＿＿.

5. The results of an experiment can be influenced by the expectations of either the subjects or the researcher. (true/false)

(continued)

6. Random assignment is used to control for:

   a. experimenter bias   c. selection bias
   b. the placebo effect   d. all of these

7. Ethical considerations can sometimes prevent researchers from using the experimental method even when they want to learn about a cause-effect relationship. (true/false)

Answers: 1. true 2. b 3. 1) c 2) b 3) d 4) a 4. placebo 5. true 6. c 7. true

Other Research Methods

The Correlational Method: Discovering Relationships, Not Causes

Question: What is the correlational method, and when is it used?

We know that researchers are interested in finding the causes of various psychological phenomena. Does stress cause illness? Does smoking cause cancer? Does heavy marijuana use cause students to lose interest in school and get lower grades? Researchers would like to have answers to these questions, but none of them can be researched by using the experimental method. It is often illegal and always unethical to randomly assign human subjects to experimental conditions that could be harmful.

To find out if smoking marijuana causes a decline in academic achievement, no researcher would randomly assign high-school students to an experimental study that would require students in the experimental groups to smoke marijuana. Can you imagine a principal notifying parents that their son or daughter had been chosen to smoke marijuana for 2 years in order to further scientific knowledge?

Much of our knowledge of the effects on human health of marijuana, cigarette smoking, or stress has been gained by performing experiments on animals or by using other research methods. When, for ethical reasons, an experimental study cannot be performed to determine cause-effect relationships, the **correlational method** is usually used. This research method determines the correlation or relationship between two characteristics, events, or behaviors. A group is selected for study, and the variables of interest are measured for each subject. For example, the variables might be the amount of marijuana used and Grade Point Average. Then a statistical formula is applied to obtain a correlation coefficient.

Question: What is a correlation coefficient?

The Correlation Coefficient: How Variables Relate A correlation coefficient is a numerical value indicating the degree and direction of the relationship between two variables. A correlation coefficient ranges from +1.00 (a perfect positive correlation) to .00 (no relationship) to −1.00 (a perfect negative correlation). The sign of a correlation coefficient (+ or −) indicates whether the two variables vary in the same or opposite directions. A positive correlation indicates that two variables vary in the same direction. In other words, an increase in the

correlational method: A research method used to determine the relationship (correlation) between two characteristics, events, or behaviors.

correlation coefficient: A numerical value that indicates the strength and direction of the relationship between two variables; ranges from +1.00 (a perfect positive correlation) to −1.00 (a perfect negative correlation).

Figure 1.2

Understanding Correlation Coefficients

Correlation coefficients can range from −1.00 (a perfect negative correlation) through .00 (no correlation) to +1.00 (a perfect positive correlation). As the arrows indicate, a negative correlation exists when an increase in one variable is associated with a decrease in the other variable. A positive correlation exists when both variables tend to either increase or decrease together.

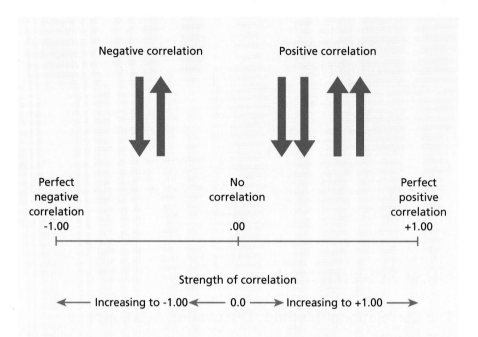

value of one variable is associated with an increase in the value of the other variable. Or, a decrease in the value of one variable is associated with a decrease in the value of the other. There is a positive but weak correlation between stress and illness, for example. When stress increases, illness is likely to increase; when stress decreases, illness tends to decrease.

A negative correlation means that an increase in the value of one variable is associated with a decrease in the value of the other variable. Think of a negative correlation as a seesaw—when one variable goes up, the other goes down. There is a negative correlation between the number of cigarettes people smoke and the number of years they can expect to live. When cigarette smoking increases, the number of years someone lives tends to decrease. The reverse is also true.

The number in a correlation coefficient indicates the relative *strength* of the relationship between two variables—the higher the number, the stronger the relationship. Therefore, a correlation of −.85 is higher than a correlation of +.64, and a correlation of −.58 is just as strong as one of +.58. A correlation of .00 indicates that no relationship exists between the variables (see Figure 1.2). Grade Point Average and height, and illness and shoe size are two sets of variables that are not correlated.

Correlation and Prediction   Correlations are useful in making predictions. The stronger the relationship between the variables, the better able we are to predict the presence or absence of one variable from the presence of the other. If correlations are high, they will be good predictors. A perfect correlation (+1.00 or −1.00) would enable you to make completely accurate predictions.

A correlation is more useful for predicting the probable performance of a group than for predicting that of an individual. Because there is a correlation between cigarette smoking and lung cancer, it can be predicted that a group of 1,000 nonsmokers will experience a lower incidence of lung cancer than a group of 1,000 two-pack-a-day smokers. But from the correlation coefficient alone you cannot accurately predict which individuals in the group will develop cancer.

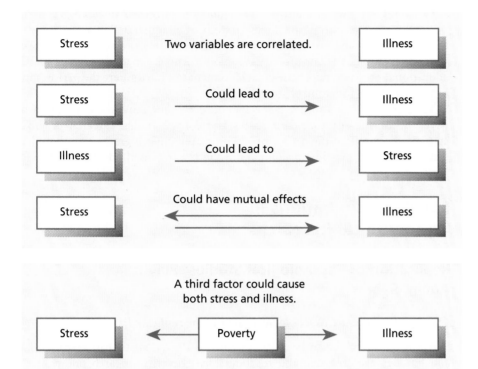

Figure 1.3

Correlation Does Not Prove Causation

A correlation between two variables does not prove that a cause-effect relationship exists between them. There is a correlation between stress and illness, but that does not mean that stress necessarily causes illness. Both stress and illness may result from another factor, such as poverty, a weak constitution, or poor general health.

The fact that there is a correlation between two variables does not mean that one variable causes the other. Only the experimental method allows us to reach conclusions about cause and effect. When two variables such as stress and illness are correlated, we cannot conclude that stress makes people sick. It might be that illness causes stress, or that a third factor such as poverty, a weak constitution, or poor general health causes susceptibility to both illness and stress as shown in Figure 1.3.

Although a correlation is not sufficient to prove cause and effect, it is one of the necessary conditions for proving it. If other evidence is gathered, then the case for cause-effect becomes stronger. For ethical reasons, the experimental method has not been used to test for a cause-effect relationship between smoking and lung cancer in humans, but animal studies have supported the hypothesis. The consistency and strength of findings in numerous studies over the years have convinced most scientists that cigarette smoking is one of the causal factors in lung cancer, in mouth and throat cancer, and in heart disease.

Psychological Tests: Assessing the Subject

Psychologists have developed a wide range of tests for measuring intelligence, scholastic achievement, aptitudes, creativity, vocational interests, personality traits, and psychiatric problems. Psychological tests are used in a variety of situations—in schools, in the workplace, and in therapeutic settings. These tests are used to evaluate or compare individuals, to measure changes in behavior, and to make predictions about behavior. Test results also provide information that can be used in educational decision making, personnel selection, and vocational guidance.

replication: The process of repeating a study using different subjects and preferably a different investigator to verify research findings.

Psychologists often use testing in conjunction with their research. Tests may be administered as part of the intensive study of an individual in a case study. In an experiment, the dependent variable might be the score on a psychological test. For example, an educational psychologist who is experimenting with a new educational program might use an achievement test to compare the performance of experimental and control subjects.

Tests are also used in correlation studies. To determine the correlation between Scholastic Aptitude Test scores and college grades, researchers had to statistically compare the SAT scores with actual college grades of the subjects tested. Table 1.1 provides a summary of the research methods discussed so far.

Some Considerations in Psychological Research

Replication of Psychological Studies: Play It Again, Sam

Question: Why must psychological research be replicated?

Psychology may claim to be a science only to the extent that its research data and findings are objective and reproducible. To verify research findings, it is necessary that studies be replicated. **Replication** is the repeating of studies by using the same procedures with different subjects and preferably different investigators. A scientific experiment is somewhat like a recipe or a set of exact instructions. It spells out in detail precisely what the researchers did, how they did it, who the subjects were, what conditions were in place, and what the researchers found.

If the results of a study are scientifically valid, a careful replication of the study should yield similar results. When the same findings occur again and again, confidence grows that the findings are indeed genuine. When replications do not yield the same findings, researchers should be suspicious of their initial results and be willing to discard their belief in them.

Human Subjects in Psychological Research

"Modern psychology has been called 'the science of the behavior of the college sophomore'" (Rubenstein, 1982, p. 83). For practical reasons, the majority of studies with human subjects in the last 30 years have used college students. They are a convenient group for college professors to study, and their participation can be encouraged by offering pay or points toward a course grade. There have also been a disproportionate number of males used in psychology studies (Gannon et al., 1992) and of whites as well (Graham, 1992).

Heavy reliance on college students presents a problem. College students are a relatively select group in terms of age, socioeconomic class, and educational level. Thus, they are not representative of the general population. But how generalizable the findings of such studies are to the general population depends on the nature of the study. Studies that investigate basic psychological processes such as sensation, perception, and memory are likely to be generalizable because these processes probably function the same way in most adults. But with research on human social behavior, there is great cultural and individual variation and thus a problem in generalizing the results to other segments of the population.

Table 1.1   Research Methods in Psychology

Method	Description	Advantages	Limitations
Naturalistic observation	Researcher observes and records behavior in its natural setting. Subjects may or may not know that they are being observed.	Good source of descriptive information. Can provide basis for hypotheses to be tested later. Behavior studied in everyday setting is more natural.	Researchers' expectations can distort observations (observer bias). Presence of researcher may influence behavior of subjects. Little or no control over conditions.
Laboratory observation	Observation under more controlled conditions where sophisticated equipment can be used to measure responses.	More control than naturalistic observation.	Possible observer bias. Behavior of subjects may be less natural than in naturalistic observation.
Case study	An in-depth study of one or a few subjects using observation, interview, and/or psychological testing.	Source of information for rare or unusual conditions or events. Can provide basis for hypotheses to be tested later.	May not be representative of condition or event. Time-consuming. Subject to misinterpretation by researcher.
Survey	Interviews and/or questionnaires used to gather information about attitudes, beliefs, experiences, or behaviors of a group of people.	Can provide accurate information about large numbers of people.	Responses may be inaccurate. Sample may not be representative. Characteristics of interviewer may influence responses.
Psychological tests	Used for measuring intelligence, scholastic achievement, aptitudes, vocational interests, personality traits, psychiatric problems.	Provide data for educational and vocational decision making, personnel selection, research, and psychological assessment.	Tests may not be reliable or valid.
Correlational method	Used to determine the relationship (correlation) between two events, characteristics, or behaviors.	Can assess strength of relationship between variables. Provides basis for prediction.	Does not demonstrate cause and effect.
Experimental method	Random assignment of subjects to groups. Manipulation of the independent variable(s) and measurement of its effect on the dependent variable.	Enables identification of cause-effect relationships.	Laboratory setting may inhibit natural behavior of subjects. Findings may not be generalizable to the real world. In some cases, experiment is unethical.

The Use of Animals in Research

Where would psychology be today without the laboratory rat, Pavlov's salivating dogs, the pigeon, and the many other species of animals used to advance scientific knowledge? Psychologists recognize the tremendous scientific contributions that laboratory animals have made and continue to make, and most psychologists favor the use of animals in research. Presently animals are used in 7 to 8 percent of psychological experiments, and 95 percent of the animals used are rodents (American Psychological Association, 1984). Many of the marvels of modern medicine would not be available today without the use of animals in research.

Most psychologists recognize that many scientific advances would not have been possible without animal research. Nevertheless, a storm of controversy surrounds the use of animals for research and other purposes.

Every disease eliminated, every vaccine developed, every method of pain relief devised, every surgical procedure invented, every prosthetic device implanted—indeed, virtually every modern medical therapy is due, in part or in whole, to experimentation using animals. (Cohen, 1986, p. 868)

Now, more than ever before, the research use of animals holds great promise for the possible cure or prevention of deadly human diseases such as AIDS and cancer. Nevertheless, a storm of controversy surrounds the research use of animals. Animal rights advocates seem to be growing in number and are becoming more militant in their efforts to stop animal research. Animal rights activists have broken into research laboratories, freed laboratory animals, destroyed research records, and wrecked laboratory equipment and other property. One animal rights group has demanded that all animal research studies be stopped immediately. Many activists are also against using animals for food, clothing, or any other purpose.

Very few psychologists favor these extreme views. The American Psychological Association (APA) has always supported the use of animals in research, and its code of ethics supports the humane treatment of animals. According to the APA guidelines governing animal research, researchers must do everything possible to minimize discomfort, pain, and illness in animal subjects (APA, 1985). Recently scientists have made great strides in improving the conditions under which animals are kept and used for research.

Ethics in Research: First and Foremost

In 1982 the APA adopted a set of ethical standards governing research with human subjects. These standards safeguard the rights of experimental subjects while supporting the goals of scientific inquiry. The United States government has also adopted specific standards for researchers receiving federal funding. At a more local level, colleges and universities usually have ethics committees that must approve any research studies proposed by professors.

Most people would agree that research must be conducted to advance scientific knowledge and that research must be an ethical enterprise. But what about deception? Is it ethical for researchers to lie to their human subjects or otherwise mislead them in order to conduct their studies? The experimental study by Lang and his associates on alcohol and expectations involved deception. The subjects were told that they were delivering electric shocks to another human being, and some of the experimental groups were deceived about the alcoholic content of their drinks. But clearly, without deception, the study could not have been conducted, nor the knowledge gained.

Can studies that use deception be justified on scientific grounds, as many psychologists believe? Not according to some psychologists who strictly oppose the use of deception under any circumstances. Diane Baumrind (1985) opposes research using deception because of the potential harm to the subjects. She also believes that such practices will damage the reputation of psychology and psychologists and cause people to lose confidence in the profession.

Even so, deception is used in many research studies. Forty percent of the research experiments in social psychology conducted in the 1970s involved deception (Hunt, 1982). Today the APA's code of ethical standards requires debriefing of subjects after they have participated in studies involving deception. The debriefing sessions are designed to erase any harmful effects of the deception and to ensure that the subjects understand that no other participants were actually harmed. In the Lang study, debriefing interviews informed subjects of the deception and revealed to them that no electric shocks were actually used. The subjects who had consumed alcohol were given a breathalyzer test to measure their blood-alcohol levels, so that no subject left the laboratory impaired to any degree by alcohol.

Memory Check 1.3

1. A correlation coefficient shows a cause-effect relationship. (true/false)

2. Which of the following describes a negative correlation?

   a. When the value of one variable increases, the value of the other variable decreases.
   b. When the value of one variable decreases, the value of the other variable decreases.
   c. When the value of one variable increases, the value of the other variable increases.
   d. both a and b

3. Which of the following correlation coefficients indicates the strongest relationship?

   a. +.65   b. −.78   c. .00   d. +.25

4. Psychological tests are sometimes used in experiments or correlational studies. (true/false)

5. The majority of psychological studies on human subjects have been conducted using college students as subjects. (true/false)

Answers: 1. false 2. a 3. b 4. true 5. true

The History of Psychology: Exploring Psychology's Roots

If we were to trace the development of psychology from the beginning, we would need to stretch far back to the earliest pages of recorded history, even beyond the early Greek philosophers, such as Aristotle and Plato. People have always had questions about human nature, and they have always tried to understand human behavior. For centuries these questions were the subject of speculation and were considered to be in the realm of philosophy. Most professors who were teaching anything resembling psychology had their appointments in philosophy.

Wilhelm Wundt: The Founding of Psychology

Question: What was Wilhelm Wundt's contribution to psychology?

It was not until experimental methods were applied to the study of psychological processes that psychology became recognized as a formal academic discipline. Three German physiologists—Ernst Weber, Gustav Fechner, and Hermann von Helmholtz—pioneered in the application of experimental methods to the study of psychological processes, and they profoundly influenced the early development of psychology.

Although a number of early researchers were contributing to the new field of psychology, Wilhelm Wundt is generally considered to be the "father of psychology." The establishment of his psychological laboratory in 1879 in Leipzig, Germany, is considered to be the official birth of psychology as a formal academic discipline. Wundt's lectures attracted many people from Europe and the United States, some of whom became important figures in psychology. But the studies and experiments that Wundt, his associates, and his students performed in that early laboratory were very different from psychology as we know it today.

For Wundt, the subject matter of psychology was experience—the actual, immediate, conscious experiences of individuals. Wundt believed that mental experiences could be reduced to their basic elements, just as the early chemists discovered water to be composed of the basic elements of hydrogen and oxygen (H_2O). In other words, Wundt was searching to find the structure of conscious experience.

A conscious experience can be observed only by the person having that experience. Therefore, research on the experience necessarily involves self-observation or introspection. Introspection as a research method involves looking inward to examine one's own conscious experience—sensations, perceptions, thoughts, images, and feelings—and then reporting that experience. Wundt's advanced psychology students were rigorously trained in introspection. It is said that they had to introspect their way through some 10,000 separate practice experiences before their reports could be considered valid.

Wundt and his associates conducted experiments on reaction time and on attention span. They also studied the perception of a variety of visual (sight), tactile (touch), and auditory (hearing) stimuli, including rhythm patterns using metronomes set at different speeds. Wundt published the results of countless experiments in the journal he founded. He wrote nearly 54,000 printed pages, yielding almost 80 volumes the size of this book. It would take you almost five years, reading 30 pages (about one chapter) every day, to read all that Wundt wrote, but we don't recommend it. Modern psychology, as you will discover, is far more fascinating than the psychology defined by Wundt and his followers.

Titchener and Structuralism: Psychology's Blind Alley

Question: What were the goals and method of structuralism, the first school of psychology?

Wundt's most famous student, an Englishman named Edward Bradford Titchener, took the new psychology to the United States, where he set up a psychological laboratory at Cornell University. Although Titchener differed from Wundt on some points, he pursued similar goals. He gave the name **structuralism** to this first school of thought in psychology, which aimed at analyzing the basic elements or the structure of conscious mental experience.

Structuralism was most severely criticized for its primary method, introspection. Introspection was not objective, even though it involved observation, measurement, and experimentation. When introspectionists were exposed to the same stimulus, such as the click of a metronome, they frequently reported different experiences from each other. Even when the same person was exposed to exactly the same stimulus at different times, he or she would often report a somewhat different experience. Structuralism was not long considered to be a viable school of thought. Later schools of thought in psychology were established, in part, as a reaction against structuralism, which collapsed with the death of its most ardent spokesperson, E. B. Titchener.

Functionalism: The First American School of Psychology

Question: What was the goal of the early school of psychology known as functionalism?

As structuralism was losing its influence in the United States in the early 1900s, a new school of psychology called functionalism was taking shape. **Functionalism** was not concerned with the structure of consciousness, but with how mental processes function, that is, how they are used by humans and animals in adapting to their environment.

The influential work of Charles Darwin, *On the Origin of Species by Means of Natural Selection* (1859), had a strong impact on the thinking of the leading proponents of functionalism. Darwin's ideas about evolution and the continuity of species were largely responsible for an increasing use of animal subjects in psychological experiments.

Another British thinker and a cousin of Charles Darwin was Sir Francis Galton. Galton did pioneering work in the study of individual differences and the role of genetic inheritance in mental abilities. In addition, he made a significant contribution in the areas of measurement and statistics. The correlation coefficient, discussed earlier, was his brainchild.

Darwin and Galton contributed important seeds of thought that helped give birth to the new school of psychology, but functionalism was primarily American in character and spirit. The famous American psychologist William James (1842–1910) was an advocate of functionalism even though he did much of his writing before this school of psychology appeared. James's best known work is his highly regarded and still popular textbook *Principles of Psychology*, published over 100 years ago (1890). James taught that mental processes are fluid and that they have continuity, rather than a rigid or fixed structure as the structuralists suggested. James spoke of the "stream of consciousness," which he said functioned to help humans adapt to their environment.

Functionalism broadened the scope of psychology to include the study of behavior as well as mental processes. Functionalism also included the study of

structuralism: The first formal school of psychology, aimed at analyzing the basic elements, or structure, of conscious mental experience through the use of introspection.

functionalism: An early school of psychology that was concerned with how mental processes help humans and animals adapt to their environments; developed in the United States as a reaction against structuralism.

William James, the first famous American psychologist, was at the forefront of the functionalist movement.

children, animals, and the mentally impaired. These groups were not subjects of study for the structuralists because they could not be trained to use introspection. Functionalism also focused on an applied, more practical use of psychology by encouraging the study of educational psychology, individual differences, and industrial psychology (adaptation in the workplace).

Behaviorism: Never Mind the Mind

Question: How did behaviorism differ from previous schools of psychology?

Psychologist John B. Watson (1878–1958) looked at the study of psychology as defined by the structuralists and functionalists and disliked virtually everything he saw. In Watson's view the study of mental processes, the concepts of mind and consciousness, and the primary investigative technique of introspection were not scientific. Watson pointed out that each person's introspection is strictly individual. He further maintained that self-reflection and internal ruminations cannot be observed, verified, understood, or communicated in objective, scientific terms. In his article "Psychology as the Behaviorist Views It" (1913), Watson argued that all the strictly subjective techniques and concepts in psychology must be thrown out. Out with introspection, the study of consciousness, and other fuzzy mentalistic concepts. Watson did not deny the existence of conscious thought or experience. He simply did not view them as appropriate subject matter for psychology.

Watson proposed a radically new approach to psychology. This new school of psychology, called **behaviorism**, redefined psychology as the "science of behavior." Behaviorism confined itself to the study of behavior because it is observable and measurable and, therefore, objective and scientific. Behaviorism also emphasized that behavior is determined primarily by factors in the environment.

B. F. Skinner: Continuing the Behaviorist Tradition   Behaviorism soon became the most influential school of thought in American psychology. It is still a major force in modern psychology, due in large part to the profound influence of B. F. Skinner (1904–1990). Skinner agreed with Watson that concepts such as mind, consciousness, and feelings were neither objective nor measurable and, therefore, were not the appropriate subject matter of psychology. Furthermore, Skinner argued that these concepts were not needed in order to explain behavior. Behavior, he claimed, can be explained by analyzing conditions that were present before a behavior occurs and by analyzing the consequences that follow the behavior.

Skinner's research on operant conditioning emphasized the importance of reinforcement in learning and in shaping and maintaining behavior. Any behavior that is reinforced—followed by pleasant or rewarding consequences—is more likely to be performed again. Skinner's work has had a powerful influence on modern psychology.

Skinner always lamented the fact "that behavior has seldom been thought of as subject matter in its own right, but rather has been viewed as the mere expression or symptom of more important happenings inside the behaving person" (1987, p. 780). Because the strict behaviorist position of Skinner and others has ignored inner, mental processes like thoughts and feelings, behaviorism has been a continuing target of criticism. Today many behaviorists do not take as extreme a view. While they still emphasize the central importance of the study of behavior, they are also willing to consider what these mental processes contribute to an explanation of behavior.

behaviorism: The school of psychology founded by John B. Watson that views observable, measurable behavior as the appropriate subject matter for psychology and emphasizes the key role of environment as a determinant of behavior.

Psychoanalysis: It's What's Down Deep That Counts

Question: What was the role of the unconscious in psychoanalysis, Freud's approach to psychology?

Although the behaviorists completely rejected unobservable mental forces in explaining behavior, this is precisely where Sigmund Freud looked in formulating his theory. Freud emphasized the importance of the unseen, unconscious mental forces as the key to understanding human nature and behavior.

Sigmund Freud (1856–1939), whose life and work you will study in the chapter on personality, developed a theory of human behavior based largely on the case studies of his patients. Freud's theory, **psychoanalysis**, maintains that human mental life is like an iceberg. The smallest, visible part of the iceberg represents the conscious mental experience of the individual. But underwater, hidden from view, floats a vast store of unconscious impulses, thoughts, wishes, and desires. Although people are not aware of them directly or consciously, these unconscious forces have the largest impact on behavior.

Freud believed that the unconscious is the storehouse for material that threatens the conscious life of the individual—disturbing sexual and aggressive impulses as well as traumatic experiences that have been repressed or pushed down to the unconscious. Once there, rather than resting quietly (out of sight, out of mind), the unconscious material festers and seethes, like "the bubbling, boiling brew in a cauldron," Freud wrote.

Freud's psychological theory does not paint a very positive or hopeful picture of human nature. He believed that we do not consciously control our thoughts, feelings, and behavior, but that they are determined by these unconscious forces that we cannot see and cannot control.

The overriding importance that Freud placed on sexual and aggressive impulses caused much controversy both inside and outside the field of psychology. The most notable of Freud's famous students—Carl Jung, Alfred Adler, and Karen Horney—broke away from their mentor and developed their own theories of personality. These three are often collectively referred to as neo-Freudians (new Freudians).

Freud's influence in the field of psychology is not nearly as strong as it once was, but he has had a tremendous impact on the popular culture. When they think of Freud, many people picture a psychiatrist using psychoanalysis with a patient on the familiar couch. The general public has heard of such concepts as the unconscious, repression, rationalization, and the Freudian slip. Such familiarity has made Sigmund Freud a larger-than-life figure rather than an obscure Austrian doctor resting within the dusty pages of history.

Gestalt Psychology: The Whole Is Greater than the Sum of Its Parts

Question: What is the emphasis of Gestalt psychology?

Although structuralism was not a major force in psychology for long, it did help give birth to other schools of thought, which arose, in part, as reactions against it. Gestalt psychology made its appearance in Germany in 1912, at almost the same time that John Watson launched behaviorism in the United States. The Gestalt psychologists objected to the central idea of structuralism, that conscious experience is best understood by reducing it to its basic elements. **Gestalt psychology** emphasized that individuals perceive objects and patterns as whole units, and that the whole thus perceived is greater than the sum of its parts. The German word *Gestalt* roughly means "whole, form, or pattern."

Sigmund Freud, perhaps the most influential psychologist of all time, believed that understanding unconscious mental forces is the key to explaining human behavior.

psychoanalysis (SY-ko-ah-NAL-ih-sis): The term Freud used for both his theory of personality and his therapy for the treatment of psychological disorders; the unconscious is the primary focus of psychoanalytic theory.

Gestalt psychology (gih-SHTALT): The school of psychology that emphasizes that individuals perceive objects and patterns as whole units and that the perceived whole is greater than the sum of its parts.

The leader of the Gestalt psychologists was Max Wertheimer (1880–1943). To support the Gestalt theory, Wertheimer presented his famous experiment demonstrating the phi phenomenon. In this experiment two light bulbs are placed a short distance apart in a dark room. The first light is flashed on and then flashed off just as the second light is flashed on. As this pattern of flashing the lights on and off continues, an observer perceives something quite different from what is actually happening. The observer sees what looks like a single light moving back and forth from one position to another. Here, said the Gestaltists, is proof that all perceptions do not arise from independent sensations as the structuralists claimed.

Perhaps you have seen flashing neon lights where you perceive figures that appear to move back and forth, but actually separate lights are being flashed on and off with precision timing as in the phi phenomenon. We perceive wholes or patterns, not collections of separate and independent sensations.

Other prominent Gestalt psychologists were Kurt Koffka and Wolfgang Kohler. Today the Gestalt psychologists continue to exert their influence in the study of perception, which will be discussed in chapter 3, "Sensation and Perception."

Humanistic Psychology: Looking at Human Potential

Question: What is the focus of humanistic psychology?

Humanistic psychology emerged in part as a reaction against behaviorism and psychoanalysis, the two major forces in psychology in the United States. In fact, its leading proponent, Abraham Maslow, called humanistic psychology the third force in psychology. **Humanistic psychology** focuses on the uniqueness of human beings and their capacity for choice, growth, and psychological health. The humanists reject the behaviorist notion that people have no free will and are shaped and controlled strictly by the environment. Humanists also reject Freud's theory that people are determined and driven from within, acting and marching to the dark drums of the unconscious.

Maslow objected to Freud's pessimistic view of human potential and pointed out that Freud had based his theory primarily on data from his disturbed patients. Maslow and other prominent humanistic psychologists, such as Carl Rogers, emphasized a much more positive view of human nature. They maintained that people are innately good and that they possess free will. The humanists believe that people are capable of making conscious, rational choices, which can lead to growth and psychological health.

Maslow proposed a theory of motivation that consists of a hierarchy of needs. He considered the need for self-actualization (developing to one's fullest potential) to be the highest need on the hierarchy. Carl Rogers developed his person-centered therapy and, with other humanists, popularized encounter groups and other techniques that are part of the human potential movement.

Table 1.2 summarizes the major schools of thought in psychology.

Memory Check 1.4

1. Match the school of psychology with its major emphasis.

    _____ 1) the scientific study of behav-   a. Gestalt psychology
           ior   b. structuralism

(continued)

Table 1.2 Schools of Thought in Psychology

School	Description
Structuralism	The first formal school of psychology. Focuses on analyzing the basic elements or structure of conscious mental experience through the use of introspection.
Functionalism	The first American school of psychology. Concerned with the study of mental processes and their role in facilitating adaptation to the environment. Broadened the scope of psychology to include the study of behavior as well as mental processes, and the study of children, the mentally impaired, and animals.
Behaviorism	Views observable, measurable behavior rather than internal mental processes as the appropriate subject matter of psychology. Stresses the key role of learning and the environment in determining behavior.
Gestalt psychology	Emphasizes that individuals perceive objects and patterns as whole units. The perceived whole is greater than the sum of its parts and is not best understood by analyzing its elemental parts (as suggested by the structuralists).
Psychoanalysis	Emphasizes the role of unconscious mental forces and conflicts in determining behavior.
Humanistic psychology	Focuses on the uniqueness of human beings and their capacity for choice, growth, and psychological health. Called the third force in psychology (behaviorism and psychoanalysis being the other two forces).

_____ 2) the perception of whole units or patterns

_____ 3) the unconscious

_____ 4) analysis of the basic elements of conscious mental experience

_____ 5) the uniqueness of human beings and their capacity for conscious choice and growth

_____ 6) the function of conscious mental experience

c. functionalism
d. psychoanalysis
e. humanistic psychology
f. behaviorism

2. Match the major figures with the appropriate school of psychology.

_____ 1) James

_____ 2) Freud

_____ 3) Watson and Skinner

_____ 4) Wundt and Titchener

_____ 5) Maslow and Rogers

a. behaviorism
b. structuralism
c. functionalism
d. psychoanalysis
e. humanistic psychology

Answers: 1. 1) f 2) a 3) d 4) b 5) e 6) c. 2. 1) c 2) d 3) a 4) b 5) e

biological perspective: A perspective that emphasizes the role of biological processes and heredity as the key to understanding behavior.

psychoanalytic perspective (SY-ko-AN-il-IT-ik): A perspective initially proposed by Freud that emphasizes the importance of the unconscious and of early childhood experiences as the keys to understanding behavior and thought.

behavioral perspective: A perspective that emphasizes the role of environment as the key to understanding behavior.

cognitive perspective: A perspective that emphasizes the role of mental processes as a key to understanding behavior.

Psychology Today

Modern Perspectives in Psychology: Current Views on Behavior and Thinking

Question: What are the five major perspectives in psychology today?

Modern psychologists are not easily categorized by a specific school of thought. There are no structuralists roaming the halls of psychology departments and, to our knowledge, no professors who call themselves functionalists. Today, rather than discussing schools of psychology, it is more appropriate to refer to psychological perspectives—points of view used for explaining people's behavior and thinking, whether normal or abnormal. Psychologists need not limit themselves to only one perspective or approach. Some take an eclectic position, choosing a combination of approaches to explain a particular behavior or psychological problem.

Psychologists who adopt the **biological perspective** emphasize the role of biological processes and heredity as the key to understanding behavior and thinking. To explain thinking, emotion, and behavior, both normal and abnormal, they study the structures of the brain and central nervous system, the functioning of the neurons, the delicate balance of neurotransmitters and hormones, and the impact of genes. For example, we know that too much or too little of different neurotransmitters in the brain are related to various mental disorders, such as schizophrenia and depression. Drugs already used in treating some of these disorders are designed to restore the brain's biochemical balance.

Researchers and theorists who adopt the biological perspective are often referred to as physiological psychologists, psychobiologists, or neuroscientists. The continuing development of medical technology in recent decades has spurred the research efforts of physiological psychologists. Many important findings in psychology have resulted from their work.

The psychoanalytic (psychodynamic) perspective in psychology is derived from the theory of Sigmund Freud. But the psychoanalytic approach has been modified considerably over the past several decades by psychologists known as neo-Freudians. The **psychoanalytic perspective** emphasizes the role of unconscious motivation and early childhood experiences in determining behavior and thought.

The biological approach looks inward to the physical and biochemical processes, and the psychoanalytic approach looks deeply inward to the unconscious to explain behavior. But the **behavioral perspective** looks in exactly the opposite direction, outward, emphasizing learning and the role of environmental factors as the keys to understanding behavior. What factors in the environment reinforce and thus maintain certain behaviors? According to the behaviorists, it is environmental factors that primarily shape behavior. These environmental factors must be analyzed in order to understand the causes of behavior and to establish programs of behavior modification to change problem behaviors.

The **cognitive perspective** considers the role of mental processes to be the key to understanding behavior. We must know more than what precedes a response and what follows it in order to understand behavior. The cognitive approach maintains that a given stimulus does not simply cause a given response. Rather, the individual consciously perceives, remembers, thinks, organizes, analyzes, decides, and then responds. To explain behavior more fully, according to the cognitive psychologists, the cognitive processes of perception, thinking, and memory must be considered.

Humanistic psychologists reject with equal vigor (1) the pessimistic view of the psychoanalytic approach, that human behavior is determined primarily by unconscious forces, and (2) the behaviorist view that behavior is determined by

Table 1.3 Modern Perspectives in Psychology

Perspective	Emphasis
Biological	The role of biological processes and structures, as well as heredity, in understanding behavior
Psychoanalytic	The role of unconscious motivation and early childhood experiences in determining behavior and thought
Behavioral	The role of learning and the environment in shaping and controlling behavior
Cognitive	The role of mental processes—perception, thinking, and memory—that underlie behavior
Humanistic	The importance of an individual's subjective experience as a key to understanding his or her behavior

humanistic perspective: A perspective that emphasizes the importance of an individual's subjective experience as a key to understanding behavior.

factors in the environment. The **humanistic perspective** views humans as capable of making rational, conscious choices. It emphasizes the importance of people's own subjective experiences as the key to understanding their behavior. Less scientific and objective than many other approaches, the humanistic approach unashamedly admits the inherent subjective nature of its position.

Table 1.3 gives a brief summary of the five perspectives in psychology today.

Psychologists at Work

Question: What are some specialists in psychology, and in what settings are they employed?

We know that psychologists have many different orientations toward the practice of psychology. Some psychologists teach at colleges and universities; others have private clinical practices and counsel patients. Psychologists work in hospitals and other medical facilities, in elementary and secondary schools, and in business and industry. Wherever you find human activity, you will likely find psychologists. Figure 1.4 shows the settings in which psychologists work.

Figure 1.4 Where Psychologists Work Psychologists work in a variety of settings. About 34 percent of psychologists work in colleges and universities, 24.5 percent work in hospitals and clinics, and 22 percent are in private practice. (Data from Howard, 1986.)

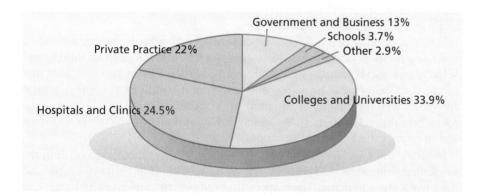

Types of Psychologists There are many specialties within the field of psychology. A few of them are briefly described in this section.

Clinical psychologists specialize in the diagnosis and treatment of mental and behavioral disorders. Some clinical psychologists also conduct research in these areas. Most clinical psychologists work in clinics, hospitals, and private practice, and many hold professorships at colleges and universities.

Counseling psychologists help people who have adjustment problems (marital, social, behavioral) that are less severe than those generally handled by clinical psychologists. Counseling psychologists may also provide academic or vocational counseling. Counselors usually work in a nonmedical setting such as a school or university, or they may have private practices. About 55 percent of all psychologists in the United States may be classified as either clinical or counseling psychologists.

Physiological psychologists, also called neuropsychologists, study the relationship between physiological processes and behavior. They study the structure and function of the brain and central nervous system, the role of the neurotransmitters and hormones, and other aspects of body chemistry to determine how physical and chemical processes affect behavior in both people and animals.

Experimental psychologists specialize in the use of experimental research methods. They conduct experiments in most fields of specialization in psychology—learning, memory, sensation, perception, motivation, emotion, and other areas as well. Some experimental psychologists study the brain and nervous system and how they affect behavior; their work overlaps with that of physiological psychologists. Experimental psychologists usually work in a laboratory, where they can exert precise control over the human or animal subjects being studied. Many experimental psychologists are faculty members who teach and conduct their research in college or university laboratories.

Developmental psychologists study how people grow, develop, and change throughout the life span. Some developmental psychologists specialize in a particular age group, such as infancy, childhood (child psychologists), adolescence, or old age (gerontologists). Others may concentrate on a specific aspect of human development such as physical, language, cognitive, or moral development. To investigate changes that occur throughout the life cycle, researchers might conduct longitudinal or cross-sectional studies. In a **longitudinal study** the same group of subjects is followed over a period of years and measured at different ages. A *cross-sectional study* is less expensive and less time-consuming. Groups of subjects of different ages are compared on certain characteristics in order to determine age-related differences. Figure 1.5 gives key aspects of longitudinal and cross-sectional studies.

Educational psychologists specialize in the study of teaching and learning. They may help train teachers and other educational professionals, or conduct research in teaching and classroom behavior. Some help prepare school curricula, develop achievement tests, or conduct evaluations of teaching and learning. School psychologists are employed by elementary and secondary schools to diagnose learning problems, to test students, and to counsel students, teachers, and parents on school-related problems.

While most other psychologists are concerned with what makes the individual function, social psychologists investigate how the individual feels, thinks, and behaves in a social setting—in the presence of others. When you are alone in a room, your behavior is probably different than it would be if another person entered. It would probably be different still if more and more people entered the room. Social psychologists study human behavior under a variety of conditions and in many different social situations.

Industry and business have found that expertise in psychology pays off in the workplace. Industrial psychologists study the relationships between people and their work environments. These specialists can benefit employers by suggesting ways to increase productivity, decrease job turnover and absenteeism, and im-

longitudinal study: A type of developmental study in which the same group of subjects is followed and measured at different ages.

cross-sectional study: A type of developmental study in which groups of subjects of different ages are compared on certain characteristics to determine age-related differences.

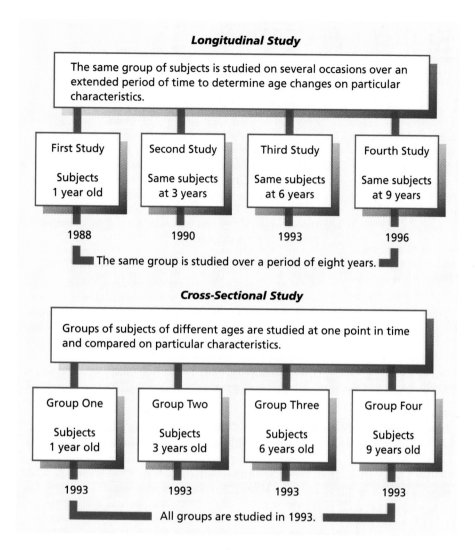

Longitudinal Study

The same group of subjects is studied on several occasions over an extended period of time to determine age changes on particular characteristics.

First Study	Second Study	Third Study	Fourth Study
Subjects 1 year old	Same subjects at 3 years	Same subjects at 6 years	Same subjects at 9 years
1988	1990	1993	1996

The same group is studied over a period of eight years.

Cross-Sectional Study

Groups of subjects of different ages are studied at one point in time and compared on particular characteristics.

Group One	Group Two	Group Three	Group Four
Subjects 1 year old	Subjects 3 years old	Subjects 6 years old	Subjects 9 years old
1993	1993	1993	1993

All groups are studied in 1993.

Figure 1.5

A Comparison of Longitudinal and Cross-Sectional Studies

To study age-related changes, longitudinal studies examine the same group of subjects over an extended period of time. Cross-sectional studies examine and compare groups of different ages at one point in time.

prove job-training programs, personnel selection, and evaluation of employees. Industrial psychologists also try to increase employee morale, job satisfaction, and motivation. The organizational psychologist is likely to work on improving the organizational structure, to advise management on effective supervision techniques, and to design programs to enhance cooperation among employees and between workers and management.

Figure 1.6 shows the percentages of psychologists who work in the specialties discussed in this section. As you can see, psychology is an enormously broad and diverse field of study. We hope that you will enjoy your explorations in the *World of Psychology*.

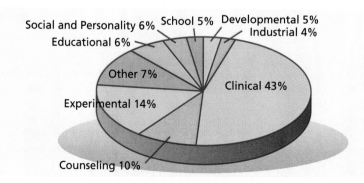

Figure 1.6

Specialties in Psychology

This chart shows the percentages of psychologists who work in various specialties in psychology. Clinical psychology is the largest specialty. (Data from Pion, Bramblett, & Wicherski, 1987.)

WORLD OF PSYCHOLOGY: APPLICATIONS

Sharpening Your Study Skills

An effective system to maximize learning is an old one, the *SQ3R* method, developed over 50 years ago by a teacher, Francis Robinson (1941). This book is organized to help you make use of S-Q-R-R-R, which stands for *Survey, Question, Read, Recite,* and *Review*. Instead of simply reading each chapter, you will learn and remember more if you faithfully follow *SQ3R*. Here is the process:

SURVEY: First scan the chapter that you plan to read. Read the chapter outline, the opening vignette, and the topic headings and study questions. Glance at the illustrations. Then read the chapter summary. This process will give you an overview of the chapter.

QUESTION: Before you actually read each section in the chapter, turn each topic heading into one or more questions. For some sections a study question is provided, but you can also add questions of your own. In other sections you alone supply the question. For example, the first topic in this chapter is *Naturalistic Observation*. The two-part study question is: "What is naturalistic observation, and what are some of its advantages and limitations?" You might add these questions: How is naturalistic observation used? What kind of information does it provide? Asking such questions helps to focus your reading.

READ: Read the information included in the first topic. As you read, try to answer the questions (the study question and your own questions). After reading the first topic, stop. If the topic is very long, or if the material seems especially difficult or complex, you should stop after reading only one or two paragraphs. Now you are ready for the second *R*.

RECITE: The second *R* means recite. After reading one topic, answer the topic question. To further grasp the material, write a short summary of the topic. If you have trouble summarizing the topic or answering the questions, scan or read the topic again before trying another time.

When you have finished the first topic, move on to the next topic (in this chapter, *Laboratory Observation*). You are back to the *Q* of *SQ3R*. Since no study question is provided, formulate your own. For example, you could ask: What is laboratory observation? How does it differ from naturalistic observation? With your questions in mind, read the topic and then recite, answering your questions or writing a brief summary as before.

REVIEW: Periodically you will find a *Memory Check* that consists of a few questions about the preceding topics. Answer the questions and check your answers. If you make errors, quickly review the preceding material until you know the answers.

When you have finished the chapter, turn to the *Chapter Summary and Review* section. Review the Key Terms. If you don't know the meaning of a Key Term, turn to the page that has the term's definition in the margin or in a table. Next review each study question in the summary and answer it in your own words. The answers provided are given only as condensed reminders, and you should be able to expand on them.

Finally, look at the three *Thinking Critically* questions: *Evaluation, Point/Counterpoint,* and *Psychology in Your Life*. Answering these questions requires more than simple memorization. The critical thinking questions give you the chance to show that you really understand the information presented in the chapter.

Study Habits That Pay Rich Dividends

- Select a quiet place, free of distractions, where you do nothing else but study. You can condition yourself to associate this environment with studying, so that entering the room or area will be your cue to begin work. Moreover, you will be less tempted to do other things while you are there.

- Research on memory has proven that spaced learning is more effective than massed practice (cramming). Instead of studying for 5 hours straight, try five study sessions of 1 hour each.

- The more active role you play in the learning process, the more you will remember. Spend some of your study time *reciting* rather than simply *rereading* the material. One effective method is to use 3″ × 5″ index cards as flash cards. Write a Key Term on the front of each card. On the back, list information from the text and lecture pertaining to that term. You should also have an index card for each study question; write the answer on the back of the card. Use these cards to help you prepare for tests. Test yourself before your professor does.

- *Overlearning* means studying beyond the point where you can just barely recite the information you are trying to memorize. For best results, don't stop studying at this point. Spend more time reviewing the information again and again until it is firmly locked in memory. If you are subject to test anxiety, overlearning will help. The overlearned information is more likely to survive an attack of nerves.

- Forgetting takes place most rapidly within the first 24 hours after you study. No matter how much you have studied for a test, *always* review shortly before you take the test. Freshening your memory will raise your grade.

- *Sleeping* immediately after you study will help you retain more of what you learned. If you can't study before you go to sleep, at least review before sleep what you studied earlier in the day. This is a good time to go through your index cards.

When you read chapter 6, "Memory," you will learn why sleep facilitates memory and why the other suggestions will help you remember more of what you study. You have an interesting journey ahead of you in the *World of Psychology*. Use the study hints you have just read, follow the *SQ3R* method as you read the chapters, and you will be off to a great start.

Memory Check 1.5

Match the psychological perspective with its major emphasis.

_____ 1) the role of biological processes and
        heredity
_____ 2) the role of learning and environmental
        factors
_____ 3) the role of mental processes
_____ 4) the role of the unconscious and early
        childhood experiences
_____ 5) understanding the individual's own
        subjective experience

a. psychoanalytic
b. biological
c. behavioral
d. cognitive
e. humanistic

Answers: 1) b 2) c 3) d 4) a 5) e

Thinking Critically _____

Evaluation

Consider the three schools of thought in psychology: behaviorism, psychoanalysis, and humanistic psychology. Which do you like most, which do you like least, and why?

Point/Counterpoint

This chapter discussed the issue of deception in research and described a study that used deception to research the effects of alcohol and expectations on aggression. Prepare convincing arguments to support each of these opinions:

a. Deception is justified in research studies.
b. Deception is not justified in research studies.

Psychology in Your Life

Having read about experimental research and survey research in this chapter, how will it affect the way you evaluate research studies in articles you read or in reports you hear in the future?

Chapter Summary and Review _____

Descriptive Research Methods

What is naturalistic observation, and what are some of its advantages and limitations?

In naturalistic observation, researchers observe and record the behavior of subjects in a natural setting without attempting to influence or control it. The limitations include the researcher's lack of control over the observed situation, and the potential for observer bias.

What is the case study method, and for what purposes is it particularly well suited?

The case study is an in-depth study of one or several subjects through observation, interview, and sometimes psychological testing. It is particularly appropriate for studying people who have rare psychological or physiological disorders.

What are the methods and purpose of survey research?

The survey is a research method in which interviews and/or

questionnaires are used to gather information about the attitudes, beliefs, experiences, or behaviors of a group of people.

What is a representative sample, and why is it essential in a survey?

A representative sample is a sample of subjects selected from the population of interest in such a way that important subgroups within the whole population are included in the same proportions in the sample. A sample must be representative for the findings to be applied to the larger population.

Key Terms

psychology (p. 3)
basic research (p. 3)
applied research (p. 3)
naturalistic observation (p. 3)
case study (p. 4)
survey (p. 4)
representative sample (p. 5)

The Experimental Method: Searching for Causes

What is the main advantage of the experimental method?

The experimental method is the only research method that can be used to identify cause-effect relationships.

What is the difference between the independent variable and the dependent variable?

In an experiment an independent variable is the condition or factor manipulated by the researcher to determine its effect on the dependent variable. The dependent variable, measured at the end of the experiment, is presumed to vary as a result of the manipulations of the independent variable.

How do the experimental and control groups differ?

The experimental group is exposed to the independent variable. The control group is similar to the experimental group and is exposed to the same experimental environment but is not exposed to the independent variable.

What is selection bias, and what technique do researchers use to control for it?

Selection bias occurs when there are systematic differences among the subject groups before the experiment begins. Random assignment—assigning subjects to groups by using a chance procedure—maximizes the probability that groups are similar at the beginning of the experiment.

What is the placebo effect, and how do researchers control for it?

The placebo effect occurs when a person's expectations influence the outcome of a treatment or experiment. To control for the placebo effect, the researcher must ensure that the subjects do not know if they are members of the experimental group (receiving the treatment) or of the control group (receiving the placebo).

What is experimenter bias, and how is it controlled?

Experimenter bias occurs when the researcher's expectations affect the outcome of the experiment. Its control is the double-blind technique, in which neither the experimenter nor the subjects know which subjects are in an experimental group and which are in a control group.

Key Terms

experimental method (p. 7)
independent variable (p. 9)
dependent variable (p. 9)
experimental group (p. 9)
control group (p. 9)
selection bias (p. 10)
random assignment (p. 10)
placebo effect (p. 11)
placebo (p. 11)
experimenter bias (p. 11)
double-blind technique (p. 11)

Other Research Methods

What is the correlational method, and when is it used?

The correlational method is used to determine the correlation or relationship between two variables. It is often used when an experimental study cannot be conducted because it is either impossible or unethical.

What is a correlation coefficient?

A correlation coefficient is a numerical value that indicates the strength and direction of the relationship between two variables.

Key Terms

correlational method (p. 13)
correlation coefficient (p. 13)

Some Considerations in Psychological Research

Why must psychological research be replicated?

Psychological research must be replicated, or repeated, in order to verify research findings.

Key Term

replication (p. 16)

The History of Psychology: Exploring Psychology's Roots

What was Wilhelm Wundt's contribution to psychology?

Wundt, considered the father of psychology, established the first psychological laboratory in 1879 and launched the study of psychology as a formal, academic discipline.

What were the goals and method of structuralism, the first school of psychology?

Structuralism's main goal was to analyze the basic elements or structure of conscious mental experience through the use of introspection.

What was the goal of the early school of psychology known as functionalism?

Functionalism was concerned with how mental processes help humans and animals adapt to their environment.

How did behaviorism differ from previous schools of psychology?

Behaviorism, the school of psychology founded by John B. Watson, views only observable, measurable behavior as the appropriate subject matter for psychology. Behaviorism also emphasizes the environment as the key determinant of behavior.

What was the role of the unconscious in psychoanalysis, Freud's approach to psychology?

According to Freud's theory of psychoanalysis, our thoughts, feelings, and behavior are determined primarily by the unconscious—the part of the mind that we cannot see and cannot control.

What is the emphasis of Gestalt psychology?

Gestalt psychology emphasizes that individuals perceive objects and patterns as whole units and that the perceived whole is greater than the sum of its parts.

What is the focus of humanistic psychology?

Humanistic psychology focuses on the uniqueness of human beings and their capacity for choice, growth, and psychological health.

Key Terms

structuralism (p. 21)
functionalism (p. 21)
behaviorism (p. 22)
psychoanalysis (p. 23)
Gestalt psychology (p. 23)
humanistic psychology (p. 25)

Psychology Today

What are the five major perspectives in psychology today?

The five major perspectives in psychology today are (1) the biological perspective, which emphasizes the role of biological processes and heredity as the key to understanding behavior and thought; (2) the psychoanalytic perspective, which focuses on the role of the unconscious and early childhood experiences; (3) the behavioral perspective, which emphasizes learning and the role of environmental factors in shaping behavior; (4) the cognitive perspective, which stresses the role of the mental processes (perceiving, thinking, remembering, etc.); and (5) the humanistic perspective, which emphasizes the importance of an individual's subjective experience.

What are some specialists in psychology, and in what settings are they employed?

There are clinical and counseling psychologists, physiological psychologists, experimental psychologists, developmental psychologists, educational and school psychologists, social psychologists, and industrial, organizational, and human factors psychologists. Psychologists are found in a number of different settings—colleges and universities, elementary and secondary schools, medical settings, business and industry, and private practice.

Key Terms

biological perspective (p. 26)
psychoanalytic perspective (p. 26)
behavioral perspective (p. 26)
cognitive perspective (p. 26)
humanistic perspective (p. 27)
longitudinal study (p. 28)

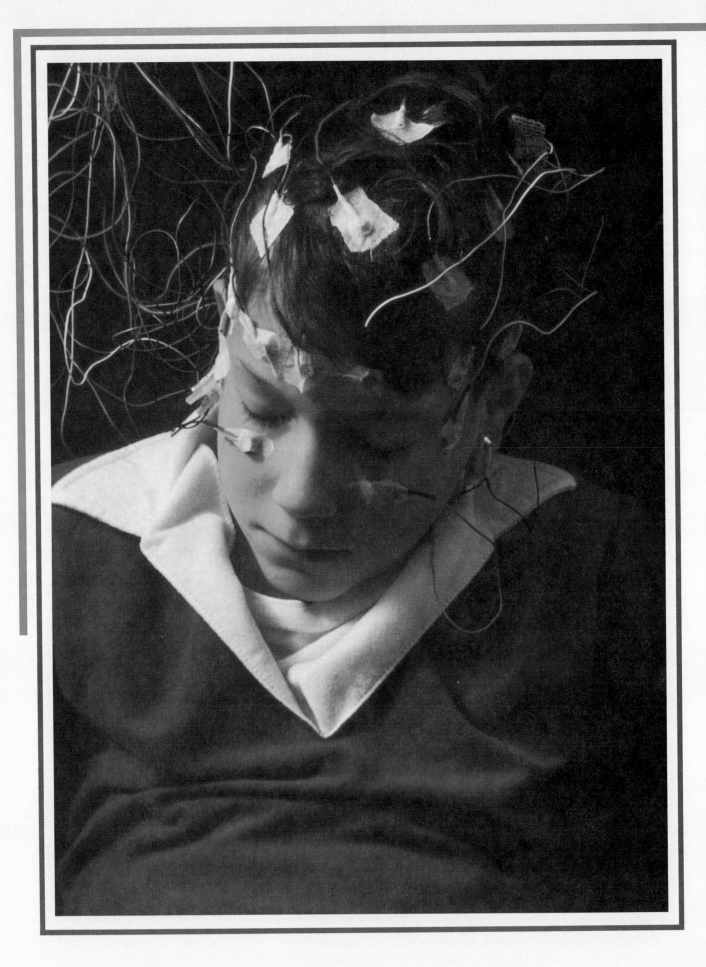

2

Biology and Behavior

CHAPTER OUTLINE

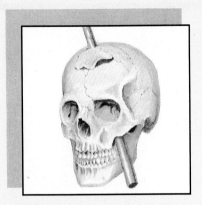

Figure 2.1

The Case of Phineas Gage

This illustration shows the area of the skull through which the crowbar passed. (From Harlow, 1848.)

On September 13, 1848, 25-year-old Phineas Gage, a foreman on a railroad construction crew, was using dynamite to blast away rock and dirt. Suddenly an unplanned explosion almost took Gage's head off, sending a 3 1/2-foot long, 13-pound metal rod under his left cheekbone and out through the top of his skull (see Figure 2.1).

Much of the brain tissue in Gage's frontal lobe was torn away, along with flesh, pieces of his skull, and other bone fragments. This should have been the end of Phineas Gage, but it wasn't. He regained consciousness within a few minutes, was loaded onto a cart, and wheeled to his hotel nearly a mile away. He got out with a little help, walked up the stairs, entered his room, and walked to his bed. He was still conscious when the doctor arrived nearly two hours later.

Gage recovered and returned home in about 5 weeks, but he was not the same man. Before the accident, he was described as a hard worker who was polite, dependable, and well liked. But the new Phineas Gage, without part of his frontal lobe, was found to be loud-mouthed and profane, rude and impulsive, and contemptuous toward others. He no longer planned realistically for the future, and was no longer motivated and industrious as he once had been. Gage lost his job as foreman and joined P. T. Barnum's circus as a sideshow exhibit at carnivals and county fairs. (Adapted from Harlow, 1848.)

ALMOST 150 YEARS HAVE PASSED since the heavy metal rod tore through Phineas Gage's brain. During that time we have learned much about the human brain—some of it puzzling and mysterious, all of it fascinating. How can the brain sustain such massive damage, as in the case of Gage, and still not kill the patient, while a small bullet fired through the brain in a number of different places can result in instant death? In this chapter you will learn how tough and resilient, yet how fragile and vulnerable this remarkable 3-pound organ really is.

In chapter 1, our introduction to the *World of Psychology*, we defined psychology as the scientific study of behavior and mental processes. Before we can gain an understanding and an appreciation of our behavior and mental processes, we must first explore the all-important biological connection. Every thought we think, every emotion we feel, every sensation we experience, every decision we reach, every move we make—in short, all of human behavior—is rooted in a biological event. Therefore we launch our exploration of psychology with the study of biology and behavior. Our story begins where the action begins, in the smallest functional unit of the brain—the nerve cell, or neuron.

The Neurons and the Neurotransmitters

The Neurons: Billions of Brain Cells

All our thoughts, feelings, and behavior can ultimately be traced to the activity of **neurons**—the specialized cells that conduct impulses through the nervous system. Most experts estimate that there may be as many as 100 billion neurons in the brain (Aoki & Siekevitz, 1988; Levine, 1988). This would mean that you have about 20 times as many neurons as there are people living on the earth right now.

Neurons perform several important tasks: (1) Afferent (sensory) neurons relay messages from the sense organs and receptors—eyes, ears, nose, mouth, and skin—to the brain or spinal cord. (2) Efferent (motor) neurons convey signals from the brain and spinal cord to the glands and the muscles, enabling us to move. (3) Interneurons, thousands of times more numerous than motor or

neuron (NEW-ron): A specialized cell that conducts impulses through the nervous system and contains three major parts—a cell body, dendrites, and an axon.

sensory neurons, carry information between neurons in the brain and between neurons in the spinal cord.

Question: What is a neuron, and what are its three parts?

Anatomy of a Neuron: Looking at Its Parts Neurons transmit signals through the nervous system. Although no two neurons are exactly alike, all are made up of three important parts: cell body (soma), dendrites, and axon. The *cell body* contains the nucleus and carries out the metabolic, or life-sustaining, functions of the neuron. Branching out from the cell body are the **dendrites,** which look much like the leafless branches of a tree (*dendrite* comes from the Greek word for "tree"). The dendrites are the primary receivers of signals from other neurons, but the cell body can also receive the signals directly.

The **axon** is the slender, taillike extension of the neuron that sprouts into many branches, each ending in a bulbous-shaped axon terminal. The axon terminals transmit signals to the dendrites, to the cell bodies of other neurons, and to muscles, glands, and other parts of the body. In humans, some axons are short—only thousandths of an inch. Others can be up to a meter—39.37 inches—long enough to reach from the brain to the tip of the spinal cord, or from the spinal cord to remote parts of the body. Figure 2.2 shows the structure of a neuron.

Question: What is a synapse?

The Synapse Remarkably, the billions of neurons that relay signals back and forth to each other and to all parts of the body are not physically connected. The axon terminals are separated from the receiving neurons by tiny, fluid-filled gaps called synaptic clefts. The **synapse** is the junction where the axon terminal of the sending (presynaptic) neuron communicates with a receiving (postsynaptic) neuron across the synaptic cleft. There may be from 10 trillion (Levine, 1988) to perhaps 100 trillion synapses in the human nervous system (Hubel, 1979; Pinel, 1990).

How big is 1 trillion? Numbers in the trillions are hard for us to conceptualize. You know what a short span of time elapses in one second. If you were to

cell body: The part of the neuron, containing the nucleus, that carries out the metabolic functions of the neuron.

dendrites (DEN-drytes): The branchlike extensions of a neuron that receive signals from other neurons.

axon (AK-sahn): The slender, taillike extension of the neuron that transmits signals to the dendrites or cell body of other neurons or to the muscles or glands.

synapse (SIN-aps): The junction where the axon of a sending neuron communicates with a receiving neuron across the synaptic cleft.

Figure 2.2 The Structure of a Neuron Neurons have three important parts: (1) a cell body, which carries out the metabolic functions of the neuron; (2) branched fibers called dendrites, which are the primary receivers of impulses from other neurons; and (3) a slender, taillike extension called an axon, the transmitting end of the neuron, which sprouts into many branches, each ending in an axon terminal. The photograph shows human neurons greatly magnified.

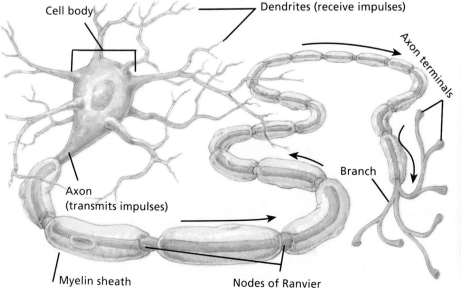

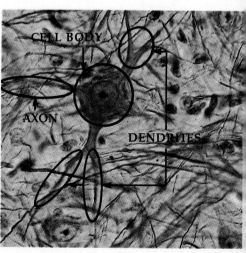

compute 1 trillion seconds, you would find that it takes almost 32,000 years for 1 trillion seconds to pass. Now try to imagine the incredible complexity of your brain if there are from 10 to 100 trillion synapses across which your neurons are passing and receiving messages.

If neurons are not physically connected, how do they communicate? How do they spread their messages throughout the brain, spinal cord, and every area of the body?

Question: What is the action potential?

The Neural Impulse: The Beginning of Thought and Action   Researchers have known for about 200 years that cells in the brain, the spinal cord, and the muscles generate electrical potentials. These tiny electric charges play a part in all bodily functions. Every time we move a muscle, experience a sensation, or have a thought or a feeling, a small but measurable electrical impulse is present.

How does this biological electricity work? Even though the impulse that travels down the axon is electrical, the axon does not transmit it the way a wire conducts an electrical current. What actually moves through the axon is a change in the permeability of the cell membrane. This process allows ions (electrically charged chemicals) to move through the membrane, into and out of the neuron. Bodily fluids contain certain types of chemical molecules known as ions, some with positive charges and others with negative charges. Like other living cells, every neuron is contained within its own thin skin, the cell membrane. Inside this membrane there are normally more negative than positive ions. When at rest (not firing), a neuron carries a negative electrical potential of about -70 millivolts (70/1,000 of a volt) in comparison to the environment outside the cell. This slight negative charge is referred to as the neuron's *resting potential*.

When a neuron is sufficiently stimulated, its resting potential becomes disturbed. As a result, the cell membrane of the neuron changes its permeability. This causes more positive ions, particularly sodium, to flow into the cell and other ions to flow out. If the disturbance reaches a minimum intensity known as the threshold, the neuron's resting membrane potential is suddenly reversed. It becomes positive, to about $+50$ millivolts for about 1/1,000 of a second (Kalil, 1989; Pinel, 1990). This sudden reversal of the resting potential is the **action potential**. The action potential operates according to the "all or none" law—the neuron either fires completely or does not fire at all. Immediately after the neuron reaches its action potential and fires, it returns to its resting potential until stimulated again. But its rest may be very short because neurons can fire up to 1,000 times per second. Figure 2.3 illustrates the movement of positive ions across the cell membrane, which stimulates the neuron to its action potential.

Neurotransmitters: The Chemical Messengers of the Brain

Question: What are neurotransmitters, and what role do they play in the transmission of signals from one neuron to another?

Once a neuron fires, how does it get its message across the synaptic cleft and on to other neurons? Messages are transmitted between neurons by one or more of a large group of chemical substances known as **neurotransmitters** (Hökfelt et al., 1984). Where are the neurotransmitters located?

Inside the axon terminal are many small, sphere-shaped containers with thin membranes called synaptic vesicles, which hold the neurotransmitters. (*Vesicle* comes from a Latin word meaning "little bladder.") When an action potential arrives at the axon terminal, synaptic vesicles move toward the cell membrane,

resting potential: The membrane potential of a neuron at rest, about -70 millivolts.

action potential: The firing of a neuron that results when the charge within the neuron becomes more positive than the charge outside the cell's membrane.

neurotransmitter (NEW-ro-TRANS-mit-er):   A chemical that is released into the synaptic cleft from the axon terminal of the sending neuron, crosses the synapse, and binds to appropriate receptor sites on the dendrites or cell body of the receiving neuron, influencing the cell either to fire or not to fire.

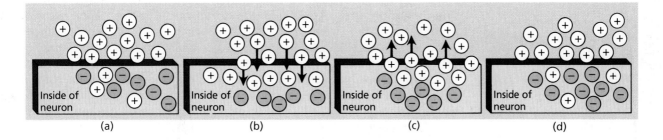

Figure 2.3   The Action Potential   (a) When a neuron is at rest (not firing), the inside of the neuron has a slight negative electrical charge compared to the outside, referred to as the neuron's resting potential. (b) When a neuron is stimulated, more positively charged particles flow into the cell, making the inside suddenly positive compared to the outside of the cell. This sudden reversal is the action potential. (c) Immediately after the neuron fires, some positive particles are actively pumped out of the cell. (d) The neuron returns to its resting potential and is ready to fire again if stimulated.

fuse with it, and release their neurotransmitter molecules. This is shown in Figure 2.4. There is evidence that the action potential opens calcium channels, permitting calcium ions (Ca^{++}) to flow into the axon terminals and trigger the release of neurotransmitters (Pinel, 1990). More recently researchers have identified a calcium sensor on the surface of the synaptic vesicles (Brose et al., 1992).

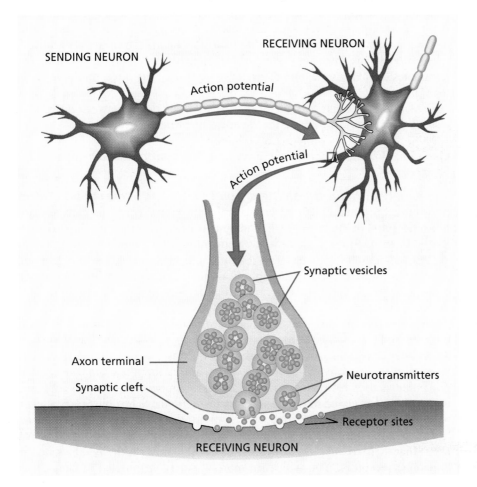

Figure 2.4

Synaptic Transmission

Sending neurons transmit their messages to receiving neurons by electrochemical action. When a neuron fires, the action potential arrives at the axon terminal and triggers the release of neurotransmitters from the synaptic vesicles. Neurotransmitters flow into the synaptic cleft and move toward the receiving neuron, which has numerous receptor sites. The receptor sites will receive only neurotransmitters with distinctive molecular shapes that match them. Neurotransmitters influence the receiving neuron only to fire or not to fire.

receptor site: A site on the dendrite or cell body of a neuron that will receive only specific neurotransmitters.

reuptake: The process by which neurotransmitter molecules are taken from the synaptic cleft back into the axon terminal for later use, thus terminating their excitatory or inhibitory effect on the receiving neuron.

The Receptor Sites: Locks for Neurotransmitter Keys Once released, neurotransmitters do not simply flow into the synaptic cleft and stimulate all the adjacent neurons. Each neurotransmitter has a distinctive molecular shape. Numerous *receptor sites* on the surfaces of dendrites and cell bodies also have distinctive shapes. Neurotransmitters can affect only those neurons that contain receptor sites designed to receive the shape of their particular molecule. In other words, each receptor site is like a locked door that only certain neurotransmitter keys can unlock.

When neurotransmitters enter receptor sites on the dendrites or cell bodies of receiving neurons, their action is either excitatory (influencing the neurons to fire) or inhibitory (influencing them not to fire). Because a single neuron may synapse with hundreds or even a thousand other neurons at the same time, there will always be both excitatory and inhibitory influences on receiving neurons. For the neuron to fire, the excitatory influences must exceed the inhibitory influences of neurotransmitter substances by a sufficient amount (the threshold).

Inhibitory influences are absolutely necessary. If the electrochemical action in a neuron caused all (or even most) of the other neurons to fire, there would be a continuous electrical storm in the brain—an unending convulsion that would make any voluntary behavior and even life itself impossible. Even though the action of the neurotransmitter is said to be either excitatory or inhibitory, there are many different neurotransmitter substances producing a variety of specific physical and psychological effects.

You may wonder how the synaptic vesicles can continue to pour out their neurotransmitters, yet have a ready supply so the neuron can respond to continuing stimulation. First, the cell body of the neuron is always working to manufacture more of the neurotransmitter substance. Second, after accomplishing its mission, the neurotransmitter may be broken down into its component molecules and reclaimed by the axon terminal to be recycled and used again. Third, by an important process called *reuptake*, the neurotransmitter substance is taken intact back into the the axon terminal, ready for immediate use. This terminates the neurotransmitters' excitatory or inhibitory effect on the receiving neuron.

The important point to remember is that signals travel between neurons by way of the neurotransmitters, the chemical messengers of the brain.

*Question: **What are some of the ways in which neurotransmitters affect our behavior?***

The Variety of Neurotransmitters: Some Excite and Some Inhibit Neurotransmitters are manufactured in the brain, the spinal cord, the glands, and a few other parts of the body. Each kind of neurotransmitter affects the activity of the brain in a different way. Some neurotransmitters regulate the actions of glands and muscles; others affect learning and memory; still others promote sleep or stimulate mental and physical alertness. Other neurotransmitters orchestrate our feelings and emotions, from depression to euphoria. Some, such as endorphins, provide relief from pain.

An imbalance in the levels of the neurotransmitters can cause a range of physical and psychological problems. For example, a deficiency in the neurotransmitter dopamine can cause Parkinson's disease, a condition characterized by tremors and rigidity in the limbs. L-dopa, a drug that the brain converts into dopamine, is used to treat Parkinson's disease. An oversensitivity to dopamine is thought to be related to some cases of schizophrenia. Schizophrenia is a severe psychotic disorder characterized by loss of contact with reality, by hallucinations (imaginary sensations such as hearing voices), and by delusions. Medications that help reduce these symptoms presumably work by blocking the dopamine receptors. You will learn more about schizophrenia in chapter 14, "Abnormal Behavior."

Neurotransmitters affect our behavior in many ways. Researchers at UCLA have found a connection between the neurotransmitter serotonin and leadership qualities in both monkeys and fraternity presidents.

The neurotransmitters serotonin and norepinephrine are related to positive moods, and a deficiency in the two has been linked to depression. Some antidepressant drugs relieve the symptoms of depression by blocking the reuptake of serotonin or norepinephrine, thus increasing its availability in the synapses.

The Rate of Neural Firing and the Speed of the Impulse

Consider this important question: If a neuron only fires or does not fire, how can we tell the difference between a very strong and a very weak stimulus? a jarring blow and a soft touch? a blinding light and a dim one? a shout and a whisper? The answer lies in the number of neurons firing at the same time and their rate of firing (the number of times per second). A weak stimulus may cause relatively few neurons to fire, while a strong stimulus may trigger thousands of neurons to fire at the same time. Also, a weak stimulus may be signaled by neurons firing very slowly, while stronger stimuli may incite the neurons to fire hundreds of times per second. Normally the firing rate is much slower, but the ability of a neuron to change from resting to action potential so many times in a single second is difficult to imagine.

Once a neuron fires, how fast do you suppose the impulse travels down the length of the axon? Impulses travel at speeds from about 1 meter per second to approximately 100 meters per second (about 224 miles per hour). The speed of the impulse is related to the size of the axon. The larger, longer axons—those that reach from the brain through the spinal cord, and from the spinal cord to remote parts of the body—send impulses at a faster speed than neurons with smaller, shorter axons. How can this be?

The most important factor in speeding the impulse on its way is the *myelin sheath*—a white, fatty coating wrapped around some axons that acts as insulation. If you look again at Figure 2.2, you will see that the coating has numerous gaps called nodes of Ranvier. These nodes cause the myelin sheath to look like links of sausage strung together. The electrical impulse is retriggered or regenerated at each node (or naked gap) on the axon. This speeds the impulse up to 100 times faster than impulses in axons without myelin sheaths.

Glial Cells: The Neurons' Helper Cells

Glial cells are specialized cells in the brain that form the myelin coating and perform many other important functions. *Glia* means "glue," and these cells hold the neurons together. Glial cells remove waste products such as dead neurons from the brain, and they handle other manufacturing, nourishing, and clean-up tasks (Rosenzweig et al., 1972). Glial cells serve another function when the brain is being formed and as it grows and develops. During this period of development, glial cells act as guides, taking the specialized neurons from where they are manufactured to where they will finally function (Rakic, 1988).

Glial cells are smaller but about five to ten times more numerous than neurons (Bloom et al., 1985). It is now known that glial cells interact with neurons in complex ways, and they play a part in creating a more efficient brain (Abbott & Raff, 1991). Marian Diamond and others (1985) analyzed four small cubes of brain tissue from different parts of Albert Einstein's brain, and comparable cubes from the brains of 11 people of average intelligence. They found that Einstein had about 73 percent more glial cells than the control subjects in one part of the left parietal lobe that is involved in analyzing information from various regions in the brain.

myelin sheath (MY-uh-lin): The white, fatty coating wrapped around some axons that acts as insulation and enables impulses to travel much faster.

glial cells (GLEE-ul): Cells that help to make the brain more efficient by holding the neurons together, removing waste products such as dead neurons, making the myelin coating for the axons, and performing other manufacturing, nourishing, and clean-up tasks.

Memory Check 2.1

1. The specialized cell that transmits signals through the nervous system is the (neuron, glial cell).

2. The part of the neuron that is the primary receiver of signals from other neurons is the (dendrite, axon).

3. The junction where the axon of a sending neuron communicates with a receiving neuron is called the:

   a. reuptake site   c. synapse
   b. receptor site   d. axon terminal

4. When a neuron fires, neurotransmitters are released into the synaptic cleft from the synaptic vesicles in the _____ terminal.

   a. dendrite   c. receptor
   b. cell body's   d. axon

5. Receptor sites on the receiving neuron:

   a. receive any available neurotransmitter molecules
   b. receive only neurotransmitter molecules of a specific shape
   c. can only be influenced by neurotransmitters from a single neuron
   d. are located only on the dendrites

6. A very strong stimulus will cause a neuron to fire (at a faster rate, more completely) than a weak stimulus.

Answers: 1. neuron 2. dendrite 3. c 4. d 5. b 6. at a faster rate

The Central Nervous System

We have discussed how neurons function individually and in groups through electrochemical action. But human functioning involves much more than the actions of individual neurons. Collections of neurons, brain structures, and organ systems also must be explored. The nervous system is divided into two parts: (1) the **central nervous system** (CNS), which is composed of the brain and the spinal cord, and (2) the peripheral nervous system, which connects the central nervous system to all other parts of the body (see Figure 2.5).

Now we will follow the spinal cord up through the brainstem and the other brain structures to the most distinctly human part of the brain—the cerebrum, with its incredible cortex. The peripheral nervous system will be discussed later in this chapter.

The Spinal Cord: An Extension of the Brain

Question: Why is an intact spinal cord important to normal functioning?

The **spinal cord** can best be thought of as an extension of the brain. Like the brain, it has gray matter as well as white matter and is loaded with glial cells. A cylinder of neural tissue about the diameter of your little finger, the spinal cord

central nervous system (CNS): The brain and the spinal cord.

spinal cord: An extension of the brain, reaching from the base of the brain through the neck and spinal column, that transmits messages between the brain and the peripheral nervous system.

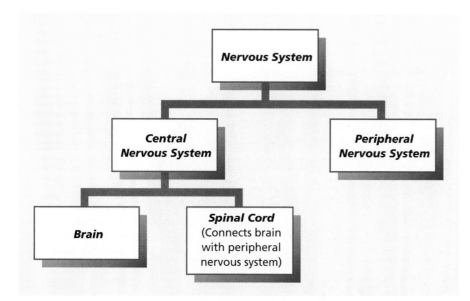

Figure 2.5

Divisions of the Human Nervous System

The human nervous system is divided into two parts: (1) the central nervous system, consisting of the brain and the spinal cord, and (2) the peripheral nervous system.

reaches from the base of the brain, through the neck, and down the hollow center of the spinal column. The spinal cord is protected by bone and also by spinal fluid, which serves as a shock absorber. The spinal cord virtually links the body with the brain. It transmits messages between the brain and the peripheral nervous system. Thus, sensory information can reach the brain, and messages from the brain can be sent to the muscles and the glands.

Although the spinal cord and the brain usually function together, the spinal cord can act without help from the brain to protect us from injury. For example, the reflex that causes you to withdraw your hand quickly from a hot stove is controlled by the spinal cord without the initial involvement of the brain. The brain, however, quickly becomes aware and involved when the pain signal reaches it. At that point, you might plunge your hand into cold water to relieve the pain.

The Brainstem: The Most Primitive Part of the Brain

Question: What are the crucial functions handled by the brainstem?

The **brainstem** begins at the site where the spinal cord enlarges as it enters the skull. The brainstem includes the medulla, the pons, and the reticular formation, as shown in Figure 2.6. The brainstem handles functions that are so critical to our physical survival that damage to it is life-threatening. The **medulla** is the part of the brainstem that controls heart rate, respiration, and blood pressure. Because the medulla handles these functions automatically, you do not have to remember to breathe or to keep your heart beating.

Extending through the brainstem into the pons is another important structure, the **reticular formation**, sometimes called the reticular activating system (RAS). Find it in Figure 2.6. The reticular formation plays a crucial role in arousal and attention. Every day our sense organs are bombarded with stimuli, but we cannot possibly pay attention to everything we see or hear. The reticular formation screens messages entering the brain. It blocks some messages and sends others on to higher brain centers for processing.

The reticular formation also determines how alert we are. When it slows down, we doze off or go to sleep. But like an alarm clock, it also can jolt us into consciousness. Thanks to the reticular formation, important messages get

brainstem: The structure that begins at the point where the spinal cord enlarges as it enters the brain and that includes the medulla, the pons, and the reticular formation.

medulla (muh-DUL-uh): The part of the brainstem that controls heartbeat, blood pressure, and respiration.

reticular formation: A structure in the brainstem that plays a crucial role in arousal and attention and that screens sensory messages entering the brain.

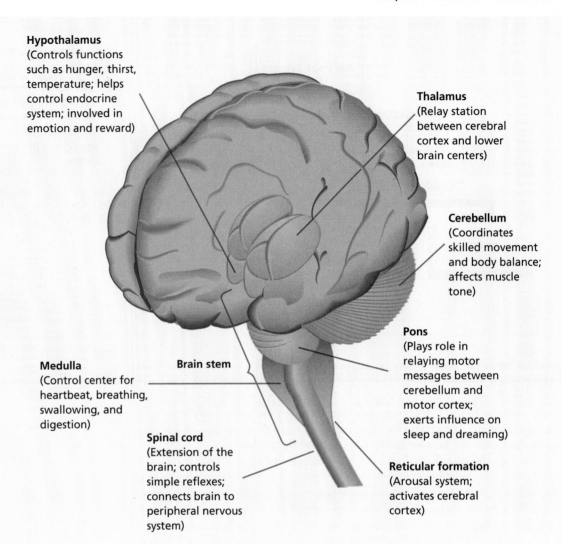

Hypothalamus
(Controls functions such as hunger, thirst, temperature; helps control endocrine system; involved in emotion and reward)

Thalamus
(Relay station between cerebral cortex and lower brain centers)

Cerebellum
(Coordinates skilled movement and body balance; affects muscle tone)

Medulla
(Control center for heartbeat, breathing, swallowing, and digestion)

Brain stem

Pons
(Plays role in relaying motor messages between cerebellum and motor cortex; exerts influence on sleep and dreaming)

Spinal cord
(Extension of the brain; controls simple reflexes; connects brain to peripheral nervous system)

Reticular formation
(Arousal system; activates cerebral cortex)

Figure 2.6 Major Structures of the Human Brain Some of the major structures of the brain are shown in the drawing, and a brief description of the function of each is provided. The brainstem contains the medulla, the reticular formation, and the pons.

through even when we are asleep (French, 1957). That is why parents may be able to sleep through a thunderstorm but will awaken to the slightest cry of their baby. (The next time you sleep through your alarm and are late for class, blame it on your reticular formation.)

Above the medulla and at the top of the brainstem is a bridgelike structure called the pons (a Latin word meaning "bridge"). The pons extends across the front top of the brainstem and connects to both the left and right halves of the cerebellum. The pons plays a role in body movement and even exerts an influence on sleep and dreaming. Hobson and McCarley (1977) report that the neurons in the pons begin firing rapidly just as a sleeper begins to dream.

The Cerebellum: A Must for Graceful Movement

Question: What are the primary functions of the cerebellum?

Cerebellum means "little cerebrum," and with its two hemispheres, the cerebellum resembles the large cerebrum, which rests above it (see Figure 2.6). Current

cerebellum (sehr-uh-BELL-um): The brain structure that executes smooth, skilled body movements and regulates muscle tone and posture.

knowledge about the cerebellum suggests that its main functions are to execute smooth, skilled movements and to regulate muscle tone and posture (Lalonde & Botez, 1990). It guides the graceful movements of the ballet dancer and the split-second timing of the skilled athlete. But more typically, the cerebellum coordinates and orchestrates the series of movements necessary to perform many everyday activities without studied, conscious effort. It enables you to guide food from the plate to your mouth without stabbing yourself with a fork. People who have suffered damage to the cerebellum must concentrate very intently, as they consciously and purposely perform each movement—pick up a fork, carefully locate the food with the fork, bring the food toward the mouth, and so on. Can you imagine trying to dance or carry on a dinner conversation without the help of the cerebellum?

The cerebellum has also been found to play a role in motor learning and in retaining memories of motor activities (Lalonde & Botez, 1990; Thompson, 1986). We will explore these functions more fully in chapter 6, "Memory."

The Thalamus: The Relay Station between Lower and Higher Brain Centers

Question: What is the primary role of the thalamus?

Above the brainstem lie two extremely important structures—the thalamus and the hypothalamus (see Figure 2.6). The **thalamus**, which looks like two egg-shaped structures, serves as the relay or switching station for virtually all the information that flows into and out of the higher brain centers. This includes sensory information from all the senses except smell. Incoming sensory information from the eyes, ears, skin, or taste buds travels first to parts of the thalamus or hypothalamus and then to the proper area of the cortex that handles vision, hearing, taste, or touch. Pain signals connect directly with the thalamus, which sends the pain message to the appropriate sensory areas of the cerebral cortex (Roland, 1992; Talbot et al., 1991).

The thalamus, or at least one small part of it, apparently affects our ability to learn new information, especially if it is verbal. This structure also plays a role in the production of language (Albert & Helm-Estabrooks, 1988a; Metter, 1991; Ojemann, 1977). Another function of the thalamus is the regulation of sleep cycles, which is thought to be accomplished in cooperation with the pons and the reticular formation. What a diverse range of activities this single brain structure performs. Now consider a much smaller structure, the hypothalamus.

The Hypothalamus: A Master Regulator

Question: What are some of the processes regulated by the hypothalamus?

Nestled directly below the thalamus and weighing only about 2 ounces, the **hypothalamus** is, ounce for ounce, the most influential structure in the brain. It regulates hunger, thirst, sexual behavior, and a wide variety of emotional behaviors. The hypothalamus also regulates internal body temperature, starting the process that causes us to perspire when we are too hot and to shiver to conserve body heat when we are too cold. Some experts believe that the hypothalamus also regulates the biological clock—our body rhythms and the timing of our sleep-wakefulness cycle (Reppert et al., 1988). As small as it is, the hypothalamus maintains nearly all our bodily functions except blood pressure, heart rhythm, and breathing.

The physiological changes in the body that accompany strong emotion are initiated by neurons concentrated primarily in the hypothalamus. You have felt

The main function of the cerebellum is to execute smooth, skilled movements.

thalamus (THAL-uh-mus): The structure, located above the brainstem, that acts as a relay station for information flowing into or out of the higher brain centers.

hypothalamus (HY-po-THAL-uh-mus): A small but influential brain structure that controls the pituitary gland and regulates hunger, thirst, sexual behavior, body temperature, and a wide variety of emotional behaviors.

these physical changes before—sweaty palms, a pounding heart, a hollow feeling in the pit of your stomach, or a lump in your throat.

The electrical stimulation of parts of the hypothalamus has elicited some unusual reactions in animals. Researcher José Delgado (1969) implanted an electrode in a particular spot in the hypothalamus of a normal bull, specifically bred for bull fighting in Spain. Delgado stood calmly in the ring as the bull charged toward him. He then pressed a remote control box that stimulated an area of the bull's hypothalamus. The bull stopped abruptly in its tracks. (Fortunately for Delgado, the batteries in the remote were working.) Apparently, aggression in animals can be turned on or off by stimulating specific areas of the hypothalamus. Not only that, even the sensations of pleasure can be produced if the right place on the hypothalamus is stimulated (Olds, 1956).

The Limbic System: Primitive Emotion and Memory

Question: What is the role of the limbic system?

The **limbic system** is composed of a group of structures in the brain, including the amygdala and the hippocampus, which are collectively involved in emotional expression, memory, and motivation. The *hippocampus* plays a central role in the formation of memories, as you will see in chapter 6, "Memory" (Squire, 1992). Autopsies performed on patients suffering from the severe memory impairment of Alzheimer's disease have revealed extensive damage to neurons in the hippocampus (Wolozin et al., 1986).

limbic system: A group of structures in the brain, including the amygdala and hippocampus, that are collectively involved in emotion, memory, and motivation.

hippocampus (hip-po-CAM-pus): A structure in the limbic system that plays a central role in the formation of long-term memories.

Memory Check 2.2

1. The brain and the spinal cord make up the (central, peripheral) nervous system.

2. The hypothalamus regulates all the following except:

   a. internal body temperature   c. coordinated movement
   b. hunger and thirst   d. the pituitary gland

3. The (amygdala, hippocampus) is the part of the limbic system primarily involved in the formation of memories.

4. Match the brain structure with its description.

   _____ 1) connects the brain with the peripheral   a. medulla
            nervous system   b. spinal cord
   _____ 2) controls heart rate, breathing, and   c. reticular
            blood pressure   formation
   _____ 3) consists of the medulla, the pons, and   d. thalamus
            the reticular formation   e. cerebellum
   _____ 4) influences attention and arousal   f. brainstem
   _____ 5) coordinates complex body movements
   _____ 6) relay station for sensory information
            flowing into the brain

Answers: 1. central 2. c 3. hippocampus 4. 1) b 2) a 3) f 4) c 5) e 6) d

The Cerebral Hemispheres

Question: What are the cerebral hemispheres, the cerebral cortex, and the corpus callosum?

The crowning achievement and the most essentially human part of the magnificent 3-pound human brain is the cerebrum and its cortex. If you could peer into your skull and look down upon your own brain, you would see a structure that resembles the inside of a huge walnut (see Figure 2.7). Like a walnut, which has two matched halves connected to each other, the **cerebrum** is composed of two **cerebral hemispheres**—a left and a right hemisphere resting side by side. The two hemispheres are physically connected at the bottom by a thick band of nerve fibers called the **corpus callosum**. This connection makes possible the transfer of information and the coordination of activity between the hemispheres. In general, the right cerebral hemisphere controls movement and feeling on the left side of the body. The left hemisphere controls the right side of the

cerebrum (seh-REE-brum): The largest structure of the human brain, consisting of the two cerebral hemispheres connected by the corpus callosum and covered by the cerebral cortex.

cerebral hemispheres (seh-REE-brul): The right and left halves of the cerebrum, covered by the cerebral cortex and connected by the corpus callosum.

corpus callosum (KOR-pus kah-LO-sum): The thick band of nerve fibers that connects the two cerebral hemispheres and makes possible the transfer of information and the synchronization of activity between them.

Figure 2.7 Two Views of the Cerebral Hemispheres The two hemispheres rest side by side like two matched halves, physically connected by the corpus callosum, shown in (a). An inside view of the left hemisphere of the cerebrum and cerebellum is shown in (b).

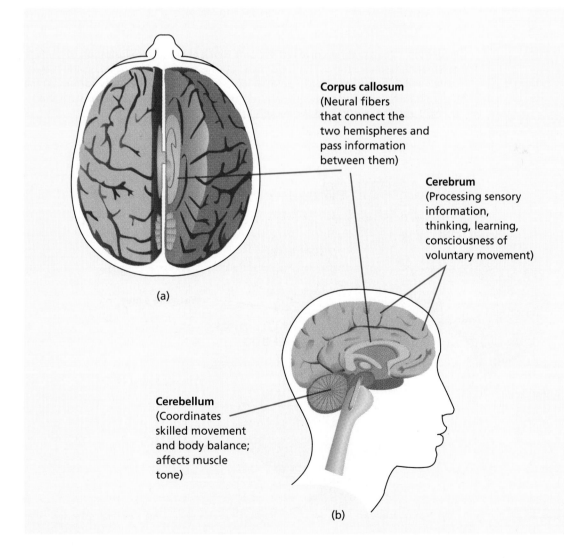

Corpus callosum
(Neural fibers that connect the two hemispheres and pass information between them)

Cerebrum
(Processing sensory information, thinking, learning, consciousness of voluntary movement)

Cerebellum
(Coordinates skilled movement and body balance; affects muscle tone)

(a)

(b)

cerebral cortex (seh-REE-brul KOR-tex): The gray, convoluted covering of the cerebral hemispheres that is responsible for higher mental processes such as language, memory, and thinking.

association areas: Areas of the cerebral cortex that house memories and are involved in thought, perception, learning, and language.

body. In over 95 percent of the population, the left hemisphere also controls the language functions (Hellige, 1990).

The cerebral hemispheres have an outer covering of gray matter about one-eighth of an inch thick called the **cerebral cortex.** The cerebral cortex accounts for approximately 40 percent of the brain's total weight (Barr, 1974). The cortex is primarily responsible for the higher mental processes of language, memory, and thinking. In humans the cortex is very large—about 2 feet by 3 feet—and is roughly three times the size of the cerebrum. For this reason, it does not fit smoothly around the cerebrum. Rather, it is arranged in numerous folds or wrinkles called convolutions. About two-thirds of the cortex is hidden from view in the folds. The cortex of less intelligent animals is much smaller in proportion to total brain size and, therefore, is much less convoluted.

The cerebral cortex contains three types of areas: (1) sensory input areas, where vision, hearing, touch, pressure, and temperature register; (2) motor areas, which control voluntary movement; and (3) **association areas,** which house our memories and are involved in thought, perception, and language.

The Lobes of the Brain

In each cerebral hemisphere there are four lobes—the frontal lobe, the parietal lobe, the occipital lobe, and the temporal lobe. Find them in Figure 2.8.

Figure 2.8   The Cerebral Cortex of the Left Hemisphere   This illustration of the left cerebral hemisphere shows the four lobes: (1) the frontal lobe, including the motor cortex and Broca's area; (2) the parietal lobe, with the somatosensory cortex; (3) the occipital lobe, with the primary visual cortex; and (4) the temporal lobe, with the primary auditory cortex and Wernicke's area.

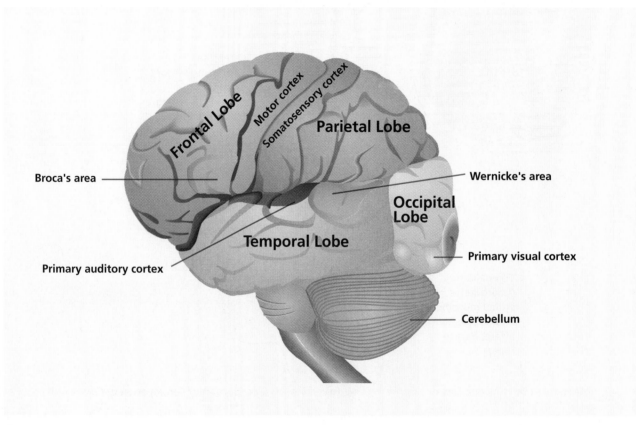

Questions: What are some of the main areas within the frontal lobes, and what are their functions?

The Frontal Lobes: For Moving, Speaking, and Thinking

Of the lobes in the brain, the frontal lobes are by far the largest. Beginning at the front of the brain, the **frontal lobes** extend to the top center of the skull. They contain the motor cortex, Broca's area, and the frontal association areas.

The Motor Cortex In 1870 two medical doctors, Fritsch and Hitzig, used a probe to apply a weak electrical current to the cortex of a dog. (The brain itself is insensitive to pain, so probing the brain causes no discomfort.) When the doctors applied electrical stimulation to various points along the rear of the frontal lobe, different parts of the dog's body moved. Fritsch and Hitzig had discovered the **motor cortex**—the area that controls voluntary body movement (see Figure 2.8). Movement in the right side of the body is controlled by the motor cortex in the left hemisphere; movement in the left side of the body is controlled by the right motor cortex.

Examine Figure 2.9. Notice the motor homunculus, or "little man," drawn next to the cross section of the motor cortex. The body parts are drawn in

frontal lobes: The lobes that control voluntary body movements, speech production, and such functions as thinking, motivation, planning for the future, impulse control, and emotional responses.

motor cortex: The strip of tissue at the rear of the frontal lobes that controls voluntary body movement.

Figure 2.9 The Motor Cortex and the Somatosensory Cortex from the Left Hemisphere The left motor cortex controls voluntary movement in the right side of the body. The left somatosensory cortex is the site where touch, pressure, temperature, and pain sensations from the right side of the body register. The more sensitive the body parts and the more capable they are of finely coordinated movements, the greater the areas of somatosensory cortex and motor cortex dedicated to those body parts. Note what large sections of cortex serve the head, face, hands, and fingers, and what small sections serve such large areas as the trunk, arms, and legs.

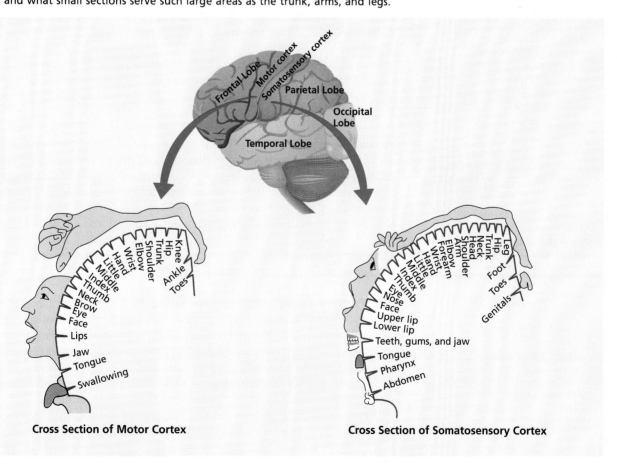

Cross Section of Motor Cortex   **Cross Section of Somatosensory Cortex**

proportion to the amount of motor cortex that controls each body part. The parts of the body that are capable of the most finely coordinated movements, such as the fingers, lips, and tongue, have a larger share of the motor cortex. Areas like the legs and the trunk of the body, which are capable only of gross movement, have a smaller amount of motor cortex. The lower parts of the body are controlled by neurons at the top of the motor cortex, while upper body parts (face, lips, and tongue) are controlled by neurons near the bottom of the motor cortex. For example, when you wiggle your right big toe, a cluster of brain cells firing at the top of the left motor cortex produces the movement.

What happens when part of the motor cortex is damaged? Depending on the severity of the damage, either paralysis or some impairment of coordination can result. Sometimes damage in the motor cortex causes the grand mal seizures of epilepsy.

Broca's Area In 1861 Paul Broca performed autopsies on two patients—one who had been totally without speech, and another who could say only four words (Jenkins et al., 1975). Broca found that both patients had damage in the left hemisphere, slightly in front of the part of the motor cortex which controls the jaw, lips, and tongue. Broca concluded that the site of damage, now called **Broca's area**, was the part of the brain responsible for speech production (see Figure 2.8). Broca's area is involved in directing the pattern of muscle movement required to produce the speech sounds.

If Broca's area is damaged, the result may be *Broca's aphasia*. **Aphasia** is a general term for a loss or impairment in the ability to use or understand language, resulting from damage to the brain (Pashek & Holland, 1988). Characteristically, patients with Broca's aphasia know what they want to say but can speak very little or not at all. If they are able to speak, their words are produced very slowly, with great effort, and are poorly articulated. One patient attempting to explain what he was doing in the hospital therapy program said, "nine o'cot, speech . . . two times . . . read . . . wr . . . ripe, er, rike, er write" (Gardner, 1975, p. 61).

Such patients who cannot speak are often able, nevertheless, to sing songs that they had previously known. Singing is normally controlled by the right hemisphere, and words to familiar songs are already stored there (Albert & Helm-Estabrooks, 1988b).

Frontal Association Areas Much of the frontal lobes consist of association areas which are involved in thinking, motivation, planning for the future, impulse control, and emotional responses. Sometimes pronounced changes in emotional responses occur when the frontal lobes are damaged. Phineas Gage, discussed in the story that opened this chapter, is one case in which damage to the frontal lobes drastically altered impulse control and emotional responses.

Question: What are the primary functions of the parietal lobes in general and the somatosensory cortex in particular?

The Parietal Lobes: Vital to Our Sense of Touch The **parietal lobes** lie directly behind the frontal lobes, in the top, middle portion of the brain. The parietal lobes are involved in the reception and processing of touch stimuli. The front strip of brain tissue in the parietal lobes is the **somatosensory cortex**, the site where touch, pressure, temperature, and pain register in the cortex (see Figure 2.8). The somatosensory cortex also makes us aware of movement in our body and the positions of our body parts at any given moment.

Dusser de Bareene discovered the function of the somatosensory cortex in 1916 when he applied a small amount of strychnine to a number of points along

Broca's area (BRO-kuz): The area in the frontal lobe, usually in the left hemisphere, that controls production of the speech sounds.

Broca's aphasia (BRO-kuz uh-FAY-zyah): An impairment in the ability to physically produce the speech sounds, or in extreme cases an inability to speak at all; caused by damage to Broca's area.

aphasia (ah-FAY-zyah): A loss or impairment of the ability to understand or communicate through the written or spoken word, which results from damage to the brain.

parietal lobes (puh-RY-uh-tul): The lobes that contain the somatosensory cortex (where touch, pressure, temperature, and pain register) and other areas that are responsible for body awareness and spatial orientation.

somatosensory cortex (so-MAT-o-SENS-or-ee): The strip of tissue at the front of the parietal lobes where touch, pressure, temperature, and pain register in the cortex.

a monkey's somatosensory cortex. The strychnine stimulated the neurons to fire. As he touched each point, the monkey scratched a different location on its skin. With this technique, de Bareene was able to map the monkey's somatosensory cortex.

If various points on your own somatosensory cortex were to be electrically stimulated, you would feel in a corresponding part of your body either a tingling sensation or a numbness. A person with damage to the somatosensory cortex of one hemisphere loses some sensitivity to touch on the opposite side of the body. If the damage is severe enough, the person might not be able to feel the difference between sandpaper and silk, or the affected part of the body might feel numb.

Like the motor cortex in the frontal lobes, the somatosensory cortex in the left and right parietal lobes are wired to opposite sides of the body. Cells at the top of the somatosensory cortex govern feeling in the lower extremities of the body. Drop a brick on your right foot, and the topmost brain cells of the left somatosensory cortex will fire and register the pain sensation. (Note, this is *not* a "Try It" exercise.) Notice in Figure 2.9 the large somatosensory areas connected to sensitive body parts such as the tongue, lips, face, and hand, particularly the thumb and index finger. Observe the small amount of cortex connected to a large area like the trunk of the body.

Other parts of the parietal lobes are responsible for spatial orientation and our sense of direction. There are association areas in the parietal lobes that house our memory of how objects feel, which explains why we can identify them by touch. People with damage to these areas could hold a pencil, scissors, or a ball in their hand but not be able to identify the object by touch alone, even if their sense of touch had not been damaged.

Question: What are the primary functions of the occipital lobes in general and the primary visual cortex in particular?

The Occipital Lobes: The Better to See You With   Behind the parietal lobes at the rear of the brain lie the **occipital lobes,** which are involved in the reception and interpretation of visual information (see Figure 2.8). At the very back of the occipital lobes is the **primary visual cortex,** the site where vision registers in the cortex (Glickstein, 1988). When this site is stimulated with an electrical probe, the subject reports seeing flashes of light.

Each eye is connected to the primary visual cortex in both the right and left occipital lobes. Look straight ahead and draw an imaginary line down the middle of what you see. Everything to the left of the line is referred to as the left visual field and registers in the right visual cortex. Everything in the right visual field registers in the left visual cortex. A person who sustains damage to one primary visual cortex will still have partial vision in both eyes.

The association areas in the occipital lobes are involved in the interpretation of visual stimuli. The association areas hold memories of past visual experiences and enable us to recognize what is familiar among the things we see. When these areas are damaged, people can lose their ability to identify objects visually although they are still able to identify the same objects by touch or through some other sense.

Question: What are the major areas within the temporal lobes, and what are their functions?

The Temporal Lobes: Hearing's Here   The **temporal lobes,** located slightly above the ears, are involved in the reception and interpretation of auditory stimuli. The site in the cortex where hearing registers is known as the **primary auditory cortex** (Aitkin, 1990; Zatorre et al., 1992). When this area is stimu-

occipital lobes (ahk-SIP-uh-tul):   The lobes that contain the primary visual cortex, where vision registers, and association areas involved in the interpretation of visual information.

primary visual cortex: The area at the rear of the occipital lobes where vision registers in the cerebral cortex.

temporal lobes: The lobes that contain the primary auditory cortex, Wernicke's area, and association areas for interpreting auditory information.

primary auditory cortex: The part of the temporal lobes where hearing registers in the cerebral cortex.

lated with an electrical probe, the subject hears bursts of sound. The primary auditory cortex in each temporal lobe receives sound inputs from both ears. Injury to one of these areas results in reduced hearing in both ears, and the destruction of both areas causes total deafness.

Wernicke's Area Adjacent to the primary auditory cortex in the left temporal lobe is **Wernicke's area,** which is the language area involved in comprehending the spoken word and in formulating coherent written and spoken language (see Figure 2.8). In less than 5 percent of the population, Wernicke's area is in the right hemisphere. When you listen to someone speak, the sound registers first in the primary auditory cortex. The sound is then sent to Wernicke's area where the speech sounds are unscrambled into meaningful patterns of words. Wernicke's area is also involved in selecting the words we use in speech and written expression.

Wernicke's aphasia is a type of aphasia resulting from damage to Wernicke's area. Although speech is fluent and words are clearly articulated, the actual message does not make sense to others. The content may be vague or bizarre and may contain inappropriate words, parts of words, or a gibberish of nonexistent words. One Wernicke's patient, when asked how he was feeling, replied, "I think that there's an awful lot of mung, but I think I've a lot of net and tunged in a little wheat duhvayden" (Buckingham & Kertesz, 1974). People with Wernicke's aphasia are not aware that anything is wrong with their speech.

Another kind of aphasia is auditory aphasia, or word deafness. It can occur if there is damage to the nerves connecting the primary auditory cortex with Wernicke's area. The person is able to hear normally but may not understand spoken language, similar to when you hear people speak a foreign language but you do not understand what they are saying.

The Temporal Association Areas The remainder of the temporal lobes consist of the association areas that house memories and are involved in the interpretation of auditory stimuli. For example, you have an association area where your memories of various sounds are stored, so you instantly recognize the sounds of running water, fire engine sirens, dogs barking, and so on. There is also a special association area where familiar melodies are stored.

Wernicke's area: The language area in the temporal lobe involved in comprehending the spoken word and in formulating coherent speech and written language.

Wernicke's aphasia: Aphasia resulting from damage to Wernicke's area in which the victim's spoken language is fluent, but the content is either vague or incomprehensible to the listener.

Memory Check 2.3

1. The thick band of fibers connecting the two cerebral hemispheres is the:

     a. cortex   c. corpus callosum
     b. cerebrum   d. motor cortex

2. The _____ is the 1/8-inch outer covering of the cerebrum.

3. Match the correct lobes with the brain areas they contain.

     _____ 1) primary auditory cortex;   a. frontal lobes
               Wernicke's area   b. parietal lobes
     _____ 2) primary visual cortex   c. occipital lobes
     _____ 3) Broca's area; motor cortex   d. temporal lobes
     _____ 4) somatosensory cortex

(continued)

4. Match the specialized area with the appropriate description of function.

_____ 1) site where hearing registers
_____ 2) site where vision registers
_____ 3) site where touch, pressure, and temperature register
_____ 4) speech production
_____ 5) voluntary movement
_____ 6) formulating and understanding the spoken and written word
_____ 7) thinking, motivation, impulse control

a. primary visual cortex
b. motor cortex
c. frontal association area
d. primary auditory cortex
e. somatosensory cortex
f. Wernicke's area
g. Broca's area

Answers: 1. c 2. cerebral cortex 3. 1) d 2) c 3) a 4) b 4. 1) d 2) a 3) e 4) g 5) b 6) f 7) c

Specialization of the Cerebral Hemispheres

Although they may look very much alike, the two cerebral hemispheres make different but complementary contributions to our mental and emotional life. We now know that some *lateralization* of the hemispheres exists; that is, each hemisphere is specialized, to some extent, to handle certain functions. Yet functions are usually not handled exclusively by one hemisphere; the two hemispheres always work together (Bradshaw, 1989; Efron, 1990).

Functions of the Left Hemisphere: Language, First and Foremost

Question: What are the main functions of the left hemisphere?

In 95 percent of right-handers and in about 62 percent of left-handers, the **left hemisphere** handles most of the language functions, including speaking, writing, reading, and understanding the spoken word (Hellige, 1990). Even sign language (ASL) used by deaf persons is clearly a left hemisphere function (Corina et al., 1992). From birth, in children of both sexes, the left hemisphere appears to be more attuned to language (Hahn, 1987; Molfese & Molfese, 1985). The left hemisphere is also specialized for mathematical abilities, particularly calculation, and it processes information in an analytical and sequential, or step-by-step, manner (Corballis, 1989). Logic is primarily, though not exclusively, a left brain specialty (Levy, 1985). The left side of Figure 2.10 shows some of the main functions of the left hemisphere.

The left hemisphere coordinates complex movements by controlling the right side of the body directly and by indirectly controlling the movements of the left side of the body. The left hemisphere accomplishes this by sending orders across the corpus callosum to the right hemisphere so that the proper movements will be coordinated and executed smoothly. Remember also that the cerebellum plays an important role in helping coordinate complex movements.

lateralization: The specialization of one of the cerebral hemispheres to handle a particular function.

left hemisphere: The hemisphere that controls the right side of the body, coordinates complex movements and, in 95 percent of the population, controls the production of speech and written language.

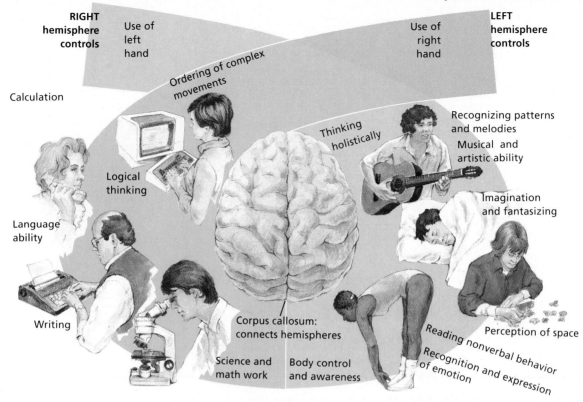

Figure 2.10   The Specialized Functions of the Two Hemispheres   The left hemisphere controls movement and sensory information for the right half of the body; the right hemisphere handles the same for the left side of the body. In most people the left hemisphere is specialized for language, logical thinking, science, and math (including calculation), while the right hemisphere specializes in creativity, musical and artistic ability, space perception, recognizing and expressing emotion, and holistic thinking.

Functions of the Right Hemisphere: The Leader in Visual-Spatial Tasks

Question: What are the primary functions of the right hemisphere?

The **right hemisphere** is generally considered to be the more adept hemisphere at visual-spatial relations. Artists, sculptors, architects, and household "do-it-yourselfers" have strong visual-spatial skills. When you put together a jigsaw puzzle, draw a picture, or assemble a piece of furniture according to instructions, you are calling primarily on your right hemisphere. The right side of Figure 2.10 shows some of the major functions of the right hemisphere.

The right hemisphere processes information holistically rather than part-by-part or piece-by-piece as the left hemisphere does (Corballis, 1989). Auditory, visual, and touch stimuli register in both hemispheres, but the right hemisphere appears to be more specialized than the left for complex perceptual tasks. Consequently, the right hemisphere is better at pattern recognition, whether of familiar voices (Van Lancker et al., 1988), melodies (Springer & Deutsch, 1985), or visual patterns.

Although the left hemisphere is generally considered the language hemisphere, the right hemisphere also makes an important contribution to our understanding of language. According to Howard Gardner (1981), the right hemisphere is involved "in understanding the theme or moral of a story, in grasping metaphor . . . and even in supplying the punch line for a joke" (p. 74). Van Lancker (1987) points out that "although the left hemisphere knows best what is being said, the right hemisphere figures out how it is meant and who is saying it" (p. 13). It is

right hemisphere: The hemisphere that controls the left side of the body and, in most people, is specialized for visual-spatial perception and understanding nonverbal behavior.

Get a meter stick or yardstick. Try balancing it across your left hand and then across your right hand. Most people are better with their dominant hand—right hand for right handers, for example. Is this true for you?

Now try this: Begin reciting the ABC's out loud as fast as you can while balancing the stick with your *left* hand. Do you have less trouble this time? Why should that be? The right hemisphere controls the act of balancing with the left hand. However, your left hemisphere, though poor at controlling the left hand, still tries to coordinate your balancing efforts. When you distract the left hemisphere with a steady stream of talk, the right hemisphere can orchestrate more efficient balancing with your left hand without interference.

the right hemisphere that is able to understand familiar idiomatic expressions such as "He is turning over a new leaf." If the right hemisphere is damaged, a person can understand only the literal meaning of the statement.

Creativity and intuition are typically considered a right hemisphere specialty, but the left hemisphere shares these functions. The right hemisphere controls singing and seems to be more specialized for musical ability in untrained musicians (Kinsella et al., 1988).

Patients with right hemisphere damage may have difficulty with spatial orientation, such as finding their way around even in familiar surroundings. They may have attentional deficits and be unaware of objects in the left visual field, a condition called unilateral neglect (Bellas et al., 1988). Unilateral neglect patients may eat only the food on the right side of their plate, read the words on the right half of a page, and even groom only the right half of their body.

The Right Hemisphere's Role in Emotion: Recognizing and Expressing Emotion The right hemisphere is also more active in the recognition and expression of emotion. Reading and interpreting nonverbal behavior, such as gestures and facial expressions, is primarily a right hemisphere task. Look at the two faces in the *Try It!* (Jaynes, 1976).

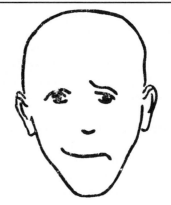 

Pick out the happy face and the sad face.

Even though the faces in the drawings are mirror images, right-handed people tend to see the face at the left as the happier face. When we look at a face, we are likely to perceive the emotional tone revealed by the part of a face to our left as we view it (McGee & Skinner, 1987). The right hemisphere processes information from the left visual field, so right-handed people tend to be more emotionally affected by the face on the left.

The right hemisphere also responds to the emotional message conveyed by another's tone of voice (Heilman et al., 1975). For example, a professor sarcastically says to a student who enters the class late, "Well, I'm so glad you could come today." A student with right hemisphere damage might respond only to the actual meaning of the words rather than the sarcastic tone.

The right hemisphere is involved in our own expression of emotion through our tone of voice and particularly our facial expression. The left side of the face, controlled by the right hemisphere, usually conveys stronger emotion than the right side of the face. Lawrence Miller (1988) describes the facial expressions and the voice inflection of people with right hemisphere damage as "often strangely blank—almost robotic" (p. 39).

The Split Brain: Separate Halves or Two Separate Brains?

Question: What is the significance of the split-brain operation?

The cerebral hemispheres, though each contributes its own important specialized functions, are always in intimate and immediate contact, thanks to the corpus callosum. There have been rare cases where people have been born with no corpus callosum or have had their corpus callosum severed in a drastic surgical procedure called the **split-brain operation**. Neurosurgeons Joseph Bogen and Philip Vogel (1963) found that patients with severe epilepsy, suffering frequent and uncontrollable grand mal seizures, could be helped by severing their corpus callosum. In this way, the pulsing waves of neural activity that occur during a seizure could be confined to one hemisphere rather than spreading across the corpus callosum and involving the entire brain.

The split-brain operation surgically separates the hemispheres, making the transfer of information between them impossible. The patient is then left with two independently functioning hemispheres. The operation has been quite successful, completely eliminating the seizures in some patients. The surgery causes no major changes in personality, intelligence, or behavior.

Research with split-brain patients by Roger Sperry (1964, 1966) and colleagues Michael Gazzaniga (1967, 1970, 1989) and Jerre Levy have expanded our knowledge of the unique capabilities of the individual hemispheres. For his work, Sperry won the Nobel Prize in Medicine in 1981. Sperry (1968) found that when surgically separated, each hemisphere continued to have individual and private experiences, sensations, thoughts, and perceptions. However, most sensory experiences are shared almost simultaneously because each ear and eye have direct sensory connections to both hemispheres.

Testing the Split-Brain Person Sperry's research revealed some fascinating findings. Look at Figure 2.11. In this illustration, a split-brain patient sits in front of a screen that separates the right and left fields of vision. If an orange is flashed to the right field of vision, it will register in the left (verbal) hemisphere. If asked what he saw, the subject will readily reply, "I saw an orange." But suppose that an apple is flashed to the left visual field and is relayed to the right (nonverbal) hemisphere. If asked what he saw, the subject will reply, "I saw nothing."

Why should this be? Sperry maintains that in split-brain patients, only the verbal left hemisphere can report what it sees. In these experiments, the left hemisphere does not see what is flashed to the right hemisphere, and the right hemisphere is unable to report verbally what it has viewed. But did the right hemisphere actually see what was flashed in the left visual field? Yes, because with his left hand (which is controlled by the right hemisphere), the patient can

split-brain operation: An operation, performed in severe cases of epilepsy, in which the corpus callosum is cut, separating the cerebral hemispheres and usually lessening the severity and frequency of grand mal seizures.

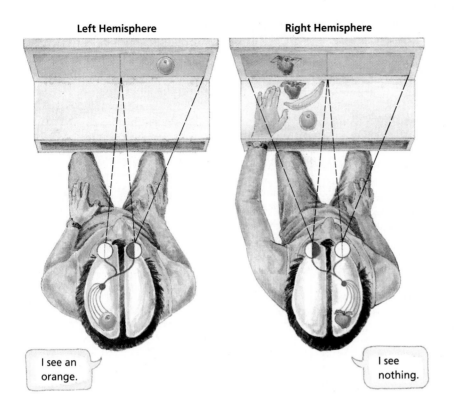

Left Hemisphere

Right Hemisphere

I see an orange.

I see nothing.

Figure 2.11

Testing a Split-Brain Person

Using special equipment, researchers are able to study the independent functioning of the hemispheres in split-brain persons. In this experiment a visual image (an orange), when flashed on the right side of the screen, is transmitted to the left (talking) hemisphere. When asked what he sees, the split-brain patient replies, "I see an orange." When an image (an apple) is flashed on the left side of the screen, it is transmitted only to the right (nonverbal) hemisphere. Because the split-brain patient's left (language) hemisphere did not receive the image, he replies, "I see nothing." But he can pick out the apple by touch if he uses his left hand, proving that the right hemisphere "saw" the apple. (After Gazzaniga, 1983.)

pick out from behind a screen any object shown to the right hemisphere. The right hemisphere knows and remembers what it sees just as well as the left, but unlike the left hemisphere, the right cannot name what it has seen. (In these experiments, images must be flashed for no more than one- or two-tenths of a second so that the subjects do not have time to refixate their eyes and send the information to the opposite hemisphere.)

On Handedness, the Hemispheres, Talents, and Problems

About 90 percent of the people around the world are right-handed, and it has evidently been that way for centuries (Coren & Porac, 1977). There are a number of explanations of how handedness develops. Some propose a genetic explanation (Annett, 1985; Levy & Nagylaki, 1972); others claim that it is learned (Blau, 1946; Collins, 1970). But none of the theories accommodates all of the facts, and most experts believe that a genetic factor is involved. Hepper and others (1990) suggest that in fetuses, a hand preference is already apparent in the womb. They found that 94.6 percent of the fetuses were sucking their right thumb and 5.4 percent, their left thumb.

On the average, left-handers have a corpus callosum that is 11 percent larger and contains as many as 25 million more nerve fibers than that of right-handers (Witelson, 1985). Researchers Geschwind and Behan (1982) found that left-handers are 12 times more likely than right-handers to stutter and have learning disabilities (dyslexia). Also, left-handers are two and one-half times more likely to have autoimmune diseases such as allergies, and are more likely to suffer from migraine headaches. Coren and Halpern (1991) even suggest that left-handers, on the average, have a shorter life span. According to Coren (1989), they are at a higher risk for accidents because of their need to accommodate themselves to an environment constructed for right-handers.

WORLD OF PSYCHOLOGY: APPLICATIONS

Discovering the Brain's Mysteries

Question: What are some methods that have been used to learn about brain function?

As you have read, the first attempts to discover the mysteries of the human brain were through autopsies, such as those performed by Paul Broca, and by clinical observations of the effects of brain injury and diseases. The next method of study was to insert electrical probes into live brains, as done by Fritsch and Hitzig in 1870.

Modern researchers need not rely solely on autopsies or wait for injuries to learn more about the brain. Today researchers are unlocking the mysteries of the human brain using electrical stimulation, the electroencephalograph (EEG), the microelectrode, and a number of modern scanning devices such as the CT scan, magnetic resonance imaging (MRI), and the PET scan (Andreasen et al., 1992).

The EEG

Question: What is the electroencephalogram (EEG), and what are three normal brain-wave patterns it reveals?

Before 1924 there was no known way to measure the electrical activity in the brain. But in that year Austrian psychiatrist Hans Berger invented the electroencephalograph (EEG), a machine that amplifies one million times the electrical activity occurring in the brain. This electrical activity, detected by electrodes placed at various points on the scalp,

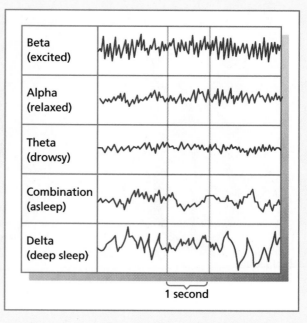

Figure 2.12   EEG Patterns Associated with Various Waking and Sleeping States   EEG patterns vary according to the level of brain activity monitored. Beta waves occur when a person is mentally or physically active.

The electroencephalograph uses electrodes placed on the scalp to amplify and record electrical activity in the brain.

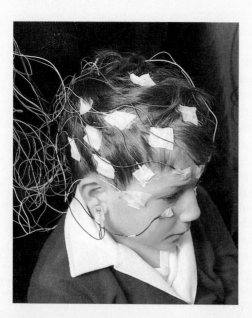

provides the power to drive a pen across a paper, producing a record of brain-wave activity called an *electroencephalogram (EEG)*. The *beta wave* is the brain-wave pattern associated with mental or physical activity. The *alpha wave* is associated with deep relaxation, and the *delta wave* with deep sleep. Figure 2.12 shows the various brain-wave patterns and their associated psychological states.

The most recent application of EEG studies employs a computerized imaging technique in which various colors are generated to represent the different levels of electrical activity occurring every millisecond in the brain. EEG imaging can show an epileptic seizure in progress and can be used to study neural activity in people with learning disabilities, schizophrenia, Alzheimer's disease, sleep disorders, and other neurological problems including brain death.

The Microelectrode

While the EEG is able to detect electrical activity in different areas of the brain, it cannot reveal what is happening in individual neurons. The microelectrode can. A *microelectrode* is a wire so small that it can be inserted into a single neuron without damaging it. Microelectrodes can be used to monitor the electrical activity of a single neuron or to stimulate activity within it. Researchers have used microelectrodes to discover the exact function of single cells within the primary visual cortex and the primary auditory cortex.

The CT Scan and Magnetic Resonance Imaging

Twenty years ago it was difficult, sometimes impossible, to diagnose many brain disorders, including tumors, without cutting into the brain to examine it. In 1973 the introduction of the *CT scan (computerized axial tomography)* changed all that. The patient undergoing a CT scan is placed inside a large, doughnut-shaped structure where an X-ray tube circles the entire head. The tube shoots pencil-thin X rays through the brain as it completes the circle. A series of computerized, cross-sectional images reveal the structures within the brain (or other parts of the body) as well as abnormalities and injuries, including tumors and old or more recent strokes.

Another technique, *MRI (magnetic resonance imaging)* produces higher resolution images without exposing patients to the hazards of X-ray photography (Jacobson, 1988). The MRI is a powerful diagnostic tool that can be used to find abnormalities in the central nervous system and in other systems of the body.

Although the CT scan and MRI do a remarkable job of showing what the brain looks like both inside and out, they

CT scans are computer-assisted X rays, which allow the brain (and other parts of the body) to be viewed in three dimensions.

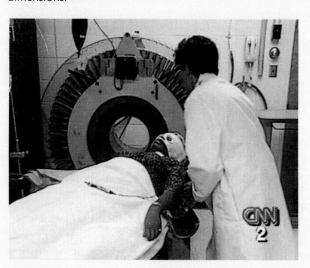

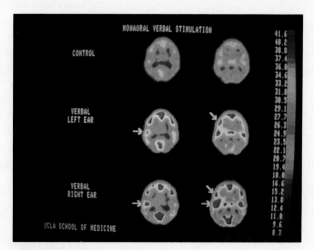

PET scans show where activity occurs in specific areas of the brain.

cannot reveal what the brain is doing. But another technological marvel can.

The PET Scan

The *PET scan (positron-emission tomography)* is a powerful instrument for identifying malfunctions that cause physical and psychological disorders and also for studying normal brain activity (Volkow & Tancredi, 1991). The PET scan can map the patterns of blood flow, oxygen use, and glucose consumption (the food of the brain). It can also show the action of drugs and other biochemical substances in the brain and other bodily organs.

The patient undergoing a PET scan either is injected with or inhales a low-level, radioactive-laced substance such as glucose or oxygen. The more active any part of the brain is, the more oxygen and glucose it consumes. The PET scan produces a computerized image of varying colors based on the amount of radioactive substance left behind as the brain uses different levels of oxygen or glucose.

Still, the PET scan can detect only *changes* in blood flow and in oxygen and glucose consumption as they occur in the various brain areas. Many parts of the brain are always active, even when a person is doing nothing observable. Petersen and others (1988, 1989) have devised an innovative technique to separate such activities as thinking, reading, and speaking from the many other ongoing brain activities that show up on the PET scan. For example, to determine which parts of the brain are involved in reading a series of words, the researchers compare the images of a subject's brain activity both before and during the time words are flashed on a screen. They then have the computer subtract the "before" images, leaving only the PET scan image of the mental activity involved in reading the words. Such creative applications of imaging techniques will continue to produce a rich store of information about the human brain.

Geschwind and Behan (1982) found a higher incidence of immune and learning disorders among first- and second-degree relatives of left-handers, leading them to hypothesize a genetic explanation. Geschwind suggested that a genetically based excess of testosterone or an increased sensitivity to testosterone slows down the growth of the left hemisphere. This allows greater development of the right hemisphere, which enables it to handle speech and language.

While it is true that left-handers have a greater risk of dyslexia or stuttering, left-handedness is also associated with some positive traits. Benbow and Stanley (1983) found that over 20 percent of the 12- to 13-year olds with exceptionally high scores in mathematics on the Scholastic Aptitude Test were left-handed. Left-handers are also overrepresented among artists, musicians, engineers, mathematicians, and major-league baseball players.

Memory Check 2.4

1. Match the hemisphere with the specialized abilities usually associated with it.

   _____ 1) visual-spatial skills   a. right hemisphere
   _____ 2) speech   b. left hemisphere
   _____ 3) recognition and expression of
            emotion
   _____ 4) singing
   _____ 5) mathematics

2. Which of these statements is *not* true of the split-brain operation?

   a. It is used for people suffering from severe epilepsy.
   b. It provides a means of studying the functions of the individual hemispheres.
   c. It causes major changes in intelligence, personality, and behavior.
   d. It makes transfer of information between the hemispheres impossible.

3. Which of these statements is *not* true of left-handers?

   a. They have a higher incidence of dyslexia and stuttering.
   b. They are more likely to be gifted in mathematics, art, and music.
   c. In most left-handers, the left hemisphere handles speech.
   d. Left-handedness is probably more attributable to learning than to heredity.

Answers: 1. 1) *a* 2) *b* 3) *a* 4) *a* 5) *b* 2. *c* 3. *d*

The Many Faces of Brain Damage

Brain damage has many causes. Head injuries, diseases, tumors, the abuse of drugs, and stroke can leave people with a variety of disabilities.

Stroke

Question: Why is a stroke so serious?

A **stroke** is the most common cause of injury to the adult brain and the third most common cause of death. Of some 500,000 people who suffer strokes each year, about 150,000 die (Alberts et al., 1990), while another 100,000 to 150,000 are severely and permanently disabled (Zivin & Choi, 1991). Stroke patients may be left with impaired intellect, loss of coordination or sensation, or paralysis. About 25 percent of stroke survivors are left with aphasia.

Stroke occurs when the blood supply to the brain is cut off, depriving the brain of oxygen and glucose and thus killing many brain cells. Stroke can be caused by a blood clot, hardening of the arteries, a cerebral hemorrhage brought on by high blood pressure.

The prevention of stroke is critical. Untreated high blood pressure, hardening of the arteries, and high doses of stimulants such as amphetamines and cocaine increase the risk of stroke.

stroke: A cardiovascular accident that occurs when the blood supply to the brain is cut off, killing many neurons; the major cause of damage to the adult brain.

plasticity: The ability of the brain to reorganize and compensate for brain damage.

Head Injury

Each year more than 300,000 Americans survive injuries that leave them with significant brain damage (Chance, 1986). Impaired motor coordination and language ability are often the most obvious results of head injury. Even more devastating is the loss of intellectual functioning—concentration, memory, reasoning, judgment, and problem-solving and decision-making abilities. Social behavior is frequently affected, as in the case of Phineas Gage, who became irritable, verbally abusive, and irresponsible. The precise disability depends largely on the area of the brain that is affected and the severity of the damage.

Many people who suffer injuries to the head develop epilepsy—a chronic brain disorder that results in recurring seizures and frequently a loss or impairment of consciousness. Grand mal seizures are marked by convulsions and loss of consciousness. Petit mal seizures involve sudden lapses of consciousness lasting several seconds, during which the victim neither falls nor has a convulsion.

Therapy for coma patients includes constant sensory stimulation, in addition to physical therapy.

Recovering from Brain Damage

Question: What must occur in the brain for there to be some recovery from brain damage?

Once neurons are completely destroyed, they are gone forever. We are born with our full supply of neurons, and those that are lost are never replaced. If neurons are damaged, however, they can sprout new dendrites and re-establish connections with other neurons to assume some of the functions of the brain cells that were lost. Axons, too, are able to regenerate and grow (Fawcett, 1992).

Some abilities lost through brain damage can be regained if areas near the damaged site take over the lost function. In the case of aphasia, the undamaged hemisphere can sometimes be trained to handle the language function but can rarely restore it to normal. The ability of the brain to reorganize and to compensate for brain damage is termed **plasticity**. Plasticity is greatest in young children before the hemispheres are completely lateralized (Bach-y-Rita & Bach-y-Rita, 1990). Some individuals who had an entire hemisphere removed early in life due to uncontrollable epilepsy have been able to lead a near normal, intellectual life (Bower, 1988). In one case, a man with only one hemisphere carried a double major in college and graduated with honors.

Memory Check 2.5

1. The (EEG, MRI) is a record of electrical activity in the brain.

2. The (CT scan, PET scan) reveals brain activity and function, rather than the structure of the brain.

3. Which of these statements is *not* true of stroke?

   a. Stroke is the main cause of injury to the adult brain.
   b. Stroke can cause paralysis and total loss of language ability.
   c. Although stroke causes many disabilities, it is not life-threatening.
   d. Stroke is caused when the blood supply to the brain is cut off.

4. Plasticity of the brain (increases, decreases) with age.

Answers: 1. EEG 2. PET scan 3. c 4. decreases

The Peripheral Nervous System

Question: What is the peripheral nervous system?

The **peripheral nervous system** (PNS) is made up of all the nerves that connect the central nervous system to the rest of the body. Without the peripheral nervous system, the brain and spinal cord, encased in their bone coverings, would be isolated and unable to send information to or receive information from other parts of the body. The peripheral nervous system has two subdivisions—the somatic nervous system and the autonomic nervous system. Figure 2.13 shows the subdivisions within the peripheral nervous system.

The Somatic Nervous System: For Sensing and Moving

The somatic nervous system consists of (1) all the sensory nerves, which transmit information from the sense receptors—eyes, ears, nose, tongue, and skin—to the central nervous system, and (2) all the motor nerves, which relay messages from the central nervous system to all the skeletal muscles of the body. In short, the nerves of the somatic nervous system make it possible for us to sense our environment and move, and they are primarily under our conscious control.

The Autonomic Nervous System: Doing Its Job without Our Conscious Thought

Question: What are the roles of the sympathetic and parasympathetic nervous systems?

peripheral nervous system (PNS) (peh-RIF-er-ul): The nerves connecting the central nervous system to the rest of the body; has two subdivisions—the autonomic and the somatic nervous systems.

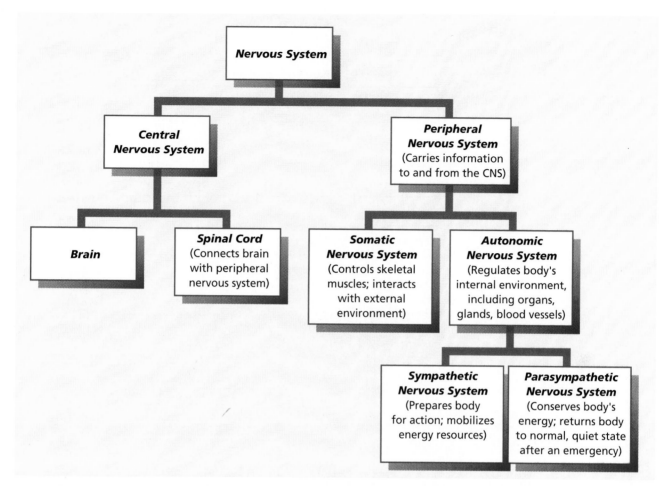

Figure 2.13   The Human Nervous System   The nervous system is divided into two parts: the central nervous system and the peripheral nervous system. The diagram shows the relationships among the parts of the nervous system and provides a brief description of the functions of those parts.

The autonomic nervous system is sometimes misread by students as "automatic," and that is not a bad synonym because the autonomic nervous system operates quite well automatically, without our being conscious of it. It transmits messages between the central nervous system and the glands, the cardiac (heart) muscle, and the smooth muscles, which are not normally under voluntary control (such as those in the large arteries, the gastrointestinal system, and the small blood vessels).

The autonomic nervous system is further divided into two parts—the sympathetic and the parasympathetic nervous systems. Any time you are under stress or faced with an emergency, the **sympathetic nervous system** automatically mobilizes the body's resources, preparing you for action. For example, what if an ominous looking stranger started following you and quickened his pace as you turned down a dark, deserted street? Your sympathetic nervous system would automatically set to work. Your heart would begin to pound, your pulse rate would increase rapidly, your breathing would quicken, and the digestive system would nearly shut down. The blood flow to your skeletal muscles would be enhanced, and all of your bodily resources would be made ready to handle the emergency—RUN.

But once the emergency is over, something must happen to bring these heightened bodily functions back to normal. The **parasympathetic nervous system** does just that. As a result of its action, your heart stops pounding and slows to

sympathetic nervous system: The division of the autonomic nervous system that mobilizes the body's resources during stress, emergencies, or heavy exertion, preparing the body for action.

parasympathetic nervous system: The division of the autonomic nervous system that is associated with relaxation and the conservation of energy and that brings the heightened bodily responses back to normal following an emergency.

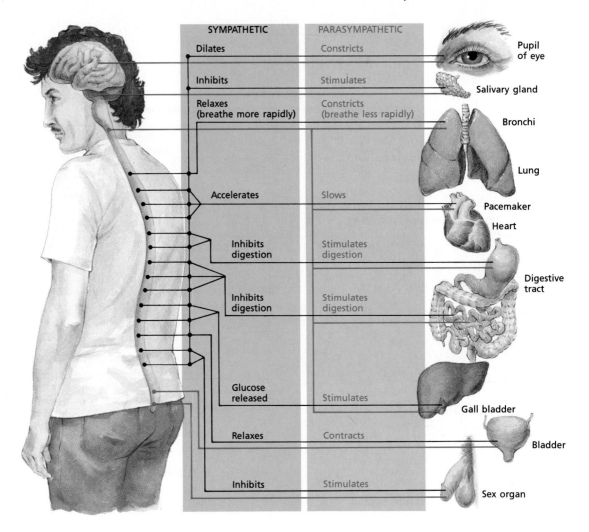

Figure 2.14   The Autonomic Nervous System   The autonomic nervous system consists of (1) the sympathetic nervous system, which mobilizes the body's resources during emergencies or during stress, and (2) the parasympathetic nervous system, which is associated with relaxation and which brings the heightened bodily responses back to normal after an emergency. This diagram shows the opposite effects of the sympathetic and parasympathetic nervous systems on various parts of the body.

normal, your pulse rate and breathing slow down, and the digestive system resumes its normal functioning. As you can see in Figure 2.14, the sympathetic and parasympathetic branches act as opposing but complementary forces in the autonomic nervous system. Their balanced functioning is essential for our health and survival.

The Endocrine System

Question: What is the endocrine system, and what are some of the glands within it?

We have seen how chemical substances called neurotransmitters exert their influence on the 100 billion or so neurons in the nervous system. There is another system in which chemical substances stimulate and regulate many other important functions in the body. The **endocrine system** is a series of glands, located in various parts of the body, that manufacture and secrete chemical substances known as hormones (from the Greek root meaning "to excite"). A chemical substance is called a **hormone** if it is manufactured and released in one part of the body but has an effect on other parts of the body. Hormones are released into the bloodstream and travel throughout the circulatory system, but they perform their assigned job only when they connect with the body cells having receptors for the specific hormone. Some of the same chemical substances that are neurotransmitters act as hormones as well—norepinephrine and vasopressin, to name two (Bergland, 1985).

Figure 2.15 shows the glands in the endocrine system and their locations in the body.

The Pituitary Gland: The Master Gland, Small as a Pea

The **pituitary gland** rests just below the hypothalamus and is controlled by it (see Figure 2.15). The pituitary is considered to be the master gland of the body because it releases the hormones that "turn on," or activate, the other glands in

endocrine system (EN-duh-krin):   A system of ductless glands in various parts of the body that manufacture and secrete hormones into the bloodstream or lymph fluids, thus affecting cells in other parts of the body.

hormone: A substance manufactured and released in one part of the body that affects other parts of the body.

pituitary gland: The endocrine gland located in the brain and often called the "master gland," which releases hormones that control other endocrine glands and also releases a growth hormone.

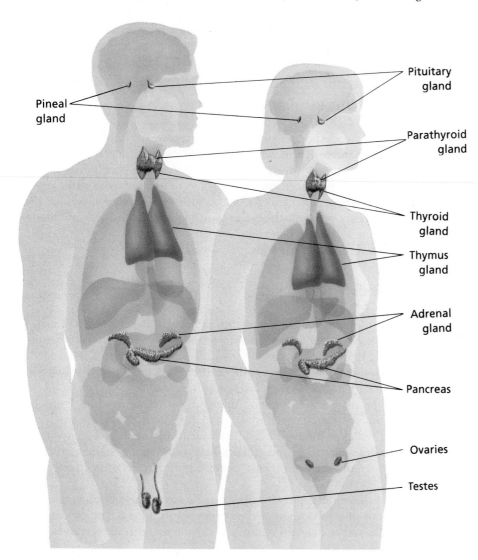

Pituitary gland

Pineal gland

Parathyroid gland

Thyroid gland

Thymus gland

Adrenal gland

Pancreas

Ovaries

Testes

Figure 2.15

The Endocrine System

The endocrine system is a series of glands, which manufacture and secrete hormones. The hormones travel through the circulatory system and have important effects on many bodily functions.

adrenal glands (ah-DREE-nal): A pair of endocrine glands that release hormones that prepare the body for emergencies and stressful situations and also release small amounts of the sex hormones.

the endocrine system—a big job for a tiny structure about the size of a pea. The pituitary also produces the hormone that is responsible for body growth. Too little of this powerful substance will make one a dwarf, while too much will produce a giant, as shown in the photograph.

The Thyroid Gland: Balancing the Body's Metabolism

The thyroid gland rests in the front, lower part of the neck just below the voice box (larynx). The thyroid produces the important hormone thyroxin, which is responsible for keeping the body's metabolism in balance. In other words, thyroxin regulates the rate at which we metabolize, or transform into energy, the food we eat. Too much thyroxin can result in hyperthyroidism, a condition in which people are nervous and excitable, find it hard to be still and relax, and are usually thin. Hypothyroidism, an underproduction of thyroxin, has just the opposite effect. An adult with hypothyroidism may feel sluggish, lack energy, and tend to be overweight.

The Adrenal Glands: Necessary for Fight or Flight

Lower in the body are the two *adrenal glands*, which rest just above the kidneys as shown in Figure 2.15. The adrenal glands produce epinephrine and norepinephrine, two hormones that activate the sympathetic nervous system. The adrenal glands also release small amounts of the sex hormones, and the corticoids, which control the important salt balance in the system.

The Pancreas: Our Insulin Factory

Curving around between the small intestine and the stomach is the pancreas (see Figure 2.15). The pancreas regulates the body's blood sugar levels by releasing the hormones insulin and glycogen into the bloodstream. In people with diabetes, too little insulin is produced. Without insulin to break down sugars in the bloodstream, the level of sugar can get dangerously high. In hypoglycemia, the opposite effect occurs—too much insulin is produced, resulting in low blood sugar. Both conditions may be controlled by diet, but in many cases the diabetic must also take daily insulin injections.

The pituitary gland is essential for body growth; an underactive pituitary may result in a dwarf, while overactivity may result in a giant.

The Sex Glands: The Gonads

The gonads are the sex glands—the ovaries in females and the testes in males (see Figure 2.15). Activated by the pituitary gland, the gonads release sex hormones that make reproduction possible and that are responsible for the secondary sex characteristics—pubic and underarm hair in both sexes, breasts in females, and facial hair and a deepened voice in males.

Androgens, the male sex hormones, influence sexual motivation. Estrogen and progesterone, the female sex hormones, help regulate the menstrual cycle. Although both males and females have androgens and estrogens, males have considerably more androgens, and females have considerably more estrogens. The sex hormones and their effects are discussed in more detail in chapter 11, "Human Sexuality and Gender."

Biology and behavior are intimately related. However, there is much more to the scientific study of behavior and mental processes than the biological connection can teach us. Other chapters in this text expand on other aspects of behavior and mental processes.

Memory Check 2.6

1. The (central, peripheral) nervous system connects the brain and the spinal cord to the rest of the body.

2. The _____ nervous system mobilizes our body's resources during times of stress; the _____ nervous system brings the heightened bodily responses back to normal when the emergency is over.

   a. somatic; autonomic   c. sympathetic; parasympathetic
   b. autonomic; somatic   d. parasympathetic; sympathetic

3. Match the endocrine gland with the appropriate description.

   _____ 1) keeps body's metabolism in balance   a. pituitary gland
   _____ 2) master gland that activates the   b. adrenal glands
          other glands   c. gonads
   _____ 3) regulates the blood sugar   d. thyroid gland
   _____ 4) makes reproduction possible   e. pancreas
   _____ 5) releases hormones that prepare the
          body for emergencies

Answers: 1. peripheral 2. c 3. 1) d 2) a 3) e 4) c 5) b

Thinking Critically _____

Evaluation

Using your knowledge about how the human brain has been studied in the past and today, point out the advantages and the disadvantages of the older investigative methods—the case study, the autopsy, the study of people with brain injuries or who have had brain surgery (including the split-brain operation). Follow the same procedure to discuss the more modern techniques—EEG, CT scan, MRI, and PET scan.

Point/Counterpoint

A continuing controversial issue is the ethical question of whether animals should be used in biological research. Review the chapter and find each occasion in which animals were used to advance our knowledge of the brain. Using what you have read in this chapter and any other information you have acquired, prepare arguments to support both of the following positions:

a. The use of animals in research projects is ethical and justifiable because of the possible benefits to humankind.
b. The use of animals in research projects is not ethical and justifiable on the grounds of possible benefits to humankind.

Psychology in Your Life

How would your life change if you had a massive stroke in your left hemisphere? How would it change if the stroke were in your right hemisphere? Which stroke would be more tragic for you, and why?

Chapter Summary and Review _____

The Neurons and the Neurotransmitters

What is a neuron, and what are its three parts?

A neuron is a specialized cell that conducts messages through the nervous system. Its three main parts are the cell body, dendrites, and axon.

What is a synapse?

A synapse is the junction where the axon terminal of a sending neuron communicates with a receiving neuron across the synaptic cleft.

What is the action potential?

The action potential is the firing of a neuron that results when the charge within the neuron becomes more positive than the charge outside the cell's membrane.

What are neurotransmitters, and what role do they play in the transmission of signals from one neuron to another?

Neurotransmitters are chemicals released into the synaptic cleft from the axon terminal of the sending neuron. They cross the synapse and bind to receptor sites on the receiving neuron, influencing the cell to fire or not to fire.

What are some of the ways in which neurotransmitters affect our behavior?

Neurotransmitters regulate the actions of our glands and muscles, affect learning and memory, promote sleep, stimulate mental and physical alertness, and influence our moods and emotions from depression to euphoria.

Key Terms

neurons (p. 36)
dendrites (p. 37)
axon (p. 37)
synapse (p. 37)
action potential (p. 38)
neurotransmitter (p. 38)

The Central Nervous System

Why is an intact spinal cord important to normal functioning?

The spinal cord is an extension of the brain connecting it to the peripheral nervous system so that sensory information can reach the brain, and messages from the brain can reach the muscles and glands.

What are the crucial functions handled by the brainstem?

The brainstem contains (1) the medulla, which controls heart rate, blood pressure, and respiration, and (2) the reticular formation, which plays a crucial role in arousal and attention.

What are the primary functions of the cerebellum?

The main functions of the cerebellum are to execute smooth, skilled movements and to regulate muscle tone and posture.

What is the primary role of the thalamus?

The thalamus acts as a relay station for information flowing into or out of the higher brain centers.

What are some of the processes regulated by the hypothalamus?

The hypothalamus controls the pituitary gland and regulates hunger, thirst, sexual behavior, body temperature, and a variety of emotional behaviors.

What is the role of the limbic system?

The limbic system is a group of structures in the brain, including the amygdala and hippocampus, which are collectively involved in emotion, memory, and motivation.

Key Terms

central nervous system (p. 42)
spinal cord (p. 42)
brainstem (p. 43)
medulla (p. 43)
reticular formation (p. 43)
cerebellum (p. 44)
thalamus (p. 45)
hypothalamus (p. 45)
limbic system (p. 46)

The Cerebral Hemispheres

What are the cerebral hemispheres, the corpus callosum, and the cerebral cortex?

The cerebral hemispheres are the two halves of the cerebrum, connected by the corpus callosum and covered by the cerebral cortex, which is responsible for higher mental processes such as language, memory, and thinking.

What are some of the main areas within the frontal lobes, and what are their functions?

The frontal lobes contain (1) the motor cortex, which controls voluntary motor activity, (2) Broca's area, which functions in speech production, and (3) the frontal association areas, which are involved in thinking, motivation, planning for the future, impulse control, and emotional responses.

What are the primary functions of the parietal lobes in general and the somatosensory cortex in particular?

The parietal lobes are involved in the reception and processing of touch stimuli. They contain the somatosensory cortex, where touch, pressure, temperature, and pain register.

What are the primary functions of the occipital lobes in general and the primary visual cortex in particular?

The occipital lobes are involved in the reception and interpretation of visual information. They contain the primary visual cortex, where vision registers in the cerebral cortex.

What are some of the main areas within the temporal lobes, and what are their functions?

The temporal lobes contain (1) the primary auditory cortex, where hearing registers in the cortex, (2) Wernicke's area, which is involved in comprehending the spoken word and in formulating coherent speech and written language, and (3) association areas, where memories are stored and auditory stimuli are interpreted.

Key Terms

cerebrum (p. 47)
cerebral hemispheres (p. 47)
corpus callosum (p. 47)
cerebral cortex (p. 48)
association areas (p. 48)
frontal lobes (p. 49)
motor cortex (p. 49)
Broca's area (p. 50)
aphasia (p. 50)
parietal lobes (p. 50)
somatosensory cortex (p. 50)
occipital lobes (p. 51)
primary visual cortex (p. 51)
temporal lobes (p. 51)
primary auditory cortex (p. 51)
Wernicke's area (p. 52)

Specialization of the Cerebral Hemispheres

What are the main functions of the left hemisphere?

The left hemisphere controls the right side of the body, coordinates complex movements, and handles most of the language functions, including speaking, writing, reading, and understanding the spoken word.

What are the primary functions of the right hemisphere?

The right hemisphere controls the left side of the body, is specialized for visual-spatial perception, and is more active in the recognition and expression of emotion.

What is the significance of the split-brain operation?

The split-brain operation involves cutting the corpus callosum, which prevents the transfer of information between the hemispheres. Research on split-brain patients has extended our knowledge of the functions of the hemispheres.

Key Terms

left hemisphere (p. 53)
right hemisphere (p. 54)
split-brain operation (p. 56)

Discovering the Brain's Mysteries

What are some methods that have been used to learn about brain function?

Researchers have learned about brain function from clinical studies of patients, through electrical stimulation of the brain, and from studies using the EEG, microelectrode, CT scan, MRI, and PET scan.

What is the electroencephalogram (EEG), and what are three normal brain-wave patterns it reveals?

The electroencephalogram (EEG) is a record of brain-wave activity. Three normal brain-wave patterns are the beta wave, alpha wave, and delta wave.

The Many Faces of Brain Damage

Why is a stroke so serious?

Stroke is the most common cause of damage to the adult brain, is the third leading cause of death, and leaves many of its victims with paralysis and/or aphasia.

What must occur in the brain for there to be some recovery from brain damage?

For some recovery from brain damage to occur, (1) damaged neurons may sprout new dendrites and re-establish connections with other neurons, (2) areas near the damaged site may take over the lost function, or (3) the undamaged hemisphere may assume the lost language function (as in aphasia).

Key Terms

stroke (p. 61)
plasticity (p. 61)

The Peripheral Nervous System

What is the peripheral nervous system?

The peripheral nervous system connects the central nervous system to the rest of the body. It has two subdivisions: (1) the somatic nervous system, which consists of the nerves that make it possible for us to sense and move, and (2) the autonomic nervous system.

What are the roles of the sympathetic and parasympathetic nervous systems?

The autonomic nervous system has two parts: (1) the sympathetic nervous system, which mobilizes the body's resources during emergencies or during stress, and (2) the parasympathetic nervous system, which is associated with relaxation and brings the heightened bodily responses back to normal after an emergency.

Key Terms

peripheral nervous system (p. 62)
sympathetic nervous system (p. 63)
parasympathetic nervous system (p. 63)

The Endocrine System

What is the endocrine system, and what are some of the glands within it?

The endocrine system is a system of glands in various parts of the body that manufacture and secrete hormones into the bloodstream. The hormones then affect cells in other parts of the body. The pituitary gland releases hormones that control other glands in the endocrine system and also releases a growth hormone. The thyroid gland produces thyroxin, which regulates metabolism. The adrenal glands release epinephrine and norepinephrine, which prepare the body for emergencies and stressful situations, and also release small amounts of the sex hormones. The pancreas produces insulin and regulates blood sugar. The gonads are the sex glands, which produce the sex hormones and make reproduction possible.

Key Terms

endocrine system (p. 65)
hormone (p. 65)
pituitary gland (p. 65)

3

Sensation and Perception

CHAPTER OUTLINE

The man called S. B. had never seen a sunrise, a flower, a smile, or even his own face, for he lost his sight in both eyes when he was only 10 months old. Despite his blindness, S. B. had managed to live a fairly full and happy life. He could get around on his own, cross streets, and even ride a bicycle with his friend's hand on his shoulder to guide him. He read braille, and he loved to make things with tools in the small shed he used as a workshop.

All his life S. B. had wondered what it would be like to see. Then, when he was 50 years old, he learned that his useless, opaque corneas could be replaced through a cornea transplant. Finally the miracle of sight he had dreamed about would be a reality.

When the surgeon first removed the bandages from S. B.'s eyes, people and objects were little more than large blurs to him. But the operation was successful, and after a few days S. B. could see quite well. He could walk up and down the hospital corridors without using a cane or holding onto the wall. Soon he was able to see and recognize objects by sight that he already knew well by touch. But all was not well.

S. B. had difficulty recognizing unfamiliar objects and things he had never touched. He never learned to read by sight, although he could recognize numbers and capital letters. S. B. had trouble perceiving distance. From the window of his hospital room he watched the cars and trucks pass in the street below. He thought his feet would touch the ground if he hung from the windowsill with his hands, yet his window was nearly 60 feet above the ground.

The ending of S. B.'s story is not a happy one. The world looked drab to him, and he was upset by the imperfections he saw. Objects he had once imagined to be perfect now had disappointing defects. He could no longer cross streets because seeing the cars whizzing by terrified him. Often he would not even bother to turn on the lights at night for he preferred to sit in his more comfortable world of darkness. As time passed, S. B. became more and more depressed and withdrawn. Within three years after the cornea transplant, he died. (Adapted from Gregory, 1978.)

---

sensation: The process through which the senses pick up visual, auditory, and other sensory stimuli and transmit them to the brain; sensory information that has registered in the brain but has not been interpreted.

perception: The process by which sensory information is actively organized and interpreted by the brain.

ARE YOU SURPRISED THAT THE MIRACLE in S. B.'s life, the gift of sight, turned out to be hardly a gift at all? The surgeons were able to give him the sensation of sight but, sadly, not the 50 years of visual perceptual experience he had missed.

Sensation and perception are intimately related in everyday experience, but they are not the same. **Sensation** is the process through which the senses detect visual, auditory, and other sensory stimuli and transmit them to the brain. **Perception** is the process by which sensory information is actively organized and interpreted by the brain. Sensation furnishes the raw material of sensory experience, while perception provides the finished product.

To a large extent we must learn to perceive, and people whose sight has been restored differ greatly in their ability to develop useful perception. S. B.'s life shows dramatically the great gap between receiving sensory information—sensation—and the ability to give it meaning, the processes of perception. For many who regain their vision, it is truly a remarkable gift, but for others like S. B., gaining sight can be a major disappointment.

In this chapter we will explore the world of sensation, with a focus on the five primary senses—vision, hearing, touch, taste, and smell—along with such secondary senses as balance and pain. You will learn how the senses detect sensory information, how this sensory information is actively organized and interpreted by the brain. We will begin with a closer look at sensation.

Sensation: The Sensory World

Our senses serve as ports of entry for all information about our world. Virtually everything we call experience is detected initially by our senses. Yet it is amazing how little of the sensory world we actually sense. For example, we see only a thin slice of the vast spectrum of electromagnetic energy. With the unaided eye we cannot see microwaves, X rays, or ultraviolet light. We cannot hear the sound of a dog whistle, and our ears can detect only a scant 20 percent of the sounds a dolphin or a bat can hear. We cannot see the outline of a warm-blooded animal from its infrared heat pattern at night, but rattlesnakes and other pit vipers can. Yet all of these sensory stimuli exist in the real, physical world.

No matter which of our senses we select for comparison, humans are not at the top of the list for quality or sensitivity. Some animals have a superior sense of hearing (bats and dolphins); others have sharper vision (hawks); still others have a superior sense of smell (bloodhounds); and so on. Nevertheless, we humans have remarkable sensory abilities and superior abilities of perception.

The Absolute Threshold: To Sense or Not to Sense

What is the softest sound you can hear, the dimmest light you can see, the most diluted substance you can taste? What is the lightest touch you can feel, the faintest odor you can smell? Researchers in sensory psychology and psychophysics have performed many experiments over the years to answer these questions. They have established measures for the senses known as absolute thresholds. Just as the threshold of a doorway is the dividing point between being outside a room and inside, the **absolute threshold** of a sense marks the difference between not being able to hear a sound (or see a light) and being just barely able to hear it (or see it). Psychologists have arbitrarily defined the absolute threshold as the minimum amount of sensory stimulation that can be detected 50 percent of the time. The absolute thresholds established for the five primary senses in humans are (1) for vision, a candle flame 30 miles away on a clear night; (2) for hearing, a watch ticking 20 feet away; (3) for taste, 1 teaspoon of sugar dissolved in 2 gallons of water; (4) for smell, a single drop of perfume in a three-room house; and (5) for touch, a bee's wing falling a distance of 1 centimeter onto your cheek.

Important as it is, the absolute threshold, once crossed, says nothing about the broad range of sensory experiences. To sense or not to sense—that is the only question the absolute threshold answers. But read on—there are other questions to be answered.

The Difference Threshold: Detecting Differences

Question: What is the difference between the absolute threshold and the difference threshold?

If you are listening to music, the very fact that you can hear it means that the absolute threshold has been crossed. But how much must the volume be turned up or down for you to notice a difference? Or, if you are carrying a load of books, how much weight must be added or subtracted for you to be able to sense that your load is heavier or lighter? The **difference threshold** is a measure of the smallest increase or decrease in a physical stimulus that is required to produce the *just noticeable difference (JND)*. The JND is the smallest change in sensation that we are able to detect 50 percent of the time. If you were holding a 5-pound weight and 1 pound were added, you could easily notice the difference. But if you were holding 100 pounds and 1 additional pound were added, you could not sense the difference. Why not? A pound is a pound, isn't it?

absolute threshold: The minimum amount of sensory stimulation that can be detected 50 percent of the time.

difference threshold: The smallest increase or decrease in a physical stimulus required to produce a difference in sensation that is noticeable 50 percent of the time.

just noticeable difference (JND): The smallest change in sensation that we are able to detect 50 percent of the time.

Weber's law: The law stating that the just noticeable difference (JND) for all our senses depends on a proportion or percentage of change in a stimulus rather than according to a fixed amount of change.

Over 100 years ago researcher Ernst Weber observed that the JND for all our senses depends on a proportion or percentage of change rather than a fixed amount of change. This observation became known as *Weber's law*. A weight we are holding must increase or decrease by a ratio of 1/50, or 2 percent, for us to notice the difference. According to Weber's law, the greater the original stimulus, the more it must be increased or decreased for us to tell the difference.

The difference threshold is not the same for all the senses. We need a very large (1/5, or 20-percent) difference to detect some changes in taste. In contrast, if you were listening to music, you would notice a difference if a tone became slightly higher or lower in pitch by only one-third of 1 percent.

Aren't some people more sensitive to sensory changes than others? Yes, the difference thresholds for the various senses are not the same for all people. In fact, there are great individual differences. Professionally trained musicians would know if they were singing or playing slightly out of tune long before the one-third of 1 percent difference in pitch appeared. Wine tasters would know if a particular vintage was a little too sweet, even if it varied by only a fraction of the 20-percent change. Actually, Weber's law best fits people with average sensitivities, and sensory stimuli that are neither very strong (loud thunder) or very weak (a faint whisper).

Transduction: Transforming Sensory Stimuli into Neural Impulses

Question: How are sensory stimuli in the environment experienced as sensations?

You may be surprised to learn that our eyes do not actually see nor do our ears hear. Our sense organs provide only the beginning point of sensation that must be completed by the brain. As you learned in chapter 2, "Biology and Behavior," certain clusters of neurons in specialized parts of the brain must be stimulated for us to see, hear, taste, and so on. Yet the brain itself cannot respond directly to light, sound waves, odors, and tastes. How, then, does it get the message? The answer is the sensory receptors.

Figure 3.1

The Processes of Sensation and Perception

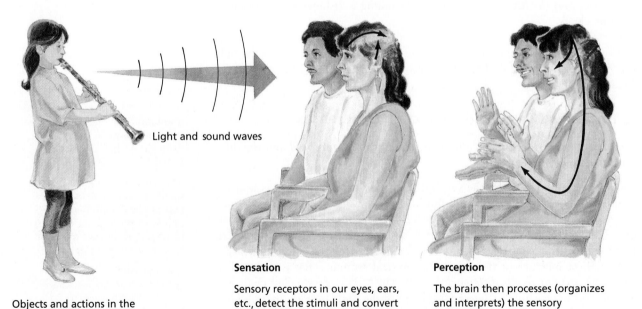

Light and sound waves

Objects and actions in the environment provide sensory stimuli.

Sensation

Sensory receptors in our eyes, ears, etc., detect the stimuli and convert them into neural impulses that the brain receives.

Perception

The brain then processes (organizes and interprets) the sensory information.

All our senses are equipped with specialized cells called **sensory receptors**, which detect and respond to one type of sensory stimuli—light, sound waves, odors, and so on. Then, through a process known as **transduction**, the receptors change or convert the sensory stimulation into neural impulses, the electrochemical language of the brain. The neural impulses are then transmitted to their own special location in the brain, such as the visual cortex for vision or the primary auditory cortex for hearing. We experience a sensation only when the appropriate part of the brain is stimulated. Our sense receptors provide the essential link between the physical sensory world and the brain (see Figure 3.1).

sensory receptors: Specialized cells in each sense organ that detect and respond to sensory stimuli—light, sound, odors, etc.—and transduce (convert) the stimuli into neural impulses.

transduction: The process by which sensory receptors convert sensory stimulation—light, sound, odors, etc.—into neural impulses.

visible spectrum: The narrow band of electromagnetic rays, 380–760 nm in length, that are visible to the human eye.

Memory Check 3.1

1. The process by which the senses pick up sensory information and transmit it to the brain is called (sensation, perception).

2. The point at which you can barely sense a stimulus 50 percent of the time is called the (absolute, difference) threshold.

3. The just noticeable difference (JND) is the same for all individuals. (true/false)

4. Sensory receptors:

   a. are structures that are specialized to detect certain sensory stimuli
   b. transduce sensory stimuli into neural impulses
   c. are located in the brain
   d. both a and b

5. The process by which a sensory stimulus is converted into a neural impulse is called (perception, transduction).

Answers: 1. sensation 2. absolute 3. false 4. d 5. transduction

Vision

For most of us, vision is our most valued sensory experience, and it is the sense that has been most investigated. Before looking at how we see, consider *what* we see. We cannot see any object unless light is reflected from it or given off by it.

Light: What We See

Light is one form of electromagnetic rays made up of tiny light particles called photons, which travel in waves. But light is only a small portion of the electromagnetic energies. They range from the shortest cosmic rays, 10 trillionths of an inch, to the progressively longer X rays, ultraviolet rays, infrared rays, radar waves, microwaves, radio waves, and other broadcast bands that are many miles long. The vast majority of these waves are either too long or too short for humans and other animals to see. Our eyes can respond only to a very narrow band of electromagnetic waves, a band called the *visible spectrum* (see Figure 3.2).

Figure 3.2

The Electromagnetic Spectrum

The electromagnetic spectrum is composed of energies ranging in wavelength from the radio and other broadcast bands (many miles long) to the shortest cosmic rays (only 10 trillionths of an inch in length). Our eyes can respond to only a very thin band of electromagnetic waves known as the visible spectrum.

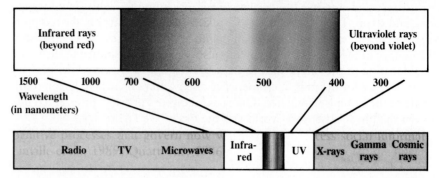

The length of a light wave primarily determines the color we perceive. The shortest light waves we can see appear violet, and the longest ones we see are red. *What* we see is confined to the visible spectrum, but *how* we see depends on the many parts of the eye and brain that bring us the world of sight.

The Eye: Window to the Visual Sensory World

The eye is our most important sensory connection to the world. Vision provides most of the information on which our brain feeds. Look at the parts of the eye (shown in Figure 3.3), and read next the role each structure plays in vision.

Question: How do the cornea, the pupil, and the iris function in vision?

The Cornea, Iris, and Pupil: Up Front in the Eye   The round, globe-shaped human eyeball measures about 1 inch in diameter. Bulging from its front surface is the **cornea**—the tough, transparent, protective layer covering the front of the eye. About the size of a dime, the cornea performs the first step in vision by

Figure 3.3   The Major Parts of the Human Eye

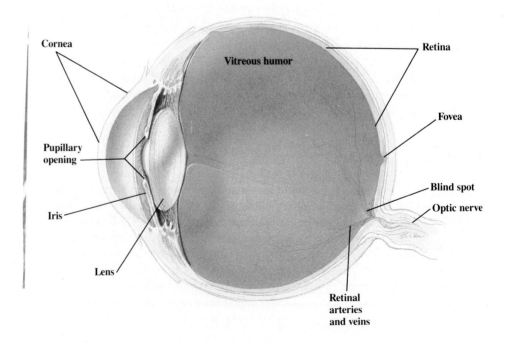

bending the light rays inward. It herds the light rays through the pupil—the small, dark opening in the center of the iris.

The iris is the circular, colored part of the eye. Two muscles in the iris dilate and contract the pupil and thus regulate the amount of light entering the eye. Although the pupil never closes completely, in very bright light it can contract to the size of the head of a pin; in very dim light it can dilate to the size of a pencil eraser (Freese, 1977). We have no control over the dilation and contraction of our pupils; the motion is a reflex, completely automatic.

The pupils respond to emotions as well as light. When we look at someone or something highly desirable, our pupils dilate as if to take in more of the pleasing view (Hess, 1965). Pupils also dilate when we are frightened, telling a lie, or sexually aroused. Our pupil size is also related to mental effort—the more intense the mental activity, the larger our pupils become (Janisse & Peavler, 1974).

Question: What are the lens and the retina?

From Lens to Retina: Focusing Images Suspended just behind the iris and the pupil, the **lens** is composed of many thin layers and looks like a transparent disc. The lens performs the task of focusing on objects closer than 20 feet. It flattens as it focuses on objects viewed at a distance, but it grows more spherical, bulging in the center, as it focuses on close objects. This flattening and bulging action of the lens is known as *accommodation*. As we grow older, the lens loses some elasticity. Hence, it loses the ability to change its shape to accommodate for near vision, a condition called presbyopia ("old eyes"). This is why most people over age 40 must hold a book or a newspaper at arm's length or use reading glasses to magnify the print. As a result of aging, disease, or injury, some people develop cataracts—a clouding of the lens that grows worse with time and can lead to blindness if not treated.

The lens focuses the image we see onto the **retina**—a membrane about the size of a small postage stamp and as thin as onion skin. The retina contains the sensory receptors for vision. The image projected onto the retina is upside down and reversed left to right. You can demonstrate this for yourself in the *Try It!*

cornea (KOR-nee-uh): The transparent covering of the colored part of the eye that bends light rays inward through the pupil.

lens: The transparent structure behind the iris that changes in shape as it focuses images on the retina.

accommodation: The changing in the shape of the lens as it focuses objects on the retina, becoming more spherical for near objects and flatter for far objects.

retina: The tissue at the back of the eye that contains the rods and the cones and onto which the retinal image is projected.

Take an ordinary tablespoon—one in which you can see your reflection. Looking at the bottom (the convex surface) of the spoon, you will see a large image of your face that is right side up—the way the image enters the eye. Turn the spoon over and look in the inside (the concave surface), and you will see your face upside down and reversed left to right—the way the image appears on the retina. The brain, however, perceives images right side up.

Try It!

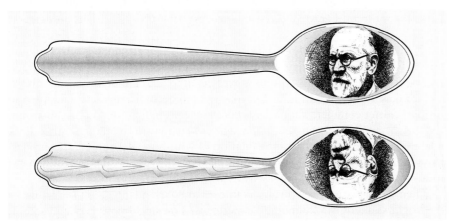

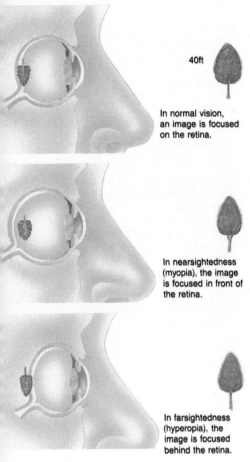

In normal vision, an image is focused on the retina.

In nearsightedness (myopia), the image is focused in front of the retina.

In farsightedness (hyperopia), the image is focused behind the retina.

Figure 3.4

Normal Vision, Nearsightedness, and Farsightedness

(From Hardman, Drew, Egan, & Wolf, 1990.)

rods: The light-sensitive receptors in the retina that provide vision in dim light in black, white, and shades of gray.

cones: The receptor cells in the retina that enable us to see color and fine detail in adequate light, but that do not function in dim light.

fovea (FO-vee-uh): A small area of the retina, 1/50 of an inch in diameter, that provides the clearest and sharpest vision because it has the largest concentration of cones.

dark adaptation: The eye's increasing ability to see in dim light resulting from the recombining of molecules of rhodopsin in the rods and the dilation of the pupils.

In some people, the distance through the eyeball (from the lens to the retina) is either too short or too long for proper focusing. Nearsightedness (myopia) occurs when the lens focuses images of distant objects in front of, rather than on, the retina. A person with this condition will be able to see near objects clearly, but distant images will be blurred. Farsightedness (hyperopia) occurs when the focal image is longer than the eye can handle, as if the image should focus behind the retina (see Figure 3.4). The individual is able to see far objects clearly, but close objects are blurred. Both conditions are correctable with eyeglasses or contact lenses.

Question: What roles do the rods and cones play in vision?

The Rods and Cones: Receptors for Light and Color   At the back of the retina is a layer of light-sensitive receptor cells—the **rods** and the **cones**. Named for their shapes, the rods look like slender cylinders and the cones appear shorter and more rounded. There are about 120 million rods and 6 million cones in each retina.

The cones are the receptor cells that enable us to see color and fine detail in adequate light, but they do not function in very dim light. There are three types of cones, each particularly sensitive to one of three colors—red, green, or blue (Livingstone, 1988). The bipolar cells and the ganglion cells in the retina begin the work that the brain completes in computing the colors we perceive and analyzing the relative activity in the three types of cones (Nathans, 1989; Schnapf et al., 1987). You will read more about color vision later in this chapter.

If we were to plot an imaginary line through the middle of your pupil, the line would strike the center of the retina in the **fovea**, a small pitlike area about the size of the period at the end of this sentence (refer to Figure 3.3). Only 1/50 of an inch in diameter, the fovea contains no rods but has nearly 50,000 cones tightly packed together. When you look directly at an object, the image of the object is focused on the center of your fovea. The clearest point of your vision, the fovea is the part of the retina that you use for fine detail work.

Rods are more plentiful and cones are more scarce as we move away from the fovea toward the periphery of the retina. The rods respond to black, white, and all other visible wavelengths but encode them in shades of gray instead of in color. The rods are more sensitive to light than the cones are, enabling us to see in very dim light and providing us with our night vision. A single rod can respond to the smallest possible quantity of light—a single photon (Stryer, 1987).

What enables us to adapt to different lighting conditions, from extremely dim to brightly illuminated? The answer lies in a reddish-purple, light-sensitive pigment in the rods called rhodopsin. Exposure to light causes the molecules of rhodopsin to split apart and become less light sensitive. In dim light or in the dark, the molecules gradually recombine, restoring their sensitivity to light.

Dark Adaptation   Step into a darkened movie theater from the bright sunlight, and at first you can hardly tell which seats are occupied and which are empty. After a few minutes in the dark your eyes begin to adapt and you can see dimly. Yet it takes about half an hour for your eyes to become completely adapted to the dark. After complete *dark adaptation*, you can see light that is 100,000 times less bright than you can see in daylight. You may have thought that dark adaptation is a direct result of the dilation of your pupils. Although this process plays a part, dark adaptation cannot occur until the rhodopsin molecules in the rods recombine, restoring their sensitivity to light.

When you leave a movie theater your eyes are dark-adapted, but the return to the bright sunlight is a "blinding" experience. You shield your eyes and squint, but it takes only seconds, not minutes, to become light-adapted again. When the light hits your eyes, the rhodopsin molecules in the rods again break apart, almost immediately causing a great reduction in your sensitivity to light.

Question: Trace the path of the neural impulse from the retina to the visual cortex.

optic nerve: The nerve that carries visual information from the retina to the brain.

From the Retina to the Brain: From Visual Sensation to Visual Perception The rods and cones are the receptors in the eye. They transduce or change light waves into neural impulses that are fed to the bipolar cells, which in turn pass the impulses along to the ganglion cells. The ganglion cells bundle together their some one million axonlike extensions in a pencil-sized cable that extends through the wall of the retina, leaving the eye on its way to the brain. Where the cable runs through the retinal wall, there can be no rods or cones, and so we are blind in that spot in each eye. After the cable leaves the retinal wall, it becomes known as the *optic nerve*. You can find your own blind spot if you perform the *Try It!*

To locate your blind spot, hold this book at arms' length. Close your right eye and look directly at the magician's eyes. Now slowly bring the book closer, keeping your eye fixed on the magician. When the rabbit disappears, you have found the blind spot in your left eye.

You might wonder why the blind spot in each eye is not perceived as a black hole in each visual field. The reason is that we usually have both eyes open, and each eye provides a slightly different view. The right eye can see the tiny area that is blind to the left eye, and vice-versa.

Try It!

Leaving the eye at the blind spot, the optic nerve cables come together at the optic chiasma, a point where some of the nerve fibers cross to the opposite side of the brain. The visual fibers from the right half of each retina go to your right hemisphere, while visual fibers from the left half of each retina go to the left hemisphere. This switching is important because it allows visual information from a single eye to be represented on the visual cortex of both hemispheres of the brain. Furthermore, it plays an important part in depth perception.

From the optic chiasma, the optic nerve travels to the thalamus. There it synapses with neural fibers that transmit the impulses to their final destination, the visual cortex.

feature detectors: Neurons in the brain that respond to specific features of a sensory stimulus (for example, to lines or angles).

Mapping the Visual Cortex: Brain Terrain for Vision   During the last few decades, researchers have learned a great deal about how the visual cortex works to produce the sensation of vision. Much of the pioneering work in this field has been conducted by researchers David Hubel and Torsten Wiesel (1959; 1979; Hubel, 1963), who won a Nobel Prize for their work in 1981. Using cats as their subjects, Hubel and Wiesel placed a microelectrode in a single cell in the animal's visual cortex. They then flashed different patterns of lines on a screen in the cat's field of vision. They observed that the neurons appeared to be highly specialized, firing only in response to particular patterns of lines.

Hubel and Wiesel moved the tiny electrode carefully and precisely from cell to cell in order to map the visual responses over a sizable area of the cat's visual cortex. They found numbers of single neurons that respond only to lines and angles. One neuron, for example, would fire only when the cat saw a vertical line, while another neuron would respond only to a horizontal line. Other neurons were responsive to nothing but right angles, while some neurons were sensitive only to lines of a certain length. These neurons are known as *feature detectors*, and according to Hubel and Wiesel, they are already coded at birth to make their unique responses.

Color Vision: A Multicolored World

Some light waves striking an object are absorbed by it, and others are reflected from it. We see only the wavelengths that are reflected, not those that are absorbed. Why does a red apple look red? If you hold a red apple in bright white light, light waves from all the different wavelengths are striking the apple, but more of the longer visible red wavelengths of light are reflected from the apple's skin. The shorter wavelengths are absorbed, so you see only the reflected red.

Figure 3.5   Hue, Saturation, and Brightness   Three dimensions combine to produce the rich world of color we experience. They are (1) hue, the actual color we see (red, green, and so on); (2) saturation, the purity of a color; and (3) brightness, the intensity of the light energy reflected from a surface. The colors in the figure are of the same hue but differ in saturation and brightness.

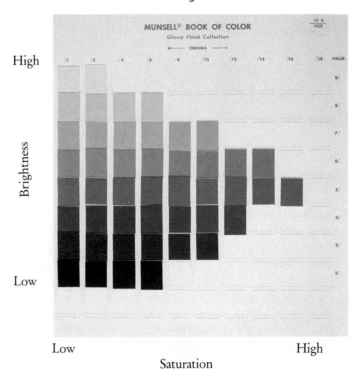

Bite into the apple and it looks white. Why? We see white because, rather than being absorbed, all the visible wavelengths of the color spectrum are reflected from the inside part of the apple. The presence of all visible wavelengths gives the sensation of white.

Our everyday visual experience goes far beyond the colors in the rainbow. We see thousands, perhaps millions, of subtle color shadings. What enables us to make these fine color distinctions? Researchers have identified three dimensions that combine to provide the rich world of color we experience. (1) The chief dimension is **hue**, which refers to the actual color we view—red, green, and so forth. (2) *Saturation* refers to the purity of a color. A color becomes less saturated, or less pure, as other wavelengths of light are mixed with it. (3) *Brightness* refers to the intensity of the light energy we perceive reflected from a surface. Figure 3.5 illustrates the dimensions of hue, saturation, and brightness.

Question: What two major theories attempt to explain color vision?

Theories of Color Vision: How We Sense Color   Two major theories have been offered to explain color vision, and both were formulated before the development of laboratory technology capable of testing them. The **trichromatic theory**, first proposed by Thomas Young in 1802, was modified by Hermann von Helmholtz about 50 years later. This theory states that there are three kinds of cones in the retina and that each kind makes its maximum chemical response to one of three colors—blue, green, or red—as shown in Figure 3.6. Research in the 1950s and the 1960s by Nobel Prize winner George Wald (1964; Wald et al., 1954) supports the trichromatic theory. Wald discovered that even though all cones have basically the same structure, the retina does indeed contain three kinds of cones.

hue: The property of light commonly referred to as color (red, blue, green, etc.), determined primarily by the wavelength of light reflected from a surface.

saturation: The degree to which light waves producing a color are of the same wavelength; the purity of a color.

brightness: The dimension of visual sensation that is dependent on the intensity of light reflected from a surface and that corresponds to the amplitude of the light wave.

trichromatic theory: The theory of color vision suggesting that there are three types of cones, which are maximally sensitive to red, green, or blue, and that varying levels of activity in these receptors can produce all of the colors.

Figure 3.6   Relative Sensitivity of the Three Types of Cones   Color vision is largely dependent on three types of cones. Each type responds maximally to a restricted range of wavelengths. The maximal response for one cone type is to short wavelengths of 450–500 nm (blue), for another type to medium wavelengths of 500–570 nm (green), and for another type to long wavelengths of 620–700 nm (red).

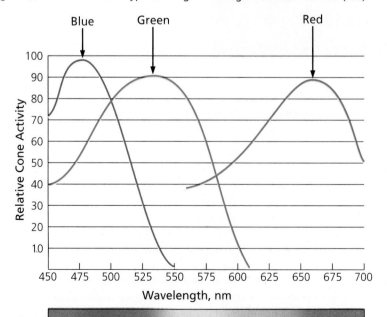

opponent-process theory:
The theory that certain cells in the visual system increase their firing rate to signal one color and decrease their firing rate to signal the opposing color (red/green, yellow/blue, white/black).

afterimage: The visual sensation that remains after a stimulus is withdrawn.

color blindness: The inability to distinguish some or all colors in vision, resulting from a defect in the cones.

The trichromatic theory alone, however, cannot explain how we are able to perceive such a rich variety of colors. Researchers now know that there must be some color-coding processes beyond the cones that combine color information in a more complex way.

The other major attempt to explain color vision is the **opponent-process theory,** which was first proposed by physiologist Ewald Hering in 1878 and revised in 1957 by researchers Leon Hurvich and Dorthea Jamison. According to the opponent-process theory, the cells respond by increasing or decreasing their rate of firing when different colors are present. The red/green cells increase their firing rate when red is present and decrease it when green is present; the yellow/blue cells have an increased response to yellow and a decreased response to blue. Another type of cell increases its response rate for white light and decreases it in the absence of light. Think of the opponent-process theory as opposing pairs of cells on a see-saw. As one goes up, the other goes down and vice-versa. The relative firing position of the three pairs of cells transmits color information to the brain. But if you look long enough at one color in the opponent-process pair and then look at a white surface, your brain will give you the sensation of the opposite color.

Does the opponent process operate in the cones, or elsewhere? Researchers now believe that the cones pass on information about wavelength (color) to higher levels of visual processing. Researchers De Valois and De Valois (1975) proposed that the opponent processes might operate at the ganglion cells in the retina and in the higher brain centers rather than at the level of the receptors, the cones.

The opponent processes are responsible for the presence of *afterimages*, which you can demonstrate in the *Try It!*

Try It!

Stare at the dot in the green, black, and yellow flag for approximately one minute. Then shift your gaze to the dot in the white space. You will see the American flag in its true colors—the opponent-process colors of red, white, and blue.

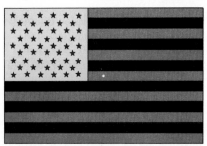

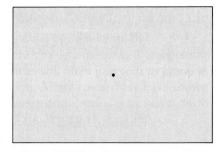

After you have stared at one color in an opponent-process pair (red/green, yellow/blue, black/white), that cell in the pair tires and the opponent cell begins to fire, producing a negative afterimage.

Color Blindness: Weakness for Sensing Certain Colors   Not all of us see the world in the same colors. If normal genes for the three color pigments are not present, there will be some form of **color blindness**—the inability to distinguish certain colors or, in rare cases, the total absence of color vision. Most color defects are actually color weaknesses or color confusion, rather than color blindness. Many people who have some type of color defect are not aware of it.

You may wonder how it is possible to know what the world looks like to a color-blind person. Some people who have normal vision in one eye but are color-blind in the other are able to explain the difference in color perception. The photograph on page 83 shows the way a scene would look to people with different types of color blindness. To a person who is completely color-blind, the whole world looks like a black-and-white movie.

The image on the left shows how the balloons would appear to a person with normal color vision. The image on the right shows how they would appear to a person with red-green color blindness, an inherited disorder.

Memory Check 3.2

1. Match the parts of the eye with their descriptions.

    _____ 1) the colored part of the eye   a. retina
    _____ 2) the opening in the iris that dilates and   b. cornea
                 constricts   c. pupil
    _____ 3) the transparent covering of the iris   d. iris
    _____ 4) the transparent structure that focuses an   e. lens
                 inverted image on the retina
    _____ 5) the thin, photosensitive membrane at the
                 back of the eye on which the lens focuses
                 an inverted image

2. The receptor cells in the retina that enable us to see in dim light are the (cones, rods); the cells that enable us to see color and sharp images are the (cones, rods).

3. Neural impulses are carried from the retina to the thalamus by the _____ and then relayed to their final destination, the _____.

    a. optic chiasma; visual cortex   c. optic nerve; visual cortex
    b. rods and cones; optic nerve   d. optic nerve; optic chiasma

4. Most people who are color-blind see no color at all. (true/false)

Answers: 1. 1) d 2) c 3) b 4) e 5) a 2. rods; cones 3. c 4. false

Hearing

More than a decade ago, the frightening science-fiction movie *Alien* was advertised this way: "In space no one can hear you scream!" Although the movie was fiction, the statement is true. Light can travel through the vast nothingness of space, a vacuum, but sound cannot. In the following section, you will learn why.

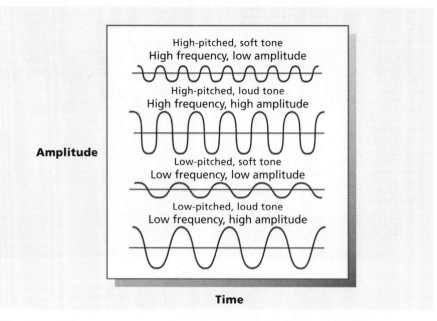

Figure 3.7 The Frequency and Amplitude of a Sound Wave The frequency of a sound wave—the number of cycles completed per second—determines the pitch of the sound. Loudness is determined by amplitude—the energy or height of the sound wave.

Sound: What We Hear

Question: What determines the pitch and the loudness of sound, and how is each quality measured?

Sound requires a medium through which to move, such as air, water, or a solid object. This fact was first demonstrated by Robert Boyle in 1660 when he suspended a ringing pocket watch by a thread inside a specially designed jar. When Boyle pumped all the air out of the jar, he could no longer hear the watch ring. But when he pumped the air back into the jar, he could hear the watch ring.

If you have ever attended a very loud rock concert, you not only heard but actually felt the mechanical vibrations. The pulsating speakers may have caused the floor, your seat, the walls, and the air around you to seem to shake or vibrate. You were feeling the moving air molecules being pushed toward you in waves as the speakers blasted their vibrations outward.

Frequency is an important characteristic of sound and is determined by the number of cycles completed by a sound wave in one second. The unit used to measure frequency, or the cycles per second, is known as hertz (Hz). The pitch, how high or low the sound, is chiefly determined by frequency—the higher the frequency (the more vibrations per second), the higher the sound.

The human ear can hear sound frequencies from low bass tones of around 20 Hz up to high-pitched sounds of about 20,000 Hz. The lowest tone on a piano sounds at a frequency of about 28 Hz and the highest tone at about 4,214 Hz. Many mammals—dogs, cats, bats, and rats—can hear tones much higher in frequency than 20,000 Hz. Amazingly, dolphins can respond to sounds up to 100,000 Hz.

The loudness of a sound is determined largely by a measure called *amplitude*. Amplitude depends on the energy of the sound wave. The force or pressure with which the air molecules are moving chiefly determines loudness. Figure 3.7 shows how sound waves vary in frequency and amplitude. We can measure the sound pressure level (loudness) of sounds, using a unit called the "bel" named for the American inventor Alexander Graham Bell. Because the bel is a rather large unit, we usually express the measure in tenths of a bel, or **decibels** (dB).

frequency: Measured in the unit hertz, the number of sound waves or cycles per second, determining the pitch of the sound.

amplitude: Measured in decibels, the magnitude or intensity of a sound wave, determining the loudness of the sound; in vision the *amplitude* of a light wave affects the brightness of a stimulus.

decibel (DES-ih-bel): A unit of measurement of the intensity or loudness of sound based on the amplitude of the sound wave.

The threshold of human hearing is set at 0 dB, which does not mean the absence of sound but the softest sound that can be heard in a very quiet setting. Each increase of 10 decibels makes a sound 10 times louder. A whisper is about 20 dB, but that is 100 times louder than 0 dB. A normal conversation, around 60 dB, is 10,000 times louder than a soft whisper at 20 dB. Figure 3.8 shows the comparative decibel levels for a variety of sounds.

The Ear: More to It Than Meets the Eye

Can people with big ears hear better than people with little ears? No. Even if your visible outer ears were cut off, your hearing would suffer very little. The part of the body that we call the ear plays only a minor role in *audition* in humans. Now we will explore this amazing structure that brings us the world of sound.

Question: How do the outer, middle, and inner ears function in hearing?

The Structure of the Ear: The Outer, Middle, and Inner Ears The oddly shaped, curved flap of cartilage and skin called the pinna is the visible part of the **outer ear** (see Figure 3.9). Inside the ear, your auditory canal is about one inch long, and its entrance is lined with hairs. At the end of the auditory canal is the eardrum (the tympanic membrane), a thin, flexible membrane about one-third of an inch in diameter. The eardrum moves in response to the sound waves that strike it.

The **middle ear** is no larger than an aspirin tablet. Inside its chamber are the ossicles, the three smallest bones in your body, each "about the size of a grain of rice" (Strome & Vernick, 1989). Named for their shapes, the three connected

audition: The sensation of hearing; the process of hearing.

outer ear: The visible part of the ear, consisting of the pinna and the auditory canal.

middle ear: The portion of the ear containing the ossicles, which connect the eardrum to the oval window and amplify the vibrations as they travel to the inner ear.

Figure 3.8 Decibel Levels of Various Sounds The loudness of a sound (its amplitude) is measured in decibels. Each increase of 10 decibels makes a sound 10 times louder. A normal conversation at 3 feet measures about 60 decibels, which is 10,000 times louder than a soft whisper of 20 decibels. Any exposure to sounds 130 dB or higher puts one at immediate risk for hearing damage.

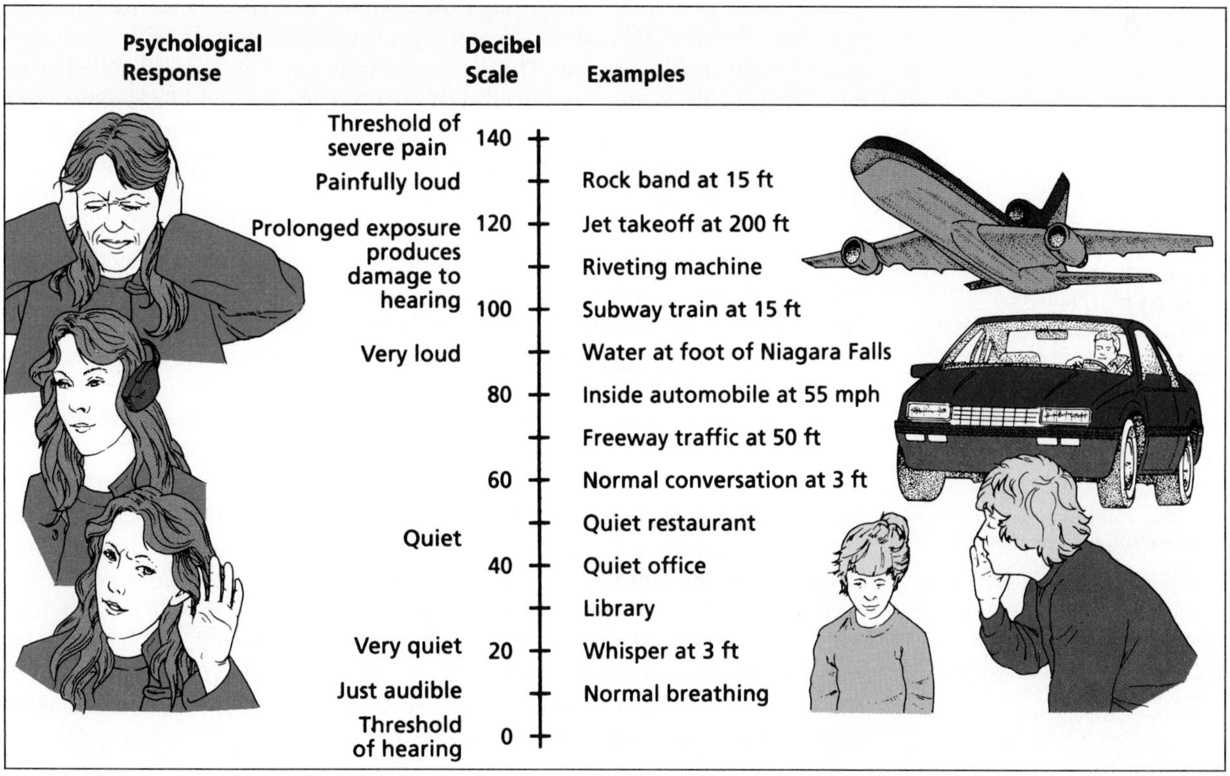

Psychological Response	Decibel Scale	Examples
Threshold of severe pain	140	
Painfully loud		Rock band at 15 ft
Prolonged exposure produces damage to hearing	120	Jet takeoff at 200 ft
		Riveting machine
	100	Subway train at 15 ft
Very loud		Water at foot of Niagara Falls
	80	Inside automobile at 55 mph
		Freeway traffic at 50 ft
	60	Normal conversation at 3 ft
		Quiet restaurant
Quiet	40	Quiet office
		Library
Very quiet	20	Whisper at 3 ft
Just audible		Normal breathing
Threshold of hearing	0	

Anatomy of the Auditory System

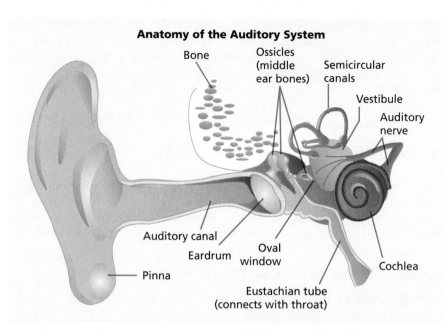

Figure 3.9   The Human Ear   Sound waves pass through the auditory canal to the eardrum, causing it to vibrate and set in motion the ossicles in the middle ear. When the stirrup pushes against the oval window, it sets up vibrations in the inner ear. This moves the fluid in the cochlea back and forth and sets in motion the hair cells, causing a message to be sent to the brain via the auditory nerve.

ossicles—the hammer, the anvil, and the stirrup—link the eardrum to the oval window (see Figure 3.9). The ossicles amplify the sound some 120 times (Coren, Porac, & Ward, 1979).

The **inner ear** begins at the inner side of the oval window on the base of the **cochlea**—a fluid-filled, snail-shaped, bony chamber. When the stirrup pushes against the oval window, it sets up vibrations that move the fluid in the cochlea back and forth in waves. The movement of the fluid sets in motion the thin basilar membrane that runs through the cochlea. Attached to the basilar membrane are about 15,000 sensory receptors called **hair cells,** each with a bundle of tiny hairs protruding from it. The tiny hair bundles are pushed and pulled by the motion of the fluid inside the cochlea. If the tip of the hair bundle is moved only as much as the width of an atom, this "changes the electrical properties of the cell and causes a message to be sent to the brain" by way of the auditory nerve (Hudspeth, 1983, p. 54).

Having two ears, one on either side of the head, enables us to determine the direction from which sounds are coming. Unless a sound is directly above, below, in front of, or behind us, it reaches one ear slightly before it reaches the other (Spitzer & Semple, 1991). The brain detects differences as small as 1/10,000 of a second and interprets them, telling us the direction of the sound (Rosenzweig, 1961). The source of a sound may also be determined by the difference in the intensity of the sound reaching each ear (Middlebrooks & Green, 1991).

Bone Conduction: Hearing Sound Vibrations through the Bones   The eardrum is not required for all the sounds we hear. We also hear through *bone conduction*—the vibrations of the bones in the face and the skull. When you click your teeth or eat crunchy food, you hear these sounds mainly through bone conduction. Some of these vibrations bypass the outer and middle ears altogether and are transmitted directly to the cochlea. If you have a watch that ticks, you can do the *Try It!* to demonstrate hearing through bone conduction without help from the outer and middle ears.

inner ear: The innermost portion of the ear, containing the cochlea, the vestibular sacs, and the semicircular canals.

cochlea (KOK-lee-uh):   The snail-shaped, fluid-filled organ in the inner ear that contains the hair cells (the sound receptors).

hair cells: Sensory receptors for hearing, found in the cochlea.

bone conduction: The transmission of vibrations along the bones of the skull or face directly to the cochlea.

Try It!

Place a ticking watch between your teeth and close your ears with your fingers. Listen and you will hear the ticking through bone conduction.

Have you ever heard a recording of your own voice? Did it sound like you? When you talk, sound waves reach your inner ear through bone conduction as well as through the auditory canal. But when you listen to a recording of your voice, there are no bone conduction vibrations in the sound you hear. You hear your voice as it sounds to other people (Békésy, 1957).

Lenhardt and others (1991) have found that humans can hear ultrasonic sounds in ranges up to 108,000 Hz through bone conduction, far beyond the normal limit of 20,000 Hz. Normal subjects and even profoundly deaf subjects could perceive, through bone conduction, some speech signals that had been converted into ultrasonic frequencies. The researchers suggest that "ultrasonic bone conduction hearing has potential as an alternative communication channel in the rehabilitation of hearing disorders" (p. 82).

Theories of Hearing: How Hearing Works

Question: What two major theories attempt to explain hearing?

In the 1860s Hermann von Helmholtz helped develop **place theory,** one of the two major theories of hearing. This theory holds that each individual pitch we hear is determined by the particular spot or place along the basilar membrane of the cochlea that vibrates the most. When we measure the amount of vibration at different places along the cochlea, we find that higher-pitched tones cause the membranes nearer the cochlea's base to vibrate most. The lower-pitched tones cause the most vibration of membranes farther along the coil toward the tip of the cochlea (Bekesy, 1957).

Another attempt to explain hearing is **frequency theory**. According to this theory, the hair cell receptors vibrate the same number of times per second as the sounds that reach them. Thus, a tone of 500 Hz would stimulate the hair cells to vibrate 500 times per second as well. Frequency theory seems valid for low- and medium-pitched tones, but it has a major problem with high-frequency tones. Individual neurons cannot fire more than about 1,000 times per second. Therefore, they could not signal to the brain the higher-pitched tones of 1,000 to 20,000 Hz.

The volley principle was put forth to suggest that groups, or volleys, of neurons, if properly synchronized, could together produce the firing rate required for higher tones (Wever, 1949). Yet even with the help of the volley principle, frequency theory is not able to explain how we hear tones with frequencies higher than about 4,000 Hz (Matlin & Foley, 1992). Today researchers believe that (1) frequency theory best explains how we perceive low frequencies, 150 Hz and below; (2) frequency theory supplements place theory in the 150- to 4,000-Hz range; and (3) place theory best accounts for how we perceive frequencies above 4,000 Hz.

place theory: The theory that sounds of different frequencies or pitch cause maximum activation of hair cells at certain locations along the basilar membrane.

frequency theory: The theory that hair cell receptors vibrate the same number of times as the sounds that reach them, thereby accounting for how variations in pitch are transmitted to the brain.

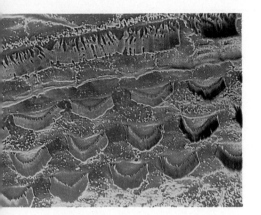

High intensity sounds, such as loud music, can permanently damage the delicate hair cells in the inner ear, causing hearing loss.

Hearing Loss: Kinds and Causes

Question: What are some major causes of hearing loss?

There are about 30 million people in the United States who have hearing problems (Catlin, 1986), and that number is growing rapidly (Dobbin, 1987). Hearing loss and deafness can be caused by disease, birth defects, injury, excessive noise, and old age. Conductive hearing loss, or conduction deafness, is usually caused by disease or injury to the eardrum or the bones of the middle ear, which prevents sound waves from being conducted to the cochlea. People with conductive hearing loss can usually be helped with a hearing aid that bypasses the middle ear and uses bone conduction to reach the cochlea.

Conventional hearing aids are useless instruments, however, for the 2 million people in this country who suffer from neural hearing loss, or nerve deafness. With this disorder the eardrum and the middle ear may be intact, but some injury or deterioration of the inner ear prevents the transduction of sound waves into neural impulses. Many people over 60 (more men than women) suffer from a gradual deterioration of the auditory nerve that results in a loss of hearing. There are some indications that life-long exposure to excessive noise may be more of a factor in hearing loss than aging is.

Older persons in one culture, the Mabaan tribe in the Sudan in Africa, don't appear to suffer much hearing loss as they age. In fact, when hearing tests were conducted on Mabaan tribe members, some 80-year-old members could hear as well as 20-year-old people in industrialized countries. The Mabaan pride themselves on their sensitive hearing, and an important tribal custom is never to raise their voices. Even their festivals and celebrations are quiet affairs, featuring dancing and soft singing accompanied by stringed instruments rather than drums. The loudest sounds they usually hear in their everyday world are made by their own domestic animals like sheep and roosters (Bennett, 1990).

Memory Check 3.3

1. Pitch is chiefly determined by (amplitude, frequency); loudness is chiefly determined by (amplitude, frequency).

2. Pitch is measured in (decibels, hertz); loudness is measured in (decibels, hertz).

3. Match the part of the ear with the structures it contains.

    _____ 1) ossicles   a. outer ear
    _____ 2) pinna, auditory canal   b. middle ear
    _____ 3) cochlea, hair cells   c. inner ear

4. The hair cells in the inner ear continuously replace themselves. (true/false)

5. Extremely loud noise can damage the:

    a. eardrum   c. hair cells in the cochlea
    b. ossicles   d. all of these

Answers: 1. frequency; amplitude 2. hertz; decibels 3. 1) b 2) a 3) c 4. false 5. d

WORLD OF PSYCHOLOGY: APPLICATIONS

Noise and Hearing Loss: Bad Vibrations

Hearing loss is increasing rapidly in the industrialized world, and the main reason for the increase is NOISE. Jet engines, power mowers, radios, firecrackers, motorcycles, chain saws, and other power tools are well-known sources of noise that can injure the ear. For centuries we have known that noise can cause hearing loss, but it was not until the early 1970s that the United States Congress passed legislation to protect employees in the workplace who are exposed regularly to hazardous noise.

Exposure to hazardous noise can begin long before we are old enough to listen to a Sony Walkman, experience a rock concert, or attend a baseball game at a covered or domed stadium. Some babies and toddlers get an early start on hearing loss with a variety of toys on the market. Researchers Axelsson and Jerson (1985) tested seven squeaking toys that, at a distance of 10 cm, squeaked out pure sound levels loud enough to put toddlers at risk for hearing loss "within minutes of exposure each day" (p. 575).

As children grow older, noise-induced hearing loss can occur within only seconds of exposure if they play with toy weapons. Researchers tested several toy weapons and found that at a distance of 50 cm, the guns produced explosive sound levels ranging from 144 to 152 dB (Axelsson & Jerson, 1985).

Firecrackers pose a particular hazard if they explode close to the ear. In another study a number of firecrackers were tested at 3 meters, and sound levels were found to range from 130 dB to an unbelievable and highly dangerous 190 dB (Gupta & Vishwakarma, 1989).

Explosions, gun blasts, and other extremely loud noises may burst the eardrum, or fracture or dislocate the tiny ossicles in the middle ear. Often these injuries can be repaired surgically, but noise injuries to the inner ear cannot. "Extremely intense sounds can rip the delicate sensory [hair] cells completely off the basilar membrane on which they normally sit, kill the cells, or merely injure them permanently" (Bennett, 1990, p. 3). (See Figure 3.10.) During the filming of a western movie, former President Ronald Reagan's hearing was damaged beyond repair by a single shot from a blank pistol fired too close to his ear.

It doesn't take an explosion to injure hair cells, or years of exposure to noise. Rock musician Kathy Peck lost 40 percent of her hearing in one evening after her band opened a stadium concert for Duran Duran.

How can you tell when noise levels are high enough to jeopardize your hearing? You are putting yourself at risk if you have difficulty talking over the noise level, or if the noise exposure leaves you with a ringing in your ears or a temporary hearing loss (Dobie, 1987).

Experts claim that exposure to noise of 90 dB (a lawn mower, for example) for more than 8 hours in a 24-hour period can damage hearing. For every increase of 5 dB, maximum exposure time should be cut in half. The Department of Labor considers 115 dB to be the maximum allowable level of "exposure to steady sound levels" (Catlin, 1986, p. 142).

In 1986 the rock group The Who entered the *Guinness Book of World Records* as the loudest rock band on record, blasting out deafening sound intensities that measured 120 dB at a distance of 164 feet from the speakers. Unless their ears were protected, every person within that 164-foot radius probably suffered some irreversible damage to the ear. And the band members? Pete Townshend of The Who has severely damaged hearing and is plagued by tinnitus, a continuous ringing in the ears.

What can you do to protect yourself from noise?

- If you must be exposed to loud noise, use ear plugs (not the kind used for swimming) or earmuffs to reduce noise by as much as 15–30 dB (Dobie, 1987).

- If you must engage in an extremely noisy activity, such as cutting wood with a chain saw, limit periods of exposure to intense noise so that stunned hair cells can recover.

- Keep the volume down on Walkman-type radios or tape players. If the volume control is numbered 1 to 10, a volume above 4 probably exceeds the federal standards for noise. If you have a ringing in your ears, if sounds seem muffled, or if you have a tickling sensation after you remove your headset, you may have sustained some hearing loss.

- Begin humming before you are exposed to loud noise. Humming will set in motion the very tiny muscles in the middle ear that will dampen the sound and provide some measure of protection (Borg & Counter, 1989).

- Put your fingers in your ears or leave the scene.

Rock musicians are at high risk for permanently damaged hearing.

olfaction (ol-FAK-shun): The sensation of smell; the process of smell.

olfactory epithelium: A one-inch square patch of tissue, at the top of the nasal cavity, that contains about 10 million receptors for smell.

olfactory bulbs: Two match-stick-sized structures above the nasal cavities, where smell sensations first register in the brain.

Smell and Taste

You have been reading how important are our abilities to sense light and sound. Now explore our chemical senses, smell and taste.

Smell: Sensing Scents

Consider what it would be like to live in a world without smell. "Not really so bad," you might say. "Although I could not smell flowers, perfume, or my favorite foods, I would never again have to endure the foul odors of life. It's a trade-off, so what's the difference?"

The difference is large indeed. Your ability to detect odors close at hand and at a distance is an aid to survival. You smell smoke and can escape before the flames of a fire envelop you. Your nose broadcasts an odor alarm to the brain when certain poisonous gases or noxious fumes are present. But the survival value of odor detection in humans does not stop there. Smell, aided by taste, is the last line of defense—your final chance to avoid putting spoiled food or drink into your body. And some research suggests that smell may even be closely tied to the sex drive.

The human olfactory system is capable of sensing and distinguishing 10,000 different odor molecules (Firestein, 1991) and more than 100,000 compounds (Dionne, 1988). Although perfumers and whiskey blenders can distinguish about 100,000 odors, the average person with training can distinguish from about 10,000 to 40,000 odors (Dobb, 1989).

Question: What path does a smell message take on its journey from the nose to the brain?

The Mechanics of Smell: How the Nose Knows *Olfaction*—the sense of smell—is a chemical sense. We cannot smell a substance unless some of its molecules vaporize (pass from a solid or liquid into a gaseous state). Heat speeds up the evaporation of molecules, which is why food that is cooking has a stronger and more distinct odor than uncooked food. When odor molecules vaporize, they become airborne and make their way up our nostrils to the **olfactory epithelium**. This one-inch-square patch of tissue at the top of the nasal cavity contains about 10 million receptor cells for smell. Have you ever wondered why dogs have a keener sense of smell than humans? Not only do some dogs have a large and long snout, some breeds have an olfactory epithelium that can be as large as the area of a handkerchief (Winter, 1976) and contain as many as 200 million receptors (Brown, 1975). Figure 3.11 shows a diagram of the human olfactory system.

The olfactory receptors are different from all other sensory receptors. Each olfactory receptor is a special type of neuron that both comes into direct contact with sensory stimuli and reaches directly into the brain. The axons of the olfactory receptor cells relay the smell message directly to the **olfactory bulbs**—two brain structures the size of matchsticks that rest above the nasal cavities (see Figure 3.11). From the olfactory bulbs, the smell message travels to different parts of the brain.

Until recently, researchers were not sure if there were many different types of olfactory receptors. Does the decoding of different odors occur mostly in the nose, or, if there are fewer different types of receptors, does the decoding task take place mainly in the brain? Researchers Buck and Axel (1991) now have evidence that more than 100 different kinds of receptors exist, and the total may be even greater. Their work suggests that the olfactory receptor is the main site for the discrimination of odors. Other recent research indicates that (1) the

Figure 3.11

The Olfactory Sense

Odor molecules travel up the nostrils to the olfactory epithelium, which contains the receptor cells for smell. Olfactory receptors are special neurons whose axons form the olfactory nerve, which relays smell messages to the olfactory bulbs and on to other parts of the brain.

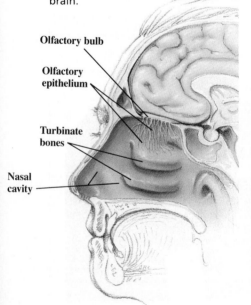

Olfactory bulb

Olfactory epithelium

Turbinate bones

Nasal cavity

number of olfactory receptors responding (firing) determines the intensity of the stimulus, that is, how strong or weak it smells, and (2) their location transmits the nature of the scent. "Each scent is expressed by a spatial pattern of receptor activity" that is transmitted to the olfactory bulb (Freeman, 1991, p. 78).

You may have noticed the distinctive odor of your own home when you first walk through the door, but after a few minutes you are not aware of it. A continuous odor will stimulate the smell receptors to respond only for a while. Then, if there is no change in the odors, the receptors will steadily diminish their firing rate, and smell adaptation will occur.

> **gustation:** The sensation of taste.
>
> **taste buds:** The structures that are composed of 60 to 100 sensory receptors for taste.

Taste: What the Tongue Can Tell

Question: What are the four primary taste sensations, and how are they detected?

A sizzling steak, a steaming lobster dipped in melted butter, chocolate cake . . . Does your sense of taste alone tell you what these foods taste like? Surprisingly, no. *Gustation*, or the sense of taste, can give you only four kinds of sensations—sweet, sour, salty, and bitter. If the sense of smell did not contribute to our enjoyment of food, there would be no gourmets and few expensive restaurants. Most of the pleasure we attribute to our sense of taste is actually due to smell, a fact researchers have known for over 75 years (Hollingworth & Poffenberger, 1917; Hornung & Enns, 1987). You can prove this for yourself in the *Try It!*

Try It!

Cover your eyes and hold your nose tightly. Have a friend present you with small pieces of food of similar texture, such as a raw potato, an apple, and an onion. See if you can identify each food by taste alone. Most people cannot.

The Taste Receptors: Taste Detectors   Look at your tongue in a mirror. You will see little bumps called papillae. There are four different types of papillae, and three of them contain **taste buds,** which cluster around the cracks and crevices between the papillae (see Figure 3.12). Each taste bud is composed of from 60 to 100 receptor cells that resemble the petals of a flower (Kinnamon, 1988). The life span of these receptor cells is only 6 or 7 days (Beidler & Smallman, 1965).

Taste buds are packed most densely on the tip of the tongue and less densely on the rear edges; they are absent from the center of the tongue (Bartoshuk, 1989). But taste is poorly localized, and taste sensations appear to come from all over the mouth rather than from only the edges and the tip of the tongue. Although aging is typically accompanied by a decline in the other senses, people lose very little of their ability to detect the four primary taste sensations as they age (Bartoshuk et al., 1986). When older people complain that food doesn't taste as good as it used to, the reason is usually a loss of smell rather than a failing sense of taste (Bartoshuk, 1989).

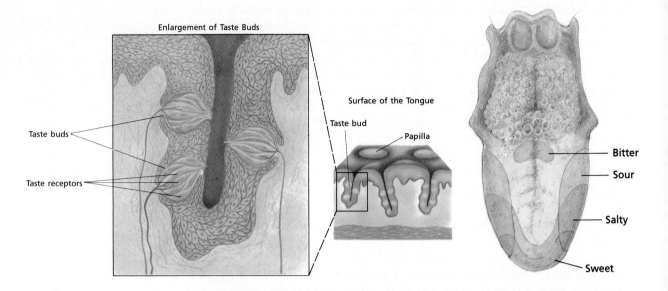

Figure 3.12   The Tongue's Taste Buds   Taste buds are sensitive only to four tastes: bitter, sour, salty, and sweet. The drawing on the right shows the areas that are most sensitive to each. The vertical cross-section enlargement shows one of the papillae. The taste buds are in the small trenches around the papillae.

Memory Check 3.4

1. The technical name for the process or the sensation of smell is (gustation, olfaction).

2. The olfactory, or smell, receptors are located in the (olfactory epithelium, olfactory tract).

3. The four primary taste sensations are _____, _____, _____, and _____.

4. Each (papilla, taste bud) contains from 60 to 100 receptor cells.

Answers: 1. olfaction   2. olfactory epithelium   3. sweet, salty, sour, bitter   4. taste bud

Our Other Senses

Other senses are our sense of touch (the tactile sense), our sense of balance (the vestibular sense), and our kinesthetic sense.

The Skin Senses: Information from Our Natural Clothing

Question: How does the skin provide sensory information?

Our own natural clothing, the skin, is the largest organ in the body. It performs many important biological functions while also yielding much of what we know as sensual pleasure. Your skin can detect heat, cold, pressure, pain, and a vast range of touch sensations—caresses, pinches, punches, pats, rubs, scratches, and the feel of many different textures, from silk to sandpaper.

The Mechanism of Touch: How Touch Works *Tactile* information is conveyed to the brain when an object touches and depresses the skin, stimulating one or more of the several distinct types of nerve cell receptors. These sensitive nerve endings in the skin send the touch message through nerve connections to the spinal cord. The message travels up the spinal cord and through the brainstem and the lower brain centers, finally reaching the brain's somatosensory cortex. Only then do we become aware of where and how hard we have been touched. Remember from chapter 2 that the somatosensory cortex is the strip of tissue at the front of the parietal lobes where touch, pressure, temperature, and pain register.

If we examine the skin from the outermost to the deepest layer, we find a variety of nerve endings that differ markedly in appearance. Most or all of these nerve endings appear to respond in some degree to all different types of stimulation.

If someone touched your skin with a sharp object like a toothpick, you could tell the exact spot where the toothpick was placed on your body, or could you? The *Try It!* may prove interesting.

> **tactile:** Pertaining to the sense of touch.

Try It!

Have someone touch the middle of your back with two toothpicks held about 1 1/2 inches apart. Do you feel one point or two? How far apart do the toothpicks have to be before you perceive them as two separate touch sensations? How far apart do they have to be on your face? on your hands? on your fingers? on your toes? Which of these body parts are the most sensitive? Which are the least sensitive?

In the 1890s one of the most prominent researchers of the tactile sense, Max von Frey, discovered the two-point threshold that measures how far apart two points must be before we feel them as two separate touches. Figure 3.13 illustrates two-point thresholds for different body parts, showing the actual distance apart at which two-point discriminations can be made by most people.

Pain: Physical Hurts

Question: What beneficial purpose does pain serve?

Although our sense of touch brings us a great deal of pleasure, it delivers pain as well.

> He has never had a headache or a toothache, never felt the pain of a cut, a bruise, or a burn. If you are thinking, "How lucky!" you are completely wrong. His arms and legs are twisted and bent. Some of his fingers are missing. A large, bloody wound covers one of his knees, and his lips are chewed raw.
>
> A battered child? No. Born with a very rare genetic defect, he is totally insensitive to pain. He does not even notice a deep cut, a burn, or a broken bone when it happens, so he continues whatever he is doing and injures himself severely. (Adapted from Wallis, 1984.)

Figure 3.13

The Two-Point Threshold

The two-point threshold measures how far apart two points must be to be felt as two separate touches. The drawing shows the average two-point thresholds for different parts of the body. The thumb and fingers, being the most sensitive, have the lowest two-point thresholds (less than 5 mm). The calves, being the least sensitive body parts, have two-point thresholds of about 45 mm. (After Weinstein, 1968.)

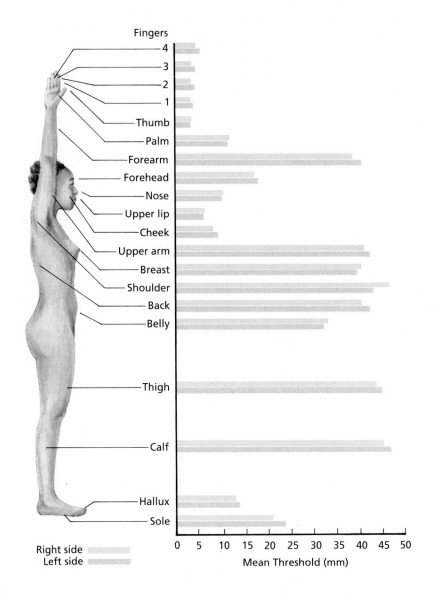

This story shows that pain functions as a valuable warning and protective mechanism. It motivates us to tend to our injuries, restrict our activity, and seek medical help if we need it. Pain also teaches us to avoid pain-producing circumstances in the future. Chronic pain, however, persists long after it serves any useful function and becomes a serious medical problem for nearly 50 to 55 million Americans (Edmund, 1990).

Question: What is the gate-control theory of pain?

The Gate-Control Theory: Conducting Pains Great and Small   Pain is probably the least understood of all the sensations. We are not certain how pain works, but one major theory seeks to explain it—the **gate-control theory** of Melzack and Wall (1965, 1983). They contend that the dorsal horn of the spinal cord is the gate through which messages from all over the body travel on the way to the brain. Only so many messages can go through the gate at any one time. This theory suggests that two types of nerve fibers are involved—the fast-conducting A fibers and the slow-conducting C fibers. The pain receptors—the

gate-control theory: The theory that the pain signals transmitted by slow-firing C fibers can be blocked at the spinal gate if the pressure-sensitive, fast-firing A fibers get their message to the spinal cord first, or if the brain itself inhibits the transmission of the pain messages.

C fibers—produce dull, throbbing, continuous pain by stimulating the dorsal horn cells in the spinal cord, which in turn open the pain gate and send the pain message to the brain.

What is the first thing you do when you stub your toe or pound your finger with a hammer? If you rub or apply gentle pressure to the injury, you are stimulating the fast-conducting A nerve fibers. The A fibers are pressure receptors. When stimulated, they inhibit the spinal cord's dorsal horn cells, thereby closing the gate and preventing the more serious pain message from reaching the brain. Melzack and Wall believe that stimulation of the fast-firing A fibers enables their message to reach the spinal cord first, thus blocking the pain message from the slower C fibers. They also state that the brain itself can inhibit the transmission of pain messages and thereby influence the perception of pain.

Question: What are endorphins?

Endorphins: Our Own Natural Pain Relievers   Americans spend more money trying to get rid of pain than for any other medical purpose. In fact, we spend over $40 billion each year on treatments for chronic pain ranging from over-the-counter medications to surgery and psychotherapy (Budiansky et al., 1987).

Our body produces its own natural painkillers, the **endorphins**, which block pain and produce a feeling of well-being (Hendler & Fenton, 1979). Endorphins are released when we are injured, when we experience stress or extreme pain, and when we laugh, cry, or exercise (Bolles & Fanselow, 1982; Terman et al., 1984). "Runner's high" and an elevated mood after exercising are often attributed to an increase in endorphin levels (Goldberg, 1988).

Sometimes hospital patients recovering from surgery are given placebos when they ask for pain medication (Benson & Epstein, 1975). A placebo can take the form of a sugar pill or an injection of saline solution. The patients believe they are receiving pain medication, but the placebos have no effect on pain. Nevertheless, 35 percent of the patients who take placebos report relief from pain (Melzack & Wall, 1983). Why? When patients believe that they have received a drug for pain, apparently that belief stimulates the release of their own natural pain relievers, the endorphins.

Acupuncture, the ancient Chinese technique for relieving pain, appears to work because the fine needles that are inserted at specific points on the body seem to stimulate the release of endorphins. But endorphins do not account for other methods of pain relief such as meditation, relaxation, distraction, or hypnosis, which we discuss in chapter 4, "Altered States of Consciousness."

The next two senses we will explore may seem minor, but they too make important contributions to our sensory world.

The Kinesthetic Sense: Keeping Track of Our Body Parts

Question: What kind of information does the kinesthetic sense provide, and how is this sensory information detected?

The **kinesthetic sense** provides information about (1) the position of our body parts in relation to each other and (2) the movement in various body parts. This information is detected by receptors in the joints, ligaments, and muscles. The other senses, especially vision, provide additional information about body position and movement, but our kinesthetic sense works well on its own. Thanks to our kinesthetic sense, we are able to perform smooth and skilled body movements without visual feedback or a studied, conscious effort. A companion sense, the vestibular sense involves equilibrium or the sense of balance.

endorphins (en-DOR-fins): Chemicals, produced naturally by the pituitary gland, that reduce pain and affect mood positively.

kinesthetic sense: The sense providing information about the position of body parts and about body movement, detected by sensory receptors in the joints, ligaments, and muscles.

The Vestibular Sense: Sensing Up and Down and Changes in Speed

Question: What is the vestibular sense, and where are its sensory receptors located?

Our **vestibular sense** detects movement and provides information about our orientation in space. The vestibular sense organs are located in the semicircular canals and the vestibular sacs in the inner ear. The **semicircular canals** sense the rotation of your head, such as when you are turning your head from side to side or when you are spinning around (see Figure 3.14). Because the canals are filled with fluid, rotating movements of the head in any direction send the fluid coursing through the tubelike semicircular canals. In the canals the moving fluid bends the hair cells, which act as receptors and send neural impulses to the brain. Because there are three canals, each positioned on a different plane, the hair cells in one canal will bend more than hair cells in the other canals depending on the direction of rotation.

The semicircular canals also play an important role in the stabilization of vision. If you move your head from side to side as you read, you can still read without losing your place. The compensatory eye movements are reflex actions that automatically move the eyes just exactly the right amount to provide a continuous, clear focus (Wallach, 1985b). The two fluid-filled, vestibular sacs in your inner ear provide information about the orientation of your head. They contain hair cells that act as motion receptors, detecting the direction of head movement. The bending of the hair cells sets up a neural impulse telling the brain in which direction you are moving (D. E. Parker, 1980). The faster you accelerate in any direction, the more the hair cells bend.

Figure 3.14

Sensing Balance and Movement

The semicircular canals, shown here, sense the rotation of the head in any direction, sending fluid coursing through the tubelike semicircular canals. The fluid bends the hair cell receptors, and they send the message to the brain.

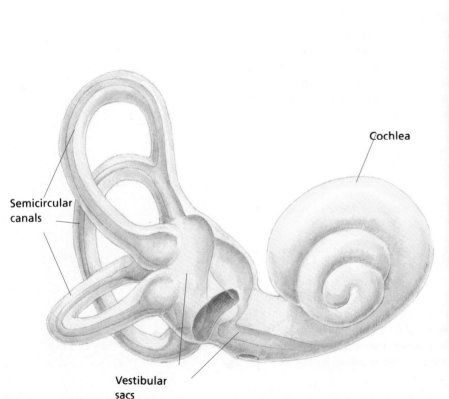

The semicircular canals and the vestibular sacs signal only *changes* in motion or orientation. If you were blindfolded and had no visual or other external cues, you would not be able to sense motion once your speed reached a constant rate. For example, you feel the take-off and landing in an airplane or sudden changes in speed. But once the pilot levels off and maintains about the same speed, your vestibular organs do not signal the brain that you are moving, even if you are traveling hundreds of miles per hour.

Memory Check 3.5

1. The two-point threshold varies for different body parts. (true/false)

2. People would be better off if they could not feel pain. (true/false)

3. (Endorphins, Placebos) are pain-relieving substances produced by the body.

4. The (kinesthetic, vestibular) sense provides information about the position of our body parts in relation to each other and about movement in those body parts.

5. The receptors for the (kinesthetic, vestibular) sense are located in the semicircular canals and vestibular sacs in the (middle ear, inner ear).

Answers: 1. true 2. false 3. Endorphins 4. kinesthetic 5. vestibular, inner ear

Perception: Ways of Perceiving

In the first part of this chapter, you learned how the senses detect visual, auditory, and other sensory information and transmit it to the brain. Now we will explore **perception**—the process by which this sensory information is actively organized and interpreted by the brain. We may *sense* sounds in hertz and decibels, but we *perceive* melodies. We may *sense* light of certain wavelengths and intensities, but we *perceive* a multicolored world of objects and people. Sensations are the raw materials of human experiences; perceptions are the finished products.

We know that physical objects can be analyzed down to their smallest parts, even to the atoms that make up the object. But can perception be analyzed and understood in the same way—broken down into its smallest sensory elements? The answer is no, according to Gestalt psychology, a school of thought that began in Germany in the early 1900s.

The Gestalt Principles of Perceptual Organization

Question: What are the Gestalt principles of perceptual organization?

The Gestalt psychologists maintained that we cannot understand our perceptual world by breaking down experiences into tiny parts and analyzing them separately. When sensory elements are brought together, something new is formed. "The whole is greater than the sum of its parts," they insisted. The German

vestibular sense (ves-TIB-yu-ler): Provides information about movement and our orientation in space through sensory receptors in the semicircular canals and the vestibular sacs that detect changes in the movement and orientation of the head.

semicircular canals: Three fluid-filled tubular canals in the inner ear that provide information about rotating head movements.

perception: The process by which sensory information is actively organized and interpreted by the brain.

Figure 3.15

Reversing Figure and Ground

In this illustration, you can see a white vase as figure against a black background, or two black faces in profile on a white background. Exactly the same visual stimulus produces two opposite figure-ground perceptions.

word *Gestalt* has no exact English equivalent, but it roughly refers to the whole form, pattern, or configuration that we perceive.

How do we organize the world of sights, sounds, and other sensory stimuli in order to perceive the way we do? The Gestalt psychologists claimed that we organize our sensory experience according to certain basic principles of perceptual organization. The principles include the figure-ground relationship and other principles of perceptual grouping.

Figure and Ground: One Stands Out

The **figure-ground** relationship is the most fundamental principle of perceptual organization and is, therefore, the best place to start analyzing how we perceive. As you view your world, some object (the figure) seems to stand out from the background (the ground).

Many psychologists believe that the figure-ground perceptual ability is *innate*, an ability that we do not have to learn. We know that figure-ground perception is present very early in life. It is also the first ability to appear in patients blind from birth who have received their sight as adults, as it was with S. B. We also know that figure-ground perception is not limited to vision. If you listen to a symphony orchestra or a rock band, the melody line tends to stand out as figure, while the chords and the rest of the accompaniment are heard as the background. An itch or a pain would immediately get your attention, while the remaining tactile stimuli you feel would fade to ground.

How can we be sure that knowing the difference between figure and ground is achieved by the perceptual system rather than being part of the sensory stimulus itself? The best proof is represented by reversible figures, where figure and ground seem to shift back and forth between two equal possibilities, as shown in Figure 3.15.

Sometimes a figure or an object blends so well with its background that we can hardly see it. When there are no sharp lines of contrast between a figure and its background, a figure is camouflaged. For many animals, camouflage provides protection from predators.

Gestalt Principles of Grouping: Perceptual Arrangements

The Gestalt psychologists believed that when we see figures or hear sounds, we organize or integrate them according to the simplest, most basic arrangement possible. They proposed the following principles of grouping: similarity, proximity, continuity, and closure (Wertheimer, 1958).

Similarity We tend to group visual, auditory, or other stimuli according to the principle of similarity. Objects that have similar characteristics are perceived as a unit. In Figure 3.16(a) dots of a similar color are perceived as belonging together to form horizontal rows in A and vertical columns in B.

Proximity Objects that are close together in space or time are usually perceived as belonging together, a principle of grouping called proximity. Because of the spacing, the lines in Figure 3.16(b) are perceived as four pairs of lines rather than eight separate lines.

Continuity The principle of continuity means that we tend to perceive figures or objects as belonging together if they appear to form a continuous pattern, as in the example in Figure 3.16(c).

Closure The principle of closure attempts to explain our tendency to complete figures with gaps in them. Even though parts of the figure in Figure 3.16(d) are missing, we use closure and perceive it as a triangle nevertheless.

Gestalt (geh-SHTALT): A German word roughly meaning "form" or "pattern."

figure-ground: A principle of perceptual organization whereby the visual field is perceived in terms of an object (figure) standing out against a background (ground).

innate: Inborn, unlearned.

perceptual constancy: The tendency to perceive objects as maintaining stable properties, such as size, shape, and brightness, despite differences in distance, viewing angle, and lighting.

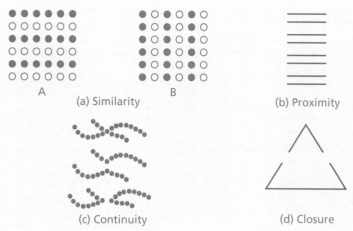

A   (a) Similarity   B

(b) Proximity

(c) Continuity   (d) Closure

Figure 3.16 Gestalt Principles of Grouping Gestalt psychologists proposed four principles of perceptual grouping: similarity, proximity, continuity, and closure.

Transparency: S&P 17
The Gestalt Principle of Proximity

Perceptual Constancy

Question: What is perceptual constancy, and what are three types?

As we view people and objects from different angles, distances, and under different lighting conditions, we tend to see them as maintaining the same shape, brightness, and color. We call this phenomenon **perceptual constancy**.

Size Constancy: When Smaller Means Farther
When you say good-bye to friends and watch them walk away, the image they cast on your retina grows smaller and smaller until they finally disappear in the distance. But the shrinking size information that the retina sends to your brain (the sensation) does not fool the perceptual system. As objects or people move farther away from us, we continue to perceive them as being about the same size. This perceptual phenomenon is known as size constancy.

We do not make a literal interpretation about the size of objects from the **retinal image**—the image projected onto the retina of objects in the visual field. If we did, we would believe that the objects we see become larger as they approach us and smaller as they move away from us. Some evidence suggests that size constancy is learned. Recall that S. B. had trouble perceiving visual sensations he had never experienced. S. B. so grossly misjudged distances that he perceived the automobiles 60 feet below his hospital window as toy cars nearby.

Shape Constancy: Seeing Round as Round from Any Angle
The shape or image of an object projected onto the retina changes according to the angle from

Figure 3.17 The Ames Room

Why does the boy in this photograph look twice as tall as the woman? The answer is that the two are standing in the famous Ames distorted room. The windows and the pattern on the floor are designed to create the illusion of a normal, rectangular room. In reality the right rear corner is much farther back than the left corner. Also, the distance from floor to ceiling is much greater in the right corner because the floor slopes steeply.

shape constancy: The tendency to perceive objects as having a stable or unchanging shape regardless of differences in viewing angle.

brightness constancy: The tendency to see objects as maintaining the same brightness regardless of differences in lighting conditions.

Figure 3.18 Shape Constancy   The door projects very different images on the retina when viewed from different angles. But due to shape constancy, we continue to perceive the door as rectangular.

which we view it. But our perceptual ability gives us *shape constancy*—the tendency to perceive objects as having a stable or unchanging shape regardless of changes in the retinal image resulting from differences in viewing angle. In other words, we perceive a door as rectangular and a plate as round from whatever angle we view them (see Figure 3.18).

Brightness Constancy: Perceiving Brightness in Sunlight and Shadow

We normally see objects as maintaining a constant level of brightness regardless of differences in lighting conditions—a phenomenon known as *brightness constancy*. Nearly all objects reflect some part of the light that falls upon them, and we know that white objects reflect more light than black objects. However, a black asphalt driveway actually reflects more light at noon in bright sunlight than a white shirt reflects indoors at night in dim lighting. Nevertheless, the driveway still looks black and the shirt still looks white. Why? We learn to infer the brightness of objects by comparing them to the brightness of all other objects viewed at the same time.

Memory Check 3.6

1. The Gestalt principle of (continuity, closure) refers to our tendency to complete figures with gaps in them.

2. Camouflage blurs the distinction between:

   a. sensation and perception   c. continuation and closure
   b. figure and ground   d. proximity and similarity

3. Which of the constancies cause us to perceive objects as being different from the actual retinal image they project?

   a. brightness and shape constancy   c. size and shape constancy
   b. brightness and size constancy   d. color and shape constancy

Answers: 1. closure 2. b 3. c

Depth Perception: Perceiving What's Up Close and Far Away

Depth perception is the ability to perceive the visual world in three dimensions and to judge distances accurately. We judge how far away from us are the objects we grasp and the people we reach out to touch. We climb and descend stairs without stumbling, and perform other visual tasks too numerous to list, all requiring depth perception.

Our depth perception ability is three-dimensional. Yet each eye is able to provide us with only a two-dimensional view. The images cast upon the retina do not contain depth; they are flat, just like a photograph. How, then, do we perceive depth so vividly?

Question: What are the binocular depth cues?

Binocular Depth Cues: The Cues Only Two Eyes Reveal Some cues to depth perception depend on our two eyes working together. These are called **binocular depth cues,** and they include convergence and binocular disparity. **Convergence** occurs when our eyes turn inward as we focus on nearby objects— the closer the object, the greater the convergence. Hold the tip of your finger about 12 inches in front of your nose and focus on it. Now slowly begin moving your finger toward your nose. Your eyes will turn inward so much that they virtually cross when the tip of your finger meets the tip of your nose. Many psychologists believe that the tension of the eye muscles as they converge conveys information to the brain that serves as a cue for distance and depth perception.

Fortunately, our eyes are just far enough apart, about 2 1/2 inches or so, to give each eye a slightly different view of the objects we focus on and consequently, a slightly different retinal image. The difference between the two retinal images, known as **binocular disparity** (or retinal disparity), provides an important cue for depth and distance. The farther away from us the objects we view (up to 20 feet or so), the less the disparity or difference between the two retinal images. The brain integrates these two slightly different retinal images and gives us the perception of three dimensions (Wallach, 1985a). Ohzawa and others (1990) suggest that there are specific neurons in the visual cortex particularly suited to detecting disparity. Ordinarily we are not aware that each eye provides a slightly different view of the objects we see, but you can prove this for yourself in the *Try It!*

depth perception: The ability to see in three dimensions and to estimate distance.

binocular depth cues: Depth cues that depend on two eyes working together; convergence and binocular disparity.

convergence: A binocular depth cue in which the eyes turn inward as they focus on nearby objects—the closer an object, the greater the convergence.

binocular disparity: A binocular depth cue resulting from differences between the two retinal images cast by objects at distances up to about 20 feet.

monocular depth cues (mah-NOK-yu-ler): Depth cues that can be perceived by only one eye.

Hold your forefinger or a pencil at arms' length straight in front of you. Close your left eye and focus on the pencil. Now quickly close your right eye at the same time that you open the left eye. Repeat this procedure, closing one eye just as you open the other. The pencil will appear to move from side to side in front of your face.

Now slowly bring the pencil closer and closer until it almost reaches your nose. The closer you bring the pencil, the more it appears to move from side to side. This is because there is progressively more disparity between the two retinal images as we view objects closer and closer.

Try It!

Convergence and binocular disparity provide depth or distance cues only for nearby objects. Fortunately, each eye by itself provides cues for objects at greater distances.

Question: What are six monocular depth cues?

Monocular Depth Cues: The Cues One Eye Can Detect Close one eye and you will see that you can still perceive depth. The visual depth cues perceived by one eye alone are called **monocular depth cues.** The following is a description of

The texture of objects can provide depth cues. Objects in the foreground appear sharp and well defined but become fuzzier as they recede into the distance.

six monocular depth cues, many of which artists have used to give the illusion of depth to their paintings.

- *Linear Perspective*   Linear perspective is a depth cue in which parallel lines that are known to be the same distance apart appear to grow closer together or converge as they recede into the distance. Linear perspective was used extensively by the Renaissance artists in the 1400s.
- *Relative Size*   Larger objects are perceived as being closer to us, and smaller objects as being farther away, as shown in Figure 3.19. We know that most adults are between 5 and 6 feet tall, so when images of the people we view are two, three, or many times smaller than their normal size, we perceive them as being two, three, or as many times farther away.
- *Texture Gradient*   Texture gradient is a depth cue in which near objects appear to have a sharply defined texture, while similar objects appear progressively smoother and fuzzier as they recede into the distance.
- *Interposition*   Some psychologists consider interposition, or overlapping, to be the most powerful depth cue of all (Haber, 1980). When one object partly blocks our view of another, we perceive the partially blocked object as farther away.
- *Shadow or Shading*   When light falls on objects, shadows are cast. We can distinguish bulges from indentions from the shadows they cast. This ability appears to be learned (Hess, 1961).
- *Motion Parallax*   When we ride in a moving vehicle and look out the side window, the objects we see outside appear to be moving in the opposite direction. The objects also seem to be moving at different speeds—those closest to us appear to be moving faster than objects in the distance. This phenomenon, called motion parallax, provides another monocular cue to depth perception. Objects very far away, such as the moon and the sun, appear to move in the *same* direction as we are moving.

The binocular and monocular depth cues can be found in Figure 3.20.

Perception of Motion

When we focus and concentrate on visual and other sensory information, we must disregard a great deal. We fix our attention on the information that is important to us and ignore the rest. There is, however, one universal, visual attention-getter: Movement gets our attention, and that of practically every

Figure 3.19

Relative Size: A Monocular Depth Cue

If we assume that these playing cards are of normal size, we perceive the largest card as being closest and the smaller cards as being progressively farther away.

Parallel lines appear to converge as they recede into the distance.

other animal. We notice motion, usually regardless of where in our visual field it occurs. When objects do move in our field of vision, they project images that move across the retina, but this alone does not explain our perception of movement. We can perceive movement, that is, *apparent motion*, even when objects do not move at all.

If several stationary lights are flashed on and off in sequence, the light will actually appear to move from one spot to the next. This type of apparent motion, called the *phi phenomenon*, was first discussed by Max Wertheimer (1912), one of the founders of Gestalt psychology. How many neon signs have you seen that caused you to perceive motion? Neon lights don't move; lights simply flash on and off in a particular sequence.

When you watch a motion picture, you are seeing apparent motion (Ramachandran & Anstis, 1986). The people or the objects appear to be moving, but in reality you are seeing stroboscopic motion, a series of still pictures of successive phases of movement. The pictures are flashed in rapid succession to give the illusion of movement.

Figure 3.20 Binocular and Monocular Depth Cues Depth cues that require two eyes working together are binocular; those that need only one eye are monocular.

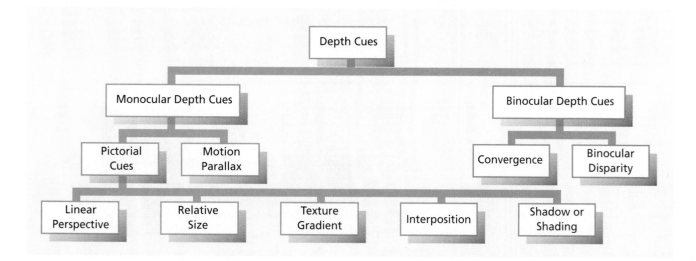

illusion: A false perception of actual stimuli involving a misperception of size, shape, or the relationship of one element to another.

Extraordinary Perceptions: Puzzling Perceptions

Not only can we perceive motion that does not exist, but we perceive impossible figures, ambiguous figures, and illusions as well.

Illusions: False Perceptions An **illusion** is a false perception or a misperception of an actual stimulus in the environment. We can misperceive size, shape, or the relationship of one element to another. We need not pay to see illusions performed by magicians. Illusions occur naturally and we see them all the time. An oar in the water appears to be bent where it meets the water. The moon looks much larger at the horizon than it does overhead. Why? One explanation involves relative size. This idea suggests that the moon looks very large on the horizon because it is viewed in comparison to trees, buildings, and other objects. When viewed overhead, the moon cannot be compared with other objects, and it appears smaller. People have been speculating about the moon illusion for 22 centuries and experimenting for 50 years to determine its cause, but there is still no agreement (Hershenson, 1989).

The Müller-Lyer Illusion Look at Figure 3.21. Which line is longer, A or B? Although they are the same length, the arrows extending outward from line B make it look considerably longer than line A, which has arrows pointing inward. British psychologist R. L. Gregory (1968) has suggested that the Müller-Lyer illusion is actually a misapplication of size constancy. The corner at A projects forward, toward the viewer, and we perceive it to be closer. The corner at B appears to be more distant because it seems to recede away from the viewer. When two lines are the same length, the line we perceive to be farther away will look longer.

Gregory also suggests that the Müller-Lyer and other such illusions probably result from our experiences with lines, edges, doors, corners, and rooms—in other words, that there is a cultural explanation for illusions. Segall and others (1966) found that the Zulus of South Africa, who have round houses and see few corners of any kind, are not fooled by the Müller-Lyer illusion. The researchers tested a group of Illinois residents and people from some 15 different cultures including the Zulus. The Illinois residents saw the Müller-Lyer illusion readily, while the Zulu natives tended not to see it.

Figure 3.21 The Müller-Lyer Illusion Lines A and B are identical in length. Line A seems to project forward and appears closer than Line B, which seems to recede in the distant corner. When two lines are the same length, the one perceived as farther away will appear longer. (After Gregory, 1978.)

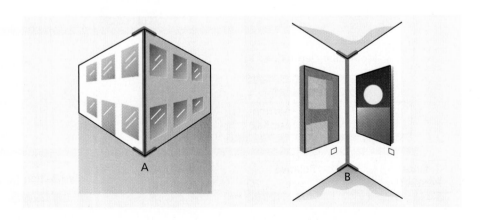

The Ponzo Illusion The Ponzo illusion also plays an interesting trick on our estimation of size. Look at the photograph in Figure 3.22. Which obstruction on the railroad tracks looks larger? You have undoubtedly guessed by now, contrary to your perceptions, that A and B are the same size. Again, our perceptions of size and distance, which we trust and which are normally accurate in perceiving the real world, can be wrong. If we saw two obstructions on real railroad tracks identical to the ones in the illusion, the one that looks larger would indeed be larger. So, the Ponzo illusion is not a natural illusion but rather a contrived one. In fact, all these illusions are really misapplications of principles that nearly always work properly in our normal, everyday experience.

Ambiguous Figures: More Than One Way to See Them

When we are faced for the first time with the ambiguous or the impossible figure, we have no experience to call on. Our perceptual system is puzzled and tries to work its way out of the quandary by seeing the ambiguous figure first one way and then another, but not both at once (Attneave, 1971). We never get closure with ambiguous figures that seem to jump back and forth beyond our control.

In some ambiguous figures, two different objects or figures are seen alternately. The best known of these, "Old Woman, Young Woman," by E. G. Boring, is shown in Figure 3.23. If you direct your gaze to the left of the drawing, you are likely to see an attractive young woman, her face turned away. But the young woman disappears when you suddenly perceive the image of the old woman. Such examples of object ambiguity offer striking evidence that our perceptions are more than the mere sum of sensory parts. It is hard to believe that the same drawing (the same sum of sensory parts) can convey such dramatically different perceptions.

Impossible Figures: This Can't Be

At first glance, the pictures of impossible figures do not seem so unusual—not until we examine them more closely. Would you invest your money in a company that manufactured three-pronged tridents as shown in Figure 3.24? Such an object could not be made as pictured because the middle prong appears to be in two different places at the same time. However, this type of impossible figure is more likely to fool the depth-perception sensibilities of people from Western cultures. Some African cultures do not represent three-dimensional visual space in their art, and they do not perceive depth in drawings that contain pictorial depth cues. These cultures see no ambiguity in drawings similar to the three-pronged trident, and they can draw it accurately from memory much more easily than subjects from Western cultures (Bloomer, 1976).

Figure 3.24 The Three-Pronged Trident This is an impossible figure because the middle prong appears to be in two places at the same time.

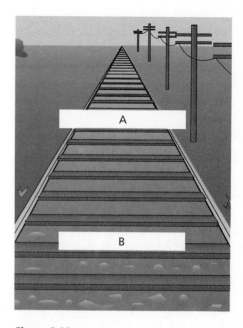

Figure 3.22

The Ponzo Illusion

The two white bars superimposed on the railroad track are identical in length. Because A appears farther away than B, we perceive it as longer. If these two white bars were actually on the railroad track, bar A would indeed be larger.

Figure 3.23

"Old Woman/Young Woman" by E. G. Boring

The most famous ambiguous figure can be seen alternately as a young woman or an old woman depending on where your eyes fixate.

perceptual set: An expectation of what will be perceived, which can affect what actually is perceived.

Memory Check 3.7

1. Retinal disparity and convergence are two (monocular, binocular) depth cues.

2. Match the appropriate monocular depth cue with each example.

    ____ 1) one building partly blocking another
    ____ 2) railroad tracks converging in the distance
    ____ 3) closer objects appearing to move faster than far objects
    ____ 4) far objects looking smaller than near objects

    a. motion parallax
    b. linear perspective
    c. interposition
    d. relative size
    e. texture gradient

3. The type of apparent motion we see in motion pictures is (motion parallax, stroboscopic motion).

4. An illusion is:

    a. an imaginary sensation
    b. an impossible figure
    c. a misperception of a real stimulus
    d. a figure-ground reversal

Answers: 1. binocular 2. 1) c 2) b 3) a 4) d 3. stroboscopic motion 4. c

Attention and Perception

Factors That Affect Our Perceptions: It's All Relative

Question: What are some factors that affect our perceptions?

We are often told that everything is relative. Nothing could be closer to the truth when we are talking about perception. We make perceptual judgments from our own individual point of reference. Other people are perceived as tall or short, young or old, depending on our own height or age (Rethlingshafer & Hinckley, 1963). Words like *intelligent, attractive, expensive, thin, successful, sensible, talented, rich, exciting, loud,* and so on, are all measured from our own perceptual point of view. Our perceptions are also affected by the value we attach to a stimulus. Most people see their boyfriend or girlfriend, husband or wife, as more attractive than others might judge them to be. And it would be a rare set of parents who truly perceived their offspring as dull or ugly.

Our **perceptual set**—what we expect to perceive—determines, to a large extent, what we actually see, hear, feel, taste, and smell. If you ordered raspberry sherbet and it was colored green, would it still taste like raspberry or might it taste more like lime? Once our expectations are set, we often bend reality to make it fit them. Psychologist David Rosenhan (1973) and some of his colleagues were admitted as patients to various mental hospitals with diagnoses of schizophrenia. Once admitted, they acted normally in every way. The purpose? They wondered how long it would take the doctors and the hospital staff to realize that they were not mentally ill. But the doctors and the staff members saw only what they expected to see and not what actually occurred. They perceived everything the pseudo-patients said and did, such as notetaking, to be symptoms of their illness. But the real patients were not fooled. They were the first to realize that the psychologists were not really mentally ill.

subliminal persuasion:
Sending persuasive messages below the recipient's level of awareness.

subliminal perception:
Perceiving sensory stimulation that is below the absolute threshold.

Subliminal Persuasion: Does It Work?

Question: Is subliminal persuasion effective in influencing behavior?

Over 30 years ago, it was reported that movie-goers in a New Jersey theater were exposed to advertising messages flashed on the screen so briefly that they were not aware of them. An advertising executive, James Vicary, claimed that the words "Eat Popcorn" and "Drink Coca-Cola" were projected on the screen for only 1/3,000 of a second every 5 seconds during the movie. The purpose of the messages was to influence the audience to buy popcorn and Coca-Cola, not by getting their conscious attention, but by sending persuasive messages below their level of awareness, a technique called *subliminal persuasion*. During the 6-week period the messages ran, popcorn sales supposedly went up by 57.5 percent, and Coca-Cola sales rose by more than 18 percent (McConnell et al., 1958).

Technically *subliminal perception* would be defined as the perception of sensory stimuli that are below the absolute threshold. But the subliminal persuasion experiment was limited to messages flashed so quickly that they could never be normally perceived at all. Can we actually perceive information that is completely below our level of awareness? Some people say that we can, and today subliminal persuasion is aimed at selling much more than popcorn and Coke. Subliminal self-help tapes, popularized by the New Age movement, are so popular that Americans now spend over $50 million a year on the tapes (Adams, 1991). There are tapes to cure virtually every ill (depression, migraine headaches), solve every problem (reduce stress, quit smoking), and meet every need (increase confidence, gain peace of mind). Embedded in the recordings of soothing music or ocean waves lapping the shore are subliminal messages for those who want to lose weight ("I eat less"), reduce stress ("I am calm"), or improve their self-image ("I am capable").

Is subliminal persuasion effective? The majority of psychologists are highly skeptical because there is no convincing evidence that subliminal persuasion is capable of influencing our behavior (McBurney & Collings, 1984; Greenwald et al., 1991). If it does not influence behavior, why do some users insist that the tapes helped them to quit smoking, lose weight, or achieve other goals? Evidently the power of suggestion, or the placebo effect, is helping them rather than the power of the tapes' subliminal persuasion. But just think of the many implications that would make life easier for psychology professors if subliminal persuasion really worked. Professors could revolutionize college life by entertaining students with interesting films, during which subliminal messages would be flashed every 5 seconds such as, "Study Psychology," "Read Psychology," and "Study Harder." If you watched enough movies, your friends and family might find it impossible to tear you away from your psychology books.

Extrasensory Perception: Does It Exist?

Question: What is extrasensory perception, and have the claims of psychics been verified scientifically?

extrasensory perception (ESP): Gaining awareness of or information about objects, events, or another's thoughts through some means other than the known sensory channels.

parapsychology: The study of psychic phenomena, which include extrasensory perception (ESP) and psychokinesis.

We know that perception refers to the process by which we organize and interpret sensory input. But is it possible to perceive information that does not come through the senses? Is there such a thing as **extrasensory perception (ESP)**—gaining information about objects, events, or another's thoughts through some means other than the known sensory channels? Can some people read minds or foretell the future? According to a 1990 Gallup poll, 49 percent of Americans believe in ESP (Gallup & Newport, 1990a). Extrasensory perception is part of a larger area of interest known as *parapsychology*, the study of psychic phenomena. Reported cases of ESP roughly fall into three categories—telepathy, clairvoyance, and precognition.

Telepathy means gaining awareness of the thoughts, the feelings, or the activities of another without the use of the senses—in other words, reading a person's mind. Clairvoyance means gaining information about objects or events without use of the senses, such as knowing the contents of a letter without opening it. Precognition refers to an awareness of an event before it occurs. Most of the reported cases of precognition in everyday life have occurred while a person was dreaming. One researcher revealed the poor record of well-known psychics who made New Year's predictions for the *National Enquirer* between 1978 and 1985. Only two of their 425 predictions proved to be accurate (Strentz, 1986). But probably the most telling blow against precognition is the failure of any of these psychics to predict some of the most astounding world events of the century—the fall of the Berlin Wall in 1989, the breakup of the Soviet Union in 1991, and the end of the cold war.

Because psychic phenomena violate what we know about the real, measurable, physical world, scientists and skeptics naturally demand proof of their existence (Hansel, 1966, 1980; Randi, 1980). Time after time trickery has been detected when investigating the claims of psychics who assert that they can read minds or contact and communicate with the dead.

Other personal reports of psychic phenomena fall into the category known as psychokinesis (PK), in which physical objects are said to be influenced by the mind alone. Uri Geller, well known for his ability to bend spoons and keys, to "read" the contents of sealed envelopes, and to perform other feats supposedly using his mind alone, was found to use magic tricks and fraud to deceive the public.

One professional magician, the Amazing Randi (1980), has gained popularity in exposing the fraudulent techniques used by Uri Geller and others who claim great powers or abilities. Randi has offered to pay $10,000 "to any person or group that can perform *one* paranormal feat of *any* kind under the proper observing conditions" (p. 3). To this day he has not found a single person able to demonstrate psychic ability under controlled conditions although the offer still stands.

What is the truth about psychic phenomena? Either they exist but have not yet been proven, or they may exist but might not be verifiable under laboratory conditions, or psychic phenomena do not exist at all. What do you believe?

Earlier we noted that sensation and perceptions are so closely linked in everyday experience that it is hard to see clearly where one ends and the other begins. But in this chapter, you have seen many examples of what is sensed and what is perceived. Our perceptual system is continuously trying to complete what we merely sense. We are always busy filling in, organizing, and making more of a complete perceptual sense out of the sensory parts that we are able to see, hear, touch, taste, and smell.

Memory Check 3.8

1. Our perceptions are affected by:

   a. our perceptual set
   b. the value we attach to a stimulus
   c. our individual point of reference
   d. all of these

2. Subliminal advertising has been proven effective in influencing consumers to buy products. (true/false)

3. Match each psychic phenomenon with its description.

   _____ 1) mind over matter
   _____ 2) reading someone's mind
   _____ 3) predicting the future
   _____ 4) "knowing" the contents of a sealed envelope

   a. clairvoyance
   b. precognition
   c. psychokinesis
   d. telepathy

4. Carefully controlled and repeatable laboratory experiments have proven the existence of extrasensory perception. (true/false)

Answers: 1. d 2. false 3. 1) c 2) d 3) b 4) a 4. false

Thinking Critically _____

Evaluation

Using what you have learned about the factors that contribute to hearing loss, prepare a statement indicating what the government should do to control noise pollution, even to the extent of banning certain noise hazards. Consider the workplace, the home, toys, machinery, rock concerts, and so on.

Point/Counterpoint

Recent polls indicate that nearly 49 percent of the population believes in ESP. Prepare a sound, logical argument supporting one of the following positions:

a. There is evidence to suggest that ESP exists.
b. There is no evidence to suggest that ESP exists.

Psychology in Your Life

Vision and hearing are generally believed to be the two most highly prized senses. How would your life change if you lost your sight? How would your life change if you lost your hearing? Which sense would you hate to lose more? Why?

Chapter Summary and Review

Sensation: The Sensory World

What is the difference between the absolute threshold and the difference threshold?

The absolute threshold is the minimum amount of sensory stimulation that can be detected 50 percent of the time. The difference threshold is a measure of the smallest increase or decrease in a physical stimulus that can be detected 50 percent of the time.

How are sensory stimuli in the environment experienced as sensations?

For each of our senses, there are sensory receptors, which detect and respond to sensory stimuli. Through a process known as transduction, the receptors convert sensory stimuli into neural impulses, which are then transmitted to their own special location in the brain.

Key Terms

sensation (p. 72)
perception (p. 72)
absolute threshold (p. 73)
difference threshold (p. 73)
sensory receptors (p. 75)
transduction (p. 75)

Vision

How do the cornea, the pupil, and the iris function in vision?

The cornea bends light rays inward through the pupil—the small, dark opening in the eye. The iris dilates and contracts the pupil to regulate the amount of light entering the eye.

What are the lens and the retina?

The lens changes its shape as it focuses images of objects from varying distances on the retina, a thin membrane containing the sensory receptors for vision.

What roles do the rods and cones play in vision?

The cones detect color, provide our sharpest vision, and function best in high illumination. The rods enable us to see in dim light. Rods respond to black and white, and they encode all other visible wavelengths in shades of gray.

Trace the path of the neural impulse from the retina to the visual cortex.

The rods and the cones transduce light waves into neural impulses that pass from the bipolar cells to the ganglion cells, whose axons form the optic nerve. At the optic chiasma, some of the fibers of the optic nerve cross to the opposite side of the brain, before reaching the thalamus. From the thalamus, the neural impulses travel to the visual cortex.

What two major theories attempt to explain color vision?

Two major theories that attempt to explain color vision are the trichromatic theory and the opponent-process theory.

Key Terms

cornea (p. 77)
lens (p. 77)
retina (p. 77)
rods (p. 78)
cones (p. 78)
fovea (p. 78)
hue (p. 81)
trichromatic theory (p. 81)
opponent-process theory (p. 82)
color blindness (p. 82)

Hearing

What determines the pitch and the loudness of a sound, and how is each quality measured?

The pitch of a sound is determined by frequency, which is measured in hertz. The loudness of a sound is determined largely by the amplitude of a sound wave and is measured in decibels.

How do the outer, middle, and inner ears function in hearing?

Sound waves enter the pinna, the visible part of the outer ear, and travel to the end of the auditory canal, causing the eardrum to vibrate. This sets in motion the ossicles in the middle ear, which amplify the sound waves. The vibration of the oval window causes activity in the inner ear, setting in motion the fluid in the cochlea and moving the hair cell receptors, which transduce the vibrations into neural impulses. The auditory nerve carries the neural impulses to the brain.

What two major theories attempt to explain hearing?

Two major theories that attempt to explain hearing are place theory and frequency theory.

What are some major causes of hearing loss?

Some major causes of hearing loss are disease, birth defects, aging, injury, and noise.

Key Terms

decibel (p. 84)
outer ear (p. 85)
middle ear (p. 85)
inner ear (p. 86)
cochlea (p. 86)
hair cells (p. 86)
place theory (p. 87)
frequency theory (p. 87)

Smell and Taste

What path does a smell message take on its journey from the nose to the brain?

The act of smelling begins when odor molecules reach the smell receptors in the olfactory epithelium at the top of the nasal cavity. The axons of these receptors form the olfactory nerve, which relays the smell message to the olfactory bulbs. From there the smell message travels to other parts of the brain.

What are the four primary taste sensations, and how are they detected?

The four primary taste sensations are sweet, salty, sour, and bitter. The receptor cells for taste are found in the taste buds on the tongue and in other parts of the mouth and throat.

Key Terms

olfactory epithelium (p. 90)
olfactory bulbs (p. 90)
taste bud (p. 91)

Our Other Senses

How does the skin provide sensory information?

Nerve endings in the skin (the sensory receptors) respond to different kinds of stimulation, including heat and cold, pressure, pain, and a vast range of touch sensations. The neural impulses ultimately register in the somatosensory cortex.

What beneficial purpose does pain serve?

Pain can be a valuable warning and protective mechanism, motivating us to tend to an injury, to restrict our activity, and to seek medical help if needed.

What is the gate-control theory of pain?

Melzack and Wall's gate-control theory holds that pain signals transmitted by slow-firing C fibers can be blocked at the spinal gate (1) if the pressure-sensitive, fast-firing A fibers get their message to the gate first, or (2) if the brain, itself, inhibits their transmission.

What are endorphins?

Endorphins, released when we are stressed or injured, are the body's natural painkillers; they block pain and produce a feeling of well-being.

What kind of information does the kinesthetic sense provide, and how is this sensory information detected?

The kinesthetic sense provides information about the position of body parts and movement in those body parts. The position or motion is detected by sensory receptors in the joints, ligaments, and muscles.

What is the vestibular sense, and where are its sensory receptors located?

The vestibular sense provides information about movement and our orientation in space. Sensory receptors in the semicircular canals and in the vestibular sacs detect changes in the movement and orientation of the head.

Key Terms

gate-control theory (p. 94)
endorphins (p. 95)
kinesthetic sense (p. 95)
vestibular sense (p. 97)
semicircular canals (p. 97)

Perception: Ways of Perceiving

What are the Gestalt principles of perceptual organization?

The Gestalt principles of perceptual organization include the figure-ground relationship and four principles of perceptual grouping—similarity, proximity, continuity, and closure.

What is perceptual constancy, and what are three types?

Perceptual constancy is the tendency to perceive objects as maintaining the same shape, size, and brightness, despite changes in lighting conditions or changes in the retinal image that result when objects are viewed from different angles and distances.

What are the binocular depth cues?

The binocular depth cues are convergence and binocular disparity, and they depend on two eyes working together for depth perception.

What are six monocular depth cues?

The monocular depth cues, those which can be perceived by one eye, include linear perspective, relative size, texture gradient, interposition, shadow or shading, and motion parallax.

Key Terms

perception (p. 97)
figure-ground (p. 98)
perceptual constancy (p. 98)
size constancy (p. 99)
retinal image (p. 99)
depth perception (p. 101)
binocular depth cues (p. 101)
convergence (p. 101)
binocular disparity (p. 101)
monocular depth cues (p. 101)
illusion (p. 104)

Attention and Perception

What are some factors that affect our perceptions?

Our perceptions are affected by our own point of reference, by the value we attach to a stimulus, and by our perceptual set—what we expect to perceive.

Is subliminal persuasion effective in influencing behavior?

In experimental studies, subliminal persuasion has not been found to influence behavior.

What is extrasensory perception, and have the claims of psychics been verified scientifically?

Extrasensory perception refers to gaining awareness of information about objects, events, and another's thoughts through some means other than known sensory channels. Experiments claiming to prove psychic phenomena have not been repeatable under carefully controlled conditions.

Key Terms

perceptual set (p. 106)
extrasensory perception (ESP) (p. 108)

4

States of Consciousness

CHAPTER OUTLINE

(© 1990 STAR TRIBUNE/Minneapolis-St. Paul)

S hortly after 6:00 A.M. one day in March 1990, Northwest Airlines Flight 650, with 91 passengers on board, left Fargo, North Dakota, bound for St. Paul, Minnesota. The flight was uneventful, and the plane landed safely.

A safe landing doesn't usually make the news, but Flight 650 did. Upon arrival, all three members of the cockpit crew—the pilot, the first officer, and the second officer—were arrested. On the night before their early morning flight, all three had been out drinking until after midnight at a tavern across the street from their motel. Although there was no evidence that any of the three was drunk, tests confirmed the presence of alcohol in their blood. Having violated Federal Aviation Administration rules against drinking alcohol within 8 hours of flying, all three fliers lost their FAA licenses.

Several years before the Flight 650 incident, a Boeing 707 took off from New York en route to Los Angeles International Airport. The flight was scheduled to arrive at 12:00 midnight. As the plane neared Los Angeles, the air traffic controllers were puzzled to see it maintaining its altitude of 32,000 feet. The flight tower continued to issue clearances to land, but the plane shot past Los Angeles and was soon 50 miles out over the Pacific Ocean, still at a high altitude. The air traffic controllers were alarmed as the plane continued flying 100 miles westward over the Pacific, because its fuel supply was running low.

What was wrong with the pilots? They had used neither drugs nor alcohol but were responding naturally to their biological clocks, which were synchronized with New York time. In New York, it was 3:00 A.M.—a time when most of us feel an urgent need to sleep. And indeed the flight crew had succumbed to their urgent need. They were all sound asleep, cruising on automatic pilot. Finally the tower was able to awaken them by activating a series of chimes in the cockpit, and the pilots returned to Los Angeles with just enough fuel to land safely. (Coleman, 1986)

THE CREWS OF THESE TWO FLIGHTS had problems because they were not flying in a state of ordinary waking consciousness. **Consciousness** is one of the most basic concepts in the study of psychology, and yet it has never been satisfactorily defined. Think of consciousness as a state of awareness—a continuous stream of perceptions, thoughts, feelings, or sensations of which we are aware from moment to moment.

Waking consciousness is said to be the state in which we are aware of what is going on around us and within us. We respond to internal and external stimuli; we are fully awake. This is our real, everyday world. Ordinary waking consciousness can be altered by unnatural means—by alcohol or drugs, for example—and by natural means, such as meditation, hypnosis, and sleep.

This chapter will explore **altered states of consciousness**. The most fundamental altered state is one in which we spend about one-third of our lives, the one we visit for several hours nearly every night—sleep.

Circadian Rhythms: Our 24-Hour Highs and Lows

Question: What is a circadian rhythm, and which rhythms are most relevant to the study of sleep?

Do you notice changes in the way you feel throughout the day—fluctuations in your energy level, moods, or efficiency? Over 100 of our bodily functions and behaviors fluctuate regularly from a high to a low point over a 24-hour period

consciousness: The continuous stream of perceptions, thoughts, feelings, or sensations of which we are aware from moment to moment.

altered state of consciousness: A mental state other than ordinary waking consciousness such as sleep, meditation, hypnosis, or a drug-induced state.

(Dement, 1974). Called **circadian rhythms** (*circa* meaning "about"; *dian* meaning "one day"), these daily fluctuations are controlled largely by the brain, apparently the suprachiasmatic nucleus in the hypothalamus (Ralph, 1989). Blood pressure, heart rate, appetite, secretion of hormones and digestive enzymes, sensory acuity, elimination, and even our body's response to medication all follow circadian rhythms. Our learning efficiency and our ability to perform a wide range of tasks also ebb and flow according to these daily rhythms.

Two circadian rhythms of particular importance to the study of sleep are the sleep/wakefulness cycle and body temperature. Normal human body temperature can range from a low of about 97 or 97.5 degrees between 4:00 and 5:00 A.M. to a high of about 98.6 degrees between 5:00 and 8:00 P.M. People sleep best when their body temperature is lowest, and they are most alert when their body temperature is at its daily high point. Alertness also follows a circadian rhythm, one that is quite separate from the sleep/wakefulness rhythm (Monk, 1989). For most of us, alertness decreases between 2:00 and 5:00 P.M. and between 2:00 and 7:00 A.M. (Mitler et al., 1988).

Are circadian rhythms strictly biological, or do environmental cues play a part? Without any environmental cues, most people naturally fall into a 25-hour schedule (Mistlberger & Rusak, 1989). But external stimuli—day and night, alarm clocks, job or school demands—cause us to modify our own biological clock's preference for a 25-hour rhythm in order to conform to a 24-hour schedule. Circadian rhythms are slightly disrupted each year when daylight saving time begins and ends. An even greater disruption occurs when people fly across a number of time zones or when they work rotating shifts.

Jet Lag: Where Am I and What Time Is It?

Suppose you fly from Chicago to London, and the plane lands at 12:00 midnight Chicago time, about the time you usually go to sleep. At the same time that it is midnight in Chicago, it is 6:00 A.M. in London, almost time to get up. The clocks, the sun, and everything else in London tell you it is early morning, but you still feel like it is 12:00 midnight. You are experiencing jet lag.

The problem is not simply the result of losing a night's sleep. You are fighting your own biological clock, which is synchronized with your usual time zone and not the time zone you are visiting (Graeber, 1989). It is difficult to try to sleep when your biological clock is telling you to wake up and feel alert. It is even harder to remain awake and alert when your internal clock is telling you to sleep.

There are people who experience a similar problem without the benefit of a trip to Europe or Asia. These people are shift workers.

Shift Work: Working Day and Night

Question: What are some problems experienced by employees who work rotating shifts?

According to the National Center of Health Statistics, "36% of working men and 25% of working women in the U.S. labor force are exposed to a variable work schedule which includes both day and night work" (Czeisler & Allan, 1988, pp. 117–118). When people must work at night, there is a disruption in the rhythms of many bodily functions normally synchronized for efficient daytime functioning. These rhythm disruptions can cause a variety of physical and psychological problems.

Not surprisingly, shift workers complain of sleepiness and sleeping difficulties. Shift workers average 5.6 hours of sleep compared to 7.5 hours for workers

circadian rhythm (sur-KAY-dee-un): Within each 24-hour period, the regular fluctuation from high to low points of certain bodily functions.

subjective night: The time during a 24-hour period when your body temperature is lowest and when your biological clock is telling you to go to sleep.

on regular shifts (Hales, 1981). Forced to remain awake when their body temperature is low, they use more caffeine. Trying to sleep when their body temperature is high, they use more alcohol and sleeping pills (Gordon et al., 1986). Moreover, digestive problems such as appetite loss, diarrhea, and irregularity are common because shift workers eat at times not in synchrony with the circadian rhythms governing appetite, elimination, and the secretion of digestive enzymes (Regestein & Monk, 1991; Vener et al., 1989).

What about performance on the job? Performance sharply deteriorates if people work during *subjective night*, when their biological clock is telling them to go to sleep (Folkard, 1990). Energy and efficiency reach their lowest point, reaction time is slowest, and productivity is diminished. A frightening fact is that "more than half of (night) shift workers in a variety of industries, including the nuclear power industry, regularly fall asleep, at least once a week while they are working at night" (Czeisler quoted in Allen, 1989, B1). In one study of 1,000 locomotive engineers, 59 percent admitted that they dozed off on most night trips (Åkerstedt, 1988).

Many air, rail, marine, and highway accidents have occurred when the shift workers in charge suffered sleep loss and fatigue because of the disruption of their circadian rhythms (Lauber and Kayten, 1988). More errors in judgment and most accidents occur during the night shift (Finn, 1981; Webb, 1975). The failure of the nuclear reactor at Three Mile Island, the Russian nuclear disaster at Chernobel, and even the Challenger disaster are thought to have occurred in part because workers on the night shift were in charge (Mitler et al., 1988). Figure 4.1 is a summary of the times of day when vehicular accidents occur.

Experts suspect that several airline crashes might have been due to pilots flying during subjective night. Already many European countries, especially Germany, have regulations requiring that biological clocks be considered when scheduling pilots. Such regulations would have prevented the perilous situation caused by the sleeping pilots who had to be awakened 100 miles over the Pacific Ocean. Sleep researcher William Dement goes so far as to suggest that naps be scheduled for pilots on long flights.

Can anything be done to make shift rotation less disruptive? Rotating work schedules from days to evenings to nights and changing work shifts every three weeks rather than every week have resulted in increased job satisfaction, health, and productivity of workers (Czeisler et al., 1982).

What are the physical and psychological effects of disturbing the normal sleep/wakefulness cycle, experienced by these shiftworkers?

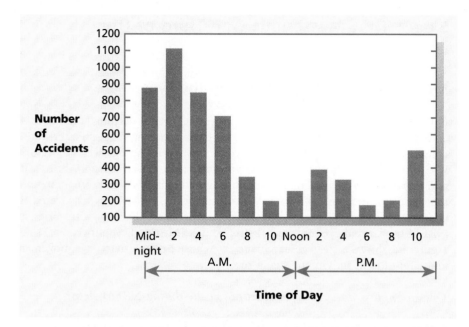

Figure 4.1

Fatigue-Related Accidents Occurring at Various Times of the Day

Both the sleep-wakefulness cycle and alertness follow circadian rhythms. The rate of vehicular accidents is dramatically higher between 10 P.M. and 6 A.M., when sleepiness is greatest, and again between 2 P.M. and 4 P.M., when alertness typically decreases. (After Mitler et al., 1988.)

In several experiments of real significance to shift workers, researchers have found that by manipulating exposure to bright light, the circadian (biological) clock could be reset and workers could adjust to shift changes in 3 days (Czeisler, Kronauer, et al., 1989; Dawson & Campbell, 1992). Industries, police departments, and hospitals should seriously consider the research in this field to facilitate the adjustment of workers to shift changes.

Memory Check 4.1

1. The regular fluctuation of certain body functions from high to low points within a 24-hour period is called a (biorhythm, circadian rhythm).

2. We sleep best when our body temperature is at its (high, low) point in our 24-hour cycle.

3. What is a common complaint of people who work rotating shifts?

   a. disturbed sleep
   b. digestive problems
   c. lowered efficiency and alertness during subjective night
   d. all of these

4. The ideal rotation schedule for shift workers is when:

   a. shifts change from days to evenings to nights
   b. shifts change from days to nights to evenings
   c. shifts are maintained for 3 weeks or longer
   d. a and c

Answers 1. circadian rhythm 2. low 3. d 4. d

NREM sleep: Non-rapid-eye-movement sleep consisting of the four sleep stages and characterized by slow, regular respiration and heart rates, an absence of rapid eye movements, and blood pressure and brain activity that are at a 24-hour-low point.

REM sleep: Sleep characterized by rapid eye movements, paralysis of large muscles, fast and irregular heart rate and respiration rate, increased brain-wave activity, and vivid dreams.

Sleep: That Mysterious One-Third of Our Lives

NREM and REM Sleep: Watching the Eyes

On the average over a lifetime, a person spends 25 years sleeping. Yet before the 1950s there was no understanding of what goes on during sleep, another state of consciousness. Then, in the 1950s, several universities set up sleep laboratories where people's brain waves, eye movements, chin-muscle tension, heart rate, and respiration rate were monitored through a night of sleep. From analyses of their sleep recordings, known as polysomnograms, researchers discovered the characteristics of the two major categories of sleep. The two categories are NREM (non-rapid eye movement) sleep and REM (rapid eye movement) sleep. Figure 4.2 shows a sleep research subject whose brain activity, eye movement, and chin-muscle activity are being recorded.

Question: How does a sleeper react physically during NREM sleep?

NREM Sleep: From Light to Deep Sleep in Stages NREM (pronounced NON-rem) **sleep** refers to the sleep in which there are no rapid eye movements. It is often called "quiet sleep" because heart rate and respiration are slow and regular, there is little body movement, and blood pressure and brain activity are at their lowest points of the 24-hour period.

There are four stages of NREM sleep—Stages 1, 2, 3, and 4—with Stage 1 being the lightest sleep and Stage 4 being the deepest. You pass gradually rather than abruptly from one stage to the next. Each stage can be identified by its brain-wave pattern as shown in Figure 4.3 (Hobson, 1989).

Question: How does the body respond physically during REM sleep?

REM Sleep: Rapid Eye Movements and Dreams Most of us envision sleep as a time of deep relaxation and calm. But **REM sleep**, sometimes called "active sleep," is anything but clam, and it constitutes 20 to 25 percent of a normal night's sleep in adults. During the REM state, there is intense brain activity, and our body reacts as if to a daytime emergency. Epinephrine (adrenaline) shoots

Figure 4.2 How Researchers Study Sleeping Subjects Researchers study subjects in a sleep laboratory or sleep clinic by taping electrodes to the subject's head to monitor brain-wave activity, eye movements, and muscle tension. (After Dement, 1974.)

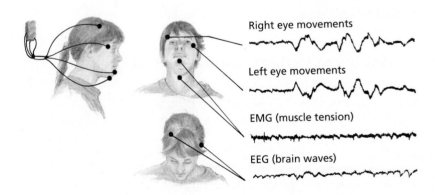

Right eye movements

Left eye movements

EMG (muscle tension)

EEG (brain waves)

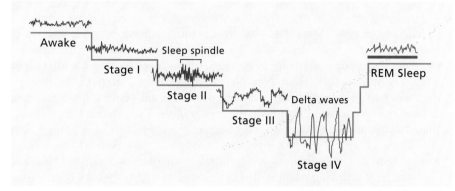

sleep cycle: A cycle of sleep lasting about 90 minutes and including one or more stages of NREM sleep followed by a period of REM sleep.

Figure 4.3   Brain-Wave Patterns Associated with Different Stages of Sleep By monitoring brain-wave activity with the EEG throughout a night's sleep, researchers have identified the brain-wave patterns associated with different stages of sleep. As sleepers progress through the four NREM stages, brain-wave pattern changes progressively from faster, low-voltage waves in Stages 1 and 2 to the slower, larger delta waves in Stages 3 and 4. Notice that the brain-wave activity during REM sleep is similar to that of the subject when awake. (After Hobson, 1989.)

into the system, blood pressure rises, and heart rate and respiration become faster and irregular. Ulcer patients may secrete from 3 to 20 times as much stomach acid as during the day and may awaken with stomach pains (Webb, 1975). In contrast to this storm of internal activity, there is an external calm during REM sleep. The large muscles of the body—arms, legs, trunk—become paralyzed (Chase & Morales, 1990). Some researchers suggest that the reason for this paralysis is to prevent us from acting out our dreams.

If you observe a sleeper during the REM state, you can see the eyes darting around under the eyelids. In 1952 Eugene Azerinsky first discovered these bursts of rapid eye movements, and William Dement and Nathaniel Kleitman (1957) made the connection between rapid eye movements and dreaming. It is during REM periods that most of our vivid dreams occur. When awakened from REM sleep, 80 percent of subjects report dreaming (Carskadon & Dement, 1989).

Almost from birth, regardless of the content of their dreams, males have a full or partial erection during REM sleep, and women experience vaginal swelling and lubrication. Because sleepers are more likely to awaken naturally at the end of a REM period than during the NREM stages of sleep, men usually wake up with an erection (Campbell, 1985). In males suffering from impotence, the presence of an erection during REM sleep indicates that the impotence is psychological; its absence indicates that the impotence is physiological in origin (Karacan et al., 1978).

If you are awakened during REM sleep and remain awake for several minutes, you will not go back into REM sleep for at least 30 minutes. This explains why most of us have experienced the disappointment of waking in the middle of a wonderful dream and trying in vain to get quickly back to sleep and into the dream.

Sleep Cycles: The Nightly Pattern of Sleep

Question: What is the progression of NREM stages and REM sleep that a person follows in a typical night of sleep?

Many people are surprised to learn that sleep follows a fairly predictable pattern each night. We sleep in cycles. During each **sleep cycle**, which lasts about 90 minutes, we have one or more stages of NREM sleep followed by a period of REM sleep. Let us take you through a typical night of sleep for a young adult.

deep sleep: Stage 3 and Stage 4 sleep.

delta wave: The slowest brain-wave pattern, associated with Stage 3 sleep and Stage 4 sleep.

Stage 4 sleep: The deepest NREM stage of sleep, characterized by an EEG pattern of more than 50 percent delta waves.

The first sleep cycle begins with a few minutes in Stage 1 sleep, sometimes called "light sleep." Stage 1 is actually a transition stage between waking and sleeping. Then sleepers descend into Stage 2 sleep, in which they are somewhat more deeply asleep and harder to awaken. About 50 percent of the total night's sleep is spent in Stage 2 sleep. Next sleepers enter Stage 3 sleep, the beginning of *deep sleep.* As sleep gradually becomes deeper, brain activity slows and more **delta waves** (the slowest brain waves) appear in the EEG. When there are more than 50 percent delta waves on the EEG, people are said to be in **Stage 4 sleep,** the deepest sleep, when people are hardest to awaken (Carskadon & Rechtschaffen, 1989). Perhaps you have taken an afternoon nap and awakened confused, not knowing whether it was morning or night, a weekday or a weekend. If so, you probably awakened during Stage 4 sleep.

After about 40 minutes in Stage 4, brain activity increases and the delta waves begin to disappear from the EEG. Sleepers make an ascent back through Stage 3 and Stage 2 and then enter the first REM period of the night, which lasts 10 or 15 minutes. At the end of this REM period, the first sleep cycle is complete, and the second sleep cycle begins. Unless people awaken after the first sleep cycle, they go directly from REM sleep into Stage 2. They then follow the same progression as in the first sleep cycle, through the NREM stages and into REM sleep.

After the first two sleep cycles of about 90 minutes each (3 hours total), the sleep pattern changes and sleepers usually get no more Stage 4 sleep. From this point on, during each 90-minute sleep cycle, people normally alternate between Stage 2 and REM sleep for the remainder of the night. With each sleep cycle, the REM periods (and therefore dreaming time) get progressively longer. At the end of the night, REM periods may last 30 minutes more. Most people sleep about five sleep cycles (7 1/2 to 8 hours) and on the average get about 1 1/2 hours of deep sleep and 1 1/2 hours of REM sleep. Figure 4.4 shows the progression through NREM and REM sleep during a typical night.

Variations in Sleep: How We Differ

There are great individual variations in patterns of sleep, and the major factor contributing to this variation is age.

Question: How do sleep patterns change over the life span?

Sleep Changes over the Life Span: The Older We Get, the Less We Get
Infants and young children have the longest sleep time and the highest percent-

Figure 4.4

The Typical Composition of Sleep Cycles for Young Adults

A typical night's sleep for young adults consists of about five sleep cycles of approximately 90 minutes each. Deep sleep occurs during the first two sleep cycles, and people spend progressively more time in REM sleep with each succeeding 90-minute cycle. (From Dement, 1974.)

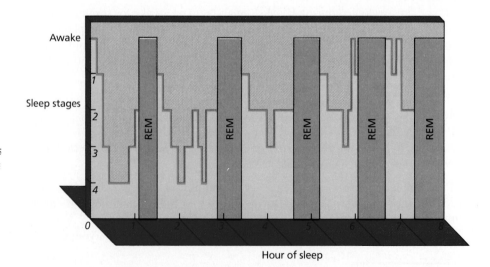

"No doubt, the most profound example of rapid eye movement during sleep that I've ever seen."

age of REM and deep sleep, but they get even more REM sleep prior to birth. The fetus spends up to 80 percent of the time in REM sleep (Hobson, 1989b).

Children from age 6 to puberty are the champion sleepers and wakers. They fall asleep easily, sleep soundly for 8 1/2 to 9 hours at night, and feel awake and alert during the day. From puberty to adolescence, teenagers average about 7 1/2 hours and typically feel the need for more sleep regardless of how much they actually sleep (Strauch & Meier, 1988).

As adults age, there is usually a decrease in both the quality and quantity of sleep. Older people have more difficulty falling asleep, and they typically have lighter sleep and more and longer awakenings than younger people (Buysee et al., 1991). They spend more time in bed but less time asleep, averaging about 6 1/2 hours of sleep (Prinz et al., 1990). Deep sleep decreases with age and may be virtually absent in one's late seventies and eighties, while the percentage of REM sleep decreases only slightly.

Larks and Owls: Early to Rise and Late to Bed Some people awaken early every morning and leap out of bed with enthusiasm, eager to start the day. Others of us fumble for the alarm clock and push in the snooze button to get a few more precious moments of sleep. Awakening, we stumble around, still in a stupor, until our morning coffee takes effect. The early risers find it hard to keep from yawning after 10 o'clock at night and have an overwhelming urge to get to bed. But this is precisely the time that the night people come to life.

Sleep researchers have names for these two types—larks and owls—and there is a physical explanation for the difference in the way they feel. About 25 percent of people are larks, people whose body temperature rises rapidly after they awaken and stays high until about 7:30 P.M. Larks turn in early and have the fewest sleep problems. Then there are the 25 percent who are owls. Their body temperature gradually rises throughout the day, peaking in the afternoon, and not dropping until later in the evening. Anderson and others (1991) found

microsleep: A momentary lapse from wakefulness into sleep, usually occurring when one has been sleep deprived.

that when subjects were tested on memory tasks at 9 A.M., 2 P.M., and 8 P.M., the performance of the larks declined as the day progressed, while that of the owls improved. The remaining 50 percent of people are neither true larks nor true owls, but somewhere in between.

"Larks see owls as lazy; owls see larks as party poopers" (Coleman, 1986, p. 15). Can an owl turn into a lark with a little self-discipline? The authors have been trying unsuccessfully to accomplish this for years. Researchers note that even when owls change their sleep schedule to match the early risers, they still *feel* like owls in the morning.

Question: What factors influence our sleep needs?

How Much Sleep Do We Need? More Than We Probably Get   Maybe you have wondered how much sleep you need in order to feel good, and perhaps you are hoping to find the answer in this chapter. When it comes to sleep, the expression "one size fits all" does not apply. Although adults average about 7 1/2 hours of sleep daily with an extra hour on weekends, this is too much for some people and too little for others. Short sleepers are the 20 percent who require less than 6 hours of sleep; long sleepers are the 10 percent who require more than 9 hours. There seems to be a limit below which most of us cannot go. In one study, not a single subject could get by with less than 4 1/2 hours of sleep, and 6 1/2 hours appears to be the minimum most people require.

What accounts for the large variation in the need for sleep? Genetics appears to play a part. Identical twins, for example, have strikingly similar sleep patterns compared to fraternal twins (Webb & Campbell, 1983). Laboratory animals have even been bred to be short or long sleepers. But genetics aside, people need more sleep when they are depressed, under stress, or experiencing significant life changes such as changing jobs or schools. Increases in mental, physical, or emotional effort also increase our need for sleep (Hartmann, 1973). Contrary to popular opinion, the amount of activity required in an occupation does not affect the amount of sleep a person needs.

Do most Americans sleep enough? Not according to the well-known sleep researcher William Dement, who claims that we have "a national sleep deficit."

Sleep Deprivation: How Does It Affect Us?

What is the longest you have ever stayed awake—one day, two days, three days, or four days? According to the *Guinness Book of World Records*, Californian Robert McDonald stayed awake 453 hours and 40 minutes (almost 19 days) in the 1986 rocking-chair marathon. Unlike McDonald, most of us have missed no more than a few consecutive nights of sleep, perhaps studying for final exams. If you have ever missed two or three nights of sleep, you might remember having had difficulty concentrating, lapses in attention, and general irritability. After 60 hours without sleep, some people even have minor hallucinations. Most people who try to stay awake for long periods of time will have *microsleeps*, 2- to 3-second lapses from wakefulness into sleep. You may have experienced a micro-sleep if you have ever caught yourself nodding off for a few seconds in class or on a long automobile trip. What suffers most from prolonged sleep loss is the motivation to sustain performance. If a task is short or interesting or demanding, we can do almost anything. But the problem is that we have difficulty making ourselves pay attention or work; we would rather be asleep.

When people are deprived of REM sleep as a result of general sleep loss, illness, too much alcohol, or other drugs, their bodies will make up for the loss by getting an increased amount of REM sleep after the deprivation (Vogel, 1975). This increase in the percentage of REM sleep to make up for REM deprivation is called a **REM rebound.** Because the intensity of REM sleep is increased during a REM rebound, nightmares often occur. Why do we need REM sleep?

The Function of REM Sleep: Necessary, but Why? Humans are not the only animals who dream. Researchers have been able to study REM sleep in other mammals, particularly rats and cats. Animal studies provide strong evidence for a relationship between REM sleep and learning (Pearlman, 1979; Smith, 1985; Winson, 1990). The fact that newborns have such a high percentage of REM sleep has led certain researchers to conclude that REM sleep is necessary for maturation of the brain in infants. Some researchers believe that REM sleep is crucial to learning complex skills. A number of others claim that REM sleep aids in the formation of permanent memories (Empsom & Clark, 1970; Glassman, 1981; Smith & Lapp, 1991). But just the opposite view is proposed by Francis Crick and Graeme Mitchison (1983). They suggest that REM sleep functions as mental housecleaning, erasing trivial and unnecessary memories and clearing overloaded neural circuits that might interfere with memory and rational thinking. In other words, they say, people dream in order to forget, particularly to reduce fantasy and obsessive thinking.

Dreaming: Mysterious Mental Activity While We Sleep

Question: How do REM and NREM dreams differ?

From earliest recorded history until the present day, people have been fascinated by dreams. The vivid dreams we remember and talk about are **REM dreams**— the type that occur almost continuously during each REM period. But there is also mental activity called *NREM dreams*, which occur during NREM sleep. REM dreams have a storylike or dreamlike quality and are more visual, vivid, and emotional than NREM dreams, which have a thoughtlike quality (Webb & Cartwright, 1978).

Have you ever heard that an entire dream takes place in an instant? Did you find that hard to believe? In fact, it is not true. Sleep researchers have discovered that it takes about as long to dream a dream as it would to experience the same thing in real life (Kleitman, 1960). Let's take a closer look at the dream state.

REM rebound: The increased amount of REM sleep that occurs after REM deprivation; often associated with unpleasant dreams or nightmares.

REM dreams: Having a dreamlike and storylike quality, the type of dream that occurs almost continuously during each REM period; more vivid, visual, emotional, and bizarre than a NREM dream.

NREM dreams: Mental activity occurring during NREM sleep that is more thoughtlike in quality than REM dreams are.

What do we dream about? REM dreams have a storylike quality and are more visual, vivid, and emotional than NREM dreams.

Dream Memories: We Remember Only a Few Sleep researchers have learned that sleepers have the best recall of a dream if they are awakened during the dream; the more time that passes after the dream ends, the poorer the recall (Kleitman, 1960). If we wake up 10 minutes or more after a dream is over, we probably will not remember it. Even the dreams we remember upon awakening will quickly fade from memory unless we mentally rehearse them or write them down. Very few dreams are memorable enough to be retained very long. Although some people insist that they do not dream at all, sleep researchers say that all people dream unless they are drinking heavily or taking drugs that suppress REM sleep.

Would we be better off if we remembered more of our dreams? Probably not. If our dream memories were as vivid as our memories of real events, we might have difficulty differentiating between events that actually happened and those we had merely dreamed about.

Try It!

Read this list of 20 common dream themes. Place a check by each one you have dreamed about.

_____ falling	_____ finding money
_____ being attacked or pursued	_____ swimming
_____ trying repeatedly to do something	_____ snakes
_____ school, teachers, studying	_____ being dressed inappropriately
_____ sexual experiences	_____ being smothered
_____ arriving too late	_____ being nude in public
_____ eating	_____ fire
_____ being frozen with fright	_____ failing an examination
_____ a loved person is dead	_____ flying
_____ being locked up	_____ seeing self as dead

Question: In general, what have researchers found regarding the content of dreams?

The Content of Dreams: Bizarre or Commonplace? What do we dream about? Sleep researchers generally agree that dreams reflect our preoccupations in waking life—our "fears, wishes, plans, hopes, and worries" (Hauri, 1982, p. 20). Since dreams are notoriously hard to remember, how do researchers know that people's dreams reflect their waking lives? Calvin Hall and Robert Van de Castle (1966) collected thousands of dream records from subjects who were asked to keep dream diaries and write down any dreams they could remember each night. Fred Snyder (1971) studied 650 dreams of subjects sleeping in the laboratory. Both studies show that dreams are less bizarre and less filled with emotion than is generally believed. Most dreams have rather commonplace settings with real people, half of whom are known to the dreamer. In general dreams are more unpleasant than pleasant, and they contain more aggression than friendly interactions and more misfortune than good fortune. Some dreams are in "living color," while others are in black and white.

Table 4.1 lists the 20 most common dream themes among 250 college students. Although the study was conducted in 1958, a study today would probably yield similar results. Compare the results of your dream themes in the *Try It!* with the results of the study shown in Table 4.1.

Some people are troubled by unpleasant, recurring dreams. The two most common themes involve being chased or falling (Stark, 1984). People who have recurring dreams seem to have more minor physical complaints, greater stress, and more anxiety and depression than other people (Brown & Donderi, 1986).

Is there anything that can be done to stop recurring dreams? Some people have been taught to use lucid dreaming to bring about satisfactory resolutions to their unpleasant recurring dreams.

You may have experienced a *lucid dream*—one during which you were aware that you were dreaming. If so, you are among the 10 percent who claim this ability. Many lucid dreamers are able to change a dream while it is in progress (La Berge, 1981; Gackenbach & Bosveld, 1989), and a few virtuosos claim to be able to dream about any subject at will (Fadiman, 1986).

lucid dream: A dream during which the dreamer is aware of dreaming and is often able to influence the content of the dream while it is in progress.

Interpreting Dreams: Are There Hidden Meanings in Our Dreams?

Sigmund Freud believed that dreams function to satisfy unconscious sexual and aggressive wishes. Because such wishes are unacceptable to the dreamer, they have to be disguised and therefore appear in a dream in symbolic form. Freud (1900/1953a) claimed that objects like sticks, umbrellas, tree trunks, and guns symbolize the male sex organ; objects like chests, cupboards, and boxes represent the female sex organ. Freud differentiated between the manifest content of the dream—the dream as recalled by the dreamer—and the underlying meaning of the dream, called the latent content, which he considered more significant.

In recent years there has been a major shift away from the Freudian interpretation of dreams. Now there is a greater focus on the manifest content, the actual dream itself, rather than on searching for symbolic meanings that can be interpreted to reveal some underlying personal conflict. The symbols in dreams, when analyzed, are now perceived as being specific to the individual rather than as having standard or universal meanings for all dreamers. Furthermore, today dreams are seen as an expression of a broad range of the dreamer's concerns rather than as primarily an expression of sexual impulses (Webb, 1975).

J. Allan Hobson (1988) rejects the notion that nature would equip us with a capability and a need to dream dreams that would require a specialist to interpret. Hobson and McCarley (1977) advanced the activation-synthesis hypothesis of dreaming. This hypothesis suggests that dreams are simply the brain's

Table 4.1 Common Dream Themes

Listed are the 20 most common dream themes reported by 250 college students and the percentage of students having each type of dream.

Type of Dream	Percentage of Students
Falling	83
Being attacked or pursued	77
Trying repeatedly to do something	71
School, teachers, studying	71
Sexual experiences	66
Arriving too late	64
Eating	62
Being frozen with fright	58
A loved person is dead	57
Being locked up	56
Finding money	56
Swimming	52
Snakes	49
Being dressed inappropriately	46
Being smothered	44
Being nude in public	43
Fire	41
Failing an examination	39
Flying	34
Seeing self as dead	33

(From Griffith, Miyago, & Tago, 1958.)

attempt to make sense of the random firing of brain cells during REM sleep. But Hobson (1989) now believes that our dreams have psychological significance, nevertheless, because they are woven from our personal experiences, remote memories, and "associations, drives, and fears" (p. 5).

Memory Check 4.2

1. State the type of sleep—NREM or REM—that corresponds to each characteristic.

   _____ 1) paralysis of large muscles   a. NREM
   _____ 2) slow, regular heart rate and respiration   b. REM
   _____ 3) rapid eye movements
   _____ 4) penile erection and vaginal swelling
   _____ 5) vivid dreams

2. The average person has about _____ sleep cycles each night.

   a. 1   b. 3   c. 5   d. 7

3. Dream memories usually do not persist for more than (5, 10) minutes after a dream has ended.

4. Which of these statements about the content of dreams is correct?
   a. Most dreams are fantastic, emotional, or bizarre.
   b. Most dreams reflect our waking preoccupations.
   c. Dreams are generally more pleasant than unpleasant.
   d. all of these

Answers 1. 1) b 2) a 3) b 4) b 5) b 2. c 3. 10 4. b

Sleep Disturbances and Disorders

So far our discussion has centered on a typical night for a typical sleeper. But one-third of American adults report sleep problems (Hauri et al., 1982), and many children also experience sleep disturbances. Sleep problems range from mild to severe and from problems that affect only sleep to those that affect a person's entire life.

Stage 4 Sleep Disturbances: Sleepwalking and Night Terrors

Question: What are some common characteristics of sleepwalking and night terrors?

somnambulism (som-NAM-bue-lism): Sleepwalking that occurs during a partial arousal from Stage 4 sleep.

night terror: A sleep disturbance in which a child partially awakens from Stage 4 sleep with a scream, dazed and groggy, in a panic state, and with a racing heart.

Somnambulism (sleepwalking) and **night terrors** are sleep disturbances that occur when there is a partial arousal during Stage 4 sleep, and the sleeper does not come to full consciousness. Most cases begin in childhood and are attributed primarily to a delayed development of the nervous system (Karacan, 1988). The disturbances are usually outgrown by adolescence, and treatment is generally not advised. If the problems persist, however, or develop later in adulthood, the origin is thought to be psychological, and treatment is recommended.

Sleepwalking (Somnambulism): Walking Around but Sound Asleep Cartoonists often depict sleepwalkers groping about with their eyes closed and their arms extended forward as if to feel their way about. Actually sleepwalkers have their eyes open with a blank stare, and rather than walking normally, they shuffle about. Their coordination is poor, and if they talk, their speech is usually unintelligible.

If an EEG recording were made during a sleepwalking episode, it would show a combination of delta waves, indicating deep sleep, and alpha and beta waves, signaling the waking state. Sleepwalkers are awake enough to carry out activities that do not require their full attention, but asleep enough not to remember having done so the following day. Sleepwalkers may get up and roam through the house, or simply stand for a short time and then go back to bed (Ferber, 1989; Karacan, 1988). Occasionally they get dressed, eat a snack, or go to the bathroom. The most important concern in sleepwalking is safety.

Finally, let us dispel a myth about sleepwalking. You might have heard that it is dangerous to awaken a sleepwalker. This piece of conventional wisdom is not true.

Question: What is a night terror?

Night Terrors: Screams in the Night Night terrors are sleep disturbances in children that usually begin with a piercing scream. The sleeper springs up in a state of panic—eyes open, perspiring, breathing rapidly, with the heart pounding at two to four times the normal rate (Karacan, 1988). Episodes usually last from 5 to 15 minutes, and then the child falls back to sleep. If not awakened during a night terror, children usually have no memory of the episode the next morning. If awakened, however, they might recall "one brief, frightening image, such as the sense of something pressing on the chest or the feeling that an intruder had entered the room" (Hartmann, 1981, p. 14).

Parents should not be unduly alarmed by night terrors in young children, but episodes that continue through adolescence into adulthood are more serious (Horner, 1992). Adult night terrors, called *incubus nightmares*, often indicate extreme anxiety and other psychological problems (Kales et al., 1980).

Other Sleep Disturbances

There are many other disturbances that can plague sleepers at various times throughout the night—anxiety nightmares and sleeptalking are two.

Anxiety Nightmares: The Worst of Dreams Anxiety **nightmares**, commonly referred to simply as nightmares, are very frightening dreams occurring during REM sleep. They are likely to be remembered in vivid detail. The most common themes are being chased, threatened, or attacked. Nightmares can be a reaction to traumatic life experiences (Hefez et al., 1987), and they are more frequent at times of high fevers, anxiety, and emotional upheaval. A REM rebound during drug withdrawal or following long periods without sleep can produce nightmares. Figure 4.5 shows that night terrors occur early in the night during Stage 4 sleep; anxiety nightmares occur toward morning, when the REM periods are longest.

Occasional nightmares are nothing to be alarmed about; most adults have had a few. Frequent nightmares may be associated with psychological maladjustment (Berquier & Ashton, 1992), although Wood and Bootzin (1990) suggest that nightmares are not that uncommon and not necessarily related to anxiety.

incubus nightmare: A night terror in an adult which, unlike one in a child, is often an indication of extreme anxiety and other psychological problems.

anxiety nightmare: A very frightening dream occurring during REM sleep.

Figure 4.5

Night Terrors and Nightmares: When They Occur

Night terrors occur during Stage 4 sleep, most often during the first sleep cycle. Nightmares occur during REM sleep, most often during the last sleep cycles. (After Hartmann, 1981.)

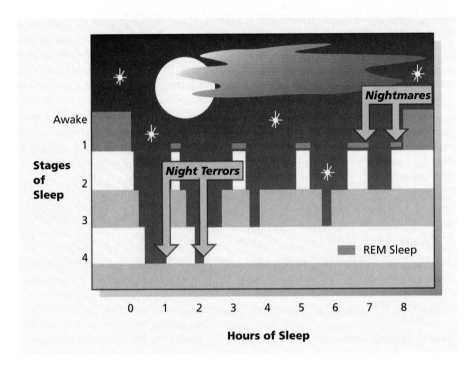

Sleeptalking (Somniloquy): Might We Reveal Secrets? Do you sometimes talk in your sleep? Are you afraid that you might confess to something embarrassing, or reveal some deep, dark secret? Relax. Sleeptalkers rarely reply to questions, and they usually mumble words or phrases that make no sense to the listener. Sleepers can talk during any sleep stage, but most often sleeptalking occurs in Stage 1 or Stage 2 sleep (Aldrich, 1989). It is more frequent in children than adults, and it is common when people have a fever. There is no evidence at all that sleeptalking is related to a physical or psychological disturbance—not even to a guilty conscience (Arkin, 1981).

Major Sleep Disorders

Some sleep disorders can be so debilitating that they affect a person's entire life. These disorders are narcolepsy, sleep apnea, and insomnia.

Question: What are the major symptoms of narcolepsy?

Narcolepsy: Sudden Attacks of REM Sleep Many people complain about having difficulty falling asleep, but a more serious problem is not being able to stay awake when we need to. **Narcolepsy** is an incurable sleep disorder characterized by excessive daytime sleepiness and uncontrollable attacks of REM sleep, lasting from a few minutes to an hour (Guilleminault, 1989). Victims—some 250,000 in the United States—are often unfairly stigmatized as lazy, depressed, and uninterested in their work.

Anything that causes an ordinary person to be tired can trigger a sleep attack in a narcoleptic—a heavy meal, sunbathing at the beach, or a boring lecture. A sleep attack can also be brought on by any situation that is exciting (narcoleptic attacks often occur during lovemaking) or that causes a strong emotion, such as anger or laughter. Many people with narcolepsy also have cataplexy—attacks

narcolepsy (NAR-co-lep-see): A serious sleep disorder characterized by excessive daytime sleepiness and sudden, uncontrollable attacks of REM sleep.

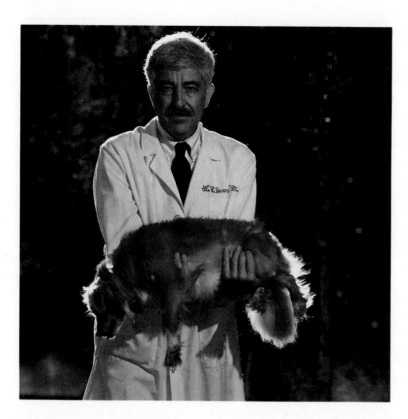

Well-known sleep researcher William Dement holds a dog during an attack of narcolepsy. Much has been learned about the disorder through research with dogs.

of muscular weakness or paralysis in which the unfortunate victim often collapses and falls to the ground (Aldrich, 1989).

Narcolepsy is easily diagnosed in the sleep laboratory because, unlike a normal sleeper, the narcoleptic tends to go into REM sleep almost immediately after sleep onset. Narcolepsy is a physiological disorder caused by an abnormality in the part of the brain that regulates sleep (Mefford et al., 1983), and it appears to have a strong genetic component (Aldrich, 1990). In serious cases stimulants can greatly reduce the frequency of attacks, but narcolepsy is "a lifelong condition for which there is no known cure" (Hauri, 1982, p. 56). Some dogs are subject to narcolepsy, and much has been learned about this disorder from research on canine subjects.

Question: What is sleep apnea?

Sleep Apnea: Can't Sleep and Breathe at the Same Time   Over one million Americans—mostly obese men—suffer from another dangerous sleep disorder, sleep apnea. **Sleep apnea** consists of periods during sleep when breathing stops, and the individual must awaken briefly in order to breathe (White, 1989). The major symptoms of sleep apnea are excessive daytime sleepiness and extremely loud snoring (as loud as a jackhammer), often accompanied by snorts, gasps, and choking noises.

A person with sleep apnea will drop off to sleep, stop breathing altogether, and then awaken struggling for breath. After gasping several breaths in a semi-awakened state, the person falls back to sleep and stops breathing again. In very severe cases, this process may be repeated throughout the night with as many as 800 partial awakenings to gasp for air. Severe sleep apnea can lead to chronic high blood pressure and heart problems, and even cause sudden death (Browman et al., 1982; Mitler et al., 1975). A relatively new device, the continuous positive airways pressure (CPAP) can now keep people breathing through the night (Zorick et al., 1990).

sleep apnea: A sleep disorder characterized by periods when breathing stops during sleep and the person must awaken briefly in order to breathe; major symptoms are excessive daytime sleepiness and loud snoring.

WORLD OF PSYCHOLOGY: APPLICATIONS

Insomnia: Symptoms and Solutions

Question: What is insomnia?

It would be unusual if you have not had at least a few nights in your life when you had difficulty falling or staying asleep. Transient *insomnia*, lasting a few weeks or less, can result from jet lag, emotional highs or lows, or a brief illness that interferes with sleep. Much more serious is chronic insomnia, which lasts for months or even years and plagues about 17 percent of the population (Gillin, 1991).

Insomniacs suffer from impaired daytime functioning and have one or more of the following symptoms (Webb & Cartwright, 1978):

- take longer than 30 minutes to fall asleep

- have five or more awakenings each night with at least 30 minutes awake

- wake up too early with less than 6 1/2 hours of sleep

- spend too much of the night in light sleep and too little in deep sleep compared with the norm for their age group

There are a number of identifiable causes of chronic insomnia, but 80 percent of the cases are believed to be primarily psychological in origin (Hauri et al., 1982). Some of the major causes include the following:

- psychological disorders, such as depression

- physical disorders, such as chronic pain

- problems with a person's biological clock

- drug use, including sleeping pills

- conditioned wakefulness, in which a person comes to associate the bed with the frustration of poor sleep

Sleeping Pills and Alcohol: Making a Bad Situation Worse Over the years, people have tried a variety of methods to induce sleep—a warm glass of milk at bedtime, counting sheep, taking sleeping pills. Helping people get to sleep is a big business. About 21 million prescriptions for sleeping pills are written annually, and another 8 million prescriptions for tranquilizers are thought to be used for sleep. Also, about 10 million people rely on over-the-counter sleep aids (Hopson, 1986). But the most widely used sleep aid of all is alcohol (Hales, 1981).

Most chemical sleep aids create more problems than they solve. Sleeping pills are addictive, and tolerance to their effects can develop within a week or so, decreasing their effectiveness. In addition, sleeping pills or a few drinks at bedtime may get you to sleep faster, but there is a price to be paid—lighter sleep, more awakenings, and less sleep overall (Hartmann, 1988).

Over-the-counter sleep products are useless in serious cases of insomnia (Kales et al., 1971) because instead of actually inducing sleep, they simply cause grogginess. These products can be dangerous if taken in higher-than-recommended doses (Webb, 1975).

Hints for a Better Night's Sleep If you associate your bed with the frustration of being unable to fall asleep, here are some tips that can help you fall asleep more easily.

- Use your bed only for sleep—not for reading, watching television, eating, or talking on the phone.

- Leave the bedroom anytime you cannot fall asleep within 10 minutes. Go to another room and read, watch TV, or listen to music. Don't return for another try until you are more tired. Repeat the process as many times as necessary until you fall asleep within 10 minutes.

- Establish a relaxing ritual that you follow each night just before bedtime (taking a warm bath, brushing your teeth, and so on).

- Set your alarm and wake up at the same time every day including weekends, regardless of how much you have slept. No naps are allowed.

- Exercise regularly but not within several hours of bedtime. Exercise raises body temperature and makes it more difficult to fall asleep.

- Establish regular mealtimes. Don't eat heavy or spicy meals close to bedtime. If you must eat then, try milk and a few crackers.

- Beware of caffeine and nicotine—they are sleep disturbers. Avoid caffeine within 6 hours and smoking within 1 or 2 hours of bedtime.

- Avoid wrestling with your problems when you go to bed. Try counting backward from 1,000 by twos or try a progressive relaxation exercise (explained on p. 132).

Memory Check 4.3

1. Which of these characteristics is *not* common to sleepwalking and night terrors?

   a. They occur during partial arousal from Stage 4 sleep.
   b. Episodes are usually forgotten the next morning.
   c. The disturbances occur most often in children.
   d. The disturbances indicate a psychological problem which should be treated by a mental health professional.

2. An anxiety nightmare occurs during (Stage 4 sleep, REM sleep).

3. Most cases of insomnia are considered to be (psychological, physiological) in origin.

4. Match the disorder with the description or the associated symptom.

   _____ 1) sleep attacks during the day   a. narcolepsy
   _____ 2) breathing stops during sleep;   b. sleep apnea
            loud snoring   c. insomnia
   _____ 3) attacks of muscular weakness
   _____ 4) difficulty falling asleep or staying
            asleep

Answers: 1. d 2. REM sleep 3. psychological 4. 1) a 2) b 3) a 4) c

There are many different methods for meditation, but all have the same goal—relaxation.

Altering Consciousness through Concentration and Suggestion

Sleep is an altered state of consciousness and a necessary one. We must sleep. But there are other forms of altered consciousness that we may enter only if we choose to do so. Meditation and hypnosis are two of these.

Meditation: Relaxing Your Way to a Different Form of Consciousness

Question: What is the purpose of meditation?

Meditation is a state of contemplation used to increase relaxation, block out worries and distractions, or foster a different form of consciousness. There are several methods, some more structured than others, but all are basically designed to achieve the same end—relaxation.

   The meditator sits in a comfortable chair with eyes closed, both feet flat on the floor, and hands in the lap or simply resting on the arms of the chair. Some people begin meditation by relaxing their muscles from the feet up, to achieve a deep state of relaxation. Other people concentrate on their breathing—slowly, rhythmically, in and out. In transcendental meditation (TM), the meditator is given a mantra, a secret word (such as "ohm") assigned by the teacher. The meditator repeats the mantra over and over during meditation to block out unwanted thoughts and facilitate the meditative state. Dr. Herbert Benson (1975) suggests that any word or sound will do. Moreover, he claims that the beneficial effects of meditation can be achieved through simple relaxation techniques. Do the *Try It!* to experience Benson's relaxation response.

Try It!

Find a quiet place and sit in a comfortable position.

1. Close your eyes.
2. Relax all your muscles deeply. Begin with your feet and move slowly upward, relaxing the muscles in your legs, buttocks, abdomen, chest, shoulders, neck, and finally your face. Allow your whole body to remain in this deeply relaxed state.
3. Now concentrate on your breathing, and breathe in and out through your nose. Each time you breathe out, silently say the word *one* to yourself.
4. Repeat this process for 20 minutes. (You can open your eyes to look at your watch periodically, but don't use an alarm.) When you are finished, remain seated for a few minutes—first with your eyes closed, and then with them open.

Benson recommends that you maintain a passive attitude. Don't try to force yourself to relax. Just let it happen. If a distracting thought comes to mind, ignore it and just repeat *one* each time you exhale. It is best to practice this exercise one or two times each day, but not within two hours of your last meal. Digestion interferes with the relaxation response.

Hypnosis: Look into My Eyes

Question: What is hypnosis, and when is it most useful?

Have you ever been hypnotized? Many people are fascinated by this unusual, somewhat mysterious altered state of consciousness. Other people doubt that it even exists.

Hypnosis has been used for a variety of purposes, including helping sports teams improve their performance.

Hypnosis is a trancelike state of concentrated and focused attention, heightened suggestibility, and diminished response to external stimuli. In the hypnotic state, subjects suspend their usual rational and logical ways of thinking and perceiving, and allow themselves to experience distortions in perceptions, memories, and thinking. Under hypnosis people may experience positive hallucinations, in which they see, hear, touch, smell, or taste things that are not present in the environment. Or they may have negative hallucinations and fail to perceive those things that are present.

From 80 to 95 percent of the population are hypnotizable to some degree, but only 5 percent can reach the deepest levels of trance in which surgery can be performed without anesthesia (Nash & Baker, 1984). The ability to become completely absorbed in imaginative activities is characteristic of highly hypnotizable people (Nadon et al., 1991).

Myths about Hypnosis: Separating Fact from Fiction   There are a number of misconceptions about hypnosis, some of which probably stem from its long and unfortunate association with stage entertainers. Have you ever believed one of these myths?

- **Subjects are not aware of what is going on during hypnosis.** When subjects are hypnotized, they know where they are and what they are doing, and they are aware that they are in a trance (Kelly & Kelly, 1985). Because many subjects expect something far different, they often have difficulty believing that they were, in fact, hypnotized.
- **Subjects will violate their moral values under hypnosis.** Generally subjects under hypnosis will not behave contrary to their true moral values. If told to violate their values, they will simply come out of the trance (Wilkes, 1986).
- **Subjects can demonstrate superhuman strength and perform amazing feats under hypnosis.** Subjects are not stronger or more powerful under hypnosis.
- **Memory is more accurate under hypnosis.** Memory is not more accurate under hypnosis (Kilstrom, 1985; Sheehan & Tilden, 1983, 1984). Hypnotized subjects supply more information and are more confident of their recollections, but the information is often inaccurate (Dywan & Bowers, 1983; Nogrady et al., 1985).
- **Subjects under hypnosis will reveal embarrassing secrets.** Hypnosis is not like a truth serum. Subjects can keep secrets or lie under hypnosis (Kelly & Kelly, 1985).
- **Subjects under hypnosis can relive an event as it occurred when they were children and can function mentally as if they were that age.** Careful reviews of studies on hypnotic age-regression have found no evidence to support this claim (Barber, 1962). "Although hypnotically regressed subjects may undergo dramatic changes in demeanor and subjective experience, their performance is not accurately childlike" (Nash, 1987, p. 50).
- **Subjects are under the complete control of the hypnotist.** Hypnosis is not something that is done to subjects. Subjects under hypnosis retain the ability to break the trance (Spiegel & Spiegel, 1978).

Medical Uses of Hypnosis: It's Not Just Entertainment   Hypnosis has come a long way from the days when it was used mainly by stage entertainers. It is now recognized as a viable technique to be used in medicine, dentistry, and psychotherapy. Hypnosis is accepted by the American Medical Association, the American Psychological Association, and the American Psychiatric Association (Orne, 1983). Hypnosis has been particularly helpful in the control of pain (Hilgard, 1975; Kilstrom, 1985). Hypnosis has also been used successfully to treat a wide range of disorders, including high blood pressure, bleeding, psoriasis, severe morning sickness, chemotherapy side-effects, and burns (Kelly &

hypnosis: A trancelike state of concentrated, focused attention, heightened suggestibility, and diminished response to external stimuli.

Kelly, 1985). Other problems that have responded well to hypnosis are asthma, severe insomnia, some phobias (Orne, 1983), and sexual dysfunction (Araoz, 1982).

For the most hypnotizable subjects, hypnosis can be used instead of a general anesthetic in surgery. In one operation "a surgeon cut through a woman's chest into her heart to enlarge one of its valves. Without chemical anesthesia, the woman was conscious and awake but suffered no pain" (Freese, 1980, p. 20).

Suppose you are overweight, or you smoke or drink heavily. Would a quick trip to a hypnotist rid you of your bad habit? Hypnosis has been only moderately effective in weight control and virtually useless in overcoming drug and alcohol abuse (Orne, 1983).

Critics' Explanations of Hypnosis: Is It Really What It Seems? Because there is no reliable way to determine whether a person is truly hypnotized, some critics offer other explanations for behavior occurring during this state. One explanation is that subjects are simply acting out the role suggested by the hypnotist (Coe & Sarbin, 1977). Although some people claiming to be hypnotized may be role-playing, this theory does not adequately explain how people can undergo surgery with hypnosis rather than a general anesthetic (Kroger & Feltzer, 1976).

Another idea is that behavior under hypnosis is no different from behavior of other highly motivated subjects. Barber (1970) found that "both hypnotic and waking control subjects are responsive to suggestions for analgesia [pain relief], age-regression, hallucinations and amnesia if they have positive attitudes toward the situation and are motivated to respond" (p. 27).

Memory Check 4.4

1. Which is not a proposed use of meditation?

   a. to promote relaxation
   b. to control pain
   c. to clear the mind of worries and distracting thoughts
   d. to alter consciousness

2. Meditation has been proven more effective than rest for promoting relaxation and reducing stress. (true/false)

3. Which of these statements is true of people under hypnosis?

   a. They will often violate their moral code.
   b. They are much stronger than in the normal waking state.
   c. They can be made to experience distortions in their perceptions.
   d. Their memory is more accurate than during the normal waking state.

4. For a moderately hypnotizable person, which use of hypnosis would probably be most successful?

   a. for relief from pain
   b. for surgery instead of a general anesthetic
   c. for treating drug addiction
   d. for improving memory

Answers: 1. b 2. false 3. c 4. a

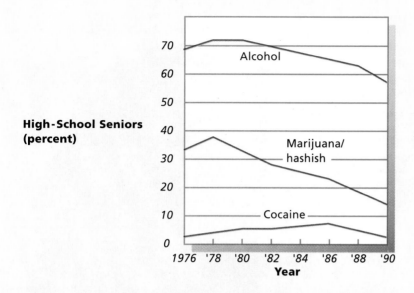

Figure 4.6 Survey Results of Alcohol, Marijuana, and Cocaine Use among High-School Seniors.   Surveys show the percentage of high-school students from 1976 through 1990, who reported having used alcohol, marijuana, or cocaine in the 30 days preceding the survey. (After Johnston, O'Malley, & Bachman, 1991.)

Altered States of Consciousness and Psychoactive Drugs

The altered states of consciousness we have examined thus far are natural ones. We will now explore psychoactive drugs, a wide range of substances that are used to modify natural consciousness. A **psychoactive drug** is any substance that alters mood, perception, or thought. Some of these drugs are legal, but most are not. When these drugs are approved for medical use only, they are called controlled substances.

Drug use among high school graduates has been falling continuously since 1980, as shown in Figure 4.6 (Johnston et al., 1991). However, the United States continues to have the highest rate of *illicit* (illegal) *drug* use of all the industrialized nations (Newcomb & Bentler, 1989). About 28 million Americans use illicit drugs (Jarvik, 1990), and 5.5 million are addicted to them (Holloway, 1991). But in terms of "damage to users, harm to society, or numbers of addicts," alcohol and tobacco are "our most serious problem drugs by far" (Goldstein & Kalant, 1990, p. 1516).

Reasons for Taking Drugs: Many Reasons, No Good Ones

Why do so many Americans use psychoactive drugs? There are many reasons for taking drugs, and users often do not recognize their real motivation. Some people take drugs to cope with or relieve anxiety, depression, or boredom (Baker, 1988). Others use drugs just to feel good, for a thrill, or because of social pressures. "Aggravating the problem are the notions prevalent in our contemporary culture . . . that (1) for every ill there's a pill, (2) the world owes me a perpetual 'high,' and (3) only 'now' counts" (Jones & Lovinger, 1985, p. 460). Table 4.2 summarizes the variables associated with adolescent involvement with psychoactive drugs.

psychoactive drug: A drug that alters normal mental functioning—mood, perception, or thought; if used medically, called a controlled substance.

illicit drug: An illegal drug.

Table 4.2

Influences on Initial Involvement with Psychoactive Drugs

Peer influences	Peers use and encourage others to use Peers provide substances
Social/Family Variables	Disadvantaged socioeconomic groups Disturbed families Adult drug users as models Lack of religious commitment
Educational Variables	Poor school performance
Psychological/behavioral variables	Low self-esteem Tolerance for deviance Deviant behaviors Lack of law abidance Need for excitement Stressful life events Depression Anxiety

Adapted from Newcomb & Bentler, 1989, and Jarvik, 1990.

Drug Dependence: Slave to a Substance

Question: What is the difference between physical and psychological dependence?

drug dependence (physical): A compulsive pattern of drug use in which the user develops a drug tolerance coupled with unpleasant withdrawal symptoms when the drug is discontinued.

drug tolerance: A condition in which the user becomes progressively less affected by the drug so that larger and larger doses are necessary to maintain the same effect.

withdrawal symptoms: The physical and psychological symptoms (usually the opposite of those produced by the drug) that occur when a regularly used drug is discontinued and that terminate when the drug is taken again.

drug dependence (psychological): A craving or irresistible urge for a drug's pleasurable effects.

The trip from first use to abuse of drugs may be a long one or a very short one. Some drugs create a physical or chemical dependence; others create a psychological dependence. **Physical dependence** comes about as a result of the body's natural ability to protect itself against harmful substances by developing a **drug tolerance**. This means that the user becomes progressively less affected by the drug and must take larger and larger doses to get the same effect or high. Tolerance occurs because the brain adapts to the presence of the drug by responding less intensely to it. In addition, more enzymes are produced by the liver to break down the drug. The various bodily processes adjust in order to continue to function with the drug in the system.

Once drug tolerance is established, a person cannot function normally without the drug. If the drug is taken away, the user begins to suffer withdrawal symptoms. The **withdrawal symptoms**, both physical and psychological, are usually the exact opposite of the effects produced by the drug. For example, withdrawal from stimulants leaves a person exhausted and depressed; withdrawal from tranquilizers leaves a person nervous and agitated.

If physical dependence alone explained drug addiction, there would be no problem with drugs long thought to be physically nonaddictive. Once the period of physical withdrawal was over, the desire for the drug would end along with the withdrawal symptoms. But this is not the case. There is more to drug addiction than physical dependence. **Psychological dependence** is a craving or irresistible urge for the drug's pleasurable effects, and it is more difficult to combat than physical dependence.

Four factors influence the addictive potential of a drug: (1) how fast the effects of the drug are felt, (2) how pleasurable the drug's effects are in producing euphoria or in extinguishing pain, (3) how long the pleasurable effects last, and (4) how much discomfort is experienced when the drug is discontinued (Medzerin, 1991). With the most addictive drugs, the pleasurable effects are felt almost immediately, and they are short-lived. For example, the intense, pleasurable effects of crack are felt in 7 seconds, and they last only about 5 minutes. The discomfort after the pleasurable effects wear off is intense, so a user is highly motivated to continue taking the drug. With any drug, the abuse potential is higher if the drug is injected rather than taken orally, and higher still if it is smoked rather than injected.

Psychoactive drugs alter consciousness in a variety of ways. We will examine the various alterations produced by the major categories of drugs: stimulants, depressants, and hallucinogens (or psychedelics).

Stimulants: Speeding Up the Nervous System

Question: How do stimulants affect the user?

Stimulants, often called "*uppers*," speed up the central nervous system, suppress appetite, and can make a person feel more awake, alert, and energetic. Stimulants increase pulse rate, blood pressure, and respiration rate, and they reduce cerebral blood flow (Mathew & Wilson, 1991). In higher doses, stimulants make people feel nervous, jittery, and restless, and they can cause shaking or trembling and interfere with sleep.

No stimulant actually delivers energy to the body. Instead, a stimulant forces the body to use some of its own stored-up energy sooner and in greater amounts than it would naturally. When the stimulant's effect wears off, the body's natural energy is depleted, leaving the person feeling exhausted and depressed.

There are legal stimulants, such as caffeine and nicotine. Illegal stimulants include amphetamines and cocaine.

Caffeine: The Most Widely Used Drug   Caffeine is the world's most widely used drug, and more than 85 percent of Americans ingest it daily in one form or another (Hughes et al., 1992). If you cannot start your day without a cup of coffee (or two, or more), you may be addicted to the stimulant caffeine. Coffee, tea, cola drinks, chocolate, and more than 100 prescription and over-the-counter drugs contain caffeine. They provide a mild jolt to the nervous system that perks us up, at least temporarily. Caffeine makes us more mentally alert and can help us stay awake. Many people use caffeine to lift their mood, but laboratory studies reveal that one hour after consuming medium or high doses of caffeine, subjects show significantly higher levels of anxiety, depression, and hostility (Veleber & Templer, 1984).

Nicotine: A Deadly Poison   Nicotine is a poison so strong that the body must develop a tolerance to it almost immediately—in only hours, rather than days or weeks for heroin, and usually months for alcohol. It is estimated that tobacco kills 390,000 Americans every year (Novello, 1990). The many health problems associated with smoking are discussed in chapter 13, "Health and Stress."

Question: What effects do amphetamines have on the user?

Amphetamines: Energy to Burn—At a Price   Amphetamines are a class of stimulants that increase arousal, relieve fatigue, suppress the appetite, and give a rush of energy. In low to moderate doses, athletic and intellectual performance may be improved. A person becomes more alert and energetic, experiences mild euphoria, and usually becomes more talkative, animated, and restless.

In high doses—100 milligrams or more—amphetamines can cause confused and disorganized behavior, extreme fear and suspiciousness, delusions and hal-

stimulants: A category of drugs that speed up activity in the central nervous system, suppress appetite, and cause a person to feel more awake, alert, and energetic.

uppers: A slang term for stimulants.

amphetamines: A class of CNS stimulants that increase arousal, relieve fatigue, and suppress the appetite.

lucinations, aggressiveness and antisocial behavior, even manic behavior and paranoia. The powerful amphetamine methamphetamine (known as "crank" or "speed") now comes in the smokable form—"ice," which is highly addictive and can be fatal.

Crashing from an amphetamine high is not a pleasant experience. The withdrawal symptoms leave a person physically exhausted, sleeping for 10 to 15 hours or more, only to awaken in a stupor, extremely depressed and intensely hungry. Stimulants constrict the tiny capillaries and the small arteries. Over time, high doses can stop the blood flow, causing hemorrhaging and leaving parts of the brain deprived of oxygen. In fact, victims of fatal overdoses of stimulants usually have multiple hemorrhages in the brain (Jones & Jones, 1977).

Question: How does cocaine affect the user?

Cocaine: Snorting White Powder, Smoking Crack
"Cocaine can make you feel brilliant, masterful, invulnerable. It can also kill you" (Mark Gold, 1986).

Cocaine, a stimulant derived from coca leaves, can be sniffed as a white powder, injected intravenously, or smoked in the form of crack. The rush of well-being is dramatically intense and powerful, but it is just as dramatically short-lived. It lasts no more than 15 to 30 minutes. In cocaine abusers, now numbering 1 to 3 million in the United States, this euphoria is followed by an equally intense *crash,* marked by depression, anxiety, agitation, and a craving for more cocaine to end the misery (Gawin, 1991).

Cocaine stimulates the reward or "pleasure" pathways in the brain, which use the neurotransmitter dopamine. With continued use, the reward systems fail to function normally. The user becomes incapable of feeling any pleasure except from the drug (Gawin, 1991). Cocaine causes a true physical addiction, but the main withdrawal symptoms are psychological: the inability to feel pleasure, and the craving for more cocaine (Gawin & Ellinwood, 1988).

Frequent cocaine snorting often dries out the delicate mucous membranes of the nose until they crack and bleed. Habitual snorters have coldlike symptoms—runny nose, sinusitis, hoarseness, and dull headaches. Heavy snorting can eat away the cartilage separating the nostrils (Gold, 1986).

Cocaine constricts the blood vessels, raises blood pressure, speeds up the heart, quickens respiration, and can even cause epileptic seizures in people who have no history of epilepsy (Pascual-Leone et al., 1990). Over time, or even quickly in high doses, cocaine can cause heart palpitations, an irregular heartbeat, and heart attacks (Lange et al., 1989). Even strong, young hearts sometimes cannot stand the strain of high doses of cocaine. In 1986 Len Bias, a promising college basketball star drafted by the Boston Celtics, died from an overdose of cocaine.

Animals become more readily addicted to cocaine than to any other drug (Geary, 1987). Given unlimited access to cocaine, animals will lose interest in everything else—food, water, and sex—and will rapidly and continuously self-administer cocaine. They die within 14 days usually from cardiopulmonary collapse (Gawin, 1991). Cocaine-addicted monkeys will press a lever as many as 12,800 times to get one cocaine injection (Yanagita, 1973).

Crack, or "rock," has made cocaine affordable, even for the very poor. Not only the cheapest but the most dangerous form of cocaine as well, crack can produce a powerful dependency in several weeks. "The rush is so intense and the crash so powerful that it keeps users—even first-time users—focused on nothing but their next hit" (Lamar, 1986, p. 17). Dr. Jeffrey Rosecan, a drug abuse consultant to the National Football League, calls cocaine "the most addicting substance known to man," and crack, he says, is "the most addicting form of the most addicting drug" (Lundgren, 1986, p. 7).

cocaine: A type of stimulant that produces a feeling of euphoria.

crash: The feelings of depression, exhaustion, irritability, and anxiety that occur following an amphetamine, cocaine, or crack high.

crack: The most potent, inexpensive, and addictive form of cocaine, and the form that is smoked.

Hallucinogens: Seeing, Hearing, and Feeling What Is Not There

Question: What are the main effects of hallucinogens, and what are three psychoactive drugs classified as hallucinogens?

The **hallucinogens,** or psychedelics, are drugs that can alter perception and mood, and produce feelings of unreality. As the name implies, hallucinogens also cause *hallucinations,* sensations that have no basis in external reality (Andreason & Black, 1991). When perceptions are distorted, the user of hallucinogens often cannot distinguish between fantasy and reality. "The records contain many reports of drug users who, while hallucinating, think they can fly or see people who are not there, who hear unreal voices, or who dissociate completely from their bodies" (Jones and Jones, 1977, p. 66).

Rather than producing a relatively predictable effect like most other drugs, hallucinogens usually magnify the mood or the frame of mind of the user at the time the drug is taken. The hallucinogens we will discuss are LSD, PCP, and the mild hallucinogen marijuana.

LSD (Lysergic Acid Diethylamide): Mind Altering, Not Mind Expanding

LSD is lysergic acid diethylamide, sometimes simply referred to as "acid." The average LSD "trip" lasts 10 to 12 hours and usually produces extreme perceptual changes—visual hallucinations and distortions. Emotions can become very intense and unstable. LSD can cause bad trips, which can be terrifying and leave the users in a state of panic, afraid of losing their sanity, and fearing that their normal perceptual world will not return. On occasion, bad LSD trips have ended tragically in accidents, death, or suicide. Some people who have taken LSD experience a *flashback*, a brief recurrence of a trip that occurs suddenly and without warning weeks or even months after the LSD use.

PCP (Phencyclidine): "Angel Dust," Unpredictable and Dangerous

Another potentially dangerous hallucinogen is phencyclidine, known as **PCP** or angel dust. The effects of PCP are unpredictable and can include intoxication, delirium, bizarre behavior, paranoia, or other psychotic reactions (Grinspoon & Bakalar, 1990). People under the influence of PCP are capable of terrifying acts of violence, making the drug dangerous for both the users and the people around them.

Question: What are some harmful effects associated with heavy marijuana use?

Marijuana: More Harmful Than We Once Believed

About 20 million people in the United States use marijuana regularly, making it the most widely used illicit drug (Andreason & Black, 1991). In general **marijuana** tends to produce a feeling of well-being, promote relaxation, relieve inhibitions, and relieve anxiety. The user may experience an increased sensitivity to sights, sounds, and touch, as well as perceptual distortions and a slowing of time.

THC (tetrahydrocannibinol), the ingredient in marijuana that produces the high, remains in the body long after it has been smoked. Even a week after use, 30 percent of the THC ingested is still in the system; 10 percent remains after 7 weeks (Jones & Jones, 1977). A person who smokes only one marijuana cigarette, or joint, every few weeks is never completely free of THC. Marijuana impairs attention and coordination and slows reaction time, and these effects make operating complex machinery such as an automobile dangerous, even after the feeling of intoxication has passed.

Marijuana interferes with the natural chemical action of the pleasure centers in the brain (Heath, 1972). With heavy marijuana use, the pleasure centers "may become incapable of responding to the pleasures of *normal* physical and

hallucinogens (hal-lu-SIN-o-jenz): A category of drugs, sometimes called psychedelics, that alter perception and mood and can cause hallucinations.

hallucination: An imaginary sensation.

LSD (lysergic acid diethylamide): A powerful hallucinogen with unpredictable effects ranging from perceptual changes and vivid hallucinations to states of panic and terror.

flashback: The brief recurrence of effects experienced while taking LSD or PCP, occurring suddenly and without warning at a later time.

PCP (phencyclidine): A potentially dangerous hallucinogen that can cause bizarre or violent behavior, paranoia, and other psychotic reactions; angel dust.

marijuana: An hallucinogen with effects ranging from relaxation and giddiness to perceptual distortions and hallucinations.

THC (tetrahydrocannabinol): The principle psychoactive ingredient in marijuana and hashish.

Researchers have found that marijuana decreases blood flow to the brain, slowing brain functioning. The long-term effects of marijuana on the brain are still unknown.

intellectual stimulation" (Nahas, 1985, p. 194). Many of the receptor sites for marijuana are in the hippocampus, which explains why memory is affected (Matsuda et al., 1990). Marijuana can interfere with concentration, logical thinking, the ability to form new memories, and the ability to hold in mind what is said. Chronic use of marijuana has been associated with a loss of motivation, a general apathy, and a decline in school performance—referred to as the amotivational syndrome (Andreason & Black, 1991).

Smoking marijuana can cause respiratory damage even faster than cigarette smoking can (Tzu-Chin et al., 1988). Heavy marijuana use in human subjects has been associated with broken chromosomes (Russell, 1983). Marijuana abuse affects the reproductive system in males, causing (1) a 20-percent impotence rate, (2) a 44-percent reduction in testosterone level (Kolodny et al., 1979), (3) a 30- to 70-percent reduction in the sperm count, and (4) an abnormal appearance of sperm cells, as shown in the photograph (Hembree et al., 1979). In women, failure to ovulate, other menstrual irregularities, and lower-birth-weight babies have been associated with heavy marijuana smoking (Hingson et al., 1982; Kolodny et al., 1979).

It is important for young people to be aware of the possible physical and psychological harm associated with psychoactive drugs. Bailey and others (1992) reported that the more concerned high school students were about the adverse physical and psychological effects of marijuana, the less likely they were to continue using it after initial experimentation.

Marijuana can adversely affect the reproductive system, as shown in this light microscope photograph of an abnormal human sperm with two tails.

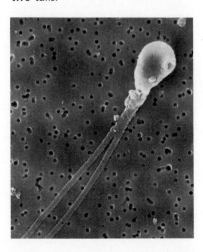

Memory Check 4.5

1. A tolerance to a drug develops when:

    a. the body adjusts to functioning with the drug in the system
    b. the user needs larger and larger doses of the drug to get the desired effect
    c. the user becomes progressively less affected by the drug
    d. all of these

2. Physical dependence is more difficult to overcome than psychological dependence. (true/false)

3. Match the stimulant with the appropriate description.

    _____ 1) responsible for the most deaths   a. caffeine
    _____ 2) used to increase arousal, relieve   b. cigarettes
              fatigue, and suppress appetite   c. amphetamines
    _____ 3) found in coffee, tea, chocolate, and   d. crack
              colas   e. cocaine
    _____ 4) snorted or injected
    _____ 5) most dangerous, potent, and addictive form of cocaine

4. People under the influence of (LSD, PCP) are capable of violent behavior.

5. Which physical problem has *not* been attributed to heavy marijuana use?

    a. heart attack
    b. respiratory damage
    c. broken chromosomes
    d. impotence in men

Answers: 1. d 2. false 3. 1) b 2) c 3) a 4) e 5) d 4. PCP 5. a

Depressants: Slowing Down the Nervous System

Question: What are some of the effects of depressants, and what drugs comprise this category?

Another class of drugs, the **depressants** (sometimes called "*downers*") decrease activity in the central nervous system, slow down body functions, and reduce sensitivity to outside stimulation. Within this category are the sedative-hypnotics (alcohol, barbiturates, and minor tranquilizers) and the narcotics, or opiates.

Alcohol: The Nation's Number One Drug Problem

Even though *alcohol* is a depressant, the first few drinks seem to relax and enliven at the same time. But the more alcohol put into the bloodstream, the more the central nervous system is depressed. As drinking increases, the symptoms of drunkenness mount—slurred speech, poor coordination, staggering. Men tend to become more aggressive (Bushman & Cooper, 1990) and more sexually aroused (Roehrich & Kinder, 1991) but less able to perform sexually (Crowe & George, 1989). Excessive alcohol can cause a person to lose consciousness, and extremely large amounts can kill. More than a few people have died playing the party game of chug-a-lugging whiskey. Table 4.3 shows the effects of various blood alcohol levels.

Alcohol is a problem substance responsible for much misery in the United States. We discuss the health consequences of alcohol abuse in detail in chapter 13, "Health and Stress." Alcohol is also a problem substance in other cultures around the world. Read about this in the boxed feature on page 142.

depressants: A category of drugs that decrease activity in the central nervous system, slow down bodily functions, and reduce sensitivity to outside stimulation.

alcohol: A central nervous system depressant.

downers: A slang term for depressants.

WORLD OF PSYCHOLOGY: MULTICULTURAL PERSPECTIVES

The Use and Abuse of Alcohol

Human societies throughout recorded history have brewed and distilled alcohol and used it for recreational purposes, in religious rites, and for social celebrations. Alcohol has also been widely abused. There is great cultural variation in drinking habits and styles, and in attitudes toward alcohol. Moderate drinking is prevalent in some American ethnic groups, most notably Jewish, Greek, Chinese, and Italian (Peele, 1984). In these cultures alcohol is used primarily in the family or larger social settings where young people are gradually included. Alcohol is rarely used excessively and is controlled by cultural norms and social customs. These cultures show strong disapproval when members of their group violate their standards for the responsible use of alcohol.

According to one stereotype, the Irish are perceived to be heavier drinkers than many other cultural groups. George Vaillant (1983) reported that in one of his samples, Irish Americans were seven times more likely to be alcoholics than the Greeks, Jews, and Italians he studied. Yet a sizable proportion of Irish Americans are total abstainers, which, as Vaillant suggested, reflects the Irish cultural view that there is no middle ground concerning alcohol. One is either a drinker (alcohol dependent) or a total abstainer.

Culture, more than genes, seems to drive the patterns of the use and abuse of alcohol. Consider the Oriental genetic heritage of Native Americans and Chinese Americans. Both groups are subject to a biological constitution in which their body metabolism has an exaggerated reaction to alcohol (Peele, 1984). Yet Native Americans have a very high rate of alcoholism, while Chinese Americans have an unusually low rate.

Matt McGue and others (1992), in a study of 356 pairs of identical and fraternal twins, report that family influences play a dominant role in drinking behavior. Genetic factors were found to play a minimal role in alcoholism in women of all ages and in men whose alcoholism appeared after adolescence. Biological factors were found to play the dominant role in males who became alcoholics early during adolescence. Thus, family influence, through which the culture is passed to future generations, appears to carry more weight than genetic influence in shaping drinking behavior.

It is well known that alcoholism has been prevalent throughout the republics that once formed the Soviet Union. In this case, cultural, economic, and political conditions may have been more powerful factors than genetics. Boris Segal (1990), a Russian psychiatrist who emigrated to the United States in 1973 at age 47, published a comparative study on alcoholism in the former Soviet Union and the United States. Segal reports that in the 1980s Soviet citizens drank two or three times more alcohol than Americans and spent five times as much money to buy it. The most shocking statistic revealed was that the Soviet death rate from acute alcohol intoxication was 278 times higher than that in the United States.

There are other cultural differences in the use of alcohol within the diverse population of the United States. Americans began the decade of the 1990s drinking less alcohol and drinking it less often than in the 1980s. According to a Gallup poll, 43 percent of Americans are total abstainers, and 57 percent define themselves as drinkers (Gallup & Newport, 1990). The poll further revealed that more men (67%) than women (51%) drink; considerably more white Americans (60%) drink than African Americans (42%); and college graduates (68%) drink more than high school graduates (57%).

In some cultures, alcohol is used in moderation within the family, but excessive use is strongly censured through social norms.

Table 4.3

Behavioral Effects Associated with Different Blood-Alcohol Levels

Blood-Alcohol Level	Behavioral Effects
.05	Altertness is lowered, judgment is impaired, inhibitions are lowered, and the user relaxes and feels good.
.10	Reaction is slowed, motor functions are impaired, and the user exercises less caution.
.15	Reaction time is slowed markedly; the user may stagger, slur speech, and act impulsively.
.20	Perceptual and motor capabilities are markedly depressed; the user shows obvious intoxication.
.25	Motor functions and sensory perceptions are severely distorted. The user may see double and fall asleep.
.30	The user is conscious but in a stupor, not able to comprehend events in the environment.
.35	The user is completely anesthetized.
.40–.80	Loss of consciousness Respiration and heartbeat stop Death (Blood level of .40 causes death for 50% of population; by .80 for the rest)

Barbiturates: Sedatives That Can Kill in Overdose Barbiturates depress the central nervous system and, depending on the dose, can act as a sedative or a sleeping pill. People who abuse barbiturates become drowsy and confused, their thinking and judgment suffer, and their coordination and reflexes are affected (Henningfield & Ator, 1986). Barbiturates can kill if taken in overdose, and a lethal dose can be as little as only three times the prescribed dose.

The Minor Tranquilizers: Prescribed by the Millions The popular **minor tranquilizers**, the benzodiazepines, came on the scene in the early 1960s and are sold under the brand names of Valium, Librium, and Dalmane, and more recently, Xanax (also used as an antidepressant). About 90 million prescriptions for minor tranquilizers are filled each year. Benzodiazepines are prescribed for a number of medical and psychological disorders and are considered to be generally effective and safe (Cole & Chiarello, 1990). They are rarely used recreationally (Woods et al., 1987). Alcohol and benzodiazepines, when taken together, are a potentially hazardous combination that can be fatal.

Question: What are the general effects of narcotics, and what are several drugs in this category?

Narcotics: Drugs from the Opium Poppy The word *narcotic* comes from a Greek word meaning "stupor." **Narcotics** produce both a pain-relieving and a calming effect. All narcotics originate from opium, a dark, gummy substance derived from the opium poppy. Opium affects mainly the brain and the bowel. It paralyzes the intestinal muscles, which is why it is used medically to treat diarrhea. If you have ever taken paregoric, you have had a little tincture of

barbiturates: A class of CNS depressants used as sedatives, sleeping pills, and anesthesia; addictive, and in overdose can cause coma or death.

tranquilizer (minor): A central nervous system depressant that calms the user (examples: Valium, Librium, Dalmane, Xanax).

narcotics: Derived from the opium poppy, a class of depressant drugs that have pain-relieving and calming effects.

WORLD OF PSYCHOLOGY: APPLICATIONS

Drugs in the Workplace

"This Bud's for you," says an Anheuser Busch commercial, but not if you are a brewery worker on the job—at least not any longer. Brewery workers used to take "beer breaks" during the working day, but the company ended that practice many years ago, presumably to improve quality control. A flat-tasting barrel of beer or a few improperly capped bottles, although costly to the company, hardly pose a major threat to society.

Are there cases in which drugs in the workplace can affect the quality and safety of products we buy, and even place our lives in jeopardy? Yes, according to many experts who find drugs in the workplace to be a major problem in the United States. Not only is 5 to 10 percent of our work force suffering from alcoholism, but 3 to 7 percent are using some type of illicit drug daily (Quale, 1983). According to estimates by the National Institute on Drug Abuse (NIDA), of those people entering the work force, almost two-thirds have used illegal drugs at some time, and 44 percent have used them within the past year (O'Keefe, 1987, p. 34). About 16 percent of the federal work force use illicit drugs regularly (Holden, 1987).

It is well known that professional baseball, football, and basketball players have used drugs on the job. But these are games, and the player-users are not a danger to the fans. Less well known are the drug abusers who hold positions in which they are responsible for the safety and the very lives of large numbers of people.

We do not know how high the three pilots' blood alcohol levels were in our opening story. But we do know that only a small amount of alcohol in a pilot's bloodstream is enough to put passengers at risk. In flight simulation tests, pilots with .075, .050, and .025 blood alcohol levels (all below the level of legal intoxication of .10 in most states) were tested for errors in planning and performance, errors in procedures, and failures in vigilance. The higher the blood-alcohol level, the more errors the pilots committed, but "serious errors increased significantly even at the lowest alcohol level studied, .025%" (Billings et al., 1991, p. 233).

Speaking of small amounts, how would one joint of marijuana affect a pilot's performance? In one study, 10 experienced pilots smoked one marijuana cigarette containing an average social dose. They had been tested on a number of maneuvers on a flight simulator before using the drug. They were then tested again—1, 4, and 24 hours later. Performance at all three times was affected. One hour after smoking marijuana, the pilots would have landed the plane an average of 32 feet from the centerline of the runway, and 24 feet from the centerline 24 hours later. Other maneuvers were affected also, but the landings could have

been disastrous considering that "some small airports have runways that are only 20 feet across" (Yesavage & Leirer, 1985).

In a later study Leirer and others (1991) found that seven out of nine pilots who smoked one marijuana cigarette (a moderate social dose) showed some impairment when tested 24 hours later. Only one of the pilots was aware of the drug's effect on his performance.

A survey of almost 600 medical students at 13 medical schools revealed that 36 percent had at some time used cocaine, 17 percent had used cocaine in the past year, and 6 percent in the previous 30 days. But even more significant is the fact that about 18 percent of the students "indicated that they probably would be using cocaine in some fashion in 5 years" (Conrad et al., 1989, p. 383). Another survey of practicing physicians and medical students revealed that 10 percent used illicit drugs recreationally (primarily marijuana and cocaine), and that 3 percent of the doctors and 5 percent of the medical students admitted drug dependence (McAuliffe et al., 1986).

For years Andrew Weil, a medical doctor and Harvard graduate, has made the point that virtually everyone uses drugs—if not marijuana, then cigarettes, and if not heroin or LSD, then chocolate or coffee. This is certainly true, but there are vast differences among these drugs. Weil claims that "there are no good or bad drugs; there are only good and bad relationships with drugs" (Weil & Rosen, 1983, p. 27). But if you were flying at 30,000 feet, would you prefer that your pilot smoke marijuana or tobacco? Would you feel safer if your air traffic controller had a "good relationship" with chocolate or with cocaine?

Drug use on the job poses a serious threat to public safety.

Table 4.4

The Effects and Withdrawal Symptoms of Various Psychoactive Drugs

Psychoactive Drug	Effects	Withdrawal Symptoms
Stimulants		
Tobacco (Nicotine)	Ranges from alertness to calmness; lowers appetite for carbohydrates; increases pulse rate and other metabolic processes.	Irritability, anxiety, increased appetite
Caffeine	Produces wakefulness and alertness; increases metabolism but slows reaction time.	Headache, depression
Amphetamines	Increased metabolism and alertness; elevated mood, wakefulness, suppressed appetite.	Fatigue, increased appetite, depression, long periods of sleep, irritability
Cocaine	Euphoric mood, energy boost, feeling of excitement, suppressed appetite.	Depression, fatigue, increased appetite, long periods of sleep, irritability
Depressants		
Alcohol	First few drinks stimulate and enliven while lowering anxiety and inhibitions; higher doses have a sedative effect, slowing reaction time, impairing motor control and perceptual ability.	Tremors, nausea, sweating, depression, weakness, irritability, and in some cases, hallucinations
Tranquilizers (e.g., Valium, Xanax)	Lowers anxiety, has calming and sedative effect, decreases muscular tension.	Restlessness, anxiety, irritability, muscle tension, difficulty sleeping
Barbiturates (e.g., phenobarbital)	Promotes sleep, has calming and sedative effect, decreases muscular tension, impairs coordination and reflexes.	Sleeplessness, anxiety; sudden withdrawal can cause seizures, cardiovascular collapse, and death
Narcotics		
Opium, Morphine, Heroin	Produces euphoria, relaxes muscles, suppresses pain, causes constipation.	Anxiety, restlessness, diarrhea, nausea, muscle spasms, chills and sweating, runny nose
Hallucinogens		
Marijuana	Most effects depend on mood and setting; generally produces euphoria, relaxation; affects ability to store new memories.	Anxiety, difficulty sleeping, decreased appetite, hyperactivity
LSD, Mescaline, Psilocybin	Produces excited exhilaration, hallucinations; experiences perceived as insightful and profound.	
PCP	Increases blood pressure and heart rate, slows reflexes, alters perceptions; may cause bizarre and violent behavior.	

opium. Because opium suppresses the cough center, it is used in some cough medicines. Both morphine and codeine, two drugs prescribed for pain, are natural constituents of opium.

A highly addictive narcotic derived from morphine is **heroin**. From 500,000 to 750,000 people in the United States are addicted to heroin. Heroin addicts describe a sudden "rush," or euphoria that is followed by drowsiness, inactivity, and impaired concentration (American Psychiatric Association, 1987). Withdrawal symptoms begin about 10 hours later, when the addict becomes physically sick. Nausea, diarrhea, depression, stomach cramps, hot and cold flashes, and pain grow worse and worse until they become intolerable . . . unless the person gets another fix.

Table 4.4 provides a summary of the effects and withdrawal symptoms of the major psychoactive drugs.

Designer Drugs: Laboratory Creations

You may have heard of designer clothes and designer perfume; now there are **designer drugs**—test-tube creations that mimic the effects of illicit substances. Designer drugs are not only easy to make, they are cheap as well—some costing as little as $10 a dose. But the laboratories that make these drugs have no stringent quality controls. Designer drugs have left their users with permanent brain damage or paralysis, and some have caused death.

The worst part of designer drugs is that they are completely legal until the Drug Enforcement Agency discovers each drug and classifies it as a controlled substance. But the chemists are usually one step ahead of the DEA. By making slight alterations in the molecular structure of a substance, they have a new drug (Shafer, 1985).

---

heroin: A highly addictive, partly synthetic narcotic derived from morphine.

designer drugs: Synthetic drugs that mimic the effects of illicit drugs and are potent, relatively inexpensive, and potentially very dangerous.

Memory Check 4.6

1. Drugs that decrease activity in the central nervous system are classified as _____.

2. Depending on the dose, alcohol and barbiturates can relax the user or cause coma or death. (true/false)

3. Which of these is not a narcotic?

   a. codeine   c. morphine
   b. heroin   d. Valium

4. Narcotics have (pain-relieving, energizing) effects.

Answers: 1. depressants 2. true 3. d 4. pain-relieving

Thinking Critically _____

Evaluation

The famous sleep researcher Wilse Webb wrote a book, *Sleep, the Gentle Tyrant.* From what you have learned about sleep, explain why this is or is not a fitting title.

Point/Counterpoint

You hear much debate about the pros and cons of legalizing drugs. Present the most convincing argument possible to support each of these positions:

a. Illicit drugs should be legalized.
b. Illicit drugs should not be legalized.

Psychology in Your Life

You have been asked to make a presentation to seventh and eighth graders about the dangers of drugs. What are the most persuasive general arguments you could give to convince them not to get involved with drugs? What are some convincing, specific arguments against using each of these drugs: alcohol, marijuana, cigarettes, and cocaine?

Chapter Summary and Review _____

Circadian Rhythms: Our 24-Hour Highs and Lows

What is a circadian rhythm, and which rhythms are most relevant to the study of sleep?

A circadian rhythm is the regular fluctuation in certain body functions from a high point to a low point within a 24-hour period. Two rhythms that are relevant to sleep are the sleep/wakefulness cycle and body temperature.

What are some problems experienced by employees who work rotating shifts?

People working rotating shifts experience a disruption in their circadian rhythms that causes sleep difficulties, digestive problems, and lowered energy, efficiency, and safety when working during subjective night.

Key Terms

consciousness (p. 114)
altered states of consciousness (p. 114)
circadian rhythm (p. 115)

Sleep: That Mysterious One-Third of Our Lives

How does a sleeper react physically during NREM sleep?

During NREM sleep, heart rate and respiration are slow and regular, blood pressure and brain activity are at a 24-hour low point, and there are no rapid eye movements.

How does the body respond physically during REM sleep?

During REM sleep, the large muscles of the body are paralyzed, respiration and heart rates are fast and irregular, brain activity increases, and the sleeper has rapid eye movements and vivid dreams.

What is the progression of NREM stages and REM sleep that a person follows in a typical night of sleep?

During a typical night, a person sleeps in sleep cycles, each lasting about 90 minutes. The first sleep cycle contains stages 1, 2, 3, 4, and REM sleep; the second contains Stages 2, 3, 4, and REM sleep. In the remaining sleep cycles, the sleeper alternates between Stage 2 and REM sleep, with each sleep cycle having progressively longer REM periods.

How do sleep patterns change over the life span?

Infants and young children have the longest sleep time and the largest percentage of REM and deep sleep. Children from age 6 to puberty sleep best. The elderly typically have shorter total sleep time, many awakenings, and a virtual lack of deep sleep.

What factors influence our sleep needs?

Factors that influence our sleep needs are heredity, the amount of stress in our lives, and our emotional state.

How do REM and NREM dreams differ?

REM dreams have a dreamlike, storylike quality and are more vivid, visual, emotional, and bizarre than the more thoughtlike NREM dreams.

In general, what have researchers found regarding the content of dreams?

Dreams usually reflect the dreamer's preoccupations in waking life. They tend to have commonplace settings, to be more unpleasant than pleasant, and to be less emotional and bizarre than generally believed.

Key Terms

NREM sleep (p. 118)
REM sleep (p. 118)
sleep cycle (p. 119)
delta wave (p. 120)
Stage 4 sleep (p. 120)
REM rebound (p. 123)
REM dreams (p. 123)

Sleep Disturbances and Disorders

What are some common characteristics of sleepwalking and night terrors?

Somnambulism (sleepwalking) and night terrors occur when there is a partial arousal from deep sleep and the person does not come to full consciousness. Episodes are rarely recalled. These disorders typically are found in children and are outgrown by adolescence.

What is a night terror?

A night terror is a sleep disturbance in which a child partially awakens from Stage 4 sleep with a scream, dazed and groggy in a panic state.

What are the major symptoms of narcolepsy?

Narcolepsy is a serious sleep disorder characterized by excessive daytime sleepiness and sudden attacks of REM sleep.

What is sleep apnea?

Sleep apnea is a serious sleep disorder in which breathing stops during sleep and the person must awaken briefly to breathe. Its major symptoms are excessive daytime sleepiness and loud snoring.

What is insomnia?

Chronic insomnia can result from barbiturates or alcohol, psychiatric or physical disorders, a biological clock that is not synchronized with society's timetable, or conditioned arousal stemming from associating the bed with the frustration of poor sleep.

Key Terms

somnambulism (p. 126)
night terror (p. 126)
anxiety nightmare (p. 127)
narcolepsy (p. 128)
sleep apnea (p. 129)

Altering Consciousness through Concentration and Suggestion

What is the purpose of meditation?

The purpose of meditation is to increase relaxation, to clear the mind of problems and distracting thoughts, and for some, to expand consciousness.

What is hypnosis, and when is it most useful?

Hypnosis, which has been used most successfully for the control of pain, is a trancelike state of consciousness characterized by focused attention, heightened suggestibility, and diminished response to external stimuli.

Key Terms

meditation (p. 131)
hypnosis (p. 133)

Altered States of Consciousness and Psychoactive Drugs

What is the difference between physical and psychological dependence?

With physical dependence, the user develops a drug tolerance so that larger and larger doses are needed to get the same effect. Withdrawal symptoms appear when the drug is discontinued and disappear when the drug is taken again. Psychological dependence involves an intense craving for the drug.

How do stimulants affect the user?

Stimulants speed up activity in the central nervous system, suppress appetite, and make a person feel more awake, alert, and more energetic.

What effects do amphetamines have on the user?

Amphetamines increase arousal, relieve fatigue, and suppress the appetite, but with continued use they result in exhaustion, depression, and agitation.

How does cocaine affect the user?

Cocaine, a stimulant, causes a feeling of euphoria and is highly addictive. Heavy use can damage the nose and throat (if snorted) and can cause heart damage, seizures, and even heart attacks.

What are the main effects of hallucinogens, and what are three psychoactive drugs classified as hallucinogens?

Hallucinogens—LSD, PCP, and marijuana—can alter perception and mood and cause hallucinations.

What are some harmful effects associated with heavy marijuana use?

There is some evidence that heavy marijuana use can cause brain and lung damage; chromosome breakage; loss of motivation; impotence, lowered testosterone level and sperm count; irregular menstrual cycles and lower-birth-weight babies.

What are some of the effects of depressants, and what drugs comprise this category?

Depressants decrease activity in the central nervous system, slow down body functions, and reduce sensitivity to outside stimulation. Depressants include sedative-hypnotics (alcohol, barbiturates, and minor tranquilizers) and narcotics (opiates).

What are the general effects of narcotics, and what are several drugs in this category?

Narcotics, which include opium, codeine, morphine, and heroin, have both pain-relieving and calming effects.

Key Terms

psychoactive drug (p. 135)
physical dependence (p. 136)
drug tolerance (p. 136)
withdrawal symptoms (p. 136)
psychological dependence (p. 136)
stimulants (p. 137)
amphetamines (p. 137)
cocaine (p. 138)
crack (p. 138)

hallucinogens (p. 139)
LSD (p. 139)
PCP (p. 139)
marijuana (p. 139)
depressants (p. 141)
barbiturates (p. 143)
minor tranquilizers (p. 143)
narcotics (p. 143)
heroin (p. 145)
designer drugs (p. 146)

5

Learning

Robert Wilson (not his real name) had it all. Born in 1960, he grew to be superior in every way—he was handsome, exceptionally bright and talented, and had an unusually charming personality. Robert completed his MBA at Harvard in 1985 when he was 25 years old, and he promptly joined a leading brokerage firm. He was ambitious and did little more than work for 2 years. Then in 1987 a senior executive with the firm who was 10 years older than Robert became his mentor and took him under his wing. Robert and his mentor were virtually inseparable at work and at play, and Robert was now on a fast track to the top.

At a party the mentor arranged, he and Robert, with some other executives, spent a long weekend with several young women. Robert was introduced to cocaine. He watched with fascination as his mentor and one of the young women took some white powder from a plastic bag and, with a razor blade, arranged it in neat lines on a mirror. They each snorted a couple of lines and seemed to enjoy it immensely.

"The first time I used cocaine, the feeling was great," said Robert. "A few days later, I wanted to do it again, and within 2 years I didn't want to do anything else. The craving was intense. The euphoria, the high, was something I could never get out of my mind. But when the high was over, I felt miserable. I would do anything to escape that feeling."

Within a short time cocaine took everything Robert had—his job, his friends, all his possessions, his self-esteem, his ambition, and finally his freedom. In 1991 he was convicted as a drug dealer and now sits in prison, far removed from the successful life he had planned.

WHAT DOES COCAINE ADDICTION have to do with learning? Our opening story provides examples of the three basic types of learning that psychologists study—classical conditioning, operant conditioning, and observational learning. In classical conditioning, an association is learned between one *stimulus* and another. In Robert's case, certain environmental cues (parties, beautiful people, a good time, drug paraphernalia) became associated with cocaine. In operant conditioning, an association is formed between a behavior and its consequences—the snorting of cocaine and the feeling of euphoria that follows. In observational learning, we learn by observing the behavior of others and then may imitate that behavior. Observational learning occurred when Robert began to use cocaine after watching his mentor, his model, use it.

These three kinds of learning are all-powerful forces that influence human thought and behavior for good or for ill. Not only were these kinds of learning involved in initiating and maintaining Robert's addiction, but also the same principles of learning can help people break addictions and improve their lives, as you will learn.

Learning may be defined as a relatively permanent change in behavior, capability, or attitude that is acquired through experience and cannot be attributed to illness, injury, or maturation. Several parts of this definition warrant further explanation. First, defining learning as a "relatively permanent change" excludes temporary changes in our behavior or attitudes that could result from illness, fatigue, or fluctuations in mood. Second, by referring to changes that are "acquired through experience," we exclude some relatively permanent, readily observable changes in behavior that occur as a result of brain injuries or certain diseases. Also, there are observable changes as we grow and mature that have nothing to do with learning. For example, a young male at puberty does not *learn* to speak in a deeper voice, but his voice changes to a lower pitch as a result of maturation.

stimulus (STIM-yu-lus): Any event or object in the environment to which an organism responds.

learning: A relatively permanent change in behavior, capability, or attitude that is acquired through experience and cannot be attributed to illness, injury, or maturation.

We cannot observe learning directly but must infer whether it has occurred. We draw our inferences from changes in observable behavior or changes in measurable capabilities and attitudes. Certainly much learning occurs that we are not able to observe or measure. As a student, you surely have experienced occasions when you had learned much more than your test scores reflected. Finally, learning does not always result in a change in behavior or performance. Sometimes we learn or acquire a capability that we may not demonstrate until we are motivated to do so.

Learning is one of the most important topics in the field of psychology, and available evidence suggests that we learn through many different avenues. This chapter explores the three basic forms of learning—classical conditioning, operant conditioning, and observational learning.

Classical Conditioning

Classical conditioning is one of the simplest forms of learning, yet it has a powerful effect on our attitudes, likes and dislikes, and emotional responses. We have all learned to respond in specific ways to a variety of words and symbols. Adolf Hitler, Saddam Hussein, the IRS, Santa Claus, and the American flag are just sounds and symbols, but they tend to evoke strong emotional responses because of their associations.

When you meet someone who has the same name as another person you like very much, the name may carry such a positive association that you like the new person from the start. The explanation for these feelings is simple—learning by association. We associate one thing with another—a positive or a negative attitude with a name, a particular gesture, a style of dress, or a manner of speaking. When we hear the name or observe the gesture, that single stimulus calls to mind the positive or negative association.

Our lives are profoundly influenced by the associations we learn through classical conditioning. We will now explore the work of Ivan Pavlov, whose research on the conditioned reflex in dogs revealed much of what we know about the principles of classical conditioning (sometimes referred to as respondent or Pavlovian conditioning).

Pavlov and Classical Conditioning

Question: What was Pavlov's major contribution to psychology?

Ivan Pavlov (1849–1936) organized and directed research in physiology at the Institute of Experimental Medicine in St. Petersburg, Russia, from 1891 until his death 45 years later. There he conducted his classic experiments on the physiology of digestion, which won him a Nobel Prize in 1904. He was the first Russian to be so honored. Pavlov's study of the conditioned reflex in dogs brought him fame, and he pursued this research from about 1898 until the end of his career. His book *Conditioned Reflexes* is one of the classic works in the field of psychology.

As with so many other important scientific discoveries, Pavlov's contribution to psychology came about quite by accident. In order to conduct his study of the salivary response, Pavlov made a small incision in the side of each experimental dog's mouth. Then he attached a tube so that the flow of saliva could be diverted from inside the animal's mouth, through the tube, and into a container, where the saliva was collected and measured.

Pavlov's purpose was to collect the saliva that the dogs would secrete naturally in response to food placed inside the mouth. But he noticed that, in many

classical conditioning: A process through which a response previously made only to a specific stimulus is made to another stimulus that has been paired repeatedly with the original stimulus.

Ivan Pavlov (1849–1936) earned fame by studying the conditioned reflex of dogs at his laboratory in St. Petersburg, Russia.

cases, the dogs would begin to salivate even before the food was presented. Pavlov observed drops of saliva collecting in the container when the dogs heard the footsteps of the laboratory assistants coming to feed them. He observed saliva collecting when the dogs only heard their dishes rattling, when they saw the person who fed them, and at the mere sight of their food. How could an involuntary response such as salivation come to be associated with the sights and sounds accompanying the act of feeding? Pavlov spent the rest of his life studying this question, and the type of learning that he studied is known today as classical conditioning.

Pavlov's Laboratory: Leaving Nothing to Chance Pavlov was a meticulous researcher; he wanted an experimental environment in which he could carefully control all the factors that could affect the dogs during the experiments. To accomplish this, Pavlov planned and built a laboratory at the Institute of Experimental Medicine in St. Petersburg. Note how advanced the laboratory was, considering that it was built nearly 100 years ago.

> The windows were covered with extra thick sheets of glass; each room had double steel doors which sealed hermetically when closed; and the steel girders which supported the floors were embedded in sand. A deep moat filled with straw encircled the building. Thus, vibration, noise, temperature extremes, odors, even drafts were eliminated. Nothing could influence the animals except the conditioning stimuli to which they were exposed. (Schultz, 1975, pp. 187–188)

The dogs were isolated inside soundproof cubicles and placed in harnesses to restrain their movements. From an adjoining cubicle, the experimenter observed the dogs through a one-way mirror. By remote control, food and other stimuli could be presented and the flow of saliva could be measured. It was in this setting that Pavlov and his colleagues conducted their studies (see Figure 5.1). What did they learn?

The Elements and Processes in Classical Conditioning

The Reflex: We Can't Help It   A *reflex* is an involuntary response to a particular stimulus. Two examples are the eyeblink response to a puff of air, and salivation to food placed in the mouth. There are two kinds of reflexes—conditioned and unconditioned. Think of the term *conditioned* as meaning "learned" and the term *unconditioned* as meaning "unlearned." Salivation in response to food is called an unconditioned reflex because this behavior is an inborn, automatic, unlearned response to a particular stimulus. Unconditioned reflexes are built into the nervous system.

When Pavlov noticed that his dogs would salivate at the sight of food or the sound of rattling dishes, he realized that this salivation reflex was the result of learning. He called these learned involuntary responses, **conditioned reflexes**.

Question: How is classical conditioning accomplished?

The Conditioned and Unconditioned Stimulus and Response   Pavlov (1927) continued to investigate the circumstances under which a conditioned reflex is formed. He used tones, bells, buzzers, lights, geometric shapes, electric shocks, and metronomes in his conditioning experiments. In a typical experiment, food powder was placed in the dog's mouth, causing salivation. Dogs do not have to be conditioned to salivate to food, so we would say that salivation is an unlearned or **unconditioned response** (UR). Any stimulus, such as food, that without learning will automatically elicit, or bring forth, an unconditioned response is called an **unconditioned stimulus** (US).

Remember, a reflex is made up of both a stimulus and a response. Following is a list of some common unconditioned reflexes, showing their two components— the unconditioned stimulus and the unconditioned response.

reflex: An involuntary response to a particular stimulus, like the eyeblink to a puff of air, or salivation to food placed in the mouth.

conditioned reflex: A learned reflex rather than a naturally occurring one.

unconditioned response (UR):   A response that is invariably elicited by the unconditioned stimulus without prior learning.

unconditioned stimulus (US):   A stimulus that elicits a specific response without prior learning.

Unconditioned Reflexes

Unconditioned Stimulus (US)	Unconditioned Response (UR)
food	salivation
onion juice	tears
heat	sweating
loud noise	startle
light in eye	contraction of pupil
puff of air in eye	eyeblink
touching hot stove	hand withdrawal

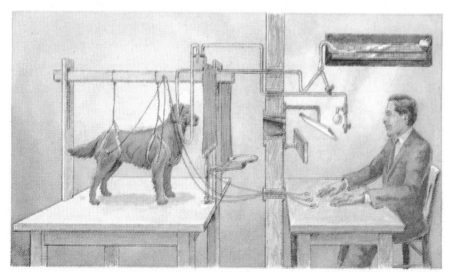

Figure 5.1

The Experimental Apparatus Used in Pavlov's Classical Conditioning Studies

In Pavlov's classical conditioning studies, the dog was restrained in a harness in the cubicle and isolated from all distractions. An experimenter observed the dog through a one-way mirror and, by remote control, presented the dog with food and other conditioning stimuli. A tube carried the saliva from the dog's mouth to a container where it was measured.

conditioned stimulus (CS): A neutral stimulus that, after repeated pairing with an unconditioned stimulus, becomes associated with it and elicits a conditioned response.

conditioned response (CR): That response that comes to be elicited by a conditioned stimulus as a result of its repeated pairing with an unconditioned stimulus.

Pavlov demonstrated that he could condition dogs to salivate to a variety of stimuli that had never before been associated with food. During the conditioning or acquisition process, a neutral stimulus such as a musical tone was presented shortly before placing food powder in the dog's mouth. The food powder would cause the dog to salivate. After pairing the tone and food many times, usually 20 or more, he found that the tone alone would elicit, or bring forth, salivation (Pavlov, 1927, p. 385). Because dogs do not naturally salivate in response to musical tones, Pavlov concluded that this salivation was a learned response. Pavlov called the tone the learned or **conditioned stimulus** (CS), and he called salivation to the tone the learned or **conditioned response** (CR). (See Figure 5.2.)

In a modern view of classical conditioning, the conditioned stimulus can be thought of as a signal that the unconditioned stimulus will follow (Schreurs, 1989). In Pavlov's experiment the tone became a signal that food would follow shortly. So, the signal (CS) gives advance warning, and a person or animal is prepared with the proper response (CR) even before the unconditioned stimulus arrives.

Figure 5.2 Classically Conditioning a Salivation Response A neutral stimulus (a tone) elicits no salivation until it is repeatedly paired with the unconditioned stimulus (food). After many pairings, the neutral stimulus (now called conditioned stimulus) alone produces salivation. Classical conditioning has occurred.

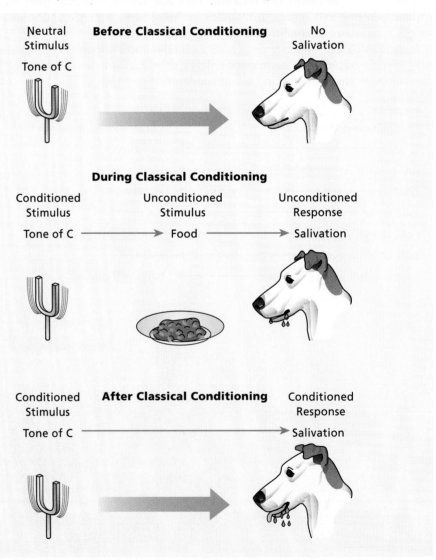

Question: How does extinction occur in classical conditioning?

Extinction and Spontaneous Recovery: Gone but Not Forgotten After conditioning an animal to salivate to a tone, what would happen if you continued to sound the tone but no longer paired it with food? Pavlov found that salivation to the tone without the food would become weaker and weaker and then finally disappear altogether—a process known as **extinction**.

By extinction, we do not mean that the conditioned response has been completely erased or forgotten. Rather, the animal learns that the tone is no longer a signal that food will follow shortly, and the old conditioned response is gradually inhibited or suppressed. Animals are better able to adapt to a changing environment if they have the ability to discard conditioned responses that are no longer useful or needed.

How did Pavlov determine whether the conditioned response, once extinguished, had been inhibited rather than permanently erased or forgotten? If, after the response had been extinguished, the dog was allowed to rest and was then brought back to the laboratory, Pavlov found that the dog would again salivate to the tone. He called this recurrence **spontaneous recovery**. The spontaneously recovered response, however, was weaker and shorter in duration than the original conditioned response. Figure 5.3 illustrates the processes of extinction and spontaneous recovery.

Question: What is generalization?

Generalization: Responding to Similarities Assume that you have conditioned a dog to salivate when it hears the tone middle C on the piano. If in your experiment, you accidentally played the tone D or E, would that note produce salivation? Or would the dog not salivate to this slightly different tone? Pavlov found that a tone similar to the original conditioned stimulus will produce the conditioned response, a phenomenon called **generalization**. If you were as careful a researcher as Pavlov, you would observe that as you move farther away from the original tone, salivation would decrease. Eventually the tone would be so different that the dog would not salivate at all (see Figure 5.4).

It is easy to see how generalization might be of value in our everyday experience. Suppose that as a child you had been bitten by a large, gray German shepherd. You would not need to see exactly the same dog or another of the same breed coming toward you in the future in order to experience fear. Your original fear would probably generalize to all large dogs of any description. Because of generalization we do not need to learn a conditioned response to every stimulus that may differ only slightly from the original one. Rather, we

extinction: The weakening and often eventual disappearance of a learned response (in classical conditioning, the conditioned response is weakened by repeated presentation of the conditioned stimulus without the unconditioned stimulus).

spontaneous recovery: The reappearance of an extinguished response (in a weaker form) when an organism is exposed to the original conditioning stimulus following a rest period.

generalization: In classical conditioning, the tendency to make a conditioned response to a stimulus similar to the original conditioned stimulus; in operant conditioning, the tendency to make the learned response to a stimulus similar to the one for which it was originally reinforced.

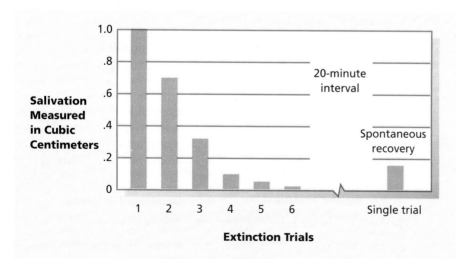

Extinction Trials

Figure 5.3

Extinction of a Classically Conditioned Response

When a classically conditioned stimulus (the tone) was presented in a series of trials without the unconditioned stimulus (the food), Pavlov's dogs salivated less and less until there was virtually no salivation. But after a 20-minute rest, with one sound of the tone the conditioned response would reappear in a weakened form (producing only a small amount of salivation), a phenomenon Pavlov called spontaneous recovery. (Data from Pavlov, 1927, p. 58.)

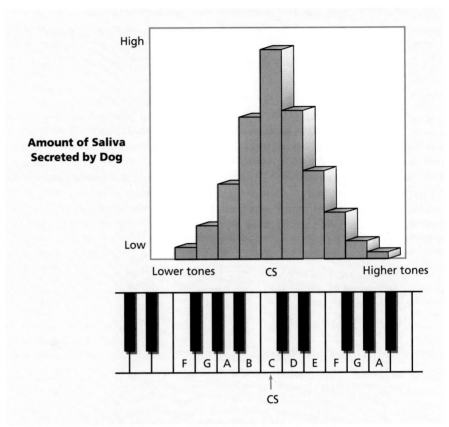

Figure 5.4   Generalization in Classical Conditioning   Due to the phenomenon of generalization, a dog conditioned to salivate to middle C on the piano also salivates to similar tones—but less and less so as the tone moves away from middle C.

learn to approach or avoid a range of stimuli similar to the one that produced the original conditioned response.

Question: What is discrimination in classical conditioning?

Discrimination: Learning That They're Not All Alike   Not only must we be able to generalize, we must also learn to distinguish between stimuli that may be very similar. Using the previous example of a dog being conditioned to a musical tone, we can trace the process of **discrimination**.

Step 1:   The dog is conditioned to tone C (assume middle C).
Step 2:   Generalization occurs, and the dog salivates to a range of musical tones above and below tone C. The dog salivates less and less as the note moves away from C.
Step 3:   The original tone C is repeatedly paired with food, but when neighboring tones are sounded, they are not followed with food. The dog is being conditioned to discriminate. Gradually, the salivation response to the neighboring tones is extinguished, while salivation to the original tone C is strengthened.

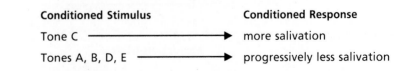

Conditioned Stimulus	Conditioned Response
Tone C ⟶	more salivation
Tones A, B, D, E ⟶	progressively less salivation

discrimination: The learned ability to distinguish between similar stimuli so that the conditioned response occurs only to the original conditioning stimulus but not to similar stimuli.

Step 4: Discrimination is achieved.

Conditioned Stimulus	Conditioned Response
Tone C ⟶	strengthened salivation response
Tones A, B, D, E ⟶	no salivation

Like generalization, discrimination has survival value. Discriminating between the odors of fresh and spoiled milk will spare you an upset stomach. Knowing the difference between a rattlesnake and a garter snake could save your life.

Memory Check 5.1

1. Classical conditioning was originally researched most extensively by _____ .

2. The dog's salivation in response to a musical tone was a(n) (conditioned, unconditioned) response.

3. The gradual weakening and disappearance of a conditioned response—when the conditioned stimulus is presented repeatedly without the unconditioned stimulus—is termed:

   a. generalization   c. extinction
   b. discrimination   d. spontaneous recovery

4. Juanita had an automobile accident on a bridge, and now she becomes very nervous whenever she has to cross any bridge. Which process accounts for this feeling?

   a. generalization   c. extinction
   b. discrimination   d. spontaneous recovery

5. Five-year-old Jesse was bitten by his neighbor's collie. He won't go near that dog but seems to have no fear of other dogs, even other collies. Which process accounts for his behavior?

   a. generalization   c. extinction
   b. discrimination   d. spontaneous recovery

Answers: 1. Ivan Pavlov 2. conditioned 3. c 4. a 5. b

John Watson, Little Albert, and Peter

Question: How did John B. Watson demonstrate that fear could be classically conditioned?

Little Albert and the Conditioned Fear Response: Learning to Fear John Watson believed that, in humans, all fears except those of loud noises and loss of

John B. Watson (1878–1958)

support are classically conditioned. In 1919 Watson and his laboratory assistant, Rosalie Rayner, conducted a now-famous study to prove that fear could be classically conditioned. The subject of the study, known as Little Albert, was a healthy and emotionally stable infant. When tested, he showed no fear except of the loud noise Watson made by striking a hammer against a steel bar near Albert's head. In this classic experiment, Watson tested whether 11-month-old Albert could be conditioned to fear a white rat by causing Albert to associate the rat with a loud noise.

In the laboratory, Rosalie presented Little Albert with a white rat. As Albert reached for the rat, Watson struck a steel bar with a hammer just behind Albert's head. This procedure was repeated, and Albert "jumped violently, fell forward and began to whimper" (Watson & Rayner, 1920, p. 4). A week later, Watson continued the experiment, pairing the rat with the loud noise five more times. Then at the sight of the white rat alone, Albert began to cry.

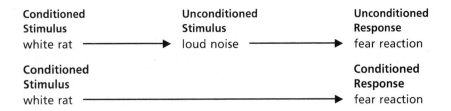

Conditioned Stimulus		**Unconditioned Stimulus**		**Unconditioned Response**
white rat	⟶	loud noise	⟶	fear reaction

Conditioned Stimulus		**Conditioned Response**
white rat	⟶	fear reaction

When Albert returned to the laboratory 5 days later, the fear had generalized to a rabbit and somewhat less to a dog, a seal coat, Watson's hair, and a Santa Claus mask. After 30 days Albert made his final visit to the laboratory, and at this time his fears remained, although they were somewhat less intense. Watson concluded that conditioned fears "persist and modify personality throughout life" (Watson & Rayner, 1920, p. 12).

Although Watson had formulated a procedure for removing conditioned fears, he apparently knew that Albert would be moving out of the city before the techniques could be tried on him. Some of Watson's ideas for removing fears were excellent, and they laid the groundwork for therapies that are used today. One method consisted of conditioning a new association between the feared object and a positive stimulus. In Albert's case, candy or other food could have been given just as the white rat was presented. Another procedure involved a modeling technique in which Albert could have observed other children playing happily with the white rat.

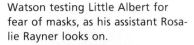

Watson testing Little Albert for fear of masks, as his assistant Rosalie Rayner looks on.

WORLD OF PSYCHOLOGY: PIONEERS

John B. Watson (1878–1958)

John B. Watson was born to a poor family on a farm near Greenville, South Carolina, in 1878. His mother was devoutly religious, while his father's three primary activities were said to be swearing, drinking, and chasing women. His father deserted the family when Watson was 13 years old, leaving him with a keen sense of loss. Watson did not see his father again for more than 30 years.

Although Watson was highly intelligent, he disliked school and was a poor student. He engaged in violent behavior and was arrested by the local authorities on two occasions. At age 15, however, Watson made a drastic change in his habits and his life. He managed to get accepted by Furman University, where he worked his way through college and became a conscientious and successful student. Watson completed his Ph.D. in psychology at the University of Chicago in 1903. Five years later he accepted a professorship at Johns Hopkins University, where he pursued a productive career.

Watson advocated a new approach to psychology, restricting its scope to the study of observable, measurable behavior. He wanted nothing to do with concepts like "mind" and "consciousness," which he claimed were neither measurable nor observable. His new school of psychology was appropriately named *behaviorism*, and its principles were set down in his works "Psychology as the Behaviorist Views It" (1913), *Psychology from the Standpoint of a Behaviorist* (1919), and *Behaviorism* (1925). Watson believed that environmental influences primarily determine human behavior.

Regrettably, Watson's academic career in psychology was cut short. When his wife discovered that he was having an affair with his laboratory assistant, Rosalie Rayner, the resulting divorce suit created a national scandal, forcing him to resign his university position in 1920.

In 1921 Watson married Rosalie Rayner and began a new career in advertising. He was so successful that by 1930 he was making nearly $70,000 a year—a tremendous salary for the time. Watson revolutionized advertising and probably originated testimonial advertising by glamorous people (Cohen, 1979). The image of purity that Watson created for Johnson's Baby Powder more than 60 years ago is still widely known today.

Even without an academic affiliation, Watson continued his research and writing on infants and children. With the publication of his *Psychological Care of the Infant and Child* (1928), he became the leading authority on child rearing. Opposed to permissive parenting, Watson developed a strict, objective, unemotional program for parents.

Watson initiated many important trends in psychology that continue today. He laid the groundwork for present-day behavior therapy techniques for removing fears, and he was a pioneer in the detailed study of infants and children. Through his research and writing, Watson freed psychology from its exclusively academic setting and made it a subject of great interest to the general public. He wrote articles for popular magazines such as *McCall's*, *Cosmopolitan*, *Collier's*, *Harper's*, and *The Nation*. One of the most colorful and influential figures in the field of psychology, John B. Watson died in 1958.

It is difficult to escape the conclusion that Watson, in his study of the conditioned fear response, showed a disregard for the welfare of Little Albert. Fortunately, the American Psychological Association (APA) now has strict ethical standards for the use of human participants and animal subjects in research experiments. The APA would not sanction such an experiment as Watson's today.

Removing Peter's Fears: The Triumph of Cookies and Patience Some 3 years passed after Watson's experiment with Little Albert. Then Watson and a colleague, Mary Cover Jones (1924), found 3-year-old Peter, who, like Albert, was afraid of white rats. He was also afraid of rabbits, a fur coat, feathers, cotton, and a fur rug. Peter's fear of the rabbit was his strongest fear, and this became the target of Watson's fear-removal techniques.

Peter was brought into the laboratory and "seated in a high chair and given food which he liked" (Jones, 1924, p. 312). A white rabbit in a wire cage was brought into the room but kept far enough away from Peter so it would not upset him. Over the course of 38 therapy sessions, the rabbit was brought closer

behaviorism: The school of psychology founded by John B. Watson that views observable, measurable behavior as the appropriate subject matter for psychology and emphasizes the key role of environment as a determinant of behavior.

and closer to Peter, who continued to enjoy his cookies. Occasionally some of Peter's friends were brought into the laboratory to play with the rabbit at a safe distance from Peter so that he could see firsthand that the rabbit did no harm. Toward the end of Peter's therapy, the rabbit was taken out of the cage and eventually put in Peter's lap. By the final session, Peter had grown fond of the rabbit. Moreover, he had lost all fear of the fur coat, cotton, and feathers, and he could tolerate the white rats and the fur rug.

So far we have considered classical conditioning primarily in relation to Pavlov's dogs and Watson's human subjects. How does classical conditioning occur in our everyday lives?

Classical Conditioning in Everyday Life

Do certain songs have special meaning because they remind you of a current or past love? Do you find the scent of a certain perfume or after-shave pleasant or unpleasant because it reminds you of a particular person? Many of our associations are the result of classical conditioning. Classical conditioning occurs when neutral cues become associated with people, objects, or situations and develop the power to elicit the same feeling as the original stimulus.

When business people wine and dine customers, they are hoping that they and their product or service will elicit the same positive response as the pleasant setting and fine food. Advertisers want to classically condition us when they show products along with beautiful or handsome models or celebrities or in situations where people are enjoying themselves. The advertisers are relying on the probability that if the "neutral" product is associated with people, objects, or situations we particularly like, then in time the product will elicit a similarly positive response. Pavlov found that presenting the tone slightly before the food was the most efficient way to condition salivation. Television advertisements, too, are most effective when the products are presented *before* the beautiful people or situations are shown (van den Hout & Merckelbach, 1991).

You might want to see just how much the principles of classical conditioning are applied in advertising with the following *Try It!*

Try It!

Some commercials simply give information about a product or place of business. Others are designed to classically condition the viewer to form a positive association. One night while you are watching TV, keep a record of the commercials you see. What proportion rely on classical conditioning? What are the kinds of cues (people, objects, or situations) with which the products are to be associated? Are the products introduced slightly before, during, or after these cues?

Factors Influencing Classical Conditioning

Question: What are four factors that influence classical conditioning?

There are four major factors that affect the strength of a classically conditioned response and the length of time required for conditioning. (1) The first factor is *the number of pairings of the conditioned stimulus and the unconditioned stimulus*. The number of pairings required varies considerably, depending on the individual characteristics of the person or animal being conditioned. But a general principle to remember is that the greater the number of pairings, the stronger the conditioned response.

(2) The second factor affecting the strength and intensity of a conditioned response is the *intensity of the unconditioned stimulus*. If a conditioned stimulus

is paired with a very strong unconditioned stimulus, the conditioned response will be stronger and will be acquired more rapidly than if it is paired with a weaker unconditioned stimulus (Gormezano, 1984). Striking the steel bar with the hammer produced stronger and faster conditioning in Little Albert than if Watson had merely clapped his hands behind Albert's head.

(3) The third and, according to Robert Rescorla (1967, 1988), the most important factor in classical conditioning is *how reliably the conditioned stimulus predicts the unconditioned stimulus*. A smoke alarm that never goes off except in response to a fire will elicit more fear than one that occasionally gives false alarms. A tone that is *always* followed by food will elicit more salivation than one that is followed by food only some of the time.

(4) Finally *the temporal relationship between the conditioned stimulus and the unconditioned stimulus* is a critical factor in classical conditioning. Conditioning takes place fastest if the conditioned stimulus occurs shortly before the unconditioned stimulus. It takes place more slowly or not at all when the two stimuli occur at the same time. Conditioning rarely takes place when the conditioned stimulus follows the unconditioned stimulus (Spooner & Kellogg, 1947; Spetch et al., 1981).

The ideal time between the presentation of the conditioned and the unconditioned stimulus is about one-half second, but this varies according to the type of response being conditioned. Some studies indicate that the age of the subject may also be a variable affecting the optimal time interval (Solomon et al., 1991). In general, if the conditioned stimulus occurs too long before the unconditioned stimulus, an association between the two will not form. One notable exception to this general principle is in the conditioning of taste aversions.

> **taste aversion:** The dislike or avoidance of a particular food that has been associated with nausea or discomfort.

Classically Conditioned Taste Aversions and Immune System Responses

Taste Aversions: That's Nauseating The experience of nausea and vomiting after eating an unfamiliar food is often enough to condition a long-lasting **taste aversion**. Taste aversions can be classically conditioned when the delay between the conditioned stimulus (food) and the unconditioned stimulus (nausea) is as long as 12 hours. Researchers believe that many taste aversions begin when we are between 2 and 3 years old, so we may not remember how our taste aversions originated (Rozin & Zellner, 1985). Taste aversions are more likely to develop to "less preferred, less familiar foods," and they can be acquired even when people are convinced that the food did not cause the nausea (Logue, 1985, p. 327). Once developed, taste aversions frequently generalize to similar foods (Logue et al., 1981). For example, an aversion to chili is likely to include Sloppy Joes as well.

Some Limits to Classical Conditioning Pavlov believed that almost any neutral stimulus could serve to condition responses, but Garcia and Kelling (1966) have demonstrated an exception to this notion. In a well-known study, groups of rats were exposed to a three-way conditioned stimulus—bright light, a clicking noise, and flavored water. For one group of rats, the unconditioned stimulus was an electric shock to their feet; for the other group, the unconditioned stimulus was either X rays or lithium chloride, either of which produces nausea and vomiting. The group receiving the electric shock continued to prefer the flavored water over unflavored water, but they would not drink at all in the presence of the bright light or the clicking sound. The rats that were made ill avoided the flavored water at all times, but they would still drink unflavored water when the bright light and the clicking sound were present. The rats in one group associated electric shock only with the light and the sound. The rats in the other group associated nausea only with the flavored water.

WORLD OF PSYCHOLOGY: APPLICATIONS

Solving Problems with Conditioned Taste Aversions

Controlling Predators by Conditioning Taste Aversions In the 1970s sheep ranchers in the western United States were plagued by wild coyotes attacking and killing their sheep. The ranchers tried to solve their problem simply by killing the coyotes, using traps or lethal poisons, and by employing bounty hunters. Such methods outraged the naturalists, who argued that such indiscriminate killing would put these wild coyotes on the endangered species list.

Applying research on conditioned taste aversion in animals, Gustavson and others (1974) devised a plan that spared the lambs and saved the coyotes. They laced lamb flesh with lithium chloride, a poison that made the coyotes extremely ill but that was not fatal. The plan was so successful that after one or two treatments, the coyotes would get sick even at the sight of a lamb.

In a similar case Cornell and Cornley (1979) came to the aid of personnel at a national park who had become worried about camper safety when a pack of coyotes began scavenging for food on the campgrounds. Again the psychologists used lithium chloride, but this time they laced a wide variety of camping foods with the substance. After a few encounters with the tainted foods, the coyotes' visits to the campgrounds ended, and even 2 years later, they had not returned.

Using Conditioned Taste Aversions to Help Cancer Patients Knowledge about conditioned taste aversion is useful in solving human problems as well. One unfortunate side effect of chemotherapy treatment in cancer patients is that nausea is often associated with foods eaten in the several hours preceding treatment. As a result, patients often develop taste aversions to normal foods in their diet, sometimes even favorite foods.

Bernstein and others (1982; Bernstein, 1985) report a technique that might help patients avoid aversions to desirable foods. A group of cancer patients were fed a novel-tasting, maple-flavored ice cream before chemotherapy. The nausea caused by the treatment resulted in a taste aversion to the ice cream. The researchers found that when an unusual or unfamiliar food becomes the "scapegoat" or target for taste aversion, other foods in the patient's diet may be protected, and the patient will continue to eat them regularly. The researchers suggest that cancer patients should refrain from eating preferred or nutritious foods prior to chemotherapy. Instead, they should be given an unusual-tasting food shortly before treatment.

Apparently animals are *prepared* to associate only certain stimuli with particular consequences (Seligman, 1970). Associating nausea with food or drink ingested beforehand has definite survival value, for rats as well as for humans. Sound and light do not produce nausea, so making such an association would not be adaptive. But electric shock, on the other hand, is likely to be accompanied by a light or a sound, so associating these stimuli would be adaptive.

Classical Conditioning and the Immune System Response The immune system itself is subject to conditioning, according to psychologist Robert Ader and immunologist Michael Cohen (Ader, 1981; Ader & Cohen, 1985). In the mid-1970s Ader was conducting a taste-aversion experiment with rats, conditioning them to avoid saccharin-sweetened water. Immediately after drinking the sweetened water (which rats consider a treat), the rats were injected with a tasteless drug that causes severe nausea. The conditioning worked, and from that time on, the rats would not drink the sweet water, with or without the drug.

Attempting to reverse the conditioned response, Ader had to force-feed the sweet water to the rats for many days; but later, unexpectedly, many of them died. Ader was puzzled because the saccharin water was in no way lethal. Checking further into the properties of the tasteless drug (cyclophosphamide), Ader learned that it suppresses the immune system. A few doses of an immune-suppressing drug paired with sweetened water had produced a conditioned response; as a result the sweet water alone continued to suppress the immune system, causing the rats to die. Ader and Cohen successfully repeated the experiment with strict controls to rule out other explanations. Later several other researchers replicated the experiment and produced the same results.

Memory Check 5.2

1. In Watson's experiment on Little Albert, the white rat was the (conditioned, unconditioned) stimulus, and Albert's crying when the hammer struck the steel bar was the (conditioned, unconditioned) response.

2. When Albert's fear transferred to the dog, the rabbit, the mask, and the fur coat, Watson said that _____ had occurred.

   a. generalization   c. extinction
   b. discrimination   d. spontaneous recovery

3. Which of the following does *not* increase the strength of the conditioned response in classical conditioning?

   a. increased pairing of the conditioned and unconditioned stimulus
   b. presenting the conditioned stimulus a long time before the unconditioned stimulus
   c. increasing the intensity of the unconditioned stimulus
   d. always following the conditioned stimulus with the unconditioned stimulus

4. Which element in classical conditioning is the signal?
   a. the conditioned response   c. the unconditioned response
   b. the conditioned stimulus   d. the unconditioned stimulus

5. Taste aversions require (fewer, more) pairings of the conditioned and the unconditioned stimulus than most other examples of classical conditioning.

Answers: 1. conditioned, unconditioned 2. a 3. b 4. b 5. fewer

Operant Conditioning

Thorndike and the Law of Effect

Before Pavlov began his experiments with dogs, American psychologist Edward Thorndike (1874–1949) was designing and conducting experiments to study animal intelligence. From his experiments, Thorndike formulated several laws of learning, the most important being the law of effect. The **law of effect** states that the consequence, or effect, of a response will determine whether the tendency to respond in the same way in the future will be strengthened or weakened. Responses closely followed by satisfying consequences are more likely to be repeated (Thorndike, 1911/1970). Thorndike's law of effect formed the conceptual starting point for B. F. Skinner's work in operant conditioning.

law of effect: Thorndike's law of learning that states that connections between a stimulus and response will be strengthened if followed by a satisfying consequence and weakened if followed by discomfort.

operant conditioning: A type of learning in which the consequences of behavior tend to modify that behavior in the future (behavior that is reinforced tends to be repeated; behavior that is ignored or punished is less likely to be repeated).

shaping: The gradual molding of a desired behavior by reinforcing responses that become progressively closer to it; reinforcing successive approximations of the desired response.

Skinner box: Invented by B. F. Skinner for conducting experiments in operant conditioning; a soundproof operant conditioning chamber with a device for delivering food and either a bar for rats to press or a disk for pigeons to peck.

successive approximations: A series of gradual training steps, with each step becoming more like the final desired response.

In the Skinner box shown here, the rat learns to press a bar through *shaping,* in which the experimenter rewards gradual, successive approximations toward the goal.

Skinner and Operant Conditioning

Question: How are responses acquired through operant conditioning?

Recall that in classical conditioning, the organism does not learn a new response. Rather, it learns to make an old or existing response to a new stimulus. Classically conditioned responses are involuntary or reflexive, and in most cases, the person or animal cannot help but respond in expected ways.

We will now examine a method for conditioning voluntary responses known as **operant conditioning.** In operant conditioning, the organism operates on the environment. Operant conditioning does not begin, as did classical conditioning, with the presentation of a stimulus to elicit a response. Rather, the response comes first, and then the consequence that follows tends to modify this behavior in the future. Behavior that is reinforced—followed by pleasant consequences—tends to be repeated. Behavior that is ignored or punished is less likely to be repeated.

Operant conditioning permits the learning of a broad range of new responses. A simple response can be operantly conditioned by merely waiting for it to appear and then reinforcing it, but this can be time consuming. The process can be speeded up with a technique called shaping.

Question: How is shaping used to condition a response?

Shaping Behavior: Just a Little Bit at a Time Shaping is a technique employed by B. F. Skinner that is particularly useful in conditioning complex behaviors. Rather than waiting for the desired response to occur prior to reinforcement, any movement in the direction of the desired response is reinforced, gradually guiding the responses closer and closer to the ultimate goal.

Skinner designed a soundproof operant-conditioning apparatus, commonly called a *Skinner box,* in which he conducted his experiments. One type of box is equipped with a lever, or bar, that a rat presses to gain a reward of food pellets or water from a dispenser. A complete record of the animal's bar-pressing responses is registered on a device called a cumulative recorder, also invented by Skinner.

Rats in a Skinner box are conditioned, through the use of shaping, to press a bar for rewards. A rat might be rewarded first for simply turning toward the bar. Once this behavior is established, the next reward comes only when the rat moves closer to the bar. Each step closer to the bar is rewarded. Next the rat might touch the bar and receive a reward; finally, the rat is rewarded only when it presses the bar.

Shaping—rewarding gradual, *successive approximations* toward the goal or terminal response—has been used effectively to condition complex behaviors in people as well as other animals. Parents might use shaping to help their children develop good table manners, praising them each time they show gradual improvements. Teachers often use shaping with disruptive children, reinforcing them at first for very short periods of good behavior and then gradually expecting them to work productively for longer and longer periods. Through shaping, circus animals have learned to perform a wide range of amazing feats, and pigeons have learned to bowl and play Ping-Pong. You might even want to try shaping your own behavior using the *Try It!*

Superstitious Behavior: Mistaking a Coincidence for a Cause Sometimes a rewarding event follows a response but is not caused by or connected with it. Superstitious behavior occurs if an individual believes that a connection exists

WORLD OF PSYCHOLOGY: PIONEERS

Burrhus Frederic Skinner (1904–1990)

Question: What was B. F. Skinner's major contribution to psychology?

Burrhus Frederic Skinner was born in 1904 in Susquehanna, Pennsylvania. He had an early interest in constructing mechanical devices and in collecting an assortment of animals, which he kept as pets. He was much impressed with the complex tricks he saw trained pigeons perform at country fairs.

Skinner reported that he always liked school, and after graduating from high school, he entered Hamilton College in upstate New York. In college he did not feel a part of student life, and he resented some of the official attempts to control his behavior, such as compulsory chapel attendance. In protest he planned and carried out a number of practical jokes, one of which greatly angered college officials. Skinner had posters printed and widely distributed

B. F. Skinner (1904–1990)

announcing that a great film star of the time, Charlie Chaplin, would appear for a performance on campus. The town railroad station and the campus were swamped with hundreds of people from miles around who had arrived for the great event. Forced to deal with angry, disappointed mobs of visitors, the college officials were not amused with Skinner's sense of humor.

In 1928 Skinner entered graduate school at Harvard, where he completed his Ph.D. in psychology in 1931. He described his life there this way:

> I would rise at six, study until breakfast, go to classes, laboratories, and libraries with no more than fifteen minutes unscheduled during the day, study until exactly nine o'clock at night and go to bed. I saw no movies or plays, seldom went to concerts, had scarcely any dates and read nothing but psychology and physiology. (Skinner, 1967, p. 398)

It was precisely this unusual degree of self-discipline that enabled Skinner to become a tireless researcher and prolific writer.

In 1936 Skinner joined the faculty at the University of Minnesota, where he conducted much of his research in operant conditioning and wrote *The Behavior of Organisms* (1938), now a classic. From 1945 to 1948, Skinner taught at Indiana University, where he received public attention for his invention of the air crib, a strictly controlled environment for the care of infants. Gaining even more attention was his first novel, *Walden Two* (1948b), which describes a fictional utopian community where reinforcement principles are used to produce happy, productive, and cooperative citizens.

In 1948 Skinner returned to Harvard and continued his research and writing. His *Science and Human Behavior* (1953) provides a description of the process of operant conditioning.

In a later and highly controversial book, *Beyond Freedom and Dignity* (1971), Skinner is critical of society's preoccupation with the notion of freedom. He maintains that free will is a myth and that our behavior is always shaped and controlled by others—parents, teachers, peers, advertising, television. He argues that rather than leaving the control of behavior to chance, society would be better served if the behavior of its members were systematically shaped for the larger good.

Skinner seemed to have a talent for provoking criticism and even outrage as a result of his writing and the application of his research to the control of human behavior. Little controversy exists, however, about the significance of his research in operant conditioning. Skinner's long career ended when he died in 1990 at the age of 86, but his strong influence in shaping the direction of modern psychology will be felt for years to come.

Try It!

Select some behavior that you would like to develop or to change. Set your goal and plan to reach it in small steps. Decide in advance to reward yourself when you reach certain points along the way. Chart your progress. This alone will provide some reinforcement for your efforts.

■ If you need to get more exercise, begin by exercising 5 minutes a day. Do this for several days and then increase it to 10 minutes. Determine how many days you will stay at each level before increasing your exercise time. Chart your progress. Set up milestones and reward yourself.

■ If you are wasting too much time watching television, record for a week how much time you spend watching TV each day. Then wean yourself gradually, perhaps by 30 minutes every few days. Set a goal for yourself, and chart your TV time.

between an act and its consequences when, in fact, there is no relationship between the two.

A gambler in Las Vegas blows on the dice just before he rolls them and wins $1,000. On the next roll, he follows the same ritual and wins again. Although this rewarding event follows the ritual of blowing on the dice, the connection between the two is accidental. Nevertheless, the gambler will probably persist in this superstitious behavior at least as long as his winning streak continues. Some professional athletes have been known to carry superstitious behavior to remarkable extremes. Baseball star Keith Hernandez reportedly wears his lucky socks (the same pair) for the entire season.

Superstitious behavior is not confined to humans. Skinner (1948a) developed superstitious behavior in pigeons by giving food rewards every 15 seconds regardless of the pigeon's behavior. Whatever response the pigeons happened to be making was reinforced, and before long each pigeon developed its own ritual, such as turning counterclockwise in the cage several times or making pendulum movements with its head.

Question: How does extinction occur in operant conditioning?

Extinction: Withholding Reinforcers   We have seen that responses followed by reinforcers tend to be repeated and that responses no longer followed by reinforcers will occur less and less frequently and eventually die out. A rat in a Skinner box will eventually stop pressing a bar when it is no longer rewarded with food pellets. In operant conditioning, **extinction** occurs when reinforcers are withheld.

In humans and other animals, extinction can lead to frustration or even rage. Consider a child having a temper tantrum. If whining and loud demands do not bring the reinforcer, the child may progress to kicking and screaming. If a vending machine takes your coins but fails to deliver candy or soda, your button-pushing or lever-pulling behavior may become erratic and more forceful. You might even shake the machine or kick it before giving up. It is what we expect and don't get that makes us angry.

The process of spontaneous recovery, which we discussed in relation to classical conditioning, also occurs in operant conditioning. A rat whose bar pressing has been extinguished may again press the bar a few times when returned to the Skinner box after a period of rest.

Generalization and Discrimination   Skinner conducted many of his experiments with pigeons placed in a Skinner box specially designed for them. The box

extinction: The weakening and often eventual disappearance of a learned response (in operant conditioning, the conditioned response is weakened by the withdrawal of reinforcement).

contained small illuminated disks that the pigeons could peck to receive bits of grain from a food tray. Skinner found that generalization occurs in operant conditioning. A pigeon reinforced for pecking at a yellow disk is likely to peck at another disk similar in color. The less similar a disk is to the original color, the lower the rate of pecking will be.

Discrimination involves learning to distinguish between a stimulus that has been reinforced and other stimuli that may be very similar. This can be accomplished by reinforcing the response to the original stimulus but not reinforcing responses to similar stimuli. For example, to encourage discrimination, the pigeon would be reinforced for pecking at the yellow disk but not for pecking at the orange or red disk.

There are certain cues that, through classical conditioning, have come to be associated with reinforcement or punishment. For example, children are more likely to ask their mother for a treat when she is smiling than when she is frowning. The stimulus that signals whether a certain response or behavior is likely to be rewarded, ignored, or punished is called a *discriminative stimulus*. If a pigeon's peck at a lighted disk results in a reward but the peck at an unlighted disk does not, the pigeon will soon be pecking at the lighted disk but not at the unlighted one. The presence or absence of the discriminative stimulus, in this case the lighted disk, will control whether or not the pecking takes place.

We may wonder why children sometimes misbehave with a grandparent but not with the parent, or why they make one teacher's life miserable but are model students for another. The children may have learned that their misbehavior in the presence of some people, the discriminative stimuli, will almost certainly lead to punishment but in the presence of certain other people may even be rewarded.

discriminative stimulus: A stimulus that signals whether a certain response or behavior is likely to be followed by reward or punishment.

Pigeons reinforced for pecking at a yellow disk learn to peck at any disks similar in color.

reinforcement: An event that follows a response and increases the strength of the response and/or the likelihood that it will be repeated.

positive reinforcement: A reward or pleasant consequence given after a response in order to increase the probability that the response will be repeated.

negative reinforcement: The termination of an unpleasant stimulus after a response in order to increase the probability that the response will be repeated.

primary reinforcer: A reinforcer that fulfills a basic physical need for survival and does not depend on learning (examples: food, water, sleep, termination of pain).

Memory Check 5.3

1. The law of effect was formulated by:

    a. Watson   c. Skinner
    b. Thorndike   d. Pavlov

2. Operant conditioning has been researched most extensively by:

    a. Watson   c. Skinner
    b. Thorndike   d. Pavlov

3. Even though the "B" that Billy wrote looked more like a "D," his teacher, Mrs. Chen, praised him because it was better than his previous attempts. Mrs. Chen is using a procedure called _____ .

4. Which of the following occur in operant conditioning?
    a. extinction, generalization, and discrimination
    b. extinction, spontaneous recovery, generalization, and discrimination
    c. generalization and discrimination
    d. extinction and generalization

Answers: 1. b 2. c 3. shaping 4. b

Reinforcement: What's the Payoff?

Question: How do positive reinforcement and negative reinforcement differ?

Positive and Negative Reinforcement: Adding the Good, Taking Away the Bad **Reinforcement** is a key concept in operant conditioning and may be defined as any event that increases the likelihood of a response. There are two types of reinforcement, positive and negative. A reward or a pleasant consequence following an act of behavior is termed a **positive reinforcement**. We have seen that a hungry rat in a Skinner box will increase its bar pressing when this response is followed by food.

An act of behavior that results in the termination of an unpleasant stimulus is also likely to be repeated. This is called **negative reinforcement**. Rats placed in Skinner boxes equipped with electric grids on the floor increase their bar pressing when it terminates a painful electric shock. Negative reinforcement is no less powerful than positive reinforcement in influencing behavior. Heroin addicts, for example, will do almost anything to obtain the heroin that terminates their painful withdrawal symptoms.

The most basic generalization concerning positive and negative reinforcement is that we will perform acts of behavior in order to gain pleasure and escape pain. But not all people or animals respond to the same reinforcers. Rat pellets would not be an effective reinforcer for your behavior. Neither would a rat's bar pressing increase if the rat were reinforced with thousands of dollars, gold and silver, or stocks and bonds.

Primary and Secondary Reinforcers: The Unlearned and the Learned A *primary reinforcer* is one that fulfills a basic physical need for survival and does not depend on learning. Food, water, sleep, and termination of pain are examples of primary reinforcers. And sex is a powerful reinforcer that fulfills a basic physical need for survival of the species. Fortunately, learning does not depend solely on primary reinforcers. If that were the case, we would need to be hungry, thirsty, or sex starved before we would respond at all. Much observed behavior in humans is in response to secondary, rather than primary, reinforcers. A *secondary reinforcer* is acquired or learned by association with other reinforcers. Money, attention, praise, good grades, prestige, fame, and signals of approval such as a smile or a kind word are all examples of secondary reinforcers.

Attention is a secondary reinforcer of great general worth. In order to obtain the reinforcers we seek from other people, we must first get their attention. Children vie for the attention of parents because they represent the main source of a child's reinforcers. But often parents reward children with attention for misbehavior and ignore their good behavior. When this happens, misbehavior is strengthened, and good behavior may be extinguished for lack of reinforcement.

Some secondary reinforcers (money, for example) can be exchanged at a later time for other reinforcers. In one study, John B. Wolfe (1936) taught chimpanzees to work for secondary reinforcers. Wolfe trained his chimps to pull a heavily weighted bar and paid them in poker chips that they could use to buy food. The chimps learned to take their poker chips and insert them into a "chimp-o-mat," which dispensed bananas and peanuts. Like humans the chimps came to value the poker chips greatly, and hoarding and stealing were reported.

Question: What are the four major schedules of reinforcement, and which schedule yields the highest response rate and the greatest resistance to extinction?

Schedules of Reinforcement: When Will I Get My Reinforcers?

In conditioning the bar-pressing response in rats, every time the rat pressed the bar, the response was reinforced with a food pellet. Reinforcing every correct response, known as *continuous reinforcement*, is the most efficient way to condition a new response. However, after a response has been conditioned, partial or intermittent reinforcement is more effective if we want to maintain or increase the rate of response (Nation & Woods, 1980). *Partial reinforcement* is operating when some but not all of an organism's responses are reinforced. Under natural conditions outside the laboratory, reinforcement is almost never continuous. Partial reinforcement is the rule.

Partial reinforcement may be administered according to different **schedules of reinforcement**. Different schedules produce distinct rates and patterns of responses, as well as varying degrees of resistance to extinction when reinforcement is discontinued. Although several varieties of reinforcement schedules are possible, the two basic types are the ratio and interval schedules. Ratio schedules require that a certain *number of responses* be made before one of the responses is reinforced. With interval schedules, a given *amount of time* must pass before a reinforcer is administered. These schedules are further subdivided into fixed and variable categories.

Following are descriptions of the four most basic schedules of reinforcement: the fixed-ratio schedule, the variable-ratio schedule, the fixed-interval schedule, and the variable-interval schedule.

The Fixed-Ratio Schedule

On a **fixed-ratio schedule**, a reinforcer is administered after a fixed number of nonreinforced responses. If the fixed ratio is set at 30 responses (FR-30), a reinforcer is given after 30 correct responses. Examples of this schedule are factory workers whose payment depends on the number of units produced and migrant farm workers paid by the bushel for the fruit they pick.

secondary reinforcer: A neutral stimulus that becomes reinforcing after repeated pairing with other reinforcers.

continuous reinforcement: Reinforcement that is administered after every desired or correct response; the most effective method of conditioning a new response.

partial reinforcement: A pattern of reinforcement in which some portion, rather than 100 percent, of the correct responses are reinforced.

schedules of reinforcement: A systematic program for administering reinforcements that has a predictable effect on behavior.

fixed-ratio schedule: A schedule in which a reinforcer is administered after a fixed number of correct responses.

These seamstresses are rewarded on a fixed-ratio schedule. Because their earnings depend entirely on the number of flags completed, they are motivated to be productive.

Note the different reactions when a response is not reinforced for people accustomed to the partial reinforcement of a casino (left) and the continuous reinforcement of a vending machine (right). It's what you expect and don't get that makes you angry.

The fixed-ratio schedule is a very effective way to maintain a high response rate because the number of reinforcers received depends directly on the response rate. The faster people respond, the more reinforcers they earn. When large ratios are used, people and animals tend to pause after each reinforcement but then return to the characteristic high rate of responding.

The Variable-Ratio Schedule The pauses after reinforcement on a high fixed-ratio schedule do not occur when the variable-ratio schedule is used. On a **variable-ratio schedule**, a reinforcer is administered after a varying number of nonreinforced responses based on an average ratio. With a variable ratio of 30 responses (VR-30), you might be reinforced one time after 10 responses, another after 50, another after 30 responses, and so on. You cannot predict exactly which responses will be reinforced, but in this example, reinforcement would average 1 in 30.

Variable-ratio schedules result in higher, more stable rates of responding than fixed-ratio schedules. Skinner (1953) reports that on this schedule "a pigeon may respond as rapidly as five times per second and maintain this rate for many hours" (p. 104). According to Skinner (1988), the variable-ratio schedule is useful because "it maintains behavior against extinction when reinforcers occur only infrequently. The behavior of the dedicated artist, writer, businessman, or scientist is sustained by an occasional, unpredictable reinforcement" (p. 174).

An insurance salesperson, working on a variable-ratio schedule, may sell policies to two clients in a row but then may have to contact 20 more prospects before making another sale. The best example of the seemingly addictive power of the variable-ratio schedule is the gambling casino. Slot machines, roulette wheels, and most other games of chance pay on this schedule. The variable-ratio schedule, in general, produces the highest response rate and the most resistance to extinction.

The Fixed-Interval Schedule On a **fixed-interval schedule**, a specific time interval must pass before a response is reinforced. For example, on a 60-second fixed-interval schedule (FI-60), a reinforcer is given for the first correct response that occurs 60 seconds after the last reinforced response. People working on a salary are reinforced on this schedule.

Unlike ratio schedules, reinforcement on interval schedules does not depend on the number of responses made, only on the one correct response made after the time interval has passed. Characteristic of the fixed-interval schedule is a

variable-ratio schedule: A schedule in which a reinforcer is administered after a varying number of nonreinforced responses based on an average ratio.

fixed-interval schedule: A schedule in which a reinforcer is administered following the first correct response after a fixed period of time has elapsed.

pause or a sharp decline in responding immediately after each reinforcement and a rapid acceleration in responding just before the next reinforcer is due.

As an example of this schedule, think of a psychology test as a reinforcer (that's a joke, isn't it?) and studying for the test as the desired response. Suppose you have four tests scheduled during the semester. Your study responses will probably drop to zero immediately after the first test, gradually accelerate and perhaps reach a frenzied peak just before the next scheduled exam, then immediately drop to zero again, and so on. As you might have guessed, the fixed-interval schedule produces the lowest response rate.

The Variable-Interval Schedule Variable-interval schedules eliminate the pause after reinforcement that is typical of the fixed-interval schedule. On a **variable-interval schedule**, a reinforcer is administered after the first correct response following a varying time of nonreinforced responses based on an average time. Rather than reinforcing a response every 60 seconds, for example, a reinforcer might be given after a 30-second interval with others following after 90-, 45-, and 75-second intervals. But the average time elapsing between reinforcers would be 60 seconds (VI-60). Although this schedule maintains remarkably stable and uniform rates of responding, the response rate is typically lower than that of the ratio schedules because reinforcement is not tied directly to the *number* of responses made.

Again, with another flight into fantasy, we could think of the psychology exam as the reinforcer and studying for the exam as the response. Rather than a regularly scheduled exam, however, we need pop quizzes to illustrate the variable-interval schedule. Because you cannot predict when a pop quiz will be given, your study responses will be more uniform and stable. Also, the response rate tends to be higher with shorter intervals and lower with longer ones. If your professor gives a pop quiz once a week on the average, your study response will be higher than if you average only one quiz per month. Table 5.1 summarizes the characteristics of the four schedules of reinforcement.

> **variable-interval schedule:** A schedule in which a reinforcer is administered after the first correct response following a varying time of nonreinforcement based on an average time.

Table 5.1

Reinforcement Schedules Compared According to Response Rate, Pattern of Responses, and Resistance to Extinction

Schedule of Reinforcement	Response Rate	Pattern of Responses	Resistance to Extinction
Fixed ratio	Very high	Steady with low ratio. Brief pause after each reinforcement with very high ratio.	The higher the ratio, the more resistance to extinction.
Variable ratio	Highest response rate	Constant response pattern, no pauses.	Most resistance to extinction.
Fixed interval	Lowest response rate	Long pause after reinforcement, followed by gradual acceleration.	The longer the interval, the more resistance to extinction.
Variable interval	Moderate	Stable, uniform response.	More resistance to extinction than fixed-interval schedule with same average.

Question: What is the partial-reinforcement effect?

The Effect of Continuous and Partial Reinforcement on Extinction One way to understand extinction in operant conditioning is to consider how consistently a response is followed by reinforcement. On a continuous schedule, a reinforcer is expected without fail after each correct response. When a reinforcer is withheld, it is noticed immediately. But on a partial-reinforcement schedule, a reinforcer is not expected after every response. Thus, no immediate difference is apparent between the partial-reinforcement schedule and the onset of extinction.

When you put money in a vending machine, pull the lever, and no candy or soda appears, you know immediately that something is wrong with the machine. But if you are playing a broken slot machine, you could have many nonreinforced responses before suspecting that the machine is malfunctioning.

Partial reinforcement results in a greater resistance to extinction than does continuous reinforcement. This result is known as the **partial-reinforcement effect**. There is an inverse relationship between the percentage of responses that have been reinforced and resistance to extinction. That is, the lower the percentage of responses that are reinforced, the longer extinction will take when reinforcement is withheld (Weinstock, 1953). The strongest resistance to extinction that we can find on record occurred in one experiment in which pigeons were conditioned to peck at a disk. According to Holland and Skinner (1961), "after the response had been maintained on a fixed ratio of 900 and reinforcement was then discontinued, the pigeon emitted 73,000 responses during the first 4 1/2 hours of extinction" (p. 124).

Parents often wonder why their children continue to nag in order to get what they want, in spite of the fact that the parents *usually* do not give in to the nagging. Unwittingly the parents are reinforcing their children's nagging on a variable-ratio schedule, which results in the most persistent behavior. For this reason experts always caution parents to be consistent. If parents *never* reward nagging, the behavior will extinguish; if they give in occasionally, it will persist and be extremely hard to extinguish.

Punishment: That Hurts!

Punishment is in many ways the opposite of reinforcement. Punishment tends to lower the probability of an undesirable response by adding an unpleasant stimulus or by removing a pleasant one when the undesirable response is made. In human behavior, punishment may be actively applied, as in spanking, scolding, disapproving looks, or imprisonment. Punishment also may be administered by removing something pleasant, for example, withholding affection and attention or taking away a privilege such as watching TV.

Students often confuse negative reinforcement and punishment. Negative reinforcement differs from punishment because it increases the probability of a desired response by removing an unpleasant stimulus when the correct response is made (see Table 5.2). "Grounding" can be used as either punishment or negative reinforcement. If teenagers fail to clean their room after many requests to do so, their parents could ground them for the weekend—a punishment. An alternative approach would be to use negative reinforcement—tell them they are grounded *until* the room is clean. Which approach would be more effective?

Question: What three factors increase the effectiveness of punishment?

Factors Influencing the Effectiveness of Punishment: Making Punishment Work Research has revealed several factors that influence the effectiveness of punishment: its *timing*, *intensity*, and the *consistency* of its application (Parke,

partial-reinforcement effect:
The greater resistance to extinction that occurs when a portion, rather than 100 percent, of the correct responses have been reinforced.

punishment: The removal of a pleasant stimulus or the application of an unpleasant stimulus, which tends to suppress a response.

Table 5.2   The Effects of Reinforcement and Punishment

Adding a Stimulus	Subtracting or Withholding a Stimulus	Effect Produced
Positive Reinforcement	**Negative Reinforcement**	
Presenting food, money, praise, or other rewards.	Removing or terminating some pain-producing or otherwise aversive stimulus such as electric shock.	Serves to increase a particular behavior.
Punishment	**Punishment**	
Delivering a pain-producing or otherwise aversive stimulus such as a spanking or an electric shock.	Removing some pleasant stimulus or taking away privileges such as TV watching, use of automobile.	Serves to decrease or suppress a particular behavior.

1977). Punishment is most effective when it is applied during the misbehavior or as soon afterward as possible. The longer the delay between the response and the punishment, the less effective it will be in suppressing the response (Azrin & Holz, 1966; Camp et al., 1967).

Animal studies have revealed that the more intense the punishment, the greater the suppression of the undesirable behavior (Church, 1963). Behavior is more effectively suppressed if the maximum intensity of punishment *appropriate* to the act is applied at the very beginning. If the initial punishment is too mild, it has no effect. If the intensity is gradually increased, the animal will adapt to it, and the unwanted behavior will persist (Solomon, 1964; Azrin & Holz, 1966). In human terms a $2.00 speeding ticket will not be much of a deterrent; a $200.00 ticket is more likely to suppress the urge to speed.

In order to be effective, punishment also needs to be applied consistently. An undesired response will be suppressed more effectively when the probability of punishment is high. Few people would speed while observing a police car in the rear-view mirror.

Question: What are some disadvantages of punishment?

The Disadvantages of Punishment: Skinner always argued that punishment does not extinguish an undesirable behavior; rather, it suppresses that behavior when the punishing agent is present. But the behavior is apt to continue in settings where punishment is unlikely. Many psychologists believe that removing the rewarding consequences of undesirable behavior is the best way to extinguish it. According to this view, extinguishing a child's temper tantrums could best be accomplished, not by punishment, but by never giving in to the child's demands during a tantrum. Problem behavior engaged in merely to get attention might best be extinguished by ignoring that behavior and giving attention to more appropriate behavior.

Another problem with punishment is that it indicates what behaviors are unacceptable but does not help people develop more appropriate behaviors. If punishment is given, it should be used in conjunction with reinforcement for appropriate behavior.

Controlling behavior by punishment has a number of other potential disadvantages. The person who is punished often becomes fearful and feels angry and hostile toward the punisher. These reactions may be accompanied by a desire to avoid or escape from the punisher and the punishing situation—or to find a way to retaliate. Punishment frequently leads to aggression, and those who administer physical punishment may become models of aggressive behavior to the person being hurt. Children of abusive, punishing parents are at greater risk than other children of becoming aggressive and abusive themselves (Widom, 1989).

Because of the many disadvantages of punishment, parents and teachers should explore other means of handling misbehavior. If a young child runs into the street, puts a finger near an electrical outlet, or reaches for a hot pan on the stove, a swift punishment may save the child from a potentially disastrous situation. But in many cases punishment is not as successful an approach as offering children rational explanations for why they should avoid certain behavior. If punishment is used, it should not be administered in anger and should *not* be excessively harsh.

Escape and Avoidance Learning

Learning to perform a behavior because it terminates an aversive event is called escape learning, and it reflects the power of negative reinforcement. Running away from a punishing situation and taking aspirins to relieve a pounding headache are examples of escape behavior. In these situations the aversive event has begun and an attempt has been made to escape it.

Avoidance learning depends on two types of conditioning. First, through classical conditioning, an event or condition comes to signal an aversive state. Drinking and driving may be associated with automobile accidents and death. Then, because of such associations, people may engage in behaviors to avoid the anticipated, aversive consequences. Making it a practice to avoid driving with people who have had too much to drink is sensible avoidance behavior.

Many avoidance behaviors are maladaptive, however, and occur in response to phobias. Students who have had a bad experience speaking in front of a class may begin to fear any situation that involves speaking before a group. They may avoid taking classes that require class presentations or taking leadership roles that necessitate public speaking. Avoiding such situations allows them to escape the dreaded consequences, so the avoidance behavior is negatively reinforced and thus strengthened through operant conditioning. Maladaptive avoidance behaviors are very difficult to extinguish because people never give themselves a chance to see that the dreaded consequences probably will not occur or are greatly exaggerated.

Factors Influencing Operant Conditioning

Question: What three factors, in addition to the schedule of reinforcement, influence operant conditioning?

We know that responses are acquired more quickly with continuous rather than partial reinforcement and that the schedule of reinforcement influences both response rate and resistance to extinction. Several other factors affect how quickly a response is acquired, response rate, and resistance to extinction.

The first factor is the *magnitude of reinforcement*. In general, as the magnitude of reinforcement increases, acquisition of a response is faster, the rate of responding is higher, and resistance to extinction is greater (Clayton, 1964).

avoidance learning: Learning to avoid events or conditions associated with dreaded or aversive outcomes.

People would be motivated to work harder and faster if they were paid $30.00 for each yard mowed rather than only $10.00. Other research indicates that level of performance is also influenced by the relationship between the amount of reinforcement expected and what is actually received (Crespi, 1942). For example, your performance on the job would undoubtedly be affected if your salary were suddenly cut in half. Also, it might improve dramatically if your employer doubled your pay.

The second factor affecting operant conditioning is the *immediacy of reinforcement*. In general, responses are conditioned more effectively when reinforcement is immediate. One reason people become addicted to crack cocaine so quickly is because its euphoric effects are felt almost instantly (Medzerin, 1991). As a rule, the longer the delay in reinforcement, the more slowly the response will be acquired (Capaldi, 1978; Perin, 1943). (See Figure 5.5.) Overweight people have difficulty changing their eating habits because of the long delay between their behavior change and the rewarding consequences of weight loss and better health.

The third factor influencing conditioning is the *level of motivation* of the learner. If you are highly motivated to learn to play tennis, you will learn faster and practice more than if you have no interest in the game. Skinner found that when food is the reinforcer, a hungry animal will learn faster than a full animal. To maximize motivation, he used rats that had been deprived of food for 24 hours and pigeons that were maintained at 75 to 80 percent of their normal body weight.

Comparing Classical and Operant Conditioning: What's the Difference?

In summary, the processes of generalization, discrimination, extinction, and spontaneous recovery occur in both classical and operant conditioning. Both depend on associative learning. In classical conditioning, an association is formed between two stimuli—for example, a tone and food, a white rat and a loud noise, or a product and a celebrity. In operant conditioning, the association

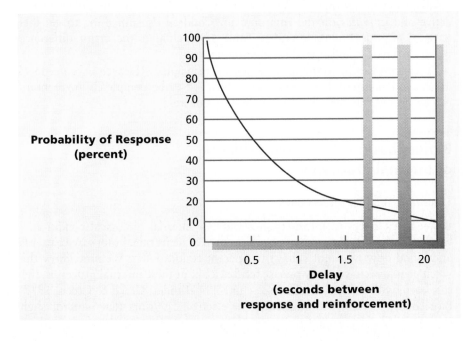

Probability of Response (percent)

Delay (seconds between response and reinforcement)

Figure 5.5

The Effect of Delay in Reinforcement on Conditioning a Response

In general, responses are conditioned more effectively when reinforcement is immediate. The longer the delay in reinforcement, the lower the probability that a response will be acquired.

Table 5.3   Classical and Operant Conditioning Compared

Characteristics	Classical Conditioning	Operant Conditioning
Type of association	Between two stimuli	Between a response and its consequence
State of subject	Passive	Active
Focus of attention	On what precedes response	On what follows response
Type of response typically involved	Involuntary or reflexive response	Voluntary response
Bodily response typically involved	Internal responses: emotional and glandular reactions	External responses: muscular and skeletal movement and verbal responses
Range of responses	Relatively simple	Simple to highly complex
Responses learned	Emotional reactions: fears, likes, dislikes	Goal-oriented responses

is established between a response and its consequences—studying hard and a high test grade, good table manners and praise from a parent, or in the world of rats and pigeons, bar pressing and food, or disk pecking and food.

In classical conditioning, the focus is on what precedes the response. Pavlov focused on what led up to the salivation in his dogs, not on what happened after they salivated. In operant conditioning, the focus is on what follows the response. If a rat's bar pressing or your studying is followed by a reinforcer, that response is more likely to occur in the future.

Generally, in classical conditioning, the subject is passive and responds to the environment rather than acting upon it. In operant conditioning, the subject is active and *operates* on the environment. Children *do* something to get their parents' attention or their praise. Table 5.3 highlights the major differences between classical and operant conditioning.

Exceptions can be found to most general principles. Research in biofeedback indicates that internal responses, once believed to be completely involuntary, can be brought under a person's voluntary control.

Biofeedback: Observable Evidence of Internal Processes

Question: What is biofeedback?

biofeedback: The use of sensitive equipment to give people precise feedback about internal physiological processes so that they can learn, with practice, to exercise control over them.

Biofeedback refers to information about our internal biological condition. It was long believed that internal responses such as heart rate, brain wave patterns, and blood flow were not subject to operant conditioning. We now know that when people are given very precise feedback about these internal processes, they can learn, with practice, to exercise control over them (Green & Green, 1977). Biofeedback devices use mechanical or electronic sensors that monitor slight changes in these internal responses and then amplify and convert them into visual or auditory signals. Thus, subjects can *see* or *hear* evidence of internal physiological processes, and by trying out various strategies (thoughts, feelings, or images), they can learn which ones routinely increase, decrease, or maintain a particular level of activity.

Biofeedback has been used to control migraine and tension headaches, heart rate, gastrointestinal disorders, asthma, anxiety tension states, epilepsy, sexual dysfunctions, and neuromuscular disorders such as cerebral palsy, spinal-cord injuries, and stroke (Kalish, 1981; Miller, 1985, 1989).

Behavior Modification: Changing Our Act

Question: What is behavior modification?

Behavior modification is a method of changing behavior through a systematic program based on the principles of learning—classical conditioning, operant conditioning, or observational learning (which we will discuss soon). Most behavior modification programs use the principles of operant conditioning.

Many institutions—schools, mental hospitals, homes for juvenile delinquents, prisons—have used behavior modification programs with varying degrees of success. Institutions lend themselves well to such techniques because they provide a restricted environment where the consequences of behavior can be more strictly controlled. Some institutions such as prisons or mental hospitals use a *token economy*—a program that motivates socially desirable behavior by reinforcing it with tokens. The tokens (poker chips or coupons) may later be exchanged for desired goods like candy or cigarettes and privileges such as weekend passes, free time, or participation in desired activities. People in the program know in advance exactly what behaviors will be reinforced and how they will be reinforced. Token economies have been used effectively in mental hospitals to encourage patients to attend to grooming, to interact with other patients, and to carry out housekeeping tasks (Ayllon & Azrin, 1965, 1968). Although the positive behaviors generally stop when the tokens are discontinued, this does not mean that the programs are not worthwhile. After all, most people who are employed would probably quit their jobs if they were no longer paid.

Classroom teachers have used behavior modification to modify undesirable behavior and to encourage learning. "Time out" is a useful technique in which a child who is misbehaving is removed for a short time from sources of positive reinforcement. (Remember, according to operant conditioning, a behavior that is no longer reinforced will extinguish.)

Some research indicates that it may be unwise to reward students for participating in learning activities they already enjoy. Reinforcement in these cases might lessen students' natural interest in the tasks, and when reinforcers are withdrawn, the natural interest might disappear (Deci, 1975; Lepper et al., 1973).

Behavior modification has been used in industry, sometimes with considerable success. Emery Freight, for example, saved $2 million with a simple program designed to encourage employees to fill all containers to 90 percent capacity rather than the previous average of 45 percent. Workers were simply informed when containers were not filled to 90 percent and were given smiles, words of encouragement, and offers of coffee when tasks were performed satisfactorily (Luthans & Kreitner, 1975).

One of the most successful applications of behavior modification has been in the treatment of psychological problems ranging from phobias to addictive behaviors. In this context behavior modification is called behavior therapy and is discussed in chapter 15, "Therapies."

behavior modification: The systematic application of the learning principles of operant conditioning, classical conditioning, or observational learning to individuals or groups in order to eliminate undesirable behavior and/or encourage desirable behavior.

token economy: A program in which socially acceptable behaviors are motivated and reinforced by administering tokens that can be exchanged for desired items or privileges.

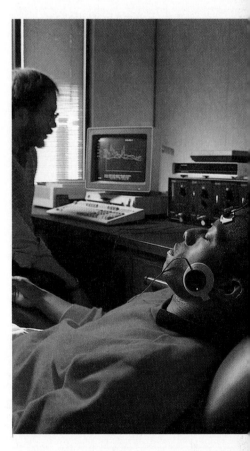

Biofeedback can teach people to achieve control over internal physiological processes such as heart rate, brain-wave activity, and muscle tension.

cognitive processes (COG-nuh-tiv): Mental processes such as thinking, knowing, problem solving, and remembering.

Memory Check 5.4

1. (Partial, Continuous) reinforcement is more effective in conditioning a new response; afterward, (partial, continuous) reinforcement is better for maintaining the response.

2. Jennifer and Ashley are both employed raking leaves. Jennifer is paid $1.00 for each bag of leaves she rakes; Ashley is paid $4.00 per hour. Jennifer is paid according to a _____ schedule; Ashley is paid according to a _____ schedule.

   a. fixed-interval; fixed-ratio
   b. variable-ratio; variable-interval
   c. variable-ratio; fixed-interval
   d. fixed-ratio; fixed-interval

3. In operant conditioning (generalization, extinction) occurs when reinforcement is withheld.

4. Punishment is roughly the same as negative reinforcement. (true/false)

5. Using sensitive electronic equipment to monitor physiological processes in order to bring them under conscious control is called (biofeedback, behavior modification).

6. Applying the principles of learning to eliminate undesirable behavior or to encourage desirable behavior is called (operant conditioning, behavior modification).

Answers: 1. Continuous; partial 2. d 3. extinction 4. false 5. biofeedback 6. behavior modification

Sultan, a chimp in Wolfgang Köhler's laboratory, solves a problem by putting two sticks together to retrieve a banana.

Cognitive Learning

Thus far, we have explored relatively simple types of learning. In classical and operant conditioning, learning is defined in terms of observable or measurable changes in behavior. Behaviorists like Skinner and Watson were not concerned with internal mental processes.

Other psychologists were unhappy with what they saw as an excessively narrow view of learning. They chose to broaden the study of learning to include mental or **cognitive processes** such as thinking, knowing, problem solving, and remembering. In discussing research on cognitive learning, we will consider the work of three leading researchers in the field—Wolfgang Köhler, Edward Tolman, and Albert Bandura.

Learning by Insight: Aha! Now I Get It

Question: What is insight, and how does it affect learning?

Wolfgang Köhler (1887–1967), a German psychologist, was the director of the anthropoid research station in the Canary Islands from 1913–1920. He studied anthropoid apes and became convinced that these animals behaved intelligently and were capable of problem solving. In his book *The Mentality of Apes* (1925), Köhler describes a series of experiments he conducted on chimpanzees confined in caged areas.

In one experiment, a bunch of bananas was hung inside the caged area but overhead, out of reach of the apes; boxes and sticks were left around the cage. Köhler observed the chimps' unsuccessful attempts to reach the bananas by jumping up or swinging sticks at them. Eventually the chimps solved the problem by piling the boxes one on top of the other until the chimps could reach the bananas.

In another experiment, Sultan, the brightest of the chimps, was given one short stick; beyond reach outside the cage was a longer stick and a bunch of bananas. After failing to reach the bananas with the short stick, Sultan used it to drag the long stick within reach. Then, finding that the long stick did not reach the bananas, Sultan finally solved the problem by fitting the two sticks together to form one long stick. With this stick, he successfully retrieved the bananas.

At times during the experiment, Köhler observed that the chimps appeared to give up in their attempts to get the bananas. However, after an interval, they returned and came up with the solution to the problem as if it had come to them in a flash of **insight**. They seemed to have suddenly discovered the relationship between the sticks or boxes and the bananas. Köhler insisted that insight, rather than trial-and-error learning, accounted for the chimps' successes, because they could easily repeat the solution and transfer this learning to similar problem situations.

Köhler's major contribution to learning is his notion of learning by insight. Learning by insight occurs when there is a sudden realization of the relationship between elements in a problem situation so that a solution becomes apparent. In human terms, a solution gained through insight is more easily learned, less likely to be forgotten, and more readily transferred to new problems than solutions learned through rote memorization (Rock & Palmer, 1990).

Latent Learning and Cognitive Maps: I Might Use That Later

Question: What is latent learning?

Like Köhler, Edward Tolman (1886–1959) differed with the prevailing ideas on learning. First, Tolman (1932) believed that learning could take place in the absence of reinforcement. Second, he differentiated between learning and performance. He maintained that **latent learning** could occur; that is, learning could occur without apparent reinforcement but not be demonstrated by performance until the organism was motivated to do so. The following experiment by Tolman and Honzik (1930) supports this position.

Three groups of rats were placed in a maze daily for 17 days. The first group always received a food reward at the end of the maze. The second group never received a reward, and the third group did not receive a food reward until the 11th day. The first group showed a steady improvement in performance over the 17-day period. The second group showed slight, gradual improvement. The third group, after being rewarded on the 11th day, showed a marked improvement the next day and throughout the experiment, outperforming the rats that had been rewarded daily (see Figure 5.6).

The marked improvement of the third group indicated to Tolman that these rats had actually learned the maze during the first 11 days. Tolman suggests that they had formed a cognitive map, or mental representation, of the maze, although the learning was not demonstrated in performance until the rats were rewarded.

insight: The sudden realization of the relationship between elements in the problem situation, which makes the solution apparent.

latent learning: Learning that occurs without apparent reinforcement but that is not demonstrated until sufficient reinforcement is provided.

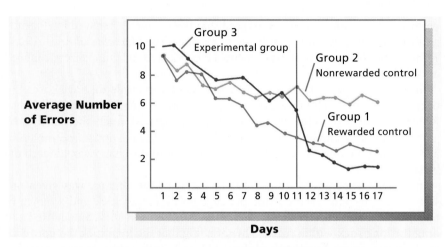

Figure 5.6   Latent Learning   Rats in Group 1 were rewarded for running the maze correctly, while rats in Group 2 were never rewarded. Group 3 rats were rewarded only on the 11th day, and thereafter outperformed the rats in Group 1. The rats had "learned" the maze but were not motivated to perform until rewarded. (From Tolman & Honzik, 1930.)

Observational Learning: Monkey See, Monkey Do

Question: What is observational learning?

In our exploration of operant conditioning, you read how people and other animals learn by directly experiencing the consequences, positive or negative, of their behavior. But must we experience rewards and punishment directly in order to learn? Not according to Albert Bandura (1986), who contends that many of our behaviors or responses are acquired through observational learning. **Observational learning**, sometimes called **modeling**, is learning that results from observing the behavior of others and the consequences of that behavior.

The person who demonstrates a behavior or whose behavior is imitated is called the **model**. Parents, movie stars, and sports personalities are often powerful models. The effectiveness of a model is related to his or her status, competence, and power. Other important factors are the age, sex, attractiveness, and ethnic status of the model. Whether or not learned behavior is actually performed depends largely on whether the observed models are rewarded or punished for their behavior and whether the individual expects to be rewarded for the behavior (Bandura, 1969, 1977).

Observational learning can be used to acquire new responses or to strengthen or weaken existing responses. Consider your native language or accent, your attitudes, gestures, personality traits, good habits (or bad habits, for that matter), moral values, food preferences. Do you share any of these with your parents? While you were growing up, their example probably influenced your behavior for better or worse. Look around the classroom, and observe the dress, hair styles, and verbal patterns of the other students. Most people have been greatly influenced by observing others.

Observational learning is particularly useful when we find ourselves in unusual situations. Picture yourself as a guest at an elaborate state dinner at the White House. More pieces of silverware extend from the plate than you have ever seen before. Which fork should be used for what? How should you proceed? You might decide to take your cue from the First Lady—observational learning.

Inhibitions can be weakened or lost as a result of observing the behavior of others. Adolescents can lose whatever resistance they may have to drinking, drug use, and sexual activity by seeing or hearing about peers engaging in these

People can learn effectively by
observing others.

behaviors. With peer pressure, there is often an overwhelming tendency to conform to the behavior and accept the values of the peer group. But inhibitions can also be strengthened through observational learning. A person does not need to experience the unfortunate consequences of dangerous behavior to avoid it. Perhaps many people decided to avoid promiscuous, unprotected sex after hearing about the tragic experience of "Magic" Johnson, a famous basketball player who contracted the HIV virus through unprotected sex.

Fears, too, can be acquired through observational learning. A parent with an extreme fear of the dentist or of thunderstorms might serve as a model for these fears in a child. Even monkeys learn specific fears by observing other monkeys (Cook et al., 1985).

Try It!

Think about everything you did yesterday from the time you woke up until the time you went to sleep. List 10 behaviors and indicate whether observational learning (OL), operant conditioning (OC), and/or classical conditioning (CC) played some role in the acquisition of each one. Remember, a behavior might originally have been learned by some combination of the three types of learning and then have been maintained by one or more of the types.

Behavior	Acquired Through			Maintained Through		
	OL	OC	CC	OL	OC	CC
Brushing teeth	X	X			X	

You probably learned to brush your teeth through a combination of observational learning (watching a parent demonstrate) and operant conditioning (being praised as your technique improved—shaping). Now the behavior is maintained through operant conditioning, specifically negative reinforcement (getting rid of the terrible taste in your mouth). Avoiding cavities and the scorn of everyone around you is an extra bonus.

Which kind of learning had the most checks on your chart?

Learning Aggression: Copying What We See Albert Bandura suspected that aggressive behavior is particularly subject to observational learning and that aggression and violence depicted on television or in cartoons tend to increase aggression in children. His pioneering work has greatly influenced current thinking on these issues. In several classic experiments, Bandura demonstrated how children are influenced by exposure to aggressive models.

One study involved three groups of preschool children. Children in one group individually observed an adult model punching, kicking, and hitting a 5-foot inflated plastic "Bobo Doll" with a mallet, while uttering aggressive words such as "Sock him in the nose . . .," "Throw him in the air . . .," "Kick him . . .," "Pow . . ." (Bandura et al., 1961, p. 576). Children in the second group observed a nonaggressive model who ignored the Bobo Doll and sat quietly assembling tinker toys. The control group was placed in the same setting with no adult present. Later, each subject was observed through a one-way mirror. Subjects exposed to the aggressive model imitated much of the aggression and also engaged in significantly more nonimitative aggression than either of the other groups. Subjects who had observed the nonaggressive models showed less aggressive behavior than the control group.

In Bandura's experiments, children imitated aggressive behavior.

A further study compared the degree of aggression in children following exposure to (1) a live aggressive model, (2) a filmed version of the episode, and (3) a film depicting an aggressive cartoon character using the same aggressive behaviors in a fantasy-like setting (Bandura et al., 1963). A control group was not exposed to any of the three situations of aggression. The groups exposed to aggressive models used significantly more aggression than the control group. The researchers concluded that "of the three experimental conditions, exposure to humans on film portraying aggression was the most influential in eliciting and shaping aggressive behavior" (p. 7).

Bandura's research provided the impetus for studying the effects of television violence and aggression both in cartoons and regular programming. Although there has been some consciousness raising about the negative impact of media violence, the amount of television violence is still excessive. The problem is compounded by the fact that the average family watches more than 7 hours of TV each day. Watching excessive violence gives people an exaggerated view of the pervasiveness of violence in our society, while making them less sensitive to the victims of violence. Media violence also encourages aggressive behavior in children by portraying aggression as an acceptable and effective way to solve problems and by teaching new forms of aggression (Wood et al., 1991). But just as children imitate the aggressive behavior they observe on television, they also imitate the prosocial, or helping, behavior they observe. Programs like "Mister Rogers' Neighborhood" and "Sesame Street" have been found to have a positive influence on children (Coats et al., 1976).

Apparently many avenues of learning are available to humans and other forms of animal life. Thankfully, our capacity to learn seems practically unlimited. Certainly our progress and advances in civilization could not have been achieved without our ability to learn.

Memory Check 5.5

1. The sudden realization of the relationship between elements in a problem situation that results in the solution to a problem is called (latent learning, insight).

2. Learning that is not translated into behavior until an organism is motivated to perform the behavior is called:

   a. learning by insight
   b. observational learning
   c. classical conditioning
   d. latent learning

3. Hayley has been afraid of snakes for as long as she can remember, and her mother has the same paralyzing fear. Hayley most likely acquired her fear through:

   a. learning by insight
   b. observational learning
   c. classical conditioning
   d. latent learning

4. Match the researcher with the subject(s) researched.

   ____ 1) Edward Tolman
   ____ 2) Albert Bandura
   ____ 3) Wolfgang Kohler

   a. observational learning
   b. cognitive maps
   c. learning by insight
   d. latent learning

Answers: 1. insight 2. d 3. b 4. 1) b, d 2) a 3) c

Thinking Critically _____

Evaluation

Prepare statements outlining the strengths and limitations of classical conditioning, operant conditioning, and observational learning in explaining how behaviors are acquired and maintained.

Point/Counterpoint

The use of behavior modification has been a source of controversy among psychologists and others. Prepare arguments supporting each of the following positions:

a. Behavior modification should be used in society to shape the behavior of others.
b. Behavior modification should not be used in society to shape the behavior of others.

Psychology in Your Life

Think of a behavior of a friend, a family member, or a professor that you would like to change. Using what you know about classical conditioning, operant conditioning, and observational learning, formulate a detailed plan for changing the behavior of the target person.

Chapter Summary and Review

Classical Conditioning

What was Pavlov's major contribution to psychology?

Ivan Pavlov's study of the conditioned reflex provided psychology with a model of learning called classical conditioning.

How is classical conditioning accomplished?

During classical conditioning, a neutral stimulus (tone) is presented shortly before an unconditioned stimulus (food), which naturally elicits or brings forth an unconditioned response (salivation). After repeated pairings, the conditioned stimulus (tone) alone will elicit the conditioned response (salivation).

How does extinction occur in classical conditioning?

If the conditioned stimulus (tone) is presented repeatedly without the unconditioned stimulus (food), the conditioned response (salivation) will become progressively weaker and eventually disappear—a process called extinction.

What is generalization?

Generalization occurs when an organism makes a conditioned response to a stimulus similar to the original conditioned stimulus.

What is discrimination in classical conditioning?

Discrimination refers to the ability to distinguish between similar stimuli, so that the conditioned response is made only to the original conditioned stimulus.

How did John B. Watson demonstrate that fear could be classically conditioned?

John Watson demonstrated that fear could be classically conditioned when, by presenting a white rat along with a loud, frightening noise, he conditioned Little Albert to fear the white rat.

What are four factors that influence classical conditioning?

Four factors influencing classical conditioning are (1) the number of pairings of conditioned stimulus and unconditioned stimulus, (2) the intensity of the unconditioned stimulus, (3) how reliably the conditioned stimulus predicts the unconditioned stimulus, and (4) the temporal relationship between the conditioned stimulus and unconditioned stimulus.

Key Terms

learning (p. 152)
classical conditioning (p. 153)
conditioned reflex (p. 155)
unconditioned response (p. 155)
unconditioned stimulus (p. 155)
conditioned stimulus (p. 156)
conditioned response (p. 156)
extinction (p. 157)
spontaneous recovery (p. 157)
generalization (p. 157)
discrimination (p. 158)
taste aversion (p. 163)

Operant Conditioning

What was B. F. Skinner's major contribution to psychology?

B. F. Skinner's major contribution to psychology was his exhaustive research on operant conditioning.

How are responses acquired through operant conditioning?

Operant conditioning is a method for conditioning voluntary responses. The consequences of behavior are manipulated to shape a new response or to increase or decrease the frequency of an existing response.

How is shaping used to condition a new response?

In shaping, rather than waiting for the desired response to be emitted, successive approximations toward the goal response are selectively reinforced until the desired response is achieved.

How does extinction occur in operant conditioning?

In operant conditioning, extinction is accomplished by withholding reinforcement.

How do positive reinforcement and negative reinforcement differ?

The probability of a response is increased with positive reinforcement by following it with a reward, or with negative reinforcement by following it with the termination of an aversive or unpleasant stimulus.

What are the four major schedules of reinforcement, and which schedule yields the highest response rate and the greatest resistance to extinction?

The four basic schedules of reinforcement are the fixed-ratio, variable-ratio, fixed-interval, and variable-interval schedules. The variable-ratio schedule provides the highest response rate and the most resistance to extinction.

What is the partial-reinforcement effect?

The partial-reinforcement effect refers to the greater resistance to extinction that occurs when responses are maintained under partial reinforcement rather than under continuous reinforcement.

What three factors increase the effectiveness of punishment?

Punishment is most effective when it is administered immediately following undesirable behavior, when it is consistently applied, and when it is fairly intense.

What are some disadvantages of punishment?

Punishment generally suppresses rather than extinguishes behavior; it does not help people develop more appropriate behaviors; and it can cause fear, anger, hostility, and aggression in the punished person.

What three factors, in addition to the schedule of reinforcement, influence operant conditioning?

In operant conditioning, acquisition of a response, response rate, and resistance to extinction are influenced by the magnitude of reinforcement, the immediacy of reinforcement, and the motivation of the organism.

What is biofeedback?

Biofeedback involves the use of sensitive equipment to give people precise feedback about internal physiological processes so that they can learn, with practice, to exercise control over them.

What is behavior modification?

Behavior modification involves the systematic application of learning principles to individuals or groups in order to eliminate undesirable behavior and/or encourage desirable behavior.

Key Terms

law of effect (p. 165)
operant conditioning (p. 166)
shaping (p. 166)
extinction (p. 168)
reinforcement (p. 170)
positive reinforcement (p. 170)
negative reinforcement (p. 170)
schedule of reinforcement (p. 171)
fixed-ratio schedule (p. 171)
variable-ratio schedule (p. 172)
fixed-interval schedule (p. 172)
variable-interval schedule (p. 173)
partial-reinforcement effect (p. 174)
punishment (p. 174)

biofeedback (p. 178)
behavior modification (p. 179)

Cognitive Learning

What is insight, and how does it affect learning?

Insight is the sudden realization of the relationship between elements in a problem situation that makes the solution apparent; this solution is easily learned and transferred to new problems.

What is latent learning?

Latent learning occurs without apparent reinforcement but is not demonstrated in performance until the organism is motivated to do so.

What is observational learning?

Observational learning is learning by observing the behavior of others, called models, and the consequences of that behavior.

Key Terms

cognitive processes (p. 180)
insight (p. 181)
latent learning (p. 181)
observational learning (p. 182)
modeling (p. 182)
model (p. 182)

6

Memory

Ronald Clauser   Father Pagano

"No, no, not me. Not me!" cried Hen Van Nguyen in halting English. This unfortunate Vietnamese immigrant, on trial for murder, protested his innocence for two full days at the trial before it was discovered that he was not the real defendant. Before the trial, Nguyen had been charged with theft and was being held in a Georgia county jail. In the same jail, was another Vietnamese man who had been accused of stabbing to death the woman he lived with.

The jailer had mistakenly delivered the wrong man to the courtroom. Yet unbelievably, during the trial, two eyewitnesses identified Nguyen and swore that he had committed the murder. Even more astonishing, the defense attorney, who had met several times with his client to prepare his defense, sat with the wrong man in the courtroom and defended him for two days. The county sheriff remarked, "How the defense attorney did not know his client, I don't know." (Adapted from "Wrong Man Tried for Murder," 1985, p. 9A.)

In this case, the defense attorney, the sheriff, and the eyewitnesses were all members of a different racial group from Mr. Nguyen. In another case, however, even though all seven eyewitnesses were of the same race as the suspect, they picked the wrong man. Look at the photographs to the left. Do these two men look alike to you?

In a famous case in Delaware, a Catholic priest was arrested for a series of armed robberies. At his trial, 53-year-old Father Pagano was identified by seven eyewitnesses and probably would have been convicted if another man, Ronald Clauser, did not confess to the robberies. The unbelievable part of this case is that the priest was shorter, thinner, bald, and 14 years older than the confessed robber, who had a full head of hair. (Adapted from Buckout, 1979.)

Do these two cases simply reflect the rare and unusual in human memory, or are memory errors common occurrences? This and many other questions you may have about memory will be answered in this chapter. We will describe three memory systems: sensory, short-term, and long-term. You will learn how much information each system holds, for how long, and in what form. You will discover why virtually everyone finds it harder to remember names than faces. Is memory like a video recorder, in which the sights and sounds we experience are captured intact and simply played back in exact detail? Or do we "reconstruct" the past when we remember, leaving out certain bits and pieces of events that actually happened and adding others that did not?

Would you like to improve your memory? You will learn some techniques that can help you study more effectively, and some mnemonic devices (memory strategies) that can be used in practical ways every day as memory aids. Now read on and . . . remember.

Research shows that babies use their memory much earlier than once thought. This 3-month-old remembers that the mobile will move when she kicks her left foot.

Remembering

Our memory is the storehouse for everything we know. It enables us to know who and where we are when we awaken each morning. Memory provides the continuity of life—the long thread to which are tied our joys and sorrows, our knowledge and skills, our triumphs and failures, and the people and places that form our lives.

Most of the current scientific efforts to understand human memory have been conducted within a framework known as the information-processing approach

(Klatzky, 1984). This approach makes use of modern computer science and other related fields to provide models or frames of reference that help us understand the processes involved in memory.

The Three Processes in Memory: Encoding, Storage, and Retrieval

Question: What three processes are involved in the act of remembering?

What must occur to enable us to remember a friend's name, a fact from history, or an incident from our past? The act of remembering requires the successful completion of three processes: encoding, storage, and retrieval. The first process, **encoding**, involves transforming information into a form that can be stored in memory. Sometimes we encode information automatically, without any effort, but often we must do something with the information in order to remember it. For example, if you met someone named George at a party, you might associate his name with George Washington or George Bush. Such simple associations, as you will see, can markedly improve your ability to recall names and other information. The careful encoding of information greatly increases the chance that you will remember it.

The second process in memory, **storage**, involves keeping or maintaining information in memory. In order for the encoded information to be stored, some physiological change in the brain must take place—a process called **consolidation**. Consolidation occurs automatically under normal circumstances, but if a person loses consciousness for any reason, the process can be disrupted and a permanent memory will not form (Deutsch & Deutsch, 1966). That is why it is not unusual for a person who has been in a serious car accident to awaken in a hospital and not remember what has happened.

The final process, **retrieval**, occurs when information stored in memory is brought to mind. Calling George by name the next time you meet him shows that you have retrieved his name from memory. To remember, we must perform all three of these processes—encode the information, store it, and then retrieve it. Memory failure can result from the failure of any one of the three processes (see Figure 6.1).

Similar steps are required in the information processing of computers. Information is encoded (entered in some form the computer is able to use), then stored on hard or floppy disks, and later retrieved on the screen or the printer.

encoding: Transforming information into a form that can be stored in short-term or long-term memory.

storage: The act of maintaining information in memory.

consolidation: The presumed process, believed to involve the hippocampus, by which a permanent memory is formed.

retrieval: The act of bringing to mind material that has been stored in memory.

Figure 6.1 The Processes Required in Remembering The act of remembering requires the successful completion of three processes: encoding, storage, and retrieval. Memory failure can result from the failure of any one of the three processes.

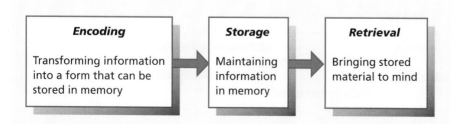

sensory memory: The memory system that holds information coming in through the senses for a period ranging from a fraction of a second to several seconds.

You would not be able to retrieve the material if you had failed to enter it, if a power failure occurred before you could save what you had entered, or if you forgot which disk or file contained the needed information. Of course, human memory is far more complex than even the most advanced computer systems, but computer processing provides a useful analogy to memory, provided we don't take it too literally.

The Three Memory Systems: The Long and the Short of It

How are memories stored? According to the Atkinson-Shiffrin model, there are three different, interacting memory systems known as sensory, short-term, and long-term memory (Atkinson & Shiffrin, 1968; Broadbent, 1958; Shiffrin & Atkinson, 1969). We will examine each of the three memory systems shown in Figure 6.2.

Question: What is sensory memory?

Sensory Memory: Images and Echoes   As information comes in through the senses, virtually everything we see, hear, or otherwise sense is held in **sensory memory**, but only for the briefest period of time. Sensory memory normally holds visual images for a fraction of a second and sounds for about 2 seconds. Visual sensory memory lasts just long enough to keep whatever we are viewing from disappearing when we blink our eyes.

We know that a motion picture is a series of still pictures presented at the proper speed to create the illusion of movement. Our visual sensory memory retains one frame until the next one arrives, enabling us to see a flow of movement rather than discrete, still pictures. You can demonstrate visual sensory memory for yourself by doing the *Try It!*

Try It!

To prove the existence of the visual sensory memory, move your forefinger back and forth rapidly in front of your face. You will see what appears to be the blurred images of many fingers. This occurs because your sensory memory briefly holds a trace of the various positions that your finger occupies as it moves.

Figure 6.2 The Three Memory Systems   According to the Atkinson-Schiffrin model, there are three separate memory systems: sensory memory, short-term memory, and long-term memory.

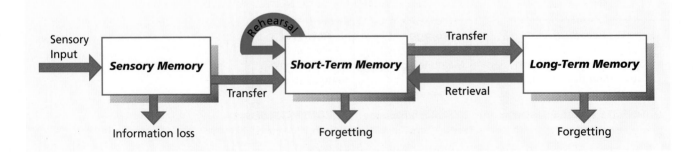

Sensory memory holds visual images, such as the moving pen light shown here, for a fraction of a second—just long enough for us to perceive a flow of movement.

Exactly how long does visual sensory memory last? In 1740 a Swedish investigator named Senger tried to answer this question. He attached a glowing ember to a rotating wheel and found that when he rotated the wheel rapidly, he could see a complete circle. When he rotated the wheel more slowly, he could see only a part of the circle. Senger then rotated the wheel at the exact speed that just allowed a complete circle to be perceived. He calculated the time of one revolution to be approximately one-tenth of a second (Baddeley, 1982).

For a fraction of a second, glance at the three rows of letters and numbers shown below and then close your eyes. How many of the items can you recall?

X B D F

M P Z G

L C N H

Most people can recall correctly only four or five of the items when they are briefly presented. Does this indicate that visual sensory memory can hold only four or five items at a time? No. Researcher George Sperling (1960) knew that our visual sensory capacity should enable us to take in most or all of the 12 items at a single glance. Could it be that sensory memory is so short-lived that while we are reporting some items, others have already faded from sensory memory? Sperling thought of an ingenious method to test this notion. He briefly flashed 12 items to his subjects. Immediately upon turning the pattern off, he sounded a high, medium, or low tone that signaled the subjects to report *only* the top, middle, or bottom row of items. Before they heard the tone, the subjects had no way of knowing which row they would have to report. Yet Sperling found that when the subjects could view the letters for 15/1,000 to 1/2 second, they could report correctly all the items in any row nearly 100 percent of the time. But the items fade from sensory memory so quickly that during the time it

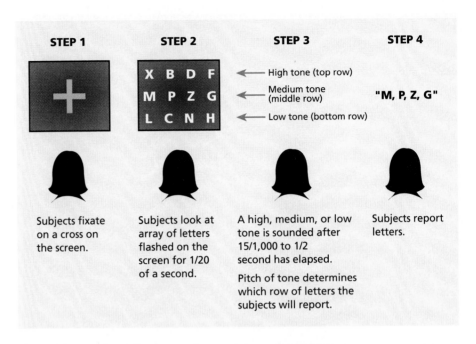

Figure 6.3 Sperling's Study of the Capacity of Sensory Memory George Sperling demonstrated that sensory memory holds more information than subjects are able to report completely because the visual afterimage fades so quickly. Sperling proved that subjects could retain 12 items in sensory memory but only long enough to report 4 items in the designated row. (Based on Sperling, 1960.)

takes to report three or four of the items, the other eight or nine have already disappeared. Figure 6.3 shows the steps involved in Sperling's research study.

Sensory memory for sound is similar to that for vision. You have experienced auditory sensory memory when the last few words someone has spoken seem to echo briefly in your head. Auditory sensory memory usually lasts about 2 seconds compared with the fraction of a second for visual sensory memory (Klatzky, 1980; Rostron, 1974).

We have seen that an abundance of information in raw, natural form can be stored briefly in sensory memory. This brief period is just long enough for us to begin to process the sensory stimuli and to select the most important information for further processing in the second memory system—short-term memory.

Question: What are the characteristics of short-term memory?

Short-Term Memory: Short Life, Small Capacity Whatever you are thinking about right now is in your **short-term memory** (STM). We use it when we carry on a conversation, solve a problem, or look up a telephone number and remember it just long enough to dial it.

Short-term memory does not hold virtually the exact sensory stimulus the way sensory memory does. Short-term memory usually codes information according to sound, that is, in acoustic form (Conrad, 1964). The letter "T" is coded as the sound "tee," not the shape of the letter **T**. Short-term memory can also hold visual images and store information in semantic form (according to meaning) as well (Scarborough, 1972; Shulman, 1972).

The Capacity of Short-Term Memory Unlike sensory memory, which can hold a vast amount of information briefly, short-term memory has a very limited

short-term memory: The second stage of memory, which holds about 7 (a range of 5 to 9) items for less than 30 seconds without rehearsal; working memory; the mental workspace we use to keep in mind tasks we are thinking about at any given moment.

capacity—about seven different items or bits of information at one time. Test the capacity of your short-term memory in the *Try It!*

Read aloud the digits in the first row (row "a" below) at a steady rate of about two per second. Then from memory, write them down on a sheet of paper. Repeat the process, row by row.

Try It!

   a. 3 8 7 1
   b. 9 6 4 7 3
   c. 1 8 3 0 5 2
   d. 8 0 6 5 9 1 7
   e. 5 2 9 7 3 1 2 5
   f. 2 7 4 0 1 9 6 8 3
   g. 3 9 1 6 5 8 4 5 1 7

How well did you do? You just learned that most people recall about seven items. This is just enough for phone numbers and the ordinary zip codes. (Nine-digit zip codes strain the capacity of most people.) When short-term memory is filled to capacity, *displacement* can occur (Waugh & Norman, 1965). In displacement, each new, incoming item pushes out an existing item, which is then forgotten.

One way to overcome the limitation of seven or so bits of information is to use a technique that psychologist George A. Miller (1956) calls chunking. Chunking means organizing or grouping separate bits of information into larger units, or chunks. A chunk is an easily identifiable unit such as a syllable, a word, an acronym, or a number (Cowan, 1988). For example, the numbers 5 2 9 7 3 1 2 5 could be chunked 52 97 31 25, leaving the short-term memory with the easier task of dealing with four chunks of information instead of eight separate bits. Complete the *Try It!* and see if chunking works for you.

Read the following letters individually at the rate of about one per second and then see if you can repeat them.

Try It!

       N-F L-C-B S-U-S A-V-C R-F-B I

Did you have difficulty? Probably so, because there are 15 different letters. But now try this:

           NFL CBS USA VCR FBI

Did you find that five chunks are easier to remember than 15 separate items?

Chunking is a very useful technique for increasing the capacity of short-term memory, but there are limits. Simon (1974) suggests that the larger the chunk, the fewer chunks we can remember.

The Duration of Short-Term Memory   Items in short-term memory are lost very quickly, in less than 30 seconds, unless we repeat them over and over to ourselves, silently or out loud, to retain them. This process is known as re-

displacement: The act that occurs when short-term memory is holding its maximum and each new item entering short-term memory pushes out an existing item.

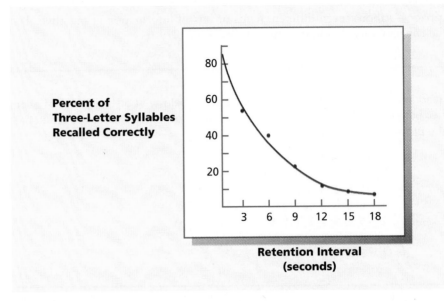

**Percent of
Three-Letter Syllables
Recalled Correctly**

**Retention Interval
(seconds)**

Figure 6.4   Results of the Peterson and Peterson Experiment   The backward-counting task kept subjects from rehearsing the consonant syllables. The longer the interval of counting, the fewer consonant syllables were recalled. At 18 seconds, recall was nearly zero. (From Peterson & Peterson, 1959.)

hearsal. We rehearse telephone numbers that we have looked up to keep them in short-term memory long enough to dial the number. But short-term memory is easily disrupted. It is so fragile, in fact, that an interruption or a distraction can cause information to be lost in just a few seconds.

Researchers have tried to determine how long short-term memory lasts if rehearsal is prevented. In a series of early studies, subjects were briefly shown three consonants, such as *H, G,* and *L,* and were then asked to count backward by threes from a given number (738, 735, 732, and so on). After intervals lasting from 3 to 18 seconds, subjects were instructed to stop their backward counting and recall the three letters (Brown, 1958; Peterson & Peterson, 1959). Following a delay of 9 seconds, the subjects could recall an average of only one of the three letters. After 18 seconds, there was practically no recall whatsoever. An 18-second distraction had completely erased the three letters from short-term memory (see Figure 6.4).

Short-Term Memory as Working Memory   Short-term memory is more than just a system that holds information received from sensory memory until we are able to store it in long-term memory. Allan Baddeley (1992, 1986, 1988) suggests that "working memory" is a more fitting term because short-term memory is used as a kind of mental work space to keep in mind the tasks we are working on or thinking about at any given moment. Sometimes it is necessary to call up material from long-term memory while we carry out our mental activities. For example, when reading a book or listening to a lecture, we are enabled by short-term memory to recall and consider information we have already learned about the topic (Waldrop, 1987). When we write a paper, every word must first be retrieved from long-term memory and then held in short-term or working memory long enough for us to write it down.

Question: What is long-term memory, and what are its subsystems?

rehearsal: The act of purposely repeating information to maintain it in short-term memory or to transfer it to long-term memory.

Long-Term Memory: As Long as a Lifetime   Some information from short-term memory makes its way into long-term memory. **Long-term memory** (LTM) is our vast storehouse of permanent or relatively permanent memories. There are no known limits to the storage capacity of long-term memory, and long-term memories last a long time, some of them for a lifetime.

When we talk about memory in everyday conversation, we are usually referring to long-term memory. Long-term memory holds all the knowledge we have accumulated, the skills we have acquired, and the memories of our past experiences. Although visual images, sounds, and odors can be stored in long-term memory, information in long-term memory is usually stored in semantic form.

But how does this vast store of information make its way from short-term memory into long-term memory? We seem to remember some information with ease, almost automatically, but other kinds of material require great effort. Sometimes, through mere repetition or rehearsal, we are able to transfer information into long-term memory. Your teachers may have used drill to try to cement the multiplication tables and other material in your long-term memory. This rote rehearsal, however, is not necessarily the best way to transfer information to long-term memory (Craik & Watkins, 1973; Woodward et al., 1973). When you relate new information to the information already safely tucked away in long-term memory and then form multiple associations, you increase the chance that you will be able to retrieve the new information. Figure 6.5 summarizes the three memory systems.

Procedural Memory and Declarative Memory   A number of experts believe that there are several systems within long-term memory itself. Researchers use different terms for these systems. They differentiate between one memory system for skills, generally referred to as **procedural memory**, and another memory system for facts, information, and personal life experiences, called **declarative memory**.

long-term memory: The relatively permanent memory system with a virtually unlimited capacity.

procedural memory: The subsystem within long-term memory that holds our memory for motor skills gained through repetitive practice.

declarative memory: The subsystem within long-term memory that stores facts, information, and personal life experiences.

Figure 6.5   Characteristics and Processes Involved in the Three Memory Systems

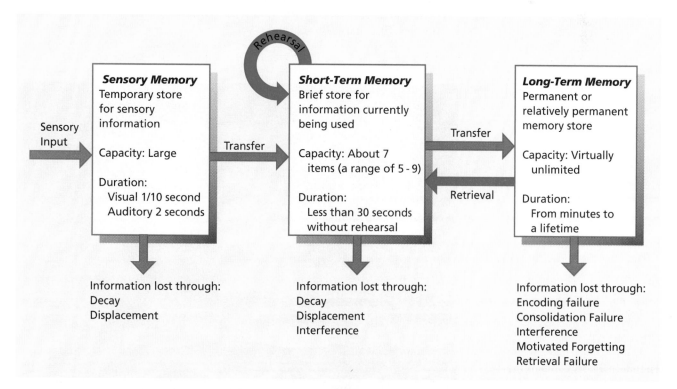

Procedural memory involves learning based on habit, including skills acquired through repetitive practice such as eating with a fork, riding a bicycle, typing, or driving a car. Once learned, these skills become habit and can be remembered and carried out with little or no conscious effort.

Declarative memory consists of facts, information, and personal life events that can be brought to mind verbally or in the form of images and then declared or stated. Declarative memory is accessible to conscious awareness. Figure 6.6 shows examples of procedural and declarative memory.

Episodic Memory and Semantic Memory Endel Tulving (1972, 1985, 1987) differentiates three systems in long-term memory—procedural, episodic, and semantic. **Episodic memory** contains the memory of events we have experienced personally. According to Tulving (1989):

> The episodic system stores and makes possible subsequent recovery of information about personal experiences from the past. It enables people to travel back in time, as it were, into their personal past, and to become consciously aware of having witnessed or participated in events and happenings at earlier times. (p. 362)

Episodic memory is somewhat like a mental diary, recording the episodes of our lives—the people we have known, the places we have seen, and the personal experiences we have had. A person would be calling on episodic memory to make the following statements:

> "Last summer I went to Florida on my vacation."
> "I did the grocery shopping this morning."
> "I took French in high school and Spanish in college."

Semantic memory is our memory for common knowledge and is made up of general facts and information. In other words, semantic memory is our mental dictionary or encyclopedia of stored knowledge.

> The three memory systems are sensory, short-term, and long-term memory.
> Dictionary is spelled d-i-c-t-i-o-n-a-r-y.
> 10 times 10 equals 100.

Episodic memory contains the memory of events we have experienced personally.

Subsystems of Long-Term Memory

Declarative memory	**Procedural memory**
Memory for facts, information, and life experiences	Memory for skills learned through practice

Information learned in school

Everyday skills

Names and faces

Athletic skills

Addresses and telephone numbers

Playing a musical instrument

Figure 6.6 Subsystems of Long-Term Memory A number of researchers have identified subsystems within long-term memory. Two subsystems are declarative memory and procedural memory.

If you have ever played the board game Trivial Pursuit, you called on semantic memory almost exclusively to answer the questions. As a rule, the semantic facts you have stored are not personally referenced to time and place like episodic memories are. You probably do not remember exactly where and when you learned to spell *dictionary* or that 10×10 equals 100.

levels-of-processing model:
A single memory system
model in which retention
depends on how deeply information is processed.

The Levels-of-Processing Model: Another View of Memory

Not all psychologists support the notion of three memory systems. Craik and Lockhart (1972) propose instead a **levels-of-processing model**. They suggest that whether we remember an item for a few seconds or a lifetime depends on how deeply we process the information. With the shallowest levels of processing, we are merely aware of the incoming sensory information. Deeper processing takes place only when we do something more with the information—when we form a relationship, make an association, or attach meaning to a sensory impression.

Craik and Tulving (1975) tested the levels-of-processing model. They had subjects answer yes or no to questions asked about words just before the words were flashed to them for one-fifth of a second. The subjects had to process the words: (1) visually (Was the word in capital letters?), (2) acoustically (Does the word rhyme with another particular word?), and (3) semantically (Does the word make sense when used in a particular sentence?). Test yourself in the *Try It!*

Try It!

	Yes	No
1. Is the word in capital letters? LARK	_____	_____
2. Does the word rhyme with sleet? speech	_____	_____
3. Would the word make sense in this sentence? park	_____	_____

The woman passed a _____ on her way to work.

The test required shallow processing for the first question, deeper processing for the second question, and the deepest processing for the third question. Later the subjects were unexpectedly given a retention test to see whether deeper levels of processing would facilitate memory. Craik and Tulving report that the deeper the level of processing, the higher the accuracy rate of memory.

Memory Check 6.1

1. The three processes required in the act of remembering are:

   a. decoding, consolidation, and recall
   b. recall, recognition, and relearning
   c. sensory, short-term, and long-term memory
   d. encoding, storage, and retrieval

2. The sensory memory holds information coming in through the senses for a period ranging from a fraction of a second to several (seconds, minutes).

3. (Declarative memory, Short-term memory) is equated with consciousness or working memory and holds about seven unrelated items for less than 30 seconds.

(continued)

4. Learning to ride a bicycle involves (declarative, procedural) memory.

5. The subpart of long-term memory that is autobiographical in nature is (episodic memory, semantic memory); the subpart that is like an encyclopedia or dictionary of stored knowledge is (episodic memory, semantic memory).

Answers: 1. d 2. seconds 3. Short-term memory 4. procedural 5. episodic memory; semantic memory

Measuring Memory

Three Methods of Measuring Memory

Question: What are three methods of measuring retention?

Psychologists have used three main methods of measuring memory: recall, recognition, and the relearning method.

Recall: Memory at Its Best   Of the three methods of measuring memory, recall tasks are usually the most difficult. In **recall** we must produce the required information by searching our memory without the help of **retrieval cues**. Trying to remember someone's name, recalling items on a shopping list, memorizing a speech or a poem word for word, and remembering appointments are all recall tasks. Test items such as essay and fill-in-the-blank questions require recall. Try to answer the following question:

The three processes involved in memory are _____, _____, and _____.

To recall, we must remember information "cold." A recall task may be made a little easier if cues are provided to jog our memory. Such cues might consist of providing the first letter of the required words for fill-in-the-blank questions. If you did not recall the three terms in the first question, try again with cued recall.

The three processes involved in memory are e_____, s_____, and r_____.

Sometimes serial recall is required; that is, information must be recalled in a specific order. This is the way you learned your ABC's, memorized poems, and learned any sequences that had to be carried out in a certain order. Often serial recall is easier than free recall—recalling the items in any order—because in serial recall, each letter, word, or task may serve as a cue for the one that follows.

We may fail to recall information in a memory task even if we are given many different retrieval cues, but this does not necessarily mean that the information is not in long-term memory. We still might be able to remember if a recognition test were used to measure memory.

Recognition: I've Seen That Before   **Recognition** is exactly what the name implies. We simply recognize something as familiar—a face, a name, a taste, a melody, or some other information. Multiple choice, matching, and true/false questions are examples of recognition test items. Consider a version of the question that was posed before:

Which of the following is *not* one of the processes involved in memory?
a.   encoding   b.   assimilation   c.   storage   d.   retrieval

recall: A measure of retention that requires one to remember material with few or no retrieval cues, as in an essay test.

retrieval cue: Any stimulus or bit of information that aids in the retrieval of particular information from long-term memory.

recognition: A measure of retention that requires one to identify material as familiar, or as having been encountered before.

relearning method: Measuring retention in terms of the percentage of time or learning trials saved in relearning material compared with the time required to learn it originally.

savings score: The percentage of time or learning trials saved in relearning material over the amount of time or number of learning trials taken in the original learning.

Was this recognition question easier than the recall version? The main difference between recall and recognition is that a recognition task does not require you to supply the information but only to recognize it when you see it. The correct answer is included along with the other items in a recognition question.

Are you better at remembering faces than names? Have you ever wondered why? Actually the task involves recognition as opposed to recall. We must recall the name but merely recognize the face and, as we have seen, recognition is easier than recall. Remembering faces would be considerably more difficult if we had to recall each feature of a person's face rather than simply recognize it as familiar. But are we better at recognizing faces than names? No. When recognition is the memory task, according to Faw (1990), there is no difference in our ability to recognize faces and names.

The Relearning Method: Learning Is Faster the Second Time Around

There is yet another way to measure memory that is even more sensitive than recognition. With the **relearning method** (the savings method), retention is expressed as the percentage of time saved when material is relearned compared with the time required to learn the material originally. Suppose it took you 40 minutes to memorize a list of words, and one month later you were tested, using recall or recognition, to see how many of the words you remembered. If you could not recall or recognize a single word, would this mean that you had absolutely no memory of anything on the test? Or could it mean that the recall and the recognition methods of testing were not sensitive enough to pick up what little information you may have stored? How could we measure a remnant of this former learning? Using the relearning method, we could time how long it would take you to relearn the list of words. If it took 20 minutes to relearn the list, this would represent a 50-percent savings over the original learning time of 40 minutes. The percentage of time saved—the *savings score*—reflects how much material remains in long-term memory.

Often parents wonder if the time they spend reading to their young children or exposing them to good music has any lasting influence. Do some traces of such early exposure remain? Many years ago, H. E. Burtt (1932) carried out a unique relearning experiment on his son Benjamin to study this question.

Every day Burtt read to his son three passages from Sophocles' *Oedipus Tyrannus* in the original Greek. He would repeat the same three passages for 3 months, and then read three new passages for the next 3 months. This procedure continued from the time Benjamin was 15 months until he was 3 years old. Nothing more was done for 5 years until the boy reached the age of eight. Then Burtt tested Benjamin by having him memorize some of the passages read to him originally and some similar passages that he had never heard before. It took Benjamin 27 percent fewer trials to memorize the original passages than the new passages. This 27 percent savings score suggests that a considerable amount of information remained in his memory for an extended period of time—information that would not have been detected using recall or recognition tests. Furthermore, the study suggests that even information we do not understand can be stored in memory. Between 15 months and 3 years of age, young Benjamin did not speak or understand Greek, yet much of the information remained in his memory for years.

Available research strongly supports the notion that the relearning method is superior to recognition and recall in measuring fully what we have learned (Nelson, 1978, 1985; Groninger & Groninger, 1980). College students demonstrate this method each semester when they study for comprehensive final exams. Relearning material for the final exams takes less time than it took to learn the materials originally.

Hermann Ebbinghaus and the First Experimental Studies on Learning and Memory

Question: What was Hermann Ebbinghaus's major contribution to psychology?

Hermann Ebbinghaus (1850–1909) conducted the first experimental studies on learning and memory. In 1885 he published his findings in a small but important volume entitled simply *Memory*. Ebbinghaus realized that some materials are easier than others to understand and remember. To study memory objectively, he was faced with the task of selecting materials that would all be equally difficult to memorize. To accomplish this task, he invented the **nonsense syllable**, which is a consonant-vowel-consonant combination that is not an actual word. Examples are *LEJ, XIZ, LUQ,* and *ZOH.* Ebbinghaus (1885) conducted his famous studies on memory using 2,300 nonsense syllables as his material and using himself as his only subject. He carried out all his experiments in the same surroundings at about the same time of day, and he kept away all possible distractions.

Ebbinghaus's method was to learn lists of nonsense syllables, repeating them over and over at a constant rate of 2.5 syllables per second, marking time with a metronome or the ticking of a watch. He repeated a list until he could recall it twice without error, a point that he called mastery.

Ebbinghaus recorded the amount of time or the number of learning trials it took to memorize his lists to mastery. Then, after different periods of time had passed and forgetting had occurred, he recorded the amount of time or the number of trials he needed to relearn the same list to mastery. Ebbinghaus compared the time or the trials required for relearning with those of the original learning and then computed the percentage of time saved, called a savings score. For him, the percentage of savings represented the percentage of the original learning that remained in memory.

Ebbinghaus learned and relearned over 1,200 lists of nonsense syllables to discover how rapidly forgetting occurs (Slamecka, 1985). His famous curve of forgetting, shown in Figure 6.7, consists of savings scores at various time intervals after the original learning.

Figure 6.7 Ebbinghaus's Curve of Forgetting After memorizing lists of nonsense syllables similar to those at the left, Ebbinghaus measured his retention after varying intervals of time using the relearning method. Forgetting was most rapid at first, as shown by his retention of only 58 percent after 20 minutes and 44 percent after one hour. Then the rate of forgetting tapered off with a retention of 34 percent after one day, 25 percent after 6 days, and 21 percent after 31 days. (Data from Ebbinghaus, 1913).

nonsense syllable: A consonant-vowel-consonant combination that does not spell a word; used to control for the meaningfulness of the material.

Hermann Ebbinghaus (1850–1909) conducted the first experimental studies on learning and memory.

HEJ	TUQ
PIW	QAM
RUJ	FOQ
MAF	CUG
LEV	PIJ
ZAD	BUP
KIR	DEG
GAK	JUC
NUH	SIW
TOV	HUQ
JAK	VUZ
WIB	LOM
KEF	NID

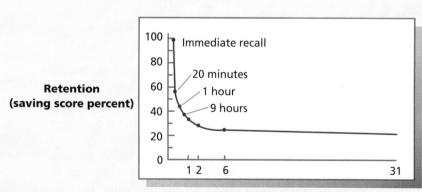

Retention (saving score percent)

Immediate recall
20 minutes
1 hour
9 hours

Elapsed Time Since Learning (days)

What does the curve of forgetting show about how rapidly this type of material is forgotten? The largest amount of forgetting occurs very quickly, then gradually tapers off. Ebbinghaus found that if he retained information as long as a day or two, very little more would be forgotten even a month later. But remember, this curve of forgetting applies to nonsense syllables. The forgetting of meaningful material usually occurs more slowly.

What Ebbinghaus learned about the rate of forgetting is relevant for all of us. Do you, like most students, cram before a big exam? If so, don't assume that everything you memorize on Monday can be held intact until Tuesday. Because a significant amount of forgetting can occur within the first 24 hours, it is wise to spend at least some time reviewing the material on the day of the test. The less meaningful the material is to you, the more forgetting you can expect and the more necessary a review will be.

Memory Check 6.2

1. The (recognition, relearning) method is the most sensitive way of measuring retention, and it can detect learning that other methods cannot.

2. Yolanda has witnessed a robbery, and the police have asked her to identify the guilty person in a police line-up. Yolanda is performing a (recall, recognition) task.

3. Alan has won his school's spelling bee by correctly spelling the word *conscious*. Alan has performed a (recall, recognition) task.

4. Ebbinghaus's curve of forgetting shows that memory loss:

   a. occurs most rapidly at first and then levels off to a slow decline
   b. begins to occur about 3 to 4 hours after learning
   c. occurs at a fairly steady rate over a month's time
   d. none of these

Answers: 1. *relearning* 2. *recognition* 3. *recall* 4. *a*

Forgetting

PATIENT: Doctor, you've got to help me. I'm sure I'm losing my memory. I hear something one minute and forget it the next. I don't know what to do!
DOCTOR: When did you first notice this?
PATIENT: Notice what?

Most of us think of forgetting as a problem to be overcome, but forgetting is not all bad. Wouldn't it be depressing if you were condemned to remember in stark detail all the bad things that ever happened to you? William James suggests that forgetting has its advantages. "In the practical use of our intellect, forgetting is as important a function as remembering. . . . If we remembered everything, we should on most occasions be as ill off as if we remembered nothing" (1892/1961, p. 167).

The Causes of Forgetting

Question: What are six causes of forgetting?

There are a number of reasons for our failure to remember. Among them are encoding failure, consolidation failure, decay, interference, motivated forgetting, and retrieval failure.

> **encoding failure:** A cause of forgetting resulting from material never having been put into long-term memory.

Encoding Failure: Never Entering Long-Term Memory   There is a distinction between forgetting and not being able to remember. Forgetting is "the inability to recall something now that could be recalled on an earlier occasion" (Tulving, 1974, p. 74). But often when we say we cannot remember, we have not actually forgotten. Our inability to remember may be a result of **encoding failure**—the information never entered our long-term memory in the first place. Of the many things we encounter every day, it is sometimes surprising how little we actually encode. Can you recall accurately, or even recognize, something you have seen thousands of times before? Read the *Try It!* to find out.

On a separate sheet of paper, draw a sketch of a U.S. penny from memory using recall. In your drawing, show the direction the President's image is facing, the location of the date, and include all the words and the images on the "heads" side of the penny. Or try the easier recognition task and see if you can recognize the real penny in the drawing provided here.

Try It!

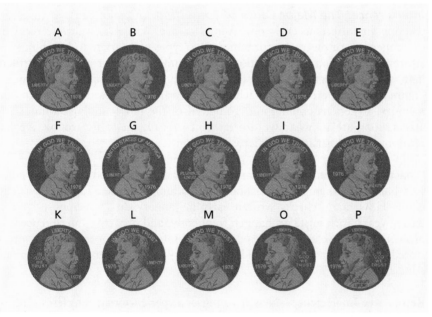

In your lifetime you have seen thousands of pennies, but unless you are a coin collector, you probably have not encoded the details of a penny. If you did poorly on this exercise, you have plenty of company. After studying a large group of subjects, Nickerson and Adams (1979) report that few people can reproduce a penny from recall. In fact, only a handful of subjects could even recognize a drawing of the real penny when it was presented along with the incorrect drawings. (The correct penny is labeled A in the drawing.)

consolidation failure: Any disruption in the consolidation process that prevents a permanent memory from forming.

retrograde amnesia (RET-ro-grade): A loss of memory for events occurring for a period of time preceding a brain trauma that caused a loss of consciousness.

decay theory: A theory of forgetting which holds that the memory trace, if not used, disappears with the passage of time.

interference: Memory loss that occurs because information or associations stored either before or after a given memory hinder our ability to remember it.

In preparing for tests, do you usually assume a passive role? Do you merely read and reread your textbook and notes and assume that this process will eventually result in learning? If you don't test yourself by reciting the material, you might find that you have been the unwitting victim of encoding failure.

Consolidation Failure: Failing to Form a Permanent Memory   Consolidation is the process by which a permanent memory is formed. When a disruption in the consolidation process occurs, a permanent memory usually does not form. **Consolidation failure** can result from anything that causes a person to lose consciousness—a car accident, a blow to the head, a grand mal seizure, or an electroconvulsive shock treatment given for severe depression. Memory loss of the experiences that occurred shortly before the loss of consciousness is called **retrograde amnesia** (Lynch & Yarnell, 1973; Stern, 1981).

Decay: Fading Away with Time   Decay theory, probably the oldest theory of forgetting, assumes that memories, if not used, fade with time and ultimately disappear entirely. The term *decay* implies a physiological change in the neural trace that recorded the experience. According to this theory, the neural trace may decay or fade within seconds, days, or much longer periods of time.

Today most psychologists would accept the notion of decay, or fading of the memory trace, as a cause of forgetting in sensory and short-term memory but not in long-term memory.

Question: What is interference, and how can it be minimized?

Interference: The Major Cause of Forgetting   A major cause of forgetting, and one that affects us every day, is **interference**. Whenever we try to recall any given memory or piece of information, two types of interference can hinder our efforts. Information or associations stored either before or after the particular item we want to remember can interfere with our success at remembering (see Figure 6.8). Interference can reach either forward or backward in time to affect memory. It gets us coming and going. Also, the more similar the interfering associations are to what we are trying to recall, the more trouble we have recalling the information (Underwood, 1964).

Proactive Interference   Laura's romance with her new boyfriend Todd got off to a bad start when she accidentally called him Dave, her former boyfriend's name. How many checks written early in January do you suppose have the wrong year? Such mistakes happen frequently, and proactive interference is the problem. Proactive interference occurs when information or experiences already stored in long-term memory hinder our ability to remember newer information (Underwood, 1957).

Retroactive Interference   New learning or experience that interferes with our ability to remember information previously stored is called retroactive interference. The more similar the new learning or experience is to the previous learning, the more interference there is.

What can we do to minimize interference? You may be surprised to learn that of all the activities we engage in, sleep interferes with previous learning the least. In one of the earliest studies of the effect of interference on memory, four subjects memorized a list of nonsense syllables (Jenkins & Dallenbach, 1924). Two subjects memorized the list to mastery late in the evening and immediately went to bed. Two other subjects memorized the list to mastery earlier in the day and then went about their normal waking activities. The researchers compared the retention of the first two subjects after 1, 2, 4, and 8 hours of sleep with the retention of the second two subjects after 1, 2, 4, and 8 hours of being awake.

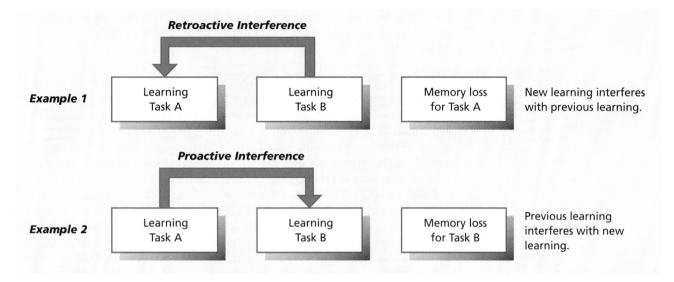

Figure 6.8 Retroactive and Proactive Interference In Example 1 retroactive interference occurs when new learning hinders the ability to recall information learned previously. In Example 2 proactive interference occurs when prior learning hinders new learning.

They found that retention scores were much higher when sleep followed learning. Subjects who stayed awake 8 hours recalled about 10 percent of the nonsense syllables, while subjects who slept for 8 hours remembered 50 to 60 percent of the material.

What can you do to lessen the effects of retroactive interference on memory?

■ When possible, study before going to sleep.
■ If you can't study before going to sleep, at least review at that time the material you need to remember.
■ Try not to study similar subjects back-to-back. Better yet, after studying one subject, take a short break before beginning the next subject.
■ Schedule your classes so that courses with similar subject matter do not follow each other.

We have discussed ways to avoid forgetting, but there are occasions in human experience when we may need to avoid remembering—times when we want to forget.

Motivated Forgetting: Don't Remind Me   Victims of rape or physical abuse, Vietnam War veterans, and survivors of an airline crash or earthquake all have had terrifying experiences that may haunt them for years. These victims are certainly motivated to forget their traumatic experiences, but even people who have not suffered any trauma use **motivated forgetting** to protect themselves from experiences that are painful, frightening, or otherwise unpleasant.

With one form of motivated forgetting, suppression, a person makes a conscious, active attempt to put a painful, disturbing, anxiety- or guilt-provoking memory out of mind, but the person is still aware that the painful event occurred. With another type of motivated forgetting, **repression**, unpleasant memories are literally removed from consciousness, and the person is no longer aware that the unpleasant event ever occurred (Freud, 1922). People who have **amnesia** that is not due to loss of consciousness or brain damage have actually repressed the events they no longer remember. Motivated forgetting is probably used by more people than any other method to deal with unpleasant memories.

motivated forgetting: Forgetting through suppression or repression in order to protect oneself from material that is too painful, anxiety- or guilt-producing, or otherwise unpleasant.

repression: Removing from one's consciousness disturbing, guilt-provoking, or otherwise unpleasant memories so that one is no longer aware a painful event occurred.

amnesia: A partial or complete loss of memory resulting from brain trauma or psychological trauma.

It seems to be a natural human tendency to forget the unpleasant circumstances of life and to remember the pleasant ones (Linton, 1979; Matlin, 1989; Meltzer, 1930).

Retrieval Failure: Misplaced Memories   How many times have these experiences happened to you? You are with a friend when you meet an acquaintance, but you can't introduce the two because you cannot recall the name of your acquaintance. Or, while taking a test, you can't remember the answer to a question that you are sure you know. Often we are certain that we know something, but we are not able to retrieve the information when we need it. This type of forgetting is called retrieval failure (Shiffrin, 1970).

Endel Tulving (1974) claims that much of what we call forgetting is really our inability to locate the information we seek. The information is in our long-term memory, but we cannot retrieve it. In his experiments, Tulving found that subjects could recall a large number of items they seemed to have forgotten if he provided retrieval cues to jog their memory. For example, odors often provide potent reminders of experiences from the past, and they can serve as retrieval cues for information learned when certain odors were present (Schab, 1990).

A common retrieval failure experience is known as the tip-of-the-tongue phenomenon (TOT) (Brown & McNeil, 1966). Surely you have experienced trying to recall a name, a word, or some other bit of information, knowing what you were searching for almost as well as your own name. You were on the verge of recalling the word or name, perhaps aware of the number of syllables and the beginning or ending letter of the word. It was on the tip of your tongue, but it just wouldn't quite come out.

Prospective Forgetting: Forgetting to Remember

Do you have trouble remembering appointments? Do you forget to mail birthday cards on time, pick up your clothes at the cleaners, pay your bills, or water your plants? If you do, you are not alone. In a study of everyday forgetting, Terry (1988) had 50 subjects keep a diary of the instances of forgetting that occurred each day. Of the 751 recorded instances of forgetting, most did not involve forgetting names, facts, or other information already known. Most instances involved prospective memory—remembering to carry out an action in the future.

Memory Check 6.3

1. When a person fails to remember because the information was never put into long-term memory, _____ has occurred.

   a. consolidation failure   c retrieval failure
   b. encoding failure   d. motivated forgetting

2. When traumatic events are removed from consciousness so that a person is no longer aware that they ever happened, (suppression, repression) has occurred.

3. Kim studied Spanish in high school and is now studying Italian in college. Her recall of a Spanish word when she is trying to write in Italian is an example of (proactive, retroactive) interference.

(continued)

4. To minimize interference, it is best to follow learning with:

    a. rest   c. sleep
    b. recreation   d. unrelated study

5. Decay is considered to be a major cause of forgetting in long-term memory. (true/false)

Answers: 1. b 2. repression 3. proactive 4. c 5. false

> **reconstruction:** A memory that is not an exact replica of an event but has been pieced together from a few highlights and using information that may or may not be accurate.

The Nature of Remembering and Forgetting

Memory as a Permanent Record: The Video Cassette Recorder Analogy

For hundreds of years people have speculated about the nature of memory. Aristotle suggested that the senses imprint memories in the brain like signet rings in wax. Sigmund Freud believed that all memories are permanently preserved, with some lying deep in the unconscious. Wilder Penfield (1969), a Canadian neurosurgeon, claimed that experiences leave a "permanent imprint on the brain . . . as though a tape recorder had been receiving it all" (p. 165). What would lead him to such a conclusion?

Penfield performed over 1,100 operations on patients with epilepsy, removing scar tissue from the cortex of the brain in an effort to reduce the frequency and the severity of their seizures. In such operations, it is necessary for the patient to be conscious so that areas of the brain can be mapped. By applying a mild electrical current to the cortex, the neurosurgeon is able to determine the function of many critical parts of the brain, which, if they were removed, would leave the patient severely impaired. Penfield found that when he stimulated parts of the temporal lobes, some of his patients reported flashback experiences as though they were actually reliving parts of their past.

Penfield's findings received considerable attention in the popular press and in psychology textbooks as well. However, while the flashback experiences are dramatic and intriguing, a closer look reveals that only 40 of Penfield's 1,132 patients (3.5 percent) actually reported such flashbacks (Penfield, 1975, p. 30).

After reviewing Penfield's findings, other researchers offer different explanations for his patients' responses. Neisser (1967) suggests that the experiences patients reported were "comparable to the content of dreams" (p. 169), rather than the recall of actual experiences.

Memory as a Reconstruction: Partly Fact and Partly Fiction

Question: What is meant by the statement "Memory is reconstructive in nature"?

Other than Penfield's work, there is no research to suggest that memory works like a video cassette recorder, capturing every part of an experience exactly as it happens. Normally what we recall is not an exact replica of an event, according to Elizabeth Loftus, a leading memory researcher. Rather, what we recall is a **reconstruction**—a memory that is pieced together from a few highlights, using information that may or may not be accurate (Loftus & Loftus, 1980). Recall is, even for those among us with the most accurate memories, partly truth and

When we recall an event, we are actually *reconstructing* it from memory by piecing together information that may or may not be totally accurate.

partly fiction. We supply what we *think* are facts to flesh out or complete those fragments of our experiences that we do recall accurately. This was the finding of another pioneer in memory research, the Englishman Sir Frederick Bartlett.

Sir Frederick Bartlett (1886–1969)   "The past is being continually remade, reconstructed in the interests of the present" (Bartlett, 1932, p. 309). We have seen that Ebbinghaus explored memory by memorizing nonsense syllables under rigidly controlled experimental conditions. In contrast, Sir Frederick Bartlett studied memory using rich and meaningful material learned and remembered under more lifelike conditions. Bartlett (1932) gave his subjects stories to read and drawings to study. Then at varying time intervals he had the subjects reproduce the original material. He found that accurate reports were rare. His subjects seemed to reconstruct the material they had learned, rather than actually remember it. They recreated the stories, making them shorter and more consistent with their own individual viewpoints. Puzzling features of the stories were rationalized to fit their expectations, and details were often changed with more familiar objects or events substituted instead. Bartlett also found that errors in memory increased with time, and that his subjects were not aware that they had partly remembered and partly invented. Ironically, the parts his subjects had created were often the very parts that they most adamantly claimed to have remembered.

Bartlett concluded that we systematically distort the facts and the circumstances of our experiences, and that we do not simply remember new experiences as isolated events. Rather, information already stored in long-term memory exerts a strong influence on how we remember new information and experiences.

Distortion in Memory   When we reconstruct our memories, we do not purposely try to distort the actual experience unless, of course, we are lying. But all of us tend to omit some facts that actually occurred and to supply other details from our own imaginations. Distortion occurs when we alter the memory of an event or of our experience in order to fit our beliefs, expectations, logic, or prejudices.

Since Bartlett's research, the tendency toward systematic distortion of actual events has been proven many times. Try your own demonstration of distortion in memory in the *Try It!* (Deese, 1959).

Try It!

Read this list of words aloud at a rate of about one word per second. Then close your book and write all the words you can remember.

| bed | rest | awake | tired | dream | wake |
| eat | night | comfort | sound | slumber | snore |

Now check your list. Did you "remember" the word *sleep*? Many people do, even though it is not one of the words on the list.

The *Try It!* shows that we are very likely to alter or distort what we see or hear to make it fit with what we believe *should* be true. All the words on the list are related to sleep, so it seems logical that *sleep* should be one of the words.

On the one hand, our tendency to distort makes our world more understandable and enables us to organize our experiences into our existing system of beliefs and expectations. On the other hand, this tendency is often responsible for gross inaccuracies in what we remember. The most dramatic examples of systematic distortion often occur in eyewitness testimony.

WORLD OF PSYCHOLOGY: APPLICATIONS

Eyewitness Testimony

When people say, "I ought to know, I saw it with my own eyes," we are likely to accept their statement almost without question. After all, seeing is believing. Or is it?

Traditionally, eyewitness testimony has been viewed as reliable by the legal system in the United States and elsewhere (Brigham & Wolfskeil, 1983). According to one estimate, each year in this country "about 77,000 individuals are suspects in cases in which the only critical evidence is eyewitness identification" (Goldstein et al., 1989, p. 71).

Recall Hen Van Nguyen and Father Pagano from our opening story, both victims of faulty eyewitness identification. Are their cases just two isolated incidents? Huff and others (1986) found that of 500 documented cases of wrongful convictions in Washington, D.C., 60 percent had been the result of eyewitness misidentification. Studies on the accuracy of human memory suggest that eyewitness testimony is highly subject to error, and that it should always be viewed with caution (Brigham et al., 1982; Loftus, 1979). But eyewitness testimony does play a vital role in our justice system. Says Elizabeth Loftus (1984), "We can't afford to exclude it legally or ignore it as jurors. Sometimes, as in cases of rape, it is the only evidence available, and it is often correct" (p. 24).

Fortunately, there are ways in which eyewitness mistakes can be minimized. Eyewitnesses to crimes typically identify suspects from a line-up. Mistakes in identification are likely to occur if eyewitnesses are shown photographs of suspects before viewing them in a line-up, or if care is not taken to have an unbiased line-up. The other subjects in a line-up should resemble the suspect in age, body build, and certainly in race.

Eyewitnesses are more likely to identify the wrong person if they are attempting to identify someone of a different race. This is particularly likely when whites try to identify blacks. Misidentification is also more likely to occur when a weapon is used in a crime. The weapon tends to monopolize the attention of eyewitnesses who may pay less attention to the physical characteristics of the criminal (Cutler et al., 1987; Ellis, 1984).

The questioning of witnesses after a crime can influence what they later remember, and leading questions can change substantially a witness's memory of the event (Loftus, 1975). Misleading information supplied after the event can result in erroneous recollections of the event itself, called the misinformation effect (Kroll et al., 1988; Loftus & Hoffman, 1989). Furthermore, witnessing a crime is stressful, and when stress is too great, our memory of events is less reliable. Unfortunately, witnesses can have great confidence in the accuracy of their testimony, even when it is grossly inaccurate (Loftus, 1984).

Hypnosis for Eyewitnesses Most of us have heard accounts of how eyewitnesses to crimes, when hypnotized, could recall important information about the crime. One such case, cited perhaps more often than any other, is the kidnaping case that occurred in Chowchilla, a small California town.

> In July 1976, a school bus was forced off the road by a gang of kidnapers. At gunpoint, 26 schoolchildren and their bus driver were herded into vans and driven to an isolated rock quarry and there, sealed inside a large tomblike area underneath the ground. After many terror-filled hours, the driver and two of the older boys were finally able to dig their way out. They called the police, and the other children were freed before the kidnapers were able to collect the ransom money.
>
> Extensive questioning of the driver and the children produced few, if any, leads in the case. But under hypnosis the driver was able to recall a license plate number. Although one digit was wrong, the rest of what the driver remembered led to the identification of a van owned by the kidnapers. One of the largest manhunts in California history ended with the arrest of the three kidnapers, who were all sentenced to life in prison. (Adapted from M. Smith, 1983.)

As a result of the publicity surrounding this well-known case and a few others, many people have taken the position of Freud and Penfield. They believed that memories are like videotape recordings, and that under hypnosis people can gain access to what is on the tape. But under controlled laboratory conditions, individuals do not show improved memory under hypnosis (Buckout et al., 1981). Hypnotized subjects supply more information and are more confident of their recollections, but they supply more inaccurate information as well (Dywan & Bowers, 1983; Nogrady et al., 1985). Because subjects are much more confident of their memories after hypnosis, they become very convincing witnesses. According to Whitehouse and others (1988), "If hypnosis is permitted to form the basis of testimony in court, the confident 'recollections' of a previously hypnotized witness could very well create a serious miscarriage of justice" (p. 294). While some critics of hypnosis are against using it in court as eyewitness testimony, they believe that it can be a valuable investigative tool as it was used in the Chowchilla case.

flashbulb memory: An extremely vivid memory of the conditions surrounding one's first hearing the news of a surprising, shocking, and highly emotional event.

Unusual Memory Phenomena

Flashbulb Memories: Extremely Vivid Memories   Most people over age 40 remember the assassination of President John F. Kennedy, and many of them claim to have unusually vivid memories of exactly when and where they received the news of the assassination. This type of extremely vivid memory is called a **flashbulb memory** (Brown & Kulik, 1977; Bohannon, 1988). Brown and Kulik suggest that a flashbulb memory is formed when an individual learns of an event that is very surprising, shocking, and highly emotional. You might have a flashbulb memory of when you received the news of the death or the serious injury of a close family member or a friend. For years to come, many people will have a vivid memory of where they were and what they were doing when Operation Desert Storm began or when they first heard the news of the Challenger explosion.

Reisberg and colleagues (1988) suggest that the vividness of a memory is related to the strength of the emotion we feel rather than to the element of surprise or whether the emotion is positive or negative (such as happiness and pleasure, or sadness and fear). Other researchers remind us that a memory remains vivid because the person has probably talked about the circumstance with others or thought about it on many occasions.

Pillemer (1990) argues that flashbulb memories do not constitute a different type of memory altogether. Rather, he suggests that all memories can vary on the dimensions of emotion, consequentiality (the importance of the consequences of the event), and rehearsal (how often people thought about the event afterwards). Flashbulb memories rank high in all three dimensions and thus are extremely memorable.

A flashbulb memory is formed when you learn of an event that is very surprising, shocking, and highly emotional, like the explosion of the space shuttle *Challenger* in 1987.

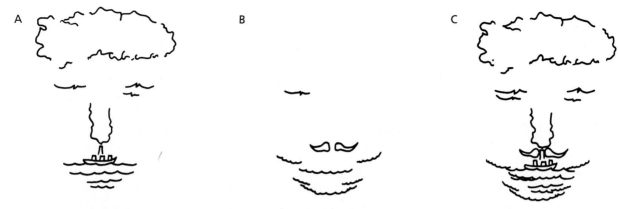

Figure 6.9 Test for Eidetic Imagery Children are tested for eidetic imagery by having them stare for 30 seconds at a picture like the one in (a). A few minutes later, the drawing in (b) is shown to the children, who are asked to report what they see. Those with eidetic imagery usually claim that they see a face and describe the composite sketch in (c). The face can be perceived only if the image of the first picture is retained and fused with the middle drawing that they are viewing. (From Haber, 1980.)

Eidetic Imagery: Almost Like "Photographic Memory" Have you ever wished that you had a photographic memory? Perhaps you have heard of someone who is able to read a page in a book and recall it word for word. More than likely, this person has developed such an enviable memory by learning and applying principles of memory improvement. Psychologists doubt that there are more than a few rare cases of a truly photographic memory, which captures all the details of any experience and retains them perfectly. But some studies do show that about 5 percent of children apparently have something akin to photographic memory that psychologists call eidetic imagery (Haber, 1980). **Eidetic imagery** is the ability to retain the image of a visual stimulus, such as a picture, for several minutes after it has been removed from view and to use this retained image to answer questions about the visual stimulus (see Figure 6.9).

Children with eidetic imagery generally have no better long-term memory than children without it, and virtually all children who have eidetic imagery lose it before adulthood. One exceptional case, however, is Elizabeth, a highly intelligent teacher and a skilled artist. Elizabeth can project on her canvas an exact duplicate of a remembered scene with all its rich detail. But even more remarkable is her ability to retain visual images other than scenes and pictures. "Years after having read a poem in a foreign language, she can fetch back an image of the printed page and copy the poem from the bottom line to the top line as fast as she can write" (Stromeyer, 1970, p. 77).

Memory Check 6.4

1. (Penfield, Bartlett) proposed that memory works like a tape recorder and that memories are stored permanently within the brain.

2. (Bartlett, James) found that people often reconstruct rather than remember experiences, systematically distorting facts to make them more consistent with past experiences.

(continued)

> **eidetic imagery** (eye-DET-ik): The ability to retain the image of a visual stimulus several minutes after it has been removed from view.

3. The confidence that eyewitnesses have in their testimony is a good indication of its accuracy. (true/false)

4. As a rule people's memories are more accurate under hypnosis. (true/false)

5. The ability to retain a visual image several minutes after it has been removed is called:

   a. photographic memory   c. eidetic imagery
   b. flashbulb memory   d. sensory memory

Answers: 1. Penfield 2. Bartlett 3. false 4. false 5. c

Factors Influencing Retrieval

Researchers in psychology have identified a number of factors that influence memory. We can control some of these factors, but not all of them.

The Serial Position Effect: To Be Remembered, Be First or Last but Not in the Middle

If you were introduced to a dozen people at a party, you would most likely recall the names of the first few people you met and the last one or two, but forget more of the names in the middle. A number of studies have revealed the **serial position effect**—the finding that for information learned in sequence, recall is better for items at the beginning and the end than for items in the middle.

We are likely to recall information at the beginning of a sequence because it already has been placed in long-term memory, and we are even more likely to recall information at the end of a sequence because it is still in short-term memory. The poorer recall of information in the middle of a sequence occurs because that information is no longer in short-term memory and has not yet been placed in long-term memory. The serial position effect lends strong support for the notion of separate systems for short-term and long-term memory (Postman & Phillips, 1965; Glanzer & Cunitz, 1966).

Environmental Context and Memory: Helping Memory by Returning to the Place Where You Learned It

Question: How does environmental context affect memory?

Have you ever stood in your living room and thought of something you needed from your bedroom, only to forget what it was when you went there? Did the item come to mind when you returned to the living room? Some research has revealed that we tend to recall information better when we are in the same location—the same environmental context—as when the information was originally encoded.

serial position effect: Upon presentation of a list of items, the tendency to remember the beginning and ending items better than the middle items.

Tulving and Thompson (1973) suggest that many elements of the physical setting in which we learn information are encoded along with the information and become part of the memory trace. If part or all of the original context is reinstated, it may serve as a retrieval cue. Then the information previously learned in that context may come to mind. This is known as the encoding specificity hypothesis.

One of the early studies of context and memory by Godden and Baddeley was prompted by the puzzling observations of a friend of the researchers who was in charge of a team of deep-sea divers. The divers were to observe the behavior of fish as they entered or tried to escape from trawl nets used by fishermen. But the divers had a problem. They found that their memory of these underwater observations failed them when they returned to the surface (Baddeley, 1982).

Why should observations made underwater be so hard to remember a short time later on dry land? Godden and Baddeley (1975) set up an experiment to answer this question. Members of a university diving club memorized a list of words when they were either 10 feet underwater or on land. They were later tested for recall of the words in the same or in a different environment. The results of the study suggest that recall of information is strongly influenced by environmental context (see Figure 6.10). Words learned underwater were best recalled underwater, and words learned on land were best recalled on land. In fact, when the scuba divers learned and recalled the words in the same context, their scores were 47 percent higher than when the two contexts were different.

The same context advantages, however, applied only to recall. Godden and Baddeley (1980) found that when memory was measured using recognition rather than recall, recognition scores were not affected by changes in context. There is a reason for the differing effects of recall and recognition. The original context seems to provide retrieval cues that make recall easier. But in a recognition task, people only have to recognize the information as being familiar, so

Figure 6.10 Context-Dependent Memory Godden and Baddeley showed the strong influence of environmental context on recall. Scuba divers who memorized a list of words, either on land or underwater, had significantly better recall in the same physical context in which the learning had taken place. (Data from Godden & Baddeley, 1975.)

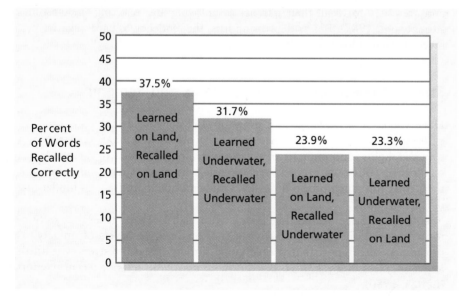

state-dependent memory effect: The tendency to recall information better if one is in the same pharmacological or psychological (mood) state as when the information was encoded.

there is less need for the extra retrieval cues that the original context provides (Eich, 1980).

Going from 10 feet underwater to dry land is a rather drastic change in context, yet some researchers find the same effects even in more subtle context changes, such as going from one room to another. Smith and others (1978) had students memorize lists of words in one room. The following day, students tested in the same room recalled 50 percent more words than those subjects tested in another room. Again there were no significant differences on recognition tests. But McDaniel and others (1989) suggest that the more completely and carefully people encode material to be remembered, the less dependent they are on reinstating the same context or environment.

The State-Dependent Memory Effect

Question: What is the state-dependent memory effect?

If, as we have stated, the external environment can affect memory, might our internal state (happy or sad, intoxicated or sober) also influence our memory performance? The answer is yes. We tend to recall information better if we are in the same internal state as when the information was encoded. Psychologists call this the **state-dependent memory effect**.

Alcohol, Other Drugs, and Memory   Some studies have shown a state-dependent memory effect for alcohol and drugs such as marijuana, amphetamines, and barbiturates (Eich, 1980). Subjects learned (encoded) material while sober or intoxicated, and later were tested in either the sober or intoxicated state. Recall was found to be best when the subjects were in the same state for both learning and testing (Weingartner et al., 1976). As in other studies, the state-dependency effect was evident for recall but not for recognition.

Mood and Memory   Several studies reveal that recall of material is better if its emotional tone is the same as the individual's current mood (Rholes et al., 1987; Snyder & White, 1982). Pleasant experiences are more likely to be recalled when people are in a happy mood, and negative experiences when people are in a negative mood (Teasdale & Fogarty, 1979). Adults who are clinically depressed tend to recall more negative life experiences (Clark & Teasdale, 1982) and are likely to recall their parents as unloving and rejecting (Lewinsohn & Rosenbaum, 1987). But as depression lifts, the tendency toward negative recall reverses itself (Lloyd & Lishman, 1975).

Stress, Anxiety, and Memory: Relax and Remember

Have you ever watched a quiz show on TV, convinced that you could have easily won the prize? Would your memory work as well under the stress of TV cameras, lights, and millions of people watching as it does in the privacy and comfort of your own home? Psychologists who study stress and memory say that either too much or too little stress and emotional arousal can hinder memory performance.

Loftus and Siegel found that people with high levels of general anxiety perform less well on memory tests than those with lower levels of anxiety. The researchers also report that people going through great life stress—death of a loved one, loss of a job, divorce—do more poorly on tests of recent memories (Loftus, 1980).

Memory Check 6.5

1. We tend to recall information better if we are in the same _____ as when we learned the information.

    a. mood   c. pharmacological state
    b. physical location   d. all of the these

2. When children learn the alphabet, they often learn the letters A, B, C, D and W, X, Y, Z before learning the letters in-between. This is called the:

    a. selective interference effect   c. serial position effect
    b. state-dependent memory effect   d. von Restorff effect

3. Scores on recognition tests, either multiple-choice or true/false, will be higher if testing and learning take place in the same physical environment. (true/false)

Answers: 1. d 2. c 3. false

Biology and Memory

We have learned a great deal about how we remember and why we forget. And we know that our vast store of information must exist physically somewhere in the brain. But where?

Brain Damage: A Clue to Memory Formation

Modern researchers are finding some specific locations in the brain that house and mediate functions and processes in memory. One important source of information comes from people who have suffered memory loss resulting from damage to specific brain areas. One such person is H.M., a man who has had a major influence on our present-day knowledge of human memory, not as a researcher but as a subject.

Question: What has the study of H.M. revealed about the role of the hippocampus in memory?

The Case of H.M.

H.M. suffered from such severe epilepsy that, out of desperation, he agreed to a radical surgical procedure. The surgeon removed the site responsible for his seizures, which included the front two-thirds of the hippocampus from both the left and right hemispheres. It was 1953, and H.M. was 27 years old.

After his surgery, H.M. remained intelligent and psychologically stable, and his seizures were drastically reduced. But unfortunately, the tissue cut from H.M.'s brain housed more than the site of his seizures. It also contained his ability to form new, conscious, long-term memories. Though his short-term memory is still as good as ever

anterograde amnesia: The inability to form long-term memories of events occurring after a brain injury or brain surgery, although memories formed before the trauma are usually intact.

hippocampus (hip-po-CAM-pus): The brain structure in the limbic system involved in the formation of memories of facts, information, and personal experiences.

and he easily remembers the events of his life stored well before the operation, H.M. suffers from *anterograde amnesia*. He has not been able to remember a single event that has occurred since the surgery some 40 years ago. As far as H.M.'s conscious long-term memory is concerned, it is still 1953 and he is still 27 years old.

Surgery affected only H.M.'s declarative, long-term memory—his ability to store facts, personal experiences, names, faces, telephone numbers, and the like. But researchers were surprised to discover that he could still form procedural memories; that is, he could still acquire skills through repetitive practice although he could not remember having done so. For example, since the surgery, H.M. has learned to play tennis and improve his game, but he has no memory of having played. (Adapted from Milner, 1966, 1970; Milner et al., 1968.)

H.M.'s case was one of the first indications that the **hippocampus** is involved in the formation of long-term memories. Other patients who, like H.M., have suffered similar damage to their brains exhibit the same types of memory loss (Squire, 1992).

Other research suggests that the hippocampus is needed for only a limited time after learning (Kim & Fanselow, 1992). The hippocampus plays a continuing role during the process of reorganization and consolidation through which memories are finally stored in other areas of the cortex. At this point, the memory can be recalled without the involvement of the hippocampus (Squire & Zola-Morgan, 1991).

Just as H.M.'s case indicates that declarative and procedural memories are processed and stored by different parts of the brain, a more recent case of amnesia suggests that different parts of the brain may be involved in episodic and semantic memory.

The Case of K.C. To support the distinction between semantic and episodic memory, Tulving (1989; Tulving et al., 1988) cites the case of K.C., who sustained a severe head injury from a motorcycle accident. K.C. suffered massive damage to his left frontal lobe and other parts of the brain as well.

> K.C.'s case is remarkable in that he cannot remember, in the sense of bringing back to conscious awareness, a single thing that he has ever done or experienced in the past. He cannot remember himself experiencing situations and participating in life's events. This total absence of personal recollections makes K.C.'s case unique; no other reports exist of amnesic patients who have been incapable of recollecting *any* personal happenings. (Tulving, 1989, p. 362)

Although his episodic memory was erased, K.C.'s semantic memory was largely spared. His storehouse of knowledge from fields such as geography, history, politics, and music is still large, enabling him to answer questions about many topics. Tulving concludes that episodic memory depends on the functioning of parts of the frontal lobe. After studying patients with frontal lobe lesions, Janowsky and others (1989) suggest that the frontal lobes might play a special role in the association of facts to the context in which they were learned.

We have described how researchers have been able to identify and locate some of the brain structures that play a part in memory. But what mechanisms and processes within these structures change, reshape, and rearrange to make new memories?

Neuronal Changes in Memory: Brain Work

Some researchers are exploring memory more minutely, by studying the actions of single neurons. Others are studying collections of neurons and their synapses, and the neurotransmitters whose chemical action begins the process of recording and storing a memory. The first close look at the nature of memory in single neurons was provided by Eric Kandel and his colleagues, who traced the effects of learning and memory in the sea slug (snail), Aplysia (Dale & Kandel, 1990; Dash et al., 1990). Using tiny electrodes implanted in several single neurons in the sea slug, Kandel and his fellow researchers have been able to map neural circuits that are formed and maintained as the animal learns and remembers. Furthermore, they have discovered the different types of protein synthesis that facilitate short-term and long-term memory (Kandel et al., 1987; Sweatt & Kandel, 1989).

But the studies of learning and memory in Aplysia reflect only simple classical conditioning, which is a type of procedural memory. Other researchers studying mammals report that physical changes occur in the neurons and synapses in brain regions involved in declarative memory. Researchers have delivered short bursts of intense, high-frequency, electrical stimulation, called long-term potentiation, to neurons in the hippocampus. They report that these short, electrical bursts make synapses more responsive to even low-level, continuing stimulation for up to weeks at a time (Bliss & Lømo, 1973).

Recently researchers have found that the threshold (the strength of stimulation required to achieve long-term potentiation) is not fixed. The threshold is strongly influenced by recent activity at the synapses where neurons communicate with each other (Huang et al., 1992). These short, intense electrical bursts appear to spark a chain of electrochemical events, which changes the shape or the structure of neurons at the synapses and allows new nerve connections to form. Long-term potentiation occurs most prominently in those structures of the brain, such as the hippocampus, that are involved in declarative memory.

Gary Lynch, a leading researcher in this area, suggests that long-term potentiation has the characteristics required of a process that is capable of forming memories (Cotman & Lynch, 1989). The final years of the 20th century promise to yield exciting information about the neurochemical nature of learning and memory.

Improving Memory

Study Habits That Aid Memory

Question: What are four study habits that can aid memory?

There are no secret formulas or magic keys for improving your memory. Remembering is a skill and, like any other skill, requires knowledge and practice. In this section, we will show you several study habits and techniques that can improve your memory. You can practice and perfect them if you have the time and the interest.

Organization: Everything in Its Place   A telephone directory would be of little use to you if the names and phone numbers were listed in random order. In a similar way you are giving your memory a task it probably will not accept if you try to remember large amounts of information in a haphazard fashion. Organizing material to be learned is a tremendous aid to memory. You can prove this for yourself by completing the *Try It!* on page 222.

WORLD OF PSYCHOLOGY: APPLICATIONS

Improving Memory with Mnemonic Devices

Question: What mnemonic devices can be used to memorize information or lists of items?

We all use external aids to help us remember. Writing notes, making lists, writing on a calendar, or keeping an appointment book is often more reliable and accurate than trusting our own memory (Intons-Peterson & Fournier, 1986). But there are times, such as when you are taking a test, when you cannot rely on external prompts. What if you need information at unpredictable times, when you do not have external aids handy?

There are several *mnemonics*, or memory devices, that have been developed over the years to aid memory (Bower, 1973; Higbee, 1977; Roediger, 1980). The different mnemonic techniques that we will explore are rhyme, the first-letter technique, the method of loci, and the link method. We are all familiar with the rhyme.

Rhyme   Many of us use rhymes to help us remember material that otherwise might be difficult to recall. Perhaps as a child you learned your ABC's by using a rhyming song:

A - B - C - D
E - F - G
H - I - J - K
L - M - N - O - P

You may repeat the verse "Thirty days hath September" when you try to recall the number of days in each month, or the saying "*i* before *e* except after *c*" when you are trying to spell a word. Rhymes are useful because they insure that information is recalled in the proper sequence. Otherwise there is no rhyme.

The First-Letter Technique   Another useful technique is to take the first letter of each item to be remembered and form either a word, a phrase, or a sentence with those letters (Matlin, 1989). For example, if you had to memorize the seven colors of the visible spectrum in their proper order, you could use the first letter of each color to form the name Roy G. Biv. Three chunks are easier to remember than seven different items.

<u>R</u>ed   <u>O</u>range   <u>Y</u>ellow   <u>G</u>reen   <u>B</u>lue   <u>I</u>ndigo   <u>V</u>iolet

As a child taking music lessons, you might have learned the saying, "<u>E</u>very <u>g</u>ood <u>b</u>oy <u>d</u>oes <u>f</u>ine," to remind you of the lines of the treble clef, and <u>F</u> <u>A</u> <u>C</u> <u>E</u> as a reminder of the spaces. To remember our license plate more easily, we think of the letters PCS as "poor civil servant."

The Method of Loci: "In the First Place"   The *method of loci* is a mnemonic device that can be used when you want to remember a list of items such as a grocery list, or when you give a speech or a class report and need to make your points in order without using notes. The word *loci* (pronounced LO-sye) is the plural form of *locus*, which means "location" or "place."

To use the method of loci, select any familiar location—your home, for example—and simply associate the items to be remembered with places in your home. You begin by picturing the first locus, for example, your driveway; the second locus, your garage; the third locus, the walk leading to your front door; and the fourth locus, perhaps the front hall closet. You progress through your house from room to room in an orderly fashion. Then you visualize the first item or idea you want to remember in its place on the driveway, the second item in your garage, the third at your front door, and so on until you have associated each word, idea, or item you want to remember with a specific place. You will probably find it helpful to conjure up exaggerated images of the items that you place at each location, as the examples in Figure 6.12 illustrate.

When you want to recall the items, take an imaginary walk starting at the first place, and the first idea will pop into your mind. When you think of the second place, the second idea will come to mind, and so on through all the places you visualize. The use of loci as a memory aid may be the origin of the phrase, "in the first place."

Research suggests that the method of loci is very effective. In one study, college students memorized a different list of 40 words, all nouns, on each of four consecutive days. They visualized each word, a noun, at specific locations on campus (Ross & Lawrence, 1968). When tested immediately after memorizing each list, the average recall was 37 out of 40 words in the exact order in which they

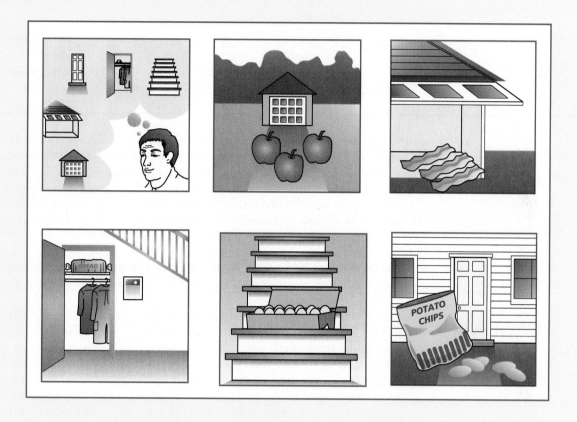

Figure 6.12   The Method of Loci   Begin by mentally picturing locations that are laid out in orderly sequence, such as certain locations in your home. Then visualize in each location one of the items to be remembered. Exaggerated images are often easier to remember. To recall the items, take an imaginary walk along the sequenced route, and the items should come to mind.

were memorized. Average recall one day later was 34 words, and average recall at the end of all four lists was 29 words per 40-word list.

The human memory is truly amazing. We hope you will use the information we have shared with you to make your memory even more amazing.

Try It!

Have a pencil and a sheet of paper handy. Read the following list of items out loud and then write down as many as you can remember.

peas	ice cream	fish	perfume	bananas
toilet paper	onions	apples	cookies	ham
carrots	shaving cream	pie	grapes	chicken

If you organize this list, the items are much easier to remember. Now read each category heading and the items listed beneath it. Write down as many items as you can remember.

Desserts	Fruits	Vegetables	Meat	Toilet Articles
pie	bananas	carrots	chicken	perfume
ice cream	apples	onions	fish	shaving cream
cookies	grapes	peas	ham	toilet paper

We tend to retrieve information from long-term memory according to the way we have organized it for storage. Almost anyone can name the months of the year in about 12 seconds, but how long would it take to recall them in alphabetical order? The same 12 items, all well-known, are much harder to retrieve in alphabetical order because they are not organized that way in memory. Organize items in alphabetical order, or according to categories, historical sequence, size, shape, or any other way that will make retrieval easier.

Overlearning: Reviewing Again, and Again, and Again Do you still remember the words to songs that were popular when you were in high school? Can you recite many of the nursery rhymes you learned as a child even though you haven't heard them in years? You probably can because of **overlearning**.

Let us say that you wanted to memorize a list of words, and you studied until you could recite them once without error. Would this amount of study or practice be sufficient? Many studies suggest that we will remember material better and longer if we overlearn it, that is, if we practice or study beyond the minimum needed to barely learn it (Ebbinghaus, 1885). A pioneering study in overlearning by Krueger (1929) showed very substantial long-term gains for subjects engaged in 50- and 100-percent overlearning (see Figure 6.11). Furthermore, overlearning makes material more resistant to interference. It is perhaps your best insurance against stress-related forgetting.

The next time you study for a test, don't stop studying as soon as you think you know the material. Spend another hour or so going over it, and you will be surprised at how much more you will remember.

Spaced versus Massed Practice: A Little at a Time Beats All at Once We have all tried cramming for examinations, but spacing study over several different sessions generally is more effective than *massed practice*—learning in one long practice session without rest periods. The spacing effect was first discovered by Ebbinghaus over 100 years ago (Dempster, 1988) and continues to be documented (Bahrick & Phelps, 1987; Glover & Corkill, 1987). The spacing effect applies to learning motor skills as well as to learning facts and information. All music students can tell you that it is better to practice for half an hour each day, every day, than to practice many hours in a row once a week.

You will remember more with less total study time if you space your study over several sessions. Long periods of memorizing make material particularly subject to interference and often result in fatigue and lowered concentration. Also, when you space your practice, you probably create a new memory that may be stored in a different place, thus increasing your chance for recall.

overlearning: Practicing or studying material beyond the point where it can be repeated once without error.

massed practice: One long learning practice session as opposed to spacing the learning in shorter practice sessions over an extended period.

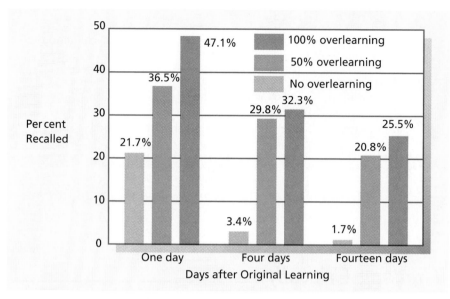

Figure 6.11 Overlearning When material is learned only to the point of one correct repetition, forgetting is very rapid. Just 21 percent is retained after one day, 3 percent after 4 days, and 2 percent after 14 days. When subjects spend 50 percent more time going over the material, retention increases to 35 percent after one day, 29 percent after 4 days, and 20 percent after 14 days. (Data from Krueger, 1929.)

Recitation versus Rereading: Recitation Wins Many students simply read and reread their textbook and notes when they study for an exam. Research over many years shows that you will recall more if you increase the amount of recitation in your study. For example, it is better to read a page or a few paragraphs and then recite or practice recalling what you have just read. Then continue reading, stop and practice reciting again, and so on. When you study for a psychology test and review the assigned chapter, try to answer each of the starred questions. Then read the material that follows each question and check to see if you answered the question correctly. This will be your safeguard against encoding failure. Don't simply read each section and assume that you can answer the question. Test yourself before your professor does.

A.I. Gates (1917) tested groups of students who spent the same amount of time in study, but who spent different percentages of their time in recitation and reading. His subjects recalled from two to three times more if they increased their recitation time up to 80 percent and spent only 20 percent of their study time rereading.

Memory Check 6.6

1. The hippocampus is the brain structure involved in the formation of permanent memories of (motor skills, facts and personal experiences).

2. When studying for an exam, it is best to spend:

   a. more time reciting than rereading
   b. more time rereading than reciting
   c. equal time rereading and reciting
   d. all of the time reciting rather than rereading

(continued)

3. Being able to recite a number of nursery rhymes from childhood is probably due mainly to:

   a. spaced practice   c. recitation
   b. organization   d. overlearning

4. Spaced practice is better than massed practice for learning:

   a. motor skills   c. both of these
   b. verbal information   d. neither of these

Answers: 1. facts and personal experiences 2. a 3. d 4. c

Thinking Critically _____

Evaluation

Some studies cited in this chapter involved only one or a few subjects.

a. **Select two of these studies and discuss the possible problems in drawing conclusions on the basis of studies using so few subjects.**
b. **Suggest several possible explanations for the researchers' findings other than those proposed by the researchers.**
c. **In your view, should such studies even be mentioned in a textbook? Why or why not?**

Point/Counterpoint

Using what you have learned in this chapter on memory, prepare an argument citing cases and specific examples to support each of these positions:

a. **Long-term memory is a permanent record of our experiences.**
b. **Long-term memory is not necessarily a permanent record of our experiences.**

Psychology in Your Life

Drawing upon your knowledge, formulate a plan that you can put into operation to help improve your memory and avoid the pitfalls that cause forgetting.

Chapter Summary and Review _____

Remembering

What three processes are involved in the act of remembering?

Three processes involved in remembering are (1) encoding—transforming information into a form that can be stored in memory, (2) storage—maintaining information in memory, and (3) retrieval—bringing stored material to mind.

What is sensory memory?

Sensory memory holds information coming in through the senses for up to several seconds, just long enough for us to begin to process the information and send some on to short-term memory.

What are the characteristics of short-term memory?

Short-term (working) memory holds about seven unrelated items of information for less than 30 seconds without rehearsal. Short-term memory also acts as our mental work space while we carry out any mental activity.

What is long-term memory, and what are its subsystems?

Long-term memory is the permanent or relatively permanent memory system with a virtually unlimited capacity. Its subsystems are (1) procedural memory, which holds memories of motor skills acquired through repetitive practice, and (2) declarative memory, which holds facts and information (semantic memory) and personal life experiences (episodic memory).

Key Terms

encoding (p. 191)
storage (p. 191)
consolidation (p. 191)
retrieval (p. 191)
sensory memory (p. 192)
short-term memory (p. 194)
rehearsal (p. 196)
long-term memory (p. 197)
procedural memory (p. 197)
declarative memory (p. 197)
episodic memory (p. 198)
semantic memory (p. 198)
levels-of-processing model (p. 200)

Measuring Memory

What are three methods of measuring retention?

Three methods of measuring retention are (1) recall where information must be supplied with few or no retrieval cues, (2) recognition, where information must simply be recognized as having been encountered before, and (3) the relearning method, which measures retention in terms of time saved in relearning material compared with the time required to learn it originally.

What was Hermann Ebbinghaus's major contribution to psychology?

Hermann Ebbinghaus conducted the first experimental studies of learning and memory. He invented the nonsense syllable, conceived the relearning method as a test of memory, and plotted the curve of forgetting.

Key Terms

recall (p. 201)
retrieval cue (p. 201)
recognition (p. 201)
relearning method (savings method) (p. 202)
nonsense syllable (p. 203)

Forgetting

What are six causes of forgetting?

Six causes of forgetting are encoding failure, consolidation failure, decay, interference, motivated forgetting, and retrieval failure.

What is interference, and how can it be minimized?

Interference occurs because information or associations stored either before or after a given memory hinder our ability to remember it. To minimize interference, follow a learning activity with sleep, and arrange learning so that similar subjects are not studied back to back.

Key Terms

encoding failure (p. 205)
consolidation failure (p. 206)
retrograde amnesia (p. 206)
decay theory (p. 206)

interference (p. 206)
motivated forgetting (p. 207)
repression (p. 207)
amnesia (p. 207)

The Nature of Remembering and Forgetting

What is meant by the statement "Memory is reconstructive in nature"?

Our memory does not work like a video recorder. We reconstruct memories, piecing them together from a few highlights and using information that may or may not be accurate.

Key Terms

reconstruction (p. 209)
flashbulb memory (p. 212)
eidetic imagery (p. 213)

Factors Influencing Retrieval

How does environmental context affect memory?

People tend to recall material more easily if they are in the same physical location during recall as during the original learning.

What is the state-dependent memory effect?

The state-dependent memory effect refers to our tendency to recall information better if we are in the same pharmacological or psychological state as when the information was learned.

Key Terms

serial position effect (p. 214)
state-dependent memory effect (p. 216)

Biology and Memory

What has the study of H.M. revealed about the role of the hippocampus in memory?

The case of H.M. reveals that the hippocampus is essential in forming declarative memories but not procedural memories.

Key Term

hippocampus (p. 218)

Improving Memory

What are four study habits that can aid memory?

Four study habits that can aid memory are organization, overlearning, the use of spaced rather than massed practice, and the use of a higher percentage of time reciting than rereading material.

What mnemonic devices can be used to memorize information or lists of items?

Memory can be improved by using mnemonics such as rhymes, the first-letter technique, and the method of loci.

Key Terms

overlearning (p. 222)

7

Intelligence, Thought, and Creativity

Marilyn vos Savant

Dr. Robert K. Jarvik

Who has the highest IQ score ever recorded on an intelligence test? The name of Albert Einstein quickly comes to mind and perhaps a host of other great thinkers of the past—mostly men. But the person with the highest IQ score ever recorded happens to be a woman.

Marilyn Mach, born in St. Louis, Missouri, in 1946, scored an amazing 230 on the Stanford-Binet IQ test when she was a 10-year-old elementary-school student. How high is a 230 IQ? The average Stanford-Binet IQ score is set at 100, and a score of 116—only about half as high as Marilyn Mach's lofty score—places a person in the top 16 percent of the population. Not only does Marilyn Mach have no peer when it comes to measured intelligence, she doesn't even have a competitor. Her score is nearly 30 points higher than that of her nearest rival.

Descended from the Austrian philosopher and physicist Ernst Mach, who did pioneering work in the physics of sound (Mach one, Mach two), Marilyn added her mother's maiden name and so as an adult became known as Marilyn Mach vos Savant. She has no college degree, but she completed about 2 years of college courses at St. Louis Community College at Meramec and Washington University in St. Louis. Her primary intellectual interest is creative writing, and she has written 12 books and 3 plays. Her first published work was the Omni IQ Quiz Contest. Now in her late forties she lives with her husband in New York, where she writes a newspaper column, lectures on intelligence, and pursues various other interests.

Now let us consider another person, Dr. Robert Jarvik, the world-famous inventor of the Jarvik artificial heart. Dr. Jarvik combined his medical knowledge and his mechanical genius to produce the world's first workable artificial heart. But his path wasn't easy. Unlike Marilyn Mach vos Savant, Jarvik was a poor test taker. In fact, he scored too low on intelligence and admissions tests to be admitted to any medical school in the United States. Eventually, despite his low test scores, he was accepted by a medical school in Italy, where he completed his studies and received his M.D. degree. Then he returned to practice in the United States and made his contribution to medical science—a contribution that has kept alive many gravely ill heart patients until a suitable heart transplant could be performed.

Perhaps, if Dr. Jarvik wishes, he can learn to score higher on IQ tests. His wife, Marilyn Mach vos Savant-Jarvik, might be willing to teach him.

A HIGH INTELLIGENCE SCORE is desirable, but a high IQ score alone is not a sufficient condition for creative accomplishment, nor is it a necessary condition. Like Dr. Jarvik, many highly creative individuals have tested poorly in school. Some of the most prominent people include the famous American inventor Thomas A. Edison; Winston Churchill, whose teachers thought he was mentally limited; and even the great Albert Einstein, who was labeled a dunce in math. We all have some notion of what intelligence is, and we have met people we believe to be more intelligent, and perhaps many others we believe to be less intelligent, than we are.

This chapter will explore intelligence, thinking skills, and creativity. You will learn about the nature of intelligence and how it is measured. Where does our intelligence come from—the genes, experiences provided by our environment, or both? We will look at the extremes in intelligence—the mentally gifted and the mentally retarded. Then we will consider how we think and examine the approaches we use to solve problems.

First, let us ask the most obvious question: What is intelligence? Scientists and laypersons alike have tried to answer this question, but even experts in the field can't agree on an answer. Probably the most generally accepted definition is that of David Wechsler (1975): "Intelligence is the global capacity of the individual to act purposefully, to think rationally, and to deal effectively with the environment." But even before a workable definition of intelligence was formulated, attempts were made to measure it.

French psychologist Alfred Binet developed the concept of mental age and published the first individual intelligence test to measure it.

Measuring Intelligence

Alfred Binet and the First Successful Intelligence Test

Question: What is Alfred Binet's major contribution to psychology?

The first successful effort to measure intelligence resulted not from a theoretical approach, but as a practical means of solving a problem in the schools of France. Around the turn of the century, the Ministry of Public Instruction in Paris was struggling with a problem—trying to find some objective means of sorting out children whose intelligence was too low for them to profit from regular classroom instruction. The ministry wanted to be sure that average or brighter children would not be wrongly assigned to special classes and that children of limited ability would not be subjected to the regular program of instruction. In 1903 a commission was formed to study the problem, and one of its members was French psychologist Alfred Binet. Read about Binet in the boxed feature on page 230.

The Intelligence Quotient or IQ: Can a Number Capture It?

Question: What does IQ mean, and how was it originally calculated?

Binet believed that children with a mental age 2 years below their chronological age were retarded and should be placed in special education classes. But there was a flaw in his thinking. A 6-year-old with a mental age of 4 is far more retarded than a 10-year-old with a mental age of 8. How could a similar degree of retardation at different ages be expressed?

German psychologist William Stern (1914) came up with the answer. In 1912 he devised a simple formula for calculating an index of intelligence—the **intelligence quotient,** or IQ. He divided a child's mental age by his or her chronological age. Then, to eliminate the decimal, he multiplied the result by 100.

$$\frac{\text{MA}}{\text{CA}} \times 100 = \text{IQ}$$

Here is how IQ is calculated:

$$\frac{\text{Mental Age } 11}{\text{Chronological Age } 8} = 1.37 \times 100 = 137 \text{ IQ (Superior IQ)}$$

$$\frac{\text{Mental Age } 8}{\text{Chronological Age } 8} = 1.00 \times 100 = 100 \text{ IQ (Normal IQ)}$$

$$\frac{\text{Mental Age } 5}{\text{Chronological Age } 8} = 0.62 \times 100 = 62 \text{ IQ (Below Normal IQ)}$$

It is interesting to note that Binet and Simon were totally against the use of an IQ score. They believed that trying to represent human intelligence with a single number was impossible and that doing so was not only misleading but dangerous (Hothersall, 1984).

intelligence quotient (IQ): An index of intelligence originally derived by dividing mental age by chronological age and then multiplying by 100.

WORLD OF PSYCHOLOGY: PIONEERS

Alfred Binet (1857–1911)

Alfred Binet was born on July 11, 1857, in Nice, France. Binet's father, a physician, and his mother, an artist, separated when Binet was young, and he was raised by his mother. Binet first studied law and then decided to follow the family tradition in medicine as his father and both his grandfathers had done. Soon his interests turned to psychology, however, and he did not complete his medical studies.

In 1890 Binet began making careful observations of the development of his two daughters—Alice, who was age 2 1/2 at the time, and Madeleine, who was age 4 1/2. Struck by the differences in their reasoning ability and memory, Binet devised tests to measure the various abilities in the girls. Binet had his daughters memorize digits and words, match colors, copy drawings, perform reasoning tasks, and play other intellectual games. As he watched them develop, he observed that the younger daughter could not perform many of the tasks that her older sister, Madeleine, could complete with ease. But two years later, Alice was able to perform the same tasks as well as her older sister had done earlier. This suggested to Binet that intelligence is developmental and progresses according to age. Perhaps tests could be constructed that would reveal what the average child could do at certain ages—5, 6, 7, and so on.

In 1903 Binet set to work on the task of developing an intelligence test that could make assessment more objective. With the help of his colleague, psychiatrist Theodore Simon, Binet began testing the school children of Paris in 1904. The two men used a wide variety of tests, some of which Binet had tried with his own daughters, and they kept only those items that discriminated well between older and younger children. Binet and Simon published their intelligence scale in 1905 and revised it in 1908 and again in 1911. The Binet-Simon Intelligence Scale was an immediate success in most Western countries.

Test items on the scale were structured according to increasing difficulty—with the easiest item first and each succeeding item becoming more and more difficult. Children went as far as they could, and then their progress was compared to others of the same age. A child with the mental ability of a normal 5-year-old could be said to have a mental level of 5. Binet and Simon used the term "mental level," but since then the term *mental age* has been used instead.

Binet, a prolific writer, authored nearly 300 published works—books, articles, reviews, and even four plays that were produced in the theaters of Paris (Siegler, 1992). In October 1911 Binet's career was ended abruptly by his untimely death at the age of 54. But his contribution—the idea of mental age and the publication of an individual intelligence test for measuring it—is still very much alive today. Binet established the concept that mental retardation and mental superiority are a function of the difference between chronological age (one's actual age) and mental age. An 8-year-old with a mental age of 8 is normal or average. An 8-year-old with a mental age of 5 is seriously deficient, while an 8-year-old with a mental age of 11 is mentally superior.

Intelligence Testing in the United States

Question: What is the Stanford-Binet Intelligence Scale?

The Stanford-Binet Intelligence Scale: A Famous IQ Test Psychologist Henry H. Goddard translated the Binet-Simon scales of 1908 and 1911 into English and made a few minor alterations in the tests. Goddard's tests became the standard intelligence test in this country until Lewis M. Terman, a psychology professor at Stanford University, published a thorough revision of the Binet-Simon scale in 1916. Terman revised and adapted the items for American children, added 36 new items, and established new **norms**. Terman's revision was the first test to make use of Stern's IQ score, and within 2 1/2 years, 4 million children had taken the test. Revised several times over the years, the test, which is known as the **Stanford-Binet Intelligence Scale**, is still highly regarded today.

Intelligence Testing for Adults: A Scale for All Ages Intelligence testing became increasingly popular in the United States in the 1920s and 1930s, but it quickly became obvious that the Stanford-Binet Intelligence Scale was not useful for testing adults. Too few of the items were appropriate for adults, and because the test had not been standardized using an adult population, no applicable norms existed. The obvious solution to the problem was to develop an adult intelligence scale.

Because intelligence is developmental and normally increases with age, the intelligence quotient MA/CA × 100 can, in most cases, reliably separate the mentally retarded or gifted children from average children. But the original IQ formula could not be applied to adults in the measurement of intelligence. At a certain age, maturity in intelligence is reached, as well as in height and other physical characteristics.

According to the original IQ formula, a 40-year-old who scored the same on an IQ test as the average 20-year-old would be mentally retarded, with an IQ of only 50 (MA/CA = 20/40 = 0.50 × 100 = 50). By the same logic, a 20-year-old who had the same score as an average 40-year-old would be a rare genius, with an IQ of 200 (MA/CA = 40/20 = 2 × 100 = 200). Obviously, something was wrong with the formula when applied to populations of all ages. Today we still use the term IQ, but it is a **deviation score** calculated by comparing an individual's score to scores of others of the *same age* on whom the test was normed. The deviation score is one of the contributions of David Wechsler, another pioneer in mental testing.

Question: What did David Wechsler's tests provide that the Stanford-Binet did not?

The Wechsler Intelligence Tests: Among the Best In 1939 psychologist David Wechsler developed the first successful individual intelligence test for adults, designed for those age 16 and older. The original test has been revised, restandardized, and renamed the **Wechsler Adult Intelligence Scale (WAIS-R)** and is now one of the most commonly used psychological tests. The test contains both verbal and performance (nonverbal) subtests, which yield separate verbal and performance IQ scores as well as an overall IQ score. This test is a departure from the Stanford-Binet scale, which yields just one IQ score. Figure 7.1 includes sample items from the WAIS-R.

Wechsler also published the Wechsler Intelligence Scale for Children (WISC) and the Wechsler Preschool and Primary Scale of Intelligence (WPPSI), which is normed for children ages 4 to 6 1/2.

Group Intelligence Tests: Testing More Than One at a Time Administering individual intelligence tests like the Stanford-Binet and the Wechsler is expensive and time-consuming. The tests must be administered to one individual at a time by a psychologist or other qualified testing professional. When large numbers of people must be tested in a short period of time on a limited budget, individual IQ testing is out of the question and group intelligence tests are the answer. A number of widely used group intelligence tests now exist, such as the California Test of Mental Maturity, the Cognitive Abilities Test, and the Otis-Lennon Mental Ability Test. You might have taken one or more of these tests, all of which are good. But not all tests are created equal.

norms: Standards based on the range of test scores of a large group of people who are selected to provide the bases of comparison for those who take the test later.

Stanford-Binet Intelligence Scale: Lewis Terman's adaptation of the Binet-Simon Scale, translated and revised for American children with new items.

deviation score: A test score calculated by comparing an individual's score to the scores of others of the same age on whom the test was normed.

Wechsler Adult Intelligence Scale (WAIS-R): An individual intelligence test for adults that yields separate verbal and performance (nonverbal) IQ scores as well as an overall IQ score.

One of the most widely used intelligence tests for children is the WISC-R, developed by David Wechsler.

Verbal Subtests	Sample Items
Information	How many wings does a bird have? Who wrote *Paradise Lost*?
Digit span	Repeat from memory a series of digits, such as 3 1 0 6 7 4 2 5, after hearing it once.
General Comprehension	What is the advantage of keeping money in a bank? Why is copper often used in electrical wires?
Arithmetic	Three men divided 18 golf balls equally among themselves. How many golf balls did each man receive? If 2 apples cost 15¢, what will be the cost of a dozen apples?
Similarities	In what way are a lion and a tiger alike? In what way are a saw and a hammer alike?
Vocabulary	This test consists simply of asking, "What is a _____?" or "What does _____ mean?" The words cover a wide range of difficulty or familiarity.

Performance Subtests	Description of Item
Picture arrangement	Arrange a series of cartoon panels to make a meaningful story.
Picture completion	What is missing from these pictures?
Block design	Copy designs with blocks (as shown at right).
Object assembly	Put together a jigsaw puzzle.
Digit symbol	

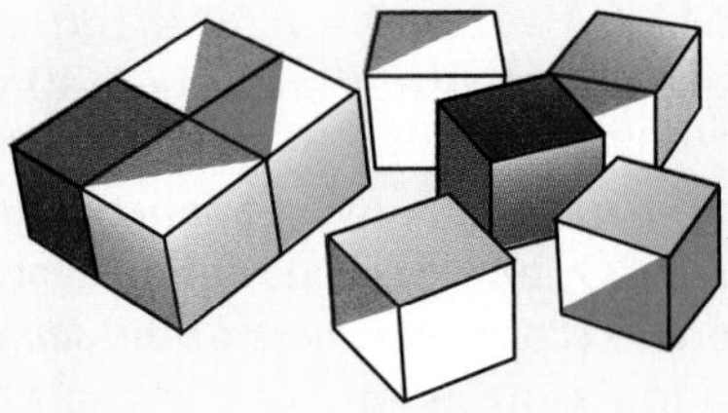

1	2	3	4
X	III	I	O

Fill in the symbols:

3	4	1	3	4	2	1	2

Figure 7.1   Sample Test Items Similar to Items on the WAIS-R

Requirements of Good Tests: Reliability, Validity, and Standardization

Question: What is meant by the terms reliability, validity, and standardization?

If your watch gains 6 minutes one day and loses 3 or 4 minutes the next day, it is not reliable. You want a watch that you can rely on to give the correct time day after day. Like a watch, an intelligence test must have **reliability**; the test must consistently yield nearly the same score when the same people are tested and then retested using the same test or an alternate form of the test. The higher the correlation between the two scores, the more reliable the test. A correlation coefficient of 1.0 would indicate perfect reliability. Most widely used tests such as the Stanford-Binet and Wechsler tests and the Scholastic Aptitude Test (SAT) all boast high reliabilities of about .90.

reliability: The ability of a test to yield nearly the same score when the same people are tested and then retested using the same test or an alternate form of the test.

Tests can be highly reliable but worthless if they are not valid. **Validity** is the ability or power of a test to measure what it is intended to measure. For example, a thermometer is a valid instrument for measuring temperature; a bathroom scale is valid for measuring weight. But no matter how reliable your bathroom scale, it will not take your temperature. It is valid only for weighing.

There are several types of validity measures, but two types—content validity and predictive validity—are most relevant for our purposes. Content validity refers to the degree to which a test contains a representative sample of the behavior or skills to be measured. For example, a well designed typing test will have content validity if it samples a person's typing ability (speed, accuracy, and so on). Predictive validity refers to a test's ability to predict performance in a given area.

Aptitude tests are designed to predict a person's probable achievement or performance at some future time. Selecting students for admission to college or to graduate and professional schools is based partly on the predictive validity of aptitude tests, such as the Scholastic Aptitude Test (SAT), American College Testing Program (ACT), and the Graduate Record Examination (GRE). How well do scores on the SAT predict success in college? Moderately at best. The correlation between SAT scores and the grades of college freshmen is about .40 (Linn, 1982).

Once a test is proven to be valid and reliable, the next requirement is **standardization**. There must be standard procedures for administering and scoring the test. Exactly the same directions must be given, whether written or oral, and the same amount of time must be allowed for every test taker. But even more important, standardization means establishing norms by which all scores are interpreted. A test is standardized by administering it to a large sample of people representative of those who will be taking the test in the future. The group's scores are analyzed, and then the average score, standard deviation, percentile rank, and other measures are computed. These comparative scores become the norms, which are used as the standard against which all other test takers will be measured. A test that successfully meets these criteria is said to be standardized.

The Range of Intelligence

Question: What are the ranges of IQ scores considered average, superior, and in the range of mental retardation?

When large populations are measured on mental characteristics such as intelligence or on physical characteristics such as height or weight, the test scores or results usually conform to the normal or bell-shaped distribution known as the normal curve. The majority of the scores cluster around the mean (average). The farther you deviate or move away from the mean, either above or below, the fewer scores there are (see Figure 7.2).

The average IQ test score for all people in the same age group is computed and arbitrarily assigned an IQ score of 100. On the Wechsler intelligence tests, approximately 50 percent of the scores are in the average range, between 90 and 109. About 68 percent of the scores fall within 80 and 115, and about 95 percent fall between 70 and 130. About 2 percent of the scores are above 130, which is considered superior, and about 2 percent fall below 70, in the range of mental retardation.

Question: According to the Terman study, how do the gifted differ from the general population?

Terman's Study of the Gifted: 1,528 Geniuses and How They Grew In 1921 Lewis M. Terman (1925) of Stanford University launched a longitudinal

validity: The ability of a test to measure what it is intended to measure.

aptitude test: A test designed to predict a person's achievement or performance at some future time.

standardization: The establishment of norms for comparing the scores of people who take the test in the future; administering tests using a prescribed procedure.

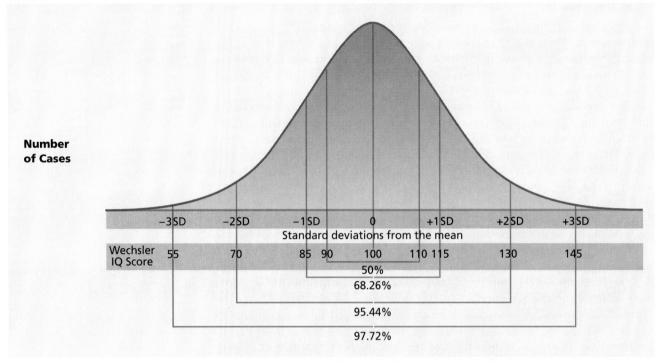

Number of Cases

Figure 7.2 The Normal Curve When a large number of test scores are compiled, they typically are distributed in a normal (bell-shaped) curve. On the Wechsler Intelligence Scale, the average or mean IQ score is set at 100. As the figure shows, about 68 percent of the scores fall between 15 IQ points (1 standard deviation) above and below 100 (from 85 to 115), and about 95 1/2 percent of the scores fall between 30 points (2 standard deviations) above and below 100 (from 70 to 130).

study, now a classic, in which he studied 1,528 gifted students. Tested on the Stanford-Binet, the subjects, 857 males and 671 females, were students who had unusually high IQs, ranging from 135 to 200, with a mean (or average) of 151.

Terman's early findings put an end to the myth that mentally superior people are more likely to be physically inferior. Terman's gifted subjects excelled in almost all of the abilities he studied—intellectual, physical, emotional, moral, and social. Terman also exploded many other myths about the mentally gifted (Terman & Oden, 1947). For example, you may have heard that there is a thin line between genius and madness. Actually Terman's gifted group enjoyed better mental health than the general population; they were less likely to end up in a mental institution. Also, you may have heard that mentally gifted people are long on "book sense" but short on "common sense." In reality Terman's group were more likely to be successful in the real, practical world than their less mentally gifted peers. Terman (1925) concluded that "there is no law of compensation whereby the intellectual superiority of the gifted is offset by inferiorities along nonintellectual lines" (p. 16).

The Terman study still continues today, with most of the subjects in their seventies and eighties. In a recent report on Terman's subjects, Shneidman (1989) states the basic findings of the study—that "an unusual mind, a vigorous body, and a relatively well-adjusted personality are not at all incompatible" (p. 687).

Who Are the Gifted? Beginning in the early 1920s, the term "giftedness" was used to describe the intellectually superior—those with IQs in the upper 2 to 3 percent of the population. Since that time, the term has been expanded to include both the exceptionally creative and those excelling in the visual or performing arts.

Most states do make some special provisions for the educational needs of the gifted and talented, but there is great variation in the quality of such programs and "in no case is it equal to the need" (Horowitz & O'Brien, 1986, p. 1147). Traditionally, special programs have involved either acceleration or enrichment. Acceleration enables students to progress at a rate that is consistent with their ability. Students may skip a grade, progress through subject matter at a faster rate, be granted advanced placement in college courses, or enter college early. Enrichment refers to broadening or extending students' knowledge by giving them special courses in foreign language, music appreciation, and the like, or by providing special experiences designed to develop more advanced thinking skills.

mental retardation: Sub-normal intelligence reflected by an IQ below 70 and by adaptive functioning severely deficient for one's age.

The Mentally Retarded   At the opposite end of the continuum from the intellectually gifted are the 2 percent of the population whose IQ scores place them in the range of **mental retardation**. Individuals are not classified as mentally retarded unless (1) their IQ score is below 70 and (2) they have a severe deficiency in everyday, adaptive functioning—the ability to care for themselves and relate to others (Grossman, 1983). There are degrees of retardation from mild to profound. Individuals with IQs ranging from 50 to 70 are considered mildly retarded; from 35 to 49, moderately retarded; from 20 to 34, severely retarded; and below 20, profoundly retarded. Table 7.1 shows the level of functioning expected for various categories of mental retardation.

Table 7.1   Description of Levels of Mental Retardation

Level of Retardation	Percentage of Retarded at Each Level	IQ Range	Characteristics of Retarded Persons at Each Level
Mild	80%	50–70	Able to grasp academic skills up to 6th grade level; can be profitably employed in vocational occupations and may become self-supporting.
Moderate	12%	35–49	Probably not able to grasp more than 2nd grade academic skills but can learn some social and occupational skills; may learn to travel unsupervised in familiar places.
Severe	7%	20–34	Through repetitive habit training can learn basic health habits; can learn to communicate verbally.
Profound	1%	Below 20	Rudimentary motor development; may learn minimal or limited self-help skills.

(Adapted from the American Psychiatric Association, 1980.)

Many children with Down Syndrome will lead satisfying and productive lives, partially as a result of improved educational opportunities.

There are many causes of mental retardation, including brain injuries, chromosomal abnormalities, chemical deficiencies, lead poisoning, and hazards present during fetal development. The latter hazards, as you will read in chapter 8, "Child Development," include maternal infections; the mother's use of alcohol, psychoactive drugs, and certain prescription drugs; and other environmental hazards. Furthermore, mental retardation can result from sensory or maternal deprivation in infancy or from other causes that are yet unknown.

Before the late 1960s, mentally retarded children were educated almost exclusively in special schools. Since then there has been a movement toward *mainstreaming*—an attempt to educate mentally retarded students in regular schools. Mainstreaming may involve placing them in classes with nonhandicapped students for part of the day or in special classrooms in regular schools.

Resources spent on training programs for the mentally retarded at several locations across the country are proving to be sound investments. These programs, which rely heavily on behavior modification techniques, are making it possible for some of our retarded citizens to become employed workers earning the minimum wage or better. Everyone benefits—the individual, the family, and society as well.

Memory Check 7.1

1. The first valid intelligence test was developed by Binet and (Terman, Simon).

2. According to Stern's formula, an individual with a mental age of 12 and a chronological age of 8 would have an IQ of (125, 150).

3. The American revision of Binet's original intelligence test is the (Binet-Simon, Stanford-Binet) Intelligence Scale.

4. Wechsler developed intelligence tests which could be given either individually or to groups. (true/false)

5. In his study of the gifted, Terman found that mentally superior individuals tend to be physically smaller and weaker. (true/false)

6. People are considered mentally retarded if their IQ is below (70, 80) and they are clearly deficient in adaptive functioning.

Answers 1. Simon 2. 150 3. Stanford-Binet 4. false 5. false 6. 70

mainstreaming: Educating mentally retarded students in regular schools by placing them in regular classes for part of the day or having special classrooms in regular rather than special schools.

The Nature of Intelligence

While Binet and Terman were working on the practical applications of intelligence testing, other researchers were struggling to discover the nature of intelligence. What is intelligence? Is it a single trait or capability? Is it many capabilities unrelated to each other? Or is it something in between? As you might expect, there are many different points of view about the nature of intelligence.

The Search for Factors Underlying Intelligence

Question: What factors underlie intelligence, according to Spearman, Thurstone, and Guilford?

Are there certain common factors that underlie intelligence? If so, what might they be?

Spearman and General Intelligence: The "g factor"
English psychologist Charles Spearman (1863–1945) observed that people who are bright in one area are usually bright in other areas as well. In other words, they tend to be generally intelligent. Spearman (1927) came to believe that intelligence is composed of a general ability, or **g factor**, which underlies all intellectual functions.

Spearman arrived at his "g theory" when he found that there were positive relationships or intercorrelations between scores on the subtests of intelligence tests. People who score high on one subtest tend to score high on the other subtests. Spearman theorized that this positive relationship between the scores on the subtests meant that the tests were measuring something in common—that general ability was being expressed to some degree in all of them. This, according to Spearman, was evidence of the g factor—general intelligence. The influence of Spearman's thinking can be seen in those intelligence tests, such as the Stanford-Binet, that yield one IQ score to indicate the level of general intelligence.

But some of the correlations between the subtests are higher than others. If the g factor alone defined the whole of what intelligence tests measure, then all of the correlations would be nearly perfect. Because they are not, some other abilities in addition to the g factor must be present. These other abilities Spearman named "*s* factors" for specific abilities. Spearman concluded that intelligence tests tap an individual's g factor, or general intelligence, and a number of s factors, or specific intellectual abilities.

Thurstone's Primary Mental Abilities: Primarily Seven
Louis L. Thurstone (1938), another famous researcher in testing, rejected Spearman's notion of an overarching general ability, or g factor. After analyzing the scores of a large number of subjects on some 50 separate ability tests, Thurstone identified seven **primary mental abilities**: verbal comprehension, numerical ability, spatial relations, perceptual speed, word fluency, memory, and reasoning. He maintained that all intellectual activities involve one or more of these primary mental abilities. Thurstone and his wife, Thelma G. Thurstone, developed their Primary Mental Abilities Tests (PMA) to measure these seven abilities.

The Thurstones believed that a single IQ score obscured more than it revealed. They suggested that a profile showing relative strengths and weaknesses on the seven primary abilities would provide a more accurate picture of a person's mental ability.

Guilford's Structure of Intellect: A Mental House with 180 Rooms
Still another effort to shed light on the nature of intelligence is J. P. Guilford's **structure of intellect**. Guilford (1967) proposed that the structure of intelligence has three dimensions: mental operations, contents, and products.

When we think, we perform a mental operation or activity. According to Guilford, that mental operation can be cognition, memory, evaluation, divergent production, or convergent production. But we can't think in a vacuum; we must think about something. The something we think about, Guilford calls "contents," which can be figural, symbolic, semantic, or behavioral. The end result of bringing some mental activity to bear on some contents is a "product."

g factor: Spearman's term for a general intellectual ability that underlies all mental operations to some degree.

primary mental abilities: According to Thurstone, seven relatively distinct abilities that singularly or in combination are involved in all intellectual activities.

structure of intellect: The model proposed by Guilford consisting of 180 different intellectual abilities, which involve all of the possible combinations of the three dimensions of intellect—mental operations, contents, and products.

Guilford (1967) hypothesized that there are 120 different intellectual abilities, depending on how these operations, contents, and products are combined in a task. Shortly before his death, Guilford (1988) expanded his theory from 120 to 180 abilities, when he divided the operation of memory into two categories (memory recording and memory retention).

Intelligence: More Than One Type?

Question: What types of intelligence did Gardner and Sternberg identify?

Some theorists, instead of searching for the factors that underlie intelligence, propose that there are different types of intelligence. Two such modern theorists are Howard Gardner and Robert Sternberg.

Gardner's Seven Frames of Mind: One Frame Is as Good as Another
Harvard psychologist Howard Gardner (1983) denies the existence of a g factor and instead proposes seven forms of intelligence, which he declares are independent and of equal importance. Gardner's multiple intelligences are as follows:

1. *Linguistic* (language skills)
2. *Logical-mathematical* (math and quantitative skills)
3. *Musical*
4. *Spatial* (skills used by painters and sculptors to manipulate and re-create forms)
5. *Bodily kinesthetic* (body control necessary in athletics, and skill and dexterity in handling objects)
6. *Interpersonal* (understanding the behavior and reading the moods, desires, and intentions of others)
7. *Intrapersonal* (understanding one's own feelings and behavior)

Gardner (1985) developed his theory of multiple intelligences from the study of patients with different types of brain damage affecting some forms of intelligence but leaving others intact. He also studied reports of individuals known as "idiot savants," who possess a strange combination of mental retardation and unusual talent or ability. Finally, Gardner considered how various abilities and skills have been valued differently in other cultures and periods of history.

Gardner's theory is criticized by those who do not believe that all seven frames of mind are of equal value in education and in life. Robert Sternberg (1985b) takes issue with Gardner and claims that "the multiple intelligences might better be referred to as multiple talents" (p. 1114). Sternberg asks whether an adult who is tone deaf and has no sense of rhythm can be considered mentally limited in the same way as another person who has never developed any verbal skills. But Sternberg is not merely a critic. He has developed his own theory of intelligence.

Sternberg's Triarchic Theory of Intelligence: The Big Three   Robert Sternberg, a psychology professor at Yale University, uses the information-processing approach to understanding intelligence. This approach involves a step-by-step analysis of the cognitive processes people employ as they acquire knowledge and use it to solve problems.

Though now a respected theorist and researcher in the area of intelligence, Sternberg admits that when he was young he never did well on traditional intelligence tests. "I really stunk on IQ tests. I was just terrible," says Sternberg (Trotter, 1986, p. 56). Believing that he possessed more intellectual power than conventional intelligence tests revealed, he made up an intelligence test of his own, the STOMA or Sternberg Test of Mental Abilities, when he was in junior high school.

Sternberg (1985a; 1986a) has formulated a **triarchic theory of intelligence,** which, as the term triarchic implies, consists of three main parts: the componential, the experiential, and the contextual. The first part, the "componential," refers to the mental abilities that are most closely related to success on conventional IQ and achievement tests. Sternberg maintains that traditional intelligence tests tap only the componential aspect of intelligence.

The second part, the "experiential," encompasses creativity and insight, although creativity has not yielded easily to conventional measurement efforts. The third leg of the triarchic theory is "contextual" or practical intelligence, which some might equate with common sense or "street smarts." People with high contextual intelligence are survivors who capitalize on their strengths and compensate for their weaknesses. They either adapt well to their environment, change the environment to help them succeed, or if necessary, find a new environment. People who have succeeded in spite of hardships and adverse circumstances probably have a great deal of contextual intelligence.

You have now read many competing explanations of how intelligence is structured and how intellectual processes work, but this is only the beginning of the controversy surrounding the concept of intelligence.

Memory Check 7.2

Match the theorists with their theory of intelligence.

_____ 1) triarchic theory of intelligence   a. Spearman
_____ 2) seven primary mental abilities   b. Thurstone
_____ 3) strucure of intellect   c. Guilford
_____ 4) seven frames of mind   d. Sternberg
_____ 5) the g factor   e. Gardner

Answers: 1) d 2) b 3) c 4) e 5) a

The IQ Controversy: Brainy Dispute

The Uses and Abuses of Intelligence Tests

From the time of Binet in the early 1900s, intelligence testing has become a major growth industry. Virtually every college and university student in America has taken one or more intelligence or aptitude tests. Increasingly, business and industry are testing prospective employees. And somehow, many Americans have come to believe that a "magical" number—an IQ score, a percentile rank, or some other derived score—unfalteringly portrays a person's intellectual capacity, ability, or potential. In many cases, the score has served as the ticket of admission or the mark of rejection to educational and occupational opportunity.

Question: For what are intelligence tests good and poor predictors?

Intelligence Test Scores: Can They Predict Success and Failure?   What can intelligence tests really tell us? IQ scores are fairly good predictors of academic achievement and success in school. The Stanford-Binet Intelligence Scale and the

triarchic theory of intelligence: Sternberg's theory that intelligence consists of three parts—the componential, the contextual, and the experiential.

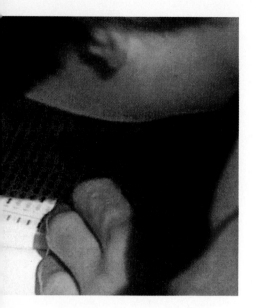

Many people believe that SATs, used by some colleges as a basis for admission, are biased against women and some minority groups.

Verbal Scale of the Wechsler tests correlate highly with school grades. This is not surprising, since success in school work and success on these intelligence tests both require the same set of skills—verbal and test-taking ability. But IQ tests and aptitude tests such as the SAT are far from infallible.

Another important question is whether there is a high correlation between IQ and success in real life. While it is true that the average IQ score of people in the professions (doctors, dentists, lawyers) tends to be higher than in lower-status occupations, the exact relationship between IQ score and occupational status is not clearly understood. IQ is not a good predictor of later occupational success among people of the same social class and level of education. In such cases, correlation may be low because attitude and motivation, critical components of success, cannot be measured by IQ tests. Furthermore, barriers to success still exist, even for intelligent and highly motivated women and minorities.

Question: What are some of the abuses of intelligence tests?

The Abuses of Intelligence Tests: Making Too Much of a Single Number

Abuses occur when scores on intelligence or aptitude tests are the only or even the major criterion for admitting people to various educational programs. Some students with very high SAT scores may leave a dismal academic record behind, while some students with lower scores may distinguish themselves in college. Intelligence tests do not measure attitude and motivation, which are critical ingredients of success. Many people are admitted to educational programs who probably should not be, but more importantly, a large number of people are denied admission to these programs who could profit from them and possibly make significant contributions to society. One good example is Dr. Robert Jarvik, described at the beginning of this chapter.

Early categorization based solely on IQ scores can doom children to slow-track educational programs that are not appropriate for them. Many poor and minority children (particularly those for whom English is a second language) and visually impaired or hearing impaired children have been dumped into special education programs. IQ tests predicted that they were not mentally able to profit from regular classroom instruction. There would be no problem if the test results were unfalteringly accurate, but in fact they are not.

In some states IQ tests are banned altogether. In others it is now illegal to place children in classes for the mentally retarded if this action is based solely on their IQ scores without also testing their level of adaptive functioning in daily life.

Many people claim that IQ tests are designed for the white middle class and that minority children and those for whom English is a second language are at a disadvantage when they are assessed with these tests. Attempts have been made to develop **culture-fair intelligence tests**. These tests are designed to minimize cultural bias; the questions do not penalize individuals whose cultural experience or language differs from that of the urban middle or upper classes. See Figure 7.3 for an example of the type of test item found on a culture-fair test.

The Nature-Nurture Controversy: Battle of the Centuries

Question: How does the nature-nurture controversy apply to intelligence?

The most vocal area of disagreement concerning intelligence has been the **nature-nurture controversy**, the debate over whether intelligence is primarily the result of heredity or environment. Sir Francis Galton (1874) initiated this debate and he coined the term. Galton, an Englishman, was born in 1822 into a family

culture-fair intelligence test: An intelligence test designed to minimize cultural bias by using questions that would not penalize individuals whose culture or language differs from that of the urban middle or upper class.

nature-nurture controversy: The debate over whether intelligence and other traits are primarily the result of heredity or environment.

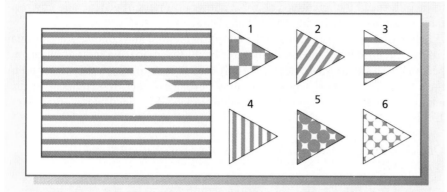

Figure 7.3   An Example of a Test Item on a Culture-Fair Test   This culture-fair test does not penalize test takers whose language or cultural experiences differ from that of the urban middle or upper classes. Subjects are to select, from the six samples on the right, the patch that would complete the pattern. Patch number 3 is the correct answer. (Adapted from the Raven Standard Progressive Matrices Test.)

line of many exceptionally able men and women, which included his cousin Charles Darwin. After studying a number of prominent families in England, Galton concluded that intelligence was inherited.

The nature-nurture controversy has raged for well over 100 years with hereditarians like Galton claiming that intelligence is largely inherited and planted at conception—the result of nature. The environmentalists, on the other hand, have insisted that intelligence is influenced mostly by a person's environment, the result of nurture. Most psychologists today agree that both nature and nurture contribute to intelligence, but they continue to debate the proportions contributed by each (Snyderman & Rothman, 1987).

Question: What is behavioral genetics, and what are the primary methods used in the field today?

Behavioral Genetics: Investigating Nature and Nurture   Behavioral genetics is a field of research that investigates the relative effects of heredity and environment on behavior and ability (Plomin & Rende, 1991). Two of the primary methods used by behavioral geneticists are the twin study method, first used by Galton (1875) in his studies of heredity, and the adoption method.

In the **twin study method, identical** (monozygotic) **twins** and **fraternal** (dizygotic) **twins** are studied to determine how much they resemble each other on a variety of characteristics. Identical twins have exactly the same genes because a single sperm cell of the father fertilizes a single egg of the mother, forming a cell that then splits and forms two human beings—"carbon copies." But fraternal twins are no more alike genetically than other siblings born to the same parents. In the case of fraternal twins, two separate sperm cells fertilize two separate eggs that happen to be released at the same time during ovulation.

Twins who are raised together, whether identical or fraternal, have similar environments. If identical twins raised together are found more alike than fraternal twins on a certain trait, then that trait is assumed to be more influenced by heredity. But if identical and fraternal twins from similar environments do not differ on a trait, that trait is assumed to be influenced more by environment. The

behavioral genetics: A field of research that investigates the relative effects of heredity and environment on behavior and ability.

twin study method: Studying identical and fraternal twins to determine the relative effects of heredity and environment on a variety of characteristics.

identical twins: Twins with identical genes; monozygotic twins.

fraternal twins: Twins who are no more alike genetically than ordinary brothers and sisters; dizygotic twins.

heritability: An index of the degree to which a characteristic is estimated to be influenced by heredity.

adoption method: A method used to study the relative effects of heredity and environment on behavior and ability in children adopted shortly after birth, by comparing them to their biological and adoptive parents.

term **heritability** is an index of the degree to which a characteristic is estimated to be influenced by heredity. Table 7.2 shows estimates of genetic and environmental factors contributing to intelligence.

Behavioral geneticists also use the **adoption method** and conduct longitudinal studies of children adopted shortly after birth. By comparing their abilities and personality traits to their adoptive family members with whom they live, and to their biological parents whom they may never have met, researchers can disentangle the effects of heredity and environment (Plomin, DeFries, & Fulker, 1988).

Question: How do twin studies support the view that intelligence is inherited?

A Natural Experiment: Identical Twins Reared Apart   Minnesota—home of the twin cities and the Minnesota Twins—is also, fittingly, the site of the most extensive American study of identical and fraternal twins. The Minnesota Center for Twin and Adoption Research at the University of Minnesota has assembled the Minnesota Twin Registry, which in 1990 included some 9,200 twin pairs (Lykken et al., 1990).

Probably the best way to assess the relative contribution of heredity and environment is to study identical twins who have been separated at birth and raised apart. When the separated twins are found to have strikingly similar

Table 7.2   Genetic and Environmental Contributions to Intelligence

Relationship	Rearing	Percentage of Genetic Similarity	Correlation
Same individual	—	100	.87
Identical twins	Together	100	.86
Fraternal twins	Together	50	.62
Siblings	Together	50	.41
Siblings	Apart	50	.24
Parent-child	Together	50	.35
Parent-child	Apart	50	.31
Adoptive parent–child	Together	?	.16

Estimates of Contributions of Genetics and Environment to Variability in Intelligence

Comparison	Genetics	Environment
Identical twins together versus fraternal twins together	.58	.28
Parent-offspring together versus parent-offspring apart	.50	.04
Siblings together versus siblings apart	.25	.25

Adapted from Henderson, N.D. A Human behavior genetics, pp. 403–440. Reproduced, with permission, from the *Annual Review of Psychology*, Volume 33. © 1982 by Annual Reviews Inc.

traits, it is assumed that heredity has been a major contributor. When identical twins differ on a given trait, the influence of the environment is thought to be greater.

Since 1979 the Minnesota researchers headed by Thomas Bouchard have studied over 100 sets of twins or triplets from many parts of the world who were reared apart. In a comparison of the similarity in IQ of identical twins reared together and apart, Bouchard and others (1990) concluded that *"general intelligence or IQ is strongly affected by genetic factors"* (p. 227). In four independent studies primarily of middle-aged adults, a heritability of .70 was found, indicating that 70 percent of the variation in IQ can be attributed to genetic factors. If the genes have such a strong influence on IQ, then it is not surprising that academic achievement, verbal ability, and spatial ability also show significant genetic influence (Plomin, 1989, 1990).

Psychologists who consider environmental factors as the chief contributors to differences in intelligence take issue with Bouchard's findings. They claim that most separated identical twins are raised by adoptive parents who have been matched as closely as possible to their actual parents. This fact, the critics say, could account for the similarity in IQ. In response to their critics, Bouchard and others (1991) point out that studies comparing nonbiologically related siblings reared in the same home reveal that IQ correlations are close to zero by the time the subjects reach adolescence (Teasdale & Owen, 1984; Scarr & Weinberg, 1978).

Further evidence for the heritability of IQ comes from adoption studies. These studies reveal that children adopted shortly after birth have IQs more closely resembling their biological parents than their adoptive parents. The family environment has an influence on IQ early in life, but that influence seems to diminish. Twin and adoption studies indicate that as subjects reach adulthood, it is the genes that are most closely correlated with IQ (Loehlin et al., 1988, 1989; McCartney et al., 1990; Plomin & Rende, 1991). Bouchard and others (1990) claim that "although parents may be able to affect their children's rate of cognitive skill acquisition, they may have relatively little influence on the ultimate level attained" (p. 225). But does this mean that the degree to which intelligence is inherited is the degree to which it is absolutely fixed and immune to environmental intervention?

Intelligence: Is It Fixed or Changeable?

Probably the most important issue in intelligence is whether IQ is fixed or changeable (Angoff, 1988). There is little doubt that the high degree of similarity in intelligence scores between identical twins reared apart makes a strong case for the powerful influence of genetics. But even Bouchard and his colleagues (1990) clearly admit that only a few of the identical twins studied were raised in impoverished environments or by illiterate parents. Consequently the researchers caution against trying to generalize their findings to people raised in disadvantaged environments. Moreover, they point out that their findings do not argue against the possibility that IQ might be enhanced in a more optimal environment.

To assert that a behavior or characteristic that is genetic in origin cannot be changed is a myth. According to Richard Weinberg (1989):

> Genes do not fix behavior. Rather, they establish a range of possible reactions to the range of possible experiences that environments can provide. . . . How people behave or what their measured IQs turn out to be or how quickly they learn depends on the nature of their environments *and* on their genetic endowments bestowed at conception" (p. 101).

Question: What are Arthur Jensen's controversial views on race and IQ?

The Controversial Views of Arthur Jensen: Race and IQ   Some studies over the past several decades have reported that, on the average, African Americans score about 15 points lower than whites on standardized IQ tests (Jensen, 1985; Loehlin et al., 1975). In 1969 psychologist Arthur Jensen published an article in the *Harvard Educational Review* in which he attributed the IQ gap to genetic differences between the races. Furthermore, he claimed that because heredity provides such a strong influence on intelligence, environmental influences cannot make a significant difference.

Almost immediately, Jensen's published views on race and intelligence sent a shock wave through the scientific community. Even today, more than 20 years later, his views continue to stimulate heated debate. Jensen's article was seen as an attack against the view held by many scientists and most educators that an enriched, stimulating environment can overcome the deficits of poverty and cultural disadvantage and thus reduce or wipe out the IQ deficit.

Question: What evidence suggests that improving a child's environment can raise IQ scores?

Evidence That IQ Can Be Changed: Enriched Environments Boost IQs
Several studies indicate that IQ test scores are not fixed but can be modified with an enriched environment.

Disputing Jensen's Claim: The Scarr-Weinberg Study   Sandra Scarr and Richard Weinberg (1976) challenged Jensen's claim that the 15-point IQ difference is due to genetic differences between the races. They studied 130 black and interracial children who had been adopted by highly educated, upper-middle-class white families; 99 of the children had been adopted in the first year of life. The adoptees were fully exposed to the middle-class cultural experiences and vocabulary, the "culture of the tests and the school" (p. 737).

A child's environment—whether deprived or enriched—has a major impact on IQ score and future achievement.

How did the children perform on IQ and achievement tests? For these children, the 15-point black-white IQ gap was bridged by an enriched environment. Compared to a mean IQ score of 90, which would be expected had these children been reared by their biological parents, the average IQ score of the 130 adoptees was 106. And their achievement test scores were slightly above the national average, not below. On the average, the earlier the children were adopted, the higher their IQs. The mean IQ score of the 99 early adoptees was 110, about 10 IQ points above the average for whites (see Figure 7.4).

Scarr and Weinberg (1976) conclude:

> If all black children had environments such as those provided by the adoptive families in this study, we would predict that their IQ scores would be 10–20 points higher than the scores are under current rearing conditions. . . . The major findings of the study support the view that the social environment plays a dominant role in determining the average IQ level of black children and that both social and genetic variables contribute to individual variation among them. (pp. 738–739)

Other Adoption Studies Reflecting Environmental Influences on Intelligence
Other studies have demonstrated that IQ scores and achievement are substantially higher when children from impoverished or lower-class environments are adopted by middle- and upper-middle-class families. Michel Schiff and his French colleagues (1978, 1982; Schiff & Lewontin, 1986) studied 35 children of lower-class mothers who had been adopted into upper-middle-class families at a young age. Their IQs were measured and compared with their siblings or half-siblings who had been reared by their birth mothers. The average IQ score of the adopted children was 109, nearly the same as the 110 IQ average of upper-middle-class children in a national sample. What about their siblings and half-siblings reared in lower-class households? Their average IQ was 95, comparable to the national sample of the children of unskilled workers. Furthermore, only 17 percent of the adoptees had been placed in remedial classes or had to repeat a grade, compared to 66 percent of their siblings or half-siblings.

Duyme (1988) studied a similar sample and reported "an important increase in cognitive performances of lower-class children adopted by upper-class families" (p. 208).

Changes in Standard of Living Further evidence that drastic changes in the environment can have major effects on intelligence stretches back more than half a century. In 1940, group IQ tests were given to 3,200 white, economically disadvantaged children from 40 schools in the Appalachian Mountains of Tennessee. Their scores were compared to the scores of other children from the same area, and many from the same families, who had been tested 10 years earlier in 1930. Within this 10-year period, the area underwent tremendous improvements in economic, educational, and cultural conditions; also, within this period average IQ scores increased from 82 in 1930 to 93 in 1940 (Wheeler, 1942). The same gene pool, after a decade of continuing environmental enrichment, had raised its average IQ by 11 points, about three-fourths of a standard deviation—a major effect, by any measure.

Researchers should not be surprised when enriched environments alter traits that are highly heritable. Consider the fact that American and British adolescents are 6 inches taller on average than their counterparts a century ago (Tanner, 1962). Height has a heritability of 0.90, yet changes in standard of living can affect this highly heritable trait. The highest heritability estimates for intelligence (.70) are far lower than those for height. It seems clear that "significant increases in average IQ might occur through the radical environmental intervention of adoption" (Plomin & Rende, 1991, p. 164).

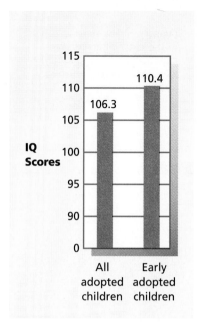

Figure 7.4

Mean IQ Scores of Black Adoptees

Scarr and Weinberg's adoption study indicates the important role of environment and economic advantage on IQ score. The 130 black children who were adopted by white, upper-middle-class families had a mean IQ score of 106.3, six points higher than the average for whites. But 99 of the 130 children who had been adopted early (in their first year of life) had a mean IQ score of 110.4. (After Scarr & Weinberg, 1976.)

imagery: The representation in the mind of a sensory experience—visual, auditory, gustatory, motor, olfactory, or tactile.

Memory Check 7.3

1. Twin studies suggest that heredity is a stronger factor than environment in shaping IQ differences. (true/false)

2. If environment played no part in IQ, then (identical, fraternal) twins would have exactly the same IQ.

3. Based on his research, Arthur Jensen believed that the black-white IQ gap should be attributed to:

   a. genetic differences in intelligence   c. discrimination
   b. environmental factors such as poverty   d. all of these

4. Most psychologists disagree with Jensen's explanation of the black-white IQ gap. (true/false)

Answers: 1. true 2. identical 3. a 4. true

Imagery and Concepts: Tools of Thinking

Whatever our IQ happens to be, we use certain skills and strategies when we think and solve problems. What are these tools of thinking?

In trying to prove his existence, the great French philosopher René Descartes (1596–1650) said, "I think, therefore I am." Unfortunately, he did not proceed to describe the act of thinking itself. All of us have an intuitive notion of what thinking is. We say, "I think it's going to rain" (a prediction); "I think this is the right answer" (a choice); "I think I will resign" (a decision). But our everyday use of the word *think* does not suggest the processes we use to perform the act itself. Sometimes our thinking is free flowing rather than goal-oriented. At other times, it is directed and aimed at a goal such as solving a problem or making a decision. Just how is the act of thinking accomplished? There is general agreement that at least two tools are commonly used when we think—images and concepts.

Imagery: Picture This—Elephants with Purple Polka Dots

Question: What is imagery?

Can you imagine hearing a recording of your favorite song or someone calling your name? Can you picture yourself jogging or walking, pouring ice water over your hands, or kissing someone you love? In your imagination, can you taste your favorite flavor of ice cream or smell body odor or ammonia? The vast majority of us are able to produce mental **imagery**; that is, we can represent or picture a sensory experience in our mind. Albert Einstein is said to have done much of his thinking in images.

In a survey of 500 adults conducted by McKellar (1972), 97 percent said they had visual images; 93 percent reported auditory images (imagine your psychology professor's voice); 74 percent claimed to have motor imagery (imagine raising your hand); 70 percent, tactile or touch images (imagine rubbing sand-

What role does imagery play in a child's ability to create?

paper); 67 percent, gustatory images (imagine the taste of a dill pickle); and 66 percent, olfactory images (imagine smelling a rose). Visual imagery is certainly the most common, although auditory imagery is not far behind.

Our images may be dimmer and less vivid than when we are experiencing the real thing, but images are not limited to time and space, size, or other physical realities. We could imagine ourselves flying though the air like an eagle, singing to the thundering applause of adoring fans, or performing all sorts of amazing feats. But normally our imaging is quite similar to the real world we are thinking about.

When we construct visual mental images, we may believe that we form the entire image all at once. But, according to Stephen Kosslyn (1988), we do not. Rather, we mentally construct the objects we image, one part at a time. Studies with split-brain patients (discussed in chapter 2, "Biology and Behavior") and normal subjects suggest that two types of processes are used in forming visual images. First, we retrieve stored memories of how parts of an object look, and then we use mental processes to arrange or assemble those parts into the proper whole. Both the left and right hemispheres participate in the processes of forming visual images. Try forming these visual images as you do the *Try It!*

Try It!

A. Picture an ant crawling on a newspaper about 3 feet away. How many legs does the ant have?
B. Picture an ant perched on the end of a toothpick right in front of your eyes. Does the ant have eyelashes?

In which mental picture is the ant larger, A or B? Which mental picture provided more detail of the ant? (After Finke, 1986.)

Kosslyn (1975, 1983) asked many such questions of research subjects and found that they answered questions concerning larger images about one-fifth of a second faster than questions about small images. It takes us slightly longer to zoom in on smaller images than on larger ones, just as it does when we actually look at real objects.

But what if we are forming new images rather than answering questions about large and small images already formed? Picture an elephant standing two feet away. Now picture a rabbit standing at the same distance. Which image took longer to form? Kosslyn (1975) discovered that it takes people longer to form large mental images than to conjure up small ones, much as it would if we had to view and consider an elephant as opposed to a rabbit. It takes longer to view the elephant because there is more of it to view, and likewise more of it to image.

Similarities in the Processes of Imaging and Perceiving Apparently we form mental images in the brain much like we actually perceive visual, auditory, and other sensory stimuli. And just like our perceptions, our imaging is subject to interference. Close your eyes, and form a mental image of your psychology professor. Now keep the visual image, and open your eyes. Doesn't the mental image fade or disappear as soon as you see a real object? But if viewing an actual object interferes with a visual image, is the reverse also true? Will a vivid visual image interfere with a real object? Segal and Fusella (1970) provided an answer to this question in their laboratory. Student subjects were asked to form either a visual image of a tree or an auditory image of the sound of a typewriter. Once the subjects were holding their assigned image (visual or auditory), the researchers made a faint sound on a harmonica or flashed a small, dimly lighted blue arrow, or did nothing at all.

Subjects who were holding the visual image of a tree were most likely to miss seeing the blue arrow but most likely to hear the harmonica. But subjects imaging the sound of a typewriter had the opposite experience. They saw the arrow but missed the sound of the harmonica. The researchers interpreted their results to mean that both perceiving and imaging probably use some of the same mental processes and that using the same processes *simultaneously* on two different tasks is difficult.

Other research indicates that both perception and imagery are handled by the same parts of the brain. Patients who have experienced damage in a particular region of the right hemisphere may have a loss of perception in the left half of their visual field. (Remember, information from the left and right visual fields is fed into the opposite brain hemispheres.) Some males with such damage will shave the right side of their face but completely ignore the left side. When these same patients are asked to produce a mental image of an object or a location they know well, they identify only the details on the right half of the object or location (Bisiach & Luzzati, 1978).

Not only do we form a mental image of an object, but we manipulate and move it around in our mind much as we would if we were actually holding and looking at the object (Cooper & Shepard, 1984). Shepard & Metzler (1971) asked eight subjects to judge some 1,600 pairs of drawings like the ones in Figure 7.5. The subjects were to pull a lever with their right hand if the objects in each pair were the same or with the left hand if they were different. Subjects had to rotate the objects in their imagination to see if they matched. In Figure 7.5 the objects in A and B are a match; those in C are not. But the important finding is that the more the objects had to be rotated in imagery, the longer it took subjects to decide whether they matched. This is precisely what would happen if the subjects had rotated real objects—the farther they needed to be rotated, the longer it would take to make the decision.

As this study demonstrates, we manipulate objects in mental imagery like we manipulate real physical objects. Does this mean that we actually store pictures

Figure 7.5

Samples of Geometric Patterns in Shepard and Metzler's Mental Rotation Study

Mentally rotate one of the patterns in each pair—A, B, and C—and decide whether the two patterns match. Do you find that the more you have to rotate the objects mentally, the longer it takes to decide if they match? (From Shepard & Metzler, 1971.)

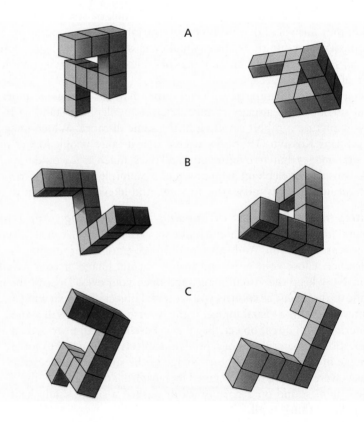

in our brain? According to some psychologists, the whole image (picture, sound, and so on) is stored intact somewhere in the brain (Shepard, 1978; Yuille & Marschark, 1983). Other researchers argue that information storage in the brain is much more abstract. Pylyshn (1984), for example, believes that images are probably stored according to verbal symbols rather than spatial or visual coding. In other words, the actual images we think about are not stored intact but are reconstructed from the coded symbols that are stored. Still others believe that information may be stored in both ways (Finke, 1985). Some evidence from split-brain patients suggests that one specific brain function may be devoted exclusively to mental imagery (Kosslyn, 1981, 1987).

Concepts: Our Mental Classification System (Is a Penguin a Bird?)

Question: What are concepts, and how are they formed?

Fortunately, thinking is not limited to conjuring up a series of pictures, sounds, touches, tastes, and smells. Humans are capable of conceptualizing as well. A **concept** is a label that represents a class or group of objects, people, or events that share common characteristics or attributes. Concepts are useful tools that help us to order our world and to think and communicate with speed and efficiency.

Imagine that you are walking down the street with a friend, and you see approaching in the distance a hairy, brown and white, four-legged animal with two eyes, two ears, its mouth open, tongue hanging out, and a long, wagging tail. You simply say to your friend, "Here comes a dog." Thanks to our ability to use concepts, we are not forced to consider and describe everything in great detail before we make an identification. We do not need a different name to identify and describe every single rock, tree, animal, or situation we meet. *Dog* is a concept that stands for a family of animals who share similar characteristics or attributes but who may differ in significant ways. Whether Great Danes, dachshunds, collies, Chihuahuas, or any other breed, we recognize all these varied creatures according to our concept *dog*.

Household pet is a broader concept, which might include dog, cat, bird, goldfish, and so on. Although other creatures may take up residence in our house—cockroach, mouse, mosquito, housefly, or bedbug—they are not likely to fit our concept of household pet.

We have concepts of abstractions as well as tangible objects and organisms. Love, beauty, and justice are abstract concepts, and we can identify and consider aspects of beauty and justice because we have formed concepts of them. Also, we use relational concepts in our thinking—larger than, smaller than, older than, younger than, and so on—to compare individuals, objects, and ideas.

Concept Formation: Learning What Fits a Concept How do we acquire concepts and how do we know what fits or does not fit a given concept? We can form concepts from a formal definition of the concept, through our experiences with positive and negative instances of the concept, by systematically memorizing a concept's common features, and through our use of prototypes.

Positive and Negative Instances We acquire many simple concepts through experiences with examples or positive instances of the concept. When children are young, parents might point out examples of a car—the family car, the neighbor's car, cars on the street, and pictures of cars in a book. If a child points to some other type of moving vehicle and says "car," the parent will say, "No, that is a truck," or "This is a bus." "Truck" and "bus" are negative instances, or

concept: A label that represents a class or group of objects, people, or events sharing common characteristics or attributes.

prototype: The example that embodies the most typical features of a particular concept.

nonexamples, of the concept "car." After experience with positive and negative instances of the concept, a child begins to grasp some of the properties of a car that distinguish it from other wheeled vehicles.

Systematic or Formal Approaches Studies have been conducted and theories proposed to explain how we form concepts. Some theorists maintain that we approach concept formation in an active, orderly, and systematic way, rather than in a random, informal, haphazard fashion (Bruner et al., 1956). Sometimes we learn a concept from a formal definition or from a formal classification system used in the sciences and other disciplines. You surely have memorized several of these formal classification systems in biology, chemistry, English, and other courses you have taken.

Prototypes Eleanor Rosch (1973, 1978) argues that formal theories of concept formation, and the experiments on which they are based, tend to be rather artificial, contrived, and not related to our actual experience. She and her colleagues have studied concept formation in its natural setting and have concluded that in real life our thinking and concept formation are somewhat fuzzy, not clear-cut and systematic. Sometimes we identify objects based on a memorized list of features or attributes that are common to members of a concept. But in addition, we are likely to picture a **prototype** of the concept—an example which embodies the most typical features of the concept.

What is your prototype for the concept *bird*? Chances are it is not a penguin, an ostrich, or a kiwi. All three are birds that cannot fly. A more likely bird prototype is a robin or perhaps a sparrow. Most birds can fly, but not all; most mammals cannot fly, but bats are mammals, have wings, and can fly. So all members within a concept do not fit it equally well. Nevertheless, the prototype most closely fits a given concept, and items and organisms belonging to the concept share more attributes with their prototype than with the prototype of any other concept.

The concepts we form do not simply exist in isolation. We form them in hierarchies. For example, the canary and the cardinal are subsets of the concept *bird;* at a higher level, birds are subsets of the concept *animal;* and at a still higher level, animals are a subset of the concept *living things.*

Memory Check 7.4

1. The two most common forms of imagery are:

   a. visual and motor imagery   c. visual and auditory imagery
   b. auditory and tactile imagery   d. visual and gustatory imagery

2. Our images are generally as vivid as the real thing. (true/false)

3. Our imaging system seems to work in much the same way as our perceptual system. (true/false)

4. A label that represents a class or a group of objects, people, or events sharing common characteristics or attributes is called a (concept, prototype).

5. A prototype is the most (unusual, typical) example of a concept.

Answers: 1. c 2. false 3. true 4. concept 5. typical

Problem Solving and Creativity

Approaches to Problem Solving: How Do We Begin?

Question: What are three problem-solving techniques, and how are they used?

All of us are faced with a variety of problems needing to be solved every day. Most of our problems are simple and mundane, like what to have for dinner or what clothing to put on when we dress in the morning. But some of our problems are more far-reaching, such as what major to choose in college, what career to pursue, how to sustain or improve a relationship, or how to stretch our income from one paycheck to the next. Then there are the problems we meet in our school work, which we must think through using problem-solving techniques. Among these techniques are trial and error, algorithms, and heuristics.

How would you go about solving the problem described in the *Try It!*?

Insert the numbers *1* through *8* in the eight boxes, one digit to a box, in such a way that no consecutive numbers will be next to each other horizontally, vertically, or diagonally. There are four possible solutions.

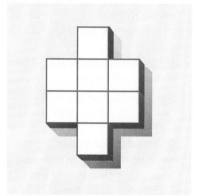

Try It!

Trial and Error: If at First You Don't Succeed . . . How did you choose to solve the problem? Some people examine the problem carefully and devise a strategy—such as placing the *1* and the *8* in the middle boxes because each of these has only *one* forbidden consecutive number (*2* and *7*) to avoid. Many people, however, simply start placing the numbers in the boxes and then change them around when a combination doesn't work. This is the *trial-and-error* approach, in which we try one solution after another, in no particular order, until we chance to hit upon the answer. Even lower animals use trial and error.

Trial and error can be very time consuming and perhaps even dangerous. Would you feel comfortable with a surgeon who operated on you using trial and error? You might not survive the errors and be able to enjoy the solution. Of course most of our problems are not life or death situations, and if all else fails in our efforts to solve a problem, we may be reduced to trial and error. But other techniques are far more effective and less time consuming.

Applying Prior Knowledge: We Don't Have to Start from Scratch Rather than beginning with a haphazard, trial-and-error approach, it is best to reflect on a problem and see if you already have any knowledge that might help in finding a solution. Some problems can be solved with only a little ready knowledge. The problem in the next *Try It!* is a good example.

trial and error: An approach to problem solving in which one solution after another is tried in no particular order until a workable solution is found.

Order the colors from least to greatest in numerical value.

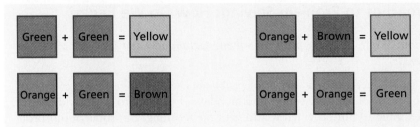

From the problem you can see that yellow is twice the value of green, and that green is twice the value of orange. Therefore, yellow is four times the value of orange. Then you can see that brown is numerically greater than either orange or green, but numerically less than yellow. Also you should know that both yellow and green must be even numbers, because any two odd numbers or any two even numbers will always equal an even number. The answer to the *Try It!* is that the colors are ordered from least value to greatest value as follows: orange, green, brown, and yellow.

Algorithms: Formulas That Can't Miss   Another major problem-solving method is the algorithm (Newell & Simon, 1972). An **algorithm** is a systematic, step-by-step procedure that guarantees a solution to a problem of a certain type if the algorithm is appropriate and executed properly. Formulas used in mathematics and other sciences are algorithms. Another type of algorithm is a systematic strategy for exploring every possible solution to a problem until the correct one is reached. In some cases there may be millions or even billions or more possibilities that would have to be tried before reaching a solution. Often computers are programmed to solve such problems because an accurate solution is guaranteed and millions of possible solutions can be tried in a few seconds.

Suppose you were a contestant on "Wheel of Fortune," trying to solve the missing letter problem: P _ Y _ _ O L _ _ _ . An exhaustive search algorithm would be out of the question—even Vanna White's smile would fade long before the nearly 9 billion possibilities could be considered.

Many problems do not lend themselves to solution by algorithms. An easier way to solve such problems is with the method of heuristics.

Heuristic Strategies in Problem Solving: Fast, But Not Infallible   An early researcher of heuristic problem solving was Karl Duncker (1945), who found or formulated a number of problems he asked students to solve. From the subjects' verbal descriptions of their problem-solving attempts, Duncker discovered some common strategies and techniques the students used, which he termed heuristics. A **heuristic** is a problem-solving method that does not guarantee success but offers a promising way to attack a problem and arrive at a solution. Chess players must use heuristics because there is not enough time in a lifetime to consider all of the moves and countermoves that would be possible in a single game of chess (Bransford et al., 1986).

Heuristic techniques are used to eliminate useless steps and to take the shortest probable path toward a solution. The missing-letter problem referred to earlier is easily solved using a simple heuristic approach that makes use of our existing knowledge of words (prefixes, roots, suffixes). Like any good contestant on the "Wheel of Fortune" quiz show, we can supply the missing letters and spell out *PSYCHOLOGY.*

algorithm: A systematic, step-by-step procedure, such as a mathematical formula, that guarantees a solution to a problem of a certain type if the algorithm is appropriate and executed properly.

heuristic (hyu-RIS-tik): A problem-solving method that offers a promising way to attack a problem and arrive at a solution, although it does not guarantee success.

Means-End Analysis   One popular heuristic strategy is *means-end analysis*, in which the current position is compared with a desired goal, and a series of steps are formulated and then taken to close the gap between the two (Sweller & Levine, 1982). Many problems are large and complex and must be broken down into smaller steps or subproblems before a solution can be reached. If your professor assigns a term paper, for example, you probably do not simply sit down and write it. You must first determine how you will deal with your topic, research the topic, make an outline, and then probably write the subtopics over a period of time. At last you are ready to assemble the complete term paper, write several drafts, and put the finished product in final form before handing it in to your professor.

Perhaps this scenario is too idealistic, but it serves to illustrate the heuristic strategy of means-end analysis. We must deal with many of life's problems in this way by accomplishing a little at a time—solving parts of a problem, step by step, until the goal is reached.

Working Backwards   Another heuristic that is effective for solving some problems is *working backwards*, sometimes called the backward search. In this approach we start with the solution, a known condition, and work our way backwards through the problem. Once our backward search has revealed the steps to be taken and their order, we can solve the problem. Try working backwards to solve the water lily problem in the *Try It!*

> **means-end analysis:**   A heuristic problem-solving strategy in which the current position is compared with the desired goal, and a series of steps are formulated and taken to close the gap between them.
>
> **working backwards:**   A heuristic strategy in which a person discovers the steps needed to solve a problem by defining the desired goal and working backwards to the current condition.

Water lilies double in area every 24 hours. At the beginning of the summer there is one water lily on a lake. It takes 60 days for the lake to become covered with water lilies. On what day is the lake half covered?

Try It!

lake is to be completely covered on the 60th day, it has to be half covered on the 59th day. realize that the most important fact is that the lilies double in number every 24 hours. If the small study. To reach a solution, they had to "selectively encode" the information given—to People who solved the water-lilies problem tended to have high IQ scores in the author's

---

Impediments to Problem Solving: Mental Stumbling Blocks

Question: What are the two major impediments to problem solving?

Sometimes the difficulty in problem solving lies not with the problem but in ourselves. The two major impediments to problem solving are functional fixedness and mental set.

functional fixedness: The failure to use familiar objects in novel ways to solve problems because of a tendency to view objects only in terms of their customary functions.

mental set: The tendency to apply a familiar strategy to the solution of a problem without carefully considering the special requirements of the problem.

artificial intelligence: Computer programming that simulates human thinking in solving problems and in making judgments and decisions.

Functional Fixedness: Every Tool Has Only One Function   Many of us are hampered in our efforts to solve problems in daily living because of **functional fixedness**—the failure to use familiar objects in novel ways to solve problems. We tend to see objects only in terms of their customary functions. Just think of all the items we use daily—tools, utensils, and other equipment—that help us perform certain functions. Often the normal functions of objects become fixed in our thinking so that we do not consider using them in new and creative ways.

Mental Set: But I've Always Done It This Way   Another impediment, similar to functional fixedness but much broader, is mental set. **Mental set** means that we get into a mental rut in our approach to solving problems, continuing to use the same old method even though another approach might be better. Perhaps we hit on a way to solve a problem once in the past and continue to use the same technique in similar situations, even though it is not highly effective or efficient. We are much more susceptible to mental set when we fail to consider the special requirements of a problem. Not surprisingly, the same people who are subject to mental set are also more likely to have trouble with functional fixedness when they attempt to solve problems (McKelvie, 1984).

Humans are not the only ones on the planet able to solve problems. We have seen that many animals can solve problems, and apparently modern machines can too.

Artificial Intelligence

Question: What is artificial intelligence?

Computer intelligence that rivals or surpasses human intelligence has long been the stuff of which science fiction is made. You may remember Hal, the uncontrollable super-intelligent computer from Arthur Clarke's novel or the movie based on it, *2001: A Space Odyssey*. Although the year 2001 is in sight, no computer anything like the sinister Hal is on the horizon.

Nevertheless, amazing progress has been made in the field of artificial intelligence since the term was first used officially by researcher John McCarthy in 1956. **Artificial intelligence** refers to computers that are programmed to simulate human thinking in solving problems and in making judgments and decisions. The first successful effort to program computers that could mimic human thinking was made by Allen Newell and Herbert A. Simon. They developed programs that could play chess as well as a human expert could (although not as well as master players). They also created a program named the "Logic Theorist," which was able to prove complex theorems in formal logic. But Newell and Simon opened the door for artificial intelligence systems able to do far more than play chess like an expert and prove mathematical theorems.

Computers are being programmed to simulate the human brain's ability to solve problems. In one such program, a computer learns to distinguish between images of females and males by analyzing hundreds of different facial features—something the human brain can do almost instantaneously.

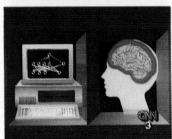

Now expert systems or programs are available that contain the collective knowledge and problem-solving strategies of the top experts in a given field. Today there are expert systems in medicine, space technology, military defense, weather prediction, and a variety of other sciences. The first of these expert systems was MYCIN, produced in the mid-1970s by computer scientist and physician Edward Shortliffe. MYCIN is a computer program that is an expert diagnostician in the area of blood diseases and meningitis. This and other programs have severe limitations, however, and so they are useful only as assistants to human experts, not as expert systems that can stand alone.

Artificial intelligence programs are designed to simulate human thinking and problem solving, and most of them now make use of heuristic problem-solving techniques, much like humans do. Both computers and humans can process information: encode, store, and retrieve data; manipulate symbols; translate information into different forms; perform logical operations; and execute other similar functions. Yet no computer can even approach the complexity and capability of the human brain. But Herbert Simon, an artificial intelligence pioneer and a 1978 Nobel prize winner in economics, believes that computers may be competing successfully with humans sooner than some of us would like to think. Simon predicted in 1957 that a chess program capable of beating any human expert would be developed within 10 years. Now, however, over 35 years later, Simon's prediction has still not come to pass.

Creativity: Unique and Useful Productions

Question: What is creativity, and what tests have been designed to measure it?

Measuring Creativity: Are There Reliable Measures? Creativity can be thought of as the ability to produce original, appropriate, and valuable ideas and/or solutions to a problem. But can creativity be measured? A number of efforts have been made to measure creativity, even though a clear definition of it has never been formulated. One well-known effort is that of J. P. Guilford, whose tests of divergent production have been used as measures of creativity. *Divergent production* is thinking aimed at producing one or more possible ideas, answers, or solutions to a problem rather than a single, correct response.

Obviously, creative thinking is divergent. But is the ability to think in divergent ways a sufficient condition for the production of creative thinking? No! All creative thought is divergent, but not all divergent thought is creative. Novelty is not synonymous with creativity. We are not surprised, then, to find that high scores on tests of divergent production do not have a very high correlation with creative production in real life. Guilford himself admitted that in studies of students from elementary through high school, the correlations of his divergent-production tests with actual creative production have not been spectacular (1967).

Other researchers have tried to design tests to measure creative ability. Mednick and Mednick (1967) reasoned that the essence of creativity consists of the creative thinker's ability to fit ideas together that might appear remote or unrelated to the noncreative thinker. They created the Remote Associates Test (RAT) as a means of measuring creative ability.

creativity: The ability to produce original, appropriate, and valuable ideas and/or solutions to problems.

divergent production: Producing one or more possible ideas, answers, or solutions to a problem rather than a single, correct response.

One indication of creativity is the ability to make associations among several elements that may be only remotely related. Test your ability to find associations for these 10 items, which are similar to those on the Remote Associates Test. Think of a fourth word that is related in some way to all three of the words in each row. For example, the words *keeper*, *text*, and *worm* are related to the word *book* and become bookkeeper, textbook, and book worm.

Try It!

1.	sales	collector	income
2.	flower	room	water
3.	red	shot	dog
4.	ball	hot	stool
5.	rock	man	classical
6.	story	true	sick
7.	news	plate	waste
8.	stuffed	sleeve	sweat
9.	class	temperature	bath
10.	wrist	man	stop

Answers: 1. tax 2. bed 3. hot 4. foot 5. music 6. love 7. paper 8. shirt 9. room 10. watch

savant syndrome: Mental retardation or autism coupled with either an ability to perform an amazing mental feat or the possession of a remarkable specific skill.

Mednick and Mednick point out that some studies show a relationship between high scores on the Remote Associates Test (RAT) and creative thinking in the workplace, but other studies have not found this relationship (Matlin, 1983). If both divergent-production tests and the Remote Associates Test measure creativity, shouldn't there be some correlation between them? Yes, but test scores on Guilford's divergent-production tests are not related to scores on the Remote Associates Test. It is not clear whether either of these two tests is actually measuring creativity, but whatever they are measuring, the two tests are not measuring the same abilities.

Creativity and Intelligence: How Do They Relate? Is creativity related to intelligence? Research to date indicates that there is a modest correlation between creativity and IQ. Highly creative people tend to be well above average in intelligence, but in the upper IQ ranges (over 120) there seems to be little correlation between IQ and creativity (Barron & Harrington, 1981).

Remember the young geniuses studied by Lewis Terman? Not a single one of them had produced a highly creative work when they were followed up over the years (Terman & Oden, 1959). No Nobel laureates, no Pulitzer prizes. Geniuses, yes; creative geniuses, no. Dr. Robert Jarvik, who in his youth tested too low for admission to medical school in this country, went on to prove his ability as a medical doctor and to establish his creative genius in conceptualizing and building mechanical medical devices.

The Savant Syndrome: Generally Retarded, Specifically a Genius

> "Arthur, how much is 6,427 times 4,234?"
>   Arthur turned his head in my direction and said, slowly but without hesitation, "27,211,918." His voice was stilted but precise. His eyes never lost their blank stare, and now he returned to gazing into space, without seeing anything, a handsome, impassive eight-year-old. (Rimland, 1978, p. 69)

Arthur can multiply multidigit numbers in his head faster than we can do them on a calculator, and he never makes a mistake. Yet his measured IQ is extremely low. People who can perform certain amazing mental feats or who possess remarkable specific skills but whose level of general intelligence is very low are known as idiot savants. But the term idiot savant, which "grates on modern sensibilities," is increasingly being replaced by the term **savant syndrome** (Treffert, 1988b, p. 29).

People who fit the savant syndrome have a curious combination of specific genius and either mental retardation or autism. Alonzo Clemons is such a person.

> He is not able to speak in complete sentences; he cannot read, and can barely count to 10. Now in his late thirties, he has the mental ability of an average 6-year-old child. Clemons lives in a facility for the retarded some 30 miles from his home in Denver. But he is making a name for himself in the art world. Alonzo, the retarded genius, is creating bronzed sculptures which collectors are eagerly buying for hundreds of dollars each, and more for special pieces (see photograph at left). Within only 4 months of his first show, Alonzo the sculptor had sold $30,000.00 worth of his work through a Denver art gallery. (After Harper, 1983.)

Of the several hundred cases reported in the literature, there are six times as many males as females. According to Treffert (1988a), "The skills can appear suddenly, without explanation, and can disappear just as suddenly" (p. 564).

The puzzling cases of the mentally retarded savants and the autistic savants are only slowly yielding their secrets to science. There is hope, however, that the unraveling of such mental mysteries will yield a clearer understanding of intelligence, thinking, and creativity.

Alonzo Clemons

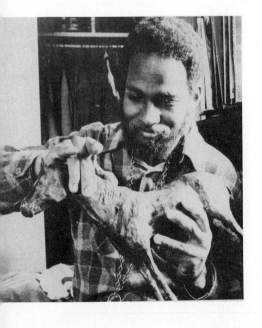

Memory Check 7.5

1. (A heuristic, An algorithm) is guaranteed to result in the correct answer to a problem.

2. Working backwards and means-end analysis are examples of (algorithms, heuristics).

3. John uses a wastebasket to keep a door from closing. He was not hindered by (functional fixedness, mental set) in solving his problem.

4. Artificial intelligence now surpasses the problem-solving ability of experts in a number of fields. (true/false)

5. Divergent-production tests and the Remote Associates Test are used to measure:

   a. imaging ability   c. problem-solving ability
   b. concept formation   d. creativity

Answers: 1. An algorithm 2. heuristics 3. functional fixedness 4. false 5. d

Thinking Critically

Evaluation

Which of the theories of intelligence best fits your notion of intelligence? Why?

Point/Counterpoint

Prepare an argument supporting each of the following positions:

a. Intelligence tests should be used in the schools.
b. Intelligence tests should not be used in the schools.

Psychology in Your Life

Give several examples of how tools of thinking (imagery and concepts) and problem-solving strategies (algorithms and heuristics) can be applied in your educational and personal life.

Chapter Summary and Review

Measuring Intelligence

What is Alfred Binet's major contribution to psychology?

Binet's major contribution to psychology is the concept of mental age and a method for measuring it—the intelligence test.

What does IQ mean, and how was it originally calculated?

IQ stands for intelligence quotient, an index of intelligence originally derived by dividing a person's mental age by his or her chronological age and then multiplying by 100.

Test Bank question 7.203 relates to material on these pages.

What is the Stanford-Binet Intelligence Scale?

The Stanford-Binet Intelligence Scale is a highly regarded intelligence test that has been revised several times since Lewis Terman's original, extensive adaptation of the Binet-Simon Intelligence Scale.

What did David Wechsler's tests provide that the Stanford-Binet did not?

David Wechsler developed the first successful individual intelligence test for adults, the Wechsler Adult Intelligence Scale (WAIS-R). His tests for adults, children, and preschoolers yield separate verbal and performance (nonverbal) IQ scores as well as an overall IQ score.

What is meant by the terms reliability, validity, and standardization?

Reliability is the ability of a test to yield nearly the same score each time a person takes the test or an alternate form of the test. Validity is the power of a test to measure what it is intended to measure. Standardization refers to prescribed procedures for administering a test and to established norms that provide a means of evaluating test scores.

What are the ranges of IQ scores considered average, superior, and in the range of mental retardation?

Fifty percent of the population have IQ scores ranging from 90 to 109; 2 percent have scores above 130, considered superior; and 2 percent have scores below 70, in the range of mental retardation.

According to the Terman study, how do the gifted differ from the general population?

Terman's long-term study revealed that, in general, the gifted enjoy better physical and mental health and are more successful than their less gifted counterparts.

Key Terms

intelligence quotient (p. 229)
norms (p. 231)
Stanford-Binet Intelligence Scale (p. 231)
deviation score (p. 231)
Wechsler Adult Intelligence Scale (WAIS-R) (p. 231)
reliability (p. 232)
validity (p. 233)
aptitude test (p. 233)
standardization (p. 233)
mental retardation (p. 235)

The Nature of Intelligence

What factors underlie intelligence, according to Spearman, Thurstone, and Guilford?

Spearman believed that intelligence is composed of a general ability (g factor), which underlies all intellectual functions, and a number of specific abilities (s factors). Thurstone points to seven primary mental abilities, which singularly or in combination are involved in all intellectual activities. Guilford's model, the structure of intellect, consists of 180 different intellectual abilities that involve all of the possible combinations of the three dimensions of intellect—mental operations, contents, and products.

What types of intelligence did Gardner and Sternberg identify?

Gardner believes that there are seven independent and equally important types of intelligence. Sternberg's triarchic theory of intelligence identifies three: the componential (conventional intelligence), the experiential (creative intelligence), and the contextual (practical intelligence).

Key Terms

g factor (p. 237)
primary mental abilities (p. 237)
structure of intellect (p. 237)
triarchic theory of intelligence (p. 239)

The IQ Controversy: Brainy Dispute

For what are intelligence tests good and poor predictors?

IQ tests are good predictors of success in school but not good predictors of attitude, motivation, or occupational success among people of the same social class and level of education.

What are some of the abuses of intelligence tests?

Abuses occur when IQ tests are the only criterion for admitting people to educational programs, for tracking children, or for placing them in classes for the mentally retarded. Many people claim that IQ tests are biased in favor of the urban middle or upper class.

How does the nature-nurture controversy apply to intelligence?

The nature-nurture controversy is the debate over whether intelligence is primarily the result of heredity or environment.

What is behavioral genetics, and what are the primary methods used in the field today?

Behavioral genetics is the field that investigates the relative effects of heredity and environment on behavior and ability. The twin study method and the adoption method are the primary methods used.

How do twin studies support the view that intelligence is inherited?

Twin studies provide evidence that intelligence is primarily inherited because identical twins are more alike in intelligence than fraternal twins, even if they have been reared apart.

What are Arthur Jensen's controversial views on race and IQ?

Arthur Jensen's controversial beliefs are that the black-white IQ gap is a function of heredity and that the influence of heredity on intelligence is too strong for the environment to make much of a difference.

What evidence suggests that improving a child's environment can raise IQ scores?

Several adoption studies have revealed that when infants from disadvantaged environments are adopted by middle- and upper-class parents, their IQ scores are raised about 15 points.

Key Terms

culture-fair intelligence test (p. 240)
nature-nurture controversy (p. 240)
behavioral genetics (p. 241)
twin study method (p. 241)
identical twins (p. 241)
fraternal twins (p. 241)

heritability (p. 242)
adoption method (p. 242)

Imagery and Concepts: Tools of Thinking

What is imagery?

Imagery is the representation in the mind of a sensory experience—visual, auditory, gustatory, motor, olfactory, or tactile.

What are concepts, and how are they formed?

Concepts are labels that represent classes or groups of objects, people, or events sharing common characteristics or attributes. We can form a concept from a formal definition of the concept, through our experiences with positive and negative instances of the concept, by systematically memorizing features or attributes common to members of a concept (as in formal classification systems), and through our use of prototypes.

Key Terms

imagery (p. 246)
concept (p. 249)
prototype (p. 250)

Problem Solving and Creativity

What are three problem-solving techniques, and how are they used?

Trial and error is an unsystematic problem-solving technique by which we try one solution after another until we hit on one that works. An algorithm is a step-by-step procedure that guarantees a solution, such as a mathematical formula or a systematic exploration of every possible solution. A heuristic method does not guarantee success but offers a promising way to solve a problem and arrive at a solution, such as working backwards or means-end analysis.

What are the two major impediments to problem solving?

Two major impediments to problem solving are functional fixedness, which is the failure to use familiar objects in novel ways to solve problems, and mental set, which is the tendency to apply familiar problem-solving strategies before carefully considering the special requirements of the problem.

What is artificial intelligence?

Artificial intelligence is a field of research in which computers are programmed to simulate human thinking in solving problems and in making judgments and decisions.

What is creativity, and what tests have been designed to measure it?

Creativity is the ability to produce original, appropriate, and valuable ideas and/or solutions to problems. Two tests used to measure creativity are divergent-production tests and the Remote Associates Test.

Key Terms

algorithm (p. 252)
heuristic (p. 252)
functional fixedness (p. 254)
mental set (p. 254)
artificial intelligence (p. 254)
creativity (p. 255)
savant syndrome (p. 256)

8

Child Development

CHAPTER OUTLINE

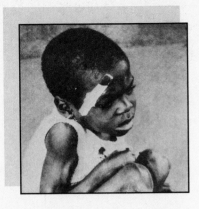

Robert, the "monkey child"

N orth of Kampala, Uganda, in Africa, the jungle is dark and dense, lush with a rich variety of exotic plant life and an abundance of animal species. But civil war has disturbed the peace and beauty of Uganda for many years, and brutal massacres have claimed the lives of many men, women, and children.

Ugandan soldiers, retreating through the jungle in 1984, came upon one of the strangest sights they had ever seen. They were accustomed to the large tribes of monkeys living in the jungle, hopping, chattering, and leaping from place to place and avoiding humans who alarmed them. But with one tribe of monkeys, they saw what appeared to be a small, dark animal unlike the others but jumping around with them. Intrigued, they came closer and were amazed to discover that this strange creature was a human child.

The soldiers captured the young boy and brought him to an orphanage in Kampala, Uganda. Here staff members named him Robert, estimated him to be between 5 and 7 years old, and were amazed by his behavior. He squealed and grunted but could not speak. He didn't walk normally, but he jumped from one place to another the way a monkey would. He scratched people when they approached him, ate grass or any other edible thing he could find, and squatted like a monkey when he was sitting still. Small for his age, Robert was only 2 1/2 feet tall when he was found, and he weighed only 22 pounds. One staff member at the orphanage said that Robert always looked miserable: no one had ever seen a smile on his face.

Foreign relief workers stationed in Uganda at the time were afraid that other "monkey children" might be living as wild creatures in the jungle where Robert was found. They suspected this because hundreds of orphaned children had been discovered wandering around in nearby villages after the civil war ended. Those who studied Robert's case believe that his parents were slaughtered when he was about one year old and that somehow he had managed to escape the massacre and make his way deep into the jungle. (Adapted from "Monkey Child," 1984.)

GENETICALLY, ROBERT IS FULLY AS HUMAN as any other human, but he behaves like a monkey. What are we to make of the tragic case of Robert?

For centuries thinkers have debated the relative influence of heredity and environment on development—a debate called the **nature-nurture controversy.** Some thinkers have taken the nature side in the debate, believing that our abilities are determined mainly by our heredity and are transmitted to us through our genes. Others take the nurture position, maintaining that our environment—the circumstances in which we are raised—determines what we become. It is true that with some physical traits, such as eye color and dimples, the influence of heredity is absolute. Other characteristics, such as the language we speak and our accent, are strictly a function of our environment.

The best possible home environment, education, and nutrition cannot produce an Einstein. However, parental neglect, poor nutrition, ill health, and lack of education can prevent even the brightest among us from becoming the best that our genes would allow. Surely nature and nurture are not opposing forces in the course of our development. They are partners, and together they wield their shared influence in forging and shaping us into the persons we become (Plomin, 1989).

How living things develop is a fascinating and remarkable process that unfolds day by day, year by year from conception to death. We will examine this amazing process in this and the next chapter. Human development begins even before birth, and we will trace its course from the very beginning.

nature-nurture controversy: The debate concerning the relative influence of heredity and environment on development.

Heredity and Prenatal Development

The Mechanism of Heredity: Genes and Chromosomes

Question: How are hereditary traits transmitted?

Genes are the biological blueprints that determine and direct the transmission of all of our hereditary traits. Genes are segments of DNA located on each of the rod-shaped structures called **chromosomes**, which are found in the nucleus of the body cells. Normal body cells, with two exceptions, have 23 pairs of chromosomes (46 chromosomes in all). The two exceptions are the sperm cells and the mature egg cells, which each have 23 single chromosomes. At conception the sperm adds its 23 single chromosomes to the 23 of the egg, and the union forms the one-celled zygote, thus providing the 46 chromosomes (23 pairs), which contain all of the genetic information needed to make a human being.

Twenty-two pairs of chromosomes (autosomes) are the same for both sexes (see Figure 8.1) and contain genes that determine various physical and mental traits. The 23rd pair are called **sex chromosomes** because they carry the genes that determine a person's sex; primary and secondary sex characteristics; and other sex-linked traits, such as red-green color blindness, male pattern baldness, and hemophilia.

The sex chromosomes of females consist of two X chromosomes (XX), while males have an X chromosome and a Y chromosome (XY). Because the egg cell always contains an X chromosome, the sex of a child will depend on whether the egg is fertilized by a sperm carrying an X chromosome, which produces a female, or a Y chromosome, which produces a male. Half of a man's sperm cells carry an X chromosome, and half carry a Y. Consequently, the chances of conceiving a boy or a girl are about equal, and it is the male's contribution that determines the sex of the child.

Each pair of chromosomes contains genes responsible for particular traits and body functions. Genes also determine the sequence of growth and the biological timetable responsible for many of the changes occurring over the life span. The majority of genes on each chromosome carry the same information in all humans, ensuring transmission of the characteristics that we all have in common. For example, we breathe through lungs rather than gills; we have four fingers and an opposable thumb, rather than claws; and so on.

In some cases a single gene from each pair of chromosomes provides the genetic influence for a particular trait. In many other cases, such as intelligence,

genes: Within the chromosomes, the segments of DNA that are the basic units for the transmission of hereditary traits.

chromosomes: Rod-shaped structures, found in the nuclei of body cells, that contain all the genes and carry all the hereditary information.

sex chromosomes: The 23rd pair of chromosomes, which carries the genes that determine one's sex and primary and secondary sex characteristics.

Figure 8.1 The 23 Pairs of Chromosomes in the Human Male and Female

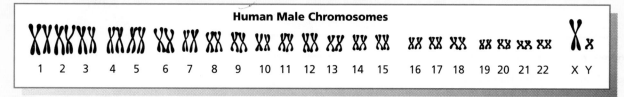

Human Male Chromosomes
1 2 3 4 5 6 7 8 9 10 11 12 13 14 15 16 17 18 19 20 21 22 X Y

Human Female Chromosomes
1 2 3 4 5 6 7 8 9 10 11 12 13 14 15 16 17 18 19 20 21 22 X X

dominant gene: The gene that is expressed in the individual.

recessive gene: A gene that will not be expressed if paired with a dominant gene but will be expressed if paired with another recessive gene.

period of the zygote: Lasting about 2 weeks, the period from conception to the time the zygote attaches itself to the uterine wall.

prenatal: Occurring between conception and birth.

embryo: The developing human organism during the period (week 3 through week 8) when the major systems, organs, and structures of the body develop.

fetus: The developing human organism during the period (week 9 until birth) when rapid growth and further development of the structures, organs, and systems of the body occur.

identical twins: Twins with exactly the same genes, who develop after one egg is fertilized by one sperm, and the ovum splits into two parts; monozygotic twins.

height, and weight, a number of genes collectively produce the genetic influence for a particular trait or ability. The Human Genome Project is aimed at identifying the function of all of the genes and locating them on the chromosomes. The ultimate goal is to decipher the complete instructions for making a human being (Jaroff, 1989).

Question: When are dominant or recessive genes expressed in a person?

Dominant and Recessive Genes: Dominants Call the Shots   When two different genes are transmitted for the same trait, one of the genes is usually a **dominant gene**, causing the dominant trait to be expressed in the individual. The gene for brown hair, for instance, is dominant over the gene for blonde hair. An individual having one gene for brown hair and one gene for blonde hair will have brown hair. And of course, two dominant genes will produce brown hair (see Figure 8.2).

The gene for blonde hair is recessive. A **recessive gene** will be expressed if it is paired with another recessive gene. Therefore, blonde-haired people have two recessive genes for blonde hair. A recessive gene will not be expressed if it is paired with a dominant gene. Yet a person still can pass either the recessive gene or the dominant gene along to his or her offspring.

The Stages of Prenatal Development: Unfolding According to Plan

Question: What are the three stages of prenatal development?

Conception occurs the moment a sperm cell fertilizes the ovum (egg cell), forming a single cell called a zygote. Conception usually takes place in one of the fallopian tubes, and within the next 2 weeks the zygote travels to the uterus and attaches itself to the uterine wall. During this 2-week period, called the **period of the zygote**, rapid cell division occurs. The zygote differentiates itself into three layers that will eventually form the various structures and organs of the body. At the end of this first stage of **prenatal** development, the zygote is only the size of the period at the end of this sentence.

The second stage of prenatal development is the period of the **embryo**, when the major systems, organs, and structures of the body develop. Lasting from week 3 through week 8, this period ends when the first bone cells form. Only 1 inch long and weighing 1/30 of an ounce, the embryo already resembles a

Figure 8.2

Gene Transmission for Hair Color

Both parents carry a gene for brown hair (B) and a gene for blonde hair (b). The chance of their having a blonde-haired child (bb) brown-haired child (BB) is 25 percent in each case. There is a 50 percent chance of having a brown-haired child who carries both the dominant gene (B) and the recessive gene (b).

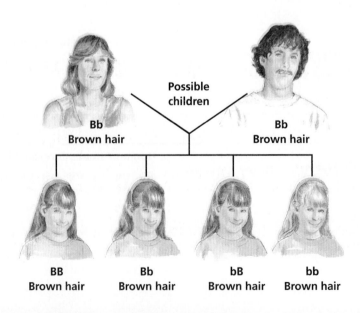

human being, with a face, limbs, fingers, toes, and many internal organs that have begun to function.

The final stage, called the period of the **fetus**, lasts from the end of the second month until birth. It is a time of rapid growth and further development of the structures, organs, and systems of the body. Table 8.1 describes the characteristics of each stage of prenatal development.

Table 8.1   Stages of Prenatal Development

Stage	Time after Conception	Major Activities of the Stage
Period of the zygote	1–2 weeks	Zygote attaches to the uterine lining. At two weeks, zygote is the size of the period at the end of this sentence.
Period of the embryo	3–8 weeks	Major systems, organs, and structures of the body develop. Period ends when first bone cells appear. At 8 weeks, embryo is about 1 inch long and weighs 1/30 of an ounce.
Period of the fetus	8 weeks to birth (38 weeks)	Rapid growth and further development of the body structures, organs, and systems.

This is how life began for most of us, with a single egg fertilized by a single sperm. But what occurs in multiple births?

Multiple Births: More Than One at a Time   In the case of **identical twins** (monozygotic twins), one egg is fertilized by one sperm, but the zygote splits and develops into two embryos with identical genetic codes. Thus, identical twins are always of the same sex. This splitting of the zygote seems to be a chance occurrence accounting for 0.4 percent of all births. Figure 8.3 shows how identical and fraternal twins occur.

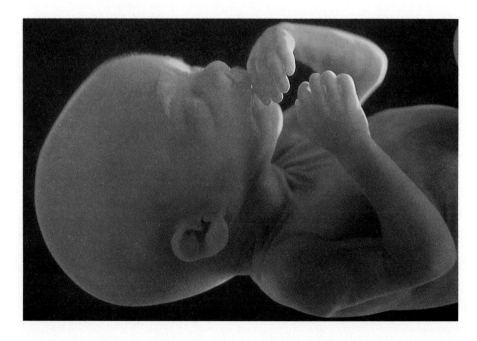

By the fifth month, the fetus has a significant heartbeat and has begun to kick.

Figure 8.3

Identical and Fraternal Twins: How They Are Formed

Because identical twins are formed by the splitting of one fertilized egg, they are always of the same sex. Fraternal twins are formed when two different eggs are fertilized by two different sperm, and they may or may not be of the same sex.

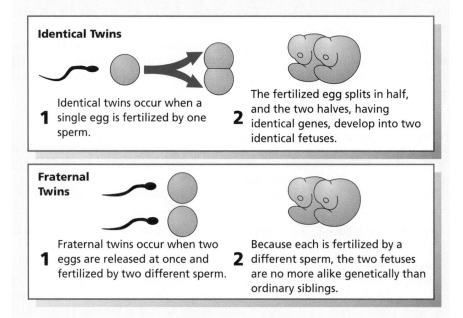

Identical Twins

1 Identical twins occur when a single egg is fertilized by one sperm.

2 The fertilized egg splits in half, and the two halves, having identical genes, develop into two identical fetuses.

Fraternal Twins

1 Fraternal twins occur when two eggs are released at once and fertilized by two different sperm.

2 Because each is fertilized by a different sperm, the two fetuses are no more alike genetically than ordinary siblings.

Fraternal twins (dizygotic twins) develop when two eggs are released during ovulation and are fertilized by two different sperm. The two zygotes develop into two siblings who are no more alike genetically than ordinary brothers and sisters. The likelihood of fraternal twins is greater if there is a family history of multiple births, if the mother is between ages 35 and 40, or if she has recently stopped taking birth control pills. Also, fertility drugs often cause the release of more than one egg. Triplets, quadruplets, and quintuplets can develop when multiple eggs are released during ovulation, when one or more eggs split before or after fertilization, or with any combination of these events.

Negative Influences on Prenatal Development: Sabotaging Nature's Plan

Question: What are some negative influences on prenatal development?

Teratogens are agents in the prenatal environment that can have a negative impact on prenatal development, causing birth defects and other problems. The impact of a teratogen depends on both its intensity and the point in time during prenatal development when it is present. Most negative influences—drugs, illnesses, and environmental hazards such as X rays or toxic waste—cause the most devastating consequences when they occur during the first 3 months of development (the first trimester). During this time there are **critical periods** when certain body structures develop. If drugs or infections interfere with development during a critical period, the structure or body part will not form properly and development will not occur at a later time (Kopp & Kaler, 1989).

In addition, some viruses can have devastating effects on the fetus during the first trimester. Probably the best known is rubella (German measles), which can cause deafness, blindness, mild retardation, heart defects, or damage to the central nervous system if contracted during the first three months of pregnancy.

Exposure to risks during the second trimester of pregnancy—the fourth to sixth month—are more likely to result in various types of intellectual and social impairments rather than physical abnormalities.

fraternal twins: Twins, no more alike genetically than ordinary siblings, who develop after two eggs are released during ovulation and fertilized by two different sperm; dizygotic twins.

teratogens: Harmful agents in the prenatal environment, which can have a negative impact on prenatal development or even cause birth defects.

critical period: A period that is so important to development that a harmful environmental influence can keep a bodily structure or behavior from developing normally.

The Hazard of Drugs: What the Pregnant Mother Takes, the Baby Gets Too Many drugs cross the placental barrier and directly affect the unborn child. Consequently, both prescription and nonprescription drugs (for example, aspirins, nose sprays, laxatives, douches, reducing aids, baking soda, and vitamin supplements) should be taken only with the consent of the doctor (Apgar & Beck, 1982). Some prescription drugs, such as certain antibiotics, tranquilizers, and anticonvulsants, are known to cause specific damage in the unborn. Most people are aware that pregnant women who take heroin, cocaine, and crack risk having babies born addicted to the drugs. Fewer people realize the potential dangers of alcohol and cigarettes.

Alcohol Few mothers would think of giving their newborns a baby bottle full of beer, wine, or hard liquor, but many mothers do not realize that even a small amount of alcohol consumed during pregnancy crosses the placental barrier. In fact alcohol levels in the fetus almost match the alcohol levels in the mother's blood (Little et al., 1989). And researchers believe that alcohol can alter brain development throughout pregnancy (Streissguth et al., 1989).

Women who drink heavily during pregnancy risk having babies with **fetal alcohol syndrome**. Babies with this syndrome are mentally retarded, abnormally small, and have facial, organ, and limb abnormalities (Becker et al., 1990; Cooper, 1987). About one-third of the babies born to chronic alcoholic women show some symptoms of fetal alcohol syndrome, and one-half show some mental deficiency (Jones et al., 1974).

Streissguth and others (1989) report that well-educated, middle-class women who consumed 1.5 ounces of alcohol daily had children who at age 4 averaged 5 IQ points lower than children of women who drank less. Moderate drinking also had adverse affects on fine and gross motor development in 4-year-old children (Barr et al., 1990). Women should abstain from drinking alcohol altogether during pregnancy.

Smoking Smoking decreases the amount of oxygen and increases the amount of carbon monoxide crossing the placental barrier. The embryo or fetus is exposed to nicotine and several thousand other chemicals as well. Smoking increases the probability that a baby will be premature or will be of low birth weight (McDonald et al., 1992). Women smoking one pack per day are at 3 times the risk for premature birth. Smoking has also been associated with higher rates of spontaneous abortion (Armstrong et al., 1992), stillbirth, infant mortality, and sudden infant death syndrome (Lincoln, 1986).

Low-Birth-Weight Babies: Newborns at High Risk The infant mortality rate in the United States is about 9.8 per 1,000 live births. The rate is 8.2 per 1,000 for white infants and more than twice as high—17.7 percent—for black infants (CDC, 1992). Sixty-five percent of these deaths occur in the 6 to 7 percent who are designated **low-birth-weight babies**—babies weighing less than 5.5 pounds. Infants of this weight born at or before the 37th week are considered **preterm infants**. The smaller and more premature the baby, the greater the risk (Hoy et al., 1988; Kopp & Kaler, 1989). According to Apgar and Beck (1982), the handicaps of prematurity range from subtle learning and behavior problems, in babies closer to normal ranges of birth weight, to "severe retardation, blindness, hearing loss, and even death," in the smallest newborns (p. 69).

Poor nutrition, poor prenatal care, smoking, drug use, maternal infection, and too short an interval between pregnancies all increase the likelihood of having a low-birth-weight baby with complications.

fetal alcohol syndrome: A condition, caused by maternal alcohol intake during pregnancy, in which the baby is mentally retarded, abnormally small, and has facial, organ, and limb abnormalities.

low-birth-weight baby: A baby weighing less than 5.5 pounds.

preterm infant: An infant born before the 37th week and weighing less than 5.5 pounds; a premature infant.

Memory Check 8.1

1. The debate concerning the relative effects of heredity and environment on development is called the _____-_____ controversy.

2. A dominant gene will be expressed if the individual carries:

   a. two dominant genes for the trait
   b. one dominant gene and one recessive gene for the trait
   c. two recessive genes for the trait
   d. both a and b

3. (Males, Females) have an X chromosome and a Y chromosome.

4. Match the stage of prenatal development with its description.

   ____ 1) first 2 weeks of life   a. period of the fetus
   ____ 2) rapid growth and further   b. period of the embryo
            development of body struc-   c. period of the zygote
            tures and systems
   ____ 3) major systems, organs, and
            structures are formed

5. Negative influences such as drugs, illness, and environmental hazards cause the most devastating consequences during the (first, middle, last) 3 months of prenatal development.

Answers: 1. nature-nurture 2. d 3. Males 4. 1) c 2) a 3) b 5. first

Physical Development and Learning in Infancy

The Neonate: Seven Pounds of Beauty?

Although **neonates** (newborn babies) may be beautiful to their parents, they do not yet resemble the babies who pose for the Gerber or Johnson & Johnson baby ads. Newborns measure about 20 inches long, weigh about 7 1/2 pounds, and have a head one-quarter the length of the body. They arrive with dry and wrinkled skin, a rather flat nose, and an elongated forehead—the temporary result of a rough journey through the birth canal. Nevertheless, newborns come equipped with an impressive range of **reflexes**, built-in behaviors needed to insure survival in their new world.

Reflexes: Built-In Responses   Sucking, swallowing, coughing, and blinking are some important behaviors that newborns can perform right away. They will move an arm, a leg, or other body part away from a painful stimulus, and they will try to remove a blanket or a cloth placed over their faces, which might hamper breathing. Stroke a baby on the cheek and you will trigger the rooting reflex—the baby's mouth opens and actively searches for a nipple. Neonates also have some reflexes that serve no apparent function, and these reflexes are believed to be remnants of our evolutionary past. As the brain develops, behaviors that were initially reflexive, controlled by the lower brain centers, gradually come under the voluntary control of the higher brain centers. The presence of

neonate: Newborn infant up to 1 month old.

reflexes: Inborn, unlearned, automatic responses to certain environmental stimuli (examples: coughing, blinking, sucking, grasping).

these reflexes at birth and their disappearance between the second and fourth months provide researchers with a means of assessing development of the nervous system.

Sensory Development in Infancy

Question: What are the sensory abilities of the newborn?

The five senses, although not fully developed, are functional at birth, and the newborn already has preferences for certain odors, tastes, sounds, and visual configurations. Robert Fantz (1961) made a major breakthrough when he realized that the interest of babies in an object can be gauged by the length of time they fixate on it. Infants' visual preferences can be assessed with eye-tracking devices that measure what a baby looks at and for how long. This and other, similar techniques have shown that newborns have clear preferences and powers of discrimination, and even memory recognition and learning ability.

Vision: What Newborns Can See

At birth, vision is about 20/150 (Dayton et al., 1964). Newborns focus best on objects about 9 inches away, and they can follow a moving object (MacFarlane, 1978). Neonates not only have an innate preference for the human face, but infants 22 to 93 hours old already indicate a preference for their own mother's face over that of an unfamiliar female (Field et al., 1984). Infants 2 to 3 months old can see all or almost all of the colors adults see, and they prefer red, blue, green, and yellow (Bornstein & Marks, 1982).

The famous **visual cliff** experiment was devised to study depth perception in infants and other animals. Gibson and Walk (1960) designed an apparatus consisting of "a board laid across a sheet of heavy glass, with a patterned material directly beneath the glass on one side and several feet below it on the other" (p. 65). This arrangement made it appear that there was a large drop off or "visual cliff" on one side. When 36 infants ranging in age from 6 to 14 months were placed on the center board, most could be coaxed by their mothers to crawl to the shallow side, but only three would crawl onto the deep side. Gibson and Walk concluded that "most human infants can discriminate depth as soon as they can crawl" (p. 64).

In another study using the visual cliff apparatus, Campos and others (1970) found that 6-week-old infants had distinct changes in heart rate when they faced the deep side of the cliff, but no change when they faced the shallow side. The change in heart rate indicated interest and showed that the infants could perceive depth.

Learning in Infancy

Question: What types of learning occur in the first few days of life?

When are babies first capable of learning? If you say from the moment of birth, you may be underestimating them. We know that learning begins even before birth because infants' experiences in the womb can affect their preferences shortly after birth. DeCasper and Spence (1986) had 16 pregnant women volunteer to read *The Cat and the Hat* to their developing fetuses twice a day during the final 6 1/2 weeks of pregnancy. The researchers used specially designed, pressure-sensitive nipples wired to electronic equipment. A few days after birth the infants could adjust their sucking to hear their mother reading either *The Cat and the Hat* or *The King, the Mice, and the Cheese*, a story they had never heard before. Which story did the infants prefer? You guessed it—their sucking behavior signaled a clear preference for the familiar sound of *The Cat and the Hat*.

visual cliff: An apparatus used to test depth perception in infants and young animals.

When placed on the visual cliff, most babies over 6 months will not crawl onto the deep side, indicating they can perceive depth.

habituation: A decrease in response or attention to a stimulus as an infant becomes accustomed to it.

maturation: Changes that occur according to one's genetically determined, biological timetable of development.

Researchers have demonstrated both classical conditioning and operant conditioning in infants in the first few days of life (Lipsitt, 1990; Rovee-Collier & Lipsitt, 1982). But probably the simplest evidence of learning in infants is the phenomenon of **habituation**. When infants are presented with a new or interesting stimulus, they respond with a general quieting, their heart rate slows, and they fixate on the stimulus. But when they become accustomed to the stimulus, they stop responding—that is, they habituate to it. Later, if the familiar stimulus is presented along with a new stimulus, infants will usually pay more attention to the new stimulus, indicating that they remember the original stimulus but prefer the new one. Memory can be measured by (1) the speed with which habituation occurs and (2) the relative amounts of time infants spend looking at a new and an old stimulus. Rovee-Collier (1990) has found that infants 2 to 3 months old can form memories of their past experience, memories lasting a period of days, and for longer time periods as the infants get older.

Amazing as it may seem, babies only 42 minutes old can even imitate gestures such as sticking out the tongue or opening and closing the mouth (Meltzoff & Moore, 1977). And infants averaging 42 hours in age can imitate head movements (Meltzoff & Moore, 1989). A recent study by Meltzoff (1988) demonstrates observational learning in 14 month-old infants. After watching an adult on TV handling "a novel toy in a particular way," the infants were able to imitate the behavior when presented with the toy 24 hours later. Perhaps parents should be more particular about the TV programs their infants watch.

Motor Development in Infancy

Babies undergo rapid change during the first few years of life. Some changes are due to maturation and some are due to learning. **Maturation** occurs naturally according to the infant's own genetically determined, biological timetable of development. Many motor skills, such as crawling, standing, and walking, do not result from learning. Rather, they are a result of maturation and are ultimately dependent on the growth and development of the central nervous system.

Although infants follow their own individual timetable, there is a sequence in which the basic motor skills appear. Physical and motor development proceeds from the head downward to the trunk and legs, so babies lift their heads before they sit, and they sit before they walk. Development also proceeds from the center of the body outward—trunk to shoulders to arms to fingers. Thus control of the arms develops before control of fingers.

The second process affecting development is learning, but learning cannot take place until particular areas of the brain mature. In other words, the child must be physically and neurologically *ready* to learn.

Figure 8.4

The Progression of Motor Development

Most infants develop motor skills in the sequence shown in the figure. The ages indicated are only averages, so normal, healthy infants may develop any of the motor skills a few months earlier or several months later than the average.

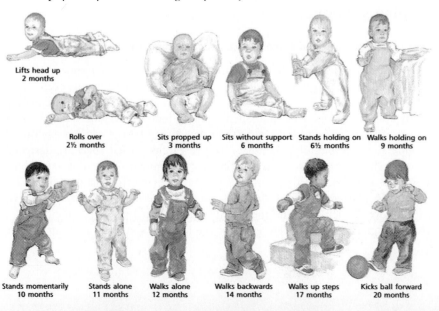

Lifts head up
2 months

Rolls over
2½ months

Sits propped up
3 months

Sits without support
6 months

Stands holding on
6½ months

Walks holding on
9 months

Stands momentarily
10 months

Stands alone
11 months

Walks alone
12 months

Walks backwards
14 months

Walks up steps
17 months

Kicks ball forward
20 months

Physical and motor development occurs naturally as a result of maturation unless an infant is subjected to extremely unfavorable environmental conditions such as severe malnutrition or maternal and sensory deprivation. Yet an ideal diet and a rich sensory environment will not enable children to walk before they are ready. Parents should be patient; babies will come to walk, talk, and be toilet trained according to their own developmental schedule. Figure 8.4 shows the sequence of motor development in the first 2 years of life.

temperament: An individual's behavioral style or characteristic way of responding to the environment.

Memory Check 8.2

1. The neonate's built-in responses, like sucking, blinking, and grasping, are called (habits, reflexes).

2. Infants can show preferences in what they want to look at, hear, taste, and smell shortly after birth. (true/false)

3. Two-month-old Michael likes to look at the soft, multicolored ball in his crib, but the new black-and-white ball has recently gained his attention. Habituation has occurred, meaning that:

   a. Michael has gotten used to a stimulus (the multicolored ball)
   b. Michael remembers the stimulus he has seen previously
   c. a simple form of learning has taken place
   d. all of these

4. Physical and motor development that occurs naturally according to the infant's own genetically determined, biological timetable of development is said to result from (reflexes, maturation).

Answers: 1. reflexes 2. true 3. d 4. maturation

Emotional Development in Infancy

Temperament: How and When Does It Develop?

Question: What is temperament, and what are the three temperament types identified by Thomas, Chess, and Birch?

Maria is usually cheerful, easygoing, and adaptable. John is always on the go, and he sticks with a problem until it is solved, but he gets upset easily. Their parents say the two children have always been that way. Are babies born with an individual behavior style or characteristic way of responding to the environment, which is referred to as **temperament**?

The New York Longitudinal Study was undertaken in 1956 to investigate temperament and its effect on development. Thomas, Chess, and Birch (1970) studied 2- to 3-month-old children and followed them for 10 years using observation, interviews with parents and teachers, and psychological tests. Three general types of temperament emerged from the study. "Easy" children—40 percent of the group—had generally pleasant moods, were adaptable, approached new situations and people positively, and established regular sleep, eating, and elimination patterns. "Difficult" children—10 percent of the group—had generally unpleasant moods, reacted negatively to new situations and people, were intense in their emotional reactions, and showed irregularity of bodily functions. "Slow-to-warm-up" children—15 percent of the group—

attachment: The strong affectionate bond a child forms with the mother or primary caregiver.

surrogate: Substitute; someone or something that stands in place of.

tended to withdraw, were slow to adapt, and were "somewhat negative in mood." The remaining 35 percent of the group were too inconsistent to categorize.

Thomas, Chess, and Birch (1970) believe that "personality is shaped by the constant interplay of temperament and environment" (p. 102). Environment can intensify, diminish, or modify these inborn behavioral tendencies.

Stability in Temperament Two striking findings emerged from the New York Longitudinal Study. First, Thomas, Chess, and Birch (1970) found that "children do show distinct individuality in temperament in the first weeks of life independently of their parents' handling or personality style" (p. 104). Second, they found that "the original characteristics of temperament tend to persist in most children over the years" (p. 104). Activity level seems to show the most consistency over time (Goldsmith et al., 1987; Korner et al., 1985; Thomas & Chess, 1977). Both twin studies (Plomin, 1986) and adoption studies (Braurigant et al., 1992) reveal a genetic influence on certain aspects of temperament—mood/extroversion, activity level, and task orientation.

The Formation of Attachment

Harlow found that infant monkeys developed a strong attachment to their cloth-covered "surrogate mothers" and little or no attachment to the wire mothers—even when the wire mothers provided their nourishment.

It is true that infants come into the world with greater capabilities than early researchers ever imagined. Yet at the same time, human newborns are among the most helpless and dependent of all animal species and cannot survive alone. Fortunately, infants form a strong **attachment** to their mothers or primary caregivers. Because their attachment is a two-way affair, the term "bonding" has been used to describe this mutual attachment (Brazelton et al., 1975).

What precisely is the *glue* that binds caregiver (usually the mother) and infant? For decades people believed that an infant's attachment to its caregiver was formed primarily because the caregiver provides the nourishment that sustains life. However, a series of classic studies conducted by Harry Harlow on attachment in rhesus monkeys suggests that life-sustaining, physical nourishment is not enough to bind infants to their primary caregivers.

Question: What did Harlow's studies reveal about maternal deprivation and attachment in infant monkeys?

Attachment in Infant Monkeys: Like Humans in So Many Ways Harry Harlow found that the behavior of monkeys deprived of mothering was not unlike that of children raised in orphanages. Motherless monkeys would "sit in their cages and stare fixedly into space, circle their cages in a repetitive stereotyped manner and clasp their heads in their hands or arms and rock for long periods of time" (Harlow & Harlow, 1962, p. 138).

To investigate systematically the nature of attachment and the effects of maternal deprivation on infant monkeys, Harlow constructed two *surrogate* (artificial) monkey mothers. One was a plain, wire-mesh cylinder with a wooden head; the other was a wire-mesh cylinder that was padded, covered with soft terry cloth, and fitted with a somewhat more monkeylike head (see photograph at left). A baby bottle could be attached to either surrogate mother for feeding.

Newborn monkeys were placed in individual cages where they had equal access to a cloth surrogate and a wire surrogate. The source of their nourishment (cloth or wire surrogate) was unimportant. "The infants developed a strong attachment to the cloth mothers and little or none to the wire mothers" (Harlow & Harlow, 1962, p. 141). Harlow found that it was contact comfort—the comfort supplied by bodily contact—rather than nourishment that formed the basis of the infant monkey's attachment to its mother.

Harlow learned that monkeys formed the same type of attachment to the cloth mother as normal monkeys did to their real mothers. In both cases the infants would cling to their mothers many hours each day and "run to them for comfort or reassurance when they are frightened" (Harlow, 1959, p. 73). If the cloth mother was not present when unfamiliar objects were placed in the cage, the monkey would huddle in the corner, clutching its head, rocking, sucking its thumb or toes, and crying in distress. But when the cloth mother was present, the infant would first cling to her and then explore and play with the unfamiliar objects.

If the infant monkeys were placed with the cloth mother for the first 5 1/2 months of life, their attachment was so strong that it persisted even after an 18-month separation. Although the infants' attachment to the cloth mother was almost identical to the attachment normal monkeys have to their real mother, their emotional development was not. Their social and sexual behavior was grossly abnormal (Harlow & Harlow, 1962). They showed inappropriate aggression and did not interact with other monkeys. They did not display normal sexual behavior, and they would not mate. If impregnated artificially, they became terrible mothers whose behavior ranged from ignoring their babies to violently abusing them (Harlow et al., 1971). The only aspect of development not affected was learning ability.

The Necessity for Love   Harlow's research reveals the disastrous effects that maternal deprivation can have on infant monkeys. Human infants, too, need love in order to grow physically and psychologically. Between 1900 and 1920 in the United States, the majority of infants under one year old who were placed in orphanages did not survive even though they were given adequate food and medical care (Montagu, 1962). Usually kept in cribs, the sides draped with sheets, these unfortunate infants were left to stare at the ceiling. Lacking a warm, close, personal caregiver and the all-important ingredient love, the infants who survived their first year failed to gain weight and grow normally—a condition known as deprivation dwarfism (Gardner, 1992).   And they were severely retarded in their mental and motor development (Spitz, 1946). For their very survival, infants need to become attached to someone. That someone can be nearly anyone, but it is most often the mother. Is the emotional bond between mother and infant present at birth?

The Development of Attachment in Humans   A strong emotional attachment between mother and infant is not present at birth, nor does it develop suddenly. Rather, as a result of the mother and the infant each responding to the other with behaviors that provide mutual satisfaction, the attachment develops gradually. The mother holds, strokes, talks, and responds to the baby's needs, and the baby gazes at and listens to the mother and even moves in synchrony with her voice (Condon & Sander, 1974; Lester et al., 1985). The baby's responses reinforce the mother's attention and care. Even crying can promote attachment because the mother is motivated to relieve the baby's distress, and she feels rewarded when she is successful. Much like Harlow's monkeys, babies cling to their mothers, and when they are old enough to crawl, they use locomotion to stay near them. The infant's attachment to the mother is usually quite strong at ages 6 to 8 months (Bowlby, 1969). Young Robert, the "monkey child" described at the beginning of this chapter, may have become attached to a mothering monkey who *adopted* him into her tribe.

Not only do infants develop attachments to parents and familiar others, they also develop anxiety when approached by strangers or when separated from their primary caregivers.

At about 6 months of age, infants develop a fear of strangers called **stranger anxiety** which increases in intensity until 12 1/2 months and then declines in the

stranger anxiety: A fear of strangers common in infants at about 6 months and increasing in intensity until 12 1/2 months, and then declining in the second year.

second year (Marks, 1987b). Stranger anxiety is greater when children are in an unfamiliar setting, when the parent is not close at hand, and when a stranger abruptly approaches or touches the child. Interestingly, stranger anxiety is not directed at unfamiliar *children* until ages 19 to 30 months (P.K. Smith, 1979).

Another type of anxiety—**separation anxiety**—occurs from ages 8 to 24 months, reaching its peak between ages 12 and 18 months (Fox & Bell, 1990). Toddlers who previously voiced no distress when their parents left them with a babysitter, now may scream when their parents leave the house.

Question: What are the three attachment patterns identified by Mary Ainsworth?

Mary Ainsworth's Study of Attachment: The Importance of Being Securely Attached   In a classic study of mother-child attachment, Mary Ainsworth (1973, 1979) observed mother-child interactions in the home during the infants' first year and then again at age 12 months in a strange laboratory situation. On the basis of infants' reactions to their mothers after two brief separations, Ainsworth identified three patterns of attachment—secure, ambivalent, and avoidant. She related these patterns to how sensitive, responsive, and accepting the mothers had been toward their infants during home observations the previous year.

Securely attached infants (65 percent of the sample) were distressed when they were separated from their mothers. They eagerly sought to re-establish contact after separation, and then showed an interest in play. The securely attached infants used their mothers as a safe base of operation from which to explore, much as Harlow's monkeys had done when unfamiliar objects were placed in their cages. Securely attached infants were the most responsive, obedient, and content, and they cried less than babies who were less strongly attached (Ainsworth et al, 1978). The mothers of securely attached infants had been the most sensitive, accepting, affectionate, and responsive to their cries and needs (Isabella et al., 1989; Pederson et al., 1990). This finding contradicts the notion that mothers who respond promptly to an infant's cries end up with spoiled babies who cry more.

Infants with an ambivalent attachment (10–15 percent of the group) both approached and then tried to avoid their mothers when they returned after the separations. These mothers had been inconsistent in their responsiveness to their babies, attending to them only when they were in the mood rather than when the child needed them.

Infants with the weakest attachment, classified as avoidant attachment (20–25 percent of the sample), actually avoided contact when they were reunited with their mothers. These mothers had shown little affection and had been generally unresponsive to their infants' needs and cries.

Securely attached infants are likely to be more sociable, more effective with peers, more interested in exploring the environment, and generally more competent than less securely attached infants (Masters, 1981; Waters et al., 1979). Furthermore, their interactions with friends tend to be more harmonious and less controlling (Park & Walters, 1989).

The Father-Child Relationship   Although mother-child rather than father-child relationships have been the traditional focus of research, this is changing due to the greater child-rearing responsibility fathers are assuming. In general fathers spend more time playing with their infants (Kotelchuck, 1976) and less time in actual caretaking—feeding, bathing, changing (Parke, 1978; Lamb, 1979). But they are just as responsive and as competent as mothers when they voluntarily assume child-rearing responsibilities (Parke et al., 1972), and their attachments can be just as strong.

separation anxiety: The fear and distress shown by toddlers when their parents leave, occurring from 8 to 24 months and reaching a peak between 12 and 18 months.

WORLD OF PSYCHOLOGY: APPLICATIONS

The Effects of Nonmaternal Care on Children

To work or not to work—that is *not* the question for well over half the women with children in the United States. Seventy percent of these women, many of whom are single parents, must work in order to produce an adequate family income (Hoffman, 1989). The United States Census Bureau estimates that by 1995, 80 percent of American women with children under 6 years old will be working outside the home (L. S. Walters, 1990). By comparison, in 1950, only 12 percent of women with children under school age were in the work force.

Where do these millions of American children go while their parents work? For children under 3 years, 27 percent are cared for in day-care centers, 54 percent in day-care homes, and 19 percent in their own home by babysitters. For children ages 3 to 5, the percentages are 57 percent, 32 percent, and 11 percent respectively (Scarr & Weinberg, 1986). It is difficult to make generalizations about the impact of day care on children because of the extreme variation in the quality and type of care available. Furthermore the characteristics of both the child and the mother affect the outcome. Early studies on the effects of child care often cited positive results, but these studies usually involved children in high quality day-care centers, such as those on university campuses. In these settings Belsky and Steinberg (1978, 1979) found no adverse effects of day care. They even claimed that children in day care tend to be more sociable and are more likely to share toys.

A decade later, when the more common, lower-quality day-care settings were studied, Belsky reversed his position. Researchers began to find that infants who are exposed to more than 20 hours per week of *any* nonmaternal care are somewhat more at risk of having an insecure attachment (Belsky, 1988; Clarke-Stewart, 1989). Furthermore, Belsky and Rovine (1988) suggest that full-time nonmaternal care is associated with a higher risk of insecure infant-father relationships as well. However, it is important to keep in mind that half the infants in these studies maintained secure relationships with their mothers, and half the boys maintained a secure relationship with their fathers. Barglow and others (1987) reported that even among middle- to upper-middle-class infants who were cared for in the home, full-time employment of the mother increased the risk of insecure-avoidant attachment.

Other researchers have found children in day care to be more aggressive, impulsive, and egocentric, and to have less tolerance for frustration (Caldwell et al., 1970; Schwartz et al., 1974). "In a number of studies, children who spend their first year in day care later were observed to be more aggressive with their peers and less compliant with

their parents" (Clarke-Stewart, 1989, p. 268).

On the plus side, say the same researchers, children in day care as infants have generally been found to do equally well or even better than children who were not in day care. Day-care and non-day-care children were compared on measures of advanced development such as "sociability, social competence, self-confidence, language, persistence, achievement, and problem solving" (Clarke-Stewart, 1989, p. 269). Finally, "day care does appear to give infants an intellectual head start—but a short lived one" (p. 269).

While research continues and opinions differ, the truth is that at present we do not know what major effects, if any, early day care has on development. But two facts are indisputable: "Bad care is never good for any child and good day care is all too hard to find" (Shell, 1988, p. 74).

Children in high-quality day-care situations may benefit socially, emotionally, and intellectually.

Memory Check 8.3

1. According to Thomas, Chess, and Birch, temperament is inborn and not influenced by the environment. (true/false)

2. Infant monkeys became attached to the surrogate that provided (nourishment, contact comfort).

3. Which of the following is *not* true of infant monkeys raised with surrogates?

   a. They showed inappropriate aggression.
   b. They would not interact with other monkeys.
   c. Their learning ability was impaired.
   d. They became abusive mothers.

4. Infants raised with adequate physical care but without the attention of a close, personal caregiver often become mentally and/or physically retarded. (true/false)

5. Ainsworth found that 65 percent of children in her study had a (secure, ambivalent, avoidant) attachment.

Answers: 1. false 2. contact comfort 3. c 4. true 5. secure

Piaget's Theory of Cognitive Development

When you consider how a child's mind differs from an adult's, you might think that the major difference is that children know less than adults. Although this is true, there are also striking differences in the actual thought processes of children and adults. Primarily as a result of the work of Swiss psychologist Jean Piaget, we have gained new insights into the cognitive, or mental, processes of children—how they think, perceive, and gain knowledge about the world.

Piaget maintains that children are active participants in their own cognitive development. Unlike empty vessels that can be filled with knowledge, children discover and construct knowledge through their own activity. According to Piaget, children's cognitive development begins with a few basic **schemas**— cognitive structures or concepts that are used to identify and interpret objects, events, and other information in the environment. When confronted with new objects, events, experiences, and information, children attempt to fit these into their existing schemas, a process known as **assimilation**. But not everything can be assimilated into the existing schemas. If children call a stranger "Daddy" or the neighbor's cat "doggie," assimilation is not appropriate. When parents and others correct them, or when they discover for themselves that something cannot be assimilated, children will use a process known as accommodation. In **accommodation**, existing schemas are modified or new schemas are created to process new information. It is through the processes of assimilation and accommodation, then, that schemas are formed, differentiated, and broadened.

schema: Piaget's term for a cognitive structure or concept used to identify and interpret information.

assimilation: The process by which new objects, events, experiences, or information are incorporated into existing schemas.

accommodation: The process by which existing schemas are modified and new schemas are created to incorporate new objects, events, experiences, or information.

The Cognitive Stages of Development: Climbing the Steps to Cognitive Maturity

Piaget formulated a comprehensive theory that systematically describes and explains how intellect develops (Piaget, 1963b, 1964; Piaget & Inhelder, 1969). Piaget claimed that cognitive development occurs in four stages, which differ not according to the knowledge children have accumulated, but in the way they reason. Each stage reflects a qualitatively different way of reasoning and understanding the world. The stages occur in a fixed sequence in which the accomplishments of one stage provide the foundation for the next one. Although children throughout the world seem to progress through the stages in the same order, there are individual differences in the rate at which they pass through them. And the rate is influenced by the child's level of maturation and experience. The transition from one stage to another is gradual, not abrupt, and children often show aspects of two stages at the same time during these transitions.

Question: What is Piaget's sensorimotor stage?

The Sensorimotor Stage (Ages Birth to 2 Years) In the first stage, the **sensorimotor stage**, infants gain an understanding of the world through their senses and their motor activities (actions or body movements), hence the name *sensorimotor*. An infant's behavior, which is mostly reflexive at birth, becomes increasingly complex and gradually evolves into intelligent behavior. At this stage, the intelligence is one of action rather than of thought, and it is confined to objects that are present and events that are directly perceived. The child learns to respond to and manipulate objects, and to use them in goal-directed activity.

At birth, infants are incapable of thought, and they are unable to differentiate themselves from others or from the environment. Living in a world of the here and now, they are aware that objects exist only when the objects actually can be seen. Take a stuffed animal away from a 5-month-old and it ceases to exist as far as the child is concerned. At this age, out of sight is always out of mind.

The major achievement of the sensorimotor period is the development of **object permanence**, which is the realization that objects (including people) continue to exist even when they are out of sight. This concept develops gradually and is complete when the child is able to mentally represent objects in their absence. This marks the end of the sensorimotor period.

Question: What cognitive limitations characterize a child's thinking during the preoperational stage?

According to Piaget, children in the sensorimotor stage learn object permanence—the understanding that objects continue to exist even when they are out of sight.

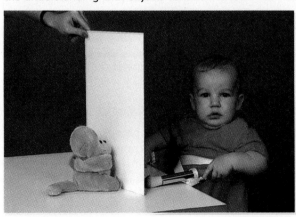

sensorimotor stage: Piaget's first stage of cognitive development (ages birth to 2 years), culminating with the development of object permanence and the beginning of representational thought.

object permanence: The realization that objects continue to exist even when they are no longer perceived.

WORLD OF PSYCHOLOGY: PIONEERS

Jean Piaget (1896–1980)

Born in Neuchatel, Switzerland, in 1896, Piaget made his professional debut in his small, French-speaking home town at the tender age of 10. Bright beyond his years and keenly interested in biology, Piaget volunteered to work as a laboratory assistant without pay, helping the director of a museum of natural history conduct his experiments on mollusks (snails, oysters, clams, and the like). The museum director, an expert on mollusks, soon died, so Piaget wrote his own description of the experiments and had them published.

Piaget's scientific papers came to the attention of many scientists, and soon a letter came offering him a job in Geneva, Switzerland, as curator of a natural history museum. But Piaget had to refuse the offer, for he was only 11 years old.

Piaget continued to study and publish his writings, and at age 22 he finished his Ph.D. in the natural sciences at the University of Neuchatel. Not sure what he wanted to do with his life, Piaget began to turn his interest to another field—psychology—and he went to Paris to continue his studies at the Sorbonne.

About a year later Henri Simon (who worked with Alfred Binet to create the first IQ test) offered Piaget a job. Piaget's work was to test French school children in order to standardize mental test items. The work seemed boring to Piaget at first, but it was destined to open the door to a distinguished career, which consumed the rest of his professional life. Strangely, it was the children's wrong answers on those test items that captured Piaget's interest. He observed that the wrong responses were not just random mistakes; instead, they seemed to reflect an unusual logic or reasoning that was systematic and shared by most children of similar ages.

Piaget had discovered a new field of research, and he began studying patterns of thinking and logical reasoning in children. His articles on the subject resulted in the offer of a new position as Director of Studies at the Rousseau Institute for Child Study and Teacher Training in Geneva. Still only 24, Piaget accepted the job, and his long, pioneering career was launched.

Using hundreds of children as subjects, including his own three children, Piaget studied the development of thinking and reasoning and language concepts in children. His books, which were based on his research, made him world-famous by the time he was 30 years old. Piaget's contribution to our knowledge of children's thinking and cognitive development is without equal in developmental psychology.

Jean Piaget

The Preoperational Stage (Ages 2–7 Years) The **preoperational stage** is a period of rapid development in language. Children become increasingly able to represent objects and events mentally with words and images. Now their thinking is no longer restricted to objects and events that are directly perceived and present in the environment. Evidence of representational thought is the child's ability to imitate the behavior of a person who is no longer present (deferred imitation). Other evidence is the child's ability to engage in imaginary play using one object to stand for another, such as using a broom to represent a horse.

Although children's thinking at the preoperational stage is more advanced than at the previous stage, it is still quite restricted. Thinking is dominated by perception, and the children at this stage exhibit egocentrism in thought. They believe that everyone sees what they see, thinks as they think, and feels as they feel.

Children at this stage also show animistic thinking, believing that inanimate objects like a tree, the sun, and a doll are alive and have feelings and intentions as well (Piaget, 1960, 1963a). That explains why 2-year-old Meghan says "hello" to her food before she eats it, and why 3-year-old Beth shows distress when her brother throws her doll into her toy box. Children also believe that all things, even the sun, the moon, and the clouds, are made for people and usually even by people.

Children at this stage are not aware that a given quantity of matter (a given number, mass, area, weight, or volume of matter) remains the same even if it is rearranged or changed in its appearance, as long as nothing has been added or taken away. This concept is know as **conservation** and is illustrated in the *Try It!*

conservation: The concept that a given quantity of matter remains the same despite rearrangement or change in its appearance as long as nothing has been added or taken away.

centration: The child's tendency during the preoperational stage to focus on only one dimension of a stimulus and ignore the other dimensions.

preoperational stage: Piaget's second stage of cognitive development (ages 2–7 years), characterized by rapid development of language, and thinking governed by perception rather than logic.

Try It!

If you know a child of preschool age, try this conservation experiment. Show the child two glasses of the same size and then fill them with the same amount of juice. After the child agrees they are the same, pour the juice from one glass into a tall, thin glass. Now ask the child if the two glasses have the same amount of juice, or if one glass has more than the other. Children at this stage will insist that the taller, thinner glass has more juice, although they will quickly agree that you neither added juice nor took it away.

Centration and irreversibility are two restrictions in children's thinking that lead them to wrong conclusions. **Centration** is the tendency to focus on only one dimension of a stimulus and ignore the other dimensions. For example, in the *Try It!*, children focused on the tallness of the glass and failed to notice that it was also thinner. At this stage, tall means more.

Preoperational children have not developed **reversibility** in thinking—the realization that any change in the shape, position, or order of matter can be returned mentally to its original state. The preoperational child in the *Try It!* cannot mentally return the juice to the original glass and realize that once again the two glasses of juice are equal.

Question: What cognitive abilities do children acquire during the concrete operations stage?

reversibility: The realization, during the concrete operations stage, that any change occurring in shape, position, or order of matter can be returned mentally to its original state.

concrete operations stage: Piaget's third stage of cognitive development (ages 7–11 years), during which a child acquires the concepts of reversibility and conservation and is able to apply logical thinking to concrete objects.

formal operations stage: Piaget's fourth and final stage, characterized by the ability to apply logical thinking to abstract problems and hypothetical situations.

The Concrete Operations Stage (Ages 7–11 or 12 Years)   In the third stage, the **concrete operations stage,** children gradually overcome the obstacles to logical thought associated with the preoperational period. Their thinking is less egocentric, and they come to realize that other people have thoughts and feelings that may be different from their own. Children acquire the ability to carry out mentally the operations essential for logical thought. They can now decenter their thinking, that is, attend to two or more dimensions of a stimulus at the same time. They can also understand the concept of reversibility, which is crucial in problem solving. Finally, during this stage children acquire the concept of conservation. Children are able to apply logical operations only to concrete problems; they cannot apply logical operations to verbal, abstract, or hypothetical problems. Surprisingly, the conservation of number, substance (liquid, mass), length, area, weight, and volume are not all acquired at once. They come in a certain sequence and usually at the ages shown in Figure 8.5.

Question: What new capability characterizes the formal operations stage?

The Formal Operations Stage (Ages 11 or 12 Years and Beyond)   The **formal operations stage** is the fourth and final stage of cognitive development. At this stage adolescents can apply reversibility and conservation to abstract, verbal, or hypothetical situations and to problems in the past, present, or future. Teenagers can comprehend abstract subjects like philosophy and politics; they become interested in the world of ideas, and they begin to formulate theories.

Not all people attain full, formal operational thinking (Kuhn, 1984; Neimark, 1981; Papalia & Bielby, 1974), but high-school math and science experience seem to facilitate it (Sharp et al., 1979). Failure to achieve formal operations has been associated with below-average scores on intelligence tests (Inhelder, 1966; Stephens et al., 1971). Piaget's four stages of development are summarized in Table 8.2.

Table 8.2   Piaget's Stages of Cognitive Development

Stage	Description
Sensorimotor (0 to 2 years)	Infants experience the world through their senses, actions, and body movements. At the end of this stage, they develop the concept of object permanence and can mentally represent objects in their absence.
Preoperational (2 to 7 years)	Children are able to represent objects and events mentally with words and images. They can engage in imaginary play (pretend), using one object to represent another. Their thinking is dominated by their perceptions, and they are unable to consider more than one characteristic of an object at the same time (centration). Their thinking is egocentric; that is, they fail to consider the perspective of others.
Concrete operational (7 to 11 or 12 years)	Children at this stage become able to think logically in concrete situations. They acquire the concepts of conservation and reversibility, can order objects in a series, and can classify them according to multiple dimensions.
Formal operational (11 or 12 years and beyond)	At this stage, adolescents learn to think logically in abstract situations, learn to test hypotheses systematically, and become interested in the world of ideas. Not all people attain full formal operational thinking.

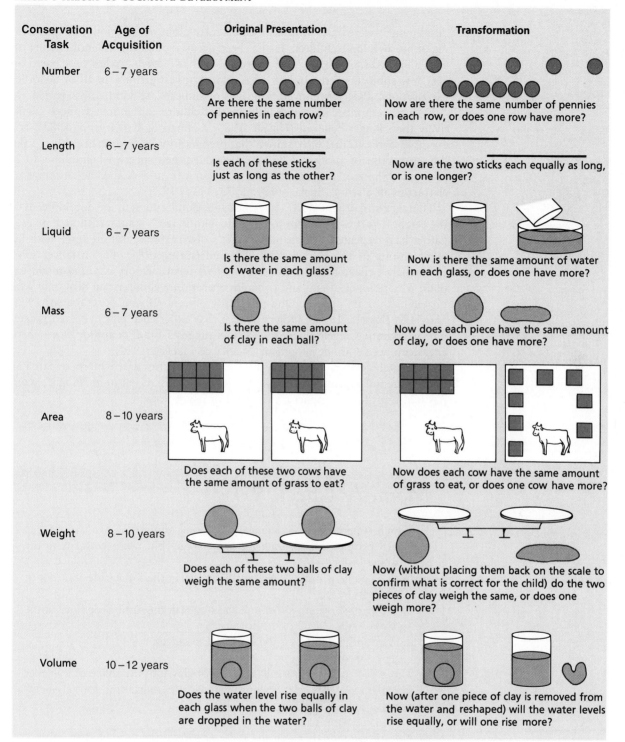

Figure 8.5 Piaget's Conservation Tasks   The ability to solve these seven conservation tasks develops over time according to the ages indicated in the figure. (From
Berk, 1991.)

An Evaluation of Piaget's Contribution

Although Piaget's genius and his monumental contribution to our knowledge of
mental development are rarely disputed, his methods and some of his findings
and conclusions have been criticized (Halford, 1989). Piaget's studies of infant

development were based primarily on his meticulous observations and questioning of his own three children. He has been accused of basing his entire theory on such a limited sample, but "the assertion . . . that Piaget's studies were based on very few subjects is true only for his infancy investigations. In all of his other explorations, Piaget employed hundreds of subjects" (Elkind, 1985, p. 11).

Even so, a number of studies indicate that children are more advanced cognitively than Piaget believed (Flavell, 1985; Gelman & Baillargeon, 1983). For example, some studies have shown that preoperational children are able to take the perspective of another. Children can adjust their speech when talking to 2-year-olds (Shatz & Gelman, 1973), and they can understand the emotions of characters in a story (Borke, 1971, 1973; Ford, 1979).

Thatcher and others (1987) have noted periodic spurts in the development of the cerebral cortex that seem to coincide with Piaget's stages. Although investigators have repeatedly confirmed Piaget's observations, not all agree with his explanations of the behavior he observed (Case, 1985). For instance, some researchers believe that a limitation in short-term memory capacity might explain why preoperational and concrete operational children can deal only with problems that are concrete and physically present (Bryant & Trabasso, 1971; Harris & Bassett, 1975). Others believe that experience plays an even greater part in cognitive development than Piaget suggests and that appropriate experiences can accelerate development (Siegler & Liebert, 1972).

Nevertheless, it is fair to say that Piaget has stimulated more research in developmental psychology than any other theorist in recent times. Piaget's work has had a profound impact on the field of psychology.

Memory Check 8.4

1. Which statement reflects Piaget's thinking about the cognitive stages?
   a. All people pass through the same stages but not necessarily in the same order.
   b. All people progress through the stages in the same order but not at the same rate.
   c. All people progress through the stages in the same order and at the same rate.
   d. Very bright children sometimes skip stages.

2. Three-year-old Kendra rolls her ball of clay into the shape of a wiener to make more clay. Her actions demonstrate (centration, formal operations).

3. Not all individuals reach the stage of formal operations. (true/false)

4. Match the stage with the relevant concept.

   _____ 1) abstract thought   a. concrete operations stage
   _____ 2) conservation, reversibility b. sensorimotor stage
   _____ 3) object permanence   c. formal operations stage
   _____ 4) egocentrism, centration   d. preoperational stage

Answers: 1. b 2. centration 3. true 4. 1) c 2) a 3) b 4) d

Language Development

At birth, the infant's only means of communication is crying, but at age 17, the average high-school graduate has a vocabulary of 80,000 words (Miller & Gildea, 1987). From age 18 months to 5 years the child acquires about 14,000 words, an amazing average of 9 new words per day (Rice, 1989).

But children do much more than simply add new words to their vocabulary. In the first five years of life, they also acquire an understanding of the way words are put together to form sentences (syntax) and the way language is used in social situations. Children acquire most of their language without any formal teaching and discover the rules of language on their own—a truly remarkable feat.

The Stages of Language Development: The Orderly Progress of Language

Question: What are the stages of language development from cooing through the acquisition of grammatical rules?

Infants begin to communicate long before they utter their first words. During their first few months, they communicate distress or displeasure through crying, although this is not actually their intent (Shatz, 1983). The cry is simply their innate reaction to an unpleasant internal state, such as hunger, thirst, discomfort, or pain. Intentional or not, the cry usually gets results from a parent or caretaker who is motivated to relieve the baby's discomfort and end the auditory assault.

Cooing and Babbling During the second or third month, infants begin cooing—repeatedly uttering vowel sounds like "ah" and "oo." Even at this young age, the mother and infant carry on conversations that consist of each vocalizing in turn, and the infant moving in synchrony with the mother's voice.

At about 6 months, infants begin **babbling**. They utter **phonemes**—the basic speech sounds of any language, which form words when combined. Consonant-vowel combinations are repeated in a string, like "ma-ma-ma" or "ba-ba-ba." During the first part of the babbling stage, infants babble all the basic speech sounds that occur in all the languages of the world. Language up to this point seems to be biologically determined because all babies throughout the world, even deaf children, vocalize this same range of speech sounds.

Then at about 8 months, babies begin to focus attention on those speech sounds (phonemes) common to their native tongue and on the rhythm and intonation of the language. Gradually they cease making the sounds not found in their native language and at this point, the babbling of a French child sounds like French, and the babbling of an American child sounds like English.

The One-Word Stage At about 1 year, the babbling stage gives way to the one-word stage, and infants utter their first real words. There is considerable similarity in the choice of first words, which usually represent objects that move or those that infants can act upon or interact with. Early words usually include food, animals, and toys—"cookie," "mama," "dada," "doggie," and "ball," to name a few (Nelson, 1973).

Sometimes infants use one word to mean a whole sentence. In these one-word sentences, called holophrases, the same word can be used to convey different meanings depending on the context. "Cookie" can mean "This is a cookie," "I want a cookie," or if the child is looking down from a high chair, "The cookie is on the floor."

By measuring brain-wave patterns, researchers have found that babies understand language far earlier than once thought.

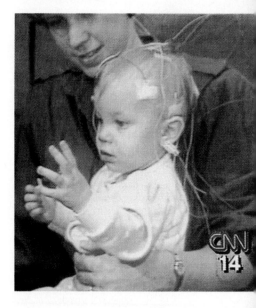

babbling: Vocalization of the basic speech sounds (phonemes), which begins between 4 and 6 months.

phonemes: The basic speech sounds in any language that, when combined, form words.

Although children acquire an average of 22 words from ages 12 to 18 months, by 2 years their vocabulary increases to about 272 words (Brown, 1973). Initially their understanding of words differs from that of an adult. On the basis of some shared feature and because they lack the correct word, children may apply a word to a broader range of objects than is appropriate. For example, any man may be called "dada," any four-legged animal, "doggie." This is known as **overextension**. *Underextension* occurs, too, when children fail to apply a word to other members of the class. Their poodle is a "doggie," but the German shepherd next door is not.

The Two-Word Stage and Telegraphic Speech   Between 18 and 20 months, when the vocabulary is about 50 words, children begin to put nouns, verbs, and adjectives together in two-word phrases and sentences. At this stage children depend to a great extent on gesture, tone, and context to convey their meaning (Slobin, 1972). Depending on intonation, their sentences may indicate questions, statements, or possession. Children adhere to a rigid word order (Slobin, 1972). You might hear "mama drink," "drink milk," or "mama milk," but not "drink mama," "milk drink," or "milk mama."

At about 2 1/2 years, short sentences are used, which may contain three or more words. Labeled **telegraphic speech** by Roger Brown (1973), these short sentences follow a rigid word order and contain only essential content words, leaving out plurals, possessives, conjunctions, articles, and prepositions. Telegraphic speech reflects the child's understanding of syntax—the rules governing how words are ordered in a sentence. When a third word is added to a sentence, it usually fills in the word missing from the two-word sentence (for example, "Mama drink milk").

Suffixes, Function Words, and Grammatical Rules   After using telegraphic speech for a time, children gradually begin to add modifiers to make words more precise. Suffixes and function words—pronouns, articles, conjunctions, and prepositions—are acquired in a fixed sequence although the rate of acquisition varies (Brown, 1973; Maratsos, 1983).

Children pick up grammatical rules intuitively, and when they learn a rule, whether for plurals or past tenses, they apply it rigidly. **Overregularization** is the kind of grammatical error that results when a grammatical rule is misapplied to a word that has an irregular plural or past tense (Brown, 1973; Kuczaj, 1978). Consequently, children who have learned and correctly used words such as "went," "came," and "did" now incorrectly apply the rule for past tenses and begin to say "goed," "comed," and "doed." What the parent sees as a regression in speech is actually an indication that the child has acquired a grammatical rule. Table 8.3 provides a summary of the early stages of language development.

Theories of Language Development: How Do We Acquire It?

Question: How do learning and the nativist position explain the acquisition of language?

There is no disagreement among theorists that children's learning of language is a truly amazing feat. But theorists do disagree about *how* children are able to accomplish such a feat. Several theories have been proposed to explain language acquisition. Some theories emphasize the role of learning and experience (nurture); some propose a biological explanation, emphasizing maturation (nature); and others suggest an interaction between maturation and experience. "There is currently no consensus of support for any one of them" (Rice, 1989, p. 150).

overextension: The act of using a word, on the basis of some shared feature, to apply to a broader range of objects than appropriate.

underextension: Restricting the use of a word to only a few, rather than to all, members of a class of objects.

telegraphic speech: Short sentences that follow a strict word order and contain only essential content words.

overregularization: The act of inappropriately applying the grammatical rules for forming plurals and past tenses to irregular nouns and verbs.

Table 8.3

Language Development during the
First 3 Years of Life

Age	Language Activity
2–3 months	Makes cooing sounds when alone; responds with smiles and cooing when talked to.
20 weeks	Makes various vowel and consonant sounds when cooing.
6 months	Begins babbling; will utter phonemes of all languages.
8 months	Focuses on the phonemes, rhythm, and intonation of native tongue.
12 months	Utters single words; mimics sounds; understands some words.
18–20 months	Uses two-word sentences; vocabulary of about 50 words; overextension common.
24 months	Vocabulary of about 270 words; suffixes and function words are acquired in a fixed sequence.
30 months	Telegraphic speech.
36 months	Overregularization common.

Learning Theory Learning theorists have long maintained that language is acquired in the same way that other behaviors are acquired—as a result of learning through reinforcement and imitation. B. F. Skinner (1957) asserted that language is shaped through reinforcement. He claimed that parents selectively criticize incorrect speech and reinforce children through praise, approval, and attention. Thus the child's utterances are progressively shaped in the direction of grammatically correct speech. Others believe that children acquire vocabulary and sentence construction mainly through imitation (Bandura, 1977).

On the surface, what the learning theorists propose appears logical, but there are a number of problems with learning theory as the sole explanation for language acquisition. Imitation cannot account for patterns of speech such as telegraphic speech or for the systematic errors such as overregularization. Children do not hear telegraphic speech in everyday life, and "I comed" and "He goed" are not forms commonly used by parents.

There are also problems with reinforcement as an explanation for language acquisition. First, parents seem to reward children more for the content of the utterance than for the correctness of the grammar (Brown et al., 1968). And parents are much more likely to correct their children for saying something untrue than for saying something grammatically incorrect. Regardless, correction does not seem to have much impact on a child's grammar.

Nevertheless, reinforcement plays an important part in language learning. Responsiveness to infants' vocalizations increases the amount of vocalization, and reinforcement can help children with language deficits improve (Lovaas, 1967; Zelazo et al., 1984).

The Nativist Position A very different theory was proposed by Noam Chomsky (1957), who believes that language ability is largely innate. Chomsky (1968) maintains that the brain contains a language acquisition device (LAD), which enables children to acquire language and discover the rules of grammar. This mechanism predisposes children to acquire language easily and naturally. Language develops in stages that occur in a fixed order and appear at about the same time in most normal children—babbling at about 6 months, the one-word stage at about 1 year, and the two-word stage at 18 to 20 months. Lenneberg

Researcher Sue Savage-Rumbaugh has taught her chimp, Kanzi, to communicate using a special keyboard. Researchers have gained valuable knowledge about the nature of language by studying chimps and other animal species.

(1967) believes that biological maturation underlies language development in much the same way that it underlies physical and motor development.

Very young infants do seem to have an innate mechanism that allows them to perceive and differentiate phonemes present in any language (Eimas, 1985). By the end of the first year, as children focus on the phonemes in their native tongue, they lose the power to distinguish the phonemes basic to many other languages.

The nativist position is better able than learning theory to account for the fact that children throughout the world go through the same basic stages in language development. It, too, can account for the similarity in errors that children make when they are first learning to form plurals, past tenses, and negatives—errors not acquired through imitation or reinforcement. However, there are several aspects of language development that the nativist position cannot explain.

Nature and Nurture   One's native language, after all, is acquired in a social setting, and experience must exert some influence on development (Bohannon & Warren-Leubecker, 1989). You remember the "monkey child," Robert, who could not speak, but whose verbal utterances were more like those of the monkeys he lived with. He vocalized what he heard in his own social setting.

Moreover, we know that parents can facilitate language development by adjusting their speech to their infant's level of development. Reading to children and reading with them supports language development and increases language. Parents should comment and expand on what the child says and encourage the child to say more by asking questions (C. P. Jones & Adamson, 1987). According to Rice (1989), "Most children do not need to be taught language, but they do need opportunities to develop language" (p. 155).

Memory Check 8.5

1. Match the linguistic stage with the appropriate example.

    _____ 1) "ba-ba-ba"   a. telegraphic speech
    _____ 2) "He eated the cookies."   b. holophrase
    _____ 3) "Mama see ball"   c. overregularization
    _____ 4) "oo," "ah"   d. babbling
    _____ 5) Calling a lion "kitty"   e. overextension
    _____ 6) Saying "ball" to mean "look at   f. cooing
            the ball"

2. Which explanation best accounts for the early stages of babbling and telegraphic speech?

    a. reinforcement   c. imitation
    b. nativist position   d. all of these

Answers: *1. 1) d 2) c 3) a 4) f 5) e 6) b 2. b*

Socialization of the Child

We are all born into a society, and in order to function effectively and comfortably within that society, we must come to know the patterns of behavior that it considers desirable and appropriate. The process of learning socially acceptable behaviors, attitudes, and values is called **socialization**. Although parents have the predominant role in the socialization process, peers, the school, the media, and religion are all important influences on socialization.

Erikson's Theory of Psychosocial Development

Question: Briefly explain Erikson's theory of psychosocial development.

Erik Erikson proposed a theory that emphasizes the role of social forces on human development throughout the life span. He was the first to stress the part that society and individuals themselves play in their own personality development, rather than focusing exclusively on the influence of parents. Erikson's is the only major theory of development to include the entire life span.

According to Erikson, individuals progress through eight **psychosocial stages** during the life span. Each stage is defined by a conflict involving the individual's relationship with the social environment that must be resolved satisfactorily in order for healthy development to occur. The stages are named for a "series of alternative basic attitudes," which result depending on how the conflict is resolved (Erikson, 1980, p. 58). Erikson believes that a healthy personality depends on acquiring the appropriate basic attitude in the proper sequence. Although failure to resolve a conflict impedes later development, resolution may occur at a later stage and reverse any damage done previously. Table 8.4 describes Erikson's first four stages.

socialization: The process of learning socially acceptable behaviors, attitudes, and values.

psychosocial stages: Erikson's eight developmental stages through the life span, each defined by a conflict that must be resolved satisfactorily in order for healthy personality development to occur.

Table 8.4 Erikson's Psychosocial Stages of Development

Stage	Ages	Description
Trust vs. Mistrust	Birth to 1 year	Infant learns to trust or mistrust depending on the degree and regularity of care, love, and affection from mother or primary caregiver.
Autonomy vs. Shame and doubt	1–3 years	Children learn to express their will and independence, to exercise some control, and to make choices. If not, they experience shame and doubt.
Initiative vs. Guilt	3–6 years	Children begin to initiate activities, to plan and undertake tasks, and to enjoy their developing motor and other abilities. If not allowed to initiate or if made to feel stupid and considered a nuisance, they may develop a sense of guilt.
Industry vs. inferiority	6 years–puberty	Children develop industriousness and feel pride in accomplishing tasks, making things, and doing things. If not encouraged, or if rebuffed by parents and teachers, they may develop a sense of inferiority.
Identity vs. Role confusion	Adolescence	
Intimacy vs. Isolation	Young adulthood	
Generativity vs. Stagnation	Middle adulthood	Described in chapter 9.
Ego integrity vs. Despair	Late adulthood	

basic trust versus basic mistrust: Erikson's first stage (ages birth–1 year), when infants develop trust or mistrust based on the quality of care, love, and affection provided.

autonomy versus shame and doubt: Erikson's second stage (ages 1–3 years), when infants develop autonomy or shame based on how parents react to their expression of will and their wish to do things for themselves.

initiative versus guilt: Erikson's third stage (ages 3–6 years), when children develop a sense of initiative or guilt depending on how parents react to their initiation of play, their motor activities, and their questions.

industry versus inferiority: Erikson's fourth stage (ages 6 years–puberty), when children develop a sense of industry or inferiority based on how parents and teachers react to their efforts to undertake projects.

Stage 1: Basic Trust versus Basic Mistrust (Ages Birth to 1 Year) During the first stage, **basic trust versus basic mistrust**, infants develop a sense of trust or mistrust depending on the degree and regularity of care, love, and affection they receive from the mother or primary caregiver. Erikson considered "basic trust as the cornerstone of a healthy personality" (Erikson, 1980, p. 58).

Stage 2: Autonomy versus Shame and Doubt (Ages 1–3 Years) During the second stage, **autonomy versus shame and doubt**, infants are developing their physical and mental abilities and want to do things for themselves. They begin to express their will or independence and develop a "sudden violent wish to have a choice" (Erikson, 1963, p. 252). "No!" is a word heard frequently from children in this stage. Erikson believes that parents must set appropriate limits and provide the control necessary for healthy development. But at the same time, they should facilitate the desire of children for autonomy by encouraging their appropriate attempts at independence. If parents are impatient or overprotective, they may make children feel shame and doubt about their efforts to express their will and explore their environment.

Stage 3: Initiative versus Guilt (Ages 3–6 Years) In the third stage, **initiative versus guilt**, children go beyond merely expressing their autonomy and begin to develop initiative. Children, enjoying their new locomotor and mental powers, begin to plan and undertake tasks "for the sake of being active and on the move" (Erikson, 1963, p. 255). They initiate play and motor activities and ask questions.

> If the child is made to feel that his motor activity is bad, that his questions are a nuisance and that his play is silly and stupid, then he may develop a sense of guilt over self-initiated activities in general that will persist through later life stages. (Elkind, 1970, pp. 87, 89)

If children's appropriate attempts at initiative are encouraged and the inappropriate attempts are handled firmly but sensitively, they will leave this stage with a sense of initiative that will form "a basis for a high and yet realistic sense of ambition and independence" (Erikson, 1980, p. 78).

Stage 4: Industry versus Inferiority (Ages 6 Years to Puberty) During the fourth stage, **industry versus inferiority**, children develop enjoyment and pride in making things and doing things.

> When children are encouraged in their efforts to make, do, or build practical things . . . , are allowed to finish their products, and are praised and rewarded for the results, then the sense of industry is enhanced. But parents who see their children's efforts at making and doing as "mischief," and as simply "making a mess," help to encourage in children a sense of inferiority. (Elkind, 1970, pp. 89–90)

The encouragement of teachers as well as parents is important for a positive resolution of the stage. The next four stages, which cover adolescence through adulthood, are discussed in the next chapter.

The Parents' Role in the Socialization Process

Parents accomplish the socialization task through the examples they set, their teachings, and their approach to discipline. Parents are usually more successful if they are loving, warm, nurturant, and supportive (Maccoby & Martin, 1983), but this alone is not enough. Some approach to discipline is needed.

Question: What are the three parenting styles discussed by Baumrind, and which did she find most effective?

Parenting Styles: What Works and What Doesn't Baumrind (1971, 1980) has identified three parenting styles—the authoritarian, the authoritative, and the permissive. She has related these styles to different patterns of behavior in nursery-school children.

Authoritarian Parents **Authoritarian parents** make the rules, expect unquestioned obedience from their children, punish misbehavior (often physically), and value obedience to authority. Rather than giving a rationale for a rule, "because I said so" is considered a sufficient reason for obedience. Parents using this parenting style tend to be uncommunicative, unresponsive, and somewhat distant. Baumrind found children disciplined in this manner to be dependent, unlikely to initiate activities, and somewhat withdrawn.

If the goal of discipline is eventually to have children internalize parental standards, the authoritarian approach leaves much to be desired. Parental failure to provide a rationale for rules makes it hard for children to see any reason for following them. When a parent says, "Do it because I said so" or "Do it or you'll be punished," the statement may succeed in making the child do what is expected when the parent is present, but it is ineffective in situations when the parent is not around. The authoritarian style seems to be particularly harmful to boys, and it has been associated with low intellectual performance and lack of social skills (Maccoby & Martin, 1983).

Authoritative Parents **Authoritative parents** set high but realistic and reasonable standards, enforce limits, and at the same time encourage open communication and independence. They are willing to discuss rules and supply rationales for them. Knowing why the rules are necessary and important makes it easier for children to internalize them and to follow them, whether in the presence of their parents or not. Authoritative parents are generally warm, nurturant, supportive, and responsive, and they show respect for their children and their opinions. Children raised in this way are the most content, self-reliant, self-controlled, assertive, socially competent, and responsible. Furthermore, this parenting style continues to be associated with higher academic performance, higher self-esteem, and internalized moral standards in middle childhood and adolescence (Dornbush et al., 1987; Steinberg et al., 1989).

Permissive Parents **Permissive parents**, although rather warm and supportive, make few rules or demands and usually do not enforce those that are made. They allow children to make their own decisions and control their own behavior. Children raised in this manner are the most immature and dependent, and they seem to be the least self-controlled and the least self-reliant.

Permissive parents also come in the indifferent, unconcerned, uninvolved variety (Maccoby & Martin, 1983). This parenting style is associated with drinking problems, promiscuous sex, delinquent behavior, and poor academic performance in adolescents.

Parenting Style and Children's Self-Esteem Stanley Coopersmith (1967, 1968) studied 10- to 12-year-old, middle-class boys and followed them through early adulthood. He found that boys with high self-esteem were successful socially and academically and had parents who "demanded high standards of behavior and were strict and consistent in enforcement of the rules" (1968, p. 99). These parents had good communication with their children and showed interest in their activities and friends. They tended to use rewards and to refrain from using corporal punishment or withdrawal of love to discipline their children.

Coopersmith (1968) found that children with low self-esteem had permissive parents, and "they took the absence of definitely stated rules and limits for their

authoritarian parents: Parents who make arbitrary rules, expect unquestioned obedience from their children, punish transgressions, and value obedience to authority.

authoritative parents: Parents who set high but realistic standards, reason with the child, enforce limits, and encourage open communication and independence.

permissive parents: Parents who make few rules or demands and allow children to make their own decisions and control their own behavior.

behavior as a sign of lack of parental interest in them" (p. 100). Coopersmith concludes: "It appears that the development of independence and self-reliance is fostered by a well-structured, demanding environment rather than by largely unlimited permissiveness and freedom to explore in an unfocused way" (p. 106).

Many of the same aspects of parenting style that Coppersmith found to be related to high self-esteem and academic success appeared again in a most unlikely place—in the children of the "boat people" from Southeast Asia. Read about this in the boxed feature on pages 290–291.

Peer Relationships

Question: How do peers contribute to the socialization process?

Infants begin to show an interest in each other at a very young age. Infants only 6 months old already demonstrate an interest in other infants by looking, reaching, touching, smiling, and vocalizing (Vandell & Mueller, 1980). Friendships begin to develop by 3 or 4 years.

Relationships with peers become increasingly important, and by middle childhood, membership in a peer group is central to a child's happiness. Peer groups are usually composed of children of the same race, sex, and social class (Schofield & Francis, 1982).

The peer group serves a socializing function by providing models of behavior, dress, and language that it considers appropriate. It is a continuing source of both reinforcement for appropriate behavior and punishment for deviant behavior. The peer group also provides an objective measure for children to evaluate their own traits and abilities—how smart or how good at sports they are. It is in the peer group that children learn how to get along with age-mates—how to share and cooperate, develop social skills, and regulate aggression.

WORLD OF PSYCHOLOGY:

MULTICULTURAL PERSPECTIVES

Cultural Values and Academic Achievement

Fleeing the political chaos and economic ruin in the aftermath of the Vietnam War, Southeast Asian refugees came by the thousands to find a better life in the United States. These Vietnamese, Laotian, Cambodian, and other immigrants, known as "boat people," knew little of Western culture and spoke little or no English when they reached America. Furthermore, the length of time required for their escape, their dangerous journey, and then long months in relocation camps meant that their children had lost months and, in some cases, years of formal schooling.

How well are these children doing in American schools? American educators are astonished by their outstanding school performance, which is even more remarkable in view of the emotional burdens they brought with them. For the most part these refugees were not the advantaged elite but common people, and "often they came with nothing more than the clothes they wore" (Caplan et al., 1992).

Researchers Caplan, Choy, and Whitmore (1992) gathered data on 6,750 Southeast Asian immigrants living in five urban areas—Boston, Chicago, Houston, Seattle, and Orange County, California. For their study, the researchers randomly selected 200 families, including 536 school-age children who were about evenly distributed in grades one through eleven. All the children were enrolled in schools located in low-income, urban areas. The researchers discovered that nearly 80 percent of these refugee children performed at the "A" or "B" range in overall school achievement. The children did even better in mathematics, where almost half of them maintained an "A" average. As expected, they did less well in subjects requiring language skills.

Was the stunning academic success limited to comparisons in the local schools they attended? No. The researchers found that their performance was exceptional when compared to nationwide norms for American students on standardized achievement tests. On the California Achievement Test in math, half the immigrant children in the study scored in the top 25 percent of test takers. Even more impressive is that 27 percent of them scored in the top 10 percent of American students nationwide. Their overall scores in language and reading skills were only slightly below the national average, even though English was not their native tongue.

How did the researchers explain this remarkable school performance? They found that the cultural values and traditions of the refugees, especially the role of central importance played by the family, strongly influenced school performance. Both parents and students identified the love of learning most often as the value that contributed most to academic success. The parents had high standards for their children, and the older children took an amazing amount of responsibility in helping their younger siblings with their homework. Every weeknight, the entire household cooperated in a joint effort to see that the children learned their assignments and finished their homework. These young Asian refugees spent between 2 1/2 and 3 hours daily on homework, twice as much as their American classmates.

Also, Asian cultural values include mutual obligations of parents toward each other and toward their children, and of children toward their parents and their brothers and sisters. Parents of successful students placed a relatively low value on seeking fun and excitement or material possessions, but a higher value on the importance of their past.

The most successful families did not reject their values and traditions in favor of the American "melting pot" but held fast to them. Yet the values and traditions that these immigrants honored and practiced are not culturally unique to the Asian people. In fact, some members of virtually every racial and ethnic group we could name hold cultural and family values very similar to those of the successful Asian boat people.

Most of the European immigrants who came to America brought strong family values, a belief in hard work, and a respect for education. Jewish culture and tradition place a high value on family and the importance of learning, which probably contributes to the academic success achieved by the Jewish people. African Americans nurtured by these same cultural values—respecting family and learning—thrive academically. "Reginald Clark of the Claremont Graduate School documented the outstanding achievement of low-income African American students in Chicago whose parents supported the school and teachers and structured their children's learning environment at home" (Caplan et al., 1992, p. 42).

This research makes a convincing argument for the importance of certain cultural values in contributing to success in school. More specifically, it points to a strong, cooperative, well-functioning family unit (which values learning more than having a good time) as a powerful influence promoting academic excellence.

Many Asian refugees are outstanding students. Researchers believe that cultural values, including an emphasis on the importance of learning, help explain their academic success.

Physical attractiveness is a major factor in peer acceptance even in children as young as 3 to 5 years, although attractiveness seems to be more important for girls than for boys (Dion & Berscheid, 1974; Krantz, 1987; Langlois, 1985). Negative traits are often attributed to unattractive children. Other qualities that are valued by the peer group are athletic ability and academic success in school. The more popular children are usually energetic, happy, cooperative, sensitive, and thoughtful.

Low acceptance by peers is an important predictor of later mental health problems (Kupersmidt et al., 1990). Excluded from the peer group are neglected children who are shy and withdrawn, and rejected children who typically exhibit aggressive and inappropriate behavior and are likely to start fights (Dodge, 1983; Dodge et al., 1990). Rejection is associated with unhappiness, alienation, and poor achievement, and in middle childhood with delinquency and dropping out of school (Kupersmidt & Coie, 1990; Parker & Asher, 1987).

Television as a Socializing Agent: Does It Help or Hinder?

Question: What are some of the positive and negative effects of television?

Television is a powerful force on young children, affecting their "knowledge, beliefs, attitudes, and behavior, for good or ill" (Huston et al., 1989, p. 424). By high-school graduation, students have spent an average of 22,000 hours watching TV—approximately twice the number of hours they have spent in school. Children with lower IQs and from low-income families tend to watch most (Huston et al., 1989). Figure 8.6 shows the average number of hours each day American children spend watching television.

The socializing effect of television begins before that of other major socializing agencies—schools, religious institutions, and peers. But television can also be an effective educational medium. "Mister Rogers' Neighborhood" has been found to increase prosocial behavior, imaginative play, and task persistency in preschoolers (Stein & Friedrich, 1975). Preschool children watching "Sesame Street" have learned their letters and number skills (Cook et al., 1975). Viewing

Figure 8.6

Average Hours per Day American Children Spend Watching Television

Research spanning 20 years reveals that children spend many hours each day watching TV. Children at ages 10 to 12 average 4 hours or more daily. (From Liebert & Sprafkin, 1988.)

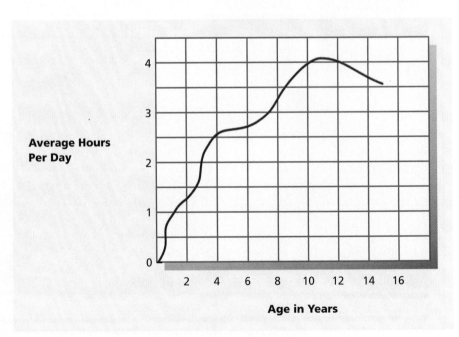

"Sesame Street" at ages 3 and 4 has been associated with larger vocabularies and better prereading skills at age 5 (Rice et al., 1987).

But television has its down side. Most studies of the effect of TV violence and aggression have found that it leads to aggressive behavior in children (Eron, 1982; Rubinstein, 1983). Television also shapes the child's view of the world, and "a major area of research suggests that heavy viewers see the world as a mean and scary place" (Rubinstein, 1983, p. 823). Television programs often promote racial and sexual stereotypes, as well as stereotypic views of the elderly and the mentally ill. Children's preferences and beliefs are easily manipulated by television (Huston et al., 1989), and it socializes children to be active consumers.

Much of children's commercial programming is marked by rapid activity and change and an "intense auditory and visual barrage" (Wright & Huston, 1983, p. 837). Singer and Singer (1979) suggest that such programming can lead to a shortened attention span. Others contend that television "promotes passive rather than active learning, induces low-level cognitive processing, and takes away time and energy from more creative or intellectually stimulating activities" (Wright and Huston, 1983, p. 835).

We have seen that many factors contribute to human development. And for all of life, from conception onward, it is the interplay of nature and nurture that drives and shapes what we become in our journey through life. In the next chapter we continue our exploration of human development, moving from adolescence through old age.

Memory Check 8.6

1. If the basic conflict of a given stage is not resolved satisfactorily, the individual:

   a. will not enter the next stage
   b. will acquire the unhealthy basic attitude associated with the stage, which will adversely affect development at the next stage
   c. will be permanently damaged regardless of future experiences
   d. b and c

2. Match the psychosocial stage with the appropriate phrase.

   _____ 1) needs regular care and love
   _____ 2) initiates play and motor activities; asks questions
   _____ 3) strives for sense of independence
   _____ 4) undertakes projects; makes things

   a. basic trust vs. mistrust
   b. industry vs. inferiority
   c. initiative vs. guilt
   d. autonomy vs. shame and doubt

3. The most effective parenting style is the (permissive, authoritative, authoritarian) style.

4. Physical appearance is a (major, minor) factor in popularity.

5. The peer group is usually a negative influence on social development. (true/false)

Answers: 1. b 2. 1) a 2) c 3) d 4) b 3. authoritative 4. major 5. false

Thinking Critically _____

Evaluation

Evaluate Erikson's first four stages of psychosocial development, explaining what aspects of the theory seem most convincing and least convincing. Support your answer.

Point/Counterpoint

Using your knowledge of both the learning theory and the nativist position on language development, prepare an argument in favor of both positions and a counterargument against both.

Psychology in Your Life

Using Baumrind's scheme, classify the parenting style used by your mother and/or father in rearing you.

a. Cite examples of techniques they used that support your classification.
b. Do you agree with Baumrind's conclusions about the effects of that parenting style on children? Why or why not?

Using Erikson's theory, try to relate the first four stages of psychosocial development to your life.

Chapter Summary and Review _____

Heredity and Prenatal Development

How are hereditary traits transmitted?

Hereditary traits are transmitted by genes, which are located on each of our 23 pairs of chromosomes.

When are dominant or recessive genes expressed in a person?

When there are alternate forms of a gene for a specific trait, the dominant gene will be expressed. A recessive gene is expressed when it is paired with another recessive gene.

What are the three stages of prenatal development?

The three stages of prenatal development are the period of the zygote, the period of the embryo, and the period of the fetus.

What are some negative influences on prenatal development?

Some common hazards in the prenatal environment include certain prescription and nonprescription drugs, psychoactive drugs, poor maternal nutrition, and maternal infections and illnesses.

Key Terms

nature-nurture controversy (p. 262)
genes (p. 263)
chromosomes (p. 263)
sex chromosomes (p. 263)
dominant gene (p. 264)
recessive gene (p. 264)
period of the zygote (p. 264)
prenatal (p. 264)
embryo (p. 264)
fetus (p. 264)
identical twins (p. 264)
fraternal twins (p. 266)

teratogens (p. 266)
critical periods (p. 266)
fetal alcohol syndrome (p. 267)
low-birth-weight babies (p. 267)
preterm infant (p. 267)

Physical Development and Learning in Infancy

What are the sensory abilities of the newborn?

All of the newborn's senses are functional at birth, and the neonate already has preferences for certain odors, tastes, sounds, and visual configurations.

What types of learning occur in the first few days of life?

Newborns are capable of habituation and can acquire new responses through classical and operant conditioning and observational learning.

Key Terms

neonate (p. 268)
reflexes (p. 268)
visual cliff (p. 269)
habituation (p. 270)
maturation (p. 270)

Emotional Development in Infancy

What is temperament, and what are the three temperament types identified by Thomas, Chess, and Birch?

Temperament refers to an individual's characteristic way of responding to the environment. Thomas, Chess, and Birch identified three temperament types—easy, difficult, and slow-to-warm-up.

What did Harlow's studies reveal about maternal deprivation and attachment in infant monkeys?

Harlow found that the basis of attachment in infant monkeys is contact comfort, and that monkeys raised with surrogates showed normal learning ability but abnormal social, sexual, and emotional behavior.

What are the three attachment patterns identified by Mary Ainsworth?

Mary Ainsworth identified three attachment patterns: secure, ambivalent, and avoidant attachment.

Key Terms

temperament (p. 271)
attachment (p. 272)
stranger anxiety (p. 273)
separation anxiety (p. 274)

Piaget's Theory of Cognitive Development

What is Piaget's sensorimotor stage?

During the sensorimotor stage (ages birth–2 years) infants gain knowledge and understanding of the world through their senses and motor activities. The major accomplishment of the stage is object permanence.

What cognitive limitations characterize a child's thinking during the preoperational stage?

Children at the preoperational stage (ages 2–7 years) are increasingly able to represent objects and events mentally, but they exhibit egocentrism, centration, and have not developed the concepts of reversibility and conservation.

What cognitive abilities do children acquire during the concrete operations stage?

When working on concrete problems, children at the concrete operations stage (ages 7–11 or 12 years) become able to decenter their thinking and to understand the concepts of reversibility and conservation.

What new capability characterizes the formal operations stage?

At the formal operations stage (ages 11 or 12 years and beyond) adolescents are able to apply logical thinking to abstract problems and hypothetical situations.

Key Terms

schemas (p. 276)
assimilation (p. 276)
accommodation (p. 276)
sensorimotor stage (p. 277)
object permanence (p. 277)
preoperational stage (p. 279)
conservation (p. 279)
centration (p. 279)
reversibility (p. 279)
concrete operations stage (p. 280)
formal operations stage (p. 280)

Language Development

What are the stages of language development from cooing through the acquisition of grammatical rules?

The stages of language development are cooing (age 2–3 months), babbling (beginning at age 6 months), single words (about age 1 year), two-word sentences (age 18–20 months), and telegraphic speech (age 2 1/2 years), followed by the acquisition of grammatical rules.

How do learning theory and the nativist position explain the acquisition of language?

Learning theory suggests that language is acquired through imitation and reinforcement. The nativist position suggests that language ability is largely innate because it is acquired in stages that occur in a fixed order at the same time in most normal children throughout the world.

Key Terms

babbling (p. 283)
phonemes (p. 283)
overextension (p. 284)
telegraphic speech (p. 284)
overregularization (p. 284)

Socialization of the Child

Briefly explain Erikson's theory of psychosocial development.

Erikson believed that individuals progress through eight psychosocial stages during the life span, each defined by a conflict with the social environment, which must be resolved. The four stages in childhood are basic trust versus basic mistrust (ages birth–2 years), autonomy versus shame and doubt (ages 1–3 years), initiative versus guilt (ages 3–6 years), and industry versus inferiority (ages 6 years–puberty).

What are the three parenting styles discussed by Baumrind, and which did she find most effective?

The three parenting styles discussed by Baumrind are the authoritarian, the permissive, and the authoritative; she found authoritative to be best.

How do peers contribute to the socialization process?

The peer group serves a socializing function by modeling and reinforcing behaviors it considers appropriate, by punishing inappropriate behavior, and by providing an objective measure against which children can evaluate their own traits and abilities.

What are some of the positive and negative effects of television?

Television can increase prosocial behavior and improve pre-reading and number skills, but it can lead to a shortened attention span, take time away from more worthwhile activities, promote sexual and racial stereotypes, and lead to aggressive behavior through exposure to TV violence.

Key Terms

socialization (p. 287)
psychosocial stages (p. 287)
basic trust versus basic mistrust (p. 287)
autonomy versus shame and doubt (p. 287)
initiative versus guilt (p. 287)
industry versus inferiority (p. 287)
authoritarian parents (p. 289)
authoritative parents (p. 289)
permissive parents (p. 289)

9

Adolescence and Adulthood

CHAPTER OUTLINE

Hulda Crooks

The sun had barely made its way over the horizon of the California desert town of Loma Linda on this beautiful day in 1988. Finishing her breakfast and pulling the 25-pound backpack onto her shoulders, Hulda Crooks set off at 6:00 A.M. to climb the highest mountain in the United States (outside of Alaska). Mt. Whitney soars 14,494 feet into a clear blue sky, and Hulda was no stranger to the mountain—she had climbed it 23 times before. "I've learned the trees and shrubs," she said. "It's like going back to see an old friend" (Innerviews, 1988, p. 64).

Hulda claimed many other "old friends" as well. She climbed California's San Gorgonio Mountain (11,502 feet) 30 times and conquered 97 different peaks, including Japan's 12,388-foot Mt. Fuji. When not busy climbing, Hulda worked at Loma Linda University doing health research and touring the country giving lectures on diet, exercise, health, and fitness.

Many other people have climbed the same mountains as Hulda. But the amazing thing is that Hulda climbed her first mountain at the age of 66. And when she stood at the top of Mt. Fuji, she was 91 years old, the oldest woman ever to climb it. When she passed 90, Hulda admitted that she had slowed down a bit. "I can tell I'm not 75 anymore," she said, but even in her nineties Hulda would take a 15-minute hike 6 days a week and spring up and down 60 steep steps from 5 to 15 times (quoted in Mills, 1987, p. 61). Even people 70 years younger had trouble keeping up with Hulda, who often left fellow hikers young enough to be her great-grandchildren huffing and puffing.

Born in 1896, Hulda lived nearly 93 rich, full, active years before she died. But she never really got old. Jim Perry, Director of the Loma Linda Lopers, the hiking club to which Hulda belonged, once said, "The package looks like it's had some wear, but inside there's an 18-year-old girl." (Reed & Fischer, 1984, p. 90)

DEVELOPMENT IS A LIFE-LONG PROCESS, as Hulda Crooks so ably proved every day of her long life. This chapter continues the study of human development, from adolescence through adulthood and old age. We will consider the ways in which we change over time and the ways in which we remain much the same. We will trace physical, cognitive, social, and personal development from adolescence to the end of life. We begin by entering the developmental world of the adolescent.

Adolescence: Physical and Cognitive Development

If you were to walk up to the average man on the street, grab him by the arm and utter the word "adolescence," it is highly probable—assuming he refrains from punching you in the nose—that his associations to this term will include references to storm and stress, tension, rebellion, dependency conflicts, peer-group conformity, black leather jackets, and the like. (Bandura, 1964, p. 224)

Is this view of adolescence supported by research? The answer might surprise you.

adolescence: The developmental stage that begins at puberty and encompasses the period from the end of childhood to the beginning of adulthood.

Adolescence is the developmental stage that spans the period from the end of childhood to the beginning of adulthood. We do not go to sleep one night as a child and awaken as an adult the next morning, at least not in contemporary

American society. But some cultures have designed elaborate ceremonies known as rites of passage or puberty rites, which publicly mark the passage from childhood to adulthood. At the end of the ceremony, the young person becomes an "instant adult," ready to assume adult responsibilities and to marry.

The concept of adolescence did not exist until the 20th century. Psychologist G. Stanley Hall first wrote about adolescence in his book by that name in 1904. He portrayed this stage in life as one of "storm and stress," the inevitable result of biological changes occurring during the period. Anna Freud (1958), daughter of Sigmund Freud, even considered a stormy adolescence a necessary part of adolescent development. But Hall and Freud were wrong.

Although some teenagers and parents may experience a stormy adolescence, for the majority the stage is not filled with turmoil and trouble (Douvan & Adelson, 1966; Offer, 1987). According to Ebata (1987), adolescent boys who experience turmoil are likely to have had difficulties before adolescence began, whereas girls are more likely to experience psychological difficulties for the first time in adolescence. In Anne Peterson's study of 335 adolescents, only 15 percent experienced a "downward spiral of trouble and turmoil" (Peterson, 1987, p. 33). A much larger study of 20,000 adolescents revealed that average adolescents "function well, enjoy good relationships with their families and friends, and accept the values of the larger society" (Offer et al., 1981, p. 116). Compelling evidence now suggests that adolescence is not typically stormy and difficult (A. C. Peterson, 1988). Psychologist Albert Bandura (1964) warns that expecting the teenage years to be difficult may become a self-fulfilling prophecy.

puberty: A period of rapid physical growth and change that culminates in sexual maturity.

adolescent growth spurt: A period of rapid physical growth that peaks in girls at about age 12 and in boys at about age 14.

secondary sex characteristics: Those physical characteristics not directly involved in reproduction but distinguishing the mature male from the mature female.

Physical Development during Adolescence: Growing, Growing, Grown

Adolescence begins with the onset of **puberty**—a period of rapid physical growth and change that culminates in sexual maturity. Although the average onset of puberty is age 10 for girls and age 12 for boys, the normal range extends from ages 7 to 14 for girls and ages 9 to 16 for boys (Chumlea, 1982). Every person's individual timetable for adolescence is influenced primarily by heredity, although environmental factors also exert some influence.

Question: What physical changes occur during puberty?

The Physical Changes of Puberty: Flooding Hormones Jump-Start Growth Puberty begins with a surge in hormone production, which in turn causes a number of physical changes.

Compelling evidence now suggests that, contrary to popular belief, adolescence is *not* typically stormy and difficult.

The Adolescent Growth Spurt The most startling change during puberty is the marked acceleration in growth known as the **adolescent growth spurt**. Who doesn't remember that time in life when the girls were towering over boys of the same age? On the average, the growth spurt occurs from ages 10 1/2 to 13 in girls and about two years later in boys, from ages 12 1/2 to 15 (Tanner, 1961). Because various parts of the body grow at different rates, the adolescent often has a lanky, awkward appearance. Girls finally attain their full height between ages 16 and 17, and boys, between ages 18 and 20 (Roche & Davila, 1972).

Other Biological Changes During puberty the reproductive organs in both sexes mature, and **secondary sex characteristics** appear—those physical characteristics not directly involved in reproduction that distinguish the mature male from the mature female. In girls the breasts develop and the hips round; in boys the voice deepens, and facial and chest hair appears; and in both sexes there is

menarche (men-AR-kee):
The onset of menstruation.

growth of pubic and underarm (axillary) hair. Figure 9.1 illustrates the physical changes that come with puberty for females and males.

The major landmark of puberty for the girl is **menarche**—the onset of menstruation—which occurs at an average age of 12 1/2, although from 10 to 15 1/2 is considered within the normal range (Hill, 1980; Zacharias et al., 1976). The major event for males is the first ejaculation, which typically occurs at age 14 or 15 in a wet dream (nocturnal emission). But males do not become capable of reproducing until sperm are present, usually a year or two later (Tanner, 1978).

Question: What are the psychological effects of early and late maturation on boys and girls?

The Timing of Puberty: Early and Late Maturation   Probably at no other time in life does physical appearance have such a strong impact on self-image, self-esteem, and general happiness as during adolescence. Girls want to be slim and sexy; boys want to be tall, broad-shouldered, and muscular. The timing of puberty can have important psychological consequences, coming as it does at a time when a sense of security is gained from being like other members of the peer group.

Early- and Late-Maturing Boys   Early maturation in males seems to provide important advantages and enhanced status in the peer group (Mussen & Jones, 1957; Peterson, 1987). Early-maturing boys, taller and stronger than their classmates, have an early advantage in sports and capture admiring glances from the girls. Not surprisingly, they are likely to feel confident, secure, independent, and happy and to be more successful academically as well (Blyth et al., 1981; Peterson, 1987). Early maturers are also viewed more favorably by adults. They are

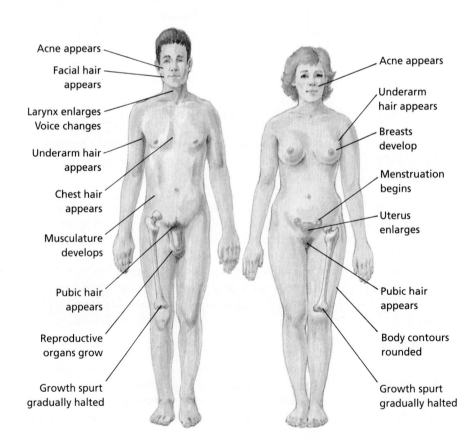

Figure 9.1

Secondary Sex Characteristics in Males and Females

During puberty the secondary sex characteristics appear. Although these physical characteristics are not directly involved in reproduction, they distinguish the mature male from the mature female.

Acne appears

Facial hair appears

Larynx enlarges Voice changes

Underarm hair appears

Chest hair appears

Musculature develops

Pubic hair appears

Reproductive organs grow

Growth spurt gradually halted

Acne appears

Underarm hair appears

Breasts develop

Menstruation begins

Uterus enlarges

Pubic hair appears

Body contours rounded

Growth spurt gradually halted

perceived as being more attractive, and they are given more responsibility and freedom than their less physically mature counterparts (Jones & Bayley, 1950).

The late-maturing boy is often at a distinct disadvantage socially and athletically and is judged as less attractive by both peers and adults. He is self-conscious about his size and lacks the physical traits of manliness—a deep voice and a developing beard. To compound the problem, he is often teased by his peers and treated like a "kid" (Frisk et al., 1966).

Early- and Late-Maturing Girls Does early and late maturation have the same social advantages and disadvantages for girls? Researchers disagree on the answer to this question. On the minus side, early-maturing girls, who may tower over their peers, feel more self-conscious about their developing bodies and their size. In addition they have to deal with the sexual advances of older boys before they are emotionally or psychologically mature (Clausen, 1975; Peterson, 1987). By later adolescence, when their peers have caught up, these girls tend to be shorter and heavier than later maturers and, therefore, are more likely to be unhappy with their physical appearance (Simmons et al., 1983; Tobin-Richards et al., 1983). For girls who aspire to be models, dancers, or gymnasts, the body changes that come with early maturation are particularly distressing (Brooks-Gunn, 1986). Some studies, though, point to advantages of early maturation. Faust (1960) found that early-maturing girls were perceived as more mature, popular, and friendly and as having more prestige among their junior high school peers.

Late-maturing girls often experience considerable stress when they fail to develop physically along with their peers. But there is a compensation for the late-maturing girl. Eventually she is likely to have a figure that is taller and slimmer than her early-maturing age mates (Jones & Mussen, 1958).

Question: What are the major symptoms of anorexia nervosa and bulimia nervosa?

In Pursuit of the Ideal Body: Living Sculptures TV, magazines, and advertisements remind us many times a day of the media's notion of the ideal male and female bodies. Teenagers and adults alike diet, exercise, and lift weights in pursuit of this ideal, but on the whole, males tend to judge their bodies more favorably than females judge theirs (Franzoi & Herzog, 1987).

Media images and female fashion models, which supposedly represent the ideal bodies for women, have over the years become increasingly thinner (Garner et al., 1980; Snow & Harris, 1985). During the same time, however, the average body weight of women under age 30 has increased (Striegel-Moore et al., 1986).

But is the media ideal what people of the opposite sex really find most appealing? Not according to Fallon and Rozin (1985), who found that both males and females make errors in estimating what the opposite sex finds most attractive. Women don't like as heavy and muscular a stature as men think they do, and contrary to what women believe, men don't like the very thin fashion figure. Although both sexes are mistaken in their beliefs about the type of body the opposite sex finds most attractive, girls are less satisfied with their body shape than boys (Allgood-Merton & Lewinsohn, 1990). Sometimes the means adolescents use to pursue the ideal body are dangerous, or even deadly. Anorexia nervosa and bulimia nervosa are two eating disorders that can have devastating consequences.

Anorexia Nervosa **Anorexia nervosa** is a severe eating disorder characterized by an irrational fear of becoming obese, compulsive dieting to the point of self-starvation, and excessive weight loss. Strangely, these victims are actually preoc-

> **anorexia nervosa** (AN-uh-REX-see-uh ner-VO-sah): A severe eating disorder characterized by excessive weight loss, compulsive dieting to the point of self-starvation, and a disturbance in body image.

cupied with food, spending inordinate amounts of time thinking about it, preparing it, or watching others eat, although they may eat only the smallest portions themselves.

Many anorectics have a gross distortion in the perception of their body size. No matter how thin they become, they typically see themselves as fat. Anorectics are so obsessed with their weight that, in addition to a starvation diet, they tend to exercise relentlessly and excessively to accelerate their weight loss. Their progressive and significant weight loss eventually results in the cessation of menstruation (amenorrhea).

Anorectics are usually so willful and steadfast in their refusal to eat that their prolonged starvation diet causes a dangerous weight loss of 20 to 25 percent of their normal body weight. Death due to starvation or related causes occurs in 15 to 21 percent of anorexia's victims (AMA, 1980). A popular singer of a decade ago, Karen Carpenter, died at age 32 in 1983 of complications from anorexia.

Anorexia nervosa typically begins in adolescence and is about 10 times more common in girls than in boys. In many cases, the anorectic is also plagued with another serious eating disorder, bulimia nervosa.

Bulimia Nervosa   Another, more common eating disorder, **bulimia nervosa,** is characterized by repeated and uncontrolled episodes of binge eating. Binging is followed by purging—self-induced vomiting and/or the use of large quantities of laxatives and diuretics. Many people with bulimia use this pattern just to maintain their weight; others also suffer from anorexia nervosa. Bulimia nervosa causes a number of health problems. The vomiting of stomach acid eats away at the teeth and leaves them rotting, and the delicate balance of body chemistry is destroyed with excessive use of laxatives and diuretics.

Compared to normal eaters in a laboratory situation where subjects were asked to eat as much as they could, bulimics "consume more calories than controls, consume them more rapidly, and yet feel more hungry immediately afterward" (Walsh et al., 1989, p. 58).

"Surveys indicate that the disorder affects 1.3% to 10.1% of American women, spanning all socioeconomic classes. Ninety percent of bulimics are female" (Schlundt & Johnson, 1990).

Cognitive Development in Adolescence: Piaget's Formal Operations Stage

Question: What cognitive abilities develop during the formal operations stage?

The most striking achievement in cognitive development during adolescence is the ability to think abstractly. Jean Piaget (1972; Piaget & Inhelder, 1969) believed that young people typically enter the final stage of cognitive development, the **formal operations stage,** at age 11 or 12 when they become able to use logical reasoning in abstract situations. Remember that according to Piaget, preadolescents are able to apply logical thought processes only in concrete situations. With the attainment of full operational thinking, they are now able to attack problems by systematically testing hypotheses and drawing conclusions through deductive reasoning.

Were you mystified by the *x*'s and *y*'s of algebra? When high-school students develop formal operational thinking, they are able to unravel the mysteries of algebra and to decipher analogies and metaphors in English literature. With formal operations comes the ability to explore the world of ideas, to look at

bulimia nervosa (boo-LEE-me-uh ner-VO-sah): An eating disorder characterized by repeated and uncontrolled periods of binge eating followed by purging—self-induced vomiting and/or the excessive use of laxatives and diuretics.

formal operations stage: Piaget's final stage of cognitive development, characterized by the ability to use logical reasoning in abstract situations.

religion and moral values in a new light, and to consider different philosophies and political systems. Formal operational thinking enables adolescents to think hypothetically; they can think of what might be. Given this new ability, it is not surprising that they begin to conceive of "perfect" solutions to the world's problems.

Formal operational thought does not develop automatically, and it may be virtually absent in some primitive cultures (Dasen, 1972). Even in the United States, the majority of adolescents and adults may not develop full formal operational thinking (Kohlberg & Gilligan, 1971). One longitudinal study of American adolescents and adults concluded that only 30 percent of the subjects attained formal operations (Kuhn et al., 1977). Not only do many people fail to show formal operational thinking, but those who do attain it usually apply it only in those areas where they are most proficient (Ault, 1983; Martorano, 1977). Some studies suggest that even very intelligent, well-educated adults think best when thinking concretely (Kuhn et al., 1977; Neimark, 1975).

Adolescent Egocentrism: On Center Stage, Unique, and Indestructible

David Elkind (1967, 1974) claims that the early teenage years are marked by adolescent egocentrism, which takes two forms—the imaginary audience and the personal fable.

Do you remember, as a teenager, picturing how your friends would react to the way you looked when you made your grand entrance at a big party? At this stage of life, it never occurred to us that most of the other people at the party were preoccupied not with us, but with the way *they* looked and the impression *they* were making. This **imaginary audience** of admirers (or critics) that adolescents conjure up exists only in their imagination; "but in the young person's mind, he/she is always on stage" (Buis & Thompson, 1989, p. 774).

Teenagers also have an exaggerated sense of personal uniqueness and indestructibility that Elkind calls the **personal fable**. They cannot fathom that anyone has ever felt as deeply as they feel or loved as they love. This compelling sense of personal uniqueness makes many adolescents believe they are somehow indestructible and protected from the misfortunes that befall others, such as unwanted pregnancies, auto accidents, or drug overdoses. Belief in the personal fable may account for much of the risk taking during adolescence.

According to David Elkind, teenagers often respond to an imaginary audience of admirers or critics.

Memory Check 9.1

1. Adolescence is a stage typically filled with turmoil and conflict with parents. (true/false)

2. The secondary sex characteristics:

    a. are directly involved in reproduction
    b. occur at the same time in all adolescents
    c. distinguish mature males from mature females
    d. all of these

3. Which of the following provides the most advantages?

    a. early maturation in girls   c. late maturation in girls
    b. early maturation in boys   d. late maturation in boys

(continued)

imaginary audience: A belief of adolescents that they are or will be the focus of attention in social situations and that others will be as critical or approving as they are of themselves.

personal fable: An exaggerated sense of personal uniqueness and indestructibility, which may be the basis of risk taking common during adolescence.

4. The ability to apply logical reasoning in abstract situations characterizes Piaget's (formal operations, concrete operations) stage.

5. The concept of the (imaginary audience, personal fable) has been suggested as an explanation for excessive risk taking in adolescence.

6. Binging and purging are the major symptoms of (anorexia, bulimia) nervosa.

Answers: 1. false 2. c 3. b 4. formal operations 5. personal fable 6. bulimia

Adolescence: Moral, Personality, and Social Development

Kohlberg's Theory of Moral Development

How do we develop our ideas of right and wrong? As children, do we acquire our moral values from our parents, from attending church or temple, from our peer group, and from other societal influences? Most of us would agree that all these forces can influence our moral values. But Lawrence Kohlberg (1981, 1984, 1985) believed, as did Piaget before him, that moral reasoning is closely related to cognitive development and that it, too, evolves in stages.

Kohlberg (1969) studied moral development by presenting a series of moral dilemmas to male subjects from the United States and other countries. Read one of his best known dilemmas, and *Try It!*

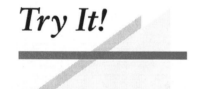
Try It!

In Europe a woman was near death from a special kind of cancer. There was one drug that the doctors thought might save her. It was a form of radium that a druggist in the same town had recently discovered. The drug was expensive to make, but the druggist was charging ten times what the drug cost him to make. He paid $200 for the radium and charged $2,000 for a small dose of the drug. The sick woman's husband, Heinz, went to everyone he knew to borrow the money, but he could only get together $1,000, which is half of what it cost. He told the druggist that his wife was dying, and asked him to sell it cheaper or let him pay later. But the druggist said, "No, I discovered the drug, and I am going to make money from it." So Heinz got desperate and broke into the man's store to steal the drug for his wife. (Colby, Kohlberg, et al., 1983, p. 77)

What moral judgment would you make about the dilemma? Should Heinz have stolen the drug? Why or why not?

Question: Briefly explain Kohlberg's three levels of moral reasoning.

Levels of Moral Reasoning   Kohlberg was less interested in whether his subjects judged Heinz's behavior right or wrong than in the *reasons* for their responses. He found that moral reasoning could be grouped into three levels, with each level having two stages. Table 9.1 describes Kohlberg's stages of moral development.

Table 9.1 Kohlberg's Stages of Moral Development

Level I: Preconventional Level (Ages 4–10) Moral reasoning is governed by the standards of others; an act is good or bad depending on its physical consequences—whether it is punished or rewarded.	**Stage 1** That which avoids punishment is right. Children obey out of fear of punishment. **Stage 2** The stage of self interest. What is right is that which benefits the individual or gains a favor in return. "You scratch my back and I'll scratch yours."
Level II: Conventional Level (Ages 10–13) The person internalizes the standards of others and judges right and wrong according to those standards.	**Stage 3** The morality of mutual relationships. The "good boy–nice girl" orientation. Acts to please and help others. **Stage 4** The morality of the social system and conscience. Oriented toward authority. Morality is doing one's duty, respecting authority, and maintaining the social order.
Level III: Postconventional Level (After age 13, at young adulthood, or never) The highest level and the mark of true morality; moral conduct is under internal control.	**Stage 5** The morality of contract, respecting individual rights and laws that are democratically agreed on. Rational valuing of the wishes of the majority and welfare of the people. Belief that society is best served if citizens obey the law. **Stage 6** The highest stage of the highest social level. The morality of universal ethical principles. The person acts according to internal standards independent of legal restrictions or opinions of others.

The Preconventional Level The first level of moral reasoning according to Kohlberg is the **preconventional level,** in which moral reasoning is governed by the standards of others rather than an individual's own internalized standards of right and wrong. An act is judged good or bad based on its physical consequences. In Stage 1 "right" is whatever avoids punishment; in Stage 2 "right" is whatever is rewarded, benefits the individual, or results in a favor being returned. "You scratch my back and I'll scratch yours" is the thinking common at this stage. Children through age 10 usually function at the preconventional level.

The Conventional Level The second level of moral reasoning is the **conventional level,** in which the individual has internalized the standards of others and judges right and wrong in terms of those standards. At Stage 3, sometimes called the *good boy–nice girl* orientation, "good behavior is that which pleases or helps others and is approved by them" (Kohlberg, 1968, p. 26). At Stage 4 the orientation is toward "authority, fixed rules, and the maintenance of the social order. Right behavior consists of doing one's duty, showing respect for authority, and maintaining the given social order for its own sake" (p. 26). Kohlberg believed that a person must have reached Piaget's concrete operational stage in order to reason morally at the conventional level. Figure 9.2 shows that this level of moral reasoning begins after age 7.

The Postconventional Level Kohlberg's highest level of moral reasoning is the **postconventional level,** which requires the ability to think at Piaget's level of formal operations. Most often this level is found among middle-class, college-educated people, according to Kohlberg. At this level, people do not simply internalize the standards of others. Instead, they weigh moral alternatives, real-

preconventional level of moral reasoning: Kohlberg's lowest level of moral reasoning, based on the physical consequences of an act; "right" is whatever avoids punishment or gains a reward.

conventional level of moral reasoning: Kohlberg's second level of moral reasoning, in which right and wrong are based on the internalized standards of others; "right" is whatever helps or is approved of by others, or whatever is consistent with the laws of society.

postconventional level of moral reasoning: Kohlberg's highest level, in which moral reasoning involves weighing moral alternatives; "right" is whatever furthers basic human rights.

Figure 9.2

The Development of Moral Reasoning

According to Lawrence Kohlberg's theory, moral development is tied to cognitive development. There are three levels of moral development: preconventional, conventional, and postconventional. There is great variation in the ages at which moral reasoning progresses, as shown in the figure. The majority of adults never reach Kohlberg's postconventional level of moral reasoning. (Data from Kohlberg, 1963.)

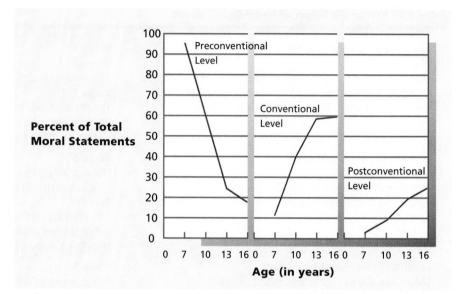

izing that at times the law may conflict with basic human rights. At Stage 5 the person believes that laws are formulated to protect both society and the individual and should be changed if they fail to do so. At Stage 6 the universal-ethical principle orientation, ethical decisions are based on universal ethical principles, which emphasize respect for human life, justice, equality, and dignity for all people. People who reason morally at Stage 6 believe that they must follow their conscience even if it results in a violation of the law.

Couldn't this kind of moral reasoning provide a convenient justification for doing anything a person feels like doing at the time? Not according to Kohlberg, who insisted that an action must be judged in terms of whether it is right and fair from the perspective of all the people involved. In other words, the person must consider the action proper even if he or she had to change positions with any individual, from the most favored to the least favored, in the society.

We should point out that Kohlberg had second thoughts about this sixth stage and was unsure whether it exists except as a matter of theoretical and philosophic speculation (Levine, Kohlberg, & Hewer, 1985).

The Development of Moral Reasoning   Kohlberg claimed that we progress through moral stages one stage at a time in a fixed order. We do not skip stages, and if movement occurs, it is to the next higher stage. Postconventional reasoning is not possible, Kohlberg said, until people fully attain Piaget's level of formal operations. They must be able to think in terms of abstract principles and be able to think through and apply ethical principles in hypothetical situations (Kohlberg & Gilligan, 1971; Kuhn et al., 1977). Attaining a high level of cognitive development, however, does not guarantee advanced moral reasoning.

Criticisms of Kohlberg's Theory   Some critics point out that moral reasoning and moral behavior are not one and the same. Kohlberg readily acknowledged that people can be capable of making mature moral judgments yet fail to live morally. But, said Kohlberg (1968), "The man who understands justice is more likely to practice it" (p. 30).

Another area of controversy concerns the apparent male sex bias in Kohlberg's stages (Gilligan, 1982). Kohlberg indicated that the majority of women remain at Stage 3, while most men attain Stage 4 reasoning. Do men typically attain a higher level of moral reasoning than women? Carol Gilligan (1982) asserts that Kohlberg's theory is sex-biased. Not only did he fail to include females in his original research, Gilligan points out, but he limited morality to abstract reasoning about moral dilemmas. Furthermore, at his highest level, Stage 6, Kohlberg emphasized justice and equality but not mercy, compassion, love, and concern for others. Gilligan suggests that females, more than males, tend to view moral behavior in terms of compassion, caring, and concern for others. Thus, she agrees that the content of moral reasoning differs between the sexes, but she contends that males and females do not differ in the complexity of their moral reasoning.

Researchers have found support for Kohlberg's invariant stages but not for sex differences in their attainment (Walker, 1989; Walker et al., 1987). Finally, some critics suggest that Kohlberg had a built-in liberal bias and claim that his theory is culture-bound, favoring Western middle-class values (Simpson, 1974; Sullivan, 1977).

There is some merit to the claim that Kohlberg's theory of moral reasoning suffers not only from gender bias but from cultural bias as well. Researchers Joan Miller and David Bersoff (1992) conducted a cross-cultural study of adults and children from India and the United States. They found great differences between the two cultures. The postconventional moral reasoning common in India stressed interpersonal responsibilities over justice obligations. In contrast, Americans tended to emphasize a personal or rights-oriented view over individual responsibilities to others. Our world would be more just if each of us, without fail, got exactly what we deserved—no more, no less. But would such a world be more moral? Are mercy and compassion less moral than objective, emotionless justice?

Regardless of whether we agree with Kohlberg's theory, most of us would agree that moral reasoning and moral behavior are critically important aspects of human development. Moral individuals make moral societies.

> **identity versus role confusion:** Erikson's fifth psychosocial stage, when adolescents need to establish their own identity and to form values to live by; failure can lead to an identity crisis.

Erikson's Psychosocial Stage for Adolescence: Identity versus Role Confusion

Erik and Joan Erikson

Question: How does Erikson explain the fifth stage of psychosocial development—identity versus role confusion?

The previous chapter described Erikson's first four psychosocial stages of development. Having weathered these four developmental stages, adolescents face a new psychosocial challenge, that of developing an identity. Erikson's eight stages are described in Table 9.2.

Erikson's fifth stage of psychosocial development, **identity versus role confusion**, is the developmental struggle of adolescence. "Who am I?" becomes the critical question at this stage, as adolescents seek to establish their identity and find values to guide their lives (Erikson, 1963). They must develop a sense of who they are, where they have been, and where they are going. Now for the first time, adolescents are seriously looking to the future and considering an occupational identity—what they will choose as their life's work. Erikson (1968) believes that "in general it is the inability to settle on an occupational identity which most disturbs young people" (p. 132). The danger at this stage, he says, is that of role confusion—not knowing who you are or where you belong.

Erikson used the term "identity crisis" to portray the disturbance adolescents experience in forging an identity. But current research does not support the notion that most young people experience a crisis (Blyth & Traeger, 1983; Offer et al., 1981). Erikson may have been projecting onto all adolescents in general the difficulties he experienced in forming his own identity.

Although Erikson (1980) considered establishing an identity to be the focus of adolescence, he recognized that "identity *formation* neither begins nor ends with adolescence: it is a lifelong development" (p. 122).

WORLD OF PSYCHOLOGY: PIONEERS

Erik Homburger Erikson (1902–   )

Erik Erikson is a personality theorist whose books sell by the hundreds of thousands and whose writings have won him a Pulitzer Prize. Yet he has neither an M.D. nor a Ph.D. in psychology. In fact, he doesn't have any kind of university degree at all.

Erikson originated the concept of "identity crisis," and in real life he had to resolve a monumental crisis of his own. Born in Frankfort, Germany, to Danish parents, Erikson did not know his biological father, who left before he was born. Not long afterward Erikson's mother married Dr. Theodore Homburger, and Erikson was raised as Erik Homburger. He did not learn that Dr. Homburger was not his real father until many years later. In fact Erikson did not take his biological father's last name until he was 37 years old. Yet Erikson did not resent his mother and stepfather for what he termed their "loving deception."

Erikson experienced other crises about who and what he was during childhood. When he started school, Erikson thought of himself as German, but the German children shunned him because he was Jewish. Yet he fared no better with his Jewish classmates, who rejected him because, as a tall, blonde Dane, he was not very Jewish in appearance. Since he did not seem to fit in very well, it is not surprising that he disliked school and made only average grades.

After he finished school, Erikson was not sure what he wanted to do or to be, and so as a young man he wandered around "trying to find himself." Eventually he went to Vienna, found Sigmund Freud, and developed a fascination for Freud's psychoanalytic theory. He entered Freud's institute and began his training in psychoanalysis, studying primarily with Freud's daughter, Anna. After he completed his training in 1933, Erikson married and then with his wife came to the United States, where he set up a practice working with children in Boston.

Erikson entered Harvard to study for his Ph.D. in psychology. He soon dropped out and accepted a position at Yale University teaching at the medical school and working with both disturbed and normal children. Interested in the development of children from diverse cultures, he conducted studies with two different American Indian tribes, as well as with other American children in Massachusetts and California. He returned to Harvard in the 1960s.

Even without a formal degree, Erikson has distinguished himself as a psychoanalyst and personality theorist, and throughout his long life he has remained prolific, productive, and influential. Now past 90 years old, Erikson continues with his wife Joan (an artist and an author in her own right) to make scholarly contributions, and they both serve as models of the successful resolution of the eight stages of life that Erikson proposed.

The Peer Group

Question: What are some of the useful functions of the adolescent peer group?

At a time when adolescents feel the need to become more independent from their parents, friends become a vital source of emotional support and approval. Adolescents usually choose friends of the same sex and race who have similar values, interests, and backgrounds (Duck, 1983; Epstein, 1983).

Interactions with peers are critical while young people are fashioning their identities. Adolescents can try out different roles and observe the reactions of their friends to their behavior and their appearance. The peer group provides teenagers with a vehicle for developing social skills, as well as a standard of comparison for evaluating their own assets.

For males and females, popularity within the peer group is based largely on good looks and personality. A boy's athletic ability is often an important factor in his popularity with both sexes (Savin-Williams, 1980). Conformity appears to be another important ingredient in popularity (Sebald, 1981), and although scholastic success is not a criterion for popularity, neither is it a liability.

Parental Relationships: Better Than You Think

Some research indicates that teens at puberty begin to distance themselves from their parents and that there is an increase in conflict, particularly with the mother (Paikoff & Brooks-Gunn, 1991; Steinberg, 1987). But despite all the talk about the generation gap, most adolescents have good relationships with their parents (Atkinson, 1988).

Bachman (1987) found that over 70 percent of high-school seniors felt that their personal values were either "very similar" or "mostly similar" to those of their parents. In a study of more than 18,000 adolescents, Curtis (1975) found that adolescents value their parents' advice even more than that of their friends. Adolescents value their parents' advice particularly on issues that affect their future—educational and occupational goals, or questions about religion, politics, morality, and the use of hard drugs (Coleman, 1980; Marcia, 1980). But on questions of dress, hairstyles, music, sex, tobacco, and alcohol, peer opinions carry more weight.

Parental influence is greatest when there is a good parent-child relationship, when parents use an authoritative, rather than authoritarian, parenting style (Baumrind, 1978), and when parents have attained some measure of professional and financial success. Furthermore, an authoritative parenting style facilitates academic achievement in adolescents (Steinberg et al., 1989).

The conventional notion that conflict between parent and child is healthy has not been supported. In fact, high conflict is related to drug abuse, dropping out of school, early pregnancy and marriage, running away, joining cults, suicide attempts, and the development of psychiatric disorders (Peterson, 1988).

Table 9.2   Erikson's Psychosocial Stages of Development

Stage	Ages	Description
Trust vs. Mistrust	Birth to 1 year	Described in chapter 8.
Autonomy vs. Shame and doubt	1–3 years	
Initiative vs. Guilt	3–6 years	
Industry vs. Inferiority	6 years–puberty	
Identity vs. Role confusion	Adolescence	Adolescents must make the transition from childhood to adulthood, establish an identity, develop a sense of self, and consider a future occupational identity. Otherwise, role confusion can result.
Intimacy vs. Isolation	Young adulthood	Young adults must develop intimacy—the ability to share with, care for, and commit themselves to another person. Avoiding intimacy brings a sense of isolation and loneliness.
Generativity vs. Stagnation	Middle adulthood	Middle-aged people must find some way of contributing to the development of the next generation. Failing this, they may become self-absorbed, personally impoverished, and reach a point of stagnation.
Ego integrity vs. Despair	Late adulthood	Individuals review their lives, and if satisfied and feel a sense of accomplishment, ego integrity will result. If dissatisfied, they may sink into despair.

Sexuality and Adolescence: The Drive Turns On

Before the 1960s the surging sex drive of adolescents was held in check primarily because most societal influences—parents, religious leaders, the schools, and the media—were all preaching the same message. Premarital sex was wrong. Then sexual attitudes began to change. According to a national survey taken in 1969 by Gallup, 68 percent of adults in the United States believed that premarital sex was wrong. By 1991, the number had dropped to 40 percent (Hugick & Leonard, 1991c).

WORLD OF PSYCHOLOGY: APPLICATIONS

Children Who Have Children Are Not the Luckiest People in the World

The United States has a higher incidence of teen pregnancy among 15- to 19-year-olds than any other developed country (Brozan, 1985). The majority of adolescents are not taking the responsibility for preventing pregnancy. In fact, one-third of the sexually active girls between ages 15 and 19 are not using contraception at all; many others use it only occasionally. Those in exclusive, committed relationships are most likely to take precautions. Those who feel guilty about their activity are less likely to use birth control because planning ahead to have sex seems more wrong to them than simply having it happen spontaneously. Some teens are embarrassed to buy contraceptives, some think that contraceptives interfere with pleasure, and many severely underestimate the risk of getting pregnant. Unfortunately, 62 percent of those who are sexually active and fail to use contraception do become pregnant (Zelnik et al., 1979).

Each year 10 percent of all adolescent girls—about 1.1 million—become pregnant (Hamburg et al., 1987). About 40 percent opt for abortion (Cullari & Mikus, 1990), and 5 percent put their babies up for adoption (Wallis, 1985). In the early 1980s two out of every three white teenage mothers and 97 percent of black teen mothers who delivered first births were unmarried when they conceived (Furstenberg et al., 1989). But the problem does not end with the pregnancy. Among those who give birth before age 18 and choose to keep their baby, half will never complete high school. As a group their earning power will be about half that of girls who did not have babies at this early age, and many will end up on welfare (Brooks-Gunn & Furstenberg, 1986). About one-third of pregnant teenagers marry the baby's father, but the divorce rate for these marriages is two to three times higher than the national average.

The babies of teen mothers are also at a disadvantage.

Teenage mothers and their babies are more likely to suffer socially, educationally, and economically.

They are twice as likely to be of low birth weight, and they are more likely to have poor health and emotional and educational problems (Brooks-Gunn & Furstenberg, 1986; Furstenberg et al., 1989). There are no winners in this disturbing trend. What will be the social, moral, and economic consequences of so many young teens—many, themselves, still children—having children?

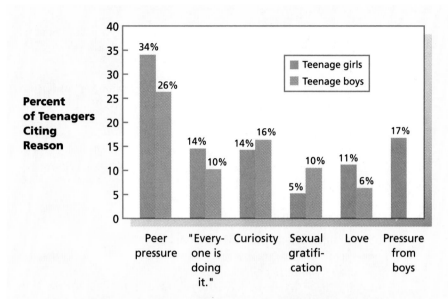

Figure 9.3

Reasons Teenagers Give for Having Intercourse

Apparently peer pressure in general, not love, is the major reason teenagers, both male and female, engage in premarital intercourse. (After "Teen Sex," 1989.)

According to the Centers for Disease Control (1992a), the incidence of premarital intercourse among high-school students is 60.8 percent for males and 48 percent for females. "Black students were significantly more likely than white or Hispanic students to ever have had intercourse (72.3 percent, 51.6 percent, and 53.4 percent, respectively)" (p. 885). Sonestein and others (1991) report that the typical pattern for males and females is serial monogamy—"a pattern of monogamous relationships that follow one another" (p. 166).

Early premarital intercourse is associated with a higher number of sexual partners and an increased risk of sexually transmitted diseases. Ostrov and others (1985) found early intercourse less prevalent among adolescents with above-average academic achievement and among those who lived with both of their natural parents and whose parents had a harmonious relationship. Figure 9.3 shows reasons given by teenage boys and girls for having intercourse.

Memory Check 9.2

1. Match Kohlberg's level of moral reasoning with the rationale for engaging in a behavior.

_____ 1) to avoid punishment or gain a reward	a. conventional
_____ 2) to ensure that human rights are protected	b. preconventional
_____ 3) to gain approval or to follow the law	c. postconventional

(continued)

2. Which of the following is *not* identified by Erikson as a developmental task in his fifth stage of psychosocial development—identity versus role confusion?

   a. forming an identity
   b. planning for an occupation
   c. forming an intimate relationship
   d. finding values to live by

3. Adolescents usually (do, do not) get along well with their parents.

4. Each year (5, 10) percent of adolescent girls in the United States become pregnant.

5. Which of these statements is *not* true of the majority of pregnant teens?

   a. They are unmarried when they become pregnant.
   b. They decide to have their babies rather than opting for abortion.
   c. They marry the father of the baby.
   d. They are more likely to have babies with poor health and with emotional and educational problems.

Answers: 1. 1) b 2) c 3) a 2. c 3. do 4. 10 5. c

Early and Middle Adulthood

The study of adult development is comparatively new. For many years developmental psychologists focused almost exclusively on childhood and adolescence. But today a number of developmental psychologists study the changes that occur during that long period of some 40 to 45 years known as adulthood. They generally divide adulthood into three parts—young or early adulthood (ages 20 to 40 or 45), middle adulthood (ages 40 or 45 to 65), and late adulthood (after age 65 or 70). These ages are only approximate because there are no biological or psychological events that neatly define the beginning or ending of a period. Bernice Neugarten, one of the most respected researchers in adult development, has said, "We seem to be moving in the direction of what might be called an age-irrelevant society; and it can be argued that age, like race or sex, is diminishing in importance as a regulator of behavior" (Neugarten & Hagestad, 1976, p. 52).

Although some things change from younger to older adulthood, in many ways older adults remain much the same as in their earlier years. For most adults (younger and older), love provides the primary source of satisfaction, followed by work (Baum & Stewart, 1990).

Physical Changes in Adulthood

Question: What are the physical changes associated with middle age?

There are varying opinions about what period should be called the "prime of life," but it is clear when the *physical* prime of life occurs. Physically, we peak early. Although most people in their twenties and thirties enjoy good general health and vitality, the decade of the twenties is the period of top physical condition. Physical strength, reaction time, reproductive capacity, and manual dexterity all peak during the twenties. In the decade of the thirties, there is a slight decline in these physical capacities, but the decline is barely perceptible to most people other than professional athletes.

Middle-aged people often complain of less stamina and a loss of physical vigor and endurance. But such losses have less to do with aging than with exercise, diet, and health habits. Some fine professional athletes, star pitcher Nolan Ryan, for example, are still competing into their forties. One change in the mid to late forties that can't be avoided is *presbyopia*, a condition in which the lens of the eyes no longer accommodates adequately for near vision, and reading glasses or bifocals are required for reading.

During middle age, people become acutely aware of their mortality and may begin to restructure life "in terms of time-left-to-live rather than time-since-birth" (Neugarten, 1968b, p. 97). By the time we reach 50, as one researcher has put it so well, "we must accept that life's seesaw has tipped; that there are now more yesterdays than tomorrows" (Vaillant, 1977, p. 233).

In middle age, people are more susceptible to diseases, especially life-threatening ones. Heart disease is responsible for more than 35 percent—and cancer, 26 percent—of all deaths among men between ages 45 and 54 (Ebersole, 1979). Cancer, usually of the breast, accounts for 44 percent of the deaths of women in this age group.

The major biological event for women during middle age is **menopause**,—the end of menstruation, which occurs between ages 45 and 55 and signifies the end of reproductive capacity. Probably the most common symptom associated with menopause and the sharp decrease in the level of estrogen is hot flashes—the sudden feelings of being uncomfortably hot. Some women also experience symptoms such as anxiety, irritability, mood swings, or depression, but most find that menopause is less upsetting than they had anticipated (Newman, 1982; Reinke, 1985). Men experience a gradual decline in their testosterone level from its peak at about age 20 until 60. During late middle age, men experience a decline in reproductive capability, called the male climacteric.

Many middle-aged people remain just as active as they were in their twenties.

Intellectual Capacity during Early and Middle Adulthood

Question: In general, can adults look forward to an increase or a decrease in intellectual performance from their twenties to forties?

Conventional wisdom has held that intellectual ability reaches its peak in the late teens or early twenties, and that it's all downhill after that. Fortunately, conventional wisdom is wrong. Although younger people tend to do better on tests requiring speed or rote memory, intellectual performance in adults continues to increase in other areas. In tests measuring general information, vocabulary, reasoning ability, and social judgment, older subjects usually do better than younger ones due to their greater experience and education (Horn, 1982; Horn & Donaldson, 1980). Adults actually continue to gain knowledge and skills over the years, particularly when they lead intellectually challenging lives.

Dennis (1968) looked at the productivity of 738 persons who had lived at least 79 years and had attained eminence as scholars or in the sciences or the arts. For almost everyone the decade of the forties was most productive. Historians, philosophers, and literary scholars enjoyed high productivity from the forties all the way through the seventies. Scientists were highly productive from their forties through sixties, but showed a significant decline in productivity in their seventies. Those in the arts peaked earliest. They were most productive in their thirties, forties, and fifties and showed a dramatic decline in their seventies. But of course, the researchers did not interview Michelangelo, Grandma Moses, Pablo Picasso, Georgia O'Keeffe, Pablo Casals, Arthur Rubinstein, Irving Berlin,

presbyopia (prez-bee-O-pee-uh): A condition, occurring in the mid to late forties, in which the lens no longer accommodates adequately for near vision, and reading glasses or bifocals are required for reading.

menopause: The end of menstruation, occurring between ages 45 and 55 and signifying the end of reproductive capacity.

intimacy versus isolation: Erikson's sixth psychosocial stage, when the young adult must establish intimacy in a relationship in order to avoid feeling a sense of isolation and loneliness.

and many others who were artistically potent and vital into their seventies, eighties, and nineties. Fortunately, we can conclude that middle age is not a time in life when we dry up and deteriorate physically, mentally, or in any other way.

Erikson's Psychosocial Stage for Early Adulthood: Intimacy versus Isolation

Question: What is Erikson's psychosocial task for early adulthood?

Erikson contends that if healthy development is to continue into young adulthood, it is necessary for the young adult to establish intimacy in a relationship. This sixth stage of psychosocial development he calls **intimacy versus isolation.**

What kind of intimacy is Erikson referring to? He means more than sexual intimacy alone. Intimacy means the ability of young adults to share with, care for, make sacrifices for, and commit themselves to another person. Erikson claims that avoiding intimacy results in a sense of isolation and loneliness.

Erikson (1980) believes that young adults must establish their own identity before true intimacy is possible. He says, "The condition of a true twoness is that one must first become oneself" (p. 101). Several studies support Erikson's notion that a stable identity is a necessary prerequisite for an intimate relationship (Tesch & Whitbourne, 1982; Vaillant, 1977).

Life-style Patterns in Adulthood

Question: What are some of the trends in life-style patterns in young adulthood?

How do you picture the average household in the United States? Although 56.5 percent of U.S. households are composed of married couples (who may or may not have children under 18), there are a number of nontraditional living patterns among Americans in early and middle adulthood in the 1990s (U.S. Bureau of the Census, 1991). Figure 9.4 illustrates the makeup of U.S. households. Let us consider some of these life-style patterns.

Figure 9.4

The Makeup of Households in the United States

Although U.S. households headed by married spouses have decreased dramatically over the last several decades, they are still in the majority (56.5 percent). Married couples with their own children under 18 now comprise only 26.6 percent of U.S. households. Females with children under age 18 comprise 7 percent of the households; males with children under 18 constitute only 1.2 percent of the households. (Data from U.S. Bureau of the Census, 1991.)

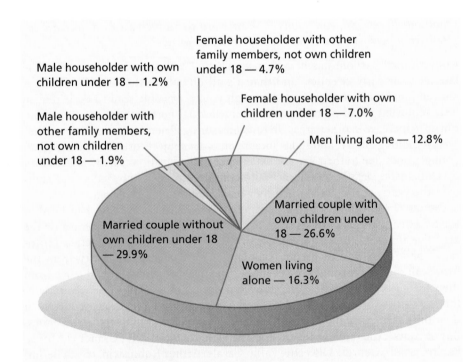

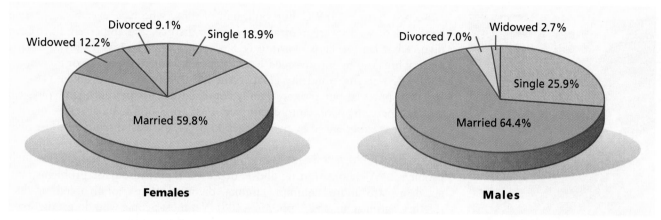

Figure 9.5   Marital Status of the U.S. Population   In the United States about 81 percent of women and 74 percent of men either are or have been married. A larger percentage of men (64.4 percent) than women (59.8 percent) are currently married. (Data from U.S. Bureau of the Census, 1991.)

Singles: Playing the Field   About 26 percent of males and 19 percent of females over age 18 are single (U.S. Bureau of the Census, 1991). Some people believe that if unburdened by a spouse, they will be able to pursue their careers and their interests and have a more interesting and exciting life. Yet the happiest singles seem to be those who have relationships that provide emotional support.

Some single people who want a relationship choose living together rather than making the commitment of marriage. The U.S. Bureau of the Census (1991) labels them "unmarried couples." From 1970 to 1989 there was a twelvefold increase in cohabitation for people under age 25. Such arrangements usually last one or two years, with one-third of the couples marrying and the rest breaking up. Surprisingly, the divorce rate among these couples is higher than the divorce rate for couples who did not live together before marriage (DeMoris & Rao, 1992).

Marriage: Tying the Knot   Despite the growing alternatives to marriage, 74 percent of men and 81 percent of women in America either are married or have been married (U.S. Bureau of the Census, 1991). (See Figure 9.5.) The difference in percentage reflects the fact that more women than men who have been married are still alive. Though the institution of marriage is still alive and well, men and women are waiting longer to tie the knot. Since 1970, the average age at first marriage has increased by almost 3 years. In 1986 the median age was 25.3 for males and 23.6 for females (U.S. Bureau of the Census, 1991).

Some research indicates that married people, in general, report higher levels of happiness. One study, relating marital status to level of happiness, found that married people were most happy, followed by the widowed, separated, or divorced. Those who had never been married were the least happy (Campbell, 1976).

Divorce: Untying the Knot   From 1970 to 1989 the divorce rate in this country increased by 34 percent (U.S. Bureau of the Census, 1991). The marriages most likely to fail are teenage marriages, those in which the bride was pregnant, and marriages of people whose parents had been divorced. And the marriages that do survive are not necessarily happy. Many couples stay together for reasons other than love—because of religious beliefs, for the sake of the children, for financial reasons, or out of fear of facing the future alone.

While parenthood can cause stress and conflict in a marriage, it is also immensely satisfying for many adults.

According to a 1989 Gallup poll, half of those who have ever been married have experienced severe marital problems or divorce, and 26 percent have been divorced at least once (Colasanto & Shriver, 1989). The reasons given for the marital breakup by the divorced were basic personality differences or incompatibility (47 percent); infidelity (17 percent); a drug or alcohol problem (16 percent); disputes about money, family, or children (10 percent); and physical abuse (5 percent) (Colasanto & Shriver, 1989, p. 36). The most severe marital discord was experienced by people ages 35 to 54, the least discord by those over age 55.

But even for the "miserable marrieds," divorce does not always solve their problems. "Alcoholism, drug abuse, depression, psychosomatic problems, and accidents are more common among divorced than nondivorced adults" (Hetherington et al., 1989, pp. 307–308). Yet most people who do get divorced are not soured on the institution of marriage; the majority do remarry.

Question: What effect does parenthood have on marital satisfaction?

Parenthood: Passing Along the Genes   In a 1990 Gallup poll, 90 percent of Americans over age 40 have had children, and despite the difficult task of raising them, only 7 percent said "they wish they had not had children" (Gallup & Newport, 1990d).

Even though most couples want children, satisfaction with marriage does tend to decline after the birth of the first child (Glenn & McLanahan, 1982; Rhyne, 1981). This decline appears to be especially true for women (Grossman et al., 1980) and particularly true for women who do not perceive themselves in sex-stereotyped ways (Belsky et al., 1986). Women in general find the period of child rearing the least satisfying time of marriage. Even though men are helping with children more than in the past, child care is still considered by most to be the primary responsibility of the woman. Ruble and others (1988) found that a woman's dissatisfaction after the birth of the first child relates to the discrepancy between how much help with child care and housework she had expected from her husband and how much help she actually receives. Several studies have revealed that when husbands in dual-earner families *do* help with child care, they too have a more negative view of their marriage, and there is an increase in marital conflict (Crouter et al., 1987).

By 1987 about 58 percent of all mothers with children under age 6 and almost 66 percent of those with children under age 18 held part-time or full-time jobs outside the home. Now, almost 54 percent of the women who give birth enter the labor force before the child is a year old (U.S. Bureau of the Census, 1991). Figure 9.6 shows the percentage of married women in the labor force according to the age of their youngest child.

Remaining Childless: No Bundles of Joy   Some couples are choosing not to have children, leaving themselves free to devote their time, energy, and money to pursuing their own interests and careers. A few studies indicate that such couples are happier and find their marriages more satisfying than couples with children (Campbell, 1975). However, this same sense of satisfaction may not continue into middle and old age, when couples may wonder if their decision to remain childless was a good one. A 1990 Gallup poll found that only about 4 percent of Americans are "anti-children"—that is, they don't have any, they don't want any, or they are glad they never had any children (Gallup & Newport, 1990d). In spite of the tremendous emotional and financial investment children require, most parents find their children provide a major source of satisfaction and meaning in their lives and that the investment has been a good one.

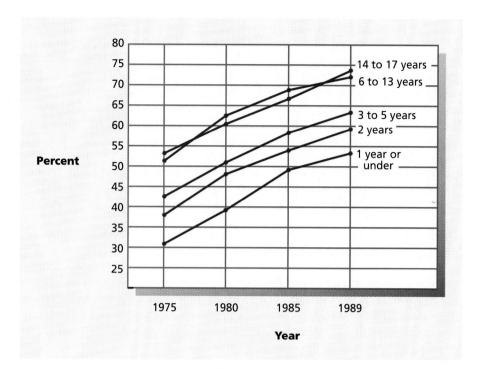

Figure 9.6

Percent of Married Women with Children in the Labor Force

The percentage of married women with children in the U.S. labor force continues to rise. Over 53 percent of women with children 1 year of age or under, and nearly 60 percent with children 2 years or under are employed. (Data from U.S. Bureau of the Census, 1991.)

Career Choice: A Critical Life Decision   Probably no other part of life is so central to identity and self-esteem as a person's occupation or profession, with the possible exception of motherhood for some women. Our career often becomes a basic part of our definition of self and a major factor in the way others define us. A career can define our life-style—the friends we choose, the neighborhood we live in, our habits, and even our ideas and opinions. Job satisfaction affects our general life satisfaction.

Although the majority of Americans seem satisfied with their jobs, job satisfaction is higher for the middle-aged than for the young adult (Kohut & DeStefano, 1989). According to a 1991 Gallup poll, 75 percent of American workers would continue to work even if it were not a financial necessity, and more than 50 percent would continue in their present job (Hugick & Leonard, 1991a).

One of the most profound changes in employment patterns has been the tremendous increase of women in the workplace. In 1989 women made up 45.2 percent of the work force (U.S. Bureau of the Census, 1991). But women are not rushing into the workplace primarily to find self-fulfillment. Most are there out of economic necessity, even though women earn on the average only about 65 percent of what men earn on the average. In spite of lower pay, sex discrimination, and fewer opportunities for advancement, most women find their jobs enjoyable and express higher self-esteem than full-time homemakers do (Baruch et al., 1983; Hoffman, 1974, 1979).

Personality and Social Development in Middle Age

Many people consider middle age the prime of life. Bernice Neugarten, a leading researcher on adult development, states that although society "may be oriented towards youth, [it] is controlled by the middle-aged" (1968b, p. 93). People aged 40 to 60 are the decision makers in industry, government, and society. Neugarten (1968b) finds that very few at this age "express a wish to be young again" (p. 97). As one of her subjects said, "There is a difference between wanting to *feel* young and wanting to *be* young" (p. 97).

generativity versus stagnation: Erikson's seventh psychosocial stage, occurring during middle age, when the individual becomes increasingly concerned with guiding and assisting the next generation rather than becoming self-absorbed and stagnating.

Reaching middle age, men and women begin to express personality characteristics that they had formerly suppressed. Men generally become more nurturant and women more aggressive (Neugarten, 1968a). Many women "feel that the most conspicuous characteristic of middle age is the sense of increased freedom" (Neugarten, 1968b, p. 96). Contrary to the conventional notion of the empty nest syndrome—that parents feel empty and depressed when their children grow up and leave home—most parents seem to be happier when their children are on their own (Campbell, 1975; Miller, 1976; Rollins & Feldman, 1970). Parents have more time and money to pursue their own goals and interests, and they are happy about it. "For the majority of women in middle age, the departure of teenage children is not a crisis, but a pleasure. It is when the children do *not* leave home that a crisis occurs (for both parent and child)" (Neugarten, 1982, p. 163). For most people, an empty nest is a happy nest!

Question: What changes does Erikson believe are essential for healthy personality development in middle age?

Erikson's Psychosocial Stage for Middle Adulthood: Generativity versus Stagnation   Erikson's seventh psychosocial stage is called **generativity versus stagnation.** Erikson (1980) believes that in order for mental health to continue into middle adulthood, individuals must develop generativity—an "interest in establishing and guiding the next generation" (p. 103).

> The person begins to be concerned with others beyond his immediate family, with future generations and the nature of the society and world in which those generations will live. Generativity does not reside only in parents; it can be found in any individual who actively concerns himself with the welfare of young people and with making the world a better place for them to live and work. (Elkind, 1970, p. 112)

People who do not develop generativity become self-absorbed and "begin to indulge themselves as if they were their own one and only child" (Erikson, 1980, p. 103). Personal impoverishment and a sense of stagnation often accompany such self-absorption. We enlarge ourselves when we have concern for others.

Memory Check 9.3

1. For most people the arrival of children brings (an increase, a decrease) in marital satisfaction.

2. People in their early twenties do better than middle-aged people on tests of general information and vocabulary and on tests requiring reasoning ability. (true/false)

3. Erikson believes the main task in young adulthood is to:

   a. develop generativity   c. start a family
   b. forge an identity   d. form an intimate relationship

4. The highest levels of life satisfaction are reported by _____; the lowest levels by _____.

   a. singles; married people   c. married people; the widowed
   b. married people; singles   d. married people; divorced people

Answers: 1. a decrease 2. false 3. d 4. b

Theories of Adulthood

There is no question that we change as we grow older. A number of experts have tried to learn how we change and develop through life, and some have identified stages of adult development.

Levinson's Seasons of Life

Question: How is Levinson's concept of life structure related to his proposed stages of development?

Daniel Levinson's stage theory of adult development emerged from his extensive interviews of 40 men between the ages of 35 and 45—"hourly workers in industry, business executives, university biologists and novelists"—who were diverse in racial, ethnic, and religious origins and in social class (Levinson et al., 1978).

Levinson found that although the lives of his subjects were unique, an underlying pattern and sequence of stages were common to all of them. He identified four eras or seasons in the life cycle: preadulthood (childhood and adolescence), early adulthood, middle adulthood, and late adulthood. Subjects went through stable periods lasting from 6 to 10 years. During these periods they made certain key choices that formed the basis of their **life structure**—the basic pattern of their life at a given time, including their relationships and activities.

Between these stable, 6- to 10-year periods were transitional periods lasting 4 to 5 years. During these transitional periods individuals would review and evaluate their life and existing life structure. A transitional period may result in minor changes in the life structure or in drastic changes, such as divorce, remarriage, changing jobs or occupations, or moving to another part of the country. When a transitional period is particularly difficult, it is called a crisis. Figure 9.7 shows "the seasons of a man's life" as proposed by Levinson.

Following are descriptions of some of Levinson's proposed stages:

- **Early Adult Transition** (ages 17 to 22): During this period of transition between adolescence and early adulthood, young people begin to separate psychologically from parents and other aspects of the preadult world in preparation for entry into the adult world.
- **Entering the Adult World** (ages 22 to 28): Young adults typically choose an occupation, form love relationships, marry and have a family, and try to turn their dream of the kind of life they want into a reality.
- **Age Thirty Transition** (ages 28 to 33): This period is a time for modifying the first adult life structure and creating "the basis for a more satisfactory structure with which to complete the era of early adulthood" (1978, p. 58).
- **Settling Down** (ages 33 to 40): Adults build a second life structure and anchor themselves more firmly in family or community. They seek to advance in their occupation and climb the ladder of success.
- **Mid-life Transition** (ages 40 to 45): During this transition period people develop "a heightened awareness of . . . mortality and a desire to use the remaining time more wisely" (1978, p. 192). Some people make few external changes, while others make drastic ones involving "divorce, remarriage, major shifts in occupation and lifestyle" (p. 194). Levinson reported that 80 percent of his subjects experienced a moderate or severe **mid-life crisis**.
- **Middle Adult Era** (ages 45 to 60): Now senior members in their own world, individuals feel a responsibility for "the development of the current generation of young adults who will soon enter the dominant generation" (Levinson, 1986, p. 6).
- **Late Adult Transition** (ages 60 to 65): A final transition into late adulthood brings a person to the last rung of Levinson's developmental ladder.

life structure: Levinson's term for the basic pattern of one's life at any given time, including one's relationships and activities and the significance they have for the individual.

mid-life crisis: A period of turmoil usually occurring in a person's forties and brought on by an awareness of one's mortality, it is characterized by a reassessment of one's life and a decision to make changes, either drastic or moderate, in order to make the remaining years better.

Figure 9.7

Levinson's Stage Theory of Adult Development

Daniel Levinson identifies four seasons in life: preadulthood (childhood and adolescence), early adulthood, middle adulthood, and late adulthood. Stable periods lasting 6 to 10 years alternate with transitional periods lasting 4 to 5 years. During a transitional period, individuals review and evaluate their life and may make minor or drastic changes in their life structure. (From Levinson et al., 1978.)

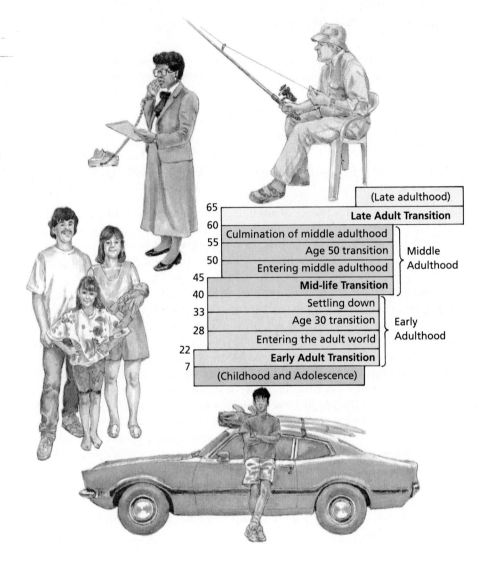

(Late adulthood)	
Late Adult Transition	65
Culmination of middle adulthood	60
Age 50 transition	55 — Middle Adulthood
Entering middle adulthood	50
Mid-life Transition	45
Settling down	40
Age 30 transition	33 — Early Adulthood
Entering the adult world	28
Early Adult Transition	22
(Childhood and Adolescence)	7

Although his first study included only men, Levinson later studied 45 women. His findings convinced him that his theory was applicable to females as well. On the basis of his research and that of others, Levinson now claims that his theory "holds for men and women of different cultures, classes, and historical epochs" (Levinson, 1986, p. 8).

Reinke, Ellicott, and Harris: The Life Course in Women

Question: What did Reinke, Ellicott, and Harris's study of middle-class women reveal about major transitional periods in the life cycle?

Reinke and others (1985) interviewed 124 middle-class women ages 30 to 60 to gain information about their marriage, family, employment, life satisfactions and dissatisfactions, and life changes. Like Levinson, the researchers found major transitional periods in which subjects seemed to reappraise their life and consider changes. Some of these changes were related to specific chronological ages, but the researchers believe that women's development is examined most profitably in relation to six phases in the family cycle: (1) the *no children phase*,

(2) the *starting a family–preschool phase*, (3) the *school age phase*, (4) the *adolescent phase*, (5) the *launching phase* (beginning when the first child leaves home and ending when the last child leaves), and (6) the *postparental phase*.

Changes were reliably associated with each of the family-cycle phases, regardless of whether women had experienced major transitions. Women experiencing a major transition at the family-preschool phase were more likely to report changes in themselves, and marital separation or divorce. The 40 percent reporting a transition at the launching phase became more introspective and assertive, but very few experienced the empty nest syndrome. One-third of the subjects had major transitions during the postparental phase, when they experienced decreased inner stability, but the transition usually ended with increased life satisfaction.

Life Stages: Fact or Fiction?

Not all researchers accept the notion of stages in adult development. Some, like Bernice Neugarten (1982), seek to develop a greater understanding of the changes that occur during the life span, rather than looking for universals and attempting to make predictions. "Adults change far more, and far less predictably, than the over-simplified stage theories suggest. . . . Choices and dilemmas do not sprout forth at ten-year intervals" (p. 162).

Neugarten warns against assuming that Levinson's findings apply to all adults. Remember that the subjects studied by Levinson and Reinke and colleagues were almost all middle or upper-middle class. Levinson found that 80 percent of his subjects experienced a mid-life crisis, but for many people in our country and around the world, life is one long crisis. For someone facing chronic unemployment, a mid-life crisis that involved choosing to change a job or vocation would be considered a luxury. Changing one's life structure to allow more time for a hobby or avocation is a concern, not for the millions of people struggling to survive, but for those people who already enjoy the necessities of life. Levinson's conclusion that his theory "holds for men and women of different cultures, classes, and historical epochs" is at least premature.

Memory Check 9.4

Match the following researchers with the appropriate statements below (you may use *a*, *b*, or *c* more than once).

a. Erikson   b. Levinson   c. Reinke, Ellicott, and Harris

_____ 1) emphasized the importance of the "life structure" as a key to understanding adult development

_____ 2) found that the most profitable way to examine life changes in a woman's life was in relation to six phases in the family cycle

_____ 3) proposed a set of stages composed of alternating stable and transitional periods that were to be applicable to both men and women

_____ 4) suggested that in middle age, mental health depends on developing an active interest in guiding the next generation

Answers: 1) b 2) c 3) b 4) a

Later Adulthood

Age 65 or 70 is generally considered the beginning of old age, and 12 percent of the United States population is now over age 65. What are your perceptions of life after 65? Complete the *Try It!* by answering *true* or *false* to the statements about older adults.

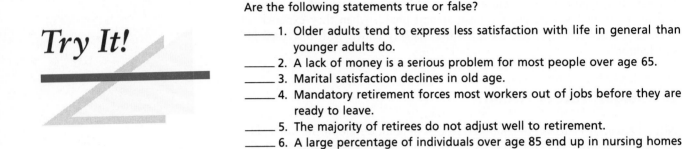

Try It!

Are the following statements true or false?

_____ 1. Older adults tend to express less satisfaction with life in general than younger adults do.

_____ 2. A lack of money is a serious problem for most people over age 65.

_____ 3. Marital satisfaction declines in old age.

_____ 4. Mandatory retirement forces most workers out of jobs before they are ready to leave.

_____ 5. The majority of retirees do not adjust well to retirement.

_____ 6. A large percentage of individuals over age 85 end up in nursing homes or institutions.

Most people give the wrong answers to questions such as these about older adults. The statements are all false. But one thing we do know is that when we reach our seventies or eighties, strenuous physical activity is definitely out for us. Right? Wrong! You remember Hulda Crooks who was climbing mountains at age 92. Many other older adults are physically (and mentally) running circles around younger people.

Physical Changes in Later Adulthood

Question: What are some physical changes generally associated with later adulthood?

As you learned in chapter 3, "Sensation and Perception," the elderly lose some of their sensory capacity. With advancing age, they typically become more farsighted and have increasingly impaired night vision (Koretz & Handelman, 1988; Long & Crambert, 1990). They suffer hearing loss in the higher frequencies and often have difficulty following a conversation when there is competing background noise (Sekuler & Blake, 1987). There may be difficulty with balance because of a deterioration in the vestibular senses.

Older bodies generally slow down. The brain takes longer to process information, and reaction time is slower (Botwinick & Birren, 1963; Butler, 1968). There is a decline in heart, lung, kidney, and muscle function, and older adults typically have less energy and stamina. Joints become stiffer, and bones lose calcium and become more brittle, increasing the risk of fractures from falls.

About 80 percent of senior citizens have one or more chronic conditions such as arthritis, rheumatism, heart problems, or high blood pressure. For both males and females, the three leading causes of death are heart disease, cancer, and stroke (U.S. Bureau of the Census, 1990). But the good news is that in spite of all of these changes, the vast majority of people over age 65 consider their health good. One-half of those aged 75 to 84 and more than one-third of those over 85 do not have to curb their activities because of health problems (Toufexis, 1988).

Although one of the greatest fears among the elderly is that of spending their last years in a nursing home, only 5 percent of those over 65 are in nursing homes or other institutions (Palmore, 1981). So, many Americans over 65 may be fit, healthy, and happy—especially if they exercise.

Fitness and Aging   Men and women in their sixties and seventies who exercise properly and regularly can have the energy and fitness of someone 20 to 30 years younger (deVries, 1986). Recent research suggests that physical exercise even enhances the performance of older adults on tests of reaction time, working memory, and reasoning (Clarkson-Smith & Hartley, 1990). "People rust out faster from disuse than they wear out from overuse" (Horn & Meer, 1987, p. 83). For most of us, the chance to remain fit and vigorous as we age, lies within our power. Even the pleasures of sex are still enjoyed by many who are well advanced in years.

Sex and the Senior Citizen   Masters and Johnson (1966) studied the sexual response in men and women at the climacteric and older, and they found that regular sexual relations are necessary to maintain effective sexual performance. In a recent survey of adults ages 80 to 102 who were not taking medication, 70 percent of the men and 50 percent of the women admitted fantasizing about intimate sexual relations often or very often. But 63 percent of men and 30 percent of the women were doing more than fantasizing—they reported having had sexual intercourse recently (McCartney, 1989). And remember, they were between 80 and 102.

Cognitive Development in Later Adulthood

*Question: **What happens to mental ability in later adulthood?***

For years it was thought that intellectual decline in late adulthood was expected and inevitable. Researchers are now finding that those who keep mentally and physically active retain their mental skills as long as their health is good (Meer, 1986). Older adults do well on tests of vocabulary, comprehension, and general information, and their ability to solve practical problems is generally higher than that of young adults. But because older adults perform tasks more slowly, they usually perform more poorly on tests requiring speed.

Another error is to equate old age with forgetfulness. When memory ability is assessed, large differences between age groups are not revealed (Crook & Larrabee, 1990). Memory failures in older adults are judged by young and old alike as signifying a more serious problem than the same memory failures in younger people (Erber et al., 1990). Two of the most common and annoying age-related memory complaints are being unable to recall a name or to think of a word needed in a conversation (Lovelace & Twohig, 1990).

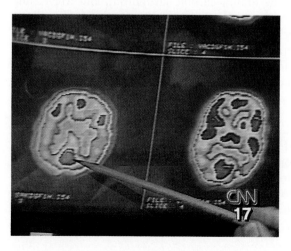

Researchers are using PET scans to help diagnose Alzheimer's disease in its early stages.

People with Alzheimer's disease function best in a stable, structured environment. Strategically placed signs can remind them of simple tasks they should perform.

Intellectual functioning can be hampered by physical problems (Manton et al., 1986) or by psychological problems such as depression. Those who continue to function at the highest levels are usually those with more education (Zabrucky et al., 1987) because they are most likely to stay mentally active, read, and use a variety of cognitive skills. Women generally show less decline than men, and interestingly, those with a high degree of intellectual functioning tend to live longer (Neugarten, 1976).

Senile Dementia   Senile dementia, commonly referred to as senility, is a state of severe mental deterioration marked by impaired memory and intellect, as well as by altered personality and behavior. "The usual estimate is that moderate to severe dementia can be found in 4% to 6% of those aged 65 and older" (Gatz & Pearson, 1988, p. 186) and in about 25 percent of those people over 85 (U.S. Congress Office of Technical Assessment, 1987).

Sometimes people who are overmedicated or who are suffering from depression have symptoms that mimic those of senility, but the symptoms usually go away when the condition is treated. True senility is caused by physical deterioration of the brain. It can result from such conditions as cerebral arteriosclerosis (hardening of the arteries in the brain), chronic alcoholism, and irreversible damage by a series of small strokes. About 50 to 60 percent of all cases of senility result from Alzheimer's disease (Terry & Katzman, 1983).

In **Alzheimer's disease** there is a progressive deterioration of intellect and personality resulting from widespread degeneration of brain cells. At first its victims show a gradual impairment in memory and reasoning, and in their efficiency in carrying out everyday tasks. Many have difficulty finding their way around in familiar locations. As the disorder progresses, Alzheimer's patients become confused and irritable, tend to wander away from home, and become increasingly unable to care for themselves. Eventually their speech becomes unintelligible, and they become incontinent (unable to control bladder and bowel function). If they live long enough they will reach a stage where they do not respond when spoken to and no longer recognize even their spouse or children. The exact cause of Alzheimer's disease is unknown although some cases appear to be hereditary. There is presently no known cure.

senile dementia: A state of mental deterioration caused by physical deterioration of the brain and characterized by impaired memory and intellect, as well as by altered personality and behavior; senility.

Alzheimer's disease (ALZ-hye-merz):   An incurable form of dementia characterized by progressive deterioration of intellect and personality, resulting from widespread degeneration of brain cells.

Personality and Social Development in Later Adulthood

Question: According to Erikson, what is the key to a positive resolution of his eighth psychosocial stage—ego integrity versus despair?

ego integrity versus despair: Erikson's eighth and final psychosocial stage, occurring during old age, when individuals look back on their lives with satisfaction and a sense of accomplishment or have major regrets about missed opportunities and mistakes.

Erikson's Final Psychosocial Stage: Ego Integrity versus Despair Psychosocial development continues into later adulthood, but its course is usually an extension of the former life pattern. In Erikson's eighth stage, **ego integrity versus despair**, the outcome depends primarily on whether a person has resolved the conflicts at the previous stages (Erikson et al., 1986). Those who have a sense of ego integrity believe their life has had meaning. They can look back on their life with satisfaction and a sense of accomplishment, and they are not burdened with major regrets.

> At the other extreme is the individual who looks back upon his life as a series of missed opportunities and missed directions; now in the twilight years he realizes that it is too late to start again. For such a person the inevitable result is a sense of despair at what might have been. (Elkind, 1970, p. 112)

Social Development and Adjustment in Later Adulthood Would you say that people are more satisfied with their marriages and with life in general when they are young adults or when they are over 65? It may surprise you to learn that several major national surveys have revealed that satisfaction and feelings of well-being are about as high in older as in younger adults (see Figure 9.8).

Life satisfaction appears to be most related to good health. In addition, it appears that "a minimum level of companionship and social activity are key elements in maintaining a sense of well-being" (Thompson & Heller, 1990, p. 541). Two studies relate happiness in career and marriage to life satisfaction in old age for men (Mussen et al., 1982; Sears, 1977). These findings provide support for Freud's definition of mental health as the ability to love and work. Another factor related to psychological and physical well-being for older adults is a feeling of control over their life (Rowe & Kahn, 1987).

Much has been said about the elderly poor. About 12 percent of older Americans live below the poverty level, and among them a disproportionately high number of black senior citizens (about one-third) live on less than $5,300 annually (McGrath, 1987). But the average income for the 65-plus group is $22,000 (Gibbs, 1988). Many older adults have homes that are paid for and no children

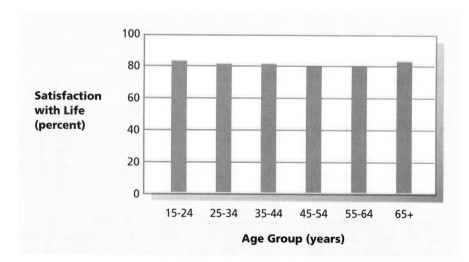

Figure 9.8

Age and Life Satisfaction

Surveys including subjects from many nationalities reveal that levels of life satisfaction and happiness remain much the same and relatively high (approximately 80 percent) throughout life. (Data from Inglehart, 1990.)

to support, so it is not surprising that people over 65 tend to view their financial situation more positively than do young adults.

Yet there is a grim side to old age. It is a period during which many losses occur, and the longer people live, the more losses they experience. Health inevitably declines, friends die, and some who do not wish to retire must do so for health reasons or because of company policies. Eventually one spouse dies, and if the other lives long enough, he or she will be increasingly dependent on others. When life becomes more burdensome than enjoyable, the older person can fall victim to depression. Depression is a major problem affecting about 15 percent of the elderly, and white males over age 75 have the highest suicide rate of any age group in our society (Roybal, 1988).

Retirement: Leaving the World of Work   To many people retirement marks the end of middle age and the beginning of old age. Younger people tend to see retirement as a time when people are forced to leave their jobs and are "put out to pasture"—an event that is seen as leading to premature death. But most retirees are happy to leave the world of work. In spite of the change in the mandatory retirement age from 65 to 70 in 1978, fewer than 12.5 percent of people over age 65 remain in the work force. Generally the people most reluctant to retire are those who are better educated, hold high-status jobs with a good income, and find fulfillment in their work. Bosse and others (1991) found that only 30 percent of retirees reported finding retirement stressful, and of those who did, most were likely to be in poor health and have financial problems.

Another misconception is that many retirees experience a sudden decline in health or die soon after retirement. Those in ill health, for the most part, were ill before they retired.

Losing a Spouse: The Hardest Blow   For most people, losing a spouse is the most stressful event in a lifetime, and more women than men experience this loss. In 1989, 48.7 percent of women over age 65 lost a spouse compared with only 14 percent of men. There were only about 69 males for every 100 females age 65 and older (U.S. Bureau of the Census, 1991). Both widow and widower are at a greater risk for health problems and have a higher mortality rate than those of the same age who are not bereaved (Kaprio et al., 1987; Wildholz et al., 1985).

Losing a spouse leaves a great void in the life of the survivor, and depression is a likely reaction (Norris & Murrell, 1990). Gone is one's best friend, companion, and lover. Not only must the remaining spouse endure the grief process alone, but survivors must restructure their lives—home life, daily routine, and social life.

Terminal Illness and Death

One of the developmental tasks for the elderly is to accept the inevitability of their own death and to prepare themselves for it. At no time does this become more critical than when people face a terminal illness.

Question: According to Kübler-Ross, what stages are experienced by terminally ill patients as they come to terms with death?

Elisabeth Kübler-Ross On Death and Dying: The Final Exit   Psychiatrist Elisabeth Kübler-Ross (1969) interviewed some 200 terminally ill people and found commonalties in their reactions to their impending death. In her book *On*

WORLD OF PSYCHOLOGY:

MULTICULTURAL PERSPECTIVES

Culture, Race, and Care for the Elderly

Every weekday morning, Willard Scott, of the "Today" show, features women and men across America who are among the oldest of the old, usually 100 years or older. Living past 100 is not as rare as in decades past. The fastest growing segment of our population consists of those 85 and older (Thomas, 1992). Where are these older Americans living? Are most people in their eighties, nineties, and hundreds sitting in nursing homes, or are they living in the same household with their adult children or other relatives? Older women are more likely than older men to live with their adult children. However, there are more older women than men because women have a longer life expectancy. Are there racial, cultural, and gender differences in the ways in which older family members are viewed, treated, and cared for?

Older African Americans as well as Asian and Hispanic Americans more often live with and are cared for by their adult children than is true of other elderly Americans. Blacks are more likely than whites to regard elderly persons with respect and to feel that children should help their older parents (Mui, 1992).

Multi-generational households are by no means commonplace among most racial groups in America. From the mid-1970s to the present, only about 18 percent of older parents live in the same household with one of their adult children (Crimmins & Ingegneri, 1990). And even in these multi-generational households, it is more often the case that adult children move into the elderly parent's home than that the older parent comes to live with one of the children. For the most part, older Americans have a strong preference for maintaining their independence and living in their own home. At the same time, the majority of older Americans, and their adult children as well, express a desire to live near each other (Bengtson et al., 1990).

The living arrangements of American families are not typical of other countries around the world. In many Latin American countries—in Columbia, Costa Rica, the Dominican Republic, Mexico, Panama, and Peru—the majority of elderly people do live in the same household with younger generations in an extended family setting (De Vos, 1990). Economic and social necessity often dictate living arrangements.

Are elderly family members accorded less respect and viewed as more of a burden to adult children and grandchildren in America than in non-Western cultures? Popular opinion holds that the elderly in Asian cultures are venerated, highly esteemed, and accorded great respect by family members and the culture in general. It is true that non-

Western cultures (Japan, for example) have carried forward traditions of long standing that value older family members. Three-generation households have been the rule rather than the exception among the Japanese. How do attitudes toward providing care for aged relatives differ between the two cultures?

Elaine Brody and others (1984) studied the attitudes of three generations of American women on providing care for their aged relatives. Her study was replicated with a comparable sample of three generations of Japanese women in Tokyo (Campbell & Brody, 1985). Only women's attitudes were studied because the care of aged relatives is typically provided by female family members in both countries. These studies yielded some surprising findings when attitudes of the American and Japanese samples were compared.

It was expected that the Japanese women would express a stronger sense of obligation toward their older family members. They did not. The American women expressed a stronger sense of obligation toward elderly members of their family, such as helping them with household chores, than the Japanese women did. The American women expressed stronger agreement that their aged parents should be able to look to them for help.

Campbell and Brody (1985) suggest that the difference in attitudes may be explained by cultural differences in the way that help is provided to older family members. Daughters typically care for their elderly parents in the United States. In Japan daughters-in-law most often care for elderly family members because those who cannot care for themselves are most likely to live in the home of their oldest son. Attitudes between daughters and parents are likely to be more positive than attitudes between daughters-in-law and their husband's parents.

Death and Dying she identifies five stages most subjects went through in coming to terms with death.

In the first stage, denial and isolation, most patients react to the initial awareness of their terminal illness with shock and disbelief. When denial can no longer be maintained, it gives way to the second stage, anger, which is marked by feelings of anger, rage, envy of those who are young and healthy, and resentment. "Why me?" is the question that rages inside. In the third stage, bargaining, the person attempts to postpone death for a specific period of time in return for a promise of "good behavior." An individual may offer God some special service or a promise to live a certain kind of life in exchange for an opportunity to attend a child's wedding or a grandchild's graduation.

Eventually the bargaining stops and gives way to the fourth stage, depression. This stage brings a great sense of loss—physical loss, loss of money due to expensive treatments, loss of ability to function in their job or in the role of mother, father, husband, or wife. The depression takes two forms—depression over past losses and over impending losses.

If enough time remains, patients usually reach the final stage, acceptance, in which they are neither depressed nor angry about their fate. They stop struggling against death and are able to contemplate its coming without fear or despair. Kübler-Ross claims that the family also goes through stages similar to those experienced by the patient. She believes the "goal should always be to help the patient and his family face the crisis together in order to achieve acceptance of this final reality simultaneously" (p. 173).

Elisabeth Kübler-Ross has made the public aware of the needs and feelings of the dying. Although other researchers acknowledge that her proposed stages often do occur, they deny their universality and their invariant sequence (Butler & Lewis, 1982; Kastenbaum & Costa, 1977).

Death and dying are not pleasant subjects, but remember that life itself is a terminal condition, and each day of life should certainly be treasured like a precious gift. Hulda Crooks, in addressing the elderly, would tell them: "We should be role models to show young people that life is worth living to the last breath" (Innerviews, 1988, p. 64). And what a role model she was!

Memory Check 9.5

1. About (5, 10) percent of people over age 65 are in nursing homes or other institutions.

2. Which of these theorists describes old age as a time of reflection?

   a. Erikson   c. Levinson
   b. Kübler-Ross   d. Kohlberg

3. People over age 65 report (more, less) satisfaction in their marriages and with life in general than do young adults.

4. The researcher known for her work on death and dying is:

   a. Erikson   c. Levinson
   b. Kübler-Ross   d. Kohlberg

Answers: 1. 5 2. a 3. more 4. b

Thinking Critically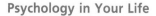

Evaluation

In your opinion, do Erikson's psychosocial stages for adolescence and early adulthood accurately represent the major conflicts of these periods of life? Why or why not?

Point/Counterpoint

Daniel Levinson has suggested a theory of adult development, for both men and women, that includes stages and transitional periods coming at certain chronological ages. Reinke, Ellicott, and Harris have suggested a stage theory for women that revolves around phases in the family cycle. Prepare an argument supporting each of the following positions:

a. Levinson's theory is superior to that of Reinke, Ellicott, and Harris in explaining development in women.
b. Reinke, Ellicott, and Harris's theory is superior to Levinson's in explaining development in women.

Psychology in Your Life

Think back to your junior high school and high school years. To what degree do you believe early or late maturation affected how boys and girls were treated by their peers, their parents, or their teachers? Did early or late maturation affect their adjustment? Explain your answer.

Chapter Summary and Review

Adolescence: Physical and Cognitive Development

What physical changes occur during puberty?

Puberty is a period marked by rapid physical growth (the adolescent growth spurt), further development of the reproductive organs, and the appearance of the secondary sex characteristics. The major event for girls is menarche, the first menstruation, and for boys, the first ejaculation.

What are the psychological effects of early and late maturation on boys and girls?

Early maturation provides enhanced status for boys because of their early advantage in sports and greater attractiveness to girls. Late maturation puts the male at a distinct disadvantage in these areas and results in a lack of confidence that may persist into adulthood. The effects for girls are less clear-cut.

What are the major symptoms of anorexia nervosa and bulimia nervosa?

The major symptoms of anorexia nervosa are compulsive dieting to the point of self-starvation and excessive weight loss. The major symptoms of bulimia nervosa are repeated and uncontrolled periods of binge eating followed by purging.

What cognitive abilities develop during the formal operations stage?

During the formal operations stage adolescents develop the ability to think abstractly, to attack problems by systematically testing hypotheses, to draw conclusions through deductive reasoning, and to think hypothetically.

Key Terms

adolescence (p. 298)
puberty (p. 299)
adolescent growth spurt (p. 299)
secondary sex characteristics (p. 299)
menarche (p. 300)
anorexia nervosa (p. 301)
bulimia nervosa (p. 302)
formal operations stage (p. 302)
imaginary audience (p. 303)
personal fable (p. 303)

Adolescence: Moral, Personality, and Social Development

Briefly explain Kohlberg's three levels of moral reasoning.

At Kohlberg's preconventional level, moral reasoning is based on the physical consequences of an act—"right" is whatever avoids punishment or gains a reward. At the conventional level, right and wrong are based on the internalized standards of others—"right" is whatever helps or is approved of by others, or whatever is consistent with the laws of society. Post-conventional moral reasoning involves weighing moral alternatives—"right" is whatever furthers basic human rights.

How does Erikson explain the fifth stage of psychosocial development—identity versus role confusion?

In Erikson's fifth psychosocial stage, identity versus role confusion, adolescents seek to establish their identity and find values to guide their lives. Difficulty at this stage can result in an identity crisis.

What are some of the useful functions of the adolescent peer group?

The adolescent peer group, usually composed of teens of the same sex, race, and similar social background, provides a vehicle for developing social skills and a standard of comparison against which their attributes can be evaluated.

Key Terms

preconventional level (p. 305)
conventional level (p. 305)
postconventional level (p. 305)
identity versus role confusion (p. 309)

Early and Middle Adulthood

What are the physical changes associated with middle age?

Physical changes associated with middle age are a need for reading glasses, a greater susceptibility to life-threatening diseases, and the menopause, or end of reproductive capacity, in women and a declining reproductive capacity in men.

In general, can adults look forward to an increase or a decrease in intellectual performance from their twenties to forties?

Although younger people tend to do better on tests requiring speed or rote memory, intellectual performance in adults continues to increase in other areas. Scholars, scientists, and those in the arts are usually most productive in their forties.

What is Erikson's psychosocial task for early adulthood?

In Erikson's sixth psychosocial stage, intimacy versus isolation, the young adult must establish intimacy in a relationship in order to avoid feeling a sense of isolation and loneliness.

What are some of the trends in life-style patterns in young adulthood?

The "traditional" family—mother, father, and several children—now comprises only 27 percent of households in the United States. Couples are waiting longer to have children, and 57 percent of women with children under age 6 hold full-time or part-time jobs outside the home.

What effect does parenthood have on marital satisfaction?

Even though most couples want children, satisfaction with marriage, particularly in women, tends to decline after children arrive. This decline can be explained in part by the unequal work load carried by mothers employed outside the home.

What changes does Erikson believe are essential for healthy personality development in middle age?

Erikson's seventh psychosocial stage, generativity versus stagnation, occurs during middle age. Individuals must develop generativity—an interest in establishing and guiding the next generation—in order to avoid stagnation.

Key Terms

menopause (p. 313)
intimacy versus isolation (p. 314)
generativity versus stagnation (p. 318)

Theories of Adulthood

How is Levinson's concept of life structure related to his proposed stages of development?

According to Daniel Levinson's stage theory of adult development, all people go through a fixed set of stages. During transitional periods individuals review and evaluate their lives and their life structure (the basic design of their life); during stable periods they make choices that form the basis of a revised life structure and then proceed to pursue their goals within it.

What did Reinke, Ellicott, and Harris's study of middle-class women reveal about major transitional periods in the life cycle?

Reinke, Ellicott, and Harris found that middle-class women went through major transitional periods that could be related more easily to phases in the family cycle than to chronological age.

Key Terms

life structure (p. 319)
mid-life crisis (p. 319)

Later Adulthood

What are some physical changes generally associated with later adulthood?

In addition to obvious changes in appearance, physical changes generally associated with later adulthood are a decline in sensory capacity; a decline in heart, lung, kidney, and muscle function; and an increase in the number of chronic conditions such as arthritis, heart problems, and high blood pressure.

What happens to mental ability in later adulthood?

Although older adults perform tasks more slowly, those who keep mentally and physically active can usually maintain their mental skills as long as their health holds out.

According to Erikson, what is the key to a positive resolution of his eighth psychosocial stage—ego integrity versus despair?

Erikson's psychosocial stage for old age, ego integrity versus despair, is a time for reflection, when people look back on their lives with satisfaction and a sense of accomplishment or have major regrets about missed opportunities and mistakes.

According to Kübler-Ross, what stages are experienced by terminally ill patients as they come to terms with death?

Elisabeth Kübler-Ross maintains that terminally ill patients go through five stages in coming to terms with death: denial, anger, bargaining, depression, and acceptance.

Key Terms

senile dementia (p. 324)
Alzheimer's disease (p. 324)
ego integrity versus despair (p. 325)

10

Motivation and Emotion

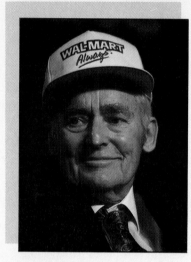

Donald Trump

Sam Walton

Picture a wheeler-dealer in grand fashion, a tycoon with a capital T, a champion of conspicuous consumption with an insatiable appetite for all things material—bigger, faster, more. Have you got the picture? You are looking at Donald Trump. At the peak of his power in 1989, he hopped from one glamorous event to another, swooping down from the sky in his French-built Super Puma jet helicopter—the only one in the United States. With his gambling casinos and hotels in New Jersey, Trump Enterprises, grand hotels, housing units, and Trump Tower in New York, Donald Trump commanded an empire valued at hundreds of millions of dollars.

How did Trump get his start? He was child of privilege. His father, Fred, amassed a 40-million-dollar fortune as a real estate developer. Through the 1970s and the 1980s, Donald Trump was able to spin those millions into a billion plus. Then his troubles began to mount. An extramarital affair with model Marla Maples caused his wife Ivana to divorce him. His bankers and other investors lost confidence in his grand schemes and in his ability to repay his loans. Falling on hard times, Trump may soon owe more than he owns.

A study in excess and exaggeration, Donald Trump has always enjoyed flaunting his wealth and bragging about his conquests. His way of life has been one of the most flamboyant "life-styles of the rich and famous." What motivates him?

Now meet a very different person. This man would rise early every morning and have a simple breakfast with his wife in their small-town home in the hilly Ozark region of Arkansas. He would climb into his beat-up 1978 Ford pickup truck and drive a few miles to his work.

This man, a child of poverty, worked his way though the University of Missouri by selling newspapers and found a job as a management trainee at a J.C. Penney store in Iowa. Then came World War II, and he was drafted in 1942. After the war, he scraped together enough money to open his own small store in rural Arkansas, but he had to close it in 1951 when the building owner would not renew his lease.

He started all over again, but more than 10 years passed before he began to achieve success in business. When someone remarked about the extent of his growing wealth, he replied, "Aw, it's only paper. All I've got is a pickup truck and some stock in Wal-Mart."

Have you heard of this man, and do you know how much paper he was talking about? Sam Walton built a merchandising empire with his Wal-Mart stores, and the "paper" he so casually dismissed was worth nearly 20 billion dollars in 1992 and is still growing. But Walton was not just another billionaire. Twice as wealthy as the second richest person on the 1988 *Forbes' 400* list of the four hundred wealthiest people, Walton split his billions with his wife and their four children in 1989. He wanted to escape the "embarrassment" of being called the richest person in America.

Sam Walton was obviously not primarily motivated by the things that money can buy. Richest of the rich in America, and yet he lived a simple, frugal life-style—no mansions, no yachts, no fleet of superjets or limousines. Only 20 billion dollars worth of paper—and a pickup truck. Sam Walton died in 1992.

motivation: The process that initiates, directs, and sustains behavior satisfying physiological or psychological needs.

PSYCHOLOGISTS HAVE ALWAYS HAD A STRONG INTEREST in trying to determine why people do the things they do. What made the life-styles of Donald Trump and Sam Walton so different? What motivated them? More importantly, what motivates us?

In our study of **motivation**, we will look at the underlying processes that initiate, direct, and sustain behavior in order to satisfy physiological and psychological needs. At any given time our behavior might be explained by one or a combination of **motives**—needs or desires that energize and direct behavior toward a goal. Motives can arise from an internal need, such as when we are hungry and are motivated to find something to eat. In this case we are pushed into action from within. Other motives originate from outside ourselves, as when some external stimulus or **incentive** pulls or entices us to act. After finishing a huge meal, some people yield to the temptation of a delicious dessert. At times like this, it is the enticement of the external tempter, not the internal need for food, that moves us.

The intensity of our motivation, which depends on the number and the strength of the motives involved, has a bearing on the effort and the persistence with which we pursue our goals. Sometimes we pursue an activity as an end in itself simply because it is enjoyable, not because any external reward is attached to it. This type of motivation is known as **intrinsic motivation**. On the other hand, when we engage in activities, not because they are enjoyable, but in order to gain some external reward or to avoid some undesirable consequence, we are pulled by **extrinsic motivation**. If you are working hard in this course solely because you find the subject interesting, then your motivation is intrinsic. But if you are studying only to meet a requirement or to satisfy some other external need, your motivation is extrinsic. In real life, the motives for many activities are both intrinsic and extrinsic. You may love your job, but you would probably be motivated to leave if your salary, an important extrinsic motivator, were taken away. Table 10.1 gives examples of intrinsic and extrinsic motivation.

What do the experts say about the motives behind our behavior? Consider some theories of motivation and find out.

motives: Needs or desires that energize and direct behavior toward a goal.

incentive: An external stimulus that motivates behavior (example: money, fame).

intrinsic motivation: The desire to perform an act because it is satisfying or pleasurable in and of itself.

extrinsic motivation: The desire to perform an act to gain a reward or to avoid an undesirable consequence.

Theories of Motivation

Do we do the things we do because of our inherent nature—the inborn, biological urges that push us from within? Or, do we act because of the incentives that pull us from without? Obviously both forces influence us, but theories of motivation differ in the relative power they attribute to each. The most thoroughly biological theories of motivation are the instinct theories.

Table 10.1

Intrinsic and Extrinsic Motivation

	Description	Examples
Intrinsic motivation	An activity is pursued as an end in itself because it is enjoyable and rewarding.	A person anonymously donates a large sum of money to a university to fund scholarships for hundreds of deserving students.
		A child reads several books each week because reading is fun.
Extrinsic motivation	An activity is pursued to gain an external reward or to avoid an undesirable consequence.	A person agrees to donate a large sum of money to a university for the construction of a building, provided it will bear the family name.
		A child reads two books each week to avoid losing television privileges.

instinct: An inborn, unlearned, fixed pattern of behavior that is characteristic of
an entire species.

instinct theory: The notion
that human behavior is motivated by certain innate tendencies, or instincts, shared
by all individuals.

drive-reduction theory: A
theory of motivation suggesting that a need creates an
unpleasant state of arousal or
tension called a drive, which
impels the organism to engage
in behavior that will satisfy
the need and reduce tension.

drive: A state of tension or
arousal brought about by an
underlying need, which motivates one to engage in behavior that will satisfy the need
and reduce the tension.

Instinct Theories of Motivation

Question: How do instinct theories explain motivation?

We have learned much about instincts by observing animal behavior. Spiders instinctively spin their intricate webs without having *learned* the technique from other spiders. It is neither a choice they make nor a task they learn, but an instinct. An **instinct** is an inborn, unlearned, fixed pattern of behavior that is characteristic of an entire species. An instinct does not improve with practice, and an animal will perform it the same way even if it has never seen another member of its species. Even when their web-spinning glands are removed, spiders still perform the complex spinning movements and then lay their eggs in the imaginary web they have spun.

But can human motivation be explained by **instinct theory**—the notion that human behavior is motivated by certain innate, unlearned tendencies or instincts that are shared by all individuals? The idea of attributing human as well as animal behavior to instincts was not seriously considered until Charles Darwin, in his *Origin of Species* (1859), suggested that humans evolved from lower animals. The notion of the continuity of the species paved the way for applying the concept of instinct to explain human behavior (Weiner, 1980).

William James (1890), the first American psychologist, claimed that human behavior is even more instinctive than the behavior of lower animals. In addition to the biological instincts, James suggested that a number of social and psychological attributes should be considered human instincts, including sociability, jealousy, fearfulness, parental love, modesty, rivalry, shyness, cleanliness—some 15 attributes in all.

Another instinct theorist, William McDougall (1908), believed that instincts were "the prime movers of all human activity." Without instincts, he claimed, humans would be incapable of and kind of activity" and would simply "lie inert and motionless" (p. 44). By 1938 McDougall had identified what he considered to be 17 instincts, including the parental instinct, curiosity, escape, reproduction, acquisitiveness, self-assertion, and pugnacity (the fighting instinct). Even Sigmund Freud believed that instincts motivated much of human behavior, but he considered instinctive sexual and aggressive urges to be the prime motivators.

Instinct theory was widely accepted by psychologists and others for the first 20 or 30 years of this century. Within those decades the list of instincts expanded until thousands of instincts were being proposed to explain human behavior. Common experience alone suggests that human behavior is too richly diverse, and too often unpredictable to be considered fixed and invariant across our species. Most present-day psychologists reject the instinct theory as an explanation of human motivation.

Drive-Reduction Theory: Striving to Keep a Balanced Internal State

Question: What is the drive-reduction theory of motivation?

Another major attempt to explain motivation, human and otherwise, is the **drive-reduction theory**, or the drive theory, popularized by Clark Hull (1943). According to Hull, all living organisms have certain biological needs that must be met if they are to survive. A need gives rise to an internal state of tension or arousal called a **drive**, and we are motivated to reduce it. For example, when we are deprived of food or go too long without water, our biological need causes a state of tension, in this case the hunger or thirst drive. We become motivated to seek food or water to reduce the drive and satisfy our biological need.

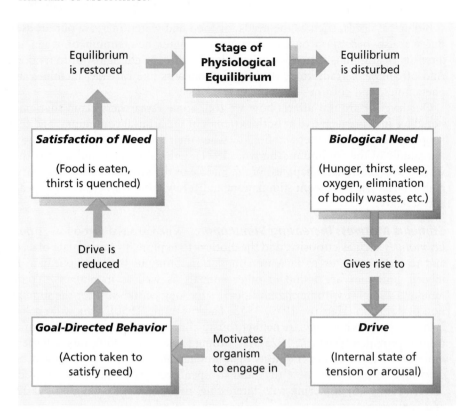

Figure 10.1

Drive-Reduction Theory

Drive-reduction theory is based on the biological concept of homeostasis—the body's natural tendency to maintain a state of internal balance, or equilibrium. When the equilibrium becomes disturbed (as when we are thirsty and need water), a drive (internal state of arousal) emerges. Then the organism is motivated to take action to satisfy the need, thus reducing the drive and restoring equilibrium.

Drive-reduction theory is derived largely from the biological concept of **homeostasis**—the tendency of the body to maintain a balanced, internal state in order to insure physical survival. Body temperature, blood sugar, water balance, oxygen—in short, everything required for physical existence—must be maintained in a state of equilibrium, or balance. When this state is disturbed, a drive is created to restore the balance, as shown in Figure 10.1. But drive theory cannot fully account for the broad range of human motivation.

It is true that we are sometimes motivated to reduce tension, as the drive-reduction theory states, but often we are just as motivated to increase it. Why do people seek activities that actually create a state of tension—hang-gliding, horror movies, or bungee-jumping? Why do animals and humans alike engage in exploratory behavior when it does not serve to reduce any primary drive?

Arousal Theory: Striving for an Optimal Level of Arousal

Question: How does arousal theory explain motivation?

Arousal theory can answer some of the puzzling questions that drive-reduction theory cannot answer. *Arousal* refers to a person's state of alertness and mental and physical activation. It ranges from no arousal (as in the comatose), to moderate arousal (when we are pursing normal day-to-day activities), to high arousal (when we are excited and highly stimulated).

Unlike drive reduction theories, **arousal theory** does not suggest that we are always motivated to reduce arousal or tension. Arousal theory states that we are motivated to maintain an optimal level of arousal. If arousal is less than the optimal level, we do something to stimulate it; if arousal exceeds the optimal level, we seek to reduce the stimulation.

homeostasis: The tendency of the body to maintain a balanced internal state with regard to oxygen level, body temperature, blood sugar, water balance, and so forth.

arousal: A state of alertness and mental and physical activation.

arousal theory: A theory suggesting that the aim of motivation is to maintain an optimal level of arousal.

Biological needs, such as the needs for food and water, increase our arousal. But we also become aroused when we encounter new stimuli or when the intensity of stimuli is increased, as with loud noises, bright lights, or foul odors. And of course, certain kinds of drugs—stimulants like caffeine, nicotine, amphetamines, and cocaine—also increase arousal.

Our level of arousal affects how we feel. Some researchers claim that emotional feelings are negative at both extremes of the arousal continuum, and that people generally feel better emotionally when their arousal level is somewhere in the middle of the continuum (Berlyne, 1971). Others disagree and suggest that we are not emotionally happiest in the middle of the arousal continuum, but at high arousal when we want stimulation, and at low arousal when we want peace and serenity.

Stimulus Motives: Increasing Stimulation   When arousal is too low, *stimulus motives* such as curiosity, and the motives to explore, to manipulate objects, and to play, cause us to increase stimulation. Stimulus motives appear to be inborn, and they are found in other animals as well as in humans. Young monkeys will play with mechanical puzzles for long periods just for the stimulation of doing so (Harlow, 1950, 1953; Harlow et al., 1950). Rats will explore intricate mazes when they are neither thirsty nor hungry and when no reinforcement is provided (Dashiell, 1925). According to Berlyne (1960), rats will spend more time exploring novel objects than familiar objects. So will humans. Children love to play with new toys and to open presents to see what is inside. Adults, too, enjoy tinkering with interesting, new objects, working on puzzles, and exploring.

Individual Differences in Arousal: Too Much for One Is Too Little for Another   We differ in the level of arousal we normally prefer. Some of us are sensation seekers, who love the thrill of new experiences and adventure and are willing, even eager, to take risks. Sensation seekers are particularly susceptible to boredom and have an aversion to predictable people and routine experiences (Weiss, 1987). Other people are the opposite and enjoy the routine and the predictable, avoid risk, and fare best when arousal is relatively low.

Where do you fit into the picture? The *Try It!* will help you determine which level of arousal you prefer.

People vary greatly in their sensation-seeking scores, and there may be gender and cultural differences in sensation-seeking tendencies. Some researchers have found that males tend to score higher on the scale than females, and white Americans tend to score higher than African Americans (Zuckerman, 1979b).

Sometimes arousal can be too low for too long for anyone, even for those who would score lowest on the scale.

Curiosity is one stimulus motive that has led this baby to explore the contents of her mother's purse.

Are you a high or a low sensation seeker?

To test your own sensation-seeking tendencies, try this shortened version of one of Marvin Zuckerman's earlier scales. For each of the 13 items, circle the choice A or B that better describes your feelings.

1 A I would like a job that requires a lot of traveling.
  B I would prefer a job in one location.
2 A I am invigorated by a brisk, cold day.
  B I can't wait to get indoors on a cold day.
3 A I get bored seeing the same old faces.
  B I like the comfortable familiarity of everyday friends.
4 A I would prefer living in an ideal society in which everyone is safe, secure, and happy.
  B I would have preferred living in the unsettled days of our history.
5 A I sometimes like to do things that are a little frightening.
  B A sensible person avoids activities that are dangerous.
6 A I would not like to be hypnotized.
  B I would like to have the experience of being hypnotized.
7 A The most important goal of life is to live it to the fullest and experience as much as possible.
  B The most important goal of life is to find peace and happiness.
8 A I would like to try parachute-jumping.
  B I would never want to try jumping out of a plane, with or without a parachute.
9 A I enter cold water gradually, giving myself time to get used to it.
  B I like to dive or jump right into the ocean or a cold pool.
10 A When I go on a vacation, I prefer the comfort of a good room and bed.
  B When I go on a vacation, I prefer the change of camping out.
11 A I prefer people who are emotionally expressive even if they are a bit unstable.
  B I prefer people who are calm and even-tempered.

12 A A good painting should shock or jolt the senses.
  B A good painting should give one a feeling of peace and security.
13 A People who ride motorcycles must have some kind of unconscious need to hurt themselves.
  B I would like to drive or ride a motorcycle.

Scoring

Count one point for each of the following items that you have circled: 1A, 2A, 3A, 4B, 5A, 6B, 7A, 8A, 9B, 10B, 11A, 12A, 13B. Add up your total and compare it with the norms below.

0–3	Very low
4–5	Low
6–9	Average
10–11	High
12–13	Very high

Source: Zuckerman, M. (1978). The search for high sensation. *Psychology Today.* February, 1978, *pp.* 38–46. Copyright © 1978 by the American Psychological Association. Reprinted by permission.

The Effects of Sensory Deprivation: Sensory Nothingness How would you like to be paid to do absolutely nothing? Bexton and others (1954) at McGill University gave student volunteers this opportunity when they studied the effects of **sensory deprivation**—a condition in which sensory stimulation is reduced to a minimum or eliminated.

Students had to lie motionless in a specially designed sensory deprivation chamber in which sensory stimulation was severely restricted. They wore translucent goggles that reduced visual input to a diffused light. Their hands were placed in cotton gloves, and cardboard cuffs were placed over their lower arms, preventing the sensation of touch. The only sound they heard was the hum of an air conditioner through a foam-rubber headpiece. The subjects could eat, drink, and go to the bathroom when they wanted to. Occasionally they would take tests of motor and mental function. Otherwise they were confined to their sensationless prison.

Did they enjoy the experience? Hardly! Half the subjects quit the experiment after the first two days. Eventually the remaining subjects became irritable, confused, and unable to concentrate. They began to have visual hallucinations. Some began to hear imaginary voices and music and felt as if they were receiving electric shocks or being hit by pellets. Their performance on motor and cognitive tasks deteriorated, and none of the subjects said they liked the experiment. Based on this study, it appears that normal mental functioning depends on a changing sensory environment. In addition, severe restrictions on sensory stimulation can have serious physical and psychological effects.

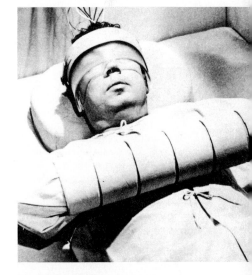

sensory deprivation: A disturbing condition in which sensory stimulation is reduced to a minimum or eliminated.

We humans are complex creatures and our motives are often baffling to other people. Mountain climbers risk life, limb, and frostbite; drug users flirt with death when they smoke crack, shoot heroin, or use similar substances. What are the motives? Where is the pleasure in such activities?

The Opponent-Process Theory: Emotions on a See-Saw

Question: What is the opponent-process theory of motivation?

Another attempt to explain why people seek high-arousal activities is the **opponent-process theory**, put forth by Richard Solomon and I. D. Corbit (1974; Solomon, 1980). You learned about the opponent-process theory of color vision in chapter 3, "Sensation and Perception."

Solomon and Corbit apply the opponent-process theory to motivation. They claim that in the opponent process, the emotional state we feel in response to certain activities or stimuli usually gives way to the opposite emotional state. Consider a frightening activity, such as parachute jumping. Solomon claims that the tremendous relief and elation following a sky-diving experience leads a person to repeat the activity in order to re-experience the feeling of elation. According to the opponent-process theory, the initial emotion gradually weakens with repetition of the activity. The opposing emotion becomes stronger and eventually provides the motivation for the activity. The terror of the free-fall gradually subsides, leaving the person to experience more of a thrill. The opposite emotion, that is, the elation and the exhilaration, intensifies and is prolonged, thus motivating the person to repeat the activity.

Solomon and Corbit propose their theory as an explanation of how people become addicted to drugs. The first few doses of an opiate such as heroin "produce a potent pleasure called the 'rush,' followed by a less intense state of euphoria" (Solomon, 1980, p. 696). Before long, euphoria gives way to the opposite emotion—a state of discomfort that leads to a craving for more of the drug. Remember, the researchers claim that as the activity is repeated, the initial emotion (the pleasure of the high) becomes weaker, and the opposite emotion (the withdrawal and the craving) becomes stronger. With successive doses, the motive for taking the drug changes. Rather than taking the drug for the high it provides, the addict wants the drug to end the withdrawal and the craving. Some research does support the opponent-process theory as it applies to drug addiction (Siegel et al., 1982).

Solomon (1980) further suggests that the opponent-process theory helps explain why "repeated pleasures lose a lot of their pleasantness" and "repeated aversive events lose a lot of their unpleasantness" (p. 709).

Maslow's Hierarchy of Needs: Putting Our Needs in Order

Question: How does Maslow's hierarchy of needs account for human motivation?

Humans have a variety of needs or motives. Clearly some needs are more critical to sustaining life than others. We could live without self-esteem, but obviously we could not live long without air to breathe, water to drink, or food to eat.

Abraham Maslow (1970) proposed a **hierarchy of needs** (Figure 10.2) to account for the range of human motivation. He placed physiological needs at the bottom of the hierarchy, stating that these needs must be adequately satisfied before higher ones can be considered.

opponent-process theory: A theory of motivation suggesting that the emotional state in response to certain activities or stimuli will usually give way to the opposite emotion; with repetition of the activity, the initial emotion gradually weakens, and the opposing emotion strengthens, eventually providing the motivation for the activity.

hierarchy of needs: Maslow's theory of motivation in which needs are arranged in order of urgency ranging from physical needs to security needs, belonging needs, esteem needs, and finally the need for self-actualization.

Self-
Actualization
Need to realize
one's fullest potential

Esteem Needs
Need to achieve, gain
competence, gain respect and
recognition from others

Belonging and Love Needs
Need to love and be loved; need to affiliate
with others and be accepted

Safety Needs
Need for safety and security

Physiological Needs
Need to satisfy the basic biological needs for food,
water, oxygen, sleep, and elimination of bodily wastes

If our physiological needs (for water, food, sleep, sex, and shelter) are adequately met, then the motives at the next higher level (the safety and the security needs) will come into play. When these needs are satisfied, we climb another level to satisfy our needs to belong and to love and be loved. Still higher are the needs for self-esteem and the esteem of others. At the top of Maslow's hierarchy is the need for **self-actualization**, the need to actualize or realize our full potential.

Although Maslow's hierarchy of needs has been a popular notion, appealing to many, it has not been verified by empirical research. The steps on the hierarchy cannot be said to be invariant, or the same for all people (Wahba & Bridwell, 1976). We know from our own experience that for some people, the desire for success and recognition is so strong that they are prepared to sacrifice safety, security, and all other relationships to achieve it. A few people are willing to sacrifice their very lives for others or for a cause to which they are committed. Perhaps they too, have a hierarchy, but one in which the order of needs is somewhat different.

Memory Check 10.1

1. When you engage in an activity in order to gain a reward or to avoid an unpleasant consequence, your motivation is (intrinsic, extrinsic).

2. (Drive-reduction, Instinct) theory suggests that human behavior is motivated by certain innate, unlearned tendencies which are shared by all individuals.

(continued)

self-actualization: The process of striving to develop one's full potential; the highest need on Maslow's hierarchy.

3. Drive-reduction theory best explains our motivation to satisfy (biological, social) needs.

4. Arousal level suggests that we seek to maintain a(n) (high, low, optimal) level of arousal.

5. The esteem needs are at the top of Maslow's hierarchy. (true/false)

6. The opponent-process theory states that if you engage in a frightening activity, you will probably feel a sense of relief or elation when it is over. The theory suggests that you will want to (avoid, engage in) the activity in the future.

Answers: 1. extrinsic 2. Instinct 3. biological 4. optimal 5. false 6. engage in

The Primary Drives: Hunger and Thirst

The drive-reduction theory, as we have seen, suggests that motivation is based largely on the **primary drives**, those which are unlearned and which satisfy biological needs. Two of the most important primary drives are thirst and hunger.

Thirst: We All Have Two Kinds

Question: Under what kinds of conditions do the two types of thirst occur?

Thirst is a basic biological drive, for all animals must have a continuous supply of fluid. Adequate fluid is critical because the body itself is about 75-percent water. Without any intake of fluids, we can survive only about 4 or 5 days.

But how do we know when we are thirsty? When we have a dry mouth and throat, or a powerful urge to drink? Yes, of course, but thirst is more complex than that. There are two types of thirst signaling us to drink. One type (extracellular thirst) occurs when fluid is lost from the body tissues rather than from the body cells. If you are exercising heavily or doing almost anything in hot weather, you will perspire and lose bodily fluid. Bleeding, vomiting, and diarrhea also rob your body of fluid. Extracellular-fluid loss takes fluid from the surrounding tissues, rather than from the body's cells. Perhaps you have heard that it is not a good idea to drink a cold beer or any other type of alcohol to quench your thirst on a very hot day. Alcohol increases extracellular-fluid loss. This is why most people awaken with a powerful thirst after drinking heavily the night before.

Another type of thirst (intracellular thirst) involves the loss of water from inside the body cells. When we eat a lot of salty food, the water-sodium balance in the blood and in the tissues outside the cells is disturbed. The salt cannot readily enter the cells, so the cells release some of their own water to restore the balance. As the body cells become dehydrated, thirst is stimulated so that we drink to increase the water volume (Robertson, 1983). Might this explain why salted peanuts and pretzels are provided at many bars free of charge?

primary drive: A state of tension or arousal arising from a biological need; one not based on learning.

The Biological Basis of Hunger: Internal Hunger Cues

We know that hunger is a biological drive operating in all animals, and we know that food is the substance that satisfies or reduces the hunger drive. You may have thought that the whole matter was very simple—when we get hungry we eat, and when we feel full we stop. But what happens in the body to make us feel hungry, and what causes satiety—the feeling of being full or satisfied?

Question: What are the roles of the lateral hypothalamus (LH) and the ventromedial hypothalamus (VMH) in the regulation of eating behavior?

The Role of the Hypothalamus: Our Feeding and Satiety Center Researchers have found two areas of the hypothalamus that are of central importance in regulating eating behavior and thus affect the hunger drive (Steffens et al., 1988). The **lateral hypothalamus (LH)** acts in part as a feeding center to excite eating. Stimulating the feeding center causes animals to eat even when they are full (Delgado & Anand, 1953). When the feeding center is destroyed, animals initially refuse to eat (Anand & Brobeck, 1951).

The **ventromedial hypothalamus (VMH)** presumably acts as a satiety center, and when active, it inhibits eating (Hernandez & Hoebel, 1989). Electrically stimulating the satiety center causes animals to stop eating (Duggan & Booth, 1986; Hoebel & Teitelbaum, 1961). If the VMH is surgically removed, experimental animals soon eat their way to gross obesity (Hetherington & Ranson, 1940; Parkinson & Weingarten, 1990). One rat whose satiety center was destroyed weighed nearly six times as much as a normal rat. In human terms this would be like a 150-pound person ballooning up to 900 pounds.

The immediate effects of gorging to obesity or refusing to eat altogether did occur with the destruction of a rat's VMH or LH; nevertheless, some time after the surgery, rats were reported to establish more normal eating patterns. But the fat rats continued to maintain an above-average body weight, and the noneating rats eventually began to eat but established a below-average body weight (Hoebel & Teitelbaum, 1966). Some researchers believe that destruction of the VMH causes animals to lose the ability to adjust their metabolism and thereby stabilize their body weight (Vilberg & Keesey, 1990).

Other organs and substances in the body also play a role in our feelings of hunger and satiety.

The Role of the Stomach: Hunger Pangs The fullness of the stomach affects our feeling of hunger. The stomach has a capacity of about 1 pint when empty and stretches to hold 2 1/2 pints when full (Avraham, 1989). Generally the more full or distended the stomach, the less hunger we feel (Pappas et al., 1989).

Stomach Contractions How do you know when you are hungry? Does your stomach growl? Do you have stomach contractions called hunger pangs? The association between hunger and stomach contractions was demonstrated in a classic experiment by Cannon and Washburn (1912).

Washburn swallowed a balloon with a long tube attached to it. The end of the tube was connected to a recording device. The balloon was then inflated while still in his stomach so that a stomach contraction would squeeze air out of the balloon and be registered on the recording device. Washburn sat in the laboratory for hours and pressed a key when he felt hungry. The results of the experiment showed a close correlation between the stomach contractions and the perception of hunger. The results do not necessarily mean that hunger is caused by stomach contractions. Additional research has confirmed that humans and

lateral hypothalamus (LH): The part of the hypothalamus that supposedly acts as a feeding center and, when activated, signals the animal to eat; when the LH is destroyed, the animal refuses to eat.

ventromedial hypothalamus (VMH): The part of the hypothalamus that presumably acts as a satiety center and, when activated, signals the animal to stop eating; when the area is destroyed, the animal overeats, becoming obese.

other animals continue to experience hunger even when it is impossible for them to feel stomach contractions. How do we know?

Experiments have revealed that rats continue to experience hunger even when all the nerves carrying hunger messages from the stomach to the brain have been cut (Morgan & Morgan, 1940), or if the entire stomach has been surgically removed (Pennick et al., 1963). Human cancer and ulcer patients who have had their entire stomach removed still report that they feel hunger pangs (Janowitz & Grossman, 1950).

If animals and humans without stomachs continue to experience hunger and satiety, then there must be other signals for hunger and satiety. The search for these signals moved from the stomach to the blood because the bloodstream is the means of transporting the products of digestion to the cells of the body.

Question: What are some of the body's hunger and satiety signals?

Other Hunger and Satiety Signals   Templeton and Quigley (1930) found that the blood of an animal that has eaten its fill is different from the blood of an excessively hungry animal. In one study, blood was taken from a very hungry dog and from a dog that had recently eaten. The blood taken from each dog was used as a transfusion to be given to the other. After the transfusions, the dog that had previously eaten began having stomach contractions even though its stomach was full. When the hungry dog that had been experiencing stomach contractions received the blood transfusion, its stomach contractions stopped.

The question is: What was in the blood that signaled hunger or satiety? Researchers began investigating factors such as the blood levels of glucose—a simple sugar remaining after carbohydrates have been digested.

Glucose and Hunger   Jean Mayer (1955) claims that the most important factor regulating hunger and satiety is glucose, which the blood must deliver to the cells. According to Mayer (1980) glucostatic theory, when glucose levels in the cells rise above a certain level, we feel satiated; when glucose levels fall below a certain level, we feel hungry.

Insulin Levels in the Blood   Insulin, a hormone produced by the pancreas, chemically converts glucose into energy that is usable by the cells. Elevations in insulin cause an increase in hunger, in food intake, and in a desire for sweets (Rodin, 1981; Rodin et al., 1985). Chronic oversecretion of insulin stimulates hunger and often leads to obesity.

Satiety Signals Released from the Gastrointestinal Tract   Some of the substances secreted by the gastrointestinal tract during digestion are released into the blood and act as satiety signals (Flood et al., 1990). The hormone cholecystokinin (CCK) is one satiety signal that causes us to limit the amount of food we eat during a meal (Woods & Gibbs, 1989). A deficiency of CCK may be involved in bulimia nervosa, a disorder in which people go on eating binges, eating immense quantities of food, only to purge the body of the food by self-induced vomiting.

We are not only pushed to eat by our hunger drive within. There are external factors as well that stimulate hunger.

Other Factors Influencing Hunger: The External Eating Cues

Question: What are some nonbiological factors that influence what and how much we eat?

Smell that aroma! Look at that mouth-watering chocolate cake. Listen to the bacon sizzling in the morning. Smell the coffee brewing. Sensory cues stimulate the appetite. Apart from our internal hunger, there are external factors influencing what, where, and how much we eat.

Susceptibility to External Eating Cues: Can You Resist Them? Are we all equally susceptible to external eating cues such as the taste, smell, and appearance of food, as well as the hands of the clock that signal mealtime is near? Stanley Schachter and colleagues suggested that overweight people are overly responsive to these external cues and are therefore more likely to overeat (Schachter & Gross, 1968). Normal-weight individuals, on the other hand, were thought to be affected by internal rather than external cues, eating when they are actually in need of food. Later studies have not supported this notion. Judith Rodin (1981), an expert in the field, found that the degree of external or internal responsiveness was not strongly correlated with the degree of overweight.

But external cues *can* trigger internal processes that motivate a person to eat. The sight and smell of appetizing food can trigger the release of insulin, particularly in those who are externally responsive (Rodin et al., 1977). Even in rats, environmental cues previously associated with food cause an increase in insulin level (Detke et al., 1989). For some individuals, "simply seeing and thinking about food" can cause an elevated level of insulin, and such people have a greater tendency to gain weight (Rodin, 1985). An extensive treatment of body weight and dieting is included in chapter 13, "Health and Stress."

The Palatability of Food: Tempting Tastes How good a particular food tastes, that is, how palatable the food is, seems to work somewhat independently of hunger and satiety in determining how much we eat (Rogers, 1990). Otherwise, most of us would refuse the pie after eating a big Thanksgiving dinner. This can explain why dieters are more tempted to go off their diets, not in response to hunger alone, but in response to the "mere exposure to the sight and smell of palatable food" (Rogers & Hill, 1989, p. 387).

Foods that are sweet and high in fat tend to stimulate the human appetite (Ball & Grinker, 1981), even when the sweetness is provided by artificial sweeteners (Blundell et al., 1988; Tordoff, 1988). In fact, even artificially sweetened chewing gum has been found to increase hunger (Tordoff & Alleva, 1990).

All cultures have their own peculiarities when it comes to food and eating. Why do you prefer the foods you like? Which are better—biscuits or bagels, egg-drop soup or creole gumbo, chicken curry or chicken and dumplings? You might say it is a matter of taste, but researchers say that taste itself is largely a matter of culture. Figure 10.3, on page 346, summarizes the factors that stimulate and inhibit eating.

Just the sight of mouth-watering foods can cause us to want to eat, even when we aren't very hungry.

Memory Check 10.2

1. Body cells lose water and become dehydrated when an individual:

   a. perspires heavily   c. has diarrhea or vomiting
   b. consumes too much salt   d. drinks too much alcohol

2. The lateral hypothalamus (LH) acts as a (feeding, satiety) center; the ventromedial hypothalamus (VMH) acts as a (feeding, satiety) center.

(continued)

3. Overweight people are overweight because they are overly responsive to external eating cues such as the taste, smell, and appearance of food. (true/false)

4. A meal with a wide variety of tasty foods stimulates the appetite more than a meal consisting of several tasty foods. (true/false)

5. Which of these is a hunger signal?

   a. high insulin level   c. CCK in the blood
   b. low glucose level in the cells   d. both a and b

Answers: 1. b 2. feeding; satiety 3. false 4. true 5. d

Figure 10.3 Factors That Stimulate and Inhibit Eating Both biological and environmental factors combine to stimulate or to inhibit eating.

Factors that Stimulate and Inhibit Eating

Factors that Stimulate Eating

Biological

- Activity in lateral hypothalamus
- Lowered glucose level in cells
- Increase in insulin
- Stomach contractions
- Stomach empty (Metabolism, set point, and fat cells are discussed in chapter 13.)

Environmental

- Aroma of food
- Sight of appetizing food
- Taste of appetizing food
- Acquired food preferences
- Being around others who are eating
- Foods high in fat and sugar
- Learned eating habits
- Reaction to boredom, stress, unpleasant emotional states

Factors that Inhibit Eating

Biological

- Activity in ventromedial hypothalamus
- Raised glucose levels in cells
- Distended (full) stomach
- CCK (hormone that acts as satiety signal)
- Sensory-specific satiety

Environmental

- Smell, taste, and appearance of unappetizing food
- Acquired taste aversions
- Learned eating habits
- Desire for thinness
- Reaction to stress, unpleasant emotional state

Social Motives

Question: What is Henry Murray's contribution to the study of motivation?

Do you have a strong need to be with other people (affiliation) or a need for power or achievement? These needs are two examples of **social motives**, which we learn or acquire through social and cultural experiences. Each of us differs in the strength of various social motives and in the priorities we assign to them. Our highest aspirations, the professions we choose, the partners we are drawn to, and the methods we use to achieve our sense of importance result primarily from our social motives.

In 1938 Henry Murray identified and defined a number of social motives or needs shown in Table 10.2. Murray believed that people have social motives in differing degrees. Which of these needs motivate you?

To investigate the strength of various needs, Murray (1938) developed the **Thematic Apperception Test (TAT)**, which consists of a series of pictures of ambiguous situations. Subjects are asked to write a story about each picture. For

social motives: Motives acquired through experience and interaction with others (example: need for achievement, need for affiliation).

Thematic Apperception Test (TAT): A projective test consisting of drawings of ambiguous human situations, which the subject describes; thought to reveal inner feelings, conflicts, and motives.

Table 10.2   Murray's List of Psychological Needs

Major Category	Need	Representative Behavior
Ambition	n Achievement	Overcoming obstacles
	n Recognition	Describing accomplishments
	n Exhibition	Attempting to shock or thrill others
	n Acquisition	Obtaining things
	n Conservance	Repairing possessions
	n Order	Making things neat and orderly
	n Retention	Hoarding things
	n Construction	Building something
Defense of status	n Inviolacy	Keeping psychological distance
	n Infavoidance	Concealing a birthmark or handicap
	n Defendance	Giving an explanation or excuse
	n Counteraction	Retaliating for something
Response to human power	n Dominance	Directing others' behavior
	n Deference	Cooperating with or obeying someone
	n Similance	Imitating others
	n Autonomy	Standing up to authority
	n Contrariance	Being oppositional
	n Aggression	Attacking or belittling others
	n Abasement	Apologizing or confessing
	n Blame avoidance	Stifling blameworthy impulses
Affection between people	n Affiliation	Spending time with others
	n Rejection	Snubbing others
	n Nurturance	Taking care of someone
	n Succorance	Being helped by another
	n Play	Seeking diversion through others
Exchange of information	n Cognizance	Asking questions of others
	n Exposition	Delivering information to others

From Carver, C. S., and Scheier, M. F. (1988). *Perspectives on Personality*. Boston: Allyn and Bacon. After Murray, 1962.

need for achievement (*n* Ach): The need to accomplish something difficult and to perform at a high standard of excellence.

each story, they are told to describe what is going on in the picture, what the person or persons pictured are thinking about, what they may be feeling, and what is likely to be the outcome of the situation. The stories are presumed to reveal the subject's needs and the strength of those needs. (The Thematic Apperception Test has also been used as a more general personality test, described in chapter 12, "Personality Theory and Assessment.")

The Need for Achievement: The Drive to Excel

Question: What is the need for achievement?

What explains why Donald Trump seems driven to build an empire? What motivated Sam Walton to bring Wal-Mart stores to happy shoppers in thousands of cities and towns all over America? Certainly not biological needs that must be satisfied or drives that must be reduced. Both men were driven by the same social motive, the need for achievement, although they chose to satisfy it in very different ways.

The **need for achievement** (abbreviated *n* Ach) is included on Murray's list of needs (Table 10.2). Murray (1938) defined the need for achievement as the motive "to accomplish something difficult. . . . To overcome obstacles and attain a high standard. To excel one's self. To rival and surpass others. To increase self regard by the successful exercise of talent" (p. 164). The need for achievement, rather than being satisfied with accomplishment, seems to grow as it is fed, rather than diminish.

The need for achievement has been researched more vigorously than any other of Murray's needs, and researchers David McClelland and John Atkinson have conducted many of these studies (McClelland et al., 1953; McClelland, 1958, 1961, 1985). Unfortunately, the subjects in these studies have been almost exclusively male.

To assess achievement motivation, McClelland and Atkinson had subjects view four to six ambiguous pictures from the Thematic Apperception Test and then write stories about them. The content of the subjects' stories was analyzed for references to achievement. Subjects who consistently included achievement themes were scored as being high in achievement motivation.

People with a high need for achievement see their success as a result of their own talent and hard work—rather than simply luck.

Atkinson's Theory of Achievement Motivation: When Do We Try?

Atkinson (1964) proposed a theory of achievement motivation to explain when individuals will attempt to accomplish certain goals. Atkinson suggests that when we approach any situation, two conflicting factors are operating—our hope for success and our fear of failure. Motivation to avoid failure can cause us to work harder at a task to try to insure success, or it can cause us to avoid the task altogether.

Whether you strive for a goal depends on three factors: (1) the strength of your need to achieve, (2) your expectation of success, and (3) the incentive value of success or failure at a particular activity (how much you value success in the activity and how distressed you would be if you failed at it). For example, whether you try to achieve an *A* in psychology would depend on how important an *A* is to you; whether you believe an *A* is possible to achieve; and how much pride you will feel in getting an *A*, as opposed to how upset you will be if you do not get an *A*.

Complete the *Try It!*, which describes a game that is said to reveal high or low achievement motivation.

Imagine yourself involved in a ring-toss game. You have three rings to toss at any of the six pegs pictured here. You will be paid a few pennies each time you are able to ring a peg.

Try It!

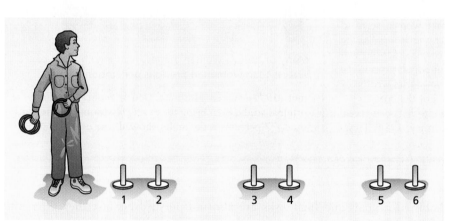

Which peg would you try to ring with your three tosses—peg 1 or 2 nearest you, peg 3 or 4 at a moderate distance, or peg 5 or 6 at the far end of the room?

Question: What are some characteristics shared by people who are high in achievement motivation?

Characteristics of Achievers: Successful People Have Them

McClelland and others (1953) found that high achievers differ from low achievers in a number of ways. People with a high *n* Ach tend to set goals of moderate difficulty. They pursue goals that are challenging yet attainable with hard work, ability, determination, and persistence. Goals that are too easy, those anyone can reach, offer no challenge and hold no interest because success would not be rewarding (Atkinson, 1958; Clark & McClelland, 1956; French, 1955). Impos-

WORLD OF PSYCHOLOGY:

MULTICULTURAL PERSPECTIVES

Gender and Fear of Success

Have you ever purposely done less than your best to avoid being called a "brain"? Are there some people who are actually afraid of success, or are there other reasons why people prefer to conceal their abilities and lower their performance?

Researcher Matina Horner (1969) reported that women stress the negative consequences of success for women, while men tend to focus on the positive aspects of success for men. Horner's subjects wrote stories based on an essay that she supplied. The essay began, "After first-term finals, Anne finds herself at the top of her medical school class" (p. 36). The women were given the "Anne" version of the essay, while the men received the same essay, except the name "John" was substituted for "Anne." Over 65 percent of the females, but only 10 percent of the males, wrote stories that expressed fear of success. On the basis of her findings, Horner (1969) concluded that women seem to have a "motive to avoid success," which she defines "as the fear that success in competitive achievement situations will lead to negative consequences such as unpopularity and the loss of femininity" (p. 38). Excerpts from stories written by Horner's subjects are shown at the end of the box.

In follow-up studies, researchers found that men reveal as much fear of success as women (Kearney, 1984; Trese-

Many of today's women are less restricted by fear of success than women in previous generations.

mer, 1977). When Hoffman (1974) replicated Horner's original study, even using the exact classrooms Horner had used, 77 percent of the males showed fear of success com-

sibly high goals and high risks are also not pursued because they offer little chance of success and are considered a waste of time. People high in *n* Ach enjoy taking moderate risks in situations that depend on their ability, but they are not gamblers. To become wealthy, business people high in achievement motivation take a number of moderate risks, ones at which they can succeed, rather than very high risks offering little or no chance of success.

People with low *n* Ach, the researchers claim, are not willing to take chances when it comes to testing their own skills and abilities. They are motivated more by their fear of failure than by their hope and expectation of success. This is why they set either ridiculously low goals, which anyone can attain, or else impossibly high goals (Geen, 1984). After all, who can fault a person for failing to reach a goal that is impossible for almost anyone?

In view of this description, which peg would people low in achievement motivation try to ring? If you guessed peg 1 or 2, or peg 5 or 6, you are right. People low in achievement motivation are likely to stand right over peg 1 so they can't possibly fail. Or they might toss the rings at peg 6, hoping that they might be lucky. But failing that, no one can blame them for not attaining a nearly impossible goal. A chance to win a few cents is certainly no incentive for people with a high need for achievement, so they tend to toss their rings at peg 3 or 4, an intermediate distance that offers some challenge. Where did you choose to stand?

pared to 65 percent of the females. In a review of 16 studies on fear of success, Zuckerman and Wheeler (1975) identified seven studies that revealed a greater fear of success in men.

One study by Balkin (1987) reports that fear of success in female college students was related to whether their close friends attended college. Of those whose friends attended college, only 10 percent showed fear of success compared to 42 percent of the subjects with few or no close friends attending college. Such results led Balkin to speculate that fear of success might involve the "fear of disapproval and rejection from significant others, namely, family and friends" (p. 40). Balkin suggests that the same explanation could apply to males. Might fear of success and possible rejection by peers be an important factor operating to keep children of the lower socioeconomic class from having greater success in school?

Some researchers doubt whether fear of success exists at all. They claim that Horner's original research might only reflect women's perceptions of the rejection and social ostracism of those who deviate from conventional, stereotyped sex roles. But times are changing. Younger women today may not fear success as much as their older sisters.

Consider the strong need for achievement expressed by one young woman, Sarah, when she was 9 years old.

On a visit to the capital city of her state, Sarah, her mother, and her aunt were driving past the governor's mansion. Sarah remarked, "Some day I want to live there."

Sarah's mother said, "Oh, you mean you want to live in a house like that."

Sarah replied, "No, I want to live in *that* house."

Her aunt chimed in, "You mean when you grow up you want to marry the governor and live there?"

Sarah responded with emphasis, "No, I mean when I grow up I want to *be* the governor."

Anne doesn't want to be number one in her class . . . she feels she shouldn't rank so high because of social reasons. She drops down to ninth in the class and then marries the boy who graduates number one.

Anne is pretty darn proud of herself, but everyone hates and envies her.

Anne is talking to her counselor. Counselor says she will make a fine *nurse*.

It was luck that Anne came out on top because she didn't want to go to medical school anyway.

John is a conscientious young man who worked hard. He is pleased with himself. John has always wanted to go into medicine and is very dedicated. . . . John continues working hard and eventually graduates at the top of his class.

Anne is pleased. She had worked extraordinarily hard and her grades showed it. "It is not enough," Anne thinks. "I am not happy." She didn't even want to be a doctor. She is not sure what she wants. Anne says to hell with the whole business and goes into social work—not hardly as glamorous, prestigious or lucrative; but she is happy.

(From Horner, 1969.)

High achievers see their success as a result of their own talents, abilities, persistence, and hard work (Kukla, 1972). They typically do not credit luck or the influence of other people for their successes, or blame luck or others for their failures. When low achievers fail, they usually give up quickly and attribute failure to their lack of ability. They believe that luck or fate, rather than effort and ability, is responsible for accomplishment (Weiner, 1972, 1974).

Some research indicates that a high or a low need for achievement becomes a fairly stable component of personality (Kagan & Moss, 1962), although the motive may find different expression as individuals age (Veroff, 1978). In a young person, the need for achievement may be expressed as a need to excel in school. Neumann and others (1988) found that high achievement motivation is related to college students' accomplishments and grades.

In adulthood those with high need for achievement are often drawn to business, sometimes starting their own, and to other occupations and professions in which their own efforts can result in high achievement. According to McClelland, it is primarily the achievement motive rather than the profit motive that drives entrepreneurs. They are interested in profits and personal income mainly because it serves as a measure of their competence. Thus the money becomes a symbol of success.

But what about those who want to be achievers, who dream of being rich and famous, yet who are not willing to put forth the effort to achieve it? The person with high *n* Ach does not fit this picture. People high in achievement motivation may indeed be dreamers, but they are "doers" as well.

Developing Achievement Motivation: Can We Learn It?   If achievement motivation, like the other social motives, is primarily learned, how is it learned? Some experts believe that child-rearing practices and values in the home are important factors in developing achievement motivation (McClelland, 1985; McClelland & Pilon, 1983). Parents may be more likely to have children with high *n* Ach if they give their children responsibilities, stress independence when they are young, and praise them for genuine accomplishments. Birth order appears to be related to achievement motivation, with first-born and only children showing higher *n* Ach than younger siblings (Falbo & Polit, 1986). Younger siblings, however, tend to be more sociable and likable than first-born or only children, and this has its rewards too.

Do some people lack achievement motivation because they are afraid of success? Read about fear of success in the boxed feature on pages 350–351.

Memory Check 10.3

1. Social motives are (learned, unlearned).

2. According to Atkinson's theory of achievement motivation, which of the following is *not* a factor in determining whether an individual approaches a goal?

   a. the strength of the individual's need to achieve
   b. the person's expectation of success
   c. how much pride the person has in achieving the goal as opposed to how upsetting failure would be
   d. the financial reward attached to the goal

3. Which of these statements is *not* true of people high in achievement motivation?

   a. They set very high goals if success is extremely difficult to obtain.
   b. They set goals of moderate difficulty.
   c. They attribute their success to their talents, abilities, and hard work.
   d. They are likely to choose careers as entrepreneurs.

Answers: 1. learned 2. d 3. a

The What and Why of Emotions

emotion: A feeling state involving physiological arousal, a cognitive appraisal of the situation arousing the state, and an outward expression of the state.

Motivation does not occur in a vacuum. Much of our motivation to act is fueled by our emotional state. In fact, the root of the word **emotion** means "to move," indicating the close relationship between motivation and emotion. Our emotions may lead us to hug someone, hit someone, run away, laugh, cry, and a whole array of other behaviors common to human experience. Emotions prepare and motivate us to respond adaptively to a variety of situations in life. Emotions enable us to communicate our feelings and intentions more effectively than just words alone and thus make it more likely that others will respond to us. But what, precisely, are emotions?

The Components of Emotions: The Physical, the Cognitive, and the Behavioral

Question: What are the three components of emotion?

Nothing more than feelings. Is that what emotions are? We say that we feel lonely or sad, happy or content, or angry, embarrassed, or afraid. We normally describe emotions in terms of feeling states, but psychologists study emotions according to their three components—the physical, the cognitive, and the behavioral.

The physical component is the physiological arousal (the internal body state) that accompanies the emotion. Without the physiological arousal, we would not feel the emotion in all its intensity. The surge of powerful feeling we know as emotion is due largely to the physiological arousal we experience. And this connection between emotion and physiological response is the principle on which the **polygraph**, or lie detector, is based.

The cognitive component, the way we perceive or interpret a stimulus or situation, determines the specific emotion we feel. If you are home alone and the wind is banging a tree limb on your roof, you may become fearful if you perceive the knocking and the banging as a burglar trying to break into your house. An emotional response to an imaginary threat is every bit as powerful as a response to a real threat. Perceptions make it so. Have you ever worked yourself up into a frenzy before a first date, a job interview, or an oral presentation for one of your classes? Then your thinking was contributing to your emotional state.

The behavioral component of emotions is the outward expression of the emotions. Our facial expressions, gestures, body posture, and tone of voice stem from and convey the emotions we are feeling within. Some of the facial expressions that accompany emotion are innate and the same across cultures. But some of our emotional expressions are more influenced by our culture and its rules for displaying emotion. Table 10.4 summarizes the components of emotions.

Theories of Emotions: Which Comes First, the Thought or the Feeling?

There is no doubt that we react to certain experiences with emotion. For example, if you think that you are making a fool of yourself in front of your friends, the emotion you feel is embarrassment, which triggers a physiological response that may cause you to blush. This type of reaction seems logical—it seems to fit our everyday experience. But is this sequence of events the course that an emotional experience really follows? Not according to psychologist William James.

Question: According to the James-Lange theory, what sequence of events occurs when we experience an emotion?

The James-Lange Theory American psychologist William James (1884) argued that the sequence of events in an emotional experience is exactly the reverse of what our subjective experience tells us. James claimed that first an event causes physiological arousal and a physical response. Only then do we perceive or interpret the physical response as an emotion. In other words, saying something stupid causes us to blush, and we interpret our physical response, the

polygraph: A device designed to pick up changes in heart rate, blood pressure, respiration rate, and galvanic skin response that typically accompany the anxiety that occurs when a person lies.

Table 10.4 The Components of Emotions

Physical component
Physiological arousal (internal bodily state accompanying the emotion)

Cognitive component
The way we interpret a stimulus or situation

Behavioral component
Outward expression of the emotion (facial expressions, gestures, body posture, tone of voice)

James-Lange theory: The theory that emotional feelings result when we become aware of our physiological response to an emotion-provoking stimulus (for example, we are afraid because we tremble).

Cannon-Bard theory: The theory that physiological arousal and the feeling of emotion occur simultaneously after an emotion-provoking stimulus is relayed to the thalamus.

blush, as an emotion, embarrassment. James (1890) went on to suggest that "we feel sorry *because* we cry, angry *because* we strike, afraid *because* we tremble" (p. 1066).

At about the same time that James proposed his theory, a Danish physiologist and psychologist, Carl Lange, independently formulated nearly the same theory. Hence, we have the **James-Lange theory** of emotion (Lange & James, 1922). The theory suggests that different patterns of arousal in the autonomic nervous system produce the different emotions we feel, and that the physiological arousal appears before the emotion is perceived. According to the theory, when a growling dog approaches you, your heart begins to pound, and you run. You perceive your physiological arousal (your pounding heart) and your behavior (running) as the emotion of fear (see Figure 10.6).

But if the physical arousal itself is the cause of what we know as emotion, there would have to be a distinctly different set of physical changes associated with each emotion. Otherwise we wouldn't know whether we were sad, embarrassed, frightened, or happy.

Question: What is the Cannon-Bard theory of emotion?

The Cannon-Bard Theory　An early theory of emotion that challenged the James-Lange theory is the Cannon-Bard theory. Walter Cannon (1927), who did pioneering work on the fight-or-flight response and the concept of homeostasis, pointed out that we often feel an emotion before we notice the physiological state of our bodies. We would not be able to experience sudden fear and panic or instant enthusiasm and joy if we had to wait for a particular pattern of physiological arousal to signal which emotion we should feel. Furthermore, Cannon claimed that the bodily changes caused by each of the emotions are not sufficiently distinct to allow people to distinguish one emotion from another.

Cannon presented his own theory that was later endorsed by one of his students, Philip Bard (1934). Known as the **Cannon-Bard theory**, it suggests that

Figure 10.6

The James-Lange Theory of Emotion

The James-Lange theory of emotion is the exact opposite of what our subjective experience tells us. If an angry pit bull growled at you, the James-Lange interpretation is the dog growled, your heart began to pound, and only by observing that your heart was pounding would you conclude that you must be afraid.

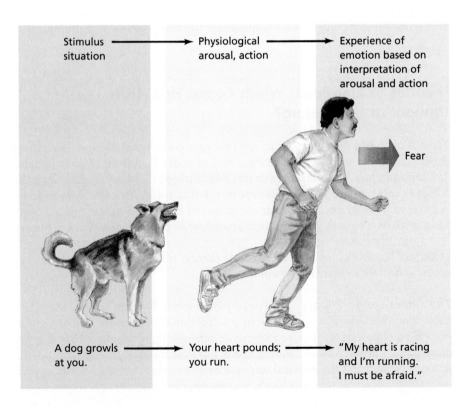

Stimulus situation ⟶ Physiological arousal, action ⟶ Experience of emotion based on interpretation of arousal and action

Fear

A dog growls at you. ⟶ Your heart pounds; you run. ⟶ "My heart is racing and I'm running. I must be afraid."

the following chain of events occurs when we feel an emotion. (1) Emotion-provoking stimuli are received by the senses and are then relayed to the thalamus in the brain. (2) The thalamus passes its information in two different directions at the same time—up to the cerebral cortex, which gives us the conscious mental experience of the emotion, and down to the internal organs of the body, which produce the physiological state of arousal. In other words, according to the Cannon-Bard theory, our feelings of emotion occur at about the same time that we experience physiological arousal. One does not cause the other, say Cannon and Bard.

Later research corrected some of the details of the Cannon-Bard theory. Instead of the thalamus, the hypothalamus apparently starts the process of physical arousal, while other areas of the limbic system are involved in the feeling or the experience of an emotion.

Question: According to the Schachter-Singer theory, what two factors must occur in order to experience an emotion?

The Schachter-Singer Theory   Stanley Schachter looked at these early theories of emotion. He concluded that they left out a critical component, our own cognitive interpretation of why we become aroused. Schachter and Singer (1962) proposed a two-factor theory suggesting that both the James-Lange and the Cannon-Bard theories are partly right. According to the **Schachter-Singer theory**, two things must happen in order to feel an emotion. (1) The person must first experience physiological arousal. (2) Then there must be a cognitive interpretation or explanation of the physiological arousal so that the person can label it as a specific emotion. Therefore, according to this theory, a true emotion can occur only if we are physically aroused and can find some reason for it. Schachter concluded that when people are in a state of physiological arousal but do not know why they are aroused, they tend to label the state as an emotion that is appropriate to their situation at the time. Figure 10.7 depicts this theory of emotion.

Schachter-Singer theory: A two-stage theory stating that, for an emotion to occur, there must be (1) physiological arousal and (2) an explanation for the arousal.

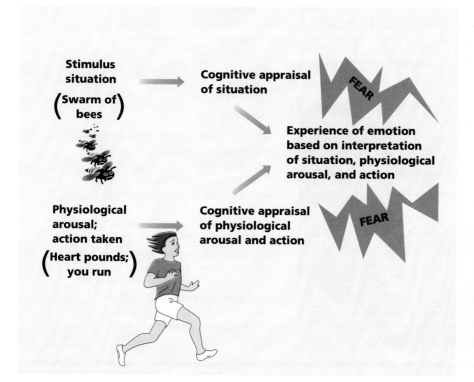

Figure 10.7

The Schachter-Singer Theory of Emotion

The Schachter-Singer theory of emotion is a two-factor theory suggesting that in order to experience emotion, (1) a person must experience physiological arousal and (2) there must be a cognitive interpretation to explain the physiological arousal. In other words, we experience a true emotion only when we become physically aroused and can identify some cause or reason for the arousal.

WORLD OF PSYCHOLOGY: APPLICATIONS

The Polygraph: Lie Detector or Emotion Detector?

Question: What does a polygraph measure?

Picture yourself in this situation. You are delighted that your application for a job with the federal government has survived the initial screening. Your job interview goes well, too, and you are informed that the job requires a security clearance. If you pass a series of tests, you are hired.

When you arrive to take your first test, you are directed to a small room where a man is seated at a table with a computer monitor and other machinery you have never seen before. As you are seated in a chair facing away from the computer, an assistant explains that you will be asked a series of questions. Then they attach electrodes to the tips of your fingers, strap a tube across your chest and over your heart, and another tube around your upper waist at your diaphragm. Already you feel like a condemned murderer being readied for execution, as a blood pressure cuff is placed around your left upper arm and is pumped up tight. Now the questions begin. The man asks, "Have you ever taken anything that did not belong to you?" Fear surges up. What do you say? You respond weakly, "Yes, but only a few times."

You know that you are taking a polygraph, or lie detector, test; but you don't know that the first question is only a control question. Whether you answer yes or no is irrelevant, but the movement of the polygraph needle reveals your level of anxiety. You answer another irrelevant question or two, revealing a baseline for your arousal. Then

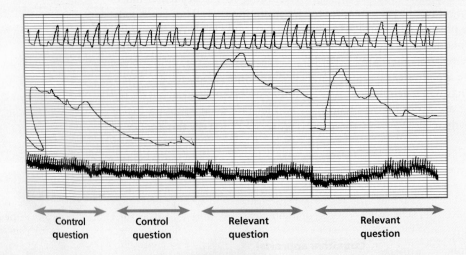

→ Control question ←   → Control question ←   → Relevant question ←   → Relevant question ←

Figure 10.4

The Polygraph

The polygraph can detect only the physiological changes associated with emotional arousal—changes in breathing (top line), galvanic skin response (middle line), and heart rate and blood pressure (lower lines). In administering a polygraph test, the examiner asks a few control questions to establish the base level of the subject's emotional arousal. Next the relevant questions are asked, and it is assumed that if the subject is lying, the emotional arousal will surge higher.

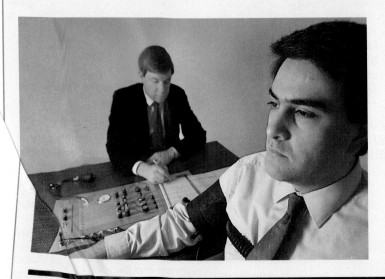

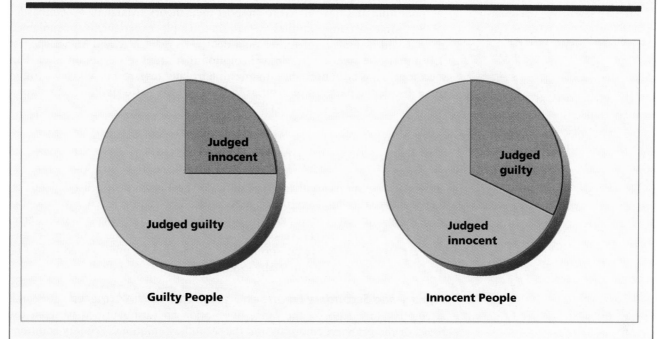

Guilty People

Innocent People

Figure 10.5   The Unreliability of Polygraphs   Polygraph tests are far from infallible. In one study, one out of four guilty people were judged innocent and one out of three innocent people were judged guilty. People who can lie easily often show little physical arousal and therefore might come across as telling the truth.

comes the big question "Did you give any false information on your job application?"

If, when you answer, the needle jumps above its peak on the control questions, the examiner will conclude that you are lying (see Figure 10.4). But couldn't the polygraph needle stay below the control peak if you are lying? And couldn't it leap above the control peak even if you are telling the truth? The answer is yes to both questions.

The polygraph is really not a lie detector. It can detect only physiological changes associated with emotional arousal. It cannot distinguish fear, sexual arousal, anxiety, anger, or general emotional arousal from lying. The assumption is that when people lie, they feel anxious, and their anxiety causes physiological changes in blood pressure, heart rate, breathing, and perspiration.

In the past, lie detector tests were used primarily by law-enforcement officers, but then they found their way into business and industry to screen prospective employees and to control employee theft. Until 1988 over one million tests a year were given in the United States (Holden, 1986a; Lykken, 1981). Then Congress passed the *Employee Polygraph Protection Act of 1988*, which put a large dent in the lie detector business by prohibiting most polygraph testing outside the government.

How accurate is the polygraph? There is as yet no definitive answer, and estimates of the accuracy of the polygraph vary considerably. In one series of studies of actual criminal suspects, 20 percent of the innocent suspects—one out of

every five—were pronounced guilty of lying on the polygraph test (Saxe et al., 1985). Other experts say the percentage of innocent people falsely accused of lying is considerably higher, with as many as one out of three innocent people labeled as a liar, as Figure 10.5 illustrates (Kleinmuntz & Szucko, 1984a). What about guilty people? One out of four guilty people who were lying were judged to be telling the truth, according to their polygraph record.

Is it possible to beat the lie detector? Inveterate, or habitual, liars—who lie easily without any emotional disturbance or physiological arousal—are more likely to come across as telling the truth. It has been suggested that failure to pay close attention, or being distracted during the questioning, also lowers physiological responses. In one study, volunteer subjects distracted themselves by counting backward by sevens throughout the examination, and they were able to lie without being detected more often than when they were not using a distraction (Waid et al., 1981). Lykken (1981) found that increasing arousal by tensing muscles and thinking about something exciting during neutral questions could alter the results. Apparently even taking tranquilizers before the test can reduce the physiological response that usually accompanies lying.

The word is out about lie detectors, and their less-than-satisfactory reliability has led to more restrictions in their use. Already evidence from the polygraph is not admissible in half the states in the U.S. (Lykken, 1985).

primary emotions: Emotions such as sadness, surprise, happiness, anger, fear, and disgust, which are presumed to be universal.

secondary emotions: Various combinations of the primary emotions, varying from culture to culture.

Attempts to replicate the findings of Schachter and Singer have been largely disappointing and have failed to support their theory (Marshall & Zimbardo, 1979). Some of these studies reveal that people experiencing unexplained arousal find it unpleasant rather than neutral as Schachter and Singer suggest (Leventhal & Tomarken, 1986). The notion that arousal is general rather than specific also has been brought into question by later researchers who have found some distinctive patterns of arousal for some of the basic emotions (Ekman et al., 1983; Schwartz et al., 1981).

The Range of Emotion: How Wide Is It?

How many emotions are there? The number of emotions people list depends on their culture, the language they speak, and other factors. Even psychologists who study emotion cannot agree on a list of primary emotions. They do agree, however, that cultures universally consider joy, liking, love, amusement, and admiration to be positive emotions and fear, sorrow, shame, and hatred to be negative emotions (Watson et al., 1984).

Primary and Secondary Emotions: The Innate and the Acquired   Research attempting to categorize the range of emotion has distinguished between the basic, or the primary, emotions and the secondary emotions. **Primary emotions** are unlearned and universal; that is, they are found in all cultures, are reflected in the same facial expressions, and emerge in children according to their own biological timetable of development. Fear, anger, disgust, surprise, joy or happiness, and sadness or distress are usually considered primary emotions. **Secondary emotions** are various combinations of the primary emotions and vary from culture to culture.

Plutchik's View of Emotion: The Many Colors of Emotions   Robert Plutchik (1980) compared the varieties of emotion with the different colors we can perceive. He claims that we experience eight primary emotions in addition to various shadings and blends of the primary emotions. According to Plutchik's analogy, the colors of red, yellow, green, and blue form the basis for the multiple

Figure 10.8

Plutchik's Emotion Circle

Robert Plutchik suggests that just as different colors (for example, red, yellow, green, and blue) can be mixed to form multiple shades and hues, so can primary emotions (shown in the center of the emotion circle) be combined to produce the many varieties of emotions we feel. The emotions shown outside the circle result from a blend of the two adjacent primary emotions inside the circle. For example, surprise and sadness yield disappointment. (From Plutchik, 1980.)

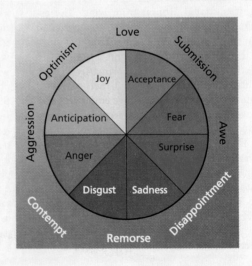

shades and hues we can distinguish, just as the primary emotions form the basis of many different emotions. He lists fear, anger, joy, disgust, anticipation, surprise, sadness, and acceptance as the primary emotions that produce the many varieties of emotions we feel.

Plutchik provides a model for his theory—the emotion circle shown in Figure 10.8. You can see that Plutchik's primary emotions inside the wheel are placed as opposites—joy opposite sadness, anger opposite fear, acceptance opposite disgust, and submission opposite anticipation. The emotions shown outside the circle result from a blend of two adjacent primary emotions inside the circle. The emotions of joy and anticipation combine to produce optimism; joy and acceptance blend to form love.

Plutchik (1980) points out that the higher the intensity of an emotion, the more likely it is to motivate behavior and move us to act. Plutchik's theory helps us understand the relationships, similarities, and differences of the many emotions we experience.

Memory Check 10.4

1. Which of these is a component of emotion?

   a. the way we perceive and think about the situation or object of our emotion
   b. the physiological arousal that accompanies emotion
   c. how the emotion is expressed in our behavior
   d. all of these

2. The *biggest* problem with lie detectors is that many innocent people are falsely accused of lying. (true/false)

3. The (Cannon-Bard, James-Lange) theory of emotion suggests that the feeling of emotion comes after our physiological response; that is, we feel fearful because we are shaking.

4. The (Cannon-Bard, Schachter-Singer) theory is the two-factor theory of emotion, which states that in order to experience or label an emotion, we must first feel physiological arousal and second have an explanation for the arousal.

5. Plutchik's emotion circle does *not* explain:

   a. varying intensities of emotions   c. various blends of emotions
   b. the origin of basic emotions   d. two of these

Answers: 1. d   2. true   3. James-Lange   4. Schachter-Singer   5. d

The Expression of Emotion

How do we learn to express our emotions? Or do we learn? There is considerable evidence that the primary emotions (fear, anger, sadness, happiness, disgust, and surprise), or the facial expressions we make when we feel them, are biologically rather than culturally determined.

The Development of Facial Expressions in Infants: Smiles and Frowns Come Naturally

Question: How does the development of facial expressions in infants suggest a biological basis for emotional expression?

Emotional expressions allow infants to communicate their feelings and needs before they are able to speak. Katherine Bridges (1932) studied emotional expression in Canadian infants over a period of months. She reported that the first emotional expression to appear is that of distress, which occurs at 3 weeks. In terms of survival, the expression of distress enables helpless newborns to get the attention of their caretakers so that their needs can be met. Bridges found that infants display all the basic or primary human emotions before they are 2 years old.

Facial expressions develop naturally just as do the motor skills of crawling and walking, according to the biological timetable of maturation (Greenberg, 1977). Carroll Izard (1990) claims that "the facial expressions of pain and the emotions of interest, enjoyment, surprise, sadness, anger, disgust, and fear are present at birth or by about 7 months of age" (p. 492).

Another strong indication that the facial expressions of emotion are biologically determined rather than learned, results from research on children who have been blind and deaf since birth. Their smiles and frowns, laughter and crying, and facial expressions of anger, surprise, and pouting were the same as those of children who could hear and see (Eibl-Eibesfeldt, 1973).

Although recent studies have contributed much to our understanding of facial expressions, the biological connection between emotions and facial expressions was first proposed many years ago. Read about it in the boxed feature on the next page.

Try It!

Look carefully at the six photographs. Which basic emotion is portrayed in each?

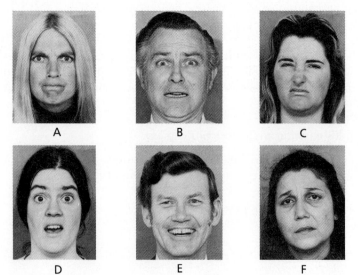

A   B   C

D   E   F

Match the letter of the photograph with the basic emotion it portrays:
   1. Happiness   2. Sadness   3. Fear   4. Anger   5. Surprise   6. Disgust

Answers: 1. E 2. F 3. B 4. A 5. D 6. C

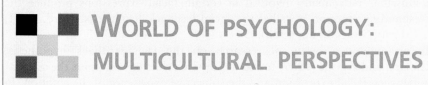

WORLD OF PSYCHOLOGY: MULTICULTURAL PERSPECTIVES

Facial Expressions for the Basic Emotions: A Universal Language

The relationship between emotions and facial expressions was first studied by Charles Darwin (1872). He believed that the facial expression of emotion was an aid to survival because it enabled people, before they developed language, to communicate their internal states and react to emergencies. Darwin maintained that most of the emotions we feel and the facial expressions that convey them are genetically inherited and characteristic of the entire human species. To test his belief, he asked missionaries and people of different cultures around the world to record the facial expressions that accompany the basic emotions. Based on those data, he concluded that facial expressions were similar across cultures. More than a hundred years later, modern researchers agree that Darwin was right.

Convincing evidence that the facial expressions of emotion are universal was provided by Ekman and Friesen (1971). They showed photographs portraying facial expressions of the primary emotions—sadness, surprise, happiness, anger, fear, and disgust—to members of the Fore tribe in a remote area in New Guinea. The Fore people were able to identify the emotional expressions of happiness, sadness, anger, and disgust, although they had difficulty distinguishing fear and surprise.

In later research Ekman and others (Ekman, 1982; Ekman & Friesen, 1975; Ekman et al., 1987) used a more culturally diverse group of subjects from different parts of the world. Subjects from the United States, Argentina, Japan, Brazil, and Chile viewed photographs showing the same basic emotions. Could people from widely diverse cultures name the emotions conveyed by the facial expressions of Americans? Yes, to an amazing degree, they could. Ekman believes that this result provides strong support for a biological explanation of facial expression. Such findings remind us that, while we acknowledge and appreciate our cultural differences and the great diversity we find within the human population, we are, after all, one species. And our facial expressions of emotion are the same around the world.

Try Ekman's test and see if you can identify the faces of emotion in the *Try It!*

The facial expressions for happiness, disgust, and anger expressed by the Fore tribe of New Guinea are the same for other cultures around the world.

The Facial-Feedback Hypothesis: Does the Face Cause the Feeling?

Question: What is the facial-feedback hypothesis?

Researcher Sylvan Tomkins (1962, 1963), like Darwin, agreed that facial expressions of the basic emotions are genetically programmed. But Tomkins went a step further. He claimed that the facial expression itself, that is, the movement of the facial muscles producing the expression, triggers both the physiological arousal and the conscious feeling associated with the emotion. The notion that the muscular movements involved in certain facial expressions produce the corresponding emotion is called the **facial-feedback hypothesis** (Izard, 1971, 1977, 1990; Strack et al., 1988).

In an extensive review of research on the facial-feedback hypothesis, Adelmann and Zajonc (1989) found impressive evidence to support the association between facial expression and the subjective experience of the emotion. In addition, they found considerable support for the notion that simply the act of making the facial expression can initiate the subjective feeling.

The Simulation of Facial Expressions: Put On a Happy Face

More than 120 years ago Darwin wrote, "Even the simulation of an emotion tends to arouse it in our minds" (1965/1872, p. 365). Ekman, Levenson, and Friesen (1983) put this notion to the test using 16 subjects (12 professional actors and 4 scientists). The subjects were guided to contract specific muscles in the face so that they could assume the facial expressions of the six basic emotions—surprise, disgust, sadness, anger, fear, and happiness. They were never actually told to smile, frown, or put on an angry face, however.

The subjects were hooked up to electronic instruments, which monitored physiological changes in heart rate, galvanic skin response (to measure perspiring), muscle tension, and hand temperature. Measurements were taken as they made each facial expression. While hooked up to the device, the subjects were also asked to imagine or relive six actual experiences in which they had felt each of the six basic emotions.

Ekman reported that the same, distinctive physiological response pattern emerged for the emotions of fear, sadness, anger, and disgust, whether the subjects relived one of their emotional experiences or simply made only the corresponding facial expression. In fact, in some cases the physiological measures of emotion were greater when the actors and scientists made the facial expression than when they imagined an actual emotional experience (Ekman et al., 1983). The researchers found that both anger and fear accelerate heart rate, while fear produces colder fingers than anger does.

Do you think that purposely simulating particular facial expressions or postures will affect your emotions? Put this idea to a test in the *Try It!*

Try It!

Try the following exercises and see whether adopting certain facial expressions and postures affects your mood.

First, make each of the following facial expressions and hold them for 15 seconds:

1) A big smile   2) A very sad face   3) An angry look   4) A look of disgust

Next stand erect, hold your head high, and walk quickly. After that, let your shoulders slump, turn your head downward, and walk slowly. Do the different postures affect your mood?

---

facial-feedback hypothesis: The idea that the muscular movements involved in certain facial expressions trigger the corresponding emotions (example: smiling makes us happy).

Were you able to make yourself feel happier by "putting on a happy face" and adopting a happy posture? Duclos and others (1989) found that assuming particular postures and facial expressions that are associated with certain emotions can actually produce the emotions.

Controlling Our Facial Expressions to Regulate Our Feelings

If facial expressions can activate emotions, is it possible that intensifying or weakening a facial expression might intensify or weaken the corresponding feeling state? In 1872 Darwin wrote:

Each culture has different display rules for expressing emotions. In Japan, people do not smile for formal wedding portraits.

The free expression by outward signs of an emotion intensifies it. On the other hand, the repression . . . of all outward signs softens our emotions. He who gives way to violent gestures will increase his rage; he who does not control the signs of fear will experience fear in greater degree. (p. 365)

Izard (1990) believes that learning to self-regulate emotional expression can enable us to gain control over our emotions. We can learn to change the intensity of an emotion by inhibiting, weakening, or amplifying its expression. Or we might change the emotion itself by simulating the expression of another emotion. Izard proposes that this approach to the regulation of emotion might be a useful adjunct to psychotherapy.

Cultural Rules for Displaying Emotion

While the facial expressions of the primary emotions are the same in cultures around the world, each culture can have very different **display rules**—cultural rules that dictate how emotions should generally be expressed and where and when their expression is appropriate (Ekman & Friesen, 1975). Often society's display rules expect us to give evidence of certain emotions that we may not actually feel. We are expected to be sad at funerals, to applaud speakers even if we do not enjoy them, and *not* to make a facial expression of disgust if the food we are served tastes bad to us.

Different cultures, neighborhoods, and even families may have very different display rules. Most of us learn them very early and abide by them most of the time. Yet we may not be fully aware that the rules we have learned dictate where, when, how, and even how long certain emotions should be expressed.

You will learn more about reading emotions and detecting the probable motives of others when we explore nonverbal behavior—the language of facial expressions, gestures, and body positions—in chapter 16, "Social Psychology."

Memory Check 10.5

1. (Display, Conventional) rules are the cultural rules that dictate how emotions should generally be expressed and when and where their expression is appropriate.

2. Children who have been blind and deaf since birth exhibit facial expressions that reflect the primary emotions. (true/false)

(continued)

display rules: Cultural rules that dictate how emotions should be expressed, and when and where their expression is appropriate.

3. Facial expressions associated with the basic emotions develop in children as a result of (learning, maturation).

4. The facial expressions conveying the basic emotions are the same from culture to culture. (true/false)

5. Some research indicates that making a happy, a sad, or an angry face can actually trigger the physiological response that accompanies these emotions. (true/false)

Answers: 1. Display 2. true 3. maturation 4. true 5. true

Thinking Critically

Evaluation

In your view, which theory or combination of theories best explains motivation: drive-reduction theory, arousal theory, opponent-process theory, or Maslow's hierarchy of needs? Which theory do you find least convincing? Support your answers.

Point/Counterpoint

Present a convincing argument for each of these positions:

a. The polygraph should not be allowed in the legal system or in business and industry.
b. The polygraph should be allowed in the legal system and in business and industry.

Psychology in Your Life

Select five of Murray's needs (shown in Table 10.2) that provide the strongest motivation for your behavior. Give specific examples of how these needs are apparent in your life.

Chapter Summary and Review

Theories of Motivation

How do instinct theories explain motivation?

Instinct theories suggest that human behavior is motivated by certain innate, unlearned tendencies, or instincts, which are shared by all individuals.

What is the drive-reduction theory of motivation?

Drive-reduction theory suggests that a biological need creates an unpleasant state of arousal or tension called a **drive**, which impels the organism to engage in behavior that will satisfy the need and reduce tension.

How does arousal theory explain motivation?

Arousal theory suggests that the aim of motivation is to maintain an optimal level of arousal. If arousal is less than optimal, we engage in activities that stimulate arousal; if arousal exceeds the optimal level, we seek to reduce stimulation.

What is the opponent-process theory of motivation?

The opponent-process theory of motivation suggests that the emotional state in response to certain activities or stimuli will usually give way to the opposite emotion. With repetition of the activity, the initial emotion gradually weakens and the opposing emotion strengthens, eventually providing the motivation for the activity.

How does Maslow's hierarchy of needs account for motivation?

Maslow's hierarchy of needs arranges needs in order of urgency ranging from physical needs (food, water, air, shelter) to security needs, belonging needs, esteem needs, and finally the need for self-actualization (developing to one's full potential) at the top of the hierarchy. Theoretically the needs at the lower levels must be satisfied adequately before a person will be motivated to fulfill the higher needs.

Key Terms

motivation (p. 334)
motives (p. 335)
incentive (p. 335)
intrinsic motivation (p. 335)
extrinsic motivation (p. 335)

instinct (p. 336)
instinct theory (p. 336)
drive-reduction theory (p. 336)
drive (p. 336)
homeostasis (p. 337)
arousal theory (p. 337)
sensory deprivation (p. 339)
opponent-process theory (p. 340)
hierarchy of needs (p. 340)
self-actualization (p. 341)

The Primary Drives: Hunger and Thirst

Under what kinds of conditions do the two types of thirst occur?

One type of thirst results from a loss of bodily fluid that can be caused by perspiring, vomiting, bleeding, diarrhea, or excessive intake of alcohol. Another type of thirst results from excessive intake of salt, which disturbs the water-sodium balance.

What are the roles of the lateral hypothalamus (LH) and the ventromedial hypothalamus (VMH) in the regulation of eating behavior?

The ventromedial hypothalamus (VMH) presumably acts as a satiety center—when activated, it signals the animal to stop eating; when the VMH is destroyed, the animal overeats, becoming obese. The lateral hypothalamus (LH) supposedly acts as a feeding center—when activated, it signals the animal to eat; when the LH is destroyed, the animal refuses to eat.

What are some of the body's hunger and satiety signals?

Some biological hunger signals are low levels of glucose utilization in the cells and high insulin levels. Some satiety signals are high glucose utilization in the cells and the presence in the blood of other satiety substances (such as CCK), secreted by the gastrointestinal tract during digestion.

What are some nonbiological factors that influence what and how much we eat?

External eating cues such as the taste, smell, and appearance of food, the variety of food offered, as well as the time of day, can cause people to eat more food than they actually need.

Key Terms

primary drives (p. 342)
lateral hypothalamus (LH) (p. 343)
ventromedial hypothalamus (VMH) (p. 343)

Social Motives

What is Henry Murray's contribution to the study of motivation?

Henry Murray defined a number of social motives, or needs, and developed the Thematic Apperception Test to assess a person's level of the needs.

What is the need for achievement?

The need for achievement (*n* Ach) is the need to accomplish something difficult and to perform at a high standard of excellence.

What are some characteristics shared by people who are high in achievement motivation?

High achievers enjoy challenges and like to compete. They tend to set goals of moderate difficulty, are more motivated by hope of success than fear of failure, attribute their success to their ability and hard work, and are most often drawn to business, frequently becoming entrepreneurs.

Key Terms

social motives (p. 347)
Thematic Apperception Test (TAT) (p. 347)
need for achievement (*n* Ach) (p. 348)

The What and Why of Emotions

What are the three components of emotions?

An emotion is a feeling state which involves physiological arousal, a cognitive appraisal of the situation arousing the emotion, and outward expression of the emotion.

What does a polygraph measure?

A polygraph monitors changes in heart rate, blood pressure, respiration rate, and galvanic skin response, which typically accompany the anxiety that occurs when a person lies.

According to the James-Lange theory, what sequence of events occurs when we experience an emotion?

According to the James-Lange theory of emotion, environmental stimuli produce a physiological response, and then our awareness of this response causes the emotion.

What is the Cannon-Bard theory of emotion?

The Cannon-Bard theory suggests that emotion-provoking stimuli received by the senses are relayed to the thalamus, which simultaneously passes the information to the cortex, giving us the mental experience of the emotion, and to the internal organs, producing physiological arousal.

According to the Schachter-Singer theory, what two factors must occur in order to experience an emotion?

The Schachter-Singer theory states that for an emotion to occur: (1) there must be physiological arousal, and (2) the person must perceive some reason for the arousal in order to label the emotion.

Key Terms

emotion (p. 352)
polygraph (p. 353)
James-Lange theory (p. 354)
Cannon-Bard theory (p. 354)
Schachter-Singer theory (p. 355)
primary emotions (p. 358)
secondary emotions (p. 358)

The Expression of Emotion

How does the development of facial expressions in infants suggest a biological basis for emotional expression?

Emotions develop in a particular sequence in infants and seem to be the result of maturation rather than learning, even in children who have been blind and deaf since birth.

What is the facial-feedback hypothesis?

The facial-feedback hypothesis suggests that the muscular movements involved in certain facial expressions trigger the corresponding emotion (for example, smiling makes us happy).

Key Terms

facial-feedback hypothesis (p. 362)
display rules (p. 363)

11

Human Sexuality and Gender

Walter Fay (Susan) Cannon

alter Fay Cannon was born into a prominent family in 1925 in Durham, North Carolina. A bright, academically talented youth, Cannon was accepted at Princeton University in 1941 when he was only 16 years old. He joined the United States Navy to serve during the last 1 1/2 years of World War II, then he returned to Princeton where he graduated in 1946. On to Harvard, where Cannon, the bright scholar, finished his Ph.D. and began a distinguished career. He was a university professor; an accomplished poet, writer, and historian; and finally a brilliant curator at the Smithsonian Institution in Washington, D.C., where he served until his retirement in 1979.

But Walter Cannon had a secret life, which was revealed only a few years before his death in 1981. He felt like and believed that he was a woman in a man's body. Though psychologically acknowledging himself as a man, Cannon had always used his body as a woman, in homosexual encounters at Princeton, when he served in the Navy, and throughout his life.

Cannon's wish to be female became even more compelling during his last years at the Smithsonian. He insisted on being called Faye rather than Walter and began carrying a purse, one colleague recalls. In 1976 Cannon began showing up for work dressed as a woman. This was a particular embarrassment to the officials at the Smithsonian because Cannon was responsible for showing visiting dignitaries around the institution. Needless to say, this eccentric behavior was not consistent with the image the Smithsonian expected of its scholars, and Cannon's early retirement was "arranged" in 1979.

Cannon did not think of himself as gay but referred to himself as a "male woman." He began taking hormone treatments and had a sex-change operation in February 1981. Now she was Susan Faye Cannon, 56 years old, in rapidly failing health and great pain.

Susan was found dead in her home from acute codeine intoxication in early November of 1981. An excerpt from Cannon's obituary notice in the *Princeton Alumni Weekly* reads: "Three months before she died, she called and told a classmate that it had been demonstrated conclusively that genetically he had always been a woman. She was very glad, because she had always suspected it and, in more recent years, known it to be a fact" (quoted in Latham & Grenadier, 1982, p. 65).

WAS HE, WALTER CANNON, A MAN, or was she, Susan Cannon, a woman? Clearly Walter had the physical body of a man, but he felt like and believed that he was a woman in a man's body. You will learn how such a condition could occur when you read about the roles the sex chromosomes and the sex hormones play in the physical formation of males and females.

Let's start at the beginning and consider all of the processes leading up to the very first announcement a parent makes—"It's a girl!" or "It's a boy!"

What Makes a Male, a Male and a Female, a Female?

Question: What are the biological factors that determine whether a person is male or female?

The Sex Chromosomes: X's and Y's

sex chromosomes: The pair of chromosomes that determines the sex of a person (XX in females and XY in males).

The first determiner of biological sex is the **sex chromosomes**, which are XX in females and XY in males. Female eggs all carry the X sex chromosome, but sperm cells in the male can carry either an X or a Y chromosome. If a Y-bearing sperm cell unites with the egg, which always carries an X chromosome, the developing embryo will be XY—a male. If a sperm cell carrying an X chromosome fertilizes the egg, the result will be XX—a female.

But this does not mean that being a male or a female is completely set at conception. Conception is only the beginning of the series of events spelling the difference between males and females. At 6 weeks after conception the primitive *gonads* (sex glands) are the same in the male and the female. During the seventh week, however, if the Y chromosome is present, the gonads develop into primitive testes. If no Y chromosome is present, the gonads develop into ovaries about 12 weeks after conception. But the story does not end here.

The Sex Hormones: Contributing to Maleness and Femaleness

In the male embryo, the primitive testes produce and secrete **androgens**, the male sex hormones that cause the male **genitals**—the penis, testes, and scrotum—to develop. If androgens are not present, female genitals—the ovaries, uterus, and vagina—will develop. In other words, the presence or absence of androgens determines whether male or female genitals—**primary sex characteristics**—develop. A genetic male (XY) can develop female genitals if androgens are absent, and a genetic female (XX) can develop male genitals if too much androgen is present. Could this be what Cannon had referred to when she told a classmate that "it had been demonstrated conclusively that genetically he had always been a woman"?

Androgens affect more than just the development of the genitals. The presence or absence of androgens in the fetus determines whether a part of the brain, the hypothalamus, becomes male or female differentiated. The hypothalamus, through its control of the pituitary (the body's master gland), plays a major part in controlling the production and release of the sex hormones.

At puberty the hypothalamus sends a signal to the pituitary, which in turn sets in motion the maturing of the internal and external genitals and the appearance of the **secondary sex characteristics**. These are the physical characteristics associated with sexual maturity—pubic and underarm hair in both sexes, breasts in females, and facial and chest hair and a deepened voice in males. Figure 11.1 shows the male and female sex organs.

gonads: The sex glands; the ovaries in females and the testes in males.

androgens: Male sex hormones.

genitals (JEN-ah-tulz): The internal and external reproductive organs.

primary sex characteristics: The internal and external reproductive organs; the genitals.

secondary sex characteristics: The physical characteristics that are not directly involved in reproduction but that develop at puberty and are associated with sexual maturity.

Figure 11.1   The Male and Female Reproductive Systems

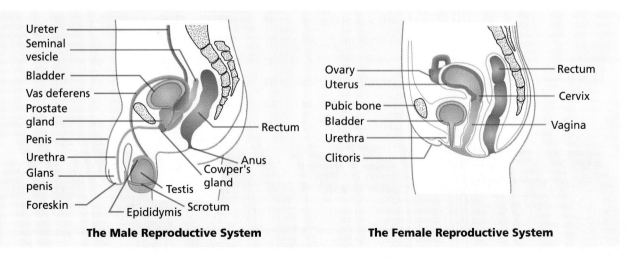

The Male Reproductive System   **The Female Reproductive System**

Sex-Role Development

Why is it that:

- by ages 15 to 26 months, children already exhibit clear preferences for toys considered appropriate for their sex.
- by age 2 1/2 years, children already have formed stereotypes concerning what boys and girls do and do not do, and what they like and dislike.
- by ages 2 to 3 years, children already consider some jobs to be for men and others for women.

What are the prevailing cultural stereotypes about the masculine and feminine sex roles—those behaviors associated with males or females? Traditionally, males have been expected to be strong, dominant, independent, competitive, assertive, logical, and unemotional; females have been expected to be warm, nurturant, caring, sensitive, supportive, emotional, passive, and dependent. Table 11.1 shows the characteristics most often used to describe men and women by respondents in a 1990 Gallup poll.

Environmental Influences on Sex Typing

Question: What is sex typing, and what are the agencies in the environment that contribute to the process?

Table 11.1

Characteristics Most Often Used to Describe Men and Women

This table shows the results of a 1990 Gallup poll in which subjects were asked to respond to the following question: "Now I want to ask about some more specific characteristics of men and women. For each one I read, please tell me whether you think it is generally more true of men or more true of women."

Characteristics Most Often Said to Describe Men				Characteristics Most Often Said to Describe Women			
		Opinions of				Opinions of	
	Total	Men	Women		Total	Men	Women
Aggressive	64%	68%	61%	Emotional	81%	79%	83%
Strong	61	66	57	Talkative	73	73	74
Proud	59	62	55	Sensitive	72	74	71
Disorganized	56	55	57	Affectionate	66	69	64
Courageous	54	55	53	Patient	64	60	68
Confident	54	58	49	Romantic	60	59	61
Independent	50	58	43	Moody	58	63	52
Ambitious	48	51	44	Cautious	57	55	59
Selfish	47	49	44	Creative	54	48	60
Logical	45	53	37	Thrifty	52	51	53
Easy-going	44	48	40	Manipulative	51	54	48
Demanding	43	39	46	Honest	42	44	41
Possessive	42	38	45	Critical	42	43	41
Funny	40	47	34	Happy	39	38	39
Level-headed	39	46	34	Possessive	37	43	32

Source: DeStefano, L., & Colastanto, D. (1990, February). Unlike 1925, today most Americans think men have it better. *Gallop Poll Monthly*, No. 293, p. 29.

sex typing: The process by which individuals acquire the traits, behaviors, attitudes, preferences, and interests that the culture considers appropriate for their biological sex.

How do individuals acquire the traits, behaviors, attitudes, preferences, and interests that the culture considers appropriate for their biological sex? This process, called **sex typing**, begins at birth, and parents, peers, television, and a number of other influences play a powerful role in promoting it.

The Parents' Role: Pink and Blue Blankets and Sex-Typed Toys Albert Bandura (1969) describes how parents attempt to influence the sex-role development of their children:

> Sex-role differentiation usually commences immediately after birth, when the baby is named and both the infant and the nursery are given the blue or pink treatment depending upon the sex of the child. Thereafter, indoctrination into masculinity and femininity is diligently promulgated by adorning children with distinctive clothes and hair styles, selecting sex-appropriate play materials and recreational activities, promoting associations with same-sex playmates, and through non-permissive parental reactions to deviant sex-role behavior. (p. 215)

Mothers tend to make fewer distinctions in the way they interact with their children based on sex. Fathers, on the other hand, play a more active role in sex typing (Power, 1985; Block, 1978). Fathers typically encourage their sons to be competent, to achieve and compete, to be assertive, and to control their emotions. Daughters are reinforced for being affectionate, nurturant, and obedient (Lamb, 1981). Boys are punished more than girls, and girls are treated with more warmth and gentleness. Boys are encouraged to engage in large muscle activities and to be more independent than girls (Fagot, 1982; Maccoby & Jacklin, 1974).

Fathers often play a more active role than mothers in sex typing their sons and daughters.

If fathers and mothers play a different role in the sex typing of their children, what happens when children are raised in single-parent homes headed by the mother? The effects of father absence seem to be most pronounced in boys under age 5 (Hetherington, 1966; Stevenson & Black, 1988). Father-present boys are more stereotypically sex typed than father-absent boys; they are more likely to choose masculine toys and activities. However, father-absent adolescents are more stereotypically sex typed and more aggressive than father-present boys. Barclay and Cusumano (1967) speculate that hypermasculinity may be an attempt to cover a basic feminine identification.

Father absence appears to have little or no effect on the sex typing of girls (Stevenson & Black, 1988). Father-absent girls tend to be slightly less feminine, but this might be the effect of having mothers who are less stereotypically feminine (Kurdek & Siesky, 1980). Hetherington (1972) found father-absent adolescent girls to be more sexually promiscuous than father-present girls.

Other Influences on Sex Typing Peers also play an important role in enforcing conformity to sex-role stereotypes. The reaction of peers to the selection of a sex-inappropriate toy can be strong indeed (Lamb & Roopnarine, 1979).

Parents, peers, and teachers put much stronger pressure on boys to avoid feminine activities, such as playing with dolls and dishes and dressing up in mother's clothes, than they put on girls to avoid masculine activities. Sissies are ostracized while tomboys are tolerated. Carol Martin (1990) suggests that adults react more negatively to cross-sex behavior in boys because they fear that boys might be less likely to outgrow it.

Psychological Theories of Sex-Role Development

Question: What are three theories of sex-role development?

Three psychological theories are currently used to explain, in part, how sex-role development occurs—social learning theory, cognitive developmental theory, and gender-schema theory.

Social Learning Theory: Observation, Imitation, and Reinforcement

According to **social learning theory,** observation, imitation, and reinforcement are the mechanisms that explain sex typing (Mischel, 1966). When children imitate behaviors considered appropriate for their **gender,** they are usually reinforced. When behaviors are not appropriate (a boy puts on lipstick, or a girl puts on shaving cream and attempts to shave), children are quickly informed, often in a tone of reprimand, that boys or girls do not do that. As a result of reinforcement and punishment, children are led to engage in sex-appropriate behavior. They need not have knowledge about gender in order to acquire sex-typed preferences.

Parents are not the only ones who serve as models or who dispense reinforcers. Children learn about sex-appropriate behaviors from TV, peers, and teachers. They observe the actions of others and the consequences of those actions. Even the praise or scorn that others receive for sex-appropriate or inappropriate actions can provide memorable lessons in what to do and what not to do.

Cognitive Developmental Theory: Understanding Gender in Stages

Cognitive developmental theory, proposed by Lawrence Kohlberg (1966; Kohlberg & Ullian, 1974) suggests that children play an active role in their own sex typing, but that an understanding of gender is a prerequisite. According to Kohlberg, children go through the following series of stages in acquiring the concept of gender. Between ages 2 and 3, children acquire gender identity and label themselves as male or female. Between ages 4 and 5, children acquire the concept of gender stability—that boys are boys and girls are girls for a lifetime. Finally, between ages 6 and 8, children acquire gender constancy—the understanding that gender does not change regardless of the activities they engage in or the clothes they wear. According to cognitive developmental theory, when children realize their gender is permanent, they are motivated to seek out same-sex models and learn to act in ways considered appropriate for their gender.

Although the attainment of gender constancy is a necessary part of sex-role development, a number of researchers have found that children have a great deal of gender-role knowledge long before they attain gender constancy (Levy & Carter, 1989; Serbin & Sprafkin, 1986). Gender constancy may occur between 6 and 8 years, but Kohlberg's theory fails to explain why many sex-appropriate behaviors and preferences are observed in children as young as age 2 or 3 (Martin & Little, 1990; Jacklin, 1989).

Gender-Schema Theory: Forming Gender Stereotypes

Gender-schema theory, proposed by Sandra Bem (1981), combines elements of both social learning and cognitive developmental theory. Like social learning theory, gender-schema theory suggests that young children are motivated to pay attention to and behave in a way consistent with gender-based standards and stereotypes of the culture. Like cognitive developmental theory, gender-schema theory stresses that children begin to use gender as a way to organize and process information. But it holds that this process occurs earlier, when gender identity rather than gender constancy is attained (Bem, 1985). According to Martin and Little (1990), "Once children can accurately label the sexes, they begin to form gender stereotypes and their behavior is influenced by these gender-associated expectations" (p. 1438). They develop strong preferences for peers of the same sex and for sex-appropriate toys and clothing. Fagot and others (1992) found gender labeling and gender stereotyping to occur in children 2 to 3 years old.

Children learn which activities and traits are most important for males and females, and they tend to evaluate themselves in relation to those traits. Children first learn the characteristics appropriate to their own sex, and later those appro-

social learning theory: A theory that explains the process of sex typing in terms of observation, imitation, and reinforcement.

gender (JEN-der): One's biological sex—male or female.

cognitive developmental theory: A theory suggesting that when children realize their gender is permanent, they are motivated to seek out same-sex models and learn to act in ways considered appropriate for their gender.

gender-schema theory: A theory suggesting that young children are motivated to attend to and behave in ways consistent with gender-based standards and stereotypes of the culture.

priate to the opposite sex (Martin et al., 1990). To a large extent, their own self-concepts and self-esteem depend on the match between their abilities and behaviors and the cultural definition of what is desirable for their gender.

> **androgyny** (an-DROJ-uh-nee): A combination of the desirable male and female characteristics in one person.

Adjustment and Sex Typing: Feminine, Masculine, or Androgynous?

Question: Do good adjustment and high self-esteem seem to be related to masculine traits, feminine traits, or androgyny?

Traditionally, masculinity and femininity have been considered opposite ends of a continuum. But must we think of masculine traits and feminine traits as mutually exclusive? Must an individual be either independent, competent, and assertive or nurturant, sensitive, and warm? Sandra Bem (1974, 1977) proposed that masculinity and femininity are separate and independent dimensions of personality rather than opposite ends of a continuum. A person can be high or low on one or both dimensions. **Androgyny** is a combination of the desirable male and female characteristics in the person who is said to be androgynous. People who are low on both dimensions are labeled undifferentiated.

Some researchers maintain that androgynous individuals have a wider range of possible behavioral characteristics at their disposal. Consequently, androgynous individuals are said to be better equipped to meet the challenges of the work world and their personal relationships (Bem, 1975). Is this true? Are androgynous individuals better adjusted than those who adopt the conventional masculine or feminine role consistent with their gender? Research suggests that for both males and females, masculine traits are most strongly associated with self-esteem and adjustment (Long, 1986; Orlofsky & O'Heron, 1987). Jones and others (1978) found that "the more adaptive, flexible, unconventional, and competent patterns of responding occurred among more masculine subjects independent of their gender" (p. 311).

Memory Check 11.1

1. The primary sex characteristics develop _____; the secondary sex characteristics develop _____.

    a. before birth; before birth   c. before birth; at puberty
    b. at puberty; at puberty   d. at puberty; before birth

2. If androgens are *not* present, (male, female) genitals will develop regardless of whether the sex chromosomes are male (XY) or female (XX).

3. The (mother, father) usually plays the major role in sex typing.

4. (Cognitive developmental theory, Gender-schema theory) is *less* able to explain sex-appropriate behaviors and preferences in 2- to 3-year-olds.

5. Research has shown androgynous individuals are better adjusted than those who adopt the masculine or feminine role. (true/false)

Answers: 1. c 2. female 3. father 4. Cognitive developmental theory 5. false

Throughout the world, a person's gender largely defines his or her destiny.

Gender Differences: Fact or Myth?

To a remarkable degree throughout recorded history and in the vast majority of cultures around the world, gender—a person's biological sex—has defined destiny. Even in the United States women did not have the right to vote in national elections until 1920. Why do issues of gender continue to mark our lives so profoundly?

Males and females are indeed different, but in what ways and to what degree? To address this question, Eleanor Maccoby and Carol Jacklin (1974a) examined 1,600 studies on gender differences and published their results in *The Psychology of Sex Differences.* They found evidence that males were generally more aggressive and had a slight advantage in mathematics and spatial skills, while females had a slight advantage in verbal ability. Maccoby and Jacklin also refuted some long-standing, unfounded beliefs about sex differences such as the notion that compared to boys, girls are more sociable or suggestible, less analytical, better at rote learning and repetitive tasks, and lower in self-esteem or achievement motivation. Table 11.2 summarizes Maccoby and Jacklin's findings on sex differences.

Gender Differences in Aggression: The Clearest Difference

Question: What is the most consistent and significant difference observed in comparative studies of gender?

Most researchers agree that greater physical aggression in males is one of the

Table 11.2   Summary of Maccoby and Jacklin's Findings on Sex Differences

Unfounded Beliefs about Sex Differences	Open Questions of Difference	Fairly Well-Established Sex Differences
Girls are more social than boys	Tactile sensitivity	Girls have greater verbal ability
Girls are more suggestible than boys	Fear, timidity, and anxiety	Boys excel in visual-spatial ability
Girls have lower self-esteem than boys	Activity level	Boys excel in mathematical ability
Girls are better at rote learning and simple repetitive tasks; boys are better at higher level cognitive processing	Competitiveness	Boys are more aggressive
Boys are more analytic than girls	Dominance	
	Compliance	
Girls are more affected by heredity; boys are more affected by environment	Nurturance and "maternal" behavior	
Girls lack achievement motivation		
Girls are more inclined toward the auditory; boys are more inclined toward the visual		

Source: Eleanor Maccoby and Carol Nagy Jacklin, *The Psychology of Sex Differences.* Stanford, CA: Stanford University Press, 1974.

WORLD OF PSYCHOLOGY: MULTICULTURAL PERSPECTIVES

Gender Differences in Cognitive Abilities

Question: For what cognitive abilities are there proven gender differences?

For many years people have been taught that, on average, females are superior to males in verbal skills, and males are superior to females in mathematics and spatial skills. What does research say about cognitive differences and gender?

Gender Differences in Verbal Ability: Is One Sex Better with Words? Maccoby and Jacklin (1974a) reported that girls performed better overall than boys in verbal abilities. But over the last few decades, the gender differences in tests of general verbal ability have virtually disappeared. Using meta-analysis, researchers Janet Hyde and Marcia Linn (1988) examined 165 studies reporting test results on verbal ability for approximately 1.5 million males and females. They found no significant gender differences in verbal ability.

Gender Differences in Math Ability: Do Males Have the Edge? Researchers Camilla Benbow and Julian Stanley (1980, 1983) conducted a series of comparative studies on males and females in the early 1980s. They compared the test scores (on the math section of the Scholastic Aptitude Test) in the United States of large groups of top-scoring seventh- and eighth-grade boys and girls. There were twice as many boys as girls scoring above 500, and 13 times as many boys as girls scoring above 700. Benbow and Stanley speculated that the explanation for the differences was biological, yet they had no biological data, and a biological connection has never been proven. Moreover, this strong male superiority was found only in a select segment of the population—the brightest of the bright in mathematics ability—and it does not hold across other ability groups.

In one of the largest studies conducted to date on gender differences in mathematics, Janet Hyde and her colleagues (1990) performed a meta-analysis of 100 studies, which together represented test results of over 3 million subjects. They found a slight superiority in female performance in the elementary- and middle-school years and a moderate male superiority in the high-school grades, which continued into adulthood.

The researchers found no significant gender difference in the understanding of mathematical concepts among the various age groups. And although females did slightly better in mathematical problem solving in elementary and middle school, males scored moderately higher in high school and college. The authors attribute the moderate superiority of males, in part, to the fact that they tend to

Researchers have found no significant gender differences in the understanding of mathematical concepts.

take more upper-level math courses in high school and college.

Parents usually expect boys to do better than girls in math, and they may communicate their expectations in subtle ways (Lummis & Stevenson, 1990). Such expectations may become a self-fulfilling prophecy, leading girls to lack confidence in their math ability and decide not to pursue advanced math courses (Eccles & Jacobs, 1986).

Gender Differences in Spatial Ability Researchers have found that, in general, males tend to perform somewhat better than females in spatial skills (Linn & Hyde, 1989; Linn & Peterson, 1985). This gender difference has been found on some but not all of the various spatial tasks, and the difference is so small that only about "5 percent of it at most can be accounted for on the basis of sex" (Fausto-Sterling, 1985, p. 33).

Gender differences in intellectual performance are small or nonexistent across cultures as well. A paper by Hanna (1988) on comparative studies in 20 countries revealed small gender differences favoring males in geometry and measurement in 10 countries, and small gender differences favoring females in algebra in 4 countries.

Try your skill at sample items used to test spatial ability. Do the *Try It!* on page 376.

testosterone (tes-TOS-tah-rone): The most powerful androgen secreted by the testes and adrenal glands in males and by the adrenal glands in females; influences the development and maintenance of male sex characteristics and sexual motivation.

most consistent and significant differences observed in comparative studies of gender. And these differences have been found in virtually every culture where aggressive behavior has been studied. Such an observation is hardly surprising. We only need to consider the number of men who are in prison for violent crimes compared to the number of women. The vast majority of the murders and beatings, and nearly all the rapes are committed by men.

Greater aggression can usually be observed in boys from the time they are 2 to 2 1/2 years old. They are more likely than girls to engage in mock-fighting and rough-and-tumble play and to have more aggressive fantasies (Maccoby & Jacklin, 1974b).

The male sex hormone **testosterone** has long been suspected as the guilty substance promoting aggression. Sex differences in aggression have been linked to testosterone levels in a number of animal studies, especially with rats and primates (Maccoby & Jacklin, 1974, 1980). Some researchers speculate that high prenatal levels of androgen may predispose males to aggressive behavior.

Gender differences are revealed most often on mental rotation tasks such as the first problem in the *Try It!*, in which three-dimensional figures must be mentally rotated quickly and accurately. Gender differences are less strong in spatial perception tasks such as the second problem, where spatial relationships must be perceived by subjects according to the orientation of their bodies.

Try It!

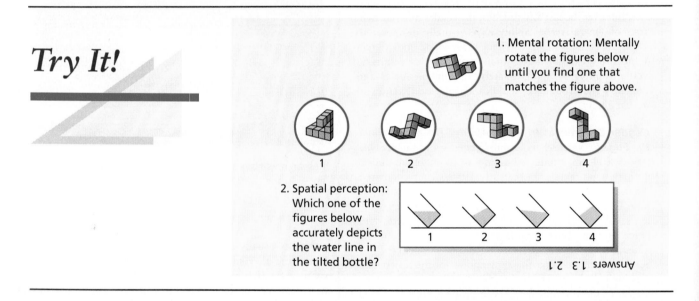

Gender Stereotyping: Who Wins? Who Loses?

A majority of the people on the planet are female, yet around the world women are vastly underrepresented in positions of power. As we have seen, gender stereotypes define males as decisive, aggressive, unemotional, logical, and ambitious. These qualities are perceived by many men and women alike as precisely the "right stuff" for leaders, decision makers, and power people at all levels of society. But women, too, can be strong, bold, and decisive leaders, like former British Prime Minister Margaret Thatcher, Golda Maier of Israel, and Indira Ghandi of India.

About 51 percent of the people in the United States today are females, yet until 1993 only 2 of the 100 U.S. senators were women, and in 1991 only 3 percent of the officers of major corporations were women (Saltzman, 1991). Strong female leaders may find a double standard when it comes to perceptions in the workplace (see Table 11.3).

Table 11.3 Double Standards in the Workplace

How to Tell a Business Man from a Business Woman

A businessman is aggressive; a businesswoman is pushy.

A businessman is good with details; a businesswoman is picky.

He loses his temper because he's so involved in his job; she's a bitch.

When he's depressed or hungover, everyone tiptoes past his office. If she's moody, it must be her time of the month.

He follows through; she doesn't know when to quit.

He's confident; she's conceited.

He stands firm; she's hard.

His judgments are her prejudices.

He is a man of the world; she's been around.

If he drinks it's because of job pressure; she's a lush.

He's never afraid to say what he thinks; she's always shooting off her mouth.

He exercises authority diligently; she's power mad.

He's close-mouthed; she's secretive.

He's a stern task master; she's hard to work for.

He climbed the ladder of success; she slept her way to the top.

Source: Doyle, J. A. (1985). *Sex and gender*. Dubuque, IA: Wm. C. Brown.

In the 1990s the negative effect that women experience due to gender stereotyping is not as bad as in decades past, but it is still a major problem for many women.

Memory Check 11.2

Indicate with an *M*, *F*, or *N* whether the abilities and traits listed below are generally more true of males, females, or neither.

_____ 1) higher verbal ability _____ 4) more sociable
_____ 2) better spatial skills _____ 5) more aggressive
_____ 3) greater mathematical ability _____ 6) lower self-esteem

Answers: 1) N 2) M 3) M 4) N 5) M 6) N

Sexual Attitudes and Behavior

Few would disagree that society's attitudes about sexual behavior are more liberal now than in decades past. In the 1940s and 1950s, virtually all societal institutions officially frowned upon sex before marriage. The topic of sex was not considered an appropriate subject for serious investigation, nor was it discussed openly in polite society. But all of that began to change when Alfred Kinsey came on the scene.

coitus: Penile-vaginal intercourse.

The Kinsey Surveys: The First In-Depth Look at Sexual Behavior

Question: What are the famous Kinsey surveys?

In the 1940s Alfred Kinsey and his associates undertook a monumental survey that helped to bring the subject of sex out in the open. They interviewed thousands of men and women about their sexual behaviors and attitudes, and their results were published in a two-volume report—*Sexual Behavior in the Human Male* and *Sexual Behavior in the Human Female*. The public was stunned by what Kinsey's subjects said they had done and were doing. It appeared that a lot of Americans had a head start on the sexual revolution way back in the 1940s and 1950s. And there was a great gulf between what people were practicing in private and what they were admitting openly.

Kinsey's interviews revealed the following:

- About 50 percent of the females and nearly 90 percent of the males reported having sexual intercourse, **coitus,** before marriage.
- Over 40 percent of the college-educated couples said they engaged in oral sex.
- The majority of women and virtually all males reported that they had masturbated.
- About 26 percent of the married women and half of the married men admitted having had extramarital affairs.

Have sexual attitudes and behavior changed much since Kinsey's survey almost 50 years ago?

Sexual Attitudes and Behavior Today: After the Sexual Revolution

A 1989 Gallup poll surveyed attitudes of a representative sample of 539 American college students from 100 public and private colleges and universities

Table 11.4   Sexual Behaviors of a National Random Sample of 1,401 Adults

Results of a 1989 Survey of Sexual Behavior

97% of adults have had sexual intercourse since age 18.

Adults had an average of 1.16 different sexual partners during the past year (males, 1.49; females, 0.91).

Adults averaged 7.2 different sexual partners since age 18 (males, 12.26; females, 3.32).

22% had no sexual intercourse within the past year (males, 14.1%; females, 28%).

1.5% of married adults had affairs during the past year (males, 2.1; females, 0.8).

65% of females and 30% of males have been faithful during their marriage.

Married couples had intercourse an average of 67 times the past year; singles and divorcees, 55 times; separated people, 66 times; and widows and widowers, 6 times.

The past year adults ages 30–39 had intercourse most often (78 times, on average) and adults over age 70 least frequently (8 times, on average).

Source: Smith, T.W. (1991). Adult sexual behavior in 1989: Number of partners, frequency of intercourse and risk of AIDS. *Family Planning Perspectives, 23,* 102–107.

(Shearer, 1989). Questioned on their own sexual practices, about 50 percent had engaged in sexual intercourse occasionally, while 26 percent engaged in it regularly. Half the students admitted to having had more than one partner, and 25 percent said they had had 5 or more partners. But the statistic that is most interesting is that 25 percent of the college students said they were virgins.

Throughout all age groups, men report having had more different sex partners than women report having. Women associate sex with love and marriage more than men do, and it may be true that women give more of themselves emotionally to the sexual union. Table 11.4 summarizes the findings of a national survey reported in 1991 of the sexual behavior of 1,401 adults age 18 and over.

In the decades before the 1960s, young men and women were less free to say yes to their sexual desires. People were constrained by virtually all of society's institutions and by the most formidable restraint of all—fear of pregnancy. But today, fear of pregnancy is less a factor because of the pill and other contraceptive methods, and abortion is legal. Peer pressure ("everybody's doing it"), films, TV, magazines, advertisements, song lyrics—all these sources of influence have combined to make it difficult for young people to say no to their sexual desires.

In a sense, then, the societal pressures that decades ago made it hard to say yes to sex have been traded for pressures that today make it just as hard to say no. Sexual freedom prevails only when we are equally free to say yes or no.

sexual response cycle: The four phases—excitement, plateau, orgasm, and resolution—that Masters and Johnson found are part of the human sexual response in both males and females.

excitement phase: The first stage in the sexual response cycle characterized by an erection in males and a swelling of the clitoris and vaginal lubrication in females.

Sexual Desire and Arousal: Factors That Drive the Sex Drive

Question: According to Masters and Johnson, what are the four phases of the human sexual response cycle?

Masters and Johnson and the Human Sexual Response Cycle Kinsey conducted the first major survey of sexual behavior, but what if the act of intercourse could be monitored while it was happening right in the laboratory? Wouldn't this be more scientific than simply relying on self reports? These were the questions asked by sex researchers Dr. William Masters and Virginia Johnson. To answer them, they planned and conducted the first laboratory investigations of the human sexual response at the Washington University School of Medicine in St. Louis in 1954. They monitored their volunteer subjects, who engaged in the sex act while connected to sophisticated (for the 1960s) electronic sensing devices.

Masters and Johnson (1966) concluded that the human sexual response is quite similar for males and females. Two major physiological changes occur in both sexes—the flow of blood into the genitals (and breasts in females) and an increase in neuromuscular tension.

Both males and females experience a **sexual response cycle** with four phases: (1) the excitement phase, (2) the plateau phase, (3) the orgasm, and (4) the resolution phase. Masters and Johnson studied over "10,000 complete cycles of sexual response" in 382 women and 312 men (1966, p. 15). They found that these phases apply not only to sexual intercourse but also to other types of sexual activity.

The Excitement Phase The **excitement phase** is the beginning of the sexual response. It can be triggered by direct physical contact as well as by psychological arousal—thoughts, emotions, and a variety of sensory stimuli. For both

William Masters & Virginia Johnson

partners, muscular tension increases, heart rate quickens, and blood pressure rises. As additional blood is pumped into the genitals, the male gets an erection and the female feels a swelling of the clitoris. Vaginal lubrication occurs as the inner two-thirds of the vagina expands and the inner lips of the vagina enlarge. In women especially, the nipples harden and stand erect.

The Plateau Phase   After the excitement phase, the couple enters the **plateau phase**, when excitement continues to mount. Blood pressure increases still more, hearts pound, breathing becomes heavy and more rapid, and muscle tension increases. The man's penis may harden even more, and his testes swell. Drops of liquid, which could contain live sperm cells, may drip from the penis during this phase.

In the female the outer part of the vagina swells as the increased blood further engorges the area, narrowing the opening by 30 percent or more. The upper two-thirds of the vagina expands still more, and the clitoris withdraws under the clitoral hood, its skin covering. The breasts become engorged with blood, increasing in size by 20 to 25 percent. Excitement builds steadily for both partners during the plateau phase. Tension and passion soar higher and higher, until the orgasm phase begins.

The Orgasm Phase   The **orgasm phase**, the shortest of the stages, is the very peak of the experience—the highest point of sexual pleasure—marked by a sudden discharge of accumulated sexual tension. Involuntary muscle contractions may seize the entire body during orgasm. All of the accompanying physiological excitements—breathing, pulse rate, and blood pressure—build and peak at orgasm. The genitals throb with rhythmic contractions.

Orgasm is a two-stage experience for the male. First is his awareness that ejaculation is near and that he can do nothing to stop it; second is the ejaculation itself, when semen is released from the penis in forceful spurts.

The experience of orgasm in women builds in much the same way as for men. Marked by powerful, rhythmic contractions, her orgasm usually lasts longer than that of the male. About 40 to 50 percent of women regularly experience orgasm during intercourse (Kinsey et al., 1953; Fisher, 1973; Wilcox & Hager, 1980). Although the vaginal orgasm and clitoral orgasm may feel different, say Masters and Johnson, the actual physiological response in the female is the same.

The Resolution Phase   The orgasm period gives way to the **resolution phase**, which is the tapering-off period, when the body returns to its unaroused state. Both partners are at rest and may feel a calm sense of well-being.

Men experience a **refractory period** in the resolution phase, during which they cannot have another orgasm. The refractory period may last only a few minutes for some men, but much longer—many hours—for others. Women do not have a refractory period and may, if restimulated, experience another orgasm right away.

Question: What are the male and female sex hormones, and how do they affect sexual desire and activity in males and females?

The Role of Hormones in Sexual Desire and Arousal: Sexual Substances

In most animal species, sexual activity does not occur unless the female is "in heat." Thus, most lower animals behave sexually in response to hormones, odors, and biologically determined sexual cycles. But humans, primarily, do not. Humans engage in far more sex than is required to continue the species, and their sexual desires can be aroused at practically any time, independent of the rhythmic biological cycles.

plateau phase: The second stage of the sexual response cycle, during which muscle tension and blood flow to the genitals increase in preparation for orgasm.

orgasm phase: The third phase in the sexual response cycle, marked by rhythmic muscular contractions and a sudden discharge of accumulated sexual tension.

resolution phase: The final stage of the sexual response cycle, during which the body returns to an unaroused state.

refractory period: The period immediately following ejaculation, when the male is unable to experience another orgasm.

The sex glands themselves manufacture hormones—**estrogens** and **progesterone** in the ovaries, and androgens in the testes. The adrenal glands in both sexes also produce small amounts of these hormones. Females have considerably more estrogens and progesterone than males do, so these are known as the female sex hormones. Males have considerably more androgens—the male sex hormones. **Testosterone**, the most important androgen, influences the development and maintenance of male sex characteristics as well as sexual motivation.

Testosterone and Sexual Desire Males must have a sufficient level of testosterone in order to maintain sexual interest and have an erection. It is more than coincidence that at puberty, when testosterone levels increase dramatically, sexual thoughts and fantasies, masturbation, and nocturnal emissions also increase significantly. Udry and colleagues (1985) found that adolescents with high blood levels of testosterone spend more time thinking about sex. Thus, they are more likely to engage in masturbation, coitus, or other sexual activity than their counterparts with lower levels of testosterone.

As men age, the level of testosterone declines, and usually there is a decline also in sexual interest and activity. Also, castration (removal of the testes, which produce 95 percent of the male's androgen) usually lowers sexual desire and activity dramatically.

Estrogen and Sexual Desire If testosterone plays an important role in male sexual desire, can we assume that estrogen does the same for females? Actually, only a minimal level of estrogen may be required to sustain sexual desire in women (Bancroft, 1984). Otherwise women would have little or no interest in sex after menopause or after ovariectomies (surgical removal of the ovaries, which produce most of a woman's estrogen and progesterone). However, when postmenopausal women or women who have lost their ovaries are given estrogen, they show an increased interest in sex and derive more pleasure from sexual activity (Dennerstein et al., 1980; Dow et al., 1983).

But it is not only hormones or other biological processes that play a major role in powering sexual arousal. Psychological arousers are potent as well.

Psychological Factors in Sexual Arousal: It All Begins in the Mind Psychological factors play a large part in sexual arousal. Part of the psychological nature of sexual behavior stems from those preferences and practices we have learned from our culture. What is perceived as sexually attractive in the male and female in one culture may differ dramatically from the standards of attractiveness in other cultures. In the United States movie stars and models are often regarded as the ultimate in sexual desirability.

Sometimes, as a result of conditioning, men and women find certain stimuli sexually arousing (Dekker & Everaerd, 1989). The stimuli might be specific settings (a romantic candlelight dinner, a walk on the beach in the evening), certain music, particular objects or articles of clothing, or even the scent of certain perfumes or after-shave.

Men and women differ in the ways they become sexually aroused. Men are more aroused by what they see; visual cues like watching a woman undress are likely to arouse them. But tender, loving touches coupled with verbal expressions of love arouse women more readily than visual stimulation. Men can become aroused almost instantly, while arousal for women is more likely to be a gradual, building process.

Men are more likely to seek out sexual stimulation and arousal in magazines such as *Playboy*, in X-rated movies, and in adult bookstores. Both males and females often use sexual fantasy to increase arousal. Ellis and Symons (1990) suggest that men's fantasies primarily reflect lust, while in women's fantasies lust is secondary to love. "Women tend to imagine themselves as objects of male

estrogens (ES-truh-jenz): A class of female sex hormones that promote the secondary sex characteristics in females and control the menstrual cycle.

progesterone (pro-JES-tah-rone): A female sex hormone that plays a role in the regulation of the menstrual cycle and prepares the lining of the uterus for possible pregnancy.

testosterone (tes-TOS-tah-rone): The most powerful androgen secreted by the testes and adrenal glands in males and by the adrenal glands in females; influences the development and maintenance of male sex characteristics and sexual motivation.

pornography: Books, pictures, films, or videos used to increase sexual arousal (hard-core *pornography* has very explicit depictions of various sex acts).

passion . . . while men tend to imagine women as responsive, lusty objects" (p. 550).

While sexual fantasy may grow out of sexual desire, at other times fantasy is used to heighten sexual desire or to increase passion (Friday, 1980). Sue (1979) found that over 60 percent of male and female college students admitted to having erotic fantasies during intercourse. The reasons they gave for doing so were to facilitate arousal, to imagine activities they do not engage in with their partner, or to increase the partner's attractiveness. They may fantasize about something morally unacceptable to them or unattainable, like having sex with an old boyfriend or girlfriend, a movie star, or some other celebrity (Crépault et al., 1977; Crépault & Conture, 1980). Many people would feel insulted if their mate needed to fantasize them out of the picture in order to gain sexual satisfaction.

Sexuality and Commitment: Where the Best Sex Is Found   The physiology of the sex act is certainly important, but there is much more to sex than the physical response. Today many people view sex as a casual recreational activity, and often it has little to do with love. Masters and Johnson have been accused of reducing the sex act to its clinical, physical components, but their book *The Pleasure Bond* (1975) argues strongly against separating the physical act of sex from the context of love and commitment. They are critical of those who "consider the physical act of intercourse as something in and of itself, a skill to be practiced and improved . . . an activity to exercise the body, or a game to be played." "To reduce sex to a physical exchange," they say, "is to strip it of richness and subtlety and, even more important, ultimately means robbing it of all emotional value."   In Masters and Johnson's view it is a couple's "total commitment, in which all sense of obligation is linked to mutual feelings of loving concern, [which] sustains a couple sexually over the years" (1975, p. 268).

The way we view ourselves as sexual beings—with special qualities, needs, gifts, and abilities—is a critical part of our human identity. Sexual relationships involve baring ourselves and revealing the most vulnerable part of our identity to one another.

Quite often the love—the emotional and personal intimacy we desire to share with another person—is missing, and we may let physical sexual intimacy alone stand as a substitute. But if sexual intimacy is practiced apart from a caring love and commitment, we may come to realize that the very essence of our sexual self was just another body to the other person, not a whole, unique, and special self.

Pornography: The Researchers' View

Question: What have researchers discovered about the effects of pornography on its viewers?

Pornography has become a lucrative industry in the United States, reaping about 4 to 6 billion dollars a year, and many people are alarmed about it. Over one-half million people, the majority of whom are middle-age and middle-class males, view pornography regularly.

There are degrees of pornography. Soft-core pornography depicts nudity and sexual acts short of intercourse. Hard-core pornography, the type commonly seen in X-rated videos, depicts very explicit sex acts, leaving little or nothing to the imagination. Women are often presented as sex objects to be degraded and dehumanized. Violent or aggressive pornography, such as the slasher films, portray women in powerless positions, victims of aggression and violence ranging from beatings and rape to dismemberment and murder.

What does research say about the effects of pornography? Following are some questions that have been studied by researchers.

Pornography may desensitize viewers to violence against women.

■ **Do sexually explicit materials increase or decrease satisfaction in a relationship?**

A number of studies reveal that people may come to value their partner and relationship less after exposure to erotic sexual material. Male college students who agreed to view sexually explicit films showing highly attractive females reported being less pleased with their wives or girlfriends than were control groups of college men who did not view such materials (Kenrick & Gutierres, 1980; Weaver et al., 1984). Also, people may feel disappointed with their own sexual performance after comparing it to the performance portrayed by actors.

■ **Does repeated exposure to pornography necessarily increase the desire to view more of it?**

Several studies have revealed that college students exposed to a steady diet of explicit sexual material find it stimulating at first and then find it boring (Howard et al., 1973; Zillmann & Bryant, 1983). But we cannot assume that all people have the same reaction to frequent viewing of pornography. Some individuals, when they no longer find X-rated films arousing, may completely turn away, while others may turn to increasingly more deviant and violent offerings. And if boredom were the most common reaction, sales and rental of pornographic materials would not be a growing multibillion-dollar market.

■ **Does frequent exposure to pornography change the viewer's sexual behavior or attitudes toward deviant sexual practices?**

A number of laboratory studies indicate that the frequent viewing of violent pornography or of scenes in which women are mistreated and degraded tends to desensitize the regular viewer to violent and deviant sexual practices. Consequently, men who view numerous violent rape scenes may become desensitized to the horror and reality of rape and have less compassion for rape victims (Donnerstein & Linz, 1984; Linz et al., 1984, 1988; Zillmann & Bryant, 1982). And "pornography that portrays sexual aggression as pleasurable for the victim increases the acceptance of the use of coercion in sexual relations" (Koop, 1987, p. 945).

Many people come to accept the *rape myth*—the unfounded belief that women who are raped ask for it, deserve it, and often enjoy it (Malamuth 1984). Even worse, Check (1984) found that after watching degrading or violent pornography, male subjects were more likely to admit that they would pressure or even rape a woman if they could be sure they would not get caught.

After reviewing numerous studies of violent and nonviolent pornography, Linz (1989) said, "Every study that has included a 'slasher' condition has found antisocial effects resulting from exposure to these films" (p. 74). But Linz did not find this effect to be true of nonviolent pornography.

Memory Check 11.3

1. The first major survey of sexual habits of American males and females was conducted by (Masters and Johnson, Kinsey).

2. The first large-scale study of the human sexual response in a laboratory setting was conducted by (Masters and Johnson, Kinsey).

(continued)

rape myth: The unfounded belief that women who are raped ask for it, deserve it, or enjoy it.

sexual orientation: The direction of one's sexual preference—toward members of the opposite sex (heterosexuality), toward one's own sex (homosexuality), or toward both sexes (bisexuality).

3. Both males and females experience a refractory period. (true/false)

4. Men and women behave sexually primarily in response to (hormonal levels, psychological factors).

5. Androgens, estrogens, and progesterone are present in both males and females. (true/false)

6. What do researchers report is an effect of repeated exposure to violent pornography?

   a. Individuals may become less repelled by deviant sex acts.
   b. Some men admit a greater willingness to force women to engage in sex.
   c. Some individuals become more accepting of the rape myth.
   d. all of these

Answers: 1. Kinsey 2. Masters and Johnson 3. false 4. psychological factors 5. true 6. d

Recent research suggests that biological factors play a part in determining a person's sexual orientation.

Homosexuality

Question: What is meant by sexual orientation?

We have said a great deal about the human sexual response and sexual arousal, but we have not considered **sexual orientation**—the direction of an individual's sexual preference, erotic feelings, and sexual activity. In heterosexuality, the human sexual response is oriented toward members of the opposite sex; in homosexuality, toward those of the same sex; and in bisexuality, toward members of both sexes.

Homosexuality has been reported in all societies throughout recorded history (Ford & Beach, 1951; Carrier, 1980). Kinsey and his associates (1948, 1953) estimated that 4 percent of the male subjects had nothing but homosexual relations throughout life, and about 2 to 3 percent of the female subjects had been in mostly or exclusively lesbian relationships. Fay and others (1989) estimate that from 3.3 to 6.2 percent of the adult male population have had adult homosexual contacts. Gay and lesbian rights groups claim that about 10 percent of the American population are predominantly homosexual. Notably, all estimates suggest that the incidence of homosexuality is at least twice as high for males as it is for females.

Until recent years, most homosexuals kept their sexual orientation a secret rather than risk shame and discrimination. But now more homosexuals are "coming out," preferring to acknowledge and express their sexual orientation rather than having to lead a double life (E.M. Gorman, 1991).

The Causes of Homosexuality: Physiological or Psychological?

Question: What are the various biological factors that have been suggested as possible causes of homosexuality?

What causes homosexuality? There is still professional debate among psychologists about whether homosexuality is biologically fixed or is acquired through learning and experience. Some experts suggest that perhaps a homosexual orientation is learned (Gagnon & Simon, 1973; Masters & Johnson, 1979). Others believe that biological factors largely determine sexual orientation (Isay, 1989). Still others lean toward an interaction—that both nature and nurture play a part.

Researchers have failed to show consistent differences in sex-hormone levels between homosexuals and heterosexuals (Meyer-Bahlburg, 1977; Griffiths et al., 1974). The effect of treating gay men with male sex hormones has been to increase sexual desire—not for the opposite sex but for members of their own sex.

It has been suggested that abnormal levels of androgens during prenatal development might predispose individuals to homosexuality. Too much or too little androgen at critical periods of brain development might masculinize or feminize the brain of the developing fetus, making it more likely that the individual will develop a homosexual orientation. A few studies have revealed an increase in the incidence of lesbianism among females who had an excess of androgens during prenatal development (Ehrhardt et al., 1968; Money & Schwartz, 1977).

Definitive answers to nature-nurture questions are always elusive, but some recent research has been reported that suggests biological factors play a part in homosexuality.

The LeVay Study: Homosexuality and a Tiny Speck in the Hypothalamus Neuroscientist Simon LeVay (1991) reported that an area in the hypothalamus governing sexual behavior is about twice as large in heterosexual men as in homosexual men. This same part of the hypothalamus, no larger than a grain of sand, is about the same size in heterosexual females as in homosexual males. Figure 11.2 shows the location of the hypothalamus where LeVay discovered the differences.

Do LeVay's findings make a strong case for a biological cause of homosexuality? No, only an interesting preliminary case. LeVay admits that his research offers no direct evidence that the brain differences he found cause homosexuality. Questions remain about the brain differences LeVay observed. Are they the cause or the consequence of sexual orientation or of variables as yet unidentified that may interact with the brain differences and sexual orientation? There is no question, however, that LeVay's research is the first to identify specific structural differences in a brain area known to be involved in the regulation of male-typical sexual behavior.

Homosexuality: Is There a Genetic Connection? Another recent study of the genetic influence on sexual orientation is a twin study conducted by researchers Bailey and Pillard (1991). The researchers determined that among 56 pairs of identical twins, 52 percent were both homosexual. Among 54 pairs of fraternal twins, 22 percent were both homosexual. Among the 57 pairs of adoptive brothers, however, only 11 percent shared a homosexual orientation.

The researchers reported estimates of heritability (genetic influence) ranging from .31 to .74. The combined environmental influence, then, could range from .69 to .26. In short, the authors believe their study shows that substantial genetic influences determine sexual orientation, but that nongenetic influences are at work as well.

Research Findings on the Developmental Experiences of Homosexuals

Considerable research suggests that sexual orientation, whether homosexual or heterosexual, is apparently established by early childhood (Marmor, 1980; Money, 1987).

Question: What does the study by Bell, Weinberg, and Hammersmith reveal about the developmental experiences of homosexuals?

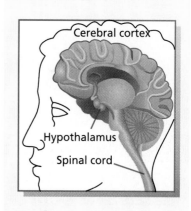

Figure 11.2

The Hypothalamus and Sexual Orientation

The hypothalamus exerts important influences on sexual behavior. Researcher Simon LeVay discovered in the hypothalamus an area no larger than a grain of sand, that is twice as large in heterosexual males as it is in females and in homosexual males. LeVay suggests that the small speck in the hypothalamus may influence sexual orientation.

homophobia: An intense, irrational hostility toward or fear of homosexuals.

The Bell, Weinberg, and Hammersmith Study   Bell, Weinberg, and Hammersmith (1981) conducted extensive face-to-face interviews with 979 homosexual subjects (293 women, 686 men) and 477 heterosexual controls. The subjects were questioned about their childhood, adolescence, and sexual experiences in an attempt to discover developmental factors associated with homosexuality. The researchers found no single condition of family life that in and of itself appeared to be a factor in either homosexual or heterosexual development. The only experience common to homosexuals was that as children they did not feel they were like others of their sex, and for this reason the researchers assume a biological predisposition.

Early Effeminate Behavior in Boys: What Does It Mean?   Other researchers have suggested that boys and girls who do not show typical gender-role behavior but rather are seen as sissies or tomboys may be more likely to become homosexual (Green, 1985, 1987; Green and Money, 1961). Zuger (1990) believes that in many cases, early and extreme effeminate behavior in boys is an early stage of homosexuality, and he states:

> The most frequent signs include cross-dressing, apparent as soon as the boy is able to indicate a preference; an expressed desire to be a girl, . . . and the child's statement that he *is*, in fact, a girl. These boys choose girls as playmates, play "girl" games, and insist on playing feminine roles in them. On the other hand, they are averse to "boy" games and sports.
>
> Boys with those characteristics are very close to their mother and show an interest in her clothes and daily activities. Conversely, they choose to have little contact with their father and are not interested in men's activities. Some boys show feminine gesturing and posturing. (p. 74)

This early effeminate pattern is not characteristic of all gay males by any means. Walter/Susan Cannon did not exhibit this pattern; in fact, Walter did not discover what he called his "womanly tendencies" until his teenage years at Princeton.

Social Attitudes toward Homosexuals: From Celebration to Condemnation

In contemporary American society, many people look on homosexuality as immoral, while others view it as simply an alternate life-style. Until 1973 the American Psychiatric Association considered homosexuality a mental disorder, but the APA now views it as such only if the individual considers it a problem. Researchers find no significant differences between homosexuals and heterosexuals in emotional stability or rate of psychiatric illness (Reiss, 1980).

Nevertheless, many people in our society could be considered homophobic. *Homophobia* is an intense, irrational hostility toward or fear of homosexuals; in its extreme form homophobia can result in ridicule, beatings, and even murder (Greer, 1986; Whitham & Mathy, 1986).

Memory Check 11.4

1. The direction of one's sexual preference—toward members of the opposite sex or toward one's own sex—is termed sexual (identification, orientation).

(continued)

2. Which of these did Bell, Weinberg, and Hammersmith's study reveal about their homosexual subjects?

a. They were likely to have been seduced or molested by adult homosexuals.
b. As children, they did not feel that they were like others of their sex.
c. As children, they had disturbed relationships with their parents.
d. There were biological differences between the homosexual and control subjects.

3. The American Psychological Association considers homosexuality to be a mental disorder. (true/false)

Answers: 1. orientation 2. b 3. false

> **impotence** (IM-puh-tents): The repeated inability of a man to get or maintain an erection that is firm enough for coitus.

Sexual Dysfunctions and Treatment

Like the course of true love, the course of sexual function does not always run smoothly. Although most people experience sexual problems some of the time, a sizable number of men and women are consistently plagued with sexual dysfunctions. What are these sexual dysfunctions, which deny or lower the pleasures of sex for men and women?

Sexual Dysfunctions in Men

Question: What are the three most common sexual dysfunctions in men?

Impotence: Ready, Willing, and Unable   The most common sexual dysfunction reported in men is **impotence** (erectile dysfunction)—the repeated inability to have or sustain an erection firm enough for coitus. Impotence can take different forms, including the inability to have an erection at all, having one but losing it, or having a partial erection that is not adequate for intercourse. Impotence can also consist of having firm erections under some conditions but not under others (as with one sexual partner but not with another, or during masturbation but not during intercourse).

Impotence does not include the failures all males have on occasion as a result of fear or anxiety, physical fatigue, illness, or drinking too much alcohol. About 10 percent of American men suffer from chronic impotence, with the percentages rising to 18 percent at age 55, 30 percent at age 65, and 55 percent at age 75 (Church, 1989a).

Impotence may be physical or psychological in origin. Over 50 percent of impotence is due to physical causes, which include diabetes, alcoholism, and drugs such as amphetamines, barbiturates, tranquilizers, and blood pressure medication (Church, 1989a). When the cause is physical, impotence usually develops gradually over a period of months or years and the man always has difficulty achieving an erection, in all circumstances (Lizza & Cricco-Lizza, 1990). But if a man suffering from impotence awakens to find himself with an erection, even occasionally, he can usually rule out a physical cause.

Resentment, guilt, fear, or anxiety are psychological factors that are suspected when the symptoms of impotence come on suddenly or when they occur in some circumstances but not in others (Lizza & Cricco-Lizza, 1990). The most common cause is performance fear. When a man fails repeatedly to achieve an erection, his worst psychological enemy is the fear that he will not be able to get an erection when he most wants one.

Premature and Retarded Ejaculation: Too Soon or Too Late   Premature **ejaculation** is a condition in which the male ejaculates too soon—before he is ready and usually long before his partner is ready. This condition sometimes results when a man feels hostility toward his partner or when his early sexual experiences called for quick ejaculation, such as hurried masturbation or fast, impersonalized sexual release with a prostitute.

Retarded ejaculation is a sexual dysfunction in which ejaculation occurs only after strenuous effort over an extremely prolonged period. Sometimes both partners may nearly collapse from exhaustion before the male finally reaches orgasm or gives up. Suspected causes are alcoholism or drug use (illicit and prescription), an overly strict religious background, stressful or traumatic life situations, or fear of impregnating one's partner (Kaplan, 1974).

Sexual Dysfunctions in Women

*Question: **What are the two most common sexual dysfunctions in women?***

Anorgasmia: The Elusive Orgasm   The most common sexual dysfunction in women is **anorgasmia** (orgasmic dysfunction)—the inability of a woman to reach orgasm. Some women have never been able to reach orgasm; others who were formerly orgasmic no longer can achieve orgasm. Some women are able to have orgasms only under certain circumstances or during certain types of sexual activity, while others have orgasm only from time to time. Women with anorgasmia may be disinterested in sex, or they may still find it exciting, satisfying, and enjoyable.

Rarely does anorgasmia result from physical causes. Often the cause is an insensitive male partner or one whose love-making techniques leave much to be desired. Dissatisfaction with the relationship, or anger and hostility toward one's partner may also be involved (Kaplan, 1974).

Vaginismus: Physical Constriction   *Vaginismus* is a sexual dysfunction in which involuntary muscle contractions create a tightening and closing of the vagina, which makes it painful or impossible to have intercourse. The problem may stem from a rigid religious upbringing, in which sex was looked on as sinful and dirty. It may stem from past experiences of extremely painful intercourse or because of a fear of men, rape, or other traumatic experiences associated with intercourse (Kaplan, 1974).

Inhibited Sexual Desire: Lacking the Interest

About 30 percent of people who see sex therapists complain of a lack of sexual desire or interest, a condition known as *inhibited sexual desire (ISD)* (Lief, 1977; Schover & LoPiccolo, 1982). These people may be unreceptive to the sexual advances of their partner or participate in spite of their lack of desire.

Usually the causes of ISD are psychological. Repeated unsuccessful attempts at intercourse (impotence or anorgasmia) may eventually lead to a loss of desire or lack of interest. In some cases, a sexual aversion develops as a result of a sexual trauma like rape or incest.

premature ejaculation: A sexual dysfunction in which a man regularly and unintentionally ejaculates too rapidly to satisfy his partner or to maintain his own pleasure.

anorgasmia: A sexual dysfunction in women marked by the inability to achieve orgasm.

vaginismus (VAJ-ah-NIZ-mus):   A sexual dysfunction in females, in which involuntary muscle contractions in the vagina make penetration either painful or impossible.

inhibited sexual desire (ISD):   A condition marked by little or no interest in sexual activity.

Sex Therapy: There Is Help

In most cases, chronic sexual dysfunctions do not just go away, but there is help for people who suffer from sexual problems. During the past 40 years or so, a number of sex therapy techniques have been developed. Therapies based on behavioral psychology teach patients to replace their old self-defeating attitudes and behaviors with more adaptive ones. In 1959 Masters and Johnson began their innovative approach to sex therapy, in which the couple rather than the individual is treated.

Biological treatments can be useful for dysfunctions caused by medical conditions. One effective treatment for impotence is the self-injection into the tissue of the penis a drug that causes the blood vessels to dilate and fill with blood (Church, 1989b; Kaplan, 1990). This treatment has enabled thousands of American men to get and sustain an erection.

Memory Check 11.5

Match the appropriate description with each sexual disorder.

___ 1) impotence
___ 2) inhibited sexual desire
___ 3) anorgasmia
___ 4) vaginismus
___ 5) premature ejaculation

a. inability to reach orgasm
b. inability to control ejaculation
c. lack of sexual interest
d. inability to have or maintain an erection
e. involuntary closing of the vagina

Answers: 1) d 2) c 3) a 4) e 5) b

Sexually Transmitted Diseases: The Price of Casual Sex

Question: What are the major bacterial infections and viral infections known as sexually transmitted diseases?

Sexually transmitted diseases (STDs) are infections spread primarily, although not exclusively, through sexual contact. The incidence of many sexually transmitted diseases has increased dramatically over the past 20 years. This can be explained in part by more permissive attitudes toward sex and an increase in sexual activity among young people, some of whom have sexual contact with multiple partners. Another factor is the greater use of nonbarrier methods of contraception such as the pill, rather than barrier methods such as a condom and vaginal spermicide, which provide some protection against STDs.

Some of the serious sexually transmitted diseases are bacterial infections such as chlamydia, gonorrhea, and syphilis, which are curable, and viral infections, such as genital herpes, HPV, and AIDS, which are not curable.

sexually transmitted diseases (STDs): Infections that are spread primarily, although not exclusively, through intimate sexual contact.

The Bacterial Infections

Question: Why do chlamydia and gonorrhea pose a greater threat to women than to men?

Chlamydia: Little Known, but Widespread   Many people have never heard of **chlamydia**—an infection that affects 4 million people in the United States every year (Stein, 1991). Today 10 percent of all college students have chlamydia, and it is highly infectious. Women have a 70-percent risk of contracting chlamydia from an infected man in any single sexual encounter; men have a 25- to 50-percent risk.

Men with chlamydia are likely to have symptoms that alert them to the need for treatment, but they suffer no adverse reproductive consequences from the infection. Women, on the other hand, typically have only mild symptoms or no symptoms at all when chlamydia begins in the lower reproductive tract. Therefore, the infection often goes untreated and spreads to the upper reproductive tract, where it can cause **pelvic inflammatory disease** (PID). PID often produces scarring of tissue in the fallopian tubes, which can result in infertility or ectopic pregnancy—a pregnancy in which the fertilized ovum is implanted outside of the uterus (Siller & Azziz, 1991; Stein, 1991).

About one out of every seven women in the United States has had PID (Grimes et al., 1986). The probability of infertility after one episode of PID is 10 to 25 percent; with two episodes, it rises to 35 to 50 percent (Stein, 1991). It is no exaggeration, then, when Aral and Holmes (1991) call chlamydia "the primary preventable cause of sterility in women" (p. 65).

The majority of infants born to mothers with chlamydia may become infected during the birth process. Fortunately, chlamydia can be cured with antibiotics, which should be given to both partners.

Gonorrhea: An Old STD Making a Comeback   There were about 720,000 cases of **gonorrhea** reported in 1988 (U.S. Bureau of the Census, 1990). A woman having intercourse one time with an infected partner runs a 50-percent risk of contracting gonorrhea (Platt, Rice, & McCormack, 1983); a male has a 20- to 25-percent chance of developing gonorrhea after one such exposure.

Within the first 2 weeks after contracting gonorrhea, 95 percent of men develop a discharge from the penis and painful urination (Schwebke, 1991a). Most seek treatment and are cured. If there are no symptoms present or if the individual does not seek treatment within 2 to 3 weeks, the infection may spread to the internal reproductive organs and eventually cause sterility.

The bad news for women is that 50 to 80 percent who contract gonorrhea do not have early symptoms. The infection spreads from the cervix through the other internal reproductive organs, causing inflammation and scarring. About 20 percent of women with untreated gonorrhea develop pelvic inflammatory disease with its risk of sterility and ectopic pregnancy (Schwebke, 1991a). Gonorrhea can be cured with large doses of penicillin or other antibiotics.

Syphilis: Another Old STD Making a Comeback   About 50,200 cases of **syphilis** were reported in the United States in 1990 (Centers for Disease Control, 1991b). The rate is particularly high "among inner city ethnic groups of low socioeconomic status" (Schwebke, 1991b, p. 44). Syphilis has been linked to the increase in illicit drug use, particularly crack, because addicts often exchange sex for drugs (Rosen, 1990; Aral & Holmes, 1991).

Left untreated, syphilis progresses in predictable stages. In the primary stage, a painless chancre (pronounced "shanker") appears where the syphilis spirochete—the microorganism that causes syphilis—enters the body. This sore may go unnoticed, but even without treatment it will heal.

chlamydia (klah-MIH-dee-uh):   The most common bacterial, sexually transmitted disease found in both sexes, and one that can cause infertility in females.

pelvic inflammatory disease (PID):   An infection in the female pelvic organs, which can result from untreated chlamydia or gonorrhea and can cause pain, scarring of tissue, and even infertility and ectopic pregnancy.

gonorrhea (gahn-ah-REE-ah):   A sexually transmitted disease that, in males, causes a puslike discharge from the penis; if untreated, females can develop pelvic inflammatory disease and possible infertility.

syphilis (SIF-ih-lis):   A sexually transmitted disease that progresses through three stages; if untreated, it can eventually be fatal.

In the second stage—secondary syphilis—a painless rash appears on the body, usually accompanied by a fever, sore throat, loss of appetite, fatigue, and headache. Again, without treatment these symptoms also eventually disappear. Then the spirochetes enter the various tissues and organs of the body, where they may be latent (inactive) anywhere from several years to a lifetime. About 30 to 50 percent of people with syphilis who remain untreated enter the final and terrible tertiary (third) stage, in which blindness, paralysis, heart failure, mental illness, and death result.

Pregnant women with any stage of syphilis will infect the fetus. But syphilis can be stopped at any point in its development, except in the final stage, with strong doses of penicillin.

Although chlamydia, gonorrhea, and syphilis are serious and potentially dangerous, they can be treated and cured. Some STDs cannot.

The Viral Infections

Question: Why is genital herpes particularly upsetting to those who have it?

Genital Herpes: Viral Blisters That Come and Go   Each year there are 1/2 to 1 million new cases of **genital herpes** (Davies, 1990). Already about 20 million Americans—20 percent of sexually active men and women—have this presently incurable virus (Apuzzio, 1990).

Genital herpes can be caused by two forms of the herpes simplex virus (HSV). The type 1 virus usually causes oral herpes—cold sores and fever blisters in the mouth—but as a result of oral sex may produce blisters on the genitals. The type 2 virus generally produces 80 to 90 percent of the cases of genital herpes and is transmitted through direct contact with infected genitals (Peter et al., 1982).

In genital herpes, painful blisters form on the genitals (or around the anus in homosexual men), fill with pus, and then burst, leaving open sores. It is at this point that the individual is most contagious. After the blisters heal, the virus travels up the nerve fibers to an area around the base of the spinal cord, where it remains in a dormant state but can flare up anew at any time. The first herpes episode is usually the most severe (Apuzzio, 1990; Davies, 1990); recurrent attacks are typically milder and briefer (Straus et al., 1984).

Women are at a greater risk than men of contracting genital herpes as a result of unprotected sex (Mertz et al., 1992). Both men and women with genital herpes are at twice the risk of contracting HIV (Hook et al., 1992).

Pregnant women with active genital herpes should have a Caesarean delivery because babies can be infected as they pass through the birth canal during delivery. About 50 percent of these infected babies die or suffer severe damage to the brain or eyes (Binkin & Alexander, 1983).

Genital Human Papillomavirus Infection: Genital Warts and Other Growths   Another common sexually transmitted viral infection is the genital **human papillomavirus infection (HPV).** According to Aral and Holmes (1991), "genital and anal HPV infections appear to be the most prevalent STDs in the U.S., and a large proportion of sexually active adults seem to be infected" (p. 66).

In 1988 over 2 million people were treated for genital warts, which are caused by several of the strains of HPV. Even after the warts are removed or disappear spontaneously, the virus remains latent in the body for years, making recurrences likely. Other strains of HPV also remain in the system and are strongly related to genital cancer, particularly cervical cancer (Tinkle, 1990).

genital herpes (HER-peez): A sexually transmitted disease caused by the herpes simplex virus (usually type 2) and resulting in painful blisters on the genitals; presently incurable, usually recurring, and highly contagious during outbreaks.

human papillomavirus infection (pap-ah-LO-mah-VI-rus): A sexually transmitted viral infection that infects a large proportion of sexually active adults; one strain of the virus causes genital warts.

Acquired Immune Deficiency Syndrome (AIDS)

Question: What happens to a person from the time of infection with HIV to the development of full-blown AIDS?

There is no sexually transmitted disease that generates more fear or has more devastating consequences than **acquired immune deficiency syndrome (AIDS)**. Although the first case was diagnosed in this country in 1981, there is still no cure for AIDS and no vaccine to protect against it. By the end of 1991, about 206,392 cases of AIDS and 133,232 deaths from AIDS had been reported to the Centers for Disease Control (1992).

AIDS is caused by **HIV**, the **human immunodeficiency virus**, commonly referred to as the AIDS virus. "Of the estimated 1 million HIV-infected persons in the United States, approximately 20% have developed AIDS" (CDC, 1992, p. 29). From 6 to 8 million people worldwide are infected with the virus (Hutman, 1990).

When a person is first infected, the AIDS virus enters the bloodstream. There is an initial infection that usually causes no symptoms, and the immune system begins to produce HIV antibodies. It is these antibodies that are detected in the AIDS test. Individuals then progress to the asymptomatic carrier state, in which they experience no symptoms whatsoever and thus can unknowingly infect others.

The AIDS virus attacks the T4 cells (T-helper cells) in the immune system until the immune system becomes essentially nonfunctional. The diagnosis of AIDS is made when the immune system is so damaged that victims develop rare forms of cancer or pneumonia or other *opportunistic infections*. Such infections would not usually affect people with a normal immune response, but in those with a very impaired immune system, these infections can be serious and even life-threatening. At this point patients typically experience progressive weight loss, weakness, fever, swollen lymph nodes, and diarrhea, and 25 percent have a rare cancer that produces reddish purple spots on the skin. Other opportunistic infections develop as the immune system weakens further.

Some people, prior to developing a full-blown case of AIDS, develop less severe immune-system symptoms such as "unexplained fevers, persistent night sweats, chronic diarrhea and wasting [weight loss]" (Redfield & Burke, 1988, p. 94). The average time from infection with HIV to advanced AIDS is from 8 to 10 years, but some studies "show that at least 25% of HIV-positive individuals remain healthy for 10–12 years" (Hutman, 1990, p. 11). The disease progresses faster in smokers, in the very young, in people over 50, and faster apparently in women than in men. Kimberly Bergalis, who contracted AIDS from her dentist, had a rather rapid progression and died at age 23. AIDS also progresses faster in those with repeated exposures to the virus and in those who were infected by someone in an advanced stage of the disease.

Currently researchers are testing drugs on people infected with the AIDS virus, and early detection of HIV infection can lead to life-prolonging medical intervention. AZT, an antiretroviral drug, is being used to treat AIDS patients in an attempt to lessen their symptoms and prolong their lives.

Question: How is AIDS transmitted?

How Is AIDS Transmitted?   The AIDS virus has been found in blood, semen, saliva, vaginal secretions, urine, and tears. But researchers believe that the AIDS virus is transmitted primarily through the exchange of blood or semen during sexual contact or when IV (intravenous) drug users share contaminated needles or syringes (Des Jarlais & Friedman, 1989).

The high rate of AIDS among gay men is not because they are gay but because they generally have more sex partners than do heterosexuals and they are likely

acquired immune deficiency syndrome (AIDS):   A devastating and incurable illness, caused by HIV, that progressively weakens the immune system, leaving its victims vulnerable to opportunistic infections that usually cause death.

HIV: Human immunodeficiency virus; the AIDS virus.

opportunistic infection: An infection that can be serious and even life-threatening in those with very impaired immune systems.

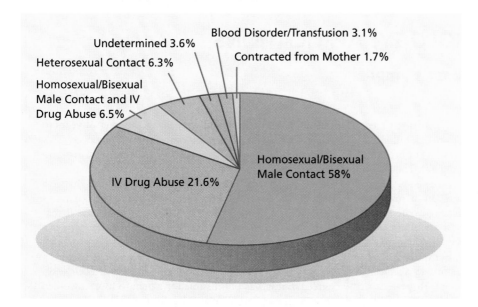

Figure 11.3

How the AIDS Virus Was Transmitted in AIDS Cases Reported in the United States

The primary means of transmission of the AIDS virus (HIV) is through homosexual/bisexual male contact (58 percent). IV drug abuse (sharing needles) accounts for 21.6 percent of the AIDS cases in the United States. (Data from Centers for Disease Control, 1991.)

to have anal intercourse. Anal intercourse is more dangerous than coitus because rectal tissue often tears during penetration, offering a ready entry of semen into the bloodstream.

It is a mistake to view AIDS as a disease confined to homosexuals. In Africa, where AIDS is believed to have originated, it strikes men and women equally, and their heterosexual activity is believed to be the primary means of transmission (Abramson & Herdt, 1990). AIDS is more easily transmitted from infected men to women than vice-versa (Hutman, 1990).

There is also a 30- to 50-percent risk that babies born to mothers with the AIDS virus will also be infected (Krajick, 1988). The blood-bank industry claims that the chance of acquiring the AIDS virus from a blood transfusion is now 1 in 40,000 (C. Gorman, 1988). Figure 11.3 shows the means of the transmission of the AIDS cases in the United States.

The Psychological Impact of HIV Infection and AIDS Consider the devastating psychological impact on a person who learns that he or she is infected with the AIDS virus. A death sentence, alone, is traumatic enough, with one's time left to live measured in a few years, but there is more. Added to the fear of rapidly declining health when full-blown AIDS arrives, there is attached to AIDS an ugly stigma paralleled by few other diseases in history. The heroic young teenager Ryan White, a hemophiliac, contracted AIDS through a blood transfusion. He died of AIDS in 1990 and was not spared the stigma of AIDS in life or even in death. Vandals spray painted "FAG" on his grave.

What are the psychological effects on people who struggle to cope with this fearsome plague? The reaction to the news that one is HIV positive is frequently a state of shock, bewilderment, confusion, or disbelief (Deuchar, 1984). Stress reactions to the news are typically so common and so acute that experts strongly recommend pretest counseling so that those who do test positive may know in advance of the consequences (Maj, 1990).

Another common reaction is anger—anger at past or present sexual partners, family members, health care professionals, or society in general. Often the response is one of guilt, leading the person to believe that he is being punished for homosexuality or drug abuse. Other patients exhibit denial, ignoring medical advice and continuing to act as if nothing has changed in their lives. Then, of course, there is fear of death; of mental and physical deterioration; of rejection by friends, family, or co-workers; of sexual rejection; of abandonment.

Other psychological symptoms follow as one struggles to cope with the condition. Depression is common and the suicide rate is high.

WORLD OF PSYCHOLOGY: APPLICATIONS

Date Rape: New Outrage on Campus

When we hear that someone has been raped, most of us picture a stranger stalking a woman on a dark, deserted street or breaking into her bedroom and raping her. The classic image of the stalking, unknown rapist is true enough, but the majority of all rapes are committed by a man the woman knows—in the act of acquaintance or date rape.

FBI statistics reveal that between 1978 and 1988, rape increased four times faster than other crimes, and that a woman is raped about every 6 minutes. But those are only the *reported* rapes. How many go unreported? According to a government-funded study, only about 16 percent of rape victims notify police (Killpatrick et al., 1992). Of the 683,000 rapes reported in 1990, only 22 percent of the perpetrators were strangers.

Many of these unreported rapes are committed right on the college campus. Koss and others (1987) conducted a study of the incidence of rape in a national sample consisting of 3,187 female and 2,972 male students from 32 colleges and universities. In their sample, 27.5 percent of the women reported being targets since age 14 of sexual acts that met the legal definition of rape. Among the college men, 7.7 percent admitted committing and attempting to commit such acts.

Who Rapes? Some researchers claim that a "macho" attitude about women and sex, while not necessarily leading to rape, does apparently relate to a greater tolerance of rape and the sexual exploitation of women. In one survey, 175 male college sophomores were asked how often they had used any of 33 acts of sexual coercion, from verbal pressure to actual physical force. Of those male sophomores, 75 percent admitted they had encouraged a date to use alcohol or drugs, for the specific purpose of having sex with the date; 69 percent had used some type of verbal coercion; over 40 percent had used anger; 13 percent had threatened to use force; and 20 percent said they had actually used force to get sex (Mosher & Anderson, 1987). According to the legal definition, many of these 175 college sophomores had actually committed rape.

So, to answer the question of who rapes, it is not only the stranger lurking in the shadows, it may also be someone sitting next to you in class. How are attitudes about rape formed?

Attitudes about Rape Zillmann and Bryant (1982) questioned both female and male subjects, after massive exposure to pornographic films depicting rape. Subjects of both sexes said they would give a rapist significantly shorter sentences for the crime than did control subjects who had not viewed such films.

Kanin and others (1987) studied attitudes toward rape of 355 unmarried undergraduate students (155 men and 200 women). Then they related their subjects' history of sexual activity—the number of different sexual partners they had had—to the number of years in prison they believed a rapist should serve. As the number of sexual partners in-

creased for both men and women, the number of years to which they would sentence a rapist significantly decreased.

Furthermore, over 71 percent of the men and, remarkably, 55 percent of the women with extensive sexual experience expressed a surprising opinion. They said that if a woman had previously engaged in any form of sexual intimacy with a man, it could not be considered rape if that man later forced her to have sex with him. But a rape is a rape whenever sexual intercourse is forced on a woman against her will. A survey of high school students revealed a surprising number of conditions under which both sexes agreed that it was permissible for a man to force a women to have sexual intercourse (Mahoney, 1983).

Effects of Rape on the Victim The effects of rape on victims vary widely, and some are quite serious, even life-threatening. Almost 20 percent of rape victims—nearly one in five—admit to a suicide attempt, a rate eight times higher than that of nonvictims ("Female victims," 1984).

A rape by a knife- or gun-wielding stranger is, of course, a terrifying experience. But the effects of date rape can be devastating as well, and victims can suffer from it for years (Parrot, 1990).

What to Do If You Are Raped

1. Report it! Date rape will continue to increase unless victims speak up and put a stop to it.

2. Usually the very first strong desire a woman has following a rape is to take a long shower. But semen, hair follicles, and many other pieces of evidence that can be used to identify the rapist should not be washed away until a medical examination has been completed.

3. Seek counseling. Many college and university campuses, as well as most cities, have rape crisis centers to help victims deal with the trauma of rape.

How to Avoid Rape

1. Know the men you date, and avoid those who lack respect for women.

2. Accepting a date with someone does not obligate you to engage in any sexual activity.

3. Avoid risky situations and settings on a first date, and be sure to tell someone where you are.

4. Alcohol and drugs are often contributing factors in date rape. Avoid drinking too much or mixing drinks.

5. Trust your instincts. If a situation does not feel right to you, change it or get away from it. Don't worry about what others might think.

6. Do not send signals that can be misinterpreted by your date. Some men assume that if a woman drinks too much, invites him to her apartment or room, or goes to his apartment, this signals that she is willing to have sex. She may feel that she is only being friendly.

7. If you are in danger, don't hesitate to run or scream.

Protection against Sexually Transmitted Diseases: Minimizing Risk

Question: What are the most effective methods of protection against sexually transmitted diseases?

There are only two foolproof ways for people to protect themselves from becoming infected with sexually transmitted disease through intimate sexual contact. The first is obvious—abstain from sexual contact. The second is to have a mutually faithful (monogamous) relationship with a partner free of infection. Anything short of these two courses of action will place a person at risk.

Discharges, blisters, sores, rashes, warts, odors, or any other unusual symptoms are warning signs of STDs. Yet we know that many people who have no visible symptoms carry sexually transmitted diseases. And what we don't know *can* hurt us. People who choose to practice risky sex cannot be safe but can reduce the risks by using a latex condom along with a spermicide such as an intravaginal contraceptive foam, jelly, or cream.

People are putting themselves at risk for AIDS when they have multiple sex partners or if they have sex with prostitutes, IV drug users, or anyone carrying the AIDS virus. This potential risk was dramatically demonstrated by basketball star Magic Johnson when he announced that he had tested positive for the AIDS virus. Several recent studies reveal that most young people, even those engaging in high risk behavior, believe they are virtually immune from AIDS (Hansen et al., 1990; Leigh, 1990). Despite the intense educational efforts to promote the use of condoms, more than half of sexually active college students still do not use condoms regularly, if at all (DeBuono et al., 1990).

People who fear that they might have been exposed should go to a doctor or clinic to be tested. Many STDs are easily treated, and serious complications can be avoided if the treatment is prompt. Obviously anyone who has a STD should tell his or her partner so that the partner can be checked and treated.

STDs were curable until herpes, HPV, and AIDS came on the scene; today engaging in sexual intimacy with multiple partners or casual acquaintances is indeed a dangerous way to satisfy the sex drive. Much has been written in recent decades about the joy of sex. It is true that the pleasures sex brings to life are many; but chlamydia, gonorrhea, syphilis, herpes, genital warts, and AIDS are not among them.

Sports superstar Magic Johnson announced that he is infected with the AIDS virus.

Memory Check 11.6

1. The proper use of condoms with a spermicide provides complete protection from sexually transmitted diseases. (true/false)

2. In addition to AIDS, (genital herpes, chlamydia) is not curable.

3. Symptoms of STDs are usually more readily apparent in (males, females), and so they are more likely to seek treatment and be cured.

4. HIV eventually causes a breakdown in the (immune, circulatory) system.

5. The incidence of AIDS in the United States is highest among homosexuals and (bisexuals, IV drug users).

Answers: 1. false 2. genital herpes 3. males 4. immune 5. IV drug users

Thinking Critically _____

Evaluation

What are some of the potential problems with information about sexual behavior and attitudes derived from surveys?

Point/Counterpoint

List the most persuasive arguments you can think of:

a. to justify sexual abstinence or having sexual intercourse only in an exclusively monogamous relationship.
b. to justify having casual sexual intercourse with a variety of partners.

Psychology in Your Life

Mary has sex with several partners, and she takes birth control pills to prevent pregnancy. She believes that she is discriminating in her choice of partners and that condoms are therefore not necessary in her case. Has Mary overlooked anything that could put her at risk?

Chapter Summary and Review _____

What Makes a Male, a Male and a Female, a Female?

What are the biological factors that determine whether a person is male or female?

At conception the sex chromosomes are set—XY in males and XX in females. The primitive gonads develop into testes if the Y chromosome is present or into ovaries if it is absent. If sufficient levels of androgens are present, male genitals develop; if not, female genitals develop.

Key Terms

sex chromosomes (p. 368)
genitals (p. 369)
androgens (p. 369)
primary sex characteristics (p. 369)
secondary sex characteristics (p. 369)

Sex-Role Development

What is sex typing, and what are the agencies in the environment that contribute to the process?

Sex typing is the process by which people acquire the traits, behaviors, attitudes, preferences, and interests that the culture considers appropriate for their biological sex. Parents, peers, the school, and the media each play a role in sex typing.

What are three theories of sex-role development?

Three theories of sex-role development are social learning theory, cognitive developmental theory, and gender-schema theory.

Do good adjustment and high self-esteem seem to be related to masculine traits, feminine traits, or androgyny?

Masculine traits appear to be related to better adjustment and high self-esteem in both males and females.

Key Terms

sex typing (p. 370)
social learning theory (p. 372)
gender (p. 372)
cognitive developmental theory (p. 372)
gender-schema theory (p. 372)
androgyny (p. 373)

Gender Differences: Fact or Myth?

What is the most consistent and significant difference observed in comparative studies of gender?

The most consistent and significant gender difference is that males tend to be more physically aggressive than females.

For what cognitive abilities are there proven gender differences?

Males are slightly better at some spatial skills, and in high school and college males perform somewhat better in mathematical problem solving. The female advantage in verbal ability has virtually disappeared over the last few decades.

Sexual Attitudes and Behavior

What are the famous Kinsey surveys?

In the 1940s and 1950s Alfred Kinsey and associates conducted the first major surveys of the sexual attitudes and behaviors of American men and women.

According to Masters and Johnson, what are the four phases of the human sexual response cycle?

The sexual response cycle consists of four phases: the excitement phase, the plateau phase, the orgasm phase, and the resolution phase.

What are the male and female sex hormones, and how do they affect sexual desire and activity in males and females?

The female sex hormones, the estrogens and progesterone, must be present in minimal amounts for sexual interest and activity to occur. Testosterone, the most important of the male sex hormones (androgens), affects sexual interest and the ability to have an erection.

What have researchers discovered about the effects of pornography on viewers?

Researchers have found that after frequent exposure to pornography, males come to value their wives and girlfriends less. Frequent viewing of violent pornography often desensitizes men to deviant sex practices and to the horror of rape, increases their acceptance of the rape myth, and possibly increases their willingness to force women to engage in sex.

Key Terms

coitus (p. 378)
sexual response cycle (p. 379)
excitement phase (p. 379)
plateau phase (p. 380)
orgasm phase (p. 380)
resolution phase (p. 380)
estrogens (p. 381)
progesterone (p. 381)
androgens (p. 381)
testosterone (pp. 376, 381)
pornography (p. 382)

Homosexuality

What is meant by sexual orientation?

Sexual orientation refers to the direction of a person's sexual preference—toward members of the opposite sex (heterosexuality), toward one's own sex (homosexuality), or toward both sexes (bisexuality).

What are the various biological factors that have been suggested as possible causes of homosexuality?

The biological factors suggested as possible causes of homosexuality are (1) abnormal levels of androgens during prenatal development, which could masculinize or feminize the brain of the developing fetus; (2) structural differences in an area of the hypothalamus of homosexual men; and (3) genetic factors.

What does the study by Bell, Weinberg, and Hammersmith reveal about the developmental experiences of homosexuals?

In comparing homosexuals to heterosexual controls, Bell, Weinberg, and Hammersmith were unable to trace differences between the two groups to problems in parental relationships. The only commonality was that as children, homosexuals did not feel that they were like others of their sex.

Key Terms

sexual orientation (p. 384)

Sexual Dysfunctions and Treatment

What are the three most common sexual dysfunctions in men?

The three most common sexual dysfunctions in males are impotence, premature ejaculation, and retarded ejaculation.

What are the two most common sexual dysfunctions in women?

The two most common female sexual dysfunctions are anorgasmia and vaginismus.

Key Terms

impotence (p. 387)
premature ejaculation (p. 388)
anorgasmia (p. 388)

Sexually Transmitted Diseases: The Price of Casual Sex

What are the major bacterial infections and viral infections known as sexually transmitted diseases?

The major sexually transmitted diseases are chlamydia, gonorrhea, and syphilis (all curable bacterial infections) and genital herpes, HPV, and AIDS (all viral infections and presently not curable).

Why do chlamydia and gonorrhea pose a greater threat to women than to men?

Chlamydia and gonorrhea pose a particular threat to women, because unlike men, they typically have no symptoms or very mild symptoms, making prompt treatment less likely. If the infection spreads, it may result in infertility or ectopic pregnancy.

Why is genital herpes particularly upsetting to those who have it?

Genital herpes causes painful blisters on the genitals, is usually recurring and highly contagious during outbreaks, and is presently incurable.

What happens to a person from the time of infection with HIV to the development of full-blown AIDS?

When a person is infected with HIV, an initial infection occurs and the body begins to produce HIV antibodies, eventually detectable in a blood test. For a period of time the victim is without symptoms, but HIV gradually renders the immune system nonfunctional. The diagnosis of AIDS is made when the person succumbs to various opportunistic infections.

How is AIDS transmitted?

AIDS is transmitted primarily through the exchange of blood or semen during sexual contact or when IV drug users share contaminated needles and syringes.

What are the most effective methods of protection against sexually transmitted diseases?

Abstinence or a monogamous relationship with a partner free of infection are the only foolproof ways to protect yourself from acquiring an STD through intimate sexual contact. Failing this, avoid sex with multiple or anonymous partners, be on the lookout for symptoms of these diseases in a potential partner, and use a latex condom with a spermicide.

Key Terms

sexually transmitted diseases (STDs) (p. 389)
chlamydia (p. 390)
pelvic inflammatory disease (PID) (p. 390)
gonorrhea (p. 390)
syphilis (p. 390)
genital herpes (p. 391)
human papillomavirus infection (HPV) (p. 391)
acquired immune deficiency syndrome (AIDS) (p. 392)
HIV (human immunodeficiency virus) (p. 392)

12

Personality Theory and Assessment

CHAPTER OUTLINE

(The Granger Collection)

W̲hat makes us the way we are? Are the personality characteristics we exhibit mainly laid down at conception, included within our own unique genetic blueprint? Or is our personality influenced more markedly by the environment in which we live, grow, and develop? Environments can be strikingly different as you know. Consider the two environments described in the next two paragraphs.

Oskar Stohr was raised as a Catholic by his grandmother in Nazi Germany. As part of Hitler's youth movement, Oskar was expected to be a "good" Nazi. Book burnings, military parades, the hatred of Jews, and the raised right hand with the greeting "Heil Hitler" were all part of Oskar's early environment. How did this environment affect his personality?

Jack Yufe, the same age as Oskar, was raised by his Jewish father on the island of Trinidad. Far removed from the goose-stepping storm troopers in Nazi Germany, Jack enjoyed all of the educational and social advantages of a good, middle-class Jewish youth. How did Jack's environment affect his personality?

Though raised in starkly different environments, Oskar and Jack are amazingly alike. They have quick tempers, are domineering toward women, enjoy surprising people by faking sneezes in elevators, and flush the toilet before using it. They both read magazines from back to front, store rubber bands on their wrists, like spicy foods and sweet liqueurs, and dip buttered toast in their coffee.

The list is much longer, but there is a good reason for the similarities between Oskar and Jack. They are identical twins. They were separated shortly after birth when their father took Jack with him to the island of Trinidad, and the maternal grandmother raised Oskar in Germany.

Researchers at the University of Minnesota are studying the effects of genetics and environment on identical twins reared apart. When Oskar and Jack first arrived at the University to take part in the study, both of them were wearing blue, double-breasted shirts with epaulets, identical neatly-trimmed mustaches, and wire-rimmed glasses. They also looked almost exactly alike physically, since identical twins have identical genes. How powerfully the genes influence personality.

Joan Gardiner and Jean Nelson are another pair of identical twins in the Minnesota study. They were also raised apart, but their environments did not differ so markedly. Joan's adoptive mother and Jean's adoptive father were sister and brother, so the twins were together quite often.

Like Oskar and Jack, Joan and Jean have many similarities and a few differences. But one difference between the twins is so unusual that researchers are especially intrigued by it. Joan is musical; Jean is not. Although her adoptive mother was a piano teacher, Jean does not play. But Joan, whose adoptive mother was not a musician, plays piano very well—so well, in fact, that she has performed with the Minnesota Symphony Orchestra. Joan's mother made her practice piano several hours every day, while Jean's mother allowed her to pursue whatever interests she chose. Duplicate genes but musical differences—how do the researchers explain it?

David Lykken, Director of the Minnesota Twin Research Center, says: "It's likely that both twins have the same genetic disposition for music, and the fact that one played and the other didn't seems clearly due to upbringing" (quoted in Lang, 1987, p. 64). How powerfully the environment influences personality.

W̲ᴇ ᴏꜰᴛᴇɴ ʜᴇᴀʀ ɪᴛ sᴀɪᴅ that no two people are exactly alike, that each of us is unique. When most people talk about someone's uniqueness, they are referring to the personality. **Personality** is defined as an individual's unique and stable pattern of characteristics and behaviors. And personalities are indeed different—Mother Teresa and Madonna, Hugh Hefner and Billy Graham, Eddie Murphy and Bill Cosby. What makes these people so different?

personality: A person's unique and stable pattern of characteristics and behaviors.

There are a number of theories that attempt to account for our personality differences and explain how we come to be the way we are. This chapter explores some of the major personality theories, and the variety of tests and inventories used to assess personality.

Sigmund Freud and Psychoanalysis

Question: What are the two aspects of Freud's work, which he called psychoanalysis?

Most textbooks begin their exploration of personality theory with Sigmund Freud, and for good reason. Freud created one of the first and most controversial personality theories. Using information gained from the treatment of his patients and from his own life experiences, Freud developed the theory of **psychoanalysis**. When you hear the term psychoanalysis, you might picture a psychiatrist treating a troubled patient on a couch. But psychoanalysis is much more than that. The term refers not only to a therapy for treating psychological disorders but also to a personality theory.

Freud's theory of psychoanalysis is neither the extension of an earlier theory nor a reaction against one. It is largely original, and it was revolutionary and shocking to the 19th and early 20th century European audience to which it was introduced. The major components of his theory, and perhaps the most controversial, are (1) the central role of the sexual instinct, (2) the concept of infantile sexuality, and (3) the dominant part played by the unconscious in moving and shaping our thought and behavior. Freud's theory assumes a psychic determinism, the view that there is a cause for our every thought, idea, feeling, action, or behavior. Nothing happens by chance or accident; everything we do and even everything we forget to do has a cause behind it.

A married man vacationing alone in Hawaii sends his wife a postcard and writes, "Having a wonderful time! Wish you were her." The husband, no doubt, would protest that he was writing hurriedly and accidentally left off the *e*. His wife might suspect otherwise, and Freud would agree. The "her" was no accident. It was a Freudian slip. Slips of the tongue, slips of the pen, and forgetting appointments—incidents we often call accidental—are not accidental at all, according to Freud (1901/1960).

Like all of us, Freud was partly a product of his environment. Read the boxed feature on page 402 to learn what kind of environment helped to shape Sigmund Freud.

The Conscious, the Preconscious, and the Unconscious: Levels of Awareness

Question: What are the three levels of awareness in consciousness?

Freud believed that there are three levels of awareness in consciousness: the conscious, the preconscious, and the unconscious. The **conscious** consists of whatever we are aware of at any given moment—a thought, a feeling, a sensation, or a memory. When we shift our attention or our thoughts, there is a change in the content of the conscious.

Freud's **preconscious** is very much like the present-day concept of long-term memory. It contains all the memories, feelings, experiences, and perceptions that we are not consciously thinking about at the moment, but that may be brought to consciousness. Where did you go to high school? In what year were you born? This information resides in your preconscious but can easily be brought to consciousness.

The most important of the three levels is the **unconscious**, which Freud believed to be the primary motivating force of our behavior. The unconscious

psychoanalysis (SY-co-ah-NAL-ih-sis): Freud's term for his theory of personality and for his therapy for the treatment of psychological disorders.

conscious (KON-shus): Those thoughts, feelings, sensations, or memories of which we are aware at any given moment.

preconscious: The thoughts, feelings, and memories that we are not consciously aware of at the moment but that may be brought to consciousness.

unconscious (un-KON-shus): Considered by Freud to be the primary motivating force of behavior, containing repressed memories as well as instincts and wishes that have never been conscious.

WORLD OF PSYCHOLOGY: PIONEERS

Sigmund Freud (1856–1939)

Sigmund Freud was born in 1856, the first of seven surviving children of Jakob and Amalie Freud. Freud resented sharing his mother's attention with his brothers and sisters, but he was her favorite child. He was the only one to have his own room, and he had the only oil lamp—the others used candles. When his sister's piano playing disturbed his studies, the piano was removed from the house. Freud later spoke of the inestimable advantage of being his mother's favorite.

As a youth, Freud was an outstanding student and proficient in eight languages. At age 17, he entered the University of Vienna to study medicine. After completing his degree, Freud began a career in biological research, which lasted only one year. He had fallen in love with Martha Bernays and wanted to marry her; since the research position paid so poorly, he decided to practice medicine instead.

In April 1886 Freud opened a private practice in Vienna, treating psychological disorders. He and Martha were married 5 months later. At the time of his marriage, Freud stood "five feet seven inches tall and weighed just over 126 pounds" (Jones, 1953, p. 151). In their life together, the couple had three sons and three daughters; one daughter, Anna, became a renowned psychoanalyst.

For about 10 years Freud suffered from a neurosis, so he began his own psychoanalysis in 1897. This provided much of the material for his major work *The Interpretation of Dreams* (1900/1953a), which sold a mere 600 copies in 8 years and brought Freud only $209.00 in royalties.

Freud's office was connected to his home. He would see patients all day and then write in his study until 1:00 A.M. or later each night. His practice grew with patients coming from all over eastern Europe and Russia. By 1922 Freud had developed a worldwide reputation, with his books being translated into many languages.

For years Freud smoked about 20 large cigars daily. Probably as a result of this habit, he developed cancer of the jaw in 1923, which required 33 operations over the course of his life. With much of his palate and inner jaw cut away, Freud had to wear a large metal device in his mouth to form a separation between his mouth and nasal cavities. The device caused him great pain, made his speech defective, and made eating difficult. Recurring infections caused nearly total deafness on the side where his jaw had been cut away.

Freud, being Jewish, was a prominent target for the Nazis, who held a public burning of his books in 1933. By 1938 Germany had conquered Austria, and Freud's home in Vienna was invaded by a Nazi gang. His daughter Anna was arrested although later released. Friends begged Freud to take his family and leave Vienna.

Finally, after the intervention of some high-ranking diplomats and the payment of a substantial sum of money, Freud moved to London with his family in 1938. He died there one year later.

holds memories that once were conscious but were so unpleasant or anxiety provoking that they were repressed (involuntarily removed from consciousness). The unconscious also contains all of the instincts (sexual and aggressive), wishes, and desires that have never been allowed into consciousness. Freud traced the roots of psychological disorders to these impulses and repressed memories.

The Id, the Ego, and the Superego: Warring Components of the Personality

Question: What are the roles of the id, the ego, and the superego?

In 1920, when he was nearly 65 years old, Freud (1923/1961) proposed a new conception of the personality, one that contained three systems—the id, the ego, and the superego. These systems do not exist physically; they are only concepts, or ways of looking at personality.

The **id** is the only part of the personality that is present at birth. It is inherited, primitive, inaccessible, and completely unconscious. The id contains (1) the life instincts, which are the sexual instincts and the biological urges such as hunger and thirst, and (2) the death instinct, which accounts for our aggressive and destructive impulses (Freud, 1933/1965). The id operates according to the **pleasure principle**, that is, to seek pleasure, avoid pain, and gain immediate gratification of its wishes. The id is the source of the **libido**, the psychic energy that fuels the entire personality, yet the id cannot act on its own. It can only wish, image, fantasize, demand.

The **ego** is the logical, rational, realistic part of the personality. The ego evolves from the id and draws its energy from the id. One of the ego's functions is to satisfy the id's urges. But the ego, which is mostly conscious, acts according to the reality principle; it must consider the constraints of the real world in determining appropriate times, places, and objects for gratification of the id's wishes. The art of the possible is its guide, and sometimes compromises must be made—a McDonald's hamburger instead of steak or lobster.

When the child is age 5 or 6, the **superego**—the moral component of the personality—is formed. The superego has two parts: (1) the "conscience" consists of all the behaviors for which we have been punished and about which we feel guilty; (2) the "ego ideal" contains the behaviors for which we have been praised and rewarded and about which we feel pride and satisfaction. At first the superego reflects only the parents' expectations of what is good and right, but it expands over time to incorporate teachings from the broader social world. In its quest for moral perfection, the superego sets moral guidelines that define and limit the flexibility of the ego. Figure 12.1 describes the three systems of the personality.

Defense Mechanisms: Protecting the Ego

Question: What is a defense mechanism?

All would be well if the id, the ego, and the superego had compatible aims. But the id's demands for sensual pleasure are often in direct conflict with the super-ego's desire for moral perfection. At times the ego needs some way to defend itself against the anxiety created by the excessive demands of the id, by the harsh judgments of the superego, or by the sometimes threatening conditions in the environment. Often the ego can relieve anxiety by solving its problems rationally and directly. When it cannot do so, it must resort to irrational defenses against anxiety called defense mechanisms. Freud's daughter Anna (1966), also a psychoanalyst, contributed much to our understanding of defense mechanisms.

A **defense mechanism** is a technique used to defend against anxiety and to maintain self-esteem, but it involves self-deception and the distortion of reality. Defense mechanisms are like painkillers. They lessen the pain of anxiety, but they do not cure the problem, and if they are to work, they must be unconscious. All of us use defense mechanisms to some degree; it is only their overuse that is considered abnormal. But there is a price to be paid. Psychic energy is required to keep defenses in place—energy that could be used more profitably in other ways.

Question: What are two ways in which repression operates?

id (IHD): The unconscious system of the personality, which contains the life and death instincts and operates on the pleasure principle.

pleasure principle: The principle by which the id operates to seek pleasure, avoid pain, and obtain immediate gratification.

libido (lih-BEE-doe): Freud's name for the psychic or sexual energy that comes from the id and provides the energy for the entire personality.

ego (EE-go): In Freudian theory, the rational and largely conscious system of the personality; operates according to the reality principle and tries to satisfy the demands of the id without violating one's moral values.

superego (sue-per-EE-go): The moral system of the personality, which consists of the conscience and the ego ideal.

defense mechanism: An unconscious, irrational means used by the ego to defend against anxiety; involves self-deception and the distortion of reality.

Figure 12.1

Freud's Conception of the Personality

According to Freud, personality is composed of three structures or systems: the id, the ego, and the superego. Their characteristics are illustrated and described here.

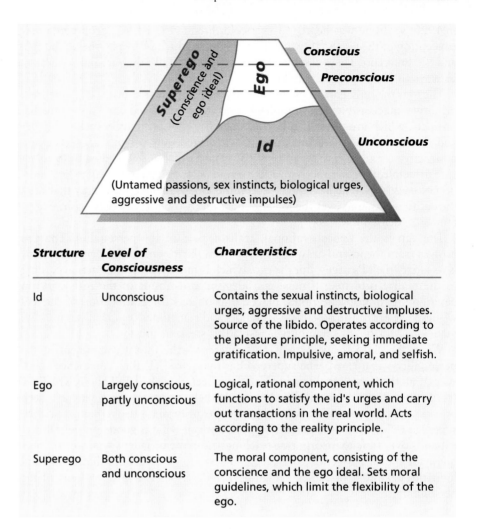

Structure	Level of Consciousness	Characteristics
Id	Unconscious	Contains the sexual instincts, biological urges, aggressive and destructive impulses. Source of the libido. Operates according to the pleasure principle, seeking immediate gratification. Impulsive, amoral, and selfish.
Ego	Largely conscious, partly unconscious	Logical, rational component, which functions to satisfy the id's urges and carry out transactions in the real world. Acts according to the reality principle.
Superego	Both conscious and unconscious	The moral component, consisting of the conscience and the ego ideal. Sets moral guidelines, which limit the flexibility of the ego.

Repression: Out of Mind, Out of Sight   According to Freud, **repression** is the most important and the most frequently used defense mechanism, and it is present to some degree in all other defense mechanisms. Repression operates in two ways: (1) it can remove painful or threatening memories, thoughts, ideas, or perceptions from consciousness and keep them in the unconscious; (2) it can prevent unconscious but disturbing sexual and aggressive impulses from breaking into consciousness.

Even though repressed, the memories lurk in the unconscious and exert an active influence on personality and behavior. In fact, Freud (1933/1965) said repressed memories are "virtually immortal; after the passage of decades, they behave as though they had just occurred" (p. 74). This is why repressed traumatic events of childhood can cause psychological disorders (neuroses) in adults. Freud believed that the way to cure such disorders is to bring the repressed material back to consciousness. This was what he tried to accomplish through his therapy, psychoanalysis (see chapter 15, "Therapies").

Question: What are some other defense mechanisms?

Other Defense Mechanisms: Excuses, Substitutions, and Denials   There are a number of other defense mechanisms that we may use from time to time. We use **projection** when we attribute our own undesirable impulses, thoughts, personality traits, or behavior to others, or when we minimize the undesirable in

Table 12.1 Defense Mechanisms

Defense Mechanism	Description	Example
Repression	The involuntary removal of an unpleasant memory from consciousness or the barring of disturbing sexual and aggressive impulses from consciousness.	John forgets a traumatic incident from childhood.
Projection	Attributing one's own undesirable traits or impulses to another.	A sex-starved middle-aged woman accuses all men of having only one thing on their mind.
Denial	Refusing to consciously acknowledge the existence of danger or a threatening situation.	Sarah sets a place at the table each night for her son who died.
Rationalization	Supplying a logical reason for an irrational or unacceptable behavior.	Fred tells his friend that he didn't get the job because he didn't have connections.
Regression	Reverting to a behavior characteristic of an earlier stage of development.	Susan bursts into tears whenever she is criticized.
Reaction formation	Denying a disturbing impulse by giving strong expression to its opposite.	Mary gives up all social activities to give her undivided attention to her 90-year-old invalid mother.
Displacement	Substituting a less threatening object for the original object of an impulse.	After being spanked by his father, Bill hits his baby brother.
Sublimation	Rechanneling of sexual and aggressive energy into pursuits that society considers acceptable or even admirable.	Tim goes to a gym to work out when he feels hostile and frustrated.

ourselves and exaggerate it in others. Projection allows us to avoid acknowledging our unacceptable traits and thereby maintain our self-esteem, but it seriously distorts our perception of the external world. A sexually promiscuous husband or wife may accuse the partner of being unfaithful. A dishonest businessman may think everyone is out to cheat him.

Denial is a refusal to consciously acknowledge or believe the existence of a danger or a threatening condition. Smokers use denial when they refuse to admit that cigarettes are a danger to their health. Many people who abuse alcohol and drugs deny that they have a problem. Yet denial is sometimes useful as a temporary means of getting through a crisis until a more permanent adjustment can be made, such as when people initially deny the existence of a terminal illness.

Rationalization occurs when we unconsciously supply a logical, rational, or socially acceptable reason rather than the real reason for a thought or action that causes us anxiety. When we rationalize, we make excuses for, or justify, our failures and mistakes. A student who did not study and then failed a test might complain, "The test was unfair." A teacher may blame students for their low grades, claiming that they are unmotivated and lazy.

Sometimes, when frustrated or anxious, we may use **regression** and revert to behavior that might have reduced anxiety at an earlier stage of development. A 5-year-old child with a new baby sister or brother may regress and suck her thumb, wet her pants, or drag a blanket around the house. An adult may have a temper tantrum, rant and rave, or throw things.

Reaction formation is at work when we deny our unacceptable impulses but give strong conscious expression to their opposite, acceptable impulses. In this way, the conscious motive masks the unconscious one. Unconscious hatred may be expressed as love and devotion. A man with unconscious feminine tendencies may overdo the macho image. A reaction formation might be suspected when a behavior is extreme, excessive, and compulsive.

Displacement occurs when we substitute a less threatening object or person for the original object of a sexual or aggressive impulse. If your boss makes you angry, you might take out your hostility on your boyfriend or girlfriend.

With **sublimation**, we rechannel sexual or aggressive energy into pursuits or accomplishments that society considers acceptable or even praiseworthy. An aggressive person may rechannel the aggression and become a football or hockey player, a boxer, a surgeon, or a butcher. Freud viewed sublimation as the only completely healthy ego defense mechanism. In fact, Freud (1930/1962) considered all advancements in civilization to be the result of sublimation. Table 12.1 describes and provides additional examples of the defense mechanisms.

Memory Check 12.1

1. Freud considered the (conscious, unconscious) to be the primary motivating force of our behavior.

2. The (id, ego, superego) is the part of the personality that would make you want to eat, drink, and be merry.

3. The (id, ego, superego) is the part of the personality that determines the most appropriate ways and means of satisfying biological urges.

4. Match the letter of the example with the corresponding defense mechanism.

   _____ 1) sublimation   a. forgetting a traumatic childhood expe-
   _____ 2) repression   rience
   _____ 3) displacement   b. supplying a logical reason for arriving
   _____ 4) rationalization   late
                             c. creating a work of art
                             d. after being punished by a parent, a boy hitting a smaller child

Answers: 1. unconscious 2. id 3. ego 4. 1) c 2) a 3) d 4) b

The Psychosexual Stages of Development: Centered on the Erogenous Zones

Question: What are the psychosexual stages, and why did Freud consider them so important in personality development?

The sex instinct, Freud said, is the most important factor influencing personality, but it does not just suddenly appear full-blown at puberty. It is present at birth and then develops through a series of **psychosexual stages**. Each stage centers around a particular erogenous zone, a part of the body that provides pleasurable sensations and around which a conflict arises (1905/1953b; 1920/1963b). If the conflict is not resolved without undue difficulty, the child may

psychosexual stages: A series of stages through which the sexual instinct develops; each stage is defined by an erogenous zone that becomes the center of new pleasures and conflicts.

develop a **fixation**. This means that a portion of the libido (psychic energy) remains invested at that stage, leaving less energy to meet the challenges of future stages. Overindulgence at a stage may leave a person unwilling psychologically to move on to the next stage. But too little gratification may leave the person trying to make up for previously unmet needs. Freud believed that certain personality characteristics develop as a result of difficulty at one or another of the psychosexual stages.

The Oral Stage (Birth–12 or 18 Months)   During the **oral stage**, the mouth is the primary source of an infant's sensual pleasure, which Freud considered to be an expression of infantile sexuality (1920/1963b). The conflict at this stage centers on weaning. Too much or too little gratification may result in an oral fixation—an excessive preoccupation with oral activities such as eating, drinking, smoking, gum-chewing, nail-biting, and even kissing. (Freud's 20-cigars-a-day habit probably qualifies as an oral fixation, according to his theory.) Freud claimed that difficulties at the oral stage can result in personality traits such as either excessive dependence, optimism, and gullibility (an individual who will swallow anything) or extreme pessimism, sarcasm, hostility, and aggression.

The Anal Stage (1 or 1 1/2–3 Years)   During the **anal stage**, children derive sensual pleasure from expelling and withholding feces. But a conflict arises when toilet training begins, because this is one of the first attempts to have children withhold or postpone gratification. When parents are harsh in their approach, children may rebel openly, defecating whenever and wherever they please. This may lead to an anal expulsive personality—someone who is sloppy, irresponsible, rebellious, hostile, and destructive. Other children may defy their parents and gain attention by withholding feces. They may develop anal retentive personalities, gaining security through what they possess and becoming stingy, stubborn, rigid, excessively neat and clean, orderly, and precise (Freud, 1933/1965). Do these patterns remind you of Felix and Oscar of the old TV series "The Odd Couple"?

Question: What is the Oedipus complex?

The Phallic Stage (3–5 or 6 Years)   During the **phallic stage**, children learn that sensual pleasure may be gained by touching their genitals, and masturbation is common. They become aware of the anatomical differences in males and females and may begin to play "Doctor."

The conflict that develops at this stage is a sexual desire for the parent of the opposite sex and a hostility toward the same-sex parent, a conflict Freud called the **Oedipus complex** (based on the Greek tragedy *Oedipus Rex*, by Sophocles). "Boys concentrate their sexual wishes upon their mother and develop hostile impulses against their father as being a rival" (1925/1963a, p. 61). But the young boy eventually develops castration anxiety—an intense fear that his father might retaliate and harm him by cutting off his penis, the offending organ (1933/1965). This fear becomes so intense, Freud believed, that the boy usually resolves the Oedipus complex by identifying with his father and repressing his sexual feelings for his mother. With identification, the child takes on his father's behaviors, mannerisms, and superego standards, and in this way the superego develops (Freud, 1930/1962a).

Girls experience a similar internal Oedipal conflict often referred to as the Electra complex, although Freud did not use that term. When young girls discover that they have no penis, they develop "penis envy," Freud claimed, and they turn to their father because he has the desired organ (1933/1965). They feel sexual desires for him and develop jealousy and rivalry toward their mother. But

fixation: Arrested development at a psychosexual stage occurring because of excessive gratification or frustration at that stage.

Oedipus complex (ED-uh-pus):   Occurring in the phallic stage, a conflict in which the child is sexually attracted to the opposite-sex parent and feels hostility toward the same-sex parent.

eventually girls, too, experience anxiety as a result of their hostile feelings. They repress their sexual feelings toward the father and identify with the mother, leading to the formation of their superego (Freud, 1920/1962).

According to Freud, failure to resolve these conflicts can have serious consequences for both boys and girls. Freud thought that tremendous guilt and anxiety could be carried over into adulthood and cause sexual problems, great difficulty relating to members of the opposite sex, and even homosexuality.

The Latency Period (5 or 6 Years–Puberty)   Following the stormy phallic stage, the **latency period** is one of relative calm. The sex instinct is repressed and temporarily sublimated in school and play activities, hobbies, and sports.

The Genital Stage (From Puberty On)   In the **genital stage**, the object of sexual energy gradually shifts to the opposite sex for the vast majority of people, culminating in heterosexual love and the attainment of full adult sexuality. Freud believed that the few who reach the genital stage without having fixations at earlier stages, can achieve the state of psychological health that he equated with the ability to love and work. Figure 12.2 provides a summary of the psychosexual stages of development.

Freud's Explanation of Personality

Question: According to Freud, what are the two primary sources of influence on the personality?

According to Freud, personality is almost completely formed at age 5 or 6, when the Oedipal conflict is resolved and the superego is formed. He believed that there are two primary sources of influence on personality: (1) the traits that develop due to fixations at any of the psychosexual stages, and (2) the relative

Figure 12.2   Freud's Psychosexual Stages of Development   In Freud's view, the sex instinct is the most important factor influencing personality, which develops through a series of psychosexual stages. Each stage is centered on a particular erogenous zone. Certain adult personality traits can result from failure to resolve problems or conflicts at the psychosexual stages.

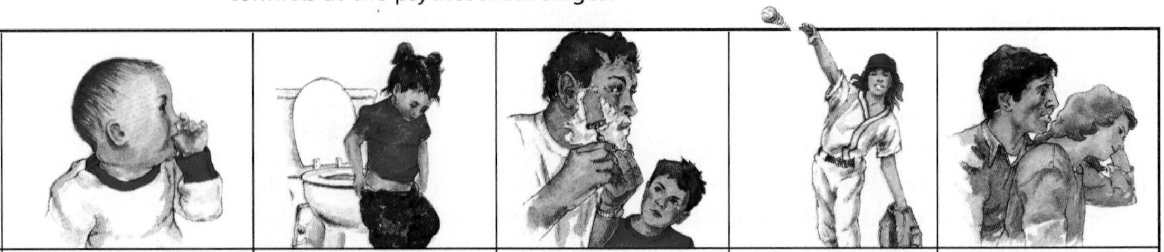

STAGE	**Oral** Birth to 12 – 18 Months	**Anal** 12 – 18 Months to 3 Years	**Phallic** 3 to 5 – 6 Years	**Latency** 5 – 6 Years to Puberty	**Genital** Puberty On
EROGENOUS ZONE	Mouth	Anus	Genitals	None	Genitals

CONFLICTS/ EXPERIENCES	Weaning
	Oral gratification
	  from sucking,
	  eating, biting
		Toilet training
		Gratification from
		  expelling and
		  withholding feces
			Oedipal conflict
			Sexual curiosity
			Masturbation
				Period of sexual
				calm; interest in
				school, hobbies,
				same-sex friends
					Sexual interests
					resurface; mature
					sexual relationships
					are established

ADULT TRAITS ASSOCIATED WITH PROBLEMS AT STAGE	Optimism, gullibility, dependency, pessimism, passivity, hostility, sarcasm, aggression	Excessive cleanliness, orderliness, stinginess, messiness, rebelliousness, destructiveness	Flirtatiousness, vanity, promiscuity, pride, chastity	—	—

strengths of the id, the ego, and the superego. In psychologically healthy people, there is a balance among the three components. If the id is too strong and the superego too weak, people will take pleasure and gratify desires, no matter who is hurt or what the cost, and not feel guilty. But a tyrannical superego will leave people with perpetual guilt feelings, unable to enjoy sensual pleasure.

Evaluating Freud's Contribution

Freud's theory is so comprehensive (he wrote more than 24 volumes) that elements of the theory must be evaluated separately. His beliefs that women are inferior to men sexually, morally, and intellectually and that they suffer penis envy seem ridiculous today. Also, research contradicts Freud's notion that personality is almost completely formed by age 5 or 6. However, we are indebted to him for pointing out the influence of early childhood experiences on later development.

Critics charge that much of Freud's theory defies scientific testing. How can a theory, they ask, based on Freud's analysis of his own life and the case histories of his disturbed patients provide a theory of personality generalizable to the larger population? The most serious flaw critics find is that Freud's theory interprets and explains behavior after the fact and lacks the power to predict behavior. In too many cases, any act of behavior or even no act of behavior at all can be interpreted to support Freud's theory.

Even so, some research in neuroscience and psychology supports the notions of unconscious mental processing (Shevrin & Dickman, 1980; Miller, 1986) and the Freudian slip (Motley, 1985, 1987). Research also finds evidence for repression, especially for memories related to feelings of fear and self-consciousness (Davis, 1987; Davis & Schwartz, 1987).

Although Freud has been a towering figure in the world of psychology, among modern psychologists he does not loom as large as in decades past. There are very few strict Freudians left, and even among most psychoanalysts, Freud's techniques constitute only a part of their therapeutic arsenal. Sigmund Freud has been both worshipped and ridiculed, but his standing as a pioneer in psychology cannot be denied.

Memory Check 12.2

1. According to Freud, the sex instinct arises at (birth, puberty).

2. Excessive concern with cleanliness and order could indicate a fixation at the (anal, phallic) stage.

3. Excessive preoccupation with eating, drinking, and smoking could have resulted from overindulgence or excessive frustration at the (oral, anal) stage.

4. When a boy develops sexual feelings toward his mother and hostility toward his father, he is experiencing the internal struggle called the (Oedipus, Electra) complex.

Answers: 1. birth 2. anal 3. oral 4. Oedipus

Carl Gustav Jung (1875–1961)

personal unconscious: In Jung's theory, the layer of the unconscious containing all of the thoughts and experiences that are accessible to the conscious, as well as repressed memories and impulses.

collective unconscious: In Jung's theory, the most inaccessible layer of the unconscious, which contains the universal experiences of mankind transmitted to each individual.

archetype (AR-keh-type): Existing in the collective unconscious, an inherited tendency to respond in particular ways to universal human situations.

The Neo-Freudians

Several personality theorists, referred to as neo-Freudians, started their careers as followers of Freud but began to disagree on some of the basic principles of psychoanalytic theory. They modified some aspects of the theory and presented their own original ideas about personality. We will discuss Carl Jung (analytical psychology), Alfred Adler (individual psychology), and Karen Horney.

Carl Gustav Jung

Question: According to Jung, what are the three components of personality?

Carl Jung (1875–1961) differed with Freud on many major points. He did not consider the sexual instinct to be the main factor in personality, nor did he believe that the personality is almost completely formed in early childhood. He claimed that middle age is an even more important period for personality development (Jung, 1933). Jung even disagreed with Freud on the basic structure of personality.

Jung's View of the Personality: A Different View of the Unconscious

Jung conceived of the personality as consisting of three parts: the ego, the personal unconscious, and the collective unconscious. He saw the ego as the conscious component of personality, which carries out our normal daily activities. Like Freud, he believed the ego to be secondary in importance to the unconscious.

The **personal unconscious** develops as a result of our own individual experience and is therefore unique to each individual. It contains all the experiences, thoughts, and perceptions accessible to the conscious, as well as repressed memories, wishes, and impulses. The personal unconscious resembles a combination of Freud's preconscious and unconscious.

The **collective unconscious** is the deepest and most inaccessible layer of the unconscious. Jung thought that the universal experiences of mankind throughout evolution are transmitted to each individual through the collective unconscious. This is how he accounted for the similarity of certain myths, dreams, symbols, and religious beliefs in cultures widely separated by distance and time. Figure 12.3 provides a summary of Jung's conception of the personality.

Archetypes: Unconscious Predispositions

The collective unconscious contains what Jung called archetypes. An **archetype** is an inherited tendency to respond to universal human situations in particular ways. Jung would say that the tendency of people to believe in a god, a devil, evil spirits, and heroes, or to have a fear of the dark or of snakes, all result from inherited archetypes.

Jung named several archetypes that exert a major influence on the personality. The persona is the public face we show to the world—"a kind of mask, designed on the one hand to make a definite impression on others, and, on the other, to conceal the true nature of the individual" (Jung, 1966, p. 192). It is consistent with the roles we play, and it helps us function socially. The persona presents no problem as long as people remain aware that it consists of the impression they are trying to make and not the real person behind it.

The shadow is a powerful archetype that represents "the 'negative side' of the personality, the sum of all those unpleasant qualities we like to hide" (Jung, 1917/1953, par. 103). To deny our shadow, or to fail to be conscious of it, gives it more power over us. The qualities we condemn most in others may be lurking in our own shadow, unadmitted and unknown.

While Jung saw differences in the psychology of males and females, he be-

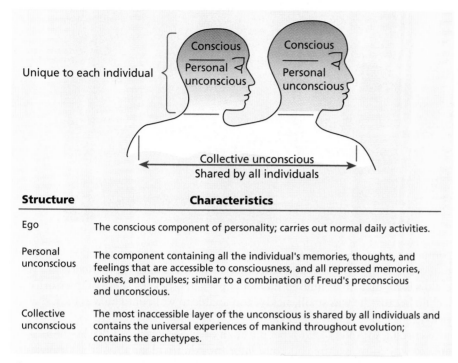

extraversion: The tendency to be outgoing, adaptable, and sociable.

introversion: The tendency to focus inward, to be reflective, retiring, and nonsocial.

Structure	Characteristics
Ego	The conscious component of personality; carries out normal daily activities.
Personal unconscious	The component containing all the individual's memories, thoughts, and feelings that are accessible to consciousness, and all repressed memories, wishes, and impulses; similar to a combination of Freud's preconscious and unconscious.
Collective unconscious	The most inaccessible layer of the unconscious is shared by all individuals and contains the universal experiences of mankind throughout evolution; contains the archetypes.

Figure 12.3 Jung's Conception of Personality Like Freud, Carl Jung saw three components in personality. The ego and the personal unconscious are unique to each individual. The collective unconscious, is shared by all individuals and accounts for the similarity of myths and beliefs in diverse cultures.

lieved that we all carry qualities and images of the opposite sex within us, although usually in an underdeveloped state. The *anima* is Jung's term for the "inner feminine figure" within the unconscious of every man, and the *animus*, the "inner masculine figure" within the unconscious of every woman (Jung, 1961, p. 186). Jung stressed that a healthy personality can develop only when both the masculine and feminine qualities are consciously acknowledged and integrated. Jung's work can be considered a forerunner of the more recent research on psychological androgyny (see chapter 11, "Human Sexuality and Gender").

The self represents the full development of the personality and is attained only when the opposing forces within are integrated and balanced. The self encompasses the conscious and the unconscious, the persona, the shadow, the masculine and feminine qualities, and the tendencies toward extraversion and introversion (terms originated by Jung). **Extraversion** is the tendency to be outgoing, adaptable, and sociable; **introversion** is the tendency to focus inward, to be reflective, retiring, and nonsocial.

Alfred Adler: Overcoming Inferiority

Question: What did Adler consider to be the driving force of the personality?

Alfred Adler (1870–1937) disagreed with most of Freud's basic beliefs; on many points his views were the exact opposite. Adler emphasized the unity of the personality rather than the separate warring components of id, ego, and superego. He believed that our behavior is motivated more by the conscious than by the unconscious and that we are influenced more by future goals than by early childhood experiences.

Unlike Freud, who claimed that sex and pleasure-seeking are our primary motives, Adler (1927, 1956) maintained that we are driven by the need to

Alfred Adler (1870–1937)

Adler believed that humans are driven by the desire to overcome and compensate for feelings of weakness.

compensate for inferiority and strive for superiority or significance. He believed that feelings of weakness and inferiority are an inevitable experience in every child's early life. Adler himself had felt a particularly keen sense of inferiority as a child because he was small, sickly, and unable to walk until he was four, due to rickets.

According to Adler (1956), people at an early age develop a "style of life"—a unique way in which the child and later the adult will go about the struggle to achieve superiority. Sometimes inferiority feelings are so strong that they prevent personal development, and Adler originated a term to describe this condition—the "inferiority complex" (Dreikurs, 1953).

Karen Horney: Champion of Feminine Psychology

Question: Why is Karen Horney considered a pioneer in psychology?

Horney's work centered on two main themes—the neurotic personality (Horney, 1937, 1945, 1950) and feminine psychology (Horney, 1967). She considered herself a disciple of Freud, accepting his emphasis on unconscious motivation and the basic tools of psychoanalysis. However, she disagreed with many of his basic beliefs. She did not accept his division of personality into id, ego, and superego, and she flatly rejected his psychosexual stages and the concepts of the Oedipus complex and penis envy. Furthermore, Horney thought Freud overemphasized the role of the sexual instinct and neglected cultural and environmental influences on personality. While she did stress the importance of early childhood experiences, Horney (1939) believed that personality could continue to develop and change throughout life. Horney argued forcefully against Freud's notion that the desire to have a child and a man are nothing more than a conversion of the unfulfilled wish for a penis.

Rather than envying the male's penis, Horney insisted that what women really want are the same opportunities, the same rights and privileges society grants to males. Although Freud did not respond directly to her arguments, he implied that Horney's challenge to his theory was merely a manifestation of her own penis envy. Horney prevailed and continued her pioneering efforts for women. She argued convincingly that women must be given the opportunity to find their own personal identities, to develop their abilities, and pursue careers if they choose.

Horney (1945) believed that in order to be psychologically healthy, we all need safety and satisfaction. But these needs can be frustrated in early childhood by parents who are indifferent, unaffectionate, rejecting, or hostile. Such early experiences may cause the child to develop basic anxiety—"the feeling a child has of being isolated and helpless in a potentially hostile world" (p. 41). In order to minimize this basic anxiety and to satisfy the need for safety, children develop coping strategies that form their basic attitude toward life—either moving toward people, moving against people, or moving away from people. If we are normal, we move in all three ways as different situations demand. But if we are neurotic, we are restricted to only one way to reduce anxiety, and we use it excessively and inappropriately.

If we cannot tolerate ourselves the way we are, said Horney, we may repress all our negative attributes and replace them with an idealized image, perfect and unblemished. As long as this image remains real to us, we feel superior and entitled to make all kinds of demands and claims. Horney (1950) believed that the idealized self brings with it the "tyranny of the should"—unrealistic demands for personal perfection, which "no human being could fulfill" (p. 66). The irrational, neurotic thinking that may spring from the "tyranny of the should" is an important part of Horney's theory. Her influence may be seen in modern-day cognitive-behavioral therapies, especially the rational-emotive therapy of Albert Ellis, which we explore in chapter 15, "Therapies."

WORLD OF PSYCHOLOGY: PIONEERS

Karen Horney (1885–1952)

Karen Horney (HOR-nye) pioneered in the introduction of feminine psychology, a perspective that until her time had been virtually excluded from the world of psychology.

Born Karen Danielsen in a small village near Hamburg, Germany, in 1885, Karen was the second child and first daughter in a financially secure, Protestant family. Her Norwegian father was a commercial ship captain who was devoutly religious, stern, and silent. Karen's mother was Dutch, bright, beautiful, vivacious, a free thinker, and 17 years younger than Captain Danielsen. Young Karen sometimes accompanied her father on long voyages at sea, visiting many ports and observing diverse cultures. This may have influenced her heavy emphasis on social and cultural forces in the formation of personality, rather than the biological forces proposed by Freud.

Karen was more heavily influenced by her mother and spent more time with her because of the long periods when her father was away at sea. An excellent student, Karen decided at age 12 to study medicine. Over the strong objections of her father but with the encouragement of her mother, Karen Danielsen, at age 21, entered medical school in Berlin. Three years later in 1909, she married Oscar Horney, a lawyer, and she finished her M.D. degree in 1911 at the age of 26. Karen Horney became a member of the Berlin Psychoanalytic Society and went into analysis with a strict Freudian, Karl Abraham, who praised her with great enthusiasm to Freud. She opened her psychoanalytic practice and became a training analyst for the Berlin Psychoanalytic Institute. Over the next several years, three daughters were born to the Horneys.

While still in Berlin Dr. Horney wrote theoretical articles, several of which were on feminine psychology. All along she had known that her male colleagues did not understand the psychology of women. In 1926 Karen Horney and her husband separated and in 1932, at the age of 47, she moved to the United States, first to Chicago and two years later to New York. There Horney established her clinical practice and published her first book, *The Neurotic Personality of Our Time,* in 1937—the same year as her divorce.

Karen Horney continued her practice and writing, and untiringly pioneered the cause of feminine psychology. She died in New York in 1952 at the age of 67.

Memory Check 12.3

1. In Jung's theory the inherited part of the personality, which stores the experiences of mankind, is the (personal, collective) unconscious.

2. (Jung, Adler) believed that our basic drive is to overcome and compensate for inferiority feelings and to strive for superiority and significance.

3. Horney traced the origin of psychological maladjustment to:

   a. the inferiority feelings of childhood
   b. basic anxiety resulting from the parents' failure to satisfy the child's needs for safety and satisfaction
   c. excessive frustration or overindulgence of the child at early stages of development
   d. the failure to balance opposing forces in the personality

Answers: 1. collective 2. Adler 3. b

Trait Theories

Question: What are trait theories of personality?

How would you describe yourself—cheerful, moody, talkative, quiet, shy, friendly, outgoing? When you describe your personality or that of someone else, you probably list several relatively stable and consistent personal characteristics called *traits*. **Trait theories** are attempts to explain personality and differences between people in terms of their personal characteristics.

Gordon Allport: Personality Traits in the Brain

Question: How does Allport differentiate between cardinal and central traits?

Gordon Allport (1897–1967) claimed that personality traits are real entities, physically located somewhere in the brain (Allport & Odbert, 1936). We each inherit our own unique set of raw materials for given traits, which are then shaped by our experiences. Traits describe the particular way we respond to the environment and the consistency of that response. If we are shy, we respond to strangers differently than if we are friendly; if we are self-confident, we approach tasks differently than if we feel inferior. As you will see later in the chapter, recent research in behavioral genetics supports the notion that certain personality characteristics are influenced by the genes.

Allport (1961) identified two main categories of traits—common traits and individual traits. Common traits are those traits we share or hold in common with most others in our own culture. For example, the quiet, polite behavior often found in Asian people is a common trait of those cultures. Far more important to Allport were three types of individual traits: cardinal, central, and secondary traits.

A **cardinal trait** is "so pervasive and so outstanding in a life that . . . almost every act seems traceable to its influence" (Allport, 1961, p. 365). It is so strong a part of the person's personality that he or she may become identified with or known for that trait. We even describe people who, to some degree, exhibit the cardinal traits of others as being Christlike or a Scrooge, for example.

trait: A personal characteristic that is used to describe or explain personality.

trait theory: A theory that attempts to explain personality and differences between people in terms of their personal characteristics.

cardinal trait: Allport's name for a personal quality that is so strong a part of the person's personality that he or she may become identified with that trait.

Central traits are those, said Allport (1961), that we would "mention in writing a careful letter of recommendation" (p. 365). Read the *Try It!* to learn more about central traits.

Which adjectives in this list best describe you? Which characterize your mother or your father? In Allport's terms you would be describing her or his central traits.

Try It!

decisive	funny	intelligent	disorganized	shy
fearful	jealous	controlled	responsible	rigid
outgoing	inhibited	religious	arrogant	loyal
competitive	liberal	friendly	compulsive	quiet
generous	sloppy	laid-back	rebellious	calm
good-natured	nervous	serious	humble	lazy
industrious	deceptive	cooperative	reckless	sad
honest	happy	selfish	organized	quiet

We also possess a number of secondary traits, but these are less obvious, less consistent, and not as critical in defining our personality as are the cardinal and central traits. Secondary traits are such things as food preferences, favorite music, and specific attitudes. We have many more secondary traits than cardinal or central traits.

Raymond Cattell's 16 Personality Factors

Question: How did Cattell differentiate between surface and source traits?

Raymond Cattell (1950) considered personality to be a pattern of traits providing the key to understanding and predicting a person's behavior. Cattell identified two types: surface traits and source traits.

If you were asked to describe your best friend, you might list such traits as kind, honest, helpful, generous, and so on. These observable qualities of personality, Cattell called **surface traits**. (Allport called these qualities central traits.) Using observations and questionnaires, Cattell studied thousands of people, and he found certain clusters of surface traits that appeared together time after time. He thought these were evidence of deeper, more general, underlying personality factors. Using a statistical technique called factor analysis, Cattell tried to identify these factors, which he called source traits.

Source traits make up the most basic personality structure and, according to Cattell, cause behavior. Even though we all possess the same source traits, we do not all possess them in the same degree. Intelligence is a source trait, and every person has a certain amount of it, but obviously not exactly the same amount or the same kind. How intelligent people are can influence whether they pursue a college degree, the profession of job they choose, what type of leisure activities they pursue, and what kind of friends they have.

Cattell found 23 source traits in normal individuals, 16 of which he studied in great detail. Cattell's Sixteen Personality Factor Questionnaire, commonly called the "16 P. F. Test," yields a personality profile (Cattell et al., 1950, 1977).

The Cattell Personality Profile can be used to provide a better understanding of a single individual or to compare one person's profile with that of others. When later researchers tried to confirm Cattell's 16 factors, no one could find more than 7 factors, and most found fewer (Digman, 1990).

central trait: Allport's name for the type of trait you would use in writing a letter of recommendation.

source traits: Cattell's name for the traits that underlie the surface traits, make up the most basic personality structure, and cause behavior.

surface traits: Cattell's name for observable qualities of personality, such as those used to describe a friend.

Try It!

Using this hypothetical personality profile as a model, circle the point along each of the 16 dimensions of bipolar traits that best describes your personality.

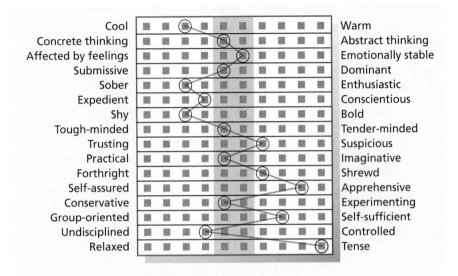

	Warm
Cool	
Concrete thinking	Abstract thinking
Affected by feelings	Emotionally stable
Submissive	Dominant
Sober	Enthusiastic
Expedient	Conscientious
Shy	Bold
Tough-minded	Tender-minded
Trusting	Suspicious
Practical	Imaginative
Forthright	Shrewd
Self-assured	Apprehensive
Conservative	Experimenting
Group-oriented	Self-sufficient
Undisciplined	Controlled
Relaxed	Tense

Hans Eysenck considered extraversion and emotional stability (neuroticism) to be the most important dimensions in assessing personality.

Hans Eysenck: Stressing Two Factors

Extraverts are sociable, outgoing, and active, whereas introverts are withdrawn, quiet, and introspective. (Jung originally introduced the terms introversion and extraversion.) Emotionally stable people are calm, even-tempered, and often easygoing, while emotionally unstable people are anxious, excitable, and easily distressed. The Eysenck Personality Questionnaire (EPQ) is a self-report instrument that assesses personality according to these two dimensions (Eysenck & Eysenck, 1975).

Eysenck (1981) believes that individual differences on the two dimensions may be partly due to differences in nervous system functioning. He suggests that extraverts have a lower level of cortical arousal than introverts and as a result seek out more stimulation to increase arousal, while introverts are more easily aroused and thus more likely to show emotional instability. Stelmack (1990) suggests that rather than having a higher base rate of arousal, "introverts exhibit greater reactivity to sensory stimulation than extraverts" (p. 293).

The 5-Factor Theories of Personality: A New View

A consensus is beginning to emerge among some trait theorists (again using factor analysis) that there are actually five dimensions underlying personality, sometimes called the "big five" (L.R. Goldberg, 1981). Although the notion of five factors began with Fiske (1949) and was supported by several researchers over the years, it received serious attention and support in the 1980s (Digman, 1990; John, 1990). Present theorists differ somewhat on the names of the five factors (Briggs, 1989), but the basic themes are extraversion, agreeableness, conscientiousness, emotionality, and intellect (Digman & Inouye, 1986; McCrae & Costa, 1987; Peabody & Goldberg, 1989). Paunonen and others (1992) have found support for the 5-factor theory in a cross-cultural study involving subjects from Canada, Finland, Poland, and Germany.

Evaluating the Trait Perspective

Do we possess stable and enduring traits that predictably guide the way we will act across time and changing situations? Critics of trait theories say no and maintain that the consistency of our behavior across situations is very low and not predictable on the basis of personality traits. Initially, one of the severest critics of the trait theory was psychologist Walter Mischel (1968). He concluded that the situation, not our traits, determines behavior. His position stimulated the person-situation debate—the question of the relative importance of factors within the person and factors within the situation that account for behavior (Rowe, 1987). Mischel (1973, 1977) eventually modified his original position (that the situation determines behavior) and now admits that behavior is influenced by both the person *and* the situation. Mischel now thinks of a trait as a conditional probability that a particular action will occur in response to a particular situation (Wright & Mischel, 1987).

After several decades of study, the weight of evidence supports the view that there are internal traits that strongly influence behavior across situations (Epstein & O'Brien, 1985; Kenrick & Funder, 1988; Carson, 1989). According to Funder & Colvin (1991), "Even though situations profoundly affect what people do, people can still manage to preserve their distinctive behavioral styles across situations" (p. 791). Additional support for the trait theorists has come from longitudinal studies. Costa & McCrea (1986, 1988) studied personality traits of subjects over time and found them to be stable after age 30. They concluded that "aging itself has little effect on personality" (1988, p. 862).

Many situations in life call forth behavior that is very similar for most of us even when our internal traits differ drastically. Even the most talkative and boisterous among us tend to be quiet during a religious service, a funeral, or other solemn occasions. Characteristic traits, according to the trait theorists, are said to determine how we behave *most* of the time, not *all* of the time. And we would agree that even the most optimistic, happy, and outgoing people have "down" days, fall ill, and frown occasionally.

Memory Check 12.4

1. Match the type of trait with its description, according to Allport's view.

   _____ 1) common trait   a. a trait one is known for
   _____ 2) central trait   b. a preference or an attitude
   _____ 3) cardinal trait   c. a trait shared by people in a culture
   _____ 4) secondary trait   d. the kind of trait used in writing a
                                                       letter of recommendation

2. According to Cattell, one can account for the differences in people by the particular source traits they possess. (true, false)

3. (Mischel, Eysenck) identified extraversion and emotional stability as the major factors underlying personality.

Answers: 1. 1) c 2) d 3) a 4) b 2. true 3. Eysenck

Learning Theories and Personality

According to the learning perspective, personality is viewed as the learned tendencies that have been acquired over a lifetime.

The Behaviorist View of B. F. Skinner

Question: How did Skinner account for what most people refer to as personality?

B. F. Skinner and other strict behaviorists have an interesting view of personality. They deny that there is any such thing. What we call personality, they believe, is nothing more nor less than a collection of learned behaviors or habits that have been reinforced in the past. Skinner denied that a personality or self initiates and directs behavior. The causes of behavior, he stated, lie outside of the person, and they are based on past and present rewards and punishments. Thus, Skinner did not use the term personality. He simply described the variables in the environment that shape an individual's observable behavior. Healthy experiences in a healthy environment make a healthy person.

But what about the psychologically unhealthy individual? Where does abnormal behavior originate? Skinner (1953) believed that psychologically unhealthy people have been reinforced by the environment for behaving abnormally. To change an individual's behavior, then, we must restructure the environment so that it will reinforce normal rather than abnormal behavior. What a contrast to psychoanalytic theory and trait theory, which see internal forces as the major shapers and determiners of behavior.

The Social-Cognitive Theorists: Expanding the Behaviorist View

Question: What processes do the social-cognitive theorists consider in explaining personality?

There is no doubt that some of our behaviors can be traced to classical and operant conditioning, but can all of personality, or even all of learning, be explained in this way? Not according to social-cognitive theorists, who consider both external and internal influences in their attempts to understand human personality. The chief advocate of the social-cognitive position is Albert Bandura (1977a, 1986).

Albert Bandura's Views on Personality   Albert Bandura agrees that the environment plays a major part in shaping our behavior, but he contends that both our thinking and our behavior can alter our environment. This mutual effect he calls reciprocal determinism. Personality and behavior can best be explained, say the social-cognitive theorists, as an interaction between the person within and the environment. They emphasize the importance of internal cognitive processes—thinking, feelings, and perceptions—and maintain that it is not merely the environment that influences our behavior but our perception and evaluation of environmental events as well (see Figure 12.4).

Bandura (1977b) suggests that how people behave in a variety of situations is influenced by their perception of their ability to perform competently and successfully in whatever is attempted, which he calls **self-efficacy**. People high in self-efficacy will approach new situations confidently and will persist in their efforts because they believe success is likely. On the other hand, people low in

self-efficacy: A person's belief in his or her ability to perform competently in whatever is attempted.

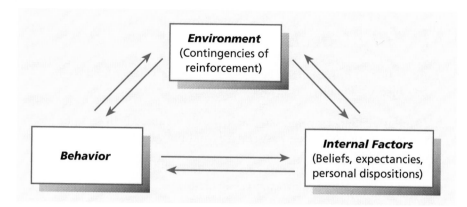

self-efficacy will expect failure and avoid challenges. In a real sense, one's sense of self-efficacy can become a self-fulfilling prophecy.

Bandura (1986) insists that we do not need to experience the effects of classical or operant conditioning directly in order to learn. Rather, we can learn merely by observing the behavior of another person (called the model) and the consequences of that behavior. If we pay close enough attention and if the behavior is not too complex, we can acquire the potential (ability) to perform the behavior. Of course there are limits to observational learning. We could not learn to play a violin by watching a violinist during a night at the symphony.

Reinforcement, as well, comes through observation. Bandura maintains we can learn through vicarious reinforcement—by observing the rewards and punishments that follow various behaviors performed by others. We can avoid disasters in our own lives by observing the misfortunes of others. Thus many of the behaviors we exhibit or inhibit can be traced to observational learning. Bandura's own research has revealed that sex-appropriate behaviors (Bussey & Bandura, 1984) and aggressive responses are readily acquired through modeling (Bandura, 1973).

Question: What does Rotter mean by the terms internal and external locus of control?

Julian Rotter and Locus of Control Julian Rotter proposes another concept—**locus of control**—which provides additional insight into why people behave as they do. Some of us see ourselves as primarily in control of our behavior and its consequences. This, Rotter (1966, 1971, 1990) defines as an internal locus of control. Others perceive that whatever happens to them is in the hands of fate, luck, or chance. They exhibit an external locus of control and may claim that it does not matter what they do because "whatever will be, will be." Rotter contends that people with an external locus of control are less likely to change their behavior as a result of reinforcement because they do not see reinforcers as being tied to their own actions.

Evaluating the Social-Cognitive Perspective The social-cognitive perspective cannot be criticized for lacking a strong research base. Yet some of its critics claim that while acknowledging certain aspects of the person within, the social-cognitive perspective continues to weigh the situation too heavily. The critics ask: What about unconscious motives or internal dispositions (traits) that we exhibit fairly consistently across many different situations? Other critics point to the accumulating evidence of a genetic influence on personality, which may explain 50 percent or more of the variation in personality characteristics (Tellegen et al., 1988).

locus of control: A concept used to explain how people account for what happens in their lives—people with an internal *locus of control* see themselves as primarily in control of their behavior and its consequences; those with an external *locus of control* perceive what happens to be in the hands of fate, luck, or chance.

humanistic psychology: An approach to psychology that stresses the uniquely human attributes and positive view of human nature.

self-actualization: Developing to one's fullest potential.

Memory Check 12.5

1. According to B. F. Skinner, behavior is initiated by inner forces, which he called personality. (true/false)

2. (Bandura, Skinner) would say that behavior is caused by forces outside the person and based on past rewards and punishments.

3. The social-cognitive theorists emphasize the role of (social forces, cognitive processes) in influencing behavior.

4. (Bandura, Rotter) proposed the concept of locus of control.

Answers: 1. false 2. Skinner 3. cognitive processes 4. Rotter

Humanistic Personality Theories

Question: Who were the two pioneers in humanistic psychology, and how did they view human nature?

Humanistic psychology seeks to give a more complete and positive picture of the human personality than the two other major forces in psychology—behaviorism and psychoanalysis. Humanistic psychologists are critical of psychoanalysis because it is based primarily on Freud's work with patients who were psychologically unhealthy. Moreover, the humanists take issue with behaviorism because of its almost exclusive concern with observable behavior, to the neglect of what is going on inside the person.

But more than simply reacting against psychoanalysis and behaviorism, humanistic psychologists have developed their own unique view of human nature, a view that is considerably more flattering. Human nature is seen as innately good, with a natural tendency toward growth and **self-actualization**—developing to one's fullest potential. The humanists largely deny a dark or evil side of human nature. They do not believe that we are shaped strictly by the environment or ruled by mysterious unconscious forces. Rather, as creative beings with an active, conscious, free will, we can chart our own course in life.

Humanistic psychology is sometimes called the "third force" in psychology. (Behaviorism and psychoanalysis are the other two forces.) The pioneering humanistic psychologists were Abraham Maslow and Carl Rogers.

Abraham Maslow: The Self-Actualizing Person

Abraham Maslow (1970) maintained that if you want to know what makes a healthy personality, you must study people who are healthy. He wrote, "the study of the crippled, stunted, immature, and unhealthy specimens can yield only a cripple psychology." So Maslow studied individuals who he believed were using their talents and abilities to their fullest—in other words, individuals who exemplified self-actualization. Maslow studied some historical figures, such as Abraham Lincoln and Thomas Jefferson, and figures who made significant contributions during his own lifetime—Albert Einstein, Eleanor Roosevelt, and Albert Schweitzer. After examining the lives of such individuals, Maslow identified characteristics that self-actualizing persons seem to share.

Maslow found self-actualizers to be accurate in perceiving reality—able to judge honestly and to quickly spot the fake and the dishonest. Self-actualizers are comfortable with life, accept themselves and others, and nature as well, with

Abraham Maslow (1908–1970)

good humor and tolerance. Most of them believe they have a mission to accomplish or the need to devote their life for some larger good, as in the case of Mother Teresa. Self-actualizers tend not to depend on external authority or other people but seem to be inner-driven, autonomous, and independent. They feel a strong fellowship with humanity, and their relationships with others are characterized by deep and loving bonds. They can laugh at themselves, and their sense of humor, though well developed, never involves hostility or criticism of others. Finally, the most telling mark of self-actualizers are frequently occurring peak experiences—experiences of deep meaning, insight, harmony within and with the universe.

Maslow came to the conclusion that each of us has the capacity for self-actualization. If we apply our talent and energy to doing our best in whatever endeavor we choose, then we, too, can lead creative lives and be considered self-actualizing.

Maslow is best remembered for his hierarchy of needs, on which his theory of motivation rests (see chapter 10, "Motivation and Emotion").

Carl Rogers: The Fully-Functioning Person

Carl Rogers (1951, 1961), like Freud, developed his theory of personality through insights gained from his patients in therapy sessions. Yet he saw something very different from what Freud and the psychoanalysts observed. Rogers viewed human nature as basically good. If left to develop naturally, he thought, people would be happy and psychologically healthy.

According to Rogers, we all live in our own subjective reality, which he called the phenomenological field. It is in this personal, subjective field (rather than in the objective, real, physical environment) that we act and think and feel. In other words, the way we see it is the way it is—for us. Gradually a part of the phenomenological field becomes differentiated as the self. The self concept emerges as a result of repeated experiences involving such terms as "I," "me," and "mine." With the emerging self comes the need for positive regard. We need such things as warmth, love, acceptance, sympathy, and respect from those people who are significant in our lives. While positive regard from others is crucial to the self, it alone is not enough. We also need positive self-regard. But the road to positive self-regard can be long and rocky indeed because we need the positive regard of others all along the way. And there are usually strings attached to positive regard from others.

Normally our parents do not view us positively, regardless of our behavior. They set up *conditions of worth*—conditions on which their positive regard hinges. Conditions of worth force us to live and act according to someone else's values rather than our own. In our efforts to gain positive regard, we deny our true self by inhibiting some of our behavior, denying and distorting some of our perceptions, and closing ourselves to parts of our experience. In so doing, we experience stress and anxiety, and our whole self-structure may be threatened.

For Rogers, a major goal of psychotherapy is to enable individuals to open themselves up to experiences and begin to live according to their own values rather than the values of others in order to gain positive regard. He called his therapy person-centered therapy, preferring not to use the term *patient* (Rogers's therapy will be discussed in chapter 15, "Therapies"). Rogers believed that the therapist must give the client *unconditional positive regard,* meaning that the therapist gives positive regard no matter what the client says, does, has done, or is thinking of doing. Unconditional positive regard is designed to reduce threat, eliminate conditions of worth, and bring the person back in tune with the true self. If successful, the therapy helps the client become what Rogers calls a fully-functioning person—one who is functioning at an optimal level and living fully and spontaneously according to his or her own inner valuing system.

conditions of worth: Conditions upon which the positive regard of others rests.

unconditional positive regard: Unqualified caring and nonjudgmental acceptance of another.

Carl Rogers believed that unconditional positive regard in childhood is essential if people are to be happy, develop normally, and become fully-functioning persons.

Evaluating the Humanistic Perspective

Humanism has become much more than a personality theory and an approach to therapy. Its influence as a social movement has spread significantly in the schools and in society in general. And some of its severest critics are religious and moral leaders who see the philosophy of humanism as a powerful threat to traditional moral values and the Judeo-Christian ethic. Others charge that an all-consuming personal quest for self-fulfillment can lead to a self-centered, self-serving, self-indulgent personality lacking moral restraint or genuine concern for others (Campbell & Specht, 1985; Wallach & Wallach, 1983, 1985).

Humanistic psychologists do not accept such criticisms as valid. By and large, they trust in the inherent goodness of human nature, and their perspective on personality is consistent with that trust. But how do humanists explain the evil we see around us—assaults, murder, rape? Where does this originate? Carl Rogers (1981) replied, "I do not find that this evil is inherent in human nature" (p. 16). Of psychological environments that nurture growth and choice, Rogers said, "I have never known an individual to choose the cruel or destructive path. . . . So my experience leads me to believe that it is cultural influences which are the major factor in our evil behaviors" (p. 16).

Even some humanists disagree about the nature of human nature. In an open letter to Carl Rogers, psychologist Rollo May (1982) wrote, "Who makes up the culture except persons like you and me? . . . The culture is not something made by fate and foisted upon us. . . . The culture is evil as well as good because we, the human beings who constitute it, are evil as well as good' (pp. 12–13).

Though the humanists have been criticized for being unscientific and for seeing, hearing, and finding no evil within the human psyche, they have inspired the study of the positive emotions—altruism, cooperation, love, and acceptance of self and others.

Personality: Is It in the Genes?

Question: What has research in behavioral genetics revealed about the influence of the genes and environment on personality?

Behavioral genetics is a field of research that investigates the relative effects of heredity and environment on behavior and ability (Plomin & Rende, 1991). One approach is the twin study method, in which identical (monozygotic, or MZ) twins and fraternal (dizygotic, or DZ) twins are studied to determine how much they resemble each other on a variety of characteristics.

An ideal way to assess the relative contribution of heredity and environment is to study identical twins who have been separated at birth and reared apart. When identical twins who were reared apart have strikingly similar traits, as in the case of Oskar and Jack introduced at the beginning of this chapter, it is assumed that heredity has been a major contributor. When twins differ on a given trait, as we saw with Joan and Jean, the influence of the environment is thought to be greater.

In the University of Minnesota twin study, Tellegen and others (1988) found that identical twins were quite similar on several personality factors regardless of whether they are raised together or apart. Figure 12.5 shows the estimated heritability of several personality factors. The term *heritability* is an index of the degree to which a characteristic is estimated to be influenced by heredity.

Plomin (1990), reports that "activity level, emotional reactivity (neuroticism), and sociability-shyness (extraversion) have accumulated the best evidence for significant genetic influence" (p. 185). Rushton and others (1986) found that altruism and aggression, traits one would expect to be strongly influenced by

behavioral genetics: The field of research that investigates the relative effects of heredity and environment on behavior and ability.

heritability: An index of the degree to which a characteristic is estimated to be influenced by heredity.

parental upbringing, were actually more strongly influenced by heredity. After studying 573 adult twin pairs, the researchers concluded that the following traits are substantially influenced by heredity: aggressiveness, nurturance, empathy, assertiveness, and altruism (see Figure 12.5).

Twin studies have also revealed a genetic influence on social attitudes such as traditionalism—whether we endorse traditional moral values and follow rules and authority (Martin et al., 1986; Tellegen et al., 1988). There even seems to be a genetic influence on the way people tend to view their environment (Plomin & Bergeman, 1991), how they perceive life events, particularly controllable ones, and their sense of well-being (Plomin & Rende, 1991).

In a study comparing identical and fraternal twins reared apart, Bouchard and McGue (1990) found that the common environment shared by twins contributes very little to personality. The only environmental factors that have a major influence on personality are those unique to each individual. This includes the special relationships each person enjoys with his or her family, rather than the common experiences shared by all the family members. Other factors influenc-

Figure 12.5   The Estimated Heritability of Personality Characteristics   Heritability is an index of the degree to which heredity influences a given trait or characteristic. Shown in the figure are the heritability estimates of a variety of personality characteristics, as derived from two different twin studies. If the heritability for a given trait is estimated to be as high as 50 percent, another 50 percent still remains as the estimated influence of environment. (Data from Tellegen et al., 1988, and Rushton et al., 1986.)

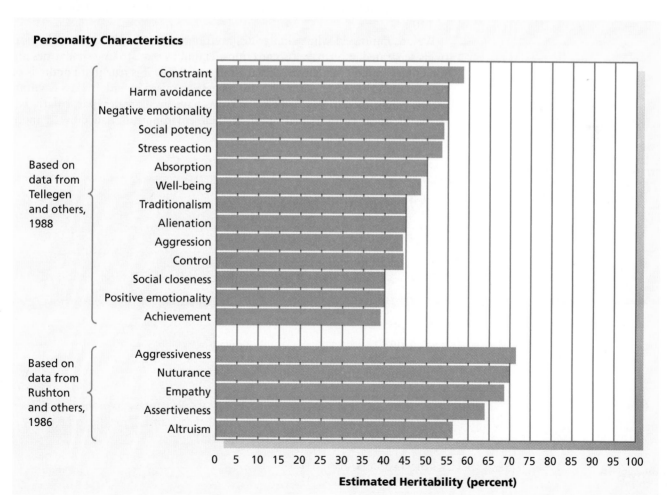

ing personality are birth order, gender differences, peer groups, accidents, and illnesses (Plomin, 1989).

Another method used to disentangle the effects of heredity and environment is to study children adopted shortly after birth—comparing their personality traits to their adoptive family members, with whom they live, and to their biological parents, whom they may never have met.

Loehlin and others (1987) assessed the personalities of 17-year-olds who had been adopted at birth and came to this startling conclusion: "Adopted children do not resemble their adoptive family members in personality, despite having lived with them from birth, but they do show a modest degree of resemblance to their genetic mothers, whom they had never known" (p. 968). When the personalities of the adopted children were compared to other children in the family, the researchers found that the shared family environment had virtually no influence on their personalities. Other researchers studying adopted children have come to the same basic conclusion (Scarr et al., 1981). Loehlin, Horne, and Willerman (1990) measured change in personality of adoptees over a 10-year period and found that children tended "to change on the average in the direction of their genetic parent's personalities" (p. 221). The prevailing thinking in behavioral genetics, then, is that the common environment plays a negligible role in the formation of personality (Loehlin et al., 1988), although there have been a few dissenting voices (Rose et al., 1988).

The genetic influences we have been discussing are not the result of one or even a few genes. Rather they involve many genes, each with small effects (Plomin, 1989, 1990). While these findings indicate that most personality traits are influenced by genes, "behavioral genetic research clearly demonstrates that both nature and nurture are important in human development" (Plomin, 1989, p. 110).

We are impressed when similarities are pointed out to us between identical twins separated at birth, but some critics remind us that striking similarities are sometimes found even between total strangers. While it is true that hundreds of pairs of twins have been studied, most have been raised in middle-class environments. Might the differences between twins have been greater, particularly between identical twins reared apart, if their environments had differed more drastically?

Memory Check 12.6

1. Humanistic psychologists say that:

   a. human nature is innately good
   b. we have a natural tendency toward self-actualization
   c. unconscious forces are important in shaping personality
   d. both a and b

2. (Maslow, Rogers) is the humanistic psychologist who stressed that individuals need unconditional positive regard in order to become fully-functioning persons.

3. When identical twins reared apart are as much alike on a trait as identical twins reared together, then that trait is thought to be influenced more by (heredity, environment).

(continued)

4. Many behavioral geneticists believe that personality may be as much as
   (25, 50) percent inherited.

Answers: 1. d 2. Rogers 3. heredity 4. 50

Personality Assessment

Question: What are the three major methods used in personality assessment?

Just as there are many different personality theories, there are many different methods for measuring personality. Various personality tests are used by clinical and counseling psychologists, psychiatrists, and counselors in the diagnosis of patients and in the assessment of progress in therapy. Personality assessment is also used in business and industry to make hiring decisions and by counselors for vocational and educational counseling.

Personality assessment methods can be grouped in a few broad categories: (1) observation, interviews, and rating scales, (2) inventories, and (3) projective tests.

Observation, Interviews, and Rating Scales

Observation All of us use observation, though informally, to form opinions about other people. Psychologists, too, use observation in personality assessment and evaluation in a variety of settings—hospitals, clinics, the schools, and the workplace.

Behaviorists, in particular, prefer observation to other methods of personality assessment. Using an observational technique known as behavioral assessment, psychologists can count and record the frequency of particular behaviors they are studying. This method is often used in behavior modification programs in settings such as mental hospitals, where psychologists may chart the progress of patients in reducing aggressive acts or other undesirable or abnormal behaviors.

Although much can be learned from observation, it has its shortcomings; it is time-consuming and expensive, and observers must be trained and paid. What is observed may be misinterpreted, and two observers can view the same event and interpret it differently. Probably the most serious limitation is that the very presence of the observer can alter the behavior that is observed.

The Interview Another personality assessment technique is the interview. Clinical psychologists and psychiatrists use interviews to help in the diagnosis and treatment of patients. Counselors use the interview to screen applicants for admission to college or other special programs, and employers use it to evaluate job applicants and employees for job promotions.

Interviewers consider not only the answers to questions but the person's tone of voice, speech, mannerisms, gestures, and general appearance as well. Psychologists and other professionals use both structured and unstructured interviews in making their assessments. In unstructured situations, the direction the interview will take and the questions to be asked are not all planned beforehand, and so the interview can be highly personalized. But the unstructured interview may be so loose that little objective information is gained. Also, it would be hard to compare people if we didn't have some questions that we asked everyone.

For this reason interviewers often use a structured interview, in which the content of the questions and even the manner in which they are asked are

halo effect: The tendency of raters to be excessively influenced by one or a few favorable or unfavorable traits in their overall evaluation of a person.

carefully planned ahead of time. The interviewer tries not to deviate in any way from the structured format so that more reliable comparisons can be made between different subjects.

Rating Scales Sometimes examiners use rating scales to record data from interviews or observations. Rating scales are useful because they provide a standardized format, including a list of traits or behaviors on which the subject is to be evaluated. The rating scale helps to focus the rater's attention on all the relevant traits to be considered so that some are not overlooked or others weighed too heavily (see Figure 12.6).

But there are problems with rating scales, too. Often there is low agreement among raters in their evaluation of the same individual. If you have watched Olympic events such as gymnastics competitions on television, you have noticed sometimes wide variations in the several judges' scoring of the same performance. One way to overcome this weakness is to train the judges or raters to a point where high agreement can be achieved when rating the same person or event.

Another problem in evaluation is the *halo effect*—the tendency of raters to be excessively influenced by one or a few favorable or unfavorable traits in their overall evaluation of a person. Often traits or attributes that are not even on the rating scale, such as physical attractiveness or similarity to the rater, heavily influence a rater's perception of a subject.

Figure 12.6 Representative Items on a Rating Scale A rating scale may be used to assess an individual's personal characteristics. Rating scales are useful because they provide a standardized format, including a list of traits or behaviors on which the person is to be evaluated. Shown here are a few items similar to those used on rating scales.

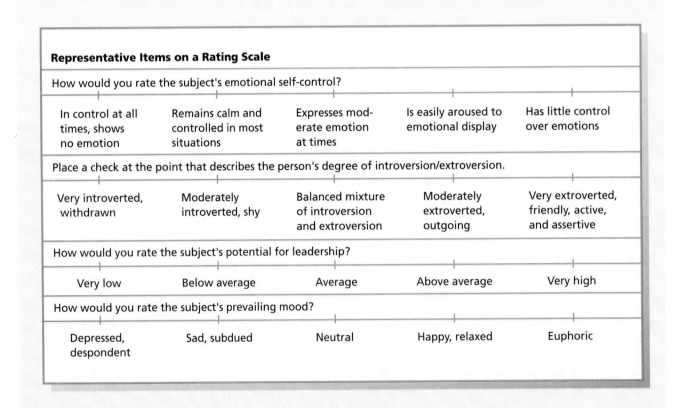

Representative Items on a Rating Scale

How would you rate the subject's emotional self-control?

| In control at all times, shows no emotion | Remains calm and controlled in most situations | Expresses moderate emotion at times | Is easily aroused to emotional display | Has little control over emotions |

Place a check at the point that describes the person's degree of introversion/extroversion.

| Very introverted, withdrawn | Moderately introverted, shy | Balanced mixture of introversion and extroversion | Moderately extroverted, outgoing | Very extroverted, friendly, active, and assertive |

How would you rate the subject's potential for leadership?

| Very low | Below average | Average | Above average | Very high |

How would you rate the subject's prevailing mood?

| Depressed, despondent | Sad, subdued | Neutral | Happy, relaxed | Euphoric |

Personality Inventories: Taking Stock

There is an objective method for measuring personality, a method in which the personal opinions and ratings of observers or interviewers do not unduly influence the results. This method is the **inventory**, a paper-and-pencil test with questions about an individual's thoughts, feelings, and behaviors, which measures several dimensions of personality and can be scored according to a standard procedure. Psychologists favoring the trait approach to personality prefer the inventory because it can assess where people fall on various dimensions of personality, and the results are plotted on a personality profile. Many personality inventories have been developed, but none is more widely used than the Minnesota Multiphasic Personality Inventory.

Question: What is the Minnesota Multiphasic Personality Inventory designed to reveal?

The Minnesota Multiphasic Personality Inventory: The Most Widely Used The **Minnesota Multiphasic Personality Inventory (MMPI)** is the most popular, the most heavily researched, and the most widely used personality test for screening and diagnosing psychiatric problems and disorders, and for use in psychological research. Published in 1943 by researchers McKinley and Hathaway, the original purpose of the MMPI was to identify tendencies toward various types of psychiatric disorders. McKinley and Hathaway gathered over 1,000 questions about attitudes, feelings, and specific psychiatric symptoms from case histories, textbooks, and other sources (Levitt & Duckworth, 1984). Then they selected groups of psychiatric patients who had been clearly diagnosed, such as paranoids, depressed patients, and others, to answer their questions. They also picked a group of normal men and women similar to the psychiatric patients in age, sex, social class, and other such variables, and had them answer the questions. Finally they compared the answers to see whether there were significant differences, which would separate the specific psychiatric groups from the normals. For the final version of the MMPI, 550 items were chosen that were to be answered "true," "false," or "cannot say." The test provides scores on 4 validity scales and 10 clinical scales, shown in Table 12.2.

Here are examples of questions on the test:

I wish I were not bothered by thoughts about sex.
When I get bored I like to stir up some excitement.
In walking I am very careful to step over sidewalk cracks.
If people had not had it in for me, I would have been much more successful.

Scoring the MMPI Scoring the MMPI can be done by computer. A high score on any of the scales does not necessarily mean that a person has a problem or a psychiatric symptom. Rather the psychologist looks at the individual's MMPI profile—the pattern of scores on all the scales (Sundberg, 1977). The profile is then compared to the profiles of normal individuals and people with various psychiatric disorders.

But what if someone lies on the test in order to appear mentally healthy? The authors considered this and have items called the L-scale embedded in the test to provide a check against lying (Dahlstrom & Welsh, 1960). If you were taking the MMPI, how would you answer these questions?

Once in a while I put off until tomorrow what I ought to do today.
I gossip a little at times.
Once in a while, I laugh at a dirty joke.

inventory: A paper-and-pencil test with questions about a person's thoughts, feelings, and behaviors, which can be scored according to a standard procedure.

Minnesota Multiphasic Personality Inventory (MMPI): The most extensively researched and widely used personality test; used to screen and diagnose psychiatric problems and disorders.

Table 12.2   The Validity and Clinical Scales of the MMPI

Scale Name	Interpretation
Validity Scales	
1. Cannot say scale (?)	High scorers were evasive in filling out the questionnaire.
2. Lie scale (L)	High scorers attempt to present themselves in a very favorable light and possibly tell lies to do so.
3. Infrequency (F)	High scorers are presenting themselves in a particularly bad way and may well be "faking bad."
4. Correction (K)	High scorers may be very defensive in filling out the questionnaire.
Clinical Scales	
1. Hypochondriasis (Hs)	High scorers reflect an exaggerated concern about their physical health.
2. Depression (D)	High scorers are usually depressed, despondent, and distressed.
3. Hysteria (Hy)	High scorers complain often about physical symptoms, with no apparent organic cause.
4. Psychopathic deviate (Pd)	High scorers show a disregard for social and moral standards.
5. Masculinity/femininity (Mf)	High scorers show "traditional" masculine or feminine attitudes and values.
6. Paranoia (Pa)	High scorers demonstrate extreme suspiciousness and feelings of persecution.
7. Psychasthenia (Pt)	High scorers tend to be highly anxious, rigid, tense, and worrying.
8. Schizophrenia (Sc)	High scorers tend to be socially withdrawn and to engage in bizarre and unusual thinking.
9. Hypomania (Ma)	High scorers are highly emotionally excitable, energetic, and impulsive.
10. Social introversion (S)	High scorers tend to be modest, self-effacing, and shy.

Minnesota Multiphasic Personality Inventory (MMPI) copyright (c) 1942, 1943 (renewed 1970), by the Regents of the University of Minnesota.

Most people would almost certainly have to answer "yes" to such questions—unless, of course, they were lying. When a person scores high on the L-scale, the test results are considered to be invalid. Another scale, the F-scale, controls for people who are faking psychiatric illness, as in the case of someone wanting to be judged not guilty of a crime by reason of insanity.

Evaluating the MMPI   How good is the MMPI at uncovering problems in people who are answering the questions honestly? The MMPI is reliable, easy to administer and score, and inexpensive to use. It is useful in research and "in the screening, diagnosis, and clinical description of psychopathology" (Faschingbauer, 1979, p. 375). On the negative side, the MMPI is not able to reveal differences among normal personalities very well, and some critics suggest that it works best in diagnosing people who are severely disturbed and people who are most like the original sample. The test is often unreliable for adolescents, African Americans, and women (Levitt & Duckworth, 1984).

Because the MMPI was published in 1943, some aspects of it were outdated. Seven years of intensive work went into revising and restandardizing the MMPI, and in 1989 the MMPI-2 was published (Butcher et al., 1989).

The MMPI-2   Over time, the original norms of the MMPI on which test score interpretations are based became outdated. This happened because the original group that was used to define average or normal no longer represented the general population (Kingsbury, 1991). The typical "normal" adult in the original sample was a 35-year-old, white, married, housewife or skilled or semi-skilled worker with an eighth-grade education living in a small town or rural area in Minnesota. The new norms are based on a sample of 2,600 men and women selected to reflect national census data, and thus the new norms achieve a geographical, racial, and cultural balance (Ben-Porath & Butcher, 1990).

Most of the original test items have been kept, but some have been deleted because they were obsolete or because they "referred to sexuality, body functions, or religious beliefs" in a way that was offensive to some people (Kingsbury, 1991, p. 8). Other items were rewritten "to update obsolete language, correct sexist or male-oriented language, or otherwise make the items more readable and understandable" (Ben-Porath & Butcher, 1989, p. 345).

New items were added to provide more adequate coverage of areas such as alcoholism, drug abuse, suicidal tendencies, eating disorders, and Type A personality. Although the MMPI-2 now has 567 items, updating the items has made it more "user friendly" and easier for the subject (Butcher & Hostetler, 1990).

The California Personality Inventory   Are there instruments to assess the personality of a normal person who may or may not be white or middle class? Yes, the *California Psychological Inventory (CPI)* is a highly regarded personality test developed especially for normal populations age 13 and older.

Similar to the MMPI, the CPI even has many of the same questions, but it does not include any questions designed to reveal psychiatric illness (Gough, 1957). The CPI deals with such personality scales as Dominance, Sociability, Self-Acceptance, Responsibility, Socialization, Self-control, Achievement-via-Conformance, Achievement-via-Independence, Flexibility, and Femininity. The CPI has been found valuable for predicting behavior, and it has been "praised for its technical competency, careful development, cross-validation and follow-up, use of sizable samples and separate sex norms" (Domino, 1984, p. 156).

Projective Tests: Projections from the Unconscious

Question: How do projective tests provide insight into personality? What are several of the most commonly used projective tests?

Responses on interviews and questionnaires are conscious responses and, for this reason, are less useful to therapists who wish to probe the unconscious (Lindzey, 1977). Such therapists may choose a completely different technique called a projective test. A **projective test** is a personality test consisting of inkblots, drawings of ambiguous human situations, or incomplete sentences for which there are no obvious correct or incorrect responses. People respond by projecting their own inner thoughts, feelings, fears, or conflicts into the test materials. Just as a movie projector projects the images on the film outward and onto a screen, so do we project our inner thoughts, feelings, fears, and conflicts into our analysis and description of inkblots and other vague or ambiguous projective test materials.

The Rorschach Inkblot Test: What Do You See?   One of the most popular and oldest projective tests is the **Rorschach Inkblot Test** developed by Swiss psychiatrist Hermann Rorschach (ROR-shok) in 1921. It consists of 10 inkblots, which the subject is asked to describe.

To develop his test, Rorschach put ink on paper and then folded it so that symmetrical patterns would result. Earlier, psychologists had used standardized series of inkblots to study imagination and other personal attributes, but Rorschach was the first to use inkblots to investigate personality (Anastasia, 1982).

California Personality Inventory (CPI):   A highly regarded personality test used to assess the normal personality.

projective test: A personality test in which people respond to inkblots, drawings of ambiguous human situations, incomplete sentences, and the like, by projecting their own inner thoughts, feelings, fears, or conflicts into the test materials.

Rorschach Inkblot Test (ROR-shok):   A projective test composed of 10 inkblots to which a subject responds; used to reveal unconscious functioning and the presence of psychiatric disorders.

Rorschach experimented with thousands of inkblots on different groups of people and found that 10 of the inkblots could be used to discriminate between different diagnostic groups. For example, manic depressives appeared to have responses characteristic of their group, paranoid schizophrenics' responses were similar to others in their group, and so on. These 10 inkblots—5 black and white, and 5 with color—were standardized and are still widely used.

Administration and Scoring of the Rorschach   The 10 inkblots are shown to the subject, who is asked to tell everything that each inkblot looks like or resembles. The examiner writes down the subject's responses and then goes through the cards again, asking questions to clarify what the subject has reported.

In scoring the Rorschach, the examiner considers whether the subject uses the whole inkblot in the description or only parts of it. The subject is asked whether the shape of the inkblot, its color, or something else prompted the response. The tester also considers whether the subject sees movement, human figures or parts, animal figures or parts, or other objects in the inkblots.

Interpreting the Responses   What difference does it make whether you describe parts or wholes, colors or movement, animals or people?

> Using the whole inkblot suggests integration and organization; many small details indicate compulsiveness and over-control. . . . The presence of much poor form, uncommon responses, and confused thinking suggests a psychotic condition. Responsiveness to color is supposed to represent emotionality. . . . Responses mentioning human movement indicate imagination, intelligence, and a rich inner life. (Sundberg, 1977, p. 208)

The main problem with the Rorschach test is that the results are too dependent on the interpretation and judgment of the examiner. One study dramatically calls the reliability of the Rorschach into question (Harrower, 1976). Experts were asked to interpret results of Rorschach tests administered shortly after World War II to 16 Nazi war criminals, including Adolf Eichmann and Hermann Goring. The experts knew whose test results they were interpreting, and the experts concluded that the responses showed the subjects to be violent and abnormal men. However, another researcher had the same Rorschach responses analyzed by other experts who did not know they were from Nazi war criminals. One expert thought the responses came from a cross-section of middle-class Americans, and another thought the responses might have been made by clergymen.

In response to criticisms such as these, Exner (1974, 1986) has developed a more reliable system of scoring. It provides some normative data so that the responses of a person taking the test can be compared to others with known personality characteristics. Although this is a positive step, reliable interpretation still remains a problem, and Anastasi (1988) suggests that perhaps the real value of the Rorschach may be not as a personality test, but as a clinical tool.

The Thematic Apperception Test: Seeing Ourselves in Scenes of Others

Another projective test is the **Thematic Apperception Test** (**TAT**) developed by Henry Murray and his colleagues in 1935 (Morgan & Murray, 1935; Murray, 1938). The TAT consists of one blank card and 19 other cards showing vague or ambiguous black-and-white drawings of human figures in various situations. The tester administers the TAT individually in an interview setting and rarely uses more than 10 scenes.

"The test is based upon the well-recognized fact that when a person interprets an ambiguous social situation he is apt to expose his own personality as much as the phenomenon to which he is attending" (Morgan & Murray, 1962, p. 531). If you were tested on the TAT, this is what you would be told:

Thematic Apperception Test (TAT):   A projective test consisting of drawings of ambiguous human situations, which the subject describes; thought to reveal inner feelings, conflicts, and motives, which are projected onto the test materials.

This is a test of your creative imagination. I shall show you a picture and I want you to make up a plot or story for which it might be used as an illustration. What is the relation of the individuals in the picture? What has happened to them? What are their present thoughts and feelings? What will be the outcome? Do your very best. Since I am asking you to indulge your literary imagination you may make your story as long and as detailed as you wish. (Morgan & Murray, 1962, p. 532)

Interpreting the Results   What does the story you write have to do with your personality or your problems or motives? The test results are analyzed according to Murray's list of needs (shown on page 347), which include the need for achievement, affiliation, and aggression. Murray (1965) stresses the importance of "an element or theme that recurs three or more times in the series of stories" (p. 432). For example, if many of a person's story themes are about illness, sex, fear of failure, aggression, power, interpersonal conflicts, and so on, such a recurring theme is thought to reveal a problem in the person's life. Murray also claims that the strength of the TAT is "its capacity to reveal things that the patient is unwilling to tell or is unable to tell because he is unconscious of them" (p. 427). Because of Murray's training as a Freudian and Jungian analyst, it is not surprising that he would develop an instrument to assess unconscious motivation (Triplet, 1992).

The TAT is time-consuming and difficult to administer and score. Although it has been used extensively in personality research, it suffers from the same weaknesses as other projective techniques: (1) It relies heavily on the interpretation skills of the examiner, and (2) it may reflect too strongly a person's temporary motivational and emotional state and not get at the more permanent aspects of personality. "Such conditions as hunger, sleep deprivation, social frustration, and the experience of failure in a preceding test situation significantly affect TAT responses" (Anastasia, 1982, p. 573).

In the Thematic Apperception Test (TAT), a person's descriptions of a series of ambiguous pictures are assumed to reflect his or her motives, problems, and unconscious conflicts.

Table 12.3   Three Approaches to Personality Assessment

Method	Examples	Description
Observation and rating	Observation Interviews Rating scales	Performance (behavior) is observed in a specific situation, and personality is assessed based on observation. In interviews, the responses to questions are taken to reveal personality characteristics. Rating scales are used to score or rate subjects on the basis of traits, behaviors, or results of interviews. Assessment is subjective, and accuracy depends largely on the ability and experience of the evaluator.
Inventories	Minnesota Multiphasic Personality Inventory-2 (MMPI-2) California Personality Inventory (CPI)	Subjects reveal their beliefs, feelings, behavior, and/or opinions on paper-and-pencil tests. Scoring procedures are standardized and responses are compared to group norms.
Projective tests	Rorschach Inkblot Test Thematic Apperception Test (TAT) Sentence Completion Test	Subjects respond to ambiguous test materials and presumably reveal elements of their own personality by what they describe in inkblots, by themes they write about scenes showing possible conflict, or by how they complete sentences. Scoring is subjective, and accuracy depends largely on the ability and experience of the evaluator.

The Sentence Completion Method: Filling in the Blanks   Another projective technique, the sentence completion method, may be one of the most valid projective techniques of all (Murstein, 1965). It consists of a number of incomplete sentences to be completed by the subject, such as these:

I worry a great deal about _____.
I sometimes feel _____.
I would be happier if _____.
My mother _____.

In a comprehensive review, Goldberg (1965) summarized 50 validity studies and concluded that sentence completion is a valuable technique appropriate for widespread clinical and research use.

The Value of Projective Tests   How effective are projective tests? Research evidence concerning the validity of projective techniques as a whole is very disappointing. There are serious problems concerning a "lack of objectivity in scoring" and a lack of adequate norms (Anastasia, 1982, p. 582). In spite of these limitations, in clinical practice projective tests continue to be a popular and valued diagnostic tool (Klopfer & Taulbee, 1976; Wade & Baker, 1977).

Table 12.3 (page 431) summarizes the different types of personality tests.

Personality Theories: A Final Comment

We have explored the major theories of personality, which are summarized in Table 12.4. The question might come to mind—which perspective best captures the elusive concept of personality? Some psychologists adhere strictly to single theories and are followers of Freud, for example, or Skinner or Rogers. It is our belief that all of the theories contribute to our knowledge, but none of them taken singly can adequately explain the whole of human personality.

Table 12.4   Summary of Four Approaches to Personality

Approach	Assumptions about Behavior	Assessment Techniques	Research Methods
Psychoanalytic	Arises mostly from unconscious conflicts between pleasure-seeking id and moral-perfectionist super-ego with reality-oriented ego as mediator.	Projective tests to tap unconscious motives; interviews for purposes of analysis.	Case studies.
Trait	Springs from personality traits that may be influenced by both heredity and environment.	Self-report inventories; adjective checklists; inventories.	Analysis of test results for identifying strength of various traits.
Learning (behaviorist and social-cognitive)	Behavior is determined strictly by environmental influences. This position modified by social-cognitive theorists, who allow for interaction between internal cognitive factors and environmental influences.	Direct observation of behavior; objective tests; interviews; rating scales; self-report.	Analyzing observations of behavior; quantifying behaviors; analysis of person-situation interactions.
Humanistic	Behavior springs from the person's own unique perception of reality and conscious choices. Humans are innately good.	Interviews and tests designed to assess the person's self-concept and perceptions of control.	Analysis of the relationship between the person's feelings or perceptions and behavior.

Memory Check 12.7

1. Match the personality test with its description.

_____ 1) MMPI-2   a. inventory used to diagnose psycho-
_____ 2) Rorschach   pathology
_____ 3) TAT   b. inventory used to assess normal
_____ 4) CPI   personality
                    c. projective test using inkblots
                    d. projective test using drawings of
                       ambiguous human situations

2. Dr. X and Dr. Y are both experts in personality assessment. They would be most likely to agree on their interpretation of results from the (Rorschach, MMPI-2).

3. The (TAT, MMPI-2) would be better able to detect Hector's unconscious resentment toward his father.

Answers: 1. 1) a 2) c 3) d 4) b 2. MMPI-2 3. TAT

Thinking Critically _____

Evaluation

In your opinion, which personality theory is the most accurate, reasonable, and realistic? Which is the least accurate, reasonable, and realistic? Support your answers.

Point/Counterpoint

Are personality characteristics mostly learned or mostly transmitted through the genes? Using what you have learned in this chapter and other evidence you can gather, make a case for both positions. Support your answers with research and expert opinion.

Psychology in Your Life

Consider your own behavior and personality attributes from the standpoint of each of the theories: psychoanalysis, trait theory, and the learning, humanistic, and genetic perspectives. Which theory or theories best explain your personality? Why?

Chapter Summary and Review _____

Sigmund Freud and Psychoanalysis

What are the two aspects of Freud's work, which he called psychoanalysis?

Psychoanalysis is the term Freud used for both his theory of personality and his therapy for the treatment of psychological disorders.

What are the three levels of awareness in consciousness?

The three levels of awareness in consciousness are the conscious, the preconscious, and the unconscious.

What are the roles of the id, the ego, and the superego?

The id is the animal-like, unconscious part of the personality, which contains the instincts and operates on the pleasure principle. The ego is the rational, largely conscious system, which operates according to the reality principle. The superego is the moral system of the personality, consisting of the conscience and the ego ideal.

What is a defense mechanism?

A defense mechanism is an unconscious, irrational means that the ego uses to defend against anxiety and to maintain self-esteem; it involves self-deception and the distortion of reality.

What are two ways in which repression operates?

Through repression (1) painful memories, thoughts, ideas, or perceptions are involuntarily removed from consciousness, and (2) disturbing sexual or aggressive impulses are prevented from breaking into consciousness.

What are some other defense mechanisms?

Other defense mechanisms are projection, denial, rationalization, regression, reaction formation, displacement, and sublimation.

What are the psychosexual stages, and why did Freud consider them so important in personality development?

Freud believed that the sexual instinct is present at birth, develops through a series of psychosexual stages, and provides the driving force for thought and activity. The psychosexual stages are the oral stage, anal stage, phallic stage (followed by the latency period), and genital stage.

What is the Oedipus complex?

The Oedipus complex, occurring in the phallic stage, is a conflict in which the child is sexually attracted to the opposite-sex parent and feels hostility toward the same-sex parent.

According to Freud, what are the two primary sources of influence on the personality?

Freud believed that differences in personality result from the relative strengths of the id, the ego, and the superego and from the personality traits that develop as a result of problems during the psychosexual stages.

Key Terms

personality (p. 400)
psychoanalysis (p. 401)
conscious (p. 401)
preconscious (p. 401)
unconscious (p. 401)
id (p. 403)
pleasure principle (p. 403)
libido (p. 403)
ego (p. 403)
superego (p. 403)
defense mechanism (p. 403)
repression (p. 405)
projection (p. 405)
denial (p. 405)
rationalization (p. 405)
regression (p. 405)
reaction formation (p. 405)
displacement (p. 405)
sublimation (p. 405)
psychosexual stages (p. 406)
fixation (p. 407)
Oedipus complex (p. 407)
oral stage (p. 408)
anal stage (p. 408)
phallic stage (p. 408)
latency period (p. 408)
genital stage (p. 408)

The Neo-Freudians

According to Jung, what are the three components of personality?

According to Jung, the personality has three parts: the ego, the personal unconscious, and the collective unconscious.

What did Adler consider to be the driving force of the personality?

Adler maintained that the predominant force of the personality is the drive to overcome and compensate for feelings of weakness and inferiority and to strive for superiority or significance.

Why is Karen Horney considered a pioneer in psychology?

Karen Horney took issue with Freud's sexist view of women and added the feminine dimension to the world of psychology.

Key Terms

personal unconscious (p. 410)
collective unconscious (p. 410)
archetype (p. 410)
extraversion (p. 411)
introversion (p. 411)

Trait Theories

What are trait theories of personality?

Trait theories of personality are attempts to explain personality and differences between people in terms of their personal characteristics.

How does Allport differentiate between cardinal and central traits?

Allport defined a cardinal trait as a personal quality that is so strong a part of a person's personality that he or she may become identified with that trait or known for it. A central trait is the type you would use in writing a letter of recommendation.

How did Cattell differentiate between surface and source traits?

Cattell used the term surface traits to refer to observable qualities of personality, which you might use in describing a friend. Source traits underlie the surface traits, make up the most basic personality structure, and cause behavior.

Key Terms

trait theories (p. 414)
cardinal trait (p. 414)
central traits (p. 415)
surface traits (p. 415)
source traits (p. 415)

Learning Theories

How did Skinner account for what most people refer to as personality?

B. F. Skinner viewed personality as simply a collection of behaviors and habits that have been reinforced in the past.

What processes do the social-cognitive theorists consider in explaining personality?

The social-cognitive theorists stress the importance of both the environment and the person's inner cognitive processes—thinking, feelings, and perceptions—in explaining personality and behavior.

What does Rotter mean by the terms internal and external locus of control?

According to Rotter, people with an internal locus of control see themselves as primarily in control of their behavior and its consequences; those with an external locus of control believe their destiny is in the hands of fate, luck, or chance.

Key Terms

self-efficacy (418)
locus of control (p. 419)

The Humanistic Perspective

Who were the two pioneers in humanistic psychology, and how did they view human nature?

Abraham Maslow and Carl Rogers, the two pioneers in humanistic psychology, believed that human nature is innately good and that people have a tendency toward self-actualization.

Key Terms

humanistic psychology (p. 420)
self-actualization (p. 420)

Personality: Is it in the Genes?

What has research in behavioral genetics revealed about the influence of the genes and environment on personality?

Research in behavioral genetics has revealed that about 50 percent of personality can be attributed to the genes.

Key Term

behavioral genetics (p. 422)

Personality Assessment

What are the three major methods used in personality assessment?

The major methods used in personality assessment are (1) observation, interviews, and rating scales; (2) inventories; and (3) projective tests.

What is the Minnesota Multiphasic Personality Inventory designed to reveal?

The Minnesota Multiphasic Personality Inventory (MMPI), the most popular and widely used personality test, is used to screen and diagnose psychiatric problems and disorders.

How do projective tests provide insight into personality? What are several of the most commonly used projective tests?

In a projective test, people respond to inkblots, drawings of ambiguous human situations, incomplete sentences, and the like by projecting their own inner thoughts, feelings, fears, or conflicts onto the test materials. Examples are the Rorschach Inkblot Test and the Thematic Apperception Test (TAT).

Key Terms

inventory (p. 427)
Minnesota Multiphasic Personality Inventory (MMPI) (p. 427)
projective test (p. 429)
Rorschach Inkblot Test (p. 429)
Thematic Apperception Test (TAT) (p. 430)

13

Health and Stress

CHAPTER OUTLINE

Researchers have found that laughter can have a remarkable effect on a person's health.

Many years ago Norman Cousins (1979), who was editor of the *Saturday Review*, was hospitalized and diagnosed with a rare and crippling disease that destroys the connective tissues of the body. The doctors gave Cousins a grim report and told him that his condition was not reversible. He could not recover. In constant pain, with his body rapidly deteriorating, he faced inevitable death. In response, Cousins decided to leave the hospital, check into a hotel, and take an active part in his own treatment. With the help of a trusted doctor and others, he followed a regimen of vitamin therapy and watched hilarious films—old "Candid Camera" television shows, Marx brothers' films, and other comedy treats. He reports in his book *Anatomy of an Illness* that the laughter inspired by the films gave him relief from pain, which made it possible for him to sleep for short periods at a time. Cousins continued his laughter therapy for several months, and he didn't grow worse and die. He walked out of his hotel room with his "incurable" disease in remission. Not only that, he lived many additional years of healthy life and, among many other activities, became a lecturer at the UCLA School of Medicine.

COUSINS'S EXPERIENCE DOES NOT SUGGEST that we can laugh all our troubles and illnesses away. Even optimists and humorists get sick and die. But his experience and that of many others suggest that the body is not a completely separate system that falls ill and either recovers or dies apart from psychological and social influences. The doctors who diagnosed Cousins's illness and pronounced him incurable were using the best medical knowledge available according to the biomedical model, the predominant view in medicine.

The biomedical model focuses on illness rather than health. It explains illness in terms of biological factors without considering psychological and social factors that might contribute to the disorder. Professionals who are committed to the biomedical model can only shake their heads in disbelief when patients like Cousins regain their health through other than conventional medical treatments.

Another approach that is gaining serious attention is the **biopsychosocial model** of health and wellness. This approach focuses on health as well as illness, and it holds that both are determined by a combination of biological, psychological, and social factors (Engel, 1977, 1980; Schwartz, 1982). It is this model that most health psychologists endorse and that guides our exploration in this chapter. The biopsychosocial model is depicted in Figure 13.1.

But first, what is health psychology? **Health psychology** is "the field within psychology devoted to understanding psychological influences on how people stay healthy, why they become ill, and how they respond when they do get ill" (Taylor, 1991, p. 6). Health psychologists study psychological factors associated with health and illness, and they promote interventions that foster good health and aid recovery from illness.

Why do people become ill in the modern age? At the beginning of the 20th century, the primary causes of death in the United States were infectious diseases such as pneumonia, diphtheria, and tuberculosis. Medical research has virtually conquered these diseases, with the exception of some new strains of tuberculosis. The health menace of modern times are diseases related to unhealthy lifestyle and stress—heart attack, stroke, hardening of the arteries, cancer, and cirrhosis of the liver (see Figure 13.2). In this chapter, we will discuss stress, disease, and behaviors that promote and compromise health.

How would you define stress? Is stress something in the environment? Is it a physiological or psychological reaction that occurs within a person? Is it some-

biopsychosocial model: A perspective that focuses on health as well as illness and holds that both are determined by a combination of biological, psychological, and social factors.

health psychology: The field concerned with the psychological factors that contribute to health, illness, and recovery.

stress: The physiological and psychological response to a condition that threatens or challenges a person and requires some form of adaptation or adjustment.

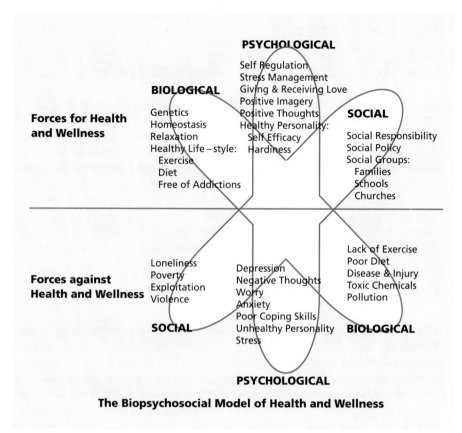

The Biopsychosocial Model of Health and Wellness

Figure 13.1

The Biopsychosocial Model of Health and Wellness

The biopsychosocial model focuses on health as well as illness and holds that both are determined by a combination of biological, psychological, and social factors. Most health psychologists endorse the biopsychosocial model. (From Green & Shellenberger, 1970.)

thing we should avoid at all costs? As with most issues in psychology, there are different ways to view stress. Some researchers emphasize the physiological effects of stress, while others focus on the role that our thinking plays in stress. Most psychologists define **stress** as the physiological and psychological response to a condition that threatens or challenges the individual and requires some form of adaptation or adjustment.

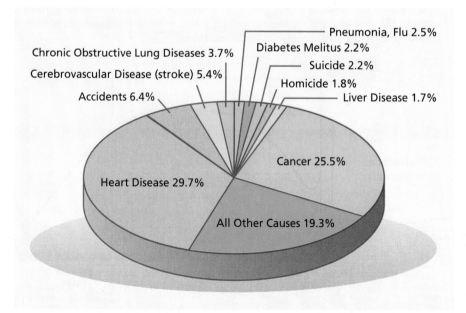

Figure 13.2

The Ten Leading Causes of Death in the United States

The two leading causes of death in the United States are heart disease (29.7 percent) and cancer (25.5 percent). Accidents (6.4 percent) are the third leading cause of death, followed by stroke (5.4 percent). (Data from U.S. Bureau of the Census, 1991.)

Hans Selye (1907–1982)

Theories of Stress

Hans Selye and the General Adaptation Syndrome

An early, classic contribution to stress research was made by Walter Cannon (1932), who described the fight-or-flight response. Cannon discovered that when any threat is perceived by an organism (animal or human), the sympathetic nervous system and the endocrine glands prepare the body to fight the threat or flee from it. Cannon considered the fight-or-flight response wonderfully adaptive because it helps the organism respond rapidly to threats. He also considered it potentially harmful in the long run, if an organism is not able to fight or flee and experiences prolonged stress and continuing physical arousal.

Hans Selye (1907–1982), the researcher most prominently associated with the effects of stress on health, established the field of stress research. Read about his work in the boxed feature on the next page.

Question: What is the general adaptation syndrome?

The General Adaptation Syndrome: A General Physical Response to Many Stressors Selye knew that all living organisms are constantly confronted with **stressors**—stimuli or events that place a demand on the organism for adaptation or readjustment. Each stressor causes both specific and nonspecific responses. Extreme cold, for example, causes the specific response of shivering. Apart from the specific response, the body makes a common or nonspecific response to a wide variety of stressors. The heart of Selye's concept of stress is the **general adaptation syndrome (GAS)**, his term for the nonspecific response to stress. The syndrome consists of three stages—the alarm stage, the resistance stage, and the exhaustion stage (Selye, 1956).

The body's first response to a stressor is the **alarm stage**, when emotional arousal occurs and the defensive forces of the body are prepared to meet the

Figure 13.3 The General Adaptation Syndrome The three stages in Hans Selye's general adaptation syndrome are (1) the alarm stage, during which there is emotional arousal and the defensive forces of the body are mobilized for fight or flight; (2) the resistance stage, in which intense physiological efforts are exerted to resist or adapt to the stressor; and (3) the exhaustion stage, when the organism fails in its efforts to resist the stressor. (Based on Selye, 1956.)

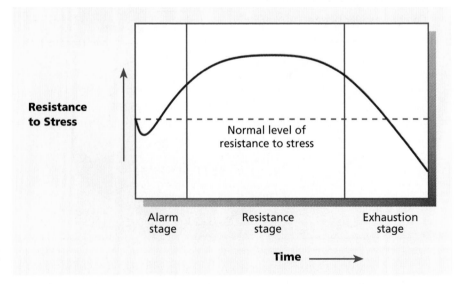

WORLD OF PSYCHOLOGY: PIONEERS

Hans Selye

Hans Selye was born in Vienna in 1907, the son of a surgeon. At age 18 he was admitted to medical school at the University of Prague in Germany, even though he had a rather undistinguished academic record. But four years later, in 1929, he earned his M.D. degree, graduating first in his class and extending his family's medical tradition to five generations. He stayed at the university two more years, earning a Ph.D. in organic chemistry in 1931.

Selye spent most of his pioneering career in Canada—at McGill University from 1932 to 1945 and at the University of Montreal from 1945 to 1977. At McGill University Selye conducted research on the effects of sex hormones. In one experiment, he injected rats with hormone-rich extracts of cow ovaries. What happened to the rats? To Selye's amazement, (1) their adrenal glands became swollen, (2) their immune system was weakened, and (3) the rats developed bleeding ulcers in their stomach and intestines. Never before had a hormone been shown to cause such clear physical symptoms. Selye, an excited and elated 28-year-old, thought he might be hot on the trail of discovering a new hormone. But further experiments proved that the same symptoms could be produced by almost anything Selye tried on the rats, including a wide variety of toxic chemicals and exposure to freezing cold temperatures. Even extreme muscle fatigue caused the same symptoms.

It seemed that Selye had not discovered anything at all. He was crushed, defeated, and he later admitted, "Suddenly all my dreams of discovering a new hormone were shattered. . . . I became so depressed that for a few days I could not do any work at all. I just sat in my laboratory, brooding" (1956, p. 24). Then brooding gave way to reflection. Selye recalled, "As I repetitiously continued to go over my ill-fated experiments and their possible interpretation, it suddenly struck me that one could look at them from an entirely different angle" (p. 25).

The different angle Selye pursued paved the way for the rest of his life's work. He realized that the body responds in much the same way to all harmful agents (toxic substances, injuries, electric shock) and a host of other stressors. The physical response was so predictable, so general, that Selye named it the *general adaptation syndrome*. As a medical student in the 1920s, Selye had been struck by the fact that patients admitted to the hospital with an amazingly wide variety of illnesses all had many of the same physical symptoms. Now he was seeing general symptoms result in rats exposed to a variety of stressors.

Selye was elated with his discovery, but the medical world was skeptical. The notion that organisms react in the same way to a wide range of dangers was completely contrary to the orthodox medical thinking of his day. Against the advice of his colleagues and without the endorsement of the medical research establishment, Selye continued to test his new theories. He prevailed, and within five years he proved that the general stress reaction was indeed the body's way of responding to stress.

Although Selye has his critics, his contribution is now widely accepted by researchers around the world. His place as a pioneer in medicine and psychology seems secure.

---

threat. If the stressor cannot be quickly conquered or avoided, the organism enters the **resistance stage**, characterized by intense physiological efforts either to resist or adapt to the stressor. Resistance may last a long time, but according to Selye, the length of the resistance stage depends both on the strength or intensity of the stressor and on the body's power to adapt.

If the organism finally fails in its efforts to resist, the final stage of the general adaptation syndrome, the **exhaustion stage**, is reached. Selye (1974) wrote, "The stage of exhaustion after a temporary demand upon the body, is reversible, but the complete exhaustion of all stores of deep adaptation energy is not" (p. 29). If exposure to the stressor continues, all the stores of deep energy are depleted, and disintegration and death follow. Figure 13.3 shows the progression of the general adaptation syndrome.

Selye claimed that any event, positive or negative, requiring a readjustment will produce stress in an organism. He did, however, differentiate between the

resistance stage: The second stage of the general adaptation syndrome, during which there are intense physiological efforts to resist or adapt to the stressor.

exhaustion stage: The final stage of the general adaptation syndrome, occuring if the organism fails in its efforts to resist the stressor.

Richard Lazarus

positive and negative aspects of stress. Eustress is positive or good stress, including exhilaration, excitement, and the thrill of accomplishment. Distress is damaging or unpleasant stress, such as that of frustration, inadequacy, loss, disappointment, insecurity, helplessness, or desperation.

Criticisms of Selye's Theory: A Missing Cognitive Factor   Thanks to Selye, the connection between extreme, prolonged stress and certain diseases is now widely accepted by medical experts, but some criticism of his work seems justified. Critics point out that Selye's general adaptation syndrome model was primarily formulated from research on laboratory rats. Although there may be some individual variation in the way rats respond to particular stressors, there is infinitely more variation in individual human responses to stress.

The major criticism is directed at Selye's claim that the intensity of the stressor determines one's physical reaction to it. His theory does not provide for a psychological component—how a person perceives and evaluates the stressor. This criticism led to the development of the cognitive theory of stress.

Richard Lazarus's Cognitive Theory of Stress

Richard Lazarus (1966; Lazarus & Folkman, 1984) contends that it is not the stressor itself that causes stress, but a person's perception of the stressor. Because Lazarus emphasizes the importance of perceptions and appraisal of stressors, his is a cognitive theory of stress and coping.

Question: What is the role of primary and secondary appraisal when people are confronted with a potentially stressful event?

The Cognitive Appraisal of Stressors: Evaluating the Stressor and Considering Your Options   When people are confronted with a potentially stressful event, they engage in a cognitive process that involves a primary and a secondary appraisal. A **primary appraisal** is an evaluation of the meaning and significance of a situation—whether its effect on our well-being is positive, irrelevant, or negative. An event appraised as negative or stressful could involve (1) harm or loss—damage that has already occurred, (2) threat—the potential for harm or loss, or (3) challenge—the opportunity to grow or to gain. An appraisal of threat, harm, or loss can occur in relation to anything important to us—a friendship, a part of the body, our property, finances, or self-esteem.

The same event can be appraised differently by different people. Some students might welcome the opportunity to give an oral presentation in class, seeing it as a challenge and a chance to impress their professor and raise their grade. Other students might feel threatened, fearing that they might embarrass themselves in front of their classmates and lower their grade in the process. Still others might view the assignment as both a challenge and a threat. When we appraise a situation as involving harm, loss, or threat, we have negative emotions such as anxiety, fear, anger, or resentment (Folkman, 1984). A challenge appraisal, on the other hand, is usually accompanied by positive emotions such as excitement, hopefulness, and eagerness. Stress for younger people is more likely to take the form of challenges; for older people, losses and threats are more common (El-Shiekh et al., 1989).

When we assess an event as stressful, we engage in a **secondary appraisal**. During secondary appraisal, if we judge the situation to be within our control, we make an evaluation of our available coping resources—physical (health, energy, stamina), social (support network), psychological (skills, morale, self-esteem), material (money, tools, equipment), and time. Then we consider our options and decide how we will deal with the stressor. The level of stress we feel

primary appraisal: Evaluating the significance of a potentially stressful event according to how it will affect one's well-being—whether it is perceived as irrelevant or as involving harm or loss, threat, or challenge.

secondary appraisal: Evaluating one's coping resources and deciding how to deal with a stressful event.

is largely a function of whether our resources are adequate to cope with the threat, and how severely our resources will be taxed in the process. Figure 13.4 summarizes the Lazarus and Folkman psychological model of stress.

Figure 13.4

Lazarus and Folkman's Psychological Model of Stress

Lazarus and Folkman emphasize the importance of a person's perceptions and appraisal of stressors. The stress response depends on the outcome of the primary and secondary appraisals, whether the person's coping resources are adequate to cope with the threat, and how severely the resources are taxed in the process. (Based on Folkman, 1984.)

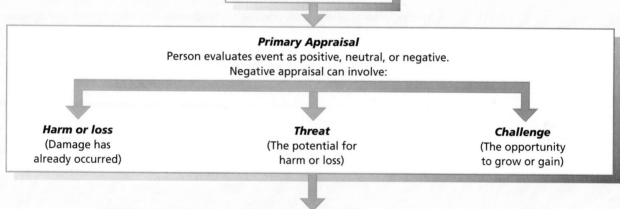

Potentially Stressful Event

Primary Appraisal
Person evaluates event as positive, neutral, or negative.
Negative appraisal can involve:

Harm or loss
(Damage has
already occurred)

Threat
(The potential for
harm or loss)

Challenge
(The opportunity
to grow or gain)

Secondary Appraisal
If the situation is judged to be within the person's control:

1. Person evaluates coping resources (physical, social, psychological, material) to determine if they are adequate to deal with stressor.
2. Person considers options in dealing with stressor.

Stress Response

Physiological
Autonomic arousal,
fluctuations in hormones

Emotional
Anxiety, fear, grief,
resentment, excitement

Behavioral
Coping behaviors (including
problem-focused and emotion-focused
coping strategies)

Question: What is the difference between problem-focused and emotion-focused coping?

Problem-Focused and Emotion-Focused Coping: Strategies for Dealing with Stress Coping strategies fall into two categories—problem-focused and emotion-focused coping (Lazarus & Folkman, 1984). **Problem-focused coping** is direct; it consists of reducing, modifying, or eliminating the source of stress itself. If you are getting a poor grade in history and appraise this as a threat, you might study harder, talk over your problem with your professor, form a study group with other class members, get a tutor, or drop the course.

But what can we do when we face stress that we cannot fight, escape from, avoid, or modify in any way? We can use **emotion-focused coping** to change the way we respond emotionally. Emotion-focused coping might involve reappraising a stressor. If you lose your job, you might decide that it isn't a major tragedy and, instead, view it as a challenge—an opportunity to find a better job with a higher salary. To cope emotionally, people may use anything from religious faith, wishful thinking, humor, or denial, to alcohol, drugs, or promiscuous sex (Lazarus & DeLongis, 1983). But misguided emotion-focused coping efforts can become additional sources of stress themselves. Table 13.1 summarizes the problem-focused and emotion-focused coping strategies.

Well-functioning people use a combination of problem-focused and emotion-focused coping in almost every stressful situation. Folkman and Lazarus (1980) studied the coping patterns of 100 subjects over a 12-month period and found that both types of coping were used in 98 percent of the 1,300 stressful life events their subjects had confronted. Not surprisingly, problem-focused coping strategies increased in situations subjects appraised as changeable, and emotion-focused coping techniques increased in situations appraised as not changeable.

The two types of coping are summed up well in an ancient prayer you may have heard: "Lord, grant me the strength to change those things which I can

Table 13.1   Problem-Focused and Emotion-Focused Coping Strategies

Coping Strategy	Definition	Examples
Problem-focused	A response aimed at reducing, modifying, or eliminating the source of stress.	Acting to remove or lessen the threat. Removing oneself from the stressful situation. Enlisting the help of others in dealing with threat. Seeking professional help or advice. Acting to prevent recurrence of similar stressful situations.
Emotion-focused	A response aimed at reducing the emotional distress caused by the stressor.	Viewing stressor as a challenge rather than a threat. Using one of these responses: prayer, denial, wishful thinking, fantasizing, humor, relaxation, biofeedback, alcohol, drugs, overeating, promiscuous sex.

change [problem-focused coping], the grace to accept those things which I cannot change [emotion-focused coping], and the wisdom to know the difference."

Memory Check 13.1

1. Selye called the predictable sequence of reactions organisms show in response to stressors the (fight-or-flight response, general adaptation syndrome).

2. Selye stresses the (physiological, psychological) aspects of stress.

3. (Selye, Lazarus) emphasized the importance of a person's evaluation of a stressor in determining the stressfulness of an event.

4. Coping aimed at reducing, modifying, or eliminating a source of stress is called _____ coping; coping aimed at reducing emotional distress is called _____ coping.

   a. emotion-focused; problem-focused   c. primary; secondary
   b. problem-focused; emotion-focused   d. secondary; primary

Answers: 1. general adaptation syndrome 2. physiological 3. Lazarus 4. b

Sources of Stress: The Common and the Extreme

Some stressors produce temporary stress while others produce chronic stress—a state of stress that continues unrelieved over time. Chronic health problems, physical handicaps, poverty, and unemployment are sources of chronic stress. The burden of chronic stress is disproportionately heavy for the poor, for minorities, and for the elderly.

Choices: Everyday Sources of Stress

Question: How do approach-approach, avoidance-avoidance, and approach-avoidance conflicts differ?

Sometimes conflicting motives can be sources of stress. When we must make a choice between two desirable alternatives, known as an **approach-approach conflict**, stress may be the result. Some approach-approach conflicts are minor, like deciding which movie to see. Others can have major consequences, such as whether to continue building a promising career or to interrupt the career to raise a child. In approach-approach conflicts, both choices are desirable.

In **avoidance-avoidance conflicts** we must choose between two undesirable alternatives. You may want to avoid studying for an exam, but at the same time want to avoid failing the test. **Approach-avoidance conflicts** include both desirable and undesirable features of the same choice. We are simultaneously drawn to and repelled by a choice—wanting to take a wonderful vacation but having to empty a savings account to do so.

approach-approach conflict: A conflict arising from having to choose between desirable alternatives.

approach-avoidance conflict: A conflict arising when the same choice has both desirable and undesirable features; one in which you are both drawn to and repelled by the same choice.

avoidance-avoidance conflict: A conflict arising from having to choose between equally undesirable alternatives.

Research shows that elderly people who are given a sense of control over their lives benefit both physically and psychologically.

Unpredictability and Lack of Control: Factors That Increase Stress

Unpredictable stressors are more difficult to cope with than predictable stressors. Laboratory tests have shown that rats receiving electric shocks without warning develop more ulcers than rats given shocks just as often but only after a warning (Weiss, 1972). Likewise, humans who are warned of a stressor before it occurs and have a chance to prepare themselves for it, experience less stress than those who cannot predict when a stressor will occur.

Our physical and psychological well-being is profoundly influenced by the degree to which we feel a sense of control over our lives (Rodin & Salovey, 1989). Langer and Rodin (1976) studied the effects of control on nursing-home residents. One group of residents were given some measure of control over their lives, such as choices in arranging their rooms and in the times they could see movies. They showed improved health and well-being and had a lower death rate than another group who were not given choices. Within 18 months, 30 percent of the residents given no choices had died compared to only 15 percent of those who had been given some control over their lives.

Several studies suggest that we are less subject to stress when we have the power to do something about it, whether we exercise that power or not. Glass and Singer (1972) subjected two groups of subjects to the same loud noise, but one group was told that they could, if necessary, terminate the noise by pressing a switch. The group that had the control suffered less stress even though they never did exercise the control they were given.

Catastrophic Events and Chronic Intense Stress

Question: How do people typically react to catastrophic events?

Environmental, social, bodily, and emotional stressors are a fact of life for most people, but some people also experience catastrophic events such as plane crashes, fires, or earthquakes. Panic reactions are rare, except in situations such

Some children who grow up surrounded by inner-city violence suffer a form of posttraumatic stress, evidenced by their rising rates of depression and suicide.

as fires in which people feel that they will survive only if they escape immediately. Many victims of catastrophic events react initially with such shock that they appear dazed, stunned, and emotionally numb. They seem disoriented and may wander about aimlessly, often unaware of their own injuries, attempting to help neither themselves nor others. Following this stage, the victims show a concern for others and although unable to act efficiently on their own, they are willing to follow the directions of rescue workers.

As victims begin to recover, the shock is replaced by generalized anxiety. Recovering victims typically have recurring nightmares and feel a compulsive need to retell the event over and over. Perhaps reexperiencing the event through dreaming and retelling helps desensitize them to the horror of the experience. Crisis-intervention therapy can provide victims with both coping strategies and realistic expectations about the problems they might face in connection with the trauma.

Question: What is posttraumatic stress disorder?

Posttraumatic Stress Disorder: The Trauma Is Over, but the Stress Remains Posttraumatic stress disorder (PTSD) is a prolonged and severe stress reaction to a catastrophic event (such as a plane crash or an earthquake) or to chronic intense stress (such as occurs in combat or imprisonment as a hostage or POW). Breslau and others (1991) found that 9 percent of a random sample of 1,007 adults ages 20 to 30 in metropolitan Detroit had suffered from posttraumatic stress syndrome from a variety of events. This statistic included 80 percent of the women who had been raped. The disorder may show up immediately, or it may not occur until 6 months or more after the traumatic experience, in which case it is called delayed posttraumatic stress disorder. More than 400,000 Vietnam veterans were found to suffer from posttraumatic stress disorder (Goldberg et al., 1990). The most serious cases of PTSD have resulted from witnessing brutal atrocities, whether among Vietnam veterans (Yehuda et al., 1992), Cambodian refugees (Carlson et al., 1992), or Holocaust survivors (Kuch & Cox, 1992).

Victims with posttraumatic stress disorder often have flashbacks, nightmares, or intrusive memories in which they feel as though they are actually reexperienc-

posttraumatic stress disorder (PTSD): A prolonged and severe stress reaction to a catastrophic or otherwise traumatic event, characterized by anxiety, psychic numbing, withdrawal from others, and the feeling that one is reliving the traumatic experience.

ing the traumatic event. They suffer from heightened anxiety and startle easily, particularly in response to anything that reminds them of the trauma (Green et al., 1985). Many survivors of war or catastrophic events experience survivor guilt because they lived while others died. Some feel that perhaps they could have done more to save others.

Memory Check 13.2

1. A feeling of control reduces stress regardless of whether the control is actually exercised. (true/false)

2. A predictable stressor is generally (more, less) stressful than an unpredictable stressor.

3. A common *initial* reaction to a catastrophic event is to be in a state of panic. (true/false)

4. Victims of catastrophic events typically want to avoid all discussion of the experience. (true/false)

5. Posttraumatic stress disorder is a prolonged and severe stress reaction that occurs in response to a number of common sources of stress that occur simultaneously. (true/false)

Answers: 1. true 2. less 3. false 4. false 5. false

Evaluating Life Stress: Major Life Changes, Hassels, and Uplifts

There are two major approaches to evaluating life stress and its relation to illness. One approach focuses on major life events, which cause life changes that require adaptation. A second approach focuses on life's daily hassles.

Holmes and Rahe's Social Readjustment Rating Scale: Adding Up the Stress Score

Social Readjustment Rating Scale (SRRS): A stress scale developed by Holmes and Rahe, which ranks 43 different life events from most to least stressful and assigns a point value to each.

Question: What was the Social Readjustment Rating Scale designed to reveal?

Interested in the relationship between life changes and illness, researchers Thomas Holmes and Richard Rahe (1967) developed the **Social Readjustment Rating Scale (SRRS)**. The SRRS is designed to measure stress by ranking different life events from most to least stressful. Each life event is assigned a point value. Life events that produce the greatest life changes and require the greatest adaptation are considered the most stressful, regardless of whether the events are positive or negative. The 43 life events range from death of a spouse, as-

Even positive life events, such as marriage, can cause stress.

signed 100 stress points, to such items as divorce (73 points), death of a close family member (63 points), marriage (50 points), pregnancy (40 points), and trouble with boss (23 points), to minor law violations such as getting a traffic ticket (11 points).

Holmes and Rahe maintain that there is a connection between the degree of life stress and major health problems. After analyzing over 5,000 medical case histories, they concluded that major life changes often precede serious illness (Rahe et al., 1964). People who score 300 or more on the inventory, the researchers claim, run about an 80-percent risk of suffering a major health problem within the next 2 years. Are Holmes and Rahe's claims justified?

Most researchers do not consider a high score on the SRRS a reliable predictor of future health problems (McCrae, 1984; Krantz et al., 1985). The correlations between major life changes and subsequent illness have, in fact, been quite small (Schroeder & Costa, 1984). One of the main shortcomings of the SRRS is that it assigns a point value to each life change without taking into account whether the change is for the better or worse. For example, life changes such as divorce, separation, pregnancy, retirement from work, and changing jobs or residences may be either welcome or unwelcome changes.

hassles: Little stressors that include the irritating demands and troubled relationships that can occur daily and that, according to Lazarus, cause more stress than do major life changes.

The Hassles of Life: Little Things Stress a Lot

Question: What roles do hassles and uplifts play in the stress of life, according to Lazarus?

Richard Lazarus disagrees with the rationale behind Holmes and Rahe's scale. He contends that life events cannot be assessed and assigned a numerical value for stressfulness without considering their meaning to the individual. Furthermore, he believes that the little stressors, which he calls **hassles,** add up to more stress than major life events.

Daily hassles are the "irritating, frustrating, distressing demands and troubled relationships that plague us day in and day out" (Lazarus & DeLongis, 1983, p. 247). Kanner, Coyne, Schaefer, and Lazarus (1981) developed the Hassles Scale to assess various categories of hassles. Unlike the Holmes and Rahe scale, the Hassles Scale takes into account that items may or may not represent stressors and that the amount of stress produced by an item varies from person to person. Consequently, people completing the scale indicate the items that have been a hassle for them and rate the items for severity on a 3-point scale.

DeLongis, Folkman, and Lazarus (1988) studied 75 American couples over a 6-month period and found that daily stress (as measured on the Hassles Scale) related significantly to present and future "health problems such as flu, sore throat, headaches, and backaches" (p. 486).

Table 13.2

The Ten Most Common Hassles for College Students and Middle-Aged Adults

College Sample (n = 34)	% of Times Checked	Middle-aged Sample (n = 100)	% of Times Checked
1. Troubling thoughts about future	76.6	1. Concerns about weight	52.4
2. Not getting enough sleep	72.5	2. Health of a family member	48.1
3. Wasting time	71.1	3. Rising prices of common goods	43.7
4. Inconsiderate smokers	70.7	4. Home maintenance	42.8
5. Physical appearance	69.9	5. Too many things to do	38.6
6. Too many things to do	69.2	6. Misplacing or losing things	38.1
7. Misplacing or losing things	67.0	7. Yard work or outside home maintenance	38.1
8. Not enough time to do the things you need to do	66.3	8. Property, investment, or taxes	37.6
9. Concerns about meeting high standards	64.0	9. Crime	37.1
10. Being lonely	60.8	10. Physical appearance	35.9

Source: Kanner, A.D., Coyne, J.C., Schaefer, C., & Lazarus, R.S. (1981). Comparison of two modes of stress measurement: Daily hassles and uplifts versus major life events. *Journal of Behavioral Medicine, 4,* 1–39.

Several studies reveal that scores on the Hassles Scale are better than SRRS scores at predicting illness (DeLongis et al., 1982; Weinberger et al., 1987) and are better predictors of psychological symptoms such as anxiety and depression (Kanner et al., 1981). Table 13.2 shows the 10 most frequent hassles reported by college students and by middle-aged adults.

According to Lazarus, "a person's morale, social functioning, and health don't hinge on hassles alone, but on a balance between the good things that happen to people—that make them feel good—and the bad" (quoted in Goleman, 1979, p. 52). Fortunately, the **uplifts**, or positive experiences in life, may neutralize or cancel out the effect of many of the hassles.

Lazarus and his colleagues also constructed an Uplifts Scale. As in the Hassles Scale, a cognitive appraisal is involved in determining what is considered an uplift. Items viewed as uplifts by some people may actually be stressors for other people. Kanner and others (1981) found that for middle-aged people, uplifts were often health- or family-related, whereas for college students uplifts came in the form of having a good time.

Would you like to learn how vulnerable you are to stress? Answer the questions in the *Try It!* to find out.

uplifts: The positive experiences in life, which can neutralize the effects of many of the hassles.

The following test was developed by psychologists Lyle H. Miller and Alma Dell Smith at Boston University Medical Center. Score each item from 1 (almost always) to 5 (never), according to how much of the time each statement applies to you.

Try It!

___ **1.** I eat at least one hot, balanced meal a day.
___ **2.** I get seven to eight hours sleep at least four nights a week.
___ **3.** I give and receive affection regularly.
___ **4.** I have at least one relative within 50 miles on whom I can rely.
___ **5.** I exercise to the point of perspiration at least twice a week.
___ **6.** I smoke less than half a pack of cigarettes a day.
___ **7.** I take fewer than five alcoholic drinks a week.
___ **8.** I am the appropriate weight for my height.
___ **9.** I have an income adequate to meet basic expenses.
___**10.** I get strength from my religious beliefs.
___**11.** I regularly attend club or social activities.
___**12.** I have a network of friends and acquaintances.
___**13.** I have one or more friends to confide in about personal matters.
___**14.** I am in good health (including eyesight, hearing, teeth).
___**15.** I am able to speak openly about my feelings when angry or worried.
___**16.** I have regular conversations with the people I live with about domestic problems, *e.g.,* chores, money and daily living issues.
___**17.** I do something for fun at least once a week.
___**18.** I am able to organize my time effectively.
___**19.** I drink fewer than three cups of coffee (or tea or cola drinks) a day.
___**20.** I take quiet time for myself during the day.

___**TOTAL**

To get your score, add up the figures and subtract 20. Any number over 30 indicates a vulnerability to stress. You are seriously vulnerable if your score is between 50 and 75, and extremely vulnerable if it is over 75.

Source: Miller, L. H., & Smith, A. D., Boston University Medical Center. In Wallis, C. (1983, June 6). Stress: Can we cope? *TIME*, p. 54.

WORLD OF PSYCHOLOGY: APPLICATIONS

Managing Stress

Question: What are some techniques for managing stress?

Anyone who is alive is subject to stress, but some of us are more negatively affected by it than others.

If stress leaves you fretting and fuming with your muscles in knots, try a few relaxation techniques that might spell relief.

Progressive Relaxation

The fight-or-flight response is our body's way of preparing us to deal with a threat, but if we can neither fight nor flee, we are left with intense physiological arousal, or stress. There are several relaxation techniques that you can use to calm yourself and relieve muscular tension. Probably the most widely used relaxation technique in the United States is *progressive relaxation* (Rice, 1987). It consists of flexing and then relaxing the different muscle groups throughout the body from the head to the toes. Here's how to do it:

1. Loosen or remove any tight-fitting clothing, take off your shoes, and situate yourself comfortably in an armchair with your arms resting on the chair's arms. Sit straight in the chair, but let your head fall forward so that your chin rests comfortably on your chest. Place your feet flat on the floor with your legs slightly apart in a comfortable position.

2. Take a deep breath. Hold the breath for a few seconds and then exhale slowly and completely. Repeat several times. Notice the tension in your chest as you hold the breath, and the relaxation as you let the breath out.

3. Flex the muscles in your right upper arm (in your left arm if you are left-handed). Hold the muscles as tight as you can for about 10 seconds. Observe the feeling of tension. Now relax the muscles completely and observe the feeling of relaxation. Repeat the flexing and the relaxing several times.

4. After completing the opening routine with your arm, use the same procedure, tensing and then relaxing a group of muscles, starting with the muscles in the forehead. Progressively work your way down through all the muscle groups in the body, ending with your feet.

Another excellent relaxation technique is Herbert Benson's relaxation response, described in chapter 4, on page 132.

Managing Mental Stress

Many of us stress ourselves almost to the breaking point by our own thinking. When we become angry, hostile, fearful, worried, and upset by things we think are going to happen, we cause our hearts to pound and our stomachs to churn. How often have you done this to yourself only to find that what you had imagined never actually materialized? The next time you begin to react to something you *think* will happen, stop yourself. Remember all the times you have become upset about things that never came to pass. Learn to use your own thinking to reduce stress, not create it. Give your body a break!

Stress-Inoculation Training Stress-inoculation training is a program designed by David Meichenbaum (1977) to help people cope with particular stressors that are troubling them. Test anxiety, stress over personal and social relationships, and various types of performance anxiety have been successfully treated with stress-inoculation. Individuals are taught to recognize their own negative thoughts ("I'll never be able to do this" or "I'll probably make a fool of myself"), and to replace negative thoughts with positive ones. They learn how to talk to themselves using positive coping statements to dispel worry and provide self-encouragement. Table 13.3 gives some examples of these coping statements.

Other Stress-Reducing Measures

Here are some additional suggestions for reducing the negative effects of stress.

- Engage in regular exercise to reduce the physiological arousal accompanying stress.
- Make time for relaxation and activities you enjoy.
- Use laughter and a positive attitude as stress relievers. Norman Cousins, the focus of the chapter's opening story, was firmly convinced that these two factors helped prolong his life.
- Rely on social support to moderate the effects of stress.
- Don't expect perfection from yourself or from other people.
- If you suffer from "hurry sickness," slow down.
- Learn patience.
- Check to see if you are responding to stress by using behaviors that increase stress in the long run, such as overeating, drinking, or using drugs.
- Eat a balanced diet and get enough sleep.
- Use caffeine in moderation. Caffeine can produce some of the same physiological responses as stress.

Table 13.3 Positive Coping Statements

Preparing for the Stressor

"I will state precisely what I have to do."

"I can come up with a plan to handle the problem."

"I refuse to worry about it. Worry doesn't help anything."

"I won't think about or make any negative or pessimistic statements."

"I'm going to think rationally and logically about this."

Facing or Confronting the Stressor

"If I take one step at a time, I know that I can handle this situation."

"The doctor told me I would feel anxious. This simply reminds me to do my coping exercises."

"I will take a few slow, deep breaths and relax."

Coping with the Stressor

"If I feel fear, I will simply pause."

"I will keep my mind focused on the present, on what is happening now, and just concentrate on what I have to do."

"It is not necessary for me to remove all of my fear. I just have to keep it under control."

When the Coping Attempt Is Finished

"This is working. It gets easier every time I use the exercises."

"This was easier than I thought it would be."

"I am really making progress."

Source: Adapted from Meichenbaum, 1975.

Memory Check 13.3

1. On the Social Readjustment Rating Scale, only negative life changes are considered stressful. (true/false)

2. According to Lazarus, hassles typically account for more stress than major life changes. (true/false)

3. Lazarus's approach to measuring hassles and uplifts (does, does not) consider individual perceptions of stressful events.

Answers: 1. false 2. true 3. does

Health and Disease

Responding to Illness

Health psychologists study the myriad ways in which we respond to illness, and the factors that affect whether we seek treatment. How do people tend to respond to illness?

The Sick Role   We have all been sick at one time or another, and most of us do not wish to be again. However, some people seem to take comfort in the "sick role." Sociologist Talcott Parsons (1979) indicated that there are benefits provided by the sick role. The ill person gets attention, sympathy, and concern, which can be very rewarding. Also, little is expected of a person who is sick. Obligations can be postponed and demands can be lifted until the person is well again. The surge in visits to college and university health services when term papers are due and when examinations begin may be partly due to students taking refuge in the sick role. How do we determine whether we are sick enough to seek treatment?

Recognizing and Interpreting Symptoms   Headache, stomach ache, sore throat, back pain, diarrhea—all are familiar symptoms that can represent nothing serious or something very critical. In many cases the first signs of serious disorders are common symptoms, familiar to us all. Symptoms that involve pain are typically interpreted as more serious than painless symptoms. And the more painful the symptom, the more likely we are to interpret it as serious and seek treatment.

Situational factors sometimes affect our tendency to recognize and interpret symptoms. For example, "medical student disease" is common among medical students who sometimes fear that they might be afflicted with the symptoms of the diseases they are learning about. Psychology students are also subject to letting their imagination run rampant when they study the symptoms of psychological disorders. Be forewarned when you study chapter 14, "Abnormal Behavior."

Seeking Treatment   When people recognize symptoms and interpret them as potentially serious, they seek treatment . . . or do they? There are several factors that determine who is more likely to seek treatment and use health services. Gender is one. Women use medical services more frequently than men. The reasons are not clear, and even when visits involving pregnancy and childbirth are factored out, women still seek health services more than men. It has been suggested that women may be more sensitive to bodily changes and detect symptoms more readily than men (Taylor, 1991). Cultural norms and expectations may partly explain why women seek treatment more than men (Bishop, 1984).

Socioeconomic class is involved in the decision to seek treatment. The lower socioeconomic classes have less to spend on health care. The poor are likely to seek treatment only in emergencies and are far less likely to have a regular physician than are the middle- and upper-socioeconomic classes.

Compliance with Medical Treatment: Following the Doctor's Orders
When we do receive medical treatment, do we always comply with the treatment regimen? Do we take all the medicine prescribed as the doctor instructed, or do we stop taking it when our symptoms disappear? A review of some 250 studies indicates that up to 50 percent of patients fail to follow what the doctor ordered (Adler & Stone, 1984). Even among patients with chronic disorders, at least half do not comply fully with their prescribed treatment regimen (Taylor, 1991).

It is even less likely that patients will comply with life-style changes that promote better health. In fact, 97 percent of patients do not adhere fully to life-style recommendations (Taylor, 1991). In other words, health professionals and researchers have discovered many more effective treatments than people are willing to follow.

Coronary Heart Disease: The Leading Cause of Death

The leading cause of death in the United States is coronary heart disease, which accounts for approximately 30 percent of all deaths (National Center for Health Statistics, 1991). For the heart muscle to survive, it requires a steady, sufficient supply of oxygen and nutrients carried by the blood. Coronary heart disease (CHD) is caused by the narrowing or the blockage of the coronary arteries—the arteries that supply blood to the heart muscle.

A health problem of modern times, coronary heart disease is largely attributable to life-style and is therefore an important field of study for health psychologists. A *sedentary life-style*—one with less than 20 minutes of exercise three times per week—is the primary modifiable risk factor contributing to death from coronary heart disease. Other risk factors are high serum-cholesterol levels, cigarette smoking, obesity, high blood pressure, and diabetes (Centers for Disease Control, 1990). Though not modifiable, another important risk factor is a family history of heart disease.

Question: What are the Type A and Type B Behavior Patterns?

The Type A and Type B Behavior Patterns: In a Hurry or Laid-Back One day *cardiologists* Meyer Friedman and Ray Rosenman (1974) asked an upholsterer to repair the chairs in their reception room. After inspecting the chairs, the upholsterer asked what kind of practice they had. The doctors explained that they were cardiologists and asked the upholsterer why he wanted to know. "'Well,' he replied, 'I was just wondering, because it's so peculiar that only the front edge of your chair seats are worn out'" (p. 71).

Apparently most of the heart patients had been literally sitting on the edge of their seats. This discovery led Friedman and Rosenman to wonder if there might be two types of personalities, one related to healthy hearts and one related to heart disease. After extensive research, they concluded that there are two types—the Type A Behavior Pattern, associated with a high rate of coronary heart disease, and the Type B Behavior Pattern, commonly found in persons unlikely to develop heart disease. Are your characteristics more like those of a Type A or Type B person? Complete the *Try It!* and find out.

sedentary life-style: One in which a person exercises less than 20 minutes three times a week.

cardiologist: A medical doctor specializing in care of the heart.

People with Type A Behavior Pattern, such as this stockbroker, are at increased risk for coronary heart disease.

Try It!

Circle *T* (true) or *F* (false) for each of these statements.

T   F   1. I forcefully emphasize key words in my everyday speech.

T   F   2. I usually walk and eat quickly.

T   F   3. I get irritated and restless around slow workers.

T   F   4. When talking to others, I get impatient and try to hurry them along.

T   F   5. I get very irritated, even hostile, when the car in front of me drives too slowly.

T   F   6. When others are talking, I often think about my own concerns.

T   F   7. I usually think of or do at least two things at the same time.

T   F   8. I get very impatient when I have to wait.

T   F   9. I usually take command and move the conversation to topics that interest me.

T   F   10. I usually feel guilty when I relax and do nothing.

T   F   11. I am usually too absorbed in my work to notice my surroundings.

T   F   12. I keep trying to do more and more in less time.

T   F   13. I sometimes punctuate my conversation with forceful gestures such as clenching my fists or pounding the table.

T   F   14. My accomplishments are due largely to my ability to work faster than others.

T   F   15. I don't play games just for fun. I play to win.

T   F   16. I am more concerned with acquiring things than with becoming a better person.

T   F   17. I usually use numbers to evaluate my own activities and the activities of others.

(Adapted from Friedman and Rosenman, 1974.)

Type A Behavior Pattern: A behavior pattern characterized by a sense of time urgency, impatience, excessive competitive drive, hostility, and easily aroused anger; believed to be a risk factor in coronary heart disease.

Type B Behavior Pattern: A behavior pattern characterized by a relaxed, easygoing manner and not associated with coronary heart disease.

People with the **Type A Behavior Pattern** have a strong sense of time urgency and are impatient, excessively competitive, hostile, and easily angered. They are "involved in a *chronic, incessant* struggle to achieve more and more in less and less time," often called the "hurry sickness" (Friedman & Rosenman, 1974, p. 84). Type A's would answer "true" to all or most of the questions in the *Try It!* The Type A person may be a driven executive, a competitive mortician, or a stressed hourly employee and may wear a white collar, a blue collar, or no collar at all.

Friedman now conducts consulting programs to help people change their Type A behavior, and he runs into some extreme cases. "One man liquefies his food in a blender so he doesn't have to waste time chewing. Another saves time going to the bathroom by keeping a bottle at his desk" (Rogers, 1989, p. 18).

In stark contrast to Type A's, people with the **Type B Behavior Pattern** are relaxed and easygoing and do not suffer from a sense of time urgency. They are not impatient or hostile and are able to relax without guilt. They play for fun and relaxation rather than to exhibit superiority over others. Yet the Type B individual may be as bright and ambitious as the Type A, and more successful as well. Type B's would answer "false" to all or most of the *Try It!* questions.

Research on Behavior Pattern and Heart Disease   Time urgency, a clear Type A trait, is a factor related to serum-cholesterol level, say Friedman and Rosenman (1974). In one study they monitored the serum-cholesterol levels in a number of accountants from January through June. The cholesterol levels rose as the income tax deadline approached and then fell after April 15, when the sense of time urgency diminished. Later the researchers compared the serum-cholesterol levels in Type A and Type B men and women and found higher levels in Type A's of both sexes.

In 1960–1961, the researchers embarked on the Western Collaborative Group Study (WCGS), a long-range study of more than 3,000 men who were classified as having either Type A or Type B Behavior Pattern but no trace of coronary heart disease. Information relating to diet, exercise patterns, blood pressure, and smoking were collected along with other biographical data. By 1969, 257 of the men had developed coronary heart disease. Neither dietary nor exercise patterns helped predict the men who developed heart disease. The researchers concluded that "the most pronounced danger signal back in 1960–1961 was, above all, the presence of Type A Behavior Pattern" (1974, p. 80). Type A subjects who were between the ages of 35 and 65 at the beginning of the study were nearly three times as likely to have heart disease within the following 10-year period as Type B subjects. Other research supports Friedman and Rosenman's conclusions (Haynes et al., 1980; Matthews, 1982; Dembroski et al., 1985).

Beginning in 1982 another series of studies failed to reveal the Type A–heart disease connection (Case et al., 1985; Shekelle et al., 1985). These more recent studies had two things in common: (1) They used a different method of assessing Type A behavior, and (2) they typically used subjects who were already at risk for CHD (Evans, 1990).

Some researchers speculate that it may not be the whole Type A Behavior Pattern that leads to heart disease. Dembroski and others (1985) point to anger and hostility as the toxic components. Redford Williams of Duke University Medical School suggests that hostility is the real culprit, particularly a cynical, mistrusting attitude (Barefoot, Dahlstrom, & Williams, 1983; Williams, 1989). Recently Rosenman has come to believe that it is the hostility rather than the "hurry sickness" that really causes the problem. Friedman, on the other hand, disagrees (he and Rosenman are no longer a team) and considers the whole Type A pattern a disorder that needs to be treated.

Cancer: A Dreaded Disease

Cancer. The word alone is frightening. Second only to heart disease as the leading cause of death, cancer causes 22 percent of the deaths in the United States (National Center for Health Statistics, 1991). Cancer strikes frequently in the adult population, and about 30 percent of Americans—over 75 million people—will develop cancer at some time in their lives. The young are not spared the scourge of cancer, for it takes the lives of more children between the ages of 3 and 14 than any other disease.

We speak of cancer as a single disease, but actually it is a complicated collection of 250 or more diseases. Cancer can invade cells in any part of a living organism—humans, other animals, and even plants. Cancer always starts small, because it is a disease of the body's cells. Normal cells in all parts of the body reproduce (divide), but fortunately they have built-in instructions about when to stop dividing. If they did not, every part of our body would continue to grow as long as we live. Unlike normal cells, cancer cells do not stop dividing. Unless they can be caught in time and destroyed, they continue to grow and spread, eventually killing the organism they have invaded.

Health psychologists warn that smoking, excessive alcohol consumption, diet, promiscuous sexual behavior, or becoming sexually active in the early teens (especially for females) are all behaviors that increase the risk of cancer. Many cancer patients report more high-stress situations occurring before their cancer was diagnosed. A considerable number of studies report a high rate of cancer in people who have suffered extended periods of depression (Persky et al., 1987), grieving, or helplessness (Sklar & Anisman, 1981).

WORLD OF PSYCHOLOGY: MULTICULTURAL PERSPECTIVES

Health in America

The quality of health and the leading health risk factors are not the same for all Americans. They differ among the various cultural and ethnic groups that make up our nation and according to gender and age as well.

African Americans As the nation's largest minority group, African Americans make up 12 percent of the population and are represented in every socioeconomic group from the poorest to the richest. But their overall poverty rate is about three times higher than that of the white population. As a result, many African Americans are at higher risk for disease and death and are more likely to suffer from inadequate health care. Their life expectancy has trailed behind that of the total U.S. population throughout the 20th century. Black infants are at twice the risk of death within their first year of life compared to white infants (CDC, 1992a). Moreover, the leading causes of death affect blacks at higher rates than whites in 8 out of 10 categories, as shown in Table 13.4 (U.S. Bureau of the Census, 1991).

High blood pressure is twice as common in African Americans as in the general population, and researchers still don't know why. If stress is a factor, the doubly stressing conditions of poverty and racism could contribute to high blood pressure. Among African Americans, the rate of AIDS is more than 3 times higher than that of whites, and black women are from 10 to 15 times more likely than white women to contract AIDS (Public Health Service, 1991).

Hispanic Americans By 1990 Hispanic Americans, the fastest growing and second largest minority group, had increased to make up about 8 percent of the total U.S. population. While many Hispanics are immigrants, over 70 percent are native-born Americans. The majority of Hispanics, about 63 percent, are Mexican Americans.

Obesity and diabetes are more prevalent in the Hispanic population, and cigarette smoking and alcohol abuse are more common among Hispanic teenagers than among other teenagers, white or black. Hispanic Americans are at high risk of death from accidental injuries (automobile and others), homicide, cirrhosis and other chronic liver diseases, and AIDS (Public Health Service, 1991).

Hispanic Americans comprise the majority of migrant farm workers. In addition to back-breaking labor and low

Table 13.4 Comparative Death Rates for the Ten Leading Causes of Death in the U.S. (deaths per 100,000 population)

	Blacks	Whites
Total deaths	**788.8**	**509.8**
Heart disease	226.6	161.5
Cancer	171.3	130.0
Accidents	43.7	34.1
Stroke	51.5	27.5
Chronic lung disease	16.6	19.8
Pneumonia	19.6	13.6
Suicide	6.8	12.2
Chronic liver disease	14.5	8.4
Diabetes	21.2	9.0
Homicide	34.1	5.3

Source: U.S. Bureau of the Census (1991). *Statistical abstract of the United States* (111th ed.). Washington, DC: U.S. Government Printing Office. No. 118, p. 81.

wages, the life expectancy of migrant farm workers is only 49 years—far below the national average of 75 years (National Migrant Resource Program and Migrant Clinicians Network, 1990).

Asian Americans There are over 11 million Asian Americans, making them the third largest minority group in the United States. Some 75 percent of Asian Americans are immigrants, among them many refugees, primarily from Southeast Asia (Laos, Cambodia, Vietnam).

Asian Americans born and well-established in the United States resemble the total population in terms of health and are better off financially than most immigrants. In stark contrast, however, are Asian immigrant groups such as Laotians, whose poverty rate is one of the highest in the nation. They and other Asian immigrant subgroups are far more likely to suffer from certain infectious diseases, such as hepatitis B and especially tuberculosis. In fact the rate of tuberculosis is 40 times higher in Southeast Asian immigrants than in the total population (Public Health Service, 1991).

Native Americans The smallest of the defined minority groups are the descendants of the original residents of North America who number about 1.6 million. A large proportion of the Native American population die before the age of 45. This fact partly accounts for their statistically low rates of heart disease and cancer, which are more common among older people.

Obesity is common among many Native American tribes and contributes to the prevalence of diabetes. According to the Indian Health Service (1988), over one-fifth of the members of some tribes suffer from diabetes. Alcohol represents a dangerous risk factor among Native Americans since cirrhosis of the liver occurs at three times the rate of the total U.S. population. About 95 percent of Native American families are affected in some way by alcohol abuse (Rhoades et al., 1987). One-fifth of all deaths among Native Americans result from injuries (motor vehicle crashes and others), and alcohol is involved in an estimated 75 percent of these fatal injuries. Furthermore, alcohol is a leading factor in their homicide rate and suicide rate, which are 60-percent higher and 28-percent higher, respectively, than in the total U.S. population (Indian Health Service, 1988).

The Gender Gap in America's Health Care Significant health disparities also exist that are related neither to poverty nor racial or ethnic differences. According to Helen Rodriguez-Trias (1992), the health of many women is threatened by "assaults by husbands, exhusbands, and lovers [who] cause more injuires to women than motor vehicle accidents, rape, and muggings combined" (p. 664). There is also a serious gender gap in health care and medical research in the United States.

Most medical research, much of it funded by the U.S. government, rejects women as subjects in favor of men. Women are slighted as well in health care and treatment. Physicians are more likely to see women's health complaints as "emotional" in nature rather than due to physical causes (Council on Ethical and Judicial Affairs, AMA, 1991). The American Medical Association released a major report in 1991 revealing that of men and women who received an abnormal reading on a heart scan, 40 percent of the men but only 4 percent of the women were referred for further testing and possible bypass surgery. Women are less likely than men to receive kidney dialysis and 30 percent less likely to receive a kidney transplant. Not only gender, but age is a factor as well. Women between the ages of 46 and 60 were only half as likely as men to get a new kidney (Council on Ethical and Judicial Affairs, AMA, 1991).

The good news is that efforts to erase the gender disparity in medical research and treatment are now underway. Dr. Bernadine Healy, the first woman to head the prestigious National Institutes of Health, reported to Congress in 1991 that NIH will launch a long-term effort to address women's health care needs. In addition, NIH no longer funds research projects that do not include women in their sample. Such an effort is long overdue.

Efforts are underway to help erase inequalities in health care among different cultural groups in the United States.

Is there such a thing as a cancer-prone personality? Some researchers claim that people who suppress or hold in their emotions—those who are *too* calm, passive, or apathetic—and people who have a tendency toward depression are more susceptible to developing cancer (Renneker, 1981; Bahnson, 1981).

The Immune System: An Army of Cells to Fight Off Disease

Have you heard of a new field of study known as psychoneuroimmunology? This nine-syllable word names a field of study in which psychologists, biologists, and medical researchers combine their expertise to learn the effects of psychological factors (emotions, thinking, and behavior) on the immune system.

Several studies provide indirect evidence that psychological factors, emotions, and stress are related to immune system functioning (O'Leary, 1990). The immune system is the body's surveillance system—an army of cells and substances guarding against bacteria, viruses, fungi, and any other foreign matter that might enter and harm the body. The immune system exchanges information with the brain, and what goes on in the brain can apparently influence the immune system for good or ill.

High periods of stress have been correlated with increased symptoms of a number of infectious diseases, including oral and genital herpes, mononucleosis, colds, and flu (Jemmott & Locke, 1984). Cohen and Williamson (1991) conclude from a review of studies that stress is associated with an increase in illness behaviors—reporting physical symptoms and seeking medical care. They found somewhat less convincing evidence that stress plays a role in the "onset of infectious diseases and reactivation of latent viruses" (p. 17).

Lowered immune response has been associated with poor marital relationships, exams and academic pressures, and sleep deprivation (Kiecolt-Glaser et al., 1987; Maier & Laudenslager, 1985). Several researchers have reported that severe, incapacitating depression is related to lowered immune activity (Irwin et al., 1987; Schleifer et al., 1983, 1985). For several months after the death of a spouse, the widow or widower suffers weakened immune system function (Bartrop et al., 1977) and is at a higher risk of mortality (Rogers & Reich, 1988).

McNaughton and others (1990) report that immune suppression in the elderly is associated with depressed mood, severe stress, and dissatisfaction with social supports, whereas improved immune functioning is related to the use of problem-focused coping. Rodin (1986) found that nursing-home residents who were given training in coping skills developed fewer illnesses, suffered less deterioration from chronic conditions, and reported less stress than a similar group not given the training.

Personal Factors Associated with Health and Illness

Question: What personal factors are associated with health and resistance to stress?

Researchers have identified two personal factors that might contribute to better health—psychological hardiness and social support.

Psychological Hardiness: Commitment, Challenge, and Control   Suzanne Kobasa (1979) wondered why some people under great stress succumb to illness while others do not. She studied 670 male executives who identified stressful life events and symptoms of illness that they had experienced in the preceding three years. Kobasa then administered personality questionnaires to the 200 executives who had ranked high on both stress and illness and to the 126 who had equally stressful life events but few symptoms of illness. She found high-stress/low-illness male subjects were more immersed in their work and social lives. They enjoyed challenge and had a greater sense of control over events than their high-stress/high illness counterparts. Two years later Kobasa, Maddi, and Kahn (1982) again looked at the same executives. The high-stress/low-illness group remained healthier and retained their attitudes of commitment, challenge, and control—three characteristics that Kobasa collectively called psychological **hardiness**.

Roth and others (1989) suggest that "hardy individuals may possess a cognitive style such that troubling life events are interpreted less negatively and thereby rendered less harmful" (p. 141).

Social Support: Help in Time of Need   Another factor that seems to contribute to better health is *social support*. It can be thought of as support provided, usually in time of need, by a spouse or other family members, friends, neighbors, colleagues, support groups, or even by members of the larger community (Johnson & Sarason, 1979). Social support can involve tangible support, information, and advice, as well as emotional support (Cohen, 1988). It can also be viewed as the feeling that we are loved, valued, esteemed, and cared for by those for whom we feel a mutual obligation (Cobb, 1976).

Social support has been shown to reduce the impact of stress from unemployment, long-term illness, retirement, and bereavement (Krantz et al., 1985). People with social support recover more quickly from illnesses and lower their risk of death from specific diseases (House et al., 1988). Social support may increase the probability of surviving a heart attack, help moderate the effects of high blood pressure, and even influence the length of survival for those stricken with cancer (Turner, 1983). In a study of 4,775 people over a 9-year period, Berkman and Syme (1979) found that people low in social support were twice as likely to die as those high in social support.

hardiness: Three psychological qualities shared by people who can undergo high levels of stress yet remain healthy—a sense of control over one's life, commitment to one's personal goals, and a tendency to view change as a challenge rather than a threat.

social support: Tangible support, information, advice, and/or emotional support provided in time of need by family, friends, and others; the feeling that we are loved, valued, and cared for.

Memory Check 13.4

1. The (Type A, Type B) Behavior Pattern is characterized by a sense of time urgency, impatience, excessive competition, anger, and hostility.

2. All major studies have found the Type A Behavior Pattern to be a predictor of coronary heart disease. (true/false)

3. Recent research suggests that the most toxic component of the Type A Behavior Pattern is (hostility, a sense of time urgency).

4. Research suggests that stress:

   a. can suppress the action of the immune system
   b. is related to many cases of coronary heart disease
   c. can hasten the spread of cancer
   d. all of these

(continued)

5. Which of these is *not* a dimension of psychological hardiness?

    a. a feeling that adverse circumstances can be controlled and changed
    b. a sense of commitment and deep involvement in personal goals
    c. close, supportive relationships with family and friends
    d. a tendency to look on change as a challenge rather than a threat

Answers: 1. Type A 2. false 3. hostility 4. d 5. c

Your Life-style and Your Health

Question: What constitutes an unhealthy life-style, and how serious a factor is it in illness and disease?

If you are not healthy and physically hardy, who or what is to blame? Of course there are a number of enemies of good health: environmental pollutants; job, family, and personal stressors; genetic and congenital defects; accidents and injury; and others. But for most Americans, health enemy number one consists of their own habits. As Figure 13.5 shows, 53.5 percent of all deaths in the United States are attributable to unhealthy behavior or life-style (Powell, 1986). What are these unhealthy behaviors? The culprits are all well known—an unhealthy diet, overeating, lack of exercise, alcohol and drug abuse, too little sleep, and so on. But the most dangerous unhealthy behavior of all is smoking.

Figure 13.5

Factors Contributing to Death before Age 65

The number one factor leading to premature death in the United States is unhealthy life-style. Fortunately our own life-style is more completely under our control than any of the other factors contributing to premature death. (Based on Powell, Spain, Christenson, & Mollenkamp, 1986.)

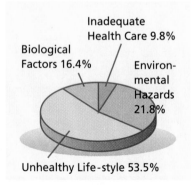

Smoking: Hazardous to Your Health

Question: Why is smoking considered the single most preventable cause of death?

"Cigarettes are among the most addictive substances of abuse and by far the most deadly" (Schelling, 1992, p. 430). According to the Centers for Disease Control (CDC) (1991), "Tobacco use is the single most preventable cause of death in the United States" (p. 617). There are 50 million Americans who smoke, and each day 3,000 more teenagers become regular smokers (Novello, 1990). Countless other millions who must breathe smoke-filled air suffer the ill effects and consequences of passive smoking. Current estimates are that smoking is directly related to 390,000 deaths annually in the United States, which means that "more than one of every six deaths in the United States are caused by smoking" (Novello, 1990, p. viii). Add to this statistic the suffering of millions from chronic bronchitis, emphysema, and other respiratory diseases; death and injury from fires caused by smoking; and low birth weight and retarded fetal development of babies born to smoking mothers (CDC, 1989). The American Cancer Society claims that compared to nonsmokers, the death rate increases 60 percent for men smoking less than half a pack of cigarettes a day, 90 percent for those smoking one to two packs a day, and 120 percent for those smoking more than two packs a day. Among women who smoke, lung cancer claims more lives than breast cancer. "Current smokers can greatly reduce their risk of cancer, especially lung cancer, if they quit smoking" (Chyou et al., 1992, p. 37).

Now for the good news: The percentage of smokers in the U.S. population is declining. A 1991 Gallup poll revealed that 30 percent of males and 27 percent of females were smoking, down from a high of 57 percent for males and 32 percent for females (Hugick & Leonard, 1991). Moreover, 76 percent of the smokers claimed that they wanted to quit, an indication that a strong, nonsmoking sentiment is increasing among Americans.

Most smokers begin smoking as teenagers, when peer pressure is strong. Adolescents tend to emulate the behavior of others to gain social acceptance (Taylor, 1991). Teens with parents and friends who smoke are at greater risk of taking up smoking themselves. Reviews of twin and adoption studies indicate that there may even be a genetic connection that influences addiction to smoking (Epstein et al., 1989).

Why do adult smokers continue the habit when the majority admit that they would prefer to be nonsmokers? Clearly, smoking is an addiction, and the U.S. Surgeon General declared in 1988 that tobacco is just as addictive as cocaine and heroin. Pomerleau and Pomerleau (1984, 1989) have provided a convincing explanation of why smokers continue, even when they have expressed the desire to quit. Smokers must struggle against both positive and negative reinforcers. Quitting smoking causes withdrawal symptoms, which motivates smokers to end the symptoms by smoking another cigarette. Then there are the satisfying, positive reinforcers that help maintain the addiction. Nicotine increases the release of acetylcholine, norepinephrine, dopamine, and other neuroregulators that improve mental alertness, sharpen memory, and reduce tension and anxiety.

This theory may explain why techniques developed to help smokers break the habit have such a high failure rate. Smokers have tried hypnosis, acupuncture, drug treatments (nicotine gum or patches), cognitive therapy, operant conditioning, aversion therapy (pairing smoking with a nauseating stimulus), and other techniques to break the habit. Many such treatments work well for a short time, but from 60 to 75 percent of the smokers who try such treatments ultimately relapse and begin smoking again (Pomerleau & Rodin, 1986). Yet many people are quitting with and without help from stop-smoking programs. More than 30 million Americans have kicked the habit—about 90 percent of them on their own (Novello, 1990).

Alcohol: A Problem for Millions

Question: What are some health risks of alcohol consumption?

Although smoking is directly related to a greater number of deaths, alcohol undoubtedly causes more misery. The health and social costs of alcohol are staggering—fatalities, medical bills, lost work, family problems. According to Rodin and Salovey (1989), alcohol "represents one of the three leading causes of death in modern societies" (p. 551). Some 18 million Americans have a serious drinking problem, and about 10 million are alcoholics (Lord et al., 1987). Alcohol abuse and dependence is three times more prevalent in males than in females (Grant et al., 1992). Although a higher percentage of white-collar workers use alcohol, the percentage of problem drinkers is higher among blue-collar workers (Harford et al., 1992). For many, alcohol provides a method of coping with life strains they feel powerless to control (Seeman & Seeman, 1992). But more and more people are turning away from alcohol altogether. About 43 percent of Americans are total abstainers (Gallup & Newport, 1990a).

Alcohol can damage virtually every organ in the body, but it is especially harmful to the liver and is the major cause of cirrhosis, which kills 14,000

controlled drinking: A behavioral approach to the treatment of alcoholism, designed to teach the skills necessary so that alcoholics can drink socially without losing control.

people each year (Desmond, 1987). Alcohol can also cause stomach problems—indigestion, nausea, diarrhea, and ulcers. One-half of heavy, long-term drinkers suffer damage to their skeletal muscles, and one-third sustain damage to their heart muscle (Urbano-Marquez et al., 1989). Alcohol increases the risk of many cancers, including cancer of the liver, mouth, throat, tongue, and voice box. Pregnant women should avoid all alcohol because of its potentially disastrous effects on the developing fetus. (See chapter 8, "Child Development," for a discussion of fetal alcohol syndrome.)

Shrinkage in the cerebral cortex of alcoholics has been revealed using magnetic resonance imaging (Jernigan et al., 1991). CAT scans also show brain shrinkage in a high percentage of alcoholics, even in young subjects and in those who appear to be intact mentally (Lishman, 1990). Moreover, heavy drinking can cause cognitive impairment (Goldman, 1983) and seizures (Ng et al., 1988). The only good news in recent studies is that some of the effects of alcohol on the brain are thought to be partially reversible with prolonged abstinence.

Alcoholism's toll goes beyond physical damage to the alcoholic. Drunk drivers cause 50 percent of the motor vehicle accidents in the United States (Koshland, 1989), killing 50,000 yearly (Mayer, 1983) and injuring 75,000 more (Nathan, 1983). Alcohol has been implicated in 70 percent of the drownings, 30 percent of the suicides, and almost one-third of the rapes, burglaries, and assaults (Desmond, 1987).

Alcoholism: Causes and Treatment   The American Medical Association and the American Psychiatric Association maintain that alcoholism is a disease, and as such, once an alcoholic, always an alcoholic. According to this view, even a small amount of alcohol is believed to cause an irresistible craving for more, leading alcoholics to lose control of their drinking (Jellinek, 1960). Thus total abstinence is seen as the only acceptable method of treatment. The medical establishment and Alcoholics Anonymous endorse both the disease concept and the total abstinence approach to treatment.

Some studies suggest a genetic factor in alcoholism and lend support to the disease model. According to Goodwin (1985), about one-half of hospitalized alcoholics have a family history of alcohol abuse. Adoption studies have revealed that "sons of alcoholics were three or four times more likely to be alcoholic than were sons of nonalcoholics, whether raised by their alcoholic biologic parents or by nonalcoholic adoptive parents" (Goodwin, 1985, p. 172).

Some experts reject the disease concept and contend that alcoholism can take various forms and have various causes (Pattison, 1983). Even in people who are genetically predisposed, some researchers caution against overlooking the environmental contribution to alcoholism (Searles, 1988). A large recent study by McGue and others (1992) involving 356 pairs of identical and fraternal twins revealed a substantial genetic influence for males when the first symptoms of alcoholism appear before age 20. Family and cultural influences are apparently the dominant factors in alcoholism among women of all ages and among men whose drinking problems appear after adolescence.

Some experts stress the role of behavioral, social, and cultural factors in alcoholism and advocate various approaches to treatment. They believe that with behavior therapy, some (not all) problem drinkers can learn the skills necessary to drink socially without losing control (Peele, 1992; Sobell & Sobell, 1978). Advocates of this treatment—*controlled drinking*—generally suggest that it is most successful with younger drinkers who have less serious drinking problems and who are not yet physically dependent on alcohol (Marlatt, 1983; Polich et al., 1981).

Abstinence is the surest, safest solution to alcoholism—our country's foremost drug problem (Nathan, 1992).

Cholesterol, Saturated Fat, and Salt: Unhealthy in Excess

Question: How much dietary fat and cholesterol is recommended for daily intake?

It is well known that good nutrition is essential to good health. But ideas about good nutrition have changed drastically over the years. A generation ago many parents urged their children to eat a hearty breakfast—crisp bacon, a large glass of whole milk, and the all-important egg, especially the yolk. Red meat was considered essential for strong, healthy bodies, and organ meats (liver, for example), which are a rich source of nutrients, were often forced on children as health foods. Then researchers discovered that diets high in cholesterol were killing us.

What is cholesterol? **Cholesterol** is a substance necessary to sustain life. It plays a vital role in forming cell membranes, in aiding digestion, and in the production of the sex hormones. Your own liver manufactures all the cholesterol you require. Food containing **saturated fat**, and to a lesser extent, foods containing cholesterol, raise blood-cholesterol levels.

Cholesterol is found only in foods of animal origin—milk, cheese, butter, eggs, red meat, poultry, and fish. Saturated fats are those which are solid at room temperature. They include butter, lard, fat in whole-milk products (cheese, ice cream, cream), fat in red meat and poultry (especially in the skin), and in the vegetable fats palm oil and coconut oil. Unsaturated fats fall into two categories—polyunsaturated fats, which include corn, sunflower, and safflower oils, and monounsaturated fats, which include olive and peanut oils.

Many food products at the supermarket are labeled "No Cholesterol," but this does not necessarily mean that they are good products to buy. When you read food labels, you should be concerned about the total grams of fat per serving and the type of fat the product contains. Try to avoid products high in saturated fat so that you can keep blood cholesterol at a healthy level.

The average American diet is about 37 percent fat, although a healthy diet should consist of no more than 30 percent dietary fat. That 30 percent should be divided evenly among saturated, polyunsaturated, and monounsaturated fats. A diet high in fat has been associated with clogged arteries, heart disease, and cancers, particularly colon and breast cancer. Table 13.5 shows the daily allotment of fat according to the number of calories one consumes in a day.

> **cholesterol:** A substance necessary for sustaining life, manufactured by the liver and found in foods of animal origin such as whole milk products, eggs, red meat, poultry, and fish.
>
> **fat (saturated):** Dietary fat that is solid at room temperature; the type of fat that elevates serum cholesterol levels.

Table 13.5

Maximum Grams of Saturated, Polyunsaturated, and Monounsaturated Fat Allowed in Order to Maintain a Diet of No More Than 30 Percent Fat

Total Calories	Daily Grams of Fat	Grams of Saturated, Polyunsaturated, Monounsaturated Fat
1,000	33	11 grams each
1,200	40	13 grams each
1,500	50	17 grams each
1,800	60	20 grams each
2,000	67	22 grams each
2,200	73	24 grams each
2,500	83	28 grams each

Cholesterol intake should be kept below 300 milligrams.

cholesterol (serum): The milligrams of cholesterol per deciliter of blood, which should be kept below 200.

aerobic exercise (ah-RO-bik): Exercise involving the use of large muscle groups in continuous, repetitive action and requiring increased oxygen intake and increased breathing and heart rates.

Serum cholesterol is measured in milligrams per deciliter of blood. The American Heart Association recommends that cholesterol levels should be kept below 200 milligrams. However, the picture is not so simple. Experts are now suggesting that although high levels of cholesterol represent a danger, the type of lipoproteins that transport the cholesterol is what really matters. Low density lipoproteins (LDL) are said to be the bad cholesterol, because they are believed to be responsible for depositing cholesterol on artery walls. High density lipoproteins (HDL) are considered to be the good cholesterol and actually beneficial in combatting heart disease. HDL apparently acts somewhat like a vacuum sweeper, removing excess cholesterol from the bloodstream. Some researchers suggest that HDL can even remove cholesterol already deposited on artery walls.

Maximum protection from heart disease, as far as diet is concerned, can be gained by simultaneously raising HDL levels and lowering high LDL levels. LDL can be lowered by reducing fat in the diet, particularly saturated fat and cholesterol, while HDL can be raised through an appropriate, regular exercise program.

Finally, try to limit your sodium (salt) intake to 2,400 milligrams per day. Further restriction is necessary for people with high blood pressure.

Exercise: Keeping Fit Is Healthy

Question: What are some benefits of regular aerobic exercise?

For years medical experts, especially health psychologists, have promoted regular exercise. Yet "only 15% of the general population is highly active, and as much as 70% of the entire population can be characterized as inactive" (Rodin & Salovey, 1989, p. 554). Many studies show that regular **aerobic exercise** pays rich dividends in the form of physical and mental fitness. Aerobic exercise (such as running, swimming, brisk walking, bicycling, rowing, and jumping rope) uses the large muscle groups in continuous, repetitive action and requires increased oxygen intake and increased breathing and heart rates. To improve cardiovascular fitness and endurance and to lessen the risk of heart attack, aerobic exercise should be performed regularly. This means 3 or 4 times a week for 20 to 30 minutes, with an additional 5- to 10-minute warm-up and cool-down period (Alpert et al., 1990; Shephard, 1986). Fewer than 20 minutes of aerobic exercise 3 times a week has "no measurable effect on the heart," and more than 3 hours per week "is not known to reduce cardiovascular risk any further" (Simon, 1988, p. 3).

The importance of regular, systematic aerobic exercise in keeping the cardiovascular system healthy for people of all ages cannot be overemphasized. Even preschoolers have been shown to receive cardiovascular benefits from planned exercise (Alpert et al., 1990). At the other end of the age spectrum, regular, planned exercise yields dramatic increases in muscle and bone strength. Older exercisers between the ages of 87 and 96 who were on a weight-lifting program for only 2 months showed the same absolute gains in rate of muscular strength as younger people (Allison, 1991). Strenuous workouts would not transform a George Burns into an Arnold Schwarzenegger, but significant increases in muscle strength have been recorded even in older exercisers pushing 100.

A large, recent study on the health benefits of physical fitness is compelling enough to convince couch potatoes of all ages to get up and get moving. Steven Blair and colleagues (1989) studied 13,344 men and women of different age groups, 20 years and older. The subjects were tested for physical fitness and then

A regular exercise program is essential for maintaining good health.

assigned to one of five physical fitness levels based on age, sex, and performance on a treadmill test. Follow-up continued for a little over 8 years, and during that time 283 subjects (240 men and 43 women) had died. The researchers found that the number of deaths from all causes for both men and women was significantly related to fitness level.

But there is some encouraging news from this large study. We do not need to become marathon runners or spend several hours a day sweating and grunting in a fitness center in order to enjoy the maximum benefits of health and longevity. Even a daily brisk walk of 30 minutes or more yields the fitness standard associated with a much lower death rate.

Researchers Lynn McCutcheon and Karen Hassani (1981) matched 74 male and 32 female runners for sex, age, and stress scores on the Social Readjustment Rating Scale with the same number of nonrunners. The researchers found that running increases resistance to illness, but that "part of the immunizing effect of running is psychological" (p. 151). And while men of different ages reaped similar health benefits from running, older women derived greater health benefits than their younger counterparts. Other researchers also report that exercise helps combat the effects of stress and lowers illness.

According to Brown (1991), "People who are physically fit are less vulnerable to the adverse effects of life stress than are those who are less fit" (p. 560). In a study of 137 stressed, male business executives, Kobasa and her colleagues (1982) found that those who exercised had lower rates of illness. The more stress the men suffered, the more important exercise was in the prevention of illness.

In case you are not yet convinced, consider the following benefits of exercise:

- Increases the efficiency of the heart, enabling it to pump more blood with each beat; reduces the resting pulse rate and improves circulation.
- Raises HDL (the good cholesterol) levels, which (1) helps rid the body of LDL (the bad cholesterol) and (2) removes plaque buildup on artery walls.
- Burns up extra calories, enabling you to lose or maintain your weight.
- Makes bones denser and stronger, helping to prevent osteoporosis in women.
- Moderates the effects of stress.
- Gives you more energy and increases your resistance to fatigue.
- Benefits the immune system by increasing natural killer cell activity (Fiatarone et al., 1988).

Memory Check 13.5

1. Which of these is the most important factor leading to disease and death?

   a. environmental hazards   c. unhealthy life-style
   b. a poor health-care system   d. genetic disorders

2. Which of these health-compromising behaviors is responsible for the most deaths each year?

   a. overeating   c. lack of exercise
   b. smoking   d. excessive alcohol use

3. (Alcohol, Smoking) damages virtually every organ in the body.

4. Serum-cholesterol levels are raised by dietary cholesterol and (saturated, unsaturated) fat.

5. In order for aerobic exercise to improve cardiovascular fitness, it should be done 20–30 minutes (daily, 3–4 times a week).

Answers: 1. c 2. b 3. Alcohol 4. saturated 5. 3–4 times a week

Understanding Body Weight: Why We Weigh What We Weigh

Pencil-thin models seen in television commercials and fashion magazines have come to represent the ideal body for many American women. But most of these models have only 10- to 15-percent body fat, far below the 22 to 26 percent considered normal for women (Brownell, 1991). Fat has become a negative term, even though some body fat is necessary. Men need 3 percent and women, 12 percent, just for survival. And in order for a woman's reproductive system to function properly, she must maintain 20 percent body fat.

Extremes in either fatness or thinness can pose health risks. An abnormal desire for thinness can result in eating disorders such as the self-starvation in anorexia nervosa, and the pattern of binging and purging found in bulimia nervosa (Lundholm & Littrell, 1986). At the other extreme are the 34 million Americans suffering from obesity with its increased risk of high blood pressure, coronary heart disease, stroke, and cancer (Whelan & Stare, 1990). The term **obesity** means excessive fatness and is applied to men whose body fat exceeds 20 percent and to women whose body fat exceeds 30 percent of their weight (S. R. Williams, 1986).

obesity (o-BEE-sih-tee): Excessive fatness; a term applied to men whose body fat exceeds 20 percent of their weight and to women whose body fat exceeds 30 percent of their weight.

Variations in Body Weight: What Causes Them?

Question: What are some factors that account for variations in body weight?

Although excessive thinness and obesity both result from a long-term imbalance between energy intake and energy expenditure, the cause is not necessarily insufficient or excessive food intake. Obesity is usually caused by a combination of factors that include heredity, metabolic rate, activity level, number of fat cells, and eating habits.

The Role of Genetic Factors in Body Weight   Adoption and twin studies reveal the strong influence of genes on body size. Genes are particularly likely to be involved when obesity begins before age 10 (Price, Stunkard, et al., 1990). Across all weight classes, from very thin to very fat, children adopted from birth tend to resemble their biological parents more than their adoptive parents in body size (Price, Cadoret, et al., 1987; Stunkard, Harris, et al., 1990). In adoptees, thinness seems to be even more influenced by genes than is obesity (Costanzo & Schiffman, 1989). Also, people may inherit their resting metabolic rate, their tendency to store surplus calories primarily as muscle or fat, and even the pattern of where fat is deposited (Bouchard et al., 1990). But these findings do not mean that childhood eating patterns are not important. There is considerable evidence to suggest that "childhood eating behavior influences whether the inherited tendency towards obesity is realized" (Sims, 1990, p. 1522).

Metabolic Rate: Burning Energy—Slow or Fast   The term "metabolism" refers to all the physical and chemical processes that are carried out in the body to sustain life. Food is the source of energy required to carry out these processes. The rate at which the body burns calories to produce energy is called the **metabolic rate**. Physical activity accounts for only about one-third of our energy use; the other two-thirds is consumed by the maintenance processes that keep us alive. When there is an imbalance between energy input (how much we eat) and output (how much energy we use), our weight changes. If our calorie intake exceeds our daily energy requirement, we gain weight. If our daily energy requirement exceeds our caloric intake, we lose weight.

Fat-Cell Theory: Tiny Storage Tanks for Fat   Fat-cell theory proposes that fatness is related to the number of **fat cells** in the body. It is estimated that we have between 30 and 40 billion fat cells (adipose cells) and that the number is determined by both our genes and our eating habits (Bennett & Gurin, 1982; Grinker, 1982). Fat cells serve as storehouses for liquefied fat. When we lose weight, we do not lose the fat cells themselves. We lose the fat that is stored in them, and the cells simply shrink (Dietz, 1989).

Researchers once believed that early eating habits had a tremendous influence on weight in adulthood, and that all the fat cells a person would ever have were formed early in life. This is no longer the accepted view. Judith Rodin maintains that when people overeat beyond the point at which the fat cells reach their capacity, the number of fat cells continues to increase (Rodin & Wing, 1988).

Question: How does set point affect body weight?

Set-Point Theory: Thin/Fat Thermostat   Set-point theory suggests that humans and other mammals are genetically programmed to carry a certain amount of body weight (Keesey, 1988). **Set point** is affected by the number of fat cells in the body and by metabolic rate, both of which are influenced by the genes (Gurin, 1989). Yet people with a genetic propensity to be thin can become very

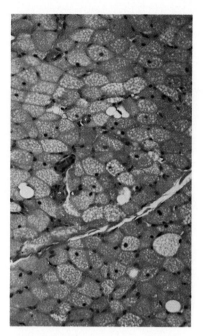

These fat cells, magnified many times, may be the result of overeating.

metabolic rate (meh-tuh-BALL-ik): The rate at which the body burns calories to produce energy.

fat cells: Numbering 30 to 40 billion, cells that serve as storehouses for liquefied fat in the body; with weight loss, they decrease in size but not in number.

set point: The weight the body normally maintains when one is trying neither to gain or lose weight (if weight falls below the normal level, appetite increases and metabolic rate decreases; if weight is gained, appetite decreases and metabolic rate increases so that the original weight is restored).

fat indeed if they continually overeat, because over the years they will develop a high set point for body fat.

According to set-point theory, an internal homeostatic system functions to maintain set-point weight, much like a thermostat works to keep temperature near the point at which it is set. Whether we are lean, fat, or average, when our weight falls below our set point, our appetite increases. When our weight climbs above our set point, our appetite decreases so as to restore the original weight.

The theory also holds that our rate of energy expenditure is adjusted to maintain the body's set-point weight (Keesey & Powley, 1986). When people gain weight, metabolic rate increases (Dietz, 1989). But when they restrict calories to lose weight, the metabolic rate lowers, causing the body to burn fewer calories and thus make further weight loss more difficult. Increasing the amount of physical activity is the one method recommended for lowering the set point so that the body will store less fat.

Dieting: A National Obsession

At any given time, one out of five adults in the United States is on some kind of reducing diet, but 51 percent of women and 43 percent of men perceive themselves as overweight (Gallup & Newport, 1990b). Most diets do produce an initial weight loss—but not once and for all. In fact, 95 percent of those who diet do not maintain the weight loss (S. R. Williams, 1986).

Question: Why is it almost impossible to maintain weight loss by cutting calories alone?

Why Diets Don't Work   To lose weight, a person must decrease calorie intake, increase exercise, or do both. Unfortunately, most people who are trying to lose weight focus only on cutting calories. At first, when overweight people begin to diet and cut their calories, they do lose weight, and fairly quickly if they are on a starvation diet. But as the calorie restriction continues, the rate of weight loss begins to decrease. After an initial shedding of pounds, the dieter's metabolic rate slows down as if to conserve the remaining fat store because fewer calories are being consumed (Weigle et al., 1988).

Then how are overweight people to succeed in reaching their desired weight? A reasonable calorie restriction must be coupled with increased exercise and activity to counteract the body's tendency toward a lower metabolic rate when fewer calories are consumed. Starvation diets are self-defeating in the long run. When calories are too severely restricted, even exercise cannot reverse the body's drastic lowering of metabolism and the natural tendency to conserve remaining fat (Ballor et al., 1990). For this reason, women should consume at least 1,000 calories a day, and men 1,500 calories a day, unless they are under a doctor's supervision.

Some encouraging news for overweight exercisers is that the more they weigh, the more calories they burn during exercise compared to a thinner person. And exercise does not increase the appetite. Sometimes exercise alone, without a restriction in diet, can result in weight loss (Frey-Hewitt et al., 1990).

Yo-Yo Dieting   Many dieters go through repeated cycles of weight gain and loss, a phenomenon called weight cycling or yo-yo dieting (Brownell, 1988). Some experts suggest that with frequent dieting the body becomes an increasingly efficient energy conserver, causing the person to gain weight more quickly and lose weight more slowly with each succeeding weight cycle (Archambault et al., 1989; Brownell et al., 1986).

Research shows that the eating habits and body weight of identical twins are amazingly similar, indicating that genetics exerts a significant influence on one's weight.

Changing Eating Habits: A Long-Term Solution   Dieting is not a long-term solution to the problem of being overweight. Many people believe that once the weight is lost, the diet is no longer necessary and old eating habits can be resumed. But because the old habits caused much of the weight problem, returning to those habits is a sure-fire formula for weight gain. It is rather like compulsive spenders who have their credit cards taken away until their bills are paid. If they resume their old spending habits, the bills will pile up again.

Evidence is accumulating to suggest that successful weight loss involves more than simply counting calories. It seems that calories eaten in the form of fat are more likely to be stored as body fat than calories eaten as carbohydrates. Miller and others (1990) found that even when obese and thin people consume the same amount of food, thin subjects consume about 29 percent of their diet in fats while the diets of the obese are 35 percent fat. The researchers believe that the composition of the diet may have as much to do with gaining weight as the amount of food eaten and the lack of exercise. Counting and limiting the grams of fat may be more beneficial than counting calories to achieve and maintain a desirable body weight. Low-fat diets are healthier, too!

Fortunately, Americans are becoming more health conscious. Millions of people are developing healthier eating habits. Dangerous drug use is declining overall among the young, and fewer people are smoking now than in decades past. Joggers are commonplace, and people everywhere are becoming more interested in physical fitness. All these trends will add up to a healthier nation. The most important point to keep in mind is that we are largely responsible for our own health. Let us aim not simply for the absence of illness, but for a high state of wellness.

Memory Check 13.6

1. Adopted children are more likely to be very thin or obese if their (biological, adoptive) parents are very thin or obese.

2. The (metabolic rate, set point) is the rate at which your body burns calories.

3. Fat cells never decrease in number. (true/false)

4. According to set-point theory, the body works to (increase, decrease, maintain) body weight.

5. Increased exercise during dieting is important to counteract the body's tendency to:

   a. increase the fat in the fat cells
   b. increase the number of fat cells
   c. lower its metabolic rate
   d. raise its metabolic rate

Answers: 1. biological 2. metabolic rate 3. true 4. maintain 5. c

Thinking Critically —————————————————

Evaluation

Using what you have learned about body weight and dieting, select any well-known weight-loss plan (for example, Weight Watchers, Jenny Craig, Slim Fast) and evaluate it, explaining why it is or is not an effective way to lose weight and keep it off.

Point/Counterpoint

Prepare two arguments, one supporting the position that alcoholism is a genetically inherited disease, and the other supporting the position that alcoholism is not a medical disease but results from learning.

Psychology in Your Life

Choose several stress-producing incidents from your own life and explain what problem-focused and emotion-focused coping strategies you used. From the knowledge you have gained in this chapter, list other coping strategies that might have been more effective.

Chapter Summary and Review —————————————————

Theories of Stress

What is the general adaptation syndrome?

The general adaptation syndrome is the predictable sequence of reactions that organisms show in response to stressors consisting of the alarm stage, the resistance stage, and the exhaustion stage.

What is the role of primary and secondary appraisal when people are confronted with a potentially stressful event?

Lazarus maintains that when we are confronted with a potentially stressful event, we engage in a cognitive appraisal process consisting of (1) a primary appraisal, to evaluate the relevance of the event to our well-being (whether it is positive, irrelevant, or involves harm or loss, threat, or challenge), and (2) a secondary appraisal to determine how we will cope with the stressor.

What is the difference between problem-focused and emotion-focused coping?

Problem-focused coping is a response aimed at reducing, modifying, or eliminating the source of stress; emotion-focused coping is aimed at reducing the emotional distress caused by the stressor.

Key Terms

biopsychosocial model (p. 438)
health psychology (p. 438)
stress (p. 438)
stressor (p. 440)
general adaptation syndrome (GAS) (p. 440)
alarm stage (p. 440)
resistance stage (p. 441)

exhaustion stage (p. 441)
primary appraisal (p. 442)
secondary appraisal (p. 442)
problem-focused coping (p. 444)
emotion-focused coping (p. 444)

Sources of Stress: The Common and the Extreme

How do approach-approach, avoidance-avoidance, and approach-avoidance conflicts differ?

In an approach-approach conflict, we must decide between equally desirable alternatives; in an avoidance-avoidance conflict, between two undesirable alternatives. In an approach-avoidance conflict, we are both drawn to and repelled by a choice.

How do people typically react to catastrophic events?

Victims of catastrophic events are initially dazed and stunned. When they begin to recover from the shock, they typically experience anxiety, nightmares, and a compulsive need to retell the event over and over.

What is posttraumatic stress disorder?

Posttraumatic stress disorder (PTSD) is a prolonged, severe stress reaction to a catastrophic event; the victim relives the trauma in flashbacks, nightmares, or intrusive memories.

Key Terms

approach-approach conflict (p. 445)
avoidance-avoidance conflict (p. 445)
approach-avoidance conflict (p. 445)
posttraumatic stress disorder (PTSD) (p. 447)

Evaluating Life Stress: Major Life Changes, Hassles, and Uplifts

What was the Social Readjustment Rating Scale designed to reveal?

The Social Readjustment Rating Scale assesses stress in terms of life events that necessitate life change. Holmes and Rahe found a relationship between degree of life stress (as measured on the scale) and major health problems.

What roles do hassles and uplifts play in the stress of life, according to Lazarus?

According to Lazarus, daily hassles typically cause more stress than major life changes. The positive experiences in life—the uplifts,—can neutralize the effects of many of the hassles.

What are some techniques for managing stress?

Several techniques for managing stress are progressive relaxation, meditation, stress-inoculation training, regular exercise, making time for enjoyable activities and laughter, and having a healthy life-style.

Key Terms

Social Readjustment Rating Scale (SRRS) (p. 448)
hassles (p. 450)
uplifts (p. 451)

Health and Disease

What are the Type A and Type B Behavior Patterns?

Type A Behavior Pattern, often cited as a risk factor for coronary heart disease, is characterized by a sense of time urgency, impatience, excessive competitive drive, hostility, and easily aroused anger. The Type B Behavior Pattern is characterized by a relaxed, easygoing manner.

What personal factors are associated with health and resistance to stress?

Personal factors related to health and resistance to stress are psychological hardiness and social support.

Key Terms

Type A Behavior Pattern (p. 456)
Type B Behavior Pattern (p. 456)
hardiness (p. 461)

Your Life-style and Your Health

What constitutes an unhealthy life-style, and how serious a factor is it in illness and disease?

Slightly over 50 percent of all deaths in this country can be attributed to an unhealthy life-style, which includes smoking, overeating, an unhealthy diet, too much coffee and alcohol, drug abuse, and/or too little exercise and rest.

Why is smoking considered the single most preventable cause of death?

Smoking is considered the single most preventable cause of death because it is directly related to 390,000 deaths each year, including deaths from heart disease, cancer, lung disease, and stroke.

What are some health risks of alcohol consumption?

Alcohol damages virtually every organ in the body, including the liver, stomach, skeletal muscles, heart, and brain, and is involved in over 50 percent of motor vehicle accidents.

How much dietary fat and cholesterol is recommended daily?

The average person should eat a diet consisting of no more than 300 milligrams of cholesterol and no more than 30 percent dietary fat—one-third each of saturated, polyunsaturated, and monounsaturated fat.

What are some benefits of regular aerobic exercise?

Regular aerobic exercise reduces the risk of cardiovascular disease, increases muscular strength, moderates the effects of stress, makes bones denser and stronger, and helps maintain a desirable weight.

Key Terms

cholesterol (p. 465)
saturated fat (p. 465)
aerobic exercise (p. 466)

Understanding Body Weight: Why We Weigh What We Weigh

What are some factors that account for variations in body weight?

Variations in body weight are influenced by heredity, metabolic rate, activity level, number of fat cells, and eating habits.

How does set point affect body weight?

Set-point theory suggests an internal homeostatic system that functions to maintain body weight by adjusting appetite and metabolic rate.

Why is it almost impossible to maintain weight loss by cutting calories alone?

It is almost impossible to maintain weight loss by cutting calories alone because the dieter's metabolic rate slows down to compensate for the lower intake of calories. Exercise both prevents the lowering of metabolic rate and burns up additional calories.

Key Terms

obesity (p. 468)
metabolic rate (p. 469)
fat cells (p. 469)
set point (p. 469)

14

Abnormal Behavior

It was early in January, and Sybil Dorsett was working with other students in the chemistry lab at Columbia University in New York. Suddenly the loud crash of breaking glass made her heart pound and her head throb. The room seemed to be whirling around, and the acrid smell of chemicals filled the air, stinging her nostrils.

That smell—so like the old drugstore back in her native Wisconsin, and the broken glass, like a half-forgotten, far-off memory at home in her dining room when she was a little girl. Again Sybil heard the accusing voice, "You broke it." Frantically she seized her chemistry notes, stuffed them into her brown zipper folder, and ran for the door with all eyes in astonishment—those of the professor and the other students following her.

Sybil ran down the long, dark hall on the third floor of the chemistry building, pushed the elevator button, and waited. Seconds seemed like hours.

The next thought that entered Sybil's awareness was that of clutching for her brown folder, but it was gone. Gone, too, were the elevator she was waiting for and the long, dark hallway. She found herself walking down a dark, deserted street in a strange city. An icy wind whipped her face, and thick snowflakes filled the air. This wasn't New York. Where could she be? And how could she have gotten here in the few seconds between waiting for the elevator and now? Sybil walked on, bewildered, and finally came to a newsstand, where she bought a local paper. She was in Philadelphia. The date on the newspaper told her that five days had passed since she stood waiting for the elevator. Where had she been? What had she done?

A victim of sadistic physical abuse since early childhood, Sybil had experienced blackouts—missing days, weeks, and even longer periods, which seemed to have been taken from her life. Unknown to Sybil, other, very different personalities emerged during those periods to take control of her mind and body. Sixteen separate selves, 14 female and 2 male, lived within Sybil, each with different talents and abilities, emotions, ways of speaking and acting, moral values, and ambitions.

After many years of working with a talented psychiatrist, Sybil's 16 personalities were integrated into one. At last she was herself alone. (Adapted from Schreiber, 1973.)

WHAT YOU HAVE JUST READ is not fiction. These and even stranger experiences are part of the real-life story of Sybil Isabel Dorsett, who suffered from an unusual psychological disorder known as multiple personality. Her life story, told in the book *Sybil*, and the life story of Chris Sizemore, told in the famous *Three Faces of Eve*, are two of the best-known cases of multiple personality disorder.

How can we know whether *our* behavior is normal or abnormal? At what point do our fears, thoughts, mood changes, and actions move from normal to mentally disturbed? This chapter explores many mental disorders, their symptoms and possible causes. But first let us ask the obvious question: What is abnormal?

What Is Abnormal?

Question: What criteria might be used to differentiate normal from abnormal behavior?

Because Sybil's case is such an extreme example, virtually everyone would agree that her behavior is abnormal. But most abnormal behavior is not so extreme and clear-cut. There are not two clearly separate and distinct kinds of human beings, one kind always mentally healthy and well adjusted, and another kind always abnormal and mentally disturbed. Behavior lies along a continuum, with most of us fairly well adjusted and experiencing only occasional maladaptive thoughts or behavior. At one extreme end of the continuum are the unusually mentally healthy; at the other extreme end are the seriously disturbed, like Sybil.

But where along the continuum does behavior become abnormal? There are several questions we might ask in determining what behavior is abnormal.

Is the behavior considered strange within the person's own culture?   Among the diverse cultures around the world, what is considered normal and abnormal in one culture would not necessarily be considered so in another. The culture generally defines what behaviors are acceptable. Even within the same culture, conceptions about what is normal can change from time to time.

Does the behavior cause personal distress?   When people experience considerable emotional distress without any life experience that warrants it, they may be diagnosed as having a psychological or mental disorder. Some people may be sad and depressed, some anxious, others agitated or excited, and still others frightened, or even terrified by delusions and hallucinations. But not all persons with psychological disorders feel distress. Some feel perfectly comfortable, even happy with the way they are and the way they feel.

Is the behavior maladaptive?   A number of experts believe that the best way to differentiate between normal and abnormal behavior is to consider whether the behavior is adaptive or maladaptive, that is, whether it leads to healthy or impaired functioning. Maladaptive behavior interferes with the quality of people's lives and can cause a great deal of distress to family members, friends, and co-workers.

Is the person a danger to self or others?   Another consideration is whether people are a threat or danger to themselves or others. In order to be committed to a mental institution, a person has to be judged both mentally ill and a danger to self or others.

Is the person legally responsible for his or her acts?   Often the term insanity is used to label those who behave abnormally. Insanity is a legal term used by the courts to declare people not legally responsible for their acts. The term insanity, however, is not used by mental health professionals. In a sanity hearing, mass murderer Jeffrey Dahmer was ruled legally responsible for his acts, yet his behavior was clearly abnormal.

Behavior that is labeled abnormal in one culture might be considered completely normal in another.

Perspectives on the Causes and Treatment of Abnormal Behavior

Question: What are five current perspectives that attempt to explain the causes of abnormal behavior?

There are several different perspectives on abnormal behavior that attempt to explain its causes and to recommend the best methods of treatment. The earliest explanation of abnormal behavior was that disturbed people were possessed by evil spirits or demons. The five current perspectives are the biological, psychodynamic, learning, cognitive, and humanistic perspectives.

The Biological Perspective   The biological perspective views abnormal behavior as a symptom of an underlying physical disorder. Just as doctors look for an organic cause of physical illness, those who hold the biological view believe that mental disorders have a physical cause such as genetic inheritance, biochemical abnormalities or imbalances, structural abnormalities within the brain, and/or infection. Consequently those holding the biological view generally favor biological treatments, which may include drugs, electroconvulsive treatment, or psychosurgery.

There are two points to keep in mind as you read this chapter. First, even when there is strong evidence of a genetic factor in a mental disorder, people do not inherit the disorder directly. They inherit a predisposition toward the disorder. Whether they actually develop the disorder will depend on other conditions in their lives. Second, when certain structural or biochemical abnormalities are associated with a mental disorder, there is the possibility that such abnormalities could be the result rather than the cause of the disorder.

The Psychodynamic Perspective   Where does the psychodynamic perspective look for the cause of abnormal behavior? Originally proposed by Freud, the psychodynamic perspective maintains that the cause of abnormal behavior lies in early childhood experiences and in unresolved, unconscious conflicts, usually of a sexual or aggressive nature. The cause assumed by the psychodynamic approach also suggests the cure—psychoanalysis—which, remember, was developed by Freud to uncover and resolve such unconscious conflicts.

The Learning Perspective   According to the learning perspective, abnormal behaviors are not symptoms of an underlying disorder, but the behavioral symptoms are themselves the disorder. Get rid of the symptoms (the abnormal behavior), and the problem is solved. Many abnormal behaviors are thought to be learned and sustained in the same way as any other behavior. According to this view, people who exhibit abnormal behavior are either victims of faulty learning or they have failed to learn appropriate patterns of thinking and acting. Advocates of the learning perspective assume that much abnormal behavior can be treated by using learning principles to eliminate the distressing behavior and to establish new, more appropriate behavior in its place.

The Cognitive Perspective   The cognitive perspective suggests that faulty thinking or distorted perceptions can contribute to some types of abnormal behavior. For example, negative thinking is intimately involved in depression and anxiety. Treatment consistent with this perspective is aimed at changing thinking and perceptions, which presumably will lead to a change in behavior.

The Humanistic Perspective   The humanistic perspective views human nature as inherently good and rational, and naturally moving toward self-actualization (the fulfillment of one's potential). According to this view, abnormal behavior results when a person's natural tendency toward self-actualization is blocked (Rogers, 1961; Maslow, 1970). Remove the psychological blocks, and the person can move toward self-actualization. Table 14.1 summarizes the perspectives on abnormality.

Which of these perspectives is correct? There are many mental disorders with a variety of causes, and none of these theories has tried to explain them all. Each view suggests an emphasis on different methods of treatment, all of which have been shown to work in some cases with some disorders. In fact, many of these methods are combined in practice. Each perspective has its place in the description, analysis, and treatment of certain mental disorders.

Although mental health professionals often disagree about the causes of abnormal behavior and the best treatments, there is less disagreement about diagnosis. A standard set of criteria has been established and is used by the majority of mental health professionals to diagnose mental disorders.

Table 14.1   Perspectives on Abnormality

Perspective	Cause of Abnormal Behavior	Treatment
Biological perspective	Abnormal behavior is a symptom of an underlying physical disorder caused by a structural or biochemical abnormality in the brain, by genetic inheritance, or by infection.	Diagnose and treat like any other physical disorder. Drugs, ECT, or psychosurgery
Psychodynamic perspective	Unconscious sexual or aggressive conflicts; imbalance among id, ego, and superego.	Bring disturbing repressed material to consciousness and work through unconscious conflicts. Psychoanalysis
Learning perspective	Abnormal behavior is learned and sustained like any other behavior.	Use of classical and operant conditioning and modeling to extinguish abnormal behaviors and to increase adaptive behavior. Behavior therapy, behavior modification
Cognitive perspective	Faulty and negative thinking can cause depression and anxiety.	Change faulty, irrational, and/or negative thinking. Beck's cognitive therapy, rational-emotive therapy
Humanistic perspective	Blocking of normal tendency toward self-actualization.	Increase self-acceptance and self-understanding; become more inner-directed. Client-centered therapy, Gestalt therapy

Defining and Classifying Mental Disorders

Question: What is the DSM-III-R?

In 1952 the American Psychiatric Association (APA) published a manual providing a diagnostic system for describing and classifying mental or psychological disorders. Over the years the manual has been revised several times. In 1987 the APA published its most recent edition—the *Diagnostic and Statistical Manual of Mental Disorders (Third Edition-Revised)*, commonly referred to as the **DSM-III-R**. The manual consists of descriptions of about 235 specific mental disorders, and it lists criteria that must be met in order to make a particular diagnosis. The *DSM-III-R* is the most widely accepted diagnostic system in the United States and is used by researchers, therapists, mental health workers, and most insurance companies. It enables a diverse group of mental health professionals to speak the same language when diagnosing, treating, researching, and conversing about a variety of mental disorders. Table 14.2 summarizes the major categories of mental disorders in the *DSM-III-R*.

You have probably heard the terms *neurotic* and *psychotic* used in relation to mental disturbances. Prior to 1980 the American Psychiatric Association grouped psychological disorders into two broad, general categories labeled neuroses and psychoses (plurals of neurosis and psychosis). Although now obsolete, the term **neurosis** was applied to disorders that cause people considerable personal distress and some impairment in functioning, without causing them to lose contact with reality or to violate important social norms.

DSM-III-R: The American Psychiatric Association's *Diagnostic and Statistical Manual of Mental Disorders, Third Edition-Revised*, which describes over 235 mental disorders and the symptoms that must be present for making a diagnosis.

neurosis (new-RO-sis): An obsolete term for a disorder causing personal distress and some impairment in functioning but not causing one to lose contact with reality or to violate important social norms.

Table 14.2   Major DSM-III-R Categories of Mental Disorders

Disorder	Symptoms	Examples
Anxiety disorders	Disorders characterized by anxiety and avoidance behavior.	Panic disorder Social phobia Obsessive compulsive disorder Post-traumatic stress disorder
Somatoform disorders	Disorders in which physical symptoms are present that are psychological in origin rather than due to physical causes.	Hypochondriasis Somatoform pain disorder Conversion disorder
Dissociative disorders	Disorders in which stress or conflict is handled by forgetting important personal information or one's whole identity, or by compartmentalizing the trauma or conflict into a split-off alter personality.	Psychogenic amnesia Psychogenic fugue Multiple personality disorder
Schizophrenia	Disorder characterized by loss of contact with reality; hallucinations, delusions, and/or disordered thought; inappropriate or flat affect; social withdrawal and bizarre behavior.	Disorganized Catatonic Paranoid Undifferentiated
Delusional (paranoid) disorders	Disorders characterized by delusions that are more believable and logical than those of schizophrenia.	Jealous type Persecutory type Grandiose type
Mood disorders	Disorders characterized by periods of extreme depression or mania or both.	Major depression Bipolar disorder
Personality disorders	Disorders characterized by long-standing, inflexible, maladaptive patterns of behavior beginning early in life and causing personal distress or problems in social and occupational functioning.	Antisocial Histrionic Narcissistic Passive aggressive Compulsive
Sexual disorders	Disorders including sexual dysfunctions (impaired sexual performance due to psychological causes) or paraphilias (sexual urges and fantasies involving unusual or bizarre images, conditions, objects, or acts).	Sexual desire disorders Orgasm disorders Fetishism Sexual masochism Voyeurism
Organic mental disorders	Disorders in which impairment of cognitive or behavioral functioning is due to temporary or permanent brain dysfunction.	Dementias Psychoactive-substance-induced organic mental disorder
Psychoactive substance use disorders	Disorders in which undesirable behavioral changes result from the abuse or dependence on drugs affecting the central nervous system.	Alcohol abuse Cocaine abuse Cannabis dependence
Disorders usually first evident in infancy, childhood, or adolescence	Include developmental disorders, disruptive behavior disorders, eating disorders, and gender identity disorders.	Conduct disorder Infantile autism Anorexia nervosa Transsexualism
Sleep disorders	Disorders including dyssomnias (disturbance in the amount, quality, or timing of sleep) and parasomnias (abnormal occurrences during sleep).	Hypersomnia disorder Insomnia disorder Sleep terror disorder Sleepwalking disorder

Source: Based on *DSM-III-R* (American Psychiatric Association, 1987).

In contrast, a **psychosis** is a more serious disturbance that greatly impairs the ability to function in everyday life. It can cause people to lose touch with reality, possibly suffer from delusions and hallucinations, and sometimes requires hospitalization. The term psychosis is still used by mental health professionals.

Memory Check 14.1

1. It is relatively easy to differentiate normal behavior from abnormal behavior. (true/false)

2. Match the perspective with its suggested cause of abnormal behavior.

   _____ 1) faulty learning
   _____ 2) unconscious, unresolved conflicts
   _____ 3) blocking the natural tendency to-
            ward self-actualization
   _____ 4) genetic inheritance, biochemical or
            structural abnormalities in the brain
   _____ 5) faulty thinking

   a. psychodynamic
   b. biological
   c. learning
   d. humanistic
   e. cognitive

3. The *DSM-III-R* is a manual published by the American Psychiatric Association and is used to (diagnose, treat) mental disorders.

Answers: 1. false 2. 1) c 2) a 3) d 4) b 5) e 3. diagnose

Anxiety, Somatoform, and Dissociative Disorders

Anxiety Disorders: When Anxiety Is Extreme

Question: When is anxiety normal, and when is it abnormal?

The most commonly occurring group of mental disorders in the general population are the **anxiety disorders**. **Anxiety** is a vague, general uneasiness or feeling that something bad is about to happen. Anxiety may be associated with a particular situation or object, or it may be free floating—not associated with anything specific. None of us are strangers to anxiety. We have all felt it.

Some anxiety is normal and appropriate. Imagine driving on a highway late at night when you notice that your gas tank is on empty. A wave of anxiety sweeps over you, and you immediately begin to look for a service station. You are feeling normal anxiety—a response to a real danger or threat. Normal anxiety prompts us to take useful action and is therefore healthy. But anxiety serves no useful purpose and is abnormal if it is all out of proportion to the seriousness of the situation, if it does not soon fade when the danger is past, or if it occurs in the absence of real danger (Goodwin, 1986). You can assess your anxiety level in the *Try It!* on page 482.

Some of the psychological disorders characterized by severe anxiety are generalized anxiety disorder, panic disorder, phobic disorder, and obsessive compulsive disorder.

psychosis (sy-CO-sis): A severe mental disorder, sometimes requiring hospitalization, in which one typically loses contact with reality, may suffer delusions and hallucinations, and whose ability to function in everyday life is seriously impaired.

anxiety: A generalized feeling of apprehension, fear, or tension that may be associated with a particular object or situation or may be free-floating, not associated with anything specific.

anxiety disorders: Disorders characterized by severe anxiety (examples: panic disorder, phobic disorders, general anxiety disorder, obsessive compulsive disorder).

The Burns Anxiety Inventory

Instructions: The symptoms of anxiety can be divided into those affecting feelings, thoughts and the body. To find out the level of your anxiety, put a check (√) in the space to the right that best describes how much that symptom or problem has bothered you during the last week. You can add up your score and interpret it according to the scale at the end. If you are troubled by anxiety, Dr. Burns suggests you might consider seeking professional help in coping with it.

	0 Not at all	1 Somewhat	2 Moderately	3 A lot
Category I: Anxious Feelings				
1. Anxiety, nervousness, worry or fear				
2. Feeling that things around you are strange, unreal or foggy	0			
3. Feeling detached from all or part of your body		1		
4. Sudden, unexpected panic spells		1		
5. Apprehension or a sense of impending doom		1		
6. Feeling tense, stressed, "uptight" or on edge				
Category II: Anxious Thoughts				
7. Difficulty concentrating				
8. Racing thoughts or having your mind jump from one thing to the next	0	1		
9. Frightening fantasies or daydreams		1		
10. Feeling that you're on the verge of losing control				
11. Fears of cracking up or going crazy	0			
12. Fears of fainting or passing out	0			
13. Fears of physical illness or heart attacks or dying				
14. Concerns about looking foolish or inadequate in front of others		1		
15. Fears of being alone, isolated or abandoned		1		
16. Fears of criticism or disapproval				
17. Fears that something terrible is about to happen				
Category III: Physical Symptoms				
18. Skipping or racing or pounding of the heart (sometimes called palpitations)	0			
19. Pain, pressure or tightness in the chest	0			
20. Tingling or numbness in the toes or fingers		1		
21. Butterflies or discomfort in the stomach		1		
22. Constipation or diarrhea				
23. Restlessness or jumpiness				
24. Tight, tense muscles		1		
25. Sweating not brought about by the heat				
26. A lump in the throat				
27. Trembling or shaking	0			
28. Rubbery or "jelly" legs	0			
29. Feeling dizzy, light-headed or off balance				
30. Choking or smothering sensations or difficulty breathing		1		
31. Headaches or pains in the neck or back		1		
32. Hot flashes or cold chills				
33. Feeling tired, weak or easily exhausted				

Interpreting your anxiety score:
5 or below: minimal; 6–15: mild; 16–30: moderate: 31–50: severe; over 50: extreme.

Total ____

Generalized Anxiety Disorder Have you known people who were constantly preoccupied with worries that seemed to have no basis in reality? **Generalized anxiety disorder** is the diagnosis given to people who experience excessive or unrealistic anxiety and worry about several areas in their lives. They may be unduly worried about their finances or their own health or the health of family members. They may worry unnecessarily about their performance at work or their ability to function socially. Their excessive anxiety may cause them to feel tense, tired, and irritable, and to have difficulty concentrating and sleeping. Their symptoms may include trembling, palpitations, sweating, dizziness, nausea, diarrhea, or frequent urination. Kendler and others (1992a) estimate the heritability of generalized anxiety disorder to be about 30 percent.

As troubling as these symptoms are, they are mild compared to what people experience in panic disorder.

Question: What are the typical symptoms a person experiences during a panic attack?

Panic Disorder

> Mindy Markowitz is an attractive, stylishly dressed, 25-year-old art director for a trade magazine . . . seeking treatment for "panic attacks" that have occurred with increasing frequency over the past year, often two or three times a day. These attacks begin with a sudden intense wave of "horrible fear" that seems to come out of nowhere, sometimes during the day, sometimes waking her from sleep. She begins to tremble, is nauseated, sweats profusely, feels as though she is gagging, and fears that she will lose control and do something crazy, like run screaming into the street. (Spitzer et al., 1989, p. 154)

Mindy suffers from **panic disorder**, which consists of attacks of overwhelming anxiety, fear, or terror. People commonly report that during panic attacks their heart is pounding, they tremble or shake uncontrollably, and they feel like they are choking or smothering. They may report being afraid that they are going to die or that they are going crazy (Lipschitz, 1988). One estimate puts the number of people in the United States with panic disorder at between 4 million and 10 million, the majority of them women (Fishman & Sheehan, 1985).

The biological perspective sheds some light on panic disorder. PET scans reveal that even in a nonpanic state, many panic-disorder patients show a greatly increased blood flow to parts of the right hemisphere of the limbic system—the part of the brain involved in emotion (Reiman et al., 1984, 1989). Although family and twin studies suggest that genetic factors play a role in panic disorder (Crowe, 1990; Togerson, 1983), there are psychological factors operating in panic disorder as well (McNally, 1990).

Faravelli and Pallanti (1989) found that high life stress, particularly in the form of significant losses or threatening events, may be the precipitating factor in the first panic attack. And once people have had an attack, they may develop extreme anxiety about the possibility that it will happen again (Gorman et al., 1989). Clark (1988) offers a cognitive theory suggesting that panic attacks are associated with a catastrophic misinterpretation of bodily sensations. Roth and others (1992) suggest that when panic-disorder patients know a stressor is coming, their anticipatory anxiety may set the stage for a panic attack.

Panic disorder can have significant social and health consequences. In one major study, a surprising 20 percent of the subjects with panic disorder reported having attempted suicide, compared with 15 percent of subjects suffering from depression (Markowitz et al., 1989; Weissman, Klerman, et al., 1989). In addition, panic-disorder patients are at increased risk for abuse of alcohol and other drugs and are more likely to suffer impaired social and marital functioning.

Question: What are the characteristics of the three categories of phobias?

generalized anxiety disorder: A disorder in which people experience excessive or unrealistic worry and anxiety about several areas in their lives.

panic disorder: An anxiety disorder in which a person experiences unpredictable attacks of overwhelming anxiety, fear, or terror.

phobia (FO-bee-ah):   A persistent, irrational fear of an object, situation, or activity that the person feels compelled to avoid.

agoraphobia (AG-or-uh-FO-bee-uh):   An intense fear of being in a situation where immediate escape is not possible or help is not immediately available in case of incapacitating anxiety.

social phobia: An irrational fear and avoidance of social situations in which people believe they might embarrass or humiliate themselves by appearing clumsy, foolish, or incompetent.

simple phobia: A catchall category for any phobia other than agoraphobia and social phobia.

This woman suffers from agoraphobia and is working with her therapist to overcome her debilitating fear of being in public places.

Phobic Disorders   People suffering from a **phobia** experience a persistent, irrational fear of some specific object, situation, or activity that poses no real danger, or the danger is blown all out of proportion. People realize the fear is irrational, but they nevertheless feel compelled to avoid the feared object or situation. Robins and others (1984) found that about 13.5 percent of the population in the United States will suffer from phobia during their lifetime. There are three classes of phobic disorders—agoraphobia, social phobia, and simple phobia.

Agoraphobia   The phobia most likely to drive people to seek professional help is **agoraphobia**—an intense fear of being in a situation where immediate escape is not possible or where help is not readily available if the person should become overwhelmed by anxiety. In some cases an individual's entire life must be planned around avoiding feared situations such as busy streets, crowded stores, restaurants, or public transportation. An agoraphobic often will not leave home unless accompanied by a friend or family member and, in severe cases, not even then.

Typically agoraphobia has its onset during the early adult years and may begin with repeated panic attacks. The intense fear of having another attack causes the person to avoid any place or situation where previous attacks have occurred. Some researchers believe that agoraphobia is actually an extreme form of panic disorder (Sheehan, 1983; Thyer et al., 1985).

Genetic factors seem to play a role in some cases of agoraphobia. A person is at greater risk of developing the disorder when other family members have it—the closer the relative, the higher the risk (Noyes et al., 1986). Some agoraphobics have been treated successfully with psychotherapy (Marks, 1987, 1988); others have responded well to antidepressants (Mavissakalian, 1990).

Social Phobia   Sufferers of **social phobia** have an irrational fear of situations in which they might embarrass or humiliate themselves in front of others—where they might shake, blush, sweat, or in some other way appear clumsy, foolish, or incompetent. They may fear eating, talking, or writing in front of others, or doing anything else that would cause people to think poorly of them. Can you imagine having a social phobia and being unable to write in front of other people? You could not cash a check, use a credit card, vote, or even take notes in class or take a written exam.

Social phobia affects about 2 percent of the population (Robins et al, 1984). The average age of onset is 15.5 years, and it rarely begins after age 25 (Schneier et al., 1992). Although less debilitating than agoraphobia, social phobia in extreme form can seriously affect people's performance at work, prevent them from advancing in their careers or pursuing an education, and severely restrict their social lives. And often those with social phobia turn to alcohol and tranquilizers to lessen their anxiety in social situations (Kushner et al., 1990; Turner & Beidel, 1989).

Simple Phobia   **Simple phobia** is a catchall category for any phobias other than agoraphobia and social phobia, and this type usually has its onset in childhood or adolescence (Emmelkamp, 1988). The most common phobias in the general population are those of dogs, snakes, insects, and mice, but claustrophobia (fear of closed spaces) and acrophobia (fear of heights) are the simple phobias treated most often by therapists.

People with simple phobias generally fear the same things others fear—thunderstorms, animals, illness, danger, and so on—but their fears are grossly exaggerated (Snaith, 1968). A fear is not considered a phobia unless it causes a great deal of distress or interferes with a person's life in a major way. Phobics experience intense anxiety when they are faced with the object or situation they fear, even to the point of shaking or screaming.

Phobics will go to great lengths to avoid the feared object or situation. Some people with blood-injury phobia will not seek medical care even if it is a matter of life and death (Marks, 1988). Few of us are thrilled at the prospect of visiting the dentist, but some people with a dental phobia will actually let their teeth rot rather than visit one.

Question: What do psychologists believe are some probable causes of phobias?

Causes of Phobias   It is likely that most simple and social phobias result from learning (Eysenck, 1987; Thyer et al., 1985). Frightening experiences, most experts agree, set the stage for phobias, although not all phobics recall the experience producing the phobia. A person with a dog phobia might be able to trace its beginning to a painful dog bite; a fear of heights might date from a frightening fall down a flight of stairs (Beck & Emory, 1985).

Phobias may be acquired, as well, through observational learning. For example, children who hear their parents talk about frightening experiences with the dentist, with bugs or snakes or thunderstorms, may develop similar fears themselves. In many cases phobias are acquired through a combination of conditioning and observational learning (Merckelbach et al., 1989, 1991; Öst, 1991).

Genes appear to play a role in simple phobia (particularly animal phobias), social phobia, and agoraphobia. Heritability estimates range from 30 to 40 percent (Kendler et al., 1990b).

From the psychodynamic perspective, phobias are viewed primarily as a defense against the anxiety experienced when sexual or aggressive impulses threaten to break into consciousness. If the anxiety can be displaced onto a feared object and if that object can be avoided, then there is less chance that the disturbing impulse will break through. For example, a single person who has strong, repressed sexual urges may develop a fear of going out at night as an unconscious defense against acting on these urges.

Question: What is obsessive compulsive disorder?

Obsessive Compulsive Disorder   What is wrong with a person who is endlessly counting, checking, or performing other time-consuming rituals over and over? Why would someone wash his hands 125 times a day until they were raw and bleeding? People with another form of anxiety disorder, **obsessive compulsive disorder** (OCD), suffer from obsessions or compulsions or both.

Obsessions   Have you had a tune or the words of a song run through your mind over and over without being able to stop it? If so, you have experienced obsessive thinking in a mild form. Imagine how miserable you would be if every time you touched something you thought you were being contaminated, or if the thought of stabbing your mother kept popping into your mind. **Obsessions** are persistent, recurring, involuntary thoughts, images, or impulses that invade consciousness and cause great distress.

Common themes of obsessions include contamination and doubt as to whether a certain act was performed (Insel, 1990). People with obsessional doubt may have a persistent fear that they failed to turn off the stove or to put out a cigarette. Other types of obsessions center upon aggression, religion, or sex. One minister reported obsessive thoughts of running naked down the church aisle and shouting obscenities to his congregation.

Do people ever act on their obsessive thoughts? It is not unheard of, but it is extremely rare for people actually to carry out their obsessive thoughts (Marks, 1978b). Yet many people are so horrified by their obsessions that they think they are losing their mind.

obsessive compulsive disorder: An anxiety disorder in which a person suffers from obsessions or compulsions or both.

obsession: A persistent, recurring, involuntary thought, image, or impulse that invades consciousness and causes great distress.

Compulsions   A person who has a **compulsion** feels literally compelled to repeat certain acts over and over or to perform specific rituals repeatedly. The individual knows such acts are irrational and senseless but cannot resist performing them without experiencing an intolerable build-up of anxiety—anxiety that can be relieved only by yielding to the compulsion. Many of us have engaged in compulsive behavior like stepping over cracks on the sidewalk, counting stairsteps, or performing little rituals from time to time. But the behavior becomes a psychological problem only when the person cannot resist performing it, when it is very time-consuming, and when it interferes with the person's normal activities and relationships with others.

Compulsions usually involve cleanliness, counting, checking, or touching objects. Sometimes compulsive acts or rituals resemble magical thinking and must be performed faithfully in order to ward off some danger. People with OCD do not enjoy the time-consuming rituals—the endless counting, checking, hand washing, or cleaning. They realize that their behavior is not normal, but they simply cannot help themselves, as shown in the following example.

> Mike, a 32-year-old patient, performed checking rituals that were preceded by a fear of harming other people. When driving, he had to stop the car often and return to check whether he had run over people, particularly babies. Before flushing the toilet, he had to check to be sure that a live insect had not fallen into the toilet, because he did not want to be responsible for killing a living thing. At home he repeatedly checked to see that the doors, stoves, lights, and windows were shut or turned off. . . . Mike performed these and many other checking rituals for an average of 4 hours a day. (Kozak, Foa, & McCarthy, 1988, p. 88)

Are there many Mikes out there, or is his case unusual? Mike's checking compulsion is quite extreme, but apparently about 2 to 3 percent of the general population (over 4 million people) suffer from obsessive compulsive disorder (Jenike, 1989). We have said that people may have obsessions only or compulsions only, but in about 70 percent of the cases both appear together. When they occur together, the compulsion is most often used to relieve the anxiety caused by the obsession. All age groups with this disorder—children, adolescents, and adults—show strikingly similar thoughts and rituals (Swedo et al., 1989). Table 14.3 shows some common compulsions.

Causes of Obsessive Compulsive Disorder   For many years obsessive compulsives were seen as extremely insecure individuals who viewed the world as threatening and unpredictable. Ritualistic behavior was thought to be their method of imposing some order, structure, and predictability on their world. From the psychodynamic perspective, obsessive compulsive behavior protects individuals from recognizing the real reasons for their anxiety—repressed hostility or unacceptable sexual urges. Thus a person, without knowing quite why, might perform compulsive acts to undo or make amends for unconscious forbidden wishes, such as compulsive handwashing to atone for "dirty thoughts."

Some evidence points to a biological basis for obsessive compulsive disorder in some patients. Several twin and family studies suggest that a genetic factor may be involved (Rasmussen & Eisen, 1990; Turner et al., 1985). PET scans have revealed abnormally high rates of glucose consumption in the left frontal lobes and basal ganglia in OCD patients (Baxter et al., 1987). But the most significant finding seems to be that many OCD patients have an imbalance in levels of the neurotransmitter serotonin (Barr et al., 1992). Such patients are often helped by an antidepressant medication, which restores the balance of the serotonin (Murphy & Pigott, 1990). But because the drug treatment does not work for all OCD patients, some researchers suggest that OCD may have several different causes (Goodman et al., 1989).

compulsion: A persistent, irresistible, irrational urge to perform an act or ritual repeatedly.

Table 14.3

The Percentage of Children and Adolescents with Obsessive Compulsive Disorder Reporting These Common Compulsions

Common Compulsions	Percent Reporting
Excessive or ritualized handwashing, showering, bathing, toothbrushing or grooming	85
Repeating rituals (going in or out of a door, up or down from a chair)	51
Checking (doors, locks, stove, appliances, emergency brake on car, paper route, homework)	46
Rituals to remove contact with contaminants	23
Touching	20
Measures to prevent harm to self or others	16
Ordering or arranging	17
Counting	18
Hoarding or collecting rituals	11
Rituals of cleaning household or inanimate objects	6
Miscellaneous rituals (such as writing, moving, speaking)	26

Source: Rapoport, J. L. (1989, March). The biology of obsessions and compulsions. *Scientific American. 260, p. 84.*

Memory Check 14.2

1. Try your skill at diagnosis. Match the disorder with the example.

_____1) René refuses to eat in front of others for fear his hand will shake.

_____2) Betty has been housebound for 4 years.

_____3) Jackson gets hysterical when a dog approaches him.

_____4) Laura has incapacitating attacks of anxiety that come on her suddenly.

a. panic disorder
b. agoraphobia
c. simple phobia
d. social phobia

2. Persistent, recurring, involuntary thoughts, images, and impulses that invade consciousness and cause great distress are called (obsessions, compulsions).

3. People with obsessive compulsive disorder realize that their compulsions are irrational and senseless. (true/false)

Answers: 1. 1) d 2) b 3) c 4) a 2. obsessions 3. true

Somatoform Disorders: Physical Symptoms with Psychological Causes

Question: What are two somatoform disorders, and what symptoms do they share?

The word *soma* means "body," and the **somatoform disorders** involve complaints of bodily symptoms even though tests show no evidence that anything is physically wrong. Although their symptoms are psychological in origin, patients are sincerely convinced that their symptoms spring from real physical disorders. They are not consciously faking illness to avoid work or other activities. Hypochondriasis and conversion disorder are two types of somatoform disorders.

Hypochondriasis   Patients diagnosed as suffering from **hypochondriasis** are overly concerned about their health. They may have many physical complaints that they fear are a sign of some serious disease, but their complaints are not usually consistent with known physical disorders. And even when a medical examination reveals no physical problem, hypochondriacs are not convinced. They may "doctor shop," going from one physician to another, seeking confirmation of their worst fears. Unfortunately, hypochondriasis is not easily treated, and there is usually a poor chance for recovery.

Conversion Disorder: When Thoughts and Fears Can Paralyze   A man is suddenly struck blind, or an arm, a leg, or some other part of his body becomes paralyzed. Extensive medical tests find nothing wrong—no physical reason that could possibly cause the blindness or the paralysis. How can this be?

A diagnosis of **conversion disorder** is made when there is a loss of functioning in some part of the body not due to a physical cause but solving a psychological problem. A patient may become blind, deaf, unable to speak, or develop a paralysis in some part of the body. Many of Freud's patients suffered from conversion disorder, and he believed they unconsciously developed a physical disability to help resolve an unconscious sexual or aggressive conflict.

Modern-day psychologists think that conversion disorder can act as an unconscious defense against any intolerable anxiety situation that the individual cannot otherwise escape. For example, a soldier who desperately fears going into battle might escape the anxiety by developing a paralysis or some other physically disabling symptom.

You would expect normal persons to show great distress if they suddenly lost their sight or hearing, or became paralyzed. But this is not true of many patients with conversion disorder who seem to exhibit a calm and cool indifference to their symptoms, called "la belle indifference." Furthermore, many seem to enjoy the attention, sympathy, and concern their disability brings them.

Dissociative Disorders: Mental Escapes

Question: What are psychogenic amnesia and psychogenic fugue?

Day in and day out we are consciously aware of who we are, and we are able to recall important events in our lives. Our memories, our identity, and our consciousness are integrated. But some people, in response to unbearable stress, develop a **dissociative disorder** and lose this integration. Their consciousness becomes dissociated from either their identity or their memories of important personal events. Dissociative disorders provide a mental escape from intolerable circumstances. Three types of dissociative disorders are psychogenic amnesia, psychogenic fugue, and multiple personality disorder.

somatoform disorders (so-MAT-uh-form):   Disorders in which physical symptoms are present that are due to psychological rather than physical causes.

hypochondriasis (HI-puh-kahn-DRY-uh-sis):   A somatoform disorder in which persons are preoccupied with their health and convinced they have some serious disorder despite reassurance from doctors to the contrary.

conversion disorder: A somatoform disorder in which a loss of functioning in some part of the body has no physical cause but solves some psychological problem.

dissociative disorders: Disorders in which, under stress, one loses the integration of consciousness, identity, and memories of important personal events.

Psychogenic Amnesia: "Who Am I?" Amnesia is the complete or partial loss of the ability to recall personal information or identify past experiences that cannot be attributed to ordinary forgetfulness. Popular books, movies, and TV shows have used amnesia as a central theme in which, usually after a blow to the head, characters cannot remember who they are or anything about their past. In **psychogenic amnesia**, however, no physical cause such as a blow to the head is present. Rather a traumatic experience—a psychological blow, so to speak—or an unbearable anxiety situation causes the person to escape by "forgetting." Patients with psychogenic amnesia can have a loss of memory about specific periods of their life or a complete loss of memory for their entire identity. For example, if a soldier experienced the very traumatic event of watching his best friend blown apart on the battlefield, he might avoid facing the trauma by developing some form of psychogenic amnesia. Yet such people do not forget everything. They forget only items of personal reference such as their name, their age, and where they live, and they may fail to recognize their parents, other relatives, and friends. But they do not forget how to read and write or solve problems, and their basic personality structure remains intact.

Psychogenic Fugue: "Where did I go and what did I do?" Even more puzzling than psychogenic amnesia is a dissociative disorder known as **psychogenic fugue**. In a fugue state, people not only forget their identity, they also leave the scene physically, travel away from home, and take on a new identity somewhere else. The fugue state may last for hours or days or, more rarely, for months or years. The fugue is usually a reaction to some severe psychological stress such as a natural disaster, a serious family quarrel, a deep personal rejection, or military battle.

For most people, recovery from psychogenic fugue is usually rapid, and a recurrence of either amnesia or fugue is unlikely. But when people recover from the fugue, they have no memory of events that occurred during the episode.

Question: What are some of the identifying symptoms of multiple personality disorder?

Multiple Personality: "How many of us are there?" Multiple personality **disorder** is an unusual disorder in which two or more distinct, unique personalities exist in the same individual, as in the case of Sybil, whom you met earlier. In 50 percent of the cases, there are more than 10 different personalities (Sybil had 16). The change from one personality to another often occurs suddenly and usually during stress (APA, 1987). The host personality is "the one who has executive control of the body the greatest percentage of time" (Kluft, 1984, p. 23). The alternate or alter personalities may differ radically in intelligence, speech, accent, vocabulary, posture, body language, hairstyle, taste in clothes, manners, and even handwriting. And incredibly, within the same individual some of the alter personalities may be male, some female, some left-handed, and some right-handed. In other cases, an alter personality may need different prescription glasses, have specific food allergies, or show different responses to alcohol or medications (Putnam et al., 1986). Many multiples report hearing voices in their head and sometimes the sounds of crying or screaming or laughter. For this reason, such patients have often been misdiagnosed as schizophrenic.

In 80 percent of the cases, the host personality does not know of the alters, but "the alter personalities will possess varying levels of awareness for one another" (Putnam, 1989, p. 114). The host and alter personalities commonly show amnesia for certain periods of time or for important episodes in their life such as their graduation, wedding, or birth of a child. There is the common complaint of "lost time"—periods for which they have no memory because they were not in control of the body.

psychogenic (SY-kuh-JEN-ik): Psychological in origin.

psychogenic amnesia: A dissociative disorder in which there is a loss of memory for limited periods in one's life or for one's entire personal identity.

psychogenic fugue (FEWG): A dissociative disorder in which one has a complete loss of memory for one's entire identity, wanders away from home, and assumes a new identity.

multiple personality disorder: A dissociative disorder in which two or more distinct personalities occur in the same individual, each taking over at different times.

Imagine how strange it would be if you, like Eve White, were a shy, serious, highly moral, nondrinker, and you awakened one morning with a hangover. Eve Black, one of your personalities unknown to you, had been out partying all night and then went "back in," leaving the host personality, Eve White, to suffer the consequences. The real Eve, Chris Sizemore, was not able to integrate the three personalities as suggested by the movie *The Three Faces of Eve*. She returned for many more years of therapy and at last count had exhibited 22 different personalities.

Causes of Multiple Personality Disorder   Multiple personality disorder usually begins in early childhood, but the condition is rarely diagnosed before adolescence (Vincent & Pickering, 1988). About 90 percent of the treated cases have been women (Ross et al., 1989). More than 95 percent of the patients have early histories of severe physical and/or sexual abuse (Putnam et al., 1986; Ross et al., 1990). "The abuse suffered by multiple personality patients tends to be far more sadistic and bizarre than that suffered by most victims of child abuse" (Putnam, 1989, p. 49). Being burned with steam irons or matches, cut with glass or razors, or locked in trunks or closets are not uncommon reports. The splitting off of separate personalities is apparently a way of coping with such intolerable abuse.

But how can we account for the 5 percent of multiple personality patients who were not abused? The psychodynamic perspective suggests that alternate personalities may come forth to express forbidden sexual or aggressive impulses that would be unacceptable to the original personality.

The Incidence of Multiple Personality Disorder   There is no general consensus on the incidence of the disorder. Some clinicians believe that it is extremely rare (Chodoff, 1987), and others believe that it is more common but often misdiagnosed or underdiagnosed (Bliss & Jeppsen, 1985; Coons et al., 1988). A survey of Swiss psychiatrists revealed that 3 percent were currently treating a multiple personality patient (Modestin, 1992). Canadian researchers Ross and others (1991) estimate that at least 5 percent of the patients admitted to Canadian psychiatric units have multiple personality disorder.

Memory Check 14.3

1. John is always afraid that he has some serious disease even though his doctors can find nothing physically wrong. His diagnosis would probably be (conversion disorder, hypochondriasis).

2. In conversion disorder, the person is actually faking the symptom. (true/false)

3. People suffering from psychogenic fugue:

   a. forget their whole personal identity   c. take on a new identity
   b. travel away from home   d. all of these

4. In multiple personality disorder, the host personality usually (is, is not) aware of the alter personalities.

Answers: 1. hypochondriasis   2. false   3. d   4. is not

Schizophrenia and Delusional Disorder

To a mild degree we can identify with most people who suffer from most mental disorders. We can imagine being anxious, fearful, depressed, or euphoric. We can picture ourselves having an obsession or a compulsion. But schizophrenia is so far removed from our common, everyday experience that it is all but impossible for us to imagine what it is like to be schizophrenic. Consider the case of Eric, whose normal childhood and youth turned into a nightmare when he lost touch with reality during his senior year in high school.

> Now in his thirties, he lives in his parents' wood-paneled basement. Usually sitting with a blanket covering his head, Eric is oblivious to the normal world. His world consists of the voices he hears inside his head and the visual hallucinations he takes to be real. Eric insists that he talks to God and to Satan, and at times he believes that he is Jesus Christ. If he refuses to take his antipsychotic medication, he is likely to become violent, and two times he has tried to take his own life. "His parents live in fear of what tomorrow will bring as they muddle through discouraging todays. There is seldom a moment without stress, an hour with peace of mind" (Bartimus, 1983, p. D1).

Schizophrenia is the most serious of the mental disorders. It affects about one person in 100, and one-half of all the mental hospital beds in this country are occupied by schizophrenic patients. Schizophrenia usually begins in adolescence or early adulthood, although it can appear later in life. It is probably the most devastating of all the mental disorders because of the social disruption and misery it causes in proportion to the number of people who suffer from it.

The Symptoms of Schizophrenia: Many and Varied

Question: What are some of the major symptoms of schizophrenia?

Although there are a number of symptoms associated with schizophrenia, any given individual with the disorder may have one or more of the major symptoms. Schizophrenia always involves either delusions, hallucinations, inappropriate or flat affect, or disturbances in thinking.

Hallucinations   One of the clearest symptoms suggesting schizophrenia is the presence of **hallucinations**—imaginary sensations. Schizophrenic patients may see, hear, feel, taste, or smell strange things in the absence of any stimulus in the environment, but hearing voices is the most common type of hallucination. Schizophrenic patients may believe they hear the voice of God or Satan, the voices of family members or friends, unknown voices, and even their own voice broadcasting aloud what they are thinking. Tiihonen and others (1992) suggest that auditory hallucinations stimulate the primary auditory cortex much like real sounds.

Most often the voices are unpleasant, accusing or cursing the patient. Sometimes they are menacing and can be dangerous if the unfortunate victims are ordered by the voices to kill someone or to take their own life.

Visual hallucinations are usually in black and white and commonly take the form of friends, relatives, God, Jesus, or the devil (Bracha et al., 1989). Schizophrenics also may experience bodily sensations that are exceedingly frightening and painful. They may feel they are being beaten, burned, or sexually violated. One schizophrenic complained "that spiders were crawling all through his heart and vessels, eating his brain, and although he could not see them, he thought he could feel them crawling on his skin" (Salama & England, 1990, p. 86).

schizophrenia (SKIT-suh-FREE-nee-ah):   A psychosis characterized by loss of contact with reality, hallucinations, delusions, inappropriate or flat affect, some disturbance in thinking, social withdrawal, and/or other bizarre behavior.

hallucination: A sensory perception in the absence of any external sensory stimulus; an imaginary sensation.

delusion: A false belief, not generally shared by others in the culture, that cannot be changed despite strong evidence to the contrary.

delusion of grandeur: A false belief that one is a famous person or one who has some great knowledge, ability, or authority.

delusion of persecution: An individual's false belief that a person or group is trying in some way to harm him or her.

delusion of reference: A false belief that certain events or objects have some special symbolic meaning.

first-degree relatives: A person's parents, children, or siblings.

Delusions   Imagine how upset you would be if you believed that every thought you had was being broadcast aloud for everyone to hear. What if you were convinced that some strange agent or force was stealing your thoughts or inserting thoughts in your head that were not your own? These are examples of **delusions**—false beliefs that are not generally shared by others in the culture. Usually patients cannot be persuaded that their beliefs are false, even in the face of strong evidence.

Delusions may be of several different types. People with *delusions of grandeur* might believe they are a famous person (the President or Jesus Christ, for example) or a powerful or important person who possesses some great knowledge, ability, or authority. Those with *delusions of persecution* have the false notion that some person or agency is trying to harass, cheat, spy on, conspire against, injure, kill, or in some other way harm them. With *delusions of reference*, patients believe that certain common events have some special symbolic meaning for them. One patient observed that "the room number of his therapist's office was the same as the number of the hospital room in which his father died and believed that this meant there was a plot to kill him" (APA, 1987, p. 396).

Some patients suffer from delusions of being controlled. They believe that their thoughts, feelings, or actions are being controlled by some external force.

Inappropriate or Flat Affect   Schizophrenics may have grossly **inappropriate affect**, that is, their facial expressions, tone of voice, and gestures do not reflect the emotion that would be expected under the circumstances. A patient might cry when watching a television comedy and laugh when watching a television news story showing bloody bodies being removed from a fatal automobile accident.

Some schizophrenic patients show flat affect—practically no emotional response at all. They may speak in a monotone, and their facial expressions may be blank and emotionless. Such patients may act and move more like robots than humans.

Disturbances in the Form of Thought   Schizophrenia is often marked by a disturbance in the form of thought. The most common type is loosening of associations, when an individual does not follow one line of thought to completion, but on the basis of vague connections shifts from one subject to another. The speech of schizophrenics is often very difficult, if not impossible, to understand. The content of the message may be extremely vague, or the individual may invent words or use them inappropriately (Chaika, 1985).

Other Symptoms of Schizophrenia   Schizophrenics tend to withdraw from normal social contacts and retreat into their own world. They have difficulty relating to people, and often their functioning is too impaired for them to hold a job or even to care for themselves. Personal hygiene often suffers, and patients might need to be reminded to bathe, shave, and change their clothing. Unusual or inappropriate motor behavior is common in schizophrenia, and it may take many forms—strange gestures, facial expressions, or postures.

Brain Abnormalities in Some Schizophrenics   A number of abnormalities in brain structure and function have been found in schizophrenic patients (Andreasen, 1988). PET scans have shown abnormally low activity in the frontal lobes (Buchsbaum et al., 1982; Weinberger, 1988). Other studies have revealed cortical atrophy (Vita et al., 1991) and abnormalities in the hippocampus (Conrad et al., 1991; Jeste & Lohr, 1989). In some schizophrenics, the ventricles—cavities in the brain filled with cerebrospinal fluid—are larger than in the normal brain (Lieberman et al., 1992; Zipursky et al., 1992). This particular abnormality was discovered in the brain of John Hinckley, Jr., the man who tried to assassinate Ronald Reagan.

It is not clear whether these differences in function and structure cause schizophrenia, or whether they are a result of the disorder itself or of the medication used to treat it (Mesulam, 1990).

Types of Schizophrenia

Although we have seen that a number of behavioral characteristics are commonly shared by schizophrenics, there are certain distinguishing features that separate one subtype of schizophrenia from another. There are four major types of schizophrenia: catatonic, disorganized, paranoid, and undifferentiated.

Persons with **catatonic schizophrenia** may display complete stillness and stupor, or great excitement and agitation. Frequently they alternate rapidly between the two. They may become frozen in a strange posture or position, as shown in the photograph on this page, and remain there for hours without moving.

Disorganized schizophrenia (formerly called hebephrenia) is the most serious type, marked by extreme social withdrawal, hallucinations, delusions, silliness, inappropriate laughter, grimaces, grotesque mannerisms, and other bizarre behavior. These patients show flat or inappropriate affect and are frequently incoherent. They often exhibit obscene behavior, may masturbate openly, and swallow almost any kind of object or material. Disorganized schizophrenia tends to occur at an earlier age than the other types, and it results in the most severe disintegration of the personality. Consequently, patients with this disorder have the poorest chance of recovery (Fenton & McGlashan, 1991).

People with **paranoid schizophrenia** usually suffer from delusions of grandeur or persecution. They may be convinced that they have an identity other than their own—that they are the President, the Virgin Mary, or God. Their delusions may include the belief that they possess great ability or talent, or that they have some special mission. They may feel that they are in charge of the hospital or on a secret assignment for the government. Paranoid schizophrenics often show exaggerated anger and suspiciousness. If they have delusions of persecution and feel that they are being harassed or threatened, they may become violent in an attempt to defend themselves against their imagined persecutors. Usually the behavior of the paranoid schizophrenic is not so obviously disturbed as that of the catatonic or disorganized types, and the chance for recovery is better (Fenton & McGlashan, 1991; Kendler et al., 1984).

Undifferentiated schizophrenia is a general catchall category for the individual who clearly has schizophrenic symptoms but whose symptoms either do not conform to the criteria of any of the other schizophrenia types or conform to more than one type.

The Causes of Schizophrenia

Question: What are some suggested causes of schizophrenia?

During the 1950s and 1960s, many psychiatrists and some researchers pointed to unhealthy patterns of communication and interaction in the entire family as the breeding ground for schizophrenia (Bateson et al., 1956; Lidz et al., 1965). However, unhealthy family interaction patterns could be the *result* rather than the *cause* of schizophrenia. Convincing evidence is not available to justify pointing the finger of blame at mothers, fathers, or other family members (Johnson, 1989; Torrey, 1983).

On the other hand, research evidence continues to mount that suggests a biological factor in many cases of schizophrenia.

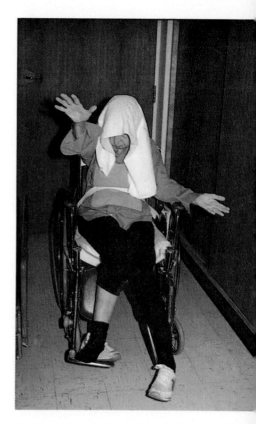

People with catatonic schizophrenia may become frozen in unusual, statuelike positions and remain there for hours without moving.

catatonic schizophrenia (KAT-uh-TAHN-ik): A type characterized by extreme stillness or stupor and/or periods of great agitation and excitement; patients may assume an unusual posture and remain in it for long periods.

disorganized schizophrenia: The most serious type marked by inappropriate affect, silliness, laughter, grotesque mannerisms, and bizarre behavior.

paranoid schizophrenia (PAIR-uh-noid): A type characterized by delusions of grandeur or persecution.

Researchers have recently identified a specific gene that predisposes persons to developing
schizophrenia.

Genetic Inheritance   Research evidence has accumulated to suggest that there
is a genetic factor operating in many cases of schizophrenia. In the general
population, the chance of a person developing schizophrenia is about 1 in 100 (1
percent). People with one schizophrenic parent, however, have about a 13 percent chance of developing the disorder; those with two schizophrenic parents
have roughly a 46 percent chance. If one identical twin develops schizophrenia,
the other twin has about a 46 percent chance of having it as well. But if one
fraternal twin has schizophrenia, the other twin has about a 14 percent chance
of developing it (Nicol & Gottesman, 1983). Figure 14.1 shows the relationship
between genetic similarity and the probability of developing schizophrenia.

Still more evidence for a genetic factor comes from adoption studies showing
that adoptees are at greater risk of developing schizophrenia if their biological
parent rather than their adoptive parent is schizophrenic. Offspring of a schizophrenic parent, adopted and raised by normal parents, will still have the same
chance of developing schizophrenia as if they had been raised by their schizophrenic, biological parent (Kendler & Gruenberg, 1984).

Exactly what is the genetic connection? What is inherited, according to the
genetic theorists, is a predisposition or tendency toward developing the disorder
(Rosenthal, 1970; Zubin & Spring, 1977). Schizophrenics are particularly vulnerable to stress, and whether people with a predisposition to schizophrenia
develop the disorder presumably may depend on their life circumstances (Johnson, 1989). Torrey and Bowler (1990) have data suggesting that schizophrenia
is more common in highly urbanized areas of the United States than in rural
areas. They speculate that the cause is the greater stressfulness of city life coupled with higher exposure to pollutants, toxins, and infectious disease.

Excessive Dopamine Activity   Abnormal activity in the brain's dopamine
systems is common in many schizophrenics, and much of the dopamine activity
occurs in the limbic system, which is involved in human emotions (Davis et al.,
1991). Drugs found to be effective in reducing the symptoms of schizophrenia
block dopamine action (Iverson, 1979; Torrey, 1983), although about one-third
of the patients do not show improvement with the drugs (Wolkin et al., 1989).

Questions still remain about the causes of schizophrenia. Most likely many
factors play an interactive role—genetic predispositions, biochemical processes,
environmental conditions, and life experiences.

Figure 14.1

**Genetic Similarity and Probability
of Developing Schizophrenia**

Research strongly indicates a
genetic factor operating in many
cases of schizophrenia. Identical
twins have identical genes, and if
one twin develops schizophrenia,
the other twin has a 46 percent
chance of developing it also. In
fraternal twins the chance is only
14 percent. A person with one
schizophrenic parent has a 13 percent chance of developing schizophrenia, but a 46 percent chance if
both parents are schizophrenic.
(Data from Nicol & Gottesman,
1983.)

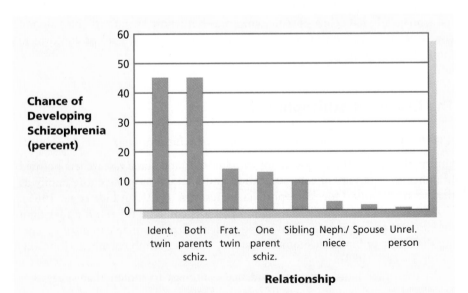

Delusional (Paranoid) Disorder: Plagued by False Beliefs

Question: How does delusional disorder differ from schizophrenia?

Another serious psychotic disorder is **delusional disorder**, formerly called paranoid disorder (Kendler et al., 1989). People with this disorder suffer from delusions, but their delusions are more specific, more logical and believable than the bizarre and fragmented delusions of the schizophrenic. They may be insanely jealous, abnormally suspicious, or feel that other individuals, groups, foreign governments, or unseen powers are plotting against them, watching their every move, or seeking to kill them. Other themes may involve the delusion that they are loved by some famous person or a person of higher status; that their spouse or lover is unfaithful (delusional jealousy); that they are related to some prominent person; or that they are themselves a prominent person.

Apart from their delusions, people with this disorder often appear logical and normal. Because their intellectual functioning remains fairly intact, they can usually continue to be employed and carry on their daily affairs. Typically it is their social and marital functioning that suffers.

Delusional disorder is relatively rare, affecting only 5 to 10 people in 1,000 (APA, 1987), and it does not tend to run in families. People with this disorder rarely seek help and are hard to treat because they are convinced that their delusions are real.

delusional disorder: A psychotic disorder characterized by delusions more believable and logical than those of schizophrenia, and in which intellectual functioning apart from the delusions usually remains intact.

Memory Check 14.4

1. Match the symptom with the appropriate example.

    _____1) Joe believes he is Moses.
    _____2) Elena thinks her family is spreading rumors about her.
    _____3) Peter hears voices cursing him.
    _____4) Marco laughs at tragedies and cries when he hears a joke.

    a. delusions of grandeur
    b. hallucinations
    c. inappropriate affect
    d. delusions of persecution

2. Ron thinks the CIA is following him because he is so important. He probably suffers from (catatonic, paranoid) schizophrenia.

3. People who are adopted at birth are at greater risk of developing schizophrenia if their (biological, adoptive) parent is schizophrenic.

4. Some researchers believe one cause of schizophrenia is excessive (norepinephrine, dopamine) activity.

5. People with delusional disorder usually (can, cannot) continue to hold a job or carry on their everyday affairs.

Answers: 1. 1) a 2) d 3) b 4) c 2. paranoid 3. biological 4. dopamine 5. can

mood disorders: Disorders characterized by extreme and unwarranted disturbances in feeling or mood, which can include depression or manic episodes or both.

depression (major): A mood disorder characterized by feelings of great sadness, despair, guilt, worthlessness, hopelessness, and in extreme cases, suicidal intentions.

seasonal affective disorder (SAD): A mood disorder in which depression comes and goes with the seasons.

Mood Disorders

Mood disorders involve moods or emotions that are extreme and unwarranted. In the most serious disorders, mood ranges from the depths of severe depression to the heights of extreme elation. Mood disorders fall into two broad categories—depressive disorders and bipolar disorders.

Depressive Disorders and Bipolar Disorder: Emotional Highs and Lows

Question: What are the symptoms of major depression?

Major Depression We all have our dark moments, and it is normal to feel blue, down, sad, or depressed in response to many of life's common experiences—death of a loved one, divorce, loss of a job, or an unhappy ending to a long-term relationship. Major depression, however, is not normal. People with **major depression** feel an overwhelming sadness, despair, and hopelessness, and they usually lose their ability to experience pleasure. They may have appetite and weight changes, sleep disturbance, loss of energy, and difficulty thinking or concentrating. Body movements and speech may be so slowed that some depressed people almost seem to be doing everything in slow motion. Some depressed patients experience the other extreme and are constantly moving and fidgeting, wringing their hands, pacing, and unable to sit still. Depression can be so severe that its victims suffer from delusions or hallucinations.

Ten times more common than schizophrenia, depression is the most common of all serious mental disorders. It strikes people of all social classes, cultures, and nations around the world. Unlike schizophrenia, depression has been recognized as a disorder for well over 2,000 years (Beck, 1967).

About 10 to 15 percent of the population develop clinical depression at some time in their lives (Akiskal, 1989), and most types of depression are twice as common in women as in men (McGrath, 1992). Burke and others (1991) have found that over the years there has been a shift in the age of onset for major depression, with increases reported in the 15 to 19 age group. Some people suffer only one major depression, but over 50 percent will have a recurrence (APA, 1987). Risk of recurrence is greatest for females (Lewinsohn et al., 1989), for those with an onset of depression before age 20 (Giles et al., 1989), and for those with a family history of mood disorders (Akiskal, 1989). Recurrences may be frequent or infrequent, and for 20 to 35 percent of patients, the episodes are chronic, lasting two years or longer. Recurring episodes tend to be increasingly more severe (Maj et al., 1992). Keitner and others (1992) report that slightly less than one-half (48.6%) of those hospitalized for major depression are fully recovered after one year. Unfortunately, about 80 percent of those suffering from depression never even receive treatment (Holden, 1986b). And in cases of major depression, suicide is a danger that must always be considered. To learn more about suicide, read the boxed feature on pages 502–503.

Many people suffer from a milder form of depression called dysthymia, which is nonetheless chronic (lasting 2 years or longer). Individuals with dysthymia suffer from depressed mood but have fewer of the associated symptoms common in major depression.

Seasonal Depression Many people find that their moods seem to change with the seasons (Kasper et al., 1989). But people suffering from **seasonal affective disorder (SAD)**, experience a significant depression that tends to come and go with the seasons (Wehr & Rosenthal, 1989). The most common type, winter depression, seems to be triggered by light deficiency. During the winter months,

People with major depression feel overwhelming sadness, despair, and hopelessness.

when the days are shorter, some people become very depressed and tend to sleep and eat more, gain weight, and crave carbohydrates (Rosenthal et al., 1986; Wurtman & Wurtman, 1989). However, during the spring and summer months, they are in higher spirits, become more energetic, and claim to function better (Wehr et al., 1986).

Reasoning that the obvious difference between the seasons was the amount and intensity of light, Rosenthal and colleagues (1985) exposed patients with winter depression to bright light, which simulated the longer daylight hours of summer. After several days of the light treatment, most of the subjects improved.

Figure 14.2 shows the difference in mood fluctuations between seasonal-affective-disorder patients and normal individuals.

Question: What are the extremes of mood suffered in bipolar disorder?

Bipolar Disorder   Another type of mood disorder is **bipolar disorder**, in which patients experience two radically different moods—extreme highs called manic episodes (or mania) and the extreme lows of major depression—usually with relatively normal periods in between. A **manic episode** is marked by excessive euphoria, inflated self-esteem, wild optimism, and hyperactivity. During a manic episode people are wound up and full of energy. They rarely sleep, are frantically engaged in a flurry of activity, and talk loud and fast, skipping from one topic to another.

You may wonder what is wrong with being euphoric, energetic, and optimistic. Obviously nothing, as long as it is warranted. But people in a manic state have temporarily lost touch with reality and frequently have delusions of grandeur along with their euphoric high. Their high-spirited optimism is not merely irrational, it is delusional. They may go on wild spending sprees or waste large sums of money on grand, get-rich-quick schemes. If family members try to stop

Light therapy has been an effective treatment for people with seasonal depression.

CNN: Exploring Seasonal Depression (2:47; videotape, videodisk) According to recent research, fewer daylight hours during the winter months may contribute to depression in some people. Light therapy is one technique to help alleviate seasonal depression.

Figure 14.2   Seasonal Mood Changes   Normally mood fluctuates with the seasons. People typically report feeling best during May and June and worst during January and February. People with seasonal affective disorder (SAD) experience wider mood fluctuations—higher highs in June, July, and August and lower lows in December, January, and February. The winter depression of seasonal affective disorder seems to be related to the light deficiency during the short winter days. An effective treatment is light therapy. (After Wurtman & Wurtman, 1989.)

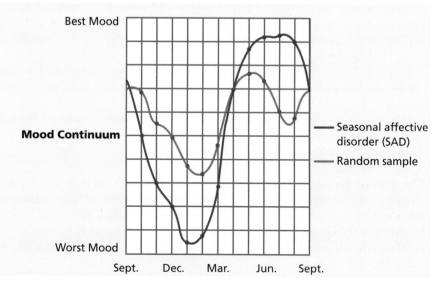

bipolar disorder: A mood disorder in which one has manic episodes alternating with periods of depression, usually with relatively normal periods in between.

manic episode (MAN-ik): A period of extreme elation, euphoria, and hyperactivity, often accompanied by delusions of grandeur and by hostility if activity is blocked.

them or talk them out of their irrational plans, they are likely to become irritable, hostile, enraged, or even dangerous. Quite often patients must be hospitalized during manic episodes to protect them and others from the disastrous consequences of their poor judgment.

The excessive euphoria, boundless energy, and delusions of grandeur are all apparent in this manic episode of Edward O, a 27-year-old high-school teacher.

> One day Edward O's behavior suddenly became bizarre. He charged into the principal's office and outlined his plan for tearing down the school building and having his students rebuild it from the ground up over the weekend. The school principal called the police and had Edward taken to a hospital. There Edward paced up and down for two days, would not sleep or eat, and spoke excitedly about his plans to take over administration of the hospital. On the third day he demanded paper and pens, and in a frenzy wrote 100 letters, one to each U.S. senator. He cursed the pens for not writing faster and threw them against the wall, demanding new ones. When staff members tried to stop him, Edward flew into a rage, so they decided to let him "run out of steam." After the fourth day he collapsed, totally exhausted. (Adapted from Goldenberg, 1977.)

People with frequent but milder mood swings, not severe enough to indicate bipolar disorder, would receive a diagnosis of cyclothymia. The highs are not so extreme as to seriously impair their social and occupational functioning, and hospitalization is not required.

Causes of Major Depression and Bipolar Disorder

Question: What are some suggested causes of major depression and bipolar disorder?

What theoretical perspectives can shed light on the possible causes of depression and bipolar disorder? The biological and cognitive perspectives offer some insight into the causes of mood disorders and suggest treatments that have proven helpful to many people suffering from these disorders.

The Biological Perspective   Biological factors such as genetic inheritance and abnormal brain chemistry play a major role in bipolar disorder and major depression.

The Role of Genetic Inheritance   Does depression tend to run in families? Apparently so, because people who have relatives with mood disorders are at higher risk of developing mood disturbances (Johnson & Leeman, 1977), and this risk is due to shared genetic factors rather than shared environmental factors (Kendler et al., 1992c). In fact, a person is 3 times more likely to develop depression if a close relative has had an early onset of depression and if the depression was recurring rather than a single episode (Bland et al., 1986; Weissman, Wickramartne, et al., 1984).

Adoption studies have shown that among adult adoptees who had developed depression, there was 8 times more major depression and 15 times more suicide in biological than in adoptive family members (Wender et al., 1986). The genetic link, however, is much stronger in bipolar disorder than in depression. The odds of developing bipolar disorder are 24 times greater in persons who have *first-degree relatives* with the disorder (Weissman, Gershon, et al., 1984).

The Role of Serotonin and Norepinephrine   We all know that mood can be altered by the substances people put into their bodies. Alcohol, caffeine, various other uppers and downers, and a host of additional psychoactive substances are known to alter mood. Researchers now know that our moods are altered and regulated by our own biochemicals, which of course include the neurotransmitters. Norepinephrine and serotonin are two neurotransmitters thought to play an important role in mood disorders. Both are localized in the limbic system and the hypothalamus, parts of the brain that help regulate emotional behavior.

Too little norepinephrine is associated with depression, and too much is related to mania (Schildkraut, 1970). It is interesting to note that amphetamines, which cause an emotional "high," are reported to stimulate the release of both serotonin and norepinephrine.

An important unanswered question remains. Do these biochemical differences in the brain *cause* psychological changes or *result* from them? Theorists who emphasize psychological causes see biochemical changes as results, not causes of mood disorders.

The Cognitive Perspective Cognitive explanations such as that of Aaron Beck (1967, 1991) maintain that depression is characterized by distortions in thinking. According to Beck, depressed individuals view themselves, their world, and their future all in negative ways. They see their interactions with the world as defeating—a series of burdens and obstacles that mostly end in failure. Depressed persons believe they are deficient, unworthy, and inadequate, and they attribute their perceived failures to their own physical, mental, or moral inadequacies. Finally, according to the cognitive theory, depressed patients believe that their future holds no hope. They may reason: "Everything always turns out wrong." "I never win." "Things will never get better." "It's no use."

In a review of a number of studies, Haaga and others (1991) found that depression is related to distortions in thinking. The cognitive perspective has much to offer for us to apply in our daily lives. Read the boxed feature on page 500.

Other Suggested Causes of Mood Disorders

The Psychodynamic Explanation The psychodynamic explanation suggests that when people cannot effectively express aggressive or negative feelings, they may turn those feelings inward (repress them) and thus experience depression.

Stress Stressful life events such as physical illness, work and family problems, legal problems, financial difficulties, retirement, difficulties in interpersonal relationships, and other life changes are also associated with depression. The incidence of depression is higher in the lower socioeconomic classes and may be related to the stress of poverty (Murphy et al., 1991). Compared to the number of stressful life events reported by nondepressed people, depressed individuals report 2 to 3 times as many occurring shortly before a depression (Greist & Jefferson, 1984). "Although the majority of individuals exposed to such circumstances do not sink into morbid despair, those predisposed to mood disorders may do so at such times" (Akiskal, 1989, p. 7). Life events that represent a major loss, such as death of a loved one or loss of a job, are associated with the onset of depression. However, life events that relate to threat are more likely to precede anxiety disorders (Monroe & Simmons, 1991). Pribor and Dinwiddie (1992) found an incidence of 88.5 percent of depression among incest victims.

Stressful life events are linked more strongly to the first episode of depression than to recurrences (Ghaziuddin et al., 1990). We know that some people suffer bouts of depression with no identifiable event or experience that could trigger it. Stressful life events may leave some people simply feeling bad, while others become clinically depressed. What accounts for the difference? Do our genes predispose us to depression? Is our brain chemistry at fault? Might our early childhood experiences be responsible? Or is it the way we interpret life events, whether optimistic or pessimistic? There is some evidence to suggest that each explanation can play a part in the puzzle of depression.

WORLD OF PSYCHOLOGY: APPLICATIONS

Thinking and Depression: Avoiding Cognitive Traps

Many people contribute to their own depressed moods by their distorted, negative thinking. Consider your own thinking habits. Are they typically positive or negative? Negative thinking can rob us of happiness, destroy our motivation, and contribute to a depressed mood. "I'll never pass this course." "She/He would never go out with me." "I can't do anything right." "I'm a failure." If such thoughts are part of your habitual repertoire, you need to develop healthier thinking habits. Self evaluations that include "never" or "always" are exaggerations, distortions of the truth.

The next time you notice yourself entertaining negative self-evaluations, or self-doubts, write them down and analyze them objectively and unemotionally. But don't sweep to the other extreme and substitute equally distorted, positive thinking or mindless "happy talk." Self-delusion in either direction is not healthy. Your goal should be to monitor your thinking and systematically make it less distorted, more rational, and more accurate and logical.

When it comes to physical health and well-being, you have probably heard it said, "You are what you eat." To a large extent, "You are what you *think*" in the area of mental health. Depression and other forms of mental misery can all be fueled by our own thoughts. One step toward healthy thinking is to recognize five cognitive traps.

Cognitive Trap No. 1: The "Tyranny of the Should"

One certain path to unhappiness is lined with unrealistic, unachievable standards that we set for ourselves. Karen Horney called this cognitive trap the "*tyranny of the should*." This list of shoulds is characterized by such words as *always, never, all, everybody,* and *everything.* Have you ever been tyrannized by any of these "shoulds"?

I should always be the perfect friend, lover, spouse, parent, student, teacher, employee.

I should be able to endure everything and like everybody.
I should never feel hurt and should always be calm.
I should know, understand, and foresee everything.
I should be able to solve all of my problems and the problems of others in no time.
I should never be tired or fall ill.

(Adapted from Horney, 1950, pp. 64–66.)

Cognitive Trap No. 2: Negative, "What If" Thinking

Much unhappiness stems from a preoccupation with what might be. Examples of "what if" thinking are: What if she (he) turns me down? What if I lose my job? What if I flunk this test? What if I can't pay my bills?

Cognitive Trap No. 3: Making Mountains Out of Molehills

A molehill becomes a mountain when a single negative event is perceived as catastrophic or when we allow it to stand as a total definition of our worth. "I failed this test" might become "I'll never pass this course," "I'll never graduate from college," or "I'm a failure."

Cognitive Trap No. 4: The Perfection-Failure Dichotomy

Only on the rarest occasions can our performance be considered absolutely perfect or a total failure. In reality, we fall somewhere on a continuum between these two extremes. But people caught in Cognitive Trap No. 4 see anything short of perfection as a total failure.

Cognitive Trap No. 5: Setting Impossible Conditions for Happiness

Don't let your happiness hinge on perfection in yourself and others. Not everyone will love you or even like you, approve of you, or agree with you. If any of these are conditions upon which your happiness depends, you are setting the stage for disappointment or even depression.

Memory Check 14.5

1. (Males, Females) are more likely to suffer from major depression.

2. Often people have to be hospitalized during a manic episode to keep them from committing suicide. (true/false)

3. The suicide rate drops for white men after age 55. (true/false)

(continued)

4. Match the theory of depression with the proposed cause.

_____ 1) negative thoughts about oneself, the world, and one's future

_____ 2) a deficiency of serotonin and norepinephrine

_____ 3) turning resentment and hostility inward

_____ 4) a family history of depression

a. psychodynamic theory
b. cognitive theory
c. genetic theory
d. biochemical theory

5. Stress appears to be unrelated to depression. (true/false)

Answers: 1. Females 2. false 3. false 4. 1) b 2) d 3) a 4) c 5. false

Other Psychological Disorders

Personality Disorders: Troublesome Behavior Patterns

Question: What characteristics are shared by most people with personality disorders?

Do you know people who are impossible to get along with—people who always seem to be at odds with themselves, their environment, their family, and others? Such people may have a **personality disorder,** a long-standing, inflexible, maladaptive pattern of behaving and relating to others, which usually begins early in childhood or adolescence (Widiger et al., 1988). They tend to have problems in their social relationships and in their work, and they may experience personal distress as well. Some people with personality disorders realize that their behavior causes problems in their lives, yet they seem unable to change. But more commonly, they are self-centered and do not see themselves as responsible for their difficulties. Instead, they tend to blame other people or situations for their problems.

The *DSM-III-R* lists 11 personality disorders, which are explained briefly in Table 14.4. We will explore a few of them.

Passive Aggressive Personality Disorder Persons with *passive aggressive personality disorder* passively resist demands to perform adequately in social relationships and at work through forgetfulness, procrastination, stubbornness, and intentional inefficiency. They are masters at bringing out anger, even hostility, in others while remaining passive and nonviolent themselves. Passive aggressive types apparently resent authority and any expectations or demands made of them. But rather than resisting or displaying their aggressive feelings openly, they use devious, passive means of rebellion. They may promise earnestly to do their part, but then they procrastinate, pout, show stubbornness, or perform poorly on purpose. They often frustrate the efforts of others in a cooperative work setting by failing to do their share of the work. They will appear late for appointments, fail to follow through on tasks, "forget" to complete assignments, and generally make life miserable for others who depend on them.

Antisocial Personality Disorder All too often we read or hear about people who commit horrible crimes and show no remorse whatsoever. After raping and

personality disorder: A long-standing, inflexible, maladaptive pattern of behaving and relating to others, which begins early in life and causes impairment in social and occupational functioning and/or personal distress.

passive aggressive personality disorder: A personality disorder in which a person passively resists demands to perform adequately through forgetfulness, procrastination, stubbornness, and intentional inefficiency.

WORLD OF PSYCHOLOGY: MULTICULTURAL PERSPECTIVES

Suicide and Gender, Race, and Age

Question: What people are at the greatest risk of committing suicide?

I n July 1990 Mitch Snyder, a well-known advocate for the homeless who had been near death several times from hunger strikes, hanged himself. He was 46 years old. Why, we ask, would any person commit the final act of desperation?

Who commits suicide? What are some of the risk factors, and what can we do to help prevent a person from committing suicide?

Who Commits Suicide?   There were 30,407 suicides reported in the United States in 1988: 24,078 males and 6,329 females (U.S. Bureau of the Census, 1991). Why do so many more males than females commit suicide? The question becomes even more complex when we consider that females are from 4 to 10 times more likely than males to *attempt* suicide (Van Fossen, 1985). More women try,

but males are almost 4 times more likely than females to *succeed* at taking their own lives (McGinnis, 1987). White males of all age groups have the highest suicide rate, 60 percent higher than the rate of African-American males. Figure 14.3 shows sex differences in methods used for suicide.

Who Is at Highest Risk for Suicide?   Older Americans are at far greater risk for suicide than younger people. White males age 85 and over have the highest recorded suicide rate, which in 1989 reached 60.4 per 100,000 population (U.S. Bureau of the Census, 1991). This is more than 5 times the average national suicide rate of 11.8 per 100,000. Poor general health, serious illness, loneliness (often due to the death of a spouse), and decline in social and economic status are conditions that may push many older Americans, especially those age 75 and over, to commit suicide (McGinnis, 1987; Rich et al., 1991).

For teenagers and young adults ages 15 through 24, suicide is now the third leading cause of death, with accidents ranking first and homicides second (U.S. Bureau of the Census, 1991). For college students, however, suicide ranks second (Silver et al., 1984). The rate of suicide among 15- to 24-year-olds nearly doubled over the last few decades, possibly due to increases in alcohol and drug abuse (Berman & Schwartz, 1990; Fowler et al., 1986), psychiatric disorders (Runeson, 1989), antisocial behavior (Shafii et

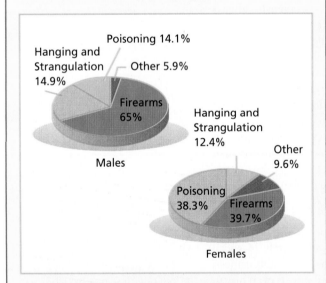

Figure 14.3   Gender Differences in Methods Used for Suicide   Males who commit suicide are far more likely to use firearms (65 percent) than any other method. Hanging and strangulation is a very distant second at 14.9 percent. Although females, too, are most likely to use firearms (39.7 percent), poisoning (38.3 percent) is a very close second. (Data from U.S. Bureau of the Census, 1991.)

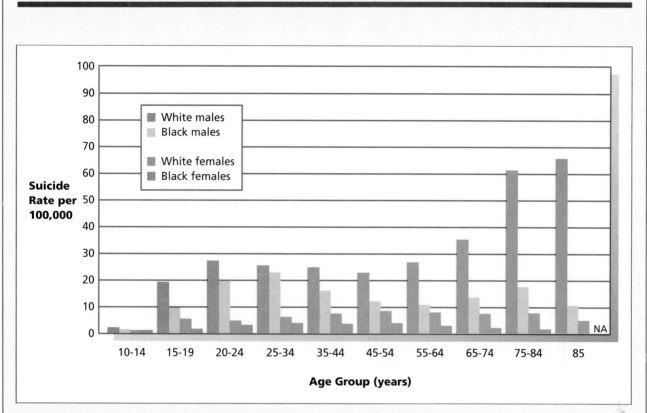

Figure 14.4 Differences in Suicide Rate According to Race, Gender, and Age In every age group the suicide rate is highest for white males and second highest for black males. The general conclusion is that males are more likely to commit suicide than females, and whites are more likely than blacks. (Data from U.S. Bureau of the Census, 1991.)

al., 1985), and disturbed home life (Holinger et al., 1987). In addition, a precipitating circumstance such as the breakup of a relationship, a disciplinary crisis, school problems, or a family crisis may push a teenager "over the edge" (Neiger & Hopkins, 1988; Rich et al., 1991; Shaffer, 1988).

Regardless of age group, suicide rates are lowest for married persons (Smith et al., 1988) and highest for persons who have made a previous suicide attempt (Beck et al., 1990). People suffering from psychiatric disorders, particularly depression, schizophrenia, panic disorder, and alcoholism, are at higher risk. In fact, half of those who commit suicide are clinically depressed at the time (Stanley & Stanley, 1990). Figure 14.4 shows the differences in suicide rates according to race, gender, and age.

Preventing Suicide Although there are cultural differences in the rates, the methods used, and the reasons for committing suicide, the warning signs are very similar across racial, gender, and age groups. Most suicidal persons communicate their intent; in fact, about 80 percent of them leave clues (Schneidman, 1987). They may communicate verbally: "You won't be seeing me again." "You won't have to worry about me anymore." "Life isn't worth living." They may leave behavioral clues such as giving away their most valued possessions; withdrawing from friends, family, and associates; taking unnecessary risks; showing personality changes; acting and looking depressed; and losing interest in favorite activities. These warning signs should always be taken seriously. Suicidal individuals need compassion, emotional support, and the opportunity to express the feelings and problems that are the source of their psychological pain.

Hopelessness is a common characteristic of suicidal individuals (Beck, Brown, et al., 1990; Wetzel & Reich, 1989). Proposing some solutions or some alternatives that could lessen hopelessness may lower the likelihood of suicide. Most people contemplating suicide are not totally committed to self-destruction. This may explain why many potential victims leave warnings or use less lethal means in attempted suicide.

But we should not be amateur psychologists if dealing with a suicidal person. Probably the best service you can render is to encourage the person to get professional help. There are 24-hour-a-day suicide hotlines all over the country. A call might save a life.

antisocial personality disorder: A disorder marked by lack of feeling for others; selfish, aggressive, irresponsible behavior; and willingness to break the law, lie, cheat, or exploit others for personal gain.

nearly beating to death a young woman jogging in New York's Central Park, one of her attackers calmly stated, "She was nothing." Another happily claimed, "It was fun!" Baffled, we ask ourselves how a person could do such a thing. Many of these people may have what psychologists call antisocial personality disorder. Ted Bundy, the infamous serial killer executed in 1990, was thought to have antisocial personality disorder.

People with **antisocial personality disorder** have a long-standing "pattern of irresponsible and antisocial behavior" beginning in childhood or early adolescence (APA, 1987, p. 342). As children they lie, steal, vandalize, initiate fights, skip school, run away from home, and may be physically cruel to others. By early adolescence they usually drink excessively, use drugs, and engage in promiscuous sex. In adulthood the antisocial personality typically fails to keep a job, to act as a responsible parent, to honor financial commitments, and to obey the law.

Many antisocial types are intelligent and may seem charming and very likable at first. They are good con men, and they are more often men—as many as 3 percent of the U.S. male population compared with less than 1 percent of the female population. One of the first researchers to study antisocial personality disorder revealed that they seem to lack the ability to love or feel loyalty and compassion toward others (Checkley, 1941). They do not appear to have a conscience, feeling little or no guilt or remorse for their actions no matter how cruel or despicable the actions might be (Hare, 1985).

Although the *DSM-III-R* does not include the following characteristics, some experts believe that antisocial types fail to experience anxiety as normal people do. They seem fearless, oblivious to danger to themselves and unconcerned

Table 14.4 DSM-III-R Categories of Personality Disorders

Disorder	Symptoms
Paranoid	Highly suspicious, untrusting, guarded, hypersensitive, easily slighted, lacking in emotion.
Schizoid	Unable to form social relationships, lacking in feeling for others, indifferent to praise or criticism, a "loner."
Schizotypal	Difficulty relating to others; odd speech, beliefs, behavior, and appearance; inappropriate affect.
Antisocial personality	Lacking in feeling for others; impulsive, selfish, aggressive, irresponsible; willingness to break law, lie, cheat, or exploit others for personal gain; failure to hold job.
Histrionic	Seeks attention and approval; overly dramatic, self-centered, shallow; demanding, manipulative; easily bored, craving excitement; often attractive and sexually seductive.
Narcissistic	Exaggerated sense of self-importance, self-centered; demanding, exploitive; craving admiration and attention, envious; lacking in empathy.
Borderline	Unstable and unpredictable in mood, behavior, self-image, and social relationships.
Passive aggressive	Passively resists demands to perform adequately in social relationships and at work through forgetfulness, procrastination, stubbornness, and intentional inefficiency.
Avoidant	Although in need of attention and affection, avoids others because of fear of rejection or humiliation.
Dependent	Dependent, submissive; turns over responsibility for making major life decisions to another, and subordinates needs or desires to that person for fear of jeopardizing the relationship.
Obsessive compulsive	Perfectionistic, rigid, lacking in warmth, judgmental, overconscientious; extremely devoted to work to the exclusion of pleasure; occupied with rules, order, and detail.

Based on DSM-III-R (American Psychiatric Association, 1987).

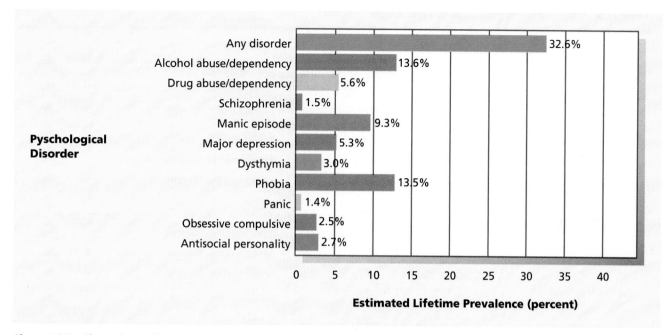

Pyschological Disorder

Figure 14.5   The Estimated Lifetime Prevalence of Psychological Disorders   The largest study ever conducted on the lifetime prevalence of psychological disorders in the United States revealed that 32.6 percent of the population will have some psychological disorder sometime during their lives. Lifetime prevalence percentages for the U.S. population are shown for a variety of psychological disorders. (Data from Robins et al., 1984.)

about the possible, even likely, consequences of their actions, and they appear unable to profit from experience (Chesno & Kilmann, 1975; Hare, 1970). Several adoption studies strongly indicate a genetic factor in antisocial personality (Stewart, 1991; Loehlin et al., 1988).

Years ago people with antisocial personality disorder were referred to as psychopaths or sociopaths. A number of con men, quack doctors, impostors, drug pushers, pimps, delinquents, and more than a few criminals could be diagnosed as having this disorder. Some come to the attention of the authorities; others do not.

Figure 14.5 shows the estimated lifetime prevalence of antisocial personality disorder and many other disorders we have discussed in the chapter.

Sexual Disorders: Problems Involving Sex

Question: What are two categories of sexual disorders?

Most psychologists define sexual disorders as those that are destructive, guilt- or anxiety-producing, compulsive, or a cause of discomfort or harm to one or both parties involved. The *DSM-III-R* has two categories of sexual disorders: sexual dysfunctions (discussed in chapter 11) and paraphilias. *Sexual dysfunctions* involve a lack of sexual desire or impaired sexual performance due to psychological causes. *Paraphilias* are disorders in which sexual urges and fantasies generally involve children, other nonconsenting partners, nonhuman objects, or the suffering or humiliation of the individual or the partner. To be diagnosed as having a paraphilia, the urges must have been acted on or must cause considerable psychological distress. *Gender identity disorders*, which involve a problem accepting one's identity as male or female, are categorized as developmental disorders rather than sexual disorders.

sexual dysfunction: Lack of or inhibited sexual desire or some impairment in sexual performance.

paraphilia: A sexual disorder in which sexual urges and fantasies generally involve children, other nonconsenting partners, nonhuman objects, or the suffering and humiliation of one or one's partner.

gender identity disorders: Disorders characterized by behaviors associated with the opposite sex and dissatisfaction with one's sexual identity as male or female.

Table 14.5   DSM-III-R Categories of Sexual Disorders

Paraphilias	Disorders in which sexual urges and fantasies involve nonhuman objects, children, other nonconsenting persons, or the suffering or humiliation of the individual or his/her partner. Diagnosis is made only if urges have been acted on or if they cause great distress.
Fetishism	A disorder in which sexual urges and fantasies involve an inanimate object, such as women's undergarments or shoes, or some body part other than the genitals (e.g., nails or hair).
Transvestic fetishism	A disorder in which sexual urges and fantasies involve cross dressing.
Pedophilia	A disorder in which sexual urges and fantasies involve sexual activity with a prepubescent child or children.
Exhibitionism	A disorder in which sexual urges and fantasies involve exposing one's genitals to an unsuspecting stranger.
Voyeurism	A disorder in which sexual urges and fantasies involve watching unsuspecting people naked, undressing, or engaging in sexual activity.
Sexual masochism	A disorder in which sexual urges and fantasies involve being beaten, humiliated, bound, or otherwise made to suffer.
Sexual sadism	A disorder in which sexual urges and fantasies involve inflicting physical or psychological pain and suffering on another.
Frotteurism	A disorder in which sexual urges and fantasies involve touching or rubbing against a nonconsenting person, usually in a crowded place.
Other paraphilias	Disorders in which sexual urges and fantasies involve, among other things, animals, feces, urine, corpses, filth, or enemas.
Psychosexual dysfunctions	Disorders involving inhibited sexual desire, inhibited sexual excitement (frigidity or impotence), or inhibited orgasm.

Based on DSM-III-R (American Psychatric Association, 1987).

Sexual sadism and sexual masochism are sexual disorders in which inflicting or receiving pain causes sexual arousal.

Table 14.5 shows a number of the sexual disorders listed in the *DSM-III-R*. Please note that homosexuality is not considered a sexual disorder unless it causes distress or guilt or is otherwise destructive to the individual.

As we have seen, there are a variety of mental disorders with a range of causes from the biological or genetic to life events and one's environment. As you will see in the following chapter, there are a variety of treatments as well.

Memory Check 14.6

1. Which of these is true of personality disorders?

   a. Personality disorders usually begin in adulthood.
   b. Persons with these disorders usually realize their problem.
   c. Personality disorders typically cause problems in social relationships and at work.
   d. Persons with these disorders typically seek professional help.

2. Tim lies, cheats, and exploits others without feeling guilty. He has (antisocial, passive aggressive) personality disorder.

3. (Sexual dysfunctions, Paraphilias) are disorders in which bizarre practices are necessary for sexual arousal.

Answers: 1. c 2. antisocial 3. Paraphilias

Thinking Critically _____

Evaluation

Some mental disorders are more common in women (depression, agoraphobia, and simple phobia), and some are more common in men (antisocial personality, substance abuse and dependence). Give some possible reasons why such gender differences exist in the incidence of mental disorders. Support your answer.

Point/Counterpoint

There is continuing controversy over whether specific psychological disorders are chiefly biological in origin (nature) or result primarily from learning and experience (nurture). Select any two disorders from this chapter and prepare an argument for both the nature and nurture positions for both disorders.

Psychology in Your Life

Review the boxed feature on cognitive traps, page 500. Formulate a specific plan for your own life that will help you to recognize and avoid these 5 traps, which contribute to unhealthy thinking. You might enlist the help of a friend to monitor your negative statements.

Chapter Summary and Review

What Is Abnormal?

What criteria might be used to differentiate normal from abnormal behavior?

Behavior might be considered abnormal if it deviates radically from what is considered normal in one's own culture, if it leads to personal distress or impaired functioning, or if it results in one's being a danger to self and/or others.

What are five current perspectives that attempt to explain the causes of abnormal behavior?

Five current perspectives on the causes of abnormal behavior are (1) the biological perspective, which views it as a symptom of an underlying physical disorder; (2) the psychodynamic perspective, which maintains that it is caused by unconscious, unresolved conflicts; (3) the learning perspective, which claims that it is learned and sustained in the same way as other behavior; (4) the cognitive perspective, which suggests that it results from faulty thinking; and (5) the humanistic perspective, which views it as a result of the blocking of one's natural tendency toward self-actualization.

What is the DSM-III-R?

The DSM-III-R, published by the American Psychiatric Association, is the system most widely used in the United States to diagnose mental disorders.

Key Terms

DSM-III-R (p. 479)
neurosis (p. 479)
psychosis (p. 481)

Anxiety, Somatoform, and Dissociative Disorders

When is anxiety normal, and when is it abnormal?

Anxiety—a generalized feeling of apprehension, fear, or tension—is healthy if it is a response to a real danger or threat, and it is unhealthy if it is inappropriate or excessive.

What are the typical symptoms a person experiences during a panic attack?

Panic disorder is marked by unpredictable attacks of overwhelming anxiety, fear, or terror, during which people experience palpitations, trembling or shaking, choking or smothering sensations, and the feeling that they are going to die or go crazy.

What are the characteristics of the three categories of phobias?

The three categories of phobic disorders are (1) agoraphobia, fear of being in situations where escape is impossible or help is not available in case of incapacitating anxiety; (2) social phobia, fear of social situations where one might be embarrassed or humiliated by appearing clumsy or incompetent; and (3) simple phobia, a catchall category for all phobias other than agoraphobia or social phobia.

What do psychologists believe are some probable causes of phobias?

Phobias result mainly from frightening experiences, through observational learning, or both. Genes may also play a role.

What is obsessive compulsive disorder?

Obsessive compulsive disorder is characterized by obsessions (persistent, recurring, involuntary thoughts, images, or impulses that cause great distress) and/or compulsions (persistent, irresistible, irrational urges to perform an act or ritual repeatedly).

What are two somatoform disorders, and what symptoms do they share?

Somatoform disorders involve complaints of bodily symptoms that patients believe are real but that are psychological rather than physiological in origin. Hypochondriasis involves persistent physical complaints, and conversion disorder involves a loss of functioning in some part of the body such as evidenced by paralysis or blindness.

What are psychogenic amnesia and psychogenic fugue?

With psychogenic amnesia, people lose their memory of important information about themselves or their entire personal identity. In psychogenic fugue people forget their entire identity, wander away from home, and assume a new identity somewhere else.

What are some of the identifying symptoms of multiple personality disorder?

Multiple personality disorder is one in which two or more distinct, unique personalities occur in the same person, each taking over at different times. Most patients are female and victims of early, severe physical and/or sexual abuse, and they typically complain of periods of "lost time."

Key Terms

anxiety disorders (p. 481)
anxiety (p. 481)
generalized anxiety disorder (p. 483)
panic disorder (p. 483)
phobia (p. 484)
agoraphobia (p. 484)
social phobia (p. 484)
simple phobia (p. 484)
obsessive compulsive disorder (OCD) (p. 485)
obsession (p. 485)
compulsion (p. 486)
somatoform disorders (p. 488)
hypochondriasis (p. 488)
conversion disorder (p. 488)
dissociative disorder (p. 488)
psychogenic amnesia (p. 489)
psychogenic fugue (p. 489)
multiple personality disorder (p. 489)

Schizophrenia and Delusional Disorder

What are some of the major symptoms of schizophrenia?

Schizophrenia is a psychotic disorder characterized by some of the following symptoms: a loss of contact with reality, hallucinations, delusions, inappropriate or flat affect, some disturbance in thought, withdrawal from contact with others, and strange or bizarre behavior.

What are some suggested causes of schizophrenia?

Some suggested causes of schizophrenia are a genetic predisposition and excessive dopamine activity in the brain.

How does delusional disorder differ from schizophrenia?

Delusional disorder is marked by delusions that are more believable and logical than those of schizophrenia; intellectual functioning apart from the delusions usually remains intact.

Key Terms

schizophrenia (p. 491)
hallucinations (p. 491)
delusions (p. 492)
inappropriate affect (p. 492)
catatonic schizophrenia (p. 493)
paranoid schizophrenia (p. 493)
delusional disorder (p. 495)

Mood Disorders

What are the symptoms of major depression?

Major depression is characterized by feelings of great sadness, despair, guilt, worthlessness, hopelessness, and in extreme cases, suicidal intentions.

What are the extremes of mood suffered in bipolar disorder?

Bipolar disorder is a mood disorder in which a person suffers from manic episodes (periods of extreme elation, euphoria, and hyperactivity) alternating with major depression, usually with relatively normal periods in between.

What are some suggested causes of major depression and bipolar disorder?

Some of the proposed causes are (1) a genetic predisposition, (2) an imbalance in the neurotransmitters norepinephrine and serotonin, (3) turning hostility and resentment inward rather than expressing it, (4) distorted and negative views of self, the world, and the future, and (5) stress.

What people are at the greatest risk of committing suicide?

Suicide rates are highest for males, whites, the elderly, people who have made previous suicide attempts, and those with psychiatric disorders such as depression, schizophrenia, panic disorder, and alcohol or drug abuse.

Key Terms

mood disorders (p. 496)
major depression (p. 496)
seasonal affective disorder (SAD) (p. 496)
bipolar disorder (p. 497)
manic episode (p. 497)

Other Psychological Disorders

What characteristics are shared by most people with personality disorders?

Personality disorders are long-standing, inflexible, maladaptive patterns of behaving and relating to others, patterns that begin early in life and cause impairment in social and occupational functioning and/or personal distress.

What are two categories of sexual disorders?

Two categories of sexual disorders are sexual dysfunctions (inhibited sexual desire or impaired sexual performance due to psychological causes) and paraphilias (the necessity for unusual or bizarre objects, conditions, or acts for sexual gratification).

Key Terms

personality disorder (p. 501)
antisocial personality disorder (p. 504)

15

Therapies

Mary Beth Olson is a young professional musician, a violinist with a promising talent who made her professional debut 3 years ago. Now considered among the best young violinists in the Midwest, she will walk on stage in less than half an hour and play the Brahms violin concerto.

Mary Beth enjoyed rave reviews and critical acclaim for the first two years of her professional career, but during the last year, she has been plagued by nagging doubts. "Can I play as well this time as I have before?" she wonders. She usually played beautifully, but lately she has struggled through longer and longer periods of performance anxiety before going on stage. She has tried tranquilizers, which calm her down but rob her playing of its technical facility, power, and intensity.

In 20 minutes the orchestra will finish its overture, and Mary Beth will make her entrance. The hall is packed, and her entire family is there, along with her beloved teacher and mentor from the Juilliard School, where she had studied. "I can't let them down," she tells herself, but as the time draws nearer her heart begins to pound and her palms to sweat.

Fortunately, Mary Beth has been undergoing cognitive behavior therapy for the past several months. In the remaining minutes, she reviews what she has learned about controlling her own thinking to combat performance anxiety. "These people are all on my side, my friends and family, my fans. I have practiced and played this concerto hundreds of times. I know I can do it. Just relax . . . take slow deep breaths. Go out there and do what you've done so many times before. Relax, breathe, concentrate on the music."

Mary Beth walks on stage, still a little anxious, but she *appears* confident and self-assured. As she plays, she loses herself in the music, which ends to thundering applause and two encores.

MANY OF US CAN RELATE to the performance anxiety that might have ruined Mary Beth Olson's promising career. We have felt similar anxiety when expected to give a talk, make a report, conduct a meeting, or take a test in class. A number of treatment approaches have been developed to control performance anxiety, including various drugs, counseling, and several behavior therapy techniques. Recent research suggests that cognitive behavior therapy is one of the most effective approaches for treating performance anxiety (Clark & Agras, 1991).

This chapter will present a variety of modern therapies designed to treat psychological disorders. We will explore the insight therapies, which use talk, thought, reasoning, understanding, and analysis to treat psychological problems. Next we will look at behavior therapies, which are based on principles of learning theory. Finally we will examine the biological therapies and learn about drug therapy, electroconvulsive therapy (ECT), and psychosurgery.

Insight Therapies

psychotherapy: The treatment for psychological disorders that uses psychological rather than biological means and primarily involves conversations between patient and therapist.

insight therapy: Any type of psychotherapy based on the notion that psychological well-being depends on self-understanding.

What comes into your mind when you hear the word *psychotherapy*? Many people picture a patient on a couch talking to a gray-haired, bearded therapist with a heavy accent. But that picture is hopelessly out of date, as you will see. **Psychotherapy** uses psychological rather than biological means to treat emotional and behavioral disorders, and it usually involves a conversation between the patient (often called a client) and the therapist. Psychotherapy has grown and changed enormously since its beginnings in the days of Freud, over 100 years ago. Now it seems that there is a therapy for every trouble, a technique for every taste—over 450 different psychotherapies (Karasu, 1986). Today, for the most part, the couch has been replaced by a comfortable chair, and instead of years of treatment, psychotherapy is usually relatively brief, averaging about 18 sessions among private therapists (Goode, 1987). Furthermore, psychotherapy in the modern age is not completely dominated by men, as more women are becoming therapists. We have come a long way since the days of Sigmund Freud.

Some forms of psychotherapy are collectively referred to as **insight therapies** because their assumption is that our psychological well-being depends on self-understanding—understanding our thoughts, emotions, motives, behavior, and coping mechanisms. The major insight therapies are psychoanalysis, person-centered therapy, existential therapy, and Gestalt therapy.

Psychodynamic Therapies: Freud Revisited

Freud originally proposed the psychodynamic perspective on abnormal behavior, which maintains that the cause of abnormal behavior lies in early childhood experiences and in unresolved, unconscious conflicts, usually of a sexual or aggressive nature. **Psychoanalysis**, the treatment approach developed by Freud, was the first formal psychotherapy, and it was the dominant influence in psychotherapy in the 1940s and 1950s (Garfield, 1981). The goals of psychoanalysis are to uncover repressed memories and to bring to consciousness the buried, unresolved conflicts believed to lie at the root of the person's problem.

Question: What are the four basic techniques of psychoanalysis, and how are they used to help disturbed patients?

Psychoanalysis: From the Couch of Freud Freudian psychoanalysis uses four basic techniques: free association, analysis of resistance, dream analysis, and analysis of transference.

Free Association The central technique of psychoanalytic therapy is **free association,** in which the patient is instructed to reveal whatever thoughts, feelings, or images come to mind no matter how terrible, embarrassing, or trivial they might appear. Freud believed that free association allows important unconscious material to surface—repressed memories, threatening impulses, and traumatic episodes of childhood.

The patient lies comfortably on a couch, with the analyst sitting out of the patient's view. This setting is presumed to minimize distractions that might interfere with the patient's free flow of thoughts and speech. The analyst pieces together the free-flowing associations, explains their meaning, and helps patients gain insight into the thoughts and behavior that are troubling them.

Analysis of Resistance How do you think you would react if an analyst told you to express *everything* that came into your mind? Would you try to avoid revealing certain painful or embarrassing thoughts? Freud's patients did, and he called this **resistance.** Freud (1920/1963b) said:

> The patient attempts to escape from it by every possible means. First he says nothing comes into his head, then that so much comes into his head that he can't grasp any of it. . . . He betrays it by the long pauses which occur in his talk. At last he admits that he really cannot say something, he is ashamed to. (p. 254)

psychoanalysis (SY-ko-uh-NAL-ul-sis): The psychotherapy that uses free association, dream analysis, and analysis of resistance and transference to uncover repressed memories, impulses, and conflicts thought to cause psychological disorder.

free association: A psychoanalytic technique used to explore the unconscious by having patients reveal whatever thoughts or images come to mind.

resistance: In psychoanalytic therapy, the patient's attempts to avoid expressing or revealing painful or embarrassing thoughts or feelings.

The famous couch used by Freud's patients during psychoanalysis.

transference: An intense emotional situation occurring in psychoanalysis when one comes to behave toward the analyst as one had behaved toward a significant figure from the past.

If the patient hesitates, balks, or becomes visibly upset about any topic touched on, the analyst assumes that the topic is emotionally important to the patient. Freud also pointed out other forms of resistance, such as "forgetting" appointments with the analyst or arriving late.

Dream Analysis Freud believed that areas of emotional concern repressed in waking life are sometimes expressed in symbolic form in dreams. Freud called dreams "the royal road to the unconscious" because they often convey hidden meanings and identify important repressed thoughts, memories, and emotions.

Analysis of Transference Freud believed that at some point during psychoanalysis, the patient inevitably begins to react to the analyst with the same feelings and attitudes that were present in another significant relationship—usually with the mother or father. This reaction he called **transference**.

> In every analytic treatment there arises . . . an intense emotional relationship between the patient and the analyst. . . . It can be of a positive or of a negative character and can vary between the extremes of a passionate, completely sensual love and the unbridled expression of an embittered defiance and hatred. (Freud, 1925/1963a, p. 71)

Transference allows the patient to relive or re-enact troubling experiences from the past with the analyst as parent substitute. Then the unresolved childhood conflicts can be replayed in the present, but this time with a parent figure who does not reject, provoke guilt, or punish as the actual parent did.

Psychodynamic Therapy Today: The New View Traditional psychoanalysis can be a long and costly undertaking. Patients attend four or five therapy sessions per week for 2 to 4 years. Today, only 2 percent of people undergoing psychotherapy go through classical psychoanalysis (Goode, 1987). This therapy is most suitable for those with average or higher intelligence who are not severely disturbed, but who are interested in extensive self-exploration (Luborsky & Spence, 1978).

Although some psychoanalysts practice traditional psychoanalysis, many practice brief psychodynamic therapy, which is also aimed at gaining insight into unconscious conflicts. The therapist assumes a more active role and places more emphasis on the present than in traditional psychoanalysis (Davanloo, 1980). Brief psychodynamic therapy may require only one or two visits per week for as few as 12 to 20 weeks (Altshuler, 1989). In a meta-analysis of 11 well-controlled studies, Chrits-Christoph (1992) found brief dynamic therapy to be as effective as other psychotherapies.

Criticisms of Psychoanalytic Therapy Traditional psychoanalysis has been criticized for its absorption in the unconscious and the past and for its virtual neglect of the conscious and the present (Applebaum, 1982). Furthermore, the emphasis on unconscious motives as the major determinants of behavior minimizes the patients' responsibility for their behavior and their choices.

The Humanistic and Existential Therapies

Based on a more optimistic and hopeful picture of human nature and human potential, humanistic and existential therapies stand in stark contrast to psychoanalysis. Individuals are viewed as unique and basically self-determining, with the ability and freedom to lead rational lives and make rational choices. Humanistic and existential therapists encourage personal growth and attempt to teach their patients how to fulfill their potential and take responsibility for their behavior and for what they become in life. The focus is primarily on current relationships and experiences (Drob, 1989).

Question: What are the role and the goal of the therapist in person-centered therapy?

Person-Centered Therapy: The Patient Becomes the Person Person-centered therapy, developed by Carl Rogers (1951), is based on the humanistic view of human nature. According to this view, people are innately good and if allowed to develop naturally, they will grow toward **self-actualization** (the realization of their inner potential).

If people grow naturally toward self-actualization, why is it that everyone is not self-actualized? The humanistic perspective suggests that abnormal behavior results when a person's natural tendency toward self-actualization is blocked. Rogers (1959) insisted that individuals block their natural tendency toward growth and self-actualization when they act in ways inconsistent with their true self in order to gain the positive regard of others.

In person-centered therapy (formerly called client-centered therapy), the focus is on conscious thoughts and feelings. The therapist attempts to create a warm, accepting climate in which clients are free to be themselves so that their natural tendency toward growth can be released. Person-centered therapy is a **nondirective therapy**. The direction of the therapy sessions is controlled by the client. The therapist acts as a facilitator of growth, giving understanding, support, and encouragement rather than proposing solutions, answering questions, and actively directing the course of therapy. Rogers rejected all forms of therapy that cast the therapist in the role of expert and clients in the role of patients who expect the therapist to tell them something or prescribe something that "cures" their problem.

According to Rogers, there are only three conditions required of therapists. First, they must have **unconditional positive regard** for, or total acceptance of, the client, regardless of the client's feelings, thoughts, or behavior. In this atmosphere of unconditional positive regard, clients will feel free to reveal their weakest points, to relax their defenses, and to begin to accept and value themselves. Second, therapists' feelings toward their clients must be genuine or con-

person-centered therapy: A nondirective, humanistic therapy in which the therapist creates a warm, accepting climate, freeing clients to be themselves and releasing their natural tendency toward positive growth; developed by Carl Rogers.

self-actualization: Developing to one's fullest potential.

nondirective therapy: An approach in which the therapist acts to facilitate growth, giving understanding and support rather than proposing solutions, answering questions, and actively directing the course of therapy.

unconditional positive regard: A condition required of person-centered therapists, involving a caring for and acceptance of clients regardless of their feelings, thoughts, or behavior.

Carl Rogers (top, right) facilitating discussion in a therapy group.

gruent—no facade, no putting up a professional front. Third, therapists must have empathy with the clients—the ability to put themselves in the clients' place. Therapists must show that they comprehend the clients' feelings, emotions, and experiences, and that they understand and see the clients' world as the clients see it. When clients speak, the therapist follows by restating or reflecting back their ideas and feelings. In this way clients begin to see themselves more clearly and eventually resolve their own conflicts and make positive decisions about their lives.

The following is an excerpt from a 21-year-old woman's first person-centered therapy session.

Therapist: I really know very little as to why you came in. Would you like to tell me something about it?

Client: It is a long story. I can't find myself. Everything I do seems to be wrong. . . . If there is any criticism or anyone says anything about me I just can't take it. . . .

Therapist: You feel things are all going wrong and that you're just crushed by criticism.

Client: Well, it doesn't even need to be meant as criticism. It goes way back. In grammar school I never felt I belonged. . . .

Therapist: You feel the roots go back a long way but that you have never really belonged, even in grammar school.

Client: Lately it's been worse. I even feel I ought to be in a sanitarium. There must be something awfully wrong with me.

Therapist: Things have been so bad you feel perhaps you're really abnormal.

(Rogers, 1977, p. 199)

In the 1940s and 1950s, person-centered therapy was the only psychotherapy other than psychoanalysis with any following among psychologists (Garfield, 1981). Since that time a number of new therapies have been introduced, and many psychologists and counselors no longer restrict themselves to the techniques of just one therapeutic approach. Nevertheless, according to a survey of 400 psychologists and counselors, "Carl Rogers heads by far the list of those who have the greatest influence on counseling and psychotherapy" (Smith, 1982, p. 808).

Question: What is the major emphasis in Gestalt therapy?

Gestalt Therapy: Getting in Touch with Your Feelings Gestalt therapy, developed by Fritz Perls (1969), emphasizes the importance of clients fully experiencing, in the present moment, their feelings, thoughts, and actions and then taking responsibility for both their feelings and behavior. Perls maintains that many of us block out aspects of our experience and are often not aware of how we really feel.

Gestalt therapy is a **directive therapy**, one in which the therapist takes an active role in determining the course of therapy sessions. The well-known phrase "getting in touch with your feelings" is an ever-present objective of the Gestalt therapist, who helps, prods, or badgers clients to experience their feelings as deeply and genuinely as possible and then admit responsibility for them.

A . . . man is tapping his finger on the table while a woman in the group talks on and on. Asked if he has anything to comment about what the woman is saying, he denies much concern with it but continues the tapping. He is asked then to intensify the tapping, to tap louder and more vigorously, and to continue until he feels more fully what he is doing. His anger mounts quickly and in a minute or so he is pounding the table and expressing vehemently his disagreement with the woman. He declares that she is "just like my wife." (Enright, 1970, p. 110)

Gestalt therapy: A therapy originated by Fritz Perls and emphasizing the importance of clients fully experiencing, in the present moment, their feelings, thoughts, and actions and taking personal responsibility for their behavior.

directive therapy: An approach to therapy in which the therapist takes an active role in determining the course of therapy sessions and provides answers and suggestions to the patient.

Perls suggests that those of us who are in need of therapy carry around a heavy load of unfinished business, which may be in the form of resentments or conflicts with parents, siblings, lovers, employers, or others. If not resolved, these conflicts are carried forward into our present relationships. One method for dealing with unfinished business is the "empty chair" technique, which is used to help clients express their true feelings about significant people in their lives. The client imagines, for example, that a wife or husband, father or mother sits in the empty chair. The client then proceeds to tell the "chair" what he or she truly feels about that person. Then the client will trade places and sit in the empty chair and role-play what the imagined person's response would be to what the client has said.

The ultimate goal of Gestalt therapy is not merely to relieve symptoms. Rather, the goal is to help the clients achieve a more integrated self and to become more authentic and self-accepting. In addition, they must learn to assume personal responsibility for their behavior rather than blame society, past experiences, parents, or others.

Existential Therapy: Finding Meaning in Life   Existential therapy helps people deal with the issues that are part of the human condition—finding meaning in life, values that are worth living and even dying for. The existential point of view tries to deal with alienation, the feeling that we are disconnected from the rest of the world, that we don't fit in, that we are lonely and stand apart.

The existential therapist stresses that we have both the freedom and the responsibility to choose the kind of person we want to become. Because each of us is unique, we must find our own personal meaning in our existence.

Memory Check 15.1

1. All insight psychotherapies share the assumption that the client's psychological well-being depends on:

    a. a focus on the present rather than on the past
    b. increased self-understanding
    c. an understanding of the unconscious
    d. all of these

2. The psychoanalytic technique whereby patients reveal every thought, idea, or image that comes to mind is called (free association, transference); the attempt to avoid revealing certain thoughts is called (transference, resistance).

3. (Person-centered, Gestalt) therapy is a directive therapy emphasizing the importance of the client fully experiencing, in the present moment, his or her thoughts, feelings, and actions.

4. (Person-centered, Gestalt) therapy is a nondirective therapy developed by Carl Rogers in which the therapist creates a warm, accepting climate so that the client's natural tendency toward positive change can be released.

Answers 1. b   2. free association; resistance   3. Gestalt   4. Person-centered

Therapies Emphasizing Interaction with Others

Some therapies look not only at the individual's internal struggles but also at the interpersonal relationships.

Question: What is the goal of interpersonal therapy, and for what disorder is it most effective?

Interpersonal Therapy: Short Road to Recovery Interpersonal therapy (IPT) is a brief psychotherapy that has proven very effective in the treatment of depression (Weissman, 1984; Weissman, Klerman, et al., 1981; Elkin et al., 1989). The therapist and the patient focus on the interpersonal conflicts and disturbed relationships that have contributed to the depression. The goal of IPT is to help the patient find solutions to current interpersonal problems (with family, friends, and/or co-workers), find ways to reduce stress at home and at work, and develop the interpersonal skills necessary to initiate and sustain relationships. To accomplish these aims, the family is engaged in the treatment.

Interpersonal therapy is designed specifically to help patients cope with four types of problems commonly associated with major depression: (1) unusual or severe responses to the death of a loved one; (2) interpersonal role disputes such as disagreement about social or sex roles; (3) difficulty in adjusting to role transitions such as divorce, career change, and retirement; and (4) deficits in interpersonal skills (Klerman et al., 1984).

Recent research indicates that patients who recover from major depression can enjoy a longer period without relapse when they continue with monthly sessions of IPT (Frank et al., 1991).

Family and Marital Therapy: Healing Our Relationships For most of us the most significant group to which we will ever belong is the family. But even the best of families sometimes have problems, and there are therapists of all types who specialize in treating the troubled family. Families who come to therapists might be those with troubled or troublesome teenagers, alcoholic parents, abusive family situations, or other problems. In **family therapy**, parents and children enter therapy as a group with one or more family therapists (called conjoint therapy). But as you can imagine, there are some things a family member might want to discuss privately with the therapist. Family therapists realize this and do not conduct every session with the entire family group together. Sometimes they work with only one or a few family members at a time.

The therapist pays attention to the dynamics of the family unit—how family members communicate, how they act toward one another, and how they view each other. Do they quarrel and fight? Is there a power struggle? Are unreasonable demands being made? The goal of the therapist is to help the family reach agreement on certain changes that will help heal the wounds of the family unit, improve communication patterns, and create more understanding and harmony within the group.

Marriages often have problems, too. Nearly half of the couples who decide to "tie the knot" will later decide to untie it. Some therapists work with married couples. They may help them resolve their difficulties and stay together, or ease the emotional turmoil if an adjustment to an irretrievably broken marriage is the best answer for the couple.

Family therapy can be beneficial in the treatment of schizophrenic patients. Patients are more likely to relapse if their family members are overprotective, overly critical, and overly intrusive (labeled high EE, or high in expressed emotion) (Falloon, 1988; Hooley, 1985). Family therapy can help family members modify their behavior.

interpersonal therapy (IPT): A brief psychotherapy designed to help depressed people understand their problems in interpersonal relationships and develop more effective ways to improve them.

family therapy: Therapy based on the assumption that an individual's problem is caused and/or maintained in part by problems within the family unit, and so the entire family is involved in therapy.

Therapists must pay attention to the dynamics of a family—how members communicate, act toward one another, and view each other.

Question: What are some advantages of group therapy?

Group Therapy: Helping One at a Time, Together Group therapy really took root in the military some 50 years ago, during World War II. The armed services ran short of therapists and tried to handle more patients with group therapy. Besides being less expensive than individual therapy, group therapy has other advantages. It gives the individual a sense of belonging and an opportunity to express feelings, to get feedback from other members, and to give and receive help and emotional support. Seeing that others share their problems leaves individuals feeling less alone and ashamed. Most of the therapies we have discussed can be used in a group setting, but there are others that are designed primarily for a group.

Psychodrama, originated by J. L. Moreno (1959) in the mid-1950s, is a technique used by many group therapists. If you entered group therapy based on this approach, you would act out your problem situation or relationship with the assistance and participation of other group members. Sometimes you would play the part of the person who is a problem in your life, a technique called role reversal. You might take the role of your parent, boyfriend, girlfriend, or spouse and in this way gain some understanding of the other person's feelings. When group members act out their own frustrations and role-play the frustrations of others, they can gain insight into the nature of their problems and troubling relationships.

Group Help of a Different Sort Large numbers of Americans are seeking help for their problems from sources other than mental health professionals. Some are attending encounter groups; millions are getting support from self-help groups.

group therapy: A form of therapy in which several clients (usually 7–10) meet regularly with one or two therapists to resolve personal problems.

psychodrama: A group therapy in which one group member acts out personal problem situations and relationships, assisted by other members, to gain insight into the problem.

encounter group: An intense emotional group experience designed to promote personal growth and self-knowledge; participants are encouraged to let down their defenses and relate honestly and openly to one another.

Encounter Groups: Where Anything Goes   Although not technically considered a therapy, **encounter groups** claim to promote personal growth and self-knowledge and to improve personal relationships through intense, emotional encounters with other group members. Groups are composed of 10 to 20 people who meet over a period of several weeks or months. Marathon encounter groups, which meet for 18 to 48 hours, provide a particularly intense form of encounter experience.

Encounter group participants are encouraged to become more open and let down their defenses so that they can reveal themselves to others and allow others to reach them. Group members are urged to express honestly their feelings about themselves and others. Not all exchanges are verbal. Relating to others nonverbally is also encouraged.

> Touching, massaging, holding, hugging, dancing, exercising, playing games, eyeball-to-eyeballing, acting out dreams and fantasies, etc. The purpose of all these activities is to loosen people up emotionally, help them get rid of their inhibitions and resistances, and "peel off their hangups." (Harper, 1979, p. 93)

Sometimes more is peeled off than just hangups—all is bared at nude encounters. Is this really therapy? How successful are these encounters? Are there any dangers involved? Some studies indicate that about one-third of the participants benefit from the experience, one-third are unaffected, and one-third have negative effects (Lieberman et al., 1973). Although encounter leaders generally agree that their groups are not appropriate for disturbed individuals, often little is done to screen applicants. About 8 to 10 percent of encounter group participants have significant negative effects from the experience (Hartley et al., 1976).

Self-Help Groups: Let's Do It Ourselves   A special type of group offering help for specific problems is the self-help group. Unlike other group therapy approaches we have discussed, self-help groups usually are not led by professional therapists. They are simply groups of people who share a common problem and meet to give and receive support from each other. About 12 million people in the United States presently participate in roughly 500,000 self-help groups (Hurley, 1988).

One of the oldest and best known self-help groups is Alcoholics Anonymous, which claims 1.5 million members worldwide (Hurley, 1988). Other self-help groups patterned after Alcoholics Anonymous have been formed to help individuals overcome many other addictive behaviors, from overeating (Overeaters Anonymous) to gambling (Gamblers Anonymous). There are self-help groups for people with a variety of physical and mental illnesses, and groups to help people deal with numerous crises from divorce and bereavement to victimization. Furthermore, there are groups to help relatives and friends of people having such problems.

Self-help groups offer comfort because people can talk about their problems with others who have "been there" and learn that their painful emotional reactions are normal. They exchange useful information, discuss their coping strategies, and gain hope by seeing people who are coping with the same problems successfully (Galanter, 1988). Lieberman (1986), after reviewing a number of studies of self-help groups, concludes that the results tend to be positive. In many cases self-help groups are as effective as psychotherapy for problems such as alcoholism and obesity (Zilbergeld, 1986). Jacobs and Goodman (1989) state that "the self-help group is becoming a serious rival to psychotherapy as a major method for coping with mental health problems" (p. 544).

Memory Check 15.2

1. (Interpersonal therapy, Gestalt therapy) focuses on improving interpersonal relationships and is effective in the treatment of depression.

2. In encounter groups, emphasis is placed on learning how to communicate feelings gently and tactfully. (true/false)

3. Psychotherapy is more beneficial than encounter groups for people with serious emotional disturbance. (true/false)

4. Self-help groups are generally ineffective because they are not led by professionals. (true/false)

Answers: 1. Interpersonal therapy 2. false 3. true 4. false

Behavior Therapy: Unlearning the Old, Learning the New

Question: What is behavior therapy?

Behavior therapy is a treatment approach associated with the learning perspective on abnormal behavior—the perspective that maladaptive behavior is learned. Behavior therapy uses the principles of operant conditioning, classical conditioning, and/or observational learning theory to eliminate inappropriate or maladaptive behaviors and replace them with more adaptive responses. Sometimes this approach is referred to as **behavior modification**.

According to the behaviorists, unless people are suffering from some physiological disorder such as brain pathology, those who seek therapy need it for one of two reasons: (1) they have learned inappropriate or maladaptive responses, or (2) they never had the opportunity to learn appropriate behavior in the first place.

Instead of viewing the maladaptive behavior as a symptom of some underlying disorder, the behavior therapist sees the behavior itself as the disorder. If a person comes to a therapist with a fear of flying, that fear of flying is seen as the problem. The goal is to change the troublesome behavior, not to change the individual's personality structure or to search for the origin of the problem behavior. "Behavior therapy is educational rather than 'healing'" (Thorpe & Olson, 1990, p. 15). The therapist's role is active and directive.

Behavior Modification Techniques Based on Operant Conditioning

Question: How do behavior therapists modify behavior using operant conditioning techniques?

Behavior modification techniques based on operant conditioning seek to control the consequences of behavior. Undesirable behavior is eliminated by taking away the reinforcement for the behavior. If children are showing off to get attention, behavior therapists might recommend ignoring the behavior. If chil-

behavior therapy: A treatment approach employing the principles of operant conditioning, classical conditioning, and/or observational learning theory to eliminate inappropriate or maladaptive behaviors and replace them with more adaptive responses.

behavior modification: The systematic application of learning principles to eliminate undesirable behaviors and/or acquire more adaptive behaviors; sometimes term is used interchangeably with behavior therapy.

dren are nagging or having temper tantrums to get their way, therapists would make sure that the nagging and temper tantrums do not pay off. As we have learned, behavior that is not reinforced will eventually stop.

Behavior therapists would also reinforce any desirable behavior in order to increase its frequency, and they would use reinforcement to shape entirely new behaviors. The process works best when it is applied consistently. Institutional settings such as hospitals, prisons, and school classrooms lend themselves well to these techniques because they provide a restricted environment where the consequences (contingencies) of behavior can be more strictly controlled.

You can readily see the use of shaping in the following case. An attractive and healthy woman at age 18 had became a 47-pound walking skeleton by the age of 37. When she was admitted to the hospital, she could not stand without assistance, and she was in critical condition, in fact, near death. She was diagnosed as suffering from anorexia nervosa—an eating disorder in which individuals eat little or nothing and yet perceive themselves to be fat in spite of excessive, sometimes life-threatening, weight loss (Bachrach et al., 1977, p. 364).

It was decided that a behavior modification program designed to get the patient to eat should be started immediately. A reinforcement schedule was set up that consisted of pleasant conversation when the patient made any movement toward eating. Then an additional reinforcer—radio, TV, and the like— would be presented when she ate any part of her meal. If the patient did not eat any of her food, there were no reinforcements of any kind, and she would be left alone until the next meal. Every day she had to eat more and more of her food in order to be reinforced, until finally she had to finish everything on her plate.

In about two months, she was discharged as an outpatient, having gained 14 pounds—a significant 30 percent weight increase. The treatment was successful and although the patient was no longer near death, the long years of starvation had taken their toll. Irreversible physical damage had been done (Bachrach et al., 1977).

Token Economies: What Would You Do for a Token?

Some behavior modification programs, called **token economies**, reward appropriate behavior with tokens such as poker chips, play money, gold stars, or the like. These tokens can later be exchanged for desired goods (candy, gum, cigarettes) and/or privileges (weekend passes, free time, participation in desirable activities). Sometimes individuals are fined a given number of tokens for undesirable behavior. Such programs are used in institutional settings like hospitals, prisons, and schools. Some mental hospitals have used token economies with chronic schizophrenics to improve self-care skills and social interaction, and with good results (Ayllon & Azrin, 1965, 1968). Patients tend to perform chores when reinforced but not to perform them in the absence of reinforcement. Schizophrenic symptoms such as delusions and hallucinations, of course, were not affected.

Time Out: All Alone with No Reinforcers

Another effective method used to eliminate undesirable behavior, especially in children and adolescents, is **time out** (Brantner & Doherty, 1983). The principle is simple. Children are told in advance that if they engage in certain undesirable behaviors, they will be removed calmly from the situation and have to pass a period of time (usually no more than 15 minutes) in a place containing no reinforcers (no TV, books, toys, friends, and so on). Theoretically, the undesirable behavior will stop if it is no longer followed by attention or any other positive consequence.

Stimulus Satiation: Too Much of a Good Thing

Another behavior modification technique, *stimulus satiation*, attempts to change problem behaviors by giving people too much of whatever they find reinforcing. The idea is that the reinforcer will lose its attraction and become something to be avoided.

token economy: A behavioral technique used to encourage desirable behaviors by reinforcing them with tokens that can be exchanged later for desired objects, activities, and/or privileges.

time out: A behavioral technique, used to decrease the frequency of undesirable behavior, that involves withdrawing the individual from all reinforcement for a period of time.

stimulus satiation (say-she-A-shun): A behavioral technique in which patients are given so much of a stimulus that it becomes something the patients want to avoid.

The stimulus satiation technique was used successfully with a 47-year-old chronic schizophrenic woman who, during her 9 years of hospitalization, would collect and hoard large numbers of towels.

> At the beginning of treatment, the nurses would bring a towel to the patient in her room several times throughout the day, and without any comment simply hand it to her. "The first week she was given an average of 7 towels daily, and by the third week this number was increased to 60" (Ayllon, 1977, p. 358). At first, she seemed to enjoy folding and stacking her towels, but finally, when the patient had 625 towels in her room, she could stand it no longer and began saying to the nurses: "Don't give me no more towels. I've got enough." "Take them towels away . . . I can't sit here all night and fold towels" (p. 359).
>
> Stimulus satiation was working well. Within a few weeks the patient was angrily demanding, "Get these dirty towels out of here." And finally after taking hundreds of towels out of her room, she remarked to the nurse, in desperation, "I can't drag any more of these towels, I just can't do it" (p. 359). During the following 12 months, no more than one or two towels could be found in the patient's room.

The Effectiveness of Operant Approaches: Do They Work? Therapies based on operant conditioning have been particularly effective in modifying some behaviors of seriously disturbed individuals (Ayllon & Azrin, 1968; Paul & Lentz, 1977). Although these techniques do not presume to cure schizophrenia, autism, or mental retardation, they can increase the frequency of behaviors that are desirable and decrease the frequency of undesirable behaviors. Sometimes modifying some of the more extreme and bizarre behaviors can make it possible for the family to accept and care for the patient themselves.

Behavior modification techniques can also be used by people who want to break bad habits such as smoking and overeating or to develop good habits like a regular exercise regime. If you want to modify any of your behaviors, devise a reward system for desirable behaviors, and remember the principles of shaping. Reward gradual changes in the direction of your ultimate goal. If you are trying to develop better eating habits, don't try to change a lifetime of bad habits all at once. Begin with a small step such as substituting margarine for butter, gradually cutting down on the amount you use. Set realistic weekly goals with a likelihood of success.

Therapies Based on Classical Conditioning

Question: What behavior therapies are based on classical conditioning?

Some behavior therapies are based mainly on the principles of classical conditioning, which can account for how we acquire many of our emotional reactions. In chapter 5, "Learning," we discussed how Little Albert came to fear the white rat when it was presented along with a frightening, loud noise (Watson & Rayner, 1920). In classical conditioning, a neutral stimulus—some object, person, or situation that initially does not elicit any strong positive or negative emotional reaction—is paired with some very positive or negative stimulus. Then, after conditioning, our strong feeling toward the positive or negative stimulus transfers to the original, neutral stimulus.

Therapies based on classical conditioning can be used to rid people of fears and other undesirable behaviors. We will discuss four types of therapy based primarily on classical conditioning: systematic desensitization, flooding, exposure and response prevention, and aversion therapy.

Question: How do therapists use systematic desensitization to rid people of fears?

systematic desensitization: A behavior therapy, used to treat phobias, that involves training clients in deep muscle relaxation and then having them confront a graduated series of anxiety-producing situations (real or imagined), until they can remain relaxed while confronting even the most feared situation.

in vivo: Confronting a feared object or situation in real life as opposed to imagining it.

Systematic Desensitization: Overcoming Fears One Step at a Time Have you ever been both afraid and relaxed at the same time? Psychiatrist Joseph Wolpe (1958, 1973) came to the conclusion that these two responses are incompatible, that is, one inhibits the other. Based on this idea, Wolpe developed a therapy to treat fears and phobias. Wolpe reasoned that if he could get you to relax and stay relaxed while you thought about a feared object, person, place, or situation, you could conquer your fear or phobia.

In Wolpe's therapy, **systematic desensitization**, clients are trained in deep muscle relaxation. Then they confront a hierarchy of fears—a graduated series of anxiety-producing situations, either *in vivo* (in real life) or in imagination—until they can remain relaxed even in the presence of the most feared situation. The therapy can be used for everything from fear of animals to acrophobia (fear of high places), claustrophobia (fear of enclosed places), test anxiety, and social and other situational fears.

What do you fear most? Many college students would say that they fear speaking in front of a group. If you went to a behavior therapist who used systematic desensitization, here is what she or he would have you do. First the therapist would ask you to identify the fear causing your anxiety and everything connected with it. Then all the aspects of the fear would be arranged on a hierarchy from least to most anxiety producing, as shown in Figure 15.1.

After preparing the hierarchy, you would be taught deep muscle relaxation, progressively relaxing parts of your body until you achieve a completely relaxed state. During the actual desensitization procedure, you would be asked to picture, as vividly as possible, the least fear-producing item on your hierarchy—reading in the syllabus that the presentation will be assigned. When you are able to remain relaxed while visualizing this item, the therapist would have you move

Figure 15.1 A Hierarchy of Fears Here are eight items that might appear in a hierarchy of fears used in systematic desensitization to help a client overcome a fear of making a class presentation. First a client is trained in deep muscle relaxation. Then the client must visualize the items on the hierarchy, beginning with the least fear-producing item, while remaining completely relaxed. Eventually the client can remain relaxed even when visualizing the most fear-producing item on the hierarchy.

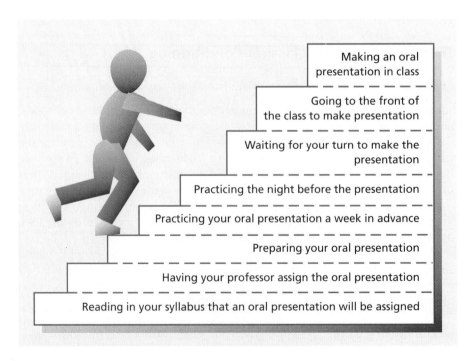

Making an oral presentation in class

Going to the front of the class to make presentation

Waiting for your turn to make the presentation

Practicing the night before the presentation

Practicing your oral presentation a week in advance

Preparing your oral presentation

Having your professor assign the oral presentation

Reading in your syllabus that an oral presentation will be assigned one step up the hierarchy and picture the next item—having your professor assign the oral presentation. This procedure is followed until you reach the top of the hierarchy and can remain calm and relaxed while you imagine vividly the most fear-producing stimulus—actually making your presentation in class. If, during the desensitization process, anxiety creeps in as you imagine items on the hierarchy, you signal the therapist. The therapist would instruct you to stop thinking about that item. You would then clear your mind, come back to a state of complete relaxation, and begin again.

How effective is systematic desensitization? "Systematic desensitization has been the most thoroughly researched, and probably the most frequently used, behavioral procedure in the treatment of simple phobia" (Marshall & Segal, 1988, p. 339). Many experiments, demonstrations, and case reports confirm that systematic desensitization is a highly successful treatment for eliminating fears and phobias in a relatively short time (Kalish, 1981; Rachman & Wilson, 1980). It has proven effective for specific problems like test anxiety, stage fright, and anxiety related to sexual disorders such as impotence and frigidity. Wolpe (1981) claims that skilled behavior therapists using systematic desensitization report marked improvement in about 80 percent of their patients. And desensitization seems to be about equally effective whether it is carried on in real-life settings or in one's imagination (James, 1985).

Is it necessary to follow strictly the techniques used by Wolpe? Not according to one researcher whose results suggest that the order of presentation of the items in the hierarchy does not matter. The only crucial element is the patient's exposure to the feared stimulus (Krapfl, 1967). Even the relaxation, an important part of Wolpe's treatment, is apparently not essential (Wilson & Davison, 1971). But relaxation does help to keep especially fearful patients from jumping up and running away from the fear-provoking stimulus.

There are several other therapies used to treat phobias and obsessive compulsive disorder that have exposure as the key therapeutic element.

Question: What is flooding?

Flooding: Confronting Our Fears All at Once   Flooding is a behavior therapy used in the treatment of phobias, in which clients are exposed to the feared object or event (or asked to vividly imagine it) for an extended period until their anxiety decreases. Flooding is almost the opposite of systematic desensitization. The person is exposed to the fear all at once, not gradually and certainly not in a state of relaxation. An individual with a fear of heights, for example, might have to go onto the roof of a tall building and remain there until the fear subsided. A person with a cat phobia might be told: "Visualize the cat all over you, perhaps scratching you, its eyes right up against yours, its hair all over you" (Sheehan, 1983, pp. 158–159).

What is the key to success in flooding? It is not that a person must be scared to death in order for flooding to work. The key to success is keeping the patients in the situation they fear long enough for them to see that none of the dreaded consequences they fear actually come to pass (Marks, 1978a). If the exposure is too brief, anxiety simply intensifies, and patients get worse instead of better. Flooding sessions typically last from 30 minutes to 2 hours and should not be terminated until patients are markedly less afraid than they were at the beginning of the session. Additional sessions are required until the fear response is extinguished or reduced to an acceptable level. Rarely are more than six treatment sessions needed (Marshall & Segal, 1988).

In vivo flooding, the real-life experience, works faster and is more effective than simply imagining the feared object, and it should be used whenever possible (Chambless & Goldstein, 1979; Marks, 1972). Flooding may be quite painful for the patient and is certainly not the treatment of choice for phobics with a weak heart. But flooding often works when other therapies have failed.

flooding: A behavioral therapy used to treat phobias, during which clients are exposed to the feared object or event (or asked to vividly imagine it) for an extended period until their anxiety decreases.

In treating fear of heights, and other phobias, the therapist gradually helps the client confront the fear.

Flooding has been found to be as effective as systematic desensitization in the treatment of phobias (Gelder et al., 1973) and particularly successful with people suffering from agoraphobia. Often, flooding can rid patients of fears in a few hours, fears that it would take months to get rid of with other treatments (Sheehan, 1983).

Question: How does exposure and response prevention help people with obsessive compulsive disorder?

Exposure and Response Prevention: Cutting the Tie That Binds Fears and Rituals Exposure and response prevention has been a successful therapy for treating obsessive compulsive disorder (Foa et al., 1984; Foa & Tillmanns, 1980; Turner & Michelson, 1984). Initially the therapist determines the thoughts, objects, or situations that trigger the compulsive ritual. Touching a door knob, a piece of unwashed fruit, or garbage might ordinarily send patients with a fear of contamination to the nearest bathroom to wash their hands or take a bath. The therapist arranges exposure sessions during which patients are gradually exposed to stimuli that generate increasing amounts of anxiety. The patients must agree not to carry out the normal ritual (hand-washing, bathing, or the like) for a specified period of time after exposure. For example, patients with excessive concern about contamination might eventually agree not to shower for a week or change clothes for 5 days. Gradually patients learn to tolerate the anxiety evoked by the various "contaminants."

A typical treatment course of about 10 sessions over a period of from 3 to 7 weeks can bring about considerable improvement in 60 to 70 percent of the patients (Jenike, 1990b). And patients treated with exposure are less likely than those treated with drugs to relapse after treatment. O'Sullivan and others (1991) found that 6 years after exposure treatment, 38 percent of the former patients had maintained their gains and 12 percent had improved further.

Systematic desensitization, flooding, and exposure help people to stop avoiding feared objects or situations. But what if the person's problem is just the opposite—bad habits, addictions, and other such behaviors that *should* be avoided? What type of therapy exists to help people learn to avoid situations, break bad habits, and overcome addictions? Aversion therapy is designed to do just that.

Question: How does aversion therapy rid people of a harmful or undesirable behavior?

exposure and response therapy: A behavior therapy that exposes obsessive compulsive disorder patients to stimuli generating increasing anxiety; patients must agree not to carry out their normal rituals for a specified period of time after exposure.

aversion therapy: A behavior therapy used to rid clients of a harmful or socially undesirable behavior by pairing it with an extremely painful, sickening, or otherwise aversive stimulus until the behavior becomes associated with pain and discomfort.

Aversion Therapy: Making Us Sick to Make Us Better Aversion therapy is used to rid clients of a harmful or socially undesirable behavior by pairing it with an extremely painful, sickening, or otherwise aversive stimulus. Electric shock, emetics (which cause nausea and vomiting), or other unpleasant stimuli are paired with the undesirable behavior time after time until a strong negative association is formed and the person comes to avoid that behavior, habit, or substance. Treatment continues until the bad habit loses its appeal because it becomes associated with pain or discomfort.

Smokers treated with aversion therapy are asked to smoke so rapidly and continuously—a puff every 6 to 8 seconds—that smoking becomes extremely distasteful. Although rapid smoking is an effective technique in getting people to quit smoking (Tiffany et al., 1986), only about 50 percent quit permanently (Hall et al., 1984). Because in rare cases cardiac complications can occur with rapid smoking, this technique should be carried out only in a medical setting (Thorpe & Olson, 1990).

Alcoholics are given a nausea-producing substance such as Antabuse, which reacts violently with alcohol and causes people to retch and vomit until their stomach is empty. Obviously the aversion therapist cannot show up at the alcoholic's house every morning with a bottle of Antabuse, but nausea-based aversion therapy has produced abstinence rates of approximately 60 percent one year after treatment (Elkins, 1991; Parloff et al., 1986).

It is even possible to eliminate a harmful or socially undesirable behavior simply by mentally associating it with some unpleasant or disgusting thought or image. Maletzky (1974) has reported success with exhibitionists—in this case, a number of men who experienced sexual satisfaction by flashing their genitals to women on the street. Maletzky tells about one patient whom he instructed to imagine the sexually deviant activity the patient found exciting and pleasurable. At the height of the patient's imagined pleasure, the therapist would describe a scene so vivid and sickening that the patient became violently ill and vomited all over himself. The therapist strengthened the technique by adding a foul-smelling substance to the revolting verbal description. At the end of a 12-month period, not one of the patients had been arrested for exposing himself, and none reported the deviant sexual urges and fantasies of the past.

Therapies Based on Observational Learning Theory: Just Watch THIS!

Question: How does participant modeling help people overcome fears?

A great deal of what we learn in life results from watching others and then copying or imitating the behaviors modeled for us. Much positive behavior is learned this way, but so are bad habits, aggressive behavior, and fears or phobias. Therapies, derived largely from the work of Albert Bandura, are based on the belief that people can overcome fears and acquire social skills through modeling.

Fears and phobias have been effectively treated by having clients watch a model (on film or in real life) responding to a feared situation in appropriate ways with no dreaded consequences. Usually the model approaches the feared object in gradual steps. Bandura describes how nursery school children lost their fear of dogs after watching a film depicting a child who was not afraid of dogs first approach a dog, then play with it, pet it, and so on (Bandura, 1967). Modeling films have been used to reduce fears of children preparing for surgery (Melamed & Siegel, 1975) and to reduce children's fear of the dentist (Adelson et al., 1972; Shaw & Thoresen, 1974).

The most effective type of therapy based upon observational learning theory is called **participant modeling** (Bandura, 1977; Bandura et al., 1975, 1977). Here the model not only demonstrates the appropriate response in graduated steps, but the client attempts to imitate the model step by step, while the therapist gives encouragement and support. This technique provides the additional benefit of exposure to the feared stimulus.

Suppose you had a snake phobia and your therapist used participant modeling. First she would calmly approach the snake's cage and encourage you to do the same. Then the therapist would show you how easy it is to handle a snake while it is in the cage. She would urge you to touch it, perhaps suggesting how surprised you will be to find that the snake does not feel at all slimy. Next she could remove the snake from the cage and have you observe her holding it for a period of time with no adverse results. In this manner your behavior would gradually imitate hers until you reached the point of allowing the snake to crawl freely on you.

Most simple phobias can be extinguished in only 3 or 4 hours of modeling therapy when the client participates. Participant modeling has proved more

Cigarette smoking can be reduced or eliminated through aversive conditioning.

participant modeling: A behavior therapy in which an appropriate response is modeled in graduated steps and the client attempts each step, encouraged and supported by the therapist.

Most simple phobias, such as fear of snakes, can be extinguished after only a few hours of modeling therapy when the client participates.

effective in curing snake phobias than simply observing a filmed or live model, and more effective than systematic desensitization (Bandura et al., 1969). In fact, 92 percent of the subjects completely lost their fear of snakes.

Memory Check 15.3

1. Techniques based on (classical, operant) conditioning try to change behavior by removing reinforcers for undesirable behavior.

2. Behavior therapies based on classical conditioning are used mainly to:

   a. shape new and more appropriate behaviors
   b. rid people of fears and undesirable behaviors or habits
   c. develop social skills
   d. all of these

3. Match the description with the therapy.

   _____ 1) flooding

   _____ 2) aversion therapy

   _____ 3) systematic desensitization

   _____ 4) participant modeling

   a. deep muscle relaxation and gradual exposure to feared object

   b. imagining painful or sickening stimuli associated with undesirable behavior

   c. direct exposure to feared object without relaxation

   d. imitating a model responding appropriately in the feared situation

Cognitive Behavior Therapies: It's the Thought That Counts

We have seen that behavior therapies based on classical and operant conditioning and modeling are effective in eliminating many types of troublesome behavior. What if the problem is not an observable, undesirable behavior but rather is in our thinking, attitudes, false beliefs, or poor self-concept? There are therapies for these problems as well. **Cognitive behavior therapies** are based on the cognitive perspective and assume that maladaptive behavior can result from irrational thoughts, beliefs, and ideas, which the therapist tries to change. The emphasis in cognitive behavior therapies is on conscious rather than unconscious processes and on the present rather than the past. According to Dobson (1988), there are at least 22 variations of cognitive behavior therapy, including rational-emotive therapy, stress-inoculation training, and Beck's cognitive therapy.

Rational-Emotive Therapy: Human Misery—The Legacy of False Beliefs

Question: What is the aim of rational-emotive therapy?

Picture this scenario: Harry received two free tickets to a concert for Saturday night featuring his favorite group. Excited and looking forward to a great time on Saturday, Harry called Sally, whom he had dated a couple of times, to ask her to share the evening with him. But she turned him down with some lame excuse like "I have to do my laundry." He was stunned, disappointed. "How could she do this to me?" he wondered. What happened? As the week dragged on, he became more and more depressed.

What caused Harry's depression? Sally turning him down, right? Not according to Albert Ellis (1961, 1977, 1987), a clinical psychologist who developed **rational-emotive therapy** in the 1950s. Rational-emotive therapy is based on Ellis's ABC theory. The *A* refers to the *activating* event, the *B* to the person's *belief* about the event, and the *C* to the emotional *consequence* that follows. Ellis claims that it is not the event that causes the emotional consequence, but rather it is the person's belief about the event. In other words, *A* does not cause *C*; *B* causes *C*. If the belief is irrational, then the emotional consequence can be extreme distress, as illustrated in Figure 15.2.

"Everyone should love me!" "I must be perfect!" Because reality does not conform to these and other irrational beliefs, patients are doomed to frustration and unhappiness. Irrational beliefs cause people to view an undesirable event as a catastrophe rather than as a disappointment or an inconvenience, leading them to say "I can't stand this" rather than "I don't like this." Irrational beliefs cause people to feel depressed, worthless, or enraged instead of simply disappointed or annoyed. And to make matters worse, they go on to feel "anxious about their anxiety" and "depressed about their depression" (Ellis, 1987, p. 369).

Rational-emotive therapy is a directive, confrontational form of psychotherapy designed to challenge clients' irrational beliefs about themselves and others. It helps them to see, rationally and logically, that their false beliefs and unrealistic expectations are the real cause of their problems. As clients begin to replace irrational beliefs with rational ones, their emotional reactions become more appropriate, less distressing, and more likely to lead to constructive behavior.

Most clients in rational-emotive therapy are seen individually, once a week, for 5 to 50 sessions. In stark contrast to person-centered therapists (and most other therapists, for that matter), "rational-emotive therapists do not believe a warm relationship between counselee and counselor is a necessary or a sufficient

cognitive behavior therapy: A therapy designed to change maladaptive thoughts and behavior, based on the assumption that maladaptive behavior can result from one's irrational thoughts, beliefs, and ideas.

rational-emotive therapy: A directive, confrontational psychotherapy designed to challenge and modify the clients' irrational beliefs thought to cause their personal distress; developed by Albert Ellis.

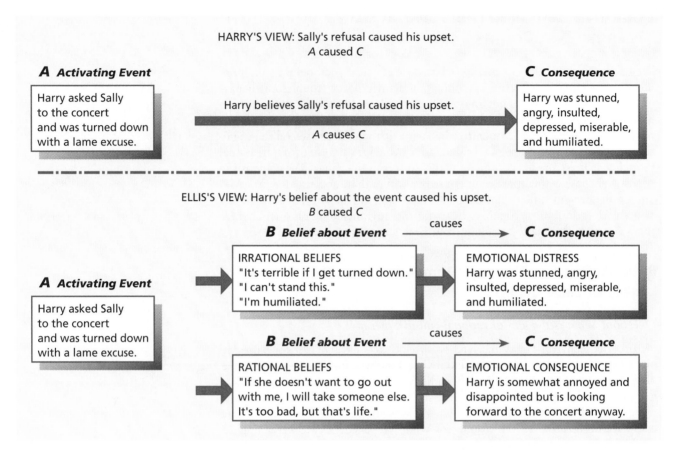

HARRY'S VIEW: Sally's refusal caused his upset.
A caused *C*

A *Activating Event*

Harry asked Sally
to the concert
and was turned down
with a lame excuse.

Harry believes Sally's refusal caused his upset.

A causes *C*

C *Consequence*

Harry was stunned,
angry, insulted,
depressed, miserable,
and humiliated.

ELLIS'S VIEW: Harry's belief about the event caused his upset.
B caused *C*

B *Belief about Event* —— causes ——> **C** *Consequence*

IRRATIONAL BELIEFS
"It's terrible if I get turned down."
"I can't stand this."
"I'm humiliated."

EMOTIONAL DISTRESS
Harry was stunned, angry,
insulted, depressed, miserable,
and humiliated.

A *Activating Event*

Harry asked Sally
to the concert
and was turned down
with a lame excuse.

B *Belief about Event* —— causes ——> **C** *Consequence*

RATIONAL BELIEFS
"If she doesn't want to go out
with me, I will take someone else.
It's too bad, but that's life."

EMOTIONAL CONSEQUENCE
Harry is somewhat annoyed and
disappointed but is looking
forward to the concert anyway.

Figure 15.2   The ABCs of Albert Ellis's Rational Emotive Therapy   Rational emotive therapy teaches clients that it is not the activating event (A) that causes their upsetting consequences (C). Rather, it is the client's beliefs (B) about the activating event. Irrational beliefs cause emotional distress, according to Albert Ellis. Rational emotive therapists help clients identify their irrational beliefs and replace them with rational ones.

Aaron T. Beck (Brad Bower/Picture Group)

condition for effective personality change" (Ellis, 1979, p. 186). In Ellis's view, "Giving a client RET with a good deal of warmth, approval and reassurance will tend to help this client 'feel better' rather than 'get better'" (p. 194).

Beck's Cognitive Therapy: Overcoming "The Power of Negative Thinking"

Question: How does Beck's cognitive therapy help people overcome depression and anxiety disorders?

"In order to be happy, I have to be successful in whatever I undertake."
"To be happy, I must be accepted (liked, admired) by all people at all times."
"My value as a person depends on what others think of me."
"If people disagree with me, it means they don't like me."

If you agree with all of these statements, you probably spend a good part of your time upset and unhappy. Psychiatrist Aaron T. Beck (1976) claims much of the misery of depressed and anxious people can be traced to **automatic thoughts**—unreasonable but unquestioned ideas that rule the person's life. Beck (1991) believes that depressed persons hold "a negative view of the present, past, and future experiences" (p. 369). They tend to view themselves as "deficient, defective, and/or undeserving"; their environment as "unduly demanding, depriving, and/or rejecting"; and their future as "without promise, value, or meaning" (Karasu, 1990a, p. 138).

Depressed persons draw negative conclusions from their erroneous assumptions about love, approval, achievement, and the like: "If I don't win X's love, I am unworthy; If disappointing event X occurs in my presence, it's my fault; If goal X is denied me once, it will never be mine" (Karasu, 1990a, p. 138).

The goal of **Beck's cognitive therapy** is to help patients stop their negative thoughts as they occur, and replace them with more objective thoughts. The focus is on the present rather than on the past, and no attempt is made to uncover hidden meanings in the patients' thoughts and responses. After challenging patients' irrational thoughts, the therapist sets up a plan and guides patients so that their own experience can provide actual evidence in the real world to refute their false beliefs. Patients are given homework assignments, such as keeping track of automatic thoughts and the feelings evoked by them and substituting more rational thoughts.

Beck's cognitive therapy is brief, usually lasting only 10 to 20 sessions, and is therefore less expensive than many other types of therapy (Beck, 1976). This therapy has been researched extensively and is reported to be highly successful in the treatment of mild to moderately depressed patients (Dobson, 1989; Thase et al., 1991). There is some evidence that depressed people who have received cognitive therapy are less likely to relapse than those who have been treated with antidepressants (Blackburn et al., 1986; Miller et al., 1989).

Cognitive therapy also seems to hold promise for generalized anxiety disorder (Clark & Beck, 1988) and panic disorder (Beck et al., 1992). When patients misinterpret bodily sensations associated with anxiety as a sign of mental or physical collapse, their anxiety escalates and causes panic (Michelson et al., 1990). Cognitive therapy teaches them to change their catastrophic interpretations of these symptoms and thereby prevent the escalation of the symptoms into panic (Sokol, Beck, et al., 1989; Klosko et al., 1990). Cognitive therapy has been effective when coupled with exposure in social phobia (Gelernter et al., 1991). We saw how Mary Beth Olson's performance anxiety was controlled by cognitive behavior therapy.

automatic thoughts: Unreasonable and unquestioned ideas that rule a person's life and lead to depression and anxiety.

Beck's cognitive therapy: A brief cognitive behavior therapy for depression and anxiety designed to help people recognize their automatic thoughts and replace them with more objective thoughts.

Memory Check 15.4

1. Cognitive behavior therapists believe that, for the most part, emotional disorders:

    a. have physical causes
    b. result from unconscious conflicts and motives
    c. result from faulty and irrational thinking
    d. all of these

2. Rational-emotive therapy is a nondirective therapy that requires a warm, accepting therapist. (true/false)

3. Beck's cognitive therapy has proven very successful in the treatment of depression and (schizophrenia, anxiety disorders).

Answers: 1. c 2. false 3. anxiety disorders

biological therapy: A therapy, based on the assumption that most mental disorders have physical causes, that attempts to change or influence the biological mechanism involved (examples: drug therapy, ECT, or psychosurgery).

antipsychotic drugs: Drugs used to control severe psychotic symptoms, such as the delusions and hallucinations of schizophrenics; the major tranquilizers.

The Biological Therapies

Question: What are the three main biological therapies?

Professionals who favor the biological perspective, the view that abnormal behavior is a symptom of an underlying physical disorder, usually favor a **biological therapy**. The three treatment categories that make up the biological therapies are drug therapy, electroconvulsive therapy (ECT), and psychosurgery.

Drug Therapy: Pills for Psychological Ills

The favorite and by far the most frequently used biological treatment is drug therapy. A major breakthrough in drug therapy came in the mid-1950s, when antipsychotic drugs, sometimes called the major tranquilizers, were introduced to treat schizophrenia. In the late 1950s antidepressants were discovered and finally, in 1970, lithium, the miracle drug for bipolar disorder, was introduced into psychiatry in the United States (Snyder, 1984). Now capable of relieving the debilitating symptoms of schizophrenia, depression, bipolar disorder, and some anxiety disorders, modern drug therapy has had a tremendous impact on the treatment of psychological disorders.

Question: How do antipsychotic drugs help schizophrenic patients?

Antipsychotic Drugs   Throughout the long course of history, efforts to treat schizophrenia have been woefully inadequate. Mental hospitals confined many patients to locked wards. Padded cells, straight jackets, and other restraints were widely used. Then, shortly after the introduction of the antipsychotic drugs in 1955, the picture suddenly changed. This breakthrough in drug therapy, coupled with the federal government's effort to reduce involuntary hospitalization of mental patients, enabled many "schizophrenics who had been warehoused in asylums" to be discharged into the community (Snyder, 1984, p. 141). In fact the mental hospital patient population has decreased from about 559,000 in 1955, when the drugs were introduced, to slightly over 100,000 by 1990, as shown in Figure 15.3.

Antipsychotic drugs include a group of drugs called the phenothiazines (sold as Thorazine, Stelazine, Compazine, and Mellaril). Prescribed mainly for schizophrenics, antipsychotic drugs are used to control severe psychotic symptoms, such as hallucinations, delusions, and other disorders in thinking. They are also effective in reducing restlessness, agitation, and excitement. The drugs apparently work by inhibiting the activity of the neurotransmitter dopamine (Baldessarini, 1988). A new but extremely expensive drug, clozapine, has been found to help many schizophrenic patients not helped by the other antipsychotics (Pickar et al., 1992).

Schizophrenics who were hospitalized in the past could expect to stay for weeks or months, but now, thanks to the antipsychotics, the average stay of such patients is usually a matter of days. But even though antipsychotic drugs help two-thirds of the patients, they do not cure schizophrenia (Wolkin et al., 1989). The drugs reduce and control many of the major symptoms so that patients are able to function, but most patients must continue to take them in order to keep the symptoms under control (Herz et al., 1991). Several cross-cultural studies have revealed that in the United States, Germany, and Japan, schizophrenic patients receiving antipsychotics at the early stages of their illness had fewer relapses and longer periods between relapses than patients who receive drug treatment later in their illness (Wyatt, 1992).

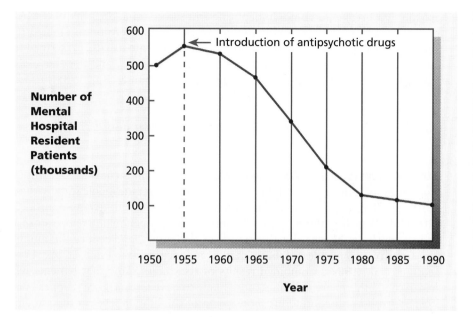

Figure 15.3

Decrease in Patient Populations in State and County Mental Hospitals (1950–1990)

State and county mental hospital patient populations peaked at approximately 560,000 in 1955. In the same year the antipsychotic drugs were introduced. The drugs coupled with the federal government's efforts to reduce involuntary hospitalization of mental patients resulted in a dramatic decrease in the patient population—down to about 100,000 in 1990.

Question: For what conditions are antidepressants prescribed?

Antidepressant Drugs Not long after the antipsychotic drugs came on the scene, another group of drugs, the **antidepressants**, were introduced. Antidepressants act effectively as mood elevators for people who are severely depressed, and they have proven helpful in the treatment of certain anxiety disorders.

Imbalances in the neurotransmitters serotonin and norepinephrine often accompany symptoms of depression. The tricyclic antidepressants, which include amitriptyline (Elavil) and imipramine (Tofranil), work against depression by blocking the reuptake of norepinephrine and serotonin into the axon terminals, thus enhancing their action in the synapses. The tricyclics are the drug treatment of first choice for major depression (Nelson, 1991), proving effective for over 60 percent of depressed patients (Karasu, 1990b). Imipramine is also effective in relieving the symptoms of panic disorder and agoraphobia (Mavissakalian, 1990). In fact, Aronson (1987) found that 88 percent of panic-disorder patients who could tolerate the drug stopped having panic attacks.

Other types of antidepressants block the reuptake of serotonin and include such drugs as fluoxetine (sold as Prozac) and clomipramine (Anafranil). Over 1 million prescriptions each month are written for Prozac, making it the most widely used antidepressant. It is most effective for less severe depression with from 50 to 60 percent of patients showing improvement (Nelson, 1991). The vast majority of its users consider it a wonder drug because it has fewer unpleasant side effects than the tricyclic antidepressants.

Antidepressants that affect the reuptake of serotonin have proven very effective in the treatment of obsessive compulsive disorder, which has been associated with a serotonin imbalance (Barr et al., 1992; Goodman et al., 1989; Rapoport, 1989). "Although some patients respond with a total resolution of symptoms, most describe a 35%–60% decrease in obsessions and compulsions after 10 weeks of treatment" (Jenike, 1990a, p. 16).

Monoamine Oxidase Inhibitors (MAO Inhibitors) Another line of treatment for depression is the monoamine oxidase inhibitors. By blocking the action of an

antidepressants: Drugs that are prescribed to treat depression and some anxiety disorders.

lithium: A drug used to control the symptoms in a manic episode and to even out the mood swings and reduce recurrence of future manic or depressive states in bipolar disorder.

enzyme that breaks down norepinephrine and serotonin in the synapses, MAO inhibitors increase the availability of norepinephrine and serotonin. These drugs (sold under the names Marplan, Nardil, and Parnate) are usually prescribed for patients who do not respond to the other antidepressants, and they have also been found effective in treating panic disorder (Sheehan & Raj, 1988).

Question: How does lithium help patients with bipolar disorder?

Lithium: A Natural Salt That Evens Moods   Lithium is considered a wonder drug for bipolar disorder, and it is said to begin to quiet the manic state within 5 to 10 days. This is a noteworthy accomplishment because the average episode, if untreated, lasts for about 3 to 4 months. The proper maintenance dose of lithium will usually even out the moods of the patient and reduce the number and severity of episodes of both mania and depression (Prien et al., 1984; Teuting et al., 1981). Combined results of six studies show that patients who discontinue lithium are 6.3 times more likely to have a recurrence (Suppes et al., 1991). Careful and continuous monitoring of the lithium level in the patient's system is absolutely necessary to guard against lithium poisoning and permanent damage to the nervous system (Schou, 1989).

The Minor Tranquilizers   The family of minor tranquilizers called benzodiazepines include Valium, Librium, and the newer drug Xanax. They are effective in relieving anxiety and in general do not reduce alertness, impair thought processes, or produce euphoria when taken in regularly prescribed doses (Goodwin, 1986). Xanax appears to be particularly effective in relieving depression as well as anxiety. Benzodiazepines are viewed by many experts as generally quite safe (Woods & Charney, 1988). In fact, they are virtually suicide proof.

Question: What are some of the problems with drug therapy?

Some Problems with Drug Therapy   So far, one might conclude that drug therapy is the simplest and possibly the most effective way of treating schizophrenia, depression, panic disorder, and obsessive compulsive disorder. There are, however, a number of potential problems with the use of drugs. Antipsychotics and antidepressants have side effects that can be unpleasant enough that a number of patients stop treatment before they have a reduction in symptoms. Other patients discontinue treatment even if they believe the drugs are helping to relieve their psychological distress. Antipsychotics commonly cause dryness in the mouth and throat, drowsiness, abnormal muscle contractions, and difficulty moving. Tricyclics frequently cause nervousness, fatigue, dry mouth, weight gain, a drop in blood pressure, and more (McLean & Carr, 1989; Thase & Shipley, 1988). According to Noyes and others (1989), progressive weight gain—an average of over 20 pounds—is the main reason people stop taking tricyclics in spite of relief from their distressing psychological symptoms. Lithium often causes weight gain, hand tremors, and excessive thirst.

Antipsychotics, antidepressants, and lithium do not cure psychological disorders, so patients usually experience a relapse if they stop taking the drugs when their symptoms lift. Maintenance doses of antidepressants following a major depression reduce the probability of recurrences (Maj et al., 1992). Maintenance doses are usually required with anxiety disorders as well, or symptoms are likely to return (Pato et al., 1988).

People who have not been helped with drug therapy may have been given too low a dosage for too short a period of time (Keller, 1989). When the same drugs are administered in the same dose to different people, there can be a 40-fold difference in blood levels of the antipsychotics (Torrey, 1983) and a 30-fold difference in blood levels of the tricyclics (Greist & Jefferson, 1984). This means that the correct dose for one patient may be too much or too little for another patient. "Many 'nonresponders' to antidepressant drugs may become responders with a higher dosage and/or longer duration of treatment" (Joyce & Paykel, 1989, p. 94).

The main problem with antidepressants is that they are relatively slow acting and, more often than not, depressed patients have to try several different antidepressants before finding one that is effective. A severely depressed patient would need at least 2 to 6 weeks to obtain relief, and 30 percent don't respond at all. This can be too risky for suicidal patients. If suicide is an imminent danger, antidepressant drugs are not the treatment of choice. In such cases many experts consider electroconvulsive therapy (ECT) the preferred treatment.

electroconvulsive therapy (ECT): A treatment in which an electric current is passed though the brain, causing a seizure; usually reserved for the severely depressed who are either suicidal or unresponsive to other treatment.

Electroconvulsive Therapy: The Controversy Continues

Question: For what purpose is electroconvulsive therapy (ECT) used?

Electroconvulsive therapy (ECT), or electric shock, as a treatment for mental disorders was introduced by two Italian physicians, Cerletti and Bini, in 1938 (Kalinowsky, 1986). ECT was widely used as a treatment for several mental disorders until the introduction of the antipsychotic and antidepressant drugs in the 1950s. ECT developed a bad reputation partly because it was misused and overused in this country in the 1940s and 1950s. Often it was misused simply to make troublesome patients easier to handle, and some patients received hundreds of shock treatments. Today electroconvulsive therapy is used mainly as a treatment for severe depression.

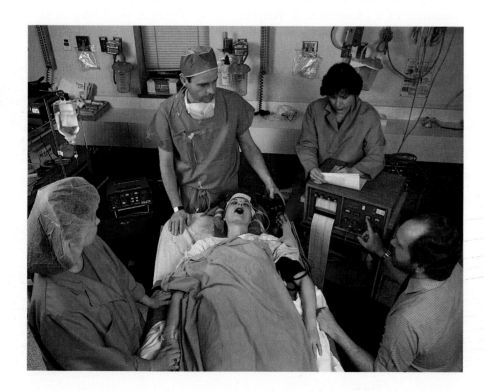

In electroconvulsive therapy a mild electronic current is passed through the brain for 1–2 seconds, causing a brief seizure.

If you were to have electroconvulsive therapy, what could you expect? Two electrodes would be placed on your head, and a mild electric current would be passed through your brain for 1 or 2 seconds. Immediately after the shock was administered, you would lose consciousness and experience a seizure lasting about 30 seconds to 1 minute. Apparently, the seizure is necessary if ECT is to have any effect (Sackeim, 1985). The complete ECT procedure takes about 5 minutes, and medical complications following the procedure are said to be rare (Abrams, 1988). Usually there is no pain associated with the treatment, and patients have no memory of the experience when they wake up. Normally ECT is given three times per week for 2 to 4 weeks (Sackeim, 1985).

Although ECT can cut depression short, it is not a cure. Experts think that the seizure temporarily changes the biochemical balance in the brain, which in turn results in a lifting of depression. ECT causes the release of beta endorphins from the pituitary (Young et al., 1991).

The Side Effects of ECT   A number of psychiatrists and neurologists have spoken out and written books and articles against the use of ECT, claiming that the procedure causes pervasive brain damage and memory loss (Breggin, 1979; Friedberg, 1976, 1977; Grimm, 1976). Even the advocates of ECT acknowledge that there are side effects, the most disturbing of which is memory loss. Typically, memory functioning is back to normal after 6 months (Squire, 1986), but on the average ECT can cause permanent gaps in memory for events occurring from 6 months before to 2 months after treatment (Squire & Slater, 1983). Fewer than 1 in 200 ECT patients claim major memory impairment (Fink, 1979).

The severity of the memory loss varies from individual to individual but seems to depend, in part, on how ECT is administered. A different type of electrical current, brief-pulse current rather than sine-wave current, became widely used in the 1980s. It requires less current overall and consequently causes less memory loss. For many years ECT was administered with electric current passing through both cerebral hemispheres (called bilateral ECT). Recent studies show that ECT can be effective and memory problems reduced (1) if a standard dose of current is administered to the right hemisphere only, a procedure known as unilateral ECT (Rosenberg & Pettinati, 1984; Weiner et al., 1986), or (2) if bilateral ECT is administered with just enough current to cause a seizure (Malitz et al., 1986; Sackeim et al., 1986).

While the pros and cons of electroconvulsive therapy continue to be hotly debated, ECT seems to be making a comeback. Current estimates are that up to 100,000 people receive ECT each year (Squire, 1987). According to the National Institute of Mental Health (1985), a majority of psychiatrists believe that there is a legitimate place for ECT in the treatment of severely depressed patients who are suicidal or who have not been helped by any other therapy.

Psychosurgery: Cutting to Cure

Question: What is psychosurgery, and for what problems is it used?

An even more drastic procedure than ECT is **psychosurgery**—brain surgery performed strictly to relieve serious psychological disorders such as severe depression, severe anxiety or obsessions, and some cases of unbearable chronic pain. We should make clear that psychosurgery is not the same as other brain surgery performed to correct a physical problem, such as removing a tumor or blood clot.

psychosurgery: Brain surgery to treat some severe, persistent, and debilitating psychological disorder or severe chronic pain.

In the 1930s experimental brain surgery was performed to calm abnormally excitable animals. The first such surgical procedure for human patients was developed by Portuguese neurologist Egas Moniz in 1935 to treat severe phobias, anxiety, and obsessions. In his technique, the **lobotomy**, the frontal lobes were surgically separated from the deeper brain centers involved in emotion, but no brain tissue was removed. At first the procedure was considered a tremendous contribution and won for Moniz the Nobel Prize in Medicine in 1949. Not everyone considered it a contribution, however. One of Moniz's lobotomized patients curtailed the surgeon's activities by shooting him in the spine, leaving him paralyzed on one side.

Neurosurgeons performed tens of thousands of these operations in the United States and elsewhere from 1935 until 1955. But eventually it became apparent that this treatment was no cure-all. Although the surgery was effective in calming many of the patients, it often left them in a severely deteriorated condition. Apathy, impaired intellect, loss of motivation, and a change in personality kept many from resuming a normal life.

In the mid-1950s, when antipsychotic drugs came into use, psychosurgery virtually stopped. Since that time there has been a "second wave" of psychosurgical procedures that are far less drastic than the lobotomies of decades past. In some of the most modern procedures there is less intellectual impairment because, rather than conventional surgery, electric currents are delivered through electrodes to destroy a much smaller, more localized area of brain tissue. In one procedure called a cingulotomy, electrodes are used to destroy the cingulum, a small bundle of nerves connecting the cortex to the emotional centers of the brain. The cingulotomy has been helpful for some extreme cases of obsessive compulsive disorder (Jenike et al., 1991).

But even today the results of psychosurgery are still not predictable, and for better or worse, the consequences are irreversible. For this reason, the procedure is considered experimental and absolutely a treatment of last resort.

Memory Check 15.5

1. For the most part, advocates of biological therapies assume that mental disorders have (physical, psychological) causes.

2. Match the disorder with the drug most often used for its treatment.

    _____ 1) panic disorder and agoraphobia   a. lithium
    _____ 2) schizophrenia   b. antipsychotic
    _____ 3) bipolar disorder   c. antidepressant
    _____ 4) depression
    _____ 5) obsessive compulsive disorder

3. ECT is typically used for (schizophrenia, severe depression).

4. The major side effect of ECT is (memory loss, loss of motivation).

5. Psychosurgery techniques are now so precise that the exact effects of the surgery can be predicted in advance. (true/false)

Answers: 1. physical 2. 1) c 2) b 3) a 4) c 5) c 3. severe depression 4. memory loss 5. false

lobotomy: A psychosurgery technique in which the nerve fibers connecting the frontal lobes to the deeper brain centers are severed.

WORLD OF PSYCHOLOGY: MULTICULTURAL PERSPECTIVES

Therapy and Race, Ethnicity, and Gender

Do psychotherapists take into account multi-cultural variables such as race, ethnicity, and gender in their therapeutic approaches? Increasingly researchers are considering the influence of racial and ethnic identity on the type of treatment for mental disorders (Flaskenrud & Hu, 1992) and are conducting cross-cultural studies as well (Compton et al., 1991). The National Institute of Mental Health (NIMH) has become interested in the part that cultural factors play in the use of mental health services and the effectiveness of different therapeutic approaches.

For many years it has been common knowledge that various racial and ethnic groups are especially susceptible to specific physical disorders, such as sickle-cell anemia in those of African heritage and Tay-Sachs disease among Eastern European Jews. Now it is known that there are significant racial differences in optimal therapeutic doses of some drugs used to treat mental disorders, including schizophrenia and bipolar disorder. Researcher Ken-Ming Lin discovered that a 2-milligram dose of the drug halperidol relieved symptoms of schizophrenia in Asian patients, but 10 times that dose was required for white American patients (Holden, 1991).

There may be gender differences in the effectiveness of drugs as well. According to Yonkers and others (1992), "Young women seem to respond better to and require lower doses of antipsychotic agents and benzodiazepines than men" (p. 587). In spite of the differences, research to establish the dosage of drugs is conducted on men even though women use the drugs more often than men.

Not only physiological but psychological differences along racial, ethnic, and gender lines must be considered as well. And when the cultures of therapist and patient (client) differ markedly, behavior normal for the patient can be misinterpreted as abnormal by the therapist. Psychologists Sue and Sue (1990) identified four cultural barriers that hinder effective counseling—language, cultural values, social class, and nonverbal communication (gestures, facial expressions, and the like). The Thematic Apperception Test discussed in chapter 12 was used with a group of Puerto Rican patients who were tested in English. Their pauses and the choice of words they used to describe the TAT pictures were interpreted as an indication of psychological problems. In fact their "problems" were not psychological at all but were problems with the language, which was not the patients' native tongue (Suarez, 1983). A group of Mexican Americans interviewed in English were perceived as having more disorders in thinking and more emotional disorders than when they were interviewed in Spanish (Martinez, 1986).

Making direct eye contact, which is presumed by many in the majority culture to connote honesty, interest, and self-confidence, is a gesture of disrespect among many Native Americans. In part the misinterpretation of this and other nonverbal communications helps explain why so many Native Americans (over 50 percent) never return to non-Native American therapists after the first visit (Heinrich et al., 1990).

Gender differences, too, get in the way of effective therapy. Even though women are choosing careers in psychology and as therapists in rapidly increasing numbers, the large majority of practicing therapists in the 1990s remain male, and the majority of their patients are female. If therapists have fixed notions about the appropriate roles of males and females, they may do their clients a disservice. "The job of a therapist is to help clients solve problems in a way that meets their individual needs and respects their cultural perspective and identity" (Ehrenberg & Ehrenberg, 1986, p. 104).

Therapists must take into account multicultural variables such as race, ethnicity, and gender when conducting psychotherapy.

Evaluating the Therapies

How effective is psychotherapy? Several hundred studies have compared the effectiveness of several psychotherapies against no treatment at all. What do these studies show on average? Researchers Smith, Glass, and Miller (1980) tried to answer this question by reanalyzing 475 of the studies, which involved 25,000 patients. Using a complex statistical method known as meta-analysis, they were able to combine the findings of the studies and compare various psychotherapies against no treatment. They concluded that "the average person who receives therapy is better off at the end of it than 80% of the persons who do not" (p. 87). Figure 15.4 shows the comparative effectiveness of various psychotherapies as reported by Smith and others (1980).

Although the study by Smith and others revealed that psychotherapy is better than no treatment, it did not indicate that one type of therapy was more effective than another. In other words the different types of therapy—behavioral, psychodynamic, and cognitive—appeared to be equally effective. Moreover, neither the length of treatment nor the therapists' years of experience appeared to be related to the effectiveness of treatment.

All these findings have led some researchers to suggest that it may be the strength of the relationship between the therapist and the patient that accounts for the effectiveness of treatment, rather than the specific techniques of the various therapies (Pilkonis et al., 1984). Furthermore, it could be the common elements that virtually all therapies share (for example, patient-therapist relationship, "acceptance and support of the patient," "the opportunity to express emotions," and so forth) rather than their differences that account for success (Altshuler, 1989, p. 311).

Figure 15.4   The Effectiveness of Different Types of Psychotherapy   Smith, Glass, and Miller (1980), using meta-analysis, were able to combine the results of 475 studies involving 25,000 patients. The researchers compared the results of various psychotherapies against no treatment and concluded that, on the average, the people receiving therapy were better off than about 80 percent of the people who received no therapy. The percentile ranks indicate how much better off the patients were who received therapy than those who did not receive therapy. (Data from Smith, Glass, & Miller, 1980.)

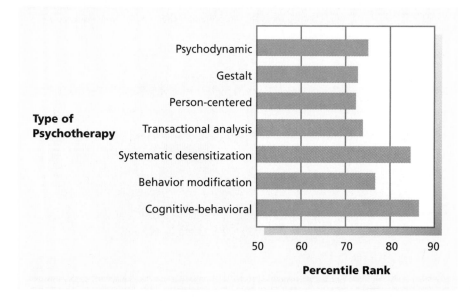

WORLD OF PSYCHOLOGY: APPLICATIONS

Selecting a Therapist: Compatibility Counts

Question: What different types of mental health professionals conduct psychotherapy?

In 1976 only 7 percent of the population had ever been to see a psychologist or psychiatrist (Grossman, 1987). Current estimates suggest that about one-third of the population will receive professional therapy at some time during their lives (Zilbergeld, 1986). During any 6-month period, almost 30 million people in the United States need professional treatment for mental illness (Sullivan, 1987); from 10 to 13 million of those Americans are receiving treatment by mental health professionals outside of hospital settings.

Although there are over 450 types of therapy (Karasu, 1986), there is a trend in psychotherapy toward eclecticism—incorporating techniques from various therapies as appropriate, rather than practicing one type of therapy exclusively. Figure 15.5 shows the percentages of clinical psychologists practicing various types of psychotherapy.

If you or someone you know were in need of a therapist, where would you look? Don't just select a therapist at random. Degrees, training, credentials are all important, but they do not guarantee that you will get quality help. A good place to start in searching for a therapist is to ask family members, friends, and your own doctor for recommendations. Another place would be the psychology or counseling department on campus or the psychiatry department of a local medical school or hospital.

For serious psychological disorders, a clinical psychologist or psychiatrist would be the best source of help. A **clinical psychologist** specializes in the assessment, treatment, and/or research of psychological problems and behavioral disturbances, and usually has a Ph.D. in clinical psychology. Clinical psychologists use various types of psy-

chotherapy to treat a variety of psychological disorders and adjustment problems. A **psychiatrist** is a medical doctor with a specialty in the diagnosis and treatment of mental disorders. Psychiatrists can prescribe drugs and other biological treatments, and many also provide psychotherapy. A **psychoanalyst** is usually, but not always, a psychiatrist with specialized training in psychoanalysis from a psychoanalytic institute.

For clients with other psychological problems, such as adjustment disorders, substance abuse, and marital or family problems, the choice of mental health professionals widens and includes counseling psychologists, counselors, and psychiatric social workers. Counseling psychologists usually have a Ph.D. in clinical or counseling psychology or a Doctor of Education (Ed.D.) with a major in counseling. Counselors typically have a masters degree in psychology or counselor education. Often employed by colleges and universities, counseling psychologists and counselors help students with personal problems and/or test or counsel them in academic or vocational areas.

Psychiatric social workers usually have a master's degree in social work (MSW) with specialized training in psychiatric problems, and they may practice psychotherapy. The entire range of mental health professionals may be found in private practice, in social agencies, or in hospital or clinic settings. Table 15.1 summarizes the different types of mental health professionals, their training, and the nature of the problems they treat.

The type of problem people have will have a bearing on the type of therapist they might select, because many therapists still practice only one type of therapy. Before engaging the services of therapists, prospective clients should ask about therapists' educational background, the nature of their supervised experience, the type of therapy they prac-

Figure 15.5

The Primary Psychotherapeutic Approach Used by a Sample of Clinical Psychologists

Of 579 clinical psychologists who are members of the American Psychological Association, the largest percentage (29 percent) are eclectic therapists. They use a variety of therapies in their practice. (Based on Norcross, Prochaska, & Gallagher, 1989.)

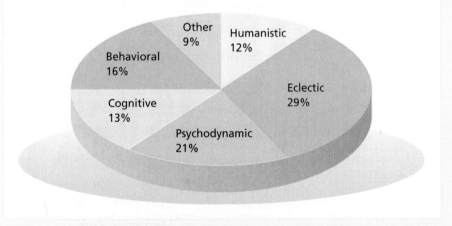

Clinical psychologists	Psychologists, usually having a Ph.D. in clinical psychology, whose training is in the diagnosis and treatment of psychological disorders. Provide various types of psychotherapy.
Counseling psychologists	Psychologists, usually having a Ph.D. or Ed.D. in counseling, who help people with problems that are considered less severe than those generally handled by clinical psychologists, or who provide vocational or academic counseling. Usually work in a nonmedical setting.
Counselors	Professionals, usually having a master's degree in psychology or counselor education, who help people with personal problems and/or test or counsel them in academic or vocational areas. Often employed by colleges and universities.
Psychiatrists	Medical doctors with 3 to 4 additional years of training in the diagnosis and treatment of psychological disorders. Treat patients with psychotherapy, drugs, and/or other biological treatment.
Psychoanalysts	Professionals, usually psychiatrists, with special training in psychoanalysis from a psychoanalytic institute.
Psychiatric social workers	Professionals with a master's degree in social work. Provide psychotherapy for psychological problems.

tice, the typical length of their treatment, and their professional fees. Because the patient-therapist relationship is an extremely important ingredient in successful therapy, clients should feel comfortable with their therapists.

Most therapies that have been proven successful—cognitive behavior therapy and interpersonal therapy for depression, and behavior therapy for fears and problem behaviors—are brief, often fewer than 20 sessions. Lengthy therapy may be good financially for therapists and may keep their hours booked so that they don't have to worry about referrals, but there is little evidence other than testimonials to suggest that lengthy therapy is better than brief therapy. As Figure 15.6 shows, the greatest benefits of psychotherapy are gained within the first 6 months.

Finally, clients should be wary of any therapist who promises overwhelming changes in their personality. Even Freud did not believe that great change in personality was possible.

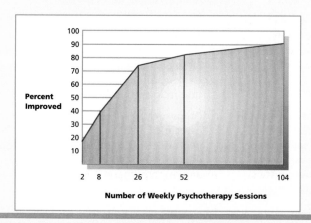

Number of Weekly Psychotherapy Sessions

Figure 15.6

The Number of Psychotherapy Sessions and Patient Improvement

About 75 percent of patients undergoing psychotherapy improve within 6 months (26 weekly sessions). After one year (52 sessions), some 80 percent of patients show improvement, and with 2 years of therapy, a little over 90 percent are improved. (After Howard, Kopta, Krause, & Orlinsky, 1986.)

Selecting a Therapy: Finding One That Fits

Question: What therapy, if any, has proven to be the most effective in treating mental disorders?

Is one therapy really better, on average, than other therapies? It seems obvious that we should ask which therapy, if any, is likely to be best for which person with a particular disorder, under which circumstances. Therapists do not treat "average" persons; they treat people individually, and some therapies are more effective than others for treating certain disorders.

Insight therapies are often more effective for general feelings of unhappiness and interpersonal problems. Various types of behavior therapy are usually best for people with a specific problem behavior they want to change, such as a fear,

Table 15.2 Summary and Comparison of Major Approaches to Therapy

Type of Therapy	Perceived Cause of Disorder	Goals of Therapy	Methods Used	Primary Disorders Treated
Psycho-analysis	Unconscious sexual and aggressive urges or conflicts; fixations; weak ego.	Bring disturbing, repressed material to consciousness and work through unconscious conflicts; strengthen ego functions.	Analysis and interpretation of dreams, free associations, resistances, and transference.	General feelings of unhappiness; unresolved problems from childhood.
Person-centered	Blocking of normal tendency toward self-actualization; incongruence between real and desired self; overdependence on positive regard of others.	Increase self-acceptance and self-understanding; become more innerdirected; increase congruence between real and desired self; personal growth.	Therapist who shows empathy, unconditional positive regard, and genuineness, and reflects client's expressed feelings back to client.	General feelings of unhappiness; interpersonal problems.
Behavior	Learning of maladaptive behaviors or failure to learn appropriate behaviors.	Extinguish maladaptive behaviors and replace with more adaptive ones; acquire needed social skills.	Methods based on classical and operant conditioning and modeling, which include systematic desensitization, flooding, aversion therapy, reinforcement, and so on.	Fears, phobias, panic disorder, obsessive compulsive disorder, bad habits.
Cognitive	Irrational and negative assumptions and ideas about self and others.	Change faulty, irrational, and/or negative thinking.	Therapist who helps client to identify irrational and negative thinking and to substitute rational thinking.	Depression, anxiety; general feelings of unhappiness.
Biological	Underlying physical disorder caused by structural or biochemical abnormality in the brain; genetic inheritance.	Eliminate or control biological cause of abnormal behavior; restore balance of neurotransmitters.	Drugs such as antipsychotics, antidepressants, lithium, and tranquilizers; ECT and psychosurgery.	Schizophrenia, depression, bipolar disorder, anxiety disorders.

phobia, bad habit, or some socially undesirable behavior. Exposure therapies, in particular, are helpful for panic disorder and obsessive compulsive disorder. Agoraphobia responds best to exposure therapy coupled with cognitive therapy (Dobson, 1989). And patients with anxiety disorders who have been treated with an appropriate behavior therapy (Jenike, 1990a, 1990b) or cognitive therapy (Klosko et al., 1990; Sokol, Beck, et al., 1989) are less likely to relapse after therapy is completed than are patients treated with drugs. Interpersonal therapy (IPT) and Beck's cognitive therapy are both effective in treating depression, and patients are less likely to relapse after therapy ends than are patients treated with antidepressants (Blackburn et al., 1986; McLean & Carr, 1989).

Antidepressants have also proven effective in the treatment of depression, panic disorder, agoraphobia, and obsessive compulsive disorder (Baldessarini, 1989); lithium for bipolar disorder; benzodiazepines (minor tranquilizers) for generalized anxiety disorder and social phobia, and even panic disorder if taken in large enough doses (Charney & Woods, 1989). There is a general consensus that antipsychotics are the best for controlling the psychotic symptoms of schizophrenia, but "family counseling, supportive therapy, rehabilitation programs and aid in solving problems of daily life can be crucially important" adjuncts to drug therapy (Baldessarini, 1988, p. 6).

Although drugs provide relief for people with many psychiatric disorders, the drugs do not cure. Relapse is likely when drugs are discontinued. For many disorders psychotherapy provides relief from symptoms and a lower likelihood of relapse after termination of treatment. Many mental health professionals see value in combining drug therapy and psychotherapy for disorders such as depression, obsessive compulsive disorder, panic disorder, and agoraphobia. A considerable number of patients respond to a combination of cognitive behavior therapy, exposure, and drugs (Mattick et al., 1990). Table 15.2 provides a summary and comparison of major approaches to therapy.

In evaluating the outcomes of various therapies, it is not only the technique specific to a particular brand of therapy but also the individual therapist's ability to establish a rapport with the patient that, in large measure, will determine the outcome. Read the boxed feature on pages 540–541 to learn how to go about selecting a therapist.

Memory Check 15.6

1. One can assume that, in general, therapy is more effective than no treatment for emotional and behavioral disorders. (true/false)

2. Researchers Smith, Glass, and Miller found that the average person receiving therapy is better off than (50%, 80%) of persons who do not receive therapy.

3. Match the problem with the most appropriate therapy.

____1) eliminating fears, bad habits   a. behavior therapy
____2) schizophrenia   b. insight therapy
____3) general unhappiness, interpersonal problems   c. drug therapy
____4) severe depression

Answers: 1. true 2. 80% 3. 1) a 2) c 3) b 4) c

Thinking Critically

Evaluation

In your opinion, what are the major strengths and weaknesses of the following approaches to therapy: psychoanalysis, person-centered therapy, behavior therapy, cognitive therapy, and drug therapy?

Point/Counterpoint

From what you have learned in this chapter, prepare a strong argument to support each of these positions:

a. Psychotherapy is generally superior to drug therapy in the treatment of psychological disorders.
b. Drug therapy is generally superior to psychotherapy in the treatment of psychological disorders.

Psychology in Your Life

In selecting a therapist for yourself or advising a friend or family member, what are some important questions you would ask a therapist to determine whether he or she would be most helpful?

Chapter Summary and Review

Insight Therapies

What are the four basic techniques of psychoanalysis, and how are they used to help disturbed patients?

The four basic techniques of psychoanalysis—free association, analysis of resistance, dream analysis, and analysis of transference—are used to uncover the repressed memories, impulses, and conflicts presumed to be the cause of the patient's problems.

What are the role and the goal of the therapist in person-centered therapy?

Person-centered therapy is a nondirective therapy in which the therapist provides a climate of unconditional positive regard where clients are free to be themselves so that their natural tendency toward positive growth will be released.

What is the major emphasis in Gestalt therapy?

Gestalt therapy emphasizes the importance of clients fully experiencing, in the present moment, their feelings, thoughts, and actions, and taking personal responsibility for their behavior.

What is the goal of interpersonal therapy, and for what disorder is it most effective?

Interpersonal therapy (IPT) is designed to help depressed people understand their problems in interpersonal relationships and develop more effective strategies for improving these relationships.

What are some advantages of group therapy?

Group therapy is less expensive than individual therapy and gives people an opportunity to express feelings and get feedback from other members, and to give and receive help and emotional support.

Key Terms

psychotherapy (p. 512)
insight therapies (p. 512)
psychoanalysis (p. 513)
free association (p. 513)
resistance (p. 513)
transference (p. 514)
person-centered therapy (p. 515)
self-actualization (p. 515)
nondirective therapy (p. 515)
unconditional positive regard (p. 515)
Gestalt therapy (p. 516)
directive therapy (p. 516)
interpersonal therapy (IPT) (p. 518)
family therapy (p. 518)
group therapy (p. 519)
encounter groups (p. 519)

Behavior Therapy: Unlearning the Old, Learning the New

What is behavior therapy?

Behavior therapy is a treatment approach that employs the principles of operant conditioning, classical conditioning, and/or observational learning theory to replace inappropriate or maladaptive behaviors with more adaptive responses.

How do behavior therapists modify behavior using operant conditioning techniques?

Operant conditioning techniques such as token economies and time out are used to eliminate undesirable behaviors by withholding reinforcement and are used to shape or increase the frequency of desirable behaviors through reinforcement.

What behavior therapies are based on classical conditioning?

Behavior therapies based on classical conditioning are systematic desensitization, flooding, exposure and response prevention, and aversion therapy.

How do therapists use systematic desensitization to rid people of fears?

Therapists using systematic desensitization train clients in deep muscle relaxation and then have them confront a series of graduated anxiety-producing situations, either real or imagined, until they can remain relaxed even in the presence of the most feared situation.

What is flooding?

With flooding, clients are exposed to the feared object or event or asked to vividly imagine it for an extended period until their anxiety decreases and they realize that none of the dreaded consequences come to pass.

How does exposure and response prevention help people with obsessive compulsive disorder?

When treated with exposure and response prevention, people with OCD are exposed to the stimuli that generate anxiety, but the clients gradually increase the time before they begin their compulsive rituals and thus learn to tolerate their anxiety.

How does aversion therapy rid people of a harmful or undesirable behavior?

Aversion therapy rids people of harmful or socially undesirable behavior by pairing it with an aversive stimulus until the bad habit becomes associated with pain or discomfort.

How does participant modeling help people overcome fears?

In participant modeling, an appropriate response is modeled in graduated steps and the client is asked to initiate each step with the encouragement and support of the therapist.

Key Terms

behavior therapy (p. 521)
behavior modification (p. 521)
token economy (p. 522)
time out (p. 522)
systematic desensitization (p. 524)
flooding (p. 525)
exposure and response prevention (p. 526)
aversion therapy (p. 526)
participant modeling (p. 527)

Cognitive Behavior Therapies: It's the Thought That Counts

What is the aim of rational-emotive therapy?

Rational-emotive therapy is a directive form of therapy designed to challenge and modify the client's irrational beliefs, which are believed to be the cause of personal distress.

How does Beck's cognitive therapy help people overcome depression and anxiety disorders?

Beck's cognitive therapy helps people overcome depression and anxiety disorders by pointing out irrational thoughts causing them misery and by helping them learn other, more realistic ways of looking at themselves and their experience.

Key Terms

cognitive behavior therapy (p. 529)
rational-emotive therapy (p. 529)
automatic thoughts (p. 531)
Beck's cognitive therapy (p. 531)

The Biological Therapies

What are the three main biological therapies?

The three main biological therapies are drug therapy, ECT, and psychosurgery.

How do antipsychotic drugs help schizophrenic patients?

Antipsychotic drugs control the major symptoms of schizophrenia by inhibiting the activity of dopamine.

For what conditions are antidepressants prescribed?

Antidepressants are prescribed for depression, panic disorder, agoraphobia, and obsessive compulsive disorder.

How does lithium help patients with bipolar disorder?

Lithium is used to control the symptoms in a manic episode and to even out the mood swings in bipolar disorder.

What are some of the problems with drug therapy?

Some problems with drugs are their unpleasant or dangerous side effects, the difficulty in establishing the proper dose, and the fact that relapse is likely if the drug is discontinued.

For what purpose is electroconvulsive therapy (ECT) used?

Electroconvulsive therapy (ECT) is a treatment of last resort for people with severe depression, and it is most often reserved for those for whom suicide is an imminent danger.

What is psychosurgery, and for what problems is it used?

Psychosurgery is brain surgery performed strictly to relieve some severe, persistent, and debilitating psychological disorder; it is considered experimental and highly controversial.

Key Terms

biological therapy (p. 532)
antipsychotic drugs (p. 532)
antidepressants (p. 533)
lithium (p. 534)
electroconvulsive therapy (ECT) (p. 535)
psychosurgery (p. 536)
lobotomy (p. 537)

Evaluating the Therapies

What therapy, if any, has proven to be the most effective in treating mental disorders?

Although, overall, one therapeutic approach has not proven generally superior, specific therapies have proven effective in treating particular disorders.

What different types of mental health professionals conduct psychotherapy?

Professionals trained to conduct psychotherapy fall into the following categories: clinical psychologists, counseling psychologists, counselors, psychiatrists, psychoanalysts, and psychiatric social workers.

Key Terms

clinical psychologist (p. 541)
psychiatrist (p. 541)
psychoanalyst (p. 541)

16

Social Psychology

Kitty Genovese was returning home alone late one night. But this was no ordinary night. Nearly 40 of her neighbors who lived in the apartment complex nearby watched as she was attacked and stabbed, but they did nothing. The attacker left. Kitty was still screaming, begging for help, and then . . . he returned. He dragged her around, stabbing her again while her neighbors watched. Some of them turned off their bedroom lights to see more clearly, pulled up chairs to the window, and they watched. Someone yelled, "Leave the girl alone," and the attacker fled again. But even then, no one came to her aid. A third time the attacker returned, more stabbing and screaming, and they watched. Finally Kitty Genovese stopped screaming. When he had finally killed her, the attacker fled for the last time. (Adapted from Rosenthal, 1964.)

WHY DID NO ONE HELP or even call the police during the attack? How can the behavior of the witnesses to this crime be explained?

Social psychology is the area of study that attempts to explain how the actual, imagined, or implied presence of others influences the thoughts, feelings, and behavior of individuals. No human being lives in a vacuum, alone and apart from other people. We are truly social animals, and our social nature—how we think about, respond to, and interact with other people—provides the scientific territory that social psychology explores. Research in social psychology provides some surprising and provocative answers to puzzling human behavior, from the atrocious to the altruistic.

This chapter explores social perception—how we form impressions of other people, and how we try to understand why they behave as they do. What are the factors involved in attraction? What draws us to other people, and in what circumstances do friendships and love relationships develop? We will look at factors influencing conformity and obedience as well as the effect the group has on performance and decision making. We will also discuss attitudes and how they can be changed. Then we will look at the conditions in which people are likely to help each other, and discuss how social psychologists explain why none of Kitty Genovese's neighbors came to her aid. Finally we will explore the factors related to aggression. To start, let us consider how social psychologists conduct their studies.

You may have seen the TV show "Candid Camera," which shows "people caught in the act of being themselves." Secretly videotaped by a hidden camera, ordinary individuals caught in various social situations provide the humorous, sometimes hilarious, material for the show.

This is precisely what researchers in social psychology must do in most of their studies—catch people in the act of being themselves. For this reason deception has traditionally played a prominent part in their research. To accomplish this deception, the researcher often must use one or more **confederates**—people who pose as subjects in a psychology experiment but are actually assisting the experimenter. The term **naive subject** refers to the actual subject who has agreed to participate but is not aware that deception is being used to conceal the real purpose of the experiment. When we explore our first topic, social perception, you will see why it is often necessary to conceal the purpose of an experiment.

social psychology: The study of how the actual, imagined, or implied presence of others influences the thoughts, the feelings, and the behavior of individuals.

confederate: Someone posing as a subject in an experiment but who is actually assisting the experimenter.

naive subject: A subject who has agreed to participate in an experiment but is not aware that deception is being used to conceal its real purpose.

Social Perception

We spend a significant portion of our lives in contact with other people. Not only do we form impressions of others, but we also attempt to understand why they behave as they do.

Impression Formation: Sizing Up the Other Person

When we meet people for the first time, we start forming impressions about them right away, and, of course, other people are busily forming impressions of us. Naturally we notice the obvious attributes first—sex, race, age, dress, and how physically attractive or unattractive they appear to us. Physical attractiveness, as shallow as it might seem, has a definite impact on our first impressions. Beyond noticing physical appearance, we may wonder: What is her occupation? Is he married? Answers to our questions, combined with a conscious or an unconscious assessment of the person's verbal and nonverbal behavior, all play their part in forming a first impression. Our own moods also play a part—when we are happy, our impressions of others are usually more positive than when we are unhappy (Forgas & Bower, 1987). First impressions are powerful and can color many of the later impressions we form about people.

Question: Why are first impressions so important and enduring?

It is difficult to avoid forming a first impression of the person pictured here.

First Impressions: Put Your Best Foot Forward—First If we gave you a list of a certain individual's characteristics or traits and asked you to write your impressions of the person, would it matter which traits were listed first? Solomon Asch (1946) gave one group of subjects the following list of traits—intelligent, industrious, impulsive, critical, stubborn, and envious. He then asked the subjects to write their impression of the person. Asch gave another group the same list but in reverse order. The subjects who responded to the list with the positive traits first, gave more favorable evaluations than subjects whose list began with the negative traits.

Why should our first impressions be so important? A number of studies reveal that our overall impression or judgment of another person is influenced more by the first information we receive about the person than by information that comes later (Luchins, 1957; Park, 1986). This phenomenon is called the **primacy effect**. It seems that we attend to initial information more carefully, and once an impression is formed, it provides the framework through which we interpret later information. Any information that is consistent with the first impression is likely to be accepted, thus strengthening the impression. Information that does not fit with the earlier information is more likely to be disregarded.

Remember, any time you list your personal traits or qualities, always list your most positive qualities first. It pays to put your best foot forward—first.

Traits That Affect Our Overall Impressions Solomon Asch (1946) believed that some traits (among them the warm/cold dimension) are so important that they can color our whole impression of a person. To test this notion, Harold Kelley (1950) set up an experiment. He told three classes at the Massachusetts Institute of Technology that they were to have a substitute teacher, and he gave the students one of two versions of a biographical summary. Each version had exactly the same description, except that in one the teacher was described as "very warm" and in the other as "rather cold."

The substitute teacher conducted a 20-minute class discussion and then left the room. The students were asked to write a description of him and rate him on 15 dimensions such as sociable-unsociable, popular-unpopular, humane-ruthless. Students who had been given the "warm" descriptor rated the teacher as "more considerate of others, more informal, more sociable, more popular, better natured, more humorous, and more humane" (p. 435). Students who read the "cold" descriptor said they found him to be more self-centered, formal, unsociable, unpopular, and irritable. Furthermore, being told in advance that the teacher was warm or cold even affected the students' willingness to partici-

primacy effect: The tendency for an overall impression or judgment of another to be influenced more by the first information received about that person than by information that comes later.

nonverbal behavior: Body language including facial expressions, gestures, posture, and body movements.

pate in class. Only 32 percent of the students given the "cold" descriptor participated, compared to 56 percent given the "warm" version. Only one word made the difference.

Expectancies: Seeing What We Expect to See   Sometimes our expectations about how other persons will act in a situation become a self-fulfilling prophecy and actually influence the way they do act. Expectations may be based on a person's sex, age, racial or ethnic group, social class, role or occupation, personality traits, past behavior, relationship to us, and so on. Once formed, our expectancies affect how we perceive the behavior of others, what we pay attention to, and what we ignore. But rarely do we consider the possibility that our expectations may color our own attitude, manner, and treatment of that person in such a way that we, ourselves, partly bring about the very behavior we expect (Jones, 1986; Miller & Turnbull, 1986).

Nonverbal Behavior: The Silent Language

Question: What is nonverbal behavior, and what does it convey?

> He that has eyes to see and ears to hear may convince himself that no mortal can keep a secret. If his lips are silent, he chatters with his fingertips; betrayal oozes out of him at every pore.
>
> —Sigmund Freud

There is some truth to the old saying "It's not what you say, it's how you say it." When we speak, what emotional impact does the verbal message alone, the words themselves, have on our listeners? Very little, according to Albert Mehrabian (1968). He claims that the emotional impact of a communication is influenced only slightly (about 7 percent) by the verbal message itself. More than five times as powerful is what he calls the vocal message—tone of voice, pronunciation, stress on words, vocal inflections, and the length and frequency of pauses—which provides 38 percent of the impact. If you were 30 minutes late for class and your professor said in a sarcastic tone, "We're so happy that you could join us today," would you believe the vocal message (the sarcastic tone) or the verbal message?

The most powerful effect of all comes, not from the verbal or the vocal message, but from **nonverbal behavior**—facial expressions, gestures, posture, and so on—which provides an amazing 55 percent of the emotional impact of a message. If the nonverbal behavior and the verbal message do not match, which one do we believe? Almost every time, the nonverbal message comes across as the real one. Figure 16.1 shows the relative effects of the verbal, vocal, and nonverbal components of a message.

Nonverbal behavior reveals a great deal about how we feel about others and how others feel about us. It can communicate anger, liking, love, happiness, sadness, anxiety, impatience, deception, and difference in status among people. But it is important to avoid attributing meaning to an isolated clue apart from its context.

We are usually best at reading nonverbal behavior that signals anger and a possible threat to our well-being. Cold stares will make almost anyone tense and uncomfortable, and there are many other gestures that we all know are not meant to wish us well. When people are interested in what we have to say, they generally lean toward us, sustain a high level of eye contact, and nod in agreement, although these gestures can be made intentionally to *seem* interested. Lovers generally spend longer gazing into each other's eyes and generally position themselves closer to each other than to friends or acquaintances.

Figure 16.1

Getting the Message Across

Researcher Albert Mehrabian claims that most of the emotional impact (55 percent) of a communication comes from nonverbal behavior (facial expressions, gestures, posture). Another large proportion of the emotional impact (38 percent) is provided by the vocal message (tone of voice, vocal inflection, pauses). The verbal message (our actual words) carries only 7 percent of the emotional impact. (Data from Mehrabian, 1968.)

Vocal Message 38%
(Tone of voice, vocal inflection, pauses)

Verbal Message 7%
(Our actual words)

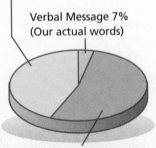

Nonverbal Behavior 55%
(Facial expressions, gestures, posture)

WORLD OF PSYCHOLOGY:

MULTICULTURAL PERSPECTIVES

Gestures: Different Meanings in Different Countries

When traveling in another country, most tourists find a phrase book indispensable, and some even make an effort to learn another language. But even if tourists learn to speak a foreign language like a native, few will recognize that the gestures they use in communicating may convey something entirely different in another country.

Paul Ekman and colleagues (1984) relate this dramatic illustration of how our gestures can get us into trouble in different cultures. Several years ago, an American tourist learned that the "A-okay" gesture (the thumb and forefinger in a circle) is not a positive signal in all cultures. After a wonderful dinner in Naples, Italy, the American, wishing to thank his waiter for fine food and expert service, flashed a big smile and the "A-okay" sign. The stunned waiter turned pale and rushed to the restaurant manager, and the two of them discussed excitedly whether they should call the police and have the American arrested for obscene and vulgar behavior in a public place.

Why did the tourist's complimentary gesture cause such an uproar? The "A-okay" gesture is not a friendly one in all cultures. It signals a lewd, insulting sexual invitation in Turkey and Greece, and it conveys the message "You are

worth zero" in France and Belgium. In parts of southern Italy (including Naples), the gesture is even more offensive and insulting. The smiling American tourist had unwittingly called his waiter a name that is a crude and vulgar reference to the anal opening.

In ancient Rome, when the gladiators battled each other to the death, the emperor gave a signal to the gladiator who held his sword at the opponent's throat. The emperor's "thumbs-up" sign meant "Let him live." The "thumbs down" sign meant "Finish the job." Today in the United States and in most western European countries, the "thumbs-up" sign means "all right." We see truck drivers, airline pilots, and other people use it as a positive gesture. But in northern Greece and parts of southern Italy, the "thumbs-up" sign is an obscene gesture that expresses the same sentiment to them as if someone were to raise a middle finger in front of your face.

Ironically, if we are trying to communicate with people who speak a different language, we are even more likely to use an abundance of gestures. Gestures are powerful communication tools, but travelers should be careful when using them in cultures other than their own, especially in Greece, Turkey, and southern Italy.

Gestures are powerful communication tools.

Touch can be a sign of warmth and intimacy, a sign of sexual interest, or a means of conveying higher status (Major et al., 1990). Higher status persons are more likely to touch lower status persons than vice versa (Henley, 1973). In nonintimate settings, men are more likely to touch women than the reverse (Major et al., 1990).

Although people often consider themselves experts in detecting deception, this is usually not the case. According to authority Paul Ekman, even professionals such as judges and law enforcement officials are no more expert than anyone else at detecting lies (Goleman, 1991). In his book *Telling Lies*, Ekman (1985) states that failure to look you in the eye is not necessarily a sign of lying but can indicate that a person is uncomfortable under scrutiny. More telling cues are overly long smiles, frowns, or looks of disbelief. Genuine expressions don't last longer than 4 or 5 seconds. Furthermore, genuine smiles are usually symmetrical in contrast to the lopsided, phony smile. True feelings often slip through in the form of fleeting microexpressions that are quickly replaced by the expression meant to deceive (Ekman et al., 1988). In deception there is a discrepancy between the verbal, vocal, and nonverbal message. Finally, when people are lying, they often have more pauses in their speech and begin sentences, stop, then begin again (Stiff et al., 1989).

Attribution: Our Explanation of Behavior

Question: What is the difference between a situational attribution and a dispositional attribution for a specific behavior?

Why do people (ourselves included) do the things they do? Why did Kitty Genovese's neighbors fail to come to her aid or call the police? To answer questions such as these, we make **attributions**—that is, we assign or attribute causes to explain the behavior of others and to explain our own behavior as well. We are particularly interested in the causes when behaviors are unexpected, when goals are not attained (Weiner, 1985), and when actions are not socially desirable (Jones & Davis, 1965).

Although we can actually observe behavior, we usually can only infer its cause or causes. Whenever we try to determine why we or someone else behaved in a certain way, we can make a **situational attribution** (an external attribution) and attribute the behavior to some external cause or factor operating within the situation. After failing an exam, we might say, "The test was unfair" or "The professor didn't teach the material well." Or we might make a **dispositional attribution** (an internal attribution) and attribute the behavior to some internal cause such as a personal trait, motive, or attitude. We might attribute our bad grade to our own lack of ability or to a poor memory.

Question: How do the kinds of attributions we tend to make about ourselves differ from those we make about other people?

Attributional Biases: Different Attributions for Ourselves and Others

There are basic differences in the way we make attributions about our own behavior and that of others (Jones & Nisbett, 1971; Jones, 1976, 1990). We tend to use situational attributions to explain our own behavior because we are aware of factors in the situation that influenced us to act as we did. We are also aware of our past behavior, so we know whether our present actions are typical or atypical.

When we try to explain the behavior of other people, however, we focus more on them personally than on the factors operating within the situation. Not knowing how they have behaved in different situations in the past, we assume a consistency in their behavior. Thus we are likely to attribute the behavior of

attribution: An inferred cause of our own or another's behavior.

situational attribution: Attributing a behavior to some external cause or factor operating in the situation.

dispositional attribution: Attributing one's own or another's behavior to some internal cause such as a personal trait, motive, or attitude; an internal attribution.

fundamental attribution error: The tendency to overemphasize internal causes and underemphasize situational factors when explaining the behavior of others.

self-serving bias: Attributing our successes to dispositional causes, and our failures to situational causes.

others to some personal quality. The tendency to overemphasize internal factors and underemphasize situational factors when we explain other people's behavior is so fundamental, so commonplace, that it has been named the **fundamental attribution error** (Ross, 1977).

In the United States, the plight of the homeless and of people on welfare is often attributed to laziness, an internal attribution, rather than to factors in the individuals' situations that might explain their condition. The fundamental attribution error is not universal, however. In India, for example, middle-class adults tend to make situational attributions for deviant behavior, attributing it to "role, status, or caste, and kin structures" rather than to internal dispositions (Pepitone & Triandis, 1987, p. 492).

There is one striking inconsistency in the way we view our own behavior—the self-serving bias. We use the **self-serving bias** when we attribute our successes to internal or dispositional causes, and blame our failures on external or situational causes (Baumgardner et al., 1986; Miller & Ross, 1975; Zuckerman, 1979b). If we interview for a job and get it, it is probably because we have the right qualifications. If someone else gets the job, it is probably because he or she knew the right people. The self-serving bias allows us to take credit for our successes and shift the blame for our failures to the situation.

Memory Check 16.1

1. We are usually (more, less) influenced by early information than by later information we receive when forming overall impressions of others.

2. If a person's verbal and nonverbal messages are inconsistent, we usually believe the (verbal, nonverbal) message.

3. When we attribute someone's behavior to a personal trait, a motive, or an attitude, we are making a (dispositional, situational) attribution.

4. We tend to make (dispositional, situational) attributions for our own behavior.

5. The fundamental attribution error consists of overemphasizing dispositional factors and underemphasizing situational factors in (our own behavior, the behavior of others).

Answers: 1. *more* 2. *nonverbal* 3. *dispositional* 4. *situational* 5. *the behavior of others*

Attraction

Think for a moment about the people you consider to be your closest friends. What causes you to like or even love one person yet ignore or react negatively to someone else? What factors influence interpersonal attraction—the degree to which we are drawn to or like another?

Factors Influencing Attraction: Magnets That Draw Us Together

Some of the factors influencing attraction are within the situation and some are within the person.

Question: Why is proximity an important factor in attraction?

Proximity: Close to You   One major factor influencing our choice of friends is physical **proximity**, or geographic closeness. If you live in an apartment complex, you are probably more friendly with people who live next door or only a few doors away (Festinger et al., 1950). The same is true in a dormitory (Priest & Sawyer, 1967). What about the people you like best in your classes? Do they sit next to you or not more than a seat or two away?

Why is proximity so important? It is much less trouble to make friends or even fall in love with people who are close at hand. Physical proximity also increases the frequency of interaction, and mere exposure to people, objects, and circumstances will probably increase our liking for them (Zajonc, 1968). The **mere-exposure effect** is the tendency to feel more positively toward stimuli with repeated exposure. People, food, songs, and styles become more acceptable the more we are exposed to them. Advertisers rely on the positive effects of repeated exposure to increase our liking for products and political candidates.

There are exceptions to the mere-exposure effect, however. If our initial reaction to a person is highly negative, frequent exposure can make us feel even more negatively toward the person (Swap, 1977). In addition, those who value privacy may react less favorably when proximity results in repeated contacts with people (Larson & Bell, 1988).

Liking through Association: A Case of Classical Conditioning   Our own mood and emotions, whether positive or negative, can influence how much we are attracted to people we meet (Cunningham, 1988). And sometimes we develop positive or negative feelings toward others simply because they are present when very good or very bad things happen to us. Through classical conditioning, other people can become associated with the pleasant or unpleasant event and the resulting good or bad feelings may rub off on them (Riordan & Tedeschi, 1983).

Reciprocal Liking: Liking Those Who Like Us   Suppose you were at a party last weekend and met several people, including Maria and Bill. Today you learned that Maria thought you were the most fascinating person at the party, but Bill found you a terrible bore. Would this information cause you to have positive feelings for Maria and anger toward Bill?

Curtis and Miller (1986) falsely led subjects to believe that another person either liked or disliked them after an initial encounter. This false information became a self-fulfilling prophecy. When the subjects met the person again, those who believed they were liked "self-disclosed more, disagreed less, expressed dissimilarity less, and had a more positive tone of voice and general attitude than subjects who believed they were disliked" (p. 284). These positive behaviors, in turn, actually caused the other person to view them positively. The moral of this story seems easy to grasp: If you want others to like you, like them first!

Question: How important is physical attractiveness in attraction?

Attractiveness: Good Looks Attract   Although people are quick to deny that mere physical appearance is the main factor that attracts them to someone

proximity: Geographic closeness; a major factor in attraction.

mere-exposure effect: The tendency of people to develop a more positive evaluation of some person, object, or other stimulus with repeated exposure to it.

initially, a substantial body of evidence indicates that it is. People of all ages have a strong tendency to prefer physically attractive people. Even 6-month-old infants, when given the chance to look at a photograph of an attractive or an unattractive woman, man, or infant, will spend more time looking at the attractive face (Langlois et al., 1991). More than 2,000 years ago Aristotle said, "Beauty is a greater recommendation than any letter of introduction." Apparently, it still is.

What constitutes physical beauty? Researchers Langlois and Rottman (1990) found that physical beauty consists not of rare physical qualities, but of facial features that are approximately the mathematical average of those features in the population. The researchers averaged the individual features of 4, 8, 16, and 32 faces, and they had a computer generate a composite of the averaged features. The larger the group that was averaged, the more attractive the computer-generated face.

Why is physical attractiveness so important? When people have one trait or quality that we either admire or dislike very much, we often assume that they also have other admirable or negative traits—a phenomenon known as the **halo effect** (Nisbett & Wilson, 1977; Thorndike, 1920). Dion and others (1972) found that people generally attribute other favorable qualities to those who are attractive. Attractive people are seen as more exciting, personable, interesting, and socially desirable than unattractive people. A study by Reis and others (1990) revealed that smiling increases the perceived attractiveness of others and makes them appear more sincere, sociable, and competent.

Eagly and others (1991) analyzed 76 studies of the physical attractiveness stereotype. They found that physical attractiveness has its greatest impact on judgments of popularity and sociability and less impact on judgments of adjustment and intellectual competence. They did find one negative, however. Attractive people are perceived as more vain and less modest than less attractive people.

Research suggests that job interviewers are more likely to recommend highly attractive people (Dipboye et al., 1975), and that attractive people have their written work evaluated more favorably (Landy & Sigall, 1974). Even the evaluation of the attractiveness of a person's voice is affected by the person's physical appearance (Zuckerman et al., 1991).

Being attractive is an advantage to children and adults, males and females, but according to some studies, women's looks contribute more to how they are judged on other personal qualities than men's looks (Bar-Tal & Saxe, 1976; Feingold, 1990). Physical attractiveness seems to have its greatest impact in the context of romantic attraction, particularly in initial encounters (Hatfield & Sprecher, 1986b; Feingold, 1988).

Does this mean that unattractive people don't have a chance? Fortunately not. Eagly and her colleagues (1991) suggest that the impact of physical attractiveness is strongest in the perception of strangers. But once we get to know people, other qualities assume more importance. In fact, as we come to like people, they begin to look more attractive to us, and those with undesirable personal qualities begin to look less attractive.

Question: Are people, as a rule, more attracted to those who are opposite or similar to them?

halo effect: The tendency to infer generally positive or negative traits in a person as a result of observing one major positive or negative trait.

Similarity: A Strong Basis of Attraction   To sum up research on attraction, the saying "Birds of a feather flock together" is more accurate than "Opposites attract." Beginning in elementary school, people are more likely to pick friends of the same age, sex, race, and socioeconomic class. These sociological variables continue to influence the choice of friends through college and later in life. Choosing friends who are similar to us could be related to proxmity—the fact that we tend to come into contact with people who are more similar to us in a variety of ways.

Not only is similarity in attitudes an important ingredient in attraction (Newcomb, 1956), but people often have negative feelings toward others whose attitudes differ from their own (Byrne et al., 1986; Rosenbaum, 1986; Smeaton et al., 1989). Liking people who have similar attitudes begins early in childhood and continues throughout life in both sexes (Griffitt et al., 1972). We are likely to choose friends and lovers who have similar views on most things that are important to us. Similar interests and attitudes toward leisure-time activities make it more likely that time spent together is rewarding. People who share our attitudes validate our judgments; those who disagree with us suggest the possibility that we are wrong and arouse negative feelings in us. It is similarities then, not differences, that usually stimulate liking and loving.

Romantic Attraction

The Matching Hypothesis: Peas in a Pod

> "Moderately attractive, unskilled, unemployed, 50-year-old, divorced man with 7 children seeks beautiful, wealthy, exciting woman between ages of 20 and 30 for companionship, romance, and possible marriage. No smokers or drinkers.

Can you imagine reading this ad in the personals column of your newspaper? Even though most of us may be attracted to handsome or beautiful people, the **matching hypothesis** suggests that we are likely to end up with someone similar to ourselves in attractiveness and other assets (Berscheid et al., 1971; Feingold, 1988; Walster & Walster, 1969). Furthermore, couples mismatched on attractiveness are more likely to end the relationship (Cash & Janda, 1984).

It has been suggested that we estimate our social assets and realistically expect to attract someone with approximately equal assets. In terms of physical attractiveness, some people might consider Tom Cruise to be the ideal man or Vanessa

The matching hypothesis suggests that we are likely to end up with someone similar to ourselves in attractiveness and other assets.

Williams the ideal woman, but they do not seriously consider the ideal to be a realistic, attainable possibility. Fear of rejection keeps people from pursuing those who are much more attractive than they are. But instead of marrying an extremely handsome man, a very beautiful woman may sacrifice physical attractiveness for money and social status. Extremely handsome men have been known to make similar "sacrifices."

What about same-sex friendships? The matching hypothesis is generally applicable in same-sex friendships (Cash & Derlega, 1978), although it is more true of males than of females (Feingold, 1988). A person's perceived attractiveness seems to be affected in part by the attractiveness of his or her friends (Geiselman et al., 1984).

Mate Selection: The Mating Game

Robert Winch (1958) proposes that men and women tend to choose mates with needs and personalities that are complementary rather than similar to their own. Winch sees complementary needs as not necessarily opposite, but as needs that supply what the partner lacks. A talkative person may seek a quiet mate who prefers to listen. The weight of research, however, does not support this notion. By and large it seems to be similarity in needs that attracts (Buss, 1984; Phillips et al., 1988). Similarity in personality as well as "physical characteristics, cognitive abilities, age, education, religion, ethnic background, attitudes and opinions, and socioeconomic status" all play a role in marital choice (O'Leary & Smith, 1991, p. 196). What's more, similarity in needs and in personality appear to be related to marital success as well as marital choice (O'Leary & Smith, 1991). Similarities wear well.

If you were to select a marital partner, what qualities would attract you? Do the *Try It!* to evaluate your own preferences.

In selecting a mate, which qualities are most and least important to you? Rank these 18 qualities from most important (1) to least important (18) in your selection of a mate.

Try It!

_____ ambition and industriousness
_____ chastity (no previous sexual intercourse)
_____ desire for home and children
_____ education and intelligence
_____ emotional stability and maturity
_____ favorable social status or rating
_____ good cook and housekeeper
_____ similar political background
_____ similar religious background

_____ good health
_____ good looks
_____ similar education
_____ pleasing disposition
_____ refinement/neatness
_____ sociability
_____ good financial prospect
_____ dependable character
_____ mutual attraction/love

Love: The Strongest Bond

We have discussed the factors influencing interpersonal attraction. Now we will consider a particularly intense form of attraction—love.

Romantic Love: Lost in Each Other   When we say we have "fallen" in love, it is probably passionate love we have fallen into. Romantic love (sometimes called passionate love) is an intense, emotional response to another person

WORLD OF PSYCHOLOGY: MULTICULTURAL PERSPECTIVES

Mate Preferences around the World

What do most people look for in a mate? Are there differences in the traits males and females value in mate selection? Do the values and preferences in mate selection vary greatly from culture to culture, or are they much the same across the entire human species?

The International Mate Selection Project (Buss et al., 1990) is the largest study ever conducted on mate preferences and is by far the most comprehensive. This cross-cultural study was designed to determine the characteristics people prefer in potential mates. Do stated preferences differ across cultures and between the sexes, or are there some mate preferences typical of the entire human species? You can compare your own ranking of mate preferences with those of the 9,474 male and female subjects from 33 countries spanning all the populated continents and five major islands around the world (see Table 16.1).

Generally men and women across cultures agree on the first four values in mate selection: (1) mutual attraction/love, (2) dependable character, (3) emotional stability and maturity, and (4) pleasing disposition. Aside from the first four values, women and men differ somewhat in the attributes they prefer. Men are more concerned that a mate have "good health" and "good looks," qualities with reproductive value in women, while women value "good financial prospect" and other qualities related to a mate's resource potential.

Buss and others report that the gender differences in mate preferences were statistically significant in virtually every sample and are among the strongest gender differences found to date across cultures. Yet when all the trait preferences were considered, the effects of gender are weaker than the effects of culture. This means, say the authors, that "there may be more similarity between men and women from the same culture than between men and men or women and women from different cultures" (p. 17). So culture accounts for more differences than gender

in mate preferences, and "chastity" is the value that varied most across cultures, although its overall average was lower than 15 other preferences. "Chastity" was valued most in China, India, Taiwan, Iran, Indonesia, and among the Palestinian Arabs, and it was considered unimportant or irrelevant in the Netherlands (Holland), Sweden, Norway, Finland, and Germany. But there was not a single culture in the study in which males rated "chastity" as less important than females did.

The desire for "home and children" and "good cook and housekeeper" also varied greatly according to culture. South Africa (Zulu), Colombia, and Estonia placed a high value on "good housekeeper," while the United States, Canada, and all cultures sampled in western Europe except Spain placed a low value on these skills.

Strong cultural variations were found for some personality variables such as "exciting personality" and "pleasing disposition." "Exciting personality" was reported to be highly desired in a potential mate in France, the United States, Japan, Brazil, Spain, and Ireland. But "exciting personality" was ranked rather low in China, South Africa (Zulu), India, and Iran.

It is always easier to observe differences than similarities among diverse cultures. But after analyzing gender and cultural differences, the researchers come to a rather surprising general conclusion. Mate preferences around the world and between the sexes are, overall, more alike than different. When mate-preference rankings were compared for all of the samples, there was an average between-country correlation of .74. The authors of the study point out that almost all samples placed "mutual attraction-love" at the top of the list, and nearly all placed great value on "dependability, emotional stability, kindness-understanding, and intelligence" (Buss et al. 1990, p. 43).

What people prefer in their mates, then, is largely typical of the human species and overrides cultural, racial, political, ethnic, geographic, and sexual diversity.

coupled with sexual arousal and a tremendous longing for that person. But when the passion fades, couples may find that they do not have similar backgrounds, attitudes, values, and interests that often form the basis for a more enduring relationship. Fortunately there is more to love than passion, important though it is. In fact passion may be only one of three parts of an ideal love relationship.

Question: How does Sternberg's triangular theory of love account for the different kinds of love?

Table 16.1 Summary of Ratings by Sex Using Entire International Sample

Ranked Value	Ratings by Males			Ratings by Females		
	Variable Name	Mean	Std. Dev.	Variable Name	Mean	Std. Dev.
1	Mutual Attraction—Love	2.81	0.16	Mutual Attraction—Love	2.87	0.12
2	Dependable Character	2.50	0.46	Dependable Character	2.69	0.31
3	Emotional Stability and Maturity	2.47	0.20	Emotional Stability and Maturity	2.68	0.20
4	Pleasing Disposition	2.44	0.29	Pleasing Disposition	2.52	0.30
5	Good Health	2.31	0.33	Education and Intelligence	2.45	0.25
6	Education and Intelligence	2.27	0.19	Sociability	2.30	0.28
7	Sociability	2.15	0.28	Good Health	2.28	0.30
8	Desire for Home and Children	2.09	0.50	Desire for Home and Children	2.21	0.44
9	Refinement, Neatness	2.03	0.48	Ambition and Industriousness	2.15	0.35
10	Good Looks	1.91	0.26	Refinement, Neatness	1.98	0.49
11	Ambition and Industriousness	1.85	0.35	Similar Education	1.84	0.47
12	Good Cook and Housekeeper	1.80	0.48	Good Financial Prospect	1.76	0.38
13	Good Financial Prospect	1.51	0.42	Good Looks	1.46	0.28
14	Similar Education	1.50	0.37	Favorable Social Status or Rating	1.46	0.39
15	Favorable Social Status or Rating	1.16	0.28	Good Cook and Housekeeper	1.28	0.27
16	Chastity (no previous experience in sexual intercourse)	1.06	0.69	Similar Religious Background	1.21	0.56
17	Similar Religious Background	0.98	0.48	Similar Poliical Background	1.03	0.35
18	Similar Political Background	0.92	0.36	Chastity (no previous experience in sexual intercourse)	0.75	0.66
	Mean	1.87	0.57	Mean	1.94	0.63

Source: Buss, D.M., et al. (1990). International preferences in selecting mates: A study of 37 cultures. *Journal of Cross-Cultural Psychology, 21*: 5–47.

Sternberg's Theory of Love: Three Components, Seven Types Robert Sternberg (1986, 1987), whose triarchic theory of intelligence was discussed in chapter 7, proposes a three-component or **triangular theory of love.** The three components are intimacy, passion, and commitment. Sternberg explains intimacy as "those feelings in a relationship that promote closeness, bondedness, and connectedness" (1987, p. 339). Passion refers to those drives in a loving relationship "that lead to romance, physical attraction, [and] sexual consummation" (1986b, p. 119). The decision/commitment component consists of (1) a

triangular theory of love: Sternberg's theory that three components—intimacy, passion and decision/commitment—singly or in various combinations produce seven different kinds of love.

consummate love: According to Sternberg's theory, the most complete form of love, consisting of three components—intimacy, passion, and decision/commitment.

short-term aspect—the decision that one person loves another, and (2) a long-term aspect—a commitment the person makes to maintaining that love over time.

Sternberg proposes that these three components, singly or in various combinations, produce seven different kinds of love, described below.

- *Liking* has only one of the love components—intimacy. In this case, liking is not used in a trivial sense. Sternberg says that this intimate liking characterizes true friendships, in which we feel a bondedness, a warmth, and a closeness with another person but not intense passion or a long-term commitment.

- *Infatuated love* consists solely of passion and is often what we feel as "love at first sight." But without the intimacy and the decision/commitment components of love, infatuated love may disappear suddenly.

- *Empty love* consists of the decision/commitment component without intimacy or passion. Sometimes a stronger love deteriorates into empty love—the commitment remains, but the intimacy and passion have died. In cultures in which arranged marriages are common, relationships often begin as empty love.

- *Romantic love* is a combination of intimacy and passion. Romantic lovers are bonded emotionally (as in liking) and physically through passionate arousal.

- *Fatuous love* has the passion and the decision/commitment components but not the intimacy. This type of love can be exemplified by a whirlwind courtship and marriage in which a commitment is motivated largely by passion without the stabilizing influence of intimacy.

- *Companionate love* consists of intimacy and commitment. This type of love is often found in marriages in which the passion has gone out of the relationship, but a deep affection and commitment remains.

- *Consummate love* is the only type that has all three components—intimacy, decision/commitment, and passion. **Consummate love** is the most complete form of love, and it represents the ideal love relationship for which many people strive but apparently few achieve. Sternberg cautions that maintaining a consummate love may be even harder than achieving it.

Figure 16.2 depicts Sternberg's triangular theory of love. Sternberg stresses the importance of translating the components of love into action. "Without expression," he warns, "even the greatest of loves can die" (1987, p. 341).

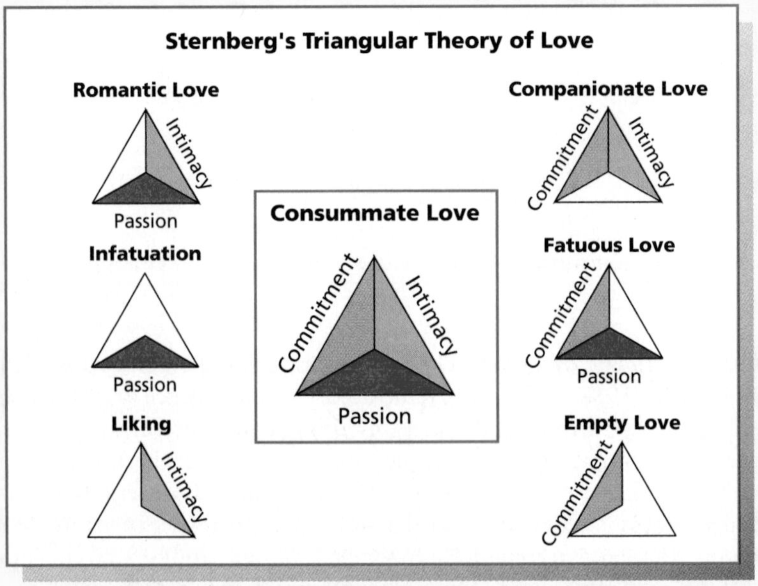

Figure 16.2

Sternberg's Triangular Theory of Love

Robert Sternberg identifies three components of love—passion, intimacy, and commitment—and shows how the three, singly and in various combinations, produce seven different kinds of love. Consummate love, the most complete form of love, has all three components. (Based on Sternberg, 1986.)

Sternberg's Triangular Theory of Love

Romantic Love

Infatuation

Liking

Consummate Love

Companionate Love

Fatuous Love

Empty Love

Memory Check 16.2

1. Attractiveness is a very important factor in initial attraction. (true/false)

2. People are usually drawn to those who are more opposite than similar to themselves. (true/false)

3. Match the term at the right with the description at the left.

   _____ 1) Brian sees Kyoko at the library often and begins to like
   her.

   _____ 2) Liane assumes that because
   Boyd is handsome, he must
   be popular and sociable.

   _____ 3) Alfonso and Carol are going
   together and are both very
   attractive.

   a. matching hypothesis
   b. halo effect
   c. mere-exposure effect

4. According to Sternberg, which of the components at the right correspond to the different types of love?

   _____ 1) consummate love
   _____ 2) infatuated love
   _____ 3) companionate love
   _____ 4) romantic love

   a. intimacy
   b. passion
   c. decision/commitment

Answers: 1. true 2. false 3. 1) c 2) b 3) a 4. 1) a,b,c 2) b 3) a,c 4) a,b

Conformity, Obedience, and Compliance

Conformity: Going Along with the Group

To conform or not to conform—that is not the question for most of us. Rather, the question is to *what* will we conform? **Conformity** is changing or adopting a behavior or an attitude in order to be consistent with the norms of a group or the expectations of other people. **Norms** are the standards of behavior and the attitudes that are expected of members of the group. Some conformity is neces-sary if we are to have a society at all. We cannot drive on any side of the street we please, park anyplace we want to, or drive as fast as we choose when we are in a hurry. Not only must we conform to and obey certain laws, but there are a whole host of conventions (unwritten laws) and ways of behaving to which we must conform if we are to be accepted by groups that are important to us.

Because we need other people to make us happy, we must conform to their expectations, to some extent, in order to have their esteem, their love, or even their company. It is easy to see why people conform to norms and standards of groups that are important to them, such as their family, peer group, social group, or team. But to an amazing degree, people also conform to the majority opinion, even when they are among a group of strangers.

conformity: Changing or adopting an attitude or be-havior to be consistent with the norms of a group or the expectations of others.

norms: The attitudes and standards of behavior ex-pected of members of a par-ticular group.

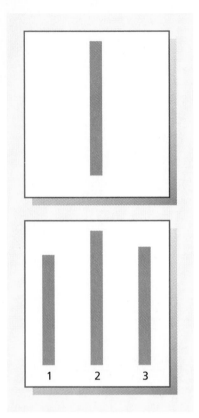

Figure 16.3

Asch's Classic Study of Conformity

If you were one of eight subjects in the Asch experiment who were asked to pick the line (1, 2, or 3) that matched the standard line shown above them, which line would you choose? If the other subjects all chose line 3, would you conform and answer line 3? Although 25 percent of the naive subjects never conformed to the incorrect answer of the majority, 70 percent conformed some of the time and 5 percent always conformed. (Based on Asch, 1955.)

Question: What did Asch find in his famous experiment on conformity?

Asch's Experiment: The Classic on Conformity   The best-known experiment on conformity was conducted by Solomon Asch (1951, 1955), who designed the simple test shown in Figure 16.3. Look at the standard line at the top. Then pick the line—1, 2, or 3—that is the same length. Did you pick line 2? Can you imagine any circumstances in which a person might tell the experimenter that either line 1 or line 3 matched the standard line? This is exactly what happened in Asch's classic experiment, even with tests so simple that subjects could pick the correct line over 99 percent of the time.

A group of eight subjects were seated around a large table and were asked, one by one, to tell the experimenter which of the three lines matched the standard line as in Figure 16.3. But only one of the eight was an actual subject; the others were confederates assisting the experimenter. There were 18 trials—18 different lines to be matched. During 12 of these trials, the confederates all gave the same wrong answer, which of course puzzled the naive subject. Would the subject continue to believe his eyes and select the correct line, or would he feel pressure to conform to the group selections and give the wrong answer himself?

Asch found that 5 percent of the subjects conformed to the incorrect, unanimous majority *all* of the time, 70 percent conformed *some* of the time, but 25 percent remained completely independent and were *never* swayed by the group.

Asch wondered how group size would influence conformity. Varying the experiment with groups of 2, 3, 4, 8, and 10–15, he found that the tendency to "go along" with the majority opinion was in full force when there was a unanimous majority of only 3 confederates. Surprisingly, unanimous majorities of 15 produced no higher conformity rate than did those of 3. Asch also discovered that the tendency to conform is not as strong if only one other person voices a dissenting opinion. When only one confederate in the group disagreed with the incorrect majority, the naive subjects' errors dropped drastically from 32 percent to 10.4 percent.

More recent research on conformity reveals that people of low status are more likely to conform than those of high status (Eagly, 1987), but contrary to the conventional wisdom, women are no more likely to conform than men (Eagly & Carli, 1981). And conformity is greater if the sources of influence are perceived as belonging to one's own group (Abrams et al., 1990).

In the Asch experiment, the unsuspecting subject (center) looks perplexed as he watches the confederates choose what he knows to be an incorrect answer.

Obedience: Following Orders

Some obedience is necessary if civilized society is to function, but unquestioned obedience can cause humans to commit unbelievably horrible acts. One of the darkest chapters in human history was due to the obedience of officials in Nazi Germany in carrying out Adolph Hitler's orders to exterminate Jews and other "undesirables." The civilized world was stunned and sickened by the revelations of the Nazi death camps, and nearly everyone wondered what type of person could be capable of committing such atrocities. Stanley Milgram, a young researcher at Yale University in 1961, wondered too. He designed a study to investigate how far ordinary citizens would go to obey orders, even if obedience meant the injury or possible death of a fellow human being.

Question: What did Milgram find in his classic study of obedience?

The Milgram Study: The Classic on Obedience   Some 30 years ago, an advertisement appeared in newspapers in New Haven, Connecticut, and other communities near Yale University.

> Wanted: Volunteers to serve as subjects in a study of memory and learning at Yale University.

Many people responded to the ad, and 40 male subjects between the ages of 20 and 50 were selected, among them "postal clerks, high school teachers, salesmen, engineers, and laborers" (Milgram, 1963, p. 372). Yet no experiment on memory and learning was to take place. Instead, a staged drama was planned in which only one actual subject at a time would participate. Imagine that you are one of the naive subjects selected for the experiment.

The researcher actually wants to know how far you would go in obeying orders to administer what you believed to be increasingly painful electric shocks to a "learner" who misses questions on a test. The cast of characters are as follows:

> *The Experimenter*: A 31-year-old high-school biology teacher dressed in a gray laboratory coat who assumes a stern and serious manner.
> *The Learner*: An accomplice of the experimenter played by a pleasant, heavyset accountant about 50 years of age.
> *The Teacher*: You—the only naive member of the cast.

The experimenter leads you and the learner into one room where the learner is then strapped into an electric-chair apparatus. You, the teacher, are delivered a sample shock of 45 volts, which stings you and is supposedly for the purpose of testing the equipment and showing you what the learner will feel. The learner complains of a heart condition and says that he hopes the electric shocks will not be too painful. The experimenter admits that the stronger shocks will hurt but hastens to add, "Although the shocks can be extremely painful, they cause no permanent tissue damage" (p. 373).

Then the experimenter takes you to an adjoining room, out of sight of the learner. The experimenter seats you in front of an instrument panel (shown in the photograph on page 564), on which 30 lever switches are set horizontally. The first switch on the left, you are told, delivers only 15 volts, but each successive switch is 15 volts stronger than the last—30 v, 45 v, and so on up to the last switch, which carries 450 volts. The instrument panel has verbal designations ranging from "Slight Shock" to "Danger: Severe Shock."

The experimenter explains that you are to read a list of word pairs to the learner and then test his memory. When the learner makes the right choice, you go on to the next pair. If he misses a question, you are to flip a switch and shock him, moving one switch to the right—delivering 15 additional volts—each time the learner misses a question. The learner does well at first but then begins missing about three out of every four questions. You begin pulling the switches, which you believe are delivering stronger and stronger shocks for each incorrect answer. When you hesitate, the experimenter urges you, "Please continue" or "Please go on." If you still hesitate, the experimenter orders you, "The experiment requires that you continue," or more strongly, "You have no other choice, you *must* go on" (p. 374).

At the 20th switch, 300 volts, the learner begins to pound on the wall and screams, "Let me out of here, let me out, my heart's bothering me, let me out!" (Meyer, 1972, p. 461). From this point on, the learner answers no more questions. Alarmed, you protest to the experimenter that the learner, who is pounding the wall frantically, does not want to continue. The experimenter answers, "Whether the learner likes it or not, you must go on" (Milgram, 1963, p. 374). Even if the learner fails to respond, you are told to count that as an incorrect response and shock him again.

Do you continue? If so, you flip the next switch—315 volts—and only groans are heard from the learner. You look at the experimenter, obviously distressed, your palms sweating, your heart pounding. The experimenter states firmly: "You have no other choice, you *must* go on" (p. 374). If you refuse at this point, the experiment is ended. Would you refuse, or would you continue to shock a silent learner nine more times until you delivered the maximum of 450 volts?

How many of the subjects do you think obeyed the experimenter to the end— 450 volts? Not a single subject stopped before the 20th switch, supposedly 300 volts, when the learner began pounding the wall. Amazingly, 26 subjects—65 percent of the sample—obeyed the experimenter to the bitter end, as shown in Figure 16.4. But this experiment took a terrible toll on the subjects. "Subjects were observed to sweat, tremble, stutter, bite their lips, groan, and dig their fingernails into their flesh. These were characteristic rather than exceptional responses to the experiment" (p. 375).

Variations of the Milgram Study Would the same results have occurred if the experiment had not been conducted at a famous university like Yale? The same experiment was carried out in a three-room office suite in a run-down building identified by a sign, "Research Associates of Bridgeport." Even there, 48 percent of subjects administered the maximum shock compared to the 65 percent in the Yale setting (Meyer, 1972).

Milgram (1965) conducted a variation of the original experiment with three teachers, two of whom were confederates and the other, a naive subject. One confederate was instructed to refuse to continue after 150 volts, and the other confederate after 210 volts. In this situation 36 out of 40 naive subjects (90

At left is the shock generator used by Milgram in his famous experiments. At right, the learner (actually an accomplice) is strapped into his chair by the experimenter and unsuspecting participant. (Copyright 1965 by Stanley Milgram. From the film OBEDIANCE, distributed by the Pennsylvania State University, Audio Visual Services.)

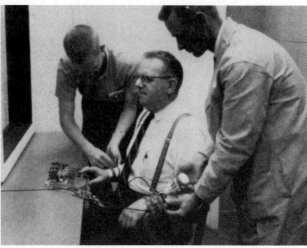

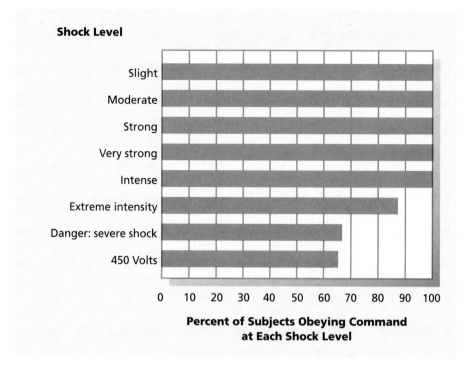

Shock Level

**Percent of Subjects Obeying Command
at Each Shock Level**

Figure 16.4

The Results of Milgram's Classic Experiment on Obedience

In his classic study, Stanley Milgram showed that a large majority of people would obey authority even if obedience caused great pain or was life-threatening to another. Milgram reported that 87.5 percent of the subjects continued to administer what they thought were painful electric shocks of 300 volts to a victim who complained of a heart condition. Amazingly, 65 percent of the subjects obeyed authority to the bitter end and continued to deliver what they thought were dangerous, severe shocks to the maximum of 450 volts. (Data from Milgram, 1963.)

percent) defied the experimenter before the maximum shock could be given, compared with only 14 subjects in the original experiment (Milgram, 1965). In Milgram's experiment, as in Asch's conformity study, the presence of another person who *refused to go along*, gave many of the subjects the courage to defy the authority.

Compliance: Giving In to Requests

Question: What are three techniques used to gain compliance?

There are many times when people act, not out of conformity or obedience, but in accordance with the wishes, suggestions, or direct requests of another person. This type of action is called **compliance**. Almost daily we are confronted by people who make requests of one sort or another. Do we comply with requests and yield to these appeals? For many of us the answer is yes, and several techniques have been used to gain our compliance.

The Foot-in-the-Door Technique: Upping the Ante   One strategy, the **foot-in-the-door technique**, is designed to secure a favorable response to a small request first. The intent is to make the subject more likely to agree later to a larger request (the request that was desired from the beginning). In one study a researcher claiming to represent a consumer's group called a number of homes and asked whether the subjects would mind answering a few questions about the soap products they used. Then a few days later, the same person called those who had agreed to the first request and asked if he could send five or six of his assistants to conduct an inventory of the products in their home. The researcher told the subjects that the inventory would take about 2 hours, and that the inventory team would have to search all drawers, cabinets, and closets in the house. Would you agree to such an imposition?

Nearly 53 percent of the foot-in-the-door group agreed to this large request compared to 22 percent of a control group who were contacted only once with the large request (Freedman & Fraser, 1966). A review of many studies on the foot-in-the-door approach suggests that it is highly effective (Beaman et al.,

compliance: Acting in accordance with the wishes, the suggestions, or the direct request of another person.

foot-in-the-door technique: A strategy designed to secure a favorable response to a small request at first, with the intent of making the subject more likely to agree later to a larger request.

door-in-the-face technique:
A strategy in which a large, unreasonable request is made with the expectation that the person will refuse but will then be more likely to respond favorably to a smaller request at a later time.

low-ball technique: A strategy to gain compliance by making a very attractive initial offer to get a person to agree to an action and then making the terms less favorable.

1983; DeJong, 1979). But strangely enough, exactly the opposite approach will work just as well.

The Door-in-the-Face Technique: An Unreasonable Request First With the **door-in-the-face technique**, a large, unreasonable request is made first. The expectation is that the person will refuse but will then be more likely to respond favorably to a smaller request later (the request that was desired from the beginning). In one of the best-known studies on the door-in-the-face technique, college students were approached on campus. They were asked to agree to serve as counselors without pay to juvenile delinquents for two hours each week for a minimum of 2 years. The researchers could not get even one person to agree to do it (Cialdini, Vincent, et al., 1975). Then the experimenters countered with a much smaller request, asking if the students would agree to take a group of juveniles on a 2-hour trip to the zoo. Half the students agreed, a fairly high compliance rate. The researchers used another group of college students as controls, asking them to respond only to the smaller request, the zoo trip. Only 17 percent agreed when the smaller request was presented alone.

The Low-Ball Technique: Not Telling the Whole Truth Up Front Another method used to gain compliance is the **low-ball technique**. A very attractive initial offer is made to get people to commit themselves to an action, and then the terms are made less favorable. College students were asked to enroll in an experimental course for which they would receive credit, but they were low-balled. Only after the students had agreed to participate were they informed that the class would meet at 7:00 A.M. But 55 percent of the low-balled group agreed to participate anyway. When another group of students were told up-front that the class would meet at 7:00 A.M., only about 25 percent agreed to take the class (Cialdini, Cacioppo, et al., 1978).

Memory Check 16.3

1. Asch found that (25, 5) percent of the subjects never conformed to the incorrect, unanimous, majority response.

2. Milgram found that (50, 65) percent of the subjects in his original obedience experiment administered what they thought was the maximum 450-volt shock.

3. Match the compliance technique with the appropriate example.

   _____ 1) Julie agreed to sign a letter
   supporting an increase in taxes
   for road construction. Later she
   agrees to make 100 phone calls
   urging people to vote for the
   measure.

(continued)

2) Rick refuses a phone request for a $24.00 donation to send four needy children to the circus but does agree to give $6.00.

3) Linda agrees to babysit for her next-door neighbors and then is informed that their three nephews will be there too.

a. door-in-the-face technique
b. low-ball technique
c. foot-in-the-door technique

Answers: 1. 25 2. 65 3. 1) c 2) a 3) b

social facilitation: Any positive or negative effect on performance due to the presence of others, either as an audience or as co-actors.

audience effects: The impact of passive spectators on performance.

co-action effects: The impact on performance caused by the presence of others engaged in the same task.

Group Influence

The Effects of the Group on Individual Performance

Our performance on tasks can be enhanced or impaired by the mere presence of others, and the decisions we reach as part of a group can be quite different from those we would make when acting alone.

Question: Under what conditions does social facilitation have either a positive or negative effect on performance?

Social Facilitation: Performing in the Presence of Others In certain cases our individual performance can be either helped or hindered by the mere physical presence of others. The term **social facilitation** refers to any effect on performance, whether positive or negative, that can be attributed to the presence of others. Research on this phenomenon has been of two types: (1) *audience effects*—the impact of passive spectators on performance, and (2) *co-action effects*—the impact on performance caused by the presence of other people engaged in the same task.

One of the first studies in social psychology was conducted by Norman Triplett (1898), who looked at co-action effects. Triplett had observed in official bicycle records that bicycle racers pedaled faster when they were pedaling against other racers than when they were racing against the clock. Was this pattern of performance peculiar to competitive bicycling? Or was it part of a more general phenomenon in which individuals would work faster and harder in the presence of others than when performing alone? Triplett set up a study in which he told 40 children to wind fishing reels as quickly as possible under two conditions—(1) alone, or (2) in the presence of other children performing the same task. He found that the children worked faster when other reel turners were present than when they performed alone.

Later studies on social facilitation found just the opposite effect—that the presence of others, whether co-acting or just watching, could hurt or diminish individual performance. Robert Zajonc (1965; Zajonc & Sales, 1966) proposed an explanation for these seemingly contradictory effects. He reasoned that we become aroused by the presence of others and that arousal facilitates the domi-

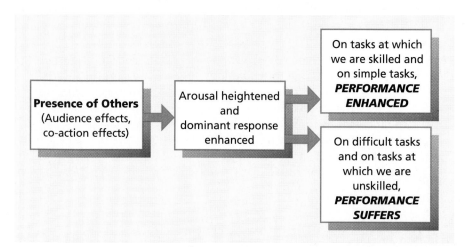

Figure 16.5   Social Facilitation: Performing in the Presence of Others   The presence of others (either as an audience or as co-actors engaged in the same task) may have opposite effects, either helping or hindering our performance. Why? Robert Zajonc explained that (1) the presence of others heightens our arousal, and (2) heightened arousal facilitates the correct response on tasks we are good at and the incorrect response on tasks that are difficult for us. (Based on Zajonc & Sales, 1966.)

nant response—the one that is most natural to us. On simple tasks and on tasks at which we are skilled, the dominant response is the correct one (not making a mistake). However, on tasks that are difficult or tasks we are first learning, the incorrect response (making a mistake) would be dominant. This reasoning accounts for the repeated findings that, in the presence of others, performance improves on tasks that people perform easily, but suffers on difficult tasks (Michaels et al., 1982). See Figure 16.5.

Other researchers have suggested that it is concern over the observers' evaluation of us that affects performance, particularly if we expect a negative evaluation (Sanna & Shotland, 1990; Seta et al., 1989).

Question: What is social loafing, and how can it be lessened or eliminated?

Social Loafing: Not Pulling Our Weight in a Group Effort   What happens in cooperative tasks in which two or more individuals are working together? Do they increase their effort or slack off? Researcher Bibb Latane used the term **social loafing** for the tendency of people to exert less effort when working with others on a common task than when they are working alone. Social loafing occurs in situations in which no one person's contribution to the group can be identified, and in which individuals are neither praised for a good performance nor blamed for a poor one (Williams et al., 1981).

In one experiment, Latane and others (1979) asked students to shout and clap as loudly as possible, first alone and then in groups. In groups of two, individuals made only 71 percent of the noise they had made alone; four persons put forth 51 percent of the effort, and six persons only 40 percent of the effort.

Harkins and Jackson (1985) found that social loafing disappeared when subjects in a group were led to believe that each person's output could be monitored and their performance evaluated. More recently Harkins and Szymanski (1989) concluded that even the potential of evaluating group performance against some standard was sufficient to eliminate the loafing effect. When group size is rela-

social loafing: The tendency to put forth less effort when working with others on a common task than when working alone.

tively small and group evaluation is important, some members will even expend extra effort if they know that some of their co-workers are either unwilling, unreliable, or incompetent (Williams & Karau, 1991). Social loafing is not likely to occur when participants can evaluate their own individual contribution (Szymanski & Harkins, 1987), when they are personally involved in the outcome, or when they feel that the task is challenging (Brickner et al., 1986; Harkins & Petty, 1982).

Social loafing is apparently not peculiar to any single culture but is typical of the human species. Some 50 studies conducted in places as diverse as Taiwan, Japan, Thailand, India, and the United States confirm that social loafing shows up when people are involved in performing cooperative tasks (Gabrenya et al., 1983).

The Effects of the Group on Decision Making

The group can have profound and predictable effects on decision making, depending on the group's attitudes before a discussion begins.

Question: How is the initial attitude of the group likely to affect its decision making?

Group Polarization: When Group Decisions Become More Extreme   It is commonly believed that groups tend to make more moderate, conservative decisions than individuals make, but some research in social psychology tells us otherwise.

Group discussion often causes members of the group to shift to a more extreme position in whatever direction they were leaning initially—a phenomenon known as **group polarization** (Isenberg, 1986; Lamm, 1988). The group, it seems, will decide to take a greater risk if they were leaning in a risky direction to begin with, but they will shift toward a less risky position if they were, on the average, somewhat cautious at the beginning of the discussion (Moscovici & Zavalloni, 1969; Myers & Lamm, 1975). Myers and Bishop (1970) found that as a result of group polarization, group discussions of racial issues can either increase or decrease prejudice.

Why, then, aren't all group decisions extreme ones? The reason is that the members of a group do not always lean in the same direction at the beginning of a discussion. When subgroups within a larger group hold opposing views, compromise rather than polarization is the likely outcome (Vinokur & Burnstein, 1978).

Groupthink: When Group Cohesiveness Leads to Bad Decisions   Group cohesiveness refers to the degree to which group members are attracted to the group and experience a feeling of oneness. **Groupthink** is the term that social psychologist Irving Janis (1982) applies to the decisions often reached by overly cohesive groups. When a tightly knit group is more concerned with preserving group solidarity and uniformity than with objectively evaluating all possible alternatives in decision making, individual members may hesitate to voice any dissent. The group may also discredit opposing views from outsiders and begin to believe it is invulnerable and incapable of making mistakes. Even plans bordering on madness can be hatched and adopted when groupthink prevails.

To guard against groupthink, Janis suggests that the group encourage an open discussion of alternative views and encourage the expression of any objections and doubts. He further recommends that outside experts sit in and challenge the views of the group. Finally, at least one group member should take the role of devil's advocate whenever a policy alternative is evaluated.

group polarization: The tendency of members of a group, after group discussion, to shift toward a more extreme position in whatever direction they were leaning initially—either more risky or more cautious.

groupthink: The tendency for members of a very cohesive group to feel such pressure to maintain group solidarity and reach agreement on an issue that they fail adequately to weigh available evidence and consider objections and alternatives.

Memory Check 16.4

1. Which of the following statements regarding the effects of social facilitation is true?

   a. Performance improves on all tasks.
   b. Performance worsens on all tasks.
   c. Performance improves on easy tasks and worsens on difficult tasks.
   d. Performance improves on difficult tasks and worsens on easy tasks.

2. Social loafing (usually, always) occurs when individuals working with others on a common task put forth less effort than when working alone.

3. When group polarization occurs following group discussion, the group will decide to take a greater risk if group members were leaning in a (cautious, risky) direction initially.

4. (Group polarization, Groupthink) occurs when members of a very cohesive group are more concerned with preserving group solidarity than with evaluating all possible alternatives in making a decision.

Answers: 1. c 2. usually 3. risky 4. Groupthink

Attitudes and Attitude Change

Attitudes: Cognitive, Emotional, and Behavioral Positions

Question: What are the three components of an attitude?

What is your attitude toward abortion? gun control? premarital sex? An **attitude** is a relatively stable evaluation of a person, object, situation, or issue. Most of our attitudes have three components: (1) a cognitive component—our thoughts and beliefs about the attitudinal object; (2) an emotional component—our feelings toward the attitudinal object; and (3) a behavioral component—how we are predisposed to act toward the object (Breckler, 1984). Figure 16.6 shows the three components of an attitude.

Attitudes enable us to appraise people, objects, and situations, thus providing structure and consistency to our social environment (Fazio, 1989). Attitudes also help us process social information (Pratkanis, 1989), guide our behavior (Sanbonmatsu & Fazio, 1990), and influence our social judgments and decisions (Devine, 1989; Jamieson & Zanna, 1989).

How do we form our attitudes? Some of our attitudes are acquired through first-hand experience with people, objects, situations, and issues. Others are acquired vicariously. When we hear parents, family, friends, and teachers express positive or negative attitudes toward certain issues or people, we may take the same attitudes as our own. The mass media, including advertising, influence our attitudes and reap billions of dollars annually for their efforts. As you might expect, however, the attitudes that we form through our own direct experience are stronger than those we acquire vicariously, and they are also more resistant to change (Wu & Schaffer, 1987). Although the attitudes of older people tend to

attitude: A relatively stable evaluation of a person, object, situation, or issue.

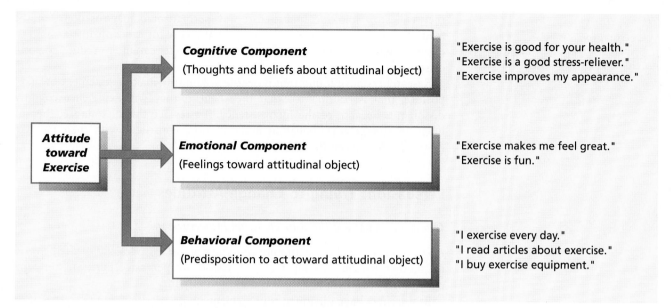

Figure 16.6   The Three Components of an Attitude   An attitude is a relatively stable evaluation of a person, object, situation, or issue. Most of our attitudes have (1) a cognitive component, (2) an emotional component, and (3) a behavioral component.

be more stable over time (Alwin et al., 1991), the lack of change seems to result from limited exposure to change-inducing experiences rather than to "an inability or unwillingness to change" (Tyler & Schuller, 1991, p. 696).

The Relationship between Attitudes and Behavior   The general consensus among social scientists initially was that attitudes govern behavior (Allport, 1935). But toward the end of the 1960s, one study after another failed to reveal a strong relationship between what people report they believe on attitude measurement scales and their actual behavior. Attitudes seemed to predict observed behavior only about 10 percent of the time (Wicker, 1969).

Why aren't attitude measures better predictors of behavior? Attitude measures may often be too general to predict specific behaviors. People may express strong attitudes toward protecting the environment and conservation of resources, yet not take their aluminum cans to a recycling center or join car pools. When attitude measures correspond very closely to the behavior of interest, they actually become good predictors of behavior (Ajzen & Fishbein, 1977). Finally, attitudes are better predictors of behavior if they are strongly held, are readily accessible in memory (Fazio & Williams, 1986; Fazio et al., 1986), and vitally affect our interests (Sivacek & Crano, 1982).

Question: What is cognitive dissonance, and how can it be resolved?

Cognitive Dissonance: The Mental Pain of Inconsistency   If we discover that some of our attitudes are in conflict with others or are not consistent with our behavior, we are likely to experience an unpleasant state. Leon Festinger (1957) called this **cognitive dissonance**. We usually try to reduce the dissonance by changing our behavior or our attitude, or by somehow explaining away the inconsistency or reducing its importance (Aronson, 1973, 1976; Festinger, 1957).

Smoking is a perfect situation for cognitive dissonance. What are smokers to do? The healthiest, but perhaps not the easiest way to reduce cognitive dissonance is to change the behavior—quit smoking. Another way is to change the attitude—to convince themselves that smoking is not as dangerous as the United States Surgeon General seems to believe. Smokers can also tell themselves that

cognitive dissonance: The unpleasant state that can occur when people become aware of inconsistencies between their attitudes or between their attitudes and behavior.

persuasion: A deliberate attempt to influence the attitudes and/or behavior of another.

they will stop smoking long before any permanent damage is done, or that medical science is advancing so rapidly that a cure for cancer is just around the corner. Figure 16.7 illustrates the methods a smoker can use to reduce cognitive dissonance.

Researchers have found that if people voluntarily make a statement or take a position that is counter to what they believe, they will experience cognitive dissonance because of the inconsistency. To resolve this dissonance, they are likely to change their belief to make it more consistent with their behavior (Festinger & Carlsmith, 1959).

Persuasion: Trying to Change Attitudes

Question: What are the four elements in persuasion?

Persuasion is a deliberate attempt to influence the attitudes and/or the behavior of another person. Attempts at persuasion are pervasive parts of our work experience, social experiences, and even family life.

Researchers have identified four elements in persuasion: (1) the source of the communication (who is doing the persuading), (2) the audience (who is being persuaded), (3) the message (what is being said), and (4) the medium (the means by which the message is transmitted).

Question: What qualities make a source most persuasive?

The Source: Look Who's Talking   Some factors that make the source (communicator) more persuasive are credibility, attractiveness, and likability. Credibility refers to how believable a source is. A credible communicator is one who has expertise (knowledge of the topic at hand) and trustworthiness (truthfulness and integrity). The influence of a credible source is even greater if the audience knows the communicator's credentials beforehand. We attach greater credibility to sources who have nothing to gain from persuading us, or better yet, sources who seem to be arguing against their own best interest. For example, arguments against pornography are more persuasive if they are made by a source known to be generally opposed to censorship.

Figure 16.7

Methods of Reducing Cognitive Dissonance

Cognitive dissonance can occur when people become aware of inconsistencies in their attitudes, or between their attitudes and their behavior. People try to reduce dissonance by (1) changing their behavior, (2) changing their attitude, (3) explaining away the inconsistency, or (4) reducing its importance. Here are examples of how a smoker could use these methods to reduce the cognitive dissonance created by his or her habit.

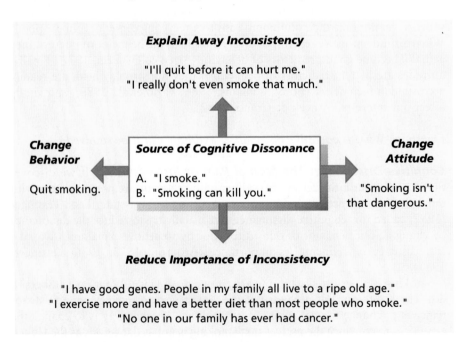

In matters that involve our own personal tastes and preferences rather than issues, attractive people and celebrities can be very persuasive (Chaiken, 1979). Movie and TV stars, athletes, and even unknown but attractive fashion models have long been used by advertisers to persuade us to buy certain products. Likable, down-to-earth, ordinary people who are perceived to be similar to the audience are sometimes more effective persuaders than famous experts, attractive models, or movie stars. Political candidates attempt to appear more likable and more like the voters when they don hard hats and visit construction sites and coal mines, kiss babies, and pose with farmers.

The Audience and the Message Persuaders must consider the nature of their audience before they attempt to persuade it. Research evidence suggests that a one-sided message is usually best if the audience is not well-informed on the issue, is not overly intelligent, or is already in agreement with the point of view. A two-sided approach works best when the audience is well-informed on the issue, fairly intelligent, or initially opposed to the point of view. Using the two-sided approach will usually sway more people than a one-sided appeal (Hovland et al., 1949; McGuire, 1969, 1985).

A message can be well-reasoned, logical, and unemotional ("just the facts"); a message can be strictly emotional ("scare the hell out of them"); or it can be a combination of the two. Which type of message works best? Arousing fear seems to be an effective method for persuading people to adopt healthier attitudes and behaviors (Robberson & Rogers, 1988). One review of many studies on fear and persuasion covering various issues—anti-smoking presentations, seat-belt safety campaigns, and appeals urging regular chest X rays—reported that high-fear appeals were more effective than low-fear appeals (Higbee, 1969). Fear appeals are most effective when the presentation outlines definite actions the audience can take to avoid the feared outcomes (Leventhal et al., 1965).

Another important factor in persuasion is repetition. The more often a product or a point of view is presented, the more people will be persuaded to buy it or embrace it. Advertisers apparently believe in the "mere exposure effect," and they repeat their message over and over (Bornstein, 1989).

Memory Check 16.5

1. The three components of an attitude are the cognitive, the emotional, and the behavioral. (true/false)

2. Cognitive dissonance can be relieved by:

   a. changing an attitude   c. explaining away the inconsistency
   b. changing a behavior   d. all of these

3. Credibility relates most directly to the expertise and (attractiveness, trustworthiness) of the communicator.

4. With a well-informed audience, (one-sided, two-sided) arguments are more persuasive.

5. Messages are more persuasive if they cause (low, high) fear and provide definite actions that can be taken to avoid the feared outcome.

Answers: 1. true 2. d 3. trustworthiness 4. two-sided 5. high

Persuasion is a deliberate attempt to influence the attitudes and behavior of another person.

bystander effect: As the number of bystanders at an emergency increases, the probability that the victim will receive help decreases, and help, if given, is likely to be delayed.

diffusion of responsibility: When bystanders at an emergency feel that the responsibility for helping is shared by the group, so each individual feels less compelled to act than if he or she alone felt the total responsibility.

Prosocial Behavior: Behavior That Benefits Others

Why did no one help or even call the police during the brutal attack on Kitty Genovese, which was discussed at the beginning of the chapter? Are we becoming a nation of selfish, cowardly, uncaring people, the news media asked, who will not aid a fellow human being screaming for help? Such charges assume a dispositional cause—a character defect in each one of the 38 neighbors who witnessed the event.

Rather than shaking their heads at the apparently callous indifference of those who watched the murder of Kitty Genovese, social psychologists Bibb Latane and John Darley looked deeper for an explanation. Perhaps certain factors in the situation itself would help explain why so many people just stood or sat there.

The Bystander Effect: The More Bystanders, the Less Likely They Are to Help

Question: What is the bystander effect, and what factors have been suggested to explain why it occurs?

If you were injured or ill and needed help, would you feel safer if one or two other people were near, or if a large crowd of onlookers were present? You may be surprised to learn of the **bystander effect.** As the number of bystanders at an emergency increases, the probability that the victim will receive help from them decreases, and the help, if given, is likely to be delayed. Why should this be?

Darley and Latane (1968a) set up a number of experiments to study helping behavior. In one study, subjects were placed one at a time in a small room and told that they would be participating in a discussion group by means of an intercom system. It was explained that because personal problems were being discussed, a face-to-face, group discussion might be inhibiting. Some subjects were told that they would be communicating with only one other subject, some believed that two other participants would be involved, and some were told that five other people would participate. There really were no other subjects in the study, only the prerecorded voices of confederates assisting the experimenter.

Shortly after the discussion began, the voice of one confederate was heard over the intercom calling for help, indicating that he was having an epileptic seizure. Of the subjects who believed that they alone were hearing the victim, 85 percent went for help before the end of the seizure. When subjects believed that one other person heard the seizure, 62 percent sought help. But when they believed that four other people were aware of the emergency, only 31 percent tried to get help before the end of the seizure. Figure 16.8 shows how the number of bystanders affects both the number of people who try to help and the speed of response.

Latane and Darley suggest two possible explanations for the bystander effect—diffusion of responsibility and the influence of apparently calm bystanders.

Diffusion of Responsibility: An Explanation for the Bystander Effect

When bystanders are present in an emergency, they generally feel that the responsibility for helping is shared by the group, a phenomenon known as **diffusion of responsibility.** Consequently each person feels less compelled to act than if she or he were alone and felt the total responsibility. Kitty Genovese's neighbors were aware that other people were watching because they saw lights go off in the other apartments. They did not feel that the total responsibility for

Why does this woman ignore the plight of the unconscious man on the sidewalk? Diffusion of responsibility is one possible explanation.

action rested only on their shoulders, or they might have thought that 'somebody else must be doing something'" (Darley & Latane, 1968a, p. 378).

The Influence of Apparently Calm Bystanders: When Faces Deceive

Sometimes real emergencies occur in rather ambiguous situations. Bystanders may not be sure if an actual emergency exists and, at the risk of appearing foolish, they often hesitate to react with alarm until they are sure that intervention is appropriate (Clark & Word, 1972). So the bystanders may stand there watching other calm-appearing bystanders and conclude that nothing is really wrong and no intervention is necessary (Darley & Latane, 1968b).

More than a few people have died while many potential helpers stood and watched passively because of the bystander effect. Picture an orthopedic surgeon's large waiting room in which eight patients are waiting to see the doctor. In one chair a middle-aged man sits slumped over, yet he does not appear to be sleeping. His position resembles that of a person who is unconscious. If you were a patient in such a setting, would you check on the man's condition or just continue sitting?

This was the actual scene one of the authors entered a few years ago as a patient. She sat down and immediately noticed the man slumped in his chair. She scanned the faces of the other waiting patients but saw no sign of alarm or even concern. Was there really no emergency, or was this a case of the bystander effect? Knowing that the reaction of onlookers is a poor indicator of the seriousness of a situation, she quickly summoned the doctor, who found that the man had suffered a heart attack. Fortunately the doctor's office was attached to a large hospital complex, and almost immediately a hospital team appeared and rushed the victim to the emergency room.

People Who Help in Emergencies

There are many kinds of **prosocial behavior**—behavior that benefits others. The term **altruism** is usually reserved for behavior aimed at helping others that requires some self-sacrifice and is not performed for personal gain. What motivates us to help or not to help in an emergency? Batson and colleagues (1988, 1989) believe that we help out of empathy—the ability to feel what another feels.

Cultures vary in their norms for helping others—that is, their social responsibility norms. According to Miller and others (1990), people in the United States tend to feel an obligation to help family, friends, and even strangers in life-threatening circumstances, but only family in moderately serious situations. In contrast, in India the social responsibility norm extends to strangers whose needs are moderately serious or even minor.

In spite of the potentially high costs of helping, we have heard accounts of people who have risked their lives to help others. During World War II, thousands of Christians risked their lives to protect Jews from extermination in Nazi Germany. Are there common factors that might explain such uncommon risks in the service of others? A study of 406 rescuers revealed that they did not consider themselves heroes, and that different motives led to their altruistic behavior. Some rescuers were motivated by strong convictions about how human beings should be treated; others, by empathy for the particular person or persons they rescued (Fogelman & Weiner, 1985; Oliner & Oliner, 1988). Still others were acting based on the norms of their family or social group that emphasized helping others.

In what conditions or circumstances might a person be more likely to receive help? People are more likely to receive help if they are physically attractive (Benson et al., 1976), if they are perceived by potential helpers as similar to them

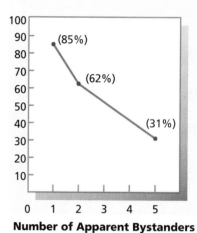

Percent of Subjects Trying to Help

Number of Apparent Bystanders

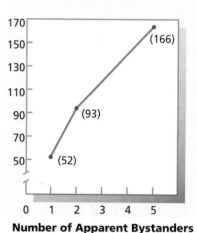

Seconds Elapsed before Subjects Tried to Help

Number of Apparent Bystanders

Figure 16.8

The Bystander Effect

In their intercom experiment, Darley and Latane showed that the more people a subject believed were present during an emergency, the longer it took the subject to respond and help a person in distress. (Data from Darley & Latane, 1968.)

prosocial behavior: Behavior that benefits others.

altruism: Behavior aimed at helping another, requiring some self-sacrifice and not designed for personal gain.

(Dovidio, 1984), and if they are not considered responsible for their plight (Reisenzein, 1986; Schmidt & Weiner, 1988). Potential helpers are more likely to help if they have specialized training in first aid or police work, are not in a hurry, have been exposed to a helpful model (Bryan & Test, 1967), are in a positive mood (Carlson et al., 1988), and if the weather is good (Cunningham, 1979).

Memory Check 16.6

1. As the number of bystanders to an emergency increases, the probability that the victim will receive help (increases, decreases).

2. Bart drives right by a woman whose car has a flat tire at the side of a busy highway. According to the concept of diffusion of responsibility:

   a. he feels less compelled to act because the responsibility for helping is shared by other people on the highway
   b. he may believe that someone else has called for help
   c. people are indifferent to the problems of others
   d. both a and b

3. In an ambiguous situation, looking at the reactions of other bystanders (is, is not) a good way to determine if an emergency exists.

4. Altruism is another word for prosocial behavior. (true/false)

Answers: 1. decreases 2. d 3. is not 4. false

Aggression: Intentionally Harming Others

We humans have a long history of **aggression**—intentionally inflicting physical or psychological harm on others. Consider the tens of millions of people killed by other humans in wars and even in times of peace. In 1990, in the United States alone, there were 23,000 homicides, 30,000 suicides, 100,000 reported rapes, 640,000 robberies, and 1 million assaults (Zimring, 1991).

What causes aggression? One of the earliest explanations of aggression was the instinct theory—human beings, along with other animal species, are genetically programmed for such behavior. Sigmund Freud believed that humans have an aggressive instinct that can be turned inward as self-destruction or outward as aggression or violence toward others. Nobel Prize-winning researcher in animal behavior, Konrad Lorenz (1966) claimed that aggression springs from an inborn, fighting instinct common in many animal species. Most psychologists, however, consider human behavior too complex to attribute to instincts.

Biological Factors in Aggression: Genes, Hormones, and Brain Damage

Question: What biological factors are thought to be related to aggression?

While rejecting the instinct theory of aggression, many psychologists do concede that biological factors are involved. Twin and adoption studies have revealed a

aggression: The intentional infliction of physical or psychological harm on another.

genetic link in criminal behavior (DiLalla & Gottesman, 1991). In a study of 573 pairs of adult twins, Rushton and others (1986) report that aggressive behavior in identical twins showed a correlation of .40 compared to a correlation of only .20 in fraternal twins.

Cloninger and others (1982) found that adoptees with a criminal biological parent were 4 times as likely to commit crimes while adoptees with a criminal adoptive parent were at twice the risk of the general population. But adoptees with both a criminal biological and a criminal adoptive parent were 14 times as likely to commit crimes.

Men are generally more physically aggressive than women, and the male hormone testosterone is thought to be involved. A correlation between high testosterone level and aggressive behavior has been found in both adolescent (Olweus, 1987) and adult males (Archer, 1991; Dabbs & Morris, 1990). Violent behavior has also been linked to low levels of the neurotransmitter serotonin (Brown & Linnoila, 1990; Burrowes et al., 1988).

Brain damage, brain tumors, and temporal lobe epilepsy have all been related to aggressive and violent behavior (Mednick et al., 1988). A study of 15 death-row inmates revealed that all had histories of severe head injuries (Lewis et al., 1986). Alcohol and aggression are also frequent partners. A meta-analysis of 30 experimental studies suggests that "alcohol does indeed cause aggression" (Bushman & Cooper, 1990, p. 341). People who are intoxicated commit the majority of murders, beatings of spouses, stabbings, and physical child abuse.

Aggression in Response to Frustration: Sometimes, but Not Always

Question: What is the frustration-aggression hypothesis?

Does *frustration*—blocking or interfering with the attainment of a goal—lead to aggression? The **frustration-aggression hypothesis** suggests that frustration produces aggression (Dollard et al., 1939; Miller, 1941). If a traffic jam kept you from arriving at your destination on time and you were frustrated, what would you do—sit on your horn, shout obscenities out of your window, or just sit patiently and wait? Frustration doesn't always cause aggression, but it is especially likely to if the frustration is intense and seems to be unjustified (Doob & Sears, 1939; Pastore, 1950). Berkowitz (1988) points out that even if frustration is justified and not aimed specifically at us, it can cause aggression if it arouses negative emotions.

Aggression in response to frustration is not always aimed at the people causing it but may be displaced if the preferred target is too threatening or not available. For example, children who are angry with their parents may take out their frustrations on a younger sibling. Sometimes minorities and others who have not been responsible for a frustrating situation become targets of displaced aggression, a practice known as **scapegoating** (Koltz, 1983).

Aggression in Response to Aversive Events: Pain, Heat, Noise, and More

Question: What kinds of aversive events and unpleasant emotions have been related to aggression?

Aggression in response to frustration is only one special case of a broader phenomenon—aggression resulting from unpleasant or aversive events in general, says a leading researcher on aggression, Leonard Berkowitz (1988, 1989). People often become aggressive when they are in pain (Berkowitz, 1983) or are

frustration: Interfering with the attainment of a goal, or blocking an impulse.

frustration-aggression hypothesis: The hypothesis that frustration produces aggression.

scapegoating: Displacing aggression onto minority groups or other innocent targets who were not responsible for the frustration causing the aggression.

exposed to loud noise, foul odors (Rotton et al., 1979), and even irritating cigarette smoke. Extreme heat has been linked to aggression in several studies (Anderson, 1989; Carlsmith & Anderson, 1979).

These and other studies lend support to the cognitive-neoassociationistic model proposed by Berkowitz (1990). He suggests that anger and aggression result from aversive events and from unpleasant emotional states like sadness, grief, and depression. "The core notion in this model is that negative affect is the basic source of anger and angry aggression" (Berkowitz, 1990, p. 494). And negative emotions (affect) tend to activate angry feelings, thoughts, and memories, as well as tendencies toward aggression or escape. The cognitive component of Berkowitz's model occurs when the angered person makes an appraisal of the aversive situation and makes attributions about the motives of the people involved. As a result of the cognitive appraisal, the initial anger reaction can be either intensified, reduced, or suppressed. This process will make it either more or less likely that the aggressive tendency will be acted on.

Several studies suggest that aggressive adolescents tend to attribute hostile intentions to others in certain social encounters, leading them to believe retaliation with aggression is appropriate (Dodge, Price, et al., 1990; Fondacaro & Heller, 1990).

The Social Learning Theory of Aggression: Learning to Be Aggressive

Question: According to social learning theory, what causes aggressive behavior?

The social learning theory holds that people learn to behave aggressively by observing aggressive models and by having their aggressive responses reinforced (Bandura, 1973). It is well known that aggression is higher in groups and subcultures that condone violent behavior and accord high status to aggressive members. A leading advocate of the social learning theory of aggression, Albert Bandura (1976) claims that aggressive models in the subculture, the family, and in the media all play a part in increasing the level of aggression in our society.

Abused children certainly experience aggression and see it modeled day after day. "One of the most commonly held beliefs in both the scholarly and popular literature is that adults who were abused as children are more likely to abuse their own children" (Widom, 1989b, p. 6). There is some truth to this belief. About 30 percent of the abused become abusers, a rate six times higher than in the general population. But nearly two-thirds of the abused do not continue a cycle of violence (Kaufman & Zigler, 1987), and "the majority of abusive parents were not abused in their own childhoods" (Widom, 1989b, p. 8). Although abused and neglected children are at higher risk of becoming delinquent, criminal, or violent, the majority do not (Widom, 1989a). Several researchers suggest that the higher risk for aggression may not be due solely to an abusive family environment but may be partly influenced by the genes (DiLalla & Gottesman, 1991). Some abused children become withdrawn and isolated rather than aggressive (Dodge, Bates, et al., 1990).

The Media and Aggression: Is There a Connection?   Bandura (1976) claims that "the modern child has witnessed innumerable stabbings, beatings, stompings, stranglings, muggings, and less blatant but equally destructive forms of cruelty before he has reached kindergarten age" (p. 125). But is there a causal link between viewing aggressive acts and committing them? Some studies say no (Freedman, 1984; Milavsky et al., 1982), but the overwhelming evidence reveals a relationship between TV violence and viewer aggression (Pearl et al., 1982; Rubinstein, 1983). Some research indicates that adults and children as young as nursery-school age show higher levels of aggression after they view media violence (Geen, 1978; Liebert et al., 1989). A study of 840 10-year-old children in Finland revealed that the more television violence children watched, the more likely they were to have aggressive fantasies and engage in aggression (Vlemerö & Paajanc, 1992).

In a longitudinal study of 600 7- to 9-year-old children launched in 1960, subjects were reinterviewed at age 19 and again at age 30 (Eron, 1987). Subjects who were most aggressive at age 8 were still aggressive at ages 19 and 30, many of them showing antisocial behavior ranging from traffic violations to criminal convictions and aggressiveness toward their spouses and children (Huesmann et al., 1984). Did media influence play a part? "One of the best predictors of how aggressive a young man would be at age 19 was the violence of the television programs he preferred when he was 8 years old" (Eron, 1987, p. 438). And the more frequently the subjects had watched TV violence at that age, "the more serious were the crimes for which they were convicted by age 30" (p. 440).

A review of 28 studies of the effects of media violence on children and adolescents revealed that "media violence enhances children's and adolescents' aggression in interactions with strangers, classmates, and friends" (Wood et al., 1991, p. 380). Media violence may lead to aggression by activating information related to aggression in memory (Bushman & Geen, 1990). It may stimulate physiological arousal, lower inhibitions, cause unpleasant feelings, and decrease sensitivity to violence and make it more acceptable to people (Wood et al., 1991).

Black and Bevan (1992) administered an aggression inventory to moviegoers attending violent and nonviolent movies. Higher aggression scores were found for moviegoers attending violent movies (both before and after the movie) than for moviegoers attending nonviolent movies. Are violent television episodes in which the "good guys" finally get the "bad guys" less harmful? Not according to Berkowitz (1964), who claims that justified aggression is the type most likely to encourage the viewer to express aggression.

Can we reduce aggression in our society? Not by letting off steam vicariously through watching aggression or violence in sports or the media and not by directly engaging in aggressive but nonviolent behavior (Berkowitz, 1964; Josephson, 1987). The best hope is to find ways to reduce aggression in families, to eliminate reinforcement for aggression, and to remove excessive violence from the media (Eron, 1980).

Memory Check 16.7

1. Social psychologists generally believe that aggression stems from an aggressive instinct in people. (true/false)

2. Frustration (always, frequently) leads to aggression.

3. The social learning theory of aggression emphasizes all of the following except that:

   a. aggressive responses are learned from the family, the subculture, and the media
   b. aggressive responses are learned through modeling
   c. most aggression results from frustration
   d. when aggressive responses are reinforced, they are more likely to continue

4. The weight of research suggests that media violence probably (is, is not) related to increased aggression.

Answers: 1. false 2. frequently 3. c 4. is

Thinking Critically _____

Evaluation

Many Americans were surprised when the majority of the people in the Soviet Union rejoiced at the downfall of the Communist system. Using what you have learned about attribution bias and conformity, try to explain why many in this country had mistakenly believed that the Soviet masses preferred the Communist system.

Point/Counterpoint

Prepare a convincing argument supporting each of the following positions:

a. Aggression results largely from biological factors (nature).
b. Aggression is primarily learned (nurture).

Psychology in Your Life

Review the factors influencing attraction and impression formation as discussed in this chapter. Prepare a dual list of behaviors indicating what you should and should not do if you wish to make a better impression on other people and to increase their liking for you.

Chapter Summary and Review _____

Social Perception

Why are first impressions so important and enduring?

First impressions are important because we attend to the first information we receive about a person more carefully, and once formed, an impression acts as a framework through which later information is interpreted.

What is nonverbal behavior, and what does it convey?

Nonverbal behavior—our gestures, facial expressions, posture, and other body language—can communicate anger, liking, loving, happiness, sadness, anxiety, impatience, deception, and differences in status.

What is the difference between a situational attribution and a dispositional attribution for a specific behavior?

An attribution is an inferred cause of our own or another's behavior. When we use situational attributions, we attribute the cause of behavior to some factor in the environment. With dispositional attributions, the inferred cause is internal—some personal trait, motive, or attitude.

How do the types of attributions we tend to make about ourselves differ from those we make about other people?

We tend to overemphasize dispositional factors when making attributions about the behavior of other people, and to overemphasize situational factors in explaining our own behavior.

Key Terms

social psychology (p. 548)
confederate (p. 548)
naive subject (p. 548)
primacy effect (p. 549)
nonverbal behavior (p. 550)
attributions (p. 552)
situational attribution (p. 552)

dispositional attribution (p. 552)
fundamental attribution error (p. 552)
self-serving bias (p. 552)

Attraction

Why is proximity an important factor in attraction?

Proximity influences attraction because it is easier to develop relationships with people close at hand. Also, proximity increases the likelihood of repeated contacts, and mere exposure tends to increase attraction (the mere-exposure effect).

How important is physical attractiveness in attraction?

Physical attractiveness is a major factor in attraction for people of all ages. People attribute other positive qualities to those who are physically attractive—a phenomenon called the halo effect.

Are people, as a rule, more attracted to those who are opposite or similar to them?

People are generally attracted to those who have similar attitudes and interests, and who are similar in economic status, race, and age.

How does Sternberg's triangular theory of love account for the different kinds of love?

In his triangular theory of love, Sternberg proposes that three components—intimacy, passion and decision/commitment—singly or in various combinations produce seven different kinds of love—infatuated, empty, romantic, fatuous, companionate, and consummate love, as well as liking.

Key Terms

proximity (p. 554)
mere exposure effect (p. 554)
halo effect (p. 555)

matching hypothesis (p. 556)
triangular theory of love (p. 559)
consummate love (p. 560)

Conformity, Obedience, and Compliance

What did Asch find in his famous experiment on conformity?

In Asch's classic study on conformity, 5 percent of the subjects went along with the incorrect, unanimous majority all the time, 70 percent went along some of the time, and 25 percent remained completely independent.

What did Milgram find in his classic study of obedience?

In Milgram's classic study of obedience, 65 percent of the subjects obeyed the experimenter's orders to the end of the experiment and administered what they believed to be increasingly painful shocks to the learner up to the maximum of 450 volts.

What are three techniques used to gain compliance?

Three techniques used to gain compliance are the foot-in-the-door technique, the door-in-the-face technique, and the low-ball technique.

Key Terms

conformity (p. 561)
norms (p. 561)
compliance (p. 565)
foot-in-the-door technique (p. 565)
door-in-the-face technique (p. 566)
low-ball technique (p. 566)

Group Influence

Under what conditions does social facilitation have either a positive or a negative effect on performance?

When others are present, either as an audience or as co-actors, one's performance on easy tasks is usually improved, but performance on difficult tasks is usually impaired.

What is social loafing, and how can it be lessened or eliminated?

Social loafing is the tendency of people to put forth less effort when they are working with others on a common task than when they were working alone. This is less likely to occur when individual output can be monitored or when people are highly involved with the outcome.

How is the initial attitude of the group likely to affect its decision making?

Following group discussions, group decisions usually shift to a more extreme position in whatever direction the members were leaning toward initially—a phenomenon known as group polarization.

Key Terms

social facilitation (p. 567)
social loafing (p. 568)
group polarization (p. 569)
groupthink (p. 569)

Attitudes and Attitude Change

What are the three components of an attitude?

Attitudes usually have a cognitive, emotional, and behavioral component.

What is cognitive dissonance, and how can it be resolved?

Cognitive dissonance is an unpleasant state that can occur when we become aware of inconsistencies between our attitudes or between our attitudes and behavior. It can be resolved by changing the attitude or the behavior, or by rationalizing away the inconsistency.

What are the four elements in persuasion?

The four elements in persuasion are the source, the audience, the message, and the medium.

What qualities make a source most persuasive?

Persuasive attempts are most successful when the source is credible (expert and trustworthy), attractive, and likable.

Key Terms

attitude (p. 570)
cognitive dissonance (p. 571)

Prosocial Behavior: Behavor that Benefits Others

What is the bystander effect and what factors have been suggested to explain why it occurs?

The bystander effect means that as the number of bystanders at an emergency increases, the probability that the victim will receive help decreases, and help, if given, is likely to be delayed. The bystander effect may be due in part to diffusion of responsibility or in ambiguous situations to the assumption that no emergency exists.

Key Terms

bystander effect (p. 574)
diffusion of responsibility (p. 574)
prosocial behavior (p. 575)
altruism (p. 575)

Aggression: Intentionally Harming Others

What biological factors are thought to be related to aggression?

Biological factors thought to be related to aggression are a genetic link in criminal behavior, high testosterone levels, low levels of serotonin, and brain damage.

What is the frustration-aggression hypothesis?

The frustration-aggression hypothesis holds that frustration produces aggression and that this aggression may be directed at the frustrater or displaced onto another target, as in scapegoating.

What kinds of aversive events and unpleasant emotions have been related to aggression?

Aggression has been associated with aversive conditions such as pain, heat, loud noise, and foul odors, and with unpleasant emotional states such as sadness, grief, and depression.

According to social learning theory, what causes aggressive behavior?

According to the social learning theory, aggressive responses are acquired by observing aggressive models in the family, the subculture, and the media, and by having aggressive responses reinforced.

Key Terms

aggression (p. 576)
frustration-aggression hypothesis (p. 577)
scapegoating (p. 577)

17

The World of Psychology: Multicultural Issues and Applications

CHAPTER OUTLINE

Dr. Charles Drew

Most people have never heard of Charles Richard Drew, but his contribution has saved millions of lives. Born in 1904, Drew became a physician and scientist, receiving his doctorate in medical science at Columbia University. His dissertation outlined techniques for blood preservation and the use of blood plasma for transfusions, and he is credited with the idea of blood transfusions. Before the United States entered World War II, Drew helped the British and French armies by showing them how to collect and dry blood plasma for use on the battlefield, thus saving many lives.

In 1941, as director of an American Red Cross program, he was appalled when the United States Armed Forces ruled that blood from white and nonwhite persons had to be stored separately. Dr. Drew continued to dispute such a ridiculous blood segregation program and presented scientific evidence that proved human blood does not differ according to race. Today we know that in blood transfusions, only the blood type matters, not the race of the donor.

In April 1950 Dr. Drew was traveling to a scientific meeting in North Carolina, when he was critically injured in an automobile accident near the town of Burlington. Only a blood transfusion would save his life. Thanks to Dr. Drew's earlier contribution, there was blood plasma in many hospitals around the country—but unfortunately not at the hospital where he lay. There was no blood plasma available for blacks at the segregated hospital in Burlington where Dr. Drew, a black American, was taken. He soon died of his injuries. Ironically, the person who had given the world an idea that continues to be the gift of life for many, died at age 46 because his gift to the world was denied him.

Our Multicultural World

DR. DREW RECOGNIZED that human blood is human blood. We are one species, although of different races and ethnic groups and from diverse cultures and many nationalities. The differences we observe among the human species—skin color, shape of the eyes, facial features, hair texture and color—though readily apparent, are superficial compared to our important biological similarities. We sense our world through identical mechanisms, and we feel and express the same range of human emotions. We grow and develop according to our species-specific timetable. We learn languages, and we pass along knowledge to our young.

By far the most important characteristic common to the human species is our ability to reason—to think and plan and solve problems. Our capacity to adapt to radically different environments, from the frozen North to the tropics, to change and reshape the natural environment for our comfort and pleasure, and to enhance our survival is truly remarkable. We are all—male or female, of whatever racial group—*Homo sapiens*, one species.

But the remarkable range of our human capabilities makes possible a virtually unlimited variety of responses to whatever type of environment we find ourselves in. Thus, diversity itself is a hallmark of the human species. Our rich diversity of customs and languages, of values and approaches to life, mark us as truly human. We are diverse because we have the ability to be so.

During the last few years we have come to recognize, more than ever before in our history, that we live in a dynamic multicultural world. The boundaries of the nations of the earth are changing so rapidly that cartographers cannot draw and redraw maps fast enough. Consider the breakup of the Soviet Union, which left many independent states to chart their own course. Here, in one of the most culturally diverse regions on the globe, live numerous ethnic and racial groups who speak different languages and practice several religions. Elsewhere we find ethnic and religious conflict and violence—the Serbians, the Croatians, and others in what was Yugoslavia; the Protestants and the Catholics in Northern Ireland; the Arabs and the Israelis; the Kurds and the Iraqis; and the warring factions in Africa.

Though times are finally changing in South Africa, the strong apartheid system requires that its people be classified as one of four official racial categories—white, colored, black, or Indian. Other minorities may be listed as Chinese, Malay, and so on. The racial classification of South Africans determines the schools they are allowed to attend, the jobs they are permitted to hold, where they are allowed to live, and whom they may marry (Yetman, 1991). That such classifications are largely arbitrary is evidenced by the fact that a person's racial category can be officially changed. And an official change brings with it all the economic, educational, and other opportunities legally extended to that racial classification.

Several years ago a South African newspaper reported a series of "racial changes":

> Nearly 800 South Africans became officially members of a different race group last year. . . . They included 518 coloreds who were officially reclassified as white, 14 whites who became colored, 7 Chinese [who are classified as "honorary whites"] who became white, 2 whites who became Chinese, 3 Malays [who are classified as colored] who became white, 1 white who became Indian, 50 Indians who became colored, 54 coloreds who became Indian, 17 Indians who became Malay, 4 coloreds who became Chinese, 1 Malay who became Chinese, 89 blacks who became colored, 5 coloreds who became black. (Usy, 1988, p. 27)

Norman Yetman (1991) points out that racial distinctions in cultures are not always related to skin color. Burundi, a small country in central Africa, has experienced waves of violence between its two major groups. The Tutsi people are tall and slender—on the average an adult male stands about 6 feet tall—while the Hutu people, of much smaller stature, average slightly over 4 feet in height. Although the taller Tutsi are a minority (about 15 percent of the population), they have for decades comprised the ruling aristocracy and forced the Hutu into the role of servant class.

When Burundi achieved its independence in 1962, the Hutu were hopeful that majority rule would put an end to Tutsi domination. But conditions remained the same, and violence erupted again in 1988. The Hutu attacks and the Tutsi counterattacks cost the lives of some 5,000 men, women, and children. To escape, thousands of the Hutu fled to Rwanda, a neighboring country where they are the tribal majority. Apparently, any discernible physical differences between peoples can lead to conflict, as can differences in values, beliefs, and religious affiliation.

Cultural diversity is on the rise in the United States as well, where the white majority is becoming less a majority. African Americans are the nation's largest racial minority, now totalling more than 30 million people. American blacks outnumber the entire population of Canada or the combined populations of Denmark, Finland, Iceland, Norway, and Sweden (Yetman, 1991). The Hispanic population in the United States now exceeds 20 million, and during the 1980s it increased by 34 percent, compared to a 13 percent growth rate for black Americans during the same period. But the most striking change among minority groups in the United States has been that of Asian Americans, whose population grew by over 70 percent in the 1980s (Yetman, 1991).

Prejudice and Discrimination

As we have seen, increasing cultural diversity is a fact of life in the modern world. And although we have one common language, the United States is among the most culturally diverse nations in the world. Can we learn to live and work peacefully with our fellow Americans, no matter what racial, ethnic, cultural, or other myriad differences exist among us? The answer is a conditional yes—if we can learn how to combat prejudice and discrimination.

The Roots of Prejudice and Discrimination

Question: What is the difference between prejudice and discrimination?

Prejudice consists of attitudes (usually negative) toward others based on their gender, religion, race, or membership in a particular group. Prejudice involves beliefs and emotions (not actions) that can escalate into hatred. **Discrimination** consists of behavior—actions (usually negative) toward members of a group. Many Americans have experienced prejudice and discrimination—minority racial groups (racism), women (sexism), the elderly (ageism), the handicapped, homosexuals, religious groups, and others. What are the roots of prejudice and discrimination?

The Realistic Conflict Theory: When Competition Leads to Prejudice   One of the oldest explanations offered for the genesis of prejudice is competition among various social groups who must struggle against each other for scarce resources—good jobs, homes, schools, and so on. Commonly called the *realistic conflict theory*, this view suggests that as competition increases, so does prejudice, discrimination, and hatred among the competing groups. Some historical evidence supports the realistic conflict theory. Prejudice and hatred were high between the American settlers and the Native Americans who struggled over land during the westward expansion. The multitudes of Irish and German immigrants who came to the United States in the 1830s and 1840s felt the sting of prejudice and hatred from other Americans who were facing economic scarcity. As many nations around the world are experiencing harder economic times in the 1990s, will we see an increase in prejudice and discrimination? The realistic conflict theory predicts that we will. But prejudice and discrimination are attitudes and actions too complex to be explained solely by economic conflict and competition. What are some other causes?

Question: What is meant by the terms in-group and out-group?

Us versus Them: Dividing the World into In-Groups and Out-Groups
Prejudice can also spring from the distinct social categories into which we divide our world—*us versus them* (Turner et al., 1987). An **in-group** is a social group with a strong feeling of togetherness and from which others are excluded. College fraternities and sororities often exhibit strong in-group feelings. The **out-group** consists of individuals or groups specifically identified by the in-group as not belonging. Us-versus-them thinking can lead to excessive competition, hostility, prejudice, discrimination, and even war.

Some leaders have achieved great national solidarity—a collective, in-group feeling—by creating hatred for another group or nation (the out-group). The leaders of Iran achieved strong national in-group sentiments by casting the United States in the role of the despised out-group—"the great Satan." During Operation Desert Storm most Americans and our allied nations, including some Arab nations, became the in-group, while Saddam Hussein and the nation of Iraq were perceived as the out-group.

prejudice: Negative attitudes toward others based on their gender, religion, race, or membership in a particular group.

discrimination: Behavior, usually negative, directed toward others based on their gender, religion, race, or membership in a particular group.

realistic conflict theory: The notion that prejudices arise when social groups must compete for scarce resources and opportunities.

in-group: A social group with a strong sense of togetherness and from which others are excluded.

out-group: A social group specifically identified by the in-group as not belonging.

But groups need not be composed of different races, religions, nations, or any other particular category for in-group/out-group hostility to develop.

The Robber's Cave Experiment A famous study by Sherif and Sherif (1967) shows how in-group/out-group conflict can escalate into prejudice and hostility rather quickly, even between groups that are very much alike. The researchers set up their experiment at the Robber's Cave summer camp. Their subjects were 22 bright, well-adjusted, white, middle-class, 11- and 12-year-old boys from Oklahoma City. Divided into two groups and housed in separate cabins, the boys were kept apart for all their daily activities and games. During the first week, in-group solidarity, friendship, and cooperation developed within each of the groups. One group called itself the *Rattlers*; the other group took the name *Eagles*.

During week two of the study, competitive events were purposely scheduled so that the goals of one group could be achieved "only at the expense of the other group" (Sherif, 1958, p. 353). The groups were happy to battle each other, and inter-group conflict quickly emerged. Name-calling began, fights broke out, and accusations were hurled back and forth. During the third week of the experiment, the researchers tried to put an end to the hostility and to turn rivalry into cooperation. They simply brought the groups together for pleasant activities such as eating meals and watching movies. "But far from reducing conflict, these situations only served as opportunities for the rival groups to berate and attack each other. . . . They threw paper, food and vile names at each other at the tables" (Sherif, 1956, pp. 57–58).

Finally the last stage of the experiment was set in motion. The experimenters manufactured a series of crises that could be solved only if all the boys combined their efforts and resources and cooperated. The water supply, sabotaged by the experimenters, could be restored only if all the boys worked together. After a week of several activities requiring cooperation, cut-throat competition gave way to cooperative exchanges. Friendships developed between groups, and peace was declared before the end of the experiment. Working together toward shared goals had turned hostility into friendship.

The seeds of prejudice are often sown early in life. (© Mike Greenlar, 1987)

Question: How does prejudice develop, according to the social learning theory?

The Social Learning Theory: Acquiring Prejudice through Modeling and Reinforcement According to the social learning theory, attitudes of prejudice and hatred are learned in the same way that other attitudes are learned. If children hear their parents, teachers, peers, and others openly express prejudices toward different racial, ethnic, and cultural groups, they may be quick to learn such attitudes. And if parents, peers, and others reward children with smiles and approval for parroting their own prejudices (operant conditioning), children may learn their prejudices even more quickly and more completely.

Oldenburg (1990) cites evidence that the seeds of prejudice are often sown very early. At a preschool class in California, a 4-year-old Korean-American boy sat down in the class circle beside a 4-year-old, blond, blue-eyed boy who yelled, "Don't touch me, Chinese!" A hush fell over the class, but teacher Kay Taus knew exactly how to handle the situation. She asked the Korean-American child if the remark hurt his feelings. He admitted that it did. The teacher told the children that in her class it was not right to make fun of a person from any race, and she continued to press her point about hurt feelings. Her lesson took root. Some months later she observed the blond boy telling some children who were pulling up the corners of their eyes to stop it because their actions hurt the feelings of Chinese children.

Question: What are stereotypes?

Social Cognition: Natural Thinking Processes Can Lead to Prejudice   Emotion- and learning-based views help explain how prejudice develops. But a more recent view suggests that *social cognition*, the ways in which we typically process social information—our natural thinking processes—play a role in giving birth to prejudice. Social cognition refers to the cognitive processes we use to notice, interpret, and remember information about our social world. The very processes we use to simplify, categorize, and order our world are the same processes by which we distort it. So prejudice may arise not only from heated negative emotions and hatred toward other social groups, but also from cooler cognitive processes that govern how we think and process social information (Linville et al., 1989; Quattrone, 1986).

Try It!

Can you list characteristics for each of the following groups?

African Americans	White, male, top-level executives
Native Americans	Homosexuals
Hispanic-Americans	Members of fundamentalist religious groups
Jews	Arabs
Italians	Germans

One way people simplify, categorize, and order their world is by using stereotypes. **Stereotypes** are widely shared beliefs about the characteristics of various social groups (racial, ethnic, religious), which include the assumption that *they* are usually all alike. Anderson and others (1990) report convincing evidence that stereotypes are intimately involved when we process social information. Their research showed that subjects could process information more efficiently and answer questions faster when stereotypes were used.

Do you believe that African Americans are good athletes and musicians but are not ambitious and industrious? Or that to be white is to be racist and filled with hatred toward blacks or other minorities? Are females nurturant and noncompetitive, while males are strong and dominant and make the best leaders? All these beliefs are stereotypes. Once developed, stereotypes strongly influence the way we attend to and evaluate incoming information about specific groups. Consequently the stereotypes we hold can powerfully affect the ways we react to and make judgments about persons in various groups.

In the *Try It!*, how many group characteristics could you list? If we can list traits thought to represent any group, we are probably demonstrating stereotypic thinking. We know that *all* members of a group do not possess the same traits or characteristics, but we tend to use stereotypic thinking nonetheless.

Newer research has revealed that social stereotypes involve more than overgeneralization about the traits or characteristics of members of certain groups (Park & Judd, 1990; Judd et al., 1991). People tend to perceive more diversity, more variability, within the groups to which they belong (in-groups), but they see more similarity among members of other groups (out-groups). Whites see more diversity among themselves but more sameness within groups of blacks and Asians. This tendency in thinking can extend from race to gender to age or any other category of persons. Another study showed that young college students believed there was much more variability or diversity in 100 of their group than in a group of 100 elderly Americans, whom the students perceived to be much the same (Linville et al., 1989). What about the elderly subjects? They perceived even more variability within their own group and less variability among 100 college students. Age stereotypes can be even more pronounced and negative than gender stereotypes (Kite et al., 1991).

Stereotypes can be positive or negative, but all are distortions of reality. One of the most insidious things about stereotypes is that we often are not even

social cognition: Mental processes that people use to notice, interpret, understand, remember, and apply information about the social world and that enable them to simplify, categorize, and order their world.

stereotypes: Widely shared beliefs about the characteristic traits, attitudes, and behaviors of various social groups (racial, ethnic, religious) and including the assumption that *they* are usually all alike.

aware that we are using them. Research conducted at Princeton University by Word and others (1974) indicates that stereotypic thinking can govern our expectancies. And often what we expect is what we get, regardless of whether our expectancies are high or low. Subjects for one study were white undergraduates who were to interview white and black job applicants (actually confederates of the experimenters). The researchers secretly videotaped the interviews and studied the tapes to see if the student interviewers had treated the black and white applicants differently. The researchers found substantial differences in the interviews based on the race of the applicants. The interviewers spent less time with the black applicants, maintained a greater physical distance from them, and generally were less friendly and outgoing. When interviewing the black applicants, the interviewers' speech deteriorated—they made more errors in grammar and pronunciation.

In a follow-up study the same researchers trained white confederates to copy the two different interview styles used in the first study. The confederates then used the different styles to interview a group of white job applicants. These interviews were videotaped as well, and later a panel of judges evaluated the tapes. The judges agreed that applicants who were subjected to the interview style for blacks were more nervous and performed more poorly than applicants interviewed according to the "white" style. The experimenters concluded that as a result of the interview style for blacks, the black confederates from the first study were not given the opportunity to demonstrate their skills and qualifications to the best of their ability. Thus they were subjected to a subtle form of discrimination in which their performance was hampered by the expectancies of the original interviewers.

Discrimination in the Workplace

Question: What did the "glass ceiling" study reveal about discrimination in corporate America?

Discrimination is also evident after the job interviews have been completed and people take their positions in the workplace. How do women and minorities fare in the world of work in the 1990s? Even though federal legislation forbids hiring, promoting, laying off, and awarding benefits to workers on the basis of sex, race, color, national origin, or religion, studies continue to show discrimination exists (Renzetti & Curran, 1992).

A barrier described as a "glass ceiling" often prevents women and minorities from attaining top management positions in corporate America.

WORLD OF PSYCHOLOGY:

MULTICULTURAL PERSPECTIVES

The "Glass Ceiling": Few Women and Minorities at the Top

In 1991 a United States Department of Labor study concluded that a barrier described as a "glass ceiling" prevents women from advancing to top management positions in corporate America. Researchers Morrison and Von Glinow (1990) agree that women and minorities, too, are blocked by a glass ceiling. They define it as "a barrier so subtle that it is transparent, yet so strong that it prevents women and minorities from moving up in the management hierarchy" (p. 200).

A survey of the Fortune 500 companies conducted in the late 1980s revealed that only 3.6 percent of their board of director positions were held by women, and a mere 1.7 percent of their corporate officers were women (Von Glinow & Krzyczkowska-Mercer, 1988). Today approximately one-third of all management positions are filled by women, but the vast majority of these positions are below the glass ceiling (middle-management and lower), and only 3 percent of the officers of major corporations are women (Saltzman, 1991). Minorities fare even worse than women in the corporate heights above the glass ceiling. One survey of 1,708 senior executives revealed only 4 blacks, 3 Hispanics, 6 Asians, and 29 women (Jones, 1986). And among the Fortune 1,000 companies, only one black CEO (chief executive officer) could be found (Leinster, 1988).

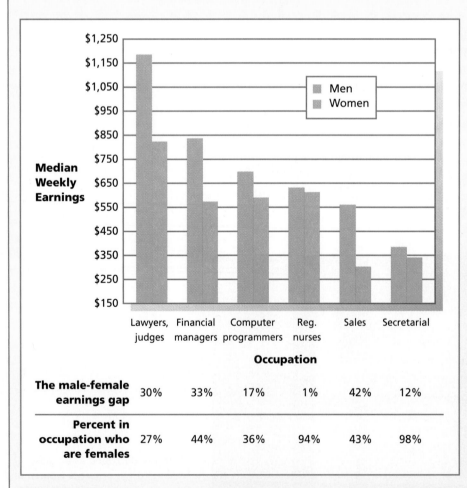

Median Weekly Earnings (chart y-axis: $150, $250, $350, $450, $550, $650, $750, $850, $950, $1,050, $1,150, $1,250)

Legend: ■ Men ■ Women

Occupation (x-axis): Lawyers, judges · Financial managers · Computer programmers · Reg. nurses · Sales · Secretarial

Occupation

	Lawyers, judges	Financial managers	Computer programmers	Reg. nurses	Sales	Secretarial
The male-female earnings gap	30%	33%	17%	1%	42%	12%
Percent in occupation who are females	27%	44%	36%	94%	43%	98%

Figure 17.1

The Male/Female Earnings Gap

The earnings gap between males and females varies from one occupation to another as indicated by the six occupational groups shown here. In sales, women make 42 percent less than men. In occupations typically held by females, the earnings gap is smaller. Female registered nurses make 1 percent less than their male counterparts. The percentage of females in each occupational group is shown at the bottom of the chart. (After Saltzman, 1991.)

Those women and minorities who do manage to break through the glass ceiling are likely to find that their salaries are lower than those of their white male counterparts. At the levels of vice-president and above, another study revealed that women were paid an average of 42 percent less than their male counterparts (Nelton & Berney, 1987). Black males in management tend to earn salaries closer to those of white males.

On the average in the United States, a female worker is paid only 70 cents for every dollar paid to a male worker (U.S. Bureau of the Census, 1990). Figure 17.1 shows the male/female earnings gap in six different occupational fields. Wage discrimination against women is not confined to the United States. Of 10 industrialized nations shown in Table 17.1, Australia has the smallest wage gap between men and women (88 cents for female workers for every dollar paid male workers). Japan has the widest wage gap, with women paid, on the average, only about half as much as men (International Labour Office, 1990).

Why So Few? Why are there so few women and minorities in upper-management, power positions in corporate America? Several explanations have been put forth. Perhaps there is no glass ceiling at all, one explanation suggests, and deficiencies in women and minorities are responsible for their not climbing the corporate ladder (a dispositional attribution).

Many corporate leaders define a good manager as tough, decisive, logical, and unemotional—the male stereotype. These qualities are perceived by men and even many women themselves, as precisely the "right stuff" for leaders and decision makers at all levels of management. People who point to the deficiencies in women claim that their personality traits and attitudes make them less suited for upper management. Yet a considerable body of research refutes the notion that sex and race deficiencies explain why so few women and minorities are in upper management (Morrison & Von Glinow, 1990).

Nevertheless, the mere perception of deficiencies, if held by the dominant corporate leaders, is sufficient to produce bias and discrimination. "Discrimination occurs in part because of the belief by white men that women and people of color are less suited for management than white men" (Morrison & Von Glinow, 1990, p. 202). The dominant group's belief that customers, employees, and others are more comfortable dealing with or working for white, male managers may lead to discrimination. In such cases these managers would be less willing to promote women and minorities to sensitive, responsible management positions.

The structure of the organization may present another problem for female managers, who are likely to be greatly outnumbered by male management colleagues. A few women among so many men in a management group are highly visible and likely to represent *women* as a category

Table 17.1 Average Earnings of Full-Time Female Workers as a Percentage of Those of Men in 10 Industrialized Countries (Nonagricultural Activities), 1980–1988

Country	Earnings Ratio (1980)	Earnings Ratio (1988)
Australia	85.9	87.9
Denmark	84.5	82.1
France	79.2	81.8*
Netherlands	78.2	76.8
Belgium	69.4	75.0
West Germany	72.4	73.5
United Kingdom	69.7	69.5**
United States	66.7***	70.2
Switzerland	67.6	76.4
Japan	53.8	50.7

*1987 data **1984 data ***1983 data

Source: Renzetti, C. M., & Curran, D. J. (1992). *Women, Men, and Society* (2nd ed.). Boston: Allyn & Bacon, p. 192.

and to be viewed as "tokens" by the dominant group (Kanter, 1977). Minority employees as well may be perceived by the white majority as "tokens," especially as they move up in the ranks of management.

Tokenism is a subtle form of discrimination in which persons are hired or promoted primarily because they represent a specific group or category rather than strictly on the basis of their qualifications. But "tokens" are interchangeable. If placed in a position solely to meet a company's affirmative action goals, one token is as good as another as long as he or she represents the *right* category. No matter how eminently qualified one might be, if an employee perceives that he or she is a token, the employee suffers and so does the organization.

According to Heilman and others (1987), women who believe that they are hired only to meet certain federal guidelines suffer low self-esteem, and their development is hampered. The organization is adversely affected, too, because the women's commitment to and satisfaction in the organization is significantly lower than that of women who rate their ability as the main reason they were hired.

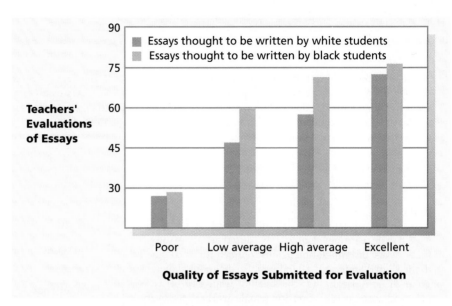

Figure 17.2   Reverse Discrimination in Grading of Essays   White teachers in a study by Fajardo practiced reverse discrimination. Essays were purposely written for the study to be of poor, low average, high average, and excellent quality. A group of white teachers were told that the essays were written either by black students or by white students. The teachers gave higher evaluations to the essays they believed were written by black students. (After Fajardo, 1985.)

Not all acts of discrimination are committed against members of specific groups. Discrimination can operate in reverse.

Question: What is reverse discrimination?

Reverse Discrimination: Bending Over Backward to Be Fair   Another subtle form of discrimination is **reverse discrimination,** in which some people bend over backward to treat members of specific groups that have been the target of discrimination more favorably than if they were not members of that particular group. Those who practice reverse discrimination may be earnestly trying to show that they are not prejudiced. But reverse discrimination is not genuine, and it insults the dignity of the group to which it is directed. It assumes that the other group is indeed inferior and only capable of achieving a lower standard.

A study by Fajardo (1985) clearly illustrates reverse discrimination. A group of teachers (all of whom were white) were asked to grade essays that were identified as having been written by either black or white students. The researchers had purposely written the essays to be poor, low average, high average, or excellent in quality. If white teachers were practicing reverse discrimination, they would rate the essays they believed were written by black students higher than those supposedly written by white students. This is exactly what happened, as you can see in Figure 17.2, especially when the quality of the essays was in the average range.

Reverse discrimination may benefit people in the short run, but it deceives them and creates false hopes, setting them up for greater disappointment and failure in the long run. Students and workers alike need and deserve objective evaluation of their work and their progress.

Prejudice and discrimination have been pervasive in human societies throughout recorded history. We have seen that these attitudes and actions may take many forms and range from bigotry and hatred to the kindness and compassion (though misplaced) of reverse discrimination.

reverse discrimination:
Giving special treatment or higher evaluations to individuals from groups that have been the target of discrimination.

Combating Prejudice and Discrimination

Question: What are several strategies for reducing prejudice and discrimination?

Given that prejudice and discrimination may grow from many roots, are there effective ways to reduce them? Many experts believe there are. One way is through education. To the extent that prejudice is learned, it can also be un-learned. We saw how Kay Taus taught her students that prejudice hurts the feelings of others, and how effectively she helped a 4-year-old boy to become more sensitive to the feelings of Asian children.

Blue Eyes, Brown Eyes: Experiencing Discrimination How would you like to be judged strictly by the color of your eyes? More than 20 years ago, elementary school teacher Jane Elliot performed a creative and dramatic experiment that is well known to psychologists and educators (Peters, 1971). One day she announced to her class that blue-eyed children were smarter, cleaner, and superior in virtually every way to brown-eyed children. The blue-eyed children were given special privileges, such as being first in line and getting second helpings in the lunch room, and they were treated with obvious favor. How did the brown-eyed children respond? Their self-esteem plummeted, their school work suffered, and they were miserable.

After 2 days the teacher announced that the brown-eyed and not the blue-eyed children were superior. All the rules were reversed. It did not take those with brown eyes long to adjust to their new, elevated status. But now the blue-eyed children suffered. Their recently inflated self-esteem collapsed, the quality of their school work fell, and they were miserable. Finally, Jane Elliot told her students that eye color has no bearing at all on performance or human worth. She said all are worthy, and there would no longer be favored treatment on the basis of eye color.

Sustained educational programs designed to increase teachers' and parents' awareness of the damage caused by prejudice and discrimination can be very effective (Aronson, 1990).

Direct Contact: Bringing Diverse Groups Together Prejudice separates us, keeping us apart from other racial, ethnic, religious, and social groups. Can we reduce our prejudices and stereotypic thinking by increasing our contact and

In Crown Heights, New York, African Americans and Hasidic Jews are reducing prejudice and shattering stereotypes through increased interaction between the groups.

contact hypothesis: The notion that prejudice can be reduced by increasing contact among members of different social groups.

interaction with others from diverse social groups? Yes, according to the *contact hypothesis*.

Increased contacts with members of groups about which we hold stereotypes can teach us that *they* are not all alike. But the contact hypothesis works to reduce prejudice only under certain conditions. In fact, if people from diverse groups are simply thrown together, prejudice and even hostility are likely to increase rather than decrease, as we learned from Sherif's Robber's Cave experiment. We also learned from Sherif the conditions under which intergroup contact reduces prejudice, and his findings have been confirmed and extended by others (Aronson, 1990; Cook, 1985; Finchilescu, 1988).

The contact hypothesis will work to reduce prejudice most effectively under the following conditions:

- Interacting groups should be approximately equal in social and economic status and in their ability on the tasks to be performed.
- The intergroup contact must be cooperative (not competitive) in nature, and work should be confined to shared goals.
- The contact should be informal so that friendly interactions develop more easily and group members get to know each other individually.
- The contact situation should be one in which the conditions favor group equality.
- The individuals involved should perceive each other as typical members of the groups to which they belong.

Us versus Them: Extending the Boundaries of Narrowly Defined Social Groups

Our tendency to separate ourselves into social categories (in-groups and out-groups) creates an us-versus-them mentality. This mentality heightens prejudice, stereotypic thinking, and discrimination—our group (our college, our state, our country, our race, our religion) is better than theirs. But the boundary lines between us and them are not eternally fixed. If such boundaries can be extended, prejudice and in-group/out-group conflict can be reduced. We saw in Sherif's study that the *Rattlers* and the *Eagles* became a larger *us* group when they were brought together to work cooperatively on shared goals.

If your college or university wins the state championship in a competitive event, then in-state rival colleges and universities will often join your *us* group as you represent the state in national competition. Many researchers have shown that working cooperatively, rather than in competition, reduces us-versus-them bias and prejudice (Gaerther et al., 1989, 1990; Wright et al., 1990).

Prejudice: Is It Increasing or Decreasing?

Few people would readily admit to being prejudiced. Gordon Allport (1954), a pioneer in research on prejudice, said, "Defeated intellectually, prejudice lingers emotionally" (p. 328). Even those who are sincerely intellectually opposed to prejudice may still harbor some prejudiced feelings (Devine, 1989b).

Is there any evidence that prejudice is decreasing in our society? According to some researchers, we are not making much progress toward reducing prejudice and discrimination (Crosby et al., 1980; Gaertner & Dovidio, 1986). But Devine and her colleagues (1991) are more optimistic. Their research suggests, "Many people appear to be in the process of prejudice reduction" (p. 829).

A recent Gallup poll reveals that whites in the United States are becoming more racially tolerant in the decade of the 1990s than they were in decades past (Gallup & Hugick, 1990). When whites were asked whether they would move if blacks were to move next door to them, 93 percent said no compared to 65 percent 25 years earlier. Even if blacks were to move into their neighborhood in great numbers, 68 percent of whites still said they would not move.

School integration, which in the past created a storm of controversy, seems not to be much of an issue for most whites today. Only 10 percent of Gallup's white respondents said they would object to sending their children to an integrated school in which up to one-half of the children were black. Also, the majority of blacks polled (two-thirds) believed that black children have the same opportunity as white children to get a good education.

Marked differences in opinions about equality of job opportunities, availability of housing, and other racial attitudes still exist between blacks and whites. When asked whether the quality of life for blacks has gotten better, stayed the same, or gotten worse over the last 10 years, 46 percent of blacks and 62 percent of whites believed conditions had improved. Twenty-five percent of both races believed the quality of life had stayed the same. But 23 percent of blacks, compared to only 6 percent of whites, believed the quality of life was worse for blacks now than it was 10 years ago.

We can make things better for all by examining our own attitudes and actions, and then by using what we have learned here to combat prejudice and discrimination in ourselves. Prejudice has no virtues. It immediately harms those who feel its sting and ultimately harms those who cause it too. Dr. Charles Drew, whose story opened this chapter, died in the prime of his life because of prejudice and discrimination. Our nation was robbed of a creative medical researcher and any further contributions he might have made to humankind.

Memory Check 17.1

1. Match the example on the left with the term on the right.

1) José was promoted because the firm needed one Hispanic manager.	a. stereotypic thinking
2) Darlene thinks all whites are racists.	b. discrimination
3) Betty's salary is $5,000 less than that of her male counterpart.	c. reverse discrimination
4) Bill can't stand Jews.	d. prejudice
5) To make his black employees feel good, Mr. Jones, who is white, gave them higher bonuses than he gave his white employees.	e. tokenism

2. The (realistic conflict theory, social learning theory) suggests that prejudice is learned through modeling and reinforcement.

3. The "glass ceiling" refers to a barrier that keeps women and minorities from being (hired, promoted to top executive positions) in corporations.

4. Researchers have found that bringing diverse social groups together almost always decreases hostility and prejudice. (true/false)

Answers 1. 1) e 2) a 3) b 4) d 5) c 2. social learning theory 3. promoted to top executive positions 4. false

Applying Psychology in the Modern World

Just as there are diverse cultures and peoples in the world, there is also great diversity in the way psychology is applied to serve the vast array of human wants and needs. **Applied psychology** is the branch of psychology that applies the methods and knowledge of the discipline to solve practical, everyday human problems. In this section we will discuss how psychologists apply their knowledge in the workplace, in the design of machines and tools, and in understanding how people use (and misuse) the environment. We will also consider the part psychologists play in our legal system, in competitive and recreational sports, and in understanding and influencing consumer behavior.

Psychology Goes to Work

Question: What are some of the activities of industrial/organizational psychologists?

Although the United States is the most technologically advanced country in the world, it ranks only fifth in international measures of productivity per person (Hatfield, 1990). Can the U.S. remain competitive with other industrialized nations, yet maintain a work setting that is satisfying and safe, both physically and psychologically, for workers? Increasingly business, industry, and government are turning to industrial/organizational psychologists for help. **Industrial/organizational psychology** (abbreviated I/O psychology) is a specialty that focuses on the relationship between the workplace or work organization and the worker. The field encompasses such areas as organizational design, decision making, work motivation, job satisfaction, communication, leadership, and personnel selection, training, and evaluation.

Personnel Selection, Training, and Evaluation   Organizations need employees who have the necessary skills and ability and who will enjoy their work and be productive. The fit between the person and the organization is significantly related to "performance, job attitudes, and turnover" (O'Reilly, 1991, p. 448). I/O psychologists can play a key role in improving personnel selection procedures and in planning a variety of training programs for new and existing employees. I/O psychologists can also assist in developing more objective criteria for evaluating specific jobs—criteria that will be acceptable to both managers and employees.

Question: What are two effective techniques for increasing work motivation?

Work Motivation and Job Performance   Work motivation can be thought of as "the conditions and processes that account for the arousal, direction, magnitude, and maintenance of effort in a person's job" (Katzell & Thompson, 1990, p. 144).

Two of the most effective approaches for increasing employee motivation and improving performance are the appropriate use of reinforcement and goal setting. I/O psychologists help business and industry design behavior modification techniques to increase performance and productivity. Some of the reinforcers or incentives that might be given are bonuses, recognition awards, praise, time off, posting individual performance, better offices, more impressive titles, or promotions. Companies might discourage or even punish ineffective behaviors through such measures as docking employees for missing work.

applied psychology: The branch of psychology that applies the methods and knowledge of the discipline to investigate and solve practical, everyday human problems.

industrial/organizational psychology: The specialty that focuses on the relationship between the workplace or work organization and the worker, including specific areas such as organizational design, decision making, work motivation, job satisfaction, communication, leadership, and personnel selection, training, and evaluation.

A second technique for increasing performance is goal setting. Establishing specific, difficult goals leads to higher levels of performance than simply telling people to do their best in the absence of assigned goals (Locke & Latham, 1990). The level of an employee's commitment to the goals also has an impact on performance. This commitment can be enhanced (1) by having employees participate in the goal-setting; (2) by making goals specific, attractive, difficult, and attainable; (3) by providing feedback on performance; and (4) by rewarding the employees for attaining the goals (Katzell & Thompson, 1990).

Question: What factors are closely related to job satisfaction?

Job Satisfaction and Performance Job satisfaction can vary on a number of dimensions including the work itself, the pay, opportunities for advancement, the benefits, the physical setting, the hours, the co-workers, and the supervision. Table 17.2 summarizes factors that are closely related to job satisfaction.

One would logically assume that increased job satisfaction results in better work performance, but this has not been supported by research (Coutts, 1991). However, job satisfaction is apparently related to lower absenteeism (Smith, 1977) and lower job turnover.

Many companies, with the help of I/O psychologists, are working to make jobs more interesting, satisfying, and attractive—an approach termed *job enrichment*. Job enrichment might involve redesigning work so that assembly-line workers become involved in the production of a whole item instead of repeating the same single task, hour after hour, day after day. In addition, workers are given a greater voice in how their work will be accomplished.

Question: What are some major sources of work stress?

Work Stress: The Many Sources of Stress on the Job Hans Selye, the pioneer in stress research, called stress the "spice of life" because within limits it can provide the challenges that make life interesting and enable us to grow.

job enrichment: Techniques used to make jobs more interesting, satisfying, and attractive.

Table 17.2 Important Factors Influencing Job Satisfaction

Factors Related to Job Satisfaction

Interesting work

Good pay

Sufficient resources and authority

Friendly, cooperative co-workers

Sufficient recognition

Opportunities for advancement

Good relationships with supervisors

Control over manner in which work is completed

Input in decisions affecting work

Job security

Excessive, unmanageable stress, however, is associated with a variety of health and psychological problems. Work stress may manifest itself in decreased job satisfaction and performance, absenteeism, low productivity, and high turnover.

For many years the National Institute for Occupational Safety and Health (NIOSH) has viewed the work environment as a potential physical threat to employees and has passed regulations to protect the health and safety of workers. Now it is looking at the adverse effects on mental health posed by factors in many work environments (Sauter et al., 1990). Following are some of the psychosocial risk factors (more commonly referred to as sources of work stress) cited by NIOSH.

- Heavy work load with little control over how work will be done
- Working rotating shifts or permanent night shifts
- Ambiguity in job role and role conflict
- Lack of job security; being passed over for promotion or promoted too quickly; fear of job obsolescence
- Poor relationships with co-workers, superordinates, or subordinates
- Jobs that consist of repetitious, narrow, invariant tasks and provide little stimulation or opportunity to use skills or creativity
- Lack of opportunity to have any say in decisions that affect their jobs

Decision Latitude: A Critical Factor in Job Stress   Whether occupational stress is the "spice of life" or the "kiss of death" for a worker depends to a great extent on the amount of decision latitude the job offers (Levi, 1990). "Decision latitude" refers to the degree to which employees have the opportunity to exercise initiative and use their skills to control working conditions. Jobs that are high in psychosocial stress and physical work load and that offer little latitude or control in the pace and manner in which the work will be completed are perceived as very stressful (Karasek & Theorell, 1990). According to Sauter and others (1990), machine-paced assembly workers report "the highest levels of anxiety, depression, and irritation, as well as more frequent somatic [bodily] complaints" (p. 1150).

In contrast are jobs like those of executives and professionals where high demand is coupled with a high degree of control over how the work will be done. In this case high demand is likely to be viewed as challenging and rewarding. Jobs with low stress are those in which people have a high degree of control coupled with a low psychological work load such as that of scientist and forester.

Additional Stress for Minorities and Women   Working in a potentially dangerous environment or in a job that sees many work-related injuries is another source of stress. Blacks and Hispanics are at greater risk of injury or job-related disease. Hispanics suffered severe disability as a result of work-related injuries at twice the rate of nonminority workers (Department of Health and Human Services, 1985). Black women and men both are at a 25 percent greater risk of dying from work-related causes than are nonminority workers (Keita & Jones, 1990).

Women often suffer the additional stress of sex discrimination and sexual harassment, as well as pay inequities based solely on gender (Ivancevich et al., 1990). And women are more likely to have a disproportionate share of child-care responsibility, which adds an additional burden of stress.

How much stress have you experienced in jobs you have had? Rate your stress in the *Try It!*

What are the sources of stress in your job? If you are not employed now, consider the last job you had. Rate your job by indicating whether there is or was too little, too much, or about the right amount of each of the following dimensions.

Try It!

Job Dimension	Too Little	About Right	Too Much
Work load			
Decision latitude			
Clarity of job description			
Task variety			
Mental challenge			
Physical demand			
Human contact			
Job status			
Job security			

(Adapted from Albrecht, 1979.)

Question: What strategies are some industries adopting to combat work stress?

Combating Work Stress: Some Help from Business and Industry   Many corporations, with the help of I/O psychologists, are beginning to address the problem of work stress. Some companies are setting up worksite stress management interventions, which can take several forms (Ivancevich et al., 1990). They may include such stress management techniques as exercise, meditation, or relaxation to help employees cope with stress. Other interventions involve changing sources of the job stress. These include redesigning jobs, changing organizational structure, improving working conditions, providing better job training, improving personnel selection and placement, or improving co-worker relations.

Policies Responsive to Families   Because of the ever-increasing presence of dual worker families and single parents in the work force, a growing number of corporations are implementing policies that are responsive to families. These include maternity and parental leaves, provision for child care, and flexibility in work schedules (Zedeck & Mosier, 1990).

In the United States relatively few corporations provide women with a paid, 3-month maternity leave, a practice which is the *minimum* in continental Europe, where even a 6-month paid leave is not uncommon (Zedeck & Mosier, 1990). But probably the most difficult problem for parents is finding reliable, affordable child care. Some companies are giving assistance that ranges from providing payment for child care as part of a benefits program to onsite day-care centers.

Alternative work schedules are attractive options for some workers. These may include job sharing, permanent part-time employment (sometimes having career potential and benefits), or flextime. In *job sharing*, two people share one full-time job (Kahne, 1985; Olmsted, 1977). Flextime refers to flexible work schedules, which may involve beginning the day several hours earlier or later than the usual work day, or working longer days and "banking" the hours so that time off can be taken later. Instead of working five 8-hour days, many nurses are now opting for three or four long days each week.

job-sharing: Employment in which two employees share one full-time job.

human factors psychology: A specialty concerned with designing and modifying machines and work environments to make them safer, easier to use, and more compatible with the user's sensory, perceptual, cognitive, and motor capabilities.

Question: What are the goals of human factors psychology?

Human Factors Psychology: Getting Along with Machines and Appliances

In a modern technological society, we use a variety of machines and appliances every day. Many of them are user-friendly, so natural and simple to operate that we hardly give them a second thought. Others may baffle, challenge, or anger us because their design is illogical, unhandy, cumbersome, and complex. Some of us have simply given up on the idea of making use of all the features on our phone, VCR, word processor, or car stereo because we can never remember how to work them.

Do you push on doors that are meant to be pulled? Have you ever been in an unfamiliar automobile and had difficulty finding the handle to open the door? Have you wasted money in copying machines because you weren't sure which buttons to push? If you answered yes to any of these questions and feel defeated by machines, you are probably not to blame. You might have been victimized by poorly designed machines.

The design of the tools and machines we use have psychological consequences, and an important applied field of psychology is human factors psychology. **Human factors psychology** is a specialty concerned with designing and modifying machines and work environments to make them more compatible with the user's sensory, perceptual, cognitive, and motor capabilities. The ultimate goal is to make machines safer and easier to use. On occasion these psychologists are involved in investigations of train or airline accidents to discover if system design led to the accident.

Human factors psychologists work "to improve the quality of working life through better design of tools, work stations, and working environment" (Heron, 1991, p. 307). They try to design work equipment so that muscles, tendons, ligaments, and joints are not subject to undue stress, which could eventually lead to permanent damage. Human factors psychologists might be asked to study the equipment and movement involved in a job if factory workers are suffering some work-related musculoskeletal problem (Heron, 1991).

Question: What are three criteria of good design?

Good Design: Features That Won't Defeat Us   Donald A. Norman (1988), a leading expert in human factors psychology, admits to fighting a losing battle with the objects in his home, car, and office. For those of us who have been fighting the same losing battle, there is some good news. According to Norman, the failure is in the design of the objects rather than in us. In fact, many of the accidents involving vehicles (airplanes, trains, automobiles) and machinery (even in nuclear power plants) in which the accident is blamed on *human error* may be partly due to poor design.

Norman insists that in well-designed devices, a button or control operates one function only. That explains why single-faucet shower knobs that control two functions have flash-frozen or nearly scalded many of us before we could adjust the water temperature. Well-designed machines should provide feedback so that we know the immediate result of any action that is taken, like the click that we hear when we hit a key on most computer keyboards. Our VCRs give us trouble because we press buttons but usually don't know what has happened as a result of our actions.

Furthermore, Norman asserts that well-designed objects have visual clues to their operation, a property he calls "visibility." Labels, pictures, or instructions should not be required for simple things. Turning on the desired burner on the stove should not pose a challenge for us. The controls for the burners should be arranged in a pattern that corresponds to the placement of the burners—for

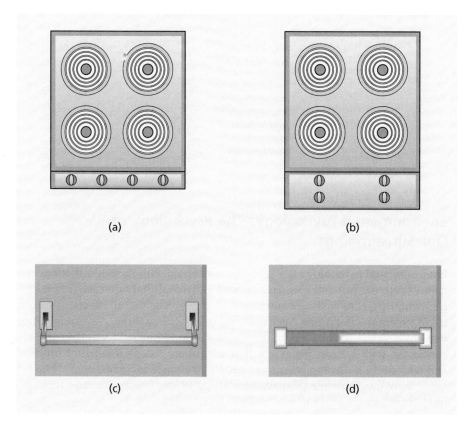

Figure 17.3 Examples of Good and Poor Design Well-designed objects have visual clues to their operation. For simple things, labels, pictures, and instructions should not be necessary. There is no confusion about the controls of stove top (b). Look at the push bars on the two doors. Which design, (c) or (d), provides the clue as to what side of the door to push?

most stoves that would be in a square rather than in a straight line as shown in Figure 17.3.

Human factors psychology has increased in importance as technology has grown, and the work of human factors psychologists has affected us all from astronauts to average citizens.

Memory Check 17.2

1. To improve employee motivation and performance, goals should be specific, attractive, attainable, and (fairly easy, difficult).

2. Increasing job satisfaction results in better work performance. (true/false)

3. In general an assembly-line worker suffers more stress than a business executive because:

   a. the work load is higher   c. the decision latitude is higher
   b. the work load is lower   d. the decision latitude is lower

(continued)

4. (Industrial/organizational, Human factors) psychologists are involved in designing or modifying machines and work environments to make them safer and easier to use.

5. In a well-designed machine, a single button or control should handle (one function, several functions).

Answers: 1. difficult   2. false   3. d   4. Human factors   5. One function

Environmental Psychology: The Psychology of Our Surroundings

Environmental psychology is a specialty concerned with the effect that environments (both natural and constructed) and individuals have on each other. Environmental psychologists are interested in the psychological effects of adverse environmental conditions such as pollution, the weather, overpopulation, crowding, noise, and other conditions in the world around us. They are also concerned with human behaviors that contribute to environmental problems and with finding ways to encourage people to change these behaviors. How do noise, crowding, our use of space, the design of our buildings, and other environmental factors affect us psychologically?

Question: What are some of the negative psychological effects that have been associated with noise pollution?

Noise: More Than Just Annoying   Why would many people find a whisper in a movie theatre more annoying than loud music at a concert? The answer lies in the definition of noise. Noise is not simply loud sound; it is unwanted sound. How annoying a noise is depends on its volume, whether it is predictable or unpredictable, and whether we can control it. The most disturbing noise is loud, unpredictable, and uncontrollable. Adding further to annoyance is the perception that the noise is unnecessary, hazardous, or caused by others who are unconcerned about its effect on us.

Of all the creatures on planet Earth, humans are by far the noisiest. And the noise created by humans and their machines produces irritating and sometimes devastating psychological and physical effects. You have already learned in chapter 3, "Sensation and Perception," that prolonged exposure to noise, or even minimal exposure to ear-splitting decibel levels, can result in major, permanent hearing loss. But apart from physical damage, how can noise harm us psychologically?

Some researchers claim that noise pollution is related to high blood pressure, distractibility in children, and less willingness on their part to persist at tasks (Cohen et al., 1980). Children continuously exposed to high levels of noise in their schools or apartment buildings were found to have impaired auditory discrimination (Cohen, Glass, & Singer, 1973) and lower reading achievement (Bronzaft, 1981; Cohen et al., 1973; Cohen et al., 1986).

More recent studies have shown that introverts (reflective, retiring, nonsocial types) and extroverts (outgoing, adaptable, sociable people) respond differently to noise. Introverts generally prefer a quiet environment (Standing et al., 1990; Weinstein, 1978). Under noisy conditions they show an increase in arousal, whereas arousal in extroverts decreases or is unchanged. Furthermore, reading comprehension was found to decrease in introverts when subjected to noise but not in extroverts. (Daoussis & McKelvie, 1986; Standing et al., 1990).

environmental psychology: The specialty concerned with the effect that environments (both natural and constructed) and individuals have on each other.

How annoying a noise is depends on its volume, whether it is predictable or unpredictable, and whether we can control it.

Question: What do the terms territory and territorial behavior mean?

Territorial Behavior: Protecting Areas We Define as Ours   People not only protect their personal space, but they protect what they consider to be their **territory**—an area defined as permanently or temporarily their own. A primary territory is one that is considered to belong to an individual or group, like a home or office. A secondary territory is one that an individual occupies regularly but shares with others, such as an assigned seat in a classroom. A public territory is one that is occupied temporarily, like a seat in a library or movie theater, or a space at the beach.

What would you do if someone moved your coat and books from a table in the library and was sitting in the area you had staked out for yourself? Just as we react negatively to invasions of our personal space, we don't like invasions into our territory. Consequently, people engage in **territorial behavior**; that is, they mark off their territory in an effort to establish control and defend it against unwelcome intrusions. Homes may be marked with fences and hedges, office doors with nameplates, and spaces at the beach with beach towels or blankets.

Question: What is the difference between density and crowding?

Density and Crowding: There Is a Difference   Most psychologists draw a distinction between **density**—the number of people occupying a defined physical space—and crowding. **Crowding** is subjective and refers to the perception that there are too many people in a defined space. A hermit would probably feel crowded if there were even one other person anywhere in sight. Psychologists further differentiate between social density and spatial density (Baum & Valins, 1977), and crowding is affected by both. Social density increases as the number of people in a fixed space increases. If five relatives came to live in your house for several weeks, social density would increase and you might feel crowded. Conversely, social density decreases as the number of people in a fixed space decreases.

territory: An area defined by a person as temporarily or permanently his or her own.

territorial behavior: Marking off a territory in an effort to establish control over it and defend it against unwelcome intrusions.

density: A measure referring to the number of people occupying a unit of space.

crowding: A subjective perception that there are too many people in a defined space.

Whether or not a person feels crowded depends on the setting: waiting in a crowded airport terminal can be stressful, while being part of a densely packed audience at a soccer game is not.

With spatial density, the number of people remains constant, but the space they occupy increases or decreases. If you have ever taken a family vacation in an automobile, you have experienced the effects of increasing spatial density. Figure 17.4 illustrates the difference between increasing social density and spatial density.

The Effects of Crowding: Too Many People, Too Little Space We have all had experiences with crowds. Sometimes it is enjoyable and exciting to be densely packed with other people at a sports event, a concert, or a party. But what if the crowd followed us home and we could not escape to our own private world even for a moment? In many parts of the world, people have little or no privacy and must live their lives under continuously crowded conditions—day and night they are subjected to the sights, the sounds, and the smells of too many other people.

Figure 17.4   Social and Spatial Density   Social density increases as the number of people in a given space increases, as illustrated in (a). Spatial density increases as the amount of space for a given number of people decreases, as shown in (b).

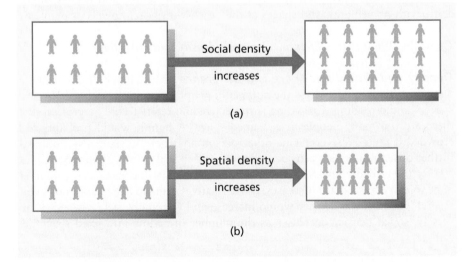

Variations in Personal Space

Question: What is personal space, and what factors influence our personal space preferences?

Personal space is an area surrounding us, much like an invisible bubble, which we consider part of us and use to regulate how closely others can interact with us. Our personal space functions to protect our privacy and to regulate our level of intimacy with others. It serves a communication function in that it determines whether intimate sensory cues like smell and touch will be exchanged or communication will be restricted to nonintimate verbal or visual channels. The size of our personal space varies according to the person or persons with whom we are interacting and the nature of the interaction.

Edward T. Hall (1966), the leading researcher on personal space, maintained that a need for personal space seems to be inborn in most animal species. For humans in general, Hall named four different types of social contact and the typical personal space distances that match them:

Intimate (From touching to 18 inches) Reserved for intimate contacts, lovers, family members, and close friends.

Personal (18 inches to 4 feet) Used in everyday interactions with people we know—friends or colleagues.

Social Distance (4 to 12 feet) For transacting business and communicating with strangers.

Public Distance (More than 12 feet) The typical distance in formal settings—between a professor and a class, a speaker and an audience.

Most people have a distinctly unpleasant feeling when their personal space is invaded. If standing, they will often step back to reestablish their space, but when this is not possible they change their body orientation and/or reduce their amount of eye contact.

Picture this: You are standing in a crowded elevator. Then someone steps in, and rather than turning to face forward, he stands face to face with you. Imagine how uncomfortable you would feel.

We usually position ourselves closer to people we perceive as similar to us in age, race, sexual preference, and status than to those we perceive as different on these dimensions. There are gender differences in personal space preferences. Researchers have found that the personal space maintained between people of the same sex varies according to gender. Pairs of females generally interact at closer distances than pairs of males (Aiello, 1987). The gender difference in personal space has been reported

Personal space is often culturally defined.

among different age groups, from children on the playground (Aiello & Jones, 1971) to simulated settings with adults (Barnard & Bell, 1982).

Personal space preferences vary most from culture to culture. Look at the conversational comfort zone in the photograph. There is hardly any space at all between these two Middle Easterners. Arabs, Hispanics, Greeks, and the French are typically comfortable with small interaction distances, while Americans, the English, the Swedish, and other Northern Europeans prefer a larger personal space (Aiello, 1987; Hall, 1966).

Personal space preferences can cause misunderstanding when people from different cultures are interacting. Hall (1968) reports how Americans in a foreign country came face to face with cultural differences in personal space preferences. "People stood 'too close' during conversations, and when the Americans backed away to a comfortable conversational distance, this was taken to mean that Americans were cold, aloof, withdrawn, and disinterested in the people of the country" (p. 84). The Americans were unwittingly insulting their foreign hosts, who were unwittingly invading the space of their American visitors.

What are the psychological effects of such wretched, inescapable, crowded conditions? With a human population, it is hard to isolate the psychological effects of crowding from other aversive environmental conditions that usually accompany it, such as poverty, noise, drug abuse, and others. Paul Paulus and others (1988) compared records from four state prisons and found that the death rates, suicides, disciplinary actions required, and psychological problems resulting in psychiatric commitment all increased as the prison population increased. The more inmates per cell, the greater the number of problems.

But we must keep in mind that a prison is an atypical environment with an atypical population. The effects of crowding vary across cultures and situations. Crowding often leads to higher physiological arousal, and males typically experience its effects more negatively than females do.

Architectural Design: More Than Just a Matter of Aesthetics

The architectural design of the buildings in which we live and work can affect our psychological well-being and behavior (Gifford, 1991). Over 30 years ago, the city of St. Louis launched a bold new venture in which extremely low-income residents could at last move into new high-rise apartments. With federal assistance, the city built 33 high-rise apartment buildings known as the Pruitt-Igoe Housing Project. But the bold new venture proved to be an urban disaster, and the urban dream became a nightmare. Vandalism, crime, prostitution, and drug dealers flourished in what should have been a model community. What went wrong?

Experts studied the Pruitt-Igoe problem, and one expert, Oscar Newman (1972), concluded that poor architectural design played an important role in facilitating the deviant behavior (crime, vandalism, and so on) that doomed the project. Each of the 33 buildings had 11 floors with a single elevator shaft in the center and extremely long corridors, which isolated the residents. Pruitt-Igoe never became a community where people mingled freely and developed friendships, because the residents were housed row on row, as in strip motel rooms, and stacked 11-floors deep.

Most of the buildings had to be demolished in the 1970s. But some still stand, empty and abandoned, in mute testimony to failed high hopes, poor architectural design, and hasty planning that ignored important principles of human psychology.

Dormitory Design

Do you live in campus housing? Some of the dormitories might have been built before architectural psychology was factored into the

The demolition of the Pruitt-Igoe Housing Project in 1972. Poor architectural design contributed to this urban disaster.

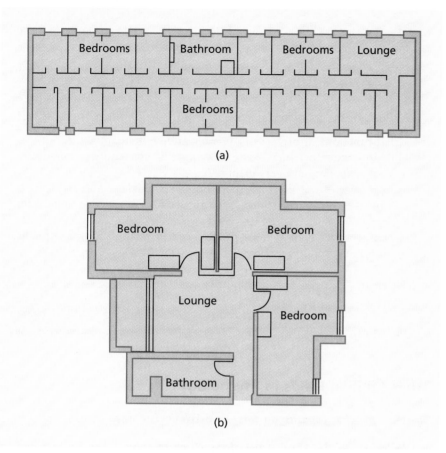

(a)

(b)

Figure 17.5 The Psychological Effects of Architectural Design A traditional corridor dorm (a) and a suite-style dorm (b) have dramatically different psychological effects on students, even when the amount of living space per student is about the same. Baum and Valins reported that students in the corridor dorms complained more than students in suite-style dorms about being crowded, being stressed, lacking privacy, and lacking control in their living arrangement. (From Baum & Valins, 1977.)

planning. Researchers Baum and Valins (1977, 1979) studied the psychological effects on students of two very different campus dormitory arrangements at the State University of New York at Stony Brook. One type was the traditional corridor dorm (Figure 17.5a), and the other consisted of clusters of suites (Figure 17.5b). The number of students per unit of space was about the same in both types of dormitories, but the psychological effects were dramatically different. Students in the corridor dormitories complained of more stress, the feeling of being crowded, lack of privacy, lack of control in their living situation, and more unsolicited social contacts than students in the suite dormitories. Also, students in the corridor dorms visited the campus health clinic with various complaints more often than did their fellow students in the suite dormitories.

But colleges and universities cannot afford to demolish all of their traditional corridor dorms and build new dorms with clusters of suites. Is there any way to solve the problem? Yes, and a very simple and inexpensive one according to Baum and Davis (1980), who did a follow-up study of a simple architectural modification of the corridor dorm. Students in the modified dorm reported feeling less crowded and less stress than students in the traditional corridor dorm. Also, they were happier and enjoyed more friendly social interactions than their fellow students in the traditional dorm.

Memory Check 17.3

1. Noise can be harmful even if it is not loud enough to damage our hearing. (true/false)

2. Which of the following statements is *not* true of our personal space?

    a. It functions to protect our privacy and regulate intimacy.
    b. How much personal space we require is affected by our culture, race, gender, and personality.
    c. The size of our personal space bubble is fixed.
    d. Invasions of our personal space are usually perceived as unpleasant.

3. Territorial behavior is most pronounced in relation to one's (public, primary, secondary) territory.

4. (Density, Crowding) is an objective concept that is measurable.

Answers: 1. true 2. c 3. primary 4. Density

Other Applied Fields in Psychology

Question: In what capacity do forensic psychologists work in the legal system?

Psychology and the Law: Psychology Goes to Court   Forensic psychology is a law-related specialty in which psychologists serve in the legal justice system as consultants or expert witnesses. The legal system in the United States operates according to many centuries of legal thought and tradition. The assumption is that the accused must be presumed innocent until proven guilty, that citizens are guaranteed a fair and impartial trial, and that justice is blind (totally unprejudiced). But psychologists and other scientists continue to present growing evidence that justice is not as blind as the ideal tradition would have us believe.

Much of the research on forming initial impressions, conformity, attitudes, and group decision making can be applied in the legal system. Members of the jury, and judges too, can be swayed by a defendant's looks, dress, attractiveness, gender, race, social class, and many other personal and social attributes. Physically attractive defendants are more likely to be found "not guilty" than unattractive defendants (Michelini & Snodgrass, 1980). In one study, subjects who viewed photographs of adults identified as sex offenders rated the least attractive persons as more dangerous and more likely to commit future crimes than the offenders who were attractive or average looking (Esses & Webster, 1988). But being physically attractive can work against a defendant if attractiveness is considered instrumental in committing a crime, as in the case of a handsome defendant accused of wooing and swindling an aging widow out of her life savings.

The Role of Psychologists in the Legal System   Psychologists are playing an increasingly influential role in matters of the law as consultants to law enforcement officials and attorneys and as researchers. They may be called on as expert witnesses to evaluate the mental state of defendants and comment on their potential for future violent behavior (Faust & Ziskin, 1988). Or they may testify on such matters as the reliability of eyewitness testimony (Kassin et al., 1989) or the reliability of lie detector tests. Psychologists sometimes assist attorneys in the jury selection process as well.

forensic psychology: A law-related specialty in which psychologists are involved in the legal justice system either as expert witnesses or as consultants to police, attorneys, defendants, judges, juries, or the penal system.

Psychologists may collect demographic data on prospective jurors—the neighborhood where they live and their social class, age, political party, occupation, amount of education, religious affiliation, and so on. Sometimes probabilities of whether a juror will be more likely to decide for acquittal or conviction can be computed from such demographic data and from attitude surveys of how a prospective juror's neighbors feel about a case to be tried (Hofer, 1991). However, a great deal of evidence suggests that such information about jurors (their age, gender, political ideology, education, occupation, and so on) does not reliably predict how they will vote (MacCoun, 1989).

Mock-Jury Research: Studying the Deliberation Process Another important line of research relates to how juries make decisions. Psychologists conduct studies using a mock-jury in which research subjects are selected randomly to act as jurors and asked to reach a verdict in a simulated legal trial (MacCoun, 1989).

One of the first findings in mock-jury research (over 50 years ago) is that many jurors tend to form early opinions about the defendant's guilt or innocence before all of the evidence is presented. This happens in spite of judges' instructions to withhold judgment until all the facts are in (MacCoun, 1989). Jurors, just like the rest of us, find it hard to lay aside their attitudes, biases, and stereotypic thinking when weighing evidence. If an attorney mentions inadmissible evidence such as a defendant's prior behavior or conviction and the jury is instructed by the judge to disregard the comment, can they? Not easily, and often it affects their decisions (Sales & Hafemeister, 1985). At the end of the trial, the fate of the defendant is in the hands of the jury.

Question: How do sports psychologists help competitive athletes as well as average citizens participating in recreational athletic programs?

Sports Psychology: More Than Playing Games The pitcher is on the mound; the batter is at the plate. The fans are cheering, excitement builds, and you are ready to settle back and enjoy America's favorite pastime. "Play ball!" yells the umpire, and the game begins. But few people are aware of the multitude of activities going on behind the scenes. Obviously the players, coaches, managers, team doctors, trainers, and other assistants have been hard at work. But in many cases, so have psychologists.

Sports psychology is a specialty concerned with improving sports performance and making participation in sports more beneficial. Sports psychologists work with a wide range of clients, from world-class teams and players to average citizens who are interested in physical activity for health reasons or simply for recreation and enjoyment (Durkin, 1991). Some sports psychologists concentrate on community-based athletic and recreation programs. They may teach both adults and children how to gain maximum physical, mental, and emotional benefits from various recreation experiences. They also help people select (and stick to) weight control and exercise programs. The work of the sports psychologists may involve identifying the conditions that facilitate learning motor skills and teaching individuals how to develop those skills.

Psychologists working with world-class and professional athletes help them develop the mental and emotional skills necessary to reach their maximal competitive performance potential. Because of their rigorous training, professional athletes are already physically prepared. Often the difference between an average and a top athletic performance is due primarily to mental and emotional factors.

Sports psychologists train athletes in relaxation, concentration, and visualization, but learning to concentrate and relax is not simple. According to Durkin (1991), "Learning to concentrate is one of the most difficult mental training tasks that the athlete faces. . . . It may often take an athlete up to a year just to

sports psychology: A specialty concerned with helping competitive athletes develop the mental and emotional skills necessary to facilitate their maximal competitive performance potential, and with helping people in recreational athletic programs attain greater physical, emotional, and mental benefits.

learn to relax and to concentrate" (p. 160). Once athletes master relaxation and concentration, sport psychologists teach them visualization techniques.

Try a concentration and visualization exercise yourself in the *Try It!*

Try It!

Imagine an orange. Do you see it inside your head? Or do you picture it on a screen in front of you? Time yourself and try to hold an image of the orange for one minute. After a few seconds, other thoughts and images will creep in, and your image of the orange will come and go. This is why developing the skill of concentration is so important. People trained in concentration can hold an image as long as they wish.

Now relax and focus your concentration by trying to visualize the orange this way: Imagine the orange again, but do something with it. Slowly remove the peel. Then break it into sections. View the sections clearly and see the juice squirting out as you separate them. Imagine how the orange smells. Now place a section in your mouth. Feel it on your tongue. Try to taste the orange section. If you notice saliva flowing, you are on the right track in learning how to visualize. (After Durkin, 1991.)

You may wonder what visualization has to do with athletics. Sports psychologists have found that athletes skilled in visualization can actually improve their performance by practicing it mentally.

Relaxation, concentration, and visualization are important elements involved in helping players to achieve peak performance. This refers to occasions when athletes are able to achieve their very best performance. It involves a psychological state akin to an altered state of consciousness accompanied by a subjective sense that they are operating in a slow-motion time frame (Browne & Mahoney, 1984). In this state, athletes are concentrating with great intensity, totally focused, oblivious to their surroundings, and not distracted in any way. They are insensitive to pain and fatigue, and filled with a sense of power and total control.

Sports psychologists may also help the coaches develop more effective teaching and human relations techniques. Through *task analysis*, they analyze the many complex skills athletes must perform, and break those skills down into their smallest parts. Then they may assist in developing better teaching and training techniques, which coaches may use in teaching the skills of the game.

Player attitude is another area of critical importance in the stressful and competitive world of sports. Sports psychologists are worth many times their salary when they can help team members develop and maintain winning attitudes and help the athletes put aside petty jealousies so that a strong team spirit can be maintained.

Question: What is the purpose of consumer psychology?

task analysis: Breaking down a job or task into its smallest component parts so that worker performance can be analyzed and evaluated and suggestions for improvement can be specific.

consumer psychology: A specialty concerned with studying, measuring, predicting, and influencing consumer behavior.

Consumer Psychology: Psychology Goes to Market   All of us are consumers, and it seems that we are bombarded incessantly with commercial messages on TV and radio, on billboards, and in newspapers and magazines. There is a great deal of psychology involved in our decision to buy certain products rather than others. What kind of car do you drive; what brand of jeans do you wear, and why? Consumer psychologists are interested in such questions, and they know much more about your buying behavior than you might imagine (Cohen & Chakravarti, 1990).

The purpose of the applied specialty **consumer psychology** is to study, measure, predict, and influence consumer behavior. Some consumer psychologists work for companies that sell products to consumers; others are employed by private organizations or government agencies responsible for consumer education and protection (Sommer & Shutz, 1992).

Consumer psychologists use their knowledge of basic psychological processes to answer such questions as "How does a label acquire name recognition? What kinds of colors and patterns have pleasant associations?" (Sommer & Shutz, 1992, pp. 197–198). Consumer psychologists may conduct market research by surveying representative samples of targeted consumer groups and asking them questions about product preferences. What do they like or dislike about certain products? Why do they choose to buy one product rather than another? What types of advertising influence them most?

Another technique is to form focus groups and consumer panels, consisting of target consumer groups selected according to age, background, education, and other variables. Focus groups are brought together to evaluate product samples and to respond to demonstrations. Consumer panel members may be asked to evaluate potential new brand names for products and rate them according to how exciting, how easy to remember, and how appealing they are to specific age groups. The consumer panel may be reassembled on repeated occasions so that consumer psychologists can learn how responses and preferences change over time (Sommer & Shutz, 1992).

Consumer psychologists are also interested in the laboratory testing of products to answer such questions as these: "Is this new paper towel stronger and more absorbent than competing brands?" "How many hours will this ball point pen write without running dry?" They also conduct blind taste tests like the old *Pepsi Challenge*, where people were asked to taste Pepsi and Coke in unmarked containers and tell which one they preferred.

Have you ever been observed by a consumer psychologist? You might have been. Often they systematically observe shoppers in stores and shopping malls to learn more about how they make buying decisions. Investigative work is the specialty of some consumer psychologists who are employed by government agencies. They may pose as customers in investigations of consumer fraud. For example, the researcher might take an automobile or VCR that needs only a minor repair to several places of business, asking for a diagnosis and repair estimate.

Consumer psychology has been around for decades, but probably the first psychologist to systematically apply psychology to advertising and consumer behavior was none other than the famous John B. Watson, the founder of behavioral psychology. When Watson's academic career ended at Johns Hopkins University in 1920, he accepted a position with the J. Walter Thompson advertising agency in New York. Watson created product images over seventy years ago, some of which still exist today—the purity of Johnson's baby powder, the good flavor of Maxwell House coffee ("Good to the last drop"), and the strength of Scott paper towels, among others.

Watson knew that sex sells and that products associated with beauty, virility, and sex appeal will move. We have come a long way in advertising and consumer psychology since the days of Watson, but the psychology that moved consumers then still moves them today.

Memory Check 17.4

1. Forensic psychology is a (law-related, business-related) specialty.

2. When working with competitive athletes, sports psychologists are concerned primarily with the (physical, mental) skills necessary for a top performance.

(continued)

3. The skills of relaxation and concentration can be learned quickly with the help of a good sports psychologist. (true/false)

4. Which of these is *not* a purpose of consumer psychology?

   a. to test new products
   b. to develop new products
   c. to influence consumer behavior
   d. to investigate consumer fraud

Answers: 1. law-related 2. mental 3. false 4. b

Thinking Critically

Evaluation

In your view, which theory of the cause of prejudice and discrimination is most convincing? Which is least convincing? Support your answer.

Point/Counterpoint

Most people would agree that minorities and women have not enjoyed equality of opportunity and access to positions of leadership and power in U.S. society. Various suggestions have been offered to correct such inequalities. One is to institute preferential practices favoring groups historically underrepresented. Prepare an argument for both sides of the issue: Preferential practices in hiring, promotion, and ascending to positions of power should be (should not be) written into law to right the wrongs of past discrimination.

Psychology in Your Life

Drawing on what you have learned in this chapter, consider all aspects of the physical environment where your psychology class meets or where you presently live. Describe in detail why the environment is or is not psychologically satisfying and conducive to learning.

Chapter Summary and Review

Prejudice and Discrimination

What is the difference between prejudice and discrimination?

Prejudice consists of attitudes (usually negative) toward others based on their gender, religion, race, or membership in a particular group. Discrimination consists of actions against others based on the same factors.

What is meant by the terms in-group and out-group?

An in-group is a social group with a strong sense of togetherness and from which others are excluded; an out-group consists of individuals or groups specifically identified by the in-group as not belonging.

How does prejudice develop, according to the social learning theory?

According to this theory, prejudice is learned in the same way as other attitudes—through modeling and reinforcement.

What are stereotypes?

Stereotypes are widely shared beliefs about the characteristics of various social groups (racial, ethnic, religious) including the assumption that *they* are usually all alike.

What did the "glass ceiling" study reveal about discrimination in corporate America?

The "glass ceiling" study revealed that subtle barriers prevent women and minorities from reaching top positions in corporate America and that female corporate executives are paid far less than their male counterparts.

What is reverse discrimination?

Reverse discrimination involves giving special treatment or higher evaluations to members of a group who have been the target of prejudice and discrimination.

What are several strategies for reducing prejudice and discrimination?

Several strategies for reducing prejudice include (1) arranging appropriate educational experiences for children, (2) providing situations where diverse social groups can interact under certain favorable conditions, and (3) extending the boundaries of narrowly defined social groups.

Key Terms

prejudice (p. 586)
discrimination (p. 586)
in-group (p. 586)
out-group (p. 586)
stereotypes (p. 588)
reverse discrimination (p. 592)

Applying Psychology in the Modern World

What are some of the activities of industrial/organizational psychologists?

Industrial/organizational psychologists work to improve personnel selection, training, and evaluation; to increase worker motivation, satisfaction, and performance; and to improve organizational design, communication, and decision making.

What are two effective techniques for increasing work motivation?

Two effective techniques for increasing work motivation are the appropriate use of reinforcement and goal setting.

What factors are closely related to job satisfaction?

Factors closely associated with job satisfaction are interesting work, good pay, having sufficient resources and authority, and having compatible co-workers.

What are some major sources of work stress?

Some major sources of work stress are a heavy work load with little control over how the work will be done (decision latitude), rotating shifts or night shifts, unclear job role and responsibilities, poor relations with co-workers and supervisors, boring and repetitive tasks, dangerous working conditions, and discrimination in the workplace.

What strategies are some industries adopting to combat work stress?

To combat work stress some companies are setting up worksite stress-management interventions to help workers deal with stress or to change aspects of the job situation that are the source of job stress. Other measures are maternity and parental leaves, provision for day care, and flexible schedules.

What are the goals of human factors psychology?

Human factors psychology is concerned with designing and modifying machines and work environments to make them safer, easier to use, and more compatible with the user's sensory, perceptual, cognitive, and motor capabilities.

What are three criteria of good design?

Well-designed objects should have controls that handle only one function, provide immediate feedback for each action taken, and have visual clues to their operation (visibility).

Key Terms

applied psychology (p. 596)
industrial/organizational psychology (p. 596)
human factors psychology (p. 600)

Environmental Psychology: The Psychology of Our Surroundings

What are some of the negative psychological effects that have been associated with noise pollution?

Negative psychological effects of noise pollution are high blood pressure, distractibility in children, less willingness to persist at tasks, impaired auditory discrimination, lower reading achievement, and increased arousal.

What is personal space, and what factors influence our personal space preferences?

Personal space is the area surrounding us that we consider part of us and that we use to regulate how closely others can interact with us. Factors influencing the size of our personal space are the nature of the interaction, the persons with whom we are interacting, and factors such as our culture, gender, and personality characteristics.

What do the terms territory and territorial behavior mean?

A territory is an area we define as permanently or temporarily our own. Territorial behavior relates to the strategies we use to establish control of our territory and to defend it against unwelcome intrusions.

What is the difference between density and crowding?

Density is an objective measure of the number of people occupying a defined physical space. Crowding is subjective and refers to the perception that there are too many people in a defined space.

Key Terms

environmental psychology (p. 602)
territory (p. 603)
territorial behavior (p. 603)
density (p. 603)
crowding (p. 603)

Other Applied Fields in Psychology

In what capacity do forensic psychologists work in the legal system?

Forensic psychologists serve the legal justice system as consultants or expert witnesses, and they conduct research on aspects of the judicial process.

How do sports psychologists help competitive athletes as well as average citizens participating in recreational athletic programs?

Sports psychologists help competitive athletes develop the mental and emotional skills necessary to facilitate their maximal competitive performance, and they help people in recreational athletic programs attain greater physical, emotional, and mental benefits.

What is the purpose of consumer psychology?

The purpose of consumer psychology is to study, measure, predict, and influence consumer behavior.

Key Terms

forensic psychology (p. 608)
sports psychology (p. 609)
consumer psychology (p. 610)

Appendix
Statistical Methods

Comedian Tim Conway, who appeared on the Carol Burnett show many years ago, once did a humorous skit as an inept sports announcer. Reporting the daily baseball scores, he said, "And now here are the scores in the National League— 6 to 4, 3 to nothing, 2 to 1, 8 to 3, and 5 to 2." Conway's report of baseball scores may have been humorous, but it was not very informative. Numbers alone tell us very little.

Psychologists must deal with mounds of data in conducting their studies. The data they compute would be just as meaningless as Tim Conway's baseball scores unless there were some methods available to organize and describe the data. Fortunately there are such methods. Statistics, a branch of mathematics, enables psychologists and other scientists to organize, describe, and draw conclusions about the quantitative results of their studies. We will explore the two basic types of statistics that psychologists use—descriptive statistics and inferential statistics.

descriptive statistics: Statistics used to organize, summarize, and describe information gathered from actual observations.

measure of central tendency: A measure or score that describes the center or middle of a distribution of scores (example: the mean, the median, and the mode).

mean: The arithmetic average of a group of scores that is computed by adding up all the single scores and dividing the sum by the number of scores.

Descriptive Statistics

Descriptive statistics are statistics used to organize, summarize, and describe information gathered from actual observations. Descriptive statistics include measures of central tendency, variability, and relationship.

Measures of Central Tendency

A **measure of central tendency** is a measure or score that describes the center or middle of a distribution of scores. The most widely used and the most familiar measure of central tendency is the mean, which is short for arithmetic mean. The **mean** is the arithmetic average of a group of scores. It is computed by adding up all the single scores and dividing the sum by the number of scores.

Carl is a student who sometimes studies and does well in his classes, but occasionally he procrastinates and fails a test. Table A.1 shows how Carl performed on the seven tests in his psychology class last semester. Carl computes his mean score by adding up all his test scores and dividing the sum by the number of tests. Carl's mean, or average, is 80.

The mean is an important and widely used statistical measure of central tendency, but it can be misleading when a group of scores contains one or several extreme scores. For example, in one group of 10 people, the mean annual income last year was $124,700.00. In this case, knowing the mean income alone covers up more than it reveals. Table A.2 lists the annual incomes of the 10 people in rank order.

When a million-dollar income is averaged with several other, more modest incomes, the mean does not provide a true picture of the group. Therefore, when one or a few individuals score far above or below the middle range of a group, a different measure of central tendency should be used. The **median** is the middle value or score when a group of scores are arranged from highest to lowest. When there are an odd number of scores, the score in the middle is the median. When there are an even number of scores, the median is the average of the two middle scores.

In the 10 salaries arranged from highest to lowest (in Table A.2), the median is $27,000, which is the average of the middle salaries $28,000 and $26,000. The median salary—$27,000—is a truer reflection of the comparative income of the group than is the $124,700 mean. It is important to select the measure of central tendency that most accurately reflects the group being studied.

Another measure of central tendency is the mode. The **mode** is easy to find because it is the score that occurs most frequently in a group of scores. The mode of the annual income group is $22,000.

**Table A.1
Carl's Psychology Test Scores**

Test 1	98
Test 2	74
Test 3	86
Test 4	92
Test 5	56
Test 6	68
Test 7	86
Sum:	560

Mean: 560 ÷ 7 = 80

Table A.2   Annual Income for 10 People

Subject	Annual Income
1	$1,000,000.
2	50,000.
3	43,000.
4	30,000.
5	28,000.
6	26,000.
7	22,000.
8	22,000.
9	16,000.
10	10,000.
Sum:	$1,247,000.

5, 6 → $27,000. ← Median

7, 8 → ← Mode

Mean: $1,247,000. ÷ 10 = $124,700.

Median: $27,000.

Mode: $22,000.

median: The middle value or score when a group of scores are arranged from highest to lowest.

mode: The score that occurs most frequently in a group of scores.

frequency distribution: An arrangement showing the frequency, or number of scores that fall within equal-sized class intervals.

Describing Data with Tables and Graphs

A researcher tested 100 students for recall of 20 new vocabulary words 24 hours after the students had memorized the list. Here are the raw scores (number of words recalled), arranged from lowest to highest, for each of the 100 students.

2	7	8	9	10	11	11	12	13	15
4	7	8	9	10	11	11	12	13	15
4	7	8	9	10	11	12	12	14	15
5	7	8	9	10	11	12	13	14	15
5	7	8	9	10	11	12	13	14	15
6	7	8	9	10	11	12	13	14	16
6	7	8	9	10	11	12	13	14	16
6	8	9	10	10	11	12	13	14	16
6	8	9	10	10	11	12	13	14	17
7	8	9	10	10	11	12	13	14	19

We can tell from the raw data that one student remembered only 2 words (the lowest score) and that one student remembered 19 words (the highest score). We can also observe that the most frequently occurring score, the mode, is 10.

The researcher organized the scores in a *frequency distribution*—an arrangement showing the frequency, or number of scores that fall within equal-sized class intervals. To organize the 100 test scores, the researcher decided to use intervals of two points each. (A different class interval—three points, for example—could have been chosen instead.) Finally, the frequency (number of scores) within each two-point interval was tallied. Table A.3 presents the resulting frequency distribution.

Table A.3 Frequency Distribution of 100 Vocabulary Test Scores

Class Interval	Tally of Scores in Each Class Interval	Number of Scores in Each Class Interval (Frequency)
1–2	|	1
3–4	||	2
5–6	ЖŦ - |	6
7–8	ЖŦ - ЖŦ - ЖŦ - |||	18
9–10	ЖŦ - ЖŦ - ЖŦ - ЖŦ - |||	23
11–12	ЖŦ - ЖŦ - ЖŦ - ЖŦ - |||	23
13–14	ЖŦ - ЖŦ - ЖŦ - ||	17
15–16	ЖŦ - |||	8
17–18	|	1
19–20	|	1

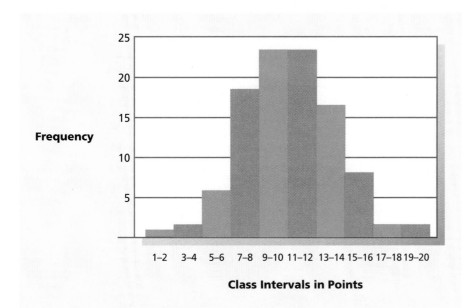

Figure A.1

A Frequency Histogram

Vocabulary test scores from the frequency distribution in Table A.3 are plotted here in the form of a frequency histogram. Class intervals of 2 points each appear on the horizontal axis. Frequencies of the scores in each class interval are plotted on the vertical axis.

The researcher then made a histogram, a more graphic representation of the frequency distribution. A **histogram** is a bar graph that depicts the frequency or number of scores within each class interval in the frequency distribution. The intervals are plotted along the horizontal axis, and the frequency of scores in each interval is plotted along the vertical axis. Figure A.1 shows the histogram for the 100 test scores.

Another common method for representing frequency data is the **frequency polygon.** As in a histogram, class intervals are plotted along the horizontal axis and the frequencies are plotted along the vertical axis. However, in a frequency polygon, a point is placed at the middle (midpoint) of a class interval so that its vertical distance above the horizontal axis shows the frequency of that interval. Lines are drawn to connect the points, as shown in Figure A.2. The histogram and the frequency polygon are simply two different ways of presenting data.

histogram: A bar graph that depicts the frequency or number of scores within each class interval in a frequency distribution.

frequency polygon: A line graph that depicts the frequency or number of scores within each class interval in a frequency distribution.

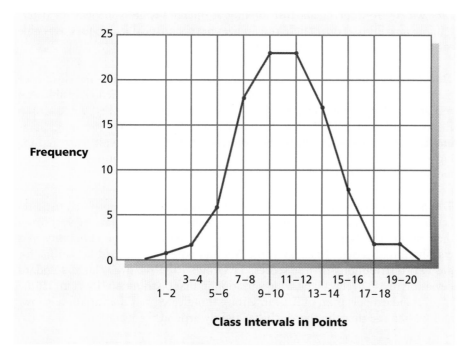

Figure A.2

A Frequency Polygon

Vocabulary test scores from the frequency distribution in Table A.3 are plotted here in the form of a frequency polygon. Class intervals of 2 points each appear on the horizontal axis. Frequencies of the scores in each class interval are plotted on the vertical axis.

Table A.4

Comparison of Range and Standard Deviation for Two Small Groups of Test Scores Having Identical Means and Median Scores

Group I				Group II	
Test	Score			Test	Score
1	99			1	83
2	99			2	82
3	98			3	81
4	80	← Median		4	80	← Median
5	72			5	79
6	60			6	79
7	52			7	76
Sum:	560			Sum:	560

Group I — Mean: $\dfrac{560}{7} = 80$ Group II — Mean: $\dfrac{560}{7} = 80$

Group I — Median: 80   Group II — Median: 80

Group I — Range: $99 - 52 = 47$ Group II — Range: $83 - 76 = 7$

Group I — Standard deviation: 18.1   Group II — Standard deviation: 2.14

Measures of Variability

Researchers usually need more information than measures of central tendency can provide. Often they need to measure the **variability** of a set of scores—how much the scores spread out, away from the mean. There can be tremendous differences in variability even when the mean and the median of two sets of scores are exactly the same, as you can see in Table A.4.

Both groups in Table A.4 have a mean and a median of 80. However, the scores in Group II cluster tightly around the mean, while the scores in Group I vary widely from the mean. Just looking at the data is not sufficient for determining variability. Fortunately researchers have statistical techniques available for measuring variability with great precision.

The Range   The simplest measure of variability is the **range**—the difference between the highest and lowest scores in a distribution of scores. Table A.4 reveals that Group I has a range of 47, indicating high variability, while Group II has a range of only 7, thus low variability. Unfortunately the range is as limited as it is simple. It tells us the difference between the lowest score and the highest score but nothing about the scores in between. A more sophisticated measure of variability is the standard deviation.

The Standard Deviation   The **standard deviation** is a descriptive statistic reflecting the average amount that scores in a distribution deviate or vary from their mean. The larger the standard deviation, the greater the variability in a distribution of scores. Refer to Table A.4 and note the standard deviations for the two distributions of test scores. In Group I the relatively large standard deviation of 18.1 reflects the wide variation in that distribution. By contrast the small standard deviation of 2.14 in Group II indicates that the variation is low, and we can see that the scores cluster tightly around the mean.

variability: How much the scores in a distribution spread out, away from the mean.

range: The difference between the highest score and the lowest score in a distribution of scores.

standard deviation: A descriptive statistic reflecting the average amount that scores in a distribution vary or deviate from their mean.

The Normal Curve

Psychologists and other scientists use descriptive statistics most often in connection with an important type of frequency distribution known as the normal curve, pictured in Figure A.3. The **normal curve** is a symmetrical, bell-shaped, theoretical curve that represents how scores are normally distributed in a population.

If a large number of people are measured on any of a wide variety of traits, the majority of scores will fall near the mean of the distribution. There will be progressively fewer and fewer scores toward the extremes either above or below the mean. Even our small distribution of the 100 test scores in the histogram in Figure A.1 would be roughly bell-shaped if we applied a curve to it. With increasingly larger numbers of scores in a distribution, the shape of the curve will more strongly resemble the ideal normal curve. On most variables we could measure (height or IQ score, for example), the great majority of values will cluster in the middle, with fewer and fewer people measuring extremely low or high on these variables. The normal distribution with its bell-shaped curve is a potent statistical concept with many very useful, practical applications.

Using the properties of the normal curve and knowing the mean and the standard deviation of a normal distribution, we can tell where any score stands (how high or low) in relation to all the other scores in the distribution. Look again at Figure A.3. You will note that slightly over 68 percent of the scores in a normal distribution fall within 1 standard deviation of the mean (34.13 percent within 1 standard deviation above the mean, and 34.13 percent within 1 standard deviation below the mean). Almost 95 1/2 percent of the scores in a normal

> **normal curve:** A symmetrical, bell-shaped frequency distribution that represents how scores are normally distributed in a population; most scores fall near the mean, and fewer and fewer scores occur in the extremes either above or below the mean.

Figure A.3   The Normal Curve   The normal curve is a symmetrical, bell-shaped curve that represents how scores are normally distributed in a population. Slightly over 68 percent of the scores in a normal distribution fall within 1 standard deviation above and below the mean. Almost 95 1/2 percent of the scores lie between 2 standard deviations above and below the mean, and about 99 3/4 percent fall between 3 standard deviations above and below the mean.

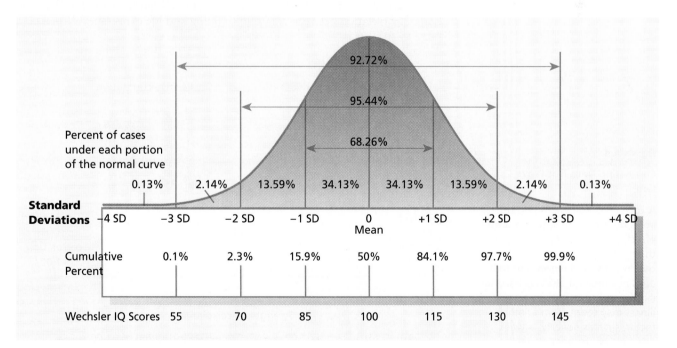

correlation coefficient: A numerical value indicating the strength and direction of relationship between two variables, which ranges from +1.00 (a perfect positive correlation) to −1.00 (a perfect negative correlation).

positive correlation: A relationship between two variables in which both vary in the same direction.

negative correlation: A relationship between two variables in which an increase in one variable is associated with a decrease in the other variable.

distribution lie between 2 standard deviations above and below the mean. Theoretically the tails of the bell-shaped curve extend indefinitely, never touching the base line of the curve. Yet the vast majority of scores in a normal distribution, almost 99 3/4 percent, fall between 3 standard deviations above and below the mean.

On the Wechsler Intelligence Scale, the mean IQ is 100 and the standard deviation is 15. Thus 99.72 percent of the population would have an IQ score within 3 standard deviations above and below the mean, ranging from an IQ of 55 to an IQ of 145. We noted that the highest IQ score ever recorded was an unbelievable 230 on the Stanford-Binet Intelligence Scale, scored by Marilyn vos Savant-Jarvik. To plot her score on the normal curve, we would have to count 8 1/2 standard deviations above the mean, so far up the right tail of the curve that her score is in a standard deviation of its own. The nearest competing score of 210 was almost 7 standard deviations above the mean.

The statistical methods we have discussed so far, the measures of central tendency and the measures of variation, are designed to consider only one variable, such as test scores. What if we are interested in knowing whether two or more different variables are related to each other? The descriptive statistic used to show relationships between variables is the correlation coefficient.

The Correlation Coefficient

A **correlation coefficient** is a number that indicates the degree and direction of relationship between two variables. Correlation coefficients can range from +1.00 (a perfect positive correlation) to .00 (no correlation) to −1.00 (a perfect negative correlation). A **positive correlation** indicates that two variables vary in the same direction. An increase in one variable is associated with an increase in the other variable, or a decrease in one variable is associated with a decrease in the other. There is a positive correlation between the number of hours students spend studying and their college grades. The more hours they study, the higher their grades are likely to be.

A *negative correlation* means that an increase in one variable is associated with a decrease in the other variable. As we pointed out in chapter 1, there is a negative correlation between cigarette smoking and life expectancy. When ciga-

Figure A.4

Correlation Does Not Prove Causation

A correlation between two variables does not prove that a cause-effect relationship exists between them. There is a correlation between stress and illness, but that does not mean that stress necessarily causes illness. Both stress and illness may result from another factor, such as poverty, a weak constitution, or poor general health.

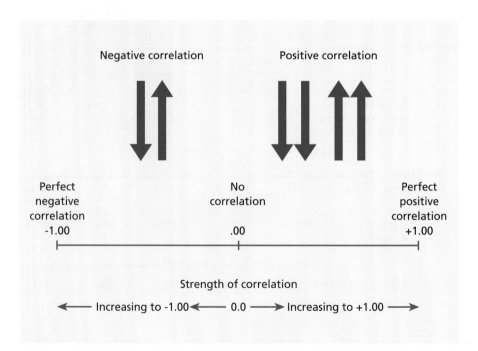

rette smoking increases, the number of years the smoker lives tends to decrease, and vice versa. There may be a negative correlation between the number of hours you spend watching television and studying. The more hours you spend watching TV, the fewer hours you might spend studying, and vice versa.

The sign + or − merely tells whether the two variables vary in the same or opposite directions. (If no sign appears, the correlation is assumed to be positive.) The number in a correlation coefficient indicates the relative *strength* of the relationship between two variables—the higher the number, the stronger the relationship. For example, a correlation of −.70 is higher than a correlation of +.56; a correlation of −.85 is just as strong as one of +.85. A correlation of .00 indicates that no relationship exists between the variables (see Figure A.4). IQ and shoe size are examples of two variables that are not correlated.

Table A.5 shows the measurements of two variables—high school GPA and college GPA for 11 college students. Most college and university admissions officers use high school grades along with standardized tests and other criteria to predict academic success in college.

Looking at the scores in Table A.5, we can observe that 6 of the 11 students had a higher GPA in high school, while 5 of the students had a higher GPA in college. A clearer picture of the actual relationship is shown by the scatterplot in Figure A.5. High school GPA (variable X) is plotted on the horizontal axis, and college GPA (variable Y) is plotted on the vertical axis.

One dot is plotted for each of the 11 students at the point where high school GPA, variable X, and college GPA, variable Y, intersect. For example, the first student's high school and college GPAs intersect at 2.0 on the horizontal (x) axis and at 1.8 on the vertical (y) axis. The scatterplot in Figure A.4 reveals a relatively high correlation between high school and college GPAs because the dots cluster near the diagonal line. It also shows that the correlation is positive because the dots run diagonally upward from left to right. The correlation coefficient for the high school and college GPAs of these 11 students is .71. If the

Table A.5

High School and College GPAs for 11 Students

Student	High School GPA Variable X	College GPA Variable Y
1	2.0	1.8
2	2.2	2.5
3	2.3	2.5
4	2.5	3.1
5	2.8	3.2
6	3.0	2.2
7	3.0	2.8
8	3.2	3.3
9	3.3	2.9
10	3.5	3.2
11	3.8	3.5

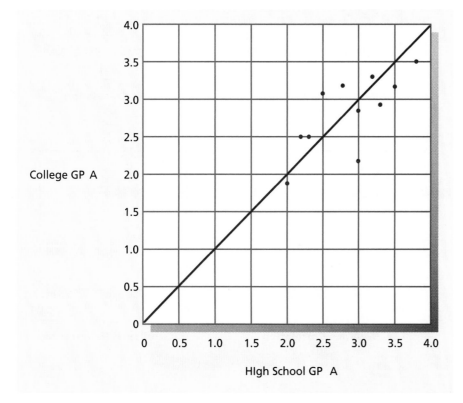

Figure A.5

A Scatterplot

A scatterplot reveals a relatively high positive correlation between the high school and college GPA's of the 11 students listed in Table A.6. One dot is plotted for each of the 11 students at the point where high school GPA (plotted on the horizontal axis) and college GPA (plotted on the vertical axis) intersect.

correlation were perfect (1.00), all the dots would fall exactly on the diagonal line.

A scatterplot shows whether a correlation is low, moderate, or high and whether it is positive or negative. Scatterplots that run diagonally up from left to right reveal a positive correlation. Scatterplots that run diagonally down from left to right indicate a negative correlation. The closer the dots are to the diagonal line, the higher the correlation. The six scatterplots in Figure A.6 depict a variety of correlations.

We have pointed out elsewhere that correlation does not demonstrate cause and effect. Even a perfect correlation (+1.00 or − 1.00) does not mean that one variable causes or is caused by the other. Correlation shows only that two variables are related.

Figure A.6   A Variety of Scatterplots   Scatterplots moving diagonally up from left to right as in (a) and (b) indicate positive correlations. Scatterplots moving diagonally down from left to right as in (d) and (e) indicate a negative correlation. The more closely the dots cluster around the diagonal line, the higher the correlation. Scatterplot (a) shows a perfect positive correlation (+1.00), while scatterplot (c) indicates no correlation. Scatterplot (f) shows a curvilinear relationship that is positive up to a point and then becomes negative. Age and strength of handgrip have a curvilinear relationship. Handgrip increases in strength up to about age 40 and then decreases with continued aging.

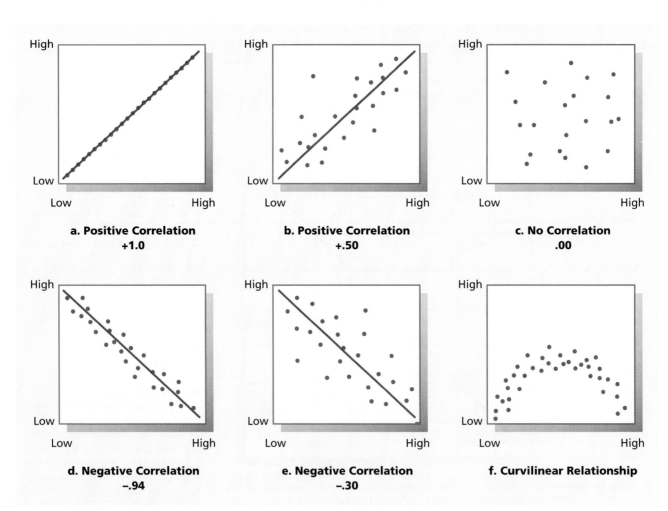

a. Positive Correlation
+1.0

b. Positive Correlation
+.50

c. No Correlation
.00

d. Negative Correlation
−.94

e. Negative Correlation
−.30

f. Curvilinear Relationship

Not all relationships between variables are positive or negative. The relationships between some variables are said to be curvilinear. A curvilinear relationship exists when two variables correlate positively (or negatively) up to a certain point and then change direction. For example, there is a positive correlation between physical strength and age up to about 40 or 45 years of age. As age increases from childhood to middle age, so does the strength of handgrip pressure. But beyond middle adulthood, the relationship becomes negative, and increasing age is associated with decreasing handgrip strength. Figure A.6f shows a scatterplot of this curvilinear relationship.

Inferential Statistics

We have learned that measures of central tendency, variability, and correlation are important in describing characteristics of data and in describing relationships between sets of data. Often, however, investigators wish to make inferences beyond the relatively small groups of subjects they actually measure. **Inferential statistics** allow researchers (1) to make inferences about the characteristics of the larger population from their observations and measurements of a sample, and (2) to derive estimates of how much faith or confidence can be placed in those inferences.

In statistical theory a **population** is the entire group of interest to researchers—it is the group to which they wish to apply their findings. For example, a population could be all the registered voters in the United States, all the members of a religious denomination or political party, and so on. On a smaller scale, a population might consist of all the female students, the entire senior class, or all of the psychology professors at your college or university. A population need not consist of persons. It can be all the chihuahuas in California, all the automobile tires manufactured in the United States, or all the oranges grown in Florida in a given year. In short, a population is all members of any group a researcher may define for study.

Usually researchers cannot directly measure and study the entire population of interest because it may be extremely large, inaccessible, or too costly in time and money. But thanks to inferential statistical methods, we can make inferences about a large population that we do not observe or measure, from the direct observations of a relatively small sample selected from the population. A *sample* is the part of a population that is selected and studied. For researchers to draw conclusions about the entire larger population of interest, the sample must be representative; that is, its characteristics must mirror those of the larger population. (See chapter 1 for more information about representative and random samples.)

Statistical Significance

Assume that a random sample of 200 psychology students was selected from the population of students at your college or university. (Remember from chapter 1 that a **random sample** is selected in such a way that every member of the population has an equal chance of being included in the sample.) Then the 200 students are randomly assigned to either the experimental group or the control group of 100 students each. Random assignment is accomplished by a chance procedure such as drawing names out of a hat. The experimental group is taught psychology using innovative learning materials for one semester. The control group receives the traditional instruction. At the end of the semester, researchers

inferential statistics: Statistical procedures that allow researchers (1) to make inferences about the characteristics of the larger population from their observations and measurements of a sample, and (2) to derive estimates of how much faith or confidence can be placed in those inferences.

population: The entire group of interest to researchers and to which they wish to generalize their findings; the group from which the sample is selected.

sample: The portion of any population that is selected for study and from which generalizations are made about the entire larger population.

random sample: A sample of subjects selected in such a way that every member of the population has an equal chance of being included in the sample; its purpose is to obtain a sample that is representative of the population of interest.

find that the mean test scores of the experimental group are considerably higher than those of the control group. Can the researchers conclude that the innovative learning program worked? No, not until they can show that the experimental results were not simply due to chance.

The researchers must use inferential statistical procedures to be confident that the results they observe are real (not chance occurrences). Tests of statistical significance yield an estimate of how often the experimental results could have occurred by chance alone. The estimates derived from tests of statistical significance are stated as probabilities. A probability of .05 means that the experimental results would be expected to occur by chance no more than 5 times out of 100. The .05 level of significance is usually required as a minimum for researchers to conclude that their findings are statistically significant. Often the level of significance reached is even more impressive, such as the .01 level. The .01 level means that the probability is no more than 1 in 100 that the results occurred by chance.

The inferences researchers make are not absolute. They are based on probability, and there is always a possibility, however small, that experimental results could occur by chance. For this reason replication of research studies is recommended.

References

Abbott, N. J., & Raff, M. C. (1991). Preface. *Annals of the New York Academy of Sciences, 633*, xiii–xv. [2]

Abrams, D., Wetherell, M., Cochrane, S., Hogg, M. A., & Turner, J. C. (1990). Knowing what to think by knowing who you are: Self-categorization and the nature of norm formation, conformity and group polarization. *British Journal of Social Psychology, 29*(Pt. 2), 97–119. [16]

Abrams, R. (1988). *Electroconvulsive therapy.* New York: Oxford University Press. [15]

Abramson, P., & Herdt, G. (1990). The assessment of sexual practices relevant to the transmission of AIDS: A global perspective. *Journal of Sex Research, 27*, 215–232. [11]

Adams, J. M. (1991, August 5). The clearest message may be: "Buy this tape." *Boston Globe*, pp. 37–40. [3]

Adelmann, P. K., & Zajonc, R. B. (1989). Facial efference and the experience of emotion. *Annual Review of Psychology, 40*, 249–280. [10]

Adelson, R., Liebert, R. M., Herskovitz, A., & Poulos, R. W. (1972, March). A modeling film to reduce children's fears of dental treatment. *International Association for Dental Research Abstracts, 114.* [15]

Ader, R. (1985). CNS immune systems interactions: Conditioning phenomena. *Behavioral and Brain Sciences, 9*, 760–763. [5]

Ader, R., & Cohen, N. (1982). Behaviorally conditioned immunosuppression and murine systemic Lupus erythematosus. *Science, 215*, 1534–1536. [5]

Adler, A. (1927). *Understanding human nature.* New York: Greenberg. [12]

Adler, A. (1956). In H. L. Ansbacher & R. R. Ansbacher (Eds.), *The individual psychology of Alfred Adler: A systematic presentation in selections from his writings.* New York: Harper & Row. [12]

Adler, N., & Stone, G. (1984). Psychology and the health system. In J. Ruffini (Ed.), *Advances in medical social science.* New York: Gordon & Breach. [13]

Aiello, J. R. (1987). Human spatial behavior. In D. Stokols & I. Altman (Eds.), *Handbook of environmental psychology* (Vol. 1, pp. 505–531). New York: Wiley-Interscience. [17]

Aiello, J. R., & Jones, S. E. (1971). Field study of the proxemic behavior of young school children in three subcultural groups. *Journal of Personality and Social Psychology, 19*, 351–356. [17]

Ainsworth, M. D. S. (1973). The development of infant-mother attachment. In B. Caldwell & H. Ricciuti (Eds.), *Review of child development research* (Vol. 3). Chicago: University of Chicago Press. [8]

Ainsworth, M. D. S. (1979). Infant-mother attachment. *American Psychologist, 34*, 932–937. [8]

Ainsworth, M. D. S., Blehar, M. C., Walters, E., & Wall, S. (1978). *Patterns of attachment.* Hillsdale, NJ: Erlbaum. [8]

Aitkin, L. (1990). *The auditory cortex: Structural and functional bases of auditory perception.* London: Chapman & Hall. [2]

Ajzen, I., & Fishbein, M. (1977). Attitude-behavior relations: A theoretical analysis and review of empirical research. *Psychological Bulletin, 84*, 888–918. [16]

Åkerstedt, T. (1988). Sleepiness as a consequence of shift work. *Sleep, 11*, 17–34. [4]

Akiskal, H. S. (1989). New insights into the nature and heterogeneity of mood disorders. *Journal of Clinical Psychiatry, 50*(5, Suppl.), 6–10. [14]

Albert, M. L., & Helm-Estabrooks, N. (1988a). Diagnosis and treatment of aphasia: Part I. *Journal of the American Medical Association, 259*, 1043–1047. [2]

Albert, M. L., & Helm-Estabrooks, N. (1988b). Diagnosis and treatment of aphasia: Part II. *Journal of the American Medical Association, 259*, 1205–1210. [2]

Alberts, M. J., Bertels, C., & Dawson, D. V. (1990). An analysis of time of presentation after stroke. *Journal of the American Medical Association, 263*, 65–68. [2]

Albrecht, K. (1979). *Stress and the manager: Making it work for you.* Englewood Cliffs, NJ: Prentice-Hall. [17]

Aldrich, M. S. (1989). Cardinal manifestations of sleep disorders. In M. H. Kry-ger, T. Roth, & W. C. Dement (Eds.), *Principles and practice of sleep medicine* (pp. 313–331). Philadelphia: W. B. Saunders. [4]

Aldrich, M. S. (1990). Narcolepsy. *New England Journal of Medicine, 323*, 389–394. [4]

Allen, W. (1989, February 20). Sleep. *St. Louis Post-Dispatch*, p. B1. [4]

Allgood-Merten, B., Lewinsohn, P. M., & Hops, H. (1990). Sex differences and adolescent depression. *Journal of Abnormal Psychology, 99*, 55–63. [9]

Allison, M. (1991, February). Improving the odds. *Harvard Health Letter, 16*, pp. 4–6. [13]

Allport, G. W. (1935). Attitudes. In C. Murchison (Ed.), *Handbook of social psychology.* Worcester, MA: Clark University Press. [16]

Allport, G. W. (1954). *The nature of prejudice.* Reading, MA: Addison-Wesley. [17]

Allport, G. W. (1961). *Pattern and growth in personality.* New York: Holt, Rinehart & Winston. [12]

Allport, G. W., & Odbert, J. S. (1936). Trait names: A psycho-lexical study. *Psychological Monographs, 47*(1, Whole No. 211), 1–171. [12]

Alpert, B., Field, T., Goldstein, S., & Perry, S. (1990). Aerobics enhances cardiovascular fitness and agility in preschoolers. *Health Psychology, 9*, 48–56. [13]

Altshuler, K. Z. (1989). Will the psychotherapies yield different results?: A look at assumptions in therapy trials. *American Journal of Psychotherapy, 43*, 310–320. [15]

Alwin, D. F., Cohen, R. L., & Newcomb, T. M. (1991). *Attitude persistence and change over the lifespan.* Madison: University of Wisconsin Press. [16]

American Psychological Association. (1984). *Survey of the use of animals in behavioral research at U. S. universities.* Washington, DC: Author. [1]

American Psychiatric Association. (1987). *Diagnostic and statistical manual of mental disorders* (3rd ed., rev.). Washington, DC: Author. [4, 14]

Anastasi, A. (1982). *Psychological testing* (5th ed.). New York: Macmillan. [12]

Anastasi, A. (1988). *Psychological testing* (6th ed.). New York: Macmillan. [17]

Anderson, C. A. (1989). Temperature and aggression: Ubiquitous effects of heat on occurrence of human violence. *Psychological Bulletin, 106*, 74–96. [16]

Anderson, M. J., Petros, T. V., Beckwith, B. E., Mitchell, W. W., & Fritz, S. (1991). Individual differences in the effect of time of day on long-term memory access. *American Journal of Psychology, 104*, 241–255. [4]

Anderson, S. M., Klatzky, R. L., & Murray, J. (1990). Traits and social stereotypes: Efficiency differences in social information processing. *Journal of Personality and Social Psychology, 59*, 192–201. [17]

Andreasen, N. C. (1988). Brain imaging: Applications in psychiatry. *Science, 239*, 1381–1388. [14]

Andreasen, N. C., & Black, D. W. (1991). *Introductory textbook of psychiatry.* Washington, DC: American Psychiatric Press. [4]

Andreasen, N. C., Cohen, G., Harris, G., Cizaldlo, T., Parkkinen, J., Rezai, K., & Swayze, V. W. (1992). Image processing for the study of brain structure and function: Problems and programs. *Journal of Neuropsychiatry and Clinical Neurosciences, 4*, 125–133. [2]

Angoff, W. H. (1988). The nature-nurture debate, aptitudes, and group differences. *American Psychologist, 43*, 713–720. [7]

Annett, M. (1985). *Left, right hand and brain: The right shift theory.* London: Lawrence Erlbaum Associates. [2]

Aoki, C., & Siekevitz, P. (1988). Plasticity in brain development. *Scientific American, 259*, 56–64. [2]

Apgar, V., & Beck, J. (1982). A perfect baby. In H. E. Fitzgerald & T. H. Carr (Eds.), *Human Development 82/83* (pp. 66–70). Guilford, CT: Dushkin. [8]

Apple, W., Streeter, L. A., & Krauss, R. M. (1979). Effects of pitch and speech rate on personal attributions. *Journal of Personality and Social Psychology, 37*, 715–727. [16]

Applebaum, S. A. (1982). Challenges to traditional psychotherapy from the "new therapies." *American Psychologist, 37*, 1002–1008. [15]

Apuzzio, J. J. (1990, February). A patient guide: Genital herpes. *Medical Aspects of Human Sexuality, 24,* 15–16. [11]

Aral, S. O., & Holmes, K. K. (1991). Sexually transmitted diseases in the AIDS era. *Scientific American, 264,* 62–69. [11]

Araoz, D. L. (1982). *Hypnosis and sex therapy.* New York: Brunner/Mazel. [4]

Archambault, C. M., Czyzewski, D., Cordua y Cruz, G. D., Foreyt, J. P., & Mariotto, M. J. (1989). Effects of weight cycling in female rats. *Physiology and Behavior, 46,* 417–421. [13]

Archer, J. (1991). The influence of testosterone on human aggression. *British Journal of Social Psychology, 82*(Pt. 1), 1–28. [16]

Arkin, A. M. (1981). *Sleep talking: Psychology and psychophysiology.* Hillsdale, NJ: Lawrence Erlbaum Associates. [4]

Armstrong, B. G., McDonald, A. D., & Sloan, M. (1992). Cigarette, alcohol, and coffee consumption and spontaneous abortion. *American Journal of Public Health, 82,* 85–87. [8]

Aronson, E. (1973, May). The rationalizing animal. *Psychology Today,* pp. 46–52. [16]

Aronson, E. (1976). Dissonance theory: Progress and problems. In E. P. Hollander & R. C. Hunt (Eds.), *Current perspectives in social psychology* (4th ed., pp. 316–328). New York: Oxford University Press. [16]

Aronson, E. (1990). Applying social psychology to desegregation and energy conservation. *Personality and Social Psychology Bulletin, 16,* 118–132. [17]

Aronson, T. A. (1987). A naturalistic study of imipramine in panic disorder and agoraphobia. *American Journal of Psychiatry, 144,* 1014–1019. [15]

Asch, S. E. (1946). Forming impressions of personality. *Journal of Abnormal and Social Psychology, 41,* 258–290. [16]

Asch, S. E. (1951). Effects of group pressure upon the modification and distortion of judgments. In H. Guetzkow (Ed.), *Groups, leadership, and men.* Pittsburgh, PA: Carnegie Press. [16]

Asch, S. E. (1955). Opinions and social pressure. *Scientific American, 193,* 31–35. [16]

Atkinson, J. W. (1958). Towards experimental analysis of human motivation in terms of motives, expectancies, and incentives. In J. W. Atkinson (Ed.), *Motives in fantasy, action, and society* (pp. 288–305). Princeton, NJ: Van Nostrand. [10]

Atkinson, J. W. (1964). *An introduction to motivation.* Princeton, NJ: Van Nostrand. [10]

Atkinson, R. (1988). *The teenage world: Adolescent self-image in ten countries.* New York: Plenum Press. [9]

Atkinson, R. C., & Shiffrin, R. M. (1968). Human memory: A proposed system and its controlled processes. In K. W. Spence & J. T. Spence (Eds.), *The psychology of learning and motivation* (Vol. 2, pp. 89–195). New York: Academic Press. [6]

Ault, R. L. (1983). *Children's cognitive development* (2nd ed.). Oxford: Oxford University Press. [9]

Avraham, R. (1989). *The digestive system.* New York: Chelsea House. [10]

Axelsson, A., & Jerson, T. (1985). Noisy toys: A possible source of sensorineural hearing loss. *Pediatrics, 76,* 574–578. [3]

Ayllon, T. (1977). Intensive treatment of psychotic behaviour by stimulus satiation and food reinforcement. In S. J. Morse & R. I. Watson, Jr. (Eds.), *Psychotherapies: A comparative casebook* (pp. 355–362). New York: Holt, Rinehart & Winston. [15]

Ayllon, T., & Azrin, N. H. (1965). The measurement and reinforcement of behavior of psychotics. *Journal of the Experimental Analysis of Behavior, 8,* 357–383. [5, 15]

Ayllon, T., & Azrin, N. (1968). *The token economy: A motivational system for therapy and rehabilitation.* New York: Appleton-Century-Crofts. [5, 15]

Azrin, N. H., & Holz, W. C. (1966). Punishment. In W. K. Honig (Ed.), *Operant behavior: Areas of research and application.* New York: Appleton-Century-Crofts. [5]

Bach-y-Rita, P., & Bach-y-Rita, E. W. (1990). Biological and psychosocial factors in recovery from brain damage in humans. *Canadian Journal of Psychology, 44,* 148–165. [2]

Bachman, J. G. (1987, July). An eye on the future. *Psychology Today,* pp. 6–8. [9]

Bachrach, A. J., Erwin, W. J., & Mohr, J. P. (1977). The control of eating behavior in an anorexic by operant conditioning techniques. In S. J. Morse & R. I. Watson, Jr. (Eds.), *Psychotherapies: A comparative casebook* (pp. 363–376). New York: Holt, Rinehart & Winston. [15]

Baddeley, A. D. (1982). *Your memory: A user's guide.* New York: Macmillan. [6]

Baddeley, A. (1986). *Working memory.* New York: Oxford University Press. [6]

Baddeley, A. (1988). Cognitive psychology and human memory. *Trends in Neurosciences, 11,* 176–181. [6]

Baddeley, A. (1992). Working memory. *Science, 255,* 556–559. [6]

Bahnson, C. B. (1981). Stress and cancer: The state of the art. *Psychosomatics, 22,* 207–220. [13]

Bahrick, H. P., & Phelps, E. (1987). Retention of Spanish vocabulary over 8 years. *Journal of Experimental Psychology: Learning, Memory, and Cognition, 13,* 344–349. [6]

Bailey, J. M., & Pillard, R. C. (1991). A genetic study of male sexual orientation. *Archives of General Psychiatry, 48,* 1089–1096. [11]

Bailey, S. L., Flewelling, R. L., & Rachal, J. V. (1992). Predicting continued use of marijuana among adolescents: The relative influence of drug-specific and social context factors. *Journal of Health and Social Behavior, 33,* 51–66. [4]

Baker, T. B. (1988). Models of addiction: Introduction to the special issue. *Journal of Abnormal Psychology, 97,* 115–117. [4]

Baldessarini, R. J. (1988, September). Update on antipsychotic agents. *Harvard Medical School Mental Health Letter, 5,* pp. 4–6. [15]

Baldessarini, R. J. (1989). Current status of antidepressants: Clinical pharmacology and therapy. *Journal of Clinical Psychiatry, 50,* 117–126. [15]

Balkin, J. (1987). Contributions of friends to women's fear of success in college. *Psychological Reports, 61,* 39–42. [10]

Ball, C. G., & Grinker, J. A. (1981). Overeating and obesity. In S. J. Mule (Ed.), *Behavior in excess* (pp. 194–220). New York: The Free Press. [10]

Ballor, D. L., Tommerup, L. J., Thomas, D. P., Smith, D. B., & Keesey, R. E. (1990). Exercise training attenuates diet-induced reduction in metabolic rate. *Journal of Applied Physiology: Respiratory, Environmental, and Exercise Physiology, 68,* 2612–2617. [13]

Bancroft, J. (1984). Hormones and human sexual behavior. *Journal of Sex and Marital Therapy, 10,* 3–21. [11]

Bandura, A. (1964). The stormy decade: Fact or fiction? *Psychology in the Schools, 1,* 224–231. [9]

Bandura, A. (1967). Behavioral psychotherapy. *Scientific American, 216,* 78–82. [15]

Bandura, A. (1969a). *Principles of behavior modification.* New York: Holt, Rinehart & Winston. [5]

Bandura, A. (1969b). Social learning theory and identificatory processes. In D. A. Goslin (Ed.), *Handbook of socialization theory and research* (pp. 213–262). Chicago: Rand McNally. [11]

Bandura, A. (1973). *Aggression: A social learning analysis.* Englewood Cliffs, NJ: Prentice-Hall. [12, 16]

Bandura, A. (1976). On social learning and aggression. In E. P. Hollander & R. C. Hunt (Eds.), *Current perspectives in social psychology* (4th ed., pp. 116–128). New York: Oxford University Press. [16]

Bandura, A. (1977a). *Social learning theory.* Englewood Cliffs, NJ: Prentice-Hall. [5, 8, 12, 15]

Bandura, A. (1977b). Self-efficacy: Toward a unifying theory of behavioral change. *Psychological Review, 84,* 191–215. [12]

Bandura, A. (1986). *Social functions of thought and action: A social-cognitive theory.* Englewood Cliffs, NJ: Prentice-Hall. [5, 12]

Bandura, A., Adams, N. E., & Beyer, J. (1977). Cognitive processes mediating behavioral change. *Journal of Personality and Social Psychology, 35,* 125–139. [15]

Bandura, A., Blanchard, E. B., & Ritter, B. J. (1969). The relative efficacy of desensitization and modeling therapeutic approaches for inducing behavioral, affective and attitudinal changes. *Journal of Personality and Social Psychology, 13,* 173–199.

Bandura, A., Jeffery, R. W., & Gajdos, E. (1975). Generalizing change through participant modeling with self-directed mastery. *Behaviour Research and Therapy, 13,* 141–152. [15]

Bandura, A., Ross, D., & Ross, S. A. (1961). Transmission of aggression through imitation of aggressive models. *Journal of Abnormal and Social Psychology, 63,* 575–582. [5]

Bandura, A., Ross, D., & Ross, S. A. (1963). Imitation of film-mediated aggressive models. *Journal of Abnormal and Social Psychology, 66,* 3–11. [5]

Bar-Tal, D., & Saxe, L. (1976). Perceptions of similarly and dissimilarly attractive couples and individuals. *Journal of Personality and Social Psychology, 33,* 772–781. [16]

Barber, T. X. (1962). Hypnotic age regression: A critical review. *Psychosomatic Medicine, 24,* 181–193. [4]

Barber, T. X. (1970, July). Who believes in hypnosis? *Psychology Today,* pp. 20–27, 84. [4]

Barclay, A., & Cusumano, D. C. (1967). Father absence, cross-sex identity, and field-dependent behavior in male adolescents. *Child Development, 38,* 243–250. [11]

Bard, P. (1934). The neurohumoral basis of emotional reactions. In C. A. Murchison (Ed.), *Handbook of general experimental psychology.* Worcester, MA: Clark University Press. [10]

Barefoot, J. C., Dahlstrom, W. D., & Williams, R. B. (1983). Hostility, CHD incidence, and total mortality: A 25-year follow-up study of 255 physicians. *Psychosomatic Medicine, 45,* 59–63. [13]

Barglow, P., Vaughn, B. E., & Molitor, N. (1987). Effects of maternal absence due to employment on the quality of infant-mother attachment in a low-risk sample. *Child Development, 58,* 945–954. [8]

Barnard, W. A., & Bell, P. A. (1982). An unobtrusive apparatus for measuring interpersonal distance. *Journal of General Psychology, 107,* 85–90. [17]

Barr, H. M., Streissguth, A. P., Darby, B. L., & Samson, P. D. (1990). Prenatal exposure to alcohol, caffeine, tobacco, and aspirin: Effects on fine and gross motor performance in 4-year-old children. *Developmental Psychology, 26,* 339–348. [8]

Barr, L. C., Goodman, W. K., Price, L. H., McDougle, C. J., & Charney, D. S. (1992). The serotonin hypothesis of obsessive compulsive disorder: Implications of pharmacologic challenge studies. *Journal of Clinical Psychiatry, 53*(4, Suppl.), 17–28. [14, 15]

Barr, M. L. (1974). *The human nervous system: An anatomical viewpoint* (2nd ed.). Hagerstown, MD: Harper & Row. [2]

Barron, F., & Harrington, D. M. (1981). Creativity, intelligence, and personality. *Annual Review of Psychology, 32,* 439–476. [7]

Bartimus, T. (1983, March 1). One man's descent into schizophrenia. *St. Louis Post-Dispatch,* pp. D1, 7. [14]

Bartlett, F. C. (1932). *Remembering: A study in experimental and social psychology.* London: Cambridge University Press. [6]

Bartoshuk, L. (1989). Taste: Robust across the age span? *Annals of the New York Academy of Sciences, 561,* 65–75. [3]

Bartoshuk, L., Rifkin, B., Marks, L. E., & Bars, P. (1986). Taste and aging. *Journal of Gerontology, 41,* 51–57. [3]

Bartrop, R. W., Lazarus, L., Luckherst, E., et al. (1977). Depressed lymphocyte function after bereavement. *Lancet, 1,* 834–836. [13]

Baruch, G., Barnett, R., & Rivers, C. (1983). *Lifeprints.* New York: McGraw-Hill. [9]

Bateson, G., Jackson, D. D., Haley, J., & Weakland, J. (1956). Toward a theory of schizophrenia. *Behavioral Science, 1,* 214–264. [14]

Batson, C. D., Batson, J. G., Griffitt, C. A., Barrientos, S., Brandt, J. R., Sprengelmeyer, P., & Bayly, M. J. (1989). Negative-state relief and the empathy-altruism hypothesis. *Journal of Personality and Social Psychology, 56,* 922–933. [16]

Batson, C. D., Dyck, J. L., Brandt, J. R., Batson, J. G., Powell, A. L., McMaster, M. R., & Griffitt, C. (1988). Five studies testing two new egoistic alternatives to the empathy-altruism hypothesis. *Journal of Personality and Social Psychology, 55,* 52–77. [16]

Baum, A., & Davis, G. E. (1980). Reducing the stress of high-density living: An architectural intervention. *Journal of Personality and Social Psychology, 38,* 471–481. [17]

Baum, A., & Valins, S. (1977). *Architecture and social behavior: Psychological studies of social density.* Hillsdale, NJ: Erlbaum. [17]

Baum, A., & Valins, S. (1979). Architectural mediation of residential density and control: Crowding and the regulation of social contact. In L. Berkowitz (Ed.), *Advances in experimental social psychology* (Vol. 12). New York: Academic Press. [17]

Baum, S. K., & Stewart, R. B., Jr. (1990). Sources of meaning through the life-span. *Psychological Reports, 67,* 3–14. [9]

Baumgardner, A. H., Heppner, P. P., & Arkin, R. M. (1986). Role of causal attribution in personal problem solving. *Journal of Personality and Social Psychology, 50,* 636–643. [16]

Baumrind, D. (1971). Current patterns of parental authority. *Developmental Psychology Monographs, 4*(1, Pt. 2). [8]

Baumrind, D. (1978). Parental disciplinary patterns and social competence in children. *Youth and Society, 9,* 239–276. [9]

Baumrind, D. (1980). New directions in socialization research. *American Psychologist, 35,* 639–652. [8]

Baumrind, D. (1985). Research using intentional deception: Ethical issues revisited. *American Psychologist, 40,* 165–174. [1]

Baxter, L. H., Jr., Phelps, M. E., Mazziotta, J. C., et al. (1987). Local cerebral glucose metabolic rates in obsessive-compulsive disorder—a comparison with rates in unipolar depression and normal controls. *Archives of General Psychiatry, 44,* 211–218. [14]

Beaman, A. L., Cole, C. M., Preston, M., Klentz, B., & Steblay, N. M. (1983). Fifteen years of foot-in-the-door research: A meta-analysis. *Personality and Social Psychology Bulletin, 9,* 181–196. [16]

Beck, A. T. (1967). *Depression: Causes and treatment.* Philadelphia: University of Pennsylvania Press. [14]

Beck, A. T. (1976). *Cognitive therapy and the emotional disorders.* New York: New American Library. [15]

Beck, A. T. (1991). Cognitive therapy: A 30-year retrospective. *American Psychologist, 46,* 368–375. [15]

Beck, A. T., Brown, G., Berchick, R. J., Stewart, B. L., & Steer, R. A. (1990). Relationship between hopelessness and ultimate suicide: A replication with psychiatric outpatients. *American Journal of Psychiatry, 147,* 190–195. [14]

Beck, A. T., & Emery, G. (with R. L. Greenberg) (1985). *Anxiety disorders and phobias: A cognitive perspective.* New York: Basic Books. [14]

Beck, A. T., Sokol, L., Clark, D. A., Berchick, R., & Wright, F. (1992). A cross-over study of focused cognitive therapy for panic disorder. *American Journal of Psychiatry, 149,* 778–783. [15]

Becker, M., Warr-Leeper, G. A., & Leeper, H. A., Jr. (1990). Fetal alcohol syndrome: A description of oral motor, articulatory, short-term memory, grammatical, and semantic abilities. *Journal of Communication Disorders, 23,* 97–124. [8]

Beeson, V., Ray, C., Coxon, A., & Kreitzman, S. (1990). The myth of the yo-yo consistent rate of weight loss with successive dieting by VLCD. *International Journal of Obesity, 13*(Suppl. 2), 135–139. [13]

Beidler, L. M., & Smallman, R. L. (1965). Renewal of cells within taste buds. *Journal of Cell Biology, 27,* 263–272. [3]

Békésy, G. von (1957). The ear. *Scientific American, 197,* 66–78. [8]

Bell, A. P., Weinberg, M. S., & Hammersmith, S. K. (1981). *Sexual preference: Its development in men and women.* Bloomington: Indiana University Press. [11]

Bellas, D. N., Novelly, R. A., Eskenazi, B., & Wasserstein, J. (1988). Unilateral displacement in the olfactory sense: A manifestation of the unilateral neglect syndrome. *Cortex, 24,* 267–275. [2]

Belsky, J. (1988). The "effects" of infant day care reconsidered. *Early Childhood Research Quarterly, 3,* 235–272. [8]

Belsky, J., Lang, M., & Huston, T. L. (1986). Sex typing and division of labor as determinants of marital change across the transition to parenthood. *Journal of Personality and Social Psychology, 50,* 517–522. [9]

Belsky, J., & Rovine, M. J. (1988). Nonmaternal care in the first year of life and the security of infant-parent attachment. *Child Development, 59,* 157–167. [8]

Belsky, J., & Steinberg, L. D. (1978). The effects of day care: A critical review. *Child Development, 49,* 929–949. [8]

Belsky, J., & Steinberg, L. D. (1979, July-August). What does research teach us about day care? A follow-up report. *Children Today,* pp. 21–26. [8]

Bem, S. L. (1974). The measurement of psychological androgyny. *Journal of Consulting and Clinical Psychology, 42,* 155–162. [11]

Bem, S. L. (1975). Sex role adaptability: One consequence of psychological androgyny. *Journal of Personality and Social Psychology, 31,* 634–643. [11]

Bem, S. L. (1977). On the utility of alternative procedures for assessing psychological androgyny. *Journal of Consulting and Clinical Psychology, 45,* 196–205. [11]

Bem, S. L. (1981). Gender schema theory: A cognitive account of sex typing. *Psychological Review, 88,* 354–364. [11]

Bem, S. L. (1985). Androgyny and gender schema theory: A conceptual and empirical integration. In T. B. Sonderegger (Ed.), *Nebraska symposium on motivation: Psychology of gender* (Vol. 32, pp. 179–226). Lincoln: University of Nebraska Press. [11]

Ben-Porath, Y. S., & Butcher, J. N. (1989). The comparability of MMPI and MMPI-2 scales and profiles. *Psychological Assessment: A Journal of Consulting and Clinical Psychology, 1,* 345–347. [12]

Benbow, C. P., & Stanley, J. C. (1980). Sex differences in mathematical ability: Fact or artifact? *Science, 210,* 1262–1264. [11]

Benbow, C. P., & Stanley, J. C. (1983). Sex differences in mathematical reasoning-ability: More facts. *Science, 222,* 1029–1031. [2, 11]

Bengtson, V., Rosenthal, C., & Burton, L. (1990). Families and aging: Diversity and heterogeneity. In R. H. Binstock & L. K. George (Eds.), *Handbook of aging and the social sciences* (3rd ed., pp. 263–287). San Diego: Academic Press. [9]

Bennett, W., & Gurin, J. (1982). *The dieter's dilemma.* New York: Basic Books. [13]

Bennett, W. I. (1990, November). Boom and doom. *Harvard Health Letter, 16,* pp. 1–4. [3]

Benson, H. (1975). *The relaxation response.* New York: Avon. [4]

Benson, H., & Epstein, M. D. (1975). The placebo effect: A neglected asset in the care of patients. *Journal of the American Medical Association, 232,* 1225–1227. [16]

Benson, P. L., Karabenick, S. A., & Lerner, R. M. (1976). Pretty pleases: The effects of physical attractiveness, race, and sex on receiving help. *Journal of Personality and Social Psychology, 12,* 409–415. [16]

Bergland, R. (1985). *The fabric of mind.* New York: Viking. [2]

Berkman, L. F., & Syme, S. L. (1979). Social networks, host resistance, and mortality: A nine-year follow-up study of Alameda County residents. *American Journal of Epidemiology, 109,* 186–204. [13]

Berkowitz, L. (1964). The effects of observing violence. *Scientific American, 210,* 35–41. [16]

Berkowitz, L. (1983). Aversively stimulated aggression: Some parallels and differences in research with animals and humans. *American Psychologist, 38,* 1135–1144. [16]

Berkowitz, L. (1988). Frustrations, appraisals, and aversively stimulated aggression. *Aggressive Behavior, 14,* 3–11. [16]

Berkowitz, L. (1989). Frustration-aggression hypothesis: Examination and reformulation. *Psychological Bulletin, 106,* 59–73. [16]

Berkowitz, L. (1990). On the formation and regulation of anger and aggression: A cognitive-neoassociationistic analysis. *American Psychologist, 45,* 494–503. [16]

Berlyne, D. E. (1971). *Aesthetics and psychobiology.* New York: Appleton-Century-Crofts. [10]

Berman, A. L., & Schwartz, R. H. (1990). Suicide attempts among adolescent drug users. *American Journal of Diseases of Children, 144,* 310–314. [14]

Bernstein, I. L. (1985). Learned food aversions in the progression of cancer and its treatment. *Annals of the New York Academy of Sciences, 443,* 365–380. [5]

Bernstein, I. L., Webster, M. M., & Bernstein, I. D. (1982). Food aversions in children receiving chemotherapy for cancer. *Cancer, 50,* 2961–2963. [5]

Berscheid, E., Dion, K., Walster, E., & Walster, G. W. (1971). Physical attractiveness and dating choice: A test of the matching hypothesis. *Journal of Experimental Social Psychology, 7,* 173–189. [16]

Bexton, W. H., Herron, W., & Scott, T. H. (1954). Effects of decreased variation in the sensory environment. *Canadian Journal of Psychology, 8,* 70–76. [10]

Billings, C. E., Demosthenes, T., White, T. R., & O'Hara, D. B. (1991). Effects of alcohol on pilot performance in simulated flight. *Aviation Space and Environmental Medicine, 62,* 233–235. [4]

Binkin, N. J., & Alexander, E. R. (1983). Neonatal herpes: How can it be prevented? *Journal of the American Medical Association, 250,* 3094–3095. [11]

Bisiach, E., & Luzzati, C. (1978). Unilateral neglect of representational space. *Cortex, 14,* 129–133. [7]

Black, S. L., & Bevan, S. (1992). At the movies with Buss and Durkee: A natural experiment on film violence. *Aggressive Behavior, 18,* 37–45. [16]

Blackburn, I. M., Eunson, K. M., & Bishop, S. (1986). A two-year naturalistic follow-up of depressed patients treated with cognitive therapy, pharmacotherapy and a combination of both. *Journal of Affective Disorders, 10*, 67–75. [15]

Blair, S. N., Kohl, H. W., III., Paffenbarger, R. S., Jr., Clark, D. G., Cooper, K. H., & Gibbons, L. W. (1989). Physical fitness and all-cause mortality: A prospective study of healthy men and women. *Journal of the American Medical Association, 262*, 2395–2401. [13]

Bland, R. C., Newman, S. C., & Orn, H. (1986). Recurrent and nonrecurrent depression: A family study. *Archives of General Psychiatry, 43*, 1085–1089. [14]

Blau, A. (1946). *The master hand.* New York: American Ortho-Psychiatric Association. [2]

Bliss, E. L., & Jeppsen, E. A. (1985). Prevalence of multiple personality among inpatients and outpatients. *American Journal of Psychiatry, 142*, 250–251. [14]

Bliss, T. V. P., & Lømo, T. (1973). Long-lasting potentiation of synaptic transmission in the dentate area of the anaesthetized rabbit following stimulation of the perforant path. *Journal of Physiology* (London), *232*, 331–356. [6]

Block, J. H. (1978). Another look at sex differentiation in the socialization of mothers and fathers. In J. Sherman & F. L. Denmark (Eds.), *Psychology of women: Future directions of research* (pp. 29–87). New York: Psychological Dimensions. [11]

Bloom, F. E., Lazerson, A., & Hofstadter, L. (1985). *Brain, mind, and behavior.* New York: W. H. Freeman. [2]

Bloomer, C. M. (1976). *Principles of visual perception.* New York: Van Nostrand Reinhold. [3]

Blundell, J. E., Rogers, P. J., & Hill, A. J. (1988). Uncoupling sweetness and calories: Methodological aspects of laboratory studies on appetite control. *Appetite, 11*(Suppl.), 54–61. [10]

Blyth, D. A., Simmons, R. G., Bulcroft, R., Felt, D., VanCleave, E. F., & Bush, D. M. (1981). The effects of physical development on self-image and satisfaction with body-image for early adolescent males. In R. G. Simmons (Ed.), *Research in community and mental health* (Vol. 2). Greenwich, CT: JAI Press. [9]

Blyth, D. A., & Traeger, C. M. (1983). The self-concept and self-esteem of early adolescents. *Theory into Practice, 22*, 91–97. [9]

Bogen, J. E., & Vogel, P. J. (1963). Treatment of generalized seizures by cerebral commissurotomy. *Surgical Forum, 14*, 431. [2]

Bohannon, J. N., III. (1988). Flashbulb memories for the Space Shuttle disaster: A tale of two theories. *Cognition, 29*, 179–196. [6]

Bohannon, J. N., & Warren-Leubecker, A. (1989). Theoretical approaches to language acquisition. In J. B. Gleason (Ed.), *The development of language* (pp. 167–223). Columbus, OH: Merrill. [8]

Bolles, R. C., & Faneslow, M. S. (1982). Endorphins and behavior. *Annual Review of Psychology, 33*, 87–101. [3]

Borg, E., & Counter, S. A. (1989). The middle-ear muscles. *Scientific American, 261*, 74–80. [3]

Borke, H. (1971). Interpersonal perception of young children: Egocentrism or empathy? *Developmental Psychology, 5*, 263–269. [8]

Borke, H. (1973). The development of empathy in Chinese and American children between 3 and 6 years of age: A cross-cultural study. *Developmental Psychology, 9*, 102–108. [8]

Bornstein, M. H., & Marks, L. E. (1982, January). Color revisionism. *Psychology Today*, pp. 64–73. [8]

Bornstein, R. F. (1989). Exposure and affect: Overview and meta-analysis of research, 1968–1987. *Psychological Bulletin, 106*, 265–289. [16]

Botwinick, J., & Birren, J. E. (1963). Mental abilities and psychomotor responses in healthy aged men. In J. E. Birren, R. N. Butler, S. W. Greenhouse, L. Sokoloff, & M. Yarrow (Eds.), *Human aging: A biological and behavioral study.* National Institute of Mental Health, PHS Publication #986. Washington, DC: U.S. Government Printing Office. [9]

Bouchard, C., Tremblay, A., Despres, J-P, Nadeau, A., Lupien, P. J., Theriault, G., Dussault, J., Moorjani, S., Pinault, S., & Fournier, G. (1990). The response to long-term overfeeding in identical twins. *New England Journal of Medicine, 322*, 1477–1482. [13]

Bouchard, T. J., Jr., Lykken, D. T., McGue, M., Segal, N. L., & Tellegen, A. (1990). Sources of human psychological differences: The Minnesota study of twins reared apart. *Science, 250*, 223–228. [7]

Bouchard, T. J., Jr., Lykken, D. T., McGue, M., Segal, N. L., & Tellegen, A. (1991). IQ and heredity: Response. *Science, 252*, 191–192. [7]

Bouchard, T. J., Jr., & McGue, M. (1990). Genetic and rearing environmental influences on adult personality: An analysis of adopted twins reared apart. *Journal of Personality, 58*, 263–292. [7]

Bower, G. H. (1973, October). How to. . . . uh . . . remember! *Psychology Today*, pp. 63–70. [6]

Bowlby, J. (1969). *Attachment and loss* (Vol. 1). New York: Basic Books. [8]

Bradley, R. M. (1971). Tongue topography. In L. M. Beidler (Ed.), *Handbook of sensory physiology* (Vol. 4, Pt. 2). New York: Springer-Verlag. [3]

Bradshaw, J. L. (1989). *Hemispheric specialization and psychological function.* New York: Wiley. [2]

Bransford, J., Sherwood, R., Vye, N., & Rieser, J. (1986). Teaching thinking and problem solving. *American Psychologist, 41*, 1078–1089. [7]

Brantner, J. P., & Doherty, M. A. (1983). A review of time out: A conceptual and methodological analysis. In S. Axelrod & J. Apsche (Eds.), *The effects of punishment on human behavior* (pp. 87–132). New York: Academic Press. [15]

Braungart, J. M., Plomin, R., DeFries, J. C., & Fulker, D. W. (1992). Genetic influence on tester-rated infant temperament as assessed by Bayley's Infant Behavior Record: Nonadoptive and adoptive siblings and twins. *Developmental Psychology, 28*, 40–47. [8]

Brazelton, T. B., Tronick, E., Adamson, L., Als, H., & Wise, S. (1975). Early mother-infant interaction. In *Parent-Infant Interaction, Ciba Symposium 33.* Amsterdam: Assoc. Science Publ. [8]

Breckler, S. J. (1984). Empirical validation of affect, behavior, and cognition as distinct attitude components. *Journal of Personality and Social Psychology, 47*, 1191–1205. [16]

Breggin, P. R. (1979). *Electroshock: Its brain-disabling effects.* New York: Springer. [15]

Breslau, N., Davis, G. C., Andreski, P., & Peterson, E. (1991). Traumatic events and posttraumatic stress disorder in an urban population of young adults. *Archives of General Psychiatry, 48*, 216–222. [13]

Brickner, M. A., Harkins, S. G., & Ostrom, T. M. (1986). Effects of personal involvement: Thought-provoking implications for social loafing. *Journal of Personality and Social Psychology, 51*, 763–769. [16]

Bridges, K. M. B. (1932). Emotional development in early infancy. *Child Development, 3*, 324–341. [10]

Briggs, S. R. (1989). The optimal level of measurement for personality constructs. In D. M. Buss & N. Cantor (Eds.), *Personality psychology: Recent trends and emerging directions* (pp. 246–260). New York: Springer-Verlag. [12]

Brigham, J. C., Maass, A., Snyder, L. E., & Spaulding, K. (1982). Accuracy of eyewitness identifications in a field setting. *Journal of Personality and Social Psychology, 42*, 673–681. [6]

Brigham, J. C., & Wolfskeil, M. P. (1983). Opinions of attorneys and law enforcement personnel on the accuracy of eyewitness identifications. *Law and Human Behavior, 7*, 337–349. [6]

Broadbent, D. E. (1958). *Perception and communication.* New York: Pergamon Press. [6]

Brody, E. M., Johnson, P. T., & Fulcomer, M. C. (1984). What should adult children do for elderly parents? Opinions and preferences of three generations of women. *Journal of Gerontology, 39*, 736–746. [9]

Bronzaft, A. L. (1981). The effect of a noise abatement program on reading ability. *Journal of Environmental Psychology, 1*, 215–222. [17]

Brooks-Gunn, J. (1986). Pubertal processes and girls' psychological adaptation. In R. M. Lerner & T. T. Foch (Eds.), *Biological-psychosocial interactions in early adolescence: A life-span perspective.* Hillsdale, NJ: Erlbaum. [9]

Brooks-Gunn, J., & Furstenberg, F. F., Jr. (1986). The children of adolescent mothers: Physical, academic, and psychological outcomes. *Developmental Review, 6*, 224–251. [9]

Brose, N., Petrenko, A. G., Südhof, T. C., & Jahn, R. (1992). Synaptotagmin: A calcium sensor on the synaptic vesicle surface. *Science, 256*, 1021–1025. [2]

Browman, C. P., Sampson, M. G., Gujavarty, K. S., & Mitler, M. M. (1982, August). The drowsy crowd. *Psychology Today*, pp. 35–38. [4]

Brown, G. L., & Linnoila, M. I. (1990). CSF serotonin metabolite (5-HIAA) studies in depression, impulsivity, and violence. *Journal of Clinical Psychiatry, 51*(Suppl.), 42–43. [16]

Brown, J. (1958). Some tests of the decay theory of immediate memory. *Quarterly Journal of Experimental Psychology, 10*, 12–21. [6]

Brown, J. D. (1991). Staying fit and staying well: Physical fitness as a moderator of life stress. *Journal of Personality and Social Psychology, 60*, 555–561. [13]

Brown, R. (1973). *A first language: The early stages.* Cambridge, MA: Harvard University Press. [8]

Brown, R., Cazden, C., & Bellugi, U. (1968). The child's grammar from I to III. In J. P. Hill (Ed.), *Minnesota symposium on child psychology* (Vol. 2, pp. 28–73). Minneapolis: University of Minnesota Press. [8]

Brown, R., & Kulik, J. (1977). Flashbulb memories. *Cognition, 5*, 73–99. [6]

Brown, R., & McNeil, D. (1966). The "tip of the tongue" phenomenon. *Journal of Verbal Learning and Verbal Behavior, 5*, 325–337. [6]

Brown, R. J., & Donderi, D. C. (1986). Dream content and self-reported well-being among recurrent dreamers, past-recurrent dreamers, and nonrecurrent dreamers. *Journal of Personality and Social Psychology, 50*, 612–623. [4]

Brown, T. S. (1975). General biology of sensory systems. In B. Scharf (Ed.), *Experimental sensory psychology* (pp. 69–111). Glenview, IL: Scott-Foresman. [3]

Browne, M. A., & Mahoney, M. J. (1984). Sport psychology. *Annual Review of Psychology, 35*, 605–625. [17]

Brownell, K. (1988, January). Yo-yo dieting. *Psychology Today*, pp. 20–23. [13]

Brownell, K. (1991). Dieting and the search for the perfect body: Where physiology and culture collide. *Behavior Therapy, 22*, 1–12. [13]

Brownell, K. D., Greenwood, M. R., Stellar, E., & Shrager, E. E. (1986). The effects of repeated cycles of weight loss and regain in rats. *Physiology and Behavior, 38*, 459–464. [13]

Brozan, N. (1985, March 13). U.S. leads industrialized nations in teen-age births and abortions. *The New York Times*, pp. 1, 22. [9]

Bruner, J. S., Goodnow, J. J., & Austin, G. A. (1956). *A study of thinking.* New York: Wiley. [7]

Bryan, J. H., & Test, M. A. (1967). Models and helping: Naturalistic studies in aiding behavior. *Journal of Personality and Social Psychology, 6*, 400–407. [16]

Bryant, P. E., & Trabasso, J. (1971). Transitive inferences and memory in young children. *Nature, 232*, 456–458. [8]

Buchsbaum, M. S., Ingvar, D. H., Kessler, R., Waters, R. N., et al. (1982). Cerebral glucography with positron tomography. *Archives of General Psychiatry*, 39, 251–259. [14]

Buck, L., & Axel, R. (1991). A novel multigene family may encode odorant receptors: A molecular basis for odor recognition. *Cell*, 65, 175–187. [3]

Buckhout, R. (1979). The mistaken seven: Eyewitness identification in the case of Delaware v. Father Bernard T. Pagano. *Social Action and the Law*, 5, 35–44. [6]

Buckhout, R., Eugenio, P., Licitra, T., Oliver, L., & Kramer, T. H. (1981). Memory, hypnosis and evidence: Research on eyewitnesses. *Social Action and the Law*, 7, 67–72. [6]

Buckingham, H. W., Jr., & Kertesz, A. (1974). A linguistic analysis of fluent aphasics. *Brain and Language*, 1, 29–42. [2]

Budiansky, S., Carey, J., Wellborn, S. N., & Silberner, J. (1987, June 29). Taking the pain out of pain. *U. S. News & World Report*, pp. 50–57. [3]

Buis, J. M., & Thompson, D. N. (1989). Imaginary audience and personal fable: A brief review. *Adolescence*, 24, 773–781. [9]

Burns, D. D. (1989). *The good feeling handbook*. New York: McMorrow. [14]

Burrowes, K. L., Hales, R. E., & Arrington, E. (1988). Research on the biologic aspects of violence. *Psychiatric Clinics of North America*, 11, 499–509. [16]

Burtt, H. E. (1932). An experimental study of early childhood memory. *Journal of Genetic Psychology*, 40, 287–295. [6]

Bushman, B. J., & Cooper, H. M. (1990). Effects of alcohol on human aggression: An integrative research review. *Psychological Bulletin*, 107, 341–354. [4, 16]

Bushman, B. J., & Geen, R. G. (1990). Role of cognitive-emotional mediators and individual differences in the effects of media violence on aggression. *Journal of Personality and Social Psychology*, 58, 156–163. [16]

Buss, D. M. (1984). Marital assortment for personality dispositions: Assessment with three different data sources. *Behavioral Genetics*, 14, 111–123. [16]

Buss, D. M., Abbott, M., Angleitner, A., Asherian, A., Biaggio, A., Blanco-Villasenor, A., Bruchon-Schweitzer, M., et al. (1990). International preferences in selecting mates: A study of 37 cultures. *Journal of Cross-Cultural Psychology*, 21, 5–47. [16]

Bussey, K., & Bandura, A. (1984). Incidence of gender constancy and social power on sex-linked modeling. *Journal of Personality and Social Psychology*, 47, 1292–1302. [12]

Butcher, J. N., Dahlstrom, W. G., Graham, J. R., Tellegen, A., & Kaemmer, B. (1989). *Manual for the restandardized Minnesota Multiphasic Personality Inventory: MMPI-2. An administrative and interpretive guide*. Minneapolis: University of Minnesota Press. [12]

Butcher, J. N., & Hostetler, K. (1990). Abbreviating MMPI item administration: What can be learned from the MMPI for the MMPI-2? *Psychological Assessment: A Journal of Consulting and Clinical Psychology*, 2, 12–21. [12]

Butler, R., & Lewis, M. (1982). *Aging and mental health* (3rd ed.). St. Louis: Mosby. [9]

Butler, R. N. (1968). The facade of chronological age: An interpretive summary. In B. L. Neugarten (Ed.), *Middle age and aging* (pp. 235–242). Chicago: University of Chicago Press. [9]

Buysse, D. J., Reynolds, C. F., III, Monk, T. H., Hoch, C. C., Yeager, A. L., & Kupfer, D. J. (1991). Quantification of subjective sleep quality in healthy elderly men and women using the Pittsburgh Sleep Quality Index (SPQI). *Sleep*, 14, 331–338. [4]

Byrne, D., Clore, G. L., & Smeaton, G. (1986). The attraction hypothesis: Do similar attitudes affect anything? *Journal of Personality and Social Psychology*, 51, 1167–1170. [16]

Byrne, D., & Nelson, D. (1965). Attraction as a linear function of proportion of positive reinforcements. *Journal of Personality and Social Psychology*, 1, 659–663. [16]

Caldwell, B. M., Wright, C. M., Honig, A. S., & Tannenbaum, J. (1970). Infant day care and attachment. *American Journal of Orthopsychiatry*, 40, 397–412. [9]

Camp, D. S., Raymond, G. A., & Church, R. M. (1967). Temporal relationship between response and punishment. *Journal of Experimental Psychology*, 74, 114–123. [5]

Campbell, A. (1975, May). The American way of mating: Marriage si, children only maybe. *Psychology Today*, pp. 37–43. [9]

Campbell, A. (1976). Subjective measures of well-being. *American Psychologist*, 31, 117–124. [9]

Campbell, D. T., & Sprecht, J. C. (1985). Altruism: Biology, culture, and religion. *Journal of Social and Clinical Psychology*, 3, 33–42. [12]

Campbell, R., & Brody, E. M. (1985). Women's changing roles and help to the elderly: Attitudes of women in the United States and Japan. *The Gerontologist*, 25, 584–592. [9]

Campbell, S. S. (1985). Spontaneous termination of ad libitum sleep episodes with special reference to REM sleep. *Electroencephalography & Clinical Neurophysiology*, 60, 237–242. [4]

Campos, J. J., Langer, A., & Krowitz, A. (1970). Cardiac responses on the visual cliff in prelocomotor human infants. *Science*, 170, 196–197. [8]

Cannon, W. B. (1927). The James-Lange theory of emotions: A critical examination as an alternative theory. *American Journal of Psychology*, 39, 106–112. [10]

Cannon, W. B. (1932). *The wisdom of the body*. New York: Norton. [13]

Cannon, W. B., & Washburn, A. L. (1912). An explanation of hunger. *American Journal of Physiology*, 29, 441–454. [10]

Capaldi, E. J. (1978). Effects of schedule and delay of reinforcement on acquisition speed. *Animal Learning and Behavior*, 6, 330–334. [5]

Caplan, N., Choy, M. H., & Whitmore, J. K. (1992). Indochinese refugee families and academic achievement. *Scientific American*, 266, 36–42. [7, 8]

Carlsmith, J. M., & Anderson, C. A. (1979). Ambient temperature and the occurrence of collective violence: A new analysis. *Journal of Personality and Social Psychology*, 37, 337–344. [16]

Carlson, E. B., & Rosser-Hogan, R. (1991). Trauma experiences, posttraumatic stress, dissociation, and depression in Cambodian refugees. *American Journal of Psychiatry*, 148, 1548–1551. [13]

Carlson, M., Charlin, V., & Miller, N. (1988). Positive mood and helping behavior: A test of six hypotheses. *Journal of Personality and Social Psychology*, 55, 211–229. [16]

Carrier, J. (1980). Homosexual behavior in cross-cultural perspective. In J. Marmor (Ed.), *Homosexual behavior* (pp. 100–122). New York: Basic Books. [11]

Carskadon, M. A., & Dement, W. C. (1989). Normal human sleep: An overview. In M. H. Kryger, T. Roth, & W. C. Dement (Eds.), *Principles and practice of sleep medicine* (pp. 3–13). Philadelphia: W. B. Saunders. [4]

Carskadon, M. A., & Rechtschaffen, A. (1989). Monitoring and staging human sleep. In M. H. Kryger, T. Roth, & W. C. Dement (Eds.), *Principles and practice of sleep medicine* (pp. 665–683). Philadelphia: W. B. Saunders. [4]

Carson, R. C. (1989). Personality. *Annual Review of Psychology*, 40, 227–248. [12]

Case, R. (1985). *Intellectual development: Birth to adulthood*. Orlando, FL: Academic Press. [8]

Case, R. B., Heller, S. S., Case, N. B., Moss, A. J., & the Multicenter Post-Infarction Research Group (1985). Type A behavior and survival after acute myocardial infarction. *New England Journal of Medicine*, 312, 737–741. [13]

Cash, T. F., & Derlega, V. J. (1978). The matching hypothesis: Physical attractiveness among same-sexed friends. *Personality and Social Psychology Bulletin*, 4, 240–243. [16]

Cash, T. F., & Janda, L. H. (1984, December). The eye of the beholder. *Psychology Today*, pp. 46–52. [16]

Catlin, F. I. (1986). Noise-induced hearing loss. *American Journal of Otology*, 7, 141–149. [3]

Cattell, R. B. (1950). *Personality: A systematic, theoretical, and factual study*. New York: McGraw-Hill. [12]

Cattell, R. B., Eber, H. W., & Tatsuoka, M. M. (1977). *Handbook for the 16 personality factor questionnaire*. Champaign, IL: Institute of Personality and Ability Testing. [12]

Cattell, R. B., Saunders, D. R., & Stice, G. F. (1950). *The 16 personality factor questionnaire*. Champaign, IL: Institute of Personality and Ability Testing. [12]

Centers for Disease Control. (1989). *Surgeon General's report on smoking: Reducing health consequences of smoking: 25 years of progress, 1964–1989*. Washington, DC: Central Office for Health Promotion and Education on Smoking and Health, U. S. Government Printing Office. [13]

Centers for Disease Control. (1990). Coronary heart disease attributable to sedentary lifestyle—Selected states, 1988. *Morbidity and Mortality Weekly Report*, 39, 541–544. [13]

Centers for Disease Control. (1991a). Premarital sexual experience among adolescent women—United States, 1970–1988. *Morbidity and Mortality Weekly Report*, 39, 929–932. [9]

Centers for Disease Control. (1991b). Primary and secondary syphilis—United States, 1981–1990. *Morbidity and Mortality Weekly Report*, 40 (No. 19), 314–323. [11]

Centers for Disease Control. (1991c). Tobacco use among high school students—United States, 1990. *Morbidity and Mortality Weekly Report*, 40, 617–619. [13]

Centers for Disease Control. (1992a). Infant mortality—United States, 1989. *Morbidity and Mortality Weekly Report*, 41(5), 81–85. [8, 13]

Centers for Disease Control. (1992b). The second 100,000 cases of acquired immunodeficiency syndrome—United States, June 1981–December 1991. *Morbidity and Mortality Weekly Report*, 41(2), 28–29. [11]

Centers for Disease Control. (1992c). Sexual behavior among high school students—United States, 1990. *Morbidity and Mortality Weekly Report*, 40(51, 52), 885–888. [9]

Chaika, E. (1985, August). Crazy talk. *Psychology Today*, pp. 30–35. [14]

Chaiken, S. (1979). Communicator physical attractiveness and persuasion. *Journal of Personality and Social Psychology*, 37, 1387–1397. [16]

Chambless, D. L., & Goldstein, A. J. (1979). Behavioral psychotherapy. In R. J. Corsini (Ed.), *Current psychotherapies* (2nd ed., pp. 230–272). Itasca, IL: F. E. Peacock. [15]

Chance, P. (1986, October). Life after head injury. *Psychology Today*, pp. 62–69. [2]

Charney, D. S., & Woods, S. W. (1989). Benzodiazepine treatment of panic disorder: A comparison of alprazolam and lorazepam. *Journal of Clinical Psychiatry*, 50, 418–423. [15]

Chase, M. H., & Morales, F. R. (1990). The atonia and myoclonia of active (REM) sleep. *Annual Review of Psychology*, 41, 557–584. [4]

Check, J. V. P. (1984). *The effects of violent and nonviolent pornography*. (Department of Supply and Services Contract No. 05SV 19200-3-0899). Ottawa, Ontario: Canadian Department of Justice. [11]

Checkley, H. (1941). *The mask of sanity*. St. Louis: Mosby. [14]

Chesno, F. A., & Killman, P. R. (1975). Effects of stimulation on sociopathic avoidance learning. *Journal of Abnormal Psychology, 84,* 144–150. [14]

Chodoff, P. (1987). More on multiple personality disorder. *American Journal of Psychiatry, 144,* 124. [14]

Chomsky, N. (1957). *Syntactic Structures.* The Hague: Mouton. [8]

Chomsky, N. (1968). *Language and mind.* New York: Harcourt, Brace & World. [8]

Chumlea, W. C. (1982). Physical growth in adolescence. In B. B. Wolman (Ed.), *Handbook of developmental psychology.* Englewood Cliffs, NJ: Prentice-Hall. [9]

Church, P. (1989a, September). Impotence, Part 1: Evaluation. *Harvard Medical School Health Letter, 14,* pp. 4–6. [11]

Church, P. (1989b, October). Impotence, Part 2: Treatment. *Harvard Medical School Health Letter, 14,* pp. 3–6. [11]

Church R. M. (1963). The varied effects of punishment on behavior. *Psychological Review, 70,* 369–402. [5]

Chyou, P. H., Nomura, A. M. Y., & Stemmermann, G. N. (1992). A prospective study of the attributable risk of cancer due to cigarette smoking. *American Journal of Public Health, 82,* 37–40. [13]

Cialdini, R. B., Cacioppo, J. T., Basset, R., & Miller, J. A. (1978). Low-ball procedure for producing compliance: Commitment then cost. *Journal of Personality and Social Psychology, 36,* 463–476. [16]

Cialdini, R. B., Vincent, J. E., Lewis, S. K., Catalan, J., Wheeler, D., & Darby, B. L. (1975). Reciprocal concessions procedure for inducing compliance: The door-in-the-fact technique. *Journal of Personality and Social Psychology, 31,* 206–215. [16]

Clark, D. B., & Agras, W. S. (1991). The assessment and treatment of performance anxiety in musicians. *American Journal of Psychiatry, 148,* 598–605. [15]

Clark, D. M. (1988). A cognitive model of panic attacks. In S. Rachman & J. D. Maser (Eds.), *Panic: Psychological perspectives* (pp. 71–89). Hillsdale, NJ: Erlbaum. [14]

Clark, D. M., & Beck, A. T. (1988). Cognitive approaches. In C. G. Last & M. Hersen (Eds.), *Handbook of anxiety disorders* (pp. 362–385). New York: Pergamon. [15]

Clark, D. M., & Teasdale, J. D. (1982). Diurnal variation in clinical depression and accessibility of memories of positive and negative experiences. *Journal of Abnormal Psychology, 91,* 87–95. [6]

Clark, R. A., & McClelland, D. C. (1956). A factor analytic integration of imaginative and performance measures of the need for achievement. *Journal of General Psychology, 55,* 73–83. [10]

Clark, R. D., III, & Word, L. E. (1972). Why don't bystanders help? Because of ambiguity? *Journal of Personality and Social Psychology, 24,* 392–400. [16]

Clarke-Stewart, K. A. (1989). Infant day care: Maligned or malignant? *American Psychologist, 44,* 266–273. [8]

Clarkson-Smith, L., & Hartley, A. A. (1990). Structural equation models of relationships between exercise and cognitive abilities. *Psychology and Aging, 5,* 437–446. [9]

Clausen, J. (1975). The social meaning of differential physical and sexual maturation. In D. Dragastin & G. Elder (Eds.), *Adolescence in the life cycle* (pp. 25–47). Washington, DC: Hemisphere Press. [9]

Clayton, K. N. (1964). T-maze choice learning as a joint function of the reward magnitudes for the alternatives. *Journal of Comparative and Physiological Psychology, 58,* 333–338. [5]

Cloninger, C. R., Sigvardsson, S., Bohman, M., & von Knorring, A. L. (1982). Predispositions to petty criminality in Swedish adoptees, II. Cross-fostering analysis of gene-environment interaction. *Archives of General Psychiatry, 39,* 1242–1249. [16]

Coates, B., Pusser, H. E., & Goodman, I. (1976). The influence of "Sesame Street" and "Mister Rogers' Neighborhood" on children's social behavior in the preschool. *Child Development, 47,* 138–144. [5]

Cobb S. (1976). Social support as a moderator of life stress. *Psychosomatic Medicine, 38,* 300–314. [13]

Coe, W. C., & Sarbin, T. R. (1977). Hypnosis from the standpoint of a contextualist. *Annals of the New York Academy of Sciences, 296,* 2–13. [4]

Cohen, C. (1986). The case for the use of animals in biomedical research. *New England Journal of Medicine, 315,* 865–870. [1]

Cohen, D. (1979). *J. B. Watson: The founder of behaviourism.* London: Routledge & Kegan Paul. [5]

Cohen, J. B., & Chakravarti, D. (1990). Consumer psychology. *Annual Review of Psychology, 41,* 243–288. [17]

Cohen, S. (1988). Psychosocial models of the role of social support in the etiology of physical disease. *Health Psychology, 7,* 269–297. [13]

Cohen, S., Evans, G. W., Krantz, D. S., & Stokols, D. (1980). Physiological, motivational, and cognitive effects of aircraft noise on children. *American Psychologist, 35,* 231–243. [17]

Cohen, S., Evans, G. W., Stokols, D., & Krantz, D. S. (1986). *Behavior, health, and environmental stress.* New York: Plenum. [17]

Cohen, S., Glass, C. D., & Singer, J. E. (1973). Apartment noise, auditory discrimination, and reading ability in children. *Journal of Experimental Social Psychology, 9,* 407–422. [17]

Cohen, S., & Williamson, G. M. (1991). Stress and infectious disease in humans. *Psychological Bulletin, 109,* 5–54. [13]

Colasanto, D., & Shriver, J. (1989, May). Mirror of America: Middle-aged face marital crisis. *Gallup Report,* No. 284, 34–38. [9]

Colby, A., Kohlberg, L., Gibbs, J., & Lieberman, M. (1983). A longitudinal study of moral judgment. *Monographs of the Society for Research in Child Development, 48*(1–2, Serial No. 200). [9]

Cole, J. O., & Chiarello, R. J. (1990). The benzodiazepines as drugs of abuse. *Journal of Psychiatric Research, 24,* 135–144. [4]

Coleman, J. (1980). Friendship and the peer group in adolescence. In J. Adelson (Ed.), *Handbook of adolescent psychology.* New York: Wiley. [9]

Coleman, R. M. (1986). *Wide awake at 3:00 a.m.: By choice or chance?* New York: W. H. Freeman. [4]

Collins, R. L. (1970). The sound of one paw clapping: An inquiry into the origins of left handedness. In G. Lindzey & D. B. Thiessen (Eds.), *Contributions to behavior-genetic analysis—The mouse as prototype.* New York: Meredith Corporation. [2]

Compton, W. M., III, Helzer, J. E., Hwu, H. G., Yeh, E. K., McEvoy, L., Tipp, J. E., & Spitznagel, E. L. (1991). New methods in cross-cultural psychiatry: Psychiatric illness in Taiwan and the United States. *American Journal of Psychiatry, 148,* 1697–1704. [15]

Conard, S., Hughes, P., Baldwin, D. C., Achenbach, K. E., & Sheehan, D. V. (1989). Cocaine use by senior medical students. *American Journal of Psychiatry, 146,* 382–383. [4]

Conrad, A. J., Abebe, T., Austin, R., Forsythe, S., & Scheibel, A. B. (1991). Hippocampal pyramidal cell disarray in schizophrenia as a bilateral phenomenon. *Archives of General Psychiatry, 48,* 413–417. [14]

Conrad, R. (1964). Acoustic confusions in immediate memory. *British Journal of Psychology, 55,* 75–84. [6]

Constanzo, P. R., & Schiffman, S. S. (1989). Thinness—not obesity—has a genetic component. *Neuroscience and Biobehavioral Reviews, 13,* 55–58. [13]

Cook, M., Mineka, S., Wolkenstein, B., & Laitsch, K. (1985). Observational conditioning of snake fear in unrelated rhesus monkeys. *Journal of Abnormal Psychology, 94,* 591–610. [5]

Cook, S. W. (1985). Experimenting on social issues: The case of school desegregation. *American Psychologist, 40,* 452–460. [17]

Cook, T. D., Appleton, H., Conner, R. F., Shaffer, A., Tamkin, G., & Weber, S. J. (1975). *Sesame Street revisited.* New York: Russell Sage. [8]

Coons, P. M., Bowman, E. S., & Milstein, V. (1988). Multiple personality disorder: A clinical investigation of 50 cases. *Journal of Nervous and Mental Disease, 176,* 519–527. [14]

Cooper, L. A., Shepard, R. N. (1984). Turning something over in the mind. *Scientific American, 251,* 106–114. [7]

Cooper, S. (1987). The fetal alcohol syndrome. *Journal of Child Psychology and Psychiatry, 28,* 223–227. [8]

Coopersmith, S. (1967). *The antecedents of self-esteem.* San Francisco: W. H. Freeman. [8]

Coopersmith, S. (1968). Studies in self-esteem. *Scientific American, 218,* 96–106. [8]

Corballis, M. C. (1989). Laterality and human evolution. *Psychological Review, 96,* 492–509. [2]

Coren, S. (1989). Left-handedness and accident-related injury risk. *American Journal of Public Health, 79,* 1–2. [2]

Coren, S., & Halpern, D. F. (1991). Left-handedness: A marker for decreased survival fitness. *Psychological Bulletin, 109,* 90–106. [2]

Coren, S., & Porac, C. (1977). Fifty centuries of right handedness: The historical record. *Science, 198,* 631–632. [2]

Coren, S., Porac, C., & Ward, L. M. (1979). *Sensation and perception.* New York: Academic Press. [3]

Corina, D. P., Vaid, J., & Bellugi, U. (1992). The linguistic basis of left hemisphere specialization. *Science, 255,* 1058–1060. [2]

Cornell, D., & Cornley, J. E. (1979). Aversive conditioning of campground coyotes in Joshua Tree National Monument. *Wildlife Society Bulletin, 7,* 129–131. [5]

Costa, P. T., Jr., & McCrae, R. R. (1986). Personality stability and its implications for clinical psychology. *Clinical Psychology Review, 6,* 407–423. [12]

Costa, P. T., Jr., & McCrae, R. R. (1988). Personality in adulthood: A six-year longitudinal study of self-reports and spouse ratings on the NEO Personality Inventory. *Journal of Personality and Social Psychology, 54,* 853–863. [12]

Cotman, C. W., & Lynch, G. S. (1989). The neurobiology of learning and memory. *Cognition, 33,* 201–241. [6]

Council on Ethical and Judicial Affairs, American Medical Association. (1991). Gender disparities in clinical decision making. *Journal of the American Medical Association, 266,* 559–562. [13]

Cousins, N. (1979). *Anatomy of an illness.* New York: Norton. [13]

Coutts, L. M. (1991). The organizational psychologist. In R. Gifford (Ed.), *Applied psychology: Variety and opportunity* (pp. 273–299). Boston: Allyn and Bacon. [17]

Cowan, N. (1988). Evolving conceptions of memory storage, selective attention, and their mutual constraints within the human information-processing system. *Psychological Bulletin, 104,* 163–191. [6]

Craik, F. I. M., & Lockhart, R. S. (1972). Levels of processing: A framework for memory research. *Journal of Verbal Learning and Verbal Behavior, 11,* 671–684. [6]

Craik, F. I. M., & Tulving, E. (1975). Depth of processing and the retention of words in episodic memory. *Journal of Experimental Psychology: General, 104,* 268–294. [6]

Craik, F. I. M., & Watkins, M. J. (1973). The role of rehearsal in short-term memory. *Journal of Verbal Learning and Verbal Behavior, 12,* 599–607. [6]

Crépault, C., Abraham, G., Porto, R., & Couture, M. (1977). Erotic imagery in women. In R. Gemme & C. C. Wheeler (Eds.), *Progress in sexology* (pp. 267–283). New York: Plenum Press. [11]

Crépault, C., & Couture, M. (1980). Men's erotic fantasies. *Archives of Sexual Behavior, 9,* 565–581. [11]

Crespi, L. P. (1942). Quantitative variation of incentive and performance in the white rat. *American Journal of Psychology, 55,* 467–517. [5]

Crick, F., & Mitchison, G. (1983). The function of dream sleep. *Nature, 304,* 408–416. [4]

Crimmins, E. M., & Ingegneri, D. G. (1990). Interaction and living arrangements of older parents and their children: Past trends, present determinants, future implications. *Research on Aging, 12,* 3–35. [9]

Crits-Christoph, P. (1992). The efficacy of brief dynamic psychotherapy: A meta-analysis. *American Journal of Psychiatry, 149,* 151–158. [15]

Cernoch, J. M., & Porter, R. H. (1985). Recognition of maternal axillary odors by infants. *Child Development, 56,* 1593–1598. [9]

Crook, T. H., III, & Larrabee, G. J. (1990). A self-rating scale for evaluating memory in everyday life. *Psychology and Aging, 5,* 48–57. [9]

Crosby, F., Bromley, S., & Saxe, L. (1980). Recent unobtrusive studies of black and white discrimination and prejudice: A literature review. *Psychological Bulletin, 87,* 546–563. [17]

Crouter, A. C., Perry-Jenkins, M., Huston, T. L., & McHale, S. M. (1987). Processes underlying father involvement in dual-earner and single-earner families. *Developmental Psychology, 23,* 431–440. [9]

Crowe, L. C., & George, W. H. (1989). Alcohol and human sexuality: Review and integration. *Psychological Bulletin, 105,* 374–386. [4]

Crowe, R. R. (1990). Panic disorder: Genetic considerations. *Journal of Psychiatric Research, 24*(Suppl. 2), 129–134. [14]

Cullari, S., & Mikus, R. (1990). Correlates of adolescent sexual behavior. *Psychological Reports, 66,* 1179–1184. [9]

Cunningham, M. R. (1979). Weather, mood, and helping behavior: Quasi experiments with the sunshine Samaritan. *Journal of Personality and Social Psychology, 37,* 1947–1956. [16]

Cunningham, M. R. (1988). Does happiness mean friendliness? Induced mood and heterosexual self-disclosure. *Personality and Social Psychology Bulletin, 14,* 283–297. [16]

Curtis, R. C., & Miller, K. (1986). Believing another likes or dislikes you: Behaviors making the beliefs come true. *Journal of Personality and Social Psychology, 51,* 284–290. [16]

Curtis, R. L. (1975). Adolescent orientations toward parents and peers: Variations by sex, age, and socioeconomic status. *Adolescence, 10,* 483–494. [9]

Cutler, B. L., Penrod, S. D., & Martens, T. K. (1987). Improving the reliability of eyewitness identification: Putting context into context. *Journal of Applied Psychology, 72,* 629–637. [6]

Czeisler, C. A., & Allan, J. S. (1988). Pathologies of the sleep-wake schedule. In R. L. Williams, I. Karacan, & C. A. Moore (Eds.), *Sleep disorders: Diagnosis and treatment* (pp. 109–129). New York: John Wiley. [4]

Czeisler, C. A., Kronauer, R. E., Allan, J. S., Duffy, J. F., Jewett, M. E., Brown, E. N., & Ronda, J. M. (1989). Bright light induction of strong (type O) resetting of the human circadian pacemaker. *Science, 244,* 1328–1333. [4]

Czeisler, C. A., Moore-Ede, M. C., & Coleman, R. M. (1982). Rotating shift work schedules that disrupt sleep are improved by applying circadian principles. *Science, 217,* 460–463. [4]

Dabbs, J. M., Jr., & Morris, R. (1990). Testosterone, social class, and antisocial behavior in a sample of 4,462 men. *Psychological Science, 1,* 209–211. [16]

Dahlstrom, W. G., & Welsh, G. S. (1960). *An MMPI handbook: A guide to use in clinical practice and research.* Minneapolis: University of Minnesota Press. [12]

Dale, N., & Kandel, E. R. (1990). Facilitatory and inhibitory transmitters modulate spontaneous transmitter release at cultured Aplysia sensorimotor synapses. *Journal of Physiology, 421,* 203–222. [6]

Daoussis, L., & McKelvie, S. (1986). Musical preference and the effects of music on a reading comprehension test for extraverts and introverts. *Perceptual and Motor Skills, 62,* 283–289. [17]

Darley, J. M., & Latané, B. (1968a). Bystander intervention in emergencies: Diffusion of responsibility. *Journal of Personality and Social Psychology, 8,* 377–383. [16]

Darley, J. M., & Latané, B. (1968b, December). When will people help in a crisis? *Psychology Today,* pp. 54–57, 70–71. [16]

Darwin, C. (1965). *The expression of emotion in man and animals.* Chicago: University of Chicago Press. (Original work published 1872). [10]

Dasen, P. R. (1972). Cross-cultural Piagetian research: A summary. *Journal of Cross-Cultural Psychology, 3,* 23–29. [9]

Dash, P. K., Hochner, B., & Kandel, E. R. (1990). Injection of the cAMP-responsive element into the nucleus of Aplysia sensory neurons blocks long-term facilitation. *Nature, 345,* 718–721. [6]

Dashiell, J. F. (1925). A quantitative demonstration of animal drive. *Journal of Comparative Psychology, 5,* 205–208. [10]

Davanloo, H. (Ed.). (1980). *Short-term dynamic psychotherapy.* New York: Jason Aronson. [15]

Davies, K. (1990). Genital herpes: An overview. *Journal of Obstetric, Gynecologic, and Neonatal Nursing, 19,* 400–406. [11]

Davis, K. L., Kahn, R. S., Ko, G., & Davidson, M. (1991). Dopamine in schizophrenia: A review and reconceptualization. *American Journal of Psychiatry, 148,* 1474–1486. [14]

Davis, P. J. (1987). Repression and the inaccessibility of affective memories. *Journal of Personality and Social Psychology, 53,* 585–593. [12]

Davis, P. J., & Schwartz, G. E. (1987). Repression and the inaccessibility of affective memories. *Journal of Personality and Social Psychology, 52,* 155–162. [12]

Dawson, D., & Campbell, S. S. (1991). Time exposure to bright light improves sleep and alertness during simulated night shifts. *Sleep, 14,* 511–516. [4]

Dayton, G. O., Jr., Jones, M. H., Aiu, R., Rossen, P. H., Steel, B., & Rose, M. (1964). Developmental study of coordinated eye movements in the human infant. I: Visual acuity in the newborn human: A study based on induced optokinetic nystagmus recorded by electro-oculography. *Archives of Opthalmology, 71,* 865–870. [8]

DeBuono, B. A., Zinner, S. H., Daamen, M., & McCormack, W. M. (1990). Sexual behavior of college women in 1975, 1986, and 1989. *New England Journal of Medicine, 322,* 821–825. [11]

DeCasper, A. J., & Spence, M. J. (1986). Prenatal maternal speech influences newborns' perception of speech sounds. *Infant Behavior and Development, 9,* 133–150. [8]

Deci, E. L. (1975). *Intrinsic motivation.* New York: Plenum. [5]

Deese, J. (1959). On the prediction of occurrence of particular verbal intrusions in immediate recall. *Journal of Experimental Psychology, 58,* 17–22. [6]

DeJong, W. (1979). An examination of self-perception mediation of the foot-in-the-door effect. *Journal of Personality and Social Psychology, 37,* 2221–2239. [16]

Dekker, J., & Everaerd, W. (1989). Psychological determinants of sexual arousal: A review. *Behaviour Research and Therapy, 27,* 353–364. [11]

Delgado, J. M. R. (1969). *Physical control of the mind: Toward a psychocivilized society.* New York: Harper & Row. [2]

Delgado, J. M. R., & Anand, B. K. (1953). Increased food intake induced by electrical stimulation of the lateral hypothalamus. *American Journal of Physiology, 172,* 162–168. [10]

DeLongis, A., Coyne, J. C., Dakof, G., Folkman, S., & Lazarus, R. S. (1982). Relationship of daily hassles, uplifts, and major life events to health status. *Health Psychology, 1,* 119–136. [13]

DeLongis, A., Folkman, S., & Lazarus, R. S. (1988). The impact of daily stress on health and mood: Psychological and social resources as mediators. *Journal of Personality and Social Psychology, 54,* 486–495. [13]

DeMaris, A., & Rao, K. V. (1992). Premarital cohabitation and subsequent marital stability in the United States: A reassessment. *Journal of Marriage and the Family, 54,* 178–190. [9]

Dembroski, T. M., MacDougall, J. M., Williams, R. B., Haney, T. I., & Blumenthal, J. A. (1985). Components of Type A, hostility, and anger in: Relationship to angiographic findings. *Psychosomatic Medicine, 47,* 219–233. [13]

Dement, W., & Kleitman, N. (1957). The relation of eye movements during sleep to dream activity: An objective method for the study of dreaming. *Journal of Experimental Psychology, 53,* 339–346. [4]

Dement, W. C. (1974). *Some must watch while some must sleep.* San Francisco: W. H. Freeman. [4]

Dement, W. C., & Carskadon, M. A. (1981). An essay on sleepiness. *Actualites en medecine experimentale* (pp. 47–71). Montpellier: Euromed. [4]

Dempster, F. N. (1988). The spacing effect: A case study in the failure to apply the results of psychological research. *American Psychologist, 43,* 627–634. [6]

Dennerstein, L., Burrows, G., Wood, C., & Hyman, G. (1980). Hormones and sexuality: Effect of estrogen and progestogen. *Obstetrics & Gynecology, 56,* 316–322. [11]

Dennis, W. (1968). Creative productivity between the ages of 20 and 80. In B. L. Neugarten (Ed.), *Middle age and aging* (pp. 106–114). Chicago: University of Chicago Press. [9]

Department of Health and Human Services. (1985). *Report of the Secretary's Task Force on Black and Minority Health: Vol. 1. Executive summary.* Washington, DC: U. S. Government Printing Office. [17]

Des Jarlais, D. C., & Friedman, S. R. (1989). AIDS and IV drug use. *Science, 245,* 578. [11]

Desmond, E. W. (1987, November 30). Out in the open: Changing attitudes and new research give fresh hope to alcoholics. *TIME,* pp. 80–90. [13]

DeStefano, L., & Colasanto, D. (1990). Unlike 1975, today most Americans think men have it better. *Gallup Poll Monthly,* No. 293, 25–36. [11]

Detke, M. J., Brandon, S. E., Weingarten, H. P., Rodin, J., & Wagner, A. R. (1989). Modulation of behavioral and insulin responses by contextual stimuli paired with food. *Physiology and Behavior, 45,* 845–851. [10]

Detterman, D. K., Thompson, L. A., & Plomin, R. (1990). Differences in heritability across groups differing in ability. *Behavioral Genetics, 20,* 369–384. [7]

Deuchar, N. (1984). AIDS in New York City with particular reference to the psycho-social aspects. *British Journal of Psychiatry, 145,* 612–619. [11]

Deutsch, J. A., & Deutsch, D. (1966). *Physiological psychology.* Homewood, IL: Dorsey. [6]

De Valois, R. L., & De Valois, K. K. (1975). Neural coding of color. In E. C.

Carterette & M. P. Friedman (Eds.), *Handbook of perception* (Vol. 5). New York: Academic. [3]

Devine, P. G. (1989a). Automatic and controlled processes in prejudice: The role of stereotypes and personal beliefs. In A. R. Pratkanis, S. J. Breckler, & A. G. Greenwald (Eds.), *Attitude structure and function* (pp. 181–212). Hillsdale, NJ: Erlbaum. [16]

Devine, P. G. (1989b). Stereotypes and prejudice: Their automatic and controlled components. *Journal of Personality and Social Psychology, 56,* 5–18. [17]

Devine, P. G., Monteith, M. J., Zuwerink, J. R., & Elliot, A. J. (1991). Prejudice with and without compunction. *Journal of Personality and Social Psychology, 60,* 817–830. [17]

De Vos, S. (1990). Extended family living among older people in six Latin American countries. *Journal of Gerontology: Social Sciences, 45,* S87–94. [9]

Diamond, M. C., Scheibel, A. B., Murphy, G. M., Jr., & Harvey, T. (1985). On the brain of a scientist: Albert Einstein. *Experimental Neurology, 88,* 198–204. [2]

Dietz, W. H. (1989). Obesity. *Journal of the American College of Nutrition,* 8(Suppl.), 139–219. [13]

Digman, J. M. (1990). Personality structure: Emergence of the five-factor model. *Annual Review of Psychology, 41,* 417–440. [12]

Digman, J. M., & Inouye, J. (1986). Further specification of the five robust factors of personality. *Journal of Personality and Social Psychology, 50,* 116–123. [12]

DiLalla, L. F., & Gottesman, I. I. (1991). Biological and genetic contributors to violence—Widom's untold tale. *Psychological Bulletin, 109,* 125–129. [16]

Dion, K., Berscheid, E., & Walster, E. (1972). What is beautiful is good. *Journal of Personality and Social Psychology, 24,* 285–290. [16]

Dion, K. K., & Berscheid, E. (1974). Physical attractiveness and peer perception among children. *Sociometry, 37,* 1–12. [8]

Dionne, V. E. (1988). How do you smell? Principle in question. *Trends in Neurosciences, 11,* 188–189. [3]

Dipboye, R. L., Fromkin, H. L., & Wilback, K. (1975). Relative importance of applicant sex, attractiveness, and scholastic standing in evaluation of job applicant resumes. *Journal of Applied Psychology, 60,* 39–43. [16]

Dobb, E. (1989, November/December). The scents around us. *The Sciences, 29,* 46–53. [3]

Dobbin, M. (1987, October 12). Loud noise from little headphones. *U.S. News & World Report,* pp. 77–78. [3]

Dobie, R. A. (1987, December). Noise-induced hearing loss: The family physician's role. *American Family Physician,* pp. 141–148. [3]

Dobson, K. S. (Ed.) (1988). *Handbook of cognitive-behavioral therapies.* New York: Guilford. [15]

Dobson, K. S. (1989). A meta-analysis of the efficacy of cognitive therapy for depression. *Journal of Consulting and Clinical Psychology, 57,* 414–419. [15]

Dodge, K. A. (1983). Behavioral antecedents of peer social status. *Child Development, 54,* 1386–1399. [8]

Dodge, K. A., Bates, J. E., & Pettit, G. S. (1990). Mechanisms in the cycle of violence. *Science, 250,* 1678–1683. [16]

Dodge, K. A., Cole, J. D., Pettit, G. S., & Price, J. M. (1990). Peer status and aggression in boys' groups: Developmental and contextual analyses. *Child Development, 61,* 1289–1309. [8]

Dodge, K. A., Price, J. M., Bachorowski, J. A., & Newman, J. P. (1990). Hostile attributional biases in severely aggressive adolescents. *Journal of Abnormal Psychology, 99,* 385–392. [16]

Dollard, J., Doob, L. W., Miller, N., Mowrer, O. H., & Sears, R. R. (1939). *Frustration and aggression.* New Haven: Yale University Press. [16]

Domino, G. (1984). California Psychological Inventory. In D. J. Keyser & R. C. Sweetland (Eds.), *Test Critiques* (Vol. 1, pp. 146–157). Kansas City: Test Corporation of America. [12]

Donnerstein, E., & Linz, D. (1984, January). Sexual violence in the media: A warning. *Psychology Today,* pp. 14–15. [11]

Doob, L. W., & Sears, R. R. (1939). Factors determining substitute behavior and the overt expression of aggression. *Journal of Abnormal and Social Psychology, 34,* 293–313. [16]

Dornbusch, S. M., Ritter, P. L., Leiderman, P. H., Roberts, D. F., & Fraleigh, M. J. (1987). The relation of parenting style to adolescent school performance. *Child Development, 58,* 1244–1257. [8]

Douvan, E., & Adelson, J. (1966). *The adolescent experience.* New York: Wiley. [9]

Dovidio, J. F. (1984). Helping behavior and altruism: An empirical and conceptual overview. In L. Berkowitz (Ed.), *Advances in experimental social psychology* (Vol. 17, pp. 361–427). New York: Academic Press. [16]

Dow, M., Hart, D., & Forrest, C. (1983). Hormonal treatments of unresponsiveness in post-menopausal women: A comparative study. *British Journal of Obstetrics and Gynecology, 90,* 361–366. [11]

Doyle, J. A. (1985). *Sex and gender.* Dubuque, IA: Wm. C. Brown [11]

Dreikurs, R. (1953). *Fundamentals of Adlerian psychology.* Chicago: Alfred Adler Institute. [12]

Drob, S. L. (1989). The dilemma of contemporary psychiatry. *American Journal of Psychotherapy, 43,* 54–67. [15]

Duck, S. (1983). *Friends for life: The psychology of close relationships.* New York: St. Martin's Press. [9]

Duclos, S. E., Laird, J. D., Schneider, E., Sexter, M., Stern, L., & Van Lighten, O. (1989). Emotion-specific effects of facial expressions and postures of emotional experience. *Journal of Personality and Social Psychology, 37,* 100–108. [10]

Duggan, J. P., & Booth, D. A. (1986). Obesity, overeating, and rapid gastric emptying in rats with ventromedial hypothalamic lesions. *Science, 231,* 609–611. [10]

Durkin, J. (1991). The sport psychologist. In R. Gifford (Ed.), *Applied psychology: Variety and opportunity* (pp. 147–170). Boston: Allyn and Bacon. [7]

Duyme, M. (1988). School success and social class: An adoption study. *Developmental Psychology, 24,* 203–209. [7]

Dywan, J., & Bowers, K. (1983). The use of hypnosis to enhance recall. *Science, 222,* 184–185. [4, 6]

Eagly, A. H. (1987). *Sex differences in social behavior: A social-role interpretation.* Hillsdale, NJ: Erlbaum. [16]

Eagly, A. H., Ashmore, R. D., Makhijani, M. G., & Longo, L. C. (1991). What is beautiful is good . . .: A meta-analytic review of research on the physical attractiveness stereotype. *Psychological Bulletin, 110,* 109–128. [16]

Eagly, A. H., & Carli, L. (1981). Sex of researchers and sex-typed communications as determinants of sex differences in influence-ability: A meta-analysis of social influence studies. *Psychological Bulletin, 90,* 1–20. [16]

Ebata, A. T. (1987). *A longitudinal study of psychological distress during early adolescence.* Unpublished doctoral dissertation, Pennsylvania State University. [9]

Ebbinghaus, H. E. (1964). *Memory: A contribution to experimental psychology* (H. A. Ruger & C. E. Bussenius, Trans.). New York: Dover. (Original work published 1885). [6]

Ebersole, P. (1979). The vital vehicle: The body. In I. M. Burnside, P. Ebersole, & H. E. Monea (Eds.), *Psychosocial caring throughout the life span.* New York: McGraw-Hill. [9]

Eccles, J. S., & Jacobs, J. E. (1986). Social forces shape math attitudes and performance. *Signs, 11,* 367–389. [11]

Edmond, S. (1990). When symptom becomes disease. *Harvard Health Letter, 16,* pp. 6–8. [3]

Efron, R. (1990). *The decline and fall of hemispheric specialization.* Hillsdale, NJ: Erlbaum. [2]

Ehrenberg, O., & Ehrenberg, M. (1986). *The psychotherapy maze: A consumer's guide to getting in and out of therapy* (rev. ed.). New York: Simon & Schuster. [15]

Ehrhardt, A. A., Evers, K., & Money, J. (1968). Influence of androgen and some aspects of sexual dimorphic behavior in women with the late-treated adrenogenital syndrome. *Johns Hopkins Medical Journal, 123,* 115–122. [11]

Eibl-Eibesfeldt, I. (1973). The expressive behavior of the deaf-and-blind-born. In M. von Cranach & I. Vine (Eds.), *Social communication and movement.* New York: Academic Press. [10]

Eich, J. E. (1980). The cue dependent nature of state-dependent retrieval. *Memory and Cognition, 8,* 157–173. [6]

Eimas, P. D. (1985). The perception of speech in early infancy. *Scientific American, 252,* 46–52. [8]

Ekman, P. (1982). *Emotion and the human face* (2nd ed.). New York: Cambridge University Press. [10]

Ekman, P. (1985). *Telling lies: Clues to deceit in the marketplace, marriage, and politics.* New York: Norton. [16]

Ekman, P., & Friesen, W. V. (1971). Constants across cultures in the face and emotion. *Journal of Personality and Social Psychology, 17,* 124–129. [10]

Ekman, P., & Friesen, W. V. (1975). *Unmasking the face: A guide to recognizing emotions from facial clues.* Englewood Cliffs, NJ: Prentice-Hall. [10]

Ekman, P., Friesen, W. V., & Bear, J. (1984, May). The international language of gestures. *Psychology Today,* pp. 64–69. [16]

Ekman, P., Friesen, W. V., & O'Sullivan, M. (1988). Smiles when lying. *Journal of Personality and Social Psychology, 54,* 414–420. [16]

Ekman, P., Friesen, W. V., O'Sullivan, M., Chan, A., Diacoyanni-Tarlatzis, I., Heider, K., Krause, R., LeCompte, W. A., Pitcairn, T., Ricci-Bitti, P. E., Scherer, K., Tomita, M., & Tzavaras, A. (1987). Universals and cultural differences in the judgments of facial expressions of emotion. *Journal of Personality and Social Psychology, 53,* 712–717. [10]

Ekman, P., Levenson, R. W., & Friesen, W. V. (1983). Autonomic nervous system activity distinguishes among emotions. *Science, 221,* 1208–1210. [10]

El-Shiekh, M., Klacynski, P. A., & Valaik, M. E. (1989). Stress and coping across the life course. *Human Development, 32,* 113–117. [13]

Elkin, I., Shea, M. T., Watkins, J. T., et al. (1989). National Institute of Mental Health Treatment of Depression Collaborative Research Program: General effectiveness of treatments. *Archives of General Psychology, 46,* 971–982. [15]

Elkind, D. (1967). Egocentrism in adolescence. *Child Development, 38,* 1025–1034. [9]

Elkind, D. (1970, April 5). Erik Erikson's eight ages of man. *The New York Times Magazine,* pp. 25–27, 84–92, 110–119. [8, 9]

Elkind, D. (1974). *Children and adolescents: Interpretive essays on Jean Piaget* (2nd ed.). New York: Oxford University Press. [9]

Elkind, D. (1985). Piaget. In H. E. Fitzgerald & M. G. Walraven (Eds.), *Human Development 85/86* (pp. 6–12). Guilford, CT: Dushkin. [8]

Elkins, R. L. (1991). An appraisal of chemical aversion (emetic therapy) approaches to alcoholism treatment. *Behaviour Research and Therapy, 29,* 387–413. [15]

Ellis, A. (1961). *A guide to rational living*. Englewood Cliffs, NJ: Prentice-Hall. [15]

Ellis, A. (1977). The basic clinical theory of rational-emotive therapy. In A. Ellis & R. Grieger (Eds.), *Handbook of rational-emotive therapy* (pp. 3–33). New York: Springer. [15]

Ellis, A. (1979). Rational-emotive therapy. In R. J. Corsini (Ed.), *Current psychotherapies* (2nd ed., pp. 185–229). Itasca, IL: F. E. Peacock. [15]

Ellis, A. (1987). The impossibility of achieving consistently good mental health. *American Psychologist, 42,* 364–375. [15]

Ellis, B. J., & Symons, D. (1990). Sex differences in sexual fantasy: An evolutionary psychological approach. *Journal of Sex Research, 27,* 527–555. [11]

Ellis, H. D. (1984). Practical aspects of face memory. In G. L. Wells & E. F. Loftus (Eds.), *Eyewitness testimony: Psychological perspectives* (pp. 12–37). Cambridge: Cambridge University Press. [6]

Emmelkamp, P. M. G. (1988). Phobic disorders. In C. G. Last & M. Herson (Eds.), *Handbook of anxiety disorders* (pp. 66–86). New York: Pergamom Press. [14]

Empson, J. A. C., & Clarke, P. R. F. (1970). Rapid eye movements and remembering. *Nature, 227,* 287–288. [4]

Engel, G. L. (1977). The need for a new medical model: A challenge for biomedicine. *Science, 196,* 126–129. [13]

Engel, G. L. (1980). The clinical application of the biopsychosocial model. *American Journal of Psychiatry, 137,* 535–544. [13]

Enright, J. B. (1970). An introduction to Gestalt techniques. In J. Fagan & I. L. Shepherd (Eds.), *Gestalt therapy now: Theory, techniques, applications* (pp. 107–124). New York: Harper & Row. [15]

Epstein, J. (1983). Examining theories of adolescent friendships. In J. Epstein & N. Karweit (Eds.), *Friends in school.* New York: Academic Press. [9]

Epstein, L. H., Grunberg, N. E., Lichtenstein, E., & Evans, R. I. (1989). Smoking research: Basic research, intervention, prevention, and new trends. *Health Psychology, 8,* 705–721. [13]

Epstein, S., & O'Brien, E. J. (1985). The person-situation debate in historical and current perspective. *Psychological Bulletin, 98,* 513–537. [12]

Erber, J. T., Szuchman, L. T., & Rothberg, S. T. (1990). Age, gender, and individual differences in memory failure appraisal. *Psychology and Aging, 5,* 600–603. [9]

Erikson, E. H. (1963). *Childhood and society* (2nd ed.). New York: Norton. [8, 9]

Erikson, E. H. (1968). *Identity: Youth and crisis.* New York: Norton. [9]

Erikson, E. H. (1980). *Identity and the life cycle.* New York: Norton. [8, 9]

Erikson, E. H., Erikson, J. M., & Kivnick, H. Q. (1986). *Vital involvement in old age: The experience of old age in our time.* New York: W. W. Norton. [9]

Eron, L. D. (1980). Prescription for reducing aggression. *American Psychologist, 35,* 244–252. [16]

Eron, L. D. (1982). Parent-child interaction, television violence, and aggression of children. *American Psychologist, 37,* 197–211. [8]

Eron, L. D. (1987). The development of aggressive behavior from the perspective of a developing behaviorism. *American Psychologist, 42,* 435–442. [16]

Esses, V. M., & Wester, C. D. (1988). Physical attractiveness, dangerousness, and the Canadian criminal code. *Journal of Applied Social Psychology, 18,* 1017–1031. [17]

Evans, P. D. (1990). Type A behaviour and coronary heart disease: When will the jury return? *British Journal of Psychology, 81,* 147–157. [13]

Exner, J. E., Jr. (1974). *The Rorschach systems.* New York: Grune & Stratton. [12]

Exner, J. E., Jr. (1986). *The Rorschach: A comprehensive system* (Vol. 1, 2nd ed.). New York: Wiley-Interscience. [12]

Eysenck, H. J. (1970). *The structure of human personality* (3rd ed.). London: Methuen. [12]

Eysenck, H. J. (1975). *The inequality of man.* San Diego: Educational and Industrial Testing Service. [12]

Eysenck, H. J. (1987). Behavior therapy. In H. J. Eysenck & I. Martin (Eds.), *Theoretical foundations of behavior therapy.* New York: Plenum Press. [14]

Eysenck, H. J., & Eysenck, S. B. G. (1975). *Manual for the Eysenck Personality Questionnaire.* San Diego: Educational and Industrial Testing Service. [12]

Fadiman, A. (1986, November). Stephen La Berge: The doctor of dreams. *LIFE,* pp. 19–20. [4]

Fagot, B. I. (1982). Adults as socializing agents. In T. M. Field (Ed.), *Review of human development.* New York: Wiley. [11]

Fagot, B. I., Leinbach, M. D., & O'Boyle, C. (1992). Gender labeling, gender stereotyping, and parenting behaviors. *Developmental Psychology, 28,* 225–230. [11]

Fajardo, D. M. (1985). Author race, essay quality, and reverse discrimination. *Journal of Applied Social Psychology, 15,* 255–268. [17]

Falbo, T., & Polit, D. F. (1986). Quantitative review of the only child literature: Research evidence and theory development. *Psychological Bulletin, 100,* 176–189. [10]

Fallon, A. E., & Rozin, P. (1985). Sex differences in perceptions of desirable body shape. *Journal of Abnormal Psychology, 94,* 102–105. [9]

Falloon, I. R. H. (1988). Expressed emotion: Current status. *Psychological Medicine, 18,* 269–274. [15]

Fantz, R. L. (1961). The origin of form perception. *Scientific American, 204,* 66–72. [8]

Faravelli, C., & Pallanti, S. (1989). Recent life events and panic disorder. *American Journal of Psychiatry, 146,* 622–626. [14]

Faschingbauer, T. R. (1979). The future of the MMPI. In C. S. Newmark (Ed.), *MMPI: Clinical and research trends.* New York: Praeger. [12]

Faust, D., & Ziskin, J. (1988). The expert witness in psychology and psychiatry. *Science, 241,* 32–35. [17]

Faust, M. S. (1960). Developmental maturity as a determinant in prestige of adolescent girls. *Child Development, 31,* 173–184. [9]

Fausto-Sterling, A. (1985). *Myths of gender.* New York: Basic Books. [11]

Faw, H. W. (1990). Memory for names and faces: A fair comparison. *American Journal of Psychology, 103,* 317–326. [6]

Fawcett, J. C. (1992). Intrinsic neuronal determinants of regeneration. *Trends in Neurosciences, 15,* 5–8. [2]

Fay, R. E., Turner, C. F., Klassen, A. D., & Gagnon, J. H. (1989). Prevalence and patterns of same-gender sexual contact among men. *Science, 243,* 338–348. [11]

Fazio, R. H. (1989). On the power and functionality of attitudes: The role of attitude accessibility. In A. R. Pratkanis, S. J. Breckler, & A. G. Greenwald (Eds.), *Attitude structure and function* (pp. 153–179). Hillsdale, NJ: Erlbaum. [16]

Fazio, R. H., Sanbonmatsu, D. M., Powell, M. C., & Kardes, F. R. (1986). On the automatic activation of attitudes. *Journal of Personality and Social Psychology, 50,* 229–238. [16]

Fazio, R. H., & Williams (1986). Attitude accessibility as a moderator of the attitude perception and attitude-behavior relations: An investigation of the 1984 presidential election. *Journal of Personality and Social Psychology, 51,* 505–514. [16]

Feingold, A. (1988). Matching for attractiveness in romantic partners and same-sex friends: A meta-analysis and theoretical critique. *Psychological Bulletin, 104,* 226–235. [16]

Feingold, A. (1990). Gender differences in effects of physical attractiveness on romantic attraction: A comparison across five research paradigms. *Journal of Personality and Social Psychology, 59,* 981–993. [16]

Female victims: The crime goes on. (1984). *Science News, 126,* 153. [11]

Fenton, W. S., & McGlashan, T. H. (1991). Natural history of schizophrenia subtypes: I. Longitudinal study of paranoid, hebephrenic, and undifferentiated schizophrenia. *Archives of General Psychiatry, 48,* 969–977. [14]

Ferber, R. (1989). Sleepwalking, confusional arousals, and sleep terrors in the child. In M. H. Kryger, T. Roth, & W. C. Dement (Eds.), *Principles and practice of sleep medicine* (pp. 640–642). Philadelphia: W.B. Saunders. [4]

Festinger, L. (1957). *A theory of cognitive dissonance.* Evanston, IL: Row, Peterson. [16]

Festinger, L., & Carlsmith, J. M. (1959). Cognitive consequences of forced compliance. *Journal of Abnormal and Social Psychology, 58,* 203–210. [16]

Festinger, L., Schachter, S., & Back, K. (1950). *Social pressures in informal groups: A study of a housing community.* New York: Harper & Row. [16]

Fiatarone, M. A., Morley, J. E., Bloom, E. T., Benton, D., Makinodan, T., & Solomon, G. F. (1988). Endogenous opioids and the exercise-induced augmentation of natural killer cell activity. *Journal of Laboratory and Clinical Medicine, 112,* 544–552. [13]

Field, T. M., Cohen, D., Garcia, R., & Greenberg, R. (1984). Mother-stranger face discrimination by the newborn. *Infant Behavior and Development, 7,* 19–25. [8]

Finchilescu, G. (1988). Interracial contact in South Africa within the nursing context. *Journal of Applied Social Psychology, 18,* 1207–1221. [17]

Fink, M. (1979). *Convulsive therapy: Theory and practice.* New York: Raven. [15]

Finke, R. A. (1985). Theories relating mental imagery to perception. *Psychological Bulletin, 98,* 236–259. [7]

Finn, P. (1981, October). The effects of shift work on the lives of employees. *Monthly Labor Review, 104,* 31–35. [4]

Firestein, S. (1991). A noseful of odor receptors. *Trends in Neurosciences, 14,* 270–272. [3]

Fisher, S. (1973). *The female orgasm.* New York: Basic Books. [11]

Fishman, S. M., & Sheehan, D. V. (1985, April). Anxiety and panic: Their cause and treatment. *Psychology Today,* pp. 26–30, 32. [14]

Fiske, D. W. (1949). Consistency of the factorial structures of personality ratings from different sources. *Journal of Abnormal and Social Psychology, 44,* 329–344. [12]

Flaskerud, J. H., & Hu, L. (1992). Racial/ethnic identity and amount and type of psychiatric treatment. *American Journal of Psychiatry, 149,* 379–384. [15]

Flavell, J. H. (1985). *Cognitive development.* Englewood, NJ: Prentice-Hall. [8]

Flood, J. F., Silver, A. J., & Morley, J. E. (1990). Do peptide-induced changes in feeding occur because of changes in motivation to eat? *Peptides, 11,* 265–270. [10]

Fluoxetine Bulimia Nervosa Collaborative Study Group. (1992). Fluoxetine in the treatment of bulimia nervosa: A multicenter, placebo-controlled, double-blind trial. *Archives of General Psychiatry, 49,* 139–147. [9]

Flying and alcohol do not mix. (1990, March 19). *Newsweek,* p. 27. [4]

Foa, E. B., Steketee, G., Grayson, J. B., Turner, R. M., & Latimer, P. R. (1984). Deliberate exposure and blocking of obsessive compulsive rituals: Immediate and long-term effects. *Behavior Therapy, 15,* 450–472. [15]

Foa, E. B., & Tillmanns, A. (1980). The treatment of obsessive-compulsive neurosis. In A. Goldstein & E. B. Foa (Eds.), *Handbook of behavioral interventions: A clinical guide* (pp. 416–500). New York: Wiley. [15]

Fogelman, E., & Wiener, V. L. (1985, August). The few, the brave, the noble. *Psychology Today*, pp. 60–65. [16]

Folkard, S. (1990). Circadian performance rhythms: Some practical and theoretical implications. *Philosophical Transactions of the Royal Society of London. Series B: Biological Sciences*, 327, 543–553. [4]

Folkman, S. (1984). Personal control and stress and coping processes: A theoretical analysis. *Journal of Personality and Social Psychology*, 46, 839–852. [13]

Folkman, S., & Lazarus, R. S. (1980). An analysis of coping in a middle-aged community sample. *Journal of Health and Social Behavior*, 21, 219–239. [13]

Fondacaro, M. R., & Heller, K. (1990). Attributional style in aggressive adolescent boys. *Journal of Abnormal Child Psychology*, 18, 75–89. [16]

Ford, C. S., & Beach, F. A. (1951). *Patterns of sexual behavior*. New York: Harper & Row. [11]

Ford, M. E. (1979). The construct validity of egocentrism. *Psychological Bulletin*, 86, 1169–1188. [8]

Forgas, J. P., & Bower, G. H. (1987). Mood effects on person-perception judgments. *Journal of Personality and Social Psychology*, 53, 53–60. [16]

Fowler, R. C., Rich, C. L., & Young, D. (1986). San Diego suicide study: II. Substance abuse in young cases. *Archives of General Psychiatry*, 43, 962–965. [14]

Fox, N. A., & Bell, M. A. (1990). Electrophysiological indices of frontal lobe development: Relations to cognitive and affective behavior in human infants over the first year of life. *Annals of the New York Academy of Sciences*, 608, 677–698. [8]

Frank, E., Kupfer, D. J., Wagner, E. F., McEachran, A. B., Cornes, C. (1991). Efficacy of interpersonal psychotherapy as a maintenance treatment of recurrent depression: Contributing factors. *Archives of General Psychiatry*, 48, 1053–1059. [15]

Franzoi, S. L., & Herzog, M. E. (1987). Judging physical attractiveness: What body aspects do we use? *Personality and Social Psychology Bulletin*, 13, 19–33. [9]

Freedman, J. L. (1984). Effects of television violence on aggressiveness. *Psychological Bulletin*, 96, 227–246. [16]

Freedman, J. L., & Fraser, S. C. (1966). Compliance without pressure: The foot-in-the-door technique. *Journal of Personality and Social Psychology*, 4, 195–202. [16]

Freeman, W. J. (1991). The physiology of perception. *Scientific American*, 264, 78–85. [3]

Freese, A. S. (1977). *The miracle of vision*. New York: Harper & Row. [3]

Freese, A. S. (1980, February). Hypnosis: A weapon against super-medicine, surgery? *Science Digest*, pp. 20–24. [4]

French, E. G. (1955). Some characteristics of achievement motivation. *Journal of Experimental Psychology*, 50, 232–236. [10]

French, J. D. (1957). The reticular formation. *Scientific American*, 196, 54–60. [2]

Freud, A. (1958). *Adolescence: Psychoanalytic study of the child* (Vol. 13). New York: Academic Press. [9]

Freud, A. (1966). *The ego and the mechanisms of defense* (rev. ed.). New York: International Universities Press. [12]

Freud, S. (1922). *Beyond the pleasure principle*. London: International Psychoanalytic Press. [6]

Freud, S. (1953a). The interpretation of dreams. In J. Strachey (Ed. and Trans.), *The standard edition of the complete psychological works of Sigmund Freud* (Vols. 4 and 5). London: Hogarth Press. (Original work published 1900). [12]

Freud, S. (1953b). Three essays on the theory of sexuality. In J. Strachey (Ed. and Trans.), *The standard edition of the complete psychological works of Sigmund Freud* (Vol. 7). London: Hogarth Press. (Original work published 1905). [12]

Freud, S. (1960). Psychopathology of everyday life. In J. Strachey (Ed. and Trans.), *The standard edition of the complete psychological works of Sigmund Freud* (Vol. 6). London: Hogarth Press. (Original work published 1901). [12]

Freud, S. (1961). The ego and the id. In H. Strachey (Ed. and Trans.), *The standard edition of the complete psychological works of Sigmund Freud* (Vol. 19). London: Hogarth Press. (Original work published 1923). [12]

Freud, S. (1962). *Civilization and its discontents* (J. Strachey, Trans.). New York: W.W. Norton. (Original work published 1930). [12]

Freud, S. (1963a). *An autobiographical study* (J. Strachey, Trans.). New York: W.W. Norton. (Original work published 1925). [12]

Freud, S. (1963b). *A general introduction to psycho-analysis* (J. Riviere, Trans.). New York: Simon & Schuster. (Original work published 1920). [12]

Freud, S. (1965). *New introductory lectures on psychoanalysis* (J. Strachey, Trans.). New York: W. W. Norton. (Original work published 1933). [12]

Frey-Hewitt, B., Vranizan, K. M., Dreon, D. M., & Wood, P. D. (1990). The effect of weight loss by dieting or exercise on resting metabolic rate in overweight men. *International Journal of Obesity*, 14, 327–334. [13]

Friday, N. (1980). *Men in love*. New York: Delacorte. [11]

Friedberg, J. M. (1976). *Shock treatment is not good for your brain*. San Francisco: Glide. [15]

Friedberg, J. M. (1977). Shock treatment, brain damage, and memory loss: A neurological perspective. *American Journal of Psychiatry*, 134, 1010–1014. [15]

Friedman, M., & Rosenman, R. H. (1974). *Type A behavior and your heart*. New York: Fawcett. [13]

Frisk, M., Tenhunen, T., Widholm, O., & Hortling, H. (1966). Psychological problems in adolescents showing advanced or delayed physical maturation. *Adolescence*, 1, 126–140. [9]

Funder, D. C., & Colvin, C. R. (1991). Explorations in behavioral consistency: Properties of persons, situations, and behaviors. *Journal of Personality and Social Psychology*, 60, 773–794. [12]

Furstenberg, F. F., Jr., Brooks-Gunn, J., & Chase-Lansdale, L. (1989). Teenaged pregnancy and childbearing. *American Psychologist*, 44, 313–320. [9]

Gabrenya, W. K., Jr., Latane, B., & Wang, Y-E (1983). Social loafing in cross-cultural perspective. *Journal of Cross-Cultural Psychology*, 14, 368–384. [16]

Gackenbach, J., & Bosveld, J. (1989, October). Take control of your dreams. *Psychology Today*, pp. 27–32. [4]

Gaertner, S. L., & Dovidio, J. F. (1986). The aversive form of racism. In J. F. Dovidio & S. L. Gaertner (Eds.), *Prejudice, discrimination, and racism* (pp. 61–89). San Diego, CA: Academic Press. [17]

Gaertner, S. L., Mann, J. A., Dovidio, J. F., & Murrell, A. J. (1990). How does cooperation reduce intergroup bias? *Journal of Personality and Social Psychology*, 59, 692–704. [17]

Gaertner, S. L., Mann, J. A., Murrell, A., & Dovidio, J. F. (1989). Reducing intergroup bias: The benefits of recategorization. *Journal of Personality and Social Psychology*, 57, 239–249. [17]

Gagnon, J. H, & Simon, W. (1973). *Sexual conduct: The social origins of human sexuality*. Chicago: Aldine. [11]

Galanter, M. C. (1988). Research on social supports and mental illness. *American Journal of Psychiatry*, 145, 1270–1272. [15]

Gallup, G., Jr., & Hugick, L. (1990). Racial tolerance grows, progress on racial equality less evident. *Gallup Poll Monthly*, No. 297, 23–32. [17]

Gallup, G., Jr., & Newport, F. (1990a). Americans now drinking less alcohol. *Gallup Poll Monthly*, No. 303, 2–6. [4, 13]

Gallup, G., Jr., & Newport, F. (1990b). The battle of the bulge: Americans continue to fight it. *Gallup Poll Monthly*, No. 303, 23–34. [13]

Gallup, G., Jr., & Newport, F. (1990c). Belief in psychic and paranormal phenomena widespread among Americans. *Gallup Poll Monthly*, No. 299, 35–43. [3]

Gallup, G. H., Jr., & Newport, F. (1990d). Virtually all adults want children, but many of the reasons are intangible. *Gallup Poll Monthly*, No. 297, 8–22. [9]

Galton, F. (1874). *English men of science: Their nature and nurture*. London: Macmillan [7]

Galton, F. (1875). The history of twins as a criterion of the relative powers of nature and nurture. *Journal of the Royal Anthropological Institute*, 5, 391–406. [7]

Gannon, L., Luchetta, R., Rhodes, K., Paradie, L., & Segrist, D. (1992). Sex bias in psychological research: Progress or complacency? *American Psychologist*, 47, 389–396. [1]

Garcia, J., & Koelling, A. (1966). Relation of cue to consequence in avoidance learning. *Psychonomic Science*, 4, 123–124. [5]

Gardner, H. (1975). *The shattered mind: The person after brain damage*. New York: Knopf. [2]

Gardner, H. (1981, February). How the split brain gets a joke. *Psychology Today*, pp. 74–78. [2]

Gardner, H. (1983). *Frames of Mind: The theory of multiple intelligence*. New York: Basic Books. [7]

Gardner, L. I. (1972). Deprivation dwarfism. *Scientific American*, 227, 76–82. [8]

Garfield, S. L. (1981). Psychotherapy: A 40-year appraisal. *American Psychologist*, 36, 174–183. [15]

Garner, D. M., Garfinkel, P. E., Schwartz, D., & Thompson, M. (1980). Cultural expectations of thinness in women. *Psychological Reports*, 47, 483–491. [9]

Gates, A. I. (1917). Recitation as a factor in memorizing. *Archives of Psychology*, 40. [6]

Gatz, M., & Pearson, C. G. (1988). Ageism revised and the provision of psychological services. *American Psychologist*, 43, 184–188. [9]

Gawin, F. H. (1991). Cocaine addiction: Psychology and neurophysiology. *Science*, 251, 1580–1586. [4]

Gawin, F. H., & Ellinwood, E. H., Jr. (1988). Cocaine and other stimulants: Actions, abuse, and treatment. *New England Journal of Medicine*, 318, 1173–1182. [4]

Gazzaniga, M. S. (1967). The split brain in man. *Scientific American*, 217, 24–29. [2]

Gazzaniga, M. S. (1970). *The bisected brain*. New York: Appleton-Century-Crofts. [2]

Gazzaniga, M. S. (1983). Right hemisphere language following brain bisection: A 20-year perspective. *American Psychologist*, 38, 525–537. [2]

Gazzaniga, M. S. (1989). Organization of the human brain. *Science*, 245, 947–952. [2]

Geary, N. (1987). Cocaine: Animal research studies. In H.I. Spitz & J.S. Rosecan (Eds.), *Cocaine abuse: New directions in treatment and research* (pp. 19–47). New York: Brunner/Mazel. [4]

Geen, R. G. (1978). Some effects of observing violence upon the behavior of the observer. In B. A. Maher (Ed.), *Progress in experimental personality research* (Vol. 8). New York: Academic Press. [16]

Geen, R. G. (1984). Human motivation: New perspectives on old problems. In

A. M. Rogers & C. J. Scheier (Eds.), *The G. Stanley Hall lecture series* (Vol. 4). Washington, DC: American Psychological Association. [10]

Geiselman, R. E., Haight, N. A., & Kimata, L. G. (1984). Context effects on the perceived physical attractiveness of faces. *Journal of Experimental Social Psychology, 20,* 409–424. [16]

Gelder, M. G., Bancroft, J. H. J., Gath, D. H., Johnston, D. W., Matthews, A. M., & Shaw, P. M. (1973). Specific and nonspecific factors in behaviour therapy. *British Journal of Psychiatry, 123,* 445–462. [15]

Gelernter, C. S., Uhde, T. W., Cimbolic, P., Arnkoff, D. B., Vittone, B. J., Tancer, M. E., & Bartko, J. J. (1991). Cognitive-behavioral and pharmacological treatments of social phobia: A controlled study. *Archives of General Psychiatry, 48,* 938–945. [15]

Gelman, R., & Baillargeon, R. (1983). A review of Piagetian concepts. In J. H. Flavell & E. M. Markman (Eds.), *Handbook of child psychology: Cognitive development* (Vol. 3). New York: Wiley. [8]

Geschwind, N., & Behan, P. O. (1982). Left handedness: Association with immune disease, migraine, and developmental learning disorders. *Proceedings of the National Academy of Sciences, 79,* 5097–5100. [2]

Ghaziuddin, M., Ghaziuddin, N., & Stein, G. S. (1990). Life events and the recurrence of depression. *Canadian Journal of Psychiatry, 35,* 239–242. [14]

Gibbs, N. R. (1988, February 22). Grays on the go. *TIME,* pp. 66–75. [9]

Gibson, E., & Walk, R. D. (1960). The "visual cliff." *Scientific American, 202,* 64–71. [8]

Gifford, R. (1991). The environmental psychologist. In R. Gifford (Ed.), *Applied psychology: Variety and opportunity* (pp. 327–352). Boston: Allyn and Bacon. [17]

Gilbert, S. (1985, March). Noise pollution. *Science Digest,* p. 28. [3]

Giles, D. E., Jarrett, R. B., Biggs, M. M., Guzick, D. S., & Rush, A. J. (1989). Clinical predictors of recurrence in depression. *American Journal of Psychiatry, 146,* 764–767. [14]

Gilligan, C. (1982). *In a different voice: Psychological theory and women's development.* Cambridge, MA: Harvard University Press. [9]

Gillin, J. C. (1991). The long and the short of sleeping pills. *New England Journal of Medicine, 324,* 1735–1737. [4]

Glanzer, M., & Cunitz, A. R. (1966). Two storage mechanisms in free recall. *Journal of Verbal Learning and Verbal Behavior, 5,* 351–360. [6]

Glass, D. C., & Singer, J. E. (1972). *Urban stress: Experiments in noise and social stressors.* New York: Academic Press. [13]

Glassman, C. (1981, July). Sleep on it: Using dreams. *Science Digest,* pp. 64–65. [4]

Glenn, N. D., & McLanahan, S. (1982). Children and marital happiness: A further specification of the relationship. *Journal of Marriage and the Family, 44,* 72–73. [9]

Glickstein, M. (1988). The discovery of the visual cortex. *Scientific American, 259,* 118–127. [2]

Glover, J. A., & Corkill, A. J. (1987). Influence of paraphrased repetitions on the spacing effect. *Journal of Educational Psychology, 79,* 198–199. [6]

Godden, D. R., & Baddeley, A. D. (1975). Context-dependent memory in two natural environments: On land and underwater. *British Journal of Psychology, 66,* 325–331. [6]

Godden, D. R., & Baddeley, A. D. (1980). When does context influence recognition memory? *British Journal of Psychology, 71,* 99–104. [6]

Gold, M. S. (1986). *800-cocaine* (rev.). Toronto: Bantam. [4]

Goldberg, J. (1988). *Anatomy of a scientific discovery.* New York: Bantam. [3]

Goldberg, J., True, W. R., Eisen, S. A., & Henderson, W. G. (1990). A twin study of the effects of the Vietnam War on posttraumatic stress disorder. *Journal of the American Medical Association, 263,* 1227–1232. [13]

Goldberg, L. R. (1981). Language and individual differences: The search for universals in personality lexicons. In L. Wheeler (Ed.), *Review of personality and social psychology* (Vol. 2, pp. 141–165). Beverly Hills, CA: Sage. [12]

Goldberg, P. A. (1965). A review of sentence completion methods in personality. In B. I. Murstein (Ed.), *Handbook of projective techniques.* New York: Basic Books. [12]

Goldenberg, H. (1977). *Abnormal psychology: A social/community approach.* Monterey, CA: Brooks/Cole. [14]

Goldman, M. S. (1983). Cognitive impairment in chronic alcoholics: Some cause for optimism. *American Psychologist, 38,* 1045–1054. [13]

Goldsmith, H. H., Buss, A. H., Plomin, R., Rothbart, M. K., Thomas, A., Chess, S., Hinde, R. A., & McCall, R. B. (1987). Roundtable: What is temperament? Four approaches. *Child Development, 58,* 504–529. [8]

Goldstein, A., & Kalant, H. (1990). Drug policy: Striking the right balance. *Science, 249,* 1513–1521. [13]

Goldstein, A. G., Chance, J. E., & Schneller, G. R. (1989). Frequency of eyewitness identification in criminal cases: A survey of prosecutors. *Bulletin of the Psychonomic Society, 27,* 71–74. [6]

Goleman, D. (1979, November). Positive denial: The case for not facing reality. *Psychology Today,* pp. 13, 44–60. [13]

Goleman, D. (1991, September 17). Non-verbal cues are easy to misinterpret. *The New York Times,* pp. C1, C9. [16]

Goode, E. E. (1987, September 28). For a little peace of mine. *U.S. News & World Report,* pp. 98–102. [15]

Goodman, W. K., Price, L. H., Rasmussen, S. A., Delgado, P. L., Heninger, G. R., & Charney, D. S. (1989). Efficacy of fluvoxamine in obsessive-compulsive disorder: A double-blind comparison with placebo. *Archives of General Psychiatry, 46,* 36–44. [14, 15]

Goodwin, D. W. (1985). Alcoholism and genetics: The sins of the fathers. *Archives of General Psychiatry, 42,* 171–174. [13]

Goodwin, D. W. (1986). *Anxiety.* New York: Oxford University Press. [14, 15]

Gordon, N. P., Cleary, P. D., Parlan, C. E., & Czeisler, C. A. (1986). The prevalence and health impact of shiftwork. *American Journal of Public Health, 76,* 1225–1228. [4]

Gorman, C. (1988, March 21). An outbreak of sensationalism. *TIME,* pp. 58–59. [11]

Gorman, E. M. (1991). Anthropological reflections on the HIV epidemic among gay men. *Journal of Sex Research, 28,* 263–273. [11]

Gorman, J. M., Liebowitz, M. R., Fyer, A. J., & Stein, J. (1989). A Neuroanatomical hypothesis for panic disorder. *American Journal of Psychiatry, 146,* 148–161. [14]

Gormezano, I. (1984). The study of associative learning with CS-CR paradigms. In D. L. Alkon & J. Farley (Eds.), *Primary neural substrates of learning and behavioral change* (pp. 5–24). New York: Cambridge University Press. [5]

Gough, H. G. (1957). *Manual for the California Psychological Inventory.* Palo Alto, CA: Consulting Psychologists Press. [12]

Graeber, R. C. (1989). Jet lag and sleep disruption. In M. H. Kryger, T. Roth, & W. C. Dement (Eds.), *Principles and practice of sleep medicine* (pp. 324–331). Philadelphia: W.B. Saunders. [4]

Graham, S. (1992). "Most of the subjects were white and middle class": Trends in published research on African Americans in selected APA journals, 1970–1989. *American Psychologist, 47,* 629–639. [1]

Grant, B. F., Harford, T. C., Chou, P., Pickering, M. S., Dawson, D. A., Stinson, F. S., & Noble, J. (1991). Prevalence of DSM-III-R alcohol abuse and dependence: United States, 1988. *Alcohol Health & Research World, 15,* 91–96. [13]

Green, B. L., Lindy, J. D., Grace, M. C. (1985). Post-traumatic stress disorder: Toward DSM-IV. *Journal of Nervous and Mental Disorders, 173,* 406–411. [13]

Green, E., & Green, A. (1977). *Beyond biofeedback.* New York: Dell. [5]

Green, J., & Shellenberger, R. (1990). *The dynamics of health and wellness: A biopsychosocial approach.* Fort Worth: Holt, Rinehart & Winston. [3]

Green, R. (1985). Gender identity in childhood and later sexual orientation: Follow-up of 78 males. *American Journal of Psychiatry, 142,* 339. [11]

Green, R. (1987). *The "sissy boy syndrome" and the development of homosexuality.* New Haven: Yale University Press. [11]

Green, R., & Money, J. (1961). Effeminacy in pubertal boys. *Pediatrics, 27,* 236. [11]

Greenberg, J. (1977, July 30). The brain and emotions: Crossing a new frontier. *Science News, 112,* 74–75. [10]

Greenwald, A. G., Spangenberg, E. R., Pratkanis, A. R., & Eskenazi, J. (1991). Double-blind tests of subliminal self-help audiotapes. *Psychological Science, 2,* 119–122. [3]

Greer, W. R. (1986, November 23). Violence against homosexuals rising, groups seeking wider protection say. *The New York Times,* p. 36. [11]

Gregory, R. L. (1978). *Eye and brain: The psychology of seeing* (3rd ed.). New York: McGraw-Hill. [3]

Greist, J. H., & Jefferson, J. W. (1984). *Depression and its treatment.* Washington, DC: American Psychiatric Press. [14, 15]

Griffith, R. M., Miyago, O., & Tago, A. (1958). The universality of typical dreams: Japanese vs. Americans. *American Anthropologist, 60,* 1173–1179. [4]

Griffiths, P. D., Merry, J., Browning, M., Eisinger, A. J., Huntsman, R. G., Lord, E. J. A., Polani, P. E., Tanner, J. M., & Whitehouse, R. H. (1974). Homosexual women: An endocrine and psychological study. *Journal of Endocrinology, 63,* 549–556. [11]

Griffitt, W., Nelson, J., & Littlepage, G. (1972). Old age and response to agreement-disagreement. *Journal of Gerontology, 27,* 269–274. [16]

Grimes, D. A., Blount, J. H., Patrick, J., & Washington, A. E. (1986). Antibiotic treatment of pelvic inflammatory disease: Trends among private physicians in the United States, 1966 through 1983. *Journal of the American Medical Association, 256,* 3223–3226. [11]

Grimm, R. J. (1976). Brain control in a democratic society. In W. L. Smith & A. Kling (Eds.), *Issues in brain/behavior control.* New York: Spectrum. [15]

Grinker, J. A. (1982). Physiological and behavioral basis for human obesity. In D. W. Pfaff (Ed.), *The physiological mechanisms of motivation.* New York: Springer-Verlag. [4]

Grinspoon, L., & Bakalar, J. (1990, January). What is phencyclidine? *Harvard Medical School Mental Health Letter, 6,* p. 8. [4]

Groninger, L. K., & Groninger, L. P. (1980). A comparison of recognition and savings as retrieval measures: A reexamination. *Bulletin of the Psychonomic Society, 15,* 263–266. [6]

Grossman, F. K., Eichler, L. S., & Winickoff, S. A. (1980). *Pregnancy, birth, and parenthood.* San Francisco: Jossey-Bass. [9]

Grossman, H. J. (Ed.). (1983). *Manual on terminology and classification in mental retardation.* Washington, DC: American Association on Mental Deficiency. [7]

Grossman, R. (1987, October 10). The changing face of psychiatry. *St. Louis Post-Dispatch,* pp. D1, 5. [15]

Guilford, J. P. (1967). *The nature of human intelligence.* New York: McGraw-Hill. [7]

Guilford, J. P. (1988). Some changes in the Structure-of-Intellect model. *Educational and Psychological Measurement, 48,* 1–4. [7]

Guilleminault, C. (1989). Narcolepsy syndrome. In M. H. Kryger, T. Roth, & W. C. Dement (Eds.), *Principles and practice of sleep medicine* (pp. 338–346). Philadelphia: W.B. Saunders. [4]

Gupta, D., & Vishwakarma, M. S. (1989). Toy weapons and firecrackers: A source of hearing loss. *Laryngoscope, 99,* 330–334. [3]

Gurin, J. (1989, June). Leaner, not lighter. *Psychology Today,* pp. 32–36. [13]

Gustavson, C. R., Garcia, J., Hankins, W. G., Rusiniak, K. W. (1974). Coyote predation control by aversive conditioning. *Science, 184,* 581–583. [5]

Haaga, D. A. F., Dyck, M. J., & Ernst, D. (1991). Empirical status of cognitive theory of depression. *Psychological Bulletin, 110,* 215–236. [14]

Haber, R. N. (1980). How we perceive depth from flat pictures. *American Scientist, 68,* 370–380. [3]

Haber, R. N. (1980, November). Eidetic images are not just imaginary. *Psychology Today,* pp. 72–82. [6]

Hahn, W. K. (1987). Cerebral lateralization of function: From infancy through childhood. *Psychological Bulletin, 101,* 376–392. [2]

Hales, D. (1981). *The complete book of sleep: How your nights affect your days.* Reading, MA: Addison-Wesley. [4]

Halford, G. S. (1989). Reflections on 25 years of Piagetian cognitive developmental psychology, 1963–1988. *Human Development, 32,* 325–327. [8]

Hall, C. S., & Van de Castle, R. L. (1966). *The content analysis of dreams.* New York: Appleton-Century-Crofts. [4]

Hall, E. T. (1966). *The hidden dimension.* Garden City, NY: Doubleday. [17]

Hall, E. T. (1968). Proxemics. *Current Anthropology, 9,* 83–107. [17]

Hall, G. S. (1904). *Adolescence: Its psychology and its relations to physiology, anthropology, sex, crime, religion and education* (Vol. 1). New York: Appleton-Century-Crofts. [9]

Hall, R. G., Sachs, D. P., Hall, S. M., & Benowitz, N. L. (1984). Two-year efficacy and safety of rapid smoking therapy in patients with cardiac and pulmonary disease. *Journal of Consulting and Clinical Psychology, 52,* 574–581. [15]

Hall, R. L. (1958). Flavor study approaches at McCormick and Co., Inc. In A. D. Little (Ed.), *Flavor research and food acceptance.* New York: Reinhold. [3]

Hamburg, D. A., Nightingale, E. O., & Takanishi, R. (1987). Facilitating the transitions of adolescence. *Journal of the American Medical Association, 257,* 3405–3406. [9]

Hanna, G. (1988, February). *Mathematics and gender differences.* Paper presented at the annual meeting of the American Association for the Advancement of Science, Boston, MA. [11]

Hansel, C. E. M. (1966). *ESP: A scientific evaluation.* New York: Charles Scribner's Sons. [3]

Hansel, C. E. M. (1980). *ESP and parapsychology: A critical reevaluation.* Buffalo, NY: Prometheus. [3]

Hansen, W. B., Hahn, G. L., & Wolkenstein, B. H. (1990). Perceived personal immunity: Beliefs about susceptibility to AIDS. *Journal of Sex Research, 27,* 622–628. [11]

Hardman, M. L., Drew, C. J., Egan, M. W., & Wolf, B. (1990). *Human exceptionality: Society, school, and family* (3rd ed.). Boston: Allyn and Bacon. [3]

Hare, R. (1985). Comparison of procedures for the assessment of psychopathy. *Journal of Clinical Psychology, 53,* 7–16. [14]

Hare, R. D. (1970). *Psychopathy: Theory and research.* New York: Wiley. [14]

Harford, T. C., Parker, D. A., Grant, B. F., & Dawson, D. A. (1992). Alcohol use and dependence among employed men and women in the United States in 1988. *Alcoholism: Clinical and Experimental Research, 16,* 146–148. [13]

Harkins, S. G., & Jackson, J. M. (1985). The role of evaluation in eliminating social loafing. *Personality and Social Psychology Bulletin, 11,* 456–465. [16]

Harkins, S.G.,& Petty, R.E.(1982).Effects of task difficulty and task uniqueness on social loafing. *Journal of Personality and Social Psychology, 43,*1214–1229.[16]

Harkins, S. G., & Szymanski, K. (1989). Social loafing and group evaluation. *Journal of Personality and Social Psychology, 56,* 941–943. [16]

Harlow, H. F. (1950). Learning and satiation of response in intrinsically motivated complex puzzle performance by monkeys. *Journal of Comparative and Physiological Psychology, 43,* 289–294. [10]

Harlow, H. F. (1953). Motivation as a factor in the acquisition of new responses. In M. R. Jones (Ed.), *Nebraska symposium on motivation.* Lincoln: University of Nebraska Press. [10]

Harlow, H. F. (1959). Love in infant monkeys. *Scientific American,200,* 68–74.[8]

Harlow, H. F., & Harlow, M. K. (1962). Social deprivation in monkeys. *Scientific American, 207,* 137–146. [8]

Harlow, H. F., Harlow, M. K., & Meyer, D. R. (1950). Learning motivated by a manipulation drive. *Journal of Experimental Psychology, 40,* 228–234. [10]

Harlow, H. F., Harlow, M. K., and Suomi, S. J. (1971). From thought to therapy: Lessons from a primate laboratory. *American Scientist, 59,* 538–549. [8]

Harlow, J. M. (1848). Passage of an iron rod through the head. *Boston Medical and Surgical Journal, 39,* 389–393. [2]

Harper, R. A. (1975). *The new psychotherapies.* Englewood Cliffs, NJ: Prentice-Hall. [15]

Harper, T. (1983, October 3). 'Idiot savant' is artist with bright future. *St. Louis Post-Dispatch,* p. 3D. [7]

Harris, P. L., & Bassett, E. (1975). Transitive inference by four year old children. *Developmental Psychology, 11,* 875–876. [8]

Harrower, M. (1976, July). Were Hitler's henchmen mad? *Psychology Today,* pp. 76–80. [12]

Hartley, D., Roback, H. B., & Abramowitz, S. I. (1976). Deterioration effects in encounter groups. *American Psychologist, 31,* 247–255. [15]

Hartmann, E. (1981, April). The strangest sleep disorder. *Psychology Today,* pp. 15, 14–18. [4]

Hartmann, E. (1988). Insomnia: Diagnosis and treatment. In R. L. Williams, I. Karacan, & C. A. Moore (Eds.), *Sleep disorders: Diagnosis and treatment* (pp. 29–46). New York: John Wiley. [4]

Hartmann, E. L. (1973). *The functions of sleep.* New Haven: Yale University Press. [4]

Hatfield, E., & Sprecher, S. (1986). *Mirror, mirror . . . The importance of looks in everyday life.* Albany, NY: State University of New York Press. [16]

Hatfield, M. O. (1990). Stress and the American worker. *American Psychologist, 45,* 1162–1164. [17]

Hauri, P. (1982). *The sleep disorders* (2nd ed.). Kalamazoo, MI: Upjohn. [4]

Hauri, P. J., Hayes, B., Sateia, M., Hellekson, C., Percy, L., & Olmstead, E. (1982). Effectiveness of a sleep disorders center: A 9-month follow-up. *American Journal of Psychiatry, 139,* 663–666. [4]

Haynes, S. G., Feinleib, M., & Kannel, W. B. (1980). The relationship of psychosocial factors to coronary heart disease in the Framingham Study: III. Eight-year incidence of coronary heart disease. *American Journal of Epidemiology, 11,* 37–58. [13]

Heath, R. G. (1972). Marihuana: Effects on deep and surface electroencephalograms of man. *Archives of General Psychiatry, 26,* 577–584. [4]

Hefez, A., Metz, L., & Lavie, P. (1987). Long-term effects of extreme situational stress on sleep and dreaming. *American Journal of Psychiatry, 144,* 344–347. [4]

Heilman, K. M., Scholes, R., & Watson, R. T. (1975). Auditory affective agnosia: Disturbed comprehension of affective speech. *Journal of Neurology, Neurosurgery and Psychiatry, 38,* 69–72. [2]

Heilman, M. E., Simon, M. C., & Repper, D. P. (1987). Intentionally favored, unintentionally harmed? Impact of sex-based preferential selection on self-perception and self-evaluation. *Journal of Applied Psychology, 72,* 62–68. [17]

Heinrich, R. K., Corbine, J. L., & Thomas, K. R. (1990). Counseling Native Americans. *Journal of Counseling and Development, 69,* 128–133. [15]

Heller, W. (1990, May/June). Of one mind: Second thoughts about the brain's dual nature. *The Sciences, 30,* 38–44. [2]

Hellige, J. B. (1990). Hemispheric asymmetry. *Annual Review of Psychology, 41,* 55–80. [2]

Hembree, W. C., III, Nahas, G. G., Zeidenberg, P., & Huang, H. F. S. (1979). Changes in human spermatozoa associated with high dose marihuana smoking. In G. G. Nahas & W. D. M. Paton (Eds.), *Marihuana: Biological effects* (pp. 429–439). Oxford: Pergamon Press. [4]

Hendler, N. H., & Fenton, J. A. (1979). *Coping with pain.* New York: Clarkson N. Potter. [3]

Henley, N. M. (1973). Status and sex: Some touching observations. *Bulletin of the Psychonomic Society, 2,* 91–93. [16]

Henningfield, J. E., & Ator, N. A. (1986). *Barbiturates: Sleeping potion or intoxicant?* New York: Chelsea House. [4]

Hepper, P. G., Shahidullah, S., & White, R. (1990). Origins of fetal handedness. *Nature, 347,* 431. [2]

Hernandez, L., & Hoebel, B. G. (1989). Food intake and lateral hypothalamic self-stimulation covary after medial hypothalamic lesions or ventral midbrain 6-hydroxydopamine injections that cause obesity. *Behavioral Neuroscience, 103,* 412–422. [10]

Heron, R. M. (1991). The ergonomist. In R. Gifford (Ed.), *Applied psychology: Variety and opportunity* (pp. 301–325). Boston: Allyn and Bacon. [17]

Hershenson, M. (1989). *The moon illusion.* Hillsdale, NJ: Erlbaum. [3]

Herz, M. I., Glazer, W. M., Mostert, M. A., Sheard, M. A., Szymanski, H. V., Hafez, H., Mirza, M., & Vana, J. (1991). Intermittent vs maintenance medication in schizophrenia. *Archives of General Psychiatry, 48,* 333–339. [15]

Hess, E. H. (1961). Shadows and depth perception. *Scientific American, 204,* 138–148. [3]

Hess, E. H. (1965). Attitude and pupil size. *Scientific American, 212,* 46–54. [3]

Hetherington, A. W., & Ranson, S. W. (1940). Hypothalamic lesions and adiposity in the rat. *Anatomical Record, 78,* 149–172. [10]

Hetherington, E. M. (1966). Effects of paternal absence on sex-typed behaviors in Negro and white preadolescent males. *Journal of Personality and Social Psychology, 4,* 87–91. [11]

Hetherington, E. M. (1972). Effects of father absence on personality development in adolescent daughters. *Developmental Psychology, 7,* 313–326. [11]

Hetherington, E. M., Stanley-Hagan, M., & Anderson, E. R. (1989). Marital transitions: A child's perspective. *American Psychologist, 44,* 303–312. [9]

Higbee, K. L. (1969). Fifteen years of fear arousal: Research on threat appeals: 1953–1968. *Psychological Bulletin, 72,* 426–444. [16]

Higbee, K. L. (1977). *Your memory: How it works and how to improve it.* Englewood Cliffs, NJ: Prentice-Hall. [6]

Hilgard, E. R. (1975). Hypnosis. *Annual Review of Psychology, 26,* 19–44. [4]

Hill, J. P. (1980). *Understanding early adolescence: A framework*. Carrboro, NC: Center for Early Adolescence. [9]

Hingson, R., Alpert, J. J., Day, N., Dooling, E., Kayne, H., Morelock, S., Oppenheimer, E., & Zuckerman, B. (1982). Effects of maternal drinking and marijuana use on fetal growth and development. *Pediatrics, 70*, 539–546. [4]

Hobson, J. A. (1988). *The dreaming brain*. New York: Basic Books. [4]

Hobson, J. A. (1989). *Sleep*. New York: Scientific American Library. [4]

Hobson, J. A., & McCarley, R. W. (1977). The brain as a dream state generator: An activation-synthesis hypothesis of the dream process. *American Journal of Psychiatry, 134*, 1335–1348. [2, 4]

Hoebel, B. G., & Teitelbaum, P. (1961). Hypothalamic control of feeding and self-stimulation. *Science, 135*, 375–377. [10]

Hoebel, B. G., & Teitelbaum, P. (1966). Weight regulation in normal and hypothalamic hyperphagic rats. *Journal of Comparative and Physiological Psychology, 61*, 189–193. [10]

Hofer, P. J. (1991). The lawyer-psychologist. In R. Gifford (Ed.), *Applied psychology: Variety and opportunity* (pp. 245–270). Boston: Allyn and Bacon. [17]

Hoffman, L. (1974). Effects of maternal employment on the child—a review of the research. *Developmental Psychology, 10*, 204–228. [9]

Hoffman, L. (1979). Maternal employment. *American Psychologist, 34*, 859–865. [9]

Hoffman, L. W. (1989). Effects of maternal employment in the two-parent family. *American Psychologist, 44*, 283–292. [8]

Hoffman, S. W. (1974). Fear of success in males and females: 1965 and 1971. *Journal of Consulting and Clinical Psychology, 42*, 353–358. [10]

Hökfelt, T., Johnasson, O., & Goldstein, M. (1984). Chemical anatomy of the brain. *Science, 225*, 1326–1334. [2]

Holden, C. (1986a). Days may be numbered for polygraphs in the private sector. *Science, 232*, 705. [10]

Holden, C. (1986b). Depression research advances, treatment lags. *Science, 233*, 723–726. [14]

Holden, C. (1987). Doctors square off on employee drug testing. *Science, 238*, 744–745. [4]

Holden, C. (1991). New center to study therapies and ethnicity. *Science, 251*, 748. [15]

Holland, J. G., & Skinner, B. F. (1961). *The analysis of behavior*. New York: McGraw-Hill. [5]

Hollingworth, H. L., & Poffenberger, A. T., Jr. (1917). *The sense of taste*. New York: Moffat, Yard. [3]

Holloway, M. (1991). Rx for addiction. *Scientific American, 264*, 94–103. [4]

Holmes, T. H., & Rahe, R. H. (1967). The social readjustment rating scale. *Journal of Psychosomatic Research, 11*, 213–218. [13]

Hook, E. W., III, Cannon, R. O., Nahmias, A. J., Lee, F. F., Campbell, C. H., Jr., Glasser, D., & Quinn, T. C. (1992). Herpes simplex virus infection as a risk factor for human immunodeficiency virus infection in heterosexuals. *Journal of Infectious Diseases, 165*, 251–255. [11]

Hooley, J. M. (1988). Expressed emotion: A review of the critical literature. *Clinical Psychology Review, 18*, 269–274. [15]

Hopson, J. L. (1986, June). The unraveling of insomnia. *Psychology Today*, pp. 20, 42–49. [4]

Horn, J. (1982). The aging of human abilities. In B. B. Wolman (Ed.), *Handbook of developmental psychology*. Englewood Cliffs, NJ: Prentice-Hall. [9]

Horn, J., & Donaldson, G. (1980). Cognitive development in adulthood. In O. Brim & J. Kagan (Eds.), *Constancy and change in human development*. Cambridge, MA: Harvard University Press. [9]

Horn, J. C., & Meer, J. (1987, May). The vintage years. *Psychology Today*, pp. 76–90. [9]

Horne, J. (1992). Annotation: Sleep and its disorders in children. *Journal of Child Psychology and Psychiatry, 33*, 473–487. [4]

Horner, M. (1969, November). Fail: Bright women. *Psychology Today*, pp. 36–38, 62. [10]

Horney, K. (1937). *The neurotic personality of our time*. New York: W. W. Norton. [12]

Horney, K. (1939). *New ways in psychoanalysis*. New York: W. W. Norton. [12]

Horney, K. (1945). *Our inner conflicts*. New York: W. W. Norton. [12]

Horney, K. (1950). *Neurosis and human growth*. New York: W. W. Norton. [12]

Horney, K. (1967). *Feminine psychology*. New York: W. W. Norton. [12]

Hornung, D. E., & Enns, M. P. (1987). Odor-taste mixtures. *Annals of the New York Academy of Sciences, 510*, 86–90. [3]

Horowitz, F. D., & O'Brien, M. (1986). Gifted and talented children: State of knowledge and directions for research. *American Psychologist, 41*, 1147–1152. [7]

Hothersall, D. (1984). *History of psychology*. Philadelphia: Temple University Press. [7]

House, J. S., Landis, K. R., & Umberson, D. (1988). Social relationships and health. *Science, 241*, 540–544. [13]

Hovland, C. I., Lumsdaine, A. A., & Sheffield, F. D. (1949). *Experiments on mass communication*. Princeton, NJ: Princeton University Press. [16]

Howard, A., Pion, G. M., Gottfredson, G. D., Flattau, P. E., Oskamp, S., Pfafflin, S. M., Bray, D. W., & Burnstein, A. G. (1986). The changing face of American psychology: A report from the committee on employment and human resources. *American Psychologist, 41*, 1311–1327.

Howard, J. L. Liptzin, M. B., & Reifler, C. B. (1973). Is pornography a problem? *Journal of Social Issues, 29*, 133–145. [11]

Howard, K. I., Kopta, S. M., Krause, M. S., & Orlinsky, D. E. (1986). The dose-effect relationship in psychotherapy. *American Psychologist, 41*, 159–164. [15]

Hoy, E. A., Bill, J. M., & Sykes, D. H. (1988). Very low birthweight: A long-term developmental impairment? *International Journal of Behavioral Development, 11*, 37–67. [8]

Huang, Y-Y., Colino, A., Selig, D. K., & Malenka, R. C. (1992). The influence of prior synaptic activity on the induction of long-term potentiation. *Science, 255*, 730–733. [6]

Hubel, D. H. (1963). The visual cortex of the brain. *Scientific American, 209*, 54–62. [3]

Hubel, D. H. (1979). The brain. *Scientific American, 241*, 45–53. [2]

Hubel, D. H., & Wiesel, T. N. (1959). Receptive fields of single neurons in the cat's striate cortex. *Journal of Physiology, 148*, 547–591. [3]

Hubel, D. H., & Wiesel, T. N. (1979). Brain mechanisms of vision. *Scientific American, 241*, 130–144. [3]

Hudspeth, A. J. (1983). The hair cells of the inner ear. *Scientific American, 248*, 54–64. [3]

Huesmann, L. R., Eron, L. D., Lefkowitz, M. M., & Walder, L. O. (1984). The stability of aggression over time and generations. *Developmental Psychology, 20*, 1120–1134. [16]

Huff, C. R., Rattner, A., & Sagarin, E. (1986). Guilty until proved innocent: Wrongful conviction and public policy. *Crime and Delinquency, 32*, 518–544. [6]

Hughes, J. R., Oliveto, A. H., Helzer, J. E., Higgins, S. T., & Bickel, W. K. (1992). Should caffeine abuse, dependence, or withdrawal be added to DSM-IV and ICD-10? *American Journal of Psychiatry, 149*, 33–40. [4]

Hugick, L., & Leonard, J. (1991a). Despite increasing hostility, one in four Americans still smokes. *Gallup Poll Monthly*, No. 315, 2–10. [13]

Hugick, L., & Leonard, J. (1991b). Job dissatisfaction grows: "Moonlighting" on the rise. *Gallup Poll Monthly*, No. 312, 2–15. [9]

Hugick, L., & Leonard, J. (1991c). Sex in America. *Gallup Poll Monthly*, No. 313, 60–73. [9]

Hull, C. L. (1943). *Principles of behavior*. New York: Appleton-Century-Crofts. [10]

Hunt, M. M. (1982, September 12). Research through deception. *The New York Times Magazine*, pp. 66–67, 138, 140–143. [1]

Hurley, G. (1988, January). Getting help from helping. *Psychology Today*, pp. 62–67. [15]

Hurvich, L. M., & Jameson, D. (1957). An opponent-process theory of color vision. *Psychological Review, 64*, 384–404. [3]

Huston, A. C., Watkins, B. A., & Kunkel, D. (1989). Public policy and children's television. *American Psychologist, 44*, 424–433. [8]

Hutman, S. (1990, December). AIDS: The year in review. *AIDS Patient Care, 11–15*. [11]

Hyde, J. S., Fenema, E., & Lamon, S. J. (1990). Gender differences in mathematics performance: A meta-analysis. *Psychological Bulletin, 107*, 139–155. [11]

Hyde, J. S., & Linn, M. C. (1988). Gender differences in verbal ability: A meta-analysis. *Psychological Bulletin, 104*, 53–69. [11]

Indian Health Service. (1988). *Indian health service chart series book*. Washington, DC: U.S. Department of Health and Human Services. [13]

Inglehart, R. (1990). *Culture shift in advanced industrial society*. Princeton, NJ: Princeton University Press. [9]

Inhelder, B. (1966). Cognitive development and its contribution to the diagnosis of some phenomena of mental deficiency. *Merrill-Palmer Quarterly, 12*, 299–319. [8]

Innerviews. (1988, June/July). *Women's Sports & Fitness*, p. 64. [9]

International Labour Office. (1990). *Yearbook of labour statistics*. Geneva: Author. [17]

Intons-Peterson, M. J., & Fournier, J. (1986). External and internal memory aids: When and how often do we use them? *Journal of Experimental Psychology: General, 115*, 267–280. [6]

Irwin, M., Daniels, M., Bloom, E. T., Smith, T. L., & Weiner, H. (1987). Life events, depressive symptoms, and immune function. *American Journal of Psychiatry, 144*, 437–441. [13]

Isabella, R. A., Belsky, J., & von Eye, A. (1989). Origins of infant-mother attachment: An examination of interactional synchrony during the infant's first year. *Developmental Psychology, 25*, 12–21. [8]

Isay, R. A. (1989). *Being homosexual: Gay men and their development*. New York: Farrar, Straus, & Giroux. [11]

Isenberg, D. J. (1986). Group polarization: A critical review and meta-analysis. *Journal of Personality and Social Psychology, 50*, 1141–1151. [16]

Ivancevich, J. M., Matteson, M. T., Freedman, S. M., & Phillips, J. S. (1990). Worksite stress management interventions. *American Psychologist, 45*, 252–261. [17]

Iverson, L. L. (1979). The chemistry of the brain. *Scientific American, 241*, 134–147. [14]

Izard, C. E. (1971). *The face of emotion*. New York: Appleton-Century-Crofts. [10]

Izard, C. E. (1977). *Human emotions*. New York: Plenum Press. [10]

Izard, C. E. (1990). Facial expressions and the regulation of emotions. *Journal of Personality and Social Psychology, 58,* 487–498. [10]

Jacklin, C. N. (1989). Female and male: Issues of gender. *American Psychologist, 44,* 127–133. [11]

Jacobs, M. K., & Goodman, G. (1989). Psychology and self-help groups: Predictions on a partnership. *American Psychologist, 44,* 536–545. [15]

Jacobson, H. G. (1988). Magnetic resonance imaging of the central nervous system. *Journal of the American Medical Association, 259,* 1211–1222. [2]

James, J. E. (1985). Desensitization treatment of agoraphobia. *British Journal of Clinical Psychology, 24,* 133–134. [15]

James, W. (1884). What is an emotion? *Mind, 9,* 188–205. [10]

James, W. (1890). *The principles of psychology.* New York: Holt. [10]

James, W. (1961). *Psychology: The briefer course.* New York: Harper and Row. (Original work published 1892). [6]

Jamieson, D. W., & Zanna, M. P. (1989). Need for structure in attitude formation and expression. In A. R. Pratkanis, S. J. Breckler, & A. G. Greenwald (Eds.), *Attitude structure and function* (pp. 383–406). Hillsdale, NJ: Erlbaum. [16]

Janis, I. L. (1982). *Groupthink: Psychological studies of policy decisions and fiascoes* (2nd ed.). Boston: Houghton Mifflin. [16]

Janisse, M. P., & Peavler, W. S. (1974, February). Pupillary research today: Emotion in the eye. *Psychology Today,* pp. 60–63. [3]

Janowitz, H. D., & Grossman, M. I. (1950). Hunger and appetite: Some definitions and concepts. *Journal of the Mount Sinai Hospital, 16,* 231–240. [10]

Janowsky, J. S., Shimamura, A. P., & Squire, L. R. (1989). Source memory impairment in patients with frontal lobe lesions. *Neuropsychologia, 27,* 1043–1056. [6]

Jaroff, L. (1989, March 20). The gene hunt. *TIME,* pp. 62–67. [8]

Jarvik, M. E. (1990). The drug dilemma: Manipulating the demand. *Science, 250,* 387–392. [4]

Jaynes, J. (1976). *The origin of consciousness and the breakdown of the bicameral mind.* Boston: Houghton Mifflin. [2]

Jellinek, E. M. (1960). *The disease concept of alcoholism.* New Brunswick, NJ: Hillhouse Press. [13]

Jemmott, J. B., III., & Locke, S. E. (1984). Psychosocial factors, immunologic mediation, and human susceptibility to infectious diseases: How much do we know? *Psychological Bulletin, 95,* 78–108. [13]

Jenike, M. A. (1989). Obsessive-compulsive and related disorders: A hidden epidemic. *New England Journal of Medicine, 321,* 539–541. [14]

Jenike, M. A. (1990a). Approaches to the patient with treatment-refractory obsessive compulsive disorder. *Journal of Clinical Psychiatry, 51*(2, Suppl.), 15–21. [15]

Jenike, M. A. (1990b, April). Obsessive-compulsive disorder. *Harvard Medical School Health Letter, 15,* pp. 4–8. [15]

Jenike, M. A., Baer, L., Ballantine, H. T., Martuza, R. L., Tynes, S., Giriunas, I., Buttolph, L., & Cassem, N. H. (1991). Cingulotomy for refractory obsessive-compulsive disorder: A long-term follow-up of 33 patients. *Archives of General Psychiatry, 48,* 548–555. [15]

Jenike, M. A., Buttolph, L., Baer, L., et al. (1989). Fluoxetine in obsessive-compulsive disorder: A positive open trial. *American Journal of Psychiatry, 146,* 909–911. [15]

Jenkins, J. G., & Dallenbach, K. M. (1924). Oblivescence during sleep and waking. *American Journal of Psychology, 35,* 605–612. [6]

Jenkins, J. J., Jimenez-Pabon, E., Shaw, R. E., & Sefer, J. W. (1975). *Schuell's aphasia in adults: Diagnosis, prognosis, and treatment* (2nd ed.). Hagerstown, MD: Harper & Row. [2]

Jensen, A. R. (1969). How much can we boost IQ and scholastic achievement? *Harvard Educational Review, 39,* 1–123. [7]

Jensen, A. R. (1985). The nature of the black-white difference on various psychometric tests: Spearman's hypothesis. *Behavioral and Brain Sciences, 8,* 193–263. [7]

Jernigan, T. L., Butters, N., DiTraglia, G., Schafer, K., Smith, T., Irwin, M., Grant, I., Schuckit, M., & Cermak, L. S. (1991). Reduced cerebral grey matter observed in alcoholics using magnetic resonance imaging. *Alcoholism: Clinical and Experimental Research, 15,* 418–427. [13]

Jeste, P. V., & Lohr, J. B. (1989). Hippocampal pathologic findings in schizophrenia: A morphometric study. *Archives of General Psychiatry, 46,* 1019–1024. [14]

John, O. P. (1990). The big-five factor taxonomy: Dimensions of personality in the natural language and in questionnaires. In L. Pervin (Ed.), *Handbook of personality theory and research* (pp. 66–100). New York: Guilford. [12]

Johnson, D. L. (1989). Schizophrenia as a brain disease: Implications for psychologists and families. *American Psychologist, 44,* 553–555. [14]

Johnson, G. F. S., & Leeman, M. M. (1977). Analysis of familial factors in bipolar affective disorders. *Archives of General Psychiatry, 34,* 1074–1077. [14]

Johnson, J. H., & Sarason, I. G. (1979). Recent developments in research on life stress. In V. Hamilton & D. M. Warburton (Eds.), *Human stress and cognition: An information processing approach* (pp. 205–233). London: Wiley. [13]

Johnston, L. D., O'Malley, P. M., & Bachman, J. G. (1991). *Drug use among American high school seniors, college students and young adults, 1975–1990: Volume 1.* [DHHS Pub. No. (ADM) 91-1813]. Washington, DC: Government Printing Office. [4]

Jones, C. P., & Adamson, L. B. (1987). Language use in mother-child and mother-child-sibling interactions. *Child Development, 58,* 357–366. [8]

Jones, E. (1953). *The life and work of Sigmund Freud: The formative years and the great discoveries (1856–1900)* (Vol. 1). New York: Basic Books. [12]

Jones, E. E. (1976). How do people perceive the causes of behavior? *American Scientist, 64,* 300–305. [16]

Jones, E. E. (1986). Interpreting interpersonal behavior: The effects of expectancies. *Science, 234,* 41–46. [16]

Jones, E. E. (1990). *Interpersonal perception.* New York: Freeman. [16]

Jones, E. E., & Davis, K. E. (1965). A theory of correspondent inferences: From acts to dispositions. In L. Berkowitz (Ed.), *Advances in experimental social psychology* (Vol. 2, pp. 219–266). New York: Academic Press. [16]

Jones, E. E., & Nisbett, R. E. (1971). *The actor and the observer: Divergent perceptions of the causes of behavior.* New York: General Learning. [16]

Jones, E. W., Jr. (1986, May–June). Black managers: The dream deferred. *Harvard Business Review,* 84–93. [17]

Jones, H. B., & Jones, H. C. (1977). *Sensual drugs: Deprivation and rehabilitation of the mind.* Cambridge: Cambridge University Press. [4]

Jones, H. C., & Lovinger, P. W. (1985). *The marijuana question.* New York: Dodd, Mead. [4]

Jones, K. L., Smith, D. W., Streissguth, A. P., & Myrionthopoulos, N. (1974). Outcome in offspring of chronic alcoholic women. *Lancet, 2,* 1076–1078. [8]

Jones, M. C. (1924). A laboratory study of fear: The case of Peter. *Pedagogical Seminary, 31,* 308–315. [5]

Jones, M. C., & Bayley, N. (1950). Physical maturing among boys as related to behavior. *Journal of Educational Psychology, 41,* 129–148. [9]

Jones, M. C., & Mussen, P. H. (1958). Self-conceptions, motivations, and interpersonal attitudes of late- and early-maturing girls. *Child Development, 29,* 491–501. [9]

Jones, W. H., Chernovetz, M. E. O'C., & Hansson, R. O. (1978). The enigma of androgyny: Differential implications for males and females? *Journal of Consulting and Clinical Psychology, 46,* 298–313. [11]

Josephson, W. L. (1987). Television violence and children's aggression: Testing the priming, social script, and disinhibition predictions. *Journal of Personality and Social Psychology, 53,* 882–890. [16]

Joyce, P. R., & Paykel, E. S. (1989). Predictors of drug response in depression. *Archives of General Psychiatry, 46,* 89–99. [15]

Judd, C. M., Ryan, C. S., & Park, B. (1991). Accuracy in the judgment of in-group and out-group variability. *Journal of Personality and Social Psychology, 61,* 366–379. [17]

Jung, C. G. (1933). *Modern man in search of a soul.* New York: Harcourt Brace Jovanovich. [12]

Jung, C. G. (1953). *The psychology of the unconscious* (R. F. C. Hull, Trans.), *Collected works* (Vol. 7). Princeton, NJ: Princeton University Press. (Original work published 1917). [13]

Jung, C. G. (1961). *Memories, dreams, reflections* (R. Winston & C. Winston, Trans.). New York: Random House. [12]

Jung, C. G. (1966). *Two essays on analytical psychology* (R. F. C. Hull, Trans.). Princeton, NJ: Princeton University Press. [12]

Kagan, J., & Moss, A. K. (1962). *Birth to maturity.* New York: Wiley. [10]

Kahne, H. (1985). *Reconceiving part-time work: New perspectives for older workers and women.* Lanham, MD: Rowman & Allanheld. [17]

Kales, A., Kales, J. D., Soldatos, C. R., Caldwell, A. B., Charney, D. S., & Martin, E. D. (1980). Night terrors: Clinical characteristics and personality patterns. *Archives of General Psychiatry, 37,* 1413–1417. [4]

Kales, J., Tan, T. C., Swearingen, C., et al. (1971). Are over-the-counter sleep medications effective? All-night EEG studies. *Current Therapeutic Research, 13,* 143–151. [4]

Kalil, R. E. (1989). Synapse formation in the developing brain. *Scientific American, 261,* 76–85. [2]

Kalinowsky, L. B. (1986). History of convulsive therapy. *Annals of the New York Academy of Sciences, 462,* 1–4. [15]

Kalish, H. I. (1981). *From behavioral science to behavior modification.* New York: McGraw-Hill. [5, 15]

Kalven, H., & Zeisel, H. (1966). *The American jury.* Boston: Little, Brown. [17]

Kandel, E. R., Castellucci, V. F., Goelet, P., & Schacher, S. (1987). 1987 cell-biological interrelationships between short-term and long-term memory. *Research Publications—Association for Research in Nervous and Mental Disease, 65,* 111–132. [6]

Kanin, E. J., Jackson, E. C., & Levine, E. M. (1987). Personal sexual history and punitive judgments for rape. *Psychological Reports, 61,* 439–442. [11]

Kanner, A. D., Coyne, J. C., Schaefer, C., & Lazarus, R. S. (1981). Comparison of two modes of stress measurement: Daily hassles and uplifts versus major life events. *Journal of Behavioral Medicine, 4,* 1–39. [13]

Kanter, R. (1977). *Men and women of the corporation.* New York: Basic Books. [17]

Kaplan, H. S. (1974). *The new sex therapy: Active treatment of sexual dysfunction.* New York: Brunner/Mazel. [11]

Kaplan, H. S. (1990). The combined use of sex therapy and intrapenile injections in the treatment of impotence. *Journal of Sex and Marital Therapy, 16,* 195–207. [11]

Kaprio, J., Koskenvuo, M., & Rita, H. (1987). Mortality after bereavement: A prospective study of 95,647 widowed persons. *American Journal of Public Health, 77,* 283–287. [9]

Karacan, I. (1988). Parasomnias. In R. L. Williams, I. Karacan, & C. A. Moore (Eds.), *Sleep disorders: Diagnosis and treatment* (pp. 131–144). New York: John Wiley. [4]

Karacan, I., Salis, P. J., & Williams, R. L. (1978). The role of the sleep laboratory in diagnosis and treatment of impotence. In R. I. Williams & I. Karacan (Eds.), *Sleep disorders: Diagnosis and treatment* (pp. 353–382). New York: Wiley. [4]

Karasek, R. A., & Theorell, T. (1990). *Healthy work*. New York: Basic Books. [17]

Karasu, T. B. (1986). The psychotherapies: Benefits and limitations. *American Journal of Psychotherapy, 40*, 324–342. [15]

Karasu, T. B. (1990a). Toward a clinical model of psychotherapy for depression, I: Systematic comparison of three psychotherapies. *American Journal of Psychiatry, 147*, 133–147. [15]

Karasu, T. B. (1990b). Toward a clinical model of psychotherapy for depression, II: An integrative and selective treatment approach. *American Journal of Psychiatry, 147*, 269–278. [15]

Kasper, S., Wehr, T. A., Bartko, J. J., Gaist, P. A., & Rosenthal, N. E. (1989). Epidemiological findings of seasonal changes in mood and behavior: A telephone survey of Montgomery County, Maryland. *Archives of General Psychiatry, 46*, 823–833. [14]

Kassin, S. M., Ellsworth, P. C., & Smith, V. L. (1989). The "general acceptance" of psychological research on eyewitness testimony: A survey of the experts. *American Psychologists, 44*, 1089–1098. [17]

Kastenbaum, R., & Costa, P. T. (1977). Psychological perspectives on death. *Annual Review of Psychology, 28*, 225–249. [9]

Katzell, R. A., & Thompson, D. E. (1990). Work motivation: Theory and practice. *American Psychologist, 45*, 144–153. [17]

Kaufman, J., & Zigler, E. (1987). Do abused children become abusive parents? *American Journal of Orthopsychiatry, 57*, 186–192. [16]

Kearney, M. (1984). A comparison of motivation to avoid success in males and females. *Journal of Clinical Psychology, 40*, 1005–1007. [10]

Keesey, R. E. (1988). The body-weight set point. What can you tell your patients? *Postgraduate Medicine, 83*, 114–18, 121–122, 127. [13]

Keesey, R. E., & Powley, T. L. (1986). The regulation of body weight. *Annual Review of Psychology, 37*, 109–133. [13]

Keita, G. P., & Jones, J. M. (1990). Reducing adverse reaction to stress in the workplace: Psychology's expanding role. *American Psychologist, 45*, 1137–1141. [17]

Keitner, G. I., Ryan, C. E., Miller, I. W., & Norman, W. H. (1992). Recovery and major depression: Factors associated with twelve-month outcome. *American Journal of Psychiatry, 149*, 93–99. [14]

Keller, M. B. (1989). Current concepts in affective disorders. *Journal of Clinical Psychiatry, 50*, 157–162. [15]

Kelley, H. H. (1950). The warm-cold variable in first impressions of persons. *Journal of Personality, 18*, 431–439. [16]

Kelly, S. F., & Kelly, R. J. (1985). *Hypnosis: Understanding how it can work for you*. Reading, MA: Addison-Wesley. [4]

Kendler, K. S., & Gruenberg, A. M. (1984). An independent analysis of the Danish Adoption Study of Schizophrenia. *Archives of General Psychiatry, 41*, 555–564. [14]

Kendler, K. S., Gruenberg, A. M., & Tsuang, M. T. (1984). Outcome of schizophrenic subtypes defined by four diagnostic systems. *Archives of General Psychiatry, 41*, 149–154. [14]

Kendler, K. S., Neale, M. C., Kessler, R. C., Heath, A. C., & Eaves, L. J. (1992a). Generalized anxiety disorder in women. *Archives of General Psychiatry, 49*, 267–272. [14]

Kendler, K. S., Neale, M. C., Kessler, R. C., Heath, A. C., & Eaves, L. J. (1992b). The genetic epidemiology of phobias in women. *Archives of General Psychiatry, 49*, 273–281. [14]

Kendler, K. S., Neale, M. C., Kessler, R. C., Heath, A. C., & Eaves, L. J. (1992c). A population-based twin study of major depression in women: The impact of varying definitions of illness. *Archives of General Psychiatry, 49*, 257–266. [14]

Kendler, K. S., Spitzer, R. L., & Williams, J. B. W. (1989). Psychotic disorders in DSM-III-R. *American Journal of Psychiatry, 146*, 953–962. [14]

Kenrick, D. T., & Gutierres, S. E. (1980). Contrast effects and judgments of physical attractiveness: When beauty becomes a social problem. *Journal of Personality and Social Psychology, 38*, 131–140. [11]

Kerlinger, F. N. (1986). *Foundations of behavioral research* (5th ed.). New York: Holt, Rinehart & Winston. [1]

Kiecolt-Glaser, J. K., Fisher, L. D., Ogrocki, P., Stout, J., Speicher, C. E., & Glaser, R. (1987). Marital quality, marital disruption, and immune function. *Psychosomatic Medicine, 49*, 13–34. [13]

Kilstrom, J. F. (1985). Hypnosis. *Annual Review of Psychology, 26*, 557–591. [4]

Kim, J. J., & Fanselow, M. S. (1992). Modality-specific retrograde amnesia of fear. *Science, 256*, 675–677. [6]

Kingsbury, S. J. (1991). Why has the MMPI been revised? *Harvard Mental Health Letter, 7*, p. 8. [12]

Kinnaman, S. C. (1988). Taste transduction: A diversity of mechanisms. *Trends in Neurosciences, 11*, 491–496. [3]

Kinsella, G., Prior, M. R., & Murray, G. (1988). Singing ability after right and left sided brain damage. A research note. *Cortex, 24*, 165–169. [2]

Kinsey, A. C., Pomeroy, W. B., & Martin, C. E. (1948). *Sexual behavior in the human male*. Philadelphia: W. B. Saunders. [11]

Kinsey, A. C., Pomeroy, W. B., Martin, C. E. & Gebhard, P. H. (1953). *Sexual behavior in the human female*. Philadelphia: W. B. Saunders. [11]

Kite, M. E., Deaux, K., & Miele, M. (1991). Stereotypes of young and old: Does age outweigh gender? *Psychology and Aging, 6*, 19–27. [17]

Klatzky, R. L. (1980). *Human memory: Structures and processes* (2nd ed.). New York: W. H. Freeman. [6]

Klatzky, R. L. (1984). *Memory and awareness: An information-processing perspective*. New York: W. H. Freeman. [6]

Kleinmuntz, B., & Szucko, J. J. (1984a). A field study of the fallibility of polygraph lie detection. *Nature, 308*, 449–450. [10]

Kleinmuntz, B., & Szucko, J. J. (1984b). Lie detection in ancient and modern times: A call for contemporary scientific study. *American Psychologist, 39*, 766–776. [10]

Kleitman, N. (1960). Patterns of dreaming. *Scientific American, 203*, 82–88. [4]

Klerman, G. L., Weissman, M. M., Rounsaville, B. J., et al. (1984). *Interpersonal psychotherapy of depression*. New York: Basic Books. [15]

Klopfer, W. G., & Taulbee, E. S. (1976). Projective tests. *Annual Review of Psychology, 27*, 543–568. [12]

Klosko, J. S., Barlow, D. H., Tassinari, R., Cerny, J. A. (1990). A comparison of alprazolam and behavior therapy in treatment of panic disorder. *Journal of Consulting and Clinical Psychology, 58*, 77–84. [15]

Kluft, R. P. (1984). An introduction to multiple personality disorder. *Psychiatric Annals, 14*, 19–24. [14]

Kobasa, S. (1979). Stressful life events, personality, and health: An inquiry into hardiness. *Journal of Personality and Social Psychology, 37*, 1–11. [13]

Kobasa, S. C. Maddi, S. R., & Kahn, S. (1982). Hardiness and health: A prospective study. *Journal of Personality and Social Psychology, 42*, 168–177. [13]

Kohlberg, L. (1963). The development of children's orientation toward a moral order: Sequence in the development of moral thought. *Vita Humana, 6*, 11–33. [9]

Kohlberg, L. (1966). A cognitive-developmental analysis of children's sex-role concepts and attitudes. In E. E. Maccoby (Ed.), *The development of sex differences* (pp. 82–173). Stanford, CA: Stanford University Press. [11]

Kohlberg, L. (1968, September). The child as a moral philosopher. *Psychology Today*, pp. 24–30. [9]

Kohlberg, L. (1969). *Stages in the development of moral thought and action*. New York: Holt, Rinehart & Winston. [9]

Kohlberg, L. (1981). *Essays in moral development, Vol. 1. The philosophy of moral development*. New York: Harper & Row. [9]

Kohlberg, L. (1984). *Essays on moral development, Vol. 2. The psychology of moral development*. San Francisco: Harper & Row. [9]

Kohlberg, L. (1985). *The psychology of moral development*. San Francisco: Harper & Row. [9]

Kohlberg, L., & Gilligan, C. (1971). The adolescent as a philosopher: The discovery of the self in a postconventional world. *Daedalus, 100*, 1051–1086. [9]

Kohlberg, L., & Ullian, D. Z. (1974). In R. C. Friedman, R. M. Richart, & R. L. Vande Wiele (Eds.), *Sex differences in behavior* (pp. 209–222). New York: Wiley. [11]

Köhler, W. (1925). The *metality of apes* (E. Winter, Trans.). New York: Harcourt Brace Jovanovich. [5]

Kolodny, R. C., Masters, W. H., & Johnson, V. E. (1979). *Textbook of sexual medicine*. Boston: Little, Brown. [11]

Koltz, C. (1983, December). Scapegoating. *Psychology Today*, pp. 68–69. [16]

Koop, C. E. (1987). Report of the Surgeon General's workshop on pornography and public health. *American Psychologist, 42*, 944–945. [11]

Kopp, C. P., & Kaler, S. R. (1989). Risk in infancy: Origins and implications. *American Psychologist, 44*, 224–230. [8]

Koretz, J. F., & Handelman, G. H. (1988). How the human eye focuses. *Scientific American, 259*, 92–99. [9]

Korner, A. F., Zeanah, C. H., Linden, J., Berkowitz, R. I., Kraemer, H. C., & Agras, W. S. (1985). The relation between neonatal and later activity and temperament. *Child Development, 56*, 38–42. [8]

Koshland, D. E., Jr. (1989). Drunk driving and statistical mortality. *Science, 244*, 513. [13]

Koss, M., Gidycz, C. A., & Wisniewski, N. (1987). The scope of rape: Incidence and prevalence of sexual aggression and victimization in a national sample of higher education subjects. *Journal of Consulting and Clinical Psychology, 55*, 162–170. [11]

Kosslyn, S. M. (1975). Information representation in visual images. *Cognitive Psychology, 7*, 341–370. [7]

Kosslyn, S. M. (1981). The medium and the message in mental imagery: A theory. *Psychological Review, 88*, 46–65. [7]

Kosslyn, S. M. (1983). *Ghosts in the mind's machine: Creating and using images in the brain*. New York: Norton. [7]

Kosslyn, S. M. (1987). Seeing and imagining in the cerebral hemispheres: A computational approach. *Psychological Review, 94*, 148–175. [7]

Kosslyn, S. M. (1988). Aspects of a cognitive neuroscience of mental imagery. *Science, 240*, 1621–1626. [7]

Kotelchuck, M. (1976). The infant's relationship to the father: Experimental evidence. In M. E. Lamb (Ed.), *The role of the father in child development*. New York: Wiley. [8]

Kozak, M. J., Foa, E. B., & McCarthy, P. R. (1988). Obsessive-compulsive disorder. In C. G. Last & M. Herson (Eds.), *Handbook of anxiety disorders* (pp. 87–108). New York: Pergamon Press. [14]

Krajick, K. (1988, May). Private passions & public health. *Psychology Today*, pp. 50–58. [11]

Krantz, D. S., Grunberg, N. E., & Baum, A. (1985). Health psychology. *Annual Review of Psychology, 36*, 349–383. [13]

Krantz, M. (1987). Physical attractiveness and popularity: A predictive study. *Psychological Reports, 60*, 723–726. [8]

Krapfl, J. E. (1967). *Differential ordering of stimulus presentations and semi-automated versus live treatment in the systematic desensitization of snake phobia*. Unpublished doctoral dissertation, University of Missouri, Columbia, MO. [15]

Kroger, W. S., & Fezler, W. D. (1976). *Hypnosis and behavior modification: Imagery conditioning*. Philadelphia: J. B. Lippincott. [4]

Kroll, N. E. A., Ogawa, K. H., & Nieters, J. E. (1988). Eyewitness memory and the importance of sequential information. *Bulletin of the Psychonomic Society, 26*, 395–398. [6]

Krueger, W. C. F. (1929). The effect of overlearning on retention. *Journal of Experimental Psychology, 12*, 71–81. [6]

Kübler-Ross, Elisabeth (1969). *On death and dying*. New York: Macmillan. [9]

Kuch, K., & Cox, B. J. (1992). Symptoms of PTSD in 124 survivors of the Holocaust. *American Journal of Psychiatry, 149*, 337–340. [13]

Kuczaj, S. A., III (1978). Children's judgments of grammatical and ungrammatical irregular past-tense verbs. *Child Development, 49*, 319–326. [8]

Kuhn, D., Kohlberg, L., Langer, J., & Haan, N. (1977). The development of formal operations in logical and moral judgment. *Genetic Psychology Monographs, 95*, 97–188. [9]

Kukla, A. (1972). Foundations of an attributional theory of performance. *Psychological Review, 79*, 454–470. [10]

Kupersmidt, J. B., & Coie, J. D. (1990). Preadolescent peer status, aggression, and school adjustment as predictors of externalizing problems in adolescence. *Child Development, 61*, 1350–1362. [8]

Kupersmidt, J. B., Coie, J. D., & Dodge, K. A. (1990). Predicting disorder from peer social problems. In S. R. Asher & J. D. Coie (Eds.), *Peer rejection in childhood*. New York: Cambridge University Press. [8]

Kurdek, L. A., & Siesky, A. E. (1980). Sex-role self concepts of single divorced parents and their children. *Journal of Divorce, 3*, 249–261. [11]

Kushner, M. G., Sher, K. J., & Beitman, B. D. (1990). The relation between alcohol problems and the anxiety disorders. *American Journal of Psychiatry, 147*, 685–695. [14]

La Berge, S. P. (1981, January). Lucid dreaming: Directing the action as it happens. *Psychology Today*, pp. 48–57. [4]

Lalonde, R., & Botez, M. I. (1990). The cerebellum and learning processes in animals. *Brain Research Reviews, 15*, 325–332. [2]

Lamar, J. V., Jr. (1986, June 2). Crack: A cheap and deadly cocaine is a spreading menace. *TIME*, pp. 16–18. [4]

Lamb, M. E. (1979). Parental influences and the father's role: A personal perspective. *American Psychologist, 34*, 938–943. [8]

Lamb, M. E., & Roopnarine, J. L. (1979). Peer influences on sex-role development in preschoolers. *Child Development, 50*, 1219–1222. [11]

Lamm, H. (1988). A review of our research on group polarization: Eleven experiments on the effects of group discussion on risk acceptance, probability estimation, and negotiation positions. *Psychological Reports, 62*, 807–813. [16]

Landy, D., & Sigall, H. (1974). Beauty is talent: Task evaluation as a function of the performer's physical attractiveness. *Journal of Personality and Social Psychology, 29*, 299–304. [16]

Lang, A. R., Goeckner, D. J., Adesso, V. J., & Marlatt, G. A. (1975). Effects of alcohol on aggression in male social drinkers. *Journal of Abnormal Psychology, 84*, 508–518. [1]

Lang, J. S. (1987, April 13). Happiness is a reunited set of twins. *U.S. News & World Report*, pp. 63–66. [12]

Lange, C. G., & James, W. (1922). *The emotions* (I. A. Haupt, Trans.). Baltimore: Williams and Wilkins. [10]

Lange, R. A., Cigarroa, R. G., Yancy, C. W., Jr., Willard, J. E., Popma, J. J., Sills, M. N., McBride, W., Kim, A. S., & Hillis, L. D. (1989). Cocaine-induced coronary-artery vasoconstriction. *New England Journal of Medicine, 321*, 1557–1562. [4]

Langer, E. J., & Rodin, J. (1976). The effects of choice and enhanced personal responsibility for the aged: A field experiment in an institutional setting. *Journal of Personality and Social Psychology, 34*, 191–198. [13]

Langlois, J. H. (1985). From the eye of the beholder to behavioral reality: The development of social behaviors and social relations as a function of physical attractiveness. In C. P. Herman (Ed.), *Physical appearance, stigma, and social behavior*. Hillsdale, NJ: Erlbaum. [8]

Langlois, J. H., Ritter, J. M., Roggman, L. A., & Vaughn, L. S. (1991). Facial diversity and infant preferences for attractive faces. *Developmental Psychology, 27*, 79–84. [16]

Larson, J. H., & Bell, N. J. (1988). Need for privacy and its effect upon interpersonal attraction and interaction. *Journal of Social and Clinical Psychology, 6*, 1–10. [16]

Latane, B., Williams, K., & Harkins, S. (1979). Many hands make light the work: The causes and consequences of social loafing. *Journal of Personality and Social Psychology, 37*, 822–832. [16]

Latham, A., & Grenadier, A. (1982, October). The ordeal of Walter/Susan Cannon. *Psychology Today*, pp. 64–72. [11]

Lauber, J. K., & Kayten, P. J. (1988). Keynote address: Sleepiness, circadian dysrhythmia, and fatigue in transportation system accidents. *Sleep, 11*, 503–512. [4]

Lazarus, R. S. (1966). *Psychological stress and the coping process*. New York: McGraw-Hill. [13]

Lazarus, R. S., & DeLongis, A. (1983). Psychological stress and coping in aging. *American Psychologist, 38*, 245–253. [13]

Lazarus, R. S., & Folkman, S. (1984). *Stress, appraisal, and coping*. New York: Springer. [13]

Leier, V. O., Yesavage, J. A., & Morrow, D. G. (1991). Marijuana carry-over effects on aircraft pilot performance. *Aviation Space and Environmental Medicine, 62*, 221–227. [4]

Leigh, B. C. (1990). The relationship of substance use during sex to high-risk sexual behavior. *Journal of Sex Research, 27*, 199–213. [11]

Lenhardt, M. L., Skellett, R., Wang, P., & Clarke, A. M. (1991). Human ultra-sonic speech perception. *Science, 253*, 82–85. [3]

Lenister, C. (1988, January 18). Black executives: How they're doing. *Fortune*, pp. 109–120. [17]

Lenneberg, E. (1967). *Biological foundations of language*. New York: Wiley. [8]

Lepper, M. R., Greene, D., & Nisbett, R. E. (1973). Undermining children's intrinsic interest with extrinsic rewards: A test of the "overjustification" hypothesis. *Journal of Personality and Social Psychology, 28*, 129–137. [5]

LeVay, S. (1991). A difference in hypothalamic structure between heterosexual and homosexual men. *Science, 253*, 1034–1037. [11]

Leventhal, H., Singer, R. P., & Jones, S. (1965). The effects of fear and specificity of recommendation upon attitudes and behavior. *Journal of Personality and Social Psychology, 2*, 20–29. [16]

Leventhal, H., & Tomarken, A. J. (1986). Emotion: Today's problems. *Annual Review of Psychology, 37*, 565–610. [10]

Levi, L. (1990). Occupational stress: Spice of life or kiss of death? *American Psychologist, 45*, 1142–1145. [17]

Levine, C., Kohlberg, L., & Hewer, A. (1985). The current formulation of Kohlberg's theory and a response to critics. *Human Development, 28*, 94–100. [9]

Levine, D. S. (1988, November/December). Survival of the synapses. *The Sciences, 28*, 46–53. [2]

Levinson, D. J. (1986). A conception of adult development. *American Psychologist, 41*, 3–13. [9]

Levinson, D. J., with Darrow, C. N., Klein, E. B., Levinson, M. H., & McKee, B. (1978). *Seasons of a man's life*. New York: Knopf. [9]

Levitt, E. E., & Duckworth, J. C. (1984). Minnesota Multiphasic Personality Inventory. In D. J. Keyser & R. C. Sweetland (Eds.), *Test critiques* (Vol. 1, pp. 466–472). Kansas City: Test Corporation of America. [12]

Levy, G. D., & Carter, D. B. (1989). Gender-schema, gender constancy, and gender-role knowledge: The roles of cognitive factors in preschoolers' gender-role stereotype attributions. *Developmental Psychology, 25*, 444–449. [11]

Levy, J. (1985, May). Right brain, left brain: Fact and fiction. *Psychology Today*, pp. 38–44. [2]

Levy, J., & Nagylaki, T. (1972). A model for the genetics of handedness. *Genetics, 72*, 117–128. [2]

Lewinsohn, P. M., & Rosenbaum, M. (1987). Recall of parental behavior by acute depressives, remitted depressives, and nondepressives. *Journal of Personality and Social Psychology, 52*, 611–619. [6]

Lewinsohn, P. M., Zeiss, A. M., & Duncan, E. M. (1989). Probability of relapse after recovery from an episode of depression. *Journal of Abnormal Psychology, 98*, 107–116. [14]

Lewis, D. O., Pincus, J. H., Feldman, M., Jackson, L., & Bard, B. (1986). Psychiatric, neurological, and psychoeducational characteristics of 15 death row inmates in the United States. *American Journal of Psychiatry, 143*, 838–845. [16]

Lidz, T., Fleck, S., & Cornelison, A. R. (1965). *Schizophrenia and the family*. New York: International Universities Press. [14]

Lieberman, J., Bogerts, B., Degreef, G., Ashtari, M., Lantos, G., & Alvir, J. (1992). Qualitative assessment of brain morphology in acute and chronic schizophrenia. *American Journal of Psychiatry, 149*, 784–794. [14]

Lieberman, M. (1986). Self-help groups and psychiatry. *American Psychiatric Association Annual Review, 5*, 744–760. [13]

Liebert, R. M., Sprafkin, J. N., & Davidson, E. S. (1988). *The early window: Effects of television on children and youth* (3rd ed.). New York: Pergamon. [16]

Lief, H. I. (1977). Inhibited sexual desire. *Medical Aspects of Human Sexuality, 11*, 94–95. [11]

Lincoln, R. (1986). Smoking and reproduction. *Family Planning Perspectives, 18*, 79–84. [8]

Lindzey, G. (1977). *Projective techniques and cross-cultural research*. New York: Irvington. [12]

Linn, M. C., & Hyde, J. S. (1989). Gender, mathematics, and science. *Educational Researcher, 18*, 17–27. [11]

Linn, M. C., & Peterson, A. C. (1985). Emergence and characterization of sex differences in spatial ability: A meta-analysis. *Child Development, 56*, 1479–1498. [11]

Linn, R. L. (1982). Ability testing: Individual differences, prediction, and differential prediction. In A. K. Wigdor & W. R. Garner (Eds.), *Ability testing: Uses, consequences, and controversies* (Part II). Washington, DC: National Academy Press. [7]

Linton, M. (1979, July). I remember it well. *Psychology Today*, pp. 80–86. [6]

Linville, P. W., Fischer, G. W., & Salovey, P. (1989). Perceived distributions of the characteristics of in-group and out-group members: Empirical evidence and a computer simulation. *Journal of Personality and Social Psychology, 57*, 165–188. [17]

Linz, D. (1989). Exposure to sexually explicit materials and attitudes toward rape: A comparison of study results. *Journal of Sex Research, 26*, 50–84. [11]

Linz, D., Donnerstein, E., & Penrod, S. (1984). The effects of multiple exposures to filmed violence against women. *Journal of Communication, 34*, 130–147. [11]

Lipschitz, A. (1988). Diagnosis and classification of anxiety disorders. In C. G. Last & M. Herson (Eds.), *Handbook of anxiety disorders* (pp. 41–65). New York: Pergamon Press. [14]

Lipsitt, L. P. (1990). Learning processes in the human newborn: Sensitization, habituation, and classical conditioning. *Annals of the New York Academy of Sciences, 608*, 113–123. [8]

Lishman, W. A. (1990). Alcohol and the brain. *British Journal of Psychiatry, 156*, 635–644. [13]

Little, R. E., Anderson, K. W., Ervin, C. H., Worthington-Roberts, B., & Clarren, S. K. (1989). Maternal alcohol use during breast-feeding and infant mental and motor development at one year. *New England Journal of Medicine, 321*, 425–430. [8]

Livingstone, M. S. (1988). Art, illusion and the visual system. *Scientific American, 258*, 78–85. [3]

Lizza, E. F., & Cricco-Lizza, R. (1990, October). Impotence—Finding the cause. *Medical Aspects of Human Sexuality, 24*, 30–40. [11]

Lloyd, G. G., & Lishman, W. A. (1975). Effect of depression on the speed of recall of pleasant and unpleasant experiences. *Psychological Medicine, 5*, 173–180. [6]

Locke, E. A., & Latham, G. P. (1990). *A theory of goal setting and task performance*. Englewood Cliffs, NJ: Prentice-Hall. [17]

Loehlin, J. C., Horn, J. M., & Willerman, L. (1989). Modeling IQ change: Evidence from the Texas Adoption Project. *Child Development, 60*, 993–1004. [7]

Loehlin, J. C., Horn, J. M., & Willerman, L. (1990). Heredity, environment, and personality change: Evidence from the Texas Adoption Project. *Journal of Personality, 58*, 221–243. [12]

Loehlin, J. C., Lindzey, G., & Spuhler, J. N. (1975). *Race differences in intelligence*. San Francisco: Freeman. [7]

Loehlin, J. C., Willerman, L., & Horn, J. M. (1987). Personality resemblance in adoptive families: A 10-year follow-up. *Journal of Personality and Social Psychology, 53*, 961–969. [12]

Loehlin, J. C., Willerman, L., & Horn, J. M. (1988). Human behavior genetics. *Annual Review of Psychology, 39*, 101–133. [7, 12, 14]

Loftus, E. (1980). *Memory: Surprising new insights into how we remember and why we forget*. Reading, MA: Addison-Wesley. [6]

Loftus, E. F. (1975). Leading questions and the eyewitness report. *Cognitive Psychology, 7*, 560–572. [6]

Loftus, E. F. (1979). *Eyewitness testimony*. Cambridge, MA: Harvard University Press. [6]

Loftus, E. F. (1984, February). Eyewitnesses: Essential but unreliable. *Psychology Today*, pp. 22–27. [6]

Loftus, E. F., & Hoffman, H. G. (1989). Misinformation and memory: The creation of new memories. *Journal of Experimental Psychology: General, 118*, 100–104. [6]

Loftus, E. F., & Loftus, G. R. (1980). On the permanence of stored information in the human brain. *American Psychologist, 35*, 409–420. [6]

Logue, A. W. (1985). Conditioned food aversion learning in humans. *Annals of the New York Academy of Sciences, 443*, 316–329. [5]

Logue, A. W., Ophir, I., & Strauss, K. R. (1981). The acquisition of taste aversions in humans. *Behaviour Research and Therapy, 19*, 319–333. [5]

Long, G. M., & Crambert, R. F. (1990). The nature and basis of age-related changes in dynamic visual acuity. *Psychology and Aging, 5*, 138–143. [9]

Long, V. O. (1986). Relationship of masculinity to self-esteem and self-acceptance in female professionals, college students, clients, and victims of domestic violence. *Journal of Consulting and Clinical Psychology, 54*, 323–327. [11]

Lord, L. J., Goode, E. E., Gest, T., McAuliffe, K., Moore, L. J., Black, R. F., & Linnon, N. (1987, November 30). Coming to grips with alcoholism. *U.S. News & World Report*, pp. 56–62. [13]

Lorenz, K. (1966). *On aggression*. New York: Harcourt, Brace, & World. [16]

Lovaas, I. (1967). A behavior therapy approach to the treatment of childhood schizophrenia. In J. P. Hill (Ed.), *Minnesota symposia on child development* (Vol. 1, pp. 108–159). Minneapolis: University of Minnesota Press. [8]

Lovelace, E. A., & Twohig, P. T. (1990). Healthy older adults' perceptions of their memory functioning and use of mnemonics. *Bulletin of the Psychonomic Society, 28*, 115–118. [9]

Luborsky, L., & Spence, D. P. (1978). Quantitative research on psychoanalytic therapy. In S. L. Garfield & A. E. Bergin (Eds.), *Handbook of psychotherapy and behavior change: An empirical analysis* (2nd ed.). New York: Wiley. [15]

Luchins, A. S. (1957). Experimental attempts to minimize the impact of first impressions. In C. I. Hovland (Ed.), *Yale studies in attitude and communication: Vol. 1. The order of presentation in persuasion* (pp. 62–75). New Haven, CT: Yale University Press. [16]

Lummis, M., & Stevenson, H. W. (1990). Gender differences in beliefs about achievement: A cross-cultural study. *Developmental Psychology, 26*, 254–263. [11]

Lundgren, C. B. (1986, August 20). Cocaine addiction: A revolutionary new treatment. *St. Louis Jewish Light*, p. 7. [4]

Lundholm, J. K., & Littrell, J. M. (1986). Desire for thinness among high school cheerleaders: Relationship to disordered eating and weight control behaviors. *Adolescence, 21*, 573–579. [13]

Luthans, F., & Kreitner, R. (1975). *Organizational behavior modification*. Glenview, IL: Scott, Foresman. [5]

Lykken, D. T. (1981). *A tremor in the blood: Uses and abuses of the lie detector*. New York: McGraw-Hill. [10]

Lykken, D. T. (1985). The probity of the polygraph. In S. M. Kassin & L. S. Wrightsman (Eds.), *The psychology of evidence and trial procedure*. Beverly Hills, CA: Sage. [10]

Lykken, D. T., Bouchard, T. J., Jr., McGue, M., Tellegen, A. (1990). The Minnesota Twin Family Registry: Some initial findings. *Acta Geneticae Medicae et Gemellologiae* (Rome), *39*, 35–70. [7]

Lynch, S., & Yarnell, P. R. (1973). Retrograde amnesia: Delayed forgetting after concussion. *American Journal of Psychology, 86*, 643–645. [6]

Maccoby, E. E., & Jacklin, C. M. (1974a). *The psychology of sex differences*. Stanford, CA: Stanford University Press. [11]

Maccoby, E. E., & Jacklin, C. N. (1974b, December). What we know and don't know about sex differences. *Psychology Today*, pp. 109–112. [11]

Maccoby, E. E., & Jacklin, C. N. (1980). Sex differences in aggression: A rejoinder and reprise. *Child Development, 51*, 964–980. [11]

Maccoby, E. E., & Martin, J. A. (1983). Socialization in the context of the family: Parent-child interaction. In P. H. Mussen (Ed.), *Handbook of child psychology* (4th ed., Vol. 4). New York: John Wiley. [8]

MacCoun, R. J. (1989). Experimental research on jury decision-making. *Science, 244*, 1046–1050. [17]

MacFarlane, A. (1978). What a baby knows. *Human Nature, 1*, 74–81. [8]

MacLachlan, J. (1979, November). What people really think of fast talkers. *Psychology Today*, pp. 113–117. [16]

Mahoney, E. R. (1983). *Human sexuality*. New York: McGraw-Hill. [11]

Maier, S. F., & Laudenslager, M. (1985, August). Stress and health: Exploring the links. *Psychology Today*, pp. 44–49. [13]

Maj, M. (1990). Psychiatric aspects of HIV-1 infection and AIDS. *Psychological Medicine, 20*, 547–563. [11]

Maj, M., Veltro, F., Pirozzi, R., Lobrace, S., & Magliano, L. (1992). Pattern of recurrence of illness after recovery from an episode of major depression: A prospective study. *Journal of Personality and Social Psychology, 62*, 795–800. [14]

Major, B., Schmidlin, A. M., & Williams, L. (1990). Gender patterns in social touch: The impact of setting and age. *Journal of Personality and Social Psychology, 58*, 634–643. [16]

Malamuth, N. M. (1986). Predictors of naturalistic sexual aggression. *Journal of Personality and Social Psychology, 50*, 953–962. [11]

Maletzky, B. M. (1974). "Assisted" covert sensitization in the treatment of exhibitionism. *Journal of Consulting and Clinical Psychology, 42*, 34–40. [15]

Malitz, S., Sackeim, H. A., Decina, P., Kanzler, M., & Kerr, B. (1986). The efficacy of electroconvulsive therapy: Dose-response interactions with modality. *Annals of the New York Academy of Sciences, 462*, 56–64. [15]

Manton, K. G., Siegler, I. C., & Woodbury, M. A. (1986). Patterns of intellectual development in later life. *Journal of Gerontology, 41*, 486–499. [9]

Maratsos, M. (1983). Some current issues in the study of the acquisition of grammar. In P. H. Mussen (Ed.), *Handbook of child psychology* (Vol. 3). New York: Wiley. [8]

Marcia, J. (1980). Identity in adolescence. In J. Adelson (Ed.), *Handbook of adolescent psychology*. New York: Wiley. [9]

Markowitz, J. S., Weissman, M. M., Ouellette, R., Lish, J. D., & Klerman, G. L. (1989). Quality of life in panic disorder. *Archives of General Psychiatry, 46*, 984–992. [14]

Marks, I. (1987a). Behavioral aspects of panic disorder. *American Journal of Psychiatry, 144*, 1160–1165. [14]

Marks, I. (1987b). The development of normal fear: A review. *Journal of Child Psychology and Psychiatry, 28*, 667–697. [8]

Marks, I. M. (1972). Flooding (implosion) and allied treatments. In W. S. Agras (Ed.), *Behavior modification*. New York: Little, Brown. [15]

Marks, I. M. (1978a). Behavioral psychotherapy of adult neurosis. In S. Garfield & A. E. Bergin (Eds.), *Handbook of psychotherapy and behavior change* (2nd ed.). New York: Wiley. [15]

Marks, I. M. (1978b). *Living with fear: Understanding and coping with anxiety*. New York: McGraw-Hill. [14]

Marlatt, G. A. (1983). The controlled-drinking controversy: A commentary. *American Psychologist, 38*, 1097–1110. [13]

Marlatt, G. A., & Rohsenow, D. J. (1981, December). The think-drink effect. *Psychology Today*, pp. 60–69, 93. [1]

Marmor, J. (Ed.). (1980). *Homosexual behavior: A modern reappraisal*. New York: Basic Books. [11]

Marshall, G. D., & Zimbardo, P. G. (1979). Affective consequences of inadequately explained physiological arousal. *Journal of Personality and Social Psychology, 37*, 970–988. [10]

Marshall, W. L., & Segal, Z. (1988). Behavior therapy. In C. G. Last & M. Hersen (Eds.), *Handbook of anxiety disorders* (pp. 338–361). New York: Pergamon. [15]

Martin, C. L. (1990). Attitudes and expectations about children and nontraditional gender roles. *Sex Roles, 22*, 151–155. [11]

Martin, C. L., & Little, J. K. (1990). The relation of gender understanding to children's sex-typed preferences and gender stereotypes. *Child Development, 61*, 1427–1439. [11]

Martin, C. L., Wood, C. H., & Little, J. K. (1990). The development of gender stereotype components. *Child Development, 61*, 1891–1904. [11]

Martin, N. G., Eaves, L. J., Heath, A. C., Jardine, R., Feingold, L. M., & Eysenck, H. J. (1986). Transmission of social attitudes. *Proceedings of the National Academy of Sciences, U.S.A., 83*, 4364–4368. [12]

Martinez, C. (1986). Hispanics: Psychiatric issues. In C. B. Wilkinson (Ed.), *Ethnic psychiatry* (pp. 61–88). New York: Plenum. [15]

Martorano, S. C. (1977). A developmental analysis of performance on Piaget's formal operations tasks. *Developmental Psychology, 13*, 666–672. [9]

Maslow, A. H. (1970). *Motivation and personality* (2nd ed.). New York: Harper & Row. [10, 12]

Masters, J. C. (1981). Developmental psychology. *Annual Review of Psychology, 32*, 117–151. [8]

Masters, W. H., & Johnson, V. E. (1966). *Human sexual response.* Boston: Little, Brown [9, 11]

Masters, W. H., & Johnson, V. E. (1975). *The pleasure bond: A new look at sexuality and commitment.* Boston: Little, Brown. [11]

Masters, W. H., & Johnson, V. E. (1979). *Homosexuality in perspective.* Boston: Little, Brown. [11]

Mathew, R. J., & Wilson, W. H. (1991). Substance abuse and cerebral blood flow. *American Journal of Psychiatry, 148*, 292–305. [4]

Matlin, M. (1983). *Cognition.* New York: Holt, Rinehart & Winston. [7]

Matlin, M. W. (1989). *Cognition* (2nd ed.). New York: Holt, Rinehart & Winston. [6]

Matlin, M. W., & Foley, H. J. (1992). *Sensation and perception* (3rd ed.). Boston: Allyn & Bacon. [3]

Matsuda, L., Lolait, S. J., Brownstein, M. J., Young, A. C., & Bonner, T. I. (1990). Structure of a cannabinoid receptor and functional expression of the cloned CDNA. *Nature, 346*, 561–564. [4]

Matthews, K. A. (1982). Psychological perspectives on the Type A behavior pattern. *Psychological Bulletin, 91*, 293–323. [13]

Mattick, R. P., Andrews, G., Hadzi-Pavlovic, D., & Christensen, H. (1990). Treatment of panic and agoraphobia: An integrative review. *Journal of Nervous and Mental Disease, 178*, 567–576. [15]

Mavissakalian, M. (1990). Sequential combination of imipramine and self-directed exposure in the treatment of panic disorder with agoraphobia. *Journal of Clinical Psychiatry, 51*, 184–188. [15]

May, R. (1982). The problem of evil: An open letter to Carl Rogers. *Journal of Humanistic Psychology, 22*, 10–21. [12]

Mayer, J. (1955). Regulation of energy intake and the body weight: The glucostatic theory and the lipostatic hypothesis. *Proceedings of the New York Academy of Sciences, 63*, 15–43. [10]

Mayer, J. (1980). Physiology of hunger and satiety. In R. S. Goodhart & M. E. Shils (Eds.), *Modern nutrition in health and disease* (6th ed., pp. 561–577). Philadelphia: Lea & Febiger. [10]

Mayer, W. (1983). Alcohol abuse and alcoholism: The psychologist's role in prevention, research, and treatment. *American Psychologist, 38*, 1116–1121. [4, 13]

McAuliffe, W. E., Rohman, M., Santangelo, S., Feldman, B., Magnuson, E., Sobol, A., & Weissman, M. A. (1986). Psychoactive drug use among practicing physicians and medical students. *New England Journal of Medicine, 315*, 805–810. [4]

McBurney, D. H., & Collings, V. B. (1984). *Introduction to sensation/perception* (2nd ed.). Englewood Cliffs, NJ: Prentice-Hall. [3]

McCarthy, P. (1989, March). Ageless sex. *Psychology Today*, p. 62. [9]

McCartney, K., Harris, M. J., & Bernieri, F. (1990). Growing up and growing apart: A developmental meta-analysis of twin studies. *Psychological Bulletin, 107*, 226–237. [7]

McClelland, D. C. (1958). Methods of measuring human motivation. In J. W. Atkinson (Ed.), *Motives in fantasy, action and society: A method of assessment and study.* Princeton, NJ: Van Nostrand. [10]

McClelland, D. C. (1961). *The achieving society.* Princeton, NJ: Van Nostrand. [10]

McClelland, D. C. (1985). *Human motivation.* Glenview, IL: Scott, Foresman. [10]

McClelland, D. C., Atkinson, J. W., Clark, R. W., & Lowell, E. L. (1953). *The achievement motive.* New York: Appleton-Century-Crofts. [10]

McClelland, D. C., & Pilon, D. A. (1983). Sources of adult motives in patterns of parent behavior in early childhood. *Journal of Personality and Social Psychology, 44*, 564–574. [10]

McConnel, J. V., Cutler, R. L., & McNeil, E. B. (1958). Subliminal stimulation: An overview. *American Psychologist, 13*, 229–242. [3]

McCrae, R. (1984). Situational determinants of coping responses: Loss, threat, and challenge. *Journal of Personality and Social Psychology, 46*, 919–928. [13]

McCrae, R. R., & Costa, P. T., Jr. (1987). Validation of the five-factor model of personality across instruments and observers. *Journal of Personality and Social Psychology, 52*, 81–90. [12]

McCutcheon, L. E., & Hassani, K. H. (1981). Running away from illness. *Journal of Sport Behavior, 4*, 151–156. [13]

McDaniel, M. A., Anderson, D. C., Einstein, G. O., & O'Halloran, C. M. (1989). Modulation of environmental reinstatement effects through encoding strategies. *American Journal of Psychology, 102*, 523–548. [6]

McDonald, A. D., Armstrong, B. G., & Sloan, M. (1992). Cigarette, alcohol, and coffee consumption and prematurity. *American Journal of Public Health, 82*, 87–90. [8]

McDougall, W. (1908). *An introduction to social psychology.* London: Methuen. [10]

McGee, A-M., & Skinner, M. (1987). Facial asymmetry and the attribution of personality traits. *British Journal of Social Psychology, 26*, 181–184. [2]

McGinnis, J. M. (1987). Suicide in America—Moving up the public health agenda. *Suicide and Life-Threatening Behavior, 171*, 18–32. [14]

McGrath, A. (1987, August 3). Living alone and loving it. *U.S. News & World Report*, pp. 52–57. [9]

McGue, M., Pickens, R. W., & Svikis, D. S. (1992). Sex and age effects on the inheritance of alcohol problems: A twin study. *Journal of Abnormal Psychology, 101*, 3–17. [13]

McGuire, W. J. (1969). The nature of attitudes and attitude change. In G. Lindzey & E. Aronson (Eds.), *Handbook of social psychology* (Vol. 3). Reading, MA: Addison-Wesley. [16]

McGuire, W. J. (1985). Attitudes and attitude change. In G. Lindzey & E. Aronson (Ed.), *Handbook of social psychology* (Vol. 2, 3rd ed.). New York: Random House. [16]

McKellar, P. (1972). Imagery from the standpoint of introspection. In P. W. Sheehan (Ed.), *The function and nature of imagery* (pp. 36–63). New York: Academic Press. [7]

McKelvie, S. J. (1984). Relationship between set and functional fixedness: A replication. *Perceptual and Motor Skills, 58*, 996–998. [7]

McKinley, J. C., & Hathaway, S. R. (1943). The identification and measurement of the psychoneuroses in medical practice: The Minnesota Multiphasic Personality Inventory. *Journal of the American Medical Association, 122*, 161–167. [12]

McLean, P. D., & Carr, S. (1989). The psychological treatment of unipolar depression: Progress and limitations. *Canadian Journal of Behavioural Science, 21*, 452–469. [15]

McNally, R. J. (1990). Psychological approaches to panic disorder: A review. *Psychological Bulletin, 108*, 403–419. [14]

McNaughton, M. E., Smith, L. W., Patterson, T. L., & Grant, I. (1990). Stress, social support, coping resources, and immune status in elderly women. *Journal of Nervous and Mental Disease, 178*, 460–461. [13]

Mednick, S. A., Brennan, P., & Kandel, E. (1988). Predisposition to violence. *Aggressive Behavior, 14*, 25–33. [16]

Mednick, S. A., & Mednick, M. T. (1967). *Examiner's manual, Remote Associates Test.* Boston: Houghton-Mifflin. [7]

Medzerian, G. (1991). *Crack: Treating cocaine addiction.* Blue Ridge Summit, PA: Tab Books. [4]

Meer, J. (1986, June). The age of reason. *Psychology Today*, pp. 60–64. [9]

Mefford, I. N., Baker, T. L., Boehme, R., Foutz, A. S., Ciaranello, R. D., Barchas, J. D., & Dement, W. C. (1983). Narcolepsy: Biogenic amine deficits in an animal model. *Science, 220*, 629–632. [4]

Mehrabian, A. (1968, September). Communication without words. *Psychology Today*, pp. 53–55. [16]

Meichenbaum, D. (1977). *Cognitive behavior modification: An integrative approach.* New York: Plenum. [13]

Melamed, B. G., & Siegal, L. J. (1975). Reduction of anxiety in children facing hospitalization and surgery by use of filmed modeling. *Journal of Consulting and Clinical Psychology, 43*, 511–521. [15]

Meltzer, H. (1930). Individual differences in forgetting pleasant and unpleasant experiences. *Journal of Educational Psychology, 21*, 399–409. [6]

Meltzoff, A. N. (1988). Imitation of televised models by infants. *Child Development, 59*, 1221–1229. [8]

Meltzoff, A. N., & Moore, M. K. (1977). Imitation of facial and manual gestures by human neonates. *Science, 198*, 75–78. [8]

Meltzoff, A. N., & Moore, M. K. (1989). Imitation in newborn infants: Exploring the range of gestures imitated and the underlying mechanisms. *Developmental Psychology, 25*, 954–962. [8]

Melzack, R., & Wall, P. D. (1965). Pain mechanisms: A new theory. *Science, 150*, 971–979. [3]

Melzack, R., & Wall, P. D. (1983). *The challenge of pain.* New York: Basic Books. [3]

Merckelbach, H., Arntz, A., & de Jong, P. (1991). Conditioning experiences in spider phobics. *Behaviour Research and Therapy, 29*, 333–335. [14]

Merckelbach, H., de Ruiter, C., van den Hout, M. A., & Hoekstra, R. (1989). Conditioning experiences and phobias. *Behaviour Research and Therapy, 27*, 657–662. [14]

Mertz, G. J., Benedetti, J., Ashley, R., Selke, S. A., & Corey, L. (1992). Risk factors for the sexual transmission of genital herpes. *Annals of Internal Medicine, 116,* 197–202. [11]

Mesulam, M-M. (1990). Schizophrenia and the brain. *New England Journal of Medicine, 322,* 842–845. [14]

Metter, E. J. (1991). Brain-behavior relationships in aphasia studied by positron emission tomography. *Annals of the New York Academy of Sciences, 620,* 153–164. [2]

Meyer, P. (1972). If Hitler asked you to electrocute a stranger, would you? In R. Greenbaum & H. A. Tilker (Eds.), *The challenge of psychology* (pp. 456–465). Englewood Cliffs, NJ: Prentice-Hall. [16]

Meyer-Bahlburg, H. F. (1977). Sex hormones and male homosexuality in comparative perspective. *Archives of Sexual Behavior, 6,* 297–325. [11]

Michaels, J. W., Bloomel, J. M., Brocato, R. M., Linkous, R. A., & Rowe, J. S. (1982). Social facilitation and inhibition in a natural setting. *Replications in Social Psychology, 2,* 21–24. [16]

Michelini, R. L., & Snodgrass, S. S. (1980). Defendant characteristics and juridic decisions. *Journal of Research in Personality, 14,* 392–350. [17]

Michelson, L., Marchione, K., Greenwald, M., Glanz, L., Testa, S., & Marchione, N. (1990). Panic disorder: Cognitive-behavioral treatment. *Behaviour Research and Therapy, 28,* 141–151. [15]

Middlebrooks, J. C., & Green, D. M. (1991). Sound localization by human listeners. *Annual Review of Psychology, 42,* 135–159. [3]

Milavsky, J. R., Kessler, R., Stipp, H., & Rubens, W. S. (1982). Television and aggression: Results of a panel study. In D. Pearl, L. Bouthilet, & J. Lazar (Eds.), *Television and behavior: Ten years of scientific progress and implications for the eighties* (Vol. 2). Washington, DC: U.S. Government Printing Office. [16]

Milgram, S. (1963). Behavioral study of obedience. *Journal of Abnormal and Social Psychology, 67,* 371–378. [16]

Milgram, S. (1965). Liberating effects of group pressure. *Journal of Personality and Social Psychology, 1,* 127–134. [16]

Miller, B. C. (1976). A multivariate developmental model of marital satisfaction. *Journal of Marriage and the Family, 38,* 643–657. [9]

Miller, D. T., & Ross, M. (1975). Self-serving biases in the attribution of causality: Fact or fiction? *Psychological Bulletin, 82,* 213–225. [16]

Miller, D. T., & Turnbull, W. (1986). Expectancies and interpersonal processes. *Annual Review of Psychology, 37,* 233–256. [16]

Miller, G. A. (1956). The magical number seven, plus or minus two: Some limits on our capacity for processing information. *Psychological Review, 63,* 81–97. [6]

Miller, G. A., & Gildea, P. M. (1987). How children learn words. *Scientific American, 257,* 94–99. [8]

Miller, I. W., Norman, W. H., & Keitner, G. I. (1989). Cognitive-behavioral treatment of depressed inpatients: Six- and twelve-month follow-up. *American Journal of Psychiatry, 146,* 1274–1279. [15]

Miller, J. G., & Bersoff, D. M. (1992). Culture and moral judgment: How are conflicts between justice and interpersonal responsibilities resolved? *Journal of Personality and Social Psychology, 62,* 541–554. [9]

Miller, J. G., Bersoff, D. M., & Harwood, R. L. (1990). Perceptions of social responsibilities in India and in the United States: Moral imperatives or personal decisions? *Journal of Personality and Social Psychology, 58,* 33–47. [16]

Miller, L. (1988, February). The emotional brain. *Psychology Today,* pp. 34–42. [2]

Miller, L. (1989, November). What biofeedback does (and doesn't) do. *Psychology Today,* pp. 22–23. [5]

Miller, N., Maruyama, G., Beaber, R. J., & Valone, K. (1976). Speed of speech and persuasion. *Journal of Personality and Social Psychology, 34,* 615–624. [16]

Miller, N. E. (1941). The frustration-aggression hypothesis. *Psychological Review, 48,* 337–342. [16]

Miller, N. E. (1985, February). Rx: Biofeedback. *Psychology Today,* pp. 54–59. [5]

Miller, W. C., Lindeman, A. K., Wallace, J., & Niederpruem, M. (1990). Diet composition, energy intake, and exercise in relation to body fat in men and women. *American Journal of Clinical Nutrition, 52,* 426–430. [13]

Mills, J. (1987, November). Life in the nineties: Grandma Whitney's climb to the top. *Women's Sports & Fitness,* p. 61. [9]

Milner, B. (1970). Memory and the medial temporal regions of the brain. In K. H. Pribram & D. E. Broadbent (Eds.), *Biology of memory.* New York: Academic Press. [6]

Milner, B. R. (1966). Amnesia following operation on the temporal lobes. In C. W. M. Whitty & O. L. Zangwill (Eds.), *Amnesia* (pp. 109–133). London: Butterworth. [6]

Milner, B., Corkin, S., & Teuber, H. L. (1968). Further analysis of the hippocampal amnesic syndrome: 14-year follow-up study of H. M. *Neuropsychologia, 6,* 215–234. [6]

Mischel, W. (1966). A social-learning view of sex differences in behavior. In E. E. Maccoby (Ed.), *The development of sex differences* (pp. 56–81). Stanford, CA: Stanford University Press. [11]

Mischel, W. (1968). *Personality and assessment.* New York: Wiley. [12]

Mischel, W. (1973). Toward a cognitive social learning reconceptualization of personality. *Psychological Review, 80,* 252–283. [12]

Mischel, W. (1977). The interaction of person and situation. In D. Magnusson & N. S. Endler (Eds.), *Personality at the crossroads: Current issues in interactional psychology.* Hillsdale, NJ: Lawrence Erlbaum. [12]

Mistlberger, R. E., & Rusak, B. (1989). Mechanisms and models of the circadian timekeeping system. In M. H. Kryger, T. Roth, & W. C. Dement (Eds.), *Principles and practice of sleep medicine* (pp. 141–152). Philadelphia: W. B. Saunders. [4]

Mitler, M. M., Carskadon, M. A., Czeisler, C. A., Dement, W. C., Dinges, D. F., & Graeber, R. C. (1988). Catastrophes, sleep, and public policy: consensus report. *Sleep, 11,* 100–109. [4]

Mitler, M. M., Guilleminault, C., Orem, J., Zarcone, V. P., & Dement, W. C. (1975, December). Sleeplessness, sleep attacks and things that go wrong in the night. *Psychology Today,* pp. 45–50. [4]

Modestin, J. (1991). Multiple personality disorder in Switzerland. *American Journal of Psychiatry, 148,* 88–92. [14]

Molfese, D. L., & Molfese, V. J. (1985). Electrophysiological indices of auditory discrimination in newborn infants: The bases for predicting later language development? *Infant Behavior and Development, 8,* 197–211. [2]

Money, J. (1987). Sin, sickness, or status? Homosexual gender identity and psychoneuroendocrinology. *American Psychologist, 42,* 384–399. [11]

Money, J., & Schwartz, M. (1977). Dating, romantic and nonromantic friendships, and sexuality in 17 early-treated adrenogenital females, aged 16–25. In P. A. Lee et al. (Eds.), *Congenital adrenal hyperplasia.* Baltimore: University Park Press. [11]

Monk, T. H. (1989). Circadian rhythms in subjective activation, mood, and performance efficiency. In M. H. Kryger, T. Roth, & W. C. Dement (Eds.), *Principles and practice of sleep medicine* (pp. 163–172). Philadelphia: W. B. Saunders. [4]

"Monkey Child" turns up in Ugandan jungle. (1986, July 4). *St. Louis Post-Dispatch,* p. 3A. [8]

Monroe, S. M., & Simons, A. D. (1991). Diathesis-stress theories in the context of life stress research: Implications for the depressive disorders. *Psychological Bulletin, 110,* 406–425. [14]

Montagu, A. (1962). *The humanization of man.* Cleveland: World. [8]

Moreno, J. L. (1959). Psychodrama. In S. Arieti et al. (Eds.), *American handbook of psychiatry* (Vol. 2). New York: Basic Books. [15]

Morgan, C. D., & Murray, H. A. (1935). A method for investigating fantasies: The Thematic Apperception Test. *Archives of Neurology and Psychiatry, 34,* 289–306. [12]

Morgan, C. D., & Murray, H. A. (1962). Thematic Apperception Test. 530–545. In H. A. Murray et al. (Eds.), *Explorations in personality: A clinical and experimental study of fifty men of college age.* New York: Science Editions. [12]

Morgan, C. T., & Morgan, J. D. (1940). Studies in hunger: II. The relation of gastric denervation and dietary sugar to the effect of insulin upon food-intake in the rat. *Journal of Genetic Psychology, 57,* 153–163. [10]

Morrison, A. M., & Von Glinow, M. S. (1990). Women and minorities in management. *American Psychologist, 45,* 200–208. [17]

Moscovici, S., & Zavalloni, M. (1969). The group as a polarizer of attitudes. *Journal of Personality and Social Psychology, 12,* 125–135. [16]

Mosher, D. L., & Anderson, R. D. (1987). Macho personality, sexual aggression, and reactions to guided imagery of realistic rape. *Journal of Research in Personality, 20,* 77–94. [11]

Motley, M. T. (1985). Slips of the tongue. *Scientific American, 253,* 116–127. [12]

Motley, M. T. (1987, February). What I meant to say. *Psychology Today,* pp. 24–28. [12]

Mui, A. C. (1992). Caregiver strain among black and white daughter caregivers: A role theory perspective. *The Gerontologist, 32,* 203–212. [9]

Murphy, J. M., Olivier, D. C., Monson, R. R., Sobol, A. M., Federman, E. B., & Leighton, A. H. (1991). Depression and anxiety in relation to social status: A prospective epidemiologic study. *Archives of General Psychiatry, 48,* 223–229. [14]

Murray, H. (1938). *Explorations in personality.* New York: Oxford University Press. [10, 12]

Murray, H. A. (1965). Uses of the Thematic Apperception Test. In B. I. Murstein (Ed.), *Handbook of projective techniques* (pp. 425–432). New York: Basic Books. [12]

Murray, J. B. (1988). Psychophysiological aspects of caffeine consumption. *Psychological Reports, 62,* 575–587. [4]

Mussen, P., Honzik, M., & Eichorn, D. (1982). Early adult antecedents of life satisfaction at age 70. *Journal of Gerontology, 37,* 315–322. [9]

Mussen, P. H., & Jones, M. C. (1957). Self-conceptions, motivations, and interpersonal attitudes of late- and early-maturing boys. *Child Development, 28,* 243–256. [9]

Myers, D. G., & Bishop, G. D. (1970). Discussion effects on racial attitudes. *Science, 169,* 778–779. [16]

Myers, D. G., & Lamm, H. (1975). The polarizing effect of group discussion. *American Scientist, 63,* 297–303. [16]

Nadon, R., Hoyt, I. P., Register, P. A., & Kilstrom, J. F. (1991). Absorption and hypnotizability: Context effects reexamined. *Journal of Personality and Social Psychology, 60,* 144–153. [4]

Nahas, G. G. (1985). *Keep off the grass.* Middlebury, VM: Paul S. Eriksson. [4]

Nakano, K. (1988). Hassles as a measure of stress in a Japanese sample: Preliminary research. *Psychological Reports, 63,* 252–254. [13]

Nash, M. (1987). What, if anything, is regressed about hypnotic age regression? A review of the empirical literature. *Psychological Bulletin, 102,* 42–52. [4]

Nash, M., & Baker, E. (1984, February). Trance encounters: Susceptibility to hypnosis. *Psychology Today,* pp. 18, 72–73. [4]

Nathan, P. E. (1983). Failures in prevention: Why we can't prevent the devastating effect of alcoholism and drug abuse. *American Psychologist, 38,* 453–467. [13]

Nathan, P. E. (1992). Peele hasn't done his homework—again: A response to "Alcoholism, politics, and bureaucracy: The consensus against controlled-drinking in America." *Addictive Behaviors, 17,* 63–65. [13]

Nation, J. R., & Woods, D. J. (1980). Persistence: The role of partial reinforcement in psychotherapy. *Journal of Experimental Psychology: General, 109,* 175–207. [5]

National Center for Health Statistics. (1991). *Vital statistics of the United States 1988, Volume II—Mortality.* Hyattsville, MD: U.S. Department of Health and Human Services. [13]

National Institute of Mental Health. (1985, June 10–12). *Consensus development conference statement: Electroconvulsive therapy: Program and abstracts.* Washington, DC: National Institute of Mental Health. [15]

National Migrant Resource Program and the Migrant Clinicians Network. (1990, April). *Migrant and seasonal farmworker, health objectives for the year 2000: Document in progress.* Austin, TX: National Migrant Resource Program. [13]

Neiger, B. L., & Hopkins, R. W. (1988). Adolescent suicide: Character traits of high-risk teenagers. *Adolescence, 23,* 469–475. [14]

Neimark, E. (1975). Intellectual development during adolescence. In F. Horowitz (Ed.), *Review of child development research* (Vol. 4). Chicago: University of Chicago Press. [9]

Neimark, E. D. (1981). Confounding with cognitive style factors: An artifact explanation for the apparent nonuniversal incidence of formal operations. In I. Sigel, D. Brodzinsky, & R. Golinkoff (Eds.), *New directions in Piagetian research and theory.* Hillsdale, NJ: Erlbaum. [8]

Neisser, U. (1967). *Cognitive psychology.* New York: Appleton-Century-Crofts. [6]

Nelson, J. C. (1991). Current status of tricyclic antidepressants in psychiatry: Their pharmacology and clinical applications. *Journal of Clinical Psychiatry, 52,* 193–200. [15]

Nelson, K. (1973). Structure and strategy in learning to talk. *Monographs of the Society for Research in Child Development, 38*(1–2, Serial No. 149). [8]

Nelson, T. O. (1978). Detecting small amounts of information in memory: Savings for nonrecognized items. *Journal of Experimental Psychology: Human Learning and Memory, 4,* 453–468. [6]

Nelson, T. O. (1985). Ebbinghaus's contribution to the measurement of retention: Savings during relearning. *Journal of Experimental Psychology: Learning, Memory, and Cognition, 11,* 472–479. [6]

Nelton, S., & Berney, K. (1987, May). Women: The second wave. *Nation's Business,* 18–27. [17]

Neugarten, B. L. (1968). The awareness of middle age. In B. Neugarten (Ed.), *Middle age and aging* (pp. 93–98). Chicago: University of Chicago Press. [9]

Neugarten, B. L. (1976). *The psychology of aging: An overview. Master lectures on developmental psychology.* Washington, DC: American Psychological Association. [9]

Neugarten, B. L. (1982). Must everything be a midlife crisis? In T. H. Carr & H. E. Fitzgerald (Eds.), *Human development 82/83* (pp. 162–163). (Reprinted from Prime Time, February 1980, 45–48). Guilford, CT: Dushkin. [9]

Neugarten, B. L., & Hagestad, G. (1976). Age and the life course. In H. Binstock & E. Shanas (Eds.), *Handbook of aging and the social sciences.* New York: Van Nostrand Reinhold. [9]

Neumann, Y., Finaly, E., & Reichel, A. (1988). Achievement motivation factors and students' college outcomes. *Psychological Reports, 62,* 555–560. [10]

Newcomb, M. D., & Bentler, P. M. (1989). Substance use and abuse among children and teenagers. *American Psychologist, 44,* 242–248. [4]

Newcomb, T. M. (1956). The prediction of interpersonal attraction. *American Psychologist, 11,* 575–587. [16]

Newell, A., & Simon, H. A. (1972). *Human problem solving.* Englewood Cliffs, NJ: Prentice-Hall. [7]

Newman, B. (1982). Mid-life development. In B. B. Wolman (Ed.), *Handbook of developmental psychology.* Englewood Cliffs, NJ: Prentice-Hall. [9]

Newman, O. (1972). *Denfensible space.* New York: Macmillan. [17]

Ng, S. K. C., Hauser, W. A., Brust, J. C. M., & Susser, M. (1988). Alcohol consumption and withdrawal in new onset seizures. *New England Journal of Medicine, 319,* 665–672. [13]

Nickerson, R. S., & Adams, M. J. (1979). Long-term memory for a common object. *Cognitive Psychology, 11,* 287–307. [6]

Nicol, S. E., & Gottesman, I. I. (1983). Clues to the genetics and neurobiology of schizophrenia. *American Scientist, 71,* 398–404. [14]

Nisbett, R. E., & Wilson, T. D. (1977). The halo effect: Evidence for unconscious alteration of judgments. *Journal of Personality and Social Psychology, 35,* 250–256. [16]

Nogrady, H., McConkey, K. M., & Campbell, P. (1985). Enhancing visual memory: Trying hypnosis, trying imagination, and trying again. *Journal of Abnormal Psychology, 94,* 195–204. [4]

Nogrady, H., McConkey, K. M., & Perry, C. (1985). Enhancing visual memory: Trying hypnosis, trying imagination, and trying again. *Journal of Abnormal Psychology, 94,* 195–204. [6]

Norcross, J. C., Prochaska, J. O., & Gallagher, K. M. (1989). Clinical psychologists in the 1980s: II. Theory, research, and practice. *Clinical Psychologist, 42,* 45–52. [15]

Norman, D. A. (1988). *The psychology of everyday things.* New York: Basic Books. [17]

Norris, F. H., & Murrell, S. A. (1990). Social support, life events, and stress as modifiers of adjustment to bereavement by older adults. *Psychology and Aging, 5,* 429–436. [9]

Novello, A. C. (1990). The Surgeon General's 1990 report on the health benefits of smoking cessation: Executive summary. *Morbidity and Mortality Weekly Report, 39* (No. RR-12). [4, 13]

Noyes, R., Jr., Crowe, R. R., Harris, E. L., Hamra, B. J., McChesney, C. M., & Chaudhry, D. R. (1986). Relationship between panic disorder and agoraphobia. *Archives of General Psychiatry, 43,* 227–232. [14]

Noyes, R., Jr., Garvey, M. J., Cook, B. L., & Samuelson, L. (1989). Problems with tricyclic antidepressant use in patients with panic disorder or agoraphobia: Results of a naturalistic follow-up study. *Journal of Clinical Psychiatry, 50,* 163–169. [15]

O'Keefe, A. M. (1987, June). The case against drug testing. *Psychology Today,* pp. 21, 34–38. [4]

O'Leary, A. (1990). Stress, emotion, and human immune function. *Psychological Bulletin, 108,* 363–382. [13]

O'Leary, K. D., & Smith, D. A. (1991). Marital interactions. *Annual Review of Psychology, 42,* 191–212. [16]

O'Reilly, C. A., III. (1991). Organizational behavior: Where we've been, where we're going. *Annual Review of Psychology, 42,* 427–458. [17]

O'Sullivan, G., Noshirvani, H., Marks, I., Monteiro, W., & Lelliott, P. (1991). Six-year follow-up after exposure and clomipramine therapy for obsessive compulsive disorder. *Journal of Clinical Psychiatry, 52,* 150–155. [15]

Offer, D. (1987). In defense of adolescents. *Journal of the American Medical Association, 257,* 3407–3408. [9]

Offer, D., Ostrov, E., & Howard, K. I. (1981). *The adolescent: A psychological self-portrait.* New York: Basic Books. [9]

Ohzawa, I., DeAngelis, G. C., & Freeman, R. D. (1990). Stereoscopic depth discrimination in the visual cortex: Neurons ideally suited as disparity detectors. *Science, 249,* 1037–1041.

Ojemann, G. A. (1977). Asymmetric function of the thalamus in man. *Annals of the New York Academy of Science, 299,* 380–396. [2]

Oldenburg, D. (1990, March 16). Children: Putting down bias: New approach to an age-old problem. *Washington Post,* p. B5. [17]

Olds, J. (1956). Pleasure centers in the brain. *Scientific American, 195,* 105–116. [2]

Oliner, S. P., & Oliner P. M. (1988). *The altruistic personality: Rescuers of Jews in Nazi Europe.* New York: Free Press. [16]

Olmsted, B. (1977). Job sharing—A new way to work. *Personnel Journal, 56,* 78–81. [17]

Olweus, D. (1987). Testosterone and adrenaline: Aggressive antisocial behavior in normal adolescent males. In S. A. Mednick, T. E. Moffitt, & S. A. Stack (Eds.), *The causes of crime: New biological approaches* (pp. 263–282). Cambridge, England: Cambridge University Press. [16]

Orlofsky, J. L., & O'Heron, C. A. (1987). Stereotypic and nonstereotypic sex role trait and behavior orientations: Implications for personal adjustment. *Journal of Personality and Social Psychology, 52,* 1034–1042. [11]

Orne, M. (1983, December 12). Hypnosis "useful in medicine, dangerous in court." *U.S. News & World Report,* pp. 67–68. [4]

Öst, L-G. (1991). Acquisition of blood and injection phobia and anxiety response patterns in clinical patients. *Behaviour Research and Therapy, 29,* 323–332. [14]

Ostrov, E., Offer, D., Howard, K. I., Kaufman, B., & Meyer, H. (1985, May). Adolescent sexual behavior. *Medical Aspects of Human Sexuality, 19,* 28–36. [9]

Paikoff, R. L., & Brooks-Gunn, J. (1991). Do parent-child relationships change during puberty? *Psychological Bulletin, 110,* 47–66. [9]

Palmore, E. B. (1981). The facts on aging quiz: Part two. *The Gerontologist, 21,* 431–437. [9]

Papalia, D., & Bielby, D. D. (1974). Cognitive functioning in middle and old age adults. *Human Development, 17,* 424–443. [8]

Pappas, T. N., Melendez, R. L., & Debas, H. T. (1989). Gastric distension is a physiologic satiety signal in the dog. *Digestive Diseases and Sciences, 34,* 1489–1493. [10]

Park, B. (1986). A method for studying the development of impressions of real people. *Journal of Personality and Social Psychology, 51,* 907–917. [16]

Park, B., & Judd, C. M. (1990). Measures and models of perceived group variability. *Journal of Personality and Social Psychology, 59,* 173–191. [17]

Park, K. A., & Waters, E. (1989). Security of attachment and preschool friendships. *Child Development, 60,* 1076–1081. [8]

Parke, R. D. (1977). Some effects of punishment on children's behavior—revisited. In E. M. Hetherington, E. M. Ross, & R. D. Parke (Eds.), *Contemporary readings in child psychology.* New York: McGraw-Hill. [5]

Parke, R. D. (1978). Children's home environments: Social and cognitive effects.

In I. Altman & J. F. Wohlwill (Eds.), *Children and the environment*. New York: Plenum. [8]

Parke, R. D., O'Leary, S. E., & West, S. (1972). Mother-father-newborn interaction: Effects of maternal mediation, labor and sex of infant. *Proceedings of the American Psychological Association, 7,* 85–86. [8]

Parker, D. E. (1980). The vestibular apparatus. *Scientific American, 243,* 98–111. [3]

Parker, G. H. (1922). *Smell, taste, and allied senses in the vertebrates.* Philadelphia: Lippincott. [3]

Parker, J. G., & Asher, S. R. (1987). Peer relations and later personal adjustment: Are low-accepted children at risk? *Psychological Bulletin, 102,* 357–389. [8]

Parkinson, W. L., & Weingarten, H. P. (1990). Dissociative analysis of ventromedial hypothalamic obesity syndrome. *American Journal of Physiology, 259,* 829–835. [10]

Parloff, M. B., London, P., & Wolfe, B. (1986). Individual psychotherapy and behavior change. *Annual Review of Psychology, 37,* 321–349. [15]

Parrot, A. (1990, April). Date rape. *Medical Aspects of Human Sexuality, 24,* 28–31. [11]

Parsons, T. (1979). Definitions of health and illness in light of the American values and social structure. In E. G. Jaco (Ed.), *Patients, physicians and illness: A sourcebook in behavioral science and health.* New York: Free Press. [13]

Pascual-Leone, A., Dhuna, A., Altafullah, I., & Anderson, D. C. (1990). Cocaine-induced seizures. *Neurology, 40,* 404–407. [4]

Pashek, G. V., & Holland, A. L. (1988). Evolution of aphasia in the first year post-onset. *Cortex, 24,* 411–423. [2]

Pastore, N. (1950). The role of arbitrariness in the frustration-aggression hypothesis. *Journal of Abnormal and Social Psychology, 47,* 728–731. [16]

Pato, M. T., Zohar-Kadouch, R., Zohar, J., & Murphy, D. L. (1988). Return of symptoms after discontinuation of clomipramine in patients with obsessive-compulsive disorder. *American Journal of Psychiatry, 145,* 1521–1525. [15]

Pattison, E. M. (1982). The concept of alcoholism as a syndrome. In E. M. Pattison (Ed.), *Selection of treatment for alcoholics.* New Brunswick, NJ: Rutgers Center of Alcohol Studies. [13]

Paul, G. L., & Lentz, R. J. (1977). *Psychosocial treatment of chronic mental patients.* Cambridge, MA: Harvard University Press. [15]

Paulus, P. B., Cox, V. C., & McCain, G. (1988). *Prison crowding: A psychological perspective.* New York: Springer-Verlag. [17]

Paunonen, S. P., Jackson, D. N., Trzebinski, J., & Fosterling, F. (1992). Personality structure across cultures: A multimethod evaluation. *Journal of Personality and Social Psychology, 62,* 447–456. [12]

Pavlov, I. P. (1960). *Conditioned reflexes: An investigation of the physiological activity of the cerebral cortex* (G. V. Anrep, Trans.). New York: Dover. (Original translation published 1927). [5]

Peabody, D., & Goldberg, L. R. (1989). Some determinants of factor structures from personality-trait descriptors. *Journal of Personality and Social Psychology, 57,* 552–567. [12]

Pearl, D., Bouthilet, L., & Lazar, J. (Eds.). (1982). *Television and behavior: Ten years of scientific progress and implications for the eighties* (Vol. 2). Washington, DC: U.S. Government Printing Office. [16]

Pearlman, C. (1979). REM sleep and information processing: Evidence from animal studies. *Neuroscience and Biobehavioral Reviews, 3,* 57–68. [4]

Pederson, D. R., Moran, G., Sitko, C., Campbell, K., Ghesquire, K., & Acton, H. (1990). Maternal sensitivity and the security of infant-mother attachment: A Q-sort study. *Child Development, 61,* 1974–1983. [8]

Peele, S. (1992). Alcoholism, politics, and bureaucracy: The consensus against controlled-drinking therapy in America. *Addictive Behaviors, 17,* 49–62. [13]

Penfield, W. (1969). Consciousness, memory, and man's conditioned reflexes. In K. Pribram (Ed.), *On the biology of learning* (pp. 129–168). New York: Harcourt Brace Jovanovich. [6]

Penfield, W. (1975). *The mystery of the mind: A critical study of consciousness and the human brain.* Princeton, NJ: Princeton University Press. [6]

Pennick, S., Smith, G., Wienske, K., & Hinkle, L. (1963). An experimental evaluation of the relationship between hunger and gastric motility. *American Journal of Physiology, 205,* 421–426. [10]

Pepitone, A., & Triandis, H. C. (1987). On the universality of social psychological theories. *Journal of Cross-Cultural Psychology, 18,* 471–498. [16]

Perin, C. T. (1943). A quantitative investigation of the delay-of-reinforcement gradient. *Journal of Experimental Psychology, 32,* 37–51. [5]

Perls, F. S. (1969). *Gestalt therapy verbatim.* Lafayette, CA: Real People Press. [15]

Persad, E. (1990). Electroconvulsive therapy in depression. *Canadian Journal of Psychiatry, 35,* 175–182. [15]

Persky, V. W., Kempthorne-Rawson, J., & Shekelle, R. B. (1987). Personality and risk of cancer: 20-year follow-up of the Western Electric Study. *Psychosomatic Medicine, 49,* 435–449. [13]

Peter, J. B., Bryson, Y., & Lovett, M. A. (1982, March/April). Genital herpes: Urgent questions, elusive answers. *Diagnostic Medicine,* 71–74, 76–88. [11]

Peters, J. (1971). *A class divided.* Garden City, NY: Doubleday. [17]

Petersen, S. E., Fox, P. T., Mintun, M. A., Posner, M. I., & Raichle, M. E. (1989). Studies of the processing of single words using averaged positron emission tomographic measurements of cerebral blood flow change. *Journal of Cognitive Neuroscience, 1,* 153–170. [2]

Petersen, S. E., Fox, P. T., Posner, M. I., Mintun, M., & Raichle, M. E. (1988).

Positron emission tomographic studies of the cortical anatomy of single-word processing. *Nature, 331,* 585–589. [2]

Peterson, A. C. (1987, September). Those gangly years. *Psychology Today,* pp. 28–34. [9]

Peterson, A. C. (1988). Adolescent development. *Annual Review of Psychology, 39,* 583–607. [9]

Peterson, L. R., & Peterson, M. J. (1959). Short-term retention of individual verbal items. *Journal of Experimental Psychology, 58,* 193–198. [6]

Phillips, K., Fulker, D. W., Carey, G., & Nagoshi, C. T. (1988). Direct marital assortment for cognitive and personality variables. *Behavioral Genetics, 18,* 347–356. [16]

Piaget, J. (1960). *The child's conception of physical causality.* Patterson, NJ: Littlefield, Adams. [8]

Piaget, J. (1963a). *The child's conception of the world.* Patterson, NJ: Littlefield, Adams. [8]

Piaget, J. (1963b). *Psychology of intelligence.* Patterson, NJ: Littlefield, Adams. [8]

Piaget, J. (1964). *Judgment and reasoning in the child.* Patterson, NJ: Littlefield, Adams. [8]

Piaget, J. (1972). Intellectual evolution from adolescence to adulthood. *Human Development, 15,* 1–12. [9]

Piaget, J., & Inhelder, B. (1969). *The psychology of the child.* New York: Basic Books. [8, 9]

Pickar, D., Owen, R. R., Litman, R. E., Konicki, P. E., Gutierrez, R., & Rapaport, M. H. (1992). Clinical and biologic response to clozapine in patients with schizophrenia: Crossover comparison with fluphenazine. *Archives of General Psychiatry, 49,* 345–353. [15]

Pilkonis, P. A., Imber, S. D., Lewis, P., & Rubinsky, P. (1984). A comparative outcome study of individual, group, and conjoint psychotherapy. *Archives of General Psychiatry, 41,* 431–437. [15]

Pillemer, D. B. (1990). Clarifying the flashbulb memory concept: Comment on McCloskey, Wible, and Cohen (1988). *Journal of Experimental Psychology: General, 119,* 92–96. [6]

Pinel, J. P. J. (1990). *Biopsychology.* Boston: Allyn and Bacon. [2]

Pion, G. M., Bramblett, J. P., Jr., & Wicherski, M. (1987). *Preliminary report: 1985 doctorate employment survey.* Washington, DC: American Psychological Association. [1]

Platt, R., Rice, P. A., & McCormack, W. M. (1983). Risk of acquiring gonorrhea and prevalence of abnormal adnexal findings among women recently exposed to gonorrhea. *Journal of the American Medical Association, 250,* 3205–3209. [11]

Plomin, R. (1989). Environment and genes: Determinants of behavior. *American Psychologist, 44,* 105–111. [7, 8, 12]

Plomin, R. (1990). The role of inheritance in behavior. *Science, 248,* 183–188. [7, 12]

Plomin, R., & Bergeman, C. S. (1991). The nature of nurture: Genetic influence on "environmental" measures. *Behavioral and Brain Sciences, 14,* 373–427. [12]

Plomin, R., DeFries, J. C., & Fulker, D. W. (1988). *Nature and nurture during infancy and early childhood.* New York: Cambridge University Press. [7]

Plomin, R., & Rende, R. (1991). Human behavioral genetics. *Annual Review of Psychology, 42,* 161–190. [7, 12]

Plutchik, R. (1980). *Emotion: A psychoevolutionary synthesis.* New York: Harper & Row. [10]

Polich, J. M., Armor, D. J., & Braiker, H. B. (1981). *The course of alcoholism: Four years after treatment.* New York: Wiley. [13]

Pomerleau, O. F., & Pomerleau, C. S. (1984). Neuroregulators and the reinforcement of smoking: Towards a biobehavioral explanation. *Neuroscience and Biobehavioral Reviews, 8,* 503–513. [13]

Pomerleau, O. F., & Pomerleau, C. S. (1989). A biobehavioral perspective on smoking. In T. Ney & A. Gale (Eds.), *Smoking and human behavior* (pp. 69–93). New York: Wiley. [13]

Pomerleau, O. F., & Rodin, J. (1986). Behavioral medicine and health psychology. In S. L. Garfield & A. E. Bergin (Eds.), *Handbook of psychotherapy and behavior change.* New York: Wiley. [13]

Postman, L., & Phillips, L. W. (1965). Short-term temporal changes in free recall. *Quarterly Journal of Experimental Psychology, 17,* 132–138. [6]

Powell, K. E., Spain, K. G., Christenson, G. M., & Mollenkamp, M. P. (1986). The status of the 1990 objectives for physical fitness and exercise. *Public Health Reports, 101,* 15–21. [13]

Power, T. G. (1985). Mother- and father-infant play: A developmental analysis. *Child Development, 56,* 1514–1524. [11]

Pratkanis, A. R. (1989). The cognitive representation of attitudes. In A. R. Pratkanis, S. J. Breckler, & A. G. Greenwald (Eds.), *Attitude structure and function* (pp. 71–93). Hillsdale, NJ: Erlbaum. [16]

Pribor, E. F., & Dinwiddie, S. H. (1991). Psychiatric correlates of incest in childhood. *American Journal of Psychiatry, 148,* 52–56. [14]

Price, R. A., Cadoret, R. J., Stunkard, A. J., & Troughton, E. (1987). Genetic contributions to human fatness: An adoption study. *American Journal of Psychiatry, 144,* 1003–1008. [13]

Price, R. A., Stunkard, A. J., Ness, R., Wadden, T., Heshka, S., Kanders, B., & Cormillot, A. (1990). Childhood onset (age less than 10) obesity has a high familial risk. *International Journal of Obesity, 14,* 185–195. [13]

Prien, R. F., Kupfer, D. J., Mansky, P. A., Small, J. G., Tuason, V. B., Voss, C. B., & Johnson, W. E. (1984). Drug therapy in the prevention of recurrences in unipolar and bipolar affective disorders. *Archives of General Psychiatry, 41,* 1096–1104. [15]

Priest, R. F., & Sawyer, J. (1967). Proximity and peership: Bases of balance in interpersonal attraction. *American Journal of Sociology, 72,* 633–649. [16]

Prinz, P. N., Vitiello, M. V., Raskind, M. A., & Thorpy, M. J. (1990). Geriatrics: Sleep disorders and aging. *New England Journal of Medicine, 323,* 520–526. [4]

Public Health Service. (1991). *Healthy people 2000: National health promotion and disease prevention objectives [Summary].* (DHHS Publication No. PHS 91-50213). Washington, DC: U.S. Department of Health and Human Services. [13]

Putnam, F. W. (1989). *Diagnosis and treatment of multiple personality disorder.* New York: Guilford Press. [14]

Putnam, F. W., Guroff, J. J., Silberman, E. K., Barban, L., & Post, R. M. (1986). The clinical phenomenology of multiple personality disorder: Review of 100 recent cases. *Journal of Clinical Psychiatry, 47,* 285–293. [14]

Pylyshyn, Z. W. (1984). *Computation and cognition.* Cambridge, MA: M.I.T. Press. [7]

Quattrone, G. A. (1986). On the perception of a group's variability. In S. Worchel & W. Austin (Eds.), *The psychology of intergroup relations* (Vol. 2, pp. 25–48). Chicago: Nelson-Hall. [17]

Quayle, D. (1983). American productivity: The devastating effect of alcoholism and drug abuse. *American Psychologist, 38,* 454–458. [4]

Rachman, S. J., & Wilson, G. T. (1980). *The effects of psychological therapy* (2nd ed.). New York: Pergamon. [15]

Rahe, R. J., Meyer, M., Smith, M., Kjaer, G., & Holmes, T. H. (1964). Social stress and illness onset. *Journal of Psychosomatic Research, 8,* 35–44. [13]

Rakic, P. (1988). Specification of cerebral cortical areas. *Science, 241,* 170–176. [2]

Ralph, M. R. (1989, November/December). The rhythm maker: Pinpointing the master clock in mammals. *The Sciences, 29,* 40–45 [4]

Ramachandran, V. S., & Anstis, S. M. (1986). The perception of apparent motion. *Scientific American, 254,* 102–109. [3]

Randi, J. (1980). *Flim-Flam: The truth about unicorns, parapsychology, and other delusions.* New York: Lippincott & Crowell. [3]

Rapoport, J. L. (1989). The biology of obsessions and compulsions. *Scientific American, 260,* 83–89. [15]

Rasmussen, S. A., & Eisen, J. L. (1990). Epidemiology of obsessive compulsive disorder. *Journal of Clinical Psychiatry, 51*(2, Suppl.), 10–13. [14]

Redfield, R. R., & Burke, D. S. (1988). HIV infection: The clinical picture. *Scientific American, 259,* 90–98. [11]

Reed, S., & Fischer, M. A. (1984, January 23). Adventure: Far from being over the hill, Hulda Crooks, at 87, is a real climber. *People Weekly,* pp. 88–90. [9]

Regestein, Q. R., & Monk, T. H. (1991). Is the poor sleep of shift workers a disorder? *American Journal of Psychiatry, 148,* 1487–1493. [4]

Reiman, E. M., Fusselman, M. J., Fox, P. T., & Raichle, M. E. (1989). Neuroanatomical correlates of anticipatory anxiety. *Science, 243,* 1071–1074. [14]

Reiman, E. M., Raichle, M. E., Butler, F. K., Herscovitch, P., & Robins, E. (1984). A focal brain abnormality in panic disorder: A severe form of anxiety. *Nature, 310,* 683–685. [14]

Reinke, B. J. (1985). Psychosocial changes as a function of chronological age. *Human Development, 28,* 266–269. [9]

Reinke, B. J., Ellicott, A. M., Harris, R. L., & Hancock, E. (1985). Timing of psychosocial changes in women's lives. *Human Development, 28,* 259–280. [9]

Reis, H. T., Wilson, I. M., Monestere, C., Bernstein, S., Clark, K., Seidl, E., Franco, M., Gioioso, E., Freeman, L., & Radoane, K. (1990). What is smiling is beautiful and good. *European Journal of Social Psychology, 20,* 259–267. [16]

Reisberg, D., Heuer, F., McLean, J., & O'Shaughnessy, M. (1988). The quantity, not the quality, of affect predicts memory vividness. *Bulletin of the Psychonomic Society, 26,* 100–103. [6]

Reisenzein, R. (1986). A structural equation analysis of Weiner's attribution-affect model of helping behavior. *Journal of Personality and Social Psychology, 50,* 1123–1133. [16]

Reiss, B. F. (1980). Psychological tests in homosexuality. In J. Marmor (Ed.), *Homosexual behavior* (pp. 296–311). New York: Basic Books. [11]

Renneker, R. (1981). Cancer and psychotherapy. In J. Goldberg (Ed.), *Psychotherapeutic treatment of cancer patients.* New York: Free Press. [13]

Renzetti, C. M., & Curran, D. J. (1992). *Women, men, and society.* Boston: Allyn and Bacon. [17]

Reppert, S. M., Weaver, D. R., Rivkees, S. A., & Stopa, E. G. (1988). Putative melatonin receptors in a human biological clock. *Science, 242,* 78–81. [2]

Rescorla, R. A. (1967). Pavlovian conditioning and its proper control procedures. *Psychological Review, 74,* 71–80. [5]

Rescorla, R. A. (1988). Pavlovian conditioning: It's not what you think it is. *American Psychologist, 43,* 151–160. [5]

Rethlingshafer, D., & Hinckley, E. D. (1963). Influence of judges' characteristics upon the adaptation level. *American Journal of Psychology, 76,* 116–119. [3]

Rhoades, E. R., Hammond, J., Welty, T. K., Handler, A. O., & Amler, R. W. (1987). The Indian burden of illness and future health interventions. *Public Health Reports, 102,* 361–368. [13]

Rholes, W. S., Riskind, J. H., & Lane, J. W. (1987). Emotional states and memory biases: Effects of cognitive priming and mood. *Journal of Personality and Social Psychology, 52,* 91–99. [6]

Rhyne, D. (1981). Bases of marital satisfaction among men and women. *Journal of Marriage and the Family, 43,* 941–955. [9]

Rice, M. L. (1989). Children's language acquisition. *American Psychologist, 44,* 149–156. [8]

Rice, M. L., Huston, A. C., Truglio, R., & Wright, J. C. (1987). *Words from Sesame Street: Learning vocabulary while viewing.* Unpublished manuscript, University of Kansas, Lawrence, KS. [8]

Rice, P. L. (1987). *Stress and health: Principles and practice for coping and wellness.* Monterey, CA: Brooks/Cole. [13]

Rich, C. L., Warstradt, G. M., Nemiroff, R. A., Fowler, R. D., & Young, D. (1991). Suicide, stressors, and the life cycle. *American Journal of Psychiatry, 148,* 524–527. [14]

Rimland, B. (1978, August). Inside the mind of the autistic savant. *Psychology Today,* p. 12, 69–80. [7]

Riordan, C. A., & Tedeschi, J. T. (1983). Attraction in aversive environments: Some evidence for classical conditioning and negative reinforcement. *Journal of Personality and Social Psychology, 44,* 683–692. [16]

Robberson, M. R., & Rogers, R. W. (1988). Beyond fear appeals: Negative and positive persuasive appeals to health and self-esteem. *Journal of Applied Social Psychology, 18,* 277–287. [16]

Robertson, G. L. (1983). Thirst and vasopressin function in normal and disordered states of water balance. *Journal of Laboratory and Clinical Medicine, 101,* 351–371. [10]

Robins, L. N., Helzer, J. E., Weissman, M. M., et al. (1984). Lifetime prevalence of specific psychiatric disorders in three sites. *Archives of General Psychiatry, 41,* 949–958. [14]

Robinson, F. P. (1941). *Effective behavior.* New York: Harper & Row. [1]

Roche, A. F., & Davila, G. H. (1972). Late adolescent growth in stature. *Pediatrics, 50,* 874–880. [9]

Rock, I., & Palmer, S. (1990). The legacy of Gestalt psychology. *Scientific American, 263,* 84–90. [5]

Rodin, J. (1981). Current status of the internal-external hypothesis for obesity: What went wrong? *American Psychologist, 36,* 361–372. [10]

Rodin, J. (1985). Insulin levels, hunger, and food intake: An example of feedback loops in body weight regulation. *Health Psychology, 4,* 1–24. [10]

Rodin, J. (1986). Aging and health: Effects of the sense of control. *Science, 233,* 1271–1276. [13]

Rodin, J., & Salovey, P. (1989). Health psychology. *Annual Review of Psychology, 40,* 533–579. [13]

Rodin, J., Slochower, J., & Fleming, B. (1977). The effects of degree of obesity, age of onset, and energy deficit on external responsiveness. *Journal of Comparative and Physiological Psychology, 91,* 586–597. [10]

Rodin, J., Wack, J., Ferrannini, E., & DeFronzo, R. A. (1985). Effect of insulin and glucose on feeding behavior. *Metabolism, 34,* 826–831. [10]

Rodin, J., & Wing, R. R. (1988). Behavioral factors in obesity. *Diabetes/Metabolism Reviews, 4,* 701–725. [13]

Rodriguez-Trias, H. (1992). Women's health, women's lives, women's rights. *American Journal of Public Health, 82,* 663–664. [13]

Roediger, H. L., III. (1980). The effectiveness of four mnemonics in ordering recall. *Journal of Experimental Psychology: Human Learning and Memory, 6,* 558–567. [6]

Roehrich, L., & Kinder, B. N. (1991). Alcohol expectancies and male sexuality: Review and implications for sex therapy. *Journal of Sex and Marital Therapy, 17,* 45–54. [4]

Rogers, C. R. (1951). *Client-centered therapy: Its current practice, implications, and theory.* Boston: Houghton Mifflin. [12, 15]

Rogers, C. R. (1959). A theory of therapy, personality, and interpersonal relationships, as developed in the client-centered framework. In S. Koch (Ed.), *Psychology: A study of a science, Vol. III. Formulations of the person and the social context* (pp. 184–256). New York: McGraw-Hill. [15]

Rogers, C. R. (1961). *On becoming a person: A therapist's view of psychotherapy.* Boston: Houghton Mifflin. [12, 14]

Rogers, C. R. (1977). The case of Mary Jane Tilden. In S. J. Morse & R. I. Watson, Jr. (Eds.), *Psychotherapies: A comparative casebook* (pp. 197–222). New York: Holt, Rinehart & Winston. [15]

Rogers, C. R. (1981). Notes on Rollo May. *Perspectives, 2*(1), 16. [12]

Rogers, J. P. (1989, April). Type A: Healing the spirit. *Psychology Today,* p. 18. [13]

Rogers, M. P., & Reich, P. (1988). On the health consequences of bereavement. *New England Journal of Medicine, 319,* 510–512. [13]

Rogers, P. J. (1990). Why a palatability construct is needed. *Appetite, 14,* 167–170. [10]

Rogers, P. J., & Hill, A. J. (1989). Breakdown of dietary restraint following mere exposure to food stimuli: Interrelationships between restraint, hunger, salivation, and food intake. *Addictive Behaviors, 14,* 387–397. [10]

Roland, P. (1992). Cortical representation of pain. *Trends in Neurosciences, 15,* 3–5. [2]

Rollins, B. C., & Feldman, H. (1970). Marital satisfaction over the family life cycle. *Journal of Marriage and the Family, 32,* 20–28. [9]

Rosch, E. H. (1973). Natural categories. *Cognitive Psychology, 4,* 328–350. [7]

Rosch, E. H. (1978). Principles of categorization. In E. H. Rosch & B. Lloyd (Eds.), *Cognition and categorization.* Hillsdale, NJ: Erlbaum. [7]

Rose, R. J., Koskenvuo, M., Kaprio, J., Sarna, S., & Langinvainio, H. (1988). Shared genes, shared experiences, and similarity of personality: Data from 14,288 adult Finnish co-twins. *Journal of Personality and Social Psychology, 54,* 161–171. [12]

Rosen, T. (1990, January). The reemergence of syphilis. *Medical Aspects of Human Sexuality, 24,* 20–22. [11]

Rosenbaum, J. F. (1990). High-potency benzodiazepines: Emerging uses in psychiatry. *Journal of Clinical Psychiatry, 51*(5, Suppl.), 3. [15]

Rosenbaum, M. E. (1986). The repulsion hypothesis: On the nondevelopment of relationships. *Journal of Personality and Social Psychology, 51,* 1156–1166. [16]

Rosenberg, J., & Pettinati, H. M. (1984). Differential memory complaints after bilateral and unilateral ECT. *American Journal of Psychiatry, 14,* 1071–1074. [15]

Rosenhan, D. L. (1973). On being sane in insane places. *Science, 179,* 250–258. [3]

Rosenthal, A. M. (1964). *Thirty-eight witnesses.* New York: McGraw-Hill. [16]

Rosenthal, D. (1970). *Genetic theory and abnormal behavior.* New York: McGraw-Hill. [14]

Rosenthal, N. E., Carpenter, C. J., James, S. P., Parry, B. L., Rogers, S. L. B., & Wehr, T. A.. (1986). Seasonal affective disorder in children and adolescents. *American Journal of Psychiatry, 143,* 356–358. [14]

Rosenthal, N. E., Sack, D. A., Carpenter, C. J., et al. (1985). Antidepressant effects of light in seasonal affective disorder. *American Journal of Psychiatry, 142,* 163–170. [14]

Rosenthal, R. (1973, September). The Pygmalion effect lives. *Psychology Today,* pp. 56–63. [1]

Rosenzweig, M. R. (1961). Auditory localization. *Scientific American, 205,* 132–142. [3]

Rosenzweig, M. R., Bennett, E. L., & Diamond, M. C. (1972). Brain changes in response to experience. *Scientific American, 226,* 22–29. [2]

Ross, L. (1977). The intuitive psychologist and his shortcomings: Distortions in the attribution process. In L. Berkowitz (Ed.), *Advances in experimental social psychology* (Vol. 10). New York: Academic Press. [16]

Ross, C. A., Anderson, G., Fleisher, W. P., & Norton, G. R. (1991). The frequency of multiple personality disorder among psychiatric inpatients. *American Journal of Psychiatry, 148,* 1717–1720. [14]

Ross, C. A., Miller, S. D., Reagor, P., Bjornson, L., Fraser, G. A., & Anderson, G. (1990). Structured interview data on 102 cases of multiple personality disorder from four centers. *American Journal of Psychiatry, 147,* 596–601. [14]

Ross, C. A., Norton, G. R., & Wozney, K. (1989). Multiple personality disorder: An analysis of 236 cases. *Canadian Journal of Psychiatry, 34,* 413–418. [14]

Ross, J., & Lawrence, K. A. (1968). Some observations on memory artifice. *Psychonomic Science, 13,* 107–108. [6]

Rostron, A. B. (1974). Brief auditory storage: Some further observations. *Acta Psychologica, 38,* 471–482. [6]

Roth, D. L., Wiebe, D. J., Filligim, R. B., & Shay, K. A. (1989). Life events, fitness, hardiness, and health: A simultaneous analysis of proposed stress-resistance effects. *Journal of Personality and Social Psychology, 57,* 136–142. [13]

Roth, W. T., Margraf, J., Ehlers, A., Taylor, B., Maddock, R. J., Davies, S., Argras, W. S. (1992). Stress test reactivity in panic disorder. *Archives of General Psychiatry, 49,* 301–310. [14]

Rotter, J. B. (1966). Generalized expectancies for internal versus external control of reinforcement. *Psychological Monographs, 80*(1, Whole No. 609). [12]

Rotter, J. B. (1971, June). External control and internal control. *Psychology Today,* pp. 37–42, 58–59. [12]

Rotter, J. B. (1990). Internal versus external control of reinforcement: A case history of a variable. *American Psychologist, 45,* 489–493. [12]

Rotton, J., Frey, J., Barry, T., Milligan, M., & Fitzpatrick, M. (1979). The air pollution experience and physical aggression. *Journal of Applied Social Psychology, 9,* 397–412. [16]

Rovee-Collier, C. (1990). The "memory system" of prelinguistic infants. *Annals of the New York Academy of Sciences, 608,* 517–576. [8]

Rovee-Collier, C. K., & Lipsett, L. P. (1982). Learning, adaptation, and memory in the newborn. In P. Stratton (Ed.), *Psychobiology of the human newborn.* New York: Wiley. [8]

Rowe, D. C. (1987). Resolving the person-situation debate: Invitation to an interdisciplinary dialogue. *American Psychologist, 42,* 218–227. [12]

Rowe, J. W., & Kahn, R. L. (1987). Human aging: Usual and successful. *Science, 237,* 143–149. [9]

Roybal, E. R. (1988). Mental health and aging: The need for an expanded federal response. *American Psychologist, 43,* 189–194. [9]

Rozin, P., & Zellner, D. (1985). The role of Pavlovian conditioning in the acquisition of food likes and dislikes. *Annals of the New York Academy of Sciences, 443,* 189–202. [5]

Rubenstein, C. (1982, July). Psychology's fruit flies. *Psychology Today,* pp. 83–84. [1]

Rubinstein, E. A. (1983). Television and behavior: Research conclusions of the 1982 NIMH report and their policy implications. *American Psychologist, 38,* 820–825. [8, 16]

Ruble, D. N., Fleming, A. S., Hackel, L. S., & Stangor, C. (1988). Changes in the marital relationship during the transition to first time motherhood: Effects of violated expectations of household labor. *Journal of Personality and Social Psychology, 55,* 78–87. [9]

Runeson, B. (1989). Mental disorder in youth suicide. DSM-III-R Axes I and II. *Acta Psychiatrica Scandinavica, 79,* 490–497. [14]

Rushton, J. P., Fulker, D. W., Neale, M. C., Nias, D. K. B., & Eysenck, H. J. (1986). Altruism and aggression: The heritability of individual differences. *Journal of Personality and Social Psychology, 50,* 1192–1198. [12, 16]

Russell, G. R. (1983). *Marijuana today: A compilation of medical findings for the layman* (rev.). New York: Myrin Institute. [4]

Sackeim, H. A. (1985, June). The case for ECT. *Psychology Today,* pp. 36–40. [15]

Sackeim, H. A., Gur, R. C., & Saucy, M. (1978). Emotions are expressed more intensely on the left side of the face. *Science, 202,* 434–436. [2]

Sackeim, H. A., Portnoy, S., Neeley, P., Steif, B. L., Decina, P., & Malitz, S. (1986). Cognitive consequences of low-dosage electroconvulsive therapy. *Annals of the New York Academy of Sciences, 462,* 326–340. [15]

Salama, A. A. A., & England, R. D. (1990). A case study: Schizophrenia and tactile hallucinations, treated with electroconvulsive therapy. *Canadian Journal of Psychiatry, 35,* 86–87. [14]

Sales, B. D., & Hafemeister, T. L. (1985). Law and psychology. In E. M. Altmeir & M. E. Meyer (Eds.), *Applied specialties in psychology.* New York: Random House. [17]

Saltzman, A. (1991, June 17). Trouble at the top. *U.S. News & World Report,* pp. 40–48. [11, 17]

Sanbonmatsu, D. M., & Fazio, R. H. (1990). The role of attitudes in memory-based decision making. *Journal of Personality and Social Psychology, 59,* 614–622. [16]

Sanna, L. J., & Shotland, R. L. (1990). Valence of anticipated evaluation and social facilitation. *Journal of Experimental Social Psychology, 26,* 82–92. [16]

Sauter, S. L., Hurrell, J. J., Jr., & Cooper, C. L. (Eds.). (1989). *Job control and worker health.* New York: Wiley. [17]

Sauter, S. L., Murphy, L. R., & Hurrell, J. J., Jr. (1990). Prevention of work-related psychological disorders: A national strategy proposed by the National Institute for Occupational Safety and Health (NIOSH). *American Psychologist, 45,* 1146–1158. [17]

Savin-Williams, R. (1980). Dominance hierarchies in groups of middle to late adolescent males. *Journal of Youth and Adolescence, 9,* 75–85. [9]

Saxe, L., Dougherty, D., & Cross, T. (1985). The validity of polygraph testing: Scientific analysis and public controversy. *American Psychologist, 40,* 355–366. [10]

Scarborough, D. L. (1972). Stimulus modality effects on forgetting in short-term memory. *Journal of Experimental Psychology, 95,* 285–289. [6]

Scarr, S., Webber, P. L., Weinberg, R. A., & Wittig, M. A. (1981). Personality resemblance among adolescents and their parents in biologically related and adoptive families. *Journal of Personality and Social Psychology, 40,* 885–898. [12]

Scarr, S., & Weinberg, R. (1976). IQ test performance of black children adopted by white families. *American Psychologist, 31,* 726–739. [7]

Scarr, S., & Weinberg, R. (1978). The influence of "family background" on intellectual attainment. *American Sociological Review, 43,* 674–692. [7]

Scarr, S., & Weinberg, R. A. (1986). The early childhood enterprise: Care and education of the young. *American Psychologist, 41,* 1140–1146. [8]

Schab, F. R. (1990). Odors and the remembrance of things past. *Journal of Experimental Psychology: Learning, Memory, and Cognition, 16,* 648–655. [6]

Schachter, S., & Gross, L. P. (1968). Manipulated time and eating behavior. *Journal of Personality and Social Psychology, 10,* 98–106. [10]

Schachter, S., & Singer, J. E. (1962). Cognitive, social, and physiological determinants of emotional state. *Psychological Review, 69,* 379–399. [10]

Schelling, T. C. (1992). Addictive drugs: The cigarette experience. *Science, 255,* 430–433. [13]

Schiff, M., Duyme, M., Dumaret, A., Stewart, J., & Tomkiewicz, S. (1982). How much could we boost scholastic achievement and IQ scores? A direct answer from a French adoption study. *Cognition, 12,* 165–196. [7]

Schiff, M., Duyme, M., Dumaret, A., Stewart, J., Tomkiewicz, S., & Feingold, J. (1978). Intellectual status of working-class children adopted early into upper-middle-class families. *Science, 200,* 1503–1504. [7]

Schiff, M., & Lewontin, R. (1986). *Education and class: The irrelevance of IQ genetic studies.* Oxford, England: Clarendon. [7]

Schildkraut, J. (1970). *Neurophychopharmacology of the affective disorders.* Boston: Little, Brown. [14]

Schleifer, S. J., Keller, S. E., Camerino, M., et al. (1983). Suppression of lymphocyte stimulation following bereavement. *Journal of the American Medical Association, 250,* 374–377. [13]

Schleifer, S. J., Keller, S. E., Siris, S. G., Davis, K. L., & Stein, M. (1985). Depression and immunity: Lymphocyte function in ambulatory depressed patients, hospitalized schizophrenic patients, and patients hospitalized for herniorraphy. *Archives of General Psychiatry, 42,* 129–133. [13]

Schlundt, D. G., & Johnson, W. G. (1990). *Eating disorders.* Boston: Allyn and Bacon. [9]

Schmidt, G., & Weiner, B. (1988). An attributional-affect-action theory of behavior: Replications of judgments of helping. *Personality and Social Psychology Bulletin, 14,* 610–621. [16]

Schnapf, J. L., Kraft, T. W., & Baylor, D. A. (1987). Spectral sensitivity of human cone photoreceptors. *Science, 325,* 439–441. [3]

Schneier, F. R., Johnson, J., Hornig, C. D., Liebowitz, M. R., & Weissman, M. M. (1992). Social phobia: Comorbidity and morbidity in an epidemiologic sample. *Archives of General Psychiatry, 49,* 282–288. [14]

Schofield, J. W., & Francis, W. D. (1982). An observational study of peer interaction in racially mixed "accelerated" classrooms. *Journal of Educational Psychology, 74,* 722–732. [8]

Schou, M. (1989). Lithium prophylaxis: Myths and realities. *American Journal of Psychiatry, 146,* 573–576. [15]

Schover, L. R., & LoPiccolo, J. (1982). Treatment effectiveness for dysfunctions of sexual desire. *Journal of Sex and Marital Therapy, 8,* 179–197. [11]

Schreurs, B. G. (1989). Classical conditioning of model systems: A behavioral review. *Psychobiology, 17,* 145–155. [5]

Schrieber, F. R. (1973). *Sybil.* Chicago: Henry Regnery. [14]

Schroeder, D. H., & Costa, P. T., Jr. (1984). Influence of life event stress on physical illness: Substantive effects or methodological flaws? *Journal of Personality and Social Psychology, 46,* 853–863. [13]

Schultz, D. (1975). *A history of modern psychology* (2nd ed.). New York: Academic Press. [5]

Schwartz, G. E. (1982). Testing the biopsychosocial model: The ultimate challenge facing behavioral medicine? *Journal of Consulting and Clinical Psychology, 50,* 1040–1052. [13]

Schwartz, G. E., Weinberger, D. A., & Singer, J. A. (1981). Cardiovascular differentiation of happiness, sadness, anger, and fear following imagery and exercise. *Psychosomatic Medicine, 43,* 343–364. [10]

Schwartz, J. C., Strickland, R. G., & Krolick, G. (1974). Infant day care: Behavioral effects at preschool age. *Developmental Psychology, 10,* 502–506. [8]

Schwebke, J. R. (1991a, March). Gonorrhea in the '90s. *Medical Aspects of Human Sexuality, 24,* 42–46. [11]

Schwebke, J. R. (1991b, April). Syphilis in the '90s. *Medical Aspects of Human Sexuality, 25,* 44–49. [11]

Sclafani, A., & Springer, D. (1976). Dietary obesity in adult rats: Similarities to hypothalamic and human obesity syndromes. *Physiology and Behavior, 17,* 461–471. [10]

Searles, J. S. (1988). The role of genetics in the pathogenesis of alcoholism. *Journal of Abnormal Psychology, 97,* 153–167. [13]

Sears, R. R. (1977). Sources of life satisfactions of the Terman gifted men. *American Psychologist, 32,* 119–128. [9]

Sebald, J. (1981). Adolescents' concept of popularity and unpopularity comparing 1960 with 1976. *Adolescence, 16,* 187–192. [9]

Seeman, M., & Seeman, A. Z. (1992). Life strains, alienation, and drinking behavior. *Alcoholism: Clinical and Experimental Research, 16,* 199–205. [13]

Segal, B. M. (1990). *The drunken society: Alcohol abuse and alcoholism in the Soviet Union. A comparative study.* New York: Hippocrene Books. [4]

Segal, S. J., & Fusella, V. (1970). Influence of imaged pictures and sounds on detection of visual and auditory signals. *Journal of Experimental Psychology, 83,* 458–464. [7]

Segall, M. H., Campbell, D. T., & Herskovitz, M. J. (1966). *The influence of culture on visual perception.* Indianapolis: Bobbs-Merrill. [3]

Sekuler, R., & Blake, R. (1987, December). Sensory underload. *Psychology Today,* pp. 48–51. [9]

Seligman, M. E. P. (1970). On the generality of the laws of learning. *Psychological Review, 77,* 406–418. [5]

Selye, H. (1956). *The stress of life.* New York: McGraw-Hill. [13]

Selye, H. (1974). *Stress without distress.* Philadelphia: Lippincott. [13]

Serbin, L. A., & Sprafkin, C. (1986). The salience of gender and the process of sex-typing in three-to seven-year-old children. *Child Development, 57,* 1188–1209. [11]

Seta, J. J., Crisson, J. E., Seta, C. E., & Wang, M. A. (1989). Task performance and perceptions of anxiety: Averaging and summation in an evaluation setting. *Journal of Personality and Social Psychology, 56,* 387–396. [16]

Shafer, J. (1985, March). Designer drugs. *Science 85,* pp. 60–67. [4]

Shaffer, D. (1988). The epidemiology of teen suicide: An examination of risk factors. *Journal of Clinical Psychiatry, 49*(9, Suppl.), 36–41. [14]

Shafii, M., Carrigan, S., Whittinghill, J. R., & Derrick, A. (1985). Psychological autopsy of completed suicide in children and adolescents. *American Journal of Psychiatry, 142,* 1061–1064. [14]

Sharp, D., Cole, M., & Lave, C. (1979). Education and cognitive development: The evidence from experimental research. *Monographs of the Society for Research in Child Development, 44*(1–2, Serial No. 178). [8]

Shatz, M. (1983). Communication. In P. H. Mussen (Ed.), *Handbook of child psychology* (Vol. 3). New York: Wiley. [8]

Shatz, M., & Gelman, R. (1973). The development of communication skills: Modifications in the speech of young children as a function of listener. *Monographs of the Society for Research in Child Development, 38*(5, Serial No. 152), 1–37. [8]

Shaw, D. W., & Thoresen, C. E. (1974). Effects of modeling and desensitization in reducing dentist phobia. *Journal of Counseling Psychology, 21,* 415–420. [15]

Shearer, L. (1989, August 6). College students: Sex, religion and lifestyles. *Parade Magazine,* pp. 12–13. [11]

Sheehan, D. V. (1983). *The anxiety disease.* New York: Charles Scribner's Sons. [14, 15]

Sheehan, D. V., & Raj, A. B. (1988). Monoamine oxidase inhibitors. In C. G. Last & M. Hersen (Eds.), *Handbook of anxiety disorders* (pp. 478–506). New York: Pergamon Press. [15]

Shekelle, R. B., Hully, S. B., Neaton, J. D., Billings, J. H., Borhani, N. O., Gerace, T. A., Jacobs, D. R., Lasser, N. L., Mittlmark, M. B., & Stamler, J. (1985). The MRFIT behavior pattern study: II. Type A behavior and incidence of coronary heart disease. *American Journal of Epidemiology, 122,* 559–570. [13]

Shell, E. R. (1988, August). Babies in day care: The controversy over whether nonmaternal care harms infants. *The Atlantic, 262,* pp. 73–74. [8]

Shepard, R. J. (1986). Exercise in coronary heart disease. *Sports Medicine, 3,* 26–49. [13]

Shepard, R. N. (1978). Externalization of mental images and the act of creation. In B. S. Randhawa & W. E. Coffman (Eds.), *Visual learning, thinking, and communication* (pp. 133–190). New York: Academic Press. [7]

Shepard, R. N., & Metzler, J. (1971). Mental rotation of three-dimensional objects. *Science, 171,* 701–703. [7]

Sherif, M. (1956). Experiments in group conflict. *Scientific American, 195,* 53–58. [17]

Sherif, M. (1958). Superordinate goals in the reduction of intergroup conflict. *American Journal of Sociology, 63,* 349–358. [17]

Shiffrin, R. M. (1970). Forgetting: Trace erosion or retrieval failure? *Science, 168,* 1601–1603. [6]

Shiffrin, R. M., & Atkinson, R. C. (1969). Storage and retrieval processes in long-term memory. *Psychological Review, 76,* 179–193. [6]

Shneidman, E. (1989). The Indian summer of life: A preliminary study of septuagenarians. *American Psychologist, 44,* 684–694. [7]

Shneidman, E. S. (1987, March). At the point of no return. *Psychology Today,* pp. 54–58. [14]

Shulman, H. G. (1972). Semantic confusion errors in short-term memory. *Journal of Verbal Learning and Verbal Behavior, 11,* 221–227. [6]

Siegel, S., Hinson, R. E., Krank, M. D., & McCully, J. (1982). Heroin "overdose" death: Contribution of drug-associated environmental cues. *Science, 216,* 436–437. [10]

Siegler, R. S. (1992). The other Alfred Binet. *Developmental Psychology, 28,* 179–190. [7]

Siegler, R. S., & Liebert, R. M. (1975). Acquisition of formal scientific reasoning by 10- and 13-year-olds: Designing a factorial experiment. *Developmental Psychology, 11,* 401–402. [8]

Siller, B., & Azziz, R. (1991, March). New ways of managing ectopic pregnancy. *Medical Aspects of Human Sexuality, 25,* 30–39. [11]

Silver, B. J., Goldstein, S. E., & Silver, L. B. (1984). The 1990 objectives for the nation for control of stress and violent behavior: Progress report. *Public Health Reports, 99,* 374–384. [14]

Simmons, R. G., Blyth, D. A., & McKinney, K. L. (1983). The social and psychological effects of puberty on white females. In J. Brooks-Gunn & A. C. Peterson (Eds.), *Girls at puberty: Biological and psychosocial perspectives.* New York: Plenum. [9]

Simon, H. A. (1974). How big is a chunk? *Science, 183,* 482–488. [6]

Simon, H. B. (1988, June). Running and rheumatism. *Harvard Medical School Health Letter, 13,* pp. 2–4. [13]

Simpson, E. L. (1974). Moral development research. *Human Development, 17,* 81–106. [9]

Sims, E. A. H. (1990). Destiny rides again as twins overeat. *New England Journal of Medicine, 322,* 1522–1524. [13]

Singer, J. L., & Singer, D. G. (1979, March). Come back, Mister Rogers, come back. *Psychology Today,* pp. 56–60. [8]

Sivacek, J., & Crano, W. D. (1982). Vested interest as a moderator of attitude-behavior consistency. *Journal of Personality and Social Psychology, 43,* 210–221. [16]

Skinner, B. F. (1938). *The behavior of organisms.* New York: Appleton-Century-Crofts. [5]

Skinner, B. F. (1948a). "Superstition" in the pigeon. *Journal of Experimental Psychology, 38,* 168–172. [5]

Skinner, B. F. (1948b). *Walden two.* New York: Macmillan. [5]

Skinner, B. F. (1953). *Science and human behavior.* New York: Macmillan. [5, 12]

Skinner, B. F. (1957). *Verbal behavior.* New York: Appleton-Century-Crofts. [8]

Skinner, B. F. (1967). Autobiography. In E. G. Boring & G. Lindzey (Eds.), *A history of psychology in autobiography* (Vol. 5, pp. 387–413). New York: Appleton. [5]

Skinner, B. F. (1971). *Beyond freedom and dignity.* New York: Knopf. [5]

Skinner, B. F. (1987). Whatever happened to psychology as the science of behavior? *American Psychologist, 42,* 780–786. [1]

Skinner, B. F. (1988). The operant side of behavior therapy. *Journal of Behavior Therapy and Experimental Psychiatry, 19,* 171–179. [5]

Sklar, L. S., & Anisman, H. (1981). Stress and cancer. *Psychological Bulletin, 89,* 369–406. [13]

Slamecka, N. J. (1985). Ebbinghaus: Some associations. *Journal of Experimental Psychology: Learning, Memory, and Cognition, 11,* 414–435. [6]

Slobin, D. (1972, July). Children and language: They learn the same all around the world. *Psychology Today,* pp. 71–74, 82. [8]

Smeaton, G., Byrne, D., & Murnen, S. K. (1989). The repulsion hypothesis revisited: Similarity irrelevance or dissimilarity bias? *Journal of Personality and Social Psychology, 56,* 54–59. [16]

Smith, C. (1985). Sleep states and learning: A review of the animal literature. *Neuroscience and Biobehavioral Reviews, 9,* 157–168. [4]

Smith, C., & Lapp, L. (1991). Increases in number of REMS and REM density in humans following an intensive learning period. *Sleep, 14,* 325–330. [4]

Smith, D. (1982). Trends in counseling and psychotherapy. *American Psychologist, 37,* 802–809. [15]

Smith, F. J. (1977). Work attitudes as predictors of attendance on a specific day. *Journal of Applied Psychology, 62,* 16–19. [17]

Smith, J. C., Mercy, J. A., & Conn, J. M. (1988). Marital status and the risk of suicide. *American Journal of Public Health, 78,* 78–80. [14]

Smith, J. E., & Krejci, J. (1991). Minorities join the majority: Eating disturbances among Hispanic and Native American youth. *International Journal of Eating Disorders, 10,* 179–186. [9]

Smith, M. C. (1983). Hypnotic memory enhancement of witnesses: Does it work? *Psychological Bulletin, 94,* 387–407. [6]

Smith, M. L., Glass, G. V., & Miller, T. I. (1980). *The benefits of psychotherapy.* Baltimore, MD: Johns Hopkins University Press. [15]

Smith, P. K. (1979). The ontogeny of fear in children. In W. Sluckin (Ed.), *Fears in animals and man* (pp. 164–168). London: Von Nostrand Reinhold. [8]

Smith, S. M., Glenberg, A., & Bjork, R. A. (1978). Environmental context and human memory. *Memory & Cognition, 6,* 342–353. [6]

Smith, T. W. (1991). Adult sexual behavior in 1989: Number of partners, frequency of intercourse and risk of AIDS. *Family Planning Perspectives, 23,* 102–107. [11]

Snaith, R. P. (1968). A clinical investigation of phobias. *British Journal of Psychiatry, 114,* 673–698. [14]

Snow, J. T., & Harris, M. B. (1985). *An analysis of weight and diet content in five women's interest magazines.* Unpublished manuscript, University of New Mexico, Albuquerque. [9]

Snyder, F. (1971). Psychophysiology of human sleep. *Clinical Neurosurgery, 18,* 503–536. [4]

Snyder, M., & White, P. (1982). Moods and memories: Elation, depression, and the remembering of the events of one's life. *Journal of Personality, 50,* 149–167. [6]

Snyder, S. H. (1984, November). Medicated minds. *Science 84,* pp. 141–142. [15]

Snyderman, M., & Rothman, S. (1987). Survey of expert opinions on intelligence and aptitude testing. *American Psychologist, 42,* 137–144. [7]

Sobell, M. B., & Sobell, L. C. (1978). *Behavioral treatment of alcohol problems.* New York: Plenum. [13]

Sokol, L., Beck, A. T., Greenberg, R. L., Wright, F. D., & Berchick, R. J. (1989). Cognitive therapy of panic disorder: A nonpharmacological alternative. *Journal of Nervous and Mental Disease, 177,* 711–716. [15]

Solomon, P. R., Blanchard, S., Levine, E., Velazquez, E., & Groccia-Ellison, M-E. (1991). Attenuation of age-related conditioning deficits in humans by extension of the interstimulus interval. *Psychology and Aging, 6,* 36–42. [5]

Solomon, R. L. (1964). Punishment. *American Psychologist, 19,* 239–253. [5]

Solomon, R. L. (1980). The opponent-process theory of acquired motivation: The costs of pleasure and the benefits of pain. *American Psychologist, 35,* 691–712. [10]

Solomon, R. L., & Corbit, J. D. (1974). An opponent-process theory of motivation: Part 1. Temporal dynamics of affect. *Psychological Review, 81,* 119–145. [10]

Sommer, R., & Shutz, H. (1991). The consumer psychologist. In R. Gifford (Ed.), *Applied psychology: Variety and opportunity* (pp. 195–214). Boston: Allyn and Bacon. [17]

Sonestein, F. L., Pleck, J. H., & Ku, L. C. (1991). Levels of sexual activity among adolescent males in the United States. *Family Planning Perspectives, 23,* 162–167. [9]

Spearman, C. (1927). *The abilities of man.* New York: Macmillan. [7]

Sperling, H. (1960). The information available in brief visual presentations. *Psychological Monographs: General and Applied, 74,* Whole No. 498, 1–29. [6]

Sperry, R. W. (1964). The great cerebral commissure. *Scientific American, 210,* 42–52. [2]

Sperry, R. W. (1966). Brain bisection and consciousness. In J. Eccles (Ed.), *Brain and conscious experience.* New York: Springer-Verlag. [2]

Sperry, R. W. (1968). Hemisphere deconnection and unity in conscious experience. *American Psychologist, 23,* 723–733. [2]

Spetch, M. L., Wilkie, D. M., & Pinel, J. P. J. (1981). Backward conditioning: A reevaluation of the empirical evidence. *Psychological Bulletin, 89,* 163–175. [5]

Spiegel, H., & Spiegel, D. (1978). *Trance and treatment: Clinical uses of hypnosis.* New York: Basic Books. [4]

Spitz, R. A. (1946). Hospitalism: A follow-up report on investigation described in volume I, 1945. *The Psychoanalytic Study of the Child, 2,* 113–117. [8]

Spitzer, M. W., & Semple, M. N. (1991). Interaural phase coding in auditory midbrain: Influence of dynamic stimulus features. *Science, 254,* 721–724. [3]

Spitzer, R. L., Gibbon, M., Skodol, A. E., Williams, J. B. W., & First, M. B. (1989). *DSM-III-R casebook.* Washington, DC: American Psychiatric Press. [14]

Spooner, A., & Kellogg, W. N. (1947). The backward conditioning curve. *American Journal of Psychology, 60,* 321–334. [5]

Springer, S. P., & Deutsch, G. (1985). *Left brain, right brain* (rev. ed.). New York: W. H. Freeman. [2]

Squire, L. R. (1986). Memory functions as affected by electroconvulsive therapy. *Annals of the New York Academy of Sciences, 462,* 307–314. [15]

Squire, L. R. (1992). Memory and the hippocampus: A synthesis from findings with rats, monkeys, and humans. *Psychological Review, 99,* 195–231. [2, 6]

Squire, L. R., Haist, F., & Shimamura, A. P. (1989). The neurology of memory: Quantitative assessment of retrograde amnesia in two groups of amnesic patients. *Journal of Neuroscience, 9,* 828–839. [6]

Squire, L. R., & Slater, P. C. (1983). Electroconvulsive therapy and complaints of memory dysfunction: A prospective three-year follow-up study. *British Journal of Psychiatry, 142,* 1–8. [15]

Squire, L. R., & Zola-Morgan, S. (1991). The medial temporal lobe memory system. *Science, 253,* 1380–1386. [6]

Squire, S. (1987, November 22). Shock therapy's return to respectability. *The New York Times Magazine,* pp. 78–89. [15]

Standing, L., Lynn, D., & Moxness, K. (1990). Effects of noise upon introverts and extroverts. *Bulletin of the Psychonomic Society, 28,* 138–140. [17]

Stanley, M., & Stanley, B. (1990). Postmortem evidence for serotonin's role in suicide. *Journal of Clinical Psychiatry, 51*(4, Suppl.), 22–28. [14]

Stark, E. (1984, October). Answer this question: Responses: To sleep, perchance to dream. *Psychology Today,* p. 16. [4]

Steffens, A. B., Scheurink, A. J., & Luiten, P. G. (1988). Hypothalamic food intake regulating areas are involved in the homeostasis of blood glucose and plasma FFA levels. *Physiology and Behavior, 44,* 581–589. [10]

Stein, A. H., & Friedrich, L. K. (1975). Impact of television on children and youth. In E. M. Hetherington (Ed.), *Review of child development research* (Vol. 5, pp. 183–256). Chicago: University of Chicago Press. [8]

Stein, A. P. (1991, February). The chlamydia epidemic: Teenagers at risk. *Medical Aspects of Human Sexuality, 25,* 26–33. [11]

Steinberg, L. (1987). Impact of puberty on family relations: Effects of pubertal status and pubertal timing. *Developmental Psychology, 23,* 451–460. [9]

Steinberg, L., Elman, J. D., & Mounts, N. S. (1989). Authoritative parenting, psychosocial maturity, and academic success among adolescents. *Child Development, 60,* 1424–1436. [8, 9]

Stelmack, R. M. (1990). Biological bases of extraversion: Psychophysiological evidence. *Journal of Personality, 58,* 293–311. [12]

Stephens, B., McLaughlin, J. A., & Mahoney, E. J. (1971). Age at which Piagetian concepts are achieved. *Proceedings, American Psychological Association,* 203–204. [8]

Stern, L. D. (1981). A review of theories of human amnesia. *Memory & Cognition, 9,* 247–262. [6]

Stern, W. (1914). *The psychological methods of testing intelligence.* Baltimore: Warwick and York. [7]

Sternberg, R. J. (1985a). *Beyond IQ: A triarchic theory of human intelligence.* New York: Cambridge University Press. [7]

Sternberg, R. J. (1985b). Human Intelligence: The model is the message. *Science, 230,* 1111–1118. [7]

Sternberg, R. J. (1986a). *Intelligence applied: Understanding and increasing your intellectual skills.* San Diego: Harcourt Brace Jovanovich. [7]

Sternberg, R. J. (1986b). A triangular theory of love. *Psychological Review, 93,* 119–135. [16]

Sternberg, R. J. (1987). Liking versus loving: A comparative evaluation of theories. *Psychological Bulletin, 102,* 331–345. [16]

Sternberg, R. J., & Davidson, J. E. (1982, June). The mind of the puzzler. *Psychology Today,* pp. 37–44. [7]

Stevenson, M. R., & Black, K. N. (1988). Paternal absence and sex-role development: A meta-analysis. *Child Development, 59,* 793–814. [11]

Stiff, J. B., Miller, G. R., Sleight, C., Mongeau, P. L., Garlick, R., & Rogan, R. (1989). Explanations for visual cue primacy in judgments of honesty and deceit. *Journal of Personality and Social Psychology, 56,* 555–564. [16]

Strack, F., Martin, L. L., & Stepper, S. (1988). Inhibiting and facilitating conditions of facial expressions: A nonobtrusive test of the facial feedback hypothesis. *Journal of Personality and Social Psychology, 54,* 768–777. [10]

Strauch, I., & Meier, B. (1988). Sleep need in adolescents: A longitudinal approach. *Sleep, 11,* 378–386. [4]

Straus, S., Seidlin, M., & Takiff, H. (1984). Management of mucocutaneous herpes simplex. *Drugs, 27,* 364–372. [11]

Streissguth, A. P., Barr, H. M., Sampson, P. D., Darby, B. L., & Martin, D. C. (1989). IQ at age 4 in relation to maternal alcohol use and smoking during pregnancy. *Developmental Psychology, 25,* 3–11. [8]

Strentz, H. (1986, January 1). Become a psychic and amaze your friends! *Atlanta Journal,* p. 15A. [3]

Striegel-Moore, R. H., Silberstein, L. R., & Rodin, J. (1986). Toward an understanding of risk factors for bulimia. *American Psychologist, 41,* 246–263. [9]

Strome, M., & Vernick, D. (1989, April). Hearing loss and hearing aids. *Harvard Medical School Health Letter, 14,* pp. 5–8. [3]

Stromeyer, C. F., III. (1970, November). Eidetikers. *Psychology Today,* pp. 76–80. [6]

Stryer, L. (1987). The molecules of visual excitation. *Scientific American, 257,* 42–50. [3]

Study finds more, younger victims of rape. (1992, April 24). *The Evansville Courier,* p. A3. [11]

Stunkard, A. J., Harris, J. R., Pedersen, N. L., & McClearn, G. E. (1990). The body-mass index of twins who have been reared apart. *New England Journal of Medicine, 322,* 1483–1487. [3]

Suarez, M. G. (1983). *Implications of Spanish-English bilingualism in the TAT stories.* Unpublished doctoral dissertation, University of Connecticut. [15]

Sue, D. (1979). Erotic fantasies of college students during coitus. *Journal of Sex Research*, *15*, 299–305. [11]

Sue, D. W., & Sue, D. (1990). *Counseling the culturally different: Theory and practice*. New York: Wiley. [15]

Sullivan, E. V. (1977). A study of Kohlberg's structural theory of moral development: A critique of liberal social science ideology. *Human Development*, *20*, 352–376. [9]

Sullivan, F. J. (1987, May 19). *Testimony before the U.S. House of Representatives Committee on Government Operations, Subcommittee on Human Resources and Intergovernmental Relations, 100th Congress, 1st Session*. Washington, DC: U.S. Government Printing Office.

Sundberg, N. D. (1977). *Assessment of persons*. Englewood Cliffs, NJ: Prentice-Hall. [12]

Sung, K. (1992). Motivations for parent care: The case of filial children in Korea. *International Journal of Aging and Human Development*, *34*, 109–124. [9]

Suppes, T., Baldessarini, R. J., Faedda, G. L., & Tohen, M. (1991). Risk of recurrence following discontinuation of lithium treatment in bipolar disorder. *Archives of General Psychiatry*, *48*, 1082–1088. [15]

Survey Research Center, University of Michigan. (1971). *Survey of working conditions*. Washington, DC: U.S. Government Printing Office. [17]

Swapp, W. C. (1977). Interpersonal attraction and repeated exposure to rewarders and punishers. *Personality and Social Psychology Bulletin*, *3*, 248–251. [16]

Sweatt, J. D., & Kandel, E. R. (1989). Persistent and transcriptionally-dependent increase in protein phosphorylation in long-term facilitation of Aplysia sensory neurons. *Nature*, *339*, 51–54. [6]

Swedo, S. E., Rapoport, J. L., Leonard, H., Lenane, M., & Cheslow, D. (1989). Obsessive-compulsive disorder in children and adolescents: Clinical phenomenology of 70 consecutive cases. *Archives of General Psychiatry*, *46*, 335–341. [14]

Sweller, J., & Levine, M. (1982). Effects of goal specificity on means-end analysis and learning. *Journal of Experimental Psychology: Learning, Memory, and Cognition*, *8*, 463–474. [6]

Szymanski, K., & Harkins, S. G. (1987). Social loafing and self-evaluation with a social standard. *Journal of Personality and Social Psychology*, *53*, 891–897. [16]

Talbot, J. D., Marrett, S., Evans, A. C., Meyer, E., Bushnell, M. C., & Duncan, G. H. (1991). Multiple representations of pain in human cerebral cortex. *Science*, *251*, 1355–1358. [2]

Tanner, J. M. (1961). *Education and physical growth*. London: University of London Press. [7]

Tanner, J. M. (1962). *Growth at adolescence* (2nd ed.). Oxford: Blackwell Press. [7]

Tanner, J. M. (1978). *Fetus into man: Physical growth from conception to maturity*. Cambridge, MA: Harvard University Press. [9]

Taylor, S. E. (1991). *Health psychology* (2nd ed.). New York: McGraw-Hill. [13]

Teasdale, J. D., & Fogarty, S. J. (1979). Differential effects of induced mood on retrieval of pleasant and unpleasant events from episodic memory. *Journal of Abnormal Psychology*, *88*, 248–257. [6]

Teasdale, T. W., & Owen, D. R. (1984). Heredity and familial environment in intelligence and educational level: A sibling study. *Nature*, *309*, 620–622. [7]

Teen sex: Not for love. (1989, May). *Psychology Today*, p. 10. [9]

Tellegen, A., Lykken, D. T., Bouchard, T. J., Jr., Wilcox, K. J., Segal, N. L., & Rich, S. (1988). Personality similarity in twins reared apart and together. *Journal of Personality and Social Psychology*, *54*, 1031–1039. [12]

Templeton, R. D., & Quigley, J. P. (1930). The action of insulin on the motility of the gastrointestinal tract. *American Journal of Physiology*, *91*, 467–474. [10]

Terman, G. W., Shavit, Y., Lewis, J. W., Cannon, J. T., & Liebeskind, J. C. (1984). Intrinsic mechanisms of pain inhibition: Activation by stress. *Science*, *226*, 1270–1277. [3]

Terman, L. M. (1925). *Genetic studies of genius, Vol. 1: Mental and physical traits of a thousand gifted children*. Stanford, CA: Stanford University Press. [7]

Terman, L. M., & Oden, M. H. (1947). *Genetic studies of genius, Vol. 4: The gifted child grows up*. Stanford, CA: Stanford University Press. [7]

Terman, L. M., & Oden, M. H. (1959). *Genetic studies of genius, Vol. 5: The gifted group at mid-life*. Stanford, CA: Stanford University Press. [7]

Terry, R. D., & Katzman, R. (1983). Senile dementia of the Alzheimer type. *Annals of Neurology*, *14*, 497–506. [9]

Terry, W. S. (1988). Everyday forgetting: Data from a diary study. *Psychological Reports*, *62*, 299–303. [6]

Tesch, S. A., & Whitbourne, S. K. (1982). Intimacy and identity status in young adults. *Journal of Personality and Social Psychology*, *43*, 1041–1051. [9]

Teuting, P., Koslow, S. H., & Hirschfeld, R. M. A. (1981). *Special report on depression research*. Rockville, MD: U.S. Department of Health & Human Services. [15]

Thase, M. E., & Shipley, J. E. (1988). Tricyclic antidepressants. In C. G. Last & M. Hersen (Eds.), *Handbook of anxiety disorders* (pp. 460–477). New York: Pergamon Press. [15]

Thase, M. E., Simons, A. D., Cahalane, J. F., & McGeary, J. (1991). Cognitive behavior therapy of endogenous depression: Part 1: An outpatient clinical replication series. *Behavior Therapy*, *22*, 457–467. [15]

Thatcher, R. W., Walker, A., & Guidice, S. (1987). Human cerebral hemispheres develop at different rates and ages. *Science*, *236*, 1110–1113. [8]

Thomas, A., & Chess, S. (1977). *Temperament and development*. New York: Brunner-Mazel. [8]

Thomas, A., Chess, S., & Birch, H. G. (1970). The origin of personality. *Scientific American*, *223*, 102–109. [8]

Thomas, D. A., & Alderfer, C. P. (1989). The influence of race on career dynamics: Theory and research on minority career experiences. In M. Arthur, D. Hall, & B. Lawrence (Eds.), *Handbook of career theory*. Cambridge, England: Cambridge University Press. [17]

Thomas, J. L. (1992). *Adulthood and aging*. Boston: Allyn and Bacon. [9]

Thompson, M. G., & Heller, K. (1990). Facets of support related to well-being: Quantitative social isolation and perceived family support in a sample of elderly women. *Psychology and Aging*, *5*, 535–544. [9]

Thompson, R. F. (1986). The neurobiology of learning and memory. *Science*, *233*, 941–947. [2]

Thorndike, E. L. (1920). A constant error in psychological ratings. *Journal of Applied Psychology*, *4*, 25–29. [16]

Thorndike, E. L. (1970). *Animal intelligence: Experimental Studies*. New York: Macmillan. (Original work published 1911). [5]

Thorpe, G. L., & Olson, S. L. (1990). *Behavior therapy: Concepts, procedures, and applications*. Boston: Allyn & Bacon. [15]

Thurstone, L. L. (1938). *Primary mental abilities*. Chicago: University of Chicago Press. [7]

Thyer, B. A., Parrish, R. T., Curtis, G. C., Neese, R. M., & Cameron, O. G. (1985). Ages of onset of DSM-III anxiety disorders. *Comprehensive Psychiatry*, *26*, 113–122. [14]

Tiffany, S. T., Martin, E. M., & Baker, T. B. (1986). Treatments for cigarette smoking: An evaluation of the contributions of aversion and counseling procedures. *Behaviour Research and Therapy*, *24*, 437–452. [15]

Tiihonen, J., Hari, R., Naukkarinen, H., Rimon, R., Jousmaki, V., & Kajola, M. (1992). Modified activity of the human auditory cortex during auditory hallucinations. *American Journal of Psychiatry*, *149*, 255–257. [15]

Tinkle, M. B. (1990, March). Genital human papillomavirus infection: A growing health risk. *Journal of Obstetric, Gynecologic, and Neonatal Nursing*, *19*, 501–507. [11]

Tobin-Richards, M. H., Boxer, A. M., & Petersen, A. C. (1983). The psychological significance of pubertal change: Sex differences in perceptions of self during early adolescence. In J. Brooks-Gunn & A. C. Peterson (Eds.), *Girls at puberty: Biological and psychological perspectives*. New York: Plenum. [9]

Togerson, S. (1983). Genetic factors in anxiety disorders. *Archives of General Psychiatry*, *40*, 1085–1089. [14]

Tolman, E. C. (1932). *Purposive behavior in animals and men*. New York: Appleton-Century-Crofts. [5]

Tolman, E. C., & Honzik, C. H. (1930). Introduction and removal of reward, and maze performance in rats. *University of California Publications in Psychology*, *4*, 257–275. [5]

Tomkins, S. (1962). *Affect, imagery, and consciousness: The positive effects* (Vol. 1). New York: Springer. [10]

Tomkins, S. (1963). *Affect, imagery, and consciousness: The negative effects* (Vol. 2). New York: Springer. [10]

Tordoff, M. G. (1988). Sweeteners and appetite. In G. M. Williams (Ed.), *Sweeteners: Health effects* (pp. 53–60). Princeton: Princeton Scientific. [10]

Tordoff, M. G., & Alleva, A. M. (1990). Oral stimulation with aspartame increases hunger. *Physiology and Behavior*, *47*, 555–559. [10]

Torrey, E. F. (1983). *Surviving schizophrenia: A family manual*. New York: Harper & Row. [14]

Torrey, E. F., & Bowler, A. (1990). Geographical distribution of insanity in America: Evidence for an urban factor. *Schizophrenia Bulletin*, *16*, 591–604. [14]

Toufexis, A. (1988, February 22). Older—but coming on strong. *TIME*, pp. 76–79. [9]

Treffert, D. A. (1988a). The idiot savant: A review of the syndrome. *American Journal of Psychiatry*, *145*, 563–572. [7]

Treffert, D. A. (1988b). An unlikely virtuoso: Leslie Lemke and the story of savant syndrome. *The Sciences*, *29*, 26–37. [7]

Tresemer, D. W. (1977). *Fear of success*. New York: Plenum. [10]

Triplet, R. G. (1992). Henry A. Murray: The making of a psychologist? *American Psychologist*, *47*, 299–307. [12]

Triplett, N. (1898). The dynamogenic factors in pacemaking and competition. *American Journal of Psychology*, *9*, 507–533. [16]

Trotter, R. J. (1986, August). Three heads are better than one: Profile: Robert J. Sternberg. *Psychology Today*, pp. 56–62. [7]

Tulving, E. (1972). Episodic and semantic memory. In E. Tulving & W. Donaldson (Eds.), *Organization of memory* (pp. 382–403). New York: Academic Press. [6]

Tulving, E. (1974). Cue-dependent forgetting. *American Scientist*, *62*, 74–82. [6]

Tulving, E. (1985). How many memory systems are there? *American Psychologist*, *40*, 385–398. [6]

Tulving, E. (1987). Multiple memory systems and consciousness. *Human Neurobiology*, *6*, 67–80. [6]

Tulving, E. (1989). Remembering and knowing the past. *American Scientist*, *77*, 361–367. [6]

Tulving, E., Schacter, D. L., McLachlan, D. R., & Moscovitch, M. (1988). Priming of semantic autobiographical knowledge: A case study of retrograde amnesia. *Brain and Cognition*, *8*, 3–20. [6]

Tulving, E., & Thompson, D. M. (1973). Encoding specificity and retrieval processes in episodic memory. *Psychological Review*, *80*, 352–373. [6]

Turner, J. C., Hogg, M. A., Oakes, P. J., Reicher, S. D., & Wetherell, M. S. (1987). *Rediscovering the social group: A self-categorization theory.* Oxford, England: Blackwell. [17]

Turner, R. J. (1983). Direct, indirect, and moderating effects of social support on psychological distress and associated conditions. In H. B. Kaplan (Ed.), *Psychosocial stress: Trends in theory and research* (pp. 105–155). New York: Academic Press. [13]

Turner, S. M., & Beidel, D. C. (1989). Social phobia: Clinical syndrome, diagnosis, and comorbidity. *Clinical Psychology Review, 9,* 3–18. [14]

Turner, S. M., Beidel, D. C., & Nathan, R. S. (1985). Biological factors in obsessive-compulsive disorders. *Psychological Bulletin, 97,* 430–450. [14]

Turner, S. M., & Michelson, L. (1984). Obsessive-compulsive disorders. In S. M. Turner (Ed.), *Behavioral theories and treatment of anxiety* (pp. 239–277). New York: Plenum. [15]

Tyler, T. R., & Schuller, R. A. (1991). Aging and attitude change. *Journal of Personality and Social Psychology, 61,* 689–697. [16]

Tzu-Chin, W., Tashkin, D. P., Djahed, B., & Rose, J. E. (1988). Pulmonary hazards of smoking marijuana as compared with tobacco. *New England Journal of Medicine, 318,* 347–351. [4]

U.S. Bureau of the Census (1990). *Statistical abstract of the United States: 1990* (110th ed.). Washington, DC: U.S. Government Printing Office. [9, 11, 17]

U.S. Bureau of the Census. (1991). *Statistical abstract of the United States: 1991* (111th ed.). Washington, DC: U.S. Government Printing Office. [9]

U.S. Congress, Office of Technology Assessment. (1987). *Losing a million minds: Confronting the tragedy of Alzheimer's disease and other dementias* (Publication No. OTA-BA-323). Washington, DC: U.S. Government Printing Office. [9]

Udry, J. R., Billy, J. O. G., Morris, N. M., Groff, T. R., & Raj, M. H. (1985). Serum androgenic hormones motivate sexual behavior in adolescent boys. *Fertility and Sterility, 43,* 90–94. [11]

Underwood, B. J. (1957). Interference and forgetting. *Psychological Review, 64,* 49–60. [6]

Urbano-Marquez, A., Estruch, R., Navarro-Lopez, F., Grau, J. M., Mont, L., & Rubin, E. (1989). The effects of alcoholism on skeletal and cardiac muscle. *New England Journal of Medicine, 320,* 409–415. [13]

Usy, P-D. (1988, September 23). Chameleons thrive under apartheid. *The New York Times,* p. 27. [17]

Vaillant, G. E. (1977). *Adaptation to life.* Boston: Little, Brown. [9]

Vaillant, G. E. (1983). *The natural history of alcoholism: Causes, patterns, and paths to recovery.* Cambridge, MA: Harvard University Press. [4]

van Dale, D., & Saris, W. H. (1989). Repetitive weight loss and weight regain: Effects on weight reduction, resting metabolic rate, and lipolytic activity before and after exercise and/or diet treatment. *American Journal of Clinical Nutrition, 49,* 409–416. [13]

Van Dalen, E. B. (1973). *Understanding educational research: An introduction* (3rd ed.). New York: McGraw-Hill. [1]

van den Hout, M., & Merckelbach, H. (1991). Classical conditioning: Still going strong. *Behavioural Psychotherapy, 19,* 59–79. [5]

Van Fossen, D. (1985, June). Preventing youth suicide. *Health Link,* 7–10. [14]

Van Lancker, D. (1987, November). Old familiar voices. *Psychology Today,* pp. 12–13. [2]

Van Lancker, D. R., Cummings, J. L., Kreiman, J., & Dobkin, B. H. (1988). Phonagnosia: A dissociation between familiar and unfamiliar voices. *Cortex, 24,* 195–209. [2]

Vandell, D. L., & Mueller, E. C. (1980). Peer play and friendships during the first two years. In H. C. Foot, A. J. Chapman, & J. R. Smith (Eds.), *Friendship and social relations in children.* New York: Wiley. [8]

Veleber, D. M., & Templer, D. I. (1984). Effects of caffeine on anxiety and depression. *Journal of Abnormal Psychology, 93,* 120–122. [4]

Vener, K. J., Szabo, S., & Moore, J. G. (1989). The effect of shift work on gastrointestinal (GI) function: A review. *Chronobiologia, 16,* 421–439. [4]

Veroff, J. (1978). Social motivation. *American Behavioral Scientist, 21,* 706–729. [10]

Viemerö, V., & Paajanen, S. (1992). The role of fantasies and dreams in the TV viewing–aggression relationship. *Aggressive Behavior, 18,* 109–116. [16]

Vilberg, T. R., & Keesey, R. E. (1990). Ventromedial hypothalamic lesions abolish compensatory reduction in energy expenditure to weight loss. *American Journal of Physiology, 258,* 476–480. [10]

Vincent, M., & Pickering, M. R. (1988). Multiple personality disorder in childhood. *Canadian Journal of Psychiatry, 33,* 524–529. [14]

Vinokur, A., & Burnstein, E. (1978). Depolarization of attitudes in groups. *Journal of Personality and Social Psychology, 36,* 872–885. [16]

Vita, A., Diece, M., Giobbio, G. M., Azzone, P., Garbarini, M., Sacchetti, E., Cesana, B. M., & Cazzullo, C. L. (1991). CT scan abnormalities and outcome of chronic schizophrenia. *American Journal of Psychiatry, 148,* 1577–1579. [14]

Vogel, G. W. (1975). A review of REM sleep deprivation. *Archives of General Psychiatry, 32,* 749–761. [4]

Volkow, N. D., & Tancredi, L. R. (1991). Biological correlates of mental activity studied with PET. *American Journal of Psychiatry, 148,* 439–443. [2]

Von Glinow, M. A., & Kryczkowska-Mercer, A. (1988, Summer). Women in corporate America: A caste of thousands. *New Management, 6,* 36–42. [17]

Wade, T. C., & Baker, T. B. (1977). Opinions and use of psychological tests: A survey of clinical psychologists. *American Psychologist, 32,* 874–882. [12]

Wahba, M. A., & Bridwell, L. G. (1976). Maslow reconsidered: A review of research on the need hierarchy theory. *Organization Behavior and Human Performance, 15,* 212–240. [10]

Waid, W. M., Orne, E. C. & Orne, M. T. (1981). Selective memory for social information, alertness, and physiological arousal in the detection of deception. *Journal of Applied Psychology, 66,* 224–232. [10]

Wald, G. (1964). The receptors of human color vision. *Science, 145,* 1007–1017. [3]

Wald, G., Brown, P. K., & Smith, P. H. (1954). Iodopsin. *Journal of General Physiology, 38,* 623–681. [3]

Waldrop, M. M. (1987). The workings of working memory. *Science, 237,* 1564–1567. [6]

Walker, L. (1989). A longitudinal study of moral reasoning. *Child Development, 60,* 157–166. [9]

Walker, L., de Vries, B., & Trevethan, S. D. (1987). Moral stages and moral orientations in real-life and hypothetical dilemmas. *Child Development, 58,* 842–858. [9]

Wallach, H. (1985a). Learned stimulation in space and motion perception. *American Psychologist, 40,* 399–404. [3]

Wallach, H. (1985b). Perceiving a stable environment. *Scientific American, 252,* 118–124. [3]

Wallach, M. A., & Wallach, L. (1983). *Psychology's sanction for selfishness: The error of egoism in theory and therapy.* New York: W. H. Freeman. [12]

Wallach, M. A., & Wallach, L. (1985, February). How psychology sanctions the cult of the self. *Washington Monthly,* pp. 46–56. [12]

Wallis, C. (1984, June 11). Unlocking pain's secrets. *TIME,* pp. 58–66. [3]

Wallis, C. (1985, December 9). Children having children. *TIME,* pp. 79–90. [9]

Walsh, B. T., Kissileff, H. R., Cassidy, S. M., & Dantzic, S. Eating behavior of women with bulimia. *Archives of General Psychiatry, 46,* 54–58. [9]

Walster, E., & Walster, G. W. (1969). The matching hypothesis. *Journal of Personality and Social Psychology, 6,* 248–253. [16]

Walters, L. S. (1990, September 10). Hi-ho, off to school wee ones go. *The Christian Science Monitor,* p. 14. [8]

Waters, E., Wippman, J., & Stroufe, L. A. (1979). Attachment, positive affect, and competence in the peer group: Two studies in construct validation. *Child Development, 50,* 821–829. [8]

Watson, D., Clark, L. A., & Tellegen, A. (1984). Cross-cultural convergence in the structure of mood: A Japanese replication and a comparison with U.S. findings. *Journal of Personality and Social Psychology, 47,* 127–144. [10]

Watson, J. B. (1913). Psychology as the behaviorist views it. *Psychological Review, 20,* 158–177. [1, 5]

Watson, J. B. (1919). *Psychology from the standpoint of a behaviorist.* Philadelphia: Lippincott. [5]

Watson, J. B. (1925). *Behaviorism.* New York: W. W. Norton. [5]

Watson J. B. (1928). *Psychological care of the infant and child.* New York: W. W. Norton. [5]

Watson, J. B., & Rayner, R. (1920). Conditioned emotional reactions. *Journal of Experimental Psychology, 3,* 1–14. [5, 15]

Waugh, N. C., & Norman, D. A. (1965). Primary memory. *Psychological Review, 72,* 89–104. [6]

Weaver, J. B., Masland, J. L., & Zillmann, D. (1984). Effect of erotica on young men's aesthetic perception of their female sexual partners. *Perceptual and Motor Skills, 58,* 929–930. [11]

Webb, W. B. (1975). *Sleep: The gentle tyrant.* Englewood Cliffs, NJ: Prentice-Hall. [4]

Webb, W. B., & Campbell, S. S. (1983). Relationships in sleep characteristics of identical and fraternal twins. *Archives of General Psychiatry, 40,* 1093–1095. [4]

Webb, W. B., & Cartwright, R. D. (1978). Sleep and dreams. *Annual Review of Psychology, 29,* 223–252. [4]

Wechsler, D. (1975). Intelligence defined and undefined: A relativistic appraisal. *American Psychologist, 34,* 135–139. [7]

Wehr, T. A., Jacobsen, F. M., Sack, D. A., et al. (1986). Phototherapy of seasonal affective disorder. *Archives of General Psychiatry, 43,* 870–875. [14]

Wehr, T. A., & Rosenthal, N. E. (1989). Seasonality and affective illness. *American Journal of Psychiatry, 146,* 829–839. [14]

Weigle, D. S., Sande, K. J., Iverius, P. H., Monsen, E. R., & Brunzell, J. D. (1988). Weight loss leads to a marked decrease in nonresting energy expenditure in ambulatory human subjects. *Metabolism, 37,* 930–936. [13]

Weil, A., & Rosen, W. (1983). *Chocolate to morphine: Understanding mind-active drugs.* Boston: Houghton Mifflin. [4]

Weinberg, R. A. (1989). Intelligence and IQ: Landmark issues and great debates. *American Psychologist, 44,* 98–104. [7]

Weinberger, D. R. (1988). Schizophrenia and the frontal lobe. *Trends in Neurosciences, 11,* 367–370. [14]

Weinberger, M., Hiner, S. L., & Tierney, W. M. (1987). In support of hassles as a measure of stress in predicting health outcomes. *Journal of Behavioral Medicine, 10,* 19–32. [13]

Weiner, B. (1972). *Theories of motivation: From mechanism to cognition.* Chicago: Rand McNally. [10]

Weiner, B. (Ed.) (1974). *Achievement motivation and attribution theory.* Norristown, NJ: General Learning Press. [10]

Weiner, B. (1980). *Human motivation.* New York: Holt, Rinehart & Winston. [10]

Weiner, B. (1985). "Spontaneous" causal thinking. *Psychological Bulletin, 97*, 74–84. [16]

Weiner, R. D., Rogers, H. J., Davidson, J. R. T., & Squire, L. R. (1986). Effects of stimulus parameters on cognitive side effects. *Annals of the New York Academy of Sciences, 462*, 315–325. [15]

Weingartner, H., Adefris, W., Eich, J. E., & Murphy, D. L. (1976). Encoding-imagery specificity in alcohol state-dependent learning. *Journal of Experimental Psychology: Human Learning and Memory, 2*, 83–87. [6]

Weinstein, N. (1978). Individual differences in reactions to noise: A longitudinal study in a college dormitory. *Journal of Applied Psychology, 63*, 458–466. [17]

Weinstein, S. (1968). Intensive and extensive aspects of tactile sensitivity as a function of body part, sex, and laterality. In D. R. Kenshalo (Ed.), *The skin senses*. Springfield, IL: Charles C. Thomas. [3]

Weinstock, S. (1954). Resistance to extinction of a running response following partial reinforcement under widely spaced trials. *Journal of Comparative and Physiological Psychology, 47*, 318–322. [5]

Weiss, J. M. (1972). Psychological factors in stress and disease. *Scientific American, 226*, 104–113. [13]

Weiss, R. (1987, July 25). How dare we? Scientists seek the sources of risk-taking behavior. *Science News, 132*, 57–59. [10]

Weissman, M. M. (1984). The psychological treatment of depression: An update of clinical trials. In J. B. W. Williams & R. L. Spitzer (Eds.), *Psychotherapy research: Where are we and where should we go?* (pp. 89–105). New York: Guilford. [15]

Weissman, M. M., Gershon, E. S., Kidd, K. K., et al. (1984). Psychiatric disorders in the relatives of probands with affective disorders: The Yale University–National Institute of Mental Health Collaborative Study. *Archives of General Psychiatry, 41*, 13–21. [14]

Weissman, M. M., Klerman, G. L., Markowitz, J. S., & Ouellette, R. (1989). Suicidal ideation and suicide attempts in panic disorder and attacks. *New England Journal of Medicine, 321*, 1209–1214. [14]

Weissman, M. M., Klerman, G. L., Prusoff, B. A., Sholomskas, D., & Padian, N. (1981). Depressed outpatients: Results one year after treatment with drugs and/or interpersonal psychotherapy. *Archives of General Psychiatry, 41*, 51–55. [15]

Weissman, M. M., Wickramartne, P., Merikangas, K. R., Leckman, J. F., Prusoff, B. A., Caruso, K. A., Kidd, K. K., & Gammon, G. D. (1984). Onset of major depression in early adulthood. *Archives of General Psychiatry, 41*, 1136–1143. [14]

Wender, P. H., Kety, S. S., Rosenthal, D., et al. (1986). Psychiatric disorders in the biological and adoptive families of adoptive individuals with affective disorders. *Archives of General Psychiatry, 43*, 923–929. [14]

Wertheimer, M. (1912). Experimental studies of the perception of movement. *Zeitschrift fur Psychologie, 61*, 161–265. [3]

Wertheimer, M. (1958). Principles of perceptual organization. In D. C. Beardslee & M. Wertheimer (Eds.), *Readings in perception* (pp. 115–135). Princeton, NJ: D. Van Nostrand. [3]

Wetzel, R. D., & Reich, T. (1989). The cognitive triad and suicide intent in depressed in-patients. *Psychological Reports, 65*, 1027–1032. [14]

Wever, E. G. (1949). *Theory of hearing*. New York: Wiley. [3]

Wheeler, L. R. (1942). A comparative study of the intelligence of East Tennessee mountain children. *Journal of Educational Psychology, 33*, 321–344. [7]

Whelan, E. M., & Stare, F. J. (1990). Nutrition. *Journal of the American Medical Association, 263*, 2661–2663. [13]

White, D. P. (1989). Central sleep apnea. In M. H. Kryger, T. Roth, & W. C. Dement (Eds.), *Principles and practice of sleep medicine* (pp. 513–524). Philadelphia: W. B. Saunders. [4]

Whitehouse, W. G., Dinges, D. F., Orne, E. C., & Orne, M. T. (1988). Hypnotic hypermnesia: Enhanced memory accessibility or report bias? *Journal of Abnormal Psychology, 97*, 289–295. [6]

Whitham, F. L., & Mathy, R. M. (1986). *Male homosexuality in four societies*. New York: Praeger. [11]

Wicker, A. W. (1969). Attitudes versus action: The relationship of verbal and overt behavioral responses to attitude objects. *Journal of Social Issues, 25*, 41–78. [16]

Widiger, T. A., Frances, A., Spitzer, R. L., & Williams, J. B. W. (1988). The DSM-III-R personality disorders: An overview. *American Journal of Psychiatry, 145*, 786–795. [14]

Widom, C. S. (1989a). The cycle of violence. *Science, 244*, 160–166. [16]

Widom, C. S. (1989b). Does violence beget violence? A critical examination of the literature. *Psychological Bulletin, 106*, 3–28. [5, 16]

Wilcox, D., & Hager, R. (1980). Toward realistic expectation for orgasmic response in women. *Journal of Sex Research, 16*, 162–179. [11]

Wildholz, M. J., Marmar, C. R., & Horowitz, M. J. (1985). A review of the research on conjugal bereavement: Impact on health and efficacy of intervention. *Comparative Psychiatry, 26*, 433–447. [9]

Wilkes, J. (1986, January). A study in hypnosis: Conversation: Ernest R. Hilgard. *Psychology Today*, pp. 23–27. [4]

Williams, K., Harkins, S. G., & Latane, B. (1981). Identifiability as a deterrent to social loafing: Two cheering experiments. *Journal of Personality and Social Psychology, 40*, 303–311. [16]

Williams, K. D., & Karau, S. J. (1991). Social loafing and social compensation: The effects of expectations of co-worker performance. *Journal of Personality and Social Psychology, 61*, 570–581. [16]

Williams, R. (1989, January/February). Curing Type A: The trusting heart. *Psychology Today*, pp. 36–42. [13]

Williams, S. R. (1986). *Essentials of nutrition and diet therapy* (4th ed.). St. Louis: Times Mirror/Mosby. [13]

Wilson, G. T., & Davison, G. C. (1971). Processes of fear reduction in systematic desensitization. *Psychological Bulletin, 76*, 1–14. [15]

Winch, R. F. (1958). *Mate selection: A study of complementary needs*. New York: Harper & Row. [16]

Winson, J. (1990). The meaning of dreams. *Scientific American, 263*, 86–96. [4]

Winter, R. (1976). *The smell book: Scents, sex, and society*. Philadelphia: J. B. Lippincott. [3]

Witelson, S. F. (1985). The brain connection: The corpus callosum is larger in left-handers. *Science, 229*, 665–668. [2]

Wolfe, J. B. (1936). Effectiveness of token-rewards for chimpanzees. *Comparative Psychology Monographs, 12*(5), 72. [5]

Wolfe, L. (1981). *The Cosmo report*. New York: Arbor House. [1]

Wolkin, A., Barouche, F., Wolf, A. P., Rotrosen, J., Fowler, J. S., Shiue, C-Y., Cooper, T. B., & Brodie, J. D. (1989). Dopamine blockade and clinical response: Evidence for two biological subgroups of schizophrenia. *American Journal of Psychiatry, 146*, 905–908. [14, 15]

Wolozin, B. L., Pruchnicki, A., Dickson, D. W., & Davies, P. (1986). A neuronal antigen in the brains of Alzheimer patients. *Science, 232*, 648–650. [2]

Wolpe, J. (1958). *Psychotherapy by reciprocal inhibition*. Stanford, CA: Stanford University Press. [15]

Wolpe, J. (1973). *The practice of behavior therapy* (2nd ed.). New York: Pergamon Press. [15]

Wolpe, J. (1981). Behavior therapy versus psychoanalysis: Therapeutic and social implications. *American Psychologist, 36*, 159–164. [15]

Wood, J. M., & Bootzin, R. (1990). The prevalence of nightmares and their independence from anxiety. *Journal of Abnormal Psychology, 99*, 64–68. [4]

Wood, W., Wong, F. Y., & Chachere, J. G. (1991). Effects of media violence on viewers' aggression in unconstrained social interaction. *Psychological Bulletin, 109*, 371–383. [5, 16]

Woods, J. H., Katz, J. L., & Winger, G. (1987). Abuse liability of benzodiazepines. *Pharmacological Reviews, 39*, 251–413. [4]

Woods, S. C., & Gibbs, J. (1989). The regulation of food intake by peptides. *Annals of the New York Academy of Sciences, 575*, 236–243. [10]

Woods, S. W., & Charney, D. S. (1988). Benzodiazepines: A review of benzodiazepine treatment of anxiety disorders: Pharmacology, efficacy, and implications for pathophysiology. In C. G. Last & M. Hersen (Eds.), *Handbook of anxiety disorders* (pp. 413–444). New York: Pergamon Press. [15]

Woodward, A. E., Bjork, R. A., & Jongeward, R. H. (1973). Recall and recognition as a function of primary rehearsal. *Journal of Verbal Learning and Verbal Behavior, 12*, 608–617. [6]

Word, C. O., Zanna, M. P., & Cooper, J. (1974). The nonverbal mediation of self-fulfilling prophecies in interracial interaction. *Journal of Experimental Social Psychology, 10*, 109–120. [17]

Wright, J. C., & Huston, A. C. (1983). A matter of form: Potentials of television for young viewers. *American Psychologist, 38*, 835–843. [8]

Wright, J. C., & Mischel, W. (1987). A conditional approach to dispositional constructs: The local predictability of social behavior. *Journal of Personality and Social Psychology, 53*, 1159–1177. [12]

Wright, S. C., Taylor, D. M., & Moghaddam, F. (1990). Responding to membership in a disadvantaged group: From acceptance to collective protest. *Journal of Personality and Social Psychology, 58*, 994–1003. [17]

Wrong man tried for murder. (1985, October 27). *St. Louis Post-Dispatch*, p. 9A. [6]

Wu, C., & Shaffer, D. R. (1987). Susceptibility to persuasive appeals as a function of source credibility and prior experience with the attitude object. *Journal of Personality and Social Psychology, 52*, 677–688. [16]

Wurtman, R. J., & Wurtman, J. J. (1989). Carbohydrates and depression. *Scientific American, 260*, 68–75. [14]

Wyatt, R. J. (1991). Neuroleptics and the natural course of schizophrenia. *Schizophrenia Bulletin, 7*, 325–351. [15]

Yanagita, T. (1973). An experimental framework for evaluation of dependence liability in various types of drugs in monkeys. *Bulletin of Narcotics, 25*, 57–64. [4]

Yehuda, R., Southwick, S. M., & Giller, E. L., Jr. (1992). Exposure to atrocities and severity of chronic posttraumatic stress disorder in Vietnam combat veterans. *American Journal of Psychiatry, 149*, 333–336. [13]

Yesavage, J. A., & Leier, V. O. (1985). Carry-over effects of marijuana intoxication on aircraft pilot performance: A preliminary report. *American Journal of Psychiatry, 142*, 1325–1329. [4]

Yetman, N. R. (Ed.). (1991). *Majority and minority: The dynamics of race and ethnicity in American life* (5th ed.). Boston: Allyn and Bacon. [17]

Yonkers, K. A., Kando, J. C., Cole, J. O., & Blumenthal, S. (1992). Gender differences in pharmacokinetics and pharmacodynamics of psychotropic medication. *American Journal of Psychiatry, 149*, 587–595. [15]

Young, E. A., Grunhaus, L., Haskett, R. F., Pande, A. C., Murphy-Weinberg, V., Akil, H., & Watson, S. J. (1991). Heterogeneity in the B-endorphin immunoreactivity response to electroconvulsive therapy. *Archives of General Psychiatry*, 48, 534–539. [15]

Yuille, J. C., & Marschark, M. (1983). Imagery effects on memory: Theoretical implications. In A. A. Sheikh (Ed.), *Imagery: Current theory, research, and application* (pp. 131–155). New York: Wiley. [7]

Zabrucky, K., Moore, D., & Schultz, N. R., Jr. (1987). Evaluation of comprehension in young and old adults. *Developmental Psychology*, 23, 39–43. [9]

Zacharias, L., Rand, W. M., & Wurtman, R. J. (1976). A prospective study of sexual development and growth in American girls: The statistics of menarche. *Obstetrical and Gynecological Survey*, 31(Suppl.), 325–337. [9]

Zajonc, R. B. (1965). Social facilitation. *Science*, 149, 269–274. [16]

Zajonc, R. B. (1968). Attitudinal effects of mere exposure. *Journal of Personality and Social Psychology, Monographs Supplement*, 9(Pt. 2), 1–27. [16]

Zajonc, R. B., & Sales, S. M. (1966). Social facilitation of dominant and subordinate responses. *Journal of Experimental Social Psychology*, 2, 160–168. [16]

Zatorre, R. J., Evans, A. C., Meyer, E., & Gjedde, A. (1992). Lateralization of phonetic and pitch discrimination in speech processing. *Science*, 256, 846–849. [2].

Zedeck, S., & Mosier, K. L. (1990). Work in the family and employing organization. *American Psychologist*, 45, 240–251. [17]

Zelazo, P. R., Kearsley, R. B., & Ungerer, J. A. (1984). *Learning to speak: A manual for parents*. Hillsdale, NJ: Erlbaum. [8]

Zelnik, M., Kim, Y. J., & Kantner, J. F. (1979). Probabilities of intercourse and conception among U.S. teenage women, 1971 and 1976. *Family Planning Perspectives*, 11, 177–183. [9]

Zilbergeld, B. (1986, June). Psychabuse. *Science 86*, pp. 48–52. [15]

Zillmann, D., & Bryant, J. (1983). Effects of massive exposure to pornography. In N. M. Malamuth & E. Donnerstein (Eds.), *Pornography and sexual aggression*. New York: Academic Press. [11]

Zillmann, D., & Bryant, J. (1982). Pornography, sexual callousness, and the trivialization of rape. *Journal of Communication*, 32, 10–21. [11]

Zimring, F. E. (1991). Firearms, violence and public policy. *Scientific American*, 265, 48–54. [16]

Zipursky, R. B., Lim, K. O., Sullivan, E. V., Brown, B. W., & Pfefferbaum, A. (1992). Widespread cerebral gray matter volume deficits in schizophrenia. *Archives of General Psychiatry*, 49, 195–205. [14]

Zivin, J. A., & Choi, D. W. (1991). Stroke therapy. *Scientific American*, 265, 56–63. [2]

Zola-Morgan, S. M., & Squire, L. R. (1990). The primate hippocampal formation: Evidence for a time limited role in memory storage. *Science*, 250, 288–290. [6]

Zorick, F. J., Roehrs, T., Conway, W., Potts, G., & Roth, T. (1990). Response to CPAP and UPPP in apnea. *Henry Ford Hospital Medical Journal*, 38, 223–226. [4]

Zubin, J., & Spring, B. J. (1977). Vulnerability: A new view of schizophrenia. *Journal of Abnormal Psychology*, 86, 103–126. [14]

Zuckerman, M. (1978, February). The search for high sensation. *Psychology Today*, pp. 38–46. [10]

Zuckerman, M. (1979a). Attribution of success and failure revisited, or: The motivational bias is alive and well in attribution theory. *Journal of Personality*, 47, 245–287. [16]

Zuckerman, M. (1979b). *Sensation seeking: Beyond the optimal level of arousal*. Hillsdale, NJ: Erlbaum. [10]

Zuckerman, M., Miyake, K., & Hodgins, H. S. (1991). Cross-channel effects of vocal and physical attractiveness and their implications for interpersonal perception. *Journal of Personality and Social Psychology*, 60, 545–554. [16]

Zuckerman, M., & Wheeler, L. (1975). To dispel fantasies about the fantasy-based measure of fear of success. *Psychological Bulletin*, 82, 932–946. [10]

Zuger, B. (1990, August). Changing concepts of the etiology of male homosexuality. *Medical Aspects of Human Sexuality*, 24, 73–75. [11]

Glossary

A

absolute threshold: The minimum amount of sensory stimulation that can be detected 50 percent of the time.

accommodation (cognitive): The process by which existing schema are modified and new schema are created to incorporate new objects, events, experiences, or information.

accommodation (eye): The changing in the shape of the lens as it focuses objects on the retina, becoming more spherical for near objects and flatter for far objects.

acquired immune deficiency syndrome (AIDS): A devastating and incurable illness, caused by the AIDS virus (HIV), that progressively weakens the immune system, leaving its victims vulnerable to rare forms of cancer and pneumonia and to other opportunistic infections that usually cause death; transmitted by intimate sexual contact, through contaminated needles and syringes of IV drug users, and through transfusions of contaminated blood.

action potential: The firing of a neuron that results when the charge within the neuron becomes more positive than the charge outside the cell's membrane.

adolescence: The developmental stage that begins at puberty and encompasses the period from the end of childhood to the beginning of adulthood.

adolescent growth spurt: A period of rapid physical growth that peaks in girls at about age 12 and in boys at about age 14.

adoption method: A method used by behavioral geneticists to study the relative effects of heredity and environment on behavior and ability in children adopted shortly after birth, comparing them to their biological and adoptive parents.

adrenal glands (ah-DREE-nal): A pair of endocrine glands, located just above the kidneys, that release hormones that prepare the body for emergencies and stressful situations and also release small amounts of the sex hormones.

aerobic exercise (ah-RO-bik): Exercise involving the use of large muscle groups in continuous, repetitive action and requiring increased oxygen intake and increased breathing and heart rates.

afterimage: The visual sensation that remains after a stimulus is withdrawn; called a positive afterimage when the sensation is the same color as the original stimulus, and called a negative afterimage when it is the complementary color of the original stimulus.

aggression: The intentional infliction of physical or psychological harm on another.

agoraphobia (AG-or-uh-FO-bee-uh): An intense fear of being in a situation where immediate escape is not possible or help is not immediately available in case of incapacitating anxiety; typically the person fears crowded or open places, enclosed places, and/or public transportation, and in severe cases may refuse to leave home.

AIDS: *See* acquired immune deficiency syndrome.

AIDS virus: *See* HIV.

alarm stage: The first stage of the general adaptation syndrome, during which there is emotional arousal and the defensive forces of the body are prepared for fight or flight.

alcohol: A central nervous system depressant.

algorithm: A systematic, step-by-step procedure, such as a mathematical formula, that guarantees a solution to a problem of a certain type if the procedure is appropriate and executed properly; in some cases, a systematic strategy for exploring every possible solution to a problem until the correct one is reached.

alpha wave: The brain wave of 8–12 cycles per second that occurs when individuals are awake but deeply relaxed with their eyes closed.

altered state of consciousness: A mental state other than ordinary waking consciousness (examples: sleep, meditation, hypnosis, drug-induced states).

altruism: Behavior aimed at helping another, requiring some self-sacrifice and not designed for personal gain.

Alzheimer's disease (ALZ-hye-merz): An incurable form of dementia characterized by progressive deterioration of intellect and personality, resulting from widespread degeneration of brain cells.

amnesia: A partial or complete loss of memory resulting from brain trauma or psychological trauma.

amphetamines: A class of central nervous system stimulants that increase arousal, relieve fatigue, and suppress the appetite, but with continued use result in exhaustion, agitation, and depression; used medically to treat narcolepsy and hyperactivity.

amplitude: Measured in decibels, the magnitude or intensity of a sound wave, determining the loudness of the sound; in vision the *amplitude* of a light wave affects the brightness of a stimulus.

anal stage: Freud's second psychosexual stage (ages 1 or 1 1/2 to 3 years), in which sensual pleasure is derived mainly from expelling and withholding feces.

androgens: A class of hormones considered the male sex hormones, which influence sexual motivation and the development of the male genitals before birth and the secondary sex characteristics at puberty; produced by the testes in males and by the adrenal glands in both sexes.

androgyny (an-DROJ-uh-nee): A combination of the desirable male and female characteristics in one person.

anorexia nervosa (AN-uh-REX-see-uh ner-VO-sah): A severe eating disorder characterized by an irrational fear of becoming obese, a disturbance in body image, compulsive dieting to the point of self-starvation, and excessive weight loss.

anorgasmia: A sexual dysfunction in women marked by the inability to achieve orgasm.

anterograde amnesia: The inability to form long-term memories of events occurring after a brain injury or brain surgery, although memories formed before the trauma are usually intact.

antidepressants: Drugs, including tricyclics and MAO (monoamine oxidase) inhibitors, that are prescribed primarily to relieve depression and in some cases to treat anxiety disorders, such as panic disorder, agoraphobia, and obsessive compulsive disorder.

antipsychotic drugs: Drugs used to control severe psychotic symptoms, such as the delusions and hallucinations of schizophrenics; sometimes called the major tranquilizers.

antisocial personality disorder: A personality disorder characterized by lack of feeling for others; by impulsive, selfish, aggressive, irresponsible behavior; by willingness to break the law, lie, cheat, or exploit others for personal gain; and by the failure to hold a job.

anxiety: A generalized feeling of apprehension, fear, or tension that may be associated with a particular object or situation or may be free-floating, not associated with anything specific.

anxiety disorders: Disorders characterized by severe anxiety (examples: panic disorder, phobic disorders, general anxiety disorder, obsessive compulsive disorder).

anxiety nightmare: A very frightening dream occurring during REM sleep.

aphasia (ah-FAY-zyah): A loss or impairment of the ability to understand or communicate through the written or spoken word, which results from damage to the brain, usually the left cerebral hemisphere.

apparent motion: The perception of motion when none is occurring (as in the phi phenomenon or in stroboscopic movement).

applied psychology: The branch of psychology that applies the methods and knowledge of the discipline to investigate and solve practical, everyday human problems.

applied research: Research conducted for the purpose of solving practical problems.

approach-approach conflict: A conflict arising from having to choose between desirable alternatives.

approach-avoidance conflict: A conflict arising when the same choice has both desirable and undesirable features; one in which you are simultaneously drawn to and repelled by the same choice.

aptitude test: A test designed to predict a person's achievement or performance at some future time.

archetype (AR-keh-type): Existing in the collective unconscious, an inherited tendency to respond in particular ways to universal human situations.

arousal: A state of alertness and mental and physical activation.

arousal theory: A theory suggesting that the aim of motivation is to maintain an optimal level of arousal.

artificial intelligence: Computer programming that simulates human thinking in solving problems and in making judgments and decisions.

assimilation: The process by which new objects, events, experiences, or information are incorporated into existing schemas.

association areas: Areas of the cerebral cortex (excluding the sensory input or motor areas) that house memories and are involved in thought, perception, learning, and language.

attachment: The strong affectionate bond a child forms with the mother or primary caregiver.

attitude: A relatively stable evaluation of a person, object, situation, or issue.

attribution: An inferred cause of our own or another's behavior.

audience effects: The impact of passive spectators on performance.

audition: The sensation of hearing; the process of hearing.

authoritarian parents: Parents who make arbitrary rules, expect unquestioned obedience from their children, punish transgressions, and value obedience to authority.

authoritative parents: Parents who set high but realistic and reasonable standards, reason with the child, enforce limits, and at the same time encourage open communication and independence.

automatic thoughts: Unreasonable and unquestioned ideas that rule a person's life and lead to depression and anxiety.

autonomy versus shame and doubt: Erikson's second psychosocial stage (ages 1–3), during which infants develop a sense of autonomy or shame depending on how parents react to their expression of will and their wish to be allowed to do things for themselves.

aversion therapy: A behavior therapy used to rid clients of a harmful or socially undesirable behavior by pairing it with an extremely painful, sickening, or otherwise aversive stimulus until the behavior becomes associated with pain and discomfort.

avoidance-avoidance conflict: A conflict arising from having to choose between equally undesirable alternatives.

avoidance learning: Learning to avoid events or conditions associated with dreaded or aversive outcomes.

axon (AK-sahn): The slender, taillike extension of the neuron that transmits signals to the dendrites or cell body of other neurons or to the muscles or glands.

B

babbling: Vocalization of the basic speech sounds (phonemes), which begins between the fourth and sixth months.

backward search: *See* working backwards.

barbiturates: A class of central nervous system depressants that are used as sedatives, sleeping pills, and anesthesia; addictive, and in overdose can cause coma or death.

basic research: Research conducted for the purpose of advancing knowledge rather than for its practical application.

basic trust versus basic mistrust: Erikson's first psychosocial stage (birth–1 year), in which the infant develops a sense of trust or mistrust depending on the degree and regularity of care, love, and affection received from the mother or primary caregiver.

Beck's cognitive therapy: A brief cognitive behavior therapy for depression and anxiety designed to help people recognize their automatic thoughts and replace them with more objective thoughts.

behavioral genetics: A field of research that investigates the relative effects of heredity and environment on behavior and ability.

behavioral perspective: A perspective that emphasizes the role of environment as the key to understanding behavior.

behaviorism: The school of psychology founded by John B. Watson that views observable, measurable behavior as the appropriate subject matter for psychology and emphasizes the key role of environment as a determinant of behavior.

behavior modification: The systematic application of the learning principles of operant conditioning, classical conditioning, or observational learning to individuals or groups in order to eliminate undesirable behavior and/or encourage desirable behavior; sometimes term is used interchangeably with behavior therapy.

behavior therapy: A treatment approach employing the principles of operant conditioning, classical conditioning, or observational learning theory to eliminate inappropriate or maladaptive behaviors and replace them with more adaptive responses.

beta wave (BAY-tuh): The brain wave of 13 or more cycles per second, occurring when one is alert and mentally or physically active.

binocular depth cues: Depth cues that depend on two eyes working together; convergence and binocular disparity.

binocular disparity: An important binocular cue to depth perception (for distances up to 20 feet) that occurs because our eyes are about 2 1/2 inches apart, resulting in slightly different views of the object and therefore slightly different retinal images; when the two images are integrated, we have the perception of three dimensions.

biofeedback: The use of sensitive equipment to give people precise feedback about internal physiological processes so that they can learn, with practice, to exercise control over those processes.

biological perspective: A perspective that emphasizes the role of biological processes and heredity as the key to understanding behavior.

biological therapy: A therapy, based on the assumption that most mental disorders have physical causes, that attempts to change or influence the biological mechanism involved, such as structural or biochemical abnormalities (examples: drug therapy, ECT, or psychosurgery).

biopsychosocial model: A perspective that focuses on health as well as illness and holds that both are determined by a combination of biological, psychological, and social factors.

bipolar disorder: A mood disorder in which a person experiences either manic episodes or manic episodes alternating with periods of depression, usually with relatively normal periods in between.

bone conduction: The transmission of vibrations along the bones of the skull or face directly to the cochlea.

brainstem: The structure that begins at the point where the spinal cord enlarges as it enters the brain and that includes the medulla, the pons, and the reticular formation.

brightness: The dimension of visual sensation that is dependent on the intensity of light reflected from a surface and that corresponds to the amplitude of the light wave.

brightness constancy: The tendency to see objects as mantaining the same level of brightness regardless of differences in lighting conditions.

Broca's aphasia (BRO-kuz uh-FAY-zyah): An impairment in the ability to physically produce the speech sounds, or in extreme cases, an inability to speak at all; caused by damage to Broca's area.

Broca's area: The area in the frontal lobe, usually in the left hemisphere, that controls production of the speech sounds; damage can result in Broca's aphasia.

bulimia nervosa (boo-LEE-me-uh ner-VO-sah): An eating disorder characterized by repeated and uncontrolled periods of binge eating followed by purging—self-induced vomiting and/or the excessive use of laxatives and diuretics.

bystander effect: As the number of bystanders at an emergency increases, the probability that the victim will receive help decreases, and help, if given, is likely to be delayed.

C

California Personality Inventory (CPI): A highly regarded personality test used to assess the normal personality.

Cannon-Bard theory: The theory of emotion stating that emotion-provoking stimuli received by the senses are relayed to the thalamus, which simultaneously passes the information to the cortex, giving us the mental experience of emotion, and to the internal organs, producing physiological arousal.

cardinal trait: Allport's name for a personal quality that is so strong a part of the person's personality that he or she may become identified with that trait or become known for it.

cardiologist: A medical doctor specializing in care of the heart.

case study: An in-depth study of one or a few subjects consisting of information gathered through observation, interview, and perhaps psychological testing; information may be collected during the course of treatment of people with psychological or physical disorders and may span a number of years.

catatonic schizophrenia (KAT-uh-TAHN-ik): A type of schizophrenia characterized by extreme stillness or stupor and/or periods of great agitation and excitement; patients may assume an unusual posture and remain in it for long periods.

cell body: The part of the neuron, containing the nucleus, that carries out the metabolic functions of the neuron and also has some receptor sites, which receive signals directly from other neurons.

central nervous system (CNS): The brain and the spinal cord.

central trait: Allport's name for the type of trait you would mention about someone in writing a letter of recommendation for that person.

centration: The child's tendency during the preoperational stage to focus on only one dimension of a stimulus and ignore the other dimensions.

cerebellum (sehr-uh-BELL-um): The brain structure that executes smooth, skilled body movements and regulates muscle tone and posture.

cerebral cortex (seh-REE-brul KOR-tex): The gray, convoluted covering of the cerebral hemispheres that is responsible for higher mental processes such as language, memory, and thinking.

cerebral hemispheres: The right and left halves of the cerebrum, covered by the cerebral cortex and connected by the corpus callosum.

cerebrum (seh-REE-brum): The largest structure of the human brain, consisting of the two cerebral hemispheres connected by the corpus callosum and covered by the cerebral cortex.

chlamydia (klah-MIH-dee-uh): The most common bacterial, sexually transmitted disease found in both sexes, and one that can cause infertility in females.

cholesterol: A substance necessary for sustaining life, manufactured by the liver and found in foods of animal origin such as whole milk products, eggs, red meat, poultry, and fish.

cholesterol (serum): The milligrams of cholesterol per deciliter of blood, which should be kept below 200.

chromosomes: Rod-shaped structures, found in the nuclei of body cells, that contain all the genes and carry all the hereditary information; the mature egg cell and sperm cell each have 23 *single* chromosomes, and other normal body cells each have 23 *pairs* of chromosomes.

circadian rhythm (sur-KAY-dee-un): Within each 24-hour period, the regular fluctuation from high to low points of certain bodily functions, evidenced, for example, in body temperature, alertness, and the sleep/wakefulness cycle.

classical conditioning: A process through which a response previously made only to a specific stimulus is made to another stimulus that has been paired repeatedly with the original stimulus.

clinical psychologist: A psychologist, usually with a Ph.D., whose training is in the diagnosis, treatment, or research of mental and behavioral disorders.

co-action effects: The impact on performance caused by the presence of others engaged in the same task.

cocaine: Derived from coca leaves, a type of stimulant that produces a feeling of euphoria; as a white powder, it is snorted, and when put into solution, it is injected.

cochlea (KOK-lee-uh): The snail-shaped, fluid-filled organ in the inner ear that contains the basilar membrane and the organ of Corti with its hair cells, which are the sound receptors; the primary organ of hearing.

cognitive behavior therapy (COG-nuh-tiv): A therapy designed to change maladaptive thoughts and behavior on the assumption that maladaptive behavior can result from one's irrational thoughts, beliefs, and ideas.

cognitive developmental theory: A theory of sex typing suggesting that when children realize their gender is permanent, they are motivated to seek out same-sex models and learn to act in ways considered appropriate for their gender.

cognitive dissonance: The unpleasant state that can occur when people become aware of inconsistencies between their attitudes or between their attitudes and behavior.

cognitive perspective: A perspective that emphasizes the role of mental processes as a key to understanding behavior.

cognitive processes: Mental processes such as thinking, knowing, problem solving, and remembering.

coitus: Penile-vaginal intercourse.

collective unconscious: In Jung's theory, the most inaccessible layer of the unconscious, which contains the universal experiences of mankind, throughout evolution, transmitted to each individual.

color blindness: The inability to distinguish some or all colors in vision, resulting from a defect in the cones.

compliance: Acting in accordance with the wishes, the suggestions, or the direct request of another person.

compulsion: A persistent, irresistible, irrational urge to perform an act or ritual repeatedly; if the impulse is resisted, anxiety increases, and if the act is completed, there is a reduction in anxiety.

computerized axial tomography: *See* CT scan.

concept: A label that represents a class or group of objects, people, or events sharing common characteristics or attributes.

concrete operations stage: Piaget's third stage of cognitive development (ages 7–11), during which a child acquires the concept of reversibility and conservation and is able to apply logical thinking to concrete objects.

conditioned reflex: A learned reflex rather than a naturally occurring one.

conditioned response (CR): That response that comes to be elicited by a conditioned stimulus as a result of its repeated pairing with an unconditioned stimulus.

conditioned stimulus (CS): A neutral stimulus that, after repeated pairing with an unconditioned stimulus, becomes associated with it and elicits a conditioned response.

conditions of worth: Conditions on which the positive regard of others rests; later, after becoming internalized, these conditions determine our own positive self-regard.

cones: The receptor cells in the retina that enable us to see color and fine detail in adequate light, but that do not function in very dim light.

confederate: Someone who poses as a subject in an experiment but is actually assisting the experimenter.

conformity: Changing or adopting an attitude or behavior in order to be consistent with the norms of a group or the expectations of others.

conscious (KON-shus): Those thoughts, feelings, sensations, or memories of which we are aware at any given moment.

consciousness: The state of being aware from moment to moment, having a continuous stream of perceptions, thoughts, feelings, and sensations.

conservation: The concept, acquired during the concrete operations stage, that a given quantity of matter—a given number, mass, area, weight, or volume of matter—remains the same despite rearrangement or change in its appearance as long as nothing has been added or taken away.

consolidation: The presumed process, believed to involve the hippocampus, by which a permanent memory is formed.

consolidation failure: Any disruption in the consolidation process that prevents a permanent memory from forming; can be caused by a blow to the head, electroconvulsive shock, or a grand mal seizure.

consumer psychology: A specialty concerned with studying, measuring, predicting, and influencing consumer behavior.

consummate love: According to Sternberg's theory, the most complete form of love, having the components of intimacy, passion, and decision/commitment.

contact hypothesis: The notion that prejudice can be reduced by increasing contact among members of different social groups.

continuous reinforcement: Reinforcement that is administered after every desired or correct response; the most effective method of conditioning a new response.

control group: In an experiment, a group that is similar to the experimental group and is exposed to the same experimental environment but is not exposed to the independent variable; used for purposes of comparison.

controlled drinking: A behavioral approach to the treatment of alcoholism, designed to teach the skills necessary so that alcoholics can drink socially without losing control.

conventional level of moral reasoning: Kohlberg's second level of moral reasoning, in which right and wrong are based on the internalized standards of others; "right" is whatever helps or is approved of by others, or whatever is consistent with the laws of society.

convergence: A binocular depth cue in which the eyes turn inward as they focus on nearby objects—the closer an object, the greater the *convergence*.

conversion disorder: A somatoform disorder in which there is a loss of functioning in some part of the body (for example, blindness, deafness, paralysis) that has no physical cause but solves some psychological problem.

cornea (KOR-nee-uh): The transparent covering of the colored part of the eye that bends light rays inward through the pupil.

corpus callosum (KOR-pus kah-LO-sum): The thick band of nerve fibers that connects the two cerebral hemispheres and makes possible the transfer of information and the synchronization of activity between them.

correlational method: A research method used to determine the relationship (correlation) between two characteristics, events, or behaviors; often used when, for ethical reasons, an experimental study cannot be performed to determine cause-effect relationships.

correlation coefficient: A numerical value that indicates the strength and direction of the relationship between two variables; ranges from +1.00 (a perfect positive correlation) to −1.00 (a perfect negative correlation). (*See also* negative correlation, positive correlation.)

CPI: *See* California Personality Inventory.

crack: The most potent, inexpensive, and addictive form of cocaine, and the form that is smoked.

crash: The feelings of depression, exhaustion, irritability, and anxiety that occur following an amphetamine, cocaine, or crack high.

creativity: The ability to produce original, appropriate, and valuable ideas and/or solutions to problems.

critical period: A period that is so important to development that a harmful environmental influence can keep a bodily structure or behavior from developing normally.

cross-sectional study: A developmental study in which groups of subjects of different ages are compared on certain characteristics to determine age-related differences.

crowding: A subjective perception that there are too many people in a defined space.

CT scan: A brain-scanning technique involving a rotating X-ray scanner and a high-speed computer analysis that produces slice-by-slice, cross-sectional images of the brain capable of revealing hidden damage or disease; computerized axial tomography.

culture-fair intelligence test: An intelligence test designed to minimize cultural bias by using questions that would not penalize individuals whose culture or language differs from that of the urban middle or upper class.

D

dark adaptation: The eye's increasing ability to see in dim light, resulting from the recombining of molecules of rhodopsin in the rods and the dilation of the pupils.

decay theory: A theory of forgetting that holds that the memory trace, if not used, disappears with the passage of time; an accepted theory for sensory and short-term memory loss.

decibel (DES-ih-bel): A unit of measurement of the intensity or loudness of sound based on the amplitude of the sound wave.

declarative memory: The hypothetical subsystem within long-term memory that stores facts, information, and personal life experiences.

deep sleep: Stage 3 and Stage 4 sleep.

defense mechanism: An unconscious, irrational means used by the ego to defend against anxiety; involves self-deception and the distortion of reality.

delta wave: The slowest brain wave, having a frequency of 1–3 cycles per second and associated with Stage 3 sleep and Stage 4 sleep (the deepest stages of sleep).

delusion: A false belief, one that is not generally shared by others in the culture and cannot be changed despite strong evidence to the contrary.

delusional disorder: A psychotic disorder characterized by delusions that are more believable and logical than those of schizophrenia, and in which intellectual functioning apart from the delusions usually remains intact.

delusion of grandeur: A false belief that one is a famous person (for example, Jesus Christ, the President) or a powerful or important person who possesses some great knowledge, ability, or authority.

delusion of persecution: A false belief that an individual or a group is trying to harass, attack, cheat, conspire against, injure, kill, or in some other way harm the disturbed person.

delusion of reference: A false belief that certain events or objects have some special symbolic meaning, usually negative, for the disturbed person.

dendrites (DEN-drytes): The branchlike extensions of a neuron that receive signals from other neurons.

denial: The act of refusing to consciously acknowledge the existence of a danger or a threatening condition.

density: A measure referring to the number of people occupying a unit of space.

dependent variable: The variable that is measured at the end of an experiment and is presumed to vary as a result of manipulations of the independent variable.

depressants: A category of drugs that decrease activity in the central nervous system, slow down bodily functions, and reduce sensitivity to outside stimulation (examples: alcohol, barbiturates, minor tranquilizers, general anesthetics, narcotics).

depression (major): A mood disorder characterized by feelings of great sadness, despair, guilt, worthlessness, hopelessness, and in extreme cases, suicidal intentions.

depth perception: The ability to see in three dimensions and to estimate distance.

descriptive research methods: Research methods that yield descriptions of behavior rather than causal explanations (examples: naturalistic and laboratory observation, the case study, the survey).

descriptive statistics: Statistics used to organize, summarize, and describe information gathered from actual observations.

designer drugs: Synthetic drugs that mimic the effects of illicit drugs and are potent, relatively inexpensive, and potentially very dangerous.

deviation score: A test score calculated by comparing an individual's score to the scores of others of the same age on whom the test was normed.

difference threshold: A measure of the smallest increase or decrease in a physical stimulus that is required to produce a difference in sensation that is noticeable 50 percent of the time.

diffusion of responsibility: When bystanders present in an emergency generally feel that the responsibility for helping is shared by the group, and consequently each individual feels less compelled to act than if he or she were alone and felt the total responsibility.

directive therapy: An approach to therapy in which the therapist takes an active role in determining the course of therapy sessions and provides answers and suggestions to the patient.

discrimination (learning): The learned ability to distinguish between similar stimuli so that the conditioned response occurs only to the original conditioning stimulus but not to similar stimuli.

discrimination (social): Behavior, usually negative, directed toward others based on their gender, religion, race, or membership in a particular group.

discriminative stimulus: A stimulus that signals whether a certain response or behavior is likely to be followed by reward or punishment.

disorganized schizophrenia: Formerly called hebephrenia, this type of schizophrenia is the most serious and is characterized by inappropriate affect, silliness, laughter, grotesque mannerisms, and bizarre behavior.

displacement (defense mechanism): Substituting a less threatening object for the original object of an impulse; taking out frustrations on objects or people who are less threatening than those who provoked us.

displacement (memory): The act that occurs when short-term memory is holding its maximum of 5–9 items and each new item entering short-term memory pushes out an existing item, which is then forgotten.

display rules: Cultural rules that dictate how emotions should be expressed, and when and where their expression is appropriate.

dispositional attribution: Attributing one's own or another's behavior to some internal cause such as a personal trait, motive, or attitude; an internal attribution.

dissociative disorders: Disorders in which, under stress, an individual loses the integration of consciousness, identity, and memories of important personal events (examples: psychogenic amnesia, psychogenic fugue, multiple personality).

divergent production: Producing one or more possible ideas, answers, or solutions to a problem rather than a single, correct response.

dizygotic twins: *See* fraternal twins.

dominant gene: The gene that is expressed in the individual.

door-in-the-face technique: A strategy in which a large, unreasonable request is made with the expectation that the person will refuse but will then be more likely to respond favorably to a smaller request at a later time (the request desired from the beginning).

double-blind technique: An experimental procedure in which neither the subjects nor the experimenter knows who is in the experimental or control groups until after the results have been gathered; the purpose is to keep the expectations of the researcher and subjects from influencing the outcome of the experiment; a control for experimenter bias.

downers: A slang term for depressants.

drive: A state of tension or arousal brought about by an underlying need, which motivates the individual to engage in behavior that will satisfy the need and reduce the tension.

drive-reduction theory: A theory of motivation suggesting that a need creates an unpleasant state of arousal or tension called a drive, which impels the organism to engage in behavior that will satisfy the need and reduce tension (example: the need for food creates the hunger drive, which motivates the individual to seek food in order to satisfy the need and reduce the drive).

drug dependence (physical): A compulsive pattern of drug use in which a user develops a drug tolerance (a need to take larger and larger doses to get the same effect) coupled with unpleasant withdrawal symptoms when the drug is discontinued.

drug dependence (psychological): A craving or irresistible urge for the drug's pleasurable effects.

drug tolerance: A condition, occurring with the persistent use of some drugs, in which the user becomes progressively less affected by the drug so that larger and larger doses are necessary to maintain the same effect; one of the two prime indicators of physical dependence.

DSM-III-R: *Diagnostic and Statistical Manual of Mental Disorders, Third Edition-Revised;* the manual developed by the American Psychiatric Association in 1987 describing over 235 mental disorders and the symptoms that must be present for a particular diagnosis to be made.

E

ego (EE-go): In Freudian theory, the rational and largely conscious system of the personality; operates according to the reality principle and tries to satisfy the demands of the id without violating the individual's moral values.

ego integrity versus despair: Erikson's eighth and final psychosocial stage, occurring during old age, when individuals look back on their lives with satisfaction and a sense of accomplishment or have major regrets about missed opportunities and mistakes.

eidetic imagery (eye-DET-ik): The ability to retain the image of a visual stimulus several minutes after it has been removed from view.

electroconvulsive therapy (ECT): A treatment in which an electric current is passed though the brain, causing a seizure; usually reserved for the severely depressed who are either suicidal or unresponsive to other treatment.

electroencephalogram (EEG) (ee-lek-tro-en-SEFF-uh-lo-gram): The record of an individual's brain-wave activity made by the electroencephalograph.

embryo: The developing human organism during the period (week 3 through week 8) when the first bone cells form and the major systems, organs, and structures of the body develop.

emotion: A feeling state involving physiological arousal, a cognitive appraisal of the situation arousing the state, and an outward expression of the state.

emotion-focused coping: A method of coping that reduces the emotional distress caused by the stressor rather than eliminating or reducing the stressor itself.

encoding: Transforming information into a form that can be stored in short-term memory or in long-term memory.

encoding failure: A cause of forgetting resulting from material never having been put into long-term memory in the first place.

encounter group: An intense emotional group experience designed to promote personal growth and self-knowledge and during which participants are encouraged to let down their defenses and relate honestly and openly to one another.

endocrine system (EN-duh-krin): A system of ductless glands in various parts of the body that manufacture and secrete hormones into the bloodstream or lymph fluids, thus affecting cells in other parts of the body.

endorphins (en-DOR-fins): Chemicals, produced naturally by the pituitary gland, that reduce pain and affect mood positively.

environmental psychology: The specialty concerned with the effect that environments (both natural and constructed) and individuals have on each other.

episodic memory (ep-ih-SOD-ik): The hypothetical subpart of memory, autobiographical in nature, that contains memories of personally experienced events.

erectile dysfunction: *See* impotence.

estrogens (ES-truh-jenz): A class of hormones considered the female sex hormones, which are produced primarily in the ovaries in females and in smaller quantities in the adrenal glands in both sexes; promote the secondary sex characteristics in females and control the menstrual cycle.

excitement phase: The first stage in the sexual response cycle in which, as a result of physical or psychological sexual arousal, there is an increase in muscular tension, heart rate, and blood pressure, and blood rushes into the genitals, causing an erection in males and a swelling of the clitoris and vaginal lubrication in females.

exhaustion stage: The third and final stage of the general adaptation syndrome, which occurs when the organism fails in its efforts to resist the stressor; if the deep stores of energy are depleted, the organism will die.

experimental group: In an experiment, the group of subjects that is exposed to the independent variable, or the treatment.

experimental method: The research method in which researchers randomly assign subjects to groups and control all conditions other than one or more independent variables, which are then manipulated to determine their effect on some behavioral measure—the dependent variable in the experiment.

experimenter bias: A phenomenon that occurs when the researcher's preconceived notions in some way influence the subject's behavior and/or the interpretation of experimental results.

exposure and response therapy: A behavior therapy in which obsessive-compulsive-disorder patients are exposed to stimuli generating increasing amounts of anxiety; the patients must agree not to carry out their normal rituals (handwashing, bathing, and so on) for a specified period of time after exposure.

extinction: The weakening and often eventual disappearance of a learned response (in classical conditioning, the conditioned response is weakened by repeated presentation of the conditioned stimulus without the unconditioned stimulus; in operant conditioning, the learned response is weakened by the withdrawal of reinforcement).

extrasensory perception (ESP): Gaining awareness of or information about objects, events, or another's thoughts through some means other than the known sensory channels.

extraversion: The tendency to be outgoing, adaptable, and sociable.

extrinsic motivation: The desire to perform an act to gain an external reward or to avoid an undesirable consequence.

F

facial-feedback hypothesis: The idea that the muscular movements involved in certain facial expressions trigger the corresponding emotions (example: smiling makes us happy).

family therapy: Therapy based on the assumption that an individual's problem is caused and/or maintained in part by problems within the family unit, and so the entire family is involved in therapy and may be seen as a group or at times individually.

fat (saturated): Dietary fat that is solid at room temperature (examples: butter; lard; the fat in whole-milk products, red meat, poultry with the skin; the vegetable fats of palm oil and coconut oil); the type of fat that elevates serum-cholesterol levels.

fat cells: Numbering 30 to 40 billion, cells that serve as storehouses for liquefied fat in the body; with weight loss, they decrease in size but not in number.

feature detectors: Neurons in the brain that respond to specific features of a sensory stimulus (for example, to lines or angles).

fetal alcohol syndrome: A condition, caused by maternal alcohol intake during pregnancy, in which the baby is mentally retarded, abnormally small, and has facial, organ, and limb abnormalities.

fetus: The developing human organism during the period (week 9 until birth) when rapid growth and further development of the structures, organs, and systems of the body occur.

figure-ground: A principle of perceptual organization whereby the visual field is perceived in terms of an object (figure) standing out against a background (ground).

first-degree relatives: A person's parents, children, or siblings.

fixation: Arrested development at a psychosexual stage occurring because of excessive gratification or frustration at that stage; a portion of the libido remains invested there, leaving less energy to meet the challenges of future stages.

fixed-interval schedule: A schedule in which a reinforcer is administered following the first correct response after a fixed period of time has elapsed.

fixed-ratio schedule: A schedule in which a reinforcer is administered after a fixed number of correct responses.

flashback: The brief recurrence of effects experienced while taking LSD or PCP, occurring suddenly and without warning at a later time.

flashbulb memory: An extremely vivid memory of the conditions surrounding one's first hearing the news of a surprising, shocking, and highly emotional event.

flooding: A behavioral therapy used in the treatment of phobias and during which clients are exposed to the feared object or event (or asked to vividly imagine it) for an extended period until their anxiety decreases.

foot-in-the-door technique: A strategy designed to secure a favorable response to a small request at first, with the intent of making the subject more likely to agree later to a larger request (the request desired from the beginning).

forensic psychology: A law-related specialty in which psychologists are involved in the legal justice system either as expert witnesses or as consultants to police, attorneys, defendants, judges, juries, or the penal system.

formal operations stage: Piaget's fourth and final stage of cognitive development, characterized by the ability to use logical reasoning in abstract situations.

fovea (FO-vee-uh): A small area of the retina, 1/50 of an inch in diameter, that provides the clearest and sharpest vision because it has the largest concentration of cones.

fraternal twins: Twins, no more alike genetically than ordinary siblings who develop after two eggs are released during ovulation and fertilized by two different sperm; dizygotic twins.

free association: A psychoanalytic technique used to explore the unconscious by having patients reveal whatever thoughts or images come to mind, no matter how terrible, embarrassing, or trivial they might appear.

frequency: Measured in the unit hertz, the number of sound waves or cycles per second, determining the pitch of the sound.

frequency distribution: An arrangement showing the frequency, or number of scores that fall within equal-sized class intervals.

frequency polygon: A line graph that depicts the frequency or number of scores within each class interval in a frequency distribution; a point is placed at the middle (midpoint) of each class interval so that its vertical distance above the horizontal axis shows the frequency of that interval, and then lines are drawn to connect the points.

frequency theory: The theory that hair cell receptors vibrate the same number of times as the sounds that reach them, thereby accounting for how variations in pitch are transmitted to the brain.

frontal lobes: The lobes of the brain that control voluntary body movements, speech production, and such functions as thinking, motivation, planning for the future, impulse control, and emotional responses.

frustration: Interfering with the attainment of a goal, or blocking an impulse.

frustration-aggression hypothesis: The hypothesis that frustration produces aggression.

functional fixedness: The failure to use familiar objects in novel ways to solve problems because of a tendency to view objects only in terms of their customary functions.

functionalism: An early school of psychology that was concerned with how mental processes help humans and animals adapt to their environments; developed in the United States as a reaction against structuralism.

fundamental attribution error: The tendency to overemphasize internal causes—character traits, motives, or attitudes—and underemphasize situational factors when explaining the behavior of others.

G

gate-control theory: The theory that the pain signals transmitted by slow-firing C fibers can be blocked at the signal gate if the pressure-sensitive, fast-firing A fibers get their message to the spinal cord first, or if the brain itself inhibits the transmission of the pain messages.

gender (JEN-der): One's biological sex—male or female.

gender identity disorders: Disorders characterized by behaviors associated with the opposite sex and dissatisfaction with one's sexual identity as male or female.

gender-schema theory: A theory that combines elements of social learning and cognitive developmental theory and suggests that young children are motivated to attend to and behave in ways consistent with gender-based standards and stereotypes of the culture.

general adaptation syndrome: The predictable sequence of reactions that organisms show in response to stressors, consisting of the alarm stage, the resistance stage, and the exhaustion stage.

generalization: In classical conditioning, the tendency to make a conditioned response to a stimulus similar to the original conditioned stimulus; in operant conditioning, the tendency to make the learned response to a stimulus similar to the one for which it was originally reinforced.

generalized anxiety disorder: A disorder in which people experience excessive or unrealistic worry and anxiety about several areas in their lives such as their finances, their health, or their work performance.

generativity versus stagnation: Erikson's seventh psychosocial stage of development, occurring during middle age, when the individual becomes increasingly concerned with guiding and assisting the next generation rather than becoming self-absorbed and stagnating.

genes: Within the chromosomes, the segments of DNA that are the basic units for the transmission of hereditary traits.

genital herpes (HER-peez): A sexually transmitted disease caused by the herpes simplex virus (usually type 2) and resulting in painful blisters on the genitals; presently incurable, usually recurring, and highly contagious during outbreaks.

genitals (JEN-ah-tulz): The internal and external reproductive organs.

genital stage: The final of Freud's psychosexual stages (from puberty on), in which for most people the object of sexual energy gradually shifts to the opposite sex, culminating in the attainment of full adult sexuality.

Gestalt (gih-SHTALT): A German word, having no exact English equivalent, which means roughly "form" or "pattern."

Gestalt psychology: The school of psychology that identified the fundamental principles of perceptual organization, emphasizing that individuals perceive objects and patterns as whole units and that a perceived whole is greater than the sum of its parts.

Gestalt therapy: A therapy originated by Fritz Perls and emphasizing the importance of clients fully experiencing, in the present moment, their feelings, thoughts, and actions and taking personal responsibility for their behavior.

g factor: Spearman's term for a general intellectual ability that underlies all mental operations to some degree.

glial cells (GLEE-ul): More numerous than the neurons in the brain, these cells help to make the brain more efficient by holding the neurons together, removing waste products such as dead neurons, making the myelin coating for the axons, and performing other manufacturing, nourishing, and clean-up tasks.

gonads: The sex glands; the ovaries in females and the testes in males.

gonorrhea (gahn-ah-REE-ah): A sexually transmitted disease that causes a puslike discharge from the penis; females often show no symptoms and, if untreated, can develop pelvic inflammatory disease and possible infertility.

group polarization: The tendency of members of a group, after group discussion, to shift toward a more extreme position in whatever direction they were leaning initially—either more risky or more cautious.

group therapy: A form of therapy in which several clients (usually 7–10) meet regularly with one or two therapists to resolve personal problems.

groupthink: The tendency for members of a very cohesive group to feel such pressure to maintain group solidarity and reach agreement on an issue that they fail adequately to weigh available evidence and consider objections and alternatives.

growth spurt: *See* adolescent growth spurt.

gustation: The sensation of taste.

H

habituation: A decrease in response or attention to a stimulus as an infant becomes accustomed to it; diminished attention to the stimulus on later occasions indicates that the infant remembers the stimulus.

hair cells: Sensory receptors for hearing, found in the cochlea.

hallucination: A sensory perception in the absence of any external sensory stimulus; an imaginary sensation (seeing, hearing, tasting, or feeling things that are not externally present).

hallucinogens (hah-lu-SIN-o-jenz): A category of drugs, sometimes called psychedelics, that alter perception and mood and can cause hallucinations (examples: LSD, PCP, psilocybin, mescaline, marijuana).

halo effect: The tendency to infer generally positive or negative traits in a person as a result of observing one major positive or negative trait (example: attributing popularity and sociability to one who is physically attractive); the tendency of raters to be excessively influenced by one or a few favorable or unfavorable traits in their overall evaluation of a person.

hardiness: Three psychological qualities shared by people who can undergo high levels of stress yet remain healthy—a sense of control over one's life, a deep sense of commitment to one's personal goals, and a tendency to look at change as a challenge rather than a threat.

hassles: Little stressors that include the irritating demands and troubled relationships that can occur daily and that, according to Lazarus, cause more stress than do major life changes.

health psychology: The area in psychology concerned with the psychological factors that contribute to health, illness, and recovery.

hemispheres: *See* cerebral hemispheres.

heritability: An index of the degree to which a characteristic is estimated to be influenced by heredity.

heroin: A highly addictive, partly synthetic narcotic derived from morphine.

heuristic (hyu-RIS-tik): A problem-solving method that offers a promising way to attack a problem and arrive at a solution, although it does not guarantee success (examples: means-end analysis, working backwards).

hierarchy of needs: A theory of motivation proposed by Abraham Maslow in which needs are arranged in order of urgency ranging from physical needs (food, water, air, shelter) to security needs, belonging needs, esteem needs, and finally, at the top of the hierarchy, the need for self-actualization (to fulfill one's potential): theoretically the needs at the lower levels must be adequately satisfied before a person will be motivated to fulfill the higher needs.

hippocampus (hip-po-CAM-pus): The brain structure in the limbic system that is involved in the formation of memories of facts, information, and personal experiences.

histogram: A bar graph that depicts the frequency or number of scores within each class interval in a frequency distribution.

HIV: Human immunodeficiency virus; the AIDS virus.

homeostasis: The tendency of the body to maintain a balanced internal state with regard to oxygen level, body temperature, blood sugar, water balance, and so forth.

homophobia: An intense, irrational hostility toward or fear of homosexuals.

hormone: A substance manufactured and released in one part of the body that affects other parts of the body.

hue: The property of light commonly referred to as color (red, blue, green, etc.), determined primarily by the wavelength of light reflected from a surface.

humanistic perspective: A perspective that emphasizes the importance of an individual's subjective experience as a key to understanding behavior.

humanistic psychology: An approach to psychology that focuses on the uniqueness of human beings and their capacity for choice, growth, and psychological health.

human papillomavirus infection (pap-ah-LO-mah-VI-rus): A sexually transmitted viral infection that infects a large proportion of sexually active adults; one strain of the virus causes genital warts.

hypnosis: A trancelike state of concentrated, focused attention, heightened suggestibility, and diminished response to external stimuli.

hypochondriasis (HI-puh-kahn-DRY-uh-sis): A somatoform disorder in which persons are preoccupied with their health and convinced they have some serious disorder despite reassurance from doctors to the contrary.

hypothalamus (HY-po-THAL-uh-mus): A small but influential brain structure, located just above the brainstem, that controls the pituitary gland and regulates hunger, thirst, sexual behavior, body temperature, and a wide variety of emotional behaviors.

hypothesis: A prediction about the relationship between two or more variables; in an experiment, the prediction of a cause-effect relationship between variables.

---

id (IHD): The only part of the personality present at birth; the animal-like, unconscious system of the personality, which contains the life and death instincts and operates on the pleasure principle.

identical twins: Twins with exactly the same genes, who develop after one egg is fertilized by one sperm, and the ovum splits into two parts; monozygotic twins.

identity versus role confusion: Erikson's fifth stage of psychosocial development, when adolescents need to establish their own identity and form values to live by; failure can lead to an identity crisis.

idiot savant: *See* savant syndrome.

illicit drug: An illegal drug.

illusion: A false perception of actual stimuli involving a misperception of size, shape, or the relationship of one element to another.

imagery: The representation in the mind of a sensory experience—visual, auditory, gustatory, motor, olfactory, or tactile.

imaginary audience: A belief of adolescents that they are or will be the focus of attention in social situations and that others will be as critical or approving as they are of themselves.

impotence (IM-puh-tents): The repeated inability of a man to get or maintain an erection that is firm enough for coitus.

inappropriate affect: A symptom common in schizophrenia in which an individual's behavior (including facial expression, tone of voice, and gestures) do not reflect the emotion that would be expected under the circumstances (for example, a person laughs at a tragedy, cries at a joke).

incentive: An external stimulus that motivates behavior (examples: money, good grades, fame).

incubus nightmare: A night terror in an adult, which, unlike one in a child, is often an indication of extreme anxiety and other psychological problems. (*See also* night terror.)

independent variable: In an experiment, the factor or condition that is manipulated by the researcher to determine its effect on another behavior or condition known as the dependent variable; sometimes called the treatment.

industrial/organizational psychology: The specialty that focuses on the relationship between the workplace or work organization and the worker, including specific areas such as organizational design, decision making, work motivation, job satisfaction, communication, leadership, and personnel selection, training, and evaluation.

industry versus inferiority: Erikson's fourth psychosocial stage (ages 6 years–puberty), during which children develop a sense of industry or inferiority depending on how parents and teachers react to their efforts to undertake projects and to build, make, or do things.

inferential statistics: Statistical procedures that allow researchers (1) to make inferences about the characteristics of the larger population from their observations and measurements of a sample, and (2) to derive estimates of how much faith or confidence can be placed in those inferences.

in-group: A social group with a strong sense of togetherness and from which others are excluded.

inhibited sexual desire (ISD): A condition marked by little or no interest in sexual activity.

initiative versus guilt: Erikson's third psychosocial stage (ages 3–6 years), during which children develop a sense of initiative or guilt depending on how parents react to their initiation of play, their motor activities, and their questions.

innate: Inborn, unlearned.

inner ear: The innermost portion of the ear containing the cochlea, which is the primary organ of hearing, and the vestibular sacs and the semicircular canals, which are the organs for the vestibular sense.

insight: The sudden realization of the relationship between elements in the problem situation, which makes the solution apparent.

insight therapy: Any type of psychotherapy based on the notion that psychological well-being depends on self-understanding—understanding one's thoughts, emotions, motives, behavior, and coping patterns (examples: psychoanalysis, person-centered therapy, Gestalt therapy).

insomnia: A sleep disorder characterized by difficulty falling or staying asleep, early termination of sleep, and/or light, unsatisfactory sleep.

instinct: An inborn, unlearned, fixed pattern of behavior that is characteristic of an entire species.

instinct theory: The notion that human behavior is motivated by certain innate tendencies or instincts shared by all individuals.

integrity versus despair: *See* ego integrity versus despair.

intelligence quotient (IQ): An index of intelligence originally derived by dividing a person's mental age by his or her chronological age and then multiplying by 100 to remove the fraction.

interference: Memory loss that occurs because information or associations stored either before or after a given memory hinder our ability to remember it.

intermittent reinforcement: *See* partial reinforcement.

interpersonal therapy (IPT): A brief psychotherapy designed to help depressed people understand their problems in interpersonal relationships and develop more effective strategies for improving them.

intimacy versus isolation: Erikson's sixth stage of psychosocial development, when the young adult must establish intimacy in a relationship in order to avoid feeling a sense of isolation and loneliness.

intrinsic motivation: The desire to perform an act because it is satisfying or pleasurable in and of itself.

introversion: The tendency to focus inward, to be reflective, retiring, and nonsocial.

inventory: A method of assessment involving a paper-and-pencil test with questions about a person's thoughts, feelings, and behaviors, which can be scored according to a standard procedure.

in vivo: Confronting a feared object or situation in real life as opposed to imagining it.

IQ: *See* intelligence quotient.

J

James-Lange theory: The theory of emotion, proposed independently by both William James and Carl Lange, stating that first environmental stimuli produce a physiological response and then our awareness of this response causes the emotion (example: we are afraid because we tremble).

job enrichment: Techniques used to make jobs more interesting, satisfying, and attractive.

job-sharing: A format of employment in which two employees share one full-time job.

just noticeable difference (JND): The smallest change in sensation that we are able to detect 50 percent of the time.

K

kinesthetic sense: The sense providing information about the position of body parts and about body movement, detected by sensory receptors in the joints, ligaments, and muscles (and supplemented with information from the other senses, especially vision).

L

latency period: The period following Freud's phallic stage (ages 5 or 6 to puberty), in which the sex instinct is largely repressed and temporarily sublimated in school and play activities.

latent learning: Learning that occurs without apparent reinforcement but is not demonstrated until sufficient reinforcement is provided.

lateral hypothalamus (LH): The part of the hypothalamus that supposedly acts as a feeding center and, when activated naturally or by electrical stimulation, signals the animal to eat; when the LH is destroyed, the animal refuses to eat.

lateralization: The specialization of one of the cerebral hemispheres to handle a particular function (example: speech is lateralized in the left hemisphere in most people).

law of effect: Thorndike's law of learning that states the connections between a stimulus and a response will be strengthened if followed by a satisfying consequence and weakened if followed by discomfort.

learning: A relatively permanent change in behavior, capability, or attitude that is acquired through experience and cannot be attributed to illness, injury, or maturation.

left hemisphere: The hemisphere that controls the right side of the body, coordinates complex movements and, in 95 percent of the population, controls the production of speech and written language.

lens: The transparent structure behind the iris that changes in shape as it focuses images on the retina.

levels-of-processing model: Craik and Lockhart's model of a single memory system (rather than short-term memory and long-term memory) in which retention depends on how deeply information is processed—shallow processing resulting in greater forgetting, deeper processing resulting in longer retention.

libido (lih-BEE-doe): Freud's name for the psychic or sexual energy that comes from the id and provides the energy for the entire personality.

life structure: Levinson's term for the basic pattern of one's life at any given time, including one's relationships and activities and the significance they have for the individual.

limbic system: A group of structures in the brain, including the amygdala and hippocampus, that are collectively involved in emotion, memory, and motivation.

lithium: A drug used to control the symptoms in a manic episode and, in maintenance therapy, to even out the mood swings and reduce recurrence of future manic or depressive states in bipolar disorder.

lobotomy: A psychosurgery technique in which the nerve fibers connecting the frontal lobes to the deeper brain centers are severed.

locus of control: A concept proposed by Julian Rotter to explain how people account for what happens in their lives—people with an internal *locus of control* see themselves as primarily in control of their behavior and its consequences; those with an external *locus of control* perceive what happens to be in the hands of fate, luck, or chance.

longitudinal study: A developmental study in which the same group of subjects is followed and measured at different ages.

long-term memory: The relatively permanent memory system with a virtually unlimited capacity.

low-ball technique: A strategy used to gain compliance that involves making a very attractive initial offer in order to get a person to agree to an action and then making the terms less favorable; if successful, the less favorable offer is accepted in spite of the change in terms.

low-birth-weight baby: A baby weighing less than 5.5 pounds.

LSD (lysergic acid diethylamide): A powerful hallucinogen with unpredictable effects ranging from perceptual changes and vivid hallucinations to states of panic and terror.

lucid dream: A dream during which the dreamer is aware of dreaming and is often able to influence the content of the dream while it is in progress.

M

magnetic resonance imaging (MRI): A diagnostic scanning technique that produces high resolution images of the structures of the brain.

mainstreaming: The movement toward educating mentally retarded students in regular schools, which may involve placing them in classes with nonhandicapped students for some part of the day or having special classrooms in regular rather than special schools.

manic episode (MAN-ik): A period of extreme elation, euphoria, and hyperactivity, often accompanied by delusions of grandeur and by hostility if activity is blocked.

marijuana: An hallucinogen with effects ranging (depending on dose, setting, and the user's mood and expectations) from relaxation and giddiness to perceptual distortions and hallucinations.

massed practice: One long learning practice session without rest periods (as opposed to spacing the learning in shorter practice sessions over an extended period).

matching hypothesis: The notion that people tend to have spouses, lovers, or friends who are approximately equivalent in social assets such as physical attractiveness.

maturation: Changes that occur according to an individual's genetically determined, biological timetable of development.

mean: The arithmetic average of a group of scores, computed by adding up all the single scores and dividing the sum by the number of scores.

means-end analysis: A heuristic problem-solving strategy in which the current position is compared with the desired goal, and a series of steps are formulated and taken to close the gap between them.

measure of central tendency: A measure or score that describes the center or middle of a distribution of scores (examples: mean, median, mode).

median: The middle value or score when a group of scores are arranged from highest to lowest.

meditation: A state of contemplation used to increase relaxation, to block our worries and distractions, and sometimes to expand consciousness.

medulla (muh-DUL-uh): The part of the brainstem that controls heartbeat, blood pressure, and respiration.

menarche (men-AR-kee): The onset of menstruation.

menopause: The end of menstruation, occurring between ages 45 and 55 and signifying the end of reproductive capacity.

mental age: The age that reflects the child's level of mental development, expressed in terms of the age at which the average child would exhibit that level of functioning.

mental retardation: Subnormal intelligence reflected by an IQ below 70 and by adaptive functioning that is severely deficient for one's age.

mental set: The tendency to apply a familiar strategy to the solution of a problem without carefully considering the special requirements of the problem.

mere-exposure effect: The tendency of people to develop a more positive evaluation of some person, object, or other stimulus with repeated exposure to it.

metabolic rate (meh-tuh-BALL-ik): The rate at which the body burns calories to produce energy.

method of loci (LO-sigh): A mnemonic technique in which items to be remembered are associated or mentally placed at various locations along a familiar route and then, to recall the items, the individual pictures each successive place on the route, calling to mind the item associated with it.

microelectrode: An electrical wire so small that it can be used either to monitor the electrical activity of a single neuron or to stimulate activity within it.

microsleep: A momentary lapse from wakefulness into sleep, usually occurring when one has been sleep deprived.

middle ear: The portion of the ear containing the ossicles (hammer, anvil, and stirrup), which connect the eardrum to the oval window and amplify the vibrations as they travel to the inner ear.

mid-life crisis: A period of turmoil usually occurring in a person's forties and brought on by an awareness of one's mortality; it is characterized by a reassessment of one's life and a decision to make changes, either drastic or moderate, in order to make the remaining years better.

Minnesota Multiphasic Personality Inventory (MMPI): The most extensively researched and most widely used personality test, consisting of over 500 questions about attitudes, feelings, and psychiatric symptoms; used to screen and diagnose psychiatric problems and disorders.

MMPI: *See* Minnesota Multiphasic Personality Inventory.

mnemonic (nih-MON-ik): A strategy used as an aid to memory.

mode: The score that occurs most frequently in a group of scores.

model: In observational learning, the person who demonstrates a behavior or who serves as an example.

modeling: Another name for observational learning. (*See also* observational learning.)

monocular depth cues (mah-NOK-yu-ler): Depth cues that can be perceived by only one eye.

monozygotic twins: *See* identical twins.

mood disorders: Disorders characterized by extreme and unwarranted disturbances in feeling or mood, which can include depression or manic episodes or both.

motivated forgetting: Forgetting through suppression or repression to protect oneself from material that is too painful, anxiety- or guilt-producing, or otherwise unpleasant.

motivation: The process that initiates, directs, and sustains behavior satisfying physiological or psychological needs.

motives: Needs or desires that energize and direct behavior toward a goal.

motor cortex: The strip of tissue at the rear of the frontal lobes that controls voluntary body movement.

multiple personality disorder: A dissociative disorder in which two or more distinct personalities occur in the same individual, each taking over at different times.

myelin sheath (MY-uh-lin): The white, fatty coating wrapped around some axons that acts as insulation and enables impulses to travel much faster.

N

naive subject: A subject who has agreed to participate in an experiment but is not aware that deception is being used to conceal the real purpose of the experiment.

narcolepsy (NAR-co-lep-see): A serious sleep disorder characterized by excessive daytime sleepiness and sudden, uncontrollable attacks of REM sleep and often accompanied by attacks of muscular weakness or paralysis called cataplexy.

narcotics: Derived from the opium poppy, a class of depressant drugs that have pain-relieving and calming effects (examples: opium, codeine, morphine, heroin).

naturalistic observation: A research method in which the researcher observes and records behavior in its natural setting, without attempting to influence or control it.

nature-nurture controversy: The debate concerning the relative influence of heredity and environment on development.

need for achievement (*n* Ach): The need to accomplish something difficult and to perform at a high standard of excellence.

negative correlation: A relationship between two variables in which an increase in one variable is associated with a decrease in the other variable (example: the relationship between drug use and academic achievement).

negative reinforcement: The termination of an unpleasant stimulus terminated after a response in order to increase the probability that the response will be repeated.

neonate: Newborn infant up to 1 month old.

neuron (NEW-ron): A specialized cell that conducts impulses through the nervous system and contains three major parts—a cell body, dendrites, and an axon.

neurosis (new-RO-sis): An obsolete term for a disorder that causes an individual considerable personal distress and some impairment in functioning but does not cause the person to lose contact with reality or to violate important social norms.

neurotransmitter (NEW-ro-TRANS-mit-er): A chemical that is released into the synaptic cleft from the axon terminal of the sending neuron, crosses the synapse, and binds to appropriate receptor sites on the dendrites or cell body of the receiving neuron, influencing the cell either to fire or not to fire.

night terror: A sleep disturbance in which a child partially awakens from Stage 4 sleep with a scream, dazed and groggy, in a panic state, and with a racing heart.

nondirective therapy: An approach to therapy during which the therapist acts as a facilitator of growth, giving understanding, support, and encouragement rather than proposing solutions, answering questions, and actively directing the course of therapy.

nonsense syllable: A consonant-vowel-consonant combination that does not spell a word; used in experiments on learning and memory to control for the meaningfulness of the material.

nonverbal behavior: Body language including facial expressions, gestures, posture, and body movements.

normal curve: A symmetrical, bell-shaped frequency distribution, which represents how scores are normally distributed in a population; as the bell shape indicates, most scores fall near the mean, and fewer and fewer scores occur in the extremes either above or below the mean.

norms (assessment): Standards based on the range of test scores of a large group of people who are selected to provide the bases of comparison for those who take the test later.

norms (behavior): The attitudes and standards of behavior that are expected of members of a particular group.

NREM dreams: Mental activity occurring during NREM sleep that is more thoughtlike in quality than REM dreams are.

NREM sleep: Non-rapid-eye-movement sleep consisting of the four sleep stages and characterized by slow, regular heart rate and respiration, an absence of rapid eye movements, and blood pressure and brain activity that are at a 24-hour low point.

O

obesity (o-BEE-sih-tee): Excessive fatness; a term applied to men whose body fat exceeds 20 percent of their weight and to women whose body fat exceeds 30 percent of their weight.

obsession: A persistent, recurring, involuntary thought, image, or impulse that invades consciousness and causes great distress.

obsessive compulsive disorder: An anxiety disorder in which a person suffers from obsessions or compulsions or both.

object permanence: The realization that objects continue to exist even when they are no longer perceived.

observational learning: Learning by observing the behavior of others and the consequences of that behavior; learning by imitation; modeling.

occipital lobes (ahk-SIP-uh-tul): The lobes of the brain that contain the primary visual cortex, where vision registers, and association areas involved in the interpretation of visual information.

Oedipus complex (ED-uh-pus): Occurring in the phallic stage, a conflict in which the child is sexually attracted to the opposite-sex parent and feels hostility toward the same-sex parent; in females, often referred to as the Electra complex.

olfaction (ol-FAK-shun): The sensation of smell; the process of smell.

olfactory bulbs: Two, matchstick-sized structures above the nasal cavities, where smell sensations first register in the brain.

olfactory epithelium: A one-inch square patch of tissue at the top of the nasal cavity, that contains about 10 million receptors for smell.

operant conditioning: A type of learning in which the consequences of behavior tend to modify that behavior in the future (behavior that is reinforced tends to be repeated; behavior that is ignored or punished is less likely to be repeated).

opponent-process theory of color vision: The theory that certain cells in the visual system increase their firing rate to signal one color and decrease their firing rate to signal the opposing color (red/green, yellow/blue, white/black).

opponent-process theory of motivation: A theory suggesting that the emotional state in response to certain activities or stimuli will usually give way to the opposite emotion; with repetition of the activity, the initial emotion gradually weakens, and the opposing emotion strengthens, eventually providing the motivation for the activity.

opportunistic infection: An infection that usually does not survive in humans with normal immune responses but can be serious and even life-threatening in humans with impaired immune systems.

optic nerve: The nerve that carries visual information from the retina to the brain.

oral stage: The first of Freud's psychosexual stages (birth to 1 or 1 1/2 years), in which sensual pleasure is derived mainly through stimulation of the mouth (examples: sucking, biting, chewing).

orgasmic dysfunction: *See* anorgasmia.

orgasm phase: The third phase in the sexual response cycle, marked by rhythmic muscular contractions and a sudden discharge of accumulated sexual tension.

outer ear: The visible part of the ear, the pinna, which collects the sound waves, and the auditory canal through which they pass on the way to the eardrum (tympanic membrane).

out-group: A social group specifically identified by the in-group as not belonging.

overextension: The act of using a word, on the basis of some shared feature, to apply to a broader range of objects than appropriate (example: calling every man "Daddy").

overlearning: Practicing or studying material beyond the point where it can be repeated once without error.

overregularization: The act of inappropriately applying the grammatical rules for forming plurals and past tenses to irregular nouns and verbs (example: saying "comed" rather than "came").

P

panic disorder: An anxiety disorder in which a person experiences unpredictable attacks of overwhelming anxiety, fear, or terror.

paranoid schizophrenia (PAIR-uh-noid): A type of schizophrenia characterized by delusions of grandeur or persecution; these patients may become dangerous.

paraphilia: A sexual disorder in which sexual urges and fantasies generally involve children, other nonconsenting partners, nonhuman objects, or the suffering and humiliation of the individual or a partner.

parapsychology: The study of psychic phenomena, which include extrasensory perception (ESP) and psychokinesis (PK).

parasympathetic nervous system: The division of the autonomic nervous system that is associated with relaxation and the conservation of energy and that brings the heightened bodily responses back to normal following an emergency.

parietal lobes (puh-RY-uh-tul): The lobes of the brain that contain the somatosensory cortex (where touch, pressure, temperature, and pain register) and other areas responsible for body awareness and spatial orientation.

partial reinforcement: A pattern of reinforcement in which some portion, rather than 100 percent, of the correct responses are reinforced.

partial-reinforcement effect: The greater resistance to extinction that occurs when a portion, rather than 100 percent, of the correct responses have been reinforced.

participant modeling: A behavior therapy in which an appropriate response is modeled in graduated steps and the client is asked to attempt each step with the encouragement and support of the therapist.

passive aggressive personality disorder: A personality disorder in which a person passively resists demands to perform adequately in social relationships and at work through forgetfulness, procrastination, stubbornness, and intentional inefficiency.

PCP (phencyclidine): A potentially dangerous hallucinogen that can cause intoxication, delirium, bizarre or violent behavior, paranoia, and other psychotic reactions; angel dust.

pelvic inflammatory disease (PID): An infection in the female pelvic organs, which can result from untreated chlamydia or gonorrhea and can cause pain, scarring of tissue, and even infertility and ectopic pregnancy.

perception: The process by which sensory information is actively organized and interpreted by the brain.

perceptual constancy: The tendency to perceive objects as maintaining stable properties, such as shape, size, brightness, and color, despite changes in lighting conditions or changes in the retinal image that result when objects are viewed from different angles and distances.

perceptual set: An expectation of what will be perceived, which can affect what actually is perceived.

period of the zygote: Lasting about two weeks, the period from conception to the time the zygote attaches itself to the uterine wall.

peripheral nervous system (PNS) (peh-RIF-er-ul): All parts of the nervous system other than the brain and the spinal cord; includes all nerves transmitting messages from sense receptors to the central nervous system and includes all nerves transmitting messages from the brain and the spinal cord to the muscles and the glands; has two subdivisions—the autonomic nervous system and the somatic nervous system.

permissive parents: Parents who make few rules or demands and usually do not enforce those that are made, allowing children to make their own decisions and control their own behavior.

personal fable: A form of adolescent egocentrism in which individuals have an exaggerated sense of personal uniqueness and indestructibility, which may be the basis of risk-taking common during adolescence.

personality: A person's unique and stable pattern of characteristics and behaviors.

personality disorder: A long-standing, inflexible, maladaptive pattern of behaving and relating to others, beginning early in life and causing impairment in social and occupational functioning and/or personal distress.

personal space: An area surrounding us, much like an invisible bubble of space, that we consider ours and that we use to regulate how closely others may interact with us.

personal unconscious: In Jung's theory, the layer of the unconscious containing all of the experiences, thoughts, and perceptions that may be accessible to the conscious, as well as repressed memories, wishes, and impulses.

person-centered therapy: A nondirective, humanistic therapy in which the therapist creates a warm, accepting climate so that clients are free to be themselves, and their natural tendency toward positive growth will be released; developed by Carl Rogers.

persuasion: A deliberate attempt to influence the attitudes and/or behavior of another.

PET scan: Positron-emission tomography; a technique in which radioactively tagged glucose or oxygen is injected or inhaled, and then a scanner and computer are used to generate colored images that reflect the amount of activity in various parts of the brain based on the amount of oxygen and glucose consumption.

phallic stage: The third of Freud's psychosexual stages (ages 3 to 5 or 6 years), during which sensual pleasure is derived mainly through touching of the genitals; the stage when the Oedipus complex arises.

phi phenomenon: An illusion of movement occurring when two or more stationary lights are flashed on and off in sequence, giving the impression that the light is actually moving from one spot to the next.

phobia (FO-bee-ah): A persistent, irrational fear of an object, situation, or activity that the person feels compelled to avoid even while realizing the fear is irrational or excessive.

phonemes: The basic speech sounds in any language that, when combined, form words.

physical dependence: *See* drug dependence (physical).

pituitary gland: The endocrine gland located in the brain and often called the "master gland," which releases hormones that control other glands in the endocrine system and also releases a growth hormone.

placebo (pluh-SEE-bo): Some inert substance, such as a sugar pill or an injection of saline solution, given to the control group in an experiment as a control for the placebo effect; sometimes given to patients by doctors hoping to treat a complaint through the power of suggestion—the patient's belief that they have received a drug for pain somehow stimulates the release of endorphins.

placebo effect (pluh-SEE-bo): The phenomenon that occurs when a person's response to a treatment or response on the dependent variable in an experiment is a function of his or her expectations regarding the treatment rather than a function of the treatment itself.

place theory: The theory that sounds of different frequencies or pitch cause maximum activation of hair cells at certain locations along the organ of Corti on the basilar membrane—the highest sounds activating the base of the organ, and the lowest sounds activating the tip.

plasticity: The ability of the brain to reorganize and compensate for brain damage.

plateau phase: The second stage of the sexual response cycle, during which muscle tension, blood flow to the genitals, heart rate, and blood pressure increase in preparation for orgasm.

pleasure principle: The principle by which the id operates to seek pleasure, avoid pain, and obtain immediate gratification of its wishes.

polygraph: A device that is used to detect lying but that actually detects emotion; designed to pick up those changes in heart rate, blood pressure, respiration rate, and galvanic skin response that typically accompany the anxiety that occurs when a person lies.

population: The entire group of interest to researchers and to which they wish to generalize their findings; the group from which the sample is selected.

pornography: Books, pictures, films, or videos used to increase sexual arousal (soft-core *pornography* depicts nudity and some sexual activity but no vaginal or anal penetration, sexual aggression, or violence; hard-core *pornography* has very explicit depictions of various sex acts).

positive reinforcement: A reward or pleasant consequence given after a response in order to increase the probability that the response will be repeated.

positive correlation: A relationship between two variables in which both vary in the same direction; an increase in one variable is associated with an increase in the other, and a decrease in one is associated with a decrease in the other (example: the relationship between cigarette smoking and lung cancer).

positron emission tomography: *See* PET scan.

postconventional level of moral reasoning: Kohlberg's highest level, in which moral reasoning involves weighing moral alternatives; "right" is whatever furthers basic human rights.

preconscious: The storehouse of thoughts, feelings, perceptions, and memories that we are not consciously thinking about at the moment but that may be brought to consciousness; similar to the concept of long-term memory.

preconventional level of moral reasoning: Kohlberg's lowest level, in which moral reasoning is based on the physical consequences of an act; "right" is whatever avoids punishment or gains a reward.

prejudice: Negative attitudes toward others based on their gender, religion, race, or membership in a particular group.

premature ejaculation: A sexual dysfunction in which a man regularly and unintentionally ejaculates too rapidly to satisfy his partner or to maintain his own pleasure.

prenatal: Occurring between conception and birth; prebirth.

preoperational stage: Piaget's second stage of cognitive development (ages 2–7 years), during which there is rapid development of language and representational thought and during which thinking is governed by perception rather than logic.

presbyopia (prez-bee-O-pee-uh): A condition, occurring in the mid to late forties, in which the lens no longer accommodates adequately for near vision, and reading glasses or bifocals are required for reading.

preterm infant: An infant born before the 37th week and weighing less than 5.5 pounds; a premature infant.

primacy effect: The tendency for an overall impression or judgment of another to be influenced more by the first information received about that person than by information that comes later.

primary appraisal: The first stage in the cognitive appraisal of a potentially stressful event, which consists of an evaluation of the significance of the event according to how it will affect the individual's well-being—whether it is perceived as irrelevant or as involving harm, loss, threat, or challenge.

primary auditory cortex: The part of the temporal lobes where hearing registers in the cerebral cortex.

primary drive: A state of tension or arousal arising from a biological need; a drive that is not based on learning.

primary emotions: Emotions such as sadness, surprise, happiness, anger, fear, and disgust, which are presumed to be universal (that is, they are reflected in the same facial expressions in all cultures and occur in children as a result of maturation rather than learning).

primary mental abilities: According to Thurstone, seven relatively distinct abilities that singularly or in combination are involved in all intellectual activities.

primary reinforcer: A reinforcer that fulfills a basic physical need for survival and does not depend on learning (examples: food, water, sleep, termination of pain).

primary sex characteristics: The internal and external reproductive organs—penis, testes, and scrotum in males, and ovaries, uterus, and vagina in females; the genitals.

primary visual cortex: The area at the rear of the occipital lobes where vision registers in the cerebral cortex.

problem-focused coping: A response aimed at reducing, modifying, or eliminating the source of stress.

procedural memory: The hypothetical subsystem within long-term memory that is not dependent on the hippocampus and that holds our memory for motor skills gained through repetitive practice.

progesterone (pro-JES-tah-rone): A female sex hormone produced in the ovaries in females and in the adrenals in both males and females; plays a role in the regulation of the menstrual cycle and prepares the lining of the uterus for possible pregnancy.

progressive relaxation: A relaxation technique that involves flexing and then relaxing the different muscle groups throughout the body from head to toes.

projection: The act of attributing our own undesirable thoughts, impulses, traits, or behaviors to others, or minimizing them in ourselves and exaggerating them in others.

projective test: A personality test in which people respond to ink-blots, drawings of ambiguous human situations, incomplete sentences, and the like, by projecting their own inner thoughts, feelings, fears, or conflicts into the test materials (examples: Rorschach Ink-blot Test, Thematic Apperception Test).

prosocial behavior: Behavior that benefits others.

prototype: The example that embodies the most typical features of a particular concept.

proximity: Geographic closeness; a major factor in attraction.

psychedelic: *See* hallucinogen.

psychiatrist: A medical doctor with a specialty in the diagnosis and treatment of mental disorders.

psychoactive drug: A drug that alters normal mental functioning—mood, perception, or thought; if used medically, called a controlled substance.

psychoanalysis (SY-ko-ah-NAL-ih-sis): The term Freud used for both his theory of personality and his therapy for the treatment of psychological disorders; the psychotherapy that uses the techniques of free association, dream analysis, and analysis of resistance and transference to uncover the repressed memories, impulses, and conflicts thought to cause psychological disorder.

psychoanalyst (SY-ko-AN-ul-ist): A professional, usually a psychiatrist, with special training in psychoanalysis.

psychoanalytic perspective (SY-ko-AN-il-IT-ik): A perspective initially proposed by Freud that emphasizes the importance of the unconscious and of early childhood experiences as the keys to understanding behavior and thought.

psychodrama: A type of group therapy in which one group member will act out his or her own problem situations and relationships with the assistance of the other members and thereby gain insight into the problem.

psychogenic (SY-kuh-JEN-ik): Psychological in origin.

psychogenic amnesia: A dissociative disorder in which there is a loss of memory for one's entire personal identity or for important personal information encompassing limited periods in one's life.

psychogenic fugue (FEWG): A dissociative disorder in which a person experiences complete loss of memory for his or her entire identity, wanders away from home, and assumes a new identity; the fugue can last from several days to years, after which no memory of the episode remains.

psychological dependence: *See* drug dependence (psychological).

psychology: The scientific study of behavior and mental processes.

psychosexual stages: A series of stages through which the sexual instinct, present at birth, develops; each stage is defined by an erogenous zone that becomes the center of new pleasures and conflicts.

psychosis (sy-CO-sis): A term used for a severe mental disorder, sometimes requiring hospitalization, in which the individual typically loses contact with reality, may suffer delusions and hallucinations, and is seriously impaired in his or her ability to function in everyday life.

psychosocial stages: Erikson's series of eight developmental stages through which an individual passes during the life span; each stage is defined by a conflict involving the individual's relationship with the social environment, which must be resolved satisfactorily in order for healthy personality development to occur.

psychosurgery: Brain surgery to treat some severe, persistent, and debilitating psychological disorder or, in some cases, severe chronic pain.

psychotherapy: The category of treatment for psychological disorders that uses psychological means (as opposed to biological treatment) and primarily involves conversations between the patient and the therapist.

puberty: A period of rapid physical growth and change that culminates in sexual maturity.

punishment: The removal of a pleasant stimulus or the application of an unpleasant stimulus that tends to suppress a response.

R

random assignment: In an experiment, the assignment of subjects to the experimental and control groups by using a chance procedure, which guarantees that all subjects have an equal probability of being placed in any of the groups; used to maximize the probability that groups are similar at the beginning of the experiment; a control for selection bias.

range: The difference between the highest and the lowest score in a distribution of scores.

rape myth: The unfounded belief that women who are raped ask for it, deserve it, or enjoy it.

rational-emotive therapy: A directive, confrontational form of psychotherapy developed by Albert Ellis and designed to challenge and modify clients' irrational beliefs about themselves and others that are believed to be the cause of their personal distress.

rationalization: The act of supplying a logical, rational, socially acceptable reason rather than the real reason for an irrational or unacceptable thought or action.

reaction formation: The process of denying an unacceptable impulse, usually sexual or aggressive, by giving strong conscious expression to its opposite (example: hostility for a child is masked by overprotection).

realistic conflict theory: The notion that prejudices arise when social groups must compete for scarce resources and opportunities.

recall: A measure of retention that requires one to remember material with few or no retrieval cues, as in an essay test.

receptor site: A site on the dendrite or cell body of a neuron that has a characteristic shape and will receive only the distinctively shaped molecules of certain neurotransmitters (drugs work by binding with certain *receptor sites* and influencing cells either to fire or not to fire).

recessive gene: A gene that will not be expressed if paired with a dominant gene but will be expressed if paired with another like itself.

recognition: A measure of retention that requires one to identify material as familiar, or as having been encountered before.

reconstruction: A memory that is not an exact replica of an event but has been pieced together from a few highlights and using information that may or may not be accurate.

reflex: An involuntary response to a particular stimulus (example: salivating when food is placed in the mouth); inborn, unlearned, automatic response to certain environmental stimuli (examples: coughing, blinking, sucking, grasping).

refractory period: Immediately following ejaculation, the period during which the male is unable to experience another orgasm; females have no such period.

regression: The act of reverting to a behavior that might have reduced anxiety at an earlier stage of development; usually occurs when individuals are frustrated or under stress.

rehearsal: The act of purposely repeating information to maintain it in short-term memory or to transfer it to long-term memory.

reinforcement: An event that follows a response and increases the strength of that response and/or the likelihood that it will be repeated.

relearning method: Measuring retention in terms of the percentage of time or learning trials saved in relearning material compared with the time required to learn it originally; the most sensitive method of measuring memory.

reliability: The ability of a test to yield nearly the same score when the same people are tested and then retested using the same test or an alternate form of the test.

REM dream: Having a dreamlike and storylike quality, the type of dream that occurs almost continuously during each REM period; more vivid, visual, emotional, and bizarre than a NREM dream.

REM rebound: The increased amount of REM sleep that occurs after REM deprivation; often associated with unpleasant dreams or nightmares.

REM sleep: Sleep characterized by rapid eye movements, paralysis of large muscles, fast and irregular heart rate and respiration, increased brain-wave activity, and vivid dreams.

replication: The process of repeating a study using different subjects and preferably a different investigator to verify existing research findings.

representative sample: A sample of subjects selected from the larger population in such a way that important subgroups within the population are included in the sample in the same proportions as they are found in the larger population.

repression: The act of removing from one's consciousness disturbing, shameful or guilt-provoking, or otherwise unpleasant memories so that one is no longer aware a painful event occurred; the most important and most frequently used defense mechanism, by which (1) painful memories, thoughts, ideas, or perceptions are involuntarily removed from consciousness, and (2) disturbing sexual or aggressive impulses are prevented from breaking into consciousness.

resistance: In psychoanalytic therapy, the patient's attempts to avoid expressing or revealing painful or embarrassing thoughts or feelings.

resistance stage: The second stage of the general adaptation syndrome, during which there are intense physiological efforts to resist or adapt to the stressor.

resolution phase: The final stage of the sexual response cycle, during which the body returns to an unaroused state.

resting potential: The membrane potential of a neuron at rest, about −70 millivolts.

reticular activating system (RAS): *See* reticular formation.

reticular formation: A structure in the brainstem that plays a crucial role in arousal and attention and that screens sensory messages entering the brain, blocking some and sending others on to higher brain centers for processing.

retina: The tissue at the back of the eye that contains the rods and the cones and onto which the retinal image is projected.

retinal image: The image of objects in the visual field projected onto the retina; although a viewed object appears relatively constant, the *retinal image* changes with every change in distance and viewing angle.

retrieval: The act of bringing to mind (consciousness) material that has been stored in memory.

retrieval cue: Any stimulus or bit of information that aids in the retrieval of particular information from long-term memory.

retrograde amnesia (RET-ro-grade): A loss of memory for events occurring for a period of time preceding a brain injury or a trauma that caused a loss of consciousness.

reuptake: The process by which neurotransmitter molecules are taken from the synaptic cleft back into the axon terminal for later use, thus terminating their excitatory or inhibitory effect on the receiving neuron.

reverse discrimination: Giving special treatment or higher evaluations to individuals from groups that have been the target of discrimination.

reversibility: The realization, during the concrete operations stage, that any change occurring in shape, position, or order of matter can be returned mentally to its original state.

right hemisphere: The hemisphere that controls the left side of the body and, in most people, is specialized for visual-spatial perception and understanding nonverbal behavior.

rods: The light-sensitive receptors in the retina that, in dim light, provide vision in black, white, and shades of gray.

Rorschach Inkblot Test (ROR-shok): A projective test composed of 10 inkblots to which a subject responds; its purpose is to reveal unconscious functioning and the possible presence of psychiatric disorders.

S

sample: The portion of any population that is selected for study and from which generalizations are made about the entire larger population.

saturation: The degree to which light waves producing a color are of the same wavelength; the purity of a color.

savant syndrome: Mental retardation or autism coupled with either an ability to perform an amazing mental feat or the possession of a remarkable specific skill, as in computation, music, or art.

savings score: The percentage of time or learning trials saved in relearning material over the amount of time or number of learning trials taken in original learning; presumed to reflect the percentage of information retained in long-term memory.

scapegoating: Displacing aggression onto minority groups or other innocent targets who have not been in any way responsible for the frustration causing the aggression.

Schachter-Singer theory: A theory stating that, for an emotion to occur, two factors must be present: (1) there must be physiological arousal, and (2) the person must perceive some reason for the arousal in order to label the emotion.

schedules of reinforcement: A systematic program for administering reinforcements that has a predictable effect on behavior.

schema: Piaget's term for a cognitive structure or concept used to identify and interpret information and that is broadened, modified, or created through the processes of assimilation and accommodation.

schizophrenia (SKIT-suh-FREE-nee-ah): A psychosis characterized by loss of contact with reality and by hallucinations, delusions, inappropriate or flat affect, some disturbance in thinking, social withdrawal, and/or other bizarre behavior.

seasonal affective disorder (SAD): A mood disorder in which depression comes and goes with the seasons (winter depression, beginning in the fall and lifting in the spring, is thought to be triggered by a decrease in light and is marked by an increase in appetite, sleep, and weight and a craving for carbohydrates; a less common type is summer depression).

secondary appraisal: The second stage in cognitive appraisal of a stressful event, which involves an evaluation of available coping resources and a plan for coping with the source of stress.

secondary emotions: Various combinations of the primary emotions, varying from culture to culture.

secondary reinforcer: A neutral stimulus that becomes reinforcing after repeated pairing with other reinforcers.

secondary sex characteristics: Those physical characteristics not directly involved in reproduction but that develop at puberty and are associated with sexual maturity (examples: pubic and underarm hair in both sexes, breasts in females, and facial hair and a deepened voice in males).

sedentary life-style: One in which a person does not exercise at least three times a week for 20 minutes each time.

selection bias: The assignment of subjects to experimental or control groups in such a way that systematic differences among the groups are present at the beginning of the experiment.

self-actualization: The process of striving to develop one's full potential; the highest need on Maslow's hierarchy, which theoretically can be developed only when the lower needs on the hierarchy have been adequately satisfied.

self-efficacy: A person's belief in his or her ability to perform competently and successfully in whatever is attempted.

self-serving bias: Attributing our successes to dispositional causes, and our failures to situational causes.

semantic memory: The hypothetical subpart of long-term memory that stores common knowledge; our mental encyclopedia or dictionary.

semicircular canals: Three fluid-filled tubular canals in the inner ear that provide information about rotating head movements.

senile dementia: A state of mental deterioration caused by physical deterioration of the brain and characterized by impaired memory and intellect, as well as by altered personality and behavior; senility.

senility: *See* senile dementia.

sensation: The process through which the senses detect visual, auditory, and other sensory stimuli and transmit them to the brain; sensory information that has registered in the brain but has not been interpreted.

sensorimotor stage: Piaget's first stage of cognitive development (ages birth to 2 years), during which infants gain knowledge and understanding of the world through their senses and motor activities, and culminating with the development of object permanence and the beginning of representational thought.

sensory deprivation: A condition in which sensory stimulation is reduced to a minimum or eliminated, causing irritability, restlessness, and temporary disturbances in thinking.

sensory memory: The memory system that holds information coming in through the senses for a period ranging from a fraction of a second to several seconds.

sensory receptors: Specialized cells in each sense organ that detect and respond to sensory stimuli—light, sound, odors, and so on—and transduce (convert) the stimuli into neural impulses.

separation anxiety: The fear and distress shown by toddlers when their parents leave, occurring from 8 to 24 months and reaching a peak between 12 and 18 months.

serial position effect: Upon presentation of a list of items, the tendency to remember the beginning and ending items better than the middle items.

set point: The weight that the body normally maintains when a person is trying neither to gain nor to lose weight (if weight falls below this normal level, the appetite will increase and metabolic rate will decrease so that the original weight is restored; if weight is gained, the appetite will decrease and metabolic rate will increase).

sex chromosomes: The 23rd pair of chromosomes (XX in females and XY in males), which carries the genes that determine a person's sex, primary and secondary sex characteristics, and other sex-linked traits.

sex typing: The process by which individuals acquire the traits, behaviors, attitudes, preferences, and interests that the culture considers appropriate for their biological sex.

sexual disorders: Disorders involving sexual dysfunction (inhibited sexual desire or impaired sexual performance due to psychological causes) or paraphilia (the need for unusual or bizarre objects, conditions, or acts in order to achieve sexual gratification).

sexual dysfunction: Lack of or inhibited sexual desire or some impairment in sexual performance.

sexually transmitted diseases (STDs): Infections that are spread primarily, although not exclusively, through intimate sexual contact.

sexual orientation: The direction of one's sexual preference—toward members of the opposite sex (heterosexuality), toward one's own sex (homosexuality), or toward both sexes (bisexuality).

sexual response cycle: The four phases—excitement, plateau, orgasm, and resolution—that Masters and Johnson found are part of the human sexual response in both males and females.

shape constancy: The tendency to perceive objects as having a stable or unchanging shape regardless of changes in the retinal image that result from differences in viewing angle.

shaping: The gradual molding of a desired behavior by reinforcing responses that become progressively closer to the desired behavior; reinforcing successive approximations of the desired response.

short-term memory: The second stage of memory, which holds about 7 (a range of 5–9) items for less than 30 seconds without rehearsal; working memory; the mental workspace we use to keep in mind tasks we are thinking about at any given moment.

simple phobia: A catchall category for any phobia other than agoraphobia and social phobia (examples: fear of insects, dogs, the dark).

situational attribution: Attributing a behavior to some external cause or factor operating within the situation; an external attribution.

size constancy: The tendency to perceive objects as maintaining the same size regardless of changes in the retinal image that result from changes in viewing distance.

Skinner box: Invented by B. F. Skinner for conducting experiments in operant conditioning; soundproof operant conditioning chamber with a device for delivering food and either a bar for rats to press or a disk for pigeons to peck.

sleep apnea: A sleep disorder characterized by periods when breathing stops during sleep and the person must awaken briefly in order to breathe; major symptoms are excessive daytime sleepiness and loud snoring.

sleep cycle: A cycle of sleep lasting about 90 minutes and including one or more stages of NREM sleep followed by a period of REM sleep.

sleep terror: *See* night terror.

sleepwalking: *See* somnambulism.

social cognition: Mental processes that people use to notice, interpret, understand, remember, and apply information about the social world and that enable them to simplify, categorize, and order their world.

social facilitation: Any positive or negative effect on performance due to the presence of others, either as an audience or as co-actors.

socialization: The process of learning socially acceptable behaviors, attitudes, and values.

social learning theory: A theory of learning that emphasizes the importance of reinforcement, observational learning, and internal cognitive processes, which influence our perception and evaluation of environmental events; the process of sex typing is explained in terms of observation, imitation, and reinforcement.

social loafing: The tendency of individuals to put forth less effort when they are working with others on a common task than when they are working alone.

social motives: Motives acquired through experience and interaction with others (examples: need for achievement, need for affiliation).

social phobia: An irrational fear and avoidance of social situations such as talking, eating, or writing in front of others, because the individuals believe they might embarrass or humiliate themselves by appearing clumsy, foolish, or incompetent.

social psychology: The area of study that attempts to explain how the actual, imagined, or implied presence of others influences the thoughts, feelings, and behavior of individuals.

Social Readjustment Rating Scale (SRRS): A stress scale developed by Holmes and Rahe, which ranks 43 different life events from most to least stressful and assigns a point value to each.

social support: Tangible support, information, advice, and/or emotional support provided in time of need by family, friends, and others; the feeling that we are loved, valued, esteemed, and cared for.

somatoform disorders (so-MAT-uh-form): Disorders in which physical symptoms are present that are psychological in origin rather than due to physical causes.

somatosensory cortex (so-MAT-o-SENS-or-ee): The strip of tissue at the front of the parietal lobes that is the site where touch, pressure, temperature, and pain register in the cortex.

somnambulism (som-NAM-bue-lism): Sleepwalking that occurs during a partial arousal from Stage 4 sleep, in which the sleepwalker is awake enough to carry out activities that do not require full attention and asleep enough to have no memory of the episode.

source traits: Cattell's name for the traits that underlie the surface traits, that make up the most basic personality structure, and that cause behavior.

spinal cord: An extension of the brain, reaching from the base of the brain through the neck and spinal column, that transmits messages between the brain and the peripheral nervous system such that sensory information can reach the brain, and messages from the brain can reach the muscles and the glands.

split-brain operation: An operation, performed in severe cases of epilepsy, in which the corpus callosum is cut, separating the cerebral hemispheres and usually lessening the severity and frequency of grand mal seizures.

spontaneous recovery: The reappearance of an extinguished response (in a weaker form) when an organism is exposed to the original conditioning stimulus following a rest period.

sports psychology: A specialty concerned with helping competitive athletes develop the mental and emotional skills necessary to facilitate their maximal competitive performance potential, and with helping people in recreational athletic programs attain greater physical, emotional, and mental benefits.

Stage 4 sleep: The stage of deepest NREM sleep, characterized by an EEG pattern of more than 50 percent delta waves; the stage in which growth hormones are secreted and during which sleepwalking and night terrors occur.

standard deviation: A descriptive statistic reflecting the average amount that scores in a distribution vary or deviate from their mean.

standardization: The establishment of norms, based on the normal distribution of scores, to provide a means of comparison for evaluating the scores of people who take the test in the future; administering tests using a prescribed procedure.

Stanford-Binet Intelligence Scale: Lewis Terman's adaptation of the Binet-Simon Scale, in which Binet's original questions were translated, revised, and adapted for American children and new items were added.

state-dependent memory effect: The tendency to recall information better when one is in the same pharmacological or psychological (mood) state as when the information was encoded.

stereotypes: Widely shared beliefs about the characteristic traits, attitudes, and behaviors of various social groups (racial, ethnic, religious) and including the assumption that *they* are usually all alike.

stimulants: A category of drugs that speed up activity in the central nervous system, suppress appetite, and cause a person to feel more awake, alert, and energetic (examples: caffeine, nicotine, amphetamines, cocaine).

stimulus (STIM-yu-lus): Any event or object in the environment to which an organism responds.

stimulus motives: Motives that cause us to increase stimulation and that appear to be unlearned (examples: curiosity; the need to explore, manipulate objects, and play).

stimulus satiation: A behavioral technique in which patients are given so much of a stimulus that it becomes something the patients want to avoid.

storage: The act of maintaining information in memory.

stranger anxiety: A fear of strangers common in infants at about 6 months and increasing in intensity until 12 1/2 months, then declining in the second year.

stress: The physiological and psychological response to a condition that threatens or challenges a person and requires some form of adaptation or adjustment.

stress-inoculation training: A program, designed to help people cope with stress, that involves replacing negative thoughts with positive ones, and learning how to talk to oneself using positive coping statements to dispel worry and provide self-encouragement.

stressor: Any event capable of producing physical or emotional stress.

stroke: A cardiovascular accident that occurs when the blood supply to the brain is cut off, depriving parts of the brain of oxygen and glucose and killing many neurons; the major cause of damage to the adult brain.

structuralism: The first formal school of psychology, aimed at analyzing the basic elements, or structure, of conscious mental experience through the use of introspection.

structure of intellect: The model proposed by Guilford and consisting of 180 different intellectual abilities, which involve all possible combinations of the three dimensions of intellect—mental operations, contents, and products.

subjective night: The time during a 24-hour period when your body temperature is lowest and when your biological clock is telling you to go to sleep.

sublimation: The rechanneling of sexual or aggressive energy to pursuits or accomplishments that society considers acceptable or even praiseworthy.

subliminal perception: Perceiving sensory stimulation that is below the absolute threshold.

subliminal persuasion: Sending persuasive messages below the recipient's level of awareness.

successive approximations: A series of gradual training steps with each step becoming more like the final desired response.

superego (sue-per-EE-go): The moral system of the personality, which consists of the conscience and the ego ideal.

surface traits: Cattell's name for observable qualities of personality such as those one might use in describing a friend.

surrogate: Substitute; someone or something that stands in place of.

survey: A research method in which interviews and/or questionnaires are used to gather information about the attitudes, beliefs, experiences, or behaviors of a group of people; usually a representative sample is studied to estimate certain characteristics in the larger population of interest.

sympathetic nervous system: The division of the autonomic nervous system that mobilizes the body's resources during stress, emergencies, or heavy exertion, preparing the body for action by increasing the heart rate and breathing rate and inhibiting digestive activity.

synapse (SIN-aps): The junction where the axon of a sending neuron communicates with a receiving neuron across the synaptic cleft.

syphilis (SIF-ih-lis): A sexually transmitted disease that progresses through three stages; if untreated it can eventually be fatal.

systematic desensitization: A behavior therapy, developed by Joseph Wolpe to treat fears and phobias, that involves training clients in deep muscle relaxation and then having them confront a graduated series of anxiety-producing situations, either real or imagined, until they can remain relaxed while confronting even the most feared situation.

T

tactile: Pertaining to the sense of touch.

task analysis: Breaking down a job or task into its smallest component parts so that worker performance can be analyzed and evaluated and suggestions for improvement can be specific.

taste aversion: The dislike or avoidance of a particular food that has been associated with nausea or discomfort.

taste buds: The structures that are composed of 60 to 100 sensory receptors for taste.

TAT: *See* Thematic Apperception Test.

telegraphic speech: Short sentences that follow a strict word order and contain only essential content words, leaving out plurals, possessives, conjunctions, articles, and prepositions.

temperament: An individual's behavioral style or characteristic way of responding to the environment.

temporal lobes: The lobes of the brain that contain the primary auditory cortex (where hearing registers), Wernicke's area (a language area usually in the left hemisphere), and association areas (where memories are stored) for interpreting auditory information.

teratogens: Harmful agents in the prenatal environment, which can have a negative impact on prenatal development or even cause birth defects.

territorial behavior: Marking off a territory in an effort to establish control over it and defend it against unwelcome intrusions.

territory: An area defined by a person as temporarily or permanently his or her own.

testosterone (tes-TOS-tah-rone): The most powerful androgen secreted by the testes and adrenals in males and by the adrenals in females; influences the development and maintenance of male sex characteristics and sexual motivation.

thalamus (THAL-uh-mus): The structure, located above the brainstem, that acts as a relay station for information flowing into or out of the higher brain centers.

THC (tetrahydrocannabinol): The principle psychoactive ingredient in marijuana and hashish.

Thematic Apperception Test (TAT): A projective test consisting of 19 drawings of ambiguous human situations and one blank card, which the subject describes; the description is thought to reveal inner feelings, conflicts, and motives being projected onto the test materials.

time out: A behavioral technique, used to decrease the frequency of undesirable behavior, that involves withdrawing the individual from all reinforcement for a period of time.

token economy: A behavioral technique used to encourage desirable behaviors by reinforcing them with tokens that can be exchanged later for desired objects, activities, or privileges.

tokenism: A subtle form of discrimination in which persons are hired or promoted primarily because they represent a specific group or category rather than strictly on the basis of their qualifications.

tolerance: *See* drug tolerance.

trait: A personal characteristic that is used to describe or explain personality.

trait theory: A theory that attempts to explain personality and differences between people in terms of their personal characteristics.

tranquilizer (minor): A central nervous system depressant that calms the user (examples: Valium, Librium, Dalmane, Xanax).

transduction: The process by which sensory receptors convert sensory stimulation—light, sound, odors, etc.—into neural impulses.

transference: An intense emotional situation that occurs during psychoanalysis when the patient comes to behave toward the analyst as he or she had behaved toward a significant figure from the past, for example, father, mother, or sibling.

trial and error: An approach to problem solving in which one solution after another is tried in no particular order until a workable solution is found.

triangular theory of love: Sternberg's theory of love, which proposes that the three components of intimacy, passion, and decision/commitment, singly or in various combinations, produce seven different kinds of love—infatuated, empty, romantic, fatuous, companionate, and consummate love, as well as liking.

triarchic theory of intelligence: The theory of intelligence proposed by Sternberg, which consists of three parts—the componential, the contextual, and the experiential.

trichromatic theory: The theory of color vision suggesting that there are three types of cones, which are maximally sensitive to red, green, or blue, and that varying levels of activity in these receptors can produce all of the colors.

twin study method: Studying identical and fraternal twins to determine the relative effects of heredity and environment on a variety of characteristics.

Type A Behavior Pattern: A behavior pattern, identified by Friedman and Rosenman, characterized by a sense of time urgency, impatience, excessive competitive drive, hostility, and easily aroused anger; believed to be a risk factor in coronary heart disease.

Type B Behavior Pattern: A behavior pattern, identified by Friedman and Rosenman, characterized by a relaxed, easygoing manner and not associated with coronary heart disease.

U

unconditional positive regard: A condition required of person-centered therapists, involving a caring for and acceptance of clients regardless of their feelings, thoughts, or behavior; unqualified caring and nonjudgmental acceptance of another.

unconditioned response (UR): A response that is invariably elicited by the unconditioned stimulus without prior learning.

unconditioned stimulus (US): A stimulus that elicits a specific response without prior learning.

unconscious (un-KON-shus): Considered by Freud to be the primary motivating force of behavior, containing repressed memories and also instincts and wishes that have never been conscious.

underextension: Restricting the use of a word to only a few, rather than to all, members of a class of objects.

uplifts: The positive experiences in life, which can neutralize or cancel out the effects of many of the hassles.

uppers: A slang term for stimulants.

V

vaginismus (VAJ-ah-NIZ-mus): A sexual dysfunction in females, in which involuntary muscle contractions in the vagina make penetration either painful or impossible.

validity: The ability of a test to measure what it is intended to measure.

variability: How much the scores in a distribution spread out, away from the mean.

variable-interval schedule: A schedule in which a reinforcer is administered after the first correct response following a varying time of nonreinforcement based on an average time.

variable-ratio schedule: A schedule in which a reinforcer is administered after a varying number of nonreinforced responses based on an average ratio.

ventromedial hypothalamus (VMH): The part of the hypothalamus that presumably acts as a satiety center and, when activated naturally or by electrical stimulation, signals the animal to stop eating (when the area is electrically stimulated, the animal stops eating; when the area is destroyed, the animal overeats, becoming obese).

vestibular sense (ves-TIB-yu-ler): Provides information about movement and our orientation in space through sensory receptors in the semicircular canals and the vestibular sacs, which detect changes in the movement and orientation of the head.

visible spectrum: The narrow band of electromagnetic rays, 380–760 nm in length, that are visible to the human eye.

visual cliff: An apparatus devised by Eleanor Gibson to test depth perception in infants and young animals (a sheet of glass covers a patterned surface; half the patterned surface appears directly under the glass, while the other half is made to simulate a steep drop or cliff).

W-X-Y-Z

Weber's law: The law stating that the just noticeable difference (JND) for all our senses depends on a proportion or percentage of change in a stimulus rather than according to a fixed amount of change.

Wechsler Adult Intelligence Scale (WAIS-R): An individual intelligence test for adults that yields separate verbal and performance (nonverbal) IQ scores as well as an overall IQ score.

weight cycling: Repeated cycles of weight gain and loss in which weight becomes progressively harder to lose and easier to regain; yo-yo dieting.

Wernicke's aphasia: Aphasia resulting from damage to Wernicke's area, in which the victim's spoken language is fluent, but the content is either vague or incomprehensible to the listener.

Wernicke's area: The language area in the temporal lobe involved in comprehending the spoken word and in formulating coherent speech and written language.

withdrawal symptoms: The physical and psychological symptoms (usually the opposite of those produced by the drug) that occur when a regularly used drug is discontinued and that terminate when the drug is taken again.

working backwards: A heuristic strategy in which a person discovers the steps needed to solve a problem by defining the desired goal and working backwards to the current condition.

working memory: *See* short-term memory.

Name Index

Coe, W. C., 134
Cohen, C., 18
Cohen, D., 161
Cohen, M., 164–165
Cohen, S., 460, 461, 602, 610
Coie, J. D., 292
Colasanto, D., 316
Colby, A., 304
Cole, J. O., 143
Coleman, J., 309
Coleman, R. M., 114, 122
Collings, V. B., 107
Collins, R. L., 57
Colvin, C. R., 417
Compton, W. M., III, 539
Condon, W. S., 273
Conrad, A. J., 492
Conrad, R., 194
Conrad, S., 144
Conture, M., 382
Conway, T., 614
Cook, M., 183
Cook, S. W., 594
Cook, T. D., 292
Coons, P. M., 490
Cooper, H. M., 141, 577
Cooper, L. A., 248
Cooper, S., 267
Coopersmith, S., 289–290
Corballis, M. C., 53, 54
Corbit, I. D., 340
Coren, S., 57, 86
Corina, D. P., 53
Corkill, A. J., 222
Cornell, D., 164
Cornley, J. E., 164
Costa, P. T., Jr., 328, 416, 449
Costanzo, 469
Cotman, C. W., 219
Counter, S. A., 89
Cousins, N., 438
Coutts, L. M., 597
Cox, B. J., 447
Coyne, J. C., 450
Craik, F. I. M., 197, 200
Crambert, R. F., 322
Crano, W. D., 571
Crepault, C., 382
Crespi, L. P., 177
Cricco–Lizza, R., 387
Crick, F., 123
Crimmins, E. M., 327
Crook, T. H., 323
Crooks, H., 298
Crosby, F., 594
Crouter, A. C., 316
Crowe, L. C., 141
Crowe, R. R., 483
Cullari, S., 310
Cunitz, A. R., 214
Cunningham, M. R., 554, 576
Curran, D. J., 592
Curtis, R. C., 554
Curtis, R. L., 309
Cusumano, D. C., 371
Cutler, B. L., 211
Czeisler, C. A., 115, 116, 117

Dabbs, J. M., Jr., 577
Dahlstrom, W. G., 427, 457
Dahmer, J., 477
Dale, N., 219
Dallenbach, K. M., 206
Danielsen, K., 413
Daoussis, L., 602
Darley, J. M., 574–575
Darwin, C., 21, 241, 336, 361, 362, 362–363
Dasen, P. R., 303
Dash, P. K., 219
Dashiell, J. F., 338
Davanloo, H., 514
Davies, K., 391
Davila, G. H., 299

Davis, G. E., 607
Davis, K. E., 552
Davis, K. L., 494
Davis, P. J., 409
Davison, G. C., 525
Dawson, D., 117
Dayton, G. O., Jr., 267, 269
de Bareene, D., 50–51
DeBuono, B. A., 395
DeCasper, A. J., 269
Deci, E. L., 179
DeFries, J. C., 242
DeJong, W., 566
Dekker, J., 381
Delgado, J. M. R., 46, 343
DeLongis, A., 444, 450, 451
Dembroski, T. M., 457
Dement, W., 115, 116, 119, 122
DeMoris, A., 315
Dempster, F. N., 222
Dennerstein, L., 381
Dennis, W., 313
Derlega, V. J., 557
Descartes, R., 246
Des Jarlais, D. C., 392
Desmond, E. W., 464
DeStefano, L., 317
Detke, M. J., 345
Deuchar, N., 393
Deutsch, D., 191
Deutsch, G., 54
Deutsch, J. A., 191
De Valois, K. K., 82
De Valois, R. L., 82
Devine, P. G., 570, 594
De Vos, S., 327
deVries, 323
Diamond, M. C., 41
Dickman, 409
Dietz, W. H., 469, 470
Digman, J. M., 415, 416
DiLalla, L. F., 578
Dinwiddie, S. H., 499
Dion, K., 292, 555
Dionne, V. E., 90
Dipboye, R. L., 555
Dobb, E., 90
Dobbin, M., 88
Dobie, R. A., 89
Dobson, K. S., 529, 531, 543
Dodge, K. A., 292, 578
Doherty, M. A., 522
Dollard, J., 577
Domino, G., 429
Donaldson, G., 313
Donderi, D. C., 124
Donnerstein, E., 383
Doob, L. W., 577
Dornbush, S. M., 289
Dorsett, S. I., 476
Douvan, E., 299
Dovidio, J. F., 576, 594
Dow, M., 381
Dreikurs, R., 412
Drew, C. R., 584
Drob, S. L., 515
Duck, S., 308
Duckworth, J. C., 427, 428
Duclos, S. E., 362
Duggan, J. P., 343
Duncan, J., 252
Duncker, K., 252
Durkin, J., 609–610
Duyme, M., 245
Dywan, J., 133, 211

Eagly, A. H., 555, 562
Ebata, A. T., 299
Ebbinghaus, H. E., 203–204, 222
Ebersole, P., 313
Eccles, J. S., 375
Edison, T. A., 228
Edmund, S., 94
Efron, R., 53
Ehrenberg, M., 539

Ehrenberg, O., 539
Ehrhardt, A. A., 385
Eibl–Eibesfeldt, I., 360
Eich, J. E., 216
Eichmann, A., 430
Eimas, P. D., 286
Einstein, A., 41, 228, 246
Eisen, J. L., 486
Ekman, P., 358, 361, 362, 363, 551, 552
El–Shiekh, M., 442
Elkin, I., 518
Elkind, D., 282, 288, 303, 318, 325
Elkins, R. L., 527
Ellicott, A. M., 320–321
Ellinwood, E. H., Jr., 138
Elliot, J., 593
Ellis, A., 413, 529–530
Ellis, B. J., 381
Ellis, H. D., 211
Emmelkamp, P. M. G., 484
Emory, G., 485
Empsom, J. A. C., 123
England, R. D., 491
Enns, M. P., 91
Enright, J. B., 516
Epstein, J., 308
Epstein, L. H., 463
Epstein, M. D., 95
Epstein, S., 417
Erber, J. T., 323
Erikson, E. H., 287–288, 307–308, 309, 314, 318, 325
Erikson, J., 308
Eron, L. D., 293, 579
Esses, V. M., 608
Everaerd, W., 381
Exner, J. E., Jr., 430
Eysenck, H. J., 416, 485
Eysenck, S. B. G., 416

Fadiman, A., 125
Fagot, B. I., 371, 372
Fajardo, D. M., 591
Falbo, T., 352
Fallon, A. E., 301
Falloon, I. R. H., 518
Fanselow, M. S., 95, 218
Fantz, R. L., 269
Faravelli, C., 483
Faschingbauer, T. R., 428
Faust, D., 608
Faust, M. S., 301
Fausto–Sterling, A., 375
Faw, H. W., 202
Fawcett, J. C., 61
Fazio, R. H., 570, 571
Fechner, G., 20
Feingold, A., 555, 556, 557
Feldman, H., 318
Feltzer, W. D., 134
Fenton, J. A., 95
Fenton, W. S., 493
Ferber, R., 127
Festinger, L., 554, 571, 572
Fiatarone, M. A., 468
Field, T. M., 269
Finchilescu, G., 594
Fink, M., 536
Finke, R. A., 247, 249
Finn, P., 116
Firestein, S., 90
Fischer, M. A., 298
Fishbein, M., 571
Fisher, S., 380
Fishman, S. M., 483
Flaskenrud, J. H., 539
Flavell, J. H., 282
Flood, J. F., 344
Foa, E. B., 526
Fogarty, S. J., 216
Fogelman, E., 575
Foley, H. J., 87
Folkard, S., 116
Folkman, S., 442–444, 450

Fondacaro, M. R., 578
Ford, C. S., 384
Ford, M. E., 282
Forgas, J. P., 549
Fournier, J., 220
Fox, N. A., 274
Francis, W. D., 291
Frank, E., 518
Franzoi, S. L., 301
Fraser, S. C., 566
Freedman, J. L., 566, 578
Freeman, W. J., 91
Freese, A. S., 77, 134
French, E. G., 349
French, J. D., 44
Freud, A., 299, 308, 403
Freud, S., 23, 125, 207, 209, 211, 308, 336, 401–409, 488, 513, 514, 576
Frey–Hewitt, B., 470
Friday, N., 382
Friedberg, J. M., 536
Friedman, S. R., 392
Friedman, R. D., 455–456, 457
Friedrich, L. K., 292
Friesen, W. V., 361, 362, 363
Frisk, M., 301
Fritsch, 49, 58
Fulker, D. W., 242
Funder, D. C., 417
Furstenberg, F. F., Jr., 310
Fusella, V., 247

Gabrenya, W. K., Jr., 569
Gackenbach, J., 125
Gaertner, S. L., 594
Gage, P., 36
Gagnon, J. H., 384
Galanter, M. C., 520
Gallup, G., Jr., 108, 142, 316, 463, 470, 594
Galton, F., 21, 240–241
Gannon, L., 16
Garcia, J., 163
Gardiner, J., 400
Gardner, L. I., 273
Gardner, H., 54, 238
Garfield, S. L., 513, 516
Garner, D. M., 301
Gates, A. I., 223
Gatz, M., 324
Gawin, F. H., 138
Gazzaniga, M. S., 56
Geary, N., 138
Geen, R. G., 350, 579
Geiselman, R. E., 557
Gelder, M. G., 526
Gelernter, C. S., 531
Geller, U., 108
Gelman, R., 282
Genovese, K., 548, 574
George, W. H., 141
Gershon, E. S., 498
Geschwind, N., 57, 60
Ghaziuddin, M., 499
Gibbs, J., 344
Gibbs, N. R., 325
Gibson, E., 269
Gifford, R., 606
Gildea, P. M., 283
Giles, D. E., 496
Gilligan, C., 303, 306, 306–307
Gillin, J. C., 130
Glanzer, M., 214
Glass, D. C., 446, 538, 602
Glassman, C., 123
Glenn, N. D., 316
Glickstein, M., 51
Glover, J. A., 222
Goddard, H. H., 230
Godden, D. R., 215
Gold, M. S., 138
Goldberg, J., 95, 447
Goldberg, L. R., 416
Goldberg, P. A., 432

Subject Index

Dark print identifies the Key Terms in this book.

progressive, 452
and sports psychology, 609–610
in systematic desensitization, 524–525
Relearning method, 202
Reliability, of tests, 232
REM dreams, 123. *See also* Dreams
Remembering. See Memory
Remote Associates Test (RAT), 255
REM rebound, 122–123
and nightmares, 127
REM sleep, 118–119. *See also* REM rebound; Sleep
and aging, 120–121
dreams during, 123
function of, 123
and narcolepsy, 128–129
Repetition, as a factor in persuasion, 573
Replication, of research studies, 16, 624
Representative sample, 5
Repression, 207, 404
Research, psychological. *See also* Research methods, psychological
animals in, 17–18
applied and basic, 3
ethics in, 18–19
goals of, 3
human subjects in, 16
replication of studies in, 16
Research methods, psychological. *See also* Research, Psychological
case study, 4
correlational, 13–15
descriptive, 3–6
experimental, 7–12
introspection, 20, 21, 22
laboratory observation, 4
naturalistic observation, 3–4
psychological tests, 15–16
survey, 4–6
table of, 17
Resistance, in psychoanalysis, 513–514
Resistance stage, in response to a stressor, 441
Resolution phase, 380
Respondent conditioning. *See* Classical conditioning
Response, conditioned versus unconditioned, 155
Resting potential, 38
Retardation, 229
categories of, 235
causes of, 236
Reticular activating system, 43–44
Reticular formation, 43–44
Retina, 77–82
Retinal disparity, 101
Retinal image, 99, 100, 101
Retirement, 326
Retrieval, of a memory, 191
Retrieval cues, 201
Retrieval failure, 208
Retroactive interference, 206–207
Retrograde amnesia, 206
Reuptake, of neurotransmitters, 40
Reverse discrimination, 592
Reversibility, 279, 280
Review, in SQ3R method, 30
Reward, 170
Rhodopsin, 78–79
Rhyme, as a mnemonic device, 220
Right handedness, 57, 60
Right hemisphere, functions of, 54–56
Robber's Cave Experiment, 587, 594
Rods, 78–79
Role reversal, 519
Romantic love, 560
Rorschach Inkblot Test, 429–430
Rubella (German measles) during pregnancy, 266
Runner's high, 95

Salivation, and classical conditioning, 153–159
Salt (sodium) intake, 466
Sample, of a population, 5, 623
Satiety signals, 344
Saturated fat, 465
Saturation, of color, 81
Savant syndrome, 256

Savings score, 202–203
Scapegoating, 577
Scatterplot, 621, 622, 623
Schachter–Singer theory, of emotion, 355, 358
Schedules of reinforcement, 171–174
fixed–interval, 172–173
fixed–ratio, 171–172
table of, 173
variable–interval, 173
variable–ratio, 172
Schemas, 276
Schizoid personality disorder, 504
Schizophrenia, 491–494
brain abnormalities in, 492
catatonic, 493
causes of, 493–494
delusions in, 492
disorganized, 493
and dopamine oversensitivity, 40
drug therapy for, 532
family therapy for, 518
genetic factors in, 494
hallucinations in, 491
paranoid, 493
symptoms of, 491–493
Schizotypal personality disorder, 504
School psychologist, 28
Schools of psychology, 21–25. *See also* specific schools
behaviorism, 22, 161
functionalism, 21
Gestalt psychology, 24, 97–98
humanistic psychology, 24, 420
psychoanalysis, 23, 401–409
table of, 25
Science and Human Behavior (Skinner), 167
Seasonal affective disorder (SAD), 496–497, 498–499
Secondary appraisal, of a stressor, 442–443
Secondary emotions, 358
Secondary reinforcer, 171
Secondary sex characteristics, 66, 299–300, 369
Sedative–hypnotics, 141–143, 145
Sedentary life–style, 455
Selection bias, 10
Self, as an archetype, 411
Self–actualization, 341, 420, 515
Self–efficacy, 418
Self–esteem
children's, and parenting styles, 289–290
on hierarchy of needs, 341
during puberty, 300–301
Self–fulfilling prophecy, 554
and experimenter bias, 11
Self–help groups, 519, 520
Self–serving bias, 553
Semantic memory, 198–199, 218
Semicircular canals, 96–97
Senile dementia, 324
Senility, 324
Sensation, 72–97. *See also* Senses
Sensation–seeking tendencies, 338, 339
Sense of direction, and the parietal lobes, 51
Senses. *See also* specific senses
absolute thresholds of, 73
difference thresholds of, 73–74
hearing, 83–89
kinesthetic, 95
smell, 90–91
taste, 91
touch (inc. pain), 93–95
and transduction, 74–75
vision, 75–83
Sensorimotor stage, 277
Sensory deprivation, 339
Sensory input areas, 48
Sensory memory, 192–194
Sensory nerves, in somatic nervous system, 62
Sensory receptors
defined, 75
for hearing, 86
for kinesthetic sense, 95
for pain, 94–95
for smell, 90

for taste, 91
for touch, 93
for vestibular sense, 96–97
for vision, 77, 78–82
Sentence completion method, 432
Separation anxiety, 274
Serial position effect, 214
Serial recall, 201
Serotonin
effects of antidepressants on, 533, 534
and mood disorders, 498–499
and moods, 41
Serum cholesterol, 466
Set point, 469–470
Sex characteristics, 66, 299–300, 369
Sex chromosomes, 263, 368–369
Sex glands, 66
differentiation in the embryo, 368
Sex hormones, 66, 369, 381
effect during prenatal development, 369
effect during puberty, 299
released by adrenal glands, 66
and sexual arousal and desire, 380–381
Sex–linked traits, 263
Sex role development, 370–373
cognitive–developmental theory of, 372
gender–schema theory of, 372–373
psychological theories of, 371–373
role of parents in, 370
role of peers in, 370
social learning theory of, 372
Sex therapy, 389
Sex typing, 370–371
Sexual arousal, 119, 379–383
human sexual response cycle, 379–380
psychological factors in, 381–382
role of hormones in, 380–381
Sexual attitudes and behavior, 377–383
Sexual Behavior in the Human Female (Kinsey), 378
Sexual Behavior in the Human Male (Kinsey), 378
Sexual disorders, 505–507
Sexual dysfunctions and treatment, 387–389. *See also* Paraphilias
anorgasmia, 388
impotence, 119, 387–388
premature and retarded ejaculation, 388
treatment for, 389
vaginismus, 388
Sexuality
and adolescence, 310–311
and gender, 367–395
Sexually transmitted diseases (STDs), 389–393
acquired immune deficiency syndrome, 392–393
chlamydia, 390
genital herpes, 391
genital warts, 391
gonorrhea, 390
pelvic inflammatory disease, 390
protection from, 395
syphilis, 390–391
Sexual masochism, 506
Sexual orientation, 384
Sexual response cycle, 379–380
Sexual sadism, 506
s factor, 237
Shadow, as archetype, 410
Shadow or shading, as a monocular depth cue, 102
Shape constancy, 99–100
Shaping, 166, 522, 523
Shift work, and circadian rhythms, 115–117
Shock. *See* Electroconvulsive therapy (ECT);
Milgram Study
Short sleepers, 122
Short–term memory (STM), 194–196
as working memory, 196
"Sick role," 454
Similarity
as a factor influencing attraction, 555–556
in perceptual grouping, 98–99
Simple phobia, 484–485
behavior therapy for, 525
Situational attribution, 552
Size constancy, 99
Skin senses, 93

The Early Window: Effects of Television on Children and Youth, Third Edition by R. M. Liebert and J. Sprafkin (Pergamon Books Ltd., 1988), p. 5. Reprinted by permission of the authors.

Chapter 9

Opener Richard Hutchings/Photo Researchers, Inc. **p. 298** AP/WIDE WORLD PHOTOS **p. 299** Bob Daemmrich/Stock Boston **p. 303** Rhoda Sidney/Stock Boston **Fig. 9.2** from Lester A. Lefton, *Psychology*, Fourth Edition. Copyright (c) 1991 by Allyn and Bacon. Reprinted with permission. **p. 307** Sarah Putnam/NYT Pictures **p. 310** Alon Reininger/Woodfin Camp & Associates **Fig. 9.3** from "Teen Sex: Not for Love" by Elizabeth Stark, *Psychology Today*, May 1989, p. 10. Reprinted with permission from Psychology Today Magazine. Copyright (c) 1989 (Sussex Publishers, Inc.). **p. 313** David Lissy/ The Picture Cube **p. 316** Spencer Grant/The Picture Cube **p. 318** excerpted material from "Erik Erikson's Eight Ages of Man" by David Elkind, *The New York Times* Magazine, April 5, 1970. Copyright (c) 1970 by The New York Times Company. Reprinted by permission. **Fig. 9.7** chart only from *The Seasons of a Man's Life* by Daniel J. Levinson. Copyright (c) 1978 by Daniel J. Levinson. Reprinted by permission of Alfred A. Knopf, Inc. and Sterling Lord Literistic, Inc. **p. 323** Courtesy of Cable News Network, Inc. **p. 324** Courtesy of Cable News Network, Inc. **p. 325** excerpted material from "Erik Erikson's Eight Ages of Man" by David Elkind, *The New York Times* Magazine, April 5, 1970. Copyright (c) 1970 by The New York Times Company. Reprinted by permission. **Fig. 9.8** Graph data from R. Inglehart, *Culture Shift in Advanced Industrial Society*. Copyright (c) 1990 by Princeton University Press. Reprinted by permission of Princeton University Press. **p. 327** James H. Simon/The Picture Cube

Chapter 10

Opener Y. Arthus Bertrand/Photo Researchers, Inc. **p. 334 (upper)** Steve Allen/Gamma Liaison **p. 334 (lower)** Diana Walker/Gamma Liaison **p. 338** Bill Bachman/Photo Researchers, Inc. **p. 340** Courtesy McGill University **p. 345** Richard Fukuhara/Woodfin Camp & Associates **Table 10.2** from Murray, *Explorations In Personality* (New York: Oxford University Press) in Charles S. Carver and Michael F. Scheier, *Perspectives on Personality*, Second Edition. Copyright (c) 1992 by Allyn and Bacon. Reprinted with permission. **p. 348** Focus on Sports **p. 350** Blair Seitz/Photo Researchers, Inc. **p. 351** excerpted material from "Fail, Bright Women" by Matina S. Horner, *Psychology Today*, November 1969. Reprinted with permission from Psychology Today Magazine. Copyright (c) 1969 (Sussex Publishers, Inc.). **p. 356 (polygraph pattern)** Courtesy Sgt. John E. Consigli, Massachusetts State Police **p. 356 (bottom)** Mike Abramson/Woodfin Camp & Associates **Fig. 10.5** data only from Kleinmuntz, B., and Szucko, J. J. (1984). Lie detection in ancient and modern times: A call for contemporary scientific study. *American Psychologist*, 39, 766-776. **Fig. 10.8** based in part on "A Language for Emotions" by R. Plutchik, *Psychology Today*, Vol. 13, No. 9, February 1980, pp. 68-78. Reprinted with permission from Psychology Today Magazine. Copyright (c) 1980 (Sussex Publishers, Inc.). **p. 360** Copyright P. Ekman, 1975 **p. 361** Copyright Paul Ekman, 1972 **p. 363** Dallas & John Heaton/Stock Boston

Chapter 11

Opener Joseph Sohm/Stock Boston **p. 368** Latham, A. & Grenadier, A. (1982, October). The ordeal of Walter/Susan Cannon. *Psychology Today*, 16(10), p. 65. **Table 11.1** from *The Gallup Poll Monthly*, February 1990, p. 29. Reprinted by permission of The Gallup

Organization, Inc. **p. 371** Bob Daemmrich/Stock Boston **Table 11.2** from *The Psychology of Sex Differences* by Eleanor Maccoby and Carol Nagy Jacklin. (Stanford, CA: Stanford University Press, 1974). Reprinted by permission. **p. 375** Rhoda Sidney/Stock Boston **p. 376 Try It!** drawings from "Emergence and Characteristics of Sex Differences in Spatial Ability: A Meta-Analysis" by M. C. Linn and A. C. Peterson, *Child Development*, Vol. 56, 1985, pp. 1479-1498. (c) The Society for Research in Child Development, Inc. **Table 11.4** Reproduced with the permission of The Alan Guttmacher Institute from Tom W. Smith, "Adult Sexual Behavior in 1989: Number of Partners, Frequency of Intercourse and Risk of AIDS," *Family Planning Perspectives*, Vol. 23, No. 3, May/June 1991. **p. 379** Jim Wilson/Woodfin Camp & Associates **p. 382** Bob Daemmrich/Stock Boston **p. 384** Owen Franken/Stock Boston **p. 395** Brad Markel/ Gamma Liaison

Chapter 12

Opener Bob Daemmrich/Stock Boston **p. 400** Courtesy Bruce Bisping **p. 402** The Granger Collection **p. 410** The Bettman Archive **p. 412** Francie Manning/The Picture Cube **p. 413** The Bettman Archive **p. 416 Try It!** profile copyright (c) 1956, 1973, 1982, 1986 by the Institute for Personality and Ability Testing, Inc., P. O. Box 1188, Champaign, Illinois, U.S.A. 61824-1188. All rights reserved. Printed in U.S.A. Adapted and reproduced by permission. **Table 12.2** scale names from the Minnesota Multiphasic Personality Inventory (MMPI) coyright (c) 1942, 1943 (renewed 1970), by the Regents of the University of Minnesota. **p. 420** The Bettman Archive **p. 429** cartoon (c) 1976 by Sidney Harris **p. 431** Martin/Custom Medical Stock Photo

Chapter 13

Opener Kindra Clineff/The Picture Cube **p. 438** Courtesy of Cable News Network, Inc. **Fig. 13.1** from THE DYNAMICS OF HEALTH AND WELLNESS: A BIOPSYCHOSOCIAL APPROACH by J. Green and R. Shellenberger. Copyright (c) 1990 by Holt, Rinehart and Winston, Inc. **p. 442** Courtesy Richard Lazarus **p.443** Charles Gupton/Stock Boston **Fig. 13.4** based on "Personal Control and Stress and Coping Processes: A Theoretical Analysis" by Susan K. Folkman, *Journal of Personality and Social Psychology*, Vol. 46, 1984, pp. 839-852. Copyright 1984 by the American Psychological Association. Reprinted by permission of the publisher and the author. **p. 446** Lawrence Migdale/Stock Boston **p. 447** Courtesy of Cable News Network, Inc. **p. 449** Bob Kramer/Stock Boston **Table 13.2** from "Comparison of Two Modes of Stress Measurement: Daily Hassles and Uplifts versus Major Life Events" by A. D. Kanner, J. C. Coyne, C. Schaefer and R. S. Lazarus, *Journal of Behavioral Medicine*, Vol. 4, 1981, pp. 1-39. Reprinted by permission of Plenum Publishing Corporation and Allen D. Kanner, Ph.D. **p. 451 Try It!** vulnerability scale from the Stress Audit, developed by Lyle H. Miller and Alma Dell Smith. Copyright 1987, Biobehavioral Associates, Brookline, MA, reprinted with permission. **p. 455** Paul Solomon/Woodfin Camp & Associates **p. 459** Bob Daemmrich/ Stock Boston **p. 467** Charles Gupton/Stock Boston **p. 469** Biophoto Associates/Photo Researchers, Inc. **p. 470** Courtesy of Cable News Network, Inc.

Chapter 14

Opener Eric Roth/The Picture Cube **p. 476** Schreiber, F. R. (1973). *Sybil*. Chicago: Henry Regency Co. **p. 477** James Holland/Stock Boston **p. 482 Try It!** chart copyright (c) 1984 by David D. Burns, M.D. Reproduced from the *Feeling Good Handbook*, Plume, New York, 1990. Do not reproduce without permission. **p. 484** Courtesy of Cable News Network, Inc. **Table 14.3** from "The Biology of Obsessions and Compulsions," by Judith J. Rapoport, *Scientific American,* March 1989, Vol. 260, pg. 84. Copyright (c) 1989 by Scientific American, Inc. All rights reserved. **p. 493** Grunnitus/Monkmeyer Press **p. 494** Courtesy of Cable News Network, Inc. **p. 496** Mark M. Walker/The Picture Cube **p. 497** Courtesy of Cable News Network, Inc. **p. 502** Nancy Hayes/Monkmeyer Press **p. 506** Bill Stanton/Magnum

Chapter 15
Opener Lori Grinker/Woodfin Camp & Associates **p. 512** John Coletti/ Stock Boston **p. 513** Reuters/Bettman Newsphotos **p. 515** Michael Rougier, LIFE Magazine, (c) Time Warner Inc. **p. 518** cartoon by S. Gross, source: *Science Digest,* February 1985. **p. 519** Will & Deni McIntyre/Photo Researchers, Inc. **p. 525** Jacques Chenet/Woodfin Camp & Associates **p. 527** Ann McQueen/Stock Boston **p. 528** Susan Rosenberg/Photo Researchers, Inc.; snake courtesy of Academy of Natural Sciences of Philadelphia **p. 530** Brad Bower/Picture Group **p. 535** James Wilson/Woodfin Camp & Associates **p. 538** Bob Daemmrich/Stock Boston **Fig. 15.6** from "The Dose-Effect Relationship in Psychotherapy" by K. I. Howard, *American Psychologist,* Vol. 41, pp. 159-164. Copyright 1986 by the American Psychological Association. Reprinted by permission of the publisher and the author.

Chapter 16
Opener Cleo/The Picture Cube **p. 549** Patrick Ward/Stock Boston **p. 551** Reuters/Bettman **p. 556** Will McIntyre/Photo Researchers, Inc. **Table 16.1** from "International Preferences in Selecting Mates: A Study of 37 Cultures" by D. M. Buss et al., *Journal of Cross-Cultural Psychology,* Vol. 21, pp. 5-47. Copyright (c) 1990 by Sage Publications, Inc. Reprinted by permission of the publisher. **p. 562** William Vandivert and *Scientific American* **p. 564** Copyright 1965 by Stanley Milgram. From the film OBEDIENCE, distributed by The Pennsylvania State University, Audio Visual Services. **p. 567** Courtesy The Henry Ford Museum, Dearborn, MI **p. 573** Spencer Grant/Stock Boston **p. 574** Freda Leinwand/Monkmeyer Press

Chapter 17
Opener Bob Daemmrich/Stock Boston **p. 584** The Granger Collection **p. 587** (c) Mike Greenlar, 1987 **p. 589** Courtesy of Cable News Network, Inc. **Table 17.1** International Labor Organization 1990:759-764; U.S. Department of Commerce 1990:405. **Fig. 17.2** data from "Reverse Discrimination in Grading of Essays" from "Author Race, Essay Quality, and Reverse Discrimination" by D. M. Fajardo, *Journal of Applied Social Psychology,* Vol. 15, 1985, pp. 255-268. Reprinted by permission of V. H. Winston & Son, Inc. **p. 593** Courtesy of Cable News Network, Inc. **p. 603** Lee Balterman/The Picture Cube **p. 604 (airport)** Wesley Bocxe/ Photo Researchers, Inc. **p. 604 (soccer)** G. Veggi/Photo Researchers, Inc. **p. 605** V. Englebert/Photo Researchers, Inc. **p. 606** AP/WIDE WORLD PHOTOS **Fig. 17.5** from *Architecture and Social Behavior: Psychological Studies of Social Density* by A. Baum and S. Valins. Copyright (c) 1977 by Lawrence Erlbaum Associates. Reprinted by permission of the publisher and the authors.

Note: Every effort has been made to locate all rightholders.